AN INTRODUCTION TO THE GRAMMAR OF THE TIBETAN LANGUAGE

AN INTRODUCTION TO THE GRAMMAR OF THE TIBETAN LANGUAGE

WITH THE TEXT OF

SITUHI SUMRTAGS,

DAG-JE SAL-WAI ME-LONG AND SITUHI SHAL-LUN

SARAT CHANDRA DAS, C. I. E.,

GYAN

Published by

Gyan Publishing House
5, Ansari Road
Daryaganj, New Delhi-110002
Phone: 011-47034999, 9811692060
E-mail: books@gyanbooks.com

Distribution Network
gyanbooks.com
India, USA, Canada, UK, Australia, France

ISBN: 978-81-212-8993-1 (PB)
First Published, 1915

2nd Impression 2023

Printed at: Gyan Press, Delhi.

AN INRODUCTION TO THE GRAMMAR OF THE TIBETAN LANGUAGE
AUTHOR: SARAT CHANDRA DAS

AN INTRODUCTION TO THE GRAMMAR OF THE TIBETAN LANGUAGE

WITH THE TEXTS OF

SITUhI SUM-rTAGs, DAG-JE SAL-WAI MÉ-LONG and SITUhI SHAL-LÛN

BY

SARAT CHANDRA DAS, C.I.E., *Rai Bahadur*,

Corresponding Member of the Imperial Archeological Society of St. Petersburg,

Associate Member of the Asiatic Society of Bengal,

Honorary Member of the Bangiya Sāhitya Parishad, Calcutta.

Winner of the Marquess of Dufferin and Ava's Silver Medal, in 1886.

,, of His Siamese Majesty King Chulālonkorn's *Tushiti Mālā* Decoration, in 1887.

,, of the Royal Geographical Society's Prize, called *The Back Premium*, in 1888.

AUTHOR OF

Narrative of a Journey to Tashi-lhunpo, in 1879.
A Journey to Lhasa and Central Tibet in 1881—1882.
A Dictionary of the Tibetan Language with Sanskrit synonyms.
Indian Paṇḍits in the Land of Snow.
Bodhisattvāvadāna Kalpalatā (*in Bengali*).

EDITOR OF

YIG-KUR NAM-SHAG, Tibetan Letter Writer.
Kṣemendra's Sanskrit Poem "The AVADANA KALPALATA" with its metrical translation by Shoṅton *Lotsava*.
KṢEMENDRA'S DARPADALAN (*in Sanskrit*).
PAGSAM JON ZANG, Pagsam Thi-shing (*in Tibetan prose*).
BUDDHIST TEXT SOCIETY'S *Journals*, &c.

Darjeeling:

PRINTED AT THE DARJEELING BRANCH PRESS.

1915.

Price—Indian Rs. 10; English 15 s.

DALAI
ཏཱ་ལའི་བླ་མ
LAMA
THUBTAN
GYAMTSHO.
H.C.DUTT

THE HON'BLE MR. W. W. ROCKHILL'S.

Description of the Present Dalai Lama.

"CONCERNING the Dalai Lama Thub-tan Gya-tsho himself, I passed a week with him during his residence at the Wut'ai Shan (རི་བོ་རྩེ་ལྔ in the Province of Shansi), and I saw him repeatedly during his stay in Peking. He is a man of undoubted intelligence and ability, of quick understanding and of force of character. He is broad-minded, possibly as a result of his varied experiences during the last few years, and of great natural dignity. He seemed deeply impressed with the great responsibilities of his office as Supreme Pontiff of his faith, more so, perhaps, than those resulting from his temporal duties. He is quick tempered and impulsive, but cheerful and kindly. At all times I found him a most thoughtful host, an agreeable talker and extremely courteous. He speaks rapidly and smoothly, but in a very low voice. He is short in stature and of slight build. His complexion is rather darker than that of the Chinese, and of a ruddier brown; his face, which is not very broad, is pitted with small-pox, but not deeply. It lights up most pleasantly when he smiles and shows his teeth, which are sound and white. In repose his face is impressive, and rather haughty and forbidding. His nose is small and slightly aquiltive, his ears large, but well set on his head. His eyes are dark brown and rather large and with considerable obliquity, and his eye-brows heavy and rising markedly towards the temples, giving him a very heavy *narquois* and wordly expression, which is further emphasized by his moustache and the small *mouche* under his lip. His hands are small and well shaped; on his left wrist he usually carried a rosary of "Red Sandalwood" beads with silver counters. When walking, he moves quickly, but he does not hold himself erect, a result of passing most of his life seated cross-legged on cushions. His usual dress is the same dark red one worn by all Lamas, with a waist-coat of gold brocade and a square of the same material covering his *Chāb-lu*, (badge of the *Gelug-pa* Yellow-Cap Sect of Tibet), and hanging down below his waist in front."

I received the ཕྱག་དབང benediction from His Holiness on June 10th, in 1882, at a religious service held on the topmost floor of Potala (see my description of it in page 17 Appendix VI.)

Mr. Rockhill, in his letter to me, dated American Embassy, Constantinople, the 15th March 1912, wrote as follows:—

My dear friend, * * * I see that the Dalai Lama has left Darjeeling for Lhasa. I hope he only acted on good advice and that he will not regret the step he has taken. He is rather opinionated and I can well imagine that he was getting very restless at the prolonged exile. As my relations with him have always been most agreeable and cordial I am very heartily his well-wisher. It may be that under the new *regimé* in China he will be able to secure for his country the autonomous Government all Tibetans wait for. I hope he may.

It will give me much pleasure to send you my photograph as soon as I can get one for you. Send me also yours. I have not seen you since 1885. What a long time!

Always sincerely yours,
W. W. Rockhill.

The Dalai Lama is seated on a chair. On his right-behind and left stand my friends *Lon-chen* Gung-thang-pa and *Lon-chen* Shol-khang-pa. The former, his *Lama* Minister wrote, at my request, the རྒྱལ་བའི or ཏཱ་ལའི་བླ་མའི་འཁྲུངས་རབས (Appendix VII) and the latter perhaps, the most thoughtful among his councillors, used often to see me in 1911, at my residence *Lhasa-Villa* in Darjeeling.

April 1914.

Sarat Chandra Das.

DEDICATED

to

THE HONOURABLE W. W. ROCKHILL,

Author of "The Land of Lamas" &c.,

(Formerly American Ambassador at Peking, Athens, St. Petersburgh and Constantinople, &c.)

AS A TOKEN OF HIGH ESTEEM.

LHASA-VILLA, DARJEELING.
April, 1914.

SARAT CHANDRA DAS.

ཞི་བའི་རྒྱ་མཚོ་ཆེན་པོའི་འགྲམ། * ཤར་ནུབ་རྒྱ་མཚོ་གཉིས་ཀྱི་བར། རྒྱལ་ཁམས་ཆེན་པོ་མེ་གོ་གནས། †

དེའི་བློན་ཆེན་རོཀ་ཧིལ་ཞབས། ‡ བདག་ལ་བཀའ་དྲིན་ཆེན་པོ་གནང་། རྒྱ་ནག་བོད་དང་ཧོར་ཡུལ་གསུམ།
རི་བོ་རྩེ་ལྔ་སྐུ་འབུམ་སོགས། གནས་མཆོག་བསྐོར་ནས་རྒྱལ་བ་མཇལ། རྒྱ་སྐད་བོད་སྐད་ལེགས་སྦྱར་སྐད།
ཡོངས་སུ་མཁྱེན་པ་ཁྱོད་ཡིན་པས། གྲོང་ཁྱེར་ཆེན་པོ་པེ་ཅིང་དུ། § བདག་གིས་ཉིད་དང་ཞལ་མཇལ་ཚེ།
མེ་གོ་ཁྲུ་ཡི་སྐུ་མཁར་ནང་། * ཕྱིན་ལ་མགྲོན་དང་གསུང་ཚ་ཆེད་གནང་། ལྷ་ས་དབུས་སོགས་བགྲོད་པའི་གཏམ། †
ཁྱོད་ཀྱིས་འབད་པས་གཏན་ལ་ཕབ། ‡ བཀའ་དྲིན་དྲན་ནས་ཕྱག་ཆུང་གིས། བད་སྒྲོད་གཞུང་དང་རྩོམ་པ་མང་།
§ ལྷག་བསམ་རྟེན་བཞིན་ལྷ་ཛས་ལྟར། སྐུ་ཉིད་ཕྱག་ལ་གུས་པས་ཕུལ། ཞེས་སྦྲི་ཤ་རད་ཙནྡ་དཱས་ཞིས།།

---

* ཞི་བའི་རྒྱ་མཚོ The Pacific Ocean.

† མེ་གོ Chinese name of America.

‡ ཞབས and རྫང are equivalents of Mr.

§ པེ་ཅིང་། Tibetan name for Peking.

* མེ་གོ་ཁྲུ Chinese name for the American Legation at Peking.

† A Journey to Lhasa and Central Tibet.

‡ Remembering kindness.

§ As a token of the fulness of heart.

བོད་ཀྱི་བརྡ་སྤྲོད་པའི་གཞུང་།

སི་ཏུའི་སུམ་རྟགས་དང་སི་ཏུའི་ཞལ་ལུང་དང་དག་བྱེད་གསལ་བའི་མེ་ལོང་བཅས།

ཨིང་ཡིཤ་སྐད་དུ་གསལ་བར་བསྟན་པ་བཞུགས་སོ།

भोट व्याकरण ।

གཙང་བཀྲ་ཤིས་ལྷུན་པོ་ཡི་མཁན་ཆེན་རྡོ་རྗེ་འཆང་བླ་མ་དམ་པ་སེང་ཆེན་རིན་པོ་ཆེ་ཡི་

སློབ་མ།

བོད་ཀྱི་ཚིག་གི་གཏེར་མཛོད་དང་ལྷ་ས་བསམ་ཡས་དཔལ་ས་སྐྱ་བཀྲ་ཤིས་ལྷུན་པོ་རྒྱལ་མཁར་རྩེ་ཡར་འབྲུག་གཡུ་མཚོ་བསམ་ཤིང་དང་ཡར་ལུང་གནས་གསུམ་རྟེན་གསུམ་དང་ སྐྱིན་སློབ་གླིང་སོགས་མཐའ་བའི་ལམ་ཡིག་དང་ཁ་བ་ཅན་དུ་རྒྱ་གར་པཎ་ཏི་ཏ་སོགས་མཛད་པ་པོ་ལོ་པཎ་

ཤྲཱི་ཤ་རཏ་ཙནྡྲ་དཱས་བརྩམས།།

རབ་བྱུང་བཅོ་ལྔ་པའི་ཤིང་སྟག་ལོ་ཡི་ཟླ་བ་གསུམ་པའི་ཚེས་བཟང་པོ་ལ་ཡུལ་བང་ག་ལའི་རྒྱལ་ས་ཆེན་པོའི་དབུར་གནས་གདན་ས་རྡོ་རྗེ་གླིང་གི་པར་ཁང་དུ་པར་དུ་

བསྒྲུབས།

ཡེ་ཤུའི་འདས་ལོ་༡༩༡༤།།

བོད་ཀྱི་བརྡ་སྤྲོད་པའི་གཞུང་སོགས་བཞུགས་སོ།

THE GRAMMAR OF TIBET, &C.

༄༅།། དཀོན་མཆོག་གསུམ་ལ་ཕྱག་འཚལ་ལོ།།

Reverence to the Three Holies—Namo, Ratna, Trayāya.

"རྨད་བྱུང་ཐུགས་བསྐྱེད་སྐྱ་རེངས་ཀྱིས། ། བྷོ་ཊའི་ཡུལ་ལྗོངས་མཁར་དབྱིངས་སུ།
རྒྱལ་བསྟན་ཉིན་མོར་བྱེད་པའི་དཔལ། ། འདྲེན་མཛད་ཐོན་མིའི་ཞབས་ལ་འདུད། "
བརྡ་སྤྲོད་གཞུང་གི་དཀའ་གནད་མང་། ། གང་གིས་དང་པོར་གསལ་བར་བསྟན།
ཨིང་ལིཤ་སྐད་དུ་བཀྲན་ལ་ཕབ། ། ཀལ་ཀ་ཏ་རུ་པར་དུ་བསྒྲུབས།
ཧུང་གེ་རི་ཡི་མཁན་པོ་མཆོག ། ཙོ་མ་ཀོ་རོ་སི་ལ་གུས།།

I bow to the feet of Thon-mi Sam Bhota, (the father of Tibetan literature) who at the dawn(-ing) of the wonderful conception of Buddhism (in the Tibetan mind) made the religion of Buddha bright, as the day, in the vast country of Bhota (Tibet).

I honour (the memory of) Csoma de Körös, the great Hungarian scholar, who first interpreted in English, the many difficult points of Tibetan grammar, arranged them and published it (grammar) in Calcutta.

"གངས་རི་རི་ཁྲོད་ཀྱི་མཁས་པ་རྣམས། ། སྨྲ་བ་རི་ངག་སྦྱར་ལ་བརྟེན་ནས།
དོན་གྱི་མཚན་ཉིད་རབ་གསལ་སྣང་། ། བརྡ་སྤྲོད་གཞུང་གིས" བསྒྲིལ་བར་བྱས།།

The learned of Tibet—Assemblage of Snowy Mountains—for making clear the essential characteristics of meanings (of things that are) based on the construction of their speech, (by interpreting བརྡ་སྤྲོད་གཞུང orthœpy and orthography), framed its grammar.

Lhasa-Villa,
Darjeeling, 1914.

SARAT CHANDRA DAS.

THE CONTENTS OF THIS VOLUME:-

CONTENTS.

CONTENTS—*concld.*

CORRIGENDA.

Some egregious mistakes have occurred in the lower half of page 15 of the *Introduction*. It is here reproduced to enable the reader see what they are. He should read this rejecting the lower half of page 15 as incorrect.

The particle ཏུ is used after ག, བ and ད་དྲག *i.e.*, when a word closes with the letter ག or བ or ད་དྲག, such as ཏྲག་ཏུ, རབ་ཏུ, ཀུནད་ཏུ, མཆོརད་ཏུ, ཕ་རོལད་ཏུ།

The ཕྲད (particles) ཏུ and དུ are used after ང, ད, ན, མ, ར, ལ final letters in a word. སུ is used after words ending in ས, such as ཐོགས་སུ, གཡས་སུ། The ཕྲད (particle) ར is used after འ (expressed or understood), such as ལྷར་གསལ།

For the use of ལ and ན one, has not to look to the nature of the closing letter in a word. They may be used after the ten རྗེས་འཇུག letters such as ག, ང, ད, ན, བ, མ, འ, ར, ལ, ས། for example:—

ཐོག་ལ, ཐོག་ན། སྟེང་ལ, སྟེང་ན། ཐོད་ལ, ཐོད་ན། གདན་ལ, གདན་ན། རབ་ལ, རབ་ན། གམ་ལ, གམ་ན།
བཀའ་ལ, བཀའ་ན། ཤར་ལ, ཤར་ན། དཔལ་ལ, དཔལ་ན། དུས་ལ, དུས་ན།

The use of ཏུ after words ending in ག, བ and ད་དྲག is in conformity with the rule ཚིག་ཚིའི་ མིང་མཐའ་འདྲེན་པའི་ཚུལ།

The use of དུ after words ending in ང, མ, འ, ར conforms to the rule ཚིག་མི་མིག་འདྲེན་པ།

དུ is used after words ending in ད simply for easy pronunciation. Its use after words ending in ན, ར, ལ is according to the rule དཀའ་མཚུངས་དང་དུ་མེད་པས་བརྗོད་བདེ་འདྲེན་པའི་ལུགས།

The use of ཏུ after words ending in ག, བ and ད་དྲག;—of དུ after words ending in ང, མ;—of ར and རུ after words ending in འ as in མཐར or མཐའ་རུ;—of སུ after words ending in ས and also of དུ after words ending in ན, ར, ལ is according to the rule མིང་མཐའ་འདྲེན་ཚུལ། &c

Preface.

The first Grammar of the Tibetan language, in English, written by Alexander Csoma de Körös was published under the patronage of the Government and the auspices of the Asiatic Society of Bengal, in 1834. The scholarship which that Hungarian Traveller displayed in it, has not, in my humble opinion, been surpassed by any subsequent student of Tibetan. In this Introduction to the Grammar of the Tibetan Language, I have followed his work, supplementing it here and there with materials drawn from Situ-Sum-Tag, the exhaustive commentary on Thon-mi Sam Bhota's *Sum-chu-pa* and *Tag-jug-pa*.

During my second sojourn, in Tibet, in 1881 and 1882, I found a manuscript copy of Situ-Sum-Tag at Tashi-lhunpo, in the library of Sengchen Lama, Prime Minister of the Tashi Lama (*Tsang Panchen Rinpo-che*) Tanpai Wang-chug.

I got it copied for my use. In 1894, its importance to students of Tibetan Literature was explained by me to Sir Alfred Croft, then Director of Public Instruction in Bengal. He obtained the sanction of the Government of Bengal to publish it at State expense. The publication of the work was, however, indefinitely delayed for the want of a second copy to collate the text. It was only, in 1911, that I could secure a block-print copy of Situ-Sum-Tag from *Ekai* Kawaguchi, the well-known Japanese Tibetan Scholar and Traveller. That good Buddhist Monk has very kindly revised the book in proof which I was unable to do owing to weak sight and the smallness of the type used in printing it.

Alexander Csoma, in the preface of his Grammar, wrote as follows:—

"Tibet being considered as the headquarters of Buddhism in the present age, these elementary works (Tibetan Grammar and Dictionary) may serve as keys to unlock the immense volumes, (faithful translations of the Sanskrit text) which are still to be found in that country, on the manners, customs, opinions, knowledge, ignorance, superstition, hopes, and fears of the great part of Asia, especially India, in former ages."

What he hoped his two works would do, eighty years ago, has, in the meantime, been partly fulfilled. Following his footsteps, in the field of Tibetan literature, I have collected a few barley corns which, in the form of this compendious compilation, I present to the learned public. It may help the reader in his endeavour to study the literature of Tibet.

Orthography being the most difficult part of the Tibetan language, access to it from any side, is as difficult as entrance to the country itself, owing to the stupendous snowy barriers which encompass it.

Patiently crossing these when a traveller has entered the snow-girt tableland of Tibet, he will love to sojourn in it, because it is the most difficult, yet delightful country to travel, on the face of the earth.

The sportsman-traveller chases on its lofty plateau the finest games—the *dong* (wild-yak), the *kyang* (wild-ass), the *ovis-polis* གཉན, the *ovis ammon*, and ibex, &c , animals that are unknown in any other part of the globe.

In like manner, the student who has entered the field of Tibetan literature will find in it new matters for study.

This compilation, it is hoped, will be useful to students going up for the Matriculation and the Bachelor of Arts Examinations of the Calcutta University, as also to Government Officers, who choose to pass High Proficiency and Honours Examinations in Tibetan.

The necessary texts for these examinations are given in it.

THE COMPILATION COMPRISES :—

Introduction to the Grammar of the Tibetan Language.
Extracts from the Yig-kur Nam-shag. *
Diary of a Journey to Lhasa from Gyan-tse, in Tibetan.
Sumpa Khan-po's Life of the Buddha (extracts from *Pagsam Jonzang*).
Kahlon Gûng-thang-pa's Life of the present Dalai Lama.
Dag-Je Salwai Melong. †
SITU SUMTAG.
Situi Shal-lûng. ‡
Tshang-yang Gya-tsho's gûl-lû.

Besides these, there are given several appendices containing specimens of composition in chaste, idiomatic Tibetan.

---

* ཡིག་བསྐུར་རྣམ་གཞག། (forms of correspondence) and *Pagsam Jonzang*, edited by Sarat Chandra Das, were published by the Government of Bengal in 1901; Bengal Secretariat Book Depôt, Calcutta.

† དག་བྱེད་གསལ་བའི་མེ་ལོང་། Metrical Spelling-Book and Dictionary.

‡ སི་ཏུའི་ཞལ་ལུང་། Commentary of the *Sum-chu-pa* and *Tag-Jug-pa* by Lama Dharma Bhadra of Ñul-chu in Tsang.

Author's Introduction

TO

Situ Sum-tag.

Reverence to Çākya Simha, who is adored by all perfected *Bodhisattvas* including the unerring Mañju ghoṣa and others, and whose very memory removes all fears from the minds of all despondent sinners.

In accordance with the prophecy of our Teacher, in the Mañju Çrī mûla Tantra, there reigned at Lha-ḻdan (Lhasa) in Central Tibet, a succesion of *Dharma Rājās* sprung from the Li-tsa-bya race.* Among them, the most illustrious was Mihilha (*Naradeva*), surnamed Sroñ-ḇtsan sgam-po the wise and just king. Among his many eminent ministers, Thu-mi SamBhoṭa ‡ was distinguished for his literary aptitude and attainments. In obedience to the command of his King, impelled by the earnest prayers (of a former life) for acquiring *Bodhi* (spiritual enlightenment) he proceeded to *Ārya deça* (India). There he studied the Arts, both of the Brāhmaṇs and the Buddhists, under *Paṇḍita* Deva-vid Simha (in Tibetan, Lha-rigpaẖi Séngé), the Brāhmaṇ Lipikara (in Tibetan Libyin *i.e.*, *Lipi-datta* and other eminent teachers.

On his return to Tibet, he resided in the castle of Maru near Lhasa where he shaped the Tibetan character after the model of the *Nāgari.* † He wrote eight grammatical works, out of which, Sum-ṟtags only is extant to this day. This work comprises two books namely, Sum-chu-pa and Ṟtags-kyi ẖjug-pa which treat of the orthography and orthoëpy of the Tibetan language.

The Sum-chu-pa is embodied in thirty verses and forms the basis of Tibetan grammar. Hence its name, in Sanskrit, is *Vyā-karaṇa mûla trimsat nāma*, in Tibetan : Luñ ston-pa ṟtsa-wa Sum-chu-pa.

After reverentially bowing to Buddha, the most rare One, the author Thu-mi SamBhoṭa begins his work with salutation to Mañju ghoṣa, the lord of speech.

Who this Mañju ghoṣa was the commentator explains with a quotation from the work Mtshan yañ-dag-par ḇrjyoḏ-pa "The master of speech is the *jñāna kāya* (ye-çes sku) of Buddha. That *jñāna kāya* is self-existent. Mañju ghoṣa is, therefore, a *Jñānasattva* (Ye-çes-sems-ḏpaẖ). He is not to be understood as being an ordinary *Bodhisattva* who has attained to the ten stages (*Daça Bhû-mi*) of *Bodhisattva* spiritual perfection.

He exists in the heart of all the *Tathāgatas i.e.*, represents the spiritual wisdom of all the Buddhas.
ཡེ་ཤེས་སེམས་དཔའ་ཞེས་བྱ་བ་དེ་བཞིན་གཤེགས་པ་ཐམས་ཅད་ཀྱི་ཐུགས་ཀ་ན་གནས་པའི་ཕྱིར་རོ།

Thu-mi then makes salutation to *Sadāçiva*, the God Maheçvara of the Brāhmaṇs, saying that he it was who first taught the Arts to them.

---

* The *Liccavi* people of Vaiçāli in Magadha, during the Buddha's time.

† The *Bengalī*, *Newarī*. and *Tibetan* characters, closely resemble one another, all three having had their origin in Mithila and having been shaped after the model of the form of *Devanagari* that was current there in the seventh century A. D. The ancient *Maithili* character bears a striking resemblance to the *Lun-tsha* (or *Rañjā*, of Nepal) or the ornamental *Deva nāgari* which was little known in India.

‡ In some grammetical works he is called Thon mi SamBhota Anubi-bu *i.e*, Thon-mi, the son of Anu. The name SamBhota signifying the good Bhota (or Tibetan) was given to him by his Indian Teachers. **Anu** was his mother. He was called Anubi bu in the manner the chief disciple of the Buddha was called *Cāriputtra* (in Tibetan Cāribi-bu) the son of *Cārī* or *Cārikā* or *Sāradhvatī.*

གང་གིས་མིང་གཞི་ཐོན་གསུངས་པ།	རྟག་ཞི་བ་ལ་ཕྱག་འཚལ་ལོ།
སློབ་སྦྱོར་ལེགས་མཛད་མཁས་རྣམས་དང་།	བླ་མ་ལ་ཡང་ཕྱག་འཚལ་ནས།
✢ ✢ ✢ ✢ ✢ ✢ ✢ ✢	ཡི་གེ འི་སྦྱོར་བ་བཤད་པར་བྱ།།

The above points to Thu-mi SamBhoṭa's having had his education in the University of Mithilā Rgya-gar lho-phyogs (India in the southern direction from Lhasa) and that under Brāhmaṇical professors. It is a remarkable coincidence that at this period the famous Chinese pilgrim-traveller Yuan-chuang should have been studying Sanskrit in the Buddhist University of Nālanda in Magadha having travelled to India by the northern route under the auspices of Emperor Tāitsung, King Sroṅ-btsan's father-in-law. Had Thu-mi SamBhoṭa been a student of Sanskrit at Nālanda at the time, he could hardly have escaped the notice of so keen an observer as the Chinese traveller.

So grateful was the earliest Tibetan student of Sanskrit that he did not forget to reverence his teacher and professors in the beginning of his grammar. He thus commences his work:—Having made profound salutations to those most skilful in orthography etc., and also to my *Guru* and holding that letters are the basis of speech, of all learning * and teachings, † and also of words and expressions, I should explain the method of their construction by the combination and collocation (of letters) §.

SUM-CHU-PA.

Letters are *Ā-li* and *Kā-li.* *Ā-li* includes the four vowels: u, i, e and o, which are based on ཨ *a.* The thirty letters of the alphabet ending in ཨ *a* are all comprised in *Kā-li.* These are arranged into seven and half groups called *sde* (*Varga*), each group consisting of four letters. They are all consonants. These are again divided into three classes: *rjes-hjug*, *sṅon-hjug* and *miṅ-gshi* letters. The ten letters ག, ང, ད, ན, བ, མ, འ, ར, ལ, ས are *rjes hjug*; out of these ག, ད, བ, མ, འ are called *sṅon-hjug.* The remaining twenty letters of the alphabet ཀ་ཁ་ཅ་ཆ་ཇ་ཉ་ཏ་ཐ་པ་ཕ་ཙ་ཚ་ཛ་ཝ་ཞ་ཟ་ཡ་ཤ་ཧ་ཨ། are called *miṅ-gshi.* These, in any sort of combination of two, three or four letters among themselves or with the four vowels never form a word, though individually they often are words themselves.

Letters are combined together to form words when no inter-syllabic point or stop ཚེག (་) occurs between them. The word ལག is a combination of the two letters, ལ and ག; ལགས is a combination of the three letters ལ, ག. and ས; འབངས is a combination of the four letters འ, བ, ང and ས. But with the twenty *miṅ-gshi* letters such combinations in two, three or four, with or without the vowels, no words in the Tibetan language can be formed; for instance, ཀཅ, ཁཆཇ, ཛཀིཚ, ཉཛྫ, ཕཞེཏ, ཚཤཀཨ, &c., are no words at all, the Tibetan tongue being not capable of pronouncing such combinations.

---

* This includes the *Vedas* of the Brāhmans. † This comprises the *Buddhist çikṣā i.e.*. the teachings of the Buddha ཡི་གེའི་སྦྱོར་བ yi-gehi byor-wa (*Akṣara yojanā.* §

TAG-JUG-PA.

རྟགས་འཇུག་པ།

The letters of the alphabet are distinguished, in consideration of the nature of their sounds, by assigning to them five genders, namely: ཕོ masculine, མ་ནིང neuter, མོ feminine, ཤིན་ཏུ་མོ very feminine and མོ་གཤམ sub-feminine or barren.

The four vowels called ཨཱ་ལི་བཞི *i*, *u*, *e*, *o* are considered as being feminine in their nature, and the thirty letters of the alphabet called ཀཱ་ལི are conventionally regarded as masculine for their combination with the vowels. It may be remembered that the thirty letters have been arranged in seven and half སྡེ series. The first letters of the first four series such as ཀ, ཅ, ཏ, and པ are classed as ཕོ masculine; the four second letters of the same series such as ཁ, ཆ, ཐ and ཕ are classed as མ་ནིང neuter; the four third letters of the four series such as ག, ཇ, ད and བ are classed as མོ feminine; and the last four letters of the same four series such as ང, ཉ, ན and མ are classed as ཤིན་ཏུ་མོ very feminine. Out of the fourteen letters of the remaining three and half series ཙ being akin to ཅ is taken as ཕོ; ཚ being like ཆ is classed as མ་ནིང and ཛ being like ཇ is taken as མོ feminine. The letter ཝ being similar in sound to བ is also classed with it as མོ feminine. The six letters ཞ, ཟ, འ, ཡ, ཤ and ས are classed as feminine. Of the remaining four letters ར, ལ, ཧ are regarded as མོ་གཤམ sub-feminine and ཨ is said to possess no gender, it being the basis of both ཨཱ་ལི and ཀཱ་ལི letters.

This distinction in gender is said to have arisen owing to the perceptible difference in the tone or accent of the letters such as hard, soft or low, &c., which is due to the place of their origin. Those that are sounded hard or strongly *i.e.* with some exertion (བྱེད་རྩོལ་ཤུགས་ཆེ་བ) are classed as ཕོ masculine, those that are sounded moderately (རན་པ) are classed as མ་ནིང neuter. Letters that are sounded low or with some ease (ཆུང་ཟད་ཆུང་བའམ་སྒྲོད are classed as མོ feminine. Those possessing still lower or softer sound are classed as ཤིན་ཏུ་མོ very feminine. The very softly sounded letters (ཤིན་ཏུ་རྩོལ་བ་སྒྲོད་ཅིང་ཞན) are classed as མོ་གཤམ sub-feminine or barren. The last letter of the alphabet ཨ is regarded as being མཚན་མེད genderless.

Among the མིང་གཞི letters ཀ་ཅ་ཏ་པ་ཙ are ཕོ masculine; ཁ་ཆ་ཐ་ཕ་ཚ are མ་ནིང neuter letters; ག་ཇ་ད་བ་ཛ་ཝ་ཞ་ཟ་འ་ཡ་ཤ་ས are མོ feminine; ང་ཉ་ན་མ are ཤིན་ཏུ་མོ very feminine; ར་ལ་ཧ are མོ་གཤམ sub-feminine or barren.

སྔོན་འཇུག་གི་རྟགས་ཀྱི་འཇུག་པ། Gender in the five སྔོན་འཇུག letters.

There is also conventional distinction, in gender, among the five སྔོན་འཇུག *prefixes* ག, ད, བ, མ and འ. The letter བ (which as a མིང་གཞི letter is མོ feminine) should be regarded as ཕོ masculine when used as a *prefix*. The letters ག and ད (which as མིང་གཞི letters were classed as མོ feminine) should be regarded as མ་ནིང neuter when used as *prefixes*. The letter འ is མོ feminine and མ is ཤིན་ཏུ་མོ very feminine. This distinction of sex in the five སྔོན་འཇུག *prefix* letters is not due to the high, strong or low tone or accentuation in the letters themselves but simply for the purpose of their combination with the མིང་གཞི letters for forming words and for determining their sounds.

On the use of the five *prefixes* སྔོན་འཇུག—ག་ད་བ་མ་འ.

The following rules are observed in attaching the five *prefix* letters to the thirty letters of the alphabet which being the basis of all words are called མིང་གཞི *basics*.

(1) ཕོ་ནི་ཕོ་དང་མོ་ལ་འཇུག། ཕོ masculine (letters) should be attached to ཕོ and མོ (masculine and feminine) letters.

(2) མོ་ནི་མོ་དང་མ་ནིང་ལ་འཇུག། མོ feminine (letters) should be attached to མོ and མ་ནིང (feminine and neuter) letters.

(3) མ་ནིང་ཡང་ནི་ཕོ་མོ་ལའོ། མ་ནིང neuter (letters) also should be attached to ཕོ and མོ (masculine and feminine) letters.

(4) ཤིན་ཏུ་མོ་ནི་མ་ནིང་དང་། མོ་དང་ཤིན་ཏུ་མོ་ཉིད་ལའོ།། ཤིན་ཏུ་མོ very feminine (letters) should be attached to མ་ནིང neuter, མོ feminine and ཤིན་ཏུ་མོ very feminine letters.

ག

The letter ག as a *Prefix*.

The letter ག as མ་ནིང (neuter) among the five སྔོན་འཇུག letters is prefixed to ཅ, ཏ, ཙ which are classed as ཕོ masculine among the seven and half *series* of the thirty མིང་གཞི letters for example: གཅིག, གཏམས, གཙང་།

ག as མ་ནིང is prefixed to ཉ, ད, ན, ཞ, ཟ, ཡ, ཤ, ས when they are རྐྱང་འཇུག used singly being classed as མོ feminine among the མིང་གཞི letters, for example: གཉེར, གདངས, གནས, གཞལ, གཟུགས, གཡས, གཤམ, གསལ།

ད

The letter ད as a *Prefix*.

The letter ད as མ་ནིང among the སྔོན་འཇུག letters is prefixed to ཀ and པ (when རྐྱང་པ་ or རྡོགས་འཕྱུལ) which are ཕོ among the མིང་གཞི letters, such as དཀོན. དཔའ། དཀྱིལ, དཀྱིགས, དཔྱད།

ད is prefixed to ག and བ (when རྐྱང་པ or འདོགས་འཛུལ) * which are མོ among the མིང་གཞི letters, for example: དགའ, དབང། དགྱེས, དགྲམ, དབྱངས, དབྱིག།

ད is prefixed to ང and མ (when རྐྱང་པ) which are མོ among the མིང་གཞི letters, for example: དངར དམར།

བ

The letter བ as a *Prefix*.

The letter བ as ཕོ masculine among the སྔོན་འཇུག letters is prefixed to words that are based on ཀ, ཅ, ཏ, ཙ which are regarded as ཕོ among the thirty མིང་གཞི letters; བ is also prefixed to words formed with ག, ང, ཇ, ཉ, ད, ན, ཛ, ཞ, ར, ཤ, ས which are classed as མོ feminine among the མིང་གཞི letters. བ may be used before ཀ and ག when they are simply joined with any of the vowels,† superscribed or subjoined, or both superscribed and subjoined ‡ for example: བཀའ, བགོས། བསྐོ, བསྐོན, བཀལ, བརྐོ། § བཀྲི, བཀྲུག, བཀྲག,། བསྐྱིད, བསྐུན, བསྐྱུད, བསྐྱིངས, བསྐྱད, བསྐྱགས།

བ is prefixed to ཏ, ཙ, ད when they are either རྐྱང་འཛུལ or བརྟགས་འཛུལ། for example: བཏགས, བཙགས, བདག། བཏུས, བརྩའ, བརྩོད, བདེ, བརྡད།

བ is prefixed to ང, ཇ, ཉ, ན, ཛ when they are only བརྟགས་འཛུལ superscribed, for example: བརྡ, བརྗགས, བརྗོད, བརྙས, བརྙིན, བརྙོག, བསྙན, བརྫང།

བ is prefixed to ཅ, ཞ, ཤ when they are only རྐྱང་པ། for example: བཅས, བཞིད, བཤད།

བ is prefixed to ཟ, ས when they are either རྐྱང་པ or འདོགས་འཛུལ། subjoined, for example: བཟང, བཟས; བསམ; བཟླས; བསླངས།

བ is prefixed to ར when it is only འདོགས་འཕྱུལ། subjoined, for example: བརླངས, བརླག།

མ

The letter མ as a *Prefix*.

The letter མ as ཤིན་ཏུ་མོ very feminine among the five སྔོན་འཇུག letters is prefixed to ཁ, ཆ, ཐ, ཚ which are མ་ནིང neuter and to ག, ཇ, ད, ཛ which are classed as མོ feminine among the མིང་གཞི letters, for example: མཁའ, མཆན, མཐོང, མཚན། མགུ, མཇེད, མདོག, མཛད

མ is prefixed to ང, ཉ, ན (when they are རྐྱང་པ) being classed as ཤིན་ཏུ་མོ among the མིང་གཞི letters, for example: མངོན, མཉམ, མནབས།

མ is prefixed to ཁ and ག when they are either རྐྱང་འཕུལ or འདོགས་འཕུལ། for example མཁྱེན, མཁྲངས, མགྱོགས, མགྲིན།

འ

THE LETTER འ AS A *Prefix.*

The letter འ as མོ feminine among the སྔོན་འཇུག letters is prefixed to ག, ཇ, ད, བ, ཛ (when རྐྱང་པ) which are classed as མོ among the མིང་གཞི letters, for example: འགོད, འཇམ, འདམ, འབོལ, འཛོམས

འ is prefixed to ཁ, ཆ, ཐ, ཕ, ཚ (when རྐྱང་པ) being classed as མ་ནིང neuter among the མིང་གཞི letters, for example: འཁོར, འཆར, འཐད, འཕགས, འཚོལ།

འ is prefixed to ཁ, ག, ཕ, བ when they are འདོགས་འཕུལ subjoined, for example: འཁྲིད འགྲིལ, འཕྲད, འབྲེལ།

HINTS ON THE USE OF CERTAIN DIACRITICAL MARKS OR STOPS CALLED ཤད (Çad)

The full-stop (.) is represented by two vertical lines (||) called ཉིས་ཤད or double-stops. The single stop (|) called ཚིག་ཤད generally represents the comma. The ཤད is broad on the top and pointed at the foot resembling a pin, and as such it is used in the block-prints of Tibet.

In prose-writings the double vertical line-mark ཉིས་ཤད is generally used at the end of a sentence or passage.

---

* རྐྱང་པ or རྐྱང་འཕུལ a letter in its simple form or when it is joined with any of the four vowel signs, (representing i, u, e and o) is called རྐྱང་འཕུལ r̲Kyan̂-h̲phul or འདོགས་ཅན།

† བརྩེགས་མ or བརྩེགས་འཕུལ a surmounted or superscribed letter such as རྐ, སྐ, ལྐ, སྣ།

‡ འདོགས་འཕུལ a subjoined letter such as ཀྱ ཀྲ, ཀླ, དྭ།

§ བརྩེགས་འདོགས་འཕུལ a letter when it is both superscribed and subjoined, such as སྒྲ (here the letter ག has ས on its head and ར at its foot.)

N.B.—When a letter in its simple or compound form is joined with any of the four vowel-signs called གི་གུ (ི), ཞབས་ཀྱུ (ུ), འགྲེང་བུ (ེ), ན་རོ (ོ) representing i, u, e and o, it is called ཕྱག་སྐྱེད་ཅན། for example: འདི, དགུ, བསྡེ, བརྗོ། In these ད, ག, ས, ར are all ཕྱག་སྐྱེད་ཅན།

The single line-mark ཚིག་ཤད also called རྐྱང་ཤད is used at the end of an expression or prose line which has not concluded but is continuing.

Tibetan grammarians consider it necessary to put ཉིས་ཤད (double-stops) at the end of each line (རྐང་པ or foot) in a verse. It is, however, usual to divide the ཉིས་ཤད into two separate ones, putting one immediately at the end of the first foot and the other at the beginning of the succeeding foot.

The ཚིག་ཤད is also used at the end of an address or vocative expression, either in prose or poetry.

The conclusion or termination of a section or chapter is marked by four vertical line-marks or བཞི་ཤད When a sentence or expression terminates in a word ending in ག or ང, it is necessary to put a ཚེག inter-syllabic point (') to the left of the ཤད in a line with its top. The use of the inter-syllabic point (') before འོ, ཙུ and འམ is optional for the purpose of metrical convenience, in poetry. It is generally not used.

The following extracts from the grammatical work called ཙང་གསལ་འབྲུལ་གྱི་སྒྲེ་མིག by དབྱངས་ཅན་དགའ་བའི་བློ་གྲོས Yangchan Gah-wai Lodoi, High-priest of the monastery of Dolonor (མཚོ་བདུན) in Mongolia (during the hierarchy of the fourth Tālahi Lama ཏཱ་ལའི་བླ་མ་ཡོན་ཏན་རྒྱ་མཚོ) illustrate the use of the ཤད and ཚིག་པར་ཚེག (stops and inter-syllabic point.)

ཚིགས་བཅད་རྐང་པའི་མཐའ་ལ་ནི། ། ཉིས་ཤད་ངེས་པར་འཐོབ་པ་ཡིན།
། ག་མཐར་ཚིག་ཤད་ང་ཡི་མཐར། ། ཤད་ཀྱི་གོང་དུ་ཕྱི་ཚེག་དགོས།

ང་ཡིག་གི་རྐང་པ་ཤད་དང་མི་འདྲེ་བའི་ཆད་ཡིན།།

ཚིགས་སླུགས་ལ་ནི་རྫོགས་ཚིག་མཐར། ། ཉིས་ཤད་རྣམ་གྲངས་སོ་སོ་དང་།
། དོན་ཚན་ཕལ་ཆེར་མཐར་དང་ནི། ། བོད་པའི་སྐབས་ལའང་ཚིག་ཤད་བྱ།
། སྡེ་ཚན་ཆེན་པོ་རྫོགས་པ་དང་། ། ལེའུའི་མཚམས་སུ་བཞི་ཤད་འཐོབ།
། རྐང་པ་སྙོང་དང་མི་སྙོང་ལས། ། འོ་ཙུ་འམ་གྱི་ཚེག་པར་ཡང་།

།འཐོབ་རྒྱལ་སྐབས་དང་སྦྱར་བར་བྱ།།

Some Hints to Readers.

It is necessary to give here some hints on the method of writing dates, which is peculiar to Tibet, as without a knowledge of it, the reader will find some difficulty in reading Tibetan correspondence and historical works.

There are two methods of reckoning time in Tibet, namely, the cycle of twelve years, called ལོ་འཁོར་བཅུ་གཉིས *Lo-khor chu-ñi* and the cycle of sixty years called ལོ་འཁོར་དྲུག་ཅུ *Lo-khor dug-chu*; the former is generally used in estimating the age of individuals, the latter in calculating the dates of all important events.

The years of the cycle, of twelve years, are named after the names of the following animals: བྱི་བ mouse, གླང ox, སྟག tiger, ཡོས, hare, འབྲུག dragon, སྦྲུལ serpent, རྟ horse, ལུག sheep, སྤྲེ ape, བྱ bird, ཁྱི dog and ཕག hog. They are counted in the following order:—

ལོ་འཁོར་བཅུ་གཉིས *Cycle of 12 years.*

Names in Tibetan.		As written.		As spoken.	Meaning.
1.	བྱི་ལོ	(byi-lo	...	*chee-lo*)	the mouse-year.
2.	གླང་ལོ	(glan-lo	...	*lang-lo*)	the ox-year.
3.	སྟག་ལོ	(stag-lo	...	*tag lo*)	the tiger-year.
4.	ཡོས་ལོ	(yos-lo	...	*yo-lo*)	the hare-year.
5.	འབྲུག་ལོ	(ẖbrul-lo	...	*dug-lo*)	the dragon-year.
6.	སྦྲུལ་ལོ	(sbrul-lo	...	*dul-lo*)	the serpent-year.
7.	རྟ་ལོ	(ṟta-lo	...	*ta-lo*)	the horse-year.
8.	ལུག་ལོ	(lug-lo	...	*loog-lo*)	the sheep-year.
9.	སྤྲེ་ལོ	(spre-lo	...	*teh-lo*)	the ape-year.
10.	བྱ་ལོ	(bya-lo	...	*chah-lo*)	the bird-year.
11.	ཁྱི་ལོ	(khyi-lo	...	*khee-lo*)	the dog-year.
12.	ཕག་ལོ	(phag-lo	...	*phag-lo*)	the hog-year.

These Tibetan names correspond to the Chinese names of the twelve animals and are said to have been first introduced in Tibet by Queen Wenchang, daughter of Emperor T'ai-tsung, who was married to King Mihi Lha surnamed Srong-tsan Gampo, in about 635 A. D. About a century later, the system of astrology then prevalent in China, which contained a cycle of sixty years, was introduced in Tibet. At a later period, in about 1026 A. D., with the introduction of *Kāla Chakra Tantras*, the Indian Cycle of sixty years called the *Vrihaspati Chakra* was brought to Tibet from S'rīdhânya Kaṭaka (དཔལ་ལྡན་འབྲས་སྤུངས Sanchi Topes ?), situated on the River Kriṣṇā near modern Amraoti, in Southern India

This cycle had a distinct name for each year of the series, but the Chinese cycle was made up by combining the names of the five elements, * namely: *wood* ཤིང, *fire* མེ, *earth* ས, *iron* ལྕགས, *water* ཆུ with those of the cycle of twelve years. These are made ten by affixing the signs of masculine and feminine genders *i.e.*, ཕོ and མོ to the elements.

The names of the years of the Indian Cycle of 60 years, in Tibetan, are as follows:—

Indian cycle of 60 years as Tibetanized. (See Appendix V).

1.	ཤིང་བྱི	(çiñ-byi)	*wood-mouse.*	2.	ཤིང་གླང	(çiñ-glañ)	*wood-ox.*
3.	མེ་སྟག	(mé-stag)	*fire-tiger.*	4.	མེ་ཡོས	(mé-yos)	*fire-hare.*
5.	ས་འབྲུག	(sa-ḫbrûg)	*earth-dragon.*	6.	ས་སྦྲུལ	(sa-sbrûl)	*earth-serpent.*
7.	ལྕགས་རྟ	(lcags-rta)	*iron-horse.*	8.	ལྕགས་ལུག	(lcags lûg)	*iron-sheep.*
9.	ཆུ་སྤྲེ	(chû spre)	*water-ape.*	10.	ཆུ་བྱ	(chu-bya)	*water-bird.*
11.	ཤིང་ཁྱི	(çiñ-khyi)	*wood-dog.*	12.	ཤིང་ཕག	(çiñ phag)	*wood-hog.*
13.	མེ་བྱི	(mé-byi)	*fire-mouse.*	14.	མེ་གླང	(mé-glañ)	*fire-ox.*
15.	ས་སྟག	(sa-stag)	*earth-tiger.*	16.	ས་ཡོས	(sa-yos)	*earth-hare.*
17.	ལྕགས་འབྲུག	(lcags-ḫbrûg)	*iron-dragon.*	18.	ལྕགས་སྦྲུལ	(lcags-sbrûl)	*iron-serpent.*
19.	ཆུ་རྟ	(chû-rta)	*water-horse.*	20.	ཆུ་ལུག	(chu-lug)	*water-sheep.*

* The Indian names of the *Pañcha bhuta* five elements are: earth, fire, air, ether or voidity and water.

21.	ཤིང་སྤྲེ	(çin̂-spre)	*wood-ape.*	22	ཤིང་བྱ	(çin̂-bya)	*wood-bird.*
23.	མེ་ཁྱི	(mé-khyi)	*fire-dog.*	24.	མེ་ཕག	(mé phag)	*fire-hog.*
25.	ས་བྱི	(sa-byi)	*earth-mouse.*	26.	ས་གླང	(sa-glan)	*earth ox.*
27.	ལྕགས་སྟག	(lcags-stag)	*iron-tiger.*	28.	ལྕགས་ཡོས	(lcags-yos)	*iron-hare.*
29.	ཆུ་འབྲུག	(chû-hbrûg)	*water-dragon.*	30.	ཆུ་སྦྲུལ	(chû sbrûl)	*water-serpent.*
31.	ཤིང་རྟ	(çin̂-rta)	*wood-horse.*	32.	ཤིང་ལུག	(çin̂ lug)	*wood-sheep.*
33.	མེ་སྤྲེ	(mé-spre)	*fire ape.*	34.	མེ་བྱ	(mé-bya)	*fire bird.*
35.	ས་ཁྱི	(sa-khyi)	*earth-dog.*	36.	ས་ཕག	(sa-phag)	*earth-hog.*
37	ལྕགས་བྱི	(lcags byi)	*iron-mouse.*	38	ལྕགས་གླང	(lcags-glan̂)	*iron-ox.*
39.	ཆུ་སྟག	(chû-stag)	*water-tiger.*	40.	ཆུ་ཡོས	(chû-yos)	*water hare.*
41.	ཤིང་འབྲུག	(çin̂-hbrûg)	*wood dragon.*	42.	ཤིང་སྦྲུལ	(çin̂ sprûl)	*wood-serpent.*
43.	མེ་རྟ	(mé rta)	*fire horse.*	44.	མེ་ལུག	(mé-lûg)	*fire-sheep.*
45.	ས་སྤྲེ	(sa-spre)	*earth-ape.*	46.	ས་བྱ	(sa-bya)	*earth bird.*
47.	ལྕགས་ཁྱི	(lcags-khyi)	*iron-dog.*	48.	ལྕགས་ཕག	(lcags-phag)	*iron-hog.*
49.	ཆུ་བྱི	(chû-byi)	*water-mouse.*	50.	ཆུ་གླང	(chu-glan)	*water-ox.*
51.	ཤིང་སྟག	(çin̂-stag)	*wood tiger.*	52.	ཤིང་ཡོས	(çin̂ yos)	*wood hare.*
53.	ས་འབྲུག	(mé-hbrûg)	*fire-dragon.*	54.	མེ་སྦྲུལ	(mé-sbrul)	*fire-serpent.*
55.	ས་རྟ	(sa-rta)	*earth-horse.*	56.	ས་ལུག	(sa lûg)	*earth-sheep.*
57.	ལྕགས་སྤྲེ	(lcags-spré)	*iron-ape.*	58.	ལྕགས་བྱ	(lcags-bya)	*iron-bird.*
59.	ཆུ་ཁྱི	(chû-khyi)	*water-dog.*	60.	ཆུ་ཕག	(chu-phag)	*water-hog.*

In the above serial enumeration of the names of the years of the *Vrihaspati Chakra* (Indian cycle), it will appear, that the name of each animal of the smaller cycle coupled with the names of the elements, occurs five times, for instance: བྱི *mouse* appears in the first year with ཤིང *wood*, 13th year with མེ *fire*, 25th year with ས *earth*, 37th year with ལྕགས *iron*, and in the 49th year with ཆུ *water*. Thus the twelve animals being joined with the five elements make up the number sixty of the cycle.

Chinese Cycle of 60 years.

1. ཤིང་ཕོ་བྱི wood *m.* mouse.
2. ཤིང་མོ་གླང wood *f.* ox.
3. མེ་ཕོ་སྟག fire *m.* tiger.
4. མེ་མོ་ཡོས fire *f.* hare.
5. ས་ཕོ་འབྲུག earth *m.* dragon.
6. ས་མོ་སྦྲུལ earth *f.* serpent.
7. ལྕགས་ཕོ་རྟ iron *m.* horse.
8. ལྕགས་མོ་ལུག iron *f.* sheep.
9. ཆུ་ཕོ་སྤྲེ water *m.* ape.
10. ཆུ་མོ་བྱ water *f.* bird.
11. ཤིང་ཕོ་ཁྱི wood *m.* dog.
12. ཤིང་མོ་ཕག wood *f.* hog.
13. མེ་ཕོ་བྱི fire *m.* mouse.
14. མེ་མོ་གླང fire *f.* ox.
15. ས་ཕོ་སྟག earth *m.* tiger.
16. ས་མོ་ཡོས earth *f.* hare.
17. ལྕགས་ཕོ་འབྲུག iron *m.* dragon.
18. ལྕགས་མོ་སྦྲུལ iron *f.* serpent.
19. ཆུ་ཕོ་རྟ water *m.* horse.
20. ཆུ་མོ་ལུག water *f.* sheep.
21. ཤིང་ཕོ་སྤྲེ wood *m.* ape.
22. ཤིང་མོ་བྱ wood *f.* bird.
23. མེ་ཕོ་ཁྱི fire *m.* dog.
24. མེ་མོ་ཕག fire *f.* hog.
25. ས་ཕོ་བྱི earth *m.* mouse.
26. ས་མོ་གླང earth *f.* ox.
27. ལྕགས་ཕོ་སྟག iron *m.* tiger.
28. ལྕགས་མོ་ཡོས iron *f.* hare.
29. ཆུ་ཕོ་འབྲུག water *m.* dragon.
30. ཆུ་མོ་སྦྲུལ water *f.* serpent.
31. ཤིང་ཕོ་རྟ wood *m.* horse.
32. ཤིང་མོ་ལུག wood *f.* sheep.
33. མེ་ཕོ་སྤྲེ fire *m.* ape.
34. མེ་མོ་བྱ fire *f.* bird.
35. ས་ཕོ་ཁྱི earth *m.* dog.
36. ས་མོ་ཕག earth *f.* hog.
37. ལྕགས་ཕོ་བྱི iron *m.* mouse.
38. ལྕགས་མོ་གླང iron *f.* ox.
39. ཆུ་ཕོ་སྟག water *m.* tiger.
40. ཆུ་མོ་ཡོས water *f.* hare.
41. ཤིང་ཕོ་འབྲུག wood *m.* dragon
42. ཤིང་མོ་སྦྲུལ wood *f.* serpent.
43. མེ་ཕོ་རྟ fire *m.* horse.
44. མེ་མོ་ལུག fire *f.* sheep.
45. ས་ཕོ་སྤྲེ earth *m.* ape.
46. ས་མོ་བྱ earth *f.* bird.
47. ལྕགས་ཕོ་ཁྱི iron *m.* dog.
48. ལྕགས་མོ་ཕག iron *f.* hog.
49. ཆུ་ཕོ་བྱི water *m.* mouse.
50. ཆུ་མོ་གླང water *f.* ox.
51. ཤིང་ཕོ་སྟག wood *m.* tiger.
52. ཤིང་མོ་ཡོས wood *f.* hare.
53. མེ་ཕོ་འབྲུག fire *m.* dragon.
54. མེ་མོ་སྦྲུལ fire *f.* serpent.
55. ས་ཕོ་རྟ earth *m.* horse.
56. ས་མོ་ལུག earth *f.* sheep.
57. ལྕགས་ཕོ་སྤྲེ iron *m.* ape.
58. ལྕགས་མོ་བྱ iron *f.* bird.
59. ཆུ་ཕོ་ཁྱི water *m.* dog.
60. ཆུ་མོ་ཕག water *f.* hog.

In the above list of the years of the Chinese cycle the introduction of ཕོ་ *male* and མོ་ *female* in six of the five elements such as ཤིང་ཕོ་, ཤིང་མོ་; མེ་ཕོ་, མེ་མོ་; ས་ཕོ་, ས་མོ་; ལྕགས་ཕོ་, ལྕགས་མོ་; ཆུ་ཕོ་, ཆུ་མོ་ differentiates it from the Indian cycle as Tibetanized. In this, the ten elements (5 males and 5 females) coupled with the twelve animals of the smaller cycle, occur six times; thus making up the number 60 of the cycle.

The Tibetans, in calculating dates, use either the Indian or the Chinese cycle; when using the Indian cycle they some times mention the individual name of the year, (in Sanskrit or in translation) but often omit it.

In page 1, Appendix I, the date of the document is mentioned in the last line which runs thus: ཤིས་པའི་ཡི་གེ་ཆུ་སྟག་ཟླ་ཚེས་དགེ་བར letter dated on an auspicious day of the month in the year *water-tiger*. The *Karmapa* Hierarch Lama Theg-pai Dorje ཐེག་པའི་རྡོ་རྗེ who issued the ངོས་འཛིན (letter of identification) lived in the 12th cycle རབ་བྱུང་བཅུ་གཉིས། The year ཆུ་སྟག *water-tiger* was the 36th year of that cycle. It may be computed thus: 24 years of the 12th cycle+60 years of the 13th cycle+60 years of the 14th cycle+48 years of the 15th cycle=192. Deducting 192 from 1914, the present year, the year 1722 A.D. is obtained (see Appendix V).

In page 2, Appendix II, the date of the document occurs in the following passage ད་ཡང་འདིར་རབ་བྱུང་བཅོ་ལྔ་པའི་ནང་གི་སྣ་ཚོགས་ཞེས་པའི་ཆུ་ཕོ་རྟའི་ལོ། Then again, (to wit) here (at Lhasa) in the year called སྣ་ཚོགས Sans. *chitra* of the 15th cycle *i.e.*, the year *water horse* རབ་བྱུང་བཅོ་ལྔ is the present cycle, ཆུ་ཕོ་རྟ་ལོ is the Chinese name of its 16th year which corresponds with the year 1882 *Anno Domini.**

In page 4, Appendix III, the date of the *Pass port* granted to *Achárya* Purangiri by the Tashi Lama Paldan Yeçes, is dated (ཤིང་སྦྲུལ་ཟླ་ཚེས)† first of the 9th month, year *wood-serpent.*
༩ ༡

This Tashi Lama lived in the 13th cycle (རབ་བྱུང་བཅུ་གསུམ). The year *wood-serpent* of that cycle may be found out in the following manner: ཤིང་སྦྲུལ was the 39th year of the 13th cycle. When 28 is taken out of 60, there remains 22. Add 60 of the 14th cycle and 48 of the present cycle. Deducting the sum 130 from 1914, the present year, the year 1784 A.D., is obtained.

---

* This was the occasion of the marriage of the present Mahārājā of Sikkim, at Lhasa, with Princess Lhading named *Lha-cham* Yeçe Dolma ཡེ་ཤེས་སྒྲོལ་མ.

† The numbers of the month and day are written below ཟླ་བ month and ཚེས date in the manner it is done here.

In page 11, Appendix VI, ཆུ་རྟ་ཟླ་བ་གསུམ་པའི་ཚེས་ལ on (an auspicious) day in the 3rd month, of the year *water-horse* The Diary commenced in the month of April (the 3rd month of the year in the Tibetan calender) 1882.

It will appear from Appendix V, where the Sanskrit names of the years of the Indian cycle are given that the first year is called *Prabhava*, in Tibetan, རབ་བྱུང (pronounced *Rab-joong*). This was the year, according to the Buddhists of Tibet, when the Buddha was born at Kapilavástu. From this name the Indian cycle is designated *Rab joong*, in Tibet. The present year 1914 called *Ánanda*, in Sanskrit and ཤིང་སྟག (*wood-tiger*) in Tibetan, is the 48th year of the 15th cycle རབ་བྱུང་བཅོ་ལྔ, reckoning the beginning of the first cycle from the year 1026 A.D., when it was introduced in Tibet by one Chilu-Pandita. The 15th cycle will terminate in the year 1926 and the sixteenth cycle རབ་བྱུང་བཅུ་དྲུག will commence in the year 1927.

The Tibetans divide the year into lunar months calling them ཟླ་བ་དང་པོ first month, ཟླ་བ་གཉིས་པ second month, ... ཟླ་བ་བཅུ་གཉིས་པ twelfth month. ཟླ་བ (zla-va) pronounced *Dá-wa* signifies the moon, hence month. ཟླ་བ་དང་པོ (*Dá-wa dang-po*) the first month of the Tibetan year begins in February. There is no particular name for each month.

In page 193, of his Grammar, Alexander Csoma has the following passage:—

"The *Kála chakra* doctrine of Adi Buddha was delivered by S'ākya, in his 80th year, at S'rīdhānya Kataka upon the request of Chandra Bhadra, a king of S'ambhala who in his 99th year visited S'ākya there. Upon his return home, he compiled the *Múla Tantra*, in accordance with what he had heard from S'ākya, and two years afterwards he died. This work is the source of all the subsequent voluminous compilations, increased modifications and interpolations. In the *Múla Tantra*, S'ākya foretells to Chandra Bhadra 25 kings, who will reign at S'ambhala, each for 100 years. The six first of them are called *Dharma* Rájás and the others are styled *Kulika*. He foretells also that after 600 years from that date *Kulika* Kīrti (Yaçokīrti or the Ephiphanes of the Greeks ?) will succeed to the throne of S'ambhala, and that 800 years afterwards the *Mleccha* or Muhamadan religion will rise at Makha (Mecca)."

He conjectured that S'ambhala must have been the capital of a kingdom that flourished in the early centuries of Christ and that S'rīdhánya Kataka was the Cuttak of modern Orissa. The last of the kings of S'ambhala is, however, not mentioned in the *Mûla Tantra*. It is stated that a king named Samudra Vijaya arrived at S'ambhala in 618 A.D., and shortly after that the period called, in the Tibetan chronology, མེ་ཁ་རྒྱ་མཚོ (Me-kha-rgya-Mtsho), commenced. It is also stated that in 622 A.D., at Makha (Mecca) the Muhamadan religion was established. From what can be gathered from Tibetan historics and works on *Kāla Chakra* it may be conjectured that this S'ambhala, very probably, was the capital of the Bactrian Empire of the Eastern Greeks who had embraced Buddhism. It is also conjectured that the modern city of Balkh must have been the site of their latest capital. The name of King Menander (in Sans. Minendra) who erected a very lofty *chaitya* has been mentioned by the Kashmirian poet Kṣemendra, in the *Avadána Kalpalatá*, a work that was finished in about 1035 A.D.

Referring to Samudra Vijaya, Alexander Csoma in a foot note remarked: "This pretended King's arrival at S'ambhala in 622 A.D., has some coincidence with *Yezdejird*, the Persian King's taking refuge in the same country; for it is affirmed, that this prince, upon the fall of Seleucia, and the conquest of Persia by the Arabs, in 636, retired to Trans-Oxiana or Ferghana".

Symbolic names for certain numerals.

As regards the explanation of the period མེ་མཁའ་རྒྱ་མཚོ (Me-kha-rgya-Mtsho), it is hardly possible to arrive at it, without a knowledge of the Indian method of expressing numerals in symbolical names or terms. These are called གྲངས་བརྡ (numerical signs), for instance: the word (མཁའ, Sans. *Çûnya* voidity or sky is expressed by a zero (0). ལག (Sans. *kara*), the hand is a symbol for 2; so are (*Netra* or *chakṣu*) eyes, *Pakṣa* (the white and the dark lunations in the month), because there are two hands in man; two eyes in all animals, two wings in birds and two lunations, white and dark, in a month. In the same manner, the གྲངས or numeral, (one) is symbolically expressed by the terms *Çurīra*, (in Tibetan གཟུགས) body, *chandra* (ཟླ་བ) the moon, *Gandára* བསེ་རུ the rhinoceros, because all animals possess only one *body*, there is only one moon, and the rhinoceros has only one horn.

The numeral 3 is expressed by the symbolical terms *Loka*, (འཇིག་རྟེན) worlds, which according to Hindu conception, are three in number, *Guṇa* (ཡོན་ཏན) qualities or attributes which are three in humanity: *Satva*, *Raja*, *Tama*, and also *Agni* (མེ) fire which according to Hindu mythology are also three in kind.

The གྲངས་བརྡ numeral sign for 4 (four) are *Samudra* (རྒྱ་མཚོ) ocean; *Pada* (རྐང་) foot; *Veda* (རིག་བྱེད) Hindu scriptures; because beasts are quadrupeds *i.e.*, possessing four feet; there are four great oceans, according to Hindu cosmogony, on the surface of the globe. These four illustrations will enable the reader to understand what is signified by the expression མེ་མཁའ་རྒྱ་མཚོ།

In the use of the གྲངས་བརྡ numeral-signs, it is usual to count or write the figures indicated by the symbolical terms from right to left. མེ (fire) expresses 3, མཁའ (sky) o, and རྒྱ་མཚོ oceans, 4. If the order is reversed in the three 3, 0, 4 by putting them as 403 the correct figure is obtained.

The period expressed by 403 years, according to the *Kála chakra Múla Tantra* commenced at the rise of the Muhamadan religion at Mecca *i.e.*, in 622 A.D. If 403 be added to 622, the first year of the *Hejira*, the year 1025 A.D., is obtained. With the year called *Prabhava* in which S'ákya is believed to have been born, the date of introduction of the Tibetan *Rabjoong* Cycle begins. Tibetan historians affirm that *Kála chakra Tantras* and the *Vrihaspati* cycle were brought from Káshmir by an Indian Buddhist named ཙི་ལུ་པཎ་ཊི་ཏ *Tsi-lu* Pandita. At this time the Máháyána Buddhism greatly flourished in that country. The Avadána Kalpalata gives abundant testimony on that point. A list of གྲངས་བརྡ terms taken from Alex. Csoma's Grammar, is here attached. They may help the reader in his studies of Tibetan works on Astronomy, Astrology and Chronology.

The number 5 (five) is expressed by the following terms:

འབྱུང (བ) *Bhútam* the elements which, in Sanskrit, are five in number: earth, air fire, water and sky.

དབང (པོ) *Indriyam* the organs of sense which are five, such as hearing, seeing, smelling, tasting, and touching.

མདའ (Sans. *Vána*) the arrows of Cupid which are five in number.

ཕུང (པོ) *Skandha* the aggregates which according to Buddhist conception, constitute the body of a living being.

The number 6 (six) is indicated by མཚམས (*Dik*) the four cardinal points: north, east, south and west, besides the zenith and the nadir.

རོ་བྲོ *Rasa* taste which are six according to Indian ideas.

དུས *Ritu* or *Samaya* the seasons, which are six in Sanskrit works.

The number 7 (seven) is expressed by the following terms:

ཀླུ (*Nága*) snake-kings who are seven in the Hindu mythology.

དྲང་སྲོང (*Risi*) the deified sages who are represented in a group of seven stars in the sky in the constellation of the Great Bear.

རིམ་གཟའ (*Graha*) the recurring planets which are represented by the days of the week.

གཏེར *Koça* treasures, they are counted seven in Hindu mythology.

The number 8 (eight) as represented in words, are as follows:

ནོར (*Vasu*) the gods of wealth who are eight, according to Hindu mythology.

སྲེད (*Trisnă*) the passions.

རི (*Parvata*) great mountains which are eight in number in the Hindu *S'astras*

The number 9 (nine) is symbolized in the following terms:

རྩ (*S'irá or múla* roots; chief veins or the pulses; they are counted nine in Hindu medical works.

གཟའ *Graha* the 7 planets, with the two comets *Rāhu* and *Ketu* are the *Nava graha* who are propitiated by the Hindus for averting calamities.

བུ་ག *Chhidra* openings or passages in the body for excretions *i.e.*, *Nava chhidra*.

སྲིན་པོ *Răksasa* the cannibal goblins who are nine according to Hindu mythology.

The number 10 (ten) is expressed by only one word:

ཕྱོགས (*Dis'a*) quarters or points, which are ten: The four cardinal points, the four corners and the two, zenith and nadir, make the *daça-diça* the ten quarters.

The number 11 (eleven) is expressed by the names, འཕྲོག་བྱེད (*Hari*), the destroyer; དྲག་པོ (*Rudra*), བདེ་འབྱུང (*Sambhú*), དབང་ཕྱུག (*Içvara*) the all powerful One. The last name, in Lamaism, is identified with that of འཇིག་རྟེན་དབང་ཕྱུག or *Lokeçvara* who is represented as possessing eleven faces བཅུ་གཅིག་ཞལ།

The number 12 (twelve) is expressed by the names:

ཉི་མ (*Súrya*) the sun, his chariot, according to Hindu mythology, being drawn by twelve horses.

ཁྱིམ (*Griha*) the Zcdiacal signs or mansions which are twelve in number.

Method of transliteration of Tibetan into English.

In Tibetan writings the intersyllabic point (˙) ཚེག་བར་ཚེག is continuously used between every two syllables, as also, between every two words in an expression or sentence. Take for instance, the first sentence in Appendix I: ཕྱོགས་དུས་རབ་འབྱམས་རྒྱལ་བ་ཀུན་གྱི་འཕྲིན་ལས་པར་དབང་བསྐུར་ཞིང་།

Here the words are: ཕྱོགས, དུས, རབ་འབྱམས, རྒྱལ་བ, ཀུན་གྱི, འཕྲིན་ལས་པར, དབང་བསྐུར་ཞིང་།

In transliterating the above sentence, a hyphen will represent the intersyllabic point (˙) which will be used to divide every two or three syllables in a word thus: རབ་འབྱམས rab-ẖbyamṣ; རྒྱལ་བ ṟgyal-wa; ཀུན་གྱི kun-gyi; འཕྲིན་ལས་པར ẖphrin-laṣ-par; དབང་བསྐུར་ཞིང ḏwan̂-ḇṣkur-shin̂ With a view to enable the reader to distinguish one word from another the passage will be transliterated thus: Phyogṣ-duṣ-rab-ẖbyamṣ-ṟgyal-wa-kun-gyi-ẖphrin-laṣ-par ḏwan̂-ḇṣkur-shin̂ instead of as Phyogṣ-duṣ-rab-ẖbamṣ-ṟgyal-wa-kun-gyi-ẖphrin-laṣ-par-ḏwan̂-ḇṣkur-shin̂.

APPENDIX I. ངོས་འཛིན *

H̱jam-gliñ Yañṣ-paẖi khyon ṣpyi-dañ [the general public of *Dsamling* (Jambu dvipa).]

Bye-brag ṣbaṣ-yul H̱braṣ-mo ḻjoñ-kyi [particularly, of the hidden land of Demojoñ (Sikkim).]

Dge-ẖdun mi-ḏwañ sa-ṣkyoñ ḇkaẖ-ḇlon ldiñ ḇu-ḏpon sogṣ [the clergy, King-Ruler, minister, captains, sergeants etc.]

Ser-ṣkya m̱thaẖ-dag gsan-ciñ ñeṣ-gyur [priests and lay class, great and low, all hearing be sure.]

Sa-ṣkyoñ Mi-ḏwañ Chos-ṟgyal Sraṣ ẖdi ḇshin [whereas this son of the King-Ruler *Dharmarājā*.]

M̱do-khamṣ Kun-m̱khyen Situ Rinpo-cheẖi ḏwon Karma Rin-chen ñes don ḇstan ẖdsin-gyi sprul-paẖi skur [nephew of *Kun-khyen* Situ Rin-po-che of Do-kham (Lower Kham Province) *Karma* Rinchen n̂e-don Tan-zin's incarnation.]

H̱di-ga ḇdag-naṣ ñoṣ ẖdsin Khri-ẖdon m̱ñaẖ-gsol ḇgyiḏ ciñ [here from me having received indentification consecration and enthronement.]

M̱tshan Karma Sgrub-ḇrgyuḏ ḇstan-ẖdsin dar-ṟgyaṣ lhun-grub ñeṣ-don ḏwañ-po [name *Karma* Dub-gyu tanzin dargyé lhun-dub n̂é-don Wang-po.]

Sheṣ gsol-shiñ dge-tshul sloñ-gi ḏñoṣ-po yañ-dag-par ṣgrub ciñ [so named having successfully passed through the orders of Ge-tshul and Ge-loñ.]

Gsañ-ṣñags gsar-ṟñiñ-gi ḏwañ rjes-gnañ du-ma dañ [having received initiation in many secrets of the new and the older mysticism.]

Zab-khriḏ-ḇkaẖ-luñ sogṣ-kyi ṣmin-par ḇgyiṣ-naṣ [being turned an adept in the deeper mysteries, precepts, &c.

Rañ-lugṣ-kyi dgon-ṣde Karma Rab-ḇrtan gliñ [of his own sect the monasteries and religious institutions (called) *Karma* Rabtanling.]

Karma Ḇkra-çiṣ choṣ-ẖkhor-gliñ, Karma ẖchi-meḏ Yañṣ-ḏwen, Karma Sgrub ḇrgyuḏ ḇstan-dar gliñ sogṣ-kyi [*Karma* Tashichoi khor-ling, *Karma* Chi-mé yang wen, *Karma* dub-gyu tandar ling of &c.]

Spyi-khyab choṣ-rje-wo dam-par [as Lord spiritual and Director-General], ḏwan̂-ṣḇkur-wa yin-paṣ [has been consecrated.]

Ḇla-ma ñiḏ-naṣ ẖchaḏ ṟtsoḏ ḇrtsam gsum [the Lama himself (will do) the three—expounding, discussing and composing (religious matters).] *thoṣ ḇsam ṣgom gsum-gyi ṣgo-naṣ* [from the three points: hearing, thinking and meditation of (spiritual things).] *riṣ-su ma-chaḏ-paẖi* [without inclining to partiality] *ṟgyal-waẖi ḇstan-pa m̱thaẖ-dag* [the entire religion of Buddha] *dar-ṟgyaṣ-su spel-waẖi thabṣ tshul gñ zab dañ* [adopting what are best means and methods for its propagation and expansion] *bye-brag Karma Ḇkaẖ ḇrgyuḏ-kyi ḇstan-pa* [especially the doctrine of the *Karma Kahgyu* School] *yar-zla ltar spel-waẖi m̱dsaḏ-ẖphrin* [like the growing crescent of the moon service to religion] *thugs-ḇskyeḏ shum-pa-meḏ-pa dañ* [will with thoughtfullness fearlessly exert himself].

Dge ẖdun-gyi ṣde-ṟnamṣ naṣ kyañ [the class of clergy also] *Ḇla-maẖi gsuñ dvanṣ len* [should receive in good spirit what the Lama says,] *ḇsgrigṣ khrimṣ ḇsruñ* [keep discipline] *ṣdomṣ-tshul ḇshin ḇgyiḏ-pa dañ* [and behave observing the vows and morals] *daḏ-ldan yon-gyi ḇdag-po ṟnamṣ-kyiṣ kyañ* [the faithful dispensers of gifts (*Dānapati*) also] *guṣ-ẖduḏ ḇsñen-ḇkur dvañṣ-len ḇgyiḏ dgoṣ ḇcaṣ* [should with reverence make homage and implicit obedience (to him.)] *thugṣ ñeṣ ẖtshal* [be sure (bear in mind as sure.)]

Sheṣ-paẖi yi-ge chu-ṣtag-gi zla tsheṣ ḏge-war [on an auspicious date (in the year (*water-tiger*) letter so written]

H̱og-min m̱tshur-phuẖi Chos grva Chen-po naṣ ṣpel [is proclaimed from the great monastery of *H̱og-min Tshur phu*.

---

* This ངོས་འཛིན n̂os-ẖdsin (letter of identification) of the *Spirit* of a deceased Lama of Lower Kham with the soul of a Sikkim Maharaja's son was issued by Lama Theg-paẖi Dorje the 14th in succession to the *Karma-pa* hierarchy, in 1722 A.D.

APPENDIX II.

གཉེན་ཡིག *Gñen-yig.*

Lha-sdiṅs [lit. the eminence where gods dwell; name of the residential house of Lhading sku-shab (སྐུ་ཞབས colloquially *Kusho*) at Lhasa.]

Lha-lcam mchog-ma Yeçes sgrol-mala [Her Highness queen Yeśe-doima.]

Gden shuhi skabs-kyi Gñen-yig [marriage-letter of the (auspicious) occasion of bringing her.]

Hdra-çus-hkhrul-mes [mistake-less copy.]

A correct copy of the marriage-letter executed on the occasion of giving away Her Highness queen Yeśe-doima in marriage.

Hail the Precious One !

Bzaṅ-pohi skal-pa hdi la dam-chos-kyis dbyar-skyes rṅa-saṅ stoṅ-du hbyin-pa-las. In this age of blessedness by Holy religion from the production of summer drum-sound (thunder noise) in void space (sky).

Sñig dus hgro-wahi gsod-gyur bdud-rtsihi char hbebs mkhas Çakyahi rgyal-pos dge legs stshol.

Grant unto us prosperity, O king of the S'ākyas, who is able to bring down the rain of nectar for healing (the sufferings) of living beings in these degenerate times.

Khams gsum dwaṅ-gyur dpal-ldan hdod-pahi rgyal ! Rgyal-wahi yum mchog Kuru kullé-la !

King of Love who has brought the three worlds under his power O, *Kuru kullé* (Venus) the great mother * of all the Buddhas !

Ma-pham hdod-dguhi † char bsñil nor-sbyin Lha, Lhahi lha-mchog-rnams-kyi rtag-tu skyoṅs.

The unsubduable wealth-giving god that draws down rains of (riches) ye the chief gods among gods, protect (us) at all times!

Bstan hgrohi mgon mdsad dam-can tshogs spyi daṅ, khyad-par raṅ rigs brgyud hgo-vahi lha.

And the hosts of *Dam-can*, in general, that support religion and living beings, and the principal gods of individual families, in particular.

Yul gshis gnas-skyoṅs sruṅ-mahi tshogs bcas-kyis dus-kun mi-gyel sruṅ skyobs gdoṅ-grogs mdsod, (ye all) together with the hosts of guardian demi-gods who protect the country, estates and holy places, at all times do guard, protect, and befriend (us) with unflagging zeal !

Hdsam gliṅ lte-wahi Bod yul chos-ldan shiṅ, hdabs hbrel lho phyogs Hbras-mo smin-pahi ljoṅs, the naval (centre) of Dsam-ling—

Tibet, the Province of Buddhism, is conterminous on the south, with Demo-jong, the land where rice ripens.

Bde skyid gyaṅ-du chags-pahi mdun-sa na sa-spyod che btsan sde-ris mṅon-hphags-pa.

In this frontier land of bounty and prosperity the king is great and strong being of sublime extraction.

Phan tshun sab-çes gñen-du hbrel-wahi mdud nam yaṅ lhod-pa med-pahi phyag rgya-yis ‡ with mutual good understanding, the marriage-tie will be kept ever unloosened by the *Mudra* (seal of solemnity).

Btab-pahi bris-yig bkra-çis re-wa-can srid-gsum kun-dgahi dpyid-gyur hdi nas pel.

It being fixed on this written letter it is hoped these (presents) (may) augment the spring (season of prosperity) that is the joy of the three worlds.

Shes çis-par brjod-pa daṅ ṅes-par brtan-pahi tshig-gi hphreṅ-wa rṅa-hi sgra dvyaṅs-kyi dge-was sñon bsus-te welcoming with the auspicious drum-sound in the (above) string of benedictory and re-assuring words.

---

* In mystic sense she (*Kuru kullé*) is the female energy or *Sakti* of all the Buddhas in the Red-Cap School. She is same with the goddess *Tārā* in the Yellow-Cap School.

† *Demo-jong* formerly comprised the eastern valley of the Kosi, the entire valleys of the Teesta and the Mu-chu rivers. It was so called being the rice-growing land, on this side of the Himalayas. Hbras is rice, ljoṅs, cultivation, field.

‡ *Phyag rgya* (Sans. *Mudrā*) the configuration on the thumb (ཐེ་ཙེ *thero*) i.e., the thumb-impression. It has been always the practice in Tibet, to put thumb-impressions on all important documents. The fixing of the seal (ཏེའུ or ཐ་མ་ག) was introduced in later times.

The following conventional system has been adopted for representing Tibetan and Sanskrit letters (the equivalents of which do not exist in English) either in Roman or in Italics:

- ā or á represents the *a* in far, fast, father.
- ē or é represents the *e* in let, met, set.
- i or ī represents the *i* in din, pin, sin.
- ō or ó represents the *o* in go, lo, so.
- u or û represents the *u* in put.
- ń represents the *Nāgari* ङ or its Tibetan equivalent ང.
- ç or s' represents the *Nāgari* श or its Tibetan equivalent ཤ.
- c or ch (as an equivalent of ཅ) represents the sound of *ch* in much, such, touch.
- ḍ represents the *Nāgari* letter ड or its Tibetan equivalent ཌ.
- g will always represent the sound of *g* in the words go, give, get, but not that of *g* in gem, gentle, germ.
- ḥ represents the sound of *h* in hour, honest, honour and the letter འ.
- ṇ represents the *Nāgari* letter ण or its Tibetan equivalent ཎ.
- ṣ represents the *Nāgari* letter ष or its Tibetan equivalent ཥ.
- ṭ represents the *Nāgari* letter ट or its Tibetan equivalent ཊ.
- v and w represent the *Nāgari* letter व or its Tibetan equivalent བ or ཝ.

Tibetan letters with their *Deva Nāgari* equivalents.

ཀ	ཁ	ག	ང	ཅ	ཏ	ཐ	ད	ན	པ	ཕ	བ
क	ख	ग	ङ	च	त	थ	द	न	प	फ	ब
མ	ཙ	ཚ	ཛ	ཝ	ཡ	ར	ལ	ཤ	ས	ཧ	ཨ།
म	च	छ	ज	व	य	र	ल	श	स	ह	अ।

Deva Nāgari letters with their Conventional Tibetan equivalents.

घ	झ	ट	ठ	ड	ढ	ण	ध	भ	ष	क्ष
གྷ	ཛྷ	ཊ	ཋ	ཌ	ཌྷ	ཎ	དྷ	བྷ	ཥ	ཀྵ

On the use of honorific terms and expressions.

In the Tibetan language, both written and colloquial, there are two methods of expression. The first is called ཞེ་སའི་སྐད and the second ཕལ་སྐད the common or vulgar language. Three words, namely, སྐུ signifying the person or body, ཕྱག hand and ཞབས foot are generally used before nouns and verbs to add a degree of politeness or respectability to them. When so used, these words lose their literal signification and acquire a quite different sense. Of the three words, སྐུ, གཟུགས, ལུས all signifying the *body*, the first *i.e.* སྐུ is *honorific*. The second and third *i.e.* གཟུགས and ལུས can be made *honorific* by prefixing to them the word སྐུ, thus:—

རྒྱལ་པོ་རིའི་སྐུ་མཛེས་པ་འདུག། རྒྱལ་པོ་རིའི་སྐུ་གཟུགས་མཛེས་པ་འདུག། རྒྱལ་པོ་རིའི་སྐུ་ལུས་མཛེས་པ་འདུག། signify the King's person is handsome.

ངའི་གཟུགས་མི་མཛེས། ངའི་ལུས་མི་མཛེས། my body is not handsome.

One, when speaking of one's own self, should not use an *honorific* word like སྐུ or སྐུ་གཟུགས or སྐུ་ལུས། Of the two words ཕྱག and ལག signifying the *hand*, ཕྱག is *honorific*: རྒྱལ་པོ་རིའི་ཕྱག་ལ་གསེར་ཡོད། there is gold in the King's hand, ངའི་ལག་ལ་གསེར་མེད there is no gold in my hand. སྐུ་ཞབས་ལ་ཕྱག་དངུལ་མི་འདུག། your honour has no silver (money.) ང་ལ་དངུལ་ཡོད I have money. The word ཕྱག is used as an *honorific*, with verbs as follows:—

བླ་མ་ཕྱག་ཕེབ། Lama come. དཀོན་མཆོག་ལ་ཕྱག་འཚལ་ལོ། Reverence be to the *Kon-chog* (Supreme One.)

Of the two words ཞབས and རྐང signifying the *foot* ཞབས is *honorific*. རྒྱལ་པོ་རིའི་ཞབས་ལ་ལྷམ་ཡོད there are shoes on the King's feet. ངའི་རྐང་པ་ལ་ལྷམ་མི་འ there are no shoes in my feet.

The words ཞབས signifying *foot* and དྲུང, *near* are equivalents of Mr. or Esquire, in English. With the *honorific* term སྐུ prefixed to them they, *i.e.* སྐུ་ཞབས and སྐུ་དྲུང signify *your honour* or *your worship*. སྐུ་ཞབས is pronounced as *Kúsho*, in conversation. ཞབས་དྲུང literally *near the feet*) is a title of dignity in Tibet. With *Rinpo-che* attached to it, it froms the exalted title, assumed by the grand Lama of Bhutan. ཞབས་དྲུང་རིན་པོ་ཆེ་ངག་དབང་རྣམ་རྒྱལ was the title which the first Bhutan Dharma Rāja had assumed, on ascending the hierarchical throne of Bhutan. ཞབས་དྲུང is evidently, an equivalent of ཉེ་གནས signifying an attendant. S'āriputtra and Maudgalyāyana were the personal attendants of the Budha. Hence the importance of the position of being *near the feet* ཞབས་དྲུང or that of the words ཞབས and དྲུང།

The following are polite expressions generally used in conversation:—

སྐུ་ཞབས་ལ་ཕྱག་འབུལ་ཞུས (colloquially, *Kûsho-la Cham-bûl-shu*)—present respects or (respectful compliments) to your honour.

དྲུང་ཆེན (དྲུང་ཡིག་ཆེན་པོ) འཆིབ་རྒྱུ་གནང་སོང་། the Secretary has gone away. འཆིབ་རྒྱུ ordinarily signifies to proceed on horseback གནང is also *honorific* to the verb སོང་།

ཨ་ནེ་དྲུང་། Mr. Ané འདིར་ཕེབས or ཕེབས་ཤིག (please) come here.

སྐུ་ཞབས་རིན་པོ་ཆེ་ལྷ་ཁང་ནང་ལ་ཞབས་འཆག་བཟང་རོགས་ན། may your precious Highness or Holiness walk into the temple.

སྐུ་ཞབས་ཀྱི་སྐུ་མདུན (*Kûsho-kee Kûmdun*) in the presence of your honour.

དབང་ལྡན་ཞབས་ལ་ཕྱག་ལས་མེད Mr. Wangdan has no work (to do). In this sentence ཕྱག does not signifying the *hand*. It is simply an *honorific* term. དགེ་རྒན་དྲུང་ལ་ཞབས་ཕྱི་མི་འདུག། Mr. Gergan (teacher or school master) has no servant.

A list of *Honorific* and *Common* terms.

Honorific.	*Common.*
ཡབ father,	ཕ
ཡུམ mother,	མ
སྲས son,	བུ
སྲས་མ daughter,	བུ་མོ
མཚན name,	མིང
དབུ the head,	མགོ
དབུ་སྐྲ the hair,	སྐྲ
དབུ་ཞྭ a hat or cap,	ཞྭ་མོ
དབུ་མཛད the head officer, workman or principal	འགོ་བ
ཞལ the month,	ཁ
ཞལ་གདོང the face,	གདོང
ཞལ་ཟད or ཞལ་ཚོས meat or food, anything to eat,	ཟས or ཁ་ཟས
ཞལ་སྐྱེམས drink,	སྐྱེམས
ཞལ་ཆེམས testament, last will,	ཁ་ཆེམས
ཞལ་གདམས advice, counsel,	གདམས or གདམས་པ
ལྗགས the tongue,	ལྕེ
ཚེམས the tooth,	སོ
ཤངས the nose,	སྣ
སྤྱན the eye,	མིག
སྤྱན་འབྲས the apple of the eye,	མིག་འབྲས
སྤྱན་ཆབ tears,	མིག་ཆུ
[illegible] the eye-lid,	མིག་ལྤགས
སྤྱན་གསྡོག the eye-lash,	མིག་གསྡོག
སྙན the ear,	རྣ་བ
སྙན་ཁུང the ear-hole,	རྣ་ཁུང
སྙན་ཤལ the flap of the ear,	རྣ་ཤལ
སྙན་གསན hearing,	རྣ་ཐོས
ཕྱག hand,	ལག or ལག་པ
ཕྱག་ངར the wrist of the hand,	ལག་ངར
ཕྱག་སོར the finger,	ལག་སོར
ཕྱག་སེན the nails of the finger,	ལག་སེན or ལག་སེན་མོ
ཞབས the foot,	རྐང་པ
ཞབས་སོར the toe,	རྐང་སོར
ཞབས་ཤུབས stocking,	རྐང་ཤུབས
ཞབས་ལྷམ shoes,	ལྷམ
ཞབས་འཆག་པ walking,	རྐང་པས་འགྲོ
ཐུགས the mind,	སྙིང or ཡིད

Certain *common* terms are made polite by prefixing to them *honorifics* like སྐུ, ཕྱག &c. These may be illustrated as follows :—

Honorific terms.	*Common* terms.	*Meanings.*
སྐུ་སྐལ	སྐལ	share, portion.
སྐུ་མཁར	མཁར	castle, fort.
སྐུ་རྒྱབ	རྒྱབ	the back.
སྐུ་བརྒྱུད	བརྒྱུད	a descendant.
སྐུ་ངལ	ངལ, ཧོ་བརྒྱལ	fatigue.
སྐུ་མཆེད	མཆེད or སྤུན	brothers or sisters.
སྐུ་ཉིད	ཉིད	you, yourself.
སྐུ་གཉེན	གཉེན	a relation, kinsman.
སྐུ་ལྟོ	ལྟོ་བ	the belly.
སྐུ་སྟོད	སྟོད	the upperpart of the body.
སྐུ་ཐང	ཐང་ཀ	picture-plate.
སྐུ་གདུང	གདུང	tomb, relic.
སྐུ་མདོག	མདོག	colour complexion.
ཕྱག་དཔེ	དཔེ	a book.
ཕྱག་ཕྱིས	ལག་ཕྱིས	handkerchief, towel.

Honorific terms.	*Common* terms.	*Meaning.*
སྐུ་ན	ན	age or stage in life.
སྐུ་འཕྲེང	འཕྲེང	rosary ; succession in royalty or hierarchy.
སྐུ་མལ	མལ	beddings.
སྐུ་སྨད	སྨད	the lower half of the body.
སྐུ་ཚེ	ཚེ	one's life or age.
སྐུ་ཚབ	ཚབ	a representative.
སྐུ་མཚལ	ཁྲག	the blood.
སྐུ་ཞང	ཞང་པོ	maternal uncle.
སྐུ་ཟླ	ཟླ་བོ	husband or wife.
སྐུ་རིམ	རིམ་འགྲོ	religious sacrifice.
སྐུ་ཁམས	ཁམས	the body.
སྐུ་ཤ	ཤ	the flesh of the body.
སྐུ་སྲིང	སྲིང་མོ	a sister.
ཕྱག་བྲིས	ལག་བྲིས or བྲིས་པ	hand-writing.
ཕྱག་དམ	དམ་ཁ or ལག་དམ	sign-manual or seal.

Some verbal adjectives are also used in honorific sense. བཞེས་གསོལ་བ་ཟན་ཟ་བ to take dinner, to eat ; the meals. གསོལ signifying *eating* is used as an *honorific* before nouns like ཇ tea, ཤ meat, སྨན medicine &c.

སྐུ་ཞབས་གསོལ་ཇ་བཞེས may your honour take tea ; བླ་མ་གསོལ་ཞིབ་ཞེས Lama, eat barley flour ; སྨན་པའི་གསོལ་སྨན physician's medicine ; གསོལ་ཤ་བཞེས please take meat. དཔོན་པོ་གསོལ་ཆང་བཞེས། my chief (or lord) take wine.

CONTENTS.

Page.

Pronoun.

Mood.

Conjugation.

INTRODUCTION

TO THE

GRAMMAR

OF THE TIBETAN LANGUAGE.

THE Alphabet of the Tibetan Language comprises thirty simple letters:—

ཀ	ཁ	ག	ང།	ཅ	ཆ	ཇ	ཉ།	ཏ	ཐ	ད	ན།
ka	*kha*	*ga*	*ña.*	*ca*	*cha*	*ja*	*ña.*	*ta*	*tha*	*da*	*na.*
པ	ཕ	བ	མ།	ཙ	ཚ	ཛ	ཝ།	ཞ	ཟ	འ	ཡ།
pa	*pha*	*ba*	*ma.*	*tsa*	*tsha*	*dsa*	*wa.*	*sha*	*za*	*ḫa*	*ya.*
ར	ལ	ཤ	ས།	ཧ	ཨ།*						
ra	*la*	*ça*	*sa.*	*ha*	*a.*						

To these may be added the four vowels *i*, *u*, *e*, *o*, formed by fixing the vowel signs ི ུ ེ ོ over the head and to the foot of the last letter ཨ།

ཨི	ཨུ	ཨེ	ཨོ།†
i	*u*	*e*	*o.*

These thirtyfour letters are divided into consonants གསལ་བྱེད thirty in number, and vowels དབྱངས which according to some Tibetan grammarians are only four.

The thirtieth letter ཨ which is inherent in all the twentynine consonants and forms the basis ངོ་བོ་ཉིད ‡ of the four vowels ཨི,ཨུ,ཨེ,ཨོ, is not considered as a distinct vowel which could be joined with the twentynine consonants for forming a syllable or word because it already exists in them. Without ཨ, it is said, the consonants would be སྲོག་མེད *srog-med i.e.*, lifeless

---

*These thirty letters are called ཀཱ་ལི (ཀ joined with the Sanskrit word ཨཱ་ལི आलि signifying འཕྲེང་བ series becomes ཀཱ་ལི *कालि) *kāli* meaning the series of letters commencing with ཀ *ka*— ཀ་ལ་སོགས་པའི་འཕྲེང་བ་གསལ་བྱེད་ཀྱི་ཡི་གེ།

†These four letters based on ཨ (when put together with ཨ) form what are called ཨཱ་ལི *āli* आलि *i.e.*, the ཨ series or vowels— ཨ་ལ་སོགས་པའི་འཕྲེང་བ་དབྱངས་ཡིག །

‡According to the grammatical works called གསལ་བའི་མེ་ལོང། and ངག་སྒྲོན་རབ་གསལ the vowels are five in number viz, ཨ་ཨི་ཨུ་ཨེ་ཨོ though the vowel signs are four.

དབྱངས་ནི་ངོ་བོ་ཨ་ལ་ཕྱད་པར་ཨི་ཨུ་ཨེ་ཨོ་དང་། དེ་ཡང་ཀ་སོགས་གསལ་བྱེད་པ། དབྱངས་ཨ་ཨི་ཨུ་ཨེ་ཨོ་དང་། བརྗོད་དོན་ཀཱ་ལི་སུམ་ཅུ་པ། ཀྱང་བ་འཕུལ་དང་མགོ་ཅན་དང་། དབྱངས་ལྔ། ཨ་ཨི་ཨུ་ཨེ་ཨོ།

The thirty simple letters called གསལ་བྱེད *gsal-byed*, are arranged in series called སྡེ *sde*, which are seven and half in number.* The first series called ཀ་སྡེ commences with ཀ *ka*, and comprises ཀ་ཁ་ག་ང། The second series begins with ཅ *ca*, and is called ཅ་སྡེ *ca-sde* :— ཅ་ཆ་ཇ་ཉ། and so on; ཏ་སྡེ:—ཏ་ཐ་ད་ན། པ་སྡེ:—པ་ཕ་བ་མ། ཙ་སྡེ:—ཙ་ཚ་ཛ་ཝ། ཞ་སྡེ:—ཞ་ཟ་འ་ཡ། ར་སྡེ:—ར་ལ་ཤ་ས། The last two letters ཧ་ཨ called ཧ་སྡེ constitute but half a series.

The four vowels *i*, *u*, *e* and *o* in uniting with the consonants lose the basic portion of their respective regular forms, for instance, ཀ when joined with ཨི becomes ཀི *ki* the basic part of the letter ཀ *i.e.*, ཨ being eliminated in the union. In the same manner, ཀ with ཨུ becomes ཀུ *ku*, with ཨེ it becomes ཀེ *ke* and with ཨོ it becomes ཀོ *ko*.

Compounds formed by joining the initial consonants with the four vowels *i*, *u*, *e*, *o* are called འདོགས་ཅན *hdogs-can*.

The vowel signs representing *i*, *u*, *e*, *o* that are fixed to the thirty གསལ་བྱེད or their compounds are called *Gi-gu*, *Shabs-kyu*, *Hgreñ-bu*, *Na-ro*.

ཀ joined with		*Gi-gu*	becomes ཀི།	ཀ joined with		*Shabs-kyu*	becomes	ཀུ།
ཀ ,, ,,		*Hgreñ-bu*,	,, ཀེ།	ཀ ,, ,,		*Na-ro*	,,	ཀོ།

In this connection Tibetan Grammarians observe that in forming compounds of consonants with the vowels the rules of *Sandhi*, as obtain in Sanskrit, are not applicable to Tibetan, where the vowel signs only represent the force of phonetic deflection of the letter ཨ *a* †

---

* སྡེ་པ་རྡངས་པོ་བདུན་དང་། ཧ་སྡེ་ཕྱེད།

† Why ཨ is classed with the consonants ?:– དབྱངས་ནི་ང་རོའི་རྣམ་པ་ཙམ་ཡིན་ཞིང་དེ་དག་ནི་གསལ་བྱེད་གཞན་ལ་མ་སྦྱར་བར་འདོན་དུ་མེད། དེ་ལྟར་མ་ཡིན་ན་ལེགས་སྦྱར་ལྟར་ཨ་ཨི་འདུས་པས་ཨེ་སོགས་སུ་འགྱུར་བར་ཁས་ལེན་དགོས།

ལེགས་པར་སྦྱར་བའི་སྐད་ལ་གསལ་བྱེད་སྲོག་ཅན་སྲོག་མེད་གཉིས་སུ་དབྱེ་བའི་སྲོག་དེ་ཡིན་ན་དབྱངས་ཡིན་པས་ཁྱབ་པའི་ཕྱིར་ཀ། ཧ་ཕྲ་སྲོག་མེད་རྐྱང་པ་བརྗོད་མི་བཏུབ་པ་ཡིན་ཞིང་བོད་དུ་འང་། ལེགས་ཟེར་བ་ལྟ་བུ་ལ་ཡིག་ཨེ་ཞུགས་ཀྱི་རྗེས་སུ་ཡས་སྲོག་མེད་ལྟར་སོགས་འཁའ་ཞིག་ལ་རིགས་འགྲེ་ནུས་ཀྱང་། སྲོག་ཅན་སྲོག་མེད་ཀྱི་དབྱེ་བ་དེ་བདེ་ཐང་མ་ཡིན་ཞིང་འཇུག་པར་དཀའ་བ་དང་། དགོས་པ་ཆུང་ཟད་མི་ཆེ་བས་དེ་ལྟའི་རྣམ་བཞག་མ་མཛད་དོ། དེ་བས་ན་བརྗོད་དུ་མེད་པའི་སྲོག་མེད་རྐྱང་པ་འདེར་མི་བརྗོད་ཅེང་ཨ་ཡིག་དེ་ཀ་ལ་སོགས་པར་ཞུགས་པའི་བ་སྐད་ཕྱུར་མེད་པས་དེས་དེ་དག་ལ་སྲ་ཞེའི་བྱ་བ་གསལ་བར་བྱེད་མ་ནུས་པའི་ཕྱིར་ཀྱ་ཞེའི་རྗེ་ཚན་དུ་འཛིན་པར་མཛད་པ་ཡིན་ནོ།

The thirty གསལ་བྱེད consonants are deflected being joined with the four vowel signs representing i, u, e and o, as follows:—

འདོགས་ཅན། Compounds with the four vowels *i*, *u*, *e* and *o*.

ཀ	ཀི	ཀུ	ཀེ	ཀོ།	ཁ	ཁི	ཁུ	ཁེ	ཁོ།
ka	*ki*	*ku*	*ke.*	*ko.*	*kha*	*khi*	*khu*	*khe*	*kho.*
ག	གི	གུ	གེ	གོ།	ང	ངི	ངུ	ངེ	ངོ།
ga	*gi*	*gu*	*ge*	*go.*	*ńa*	*ńi*	*ńu*	*ńe*	*ńo.*
ཅ	ཅི	ཅུ	ཅེ	ཅོ།	ཆ	ཆི	ཆུ	ཆེ	ཆོ།
ca	*ci*	*cu*	*ce*	*co.*	*cha*	*chi*	*chu*	*che*	*cho.*
ཇ	ཇི	ཇུ	ཇེ	ཇོ།	ཉ	ཉི	ཉུ	ཉེ	ཉོ།
ja	*ji*	*ju*	*je*	*jo.*	*ña*	*ñi*	*ñu*	*ñe*	*ño.*
ཏ	ཏི	ཏུ	ཏེ	ཏོ།	ཐ	ཐི	ཐུ	ཐེ	ཐོ།
ta	*ti*	*tu*	*t*[illegible]	*to.*	*tha*	*thi*	*thu*	*the*	*tho.*
ད	དི	དུ	དེ	དོ།	ན	ནི	ནུ	ནེ	ནོ།
da	*di*	*du*	*de*	*do.*	*na*	*ni*	*nu*	*ne*	*no.*
པ	པི	པུ	པེ	པོ།	ཕ	ཕི	ཕུ	ཕེ	ཕོ།
pa	*pi*	*p*[illegible]	*pe*	*po.*	*pha*	*phi*	*phu*	*phe*	*pho.*
བ	བི	བུ	བེ	བོ།	མ	མི	མུ	མེ	མོ།
ba	*bi*	*bu*	*be*	*bo.*	*ma*	*mi*	*mu*	*me*	*mo.*
ཙ	ཙི	ཙུ	ཙེ	ཙོ།	ཚ	ཚི	ཚུ	ཚེ	ཚོ།
tsa	*tsi*	*tsu*	*tse*	*tso.*	*tsha*	*tshi*	*tshu*	*tshe*	*tsho.*
ཛ	ཛི	ཛུ	ཛེ	ཛོ།	ཝ	ཝི	ཝུ	ཝེ	ཝོ།
dsa	*dsi*	*dsu*	*dse*	*dso.*	*wa*	*wi*	*wu*	*we*	*wo.*
ཞ	ཞི	ཞུ	ཞེ	ཞོ།	ཟ	ཟི	ཟུ	ཟེ	ཟོ།
sha	*shi*	*shu*	*she*	*sho.*	*za*	*zi*	*zu*	*ze*	*zo.*
འ	འི	འུ	འེ	འོ།	ཡ	ཡི	ཡུ	ཡེ	ཡོ།
ḥa	*ḥi*	*ḥu*	*ḥe*	*ḥo.*	*ya*	*yi*	*yu*	*ye*	*yo.*
ར	རི	རུ	རེ	རོ།	ལ	ལི	ལུ	ལེ	ལོ།
ra	*ri*	*ru*	*re*	*ro.*	*la*	*li*	*lu*	*le*	*lo.*
ཤ	ཤི	ཤུ	ཤེ	ཤོ།	ས	སི	སུ	སེ	སོ།
ça	*çi*	*çu*	*çe*	*ço.*	*sa*	*si*	*su*	*se*	*so.*
ཧ	ཧི	ཧུ	ཧེ	ཧོ།	ཨ	ཨི	ཨུ	ཨེ	ཨོ།
ha	*hi*	*hu*	*he*	*ho.*	*a*	*i*	*u*	*e*	*o.*

སྣད་འཛོགས Subjoined letters.

Compounds with the four consonants, ཡ, ར, ལ and ཝ

Some consonants are joined with the liquids ཡ, ར, ལ, and ཝ which are then called ཡ་བཏགས * *ya-btags*, ར་བཏགས *ra-btags*, ལ་བཏགས *la-btags*, and ཝ་བཏགས *wa-btags*.

The letter ཡ when sub joined to the seven consonants ཀ, ཁ, ག, པ, ཕ, བ, མ, takes the form ྱ།

ཡ་བཏགས་བདུན་ནི། the seven *ya-btags* letters having a subjoined ཡ *y* are ཀ, ཁ, ག, པ, ཕ, བ, མ།

ཀ with the ྱ *yu-btags*, subjoined becomes ཀྱ *kya*. Similarly ཁྱ *khya*, གྱ *gya*, པྱ *pya*, ཕྱ *phya*, བྱ *bya*, མྱ *mya* are formed. In these compounds both the letters are pronounced.

ར་བཏགས་བཅུ་གསུམ་ནི། the thirteen *ra-btags* letters:—ཀ, ཁ, ག, ཏ, ཐ, ད, པ, ཕ, བ, མ, ཤ, ས, ཧ། When the letter ར is subjoined to the above thirteen letters it assumes the form ྲ and is called *ra-btags* ར་བཏགས

ཀ [with the] *ra-btags* ྲ subjoined becomes

ཀྲ *kra* pronounced *ṭa*.

ཁྲ	*khra*	*ṭha*	གྲ	*gra*	*ṭa* or *ḍa*	ཏྲ	*tra*	or	*ṭa*
ཐྲ	*thra*	*ṭha*	དྲ	*dra*	*ḍa*	པྲ	*pra*	,,	*ṭa*
ཕྲ	*phra*	*ṭha*	བྲ	*bra*	*ṭa* or *ḍa*	མྲ	*mra*	,,	*mra*
ཤྲ	*çra*	*ça*	སྲ	*sra*	*sa* or *hra*	ཧྲ		,,	*hra*

ལ་བཏགས་དྲུག་ནི། the six *la-btags* letters.

The letter ལ is subjoined to the following six consonants:—ཀ, ག, བ, ཟ, ར, ས། ཀླ *kla*, གླ *gla*, བླ *bla*, ཟླ *zla*, རླ *rla*, སླ *sla*. The compounds so formed are all pronounced as ལ *la* with the exception of ཟླ *zla*, which is pronounced as *da*: The surmounting letters become silent when joined with ལ *la*. *

The letter ཝ *wa* is subjoined to certain consonants. The form it takes in the compounds so formed resembles a triangle ྭ. It is then called ཝ་ཟུར *wa-zur*, *wa*—corner.

ཝ་ཟུར་བཏགས་པ་བཅུ་དྲུག་ནི།

ཀྭ	ཁྭ	གྭ	ཅྭ	ཉྭ	ཏྭ	དྭ	ཙྭ	ཚྭ	ཞྭ	ཟྭ	རྭ	ལྭ	ཤྭ	སྭ	ཧྭ།
kwa	*khwa*	*gwa*	*cwa*	*ñwa*	*twa*	*dwa*	*tswa*	*tshwa*	*shwa*	*zwa*	*rwa*	*lwa*	*çwa*	*swa*	*hwa*.

* The silent letters have been underlined.

Of the sixteen compounds with ཝ་ཟུར only nine, namely ཀྭ, ཁྭ, དྭ, ཙྭ, ཚྭ, ཞྭ, རྭ, ལྭ and ཤྭ are in general use in Tibetan. In these the initial and the subjoined letters are both sounded.

The ཝ་ཟུར (ྭ) is obscurely sounded in དྭ, ཙྭ, ཚྭ and ཞྭ.

II

Letters are classified under four denominations, namely :—

1. མིང་གཞི *Miṅ-gshi** initial letters which generally form the roots of words.

2. རྐྱང་པ *ṟkyaṅ-pa*‡ These comprise the initial letters, *ḥdogs-can* and the compounds formed with the སྨྲད་འདོགས signs representing:- ཡ, ར, ལ, ཝ, *y*, *r*, *l*, *w*, which are subjoined to them.

3. མགོ་ཅན *ṃgo-can* :—Letters which are surmounted by ར,ལ,ས (*r*,*l*,*s*).

4. འཕུལ་ཅན *Ḫphul-can*§ The initial letter in a word (either simple or compound) is so called when it has any of the five letters ག,ད,བ,མ,འ fixed before it for forming a word.

མགོ་ཅན Surmounted letters.

The letters ར,ལ,ས are fixed on the heads of certain simple and compound letters. They are then called *ṃgo-can* surmounted letters or རྩེགས་གསུམ *ṟ's gs-gsum,* the triplepiled up letters. The compounds so formed are called མགོ་ཅན་གསུམ།

The superscribed letter which is seldom pronounced, will be represented by a line underneath it.

---

* གསལ་བྱེད་ཀ་སོགས་སུམ་ཅུ་སྟེ། དབྱངས་གསལ་ཀུན་ཀྱང་མིང་གཞིའོ། (མི་འོང་།)

‡ དབྱངས་ཨ་ཨི་ཨུ་ཨེ་ཨོ་དང་། ཡ་ར་ལ་ཝའི་སྨྲད་འདོགས་རྣམས། ཡང་དུང་ཡོད་ཀྱང་འཕུལ་དང་ར་མགོ། མེད་ན་ཐམས་ཅད་རྐྱང་པ་ཡིན།།

§ སྔོན་འཇུག་ག་ད་བ་མ་འ། ཡོད་པ་ཐམས་ཅད་འཕུལ་ཅན་ཡིན།།

The twelve basic consonants with ར over their heads:—

ར་མགོ་བཅུ་གཉིས་ནི།

རྐ རྒ རྔ རྙ རྟ རྡ རྣ རྦ རྨ རྩ རྫ རླ།

ṛka ṛga ṛña ṛña ṛta ṛda ṛna ṛba ṛma ṛtsa ṛdsa ṛla.

These retain their respective sounds in the combination with the exception of ག which then turns like the English g (hard) and also of བ which then sounds as b. In the words རྡོ་རྗེ and ཨུ་རྒྱན the ར over the heads of ཇ and ག are sounded.

The ten basic consonants with the letter ལ surmounting them:— ཀ, ག, ང, ཅ, ཇ, ཏ, ད, པ, བ, ཧ།

ལ་མགོ་བཅུ་ནི།

ལྐ ལྒ ལྔ ལྕ ལྗ ལྟ ལྡ ལྤ ལྦ ལྷ།

lka lga lña lca lja lta lda lpa lba lha.

The surmounting letter ལ *la,* is silent except in the word ལྷ signifying a god.

In the last compound *i.e.,* in ལྷ *lha* both the letters are pronounced. The letters ག, ཇ, ད, བ with the surmounting ལ are sounded harder than in their simple state.

The letter ས is fixed on the top of eleven སྐྱང་པ letters:— ཀ, ག, ང, ཉ, ཏ, ད, ན, པ, བ, མ, ཙ། In the compounds so formed the surmounting letter ས is not pronounced.

ས་མགོ་བཅུ་གཅིག་ནི།

སྐ སྒ སྔ སྙ སྟ སྡ སྣ སྤ སྦ སྨ སྩ།

ṣka ṣga ṣña ṣña ṣta ṣda ṣna ṣpa ṣba ṣma ṣtsa.

འཕྲུལ་ཅན།

Combination of letters to form words.

རྗེས་འཇུག་སྔོན་འཇུག་མི་འཇུག་མིང་གཞི།

Out of the thirty letters called མིང་གཞི *miṅ-gshi,* inasmuch as they individully form the basis of a syllable or word, the ten ག, ང, ད, ན, བ, མ, འ, ར, ལ, ས། are called རྗེས་འཇུག affixes or closing letters, from their being affixed to the basis of a word or syllable.

Out of these ten final letters the two, ད and ས are called ཡང་འཇུག secondary affixes. Again, out of the ten རྗེས་འཇུག affixes the five letters ག, ད, བ, མ, འ are used as སྔོན་འཇུག prefixes; so called from their being put before the basis of a syllable for forming a word.

The twenty remaining གསལ་བྱེད consonants—

ཀ, ཁ, ཅ, ཆ, ཇ, ཉ, ཏ, ཐ, པ, ཕ, ཙ, ཚ, ཛ, ཝ, ཞ, ཟ, ཡ, ཤ, ཧ, ཨ།

are called མི་འཇུག་མིང་གཞི། *mi-hjug miṅ-gshi.* These never occur as final letters in words or after any vowel. No compounds or combinations of these letters are made for forming words in the Tibetan language. The ten consonants ག, ང, ད, ན, བ, མ, འ, ར, ལ, ས, are the only letters that close any syllable, or follow the vowel, whether inherent or expressed. Accordingly, combinations like ཙཀ་,ཚཁ་,ཕཟལ, form no words in Tibetan. These twenty letters stand as initials in a syllable or word.

Some of the twenty མི་འཇུག་མིང་གཞི letters are words in themselves:— ཀ *ka*, pillar ཁ *kha*, mouth or snow; ཆ *cha*, part, fraction, or a pair; ཇ *ja*, tea; ཉ *ña*, fish; པ *pa*, the syllable expressing ownership; ཕ *pha*, father; ཙ *tsa*, time ཙ་ནས from the time; ཚ *tsha*, hot, fever *dsa*, an earthen vessel for cooking or for heating; ཝ *wa* fox; ཞ *sha* lead; ཟ *za* food, or to eat; ཡ *ya*, an equal or match, above, up; ཤ *ça*, flesh, meat; ཧ *ha*, breath, yonder. These letters form the basis འཇུག་ཡུལ to which the སྔོན་འཇུག and རྗེས་འཇུག letters are prefixed and affixed.

The use of the ten letters ག, ང, ད, ན, བ, མ, འ, ར, ལ, ས, called རྗེས་འཇུག closing letters may be illustrated thus: in the word ལག the letter ག is a རྗེས་འཇུག། Here the letters ལ and ག are joined so as to form a syllable in consequence of which there is no ཚེག (·) intersyllabic point between them. By this combination ག has lost its inherent ཨ *a.* Accordingly, the word ལག is pronounced *lag* and not *la-ga*; in the same manner, in the words གང་ *gaṅ*, ནད *nad*, ངན *ṅan*, ལབ *lab*, ལམ *lam*, མར *mar*, རལ *ral*, ལས *las*, the letters ང, ད, ན, བ, མ, ར, ལ, ས, are all རྗེས་འཇུག.

In the syllables ངས, པས, བས the letter ས is not strictly a རྗེས་འཇུག closing letter though it is fixed after རྗེས་སུ་འཇུག་པ for forming a grammatical termination and closes a word or syllable.

In some words the letters ད and ས are affixed to the རྗེས་འཇུག letters such as ར, ག when they are called ཡང་འཇུག In the words ཞེགས and སྒྱུརད the letters ག and ར are རྗེས་འཇུག but ད and ས, are ཡང་འཇུག། Here ག and ར have lost the ཨ that was inherent in them, in consequence of their union with ས and ད which are seldom pronounced.

The combinations གས, ངས, བས, མས are infact double affixes. (རྗེ་འཇུག་དང་ཡང་འཇུག) ནད རད, ལད also occur as double affixes in older orthography, but though the use of ད (called དདྲག) is the more correct form for designing the past tense yet in modern Tibetan this practice is seldom resorted to.

The སྔོན་འཇུག, རྗེས་འཇུག. and ཡང་འཇུག letters where silent will be represented by underlined italics.

The tendency of the Tibetan language being towards monosyllabic pronunciation the རྗེས་འཇུག and ཡང་འཇུག letters * are either softly pronounced or not sounded at all. ག and བ in the expression ཕྱག་ཚལ sound softly. Sometimes they are silent as in ནས, ནུས, ལས, ལུས, གུས, དུས, ཆོས, ཤེས། yet in their phonetical silence they slightly deflect the vowels that precede them; ནད *nad* is pronounced as *neh*, ནུས *nus* as *nui*, ལུས *lus* as *lui*, ཆོས *chos*, as *choi*, ཤེས *çes*, is pronounced as *sheh*, དད *dad* is pronounced as *deh*, and ཤད *çad* is pronounced as *sheh* and so on.

This peculiarity is more marked in the colloqual of Lhasa, *i. e.* Central Tibet, than in that of Western Tibet. In the following illustrations of the ten single affixes and four double affixes the letters that are not pronouned are underlined.

ག in ནག *nag* (meaning black), in ནགས *nags* meaning forest.

ང in རང *rañ* (meaning self), in རངས *rañs* meaning entire.

ད in ནད *nad*, མེད *med*, ཡིད *yid*, ཡོད *yod*, ལུད *lud* and so on, is never pronounced, though it slightly deflects the preceding vowel.

ན in ཀུན *kun*, དོན *don*, རིན *rin*, ལན *lan*, ལེན *len* and so on, is fully pronounced.

བ in ཐུབ *thub*, ཐོབ *thob*, རབ *rab*, རིབ *rib*, ལེབ *leb* and so on, is pronounced.

མ in གམ *gam* ངམ *nam*, དམ *dam*, ལམ *lam*, ཚམ *tsam* etc., is fully pronounced.

འ in དཀའ *dkah*, བཀའ *bkah*, is pronounced as the silent h in English.

ར in མར *mar*, དར *dar*, བར *bar*, སར *sar*, གུར *gur*, ནོར *nor* is pronounced.

ལ in བལ *bal*, རིལ *ril*, ཡུལ *yul*, ཤེལ *çel*, ཡོལ *yol* l is softly pronounced.

ས in ལས *las*, རིས *ris*, ལུས *lus*, ལེས *les*, གོས *gos* etc. is never pronounced. though it slightly changes the preceding vowel.

In all double affixes the terminating letter ས is silent—

གས in པགས *pags*, ལགས *lags*, ལེགས *legs*, ཆུགས *chugs*, དོགས *dogs* etc.

ངས in སངས *sans*, ཧོངས *hons*, རངས *rañs*, དངས *dañs* ལོངས *loñs*, etc.

བས in ཐབས *thabs*, ཆིབས *chibs*, ཤུབས *cubs*, ཁེབས *khebs*, ཧོབས *hobs*, etc.

མས in ཐམས *thams*, རིམས *rims*, ཤུམས *çums*, སེམས *sems*, སོམས *soms* etc.

According to older orthography, བརྡ་རྙིང both the letters in the three double affixes ནད, རད, ལད, are pronounced.

---

* Regarding the pronunciation of these letters, Alex. Csoma de Koros remarks :—

"They should always be sounded accordingly, since the Tibetan Grammarians say, that these letters are affixed expressly to render the words sonorous and significant."

He, however, added :—

"Some of the affixes are only obscurely heard; some are left entirely silent (as the ས in གས, ངས, བས, མས), and some change the preceding vowel."

In composition, all words not ending in a རྗེས་འཇུག letter *i.e.*, those that have vowel terminations only should be taken as if ending in འ: མི combined with འ as མིའ; ཏི as ཏིའ and so on.* This འ is only a changed form of the basic inherent ཨ. The use of འ (by fixing it at the foot) is generally made in transcribing Sanskrit terms, to lengthen or increase the power of the vowel termination of a word, in the manner the Sanskrit अ is made long, when necessary, by the addition of a stroke after it such as आ, for instance the word *Ācārya* will be written in Tibetan as ཨཱ་ཙཱརྱ། Içvara, as ཨཱི་ཤྭ་ར།

In words formed with རྗེས་འཇུག and ཡང་འཇུག *i.e.*, secondary affixes the རྗེས་འཇུག letters are pronounced, but the ཡང་འཇུག letters are not pronounced. In ཞལས *shals*, ལེགས *legs*, དོངས *hoṅs* the letter ས *s* is seldom heard.

The སྔོན་འཇུག letters ག, ད, བ, མ, འ† are put before a syllable or a radical letter to form words. They are also used to modify the meaning of a word, and for forming the present, past and future tenses of a verb. These five letters are called འཛུལ or prepositive letters when they are used as སྔོན་འཇུག།

སྦྱོར་ཚུལ METHOD OF COMBINATION.

གས་འཕུལ་ཡི་གེ་བཅུ་གཅིག་ལ། the eleven initial letters which have ག prefixed to them are ཅ. ཉ. ཏ. ད. ན, ཙ. ཞ, ཟ, ཡ. ཤ, ས། The syllables ཅའ *chah*, ཉའ *ñah*, ཏའ *tah*, དའ *dah*, ནའ *nah*, ཙའ *tsah*, ཞའ *shah*, ཟའ *xah*, ཡའ *yah*, ཤའ *çah*, སའ *sah*, would not form words in themselves if the letter ག was not prefixed, to them. With ག prefixed they are words :—གཅའ signifying drink, གཉའ neck, གཏའ pawn, དགའ pleasure, གནའ antelope, གཙའ rust, blight; གཞའ to joke, གཟའ a planet, གཡའ oxide (of a metal); གཤའ becoming fit, གསའ the snow leopard of Tibet. The prefix ག remains silent in the manner the letter k is in the English words "knife", "knee" or "know."

It is to be noted here that the prefix ག is not used before any མགོ་ཅན or སྦྲད་འདོགས compound letters formed by surmounting or subjoining one consonant with another.

དས་འཕུལ་ཡི་གེ་རྣམས། The letter ད is prefixed to the following fifteen ཀྱང་པ། and སྦྲད་འདོགས། letters: ཀ, ག, ང, པ, བ, མ,། ཀྱ, ཀྲ, གྱ, གྲ, པྱ, པྲ, བྱ, བྲ, མྱ; thus དཀའ, དགའ, དངའ, དཔའ, དབའ, དམའ, དཀྱ, དཀྲ, དགྱ, དགྲ, དཔྱ, དཔྲ, དབྱ, དབྲ, དམྱ།

ད is never prefixed to མགོ་ཅན letters. Its use in some verbs indicates that they are in the future tense.

བས་འཕུལ་གྱི་གེ་རྣམས། The letters with the prefix བ:—བ is put before ཀྱང་པ and མགོ་ཅན letters in a syllable to form words and also to form the preterite and future tenses in some verbs.

---

* མིང་མཐར་རྗེས་འཇུག་མེད་ཀུན་ཀྱང་། འ་མཐའ་ཅན་དུ་གཟུང་བར་བྱ།

† རྗེས་འཇུག་ལས་ག་ད་བ་མ་འ། ཐུ་བོ་རྗེ་ཉིད་དབང་འཇུག་པ་སྟེ།།

The twenty ཀྱང་པ letters to which the letter བ may be prefixed are as follows: ཀ, ཀྱ, ཀྲ, ཀླ། ག, གྱ, གྲ། ཙ, ཏ, ད, ཙ, ཞ. ཟ, ཟླ, ཟླ, ཤ. ས, སྲ, སླ། The twenty-five མགོ་ཅན letters to which the letter བ may also be prefixed are as follows: རྐ, རྐྱ. སྐ. སྐྱ. སྐྲ, རྒ, རྒྱ, སྒ, སྒྱ, སྒྲ, ང, ཛ, རྗ, རྙ, སྙ, རྟ, སྟ, རྡ, སྡ. རྣ. སྣ, རྩ, སྩ, ཛྫ། For example: བཀར, བཀྱ, བཀྲ, བཀླ། བགར, བགྱ, བགྲ! བཙར, བཏར, བདར, བཞར, བཟར, བཤར, བསར། བཟླ. བཟླ, བསྲ, བསླ། བརྐ. བརྐྱ, བསྐ, བསྐྱ. བསྐྲ། བརྒ, བརྒྱ, བསྒ, བསྒྱ, བསྒྲ! བརྔ, བསྔ། བརྗ, བརྙ, བསྙ, བརྟ, བསྟ, བརྡ, བསྡ. བརྣ. བསྣ། བརྩ, བསྩ། བརྫ།

The above forty-five simple and compound letters may also be འདོགས་ཅན *i.e.*, joined with the four vowels.

མས་འཇུག་ཡི་གེ་རྣམས། The letter མ is prefixed to the following fifteen ཀྱང་པ letters: ཁ, ཁྱ, ཁྲ, ག, གྱ, གྲ, ང, ཆ, ཇ, ཉ, ཐ, ད, ན, ཚ, ཛ། For instance: མཁར, མཁྱ, མཁྲ, མགར, མགྱ, མགྲ, མངར, མཆར, མཇར, མཉར, མཐར, མདར, མནར,, མཚར, མཛར།

འས་འཇུག་ཡི་གེ་རྣམས། The letter འ is prefixed to the following nineteen ཀྱང་པ letters: ཁ, ཁྱ, ཁྲ, ག. གྱ, གྲ, ཆ, ཇ, ཐ, ད, དྲ, ཕ, ཕྱ, ཕྲ, བ, བྱ, བྲ, ཚ, ཛ། Thus འཁར, འཁྱ, འཁྲ, འགར, འགྱ, འགྲ, འཆར, འཇར, འཐར, འདར, འདྲ, འཕར, འཕྱ. འཕྲ, འབར, འབྱ, འབྲ, འཚར, འཛར॥

The proper method of spelling Tibetan words is illustrated in the work called དག་བྱེད་གསལ་བའི་མེ་ལོང་། which begins with the following lines: བརྗོད་བྱེད་ཚིག་གི་སྒྲ་འདྲ་ཡང་། བརྗོད་བྱ་དོན་ལ་ཁྱད་པར་ཡོད། དེ་ཕྱིར་ཡི་གེའི་དག་བྱེད་དགོས॥

(In this language) though words sound alike, in expressing there is distinction in the meanings conveyed by them; therefore, correctness in spelling is essential. The orthoepy of this peculiar language of monosyllabic origin is of little help to its orthography. In the above quotation there are two words of similar sound, namely: སྒྲ (*sgra*) meaning sound, and འདྲ (*h̲dr̲a*), meaning like or similar. Both are pronounced as "da". In their spelling they are so different, one is *sgra* and the other is *hdra*! The author then proceeds on thus: དེ་ཡང་ཀ་སོགས་གསལ་བྱེད་ལ། དབྱངས་ཨ་ཨི་ཨུ་ཨེ་ཨོ་དང་།

ཡ་ར་ལ་ཝ་སྣད་འདོགས་རྣམས། གང་རུང་ཡོད་ཀྱང་འཕུལ་དང་མགོ། མེད་ན་ཐམས་ཅད་ཀྱང་པ་ཡིན། སྔོན་འཇུག་ག་ད་བ་མ་འ།
ཡོད་ན་ཐམས་ཅད་འཕུལ་ཅན་ཡིན། སོ་དྲུ་ར་ལ་ས་གསུམ་པོ། ཡོད་པ་ཐམས་ཅད་མགོ་ཅན་ཡིན॥ explaining how the thirty letters of the alphabet beginning with ཀ are joined with the five vowels *a*, *i*, *u*, *e*, *o*—subjoined with *y*, *r*, *l*, *w*—surmounted by *r*, *l*, *s* and combined with the འཕུལ prefixes ག *g*, ད *d*, བ *b*, མ *m* and འ *h̲*.

Pronunciation

of the

མིང་གཞི *miń-gshi*, སྨད་འདོགས *smad-hdogs* and མགོ་ཅན *mgo-can* letters.

1. མིང་གཞི་ཡི་གེ། The simple letters:—

ཀ *k*	in kill, seek.	ཁ *ks*	in inkhorn.
ག *g*	in gun, go, dog.	ང *ń* (*ng*)	in sing, king.
ཅ *c* (*ch*)	in porch.	ཆ *ch*(*chh*)	in church-hill.
ཇ *j*	in jet, jump.	ཉ *ń* (*n*)	in singe.
ཏ *t*	in water (in Ireland).	ཐ *th*	in nut-hook.
ད *d*	in dice (more like *th* in this).	ན *n*	in not, nut.
པ *p*	in pull, page.	ཕ *ph*	in up-hill.
* བ *b*	in ball, boy, bard.	མ *m*	in man, map.
ཙ *ts*	in parts.	ཚ *tsh*	*ts* aspirated.
ཛ *ds*	in guards.	ཝ *w*	in waft, wave.
ཞ *sh*	in shone or s in leisure.	ཟ *z*	in azure or s in as.
འ *h*	in hour, honour.†	ཡ *y*	in yard, year.
ར *r*	in ray, rope.	ལ *l*	in last, large.
ཤ *ç* sh,	in sharp.	ས *s*	in same, soon.
ཧ *h*	in half, help.	ཨ *a*	in far.

In all the above twenty-nine letters the last letter ཨ is inherent, for which reason the Tibetan Grammarians have included it among consonants as a basis both for vowels and consonants. The letter འ *ḥ* called ཨ་ཆུང the little ཨ *a* is generally joined to the basic-vowel of a letter to make its pronunciation long. When it is subjoined to the letter ཨ the compound so formed becomes equivalent to the Sanskrit आ *ā* and is pronounced as *a* in tar, far, or father. When it is subjoined to the vowel ཨི the compound so formed resembles the Sanskrit ई and is pronounced like *i* in police .

---

* བ is sometimes differently sounded as *p*, *v* or *w*. As an initial word or when it begins a word it is pronounced like *p*; བ *pa*, a cow; བོད Tibet, to call. As an additional syllable, or particle after ང, འ, ར, ལ final letters, or when it has a ད prefix, it is generally pronounced as *wa*: ན་བ *na-wa*, illness; རེ་བ *re-wa* hope; བདེ་བ *bde-wa* happiness; when used as a final particle in a verb or adjective it is also pronounced as *w*: དགྲོ་བ *dgro-wa*, འདྲ་བ *ḥdra-wa*. In the words དབུ *dvu*, དབོ *dvo*, ཆུ་བོ *chu-vo*, it is sounded as *w* or *v*; with any of the surmounting letters ར, ལ, ས or with འ as a preceding letter, it is sounded as *b* རྦ *rba*, a wave; ལྦ *lba*, goitre; སྦ *sba*, to hide; འབང *ḥbań*, to soak.

† In the early stage of Tibetan literature the letter འ used to be added to every radical syllable ending in the vowel *a*, *i*, *u*, *e*, or *o*, thus: ཀའ, གིའ, གུའ, གེའ, གོའ. In being so used འ simply represented the vowel ཨ which in modern Tibetan is left out or retained only in those syllables in which the radical letter is preceded by a སྔོན་འཇུག་ prefix, and where there is no closing consonant after the inherent ཨ. But when there is a closing consonant, the འ is dropped; as in the past tense of འདའ *i. e.*, in the word འདས. signifying gone away.

2. སྦྱད་འདོགས Subjoined letters:—

The four compounds of this class which in their pronunciation, in modern Tibetan, resemble the four simple letters ཅ, ཆ, ཇ, ཉ:

པྱ	*pya*	is pronounced as	ཅ *ca*.	ཕྱ	*phya*	is pronounced as	ཆ *cha*.
བྱ	*bya*	,, ,,	,, ཇ *ja*.	མྱ	*mya*	,, ,,	,, ཉ *ña*.

In nine, out of the thirteen basic consonants, to which the letter ར *r* may be subjoined, the basic constituent is seldom pronounced in Tibet proper, but the compounds so formed have a pronunciation altogether different from that of any of the constituents:

ཀྲ	ཁྲ	གྲ	ཏྲ	ཐྲ	དྲ	པྲ	ཕྲ	བྲ
kra,	*khra*,	*gra*,	*tra*,	*thra*,	*dra*,	*pra*,	*phra*,	*bra*,
(*ṭa*),	(*ṭha*),	(*ṭa* or *ḍa*),	(*ṭa*),	(*ṭha*),	(*ḍa*),	(*ṭa*),	(*ṭha*),	(*ṭa* or *ḍa*),

In the four compounds མྲ *mra*, ཤྲ *çra*, སྲ *sra*, ཧྲ *hra*—the constituents are more or less pronounced.*

The nine compounds of which the pronunciation resembles that of the Sanskrit cerebrals ट, ठ, ड represented by the (ལོག་ཡིག inverted letters ཊ, ཋ, ཌ:—

ཀྲ *kra*	(*ṭa*)	ཏྲ *tra*	(*ṭa*)	པྲ *pra*	(*ṭa*)	ཁྲ *khra*	(*ṭha*)
						ཐྲ *thra*	(*ṭha*)
གྲ *gra*	(*ḍa*)	དྲ *dra*	(*ḍa*)	བྲ *bra*	(*ḍa*)	ཕྲ *pra*	(*ḍa*)

ཐྲ is seldom used in Tibetan except in transcribing Sanskrit words.

The pronunciation of the six basic consonants to which the letter ལ may be subjoined, has been explained in page 4.

3. མགོ་ཅན Superscribed letters:—

The pronunciation of these compound letters has been explained in page 6. The letters ག, ཇ, ད. བ, when surmounted by ར, ལ, ས are pronounced like g (hard), j, d and b.

---

* In Tsang སྲ is pronounced as ས *sa* this pronunciation in markedly so in the word སྲས signifying a son. In the word སྲེ (name of a streamlet on the bank of which is situated the *Sre rgyuḍ-paḥi ḍgon-pa*) the pronunciation is Rhé. In the word སྲམ, signifying an otter, the pronunciation is *rham*.

ཚེག (་)

Between the two syllables of a dissyllabic word a triangular point called ཚེག (inter-syllabic stop) intervenes being placed on the top, as in the words དམ་པ། དགེ་བ། སྡིག་པ། This point is also used in separating one word from another in an expression or sentence; as for instance, in the expression དམ་པ་རྣམས་ལ། (to the holy ones), there are three such stops; between the words དམ་པ and རྣམས there is a ཚེག and between རྣམས and ལ there is another; but no ཚེག should be placed after ལ no matter whether a ཤད (།) the perpendicular stroke representing a comma, is put or not after the expression. In དགེ་བའི་ལས (a pious deed), there are two; in སྡིག་པ་ཅན་གྱི་བྱ་བ (a sinner's doings), there are five ཚེག། No ཚེག should be placed after the closing letter of a monosyllabic word when ending an expression or sentence. In a dissyllabic word the closing letter of the second syllable, unless it be ང, should not be followed by a ཚེག། When at the end of an expression or sentence, a word terminates in ང the ཚེག must be placed in the event a ཤད (།) has been put. If no ཚེག intervenes between ང and the ཤད the two placed in close proximity of each other, would form the letter ག། Hence the necessity of putting a ཚེག between ང and །. The use of the ཚེག between words as well, in an expressien or sentence, *i.e.*, ཚེག་བར་ཚེག discloses the monosyllabic origin of the Tibetan language.

ཚིག་ཕྲད།

The Tibetan, though it abounds in monosyllabic words, is in fact a dissyllabic language.* The formation of the second syllable in a word of two syllables is governed by the final letter of the preceding syllable, *i.e.*, the first syllable which in itself is a word. The second syllable is generally an additive or deflective particle called ཚེག་ཕྲད which often modifies the meaning of the preceding part of the word.

These additive particles chiefly indicate the different parts of speech. They are generally used in the formation of cases and in the declension of verbs and pronouns.

The first part of a dissyllabic word or ཚེག is the root-word. It is called མིང་གཞི། The word itself is called ཚེག, མིང or མིང་ཚེག when it is grammatically formed. The second part of it called ཕྲད or འཕྲད independently is never a word.

Words apparently trisyllabic are not rare in this language: སྡིག་པ་ཅན། དགེ་བ་ཅན། དཀར་ལྡན་པ། etc., those which occur largely in the sacred books are generally literal translations from the Sanskrit, such as ཡང་དག་པ (*Samyak*), རྣམ་པ་ཅན། སངས་རྒྱས་པ། བཅོམ་ལྡན་འདས། These are but expressions rather than words.

སྒྲ Sound.

Sounds སྒྲ are ཤེས་པ *i.e.*, articulate and མ་ཤེས་པ inarticulate. An articulate sound when represented by a letter or by a grammatical combination of two or more letters is called ཚེག། The particle which is added to a monosyllabic ཚེག to form a complete word is called ཕྲད་སྒྲ། Either of the syllables in a dissyllabic word or ཚེག or a postpositive particle like ཏུ, དུ, རུ, ལ or སུ etc., is also sometimes called སྒྲ signifying a term.

---

* The Tibetan tongue is incapable of pronouncing monosyllabic words like school, full, rule, fame, etc. A Tibetan will read the word "school" as *i-si coo-li*; "full" as *ful-li*; "rule" as *ru-le*; "fame" as *fa-me*, etc.

EXAMPLES OF ཚིག་ཕྲད།།

ཀ as in དཔྱིད་ཀ ནུབ་ཀ གཉིས་ཀ། ཁ as in དབྱར་ཁ རྒྱལ་ཁ སྟོན་ཁ།

ག „ རི་ག ཡོང་ག ལམ་ག། ཏུ „ ཤིན་ཏུ ཀུན་ཏུ རབ་ཏུ།

དུ „ ཐུང་དུ ལམ་དུ བོད་དུ། རུ „ འདི་རུ དེ་རུ མཁའ་རུ།

སུ „ གཡས་སུ ཕྱུགས་སུ ཕོགས་སུ། ཏེ „ གསན་ཏེ འཁྱུར་ཏེ ཉལ་ཏེ།

དེ „ ཡོད་དེ བྱེད་དེ དགོད་དེ། སྟེ „ འདུག་སྟེ སྨྲ་སྟེ སློབ་སྟེ།

པ „ ལག་པ སྒྲོག་པ དམ་པ། བ „ ཀ་བ འོང་བ རྒྱལ་བ།

མ „ བླ་མ བར་མ སྐར་མ། པོ „ རྒྱལ་པོ སྔོན་པོ སྣང་པོ།

བོ „ ཆུ་བོ ནུ་བོ རི་བོ། མོ „ མ་མོ བརྟན་མོ རྒྱལ་མོ།

ཀྱི „ ནུབ་ཀྱི བོད་ཀྱི སེམས་ཀྱི། གི „ བདག་གི ཤིང་གི རང་གི།

གྱི „ རིན་གྱི ལམ་གྱི གསེར་གྱི། འི „ མིའི ལ་འི བླ་མའི།

ཡི „ མེ་ཡི ས་ཡི ཕྱི་ཡི། གོ, ངོ, དོ, ནོ, བོ, མོ, འོ, རོ, ལོ, སོ, ཏོ!

འདུག་གོ, སོང་ངོ, ཡོད་དོ, ཡིན་ནོ, ཐོབ་བོ, ལམ་མོ, མི་འོ, འགྱུར་རོ, གསལ་ལོ, ལེགས་སོ, གསནད་ཏོ

པར as in ལག་པར མགྱོགས་པར སྒྲོག་པར། བར as in ཉེ་བར འོང་བར གསལ་བར།

ཅིག ཕྱུག་ཅིག སྡོད་ཅིག ནུབ་ཅིག། * ཞིག „ གང་ཞིག མི་ཞིག མཁར་ཞིག།

ཤིག „ ཟོས་ཤིག སེམས་ཤིག སྦྱོས་ཤིག། ཅིང „ སྒྲོག་ཅིང སྒྱུར་ཅིང གསན་ཅིང།

ཞིང „ སྨྲ་ཞིང འགྱུར་ཞིང འཚང་ཞིང། ཤིང „ སླུས་ཤིང བཀྲུགས་ཤིང ཞུས་ཤིང།

---

* ཅིག་སྒྲ *i.e.*, ཅིག in the words ཁ་ཅིག, ལྷན་ཅིག, ཐབས་ཅིག, ལན་ཅིག is not to be considered as an additive particle ཚིག་ཕྲད། In these it forms a part of the word itself.

ཁ་ཅིག་ལྷན་ཅིག་ཐབས་ཅིག་དང་། ལན་ཅིག་སོགས་ཀྱི་ཅིག་སྒྲ་དེ། མིང་གི་ཆ་ཤས་ཡིན་པས་ན། ཚིག་ཕྲད་གྲངས་སུ་མ་ཆུད་བཅེས།།

ON THE USE OF ཕྲད (additive particles).

The seven ཚིག་ཕྲད *viz.*, སུ,ར,རུ,དུ,ན,ལ, and also ཏུ used after ད་དྲག or not are called ལ་དོན་གྱི་རྣམ་དབྱེ། Their use in forming cases after nouns and pronouns is illustrated as follows:—

In the expression སྐྱབས་སུ་མཆིའོ I take refuge (in Buddha), the ཕྲད (particle) སུ is called ལས་ཀྱི་སྒྲ and shows that the word སྐྱབས is in the objective case.

In the expression དབུལ་ཕོངས་ལ་སྦྱིན་པ་གཏོང་། Give alms to the indigent, and helpless. The use of the ཕྲད (particle) ལ puts དབུལ་ཕོངས in the dative case. Here ལ is called དགོས་ཆེད་ཀྱི་སྒྲ *i. e.*, the term expressing necessity.

In the expression ཤར་ཕྱོགས་སུ་ཡོད signifying is or exists in the East, the use of the ཕྲད (particle) སུ points to (eastward) ཤར་ཕྱོགས which is put in the locative case. སུ is here called རྟེན་གནས་ཀྱི་སྒྲ the term showing location.

In the expression འོད་དུ་གསལ illuminates or brightens in or with light, the ཕྲད particle དུ signifies in or with. Here though the word འོད (light) is in the objective case the ཕྲད particle དུ is called དེ་ཉིད་ཀྱི་སྒྲ the term signifying state of that or "*that itself*".

In the expression ཉི་མ་ཤར་བ་ན་ཆོས་བརྗོད། Ejaculate religious formulas at sun-rise *i,e.*, when the sun rises, the ཕྲད particle, ན signifying "at" or "when" puts ཉི་མ་ཤར་བ in the locative case. Being indicative of time it is also called ཚེ་སྐབས་ཀྱི་སྒྲ།

In this manner the ཕྲད (particles) སུ,ར,རུ,དུ,ཏུ,ན and ལ all go under the name of ལ་སྒྲ། and are used for དོན་ཅན་ལྔ five purposes.*

The particle ཏུ is used after ག,བ and ད་དྲག *i.e.*, when a word closes with the letter ག or བ or ད་དྲག. such as མཆོད་ཏུ།

The ཕྲད (particles) སུ and དུ are used after ང,ད,ན,མ,ར,ལ final letters in a word. ཐུག་ཏུ, རབ་ཏུ, ཀུན་དུ, ཕ་རོལ་ཏུ,

སུ is used after words ending in ས. such as ཕྱོགས་སུ, གཡས་སུ། The ཕྲད (particle) ར is used after འ (express or understood) such as ལྷར་གསལ།

For the use of ལ and ན one has not to look to the nature of the losing letter in a word. They may be used after the ten རྗེས་འཇུག letters such as ག,ང,ད,ན,བ,མ,འ,ར,ལ,ས། for example :—

གང་དུ, གང་ལ; ཐམས་ཅད་དུ, ཐམས་ཅད་ལ; གདན་དུ, གདན་ལ; དཔལ་དུ, དཔལ་ལ; ནམ་དུ, ནམ་ལ;
ཤར་དུ, ཤར་ལ; རང་ཉིད་ཡིད་དམ་ལྷ་རུ་གསལ། ཐོག་ལ, ཐོག་ན, སྙིང་ལ, སྙིང་ན།

The use of ཏུ after words ending in ག,བ and ད་དྲག is in conformity with the rule ཕོས་ཕོའི་མིང་མཐའ་འཇུག་པའི་ཚུལ།

The use of དུ after words ending ང, མ, འ, ས, conform to the rule མོས་མོ་ཡིག་འཇུག་པ། དུ is used after words ending in ད simply for erephoy or easy pronunciation. Its use after words ending in ན,ར,ལ is according to the rule རྟགས་མཚུངས་དང་དུ་མེད་པས་བརྗོད་བདེ་འཇུག་པའི་ལུགས། The use of ཏུ after words ending in ག,བ and ད་དྲག; of དུ after word sending in ང,མ; after words ending in འ as in མཐའ་དུ; of སུ after words ending in ས and also of དུ after words ending in ན,ར,ལ is according to the rule མིང་མཐའ་འཇུག་ཚུལ།

* ༡ ལས་ཀྱི་སྒྲ, ༢ དགོས་ཆེད་ཀྱི་སྒྲ, ༣ རྟེན་གནས་ཀྱི་སྒྲ, ༤ དེ་ཉིད་ཀྱི་སྒྲ, ༥ ཚེ་སྐབས་ཀྱི་སྒྲ།

ལ or ན are never used to express དེ་ཉིད། The remaining five ཕྲད additine particles སུ་ར་རུ་དུ་ཏུ, as in the following illustrations all express ལ་དོན། ཤར་ཕྱོགས་སུ་འགྲོ – ཤར་ཕྱོགས་ལ་འགྲོ། go towards East. རྡོ་བར་གཟུགས་བརྙན་བྱེད། make imag on stone, རབ་ཏུ་སོང་། gone to excellence *i.e.*, become excellent.

གང་གིས་དགེ་བ་མཐའ་རུ་འཁྱོལ། by whom piety has been carried to the limit. རྒྱ་གར་དུ་འགྲོ། proceed to India.

སླར་བསྡུ་བ།

Reduplication of terminal letters.

When the closing consonant of a monosyllabic word (noun, pronoun or adjective), is reduplicated and the two letters are separated by a ཚེག (་) and the vowel o (ོ) is placed on the duplicate letter, the second syllable so formed is called སླར་བསྡུ བླ་བསྡུ or རྫོགས་ཚིག།* It does the function of the verb to be. For instance: བདག་གོ I am, འདི་སྨན་ནོ this is medicine; དེ་ལམ་མོ that is road or way; དོན་ནོ is the meaning or sense; ཁོང་ངོ, he is; བཟང་ངོ is good; ངན་ནོ is bad; བདེན་ནོ is true.

Words closing with the vowels *a*, *i*, *u*, *e* and *o* being supposed to be འ་མཐའ་ཅན *i.e.*, those that have got the letter འ after them, expressed or understood, do not undergo the process of reduplication of the final འ letter. The vowel o is only put on its head; for example: ངའོ. I am; འདིའོ this is; སུའོ, who is; དེའོ, that is; ཁོའོ he is; བཀའོ is precept or command, མཐའོ is the end or limit.

In dissyllabic words when the second syllable consists of a single letter with the vowel termination (simple or འདོགས་ཅན) the letter འ with the vowel o (ོ) is joined to it. The འོ also then acts as the verb to be. For example, བདེན་པའོ is true; བདེ་བའོ is happiness; དེ་སྲིན་བུའོ that is worm; འདི་སྲིན་པོའོ། སྲིན་མོའོ this is *Rākṣasa* or *Rāksasī*; རིང་པོའོ is long, or distant, ཐུང་ངུའོ is short. If the second syllable, in a word of two syllables, be formed of two or three letters the closing consonant in it is reduplicated as with monosyllabic words. དེ་སེམས་ཅན་ནོ that is animal; དོན་ལྡན་ནོ is significant, or is with meaning.

When words ending in ན,ར,ལ close with ད according to བརྡ་རྙིང (old orthography) the ཕྲད, particle ཏོ should used: as in བསམནད་ཏོ, འགྱུརད་ཏོ. གསལད་ཏོ, This practice is now seldom followed.*

The reduplication of the closing letter in a verb indicates that it is in the indicative mood present, future or perfect tense. འདོད་དོ wishes, ཐོབ་བོ got or has got; འགྱུར་རོ become, གྱུར་རོ has become; འཚོལ་ལོ I seek or wish.

---

* གོ ངོ དོ ནོ བོ མོ འོ། རོ ལོ སོ་རྣམས་རྫོགས་ཚིག་སྟེ། སླར་སྡུད་བླ་སྡུད་ཅེས་ཀྱང་བྱ། * ན་ར་ལ་གསུམ་རྗེས་སུ་ནི། ད་དྲག་ཐོབ་ཚེ་ཏོ་ཞེས་བྱར།

ARTICLE.

There are three definite articles and three indefinite articles in the Tibetan language. ཀ, ཁ, ག are definite articles signifying "the". ཅིག, ཞིག, ཤིག signifying a, an, any, some, certain (indeterminate) are indefinite articles. These are attached to words as ཚིག་ཕྲད additive particles.

The letter ཀ signifying "the" is used after words ending in ག, ད, བ, ས; for instance དྲུག་ཀ, the six; དཔྱིད་ཀ the spring; ནུབ་ཀ the evening; གཉིས་ཀ the two.

ཁ is used after ན, ར, ལ; as in སྟོན་ཁ the autumn; དབྱར་ཁ the summer; ཡུལ་ཁ the country.

ག is used after ང, མ; and འ (expressed or understood) or after any vowel; as in གླིང་ག the grove; གསུམ་ག the three; ན་ག the grassy plain or green; གཞི་ག the estate.

The indefinite article ཅིག is attached to words ending in ག, ད, བ; and also after the inherent ས thus: དམག་ཅིག a war; སྣོད་ཅིག a vessel; ནུབ་ཅིག a night. ཅིག is different from གཅིག signifying "one".

ཞིག is used with words ending in ང, ན, མ, འ, ར, ལ; thus: ཁང་ཞིག a house; ལན་ཞིག an answer; ལམ་ཞིག a road; འགའ་ཞིག some, or any body; མི་ཞིག a man; མཁར་ཞིག a castle; གར་ཞིག a camp; ཤེལ་ཞིག a crystal; རིན་ཞིག a price.

ཤིག is attached to words closing with ས thus: གོས་ཤིག a robe or garment; ལུས་ཤིག a body.

གེ in སེང་གེ, ང in [illegible], ཊ in [illegible], ཉི in མི་ཉི, བ in ཀ་བ, མ in ཞ་མ or ཟླ་མ, དགོན་པ་མ or འགྲོ་བ་མ and མོ in མ་མོ, འགྲོ་བ་མོ or བྱེད་པ་མོ are ཚིག་ཕྲད additive particles; they are not to be taken as Articles. The word སེང་གེ is a corrupt form of the Sanskrit *simha* signifying "lion". མ་མོ is the Tibetan for Sanskrit *Mātrikā*. ཉི in མི་ཉི is a particle of emphasis like "the" in the expression 'he is *the* man for such a work'. It is equivalent to Sanskrit *hi*.

མིང or མིང་ཚིག NOUN.

Substantive nouns are generally monosyllabic words though they may be formed of one or more letters; for instance, ཁ mouth, ཇ tea, ཉ fish, ཕ father, མ mother, བ cow, ཝ fox, ར goat ལ a high mountain, ཤ flesh, ས earth, etc., ཆུ water, རྟ horse, ཚྭ salt, ཞྭ a hat or cap, རྭ a horn ཕོ male, བུ son, མོ female, མི man, ཚེ life, ཞོ curds, འོ kiss, རི hill, རོ corpse, taste; ལི bell-metal, སོ tooth, མིག eye, ནམ sky, ལམ way, གཏམ discourse, ངག speech, དོན meaning, སེམས mind, ཡིད heart, ཤིང tree or wood; གླུ song.

Nouns formed with ཚིག་ཕྲད *i. e.*, additive particles are as follows: ལག་པ hand, རྐང་པ foot, ཀོ་བ skin, hide-boat; ཁང་པ house; ཁང་བུ cell; མཐེ་བུ thumb; ཕྲུ་གུ child or young one; ཁ་བ snow; ཀ་བ pillar, རྒྱལ་པོ king, ཉི་མ sun, ཐིགས་པ drop, ཕག་པ hog, གླང་པོ ox, བོང་བོ donkey, བློན་པོ minister. In the foregoing words the particles གུ, པ, པོ, བ, བུ མོ do not act the part of an Article. They make the full word of a monosyllabic term. In composition, they are sometimes omitted. The expression རྒྱལ་བློན is same as རྒྱལ་པོ king and བློན་པོ minister; རྐང་ལག is same as རྐང་པ foot and ལག་པ hand; དཀར་ནག is same as དཀར་པོ white and ནག་པོ black.

When attached to some monosyllabic terms they ཚིག་ཕྲད sometimes make difference in the meaning.

The word ངོ signifies "self" but joined with the particle བོ *i.e.*, ངོ་བོ signifies "nature." དང means "and" but དང་པོ signifies "first." བལ means "wool," བལ་པོ signifies a Nepalese.

Adjective nouns are also formed with ཚིག་ཕྲད attached to the adjective monosyllabic terms, such as བཟང་པོ the good, ངན་པ the wicked or the evil one. The expression བཟང་ངན signifies good and bad and also the good and the bad.

The use of ཚིག་ཕྲད additive particles with some nouns causes distinction in their signification as to size, &c.

In the following examples the use of བོ and ཅུ is thus illustrated:— མི is man; མི་བོ a great man (either in stature or position); མི་ཅུ a little man or dwarf. ཉ fish, ཉ་བོ great fish, ཉི་ཅུ little fish. ཤ antelope, ཤ་བོ big antelope, ཤ་ཅུ small antelope; ང drum, ང་བོ large drum, ངེ་ཅུ drumlet; མདའ arrow, མདའ་བོ large and long arrow, མདེ་ཅུ small arrow; རྡོ stone, རྡོ་བ huge stone, boulder or rock, རྡེ་ཅུ small boulder or pebble; རྫ earthen vessel or pot, རྫ་བོ large earthen pot or vessel, རྫེ་ཅུ small earthen pot or vessel.

In the above examples, the substantives (དངོས་པོ) such as མི, ཉ, ཤ etc., when unaccompanied by ཚིག་ཕྲད express the ordinary meaning, man, fish, antelope etc*. When joined with བོ they convey a magnifying sense; with ཅུ they become diminutives.

In the following examples the use of the ཚིག་ཕྲད additive particles ཅུ and གུ with some nouns expresses "the young one"† but nothing diminutive: ང་མོང camel, ངེ་ཅུ young camel; རྟ horse or pony, རྟེ་ཅུ colt; ཤ antelope, ཤེ་ཅུ young antelope, (ཤ་ཅུ meaning small size antelope); བ cow, བེ་ཅུ calf; ར goat, རེ་ཅུ kid; ཁྱི dog, ཁྱི་ཅུ pup; ལུག sheep, ལུག་གུ lamb.

PLURAL NUMBER མང་ཚིག།

The ཚིག་ཕྲད (additive particles) ཚོ, རྣམས, དག, ཅག are used as plural terminations. They are attached to nouns and pronouns in the singular number to express plurality. ཚོ is seldom attached to nouns. Its use is confined to pronouns. དག is attached to both nouns and pronouns. རྣམས is seldom attached to pronouns. Though there is no dual in the Tibetan language, yet the Sanskrit duals have been generally rendered by the termination དག in Tibetan. ང is the personal pronoun signifying I; ང་ཚོ signifies "we". It is not usual to express the meaning "we" by the word ང་རྣམས།

ཁོང means "he"; ཁོང་ཚོ signifies "they". ཁྱོད or ཁྱེད means "you" or "thou"; ཁྱོད་ཅག or ཁྱེད་ཚོ signifies "you". དེ signifies "that"; དེ་ཚོ or དེ་དག signifies "those".

མི is man; མི་རྣམས signifies "men". སེམས་ཅན animal; སེམས་ཅན་རྣམས animals. ཀུན, དགུ, བཅུ, མཐའ་དག, ཐམས་ཅད, ཡོངས, སོགས, ཚོགས are but words signifying many, all, collection, etc. They are never used as plural terminations in the manner the additive particles ཚོ, རྣམས, དག and ཅག are used. The two words མི་ཀུན signify "all men". The expression རི་དགུ་ལུང་དགུ comprising of four words signifies "many hills and many valleys". If it was divided into two parts རི་དགུ and ལུང་དགུ, རི་དགུ, would mean nine hills and ལུང་དགུ nine valleys. རི་རྣམས signifying "hills" is only one word; the expression རི་ཐམས་ཅད comprising of the two words, རི and ཐམས་ཅད signifies "all hills".

---

* དང་པོ་དངོས་པོ་རང་བབ་དང་། བར་པ་ཆེན་པོའམ་མཆོག་ལ་འཇུག། ཐ་མ་ཆུང་ངུ་དམན་པའི་མིང་།

† ཕྲ་མ་སེམས་ཅན་རང་མིང་དང་། ཕྱི་མ་ཕྲུ་གུའི་མིང་དུ་གྲགས།།

ཕོ་མོའི་མཚན་ or རྟགས GENDER.

ཕོ་མཚན་ is masculine gender; མོ་མཚན་ feminine gender, and མཚན་མེད་ signifies the neuter or no gender.

ཕོ signifies male, མོ female. Monosyllabic nouns in the masculine gender generally take the ཚིག་ཕྲད (additive particles) མ and མོ as feminine terminations; such as, བུ son or boy, བུ་མོ daughter or girl; ཁྱི dog, ཁྱི་མོ bitch; སྲས son, སྲས་མོ daughter; ཝ fox, ཝ་མོ vixen; སྟག tiger, སྟག་མོ tigress; ལྷ god, ལྷ་མོ goddess; ནུ younger brother, ནུ་མོ younger sister; ར goat, ར་མོ she-goat; མཁའ་འགྲོ one moving in the sky, མཁའ་འགྲོ་མ female angel.

The feminine of some monosyllabic nouns is expressed by different words: such as, མི man, བུད་མེད woman; འབྲི yak-cow, གཡག yak-bull of Tibet; it is incorrect to say ཕོ་གཡག; ཕ་གཡག (father-yak) *i.e.*, yak that is kept for breeding purpose. རྟ is horse, ཕ་རྟ stallion, རྒོད་མ mare; it is incorrect to say ཕོ་རྟ or རྟ་ཕོ; the use of ཕོ before or after རྟ being redundant. གླང signifies a bull, so it is incorret to say ཕོ་གླང or གླང་ཕོ། བ signifies cow; so it is incorrect to say བ་མོ། To dissyllabic words པ or པོ is added to signify the masculine; such as རྣལ་འབྱོར་པ (Sans. *Yogi*) and མ or མོ indicates the feminine, such as རྣལ་འབྱོར་མ (*Yoginī*).

In dissyllabic nouns the ཚིག་ཕྲད (additive particles) པ, པོ or བ, བོ are used as masculine terminations. These are changed into མ and མོ for feminine terminations, such as, གནས་པོ host, གནས་མོ hostess; ཕག་པ hog, ཕག་མོ sow, swine; ཚོང་པ trader, ཚོང་མ female seller; བཙུན་པ monk, བཙུན་མ nun; དབང་པོ ever-lord, དབང་མོ lady; རྒྱལ་པོ king, རྒྱལ་མོ queen; སྲུང་པ guard, སྲུང་མ female guard; དཔོན་པོ chief, དཔོན་མོ chief's wife or lady-chief; གཙོ་བོ lord, གཙོ་མོ lady; བོད་པ a Tibetan (male), བོད་མོ a Tibetan woman; དཔའ་བོ hero, དཔའ་མོ heroine; བླ་མ signifying one above (in Sans. *Guru*) is used in both the genders; so also གོང་མ, a superior; མ and མོ are sometimes used as female terminations and as such are attached to dissyllabic nouns, such as, དབྱངས་ཅན he with (good) voice, དབྱངས་ཅན་མ she with good voice (*Svara-svati*), དགེ་སློང ordained monk (Sans.) *Bhikṣu*), དགེ་སློང་མ ordained nun, (*Bhikṣuni*); གླང་ཆེན elephant, གླང་ཆེན་མོ she-elephant, བཅོམ་ལྡན་འདས he, the victorious one; བཅོམ་ལྡན་འདས་མ she, the victorious one.

Nouns having no gender also terminate with the ཚིག་ཕྲད additive particles པ, བུ, པོ, མ and མོ, such as ཐིགས་པ, ཐིགས་མ, ཐིགས་པོ, ཐིགས་བུ all signifying drop; སྒོ་པོ, སྒོ་མ, door or gate; གསར་པ or གསར་མ, new or novel ལྷག་པ or ལྷག་མ, additional or remnant.

Some words with མ or མོ, termination are used in both neuter and feminine genders: ནང་མ, inner also the inner one *i.e.*, wife. ཕྱི་མ the outer or the later one; འོག་མ, the lower or subodinate. སྟོན་མོ banquet, show.

Some adjective nouns ending in མ are used only in the feminine gender; such as, ཆུང་མ, wife, མཛེས་མ, a beauty (Sans. *Sundarī*), handsome woman; things inanimate (except lakes, rivers and mountains) are put in the neuter gender. They terminate irregularly and also in པ, པོ; མ, མོ; such as ཟམ་པ a bridge, ཐག་པ rope སྨིན་པོ the accomplished (one;) པར་མ printed (thing); གཏོར་མ oblation; སྒོར་མོ the (Indian) *Rupee*; སློང་མོ (Sans. *Bhikṣā*) alms, begging.

རྣམ་དབྱེ CASE.

SANS. *Vibhakti*)

There are eight cases in the Tibetan language. They are arranged in the following order:—

1.	Nominative	རྣམ་དབྱེ་དང་པོ།	མིང་ཙམ་སྟོན་པ།	The person or thing is simply named.
2.	Accusative or Objective	,, ,, གཉིས་པ།	ལས་སུ་བྱ་བ་སྟོན་པ།	Shows the object of a transitive verb.
3.	Agentive or Instrumentive	,, ,, གསུམ་པ།	བྱེད་པ་པོ་སྟོན་པ།	Indicates the agent (involving) the notion of *by* or *with*).
4.	Dative or Necessitative	,, ,, བཞི་པ།	དགོས་ཆེད་སྟོན་པ།	Expresses necessity and is indicated by *to* or *for*.
5.	Ablative or Originative	,, ,, ལྔ་པ།	འབྱུང་ཁུངས་སྟོན་པ།	Expresses source or *direction from* or *time*.
6.	Possessive or Genitive	,, ,, དྲུག་པ།	འབྲེལ་བ་སྟོན་པ།	Indicates possession or connection.
7.	Locative	,, ,, བདུན་པ།	གནས་གཞི་སྟོན་པ།	Indicates place.
8.	Vocative	,, ,, བརྒྱད་པ།	བོད་པ་སྟོན་པ།	Indicates calling or addressing a person.

In the declension of nouns, pronouns, adjectives, numerals, and participles, several secondary ཚིག་ཕྲད (additive particles) are used. They are attached to monosyllabic words or to the ཚིག་ཕྲད, such as པ in ལག་པ or མ in ཟླ་མ, in dissyllabic words or to the plural signs or postpositive particles like ཚོ, རྣམས, དག &c. They are as follows: ཀྱི, ཀྱིས, གི, གིས, གྱི, གྱིས, ཏུ, དུ, འི, འིས, ཡི, ཡིས, ར, རུ, ས, སུ, and ལ.

In the Nominative and Vocative cases, singular or plural, no secondary particles indicative of case, are attached.

ON THE USE OF SECONDARY ADDITIVE PARTICLES.

ཀྱི and ཀྱིས (ད་བ་ས་ཡི་རྗེས་སུ་ཀྱི or ཀྱིས) are attached to words ending in ད, བ, or ས: ཁྱོད་ཀྱི of you; ཡབ་ཀྱིས by father; ལུས་ཀྱི of body, དུས་ཀྱིས by time.

གི and གིས (ག་དང་ང་ཡི་རྗེས་སུ་གི or གིས) are attached to words terminating in ག or ང, such as ལུག་གི of sheep, མིང་གི of name. དུག་གིས by or with poison; དུང་གིས by or with conch-shell trumpet.

གྱི and གྱིས (ན་མ་ར་ལ་འི་རྗེས་སུ་གྱི or གྱིས) are attached to words ending in ན, མ, ར, or ལ, such as དོན་གྱི of meaning; ནམ་གྱིས by heaven; ནོར་གྱིས by wealth; ཡུལ་གྱི of country.

ཏུ (ག་བ་ནད་རད་ལད་ཀྱི་མཐའ་ཏུ་ཏུ) is attached to words terminating in ག or བ or in ད་དྲག (expressed or understood), for example: ལག་ཏུ in or to hand ; ནུབ་ཏུ to the west or in the west. According to བརྡ་རྙིང old orthography the spelling of ཀུནད་ཏུ, ཤརད་ཏུ, ཕ་རོལད་ཏུ etc., words ending in ད called ད་དྲག is correct. In modern Tibetan, these are written as ཀུན་ཏུ, ཤར་ཏུ, ཕ་རོལ་ཏུ, the ད་དྲག being understood, though not expressed after ན, ར and ལ.

དུ (ང་ད་ན་མ་ར་ལའི་མཐའ་དུ་དུ) is attached to words ending in ང, ད, ན, མ, ར, or ལ, such as མིང་དུ in or by name ; བོད་དུ in or to Tibet ; རིན་དུ for or in price ; ལམ་དུ on the way ; གསེར་དུ in or to gold ; ཡུལ་དུ into country or place.

འི, ཡི, འིས, ཡིས, or ས is attached to words ending in any vowel ; མའི of mother ; མི་ཡི of man ; ཆུ་ཡི of water ; ཕོ་ཡི of male ; མེས by fire ; ལྷ་ཡི by god ; དེ་འི of that.

ར, or རུ is attached to words ending in འ or in any vowel : ལྷར or ལྷ་རུ in or to god ; མིར or མི་རུ in or into man ; ཆུར or ཆུ་རུ into water ; མེར into fire ; ལྷོར or ལྷོ་རུ to (the) south.

ལ is the general sign of Accusative and Dative cases; signifying *to*. It is applied to any Nominative for forming those cases.

སུ is attached to words terminating in ས : གཡས་སུ to (the) right : ལས་སུ in (the) work, གྲོགས་སུ in friendship.

ཀྱེ signifying O, (Sans. *Bho*); ཀྱེ་ཧུད (Sans. *Ahovata*) &c., are words, (not particles) that are placed before Nominatives for forming the Vocative case.

ལ, ཏུ, དུ, ར, རུ and སུ signifying to, on, upon, into, unto, with regard or respect to, for, &c., are attached to the Nominative for forming the Accusative and Dative cases. The use of the above particles after the Nominative, according to its final letter, also indicate motion or progression to, into, or change, turn into promotion, &c.

གྱིས, གིས, ཀྱིས, འིས, ཡིས, or ས signifying by, with, is attached to the Nominative for forming the Agentive or Instrumentive case.

ཀྱི, གི, གྱི, འི, or ཡི signifying of, pertaining, relating, belonging to, and also the possessive sign *'s* is attached to the Nominative for forming the Genitive or Possessive case.

ནས or ལས signifying of, out of, from, is attached to the Nominative for forming the Ablative case.

ན or ལ signifying rest in, at, on, a place, also motion to, or towards a place, is attached to the Nominative for forming the Locative case.

Example of declension according to Tibetan methods.

	Singular.	Dual or Plural.*	Plural.
Nominative	སངས་རྒྱས Buddha,	སངས་རྒྱས་དག Buddhas,	སངས་རྒྱས་རྣམས Buddhas.
Accusative	སངས་རྒྱས་ལ་ (བརྟེན),	སངས་རྒྱས་དག་ལ་ (བརྟེན)།	སངས་རྒྱས་རྣམས་ལ་ (བརྟེན)།
	Depend on Buddha.	Depend on (both the) Buddhas.	Depend on Buddhas.
Agentive	སངས་རྒྱས་ཀྱིས་ (གསུངས)།	སངས་རྒྱས་དག་གིས་ (གསུངས)	སངས་རྒྱས་རྣམས་ཀྱིས་ (གསུངས)།
	By Buddha said.	By (both the) Buddhas said.	By Buddhas said.
Dative	(སེམས་ཅན་གྱི་དོན་) དུ་སངས་རྒྱས་ (བསྒྲུབས)།	སངས་རྒྱས་དག་ (བསྒྲུབས)།	སངས་རྒྱས་རྣམས་ (བསྒྲུབས)།*
	(Attained) to Buddha (hood) for (the good of animate beings).	(Propitiated) Buddhas for...	(Propitiated both the) Buddhas for ...
Ablative	སངས་རྒྱས་ལས་ (ཆོས)།	སངས་རྒྱས་དག་ལས།	སངས་རྒྱས་རྣམས་ལས།
	From Buddhas (come the scriptures).	From (both the) Buddhas come ...	From Buddhas come ...
Genitive	སངས་རྒྱས་ཀྱི་ (ཆོས)།	སངས་རྒྱས་དག་གི་ (ཆོས)།	སངས་རྒྱས་རྣམས་ཀྱི་ (ཆོས)།
	Doctrine of Buddha or Buddha's doctrine.	Doctrine of (both the) Buddhas or	Doctrine of Buddhas or Buddhas' doctrine.
Locative	སངས་རྒྱས་སུ་ (ཆོས)།	སངས་རྒྱས་དག་སུ་ (ཆོས)།	སངས་རྒྱས་རྣམས་སུ་ (ཆོས)།
	Doctrine in Buddha.	Doctrine in (both the) Buddhas.	Doctrine in Buddhas.
Vocative*	ཀྱེ་སངས་རྒྱས།	ཀྱེ་སངས་རྒྱས་དག།	ཀྱེ་སངས་རྒྱས་རྣམས།
	O, Buddha.	O, (both the) Buddhas.	O, Buddhas.

---

* In this case, as in the Nominative, no case-sign is attached. The use of Vocative terms བོད་པའི་སྒྲ like ཀྱེ, ཀྱེ་ཧོ signifying O, Oh ! (Sans. *Bho* or *Aho*) generally at the beginning of an expression, differentiates the Vocative case from the Nominative, but in general address such terms are often omitted.

༡ རྣམ་དབྱེ་དང་པོ་མིང་ཙམ་སྟོན་པ། ༢ བྱེད་པ་པོས་བྱ་བ་ལ་སྦྱོར་བ་ན་བྱ་བའི་ཡུལ་ལས་ལས་ཀྱི་ཚིག་གཙོ་བོར་བྱས་པ། ༣ བྱེད་པ་པོས་བྱ་བ་ལ་སྦྱོར་བའི་ཚིག་གཙོ་བོར་བྱས་པ། ༤ བྱེད་པ་པོས་བྱ་བ་ལ་སྦྱོར་བ་ན་བྱ་བའི་ཡུལ་དེའམ་དེ་དང་འབྲེལ་བའི་ལས་ལ་ཕན་འདོགས་པའི་དགོས། ༥ དངོས་པོ་གང་ཡིན་པ་དེ་དེ་ལས་བྱུང་ཞེས་འབྱུང་ཁུངས་སྟོན་པ། ༦ དངོས་པོ་གཉིས་ཁྱད་གཞི་ཁྱད་ཆོས་ཀྱི་ཚུལ་དུ་འབྲེལ་བ་བརྗོད་པ། ༧ དེ་ན་དེ་གནས་པའམ་དེ་ན་དེ་ཡོད་པ་ཙམ་བརྗོད་པ།། * The secondary ཚིག་ཕྲད particle ལ is understood after སངས་རྒྱས།

Examples of Declension.

Nouns terminating in ག and ང may be declined as follows:—

		Singular.	Dual or Plural.	Plural.
1.	Nominative	མིག	མིག་དག	མིག་རྣམས
		(the) eye.	both eyes.	(the) eyes.
2.	Accusative	མིག་ལ	མིག་དག་ལ	མིག་རྣམས་ལ
		in, with or to (the) eye.	in, with or to both eyes.	in, with or to (the) eyes.
3.	Agentive	མིག་གིས	མིག་དག་གིས	མིག་རྣམས་ཀྱིས
		by or with (the) eye.	by or with both eyes.	by or with (the) eyes.
4.	Dative	མིག་ལ	མིག་དག་ལ	མིག་རྣམས་ལ
		for or to the eye.	to both eyes.	to the eyes.
5.	Ablative	མིག་ནས or མིག་ལས	མིག་དག་ནས or མིག་དག་ལས	མིག་རྣམས་ནས or མིག་རྣམས་ལས
		from the eye.	from both eyes.	from the eyes.
6.	Genitive	མིག་གི	མིག་དག་གི	མིག་རྣམས་ཀྱི
		of the eye.	of both eyes.	of the eyes.
7.	Locative	མིག་ཏུ	མིག་དག་ཏུ	མིག་རྣམས་སུ
		in the eye.	in both eyes.	in the eyes.

		Singular.	Dual or Plural.	Plural.
1.	Nominative	མིང	མིང་དག	མིང་རྣམས
		(the) name.	both names.	(the) names.
2.	Accusative	མིང་ལ	མིང་དག་ལ	མིང་རྣམས་ལ
		to the name.	to both names.	to the names.
3.	Agentive	མིང་གིས	མིང་དག་གིས	མིང་རྣམས་ཀྱིས
		by or with the name.	by or with both names.	by or with the names.
4.	Dative	མིང་ལ	མིང་དག་ལ	མིང་རྣམས་ལ
		for or to the name.	for or to both names.	for or to the names.
5.	Ablative	མིང་ནས or མིང་ལས	མིང་དག་ནས or མིང་དག་ལས	མིང་རྣམས་ནས or མིང་རྣམས་ལས
		from the name.	from both names.	from the names.
6.	Genitive	མིང་གི	མིང་དག་གི	མིང་རྣམས་ཀྱི
		of the name.	of both names.	of the names.
7.	Locative	མིང་དུ	མིང་དག་ཏུ	མིང་རྣམས་སུ
		in the name.	in both names.	in the names.

There is no Article attached to the nouns མིག and མིང but English idiom requires the definite Article ***the*** to be put before the nouns *eye* and *name*; so it has been placed before them where necessary,

Words ending in ད, བ or ས may be declined as follows:—

བུད་མེད

	Case	Singular.	Dual or Plural.	Plural.
1.	Nom.	བུད་མེད the woman,	བུད་མེད་དག (both)* women,	བུད་མེད་རྣམས the women.
2.	Accus.	བུད་མེད་ལ to the woman,	བུད་མེད་དག་ལ to (both) women,	བུད་མེད་རྣམས་ལ to the women.
3.	Agent.	བུད་མེད་ཀྱིས by the woman,	བུད་མེད་དག་གིས by (both) women,	བུད་མེད་རྣམས་ཀྱིས by the women.
4.	Dat.	བུད་མེད་ལ to or for the woman,	བུད་མེད་དག་ལ to or for (both) women,	བུད་མེད་རྣམས་ལ to or for the women.
5.	Ablat.	བུད་མེད་ལས from the woman,	བུད་མེད་དག་ལས from (both) women,	བུད་མེད་རྣམས་ལས from the women.
6.	Genit.	བུད་མེད་ཀྱི of the woman,	བུད་མེད་དག་གི of (both) women,	བུད་མེད་རྣམས་ཀྱི of the women.
7.	Loc.	བུད་མེད་དུ in the woman,	བུད་མེད་དག་ཏུ in (both) women,	བུད་མེད་རྣམས་སུ in the women.
8.	Voc.	བུད་མེད or ཀྱེ་བུད་མེད O, woman!	བུད་མེད་དག or ཀྱེ་བུད་མེད་དག O, (both) women!	བུད་མེད་རྣམས or ཀྱེ་བུད་མེད་རྣམས O, women!

ཡབ

	Case	Singular.	Dual or Plural.	Plural.
1.	Nom.	ཡབ the father,	ཡབ་དག to both the fathers,	ཡབ་རྣམས the fathers.
2.	Accus.	ཡབ་ལ to father,	ཡབ་དག་ལ both fathers,	ཡབ་རྣམས་ལ to fathers.
3.	Agent.	ཡབ་ཀྱིས by father,	ཡབ་དག་གིས by both fathers,	ཡབ་རྣམས་ཀྱིས by fathers.
4.	Dat.	ཡབ་ལ to or for father,	ཡབ་དག་ལ to or for both fathers,	ཡབ་རྣམས་ལ to or for fathers.
5.	Ablat.	ཡབ་ལས from father,	ཡབ་དག་ལས from both the fathers,	ཡབ་རྣམས་ལས from fathers.
6.	Genit.	ཡབ་ཀྱི of father,	ཡབ་དག་གི of both the fathers,	ཡབ་རྣམས་ཀྱི of fathers.
7.	Loc.	ཡབ་ཏུ in father,	ཡབ་དག་ཏུ in both the fathers,	ཡབ་རྣམས་སུ in fathers.
8.	Voc.	ཡབ or ཀྱེ་ཡབ O, father!	ཡབ་དག or ཀྱེ་ཡབ་དག O, both the fathers!	ཡབ་རྣམས or ཀྱེ་ཡབ་རྣམས O, fathers!

དུས

	Case	Singular.	Dual or Plural.	Plural.
1.	Nom.	དུས the time,	དུས་དག both the times,	དུས་རྣམས the times.
2.	Accus.	དུས་ལ to or at time,	དུས་དག་ལ to or at both times,	དུས་རྣམས་ལ at or to times.
3.	Agent.	དུས་ཀྱིས by time,	དུས་དག་གིས by both times,	དུས་རྣམས་ཀྱིས by times.
4.	Dat.	དུས་ལ to or for time,	དུས་དག་ལ to or for both times,	དུས་རྣམས་ལ to or for times.
5.	Ablat.	དུས་ནས from time,	དུས་དག་ནས from both the times,	དུས་རྣམས་ནས from times.
6.	Genit.	དུས་ཀྱི of time,	དུས་དག་གི of both times,	དུས་རྣམས་ཀྱི of times.
7.	Loc.	དུས་སུ at the time,	དུས་དག་ཏུ at both the times,	དུས་རྣམས་སུ at the times.

བཀའ

	Case	Singular.	Dual or Plural.	Plural.
1.	Nom.	བཀའ command,	བཀའ་དག both the commands,	བཀའ་རྣམས commands.
2.	Accus.	བཀའ་ལ to command,	བཀའ་དག་ལ to both the commands,	བཀའ་རྣམས་ལ to commands.
3.	Agent.	བཀས or བཀའ་ཡིས by the command,	བཀའ་དག་གིས by both the commands,	བཀའ་རྣམས་ཀྱིས by the commands.
4.	Dat.	བཀའ་ལ to or for the command,	བཀའ་དག་ལ for both the commands,	བཀའ་རྣམས་ལ for the commands.
5.	Ablat.	བཀའ་ལས from the commands,	བཀའ་དག་ལས from both the commands,	བཀའ་རྣམས་ལས from the commands.
6.	Genit.	བཀའི of the commad,	བཀའ་དག་གི of both the commands,	བཀའ་རྣམས་ཀྱི of the commands.
7.	Loc.	བཀའ་ཏུ in the command,	བཀའ་དག་ཏུ in both the commands,	བཀའ་རྣམས་སུ in the commands.

ལོ

	Case	Singular.	Dual or Plural.	Plural.
1.	Nom.	ལོ the year,	ལོ་དག both the years,	ལོ་རྣམས years.
2.	Accus.	ལོ་ལ to the year,	ལོ་དག་ལ to both the years,	ལོ་རྣམས་ལ to the years.
3.	Agent.	ལོས or ལོ་ཡིས by or with the year,	ལོ་དག་གིས by both the years,	ལོ་རྣམས་ཀྱིས by or with the years.
4.	Dat.	ལོ་ལ to or for the year,	ལོ་དག་ལ to both the years.	ལོ་རྣམས་ལ to the years.
5.	Ablat.	ལོ་ལས or ལོ་ནས from the year,	ལོ་དག་ལས or ལོ་དག་ནས from both the years,	ལོ་རྣམས་ལས or ལོ་རྣམས་ནས from the years.
6.	Genit.	ལོའི of the year,	ལོ་དག་གི of both the years,	ལོ་རྣམས་ཀྱི of the years.
7.	Loc.	ལོ་ཏུ in the year,	ལོ་དག་ཏུ in both the years,	ལོ་རྣམས་སུ in the years.

All words ending in འ or any of the five vowels may be declined in manner of བཀའ and ལོ.

---

* The word "both" may or may not be used to signify the "dual".

མིང་ཚབ or མིང་གི་ཚབ་ཚིག PRONOUN.

THE PERSONAL PRONOUNS.

The first person singular ང signifying I is in general use, in Central Tibet. In Tsang, བདག is used in the place of ང. In book language and correspondence, the use of བདག is more general than that of ང. ཁྱོད signifies thou, and ཁོ he.

First Person Singular.		Plural.	
ང ངེད བདག ཁོ་བོ ཁོ་མོ	I.	ང་ཅག or ང་ཚོ རང་ཅག བདག་ཅག བདག་ཚོ	We.
ང་རང བདག་རང ང་ཉིད ངེད་ཉིད བདག་ཉིད	I myself.	ང་རང་ཚོ བདག་ཉིད་ཚོ	Ourselves.
Second Person Singular.		**Plural.**	
ཁྱོད or ཁྱེད *hon.*	Thou, you.		
ཁྱོད་རང or ཁྱེད་ཉིད ཁྱེད་རང also ཉིད	Thyself, thou or you; yourself.	ཁྱོད་ཅག or ཁྱོད་རང་ཚོ ཁྱེད་རང་ཚོ	You.
Third Person Singular.		**Plural.**	
ཁོ *com.* ཁོ་པ *m.* ཁོ་མ *f.* ཁོང *com. hon.*	He, she.	ཁོ་ཅག or ཁོང་ཚོ	They.
ཁོ་རང, ཁོ་ཉིད ཁོང་རང or ཁོང་ཉིད	He, himself; she, herself.	ཁོ་རང་ཚོ	They, themselves.

Alexander Csoma de Körös, in page 65 of his Grammar, marked the words ངེད, ངེད་རང, ངེད་ཉིད as

Demonstrative Pronouns.

They are འདི signifying "this" and དེ "that" འདི with the ཚིག་ཕྲད adlitive particle པ, *i.e.*, འདི་པ signifies "of this place," འདི་རང or འདི་ཉིད signifies "this itself." འདི་ཀ or འདི་ཀོ also signify "this" with emphasis *i.e.* signifying this (very).

དེ་ཀ, དེ་ཀོ, དེ་ག, or དེ་ཉི signifies that (very); དེ་ཉིད, དེ་ཁོན, or དེ་ཁོན་ཉིད signifies "that itself."

Relative Pronouns.

གང signifies which or what. སུ signifies who, which, or what. མི་གང, what man, བུད་མེད་སུ what or which woman; བུད་མེད་གང which woman. ཇི or ཅི signifies what. They are used alone or with གང, such as གང་ཅི that which, སུ་ཞིག signifying whoever.

Interrogative Pronouns.

These are: སུ, who? གང which? ཅི what? To these the undeterminate particle ཞིག is attached to signify whoever, whichever or whatever, such as སུ་ཞིག, གང ཞིག or ཅི་ཞིག།

Reciprocal Pronouns

The reciprocals are རང, བདག, རང་ཉིད, བདག་ཉིད signifying self, one's self.

Declension of the Personal Pronouns.

		Singular.		Plural.	
1.	Nominative	ང	I,	ང་ཅག or ང་ཚོ	we.
2.	Accusative	ང་ལ	to me,	ང་ཅག་ལ or ང་ཚོ་ལ	to or for us.
3.	Agentive	ངས or ང་ཡིས	by me,	ང་ཅག་གིས or ང་ཚོས or ང་ཚོ་ཡིས	by us.
4.	Dative	ང་ལ	to me or from me;	ང་ཅག་ལ or ང་ཚོ་ལ	to us or for us.
5.	Ablative	ང་ནས or ང་ལས	from me,	ང་ཅག་ལས or ང་ཚོ་ལས	from us.
6.	Genitive	ངའི or ང་ཡི	of me or mine;	ང་ཅག་གི or ང་ཚོའི	of us.
7.	Locative	ང་ལ	in me,	ང་ཅག་ལ	in us.

The nominative plural of the first person is seldom formed by attaching to it the plural particles དག and རྣམས. In the second and third persons they are often used. དག is seldom attached to the second person plural.

---

honorific terms. In Tibet, a person either in conversation or writing, never applies a respectful term to himself. The use of these terms, however, indicates a degree of civility or politeness in the speaker, in consequence of which, they are preferred to ང, ང་རང or ང་ཉིད which are of common use.

The first person plural is sometimes expressed by ང་སྐོལ or ང་ཅག།

		Singular.		Plural.	
1.	Nominative	བདག	I,	བདག་ཅག	we.
2.	Accusative	བདག་ལ	to me,	བདག་ཅག་ལ	to us.
3.	Agentive	བདག་གིས	by me,	བདག་ཅག་གིས	by us.
4.	Dative	བདག་ལ	to me or for me,	བདག་ཅག་ལ	to us or for us.
5.	Ablative	བདག་ལས	from me,	བདག་ཅག་ལས	from us.
6.	Genitive	བདག་གི	of me or mine,	བདག་ཅག་གི	of us, our.
7.	Locative	བདག་ཏུ	in me,	བདག་ཅག་ཏུ	in us.

Second Person.

1.	Nominative	ཁྱོད	thou,	ཁྱོད་ཅག	you or ye.
2.	Accusative	ཁྱོད་ལ	to thee,	ཁྱོད་ཅག་ལ	to you.
3.	Agentive	ཁྱོད་ཀྱིས	by thee or by you,	ཁྱོད་ཅག་གིས	by you.
4.	Dative	ཁྱོད་ལ	to thee or you, for you,	ཁྱོད་ཅག་ལ	to you or for you.
5.	Ablative	ཁྱོད་ལས	from or than you,	ཁྱོད་ཅག་ལས	from you.
6.	Genitive	ཁྱོད་ཀྱི	of thee, you; your,	ཁྱོད་ཅག་གི	your.
7.	Locative	ཁྱོད་དུ	in you,	ཁྱོད་ཅག་ཏུ or ཁྱོད་རྣམས་སུ	in you.

Third Person.

1.	Nominative	ཁོ or ཁོ་མོ	he, she,	ཁོ་ཅག	they.
2.	Accusative	ཁོ་ལ	to him, her,	ཁོ་ཅག་ལ	to them.
3.	Agentive	ཁོས or ཁོ་ཡིས	by him, her,	ཁོ་ཅག་གིས	by them.
4.	Dative	ཁོ་ལ	to him or for him,	ཁོ་ཅག་ལ	to them or for them.
5.	Ablative	ཁོ་ལས or ཁོ་ནས	from or than him,	ཁོ་ཅག་ལས	from them.
6.	Genitive	ཁོའི	his, her,	ཁོ་ཅག་གི	their.

1.	Nominative	ཁོང (*hon.*)	he or she,	ཁོང་ཚོ	they.
2.	Accusative	ཁོང་ལ	to him, her,	ཁོང་ཚོ་ལ	to them.
3.	Agentive	ཁོང་གིས	by him or her,	ཁོང་ཚོས or ཁོང་ཚོ་ཡིས	by them.
4.	Dative	ཁོང་ལ	to or for him, her,	ཁོང་ཚོ་ལ	to them or for them.
5·	Ablative	ཁོང་ནས or ལས	from him, her,	ཁོང་ཚོ་ནས or ལས	from them.
6.	Genitive	ཁོང་གི	of him, his, her,	ཁོང་ཚོའི	their or theirs.

Declension of the Demonstrative Pronouns.

		Singular.		Plural.	
1.	Nominative	འདི	this,	འདི་དག	these.
2.	Accusative	འདི་ལ	to this or with this,	འདི་དག་ལ	to these or with these.
3.	Agentive	འདི་ཡིས	by this,	འདི་དག་གིས	by these.
4.	Dative	འདི་ལ	to or for this,	འདི་དག་ལ	to or for these.
5.	Ablative	འདི་ནས	from this, hence,	འདི་དག་ལས	from these.
6.	Genitive	འདི་ཡི	of this,	འདི་དག་གི	of these.
7.	Locative	འདིར, འདི་དུ།	in this or here,	འདི་དག་ཏུ	in these.
1.	Nominative	དེ	that,	དེ་དག	those.
2.	Accusative	དེ་ལ	to that or in that,	དེ་དག་ལ	to or in those.
3.	Agentive	དེ་ཡིས	by that or with that,	དེ་དག་གིས	by those.
4.	Dative	དེ་ལ	to that or for that,	དེ་དག་ལ	to those or for those.
5.	Ablative	དེ་ལས or དེ་ནས	from that or then,	དེ་དག་ལས	from those.
6.	Genitive	དེའི	of that,	དེ་དག་གི	of those.
7.	Locative	དེར or དེ་དུ	to, at or in that, there,	དེ་དག་ཏུ	to, at or in those.

Declension of the Interrogative Pronouns.

1.	Nominative	སུ	who ?	སུ་དག	who or who both ?
2.	Accusative	སུ་ལ	to whom ?	སུ་དག	to whom ? to whom both ?
3.	Agentive	སུས or སུ་ཡིས	by whom ?	སུ་དག་གིས	by whom ?
4.	Dative	སུ་ལ	for or to whom ?	སུ་དག་ལ	for or to whom ?
5.	Ablative	སུ་ནས or སུ་ལས	from whom, which or what ?	སུ་དག་ལས	from whom ?
6.	Genitive	སུའི or སུ་ཡི	of whom ?	སུ་དག་གི	of whom ?
1.	Nominative	གང	which, what ?	གང་དག	which two, which all ?
2.	Accusative	གང་ལ	to which, with what ?	གང་དག་ལ	to which, with what ?
3.	Agentive	གང་གིས	by which, whom ?	གང་དག་གིས	by which ? by what ?
4.	Dative	གང་ལ	for which or to what ?	གང་དག་ལ	for which ? with what ?
5.	Ablative	གང་ནས or གང་ལས	from what or where ?	གང་དག་ལས	from whom, what or which ?
6.	Genitive	གང་གི	of whom, which or what ?	གང་དག་གི	of whom, which or what ?
7.	Locative	གང་དུ	in which or what, where ?	གང་དག་ཏུ	in which two ? where ?

			Singular.		Dual or Plural.	
1.	Nominative	ཅི	what ?	ཅི་དག	what two ?
2.	Accusative	ཅི་ལ	to or with what ?	ཅི་དག་ལ	to or with what ?
3.	Agentive	ཅིས or ཅི་ཡིས	by what ?	ཅི་དག་གིས	by what ?
4.	Dative	ཅི་ལ	for or to what ?	ཅི་དག་ལ	for or to what ?
5.	Ablative	ཅི་ནས or ཅི་ལས	from what ?	ཅི་དག་ལས	from what ?
6.	Genitive	ཅིའི or ཅི་ཡི	of what ?	ཅི་དག་གི	of what or of what two ?
7.	Locative	ཅི་རུ	to or in what, where ?	ཅི་དག་ཏུ	where, in what ?

When these interrogatives assume indeterminate forms, the particle ཞིག should be attached to them སུ་ཞིག who, whoever ? གང་ཞིག whichever ? ཅི་ཞིག whatever ?

Declension of Reciprocals.

1.	Nominative	རང	self, one's self,	རང་ཅག	ourselves, thyself or themselves
2.	Accusative	རང་ལ	to self or with self,	རང་ཅག་ལ	to ourselves or themselves.
3.	Agentive	རང་གིས	by myself,	རང་ཅག་གིས	by ourselves, &c.
4.	Dative	རང་ལ	for or to myself,	རང་ཅག་ལ	for or to ourselves, &c.
5.	Ablative	རང་ལས or རང་ནས	from myself,	རང་ཅག་ལས	from ourselves, &c.
6.	Genitive	རང་གི	of myself,	རང་ཅག་གི	of ourselves, &c.
7.	Localitive	རང་དུ	in myself,	རང་ཅག་ཏུ	to or in ourselves.

Pronomial Adjectives.

The following words are used as Pronomial Adjectives :— ཁ་ཅིག some one ; ཁ་ཤས a few, གང་ཡང, either, གང་རེ each, or what each. གང་ཡང་རུང whichever or whichsoever.

འགའ some, འགའ་ཞིག, some one, some body, འགའ་ཡང any, some, ཅི་ཞིག any thing, ཅི་ཡང every thing, ཅི་ཡང་རུང whatever, འབའ་ཞིག mere, གཞན other, གཞན་ཞིག another, ལ་ལ some (among many).

ལ་ལ་ཞིག some one, སུ་ཡང every one, སུ་ཡང་རུང whoever, whosoever. གང་ཡང, ཅི་ཡང, and སུ་ཡང, when followed by མ, མི, མེད, or མིན, signify none or no one, neither or nothing.

བྱེ་བྲག་བྱེད or བྱེ་བྲག་བྱས་པའི་ཚིག ADJECTIVE.

(Sans. *Viçeṣaṇa*).

Adjectives resemble nouns in their formation. It is from their meaning or context that they can be distinguished from each other. The Adjectives, generally follow singular nouns and precede the verbs in an expression or sentence: མི་ངན or མི་ངན་པ bad man; here ངན, or ངན་པ is an Adjective qualifying the noun མི man. བློ་བཟང་ or བློ་བཟང་པོ (Sans. *Sumati*) good heart; here བློ is heart, བཟང or བཟང་པོ signifies good. The particles པ and པོ in the words ངན་པ and བཟང་པོ are not Articles. The sentence "snow is white" will be rendered in Tibetan: ཁ་བ་དཀར་པོ་ཡིན (snow white is). In some words which are, mostly, translations of Sanskrit terms, Adjectives precede nouns, for instance: དཀར་ཕྱོགས (*Çukla pakṣa*) the white lunation *i.e.*, the period after the new-moon to the full-moon; ནག་ཕྱོགས (*Krisṇa Pakṣa*) the dark lunation *i.e.*, the period after the full-moon to the new-moon; སྐམ་ས dry-land; གཙང་ཁང holy or pure house or sanctuary; བཙོན་ཁང prison-house; when an Adjective is so placed it indicates relation rather than the qualification of the substantive it precedes: བཙོན་ཁང is same as བཙོན་པའི་ཁང་པ the house of prisoners or of imprisonment; གཙང་ཁང is same as གཙང་བའི་ཁང་པ the house of purity; སྐམ་ས is same as སྐམ་པའི་ས the land of dryness; ནག་ཕྱོགས is same as ནག་པོའི་ཕྱོགས the side or period of darkness; དཀར་ཕྱོགས is same as དཀར་པོའི་ཕྱོགས the side or period of light.

Some Adjectives, though derived from adjective roots are also used as substantives; སྔ་མ former or prior may mean the former or the prior; ཕྱི་མ latter, posterior, outer; for example: འགྲེལ་བྱེད་སྔ་མ་རྣམས the former commentators; འགྲེལ་བྱེད་ཕྱི་མ་རྣམས the later commentators; here སྔ་མ and ཕྱི་མ are Adjectives qualifying འགྲེལ་བྱེད commentators. སྔ་མ་རྣམས and ཕྱི་མ་རྣམས would mean the former and the later ones. ནང་མ inner or interior; the inner one; འོག་མ inferior, subordinate; the inferior or subordinate; གོང་མ or བླ་མ upper or superior, senior or junior, the senior or the junior.

When Adjectives are placed before substantives they are invariable in both singular and pluarl numbers. Though an Adjective follows the noun (in the singular number) which it qualifies, yet in the plural it precedes the plural sign. མི is singular, མི་རྣམས, མི་དག or མི་ཚོ is plural. མི་བཟང་པོ signifies good man, མི་བཟང་པོ་རྣམས or མི་བཟང་པོ་དག or མི་བཟང་པོ་ཚོ signifies good men.

In declining the expressions མི་བཟང་པོ and མི་བཟང་པོ་རྣམས the case-signs such as འི, ཀྱི, ཀྱིས, གི, གྱི, གྱིས &c., are attached to the Adjectives in the case of singular nouns and to the plural signs only in the case of plural nouns: མི་ངཟང་པོའི of good man, མི་བཟང་པོ་རྣམས་ཀྱི of good men; also མི་བཟང་དག་གི or མི་བཟང་པོ་ཚོའི of good men.

When numerals are used to qualify nouns, they follow them in both singular and plural numbers: མི་གསུམ, (man three) three men; མི་དག་གསུམ (men three) three men, this latter being more correct.

There are some adjective ཚིག་ཕྲད, (additive particles) such as ཅན and ལྡན signifying possessed of, full of. These resemble, in their use, the English particles or signs such as *ed*, *ful*, *eous*, *ous*, *y*, which are attached to monosyllabic nouns: གངས་ཅན (Sans. *Himavata*) snowful or snowy; དབང་ལྡན powerful; ནོར་ལྡན wealthy; རིན་ཅན precious; ལྷ་ལྡན * possessing god.

The words བཅས, མངའ, ཡོད signifying with, possessing or having are also placed after substantives to qualify them in the manner of ཅན and ལྡན, such as: གནས་བཅས (Sans. *Sāketa*) with habitations; ནོར་མངའ same as ནོར་ལྡན, possessing riches; ཉན་ཡོད (Sans. *Çrāvasti*) having listners. †

བྲལ and ཡས signifying less, or without, are Adjectives of negation, for example: དོན་བྲལ meaningless, སྐྱོན་བྲལ defectless; མཐའ་ཡས limitless or boundless; གཞལ་ཡས (Sans. *Vimāna*) immeasurable, (a name for the sky). བསམ་ཡས inconceivable. ‡

མིན and མེད signifying less, not or not having, are formed of the Adverbs of negation མ and མི with the verbs ཡིན and ཡོད: མ་ཡིན is མིན; མི་ཡོད is མེད. They are used as Adjectives and correspond in their use to *dis*, *il*, *im*, *in*, *ir*, and *un*, with the difference that they are affixed to nouns instead of being prefixed to them as in English: དོན་མིན unmeaning or without meaning; དོན་མེད is the opposite of དོན་ཡོད (meaningful) and signifies meaningless; འཆི་མེད immortal or deathless; འགྱུར་མེད unchangeable or changeless; འོས་མིན unfit or unbecoming; ཚུལ་མིན immodest or characterless.

བསྡུན་པ COMPARISON.

The ཚིག་ཕྲད (additive particles) ལས, པས or བས signifying *than* or *more*; *than* is put after the name of the person or pronoun or thing to which comparison is made: བདག་ལས་ཁྱོད་ཆེ thou art greater than myself; ང་བས་ཁོང་བཟང he is better than I; འདི་ལས་དེ་མཐོ that is higher than this.

The word ཤོས attached to an Adjective expresses the superlative degree. It is equivalent to (Sans. *tama*) signifying the superlative degree: ལེགས good, ལེགས་ཤོས best; ཡག་པོ fine, ཡག་ཤོས finest; ཆུང small, ཆུང་ཤོས smallest.

---

* A name of the City of Lhasa.

† Name of a City in Koçala, Ancient India, where the Buddha had resided for twentythree years and preached his doctrine to an immense number of listners (*Çrāvaka*).

‡ བསམ་ཡས་དགོན་པ (Sans. *Acintya Vihāra*) name of the oldest Buddhist Monastery in Tibet.

NUMERAL ADJECTIVES.

The cardinal numbers are as follows:—

གཅིག	one,	གཉིས	two,	གསུམ	three,
༡	1	༢	2	༣	3
བཞི	four,	ལྔ	five,	དྲུག	six,
༤	4	༥	5	༦	6
བདུན	seven,	བརྒྱད	eight	དགུ	nine,
༧	7	༨	8	༩	9
བཅུ or བཅུ་ཐམ་པ	ten,	བཅུ་གཅིག	eleven,	བཅུ་གཉིས	twelve,
༡༠	10	༡༡	11	༡༢	12
བཅུ་གསུམ	thirteen.	བཅུ་བཞི	fourteen,	བཅོ་ལྔ	fifteen,
༡༣	13	༡༤	14	༡༥	15
བཅུ་དྲུག	sixteen,	བཅུ་བདུན	seventeen,	བཅོ་བརྒྱད	eighteen,
༡༦	16	༡༧	17	༡༨	18
བཅུ་དགུ	nineteen,	ཉི་ཤུ or ཉི་ཤུ་ཐམ་པ	twenty,	ཉི་ཤུ་རྩ་གཅིག or ཉི་ཤུ་ཉེར་གཅིག	twenty one,
༡༩	19	༢༠	20	༢༡	21
ཉི་ཤུ་རྩ་གཉིས*	twenty two,	ཉི་ཤུ་གསུམ	twenty three,	ཉི་ཤུ་བཞི	twenty four,
༢༢	22	༢༣	23	༢༤	24
ཉི་ཤུ་ལྔ	twenty five,	ཉི་ཤུ་དྲུག	twenty six,	ཉི་ཤུ་བདུན	twenty seven,
༢༥	25	༢༦	26	༢༧	27
ཉི་ཤུ་བརྒྱད	twenty eight,	ཉི་ཤུ་དགུ	twenty nine,	སུམ་ཅུ or སུམ་ཅུ་ཐམ་པ	thirty,
༢༨	28	༢༩	29	༣༠	30
སུམ་ཅུ་གཅིག or གསུམ་ཅུ་སོ་གཅིག	thirty one,	སུམ་ཅུ་གཉིས	thirty two,	སུམ་ཅུ་གསུམ	thirty three,
༣༡	31	༣༢	32	༣༣	33
སུམ་ཅུ་བཞི	thirty four,	སུམ་ཅུ་ལྔ	thirty five,	སུམ་ཅུ་དྲུག	thirty six,
༣༤	34	༣༥	35	༢༦	36
སུམ་ཅུ་བདུན	thirty seven,	སུམ་ཅུ་བརྒྱད	thirty eight,	སུམ་ཅུ་དགུ	thirty nine,
༣༧	37	༣༨	38	༣༩	39
བཞི་བཅུ or བཞི་བཅུ་ཐམ་པ	forty,	བཞི་བཅུ་གཅིག	forty one,	བཞི་བཅུ་གཉིས	forty two,
༤༠	40	༤༡	41	༤༢	42

---

* The word རྩ signifying "with" is generally used in counting 21 (ཉི་ཤུ་རྩ་གཅིག), to 29 (ཉི་ཤུ་རྩ་དགུ), to 31 (སུམ་ཅུ་རྩ་གཅིག,, to 39 (སུམ་ཅུ་རྩ་དགུ) to 41 to 49, 51 to 59, 61 to 69, 71 to 79, 81 to 89, 91 (དགུ་བཅུ་རྩ་གཅིག) to 99 (དགུ་བཅུ་རྩ་དགུ).

བཞི་བཅུ་གསུམ ༤༣	forty three, 43	བཞི་བཅུ་བཞི ༤༤	forty four, 44	བཞི་བཅུ་ལྔ ༤༥	forty five, 45
བཞི་བཅུ་དྲུག ༤༦	forty six, 46	བཞི་བཅུ་བདུན ༤༧	forty seven, 47	བཞི་བཅུ་བརྒྱད ༤༨	forty eight, 48
བཞི་བཅུ་དགུ ༤༩	forty nine, 49	ལྔ་བཅུ or ལྔ་བཅུ་ཐམ་པ ༥༠	fifty, 50	ལྔ་བཅུ་གཅིག or ལྔ་བཅུ་ང་གཅིག ༥༡	fifty one, 51
ལྔ་བཅུ་གཉིས ༥༢	fifty two, 52	ལྔ་བཅུ་གསུམ ༥༣	fifty three, 53	ལྔ་བཅུ་བཞི ༥༤	fifty four, 54
ལྔ་བཅུ་ལྔ ༥༥	fifty five, 55	ལྔ་བཅུ་དྲུག ༥༦	fifty six, 56	ལྔ་བཅུ་བདུན ༥༧	fifty seven, 57
ལྔ་བཅུ་བརྒྱད ༥༨	fifty eight, 58	ལྔ་བཅུ་དགུ ༥༩	fifty nine, 59	དྲུག་ཅུ or དྲུག་ཅུ་ཐམ་པ ༦༠	sixty, 60

The word ཐམ་པ is used after the tens up to one hundred.

It is usual to count after ཉི་ཤུ་ཐམ་པ as ཉི་ཤུ་རྩ་གཅིག or ཉི་ཤུ་ཉེར་གཅིག or simply རྩ་གཅིག or ཉེར་གཅིག to signify 21 ཉི་ཤུ་རྩ་གཉིས་ or ཉི་ཤུ་ཉེར་གཉིས or simply རྩ་གཉིས or ཉེར་གཉིས to express 22, and so on.

After གསུམ་ཅུ་ཐམ་པ one has to count as གསུམ་ཅུ་སོ་གཅིག or simply སོ་གཅིག, 31, སོ་གཉིས, 32, སོ་གསུམ, 33, སོ་བཞི 34 &c.

It is to be noted here that in writing the words གསུམ་ཅུ and བཞི་བཅུ the prefix (སྔོན་འཇུག) བ of བཅུ has been mited in the former and retained in the latter. This conforms to the rule that བ of the word བཅུ is to be dropped only when it is used after a consonant such as: དྲུག་ཅུ, བདུན་ཅུ, བརྒྱད་ཅུ.

After བཞི་བཅུ་ཐམ་པ it is usual to count as བཞི་བཅུ་ཞེ་གཅིག, བཞི་བཅུ་ཞེ་གཉིས or simply ཞེ་གཅིག, ཞེ་གཉིས &c., to, express 41, 42 and so on.

After ལྔ་བཅུ་ཐམ་པ it is usual to count as ལྔ་བཅུ་ང་གཅིག or simply ང་གཅིག, ང་གཉིས, ང་གསུམ,&c., to express 51, 52 53 and so on.

དྲུག་ཅུ་གཅིག, དྲུག་ཅུ་རེ་གཅིག ༦༡	sixty one, 61	དྲུག་ཅུ་གཉིས ༦༢	sixty two, 62	དྲུག་ཅུ་གསུམ ༦༣	sixty three, 63
དྲུག་ཅུ་བཞི ༦༤	sixty four, 64	དྲུག་ཅུ་ལྔ ༦༥	sixty five, 65	དྲུག་ཅུ་དྲུག ༦༦	sixty six, 66
དྲུག་ཅུ་བདུན ༦༧	sixty seven, 67	དྲུག་ཅུ་བརྒྱད ༦༨	sixty eight, 68	དྲུག་ཅུ་དགུ ༦༩	sixty nine, 69
བདུན་ཅུ or བདུན་ཅུ་ཐམ་པ ༧༠	seventy, 70	བདུན་ཅུ་གཅིག ༧༡	seventy one, 71	བདུན་ཅུ་གཉིས ༧༢	seventy two, 72

བདུན་ཅུ་གསུམ	seventy three,	བདུན་ཅུ་བཞི	seventy four,	བདུན་ཅུ་ལྔ	seventy five,
༧༣	73	༧༤	74	༧༥	75
བདུན་ཅུ་དྲུག	seventy six,	བདུན་ཅུ་བདུན	seventy seven,	བདུན་ཅུ་བརྒྱད	seventy eight,
༧༦	76	༧༧	77	༧༨	78
བདུན་ཅུ་དགུ	seventy nine,	བརྒྱད་ཅུ or བརྒྱད་ཅུ་ཐམ་པ	eighty,	བརྒྱད་ཅུ་གཅིག	eighty one,
༧༩	79	༨༠	80	༨༡	81
བརྒྱད་ཅུ་གཉིས	eighty two,	བརྒྱད་ཅུ་གསུམ	eighty three,	བརྒྱད་ཅུ་བཞི	eighty four,
༨༢	82	༨༣	83	༨༤	84
བརྒྱད་ཅུ་ལྔ	eighty five,	བརྒྱད་ཅུ་དྲུག	eighty six,	བརྒྱད་ཅུ་བདུན	eighty seven,
༨༥	85	༨༦	86	༨༧	87
བརྒྱད་ཅུ་བརྒྱད	eighty eighty,	བརྒྱད་ཅུ་དགུ	eighty nine,	དགུ་བཅུ or དགུ་བཅུ་ཐམ་པ	ninety,
༨༨.	88	༨༩	89	༩༠	90
དགུ་བཅུ་གཅིག	ninety one,	དགུ་བཅུ་གཉིས	ninety two	དགུ་བཅུ་གསུམ	ninety three
༩༡	91	༩༢	92	༩༣	93
དགུ་བཅུ་བཞི	ninety four	དགུ་བཅུ་ལྔ	ninety five,	དགུ་བཅུ་དྲུག	ninety six,
༩༤	94	༩༥	95	༩༦	96
དགུ་བཅུ་བདུན	ninety seven,	དགུ་བཅུ་བརྒྱད	ninety eighty,	དགུ་བཅུ་དགུ	ninety nine,
༩༧	97	༩༨	98	༩༩	99
		བརྒྱ or བརྒྱ་ཐམ་པ	one hundred.		
		༡༠༠	100		

After དྲུག་ཅུ་ཐམ་པ one has to count as དྲུག་ཅུ་རེ་གཅིག or simply རེ་གཅིག, རེ་གཉིས, རེ་གསུམ, རེ་བཞི and so on to express 61, 62, 63, 64, &c.

After བདུན་ཅུ་ཐམ་པ one usually counts as བདུན་ཅུ་དོན་གཅིག, or simply དོན་གཅིག, དོན་གཉིས, དོན་གསུམ, དོན་བཞི and so on to express 71, 72, 73, 74, &c.

After བརྒྱད་ཅུ་ཐམ་པ it is usual to count as བརྒྱད་ཅུ་གྱ་གཅིག or simply གྱ་གཅིག, གྱ་གཉིས, གྱ་གསུམ, གྱ་བཞི and so on to express 81, 82, 83, 84, &c.

After དགུ་བཅུ་ཐམ་པ one has to count as དགུ་བཅུ་གོ་གཅིག, དགུ་བཅུ་གོ་གཉིས or simply གོ་གཅིག, གོ་གཉིས, གོ་གསུམ and so on to express 91, 92, 93 and so on.

In counting 101 ༡༠༡, 102 ༡༠༢, 103 ༡༠༣, and so on, it is usual to say *i.e.*, བརྒྱ་དང་གཅིག one hundred and one, one hundred and two, one hundred and three, and so on. To express one hundred, two hundred, three hundred, and so on, it is usual to say བརྒྱ་ཐམ་པ or བརྒྱ་ཕྲག་གཅིག, གཉིས་བརྒྱ or བརྒྱ་ཕྲག་གཉིས, གསུམ་བརྒྱ or བརྒྱ་ཕྲག་གསུམ and so on.

སྟོང or སྟོང་ཕྲག is 1000 ༡༠༠༠; in counting 1001 ༡༠༠༡, 1 02 ༡༠༠༢, 1003 ༡༠༠༣, and so on, one should say སྟོང་དང་གཅིག, སྟོང་དང་གཉིས, སྟོང་དང་གསུམ and so on.

གཅིག་སྟོང or ཅིག་སྟོང or སྟོང་གཅིག or སྟོང་ཕྲག་གཅིག signifies one thousand ༡༠༠༠, ཁྲི or ཁྲི་ཚོ ten thousand ༡༠,༠༠༠, འབུམ or འབུམ་ཚོ is one hundred thousand ༡༠༠༠༠༠. It is, however, not unusual to count as ཁྲི་ཕྲག and འབུམ་ཕྲག ༡༠,༠༠༠ and ༡༠༠,༠༠༠.

ས་ཡ, a million; བྱེ་བ, ten millions; དུང་ཕྱུར, a hundred millions; ཐེར་འབུམ, a thousand millions.

Cardinal Figures in Serial Order.

༡ 1,	༡༡ 11,	༢༡ 21,	༣༡ 31,	༤༡ 41,	༥༡ 51,	༦༡ 61,	༧༡ 71,	༨༡ 81,	༩༡ 91
༢ 2,	༡༢ 12,	༢༢ 22,	༣༢ 32,	༤༢ 42,	༥༢ 52,	༦༢ 62,	༧༢ 72,	༨༢ 82,	༩༢ 92
༣ 3,	༡༣ 13,	༢༣ 23,	༣༣ 33,	༤༣ 43,	༥༣ 53,	༦༣ 63,	༧༣ 73,	༨༣ 83,	༩༣ 93
༤ 4,	༡༤ 14,	༢༤ 24,	༣༤ 34,	༤༤ 44,	༥༤ 54,	༦༤ 64,	༧༤ 74,	༨༤ 84,	༩༤ 94.
༥ 5,	༡༥ 15,	༢༥ 25,	༣༥ 35,	༤༥ 45,	༥༥ 55,	༦༥ 65,	༧༥ 75,	༨༥ 85,	༩༥ 95.
༦ 6,	༡༦ 16,	༢༦ 26,	༣༦ 36,	༤༦ 46,	༥༦ 56,	༦༦ 66,	༧༦ 76,	༨༦ 86,	༩༦ 96.
༧ 7,	༡༧ 17,	༢༧ 27,	༣༧ 37,	༤༧ 47,	༥༧ 57,	༦༧ 67,	༧༧ 77,	༨༧ 87,	༩༧ 97.
༨ 8,	༡༨ 18,	༢༨ 28,	༣༨ 38,	༤༨ 48,	༥༨ 58,	༦༨ 68,	༧༨ 78,	༨༨ 88,	༩༨ 98.
༩ 9,	༡༩ 19,	༢༩ 29,	༣༩ 39,	༤༩ 49,	༥༩ 59,	༦༩ 69,	༧༩ 79,	༨༩ 89,	༩༩ 99.
༡༠ 10,	༢༠ 20,	༣༠ 30,	༤༠ 40,	༥༠ 50,	༦༠ 60,	༧༠ 70,	༨༠ 80,	༩༠ 90,	༡༠༠ 100

The cardinal numbers re-duplicated signify that they are in multiples: གཅིག་གཅིག one by one, is one; གཉིས་གཉིས་བཞི two by two (is) four; གསུམ་གསུམ་དགུ three by three is nine. When the word དང signifying *with* joins the reduplicated numbers they imply that one (is) added to the other: གསུམ་དང་གསུམ་དྲུག three and three make six, and so on.

Ordinal Adjectives.

The Ordinal Adjectives are formed from the cardinals by attaching to them the ཚིག་ཕྲད additive particle པ, such as གཉིས་པ second; གསུམ་པ third; གཅིག་པ is seldom used to mean first; the word དང་པོ signifies first.

In the arrangement of books in a library or of books in a volume, they are marked by the letters of the alphabet in a serial order, such as, volume ཀ, volume ཁ, volume ག and so on up to the 30th volume, which is marked with ཨ the last letter of the alphabet; then the four vowel signs are put on the alphabets, in serial order, to mark the volumes, such as, ཀི, ཁི, གི.........ཨི། signifying 31st, 32nd, 33rd......60th volume or book, ལེ་བམ་ཀ་པ signifies, the volume marked with ཀ; ཁ་པ signifies the volume marked with ཁ and so on.

The words གཅིག, གཉིས and གསུམ when used as qualifying adjectives of nouns, of numerals or of any high number like བརྒྱ. སྟོང, ཁྲི or འབུམ and as such are placed before them, lose the སྔོན་འཇུག prefix letter ག. The ཅ of the word གཅིག is also changed into ཆ.

Thus it is usual to write ཆིག་ཤད to signify single line-mark or stop (།); ཉིས་ཤད double stops (༎); ཆིག་བརྒྱ (༡༠༠), ཉིས་བརྒྱ (༢༠༠), སུམ་བརྒྱ (༣༠༠), ཆིག་ལན once or one time; ཉིས་ལན twice or two times; གསུམ་ལན thrice or three times; ཆིག་སྟོང (1000), ཉིས་སྟོང (2000), སུམ་སྟོང (3000), also སུམ་ཅུ (30), སུམ་ཅུ་སོ་གཅིག (31), སུམ་ཅུ་སོ་གཉིས (32) སུམ་ཅུ་སོ་དགུ (39).

No change, however, takes place in them when they follow any noun or which they may qualify, thus བརྒྱ་གཅིག means 100; བརྒྱ་གཉིས, 200; བརྒྱ་གསུམ 300; སྟོང་གཅིག 1000; སྟོང་གཉིས 2000; སྟོང་གསུམ 3000. When the word དང signifying *with* is introduced between two numbers it becomes equivalent to *plus*: གཅིག་དང་གཅིག is equivalent to $1+1$ and expresses the sum of two; གཅིག་དང་གཉིས$=1+2=3$, བརྒྱ་དང་གཅིག$=100+1=101$, སྟོང་དང་བརྒྱ 1100, ཁྲི་དང་བརྒྱ 10,100.

Numeral adjectives are formed by attaching to such words the ཚིག་ཕྲད (additive particles) པ, པོ, མ: གཅིག་པོ signifies single or singly, གཉིས་པོ, both or the two; གསུམ་པོ the three, ལེའུ་བཞི་མ signifies (the book of) three chapters; སུམ་ཅུ་པ signifies (the book of) thirty verses or *Çloka* or simply "of thirty."

བརྒྱད་སྟོང་པ (*Aṣṭa sahasrikā*) the book of eight thousand verses. The word སྟོང when used as a numeral signifies one thousand, but its ordinary meaning, whether it is used with or without པ is *empty* or *void*, hence སྟོང་པ when used alone does not signify one thousandeth. The word ཁྲི ordinarily signifies *chair*, and as a numeral means ten thousand. The word ཁྲི་པ one in the chair, *i.e.*, chairman or president is therefore, seldom used as an Ordinal.

བྱ་བ VERB.

SANS. *Kriyā*.

A Tibetan verb is always a dissyllabic word consisting of a monosyllabic verbal root and an additive particle པ or བ. In its simple form which is invariably participle present, it is a verbal noun. Take for instance, the words, བྱ་བ, བགྱི་བ; signifying doing; བྱེད་པ, བགྱིད་པ action or acting; འགྲོ་བ, འགྲོད་པ going. In these བྱ, བགྱི, བྱེད, འགྲོ or འགྲོད are verbal roots or root-verbs. In verbs the roots are only affected by the addition of the སྔོན་འཇུག (ག, ད, བ, མ, འ) and the ཡང་འཇུག (ད, ས) letters in the formation of certain tenses and moods. A verbal root with the auxiliary བྱ attached to it is generally put in the infinitive mood. The infinitive present conveys the idea of futurity, hence བྱ is attached also to the verbal roots, in the future tense.

བྱ་བ or བགྱི་བ *hon.* as a verbal noun signifies action, deed; as a verb (participle present) signifies doing. བྱ་བར, བགྱི་བར conveys the meaning "to do."

In the expression གཅད་བྱའི་ཤིང (the) tree to cut (or to be cut) བཅད་བྱ is in the infinitive present. It is called ལས་ཀྱི་སྒྲ the term for work, because cutting is the work conveyed by བཅད་བྱ།

Tibetan verbs are generally expressed in three tenses: the present tense called ད་ལྟ་བ, past or preterite called འདས་པ and future called མ་འོང་བ. Tibetan Grammarians include the completive or perfect tense in the past tense. There is mention of two moods in Tibetan grammars: the indicative and the hortative or imperative.

In the sentence ཤིང་མཁན་གྱིས་གཅད་པར་བྱ་དང་བཅད་པར་བྱས། ཤིང་མཁན is the agent (བདག), གཅད་པར་བྱ and བཅད་པར་བྱས are verbs. གཅད་པར་བྱ will cut, (or must or should cut), is in the future tense. བཅད་པར་བྱས signifying done cutting or is cut, is in the preterite or past tense.

In the sentence ཤིང་མཁན་གྱིས་སྟ་རེས་ཤིང་གཅོད་པ (by carpenter with axe tree (is) cut, ཤིང་མཁན carpenter is the principal agent or doer (བྱེད་པ་པོ་གཙོ་བོ); སྟ་རེ axe is the minor or secondary agent or doer (བྱེད་པ་པོ་ཕལ་པ); both ཤིང་མཁན and སྟ་རེ are agents. They are, therefore, put in the Agentive case by the use of the secondary particle or case-signs གྱིས after ཤིང་མཁན and ས after སྟ་རེ། According to Tibetan Grammarians ཤིང tree which is acted upon by both (the) carpenter and (the) axe is the object called གཞན། གཅོད་པ is the verb (in the indicative present) signifying cut. ཤིང་མཁན་གྱིས་སྟ་རེས་ཤིང་གཅོད་པ should be translated in English thus:— *(the) carpenter cuts tree (or wood) with (an) axe.*

In the passage མིག་གིས་གཟུགས་ལ་ལྟ་བ eye with body to seeing. Here མིག is བྱེད་པ་པོ་ཕལ་པ the secondary agent, (the person seeing being the principal agent གཙོ་བོ) གིས sign of the Instrumental case, གཟུགས is the object (གཞན); ལ is the sign of the Accusative case; ལྟ་བ seeing or to see is the verb. མིག་གིས་གཟུགས་ལ་ལྟ་བ should be translated as *seeing body with (the) eyes.* In the above two passages གཅོད་པ and ལྟ་བ being verbs are called ལས་ཀྱི་སྒྲ terms of action or work, *i.e.* cutting and seeing, *i.e.* བྱ་བ action indicated by them.

The verb (བྱ་བ) when the action (བྱ་བ or ལས) is being done (བྱེད་བཞིན་པ) is put in the present tense (ད་ལྟ་བ); when the action has been done (བྱེད་ཟིན་པ) it is in the preterite or past tense (འདས་པ); when the action, it is inderstood, will be done བྱེད་འགྱུར it is in the future tense (མ་འོང་བ).

The roots of the verbs like འགྲོ in འགྲོ་བ, བྱེད in བྱེད་པ, སྒོག in སྒོག་པ, ལྟ in ལྟ་བ &c, are always in the Indicative present.

When in the root-verb the terminating letter is reduplicated and the vowel *o* is put on the duplicate letter, the verb so formed is also put in the Indicative present, for example: བྱེད་དོ (he) does, འགྲོའོ (he) goes, འདུག་གོ (he) is or sits, ཡོད་དོ (there) is, ཡིན་ནོ (it) is, སྨྲའོ (he) speaks. The verb to *be* when expressed in the above manner *i.e.*, as བསྡུར་བསྡུ་བ (reduplication of the final letter in a noun, pronoun, adjective or verb, and the vowel *o* being fixed on the duplicate letter), is always put in the Indicative mood, present tense: མིའོ (he) is man, འདི་ལུག་གོ this is sheep, ངའོ I am, བདག་གོ I am, བཟང་ངོ is good, ངན་ནོ is bad, ཡིན་ནོ it is, &c. The auxiliary words བྱེད or བྱེད་པ, བཞིན or བཞིན་པ, གདུག or གདུག་པ, སྣང and གྱིན, གིན, ཀྱིན, འིན or ཡིན may be also attached to the root verb in the Indicative present, for example: བྱེད in འགྲོ་བྱེད or in འགྲོ་བར་བྱེད signifying moves or does moving; བྱེད་བཞིན་པ does, བྱེད་གྱིན་འདུག, བྱེད་གྱིན་སྣང, is doing; འགྲོ་བཞིན་པ goes, འགྲོ་འིན or འགྲོ་ཡིན is going or moving.

ས is generally affixed to the verbal root in the Indicative, present tense for forming the preterite or past tense. The word གསུང signifying say or tell is in the Indicative present; གསུངས is in the preterite or past tense.

In some verbal roots the prefix འ is dropt in the past tense: འབྱུང, *pres.* བྱུང, *pret.* འགྱུར, *pres.* གྱུར, *pret.* འབྱོར, *pres.* བྱོར *pret.*

The perfect tense is formed by adding the auxiliaries ཟིན, གྱུར, ཡིན, ཚར, བྱུང, འདུག, སོང to the verbal roots in the preterite; བརྗོད spoke is *pret.* བརྗོད་ཟིན has spoken is in the *perf.* རྗོད speak, is in the *pres.* It would be incorrect to write རྗོད་ཟིན། The verbal root འཕྲོག meaning deprive or snatch away is in the *pres.*; ཕྲོགས *pret.* ཕྲོགས་ཟིན has snatched away, *perf.* It is incorrect to write འཕྲོག་ཟིན.

In the formation of the preterite and perfect tenses, in some verbs, the སྔོན་འཇུག (prefix letter) བ is put at the beginning of the root and in most cases the རྗེས་འཇུག letter ས is affixed at the end: ནོར་བསྒྲུབས gained or acquired wealth; ནོར་བསྒྲུབས་ཟིན་པ has acquired wealth or ནོར་བསྒྲུབས་པར་གྱུར་པ wealth has been acquired.

ལྷ་བསྒོམས meditated on god; ལྷ་བསྒོམས་ཟིན་པ or བསྒོམས་གྱུར་པ has meditated on god; ཚུལ་ཁྲིམས་བསྲུངས preserved character; ཡིད་ལ་བཙངས strove or exerted at heart; ཆོས་བསྒྲགས preached or proclaimed religion; བདུད་བཅོམ subdued the devil, བདུད་བཅོམ་ཟིན་པ has subdued the devil; ཆོས་བསྟན expounded religion, ཆོས་བསྟན་པར་གྱུར has explained religion.

Verbal roots that are based on the ten མིང་གཞི letters ཁ, ག, ཆ, ཇ, ཐ, ད, ཕ, བ, ཚ, ཛ are preceded by tho སྔོན་འཇུག *prefix* འ in the Indicative present, for example: འཁུར་བ carrying; འགོད་པ constructing or directing; འཆད་པ telling or explaining; འཇུག་པ putting; འཐུང་བ drinking; འདིང་བ spreading; འཕྲོག་པ depriving or taking away by force; འབུལ་བ giving or offering; འཚེམ་པ sewing; འཛིན་པ holding. The changes that occur in such verbal roots in the formation of the several tenses and moods are illustrated in the following ten groups of examples.

No. I.

Indicative mood.

Verb active, participle.	*Pres.*	*pret.*	*fut.*	*Imperat.*	*Hortative.*
འཁལ་བ spinning,	འཁལ or འཁལ་བཞིན་པ	བཀལ	བཀལ or འཁལ་འགྱུར	ཁོལ	ཁོལ་ཞིག
འཁུར་བ carrying,	འཁུར or འཁུར་བཞིན་པ	བཀུར	བཀུར or འཁུར་འགྱུར	ཁུར	ཁུར་ཞིག
འཁྱིག་པ binding,	འཁྱིག or འཁྱིག་བཞིན་པ	བཀྱིགས	བཀྱིག or འཁྱིག་འགྱུར	ཁྱིག	ཁྱིག་ཅིག
འཁྲིད་པ leading,	འཁྲིད or འཁྲིད་བཞིན་པ	བཀྲིས	བཀྲི ས or འཁྲིད་འགྱུར	ཁྲིད	ཁྲིད་ཅིག
འཁྲུད་པ washing,	འཁྲུད or འཁྲུད་བཞིན་པ	བཀྲུས	བཀྲུ or འཁྲུད་འགྱུར	ཁྲུད	ཁྲུད་ཅིག

In verbs like འཁལ which are based on the letter ཁ the imperative and བསྐུལ་ཚིག (hortative, &c.) are formed. from the Indicative present, by dropping the འ *prefix*, and changing the inherent *a* into the expressed *o* vowel The future, is formed from the Indicative present by changing the འ into བ *prefix* and the letter ཁ into ཀ. It is also formed by the addition of the auxiliary འགྱུར or འགྱུར་བར to the Indicative present. The preterite is formed, in the same manner, by changing the འ into བ and affixing the རྗེས་འཇུག letter ས to the final ག in the root or by changing the final ད into ས།

No. II.

Indicative mood.

Verb active, participle.	*Pres.*	*Pret.*	*Fut.*	*Imperat.*	*Hortative.*
འགུག or འགུགས་པ calling	འགུགས or འགུག་བཞིན་བ	བཀུག	དགུག or འགུག་འགྱུར	ཁུག	ཁུག་ཅིག
འགུམ་པ killing,	འགུམ or འགུམ་བཞིན་པ	བཀུམ	དགུམ or འགུམ་འགྱུར	ཁུམ	ཁུམ་ཞིག
འགེགས་པ hindering,	འགེགས or འགེགས་འཞིན་པ	བཀག	དགག or འགེགས་འགྱུར	ཁོག	ཁོག་ཅིག
འགེངས་པ filling,	འགེངས or འགེངས་འཞིན་པ	བཀང	དགང or འགེངས་འགྱུར	ཁོང	ཁོང་ཞིག
འགེབས་བ covering,	འགེབས or འགེབས་བཞིན་པ	བཀབ	དགབ or དགེབས་འགྱུར	ཁོབ	ཁོབ་ཅིག
འགེལ་བ loading,	འགེལ or འགེལ་བཞིན་པ	བཀལ	དགལ or དཀེལ་འགྱུར	ཁོལ	ཁོལ་ཞིག
འགེས་བ splitting,	འགེས or འགེས་བཞིན་པ	བཀས	དགས or དགེས་འགྱུར	ཁོས	ཁོས་ཤིག
འགོད་པ directing,	འགོད or འགོད་བཞིན་པ	བཀོད	དགོད or འགོད་འགྱུར	ཁོད	ཁོད་ཅིག
འགྲེམ་པ scattering,	འགྲེམ	བཀྲམ	དགྲམ or འགྲེམ་འགྱུར	ཁྲོམ	ཁྲོམ་ཞིག
འགྲོལ་བ unfolding,	འགྲོལ or འགྲོལ་བཞིན་པ	བཀྲོལ	དགྲོལ or འགྲོལ་འགྱུར	ཁྲོལ	ཁྲོལ་ཞིག

In verbs based on ག the future is formed from the Indicative present by changing འ into ད and the expressed *e* into inherent *a*, and by dropping the ཡང་འཇུག letter ས if there is any. The preterite is formed from the future by changing the ད into བ, and the ག into ཀ. The Hortative བསྐུལ་ཚིག is formed from the Indicative present by dropping the འ and ས and also by changing ག into ཁ and *e* into *o*.

No. III.

འཆག་པ passing, visiting,	འཆག or འཆག་བཞིན་པ	བཅགས	བཅག or འཆག་འགྱུ	ཆོག or ཤོག	ཤོག་ཅིག
འཆང་བ holding,	འཆང or འཆང་བཞིན་པ	བཅངས	བཅང or འཆང་འགྱུར	ཆོང	ཆོང་ཞིག
འཆད་པ telling,	འཆད or འཆད་བཞིན་པ	བཤད	བཤད or འཆད་འགྱུར	ཤོད	ཤོད་ཅིག
འཆབ་པ hiding,	འཆབ ro འཆབ་བཞིན་པ	བཅབས	བཅབ or འཆབ་འགྱུར	ཆོབ	ཆོབ་ཅིག
འཆའ་བ making ready,	འཆའ or འཆའ་འཞིན་པ	བཅས	བཅའ	ཆོས	ཆོས་ཤིག
འཆིང་བ binding,	འཆིང or འཆིང་བཞིན་བ	བཅིངས	བཅིང or འཆིང་འགྱུར	ཆིང	ཆིང་ཞིག
འཆིབ་པ riding, mounting,	འཆིབ or འཆིབ་བཞིན་པ	བཅིབས	བཅིབ or འཆིབ་འགྱུར	ཆིབ	ཆིབ་ཅིག
འཆུ་པ irrigating,	འཆུ or འཆུ་བཞིན་པ	བཅུས	བཅུ	ཆུས	ཆུས་ཤིག
འཆེ་བ assuring,	འཆེ or འཆེ་བཞིན་བ	བཅེས	བཅེ	ཆས	ཆས་ཤིག
འཆེག་པ confessing,	འཆེག or འཆེག་བཞིན་པ	བཤགས	བཤག or འཆེག་འགྱུར	ཤོག	ཤོག་ཅིག
འཆོ་བ preparing,	འཆོ cr འཆོ་བཞིན་བ	བཅོས	བཅོ or འཆོ་འགྱུར	ཆོས	ཆོས་ཤིག

The Imperative and Hortative of འཆག་པ is the common word ཤོག come or ཤོག་ཅིག, please come, or let him come.

The preterite of འཆད are the common words བཤད told and ཤོད tell or please tell.

The preterite of འཆེག is བཤགས confessed. Its future and hortative are བཤག and ཤོག.

No. IV.

Indicative mood.

Verb active, participle.	*Pres.*	*Pret.*	*Fut.*	*Imperat.*	*Hortative.*
འཇལ་བ weighing,	འཇལ or འཇལ་བཞིན་པ	བཅལ	གཞལ	འཇོལ	འཇོལ་ཞིག
འཇིག་པ destroying,	འཇིག or འཇིག་བཞིན་པ	བཤིག	གཞིག or འཇིག་འགྱུར	ཤིག	ཤིག་ཅིག
འཇིབ་པ sucking,	འཇིབ or འཇིབ་བཞིན་པ	བཞིབས	བཞིབ་གྱུར	ཞིབ	ཞིབ་ཅིག
འཇིལ་བ deposing,	འཇིལ or འཇིལ་བཞིན་པ	བཅིལ	གཞིལ or འཇིལ་འགྱུར	ཆིལ	ཆིལ་ཞིག
འཇུ་བ digesting,	འཇུ or འཇུ་བཞིན་པ	བཞུས	བཞུ or འཇུ་འགྱུར	འཇུས	འཇུས་ཤིག
འཇུག་པ putting,	འཇུག or འཇུག་བཞིན་པ	བཅུག་པ	གཞུག or འཇུག་འགྱུར	ཆུག	ཆུག་ཅིག
འཇུན་པ taming,	འཇུན or འཇུན་བཞིན་པ	བཅུན	གཞུན or འཇུན་གྱུར	ཆུན	ཆུན་ཞིག
འཇོ་བ milching,	འཇོ or འཇོ་བཞིན་པ	བཞོས	བཞོ	འཇོས	འཇོས་ཤིག
འཇོག་པ placing,	འཇོག or འཇོག་བཞིན་པ	བཞག	གཞག	ཞོག	ཞོག་ཅིག
འཇོམས་པ conquering,	འཇོམས or འཇོམས་བཞིན་པ	ཅོམ	གཞོམ or འཇོམས་འགྱུར	ཆོམ	ཆོམ་ཞིག

The preterite of འཇོམས་ is བཅོམ subdued. This word, in a substantive form, is found in the name བཅོམ་ལྡན་འདས་ the accepted Tibetan equivalent of the Sanskrit word *Bhagavan*. The preterite of འཇོ is བཞོས milched. This word in an adjective form *i.e.*, བཞོས་མ is commonly applied to cows or *yaks* such as བ་བཞོས་མ milch-cow or འབྲི་བཞོས་མ, milch-*yak*.

No. V.

Verb active, participle.	*Pres.*	*Pret.*	*Fut.*	*Imperat.*	*Hortative.*
འཐགས་པ grinding or weaving,	འཐགས or འཐགས་བཞིན་པ	བཏགས	བཏག or འཐགས་འགྱུར	ཐོག	ཐོག་ཅིག
འཐིག་པ falling or drops,	འཐིག or འཐིག་བཞིན་པ	བཏིགས	བཏིག or འཐིགས་འགྱུར	ཐིག	ཐིག་ཅིག
འཐུང་བ drinking,	འཐུང or འཐུང་བཞིན་པ	བཏུངས	བཏུང or འཐུང་འགྱུར	འཐུང	འཐུང་ཤིག
འཐུབ་པ cutting in pieces,	འཐུབ or འཐུབ་བཞིན་པ	བཏུབས	གཏུབ	འཐུབ	འཐུབ་ཅིག
འཐོར་བ diffusing or scattering,	འཐོར or འཐོར་བཞིན་པ	བཏོར	གཏོར	འཐོར	འཐོར་ཤིག

In the above examples the མིང་གཞི letter ཐ of the Indicative present changes into ཏ in the preterite and future, the འ *prefix* being changed into བ and ག respectively.

No. VI.

Verb active, participle.	*Pres.*	*Pret.*	*Fut.*	*Imperat.*	*Hortative.*
འདིང་བ spreading,	འདིང or འདིང་བཞིན་པ	བཏིང	གདིང or འདིང་འགྱུར	ཐིང	ཐིང་ཞིག
འདུལ་བ subduing,	འདུལ or འདུལ་བཞིན་པ	བཏུལ	གདུལ	ཐུལ	ཐུལ་ཤིག
འདེགས་པ lifting up,	འདེགས or འདེགས་བཞིན་པ	བཏེག	གདེག	ཐེག	ཐེག་ཅིག
འདེབས་པ throwing,	འདེབས or འདེབས་བཞིན་པ	བཏབ	གདབ	ཐོབ	ཐོབ་ཅིག
འདོགས་པ binding,	འདོགས or འདོགས་བཞིན་པ	བཏགས	གདག	ཐོགས	ཐོགས་ཤིག
འདོན་པ uttering,	འདོན or འདོན་བཞིན་པ	བཏོན	གདོན	ཐོན	ཐོན་ཤིག

In the above examples the མིང་གཞི letter ད changes into ཏ only in the preterite. It is retained in the future. The *prefix* འ is changed into ག in the future.

In the Imperative and Hortative, the ད of the Indicative present changes into ཐ.

No. VII.

Participial form.	Pres.	Pret.	Fut.	Imperat.	Hortative.
འབྲལ་བ separating,	འབྲལ or འབྲལ་བཞིན་པ	ཕྲལ	དབྲལ	ཕྲོལ	ཕྲོལ་ཞིག
འཕྲི་བ subtracting, diminishing,	འཕྲི or འཕྲི་བཞིན་པ	ཕྲི	འཕྲི	ཕྲི	ཕྲི་ཅིག
འཕྲོག་པ taking away (by force),	འཕྲོག or འཕྲོག་བཞིན་པ	ཕྲོག	དབྲོག	ཕྲོག	ཕྲོག་ཅིག

In the above examples the འ of the Indicative present disappears in the preterite and in the Insperative and Hortative.

No. VIII.

Participial form.	Pres.	Pret.	Fut.	Imperat.	Hortative.
འབིགས་པ piercing,	འབིགས or འབིགས་བཞིན་པ	ཕིག	དབིག	ཕིག	ཕིག་ཅིག
འབུགས་པ boring,	འབུགས or འབུགས་བཞིན་པ	ཕུག	དབུག	ཕུག	ཕུག་ཅིག
འབུད་པ putting off,	འབུད or འབུད་བཞིན་པ	ཕུད	དབུད	ཕུད	ཕུད་ཅིག
འབུབས་པ vaulting,	འབུད or འབུད་བཞིན་པ	ཕུབ	དབུབ	ཕུབ	ཕུབ་ཅིག
འབུལ་བ offering, presenting with,	འབུལ or འབུལ་བཞིན་པ	ཕུལ	དབུལ	ཕུལ	ཕུལ་ཞིག
འབེབས་པ descending, letting down,	འབེབས or འབེབས་བཞིན་པ	ཕབ	དབབ or འབེབས་འགྱུར	ཕོབ	ཕོབ་ཅིག
འབྱིན་པ drawing or pulling out,	འབྱིན or འབྱིན་བཞིན་པ	ཕྱུང	དབྱུང or འབྱིན་འགྱུར	ཕྱུང	ཕྱུང་ཞིག
འབྱེད་པ opening or dividing,	འབྱེད or འབྱེད་བཞིན་པ	ཕྱེ	དབྱེ	ཕྱེ	ཕྱེ་ཅིག

In the above examples the root letter བ of the Indicative present is also retained in the future. It is changed into ཕ both in the preterite and Hortative. The འ disappears in the preterite and Hortative and changes into ད in the future.

The Indicative of འབྱེད *i.e.*, the word དབྱེ is found in the word རྣམ་དབྱེ (in Sans. *Vibhakti*) signifying "case."

No. IX.

Participial form.	Pres.	Pret.	Fut.	Imperat.	Hortative.
འཚག་པ sifting,	འཚག or འཚག་བཞིན་པ	བཙགས	བཙ or འཚག་འགྱུར	ཚག	ཚག་ཅིག
འཚབ་པ giving on equivalent,	འཚབ or འཚབ་བཞིན་པ	ཚབས, བསབབ	བསབ or འཚབ་འགྱུར	ཚོབ, །སོབ	ཚོབ་ཅིག
འཚིར་བ squeezing,	འཚིར or འཚིར་བཞིན་པ	བཙིར	གཙིར or འཚིར་འགྱུར	ཚིར	ཚིར་ཞིག
འཚེ་བ hurting, harming,	འཚེ or འཚེ་བཞིན་པ	བཙེས	བཙེ or གཙེ or འཚེ་འགྱུར	ཚེས	ཚེས་ཞིག
འཚེད་པ or འཚོད་པ boiling,	འཚོད, འཚོད་བཞིན་པ	བཙོས, བཙས	བཙོ or འཚོད་འགྱུར	ཚོས	ཚོས་ཤིག
འཚེམ་པ sewing,	འཚེམ, འཚེམ་བཞིན་པ	བཙེམས	བཙེམ or འཚེམ་འགྱུར	ཚེམ	ཚེམས་ཞིག
འཚོ་བ feeding or keeping alive,	འཚོ or འཚོ་བཞིན་པ	གསོས	གསོ or འཚོ་འགྱུར	སོས	སོས་ཤིག
འཚོག་པ cutting,	འཚོག, འཚོག་བཞིན་པ	བཙོགས	བཙོག	ཚོག	ཚོག་ཅིག
འཚོང་བ selling,	འཚོང or འཚོང་བཞིན་པ	བཙོངས།	བཙོང or འཚོང་འགྱུར	ཚོང	ཚོང་ཅིག
འཚོལ་བ seeking or searching,	འཚོལ or འཚོལ་བཞིན་པ	བཙལ	བཙལ	ཚོལ	ཚོལ་ཞིག

In the above examples the ཚ changes into ཙ in the preterite and future and also in the Hortative of འཚབ and འཚོ it changes into ས. This changing, according to some Grammarians, is optional.

No. X.

Participial form.	*Pres.*	*Pret.*	*Fut.*	*Imperet.*	*Hortative.*
འཛིན་པ holding, seizing,	འཛིན or འཛིན་བཞིན་པ	བཟུང	གཟུང or འཛིན་འགྱུར	ཟུང	ཟུང་ཅིག
འཛུག་པ setting or planting,	འཛུག or འཛུག་བཞིན་པ	བཙུག	གཟུག or འཛུག་འགྱུར	ཟུག	ཟུག་ཅིག
འཛུད་པ entering into,	འཛུད or འཛུད་བཞིན་པ	བཙུད	གཟུད or འཛུད་འགྱུར	ཟུད	ཟུད་ཅིག
འཛུམ་པ closing,	འཛུམ or འཛུམ་བཞིན་པ	བཟུམ	གཟུམ or འཛུམ་འགྱུར	ཟུམ	ཟུམ་ཤིག
འཛུར་བ avoiding,	འཛུར or འཛུར་བཞིན་པ	བཟུར	གཟུར or འཛུར་འགྱུར	ཟུར	ཟུར་ཞིག
འཛུལ་བ creeping in,	འཛུལ or འཛུལ་བཞིན་པ	བཟུལ	གཟུལ or འཛུལ་འགྱུར	ཟུལ	ཟུར་ཞིག
འཛེད་པ keeping or receiving,	འཛེད or འཛེད་བཞིན་པ	བཟེད	གཟེད or འཛེད་འགྱུར	ཟེད	ཟེད་ཅིག
འཛེམ་པ blushing,	འཛེམ or བཛེམ་བཞིན་པ	བཟེམ	གཟེམ or འཛེམ་འགྱུར	ཟེམ	ཟེམ་ཤིག

The letter ཛ in all the examples mentioned above changes into ཟ with the exception in the preterite of འཛུག and འཛུད།

ON THE USE OF THE FIVE སྔོན་འཇུག *Prefixes* :

ག, ད, བ, མ, འ, (in the formation of the several tenses and moods) when they begin verbal roots such as, གཅི, དཔོག, བསྒོད, མཆི, འདུ།

THE USE OF ག AS A *Prefix* IN VERBS.

གཅི་བ making water,	གཅི or གཅི་བཞིན་པ	གཅིས	གཅི or གཅི་བར་འགྱུར	གཅིས	གཅིས་ཤིག
གཡོག་པ covering,	གཡོག or གཡོག་བཞིན་པ	གཡོགས	གཡོག or གཡོག་པར་འགྱུར	གཡོགས	གཡོགས་ཤིག
གསུང་བ saying or speaking,	གསུང or གསུང་བཞིན་པ	གསུངས	གསུང or གསུང་བར་འགྱུར	གསུང	གསུང་ཤིག
གནས་པ dwelling,	གནས or གནས་བཞིན་པ	གནས	གནས or གནས་པར་འགྱུར	གནས	གནས་ཤིག

In the above examples the use of the *prefix* ག is regular, it being retained with the verbal-roots in all the tenses.

གཅོད་པ cutting or chopping off,	གཅོད or གཅོད་བཞིན་པ	བཅད	གཅད or གཅོད་པར་འགྱུར	ཆོད or གཅོད	ཆོད་ཅིག
གཏོང་བ giving,	གཏོང or གཏོང་བཞིན་པ	བཏང	གཏང or གཏང་བར་འགྱུར	ཐོང	ཐོང་ཞིག
གཏོད་པ entrusting,	གཏོད or གཏོད་བཞིན་པ	བཏད	གཏད or གཏོད་པར་འགྱུར	ཐོད	ཐོད་ཅིག
གསོད་པ killing, slaying,	གསོད or གསོད་བཞིན་པ	བསད	གསད or གསོད་པརའགྱུར	སོད or གསོད	སོད་ཅིག
གསོན་པ hearing or listening,	གསོན or གསོན་བཞིན་པ	བསན	གསན or གསོན་པར་འགྱུར	གསོན	གསོན་ཞིག

THE USE OF ད AS A *Prefix* IN VERBS.

དཔོག་པ measuring or pondering,	དཔོག or དཔོག་བཞིན་པ	དཔགས	དཔག or དཔོག་པར་འགྱུར	དཔོག	དཔོག་ཅིག
དཔོར་པ dictating,	དཔོར or དཔོར་བཞིན་པ	དཔར	དཔར or དཔོར་བར་འགྱུར	དཔོར	དཔོར་ཞིག
དཔྱོང་བ hanging,	དཔྱོང or དཔྱོང་བཞིན་པ	དཔྱངས	དཔྱང or དཔྱོང་བར་བགྱུར	དཔྱོང	དཔྱོང་ཞིག
དཔྱོད་པ examining,	དཔྱོད or དཔྱོད་བཞིན་པ	དཔྱད	དཔྱད or དཔྱོད་བར་འགྱུར	དཔྱོད	དཔྱོད་ཅིག

In the above examples ད is retained in all tenses and moods.

The use of བ as a *Prefix* in Verbs.

Participial form.	*Pres.*	*Pret.*	*Fut.*	*Imperet.*	*Hortative.*
བགོད་པ dividing,	བགོད or བགོད་བཞིན་པ	བགོས	བགོ or བགོད་པར་འགྱུར	བགོས	བགོས་ཤིག
བགྱིད་པ doing,	བགྱིད or དགྱིད་བཞིན་པ	བགྱིས	བགྱི or བགྱིད་པར་འགྱུར	གྱིས	གྱིས་ཤིག
བསྒྲུད་པ cleansing rice by beating,	བསྒྲུད or བསྒྲུད་བཞིན་པ	བསྒྲུས	བསྒྲུ	སྒྲུས	སྒྲུས་ཤིག

བ is prefixed to most verbs in the preterite.

The use of མ as a *Prefix* in Verbs.

མཆི་བ *v. n.* coming,	མཆི or མཆི་བཞིན་པ	མཆིས	མཆི or མཆི་བར་འགྱུར		
མཐོང་བ seeing or looking,	མཐོང or མཐོང་བཞིན་པ	མཐོང	མཐོང	མཐོང་ཤིག	

The མ *prefix* is retained in all the tenses in some verbs.

The use of འ as a *Prefix* in Verbs.

In some verbs འ is retained in all the tenses but in most verbs it is used in the Indicative present.

འཁྲིག་པ *v. n.* sticking together, coupling,	འཁྲིག or འཁྲིག་བཞིན་པ	འཁྲིགས	འཁྲིག or འཁྲིག་པར་འགྱུར	འཁྲིག	འཁྲིག་ཅིག
འཁྲུལ་པ *v. n.* fighting or stirring,	འཁྲུག or འཁྲུག་བཞིན་པ	འཁྲུགས or དཀྲུགས	འཁྲུག་པར་འགྱུར	འཁྲུག	
འཁྲོལ་བ *v. a.* playing music,	འཁྲོལ or འཁྲོལ་བཞིན་པ	དཀྲོལ	དཀྲོལ	ཁྲོལ	ཁྲོལ་ཤིག
འགག་པ *v. n.* stopping or staying,	འགག or འགག་བཞིན་པ	འགགས	འགག or འགག་པར་འགྱུར		
འཐུང *v. a.* drinking,	འཐུང or འཐུང་བཞིན་པ	འཐུངས	འཐུང or འཐུང་བར་འགྱུར	འཐུང	འཐུང་ཤིག
འདའ་བ *v. n.* passing away,	འདའ	འདས	འདའ་བར་འགྱུར		
འདུབ་ *v. n.* assembing, gathering,	འདུ or འདུ་བཞིན་པ	འདུས	འདུ་པར་འགྱུར		

In some verbs འ is dropped in the preterite.

འཁྱེར་བ carrying,	འཁྱེར or འཁྱེར་བཞིན་པ	ཁྱེར	འཁྱེར་བར་འགྱུར		
འཁྲིད་བ leading,	འཁྲིད or འཁྲིད་བཞིན་པ	ཁྲིད	འཁྲིད་པར་འགྱུར	ཁྲིད	ཁྲིད་ཅིག
འགས་པ splitting,	འགས or འགས་བཞིན་པ	གས	[འགས་པར་འགྱུར		
འགྱུར་པ becoming,	འགྱུར or འགྱུར་བཞིན་པ	གྱུར	འགྱུར་བར་འགྱུར		
འཛོད་པ sending,	འཛོད or འཛོད་བཞིན་པ	ཟད	འཛོད་པར་འགྱུར		

Examples of neuter verbs from which active forms may be derived.

		Pres.	*Pret.*	*Fut.*	*Meaning.*
v. n.	འཁྲུམ་པ	འཁྲུམ	ཁྲུམས	འཁྲུམ་ or འཁྲུམ་པར་འགྱུར	shrinking, contracting.
v. a.	སྐུམ་པ	སྐུམ	བསྐུམས	བསྐུམ	
v. n.	འཁོད་པ	འཁོད	འཁོད	འཁོད་པར་འགྱུར	settling or sitting.
v. a.	འཁོད་པ	འགོད	བཀོད	དགོད	

		Pres.	*Pret.*	*Fut.*	*Meaning,*
v. n.	འཁོར་བ	འཁོར	འཁོར	འཁོར་བར་འགྱུར	walking round.
v. a.	སྐོར་བ	སྐོར	བསྐོར	བསྐོར	encircling, surrounding.
v. n.	འགས་པ	འགས	གས	འགས་པར་འགྱུར	cleaving.
v. a.	འགེས་པ	བགེས	བཀས	དགས	
v. n.	འགག་པ	འགག	འགགས	འགག་པར་འགྱུར	hindering.
v. a.	འགེགས་པ	འགེགས	བཀག	དགག	
v. n.	འགུམ་པ	འགུམ	གུམ	འགུམ་པར་འགྱུར	perishing, extinguishing.
v. a.	འགུམ་པ	འགུམ	བགུམ	འགུམ་པར་འགྱུར	
v. n.	འགུལ་བ	འགུལ or འགུལ་བཞིན་པ	འགུལ	འགུལ་བར་འགྱུར	quaking or shaking.
v. a.	སྒུལ་བ	བསྒུལ་བཞིན་པ	འགུལ	དསྒུལ	
v. n.	འགྱུར་པ	འགྱུར	གྱུར	འགྱུར་ངར་འགྱུར	changing or translating.
v. a.	སྒྱུར་བ	སྒྱུར	བསྒྱུར	དསྒྱུར	
v. n.	འགྱེ་བ	འགྱེ	གྱེས	འགྱེ་བར་འགྱུར	going asunder, diffusing.
v. a.	འགྱེད་པ	འགྱེད	བགྱེས	བགྱེ	
v. n.	འགྱེལ་བ	འགྱེལ	གྱེལ	འགྱེལ་བར་འགྱུར	turning upside down.
v. a.	སྒྱེལ་བ	སྒྱེལ	བསྒྱེལ	བསྒྱེལ or སྒྱེལ་པར་འགྱུར	
v. n.	འགྲིག་པ	འགྲིག	གྲིག	འགྲིག་པར་འགྱུ	agreeing.
v. a.	སྒྲིག་བ	སྒྲིག	བསྒྲིགས	བསྒྲིག or སྒྲིག་པར་འགྱུར	
v. n.	འགྲིབ་པ	འགྲིབ	གྲིབ	འགྲིབ་བར་འགྱུར	darkening.
v. n.	སྒྲིབ་པ	སྒྲིབ	བསྒྲིབས	བསྒྲིབ or སྒྲིབ་པར་འགྱུར	
v. n.	འགྲིལ	འགྲིལ	གྲིལ	འགྲིལ་བར་འགྱུར	rolling or wrapping up.
v. a.	སྒྲིལ་བ	སྒྲིལ	བསྒྲིལ	བསྒྲིལ	
v. n.	འགྲུབ་པ	འགྲུབ	གྲུབ	འགྲུབ་པར་འགྱུར	accomplishing, making ready.
v. a.	སྒྲུབ་པ	སྒྲུབ	བསྒྲུབས	བསྒྲུབ	
v. n.	འགྲེང་བ	འགྲེང	འགྲེངས	འགྲེང་བར་འགྱུར	arising or raising.
v. a.	སྒྲེང་བ	སྒྲེང	བསྒྲེངས	བསྒྲེང	
v. n.	འགྲོལ་བ	འགྲོལ	གྲོལ or བཀྲོལ	འགྲོལ་བར་འགྱུར or དགྲོལ	loosening or delivering.
v. a.	སྒྲོལ་བ	སྒྲོལ	བསྒྲལ	བསྒྲལ	

		Pres.	Pret.	Fut.	Meaning.
v. n.	འཆག་པ	འཆག	ཆག	འཆག་པར་འགྱུར	breaking.
v. a.	གཅོག་པ	གཅོག	བཅག	གཅོག་པར་འགྱུར	
v. n.	འཆད་པ	འཆད	ཆད	འཆད་པར་འགྱུར	dissolving or cutting off.
v. a.	གཅོད	གཅོད	བཅད	གཅད	
v. n.	འཐོན	འཐོན	ཐོན	འཐོན་པར་འགྱུར	issuing, uttering.
v. a.	འདོན་པ	འདོན	བཏོན	གདོན	
v. n.	འདུ་བ	འདུ	འདུས	འདུ་བར་འགྱུར	gathering together.
v. a.	སྡུད་པ	སྡུད	བསྡུས	བསྡུ	
v. n.	འདུམ་པ	འདུམ	དུམ	འདུམ་པར་འགྱུར	agreeing, reconcile.
v. a.	སྡུམ་པ	སྡུམ	བསྡུམས	བསྡུམ	
v. n.	འཕེལ་བ	འཕེལ	ཕེལ	འཕེལ་བར་འགྱུར	increasing, augmenting.
v. a.	སྤེལ་བ	སྤེལ	སྤེལ	སྤེལ་བར་འགྱུར	
v. n.	འཕོ་བ	འཕོ	འཕོས	འཕོ་བར་འགྱུར	changing or transforming.
v. a.	སྤོ་བ	སྤོ	སྤོས	སྤོ་བར་འགྱུར	
v. n.	འབྲལ་བ	འབྲལ	བྲལ	འབྲལ་བར་འགྱུར	separating.
v. a.	འཕྲལ་བ	འཕྲལ	ཕྲལ	དབྲལ	
v. n.	འབྲི	འབྲི	བྲི	འབྲི་བར་འགྱུ	growing less.
v. a.	འཕྲི	འཕྲི	ཕྲི	དབྲི	subtracting
v. n.	འབབ་པ	འབབ	བབ or བབས	འབབ་པར་འགྱུར	descending.
v. a.	འབེབས་པ	འབེབས	ཕབ	དབབ	letting down.
v. n.	འབྱུང་བ	འབྱུང	བྱུང	འབྱུང་བར་འགྱུར	comeforth or become.
v. a.	འབྱིན་པ	འབྱིན	ཕྱུང	དབྱུང	drawing or pulling out.
v. n.	འབྱེ་བ	འབྱེ	བྱེ	འབྱེ་བར་འགྱུར	opening.
v. a.	འབྱེད་པ	འབྱེད	ཕྱེ	འབྱེ་བར་འགྱུར	
v. n.	འཛག་པ	འཛག	ཛགས	འཛག་པར་འགྱུར	dropping down or leaking.
v. a.	འཚག་པ	འཚག	བཙགས	བཙག or གཙག	borning.
v. n.	སྐྱེ་བ	སྐྱེ	སྐྱེས	སྐྱེ་བར་འགྱུར	straining.
v. a.	སྐྱེད་པ	སྐྱེད	བསྐྱེད	བསྐྱེད	glowing, producing.
v. n.	ནུབ་པ	ནུབ	ནུབ	ནུབ་པར་འགྱུར	setting.
v. a.	སྣུབ་པ	སྣུབ	བསྣུབས	བསྣུབ	destroying.

Certain root-verbs are used both in conversation and writing to express a degree of politeness in address to inferiors, equals, or superiors. Being the various forms of the verb to *be i.e.*, ཡིན and ཡོད; they generally signify am, art, is, are; there is, there are &c., and are as follows:—

འདུག, བཞུགས, མཆིས, ལགས, མངའ མད, མོད, འཚལ, གནས, སྣང, བཞིན་པ། when used with the negatives མ and མི they stand thus: མིན་ (for མ་ཡིན), མེད (for མི་ཡོད) མི་འདུག, མི་བཞུགས, མ་མཆིས, མ་ལགས, མི་མངའ, མི་གདའ. ཡོད་མིན, མི་འཚལ, མི་གནས, མི་སྣང, མི་གཞིན་པ།

These root-verbs have no variation in inflection in the several tenses, and also in respect of person and number.

They are invariable in the Indicative present, after every person of both numbers.

The use of these root-verbs is illustrated as follows:—

བླ་མ་ཆེན་པོ་ཡིན Lama is great; དེ་ལྟར་ཡིན་ནོ it is so, it is like that; སུ་འདུག who is there? ཅི་འདུག what is there? ཅི་ཙམ་འདུག how much is there; མང་པོ་འདུག there are many; རྒྱལ་པོ་གང་ན་བཞུགས where is the king; ཕོ་བྲང་ལ་བཞུགས་སོ (he) is in the palace; འདི་ནང་སྐུ་མང་པོ་མཆིས herein there are many images. བརྒྱ་ཙམ་མཆིས་སོ there are about one hundred; ང་ནི་རྒྱལ་རིགས་ལགས་སོ I am of the royal race; ཁོང་ལ་ནད་མི་མངའ there is no disease in him; འདི་ལྟར་ལགས (it is) like this; སངས་རྒྱས་ལ་ཡོན་ཏན་མཆོག་མངའ་འོ, Buddha has the supreme attributes; དེ་ན་ཅི་གདའ what is there; མད་དོ it is true, it is so; དེ་ལྟར་མོད, it is even so; བདག་གིས་ཞུ་འཚལ་ལོ I do beg or entreat; མི་གནས་སོ there is not; བླ་མས་ཀློག་གིན་སྣང the Lama is reading; སྐུ་ཞབས་སྐུ་བཞིན་པ when your honour is speaking.

CONJUGATION.

The conjugation of Tibetan verbs is simply a participial variation.

All the tenses of the verbal roots or of verbs, in general, may be formed and conjugated by the aid of the root-verbs ཡིན and ཡོད or their equivalents: འདུག, བཞུགས, མཆིས, ལགས, མངའ, མད, མོད, འཚལ, གནས, སྣང, བཞིན་པ; as also by that of the two auxiliary verbs བྱེད and འགྱུར.

CONJUGATION of the verb *to be* ཡིན་པར or its participial form ཡིན་པ *being.*

INDICATIVE MOOD.

	Singular.	Plural.
1.	*Person.* ང་ཡིན I am,	ང་ཅག་ཡིན we are.
2.	„ ཁྱོད་ཡིན Thou art,	ཁྱོད་ཅག་ཡིན you or ye are.
3.	„ ཁོ or ཁོང་ཡིན he is,	ཁོ་ཅག or ཁོང་ཚོ་ཡིན they are.

The verb *to have* ཡོད་པར or its participial form ཡོད་པ *having.*

1.	*Person.* ང་ལ་ཡོད I have,	ང་ཅག་ལ་ཡོད we have.
2.	„ ཁྱོད་ལ་ཡོད Thou hast,	ཁྱོད་ཅག་ལ་ཡོད ye have.
3.	„ ཁོ or ཁོང་ལ་ཡོད he has,	ཁོ་ཅག or ཁོང་ཚོ་ལ་ཡོད they have.

The verb *to do* བྱེད་པར or its participial form བྱེད་པ། *doing*.

Present tense.

		Singular.	Plural.
1.	*Person.*	ང་བྱེད or བདག་བྱེད I do,	ང་ཚག་བྱེད we do.
2.	„	ཁྱེད་བྱེད Thou doest,	ཁྱེད་ཚག་བྱེད you or ye do.
3.	„	ཁོ or ཁོང་བྱེད he does.	ཁོ་ཚག or ཁོང་ཚོ་བྱེད they do.

Past tense.

1.	„	ང་བྱས or བྱས་སོ I did,	ང་ཚག་བྱས we did.
2.	„	ཁྱེད་བྱས Thou didst,	ཁྱེད་ཚག་བྱས ye or you did.
3.	„	ཁོང་བྱས he did,	ཁོ་ཚག or ཁོང་ཚོ་བྱས they did.

Future tense.

1.	*Person.*	ང་བྱ, བྱོར, or བྱེད་རྒྱུ or བྱེད་པར་འགྱུར I shall do,	ང་ཚག་བྱེད་རྒྱུ or བྱེད་པར་འགྱུར we shall do.
2.	„	ཁྱེད་བྱེད་པར་འགྱུར Thou shalt do,	ཁྱེད་ཚག་བྱེད་རྒྱུ or བྱེད་པར་འགྱུར ye shall do.
3.	„	ཁོ or ཁོང་བྱེད་པར་འགྱུར	ཁོ་ཚག or ཁོང་ཚོ་བྱེན་རྒྱུ or བྱེད་པར་འགྱུང they shall do.

Imperative.	Hortative.	Conditional *present*.
བྱོས do or let him do,	བྱོས་ཤིག pray do, or let him do,	བྱེད་ན if I do, or he does.

Conditional *past* བྱས་ན if I did or he did. *Future* བྱས་པར་འགྱུར་ན if I or he shall have done.

Infinitive future, བྱེད་དུ, བྱར, བྱ་དུ, for doing, to do.

Participial form: བྱེད་ཅིང or བྱེད་དེ, when doing; བྱས་ཏེ, བྱས་ནས, བྱས་པས having done; བྱོས་ལ after having done.

The verb ཤེས་པར to know or ཤེས་པ knowing.

1.	*Person.*	ང་ཤེས I know,	ང་ཚག or ང་ཚོ་ཤེས we know.
2.	„	ཁྱེད་ཤེས you know, Thou knowest,	ཁྱེད་ཚག་ཤེས you or ye know.
3.	„	ཁོ or ཁོང་ཤེས he knows,	ཁོ་ཚག or ཁོང་ཚོ་ཤེས they know.

The verb འགྲོ་བར to go or འགྲོ་བ going.

Present tense.

1.	*Person.*	ང་འགྲོ I go,	ང་ཚག་འགྲོ we go.
2.	„	ཁྱེད་འགྲོ you go or Thou goest,	ཁྱེད་ཚག་འགྲོ ye or you go.
3.	„	ཁོང་འགྲོ he goes,	ཁོང་ཚོ་འགྲོ they go.

Past tenee.

1. ,, ང་སོང I went, ང་ཅག་སོང we went.
2. ,, ཁྱོད་སོང you went, ཁྱོད་ཅག་སོང ye or you went.
3. ,, ཁོ or ཁོང་སོང he went, ཁོང་ཚོ་སོང they went.

Future tense.

1. ,, ང་འགྲོ་ཀྱུ I shall or will go, ང་ཅག་འགྲོ་ཀྱུ we shall go.
2. ,, ཁྱོད་འགྲོ་གྲོ Thou shalt go, ཁྱོད་ཅག་འགྲོ་ཀྱུ ye shall go.
3. ,, ཁོ or ཁོང་ཀྱུ he will go, ཁོང་ཚོ་འགྲོ་ཀྱུ they shall or will go.

ཀྱུ is evidently used in the place of the auxiliary འགྱུར.

The verb མཐོང་བར to see or མཐོང་བ seeing.

1. *Person.* ང་འཐོང I see, ང་ཅག་མཐོང we see.
2. ,, ཁྱོད་མཐོང you see, ཁྱོད་ཅག་མཐོང ye or you see.
3. ,, ཁོང་མཐོང he sees, ཁོ་ཅག or ཁོང་ཚོ་མཐོང they see.

The verb འགྱུར་བར to become or its participle འགྱུར་བ becoming.

INDICATIVE.

Present.

1. *Person.* ང་འགྱུར I become, ང་ཅག་འགྱུར we become.
2. ,, ཁྱོད་འགྱུར Thou becomest, ཁྱོད་ཅག་འགྱུར ye become.
3. ,, ཁོ་འགྱུར he becomes, ཁོ་ཅག་འགྱུར they become.

Past.

1. ,, ང་གྱུར I became, ང་ཅག་གྱུར we became.
2. ,, ཁྱོད་གྱུར you became, ཁྱོད་ཅག་གྱུར ye became.
3. ,, ཁོ or ཁོང་གྱུར he became. ཁོ་ཅག་གྱུར they became.

Future. འགྱུར་ཀྱུ shall become.

Imperative. གྱུར or གྱུར་ཅིག be or let it be or become.

Conditional. འགྱུར་ན should he become, if ho be, གྱུར་ན if he became.

Gerund. འགྱུར་དུ for becoming.

Participial Expressions.

Present and future. འགྱུར་ཞིང when becoming, changing.

Past. གྱུར་ཏེ, གྱུར་ནས, གྱུར་པས or གྱུར་པ having become.

The verb མཛད་པ (when used as a respectful term for བྱེད་པ) has only one variation: in the Imperative and Hortative it is མཛོད།

The verb བགྱིད་པ, honorific also for བྱེད་པ is used by a person speaking for himself, or of others, before a superior.

Indicative Present. བགྱིད he does, *Pret.* བགྱིས he did. *Future.* བགྱི shall or will do.

Imperat. གྱིས do. *Hortative.* གྱིས་ཤིག pray do.

Participles.

Among verbs the participles form the roots of the Indicative present, past and future tenses; as སྨྲ, སྨྲས, སྨྲ་བྱ། As nouns they may all be used substantively, such as སྨྲ་བ speaking or speech; སྨྲས་པ spoken, a spoken thing; སྨྲ་བྱ a thing to be said or spoken of.

The participles terminating in པ or བ according to their final letter in the roots, take the genitive form (པའི, བའི) when used before a noun: ལས་བྱེད་པ working, doing work; ལས་བྱེད་པའི་མི a working man; མང་པོ་སྨྲ་བ or མང་སྨྲ་བ much talking; མང་པོ་སྨྲ་བའི་མི a man that talks much.

When, in the participle present, the པ or བ termination is dropped, and བྱེད or མཁན, or བྱེད་མཁན is attached to it, it becomes a noun signifying an actor or agent, an instrument or organ; as སྨྲ་བྱེད། སྨྲ་མཁན། སྨྲ་བྱེད་མཁན། a speaker; རྡུང་བྱེད, that does beat, the beater; མཐོང་བྱེད or མཐོང་མཁན that does seeing or makes one see, the eye.

The following participial terminations ཅིང, ཞིང ཤིང། གྱི, གི, ཀྱི, འི, ཡི། གྱིན, གིན, ཀྱིན, འིན, ཡིན། ཏེ, དེ, སྟེ put after the root of the present participle, correspond to the English termination—*ing*: ཞེས་སྨྲ་ཞིང so saying, thus saying; དེ་ལྟར་མོད་ཀྱི it being so; ཀློག་གིན་འདུག (he) is reading; ཟ་ཞིང་མི་སྨྲ. (he) does not speak when eating.

The participle future terminates in བྱ or བྱ་བ (taken absolutely, or after a substantive), and in བྱའི or བྱ་བའི (taken conjunctively, or before a substantive) such as, ཟ་བྱ edible, anything to be eaten; ཟ་བྱའི་ཤ flesh to be eaten; བཀླག་པར་བྱ་བ to be read over, that must be read over; བཀླག་པར་བྱ་བའི་བསྟན་བཅོས a literary work (*Çástra*) to be perused.

The past participle is expressed by any of the following secondary particles or case—signs (put after the root in the preterite, having regard to its final letter) པས, ནས། གྱིས, གིས, ཤིས or ས or ཡིས། ཏེ, སྟེ, དེ། ཅིང, ཞིང, ཤིང and ལ། they are used like 'having'—'ed' or 'being—ed' in English (for joining two or more members of a sentence); as, སྨྲས་པས། སྨྲས་ནས། སྨྲས་ཏེ། སྨྲས་ཀྱིས། སྨྲས་ཤིང། having spoken or said; སོང་ལ་ཁོ་ལ་ཟེར having gone tell him (go and tell him).

On the use of ཅིག, ཞིག, ཤིག with verbs in the Imperative Mood and Conjunctive Present.

ཅིག, ཞིག, and ཤིག are all of the same power and signification.

ཅིག is attached to verbal roots, terminating in ག, ད, བ། for instance: ཀློག་ཅིག read, let him read, he may read; ཤོད་ཅིག explain, tell, let him explain; སྒྲུབ་ཅིག make ready, prepare, let him accomplish.

ཞིག is attached to verbal roots ending in ང, ན, མ, འ, ར, ལ thus: སློང་ཞིག beg or ask for, let him beg; གསོན་ཞིག (for གསོནད་ཅིག) (please) hear, let him hear; ཤུམ་ཞིག let him die, perish; མ་ཟླ་ཞིག say not, let him not say; སྐོར་ཞིག (for སྐོརད་ཅིག) turn round, let him turn; གསོལ་ཞིག (for གསོལད་ཅིག) ask for, (please ask, let him beg.

ཤིག is attached to verbal roots ending in ས thus: སེམས་ཤིག think, let him mind; གཟིགས་ཤིག please see.

བསྒྲུབ་ཚིག་ལ་བས་འཕུལ་མེད་ཅིང་ཡང་འཇུག་འཐོབ་སྟེ། The བ *Prefix* is not put before verbal roots in the Imperative and Hortative Moods, but they receive the ཡང་འཇུག secondary *affix* ས at the end, as in སེམས་ཤིག།

On the use of གོ, ངོ, དོ, ནོ, བོ, མོ, འོ, རོ, ལོ, སོ and ཏོ།

These are, likewise all of the same power and signification, and are formed of the preceding word, by the reduplication of its final letter, and adding the vowel sign *o*. They have the power of the verbs ཡིན and ཡོད signifying am, art, is, are; do, have. They are frequently used with the present, perfect, and future tenses. འདུག་གོ is, there is; སོང་ངོ is gone; རིང་ངོ it is long, distant; ཡོད་དོ there is, is; ཡིན་ནོ it is; ཐོབ་བོ has got or found; ཤུམ་མོ has killed; འགྲོའོ go or am going; འགྱུར་རོ will become; གསོལ་ལོ I beg, I request; ལགས་སོ it is so (yes, sir,). The particle ཏོ should be used only in the perfect tense, after ན, ར, ལ (for the ད་དྲག in ནད, རད, ལད): for example: གསན་ཏོ (for གསནད་ཏོ) I have heard; གྱུར་ཏོ (for གྱུརད་ཏོ) has become; གསོལ་ཏོ (for གསོལད་ཏོ) has begged.

On the use of ཏེ, སྟེ, དེ in Verbs.

ཏེ is used after verbal roots ending in ན, ར, ལ, ས། for example: གསན་ཏེ hearing; འཁུར་ཏེ carrying; ཉལ་ཏེ lying (on the ground); སེམས་ཏེ thinking; ཡི་གེ་ཤེས་ཏེ་དོན་གྱང་ཤེས།

སྟེ is used after verbal roots ending in ག, ང, བ, མ, འ། thus: རྒྱུག་སྟེ running, འགྲེང་སྟེ standing, སློབ་སྟེ teaching སྒོམ་སྟེ meditating, ཟླ་སྟེ saying; མདའ་འཕང་སྟེ་ཐོག having shot (the arrow) it hit.

དེ is used after verbal roots ending in ད། ཡོད་དེ being, དད་དེ believing.

ལྷག་བཅས་སྒྲ་སྟེ་ཤུགས་བསྣན་ཏེ།   དེ་བཅས་ག་ང་བ་མ་འར།
ས་སྟེ་ན་ར་ལ་ས་དང་།   ད་དྲག་ཏེ་རྒྱང་དུ་མཐར་དེའོ།།
བྱེད་དང་བྱ་ཚིག་མཚམས་སྦྱོར་དང་།   ཕྱི་ཚིག་འདྲེན་པའི་དམ་བཅའ་དང་།
དེ་དག་ལྷོག་པ་ལྷག་མ་ཙམ།   འདྲེན་པའི་ལྷག་བཅས་དོན་ལ་འཇུག།

On the use of གམ, ངམ, དམ, ནམ, བམ, མམ, སམ and ཏམ།

These terminations are all of the some power and signification. They are formed of the preceding word or root-verb by reduplicating its final letter, and affixing the letter ས to it. They are interrogative signs, or express a doubt; whether, whether or not ?

The particle ཏམ is used only in the perfect tense after verbal roots ending in ན, ར, ལ (forནད, རད, ལད); as for example: འདུག་གམ is there ? སོང་ངམ is (he) gone ? ཡོད་དམ is there ? ཡིན་ནམ is it ? ཐོབ་བམ have you found ? ང་འགྲོ་འམ shall I go or should I go or whether I go ? གསེར་རམ་དངུལ whether it is gold or silver ? དངུལ་ལམ་ཟངས it is silver or copper ? ཤེས་སམ do you know ? གསན་ཏམ (for གསནད་ཏམ) have you heard ? གསོལ་ཏམ for གསོལད་ཏམ) has he askd ?

On the use of ཅིང, ཞིང, ཤིང with Verbs.

These particles are all of the same power and signification and express the participial termination—*ing*, in English. They are used after such letters as have been stated under ཅིག, ཞིག and ཤིག། for example: ཀློག་ཅིང reading; བཀླགས་ཤིང having read over; སྨྲ་ཞིང or སྨྲས་ཤིང having spoken or said.

On the use of པས and བས with Verbs.

These are comparative signs signifying: than, more than, but they are often used with verbs in their perfect participial form, for example: ཞེས་སྨྲས་པས thus having said; ཕྱག་ཏུ་ཕུལ་བས having given or placed in his hand or having presented to him.

Adverbs.

In Tibetan, the Adverbs generally precede the verbs and adjectives which they qualify, for example: ཅེས་སྨྲས་སོ (he) said so, or said thus: དེ་ལྟར་ལགས so (it) is; ཤིན་ཏུ་བཟང very good.

There are three premitive adverbial roots in the Tibetan language, namely: ཅེ, ཞེ, ཤེ། which are all of the same power and meaning. Whether used alone or with the *affix* (རྗེས་འཇུག) ས affixed to them or with the additive particles པ, ོ, འམ, ན attached to them, they signify *so*, *thus*. They are the following:—ཅེ་ན; ཞེ་ན; ཤེ་ན; ཅེས, ཞེས, ཤེས; ཅེས་པ, ཞེས་པ, ཤེས་པ; ཅེ་འོ, ཞེ་འོ, ཤེ་འོ; ཅེ་འམ, ཞེ་འམ, ཤེ་འམ། The use of these terms is explained thus: ག་ད་བ་དང་ད་དྲག་མཐར། ཅིང་ཅེས་ཅེའོ་ཅེ་ན་ཅིག། ང་ན་མ་འ་ར་ལ་དང་། རྗེས་འཇུག་མེད་པའི་མིང་མཐའ་རུ། ཞིང་ཞེས་ཞེའོ་ཞེ་ན་ཞིག། ས་མཐར་དགོས་གསལ་ཞེས་མ་གཏོགས། ཤིག་ཤེ་འོ་ཤེ་ན་འཐོབ། ཤེས་སྦྱར་ན་སློ་འི ཤེས་པར་འཇུག་པ་འབྱུང་། མ་ཡུ་གསུང་།།

There are also certain additive terms which are used both, as Adverbs and Postpositions (Prepositions in English). When used adverbially they are put before the verb. Some of these words are:—

ནང་དུ, ནང་ན, ནང་ནས; ཕྱི་ན, ཕྱི་ནས, ཕྱིར; འོག་ཏུ, རྒྱེན་དུ, སྔ་ན; མདུན་དུ: མདུན་དུ་བཞུགས sit forward; རྒྱབ་ཏུ, རྒྱབ་ཏུ་ཕྱོགས move backward; གཡས་སུ, གཡས་སུ་འཁྱིལ wind to the right; ཕྱོགས་སུ towards; ཆོས་ཕྱོགས་སུ་དཀའ་བ་སྤྱད། work hard in the direction of religion; སྟེང་ལ on above or upwards;

ན་སྒྲ the term ན when used after a verb or adverb expresses conditionality: ལས་བྱེད་ན་གསོལ་རས་འཐོབ gets remuneration if he works; ངེས་པར་ན if certain: certainly.

འདི་ཡོད་ན་འདི་འབྱུང་། if this exists, this arises.

ནི་སྒྲ the term ནི (equivalent of हि *hi*, in Sanskrit) expresses emphasis: it also separates the དངོས (subject) of a sentence from the predicate སྒྲུབ། ནི་སྒྲ་ནན་ཏུ་བསྣན་པའི་ཚིག། དམིགས་སུ་དགར་བའི་དོན་ལ་འཇུག།

The ཚིག་རྒྱན་ additive particles པར and བར are some times attached to certain adjectives to give them an adverbial sense in the manner *ly* does in English, for example: མགྱོགས་པར་འགྲོ go quickly, གསལ་བར་བསྟན showed clearly; དམན་པར་བརྩེ shows kindness towards the low.

The adverbs of negation called དགག་སྒྲ are the following :—

(1) མ, མི are used before the verb or adjective which they qualify, as in མ་འཇིགས fear not; མ་གནང (please) do not give: མི་བདེན not true; ང་མི་ཤེས I do not know.

(2) མེད, མིན are used after the verb or adjective, as in སྟ་ན་མེད (there is) nothing above. ནང་ན་ཅི་ཡང་མེད there is nothing inside; དེ་མིན་གཞན not that, another.

མ་མི་མིན་མེད་དགག་པའི་སྒྲ། མ་མི་གཉིས་ནི་ཚིག་མ་དང་། མིན་མེད་གཉིས་པོ་རྗེས་ལ་སྦྱར།།

Adverbs of Place.

གང་དུ, གང་ན where? Whether? གང་དུའང everywhere, གང་ནའང་རུང where-so-ever. གང་ནས whence?
གང་དུ་ཀྱང་རུང whither-so-ever; གང་ནས་ཀྱང་རུང whence-so-ever. འདི་ན, འདིར, འདི་རུ, here; འདི་ནས from here, hence.
དེ་ན, དེར, དེ་རུ there; དེ་ནས, from there, then, thence. ནང་དུ, ནང་ན, within, into; ཕྱི་ན, ཕྱི་རུ, ཕྱིར, outside.
ཕྱི་རོལ་དུ, ཕྱི་རོལ་ན outside, beyond, outward.
མདུན་དུ, མདུན fore, before; མདུན་ནས from the fore, from the presence of.
སྔོན་དུ་སྔོན་ལ before; རྒྱབ་ཏུ, རྒྱབ་ལ backward, afterwards; རྒྱབ་ནས, from behind, from the back. གོང་དུ, གོང་ན, གོང་ལ on, up, upon, over; above. གོང་ནས from above; སྟེང་དུ, སྟེང་ན, སྟེང་ལ above, on high. སྟེང་ནས from above.
སྟ་ན above, on high. གྱེན་དུ upwards, uphill. ཐུར་དུ, ཐུར་ལ downwards, down-hill.
ཉེ, ཉེ་མོར near; ཚུར or ཚུ་བར near, at; ཉེ་མོ་ནས from near. ཐག་རིང་དུ, ཐག་རིང་ན, ཐག་རིང་ལ, far, remotely, at a distance;
ཀུན་ཏུ every where; འོག་ཏུ, འོག་ན, འོག་ལ below; འོག་ནས from below. ཐག་རིང་ནས from a distance, from a far.

Adverbs of Time.

གང་དུས, གང་ཚེ when? ནམ, when? ནམ་ཡང whenever. འདི་དུས, འདི་ཚེ this time, at such time.
དེ་དུས, དེ་ཚེ at that time. སྔོན, སྔོན་དུས, སྔོན་ཚེ, སྔོན་རོལ་ཏུ formerly, of old, anciently.
རྒྱུན་དུ རྟག་ཏུ, གཏན་དུ, དུས་རྒྱུན་དུ continually, always, perpetually, ever. ནམ་ཡང་མེད never.
ཐོག་མར first, in the beginning; བར་དུ in the middle; ཐ་མར lastly, ultimately, at the end.
གསར་དུ recently; གློ་བུར་དུ suddenly. བར་བར་དུ, at intervals, occasionally.
དེ་མ་ཐག, དེ་མ་ཐག་ཏུ, immediately. ནམ་ཞིག, ནམ་ཞིག་ན at a certain time.
དུས་དུས་སུ at times, sometimes. སྐབས་སྐབས་སུ occasionly; བར་སྐབས་སུ in the meantime.
རེ་ཞིག for a while. སླད, སླད་ཀྱིས, སླད་མར after, afterwards, subsequently.
དང་པོར, first, the first time; གཉིས་པར, second, secondly. དེང, དེང་དུས, དེ་ཚེ now, at this.
དེང་སང, དེང་སང now-a-days. ད་དུང yet more, still, as yet. ད་དུང་ཡང now too.
ད, ད་ལྟ, ད་ལྟ་ཉིད་དུ now, this very time, presently.

དེ་རིང this day, today; མདང or མདངས yesterday; ཁ་སང day before yesterday. སང tomorrow; ནངས, གནངས day after tomorrow; གཞེས after three days or three days hence.

དགུས four days hence; ཆུས five days hence. ཞག་དང་ཞག every day, day after day.

ཟླ་དང་ཟླ every month. ལོ་རེ, ལོ་དང་ལོ, ལོ་ལྟར every year, year by year.

ལོ་ཆག every second year. ད་ལོ this year, current year. ན་ནིང last year; ཞེ་ནིང year before last. དགུ་ནིང three years ago. ཆུས་ནིང four years ago.

ཉིན་པར by day, in the day time. ཉིན་མོ by day, མཚན་མོར by night, at night. ཉིན་མཚན་དུ day and night.

སྔ་དྲོ in the morning: ཕྱི་དྲོ in the afternoon.

སྔ་མོ in the morning, early. ནང་མོ tomorrow morning. ཉིན་དགུང་ལ at midday, when the sun is on the meridian.

ནུབ་མོ་ལ in the evening, at sunset. ད་ནུབ this evening. ཁ་ནུབ last evening.

ADVERBS OF NUMBER AND TIMES.

ལན་ཅི་ཙམ how many times; ལན་གཅིག once, ལན་གཉིས twice, ལན་རེ each time, ལན་རེ་རེ at each time, every time; ལན་དུ་མར, ལན་མང་དུ many times; ལན་འགའ sometime, ལན་འགའ་ཞིག sometimes; རེས་འགའ or འགའ་རེས some time, other time; ལན་འགའ་ཡང (མེད) not a single time, never. མཐའ་ཡས་པར infinitely.

ADVERBS OF QUANTITY.

ཙམ how much? How many? འདི་ཙམ this much; དེ་ཙམ that much; ཅི་ཙམ what much. མང་ཙམ many, much about.

མང་པོ, མང་དུ, many, much, in large quantity. ཉུང་དུ little, few; ཉུང་ཙམ in a small quantity.

ཕྱེད half, a half, ཧ་ཅང to much, too many. ཚད enough; ཆོག, ཆོག་ཆོག it is enough, sufficient.

ཚད་མེད or ཚད་མེད་པར, immense, immeasurable; དཔག་མེད་པར inconceivably (great or large).

ADVERBS OF QUALITY.

ཀུན་ཏུ entirely, altogether; ཁ་རོག་ཏུ silently, mutely; ཁྱད་པར་དུ specially, particularly; འཁྲུལ་མེད་དུ, འཁྲུལ་མེད་པར infallibly; ག་ལེ slowly; མགྱོགས་པར quickly, swiftly; འགྱུར་བ་མེད་པར immutably; རྒྱས་པར amply, copiously; འགྲུལ་ཏེ walking; ངོ་བོ་ཉིད་ཀྱིས naturally; ངོས་སུ openly, on the face; དངོས་སུ really, materially; ངན་པར ill, badly;

མངོན་པར conspicuosly; མངོན་སུམ་དུ evidently; ཅིག་པར, གཅིག་པར at once; ཅི་ལྟར, ཅི་ཙུག how? In what manner? ཇི་ལྟར, ཇི་ཙུག how? In what manner? རྗེས་སུ afterwards; ཉལ་ཏེ lying;

ཉམས་པར alike; ཉེས་པར viciously, faultily; གཏང་སྙོམས་པར indifferently; ཐ་མལ་པར vulgarly; ཐེ་ཚོམ་མེད་པར undoubtedly;

ཐམས་ཅད་དུ wholly, in every way; དེ་ལྟར, དེ་ཙུག so, in that manner; འདི་ཙུག, འདི་ལྟར thus, so, in this manner; དལ་བར, དལ་བུས gently, by degrees; དངས་པོར, brightly; དྲང་པོར straightly, rightly, honestly; བདེ་བར happily; བདེན་པར truly;

འདར་འདར་པོར trembling, quakingly; འདུག་སྟེ sitting; འད་བར alike, like wise; གདོན་མི་ཟ་བར undoubtedly; བསྡུས་ཏེ shortly, briefly; མདོར་བསྡུས་ཏེ concisely, abridgedly; རྣམ་པར especially; ནན་ཏན་དུ earnestly; སྤྱིར generally; ཕལ་ཆེར, ཕལ་མོ་ཆེར mostly, for the most part; ཤུལ་ཏུ egregiously, exceedingly; ཕག་ཏུ secretly, privately; མྱུར་ཏུ quickly; བག་ཡོད་པར modestly, chastely; བག་མེད་པར, immodestly;

བབ་ཅོལ་ཏུ inconsiderately; དབེན་པར retiredly, solitarily; ཐེ་ཐག་ཏུ especially, particularly;

སྒྱུར་དུ, སྒྱུར་བར swiftly, speedily; མི་རུང་བར indecently, unbecomingly: མི་འོས་པར nnworthily, unsuitably; མི་རིགས་པར unreasonably, unjustly; གཙོ་བོར principally; མཚུངས་པར equally, like wise; མཛེས་པར beautifully; རྫུན་དུ, བརྫུན་དུ falsely; གཞན་དུ otherwise, else; བཟང་པོར well; འོས་པར worthily becomingly; ཡོངས་སུ wholely, entirely; ཡང་དག་པར thoroughly; ཡང again; ཡང་ཡང, ཡང་དང་ཡང, ཡང་དང་ཡང་དུ again and again; རབ་ཏུ eminently; རང་བཞིན་གྱིས by itself, spontaneously; རིངས་པར hastily, speedily; རིམ་གྱིས gradually; རིམ་པ་བཞིན་དུ by degrees, in order;

རུང་བར decently; རིགས་པ reasonably, justly; ཚོག་པར amiss; ལེགས་པར well, elegantly; ཤིན་ཏུ very; ཤེས་བཞིན་དུ knowingly, designedly; གསལ་པོར, གསལ་བར clearly, lucidly; སོ་སོར, asunder; སླར aga.n;

གསང་བར confidentially, secretly; སླུ་བ་མེད་པར, infallibly; ལྷག་པར in access, beyond, in a high degree.

Prepositions.

There are no Prepositions in the Tibetan language. Certain postpositive particles or Postpositions, do the function of the English *Preposition.* They are ཏུ, དུ, ན, ར, རུ. ལ, སུ། གྱི, གི &c. གྱིས, གིས &c. ནས, ལས &c.

The use of these particles has been partly explained in page 15. The Postpositions, however, do not form a part of speech. They are, but, parts of words under declension.

There are simple and compound Postpositions.

The simple ones are: 1st. གྱི, གི, ཀྱི འི or ཡི signifying: *of*, *'s*; these are genitive case-signs. 2ndly གྱིས, གིས, ཀྱིས འིས, ཡིས, ས signifying *by*, *with*. These are the signs of the Agentive or Instrumentive case. ལ is the sign both of the Accusative and the Dative cases and signifies *to*, *for*.

ནས is the sign both of the Nominative and the Ablative cases; and ལས is the sign of the Ablative. As Ablative signs they signify *from of*, *out of*; ཤར་ནས་འོད་སྣང་རི་ལས་ལྷུངས། Light shone *from* the east; (he) fell *from* the hill;

དུ་ལས་མེར་ཤེས་བྱུང་། *from* smoke knows fire;

ས་བོན་ལས་སྨྱུ་གུ་བྱུང་། *from* seeds, the seedlings grew;

ལྷའི་ནང་ནས་བརྒྱ་བྱིན་མཆོག། *among* the Gods, Indra is chief;

སྐྱབས་འགྲོ་ནས་ཤིས་བརྗོད་པར *from* (the time) of taking refuge, till saying benediction.

ལྷ་ལས་མི་དམན man is inferior *to* god or lower than god.

བ་ལས་འོ་མ milk *from* the cow.

The additive particles ཏུ, དུ, ར, ཏུ, སུ (put after the Nominative with respect to its final letter) denote motion, progression to, or towards a place; or change, turn, promotion, transformation into another state. They are the signs of the Locative case.

The compound postpositions generally require the genitive case before them. The terms ཕྱིར or ཕྱིར་དུ as in the expressions ངའི་ཕྱིར or ངའི་ཕྱིར་དུ for my sake; ཆེད or ཆེད་དུ། ཅི་ཡི་ཆེད, or ཅི་ཡི་ཆེད་དུ for what? why? དོན་དུ or དོན for the purpose of or cause: གཞན་གྱི་དོན་དུ for other's sake. སླད or སླད་དུ in behalf of, for the sake of: སུའི་སླད for whom? དྲུང་དུ to or near, at; ནང་ན in, at, among; ནང་ནས from, out of, from among; ནང་དུ into, or in side; དྲུང་ན near, by; དྲུང་ནས from near; གན or གམ, at; གན་དུ or གམ་དུ near, to, towards; གོང་དུ on, upon; གོང་ན upon, above གོང་ནས from above; ཁྲོངས་ན among, ཁྲོངས་ནས from among; ཁྲོངས་སུ into, within; among; གོན་ན near to. རྒྱབ་ཏུ, རྒྱབ་ན behind; ཐུག till, as for as; མཐར་དུ to the limit; ཐོག or ཐོག་ཏུ on, on above.

Some Postpositions illustrated with examples:

རྒྱབ་ནས from the back: རིའི་རྒྱབ་ནས from behind the hill;

སྟེང་དུ: དེའི་སྟེང་དུ above that; སྟེང་ན: དེའི་སྟེང་ན on or above that; སྟེང་ནས: དེའི་སྟེང་ནས from on that.

རྗེས་ནས or རྗེང་ནས from behind: ངའི་རྗེས་ནས from behind me; རྗེས་ན behind: ངའི་རྗེས་ན behind me.

ཕྱད་དུ. ཕྱད་ན in the direction of: དེའི་ཕྱད་ན in that direction; བར་དུ, བར་ན in the middle of, betwixt: གཉིས་ཀའི་བར་དུ between the two; མདུན་དུ. མདུན་ན before: ཁྱོད་ཀྱི་མདུན་དུ before thee, or in your presence.

སྤྱན་སྔར in the sight of: བླ་མའི་སྤྱན་སྔར before the Lama or in the Lama's presence, མཉམ་དུ with, together with: བླ་མ་དང་མཉམ་དུ with the Lama; རྒྱལ་པོ་དང་ལྷན་ཅིག in the company of the king.

Relation of Prepositions and Postpositions.

རྒྱ་མཚོ་ལ or རྒྱ་མཚོར to the ocean or sea; ལ signifying *to.*

རྒྱ་མཚོ་ན or རྒྱ་མཚོ་ནང་དུ in or on the ocean or sea; ན or ནང་དུ signifying *on* or *in.*

རྒྱ་མཚོ་ནས or རྒྱ་མཚོ་ལས out of, or from the ocean; ནས or ལས *out of* or *from.*

རི་ལ or རི་ན or རི་སྟེང to, on, upon the hill; ལ, ན, སྟེང *to, on, upon.*

རི་ནས or རི་ལས from or from on the hill; ནས or ལས, *from, from on.*

རྟ་ལ་བཞོན་པར to ride on horse; ལ signifying *to* is also the sign of the Infinitive.

རྟ་ན་འདུག་པ or རྟ་རྒྱབ་ཏུ་འདུག་པ sitting on a horse or on horse-back; ན or རྒྱབ་ཏུ *on* or *on the back.*

རྟ་ལས་འབབ་པ descending from the horse; ལས *from.* ལག་པས་བརྡུང་བར to beat with the hand; པས signifying *with.*

ཁྱོད་དང་ལྷན་ཅིག་འགྲོ་བར to go together with you; ལྷན་ཅིག *together.* ངའི་མདུན་དུ་ཤོག come before me;

མདུན་དུ *before, in the presence of.* ལམ་ན་མ་སྡོད stay not in the way; ན signifying *in* or *on.*

ཁྱོད་དེ་སུ་ནས་ཐོབ from whom have you got it or that? ནས *from.*

ངའི་ཕྱིར་དུ for me or for my sake; ཕྱིར་དུ signifying *for* or *for the sake of.*

ཁྱོད་ཀྱི་དྲུང་དུ to or near thee or you; དྲུང་དུ signifying *to* or *near.*

གྲོང་ཁྱེར་ནས from the town; ནས signifying *from.* གྲོང་ཁྱེར་དུ to the town; དུ signifying *to.*

གནམ་ན་བཞུགས་པར going to heaven; ན signifying *to* or *in.*

ལྷ་ལས་འབབ་པ descending from among the gods; ལས *from among.*

The following Tibetan equivalents of the Sanskrit prepositive particles are generally used with or before nouns and adjectives and verbs: ངན་པར་ दुर् *dur* bad; རིང་པར་ दूर *dúra* far; མཆོག་ཏུ་ परा *pará* chiefly, परम *param* highly; ངེས་པར་ नि *ni* surely; མངོན་པར་ अभि *abhi*, fully; རྗེས་སུ་ *anu* after; ཉེ་བར་ उप *upa* near; མཐོ་བའི་ उत् *ut* up; ཕྱལ་དུ་, དཀའ་པར་ अति *ati* beyond; ཕྱིར་དུ་ अव *ava* from; རྣམ་པར་ वि *vi* in high degree; བདེ་བར་ सु *su* well; ཕྱུང་བ་ निर् *nir* out; ཡོངས་སུ་ परि *pari* fully, round; ཡང་དག་པར་ सम् *sam* with; རབ་ཏུ་ प्र *pra* forth, well; སོ་སོར་ प्रति *prati* re, separately; ལེགས་པར་ आ *á* unto, greatly.

CONJUNCTION.

སྡུད་པའི་ཚིག།

དང་ signifying *and* is used in five different senses; སྡུད་འབྱེད་ as conjunction, for example: ལྷ་དང་མི god and man; ས་དང་ཆུ earth and water.*

There are three primitive conjunctions namely: ཀྱང, འང and ཡང which are all of the same power and signification. They are called འཕྲོས་ཐུང་སྒྲ † continutive terms or words expressive of continuity.

ཀྱང signifying too, also; though, although; even, is used after words ending in ག, ད, བ, ས and also after ད་དྲག། for example: བྱག་ཀྱང་། བཅད་ཀྱང་། བཀབ་ཀྱང་། བྱས་ཀྱང་། བརྙེད་ཀྱང་། འབྱོརད་ཀྱང་། རྒྱལད་ཀྱང་། འདུག་ཀྱང though there is; ཁྱོད་ཀྱང thou too or also; ཐོབ་ཀྱང though (he) got; ཤེས་ཀྱང although (he) knows.

འང is used after any vowel and after words ending in འ either expressed or understood. In being so used འང is rather joined with than attached to the words or syllable it follows:—

> ངའང I also; མིའང, man also; བུའང, the son also; མེའང, fire too; འགྲོའང, though he goes, བཀའང, the order even or also; ང with འང forms one syllable, བཀའང (formed of བཀའ and འང) is also one syllable. When it becomes necessary (in poetry for the sake of metre) to divide this one syllable into two the འང is changed into ཡང་།

ཡང is used after words or syllables ending in ང, ན, མ, འ, ར, ལ or any vowel or in འ, for example:

> གང་ཡང, དོན་ཡང, ལམ་ཡང, མཐའ་ཡང, དཀར་ཡང, གསལ་ཡང; (ང་ཡང, I also; མར་ཡང butter also; ཡུལ་ཡང་མི་འདུག (there) is even no village) བདུད་ལ་ཁྲོ་ཡང་འགྲོ་ལ་བྱམས though wrathful to the devil, yet kind to all.

ཀྱང་ signifies *as well* or *yet*; ཉམས་རྟོགས་ཀྱང་ལྡན་ལ་མཐུ་ཡང་ཆེ།

When ཀྱང, འང or ཡང is used between two similar or same adjectives, it signifies *more* or ***still more i.e.***, in a higher measure or degree. གསལ་ཡང་གསལ clear and clearer still; མཛེས་ཀྱང་མཛེས handsome and still more handsome.

---

* དང་སྒྲ is used in five different senses: 1. སྡུད་འབྱེད 2. རྒྱུ་མཚན 3. ཚེ་སྐབས 4. གདམས 5. དགུ།

† འཕྲོས་ཐུང་ཀྱང་འང་ཡང་སྒྲ་གསུམ། ག་ད་བ་ས་ད་དྲག་ཀྱང༌། འ་མཐའ་འང་དང་དེ་སྐབས་དགར། ང་ན་མ་ར་ལ་མཐར་ཡང༌། དེ་དག་ཚིག་རྫོགས་ཟླ་ཕྱི་དག། མཐུན་དང་མི་མཐུན་རྒྱུན་གཉིས་དང༌། གཞི་གཅིག་ཆོས་དོན་གཉིས་སོགས་སམ། མི་མཐུན་འགལ་དོན་སྡུད་པར་འཇུག།

When ཀྱང་, འང་ or ཡང་ is used between two adjectives of opposite meanings, it shows the contrast or points to the difference in their significations. དྲིས་ཀྱང་མ་དྲིས། དྲིས་ཀྱང་དྲིས།

མཛའང་བསླུ though friendly yet deceptive; བཀུར་ཀྱང་ཁྲོ though respectful yet furious.

མཛེས་ཤིང་འོད་ཀྱང་འཕྲོ། graceful, it also sheds lustre. ཨུཏྤལ་ཡིན་ལ་སྔོན་པོའང་ཡིན being lily, it was also blue.

འབྱེད་སྡུད་ཀྱི་སྒྲ། disjunctive conjunctions.

ཡང་ན signifying *or*, or *or else* is the only disjunctive, in this language, which is in general use.

མ་ཟད nay, rather; what is more; moreover, yet more, མིར་མ་ཟད་ལྷས་ཀྱང་བཏུད man's (not to speak of man) what is more, gods even bowed.

འོན་ཀྱང་, འོན་ཏང་ or འོན་དང་ signifies, though, although, albeit, notwithstanding.

མོད་ཀྱང་ or མད་ཀྱང་ signifies, though, although. མོད་ཀྱང་ད་དུང་, although—yet, ད་དུང་ yet, as yet, but yet.

ད་དུང་ཡང་ now too, still. འོན་ཏེ་ or འོན་ཏེ་ན,, signifies *if*, *but if*. གལ་ཏེ་ or གལ་སྲིད but or if but; དེ་ལྟ་ན or དེ་ཙེ then, so.

ཇི་སྟེ signifies *if*; དེ་སྟེ if then. ཐ་ན not even, not-even so much as, ཅེ་ན, ཤེ་ན, ཞེ་ན for, because.

གམ, ངམ, དམ, ནམ, བམ, མམ, འམ, རམ, ལམ, སམ, ཏམ are interrogative signs, expressing a doubt, whether, or? They may be formed of any word, by reduplicating its final letter, and adding a མ; as in བདག་གམ་ཁོང, ངའམ་ཁོ whether I or he; I or he?

ཅེ་འམ, ཤེ་འམ or ཞེ་འམ signifies *or*, or *so*. འོ་ན, འོ་ན་ནི or འོ་ན་ཡང་ signifies then, therefore, nevertheless.

INTERJECTION.

འབོད་པའི་ཚིག།

ཀྱེ *Kye* is the polite vocative particle signifying *o* or *oh* which is, in general use, both colloquially and in writing. It is equivalent to Sanskrit *Bho* (in Tibetan འབོད *bod* to address or call) from which the *Hindi* name *Bhoṭa* signifying Tibet, has been derived. ཀྱེ is generally used at the beginning of an expression or sentence for example: ཀྱེ་ལྷའི་ལྷ། O, the god of gods! ཀྱེ་ཁ་ལོ་སྒྱུར་བ O, charioteer!*

ཀྱེ is also used in the middle or at the end of a sentence, for example: འཇམ་དབྱངས་མགོན་ཀྱི་བདག་ལ་བློ་གྲོས་སྩོལ། O Patron Jamyang, grant unto me intellect! བུ་ཀྱེ་གཏང་བར་མི་རུང་ངོ་། O son, to renounce is improper! བདག་ལ་སྐྱོངས་ཤིག་ཁྱབ་འཇུག་ཀྱེ O, Viṣṇu! protect me.

བདག་ལ་དགོངས་ཤིག་མགོན་པོ་ཀྱེ O Patron pray think of me.

† ཀྭ་ཡེ, ཀྭའི or ཀྭ are vocative particles used in addressing inferior persons. Their use is general in dramatic writings and performances, and also in songs.

ཨ་ཡེ and མ་ཡེ are vulgar vocative expressions or *interjections* used before the name of the person addressed.‡

---

* བོད་སྐད་ཀྱི་ནི་ཡུལ་མཆོག་ལ། དམན་པར་བུགས་བརྟན་ཀྭ་ཡེ་ཀྭ། †

གྲོང་ཚིག་ཨ་ཡེ་མ་ཡེ་སོགས། མིང་གི་ཡ་ཐོག་གསུངས་པ་ནི། ‡

ཨོཾ, ཨཱཿ (or ཨཿ) and ཧཱུྃ are the three mystical interjections used in addressing the Buddhist Triad or in invoking the Lamaic chiefs of the *Vajra-yāna mystic* cult.

The following vocative terms or expressions signifying sir, yes ; o, holla are in general use colloquially.

ལགས or ཀྱེ་ལགས (sir oh! or o, sir) is used in addressing or in responding to a call in polite language ; ཀྭ, ཀྭེ or ཀྭ་ཡེ is used in addressing inferiors. ཧེ ; ཧེ་ཧེ, ཨ་རེ in addressing some one of out of scorn. ཨ་ཙི, ཙ, ཙ་ལེ are expressions of wonder. ཁྲོ་རེ expression used in threat or anger.

ཀྱི་མ། ཀྱི་ཧུ། ཨ་རོད། ཧུ་ཧུ signifying Oh ! Alas ! Woe ! are expressions of grief and sorrow.

ཨེ་མ། ཨེ་མ་ཧོ are *interjections* of admiration. ཨ་ལ་ལ། ཨ་ལ་ལ་ཧོ are expressions of wonder.

ཨ་ལ་ལ་ཨ་ལ་ལ expresses great joy. ཧ་ཧ is an *interjiction* of joy and admiration. ཨེ་ཨེ། ཡ་ཡ signifying ho !, yes are *interjections* of recollection. ཨ་ཁ། ཨ་ཁ་ཁ disapprobation, displeasure ; expressive of loss.

དགའ་བོ། ཨ་བོ། འབར་རེ། དགོས་སེ། ཤུ་ཤུ are *interjections* of endearment or affection.

ཨ་ཏ་ཏ། ཏ་ཏ་བ *interjections* of excessive pain. ཨ་ན་ན། ཨ་ར་ར are expressive of sorrow or anguish.

ཨ་ཙུ། ཨ་ཙུ་ཙུ are expressions of pain from cold. ཨ་ཚ། ཨ་ཚ་ཚ are expressions of pain from heat.

ཨ་ཇི། ཨ་ཅེ་ཇི are expressions of fright, horror or dread.

The following expressions denote approbation, confirmation, endorsement, &c.

ལེགས་སོ། ལེགས་ཧ་ལེགས་སོ Very well ! Well done ! མད་དོ། དེ་བཞིན་ནོ། དེ་དེ་བཞིན་ནོ། Well, it is just so ! exactly !

ཡིན་ནོ། yes. བདེན་ནོ true, truth ! ངེས་སོ yes, certainly. རིགས་སོ well done ! བསྟོད་དོ be praised !

SYNTAX.

The arrangement of the words of the several parts of speech, in Tibetan expressions and sentences, does not resemble that of the same in English or Sanskrit. It is rather the reverse of the English. The nouns and pronouns including the Nominative, precede their attributes, and the verbs stand at the end of the sentence. In the sentence ཤར་ཙན་དྲས་ལྷ་ལྡན་ཕྱོགས་སུ་གནས་བསྐོར་འགྲོ་སྐབས་ལ། on the occasion of going, on pilgrimage, towards Lha-ldan (Lhasa) by Sarat Chandra, རྡོ་རྗེ་འཆང་ཆེན་པོ * ནས † ལྷ་ལྕམ་སྐུ་ཞབས་ཆེན་པོར་འདི་རྣམས་ལ། ‡ གང་ཅིའི་ཐད་མགོ་འདྲེན་གནང་རོགས་པ་གསུངས་པས།། (See Appendix VI.)

R̲dorje Chañ Chen-po said (བསྒུངས་པས): grant patronage མགོ་འདྲེན་གནང in every way གང་ཅིའི་ཐད to these འདི་རྣམས་ལ (addressing Her Ladyship the Lha-lcam ལྷ་ལྕམ་སྐུ་ཞབས་ཆེན་པོར། Her Ladyship also ལྷ་ལྕམ་སྐུ་ཞབས * ནས † ཀྱང་། receiving this kind request བཀའ་བཞེས་བཟང་པོ་འཕེབ་སྐྱེ། proceded to R̲gyal-r̲tse (Gyan-tse) རྒྱལ་རྩེར་ཐེབས། on the 21st day of the above month གོང་ཟླའི་ཚེས་ཉེར།

---

* ཆེན་པོ and སྐུ་ཞབས are adjectives qualifying the nouns in the Nominative case རྡོ་རྗེ་འཆང and ལྷ་ལྕམ respectively.

† The Ablative case-sign ནས *from i.e.*, signifying origination, is generally used, in modern idiomatic Tibetan, after the Nominative. In these two instances རྡོ་རྗེ་འཆང and ལྷ་ལྕམ are Nominatives, བསྒུངས་པས and འཕེབ་སྐྱེ are verbs.

‡ གང་སྒྲ the term གང is generally used with the pronouns ཅི, དེ, འདི, and adverbs ལྟར, ཚོ and the conjunction ཡང it being placed before them, such as གང་ཅིག ; གང་དེ ; གང་འདི ; གང་ལྟར ; གང་ཚོ ; གང་ཡང་།

Verbs occur at the end of sentences, thus: ང་ནི་དེ་མི་ཤེས། I do not know that; ཁྱོད་ལ་དེ་སུས་ཟེར who told that to you; སངས་རྒྱས་ལ་ཕྱག་འཚལ་ལོ། make reverence to Buddha; སྐུ་ཞབས་ཚེ་རིང་དུ་འཚོ་བར་གྱུར་ཅིག your honour may live long or have long life!

The auxiliaries which follow the principial verb are only conjugated in the several tenses and moods, the root verb being invariable: as in བྱེད་དུ་འཇུག་པར to cause (one) make; བྱེད་ནུས་པར to make (one) can, able; ད་འདོད་པར to wish to do.

Nouns generally precede their attributes, and then it is only the last of them that is declined in the several cases; as in མི་ཆེན་འདི་དག these great men.

A noun denoting possession, is placed in the genitive and alway precedes the thing possessed: མིའི་ལུས་པོ man's body. Such genitives are also expressed adjectively, as in English: མི་ལུས the human body; ཤིང་ཕོར wooden cup; ཆུ་ཐིགས water drops.

The genitive case-sign is sometimes dropt, in nouns, denoting possession: སངས་རྒྱས་བསྟན་པ for སངས་རྒྱས་ཀྱི་བསྟན་པ། འཇིག་རྟེན་མགོན་པོ for འཇིག་རྟེན་གྱི་མགོན་པོ།

When several nouns in the agentive or genitive case are placed together with or without the word ལ་སོགས signifying *et cetera* at the end, the case-sign is attached to the last noun or to སོགས, for example: ལྷ་ཀླུ་མི་ལ་སོགས་ཀྱིས་སངས་རྒྱས་ལ་ཕྱག་བྱས་སོ། the gods, *Nāgā* men et cetera, paid reverence to Buddha. རྒྱལ་བློན་འབངས་ཐམས་ཅད་ཀྱི་སྐྱབས་གནས, the place of refuge of the king, ministers, and of all the subjects. རང་གི་ཕ་མ་དང་མི་གཞན་ཀུན་ལ to my parents and every other person.

When the adjectives precede the nouns they are intended to qualify, they are invariable in all the cases: དམ་ཆོས signifies དམ་པའི་ཆོས། སྨས་ས stands for སྨས་པོའི་ས། cardinals, expressive of any great number or quantity, require, that the preceding noun be in the sigular: མི་བཅུ ten men; ལོ་བརྒྱ a hundred years; དམག་མི་སྟོང་ཕྲག་བརྒྱ a hundred thousand war-men or warriors. གྲོང་ཁྱིམ་ཁྲི་གཅིག a myriad houses; གྲོང་ཁྱེར་འབུམ་ཕྲག a hundred thousand towns; གྲོང་མི་ས་ཡ a million of inhabitants.

The case denoting the agent, by whom, or the instrument, with which, any action is produced, is called the Instrumentive. This occurs very frequently, since it is used both before the active and passive verbs, or before every verb denoting a transitive action on an object or person.

Active and passive verbs ending བྱེད or བྱེད་དོ། can be discriminated only by the instrumentive and the nominative cases expressed before them.

ངས་བརྡུང་བར་བྱེད by me (he) is beaten; ང་བརྡུང་བར་བྱེད I am beaten.

Active and Causal verbs require before them, the Instrumentive case *i.e.* the Nominative with any of these case-signs གྱིས, ཀྱིས, གྱིས, --ས or ཡིས or འིས, according to the final letter of the word in the Nominative case, and the neuters and passives, in like manner, require the Nominative or Objective case. But, when the active verb is intransitive, the Nominative is used ; as in ཁོང་ཞབས་འཆག་བྱེད། he walks; ང་མི་འགྲུལ I do not walk or go. Instead of the Instrumentive case, the Nominative is also used with the emphatical I (ང་ནི) ; as in ང་ནི་མ་སྨྲས་སོ I have not said that. As also, when the Objective case takes the ལ particle, the Nominative (or Accusative) is used, instead of the Instrumentive ; as in ངས་ཁྱོད་ལ་ཟེར I have told you, for བདག་གིས་ཁྱོད་ལ་ཟེར by me it has been said to you. (See Csoma's Grammar).

PROSODY.

སྙན་ངག་ས། *Kāvya.*

Tibetan verses are free from the fetters of rhyme and metre. All the poetical pieces in Tibetan, originals or translations from Sanskrit, are in a sort of blank verse or prose in flowing motion. There is no distinction of vowels into long and short, accented or emphatical, in Tibetan versification. All poetical compositions differ from one another only in the number of syllables. There are feet but not metrical ones, measured by short and long vowels or syllables. The several poetical pieces occurring in the *Kah-gyur* and *Stangyur*, all of which are faithful translations from the Sanskrit Buddhist works of India, have been rendered in blank verse, consisting of two or four lines, each of seven, nine, eleven, thirteen, fifteen, seventeen, nineteen or twentyone syllables.

The *Avadāna Kalpalatā*, in Tibetan and Sanskrit, which has been published in the *Bibliotheca Indica* series by the Asiatic Society of Bengal, contains numerous examples of such poetical compositions.

In the repartee songs of Tibet which generally consist of verses of two lines of six syllables each, there is rhythm ; (see Appendix IX) but poetry (སྙན་བཅད) *i.e.*, versification is seldom done in lines of six syllables.

In lyric songs the distinction of number in the syllables of a line is, however, seldom observed. They are composites, sometimes irregularly done, of lines of six, seven and two syllables. These are, at the time of singing, lengthened by the intersyllabic addition of ལ, ཟེ (for ཟེར) &c., such as in སྐྱིད་མ (སྐྱིད་ལ་མ); ལེགས་པ (ལེགས་ལ་པ) ཡོད་ལ (ཡོད་ལ་ཟེ). See Appendix X.

INDEX.

(References are to the pages and lines).

BOOK I.

SPECIMENS OF TIBETAN COMPOSITION.

ILLUSTRATIONS.

CONTENTS.

APPENDIX I.

ངོས་འཛིན།།

ཧཱུྃ ཕྱོགས་དུས་རབ་འབྱམས་རྒྱལ་བ་ཀུན་གྱི་འཕྲིན་ལས་པར་དབང་བསྒྱུར་ཞིང་། འཇམ་དབྱངས་གོང་མ་ཆེན་པོ་རེ་ལུང་གི་གཞུ་ལའི་ཧྲ་པའུ་བ་ཡང་ཤྲི་ཧེན་ཙྪེ་ཙའུ་ཀུའེ་ཞེས་འབོད་པ། དཔལ་ཀརྨ་པའི་སྐྱེ་འཕྲེང་རིམ་བྱོན་ལས་བཅུ་བཞི་པ་ཨཱུ་ན་པ་ར་མ་བཛྲ་སྭ་སྟི་རིག་པ་མཆོག་གི་རྡོ་རྗེར་འབོད་པས་བཏམ།

Official Seal.

ཧཱུྃ འཛམ་གླིང་ཡངས་པའི་ཁྱོན་སྤྱི་དང་། བྱེ་བྲག་སྲས་ཡུལ་འབྲས་མོ་ལྗོངས་ཀྱི་བླ་མ་དགེ་འདུན། མི་དབང་། ས་སྐྱོང་། བཀའ་བློན་ཞིང་བཙུ་དཔོན་སོགས་སེར་སྐྱ་མཆོག་དམན་མཐའ་དག་གི་གསན་ཅིང་ངེས་གྱུར། ས་སྐྱོང་མི་དབང་ཆོས་རྒྱལ་གྱི་སྲས་འདི་བཞིན་མཛད་ཁམས། ཀུན་མཁྱེན་སི་ཏུ་རིན་པོ་ཆེའི་དགོན་ཀརྨ་རིན་ཆེན་ངེས་དོན་བསྟན་འཛིན་གྱི་རྫུ་ལ་པའི་སྐུར་འདི་ག

བདག་ནས་ངོས་འཛིན་ཁྲི་འདོན་མངའ་གསོལ་བགྱིད་ཅིང་མཚན་ཀརྨ་སྒྲུབ་བརྒྱུད་བསྟན་འཛིན་དར་རྒྱས་ལྷུན་གྲུབ་ངེས་དོན་དབང་པོ་ཞེས་གསོལ་ཞིང་དགེ་ཚུལ་སྡོམ་གྱི་དངོས་པོ་ཡང་དག་པར་སྩལ་ཅིང་། གསང་སྔགས་གསར་རྙིང་གི་དབང་རྗེས་གནང་དུ་མ་དང་། ཟབ་ཁྲིད་བཀའ་ལུང་སོགས་ཀྱིས་སྨིན་པར་བགྱིས་ནས་རང་ལུགས་ཀྱི་དགོན་སྡེ་ཀརྨ་རབ་བརྟན་གླིང་ཀརྨ་བཀྲ་ཤིས་ཆོས་འཁོར་གླིང་ཀརྨ་ཆོས་འཁོར་གླིང་། ཀརྨ་འཆི་མེད་ཡངས་དབེན། ཀརྨ་སྒྲུབ་བརྒྱུད་བསྟན་དར་གླིང་སོགས་ཀྱི་སྤྱི་ཁྱབ་ཆོས་ཀྱི་རྗེ་བོ་དམ་པར་དབང་བསྒྱུར་བ་ཡིན་པས་བླ་མ་ཉིད་ནས་ཀྱང་འཆད་རྩོད་བརྩོམ་གསུམ། ཐོས་བསམ་སྒོམ་གསུམ་གྱི་སྒོ་ནས་རིས་སུ་མ་ཆད་པའི། རྒྱལ་བའི་བསྟན་པ་མཐའ་དག་དར་རྒྱས་སུ་སྤེལ་བའི་ཐབས་ཚུལ་གང་ཟབ་དང་། ཁྱེ་བྲག་ཀརྨ་བཀའ་བརྒྱུད་ཀྱི་བསྟན་པ་ཡར་ཟླ་ལྟར་འཕེལ་བའི་མཛད་འཕྲིན་ཐུགས་བསྐྱེད་ཞུམ་པ་མེད་པ་དང་། དགེ་འདུན་གྱི་སྡེ་རྣམས་ནས་ཀྱང་བླ་མས་ཅི་གསུང་དྲངས་ལེན། བསླབ་པ་ཁྲིམས་བསྲུང་ཉམས་ཚུལ་བཞིན་བགྱིད་པ་དང་དད་ལྡན་ཡོན་གྱི་བདག་པོ་རྣམས་ཀྱིས་ཀྱང་། གུས་འདུད་བསྙེན་བཀུར་དྲངས་ལེན་བགྱིད་དགོས་པ་བཅས་ཐུགས་ངེས་འཚལ། ཞེས་པའི་ཡི་གེ་ཀྱུ་སྟག་ཟླ་ཚེས་དགེ་བར། འོག་མིན་མཚུར་ཕུའི་ཆོས་གྲྭ་ཆེན་པོ་ནས་ཕྲིལ།

Official Seal.

APPENDIX II.

གཉེར་ཡིག།

A Tibetan Marriage Deed.

ལྷ་ཕྱིངས་ལྷ་ལྕམ་མཆོག་མ་ཡེ་ཤེས་སྒྲོལ་མ་ལ་གཉེར་ཞུའི་སྐབས་ཀྱི་གཉེར་ཡིག་འདྲ་ཤུས་འཁྲུལ་མེད་དགེ།། +

༄༅།། ཨོཾ་སྭསྟི་སི་དྡྷམ།

བཟང་པོའི་སྐལ་པ་འདི་ལ་དམ་ཆོས་ཀྱིས། དབྱར་སྐྱེས་ཛ་སང་སྡོང་དུ་འཕྲིན་པ་ལས།

སྙིགས་དུས་འགྲོ་བའི་གསོས་གྱུར་བདུད་རྩི་འི་ཆར། འཕེབ་མཁས་ཤཱ་ཀྱའི་རྒྱལ་པོས་དགེ་ལེགས་སྩོལ།

ཁམས་གསུམ་དབང་གྱུར་དཔལ་ལྡན་འདོད་པའི་རྒྱལ། རྒྱལ་བའི་ཡུམ་མཆོག་ཀུ་རུ་ཀུ་ལླེ་ལ།

མ་ཕམ་འདོད་དགུའི་ཆར་བསྙིལ་ནོར་སྦྱིན་ལྷ། ལྷ་ཡི་ལྷ་མཆོག་རྣམས་ཀྱིས་རྟག་ཏུ་སྐྱོངས།

བསྟན་འགྲོའི་མགོན་མཛད་དམ་ཅན་ཚོགས་ཀྱི་དང་། ཁྱད་པར་རང་རང་རིགས་བརྒྱུད་འགོ་བའི་ལྷ།

ཡུལ་གཞིས་གནས་སྐྱོངས་སྲུང་མའི་ཚོགས་བཅས་ཀྱིས། དུས་ཀུན་མི་གཡེལ་སྲུང་སྐྱོབས་གདོང་གྲོགས་མཛོད།

འཛམ་གླིང་ཕྱི་བའི་བོད་ཡུལ་ཆོས་ལྡན་ཞིང་། འདབས་འབྲེལ་ལྷོ་ཕྱོགས་འབྲས་མོ་ཀླན་པའི་ལྗོངས།

བདེ་སྐྱིད་གཡང་དུ་ཆགས་པའི་མདུན་ས་ན། ས་སྐྱོང་ཆེ་བཙན་སྡེ་རིས་ཆ་རྡོན་འཕགས་པ།

ཕན་ཚུན་ཟབ་ཞེས་གཉེན་དུ་འབྲེལ་བའི་མདུད། ནམ་ཡང་གྲོད་པ་མེད་པའི་ཕྱག་རྒྱ་ཡིས།

བཏབ་པའི་བྲིས་ཡིག་བཀྲ་ཤིས་རི་བ་ཅན། སྲིད་གསུམ་ཀུན་དགའི་དཔྱིད་གྱུར་འདི་ན་སྤེལ།

ཞེས་ཤིས་པར་བརྗོད་པ་དང་ངེས་པར་བརྟན་པའི་ཚིག་གི་འཕྲེང་བ་ཙའི་སྒྲ་དབྱངས་ཀྱི་དགེ་བས་སྔོན་བསུས་ཏེ། དེ་ཡང་འདིར་རབ་བྱུང་བཅོ་ལྔ་པའི་ནང་གི་ཆུ་ཚོགས་ཞེས་པ་ཆུ་མོ་རྟའི་ལོ་ཧོར་ཟླ་དཔྱིད་ར་ཟླ་གི་ཟླ་བ་ངེས་དོན་ཉི་མ་བྱུང་བསྒྲོད་ཀྱི་ལོ་མགོ་གསར་དུ་ཚེས་པའི་སྐབས་དང་འབྲེལ་བར་རྒྱ་གར་འཕགས་པའི་ཡུལ་ནས་དཔག་ཚད་བརྒྱ་ཕྲག་གི་ཞལ་བའི་བྱང་ཕྱོགས་འཕགས་ཆེན་ཐུགས་རྗེའི་གཏེར་གྱི་གདུལ་ཞིང་བོད་ཡུལ་ཆོལ་ཁ་གསུམ་གྱི་ས་ཚིགས་སུ་ནམ་པར་ཕྱེ་བ་ལས་དབུས་གཙང་ཆོས་ཀྱི་ཆོལ་ཁ་དང་འདབ་འབྲེལ་བའི་ལྷོ་རོང་འབྲས་མོ་ལྗོངས་པའི་འདུན་ས་སྲས་གནས་དཀར་མོ་ལྗོངས་ཀྱི་ས་ལ་སྐྱོང་པའི་རྒྱལ་སྲས་མཆེད་ཟུང་གི་ཐབ་ཤེས་ཐུགས་འདུན་གནམ་བསྐོས་དཀའ་བ་བརྒྱ་ལྡན་པོ་བྲང་པ་ཆེན་པོའི་སྲིད་ཞུའི་ཞབས་འདེགས་དྲུང་རིགས་སྤྱིང་ཁྱུངས་ཕག་མོ་ལྷ་ཕྱིངས་པར་གྲགས་མཆོག་བརྒྱུད་པ་ཆེན་པོའི་སྨྲའི་རིང་ལ་ཡབ་མེས་གོང་མ་རྗེ་ཡུབ་ཆེ་དབང་ནས་སྐྱ་ཕྱིར་ཞི་དྲག་གི་ཞབས་འཇུར་ལ་བརྟེན་པའི་མདུན་ན་འདོན་གྱི་གོ་གནས་དང་དར་ལྡན་གྱི་ཚེ་བོའི་གཟེང་བསྟོད་ཀུང་རྒྱལ་བས་མཆོད་མི་རབ་གོང་མ་རིམ་ཅན་ནས་དུ་ཟླའི་བར་ནང་མའི་ལས་ཚན་གྱི་ཞབས་ཞུ་རིམ་ཅན་ཟམ་མི་ཆད་པ་བཅས་ཀྱིས་མཛད། གཞུང་དྲུང་སྤྱིང་ཁྱུངས་གཞིས་

\+ A correct copy of the Marriage Deed of the Mahārāni of Sikkim, late Lha-cham Yeçe Dolma ལྷ་ལྕམ་ཡེ་ཤེས་སྒྲོལ་མ། executed at Lhasa, in 1882.

ཆགས་ཀྱི་ཐོག་ཀྱུ་གར་ཤཱ་ཀྱའི་གདུང་བརྒྱུད་དྲི་མ་མེད་པ་ཤྲཱི་དཔོན་ང་ཐོད་པའི་སྲས་བརྒྱུད་ཀོང་པོ་འབྲུག་ལྷ་མཁན་ཆེན་གྱི་སྐུ་མཆེད་དུ་གཏོགས་པའི་ཀ་དྲུས་ལས་ནང་ཁྲུལ་གཉེན་སྤྲེལ་གྱི་སྲས་རྣམ་རྒྱལ་རྡོ་རྗེ་དང་། མི་བརྒྱུད་གཞུང་དྭང་སྙིང་ཁུངས་མདོ་སྨད་འབབ་ཁྲུལ་དུ་གོང་མ་བདག་པོ་ཆེན་པོའི་བུ་སིའི་གོ་མིང་འཛིན་པའི་གཉིས་ཆགས་ལ་བརྟེན་རྒྱལ་མཆོག་བདུན་པ་ཆེན་པོས་མདོ་ཁམས་ཀྱི་ས་ཡུལ་རྣམས་གོང་མ་རྒྱ་གཞུང་གི་ལྷ་འབངས་སུ་འབུལ་གནང་ཁོངས་ཚོད་ཀྱང་ལྷུགས་ཕག་གོར་བོད་ཕྱི་གཟར་སྐབས་བུ་སི་ཡབ་རྗེ་འཕྲིན་ལས་མགོན་པོ་ནས་ཧོར་ལེ་ཀྲུང་ཐང་ཆེན་པོའི་ཞབས་འདེགས་དམག་དོན་ཞབས་འགྱུར་ལ་ཟལ་ཐོན་གྱི་བདག་རྐྱེན་དུ་རིམ་པ་གཉིས་པའི་ཏོག་དང་སྨྱོ་ཤིག་གཉིས་པའི་གོ་གནས་ཐེའི་ཙེའི་དཔལ་བུ་ལྷུའི་ཆོ་ལོ་བཅས་གོང་མ་ཆེན་པོའི་དཔོན་གནས་མི་རབ་བརྒྱུད་འཛུགས་སུ་སྩལ་ཞིང་། རྒྱལ་མཆོག་བརྒྱད་པ་ཆེན་པོས་ཀྱང་འབར་ཝེ་བོད་ཁོངས་སུ་དྭང་སྙིང་ལར་དགོངས་ཀྱི་གཞུང་ཁོངས་ཞབས་ཕྱུར་འཇོར་རིགས་དྭང་དུག་ཁོངས་བཙོད་ཐུས་གཟིགས་གསོས་དང་འབྲེལ་བ་བཅས་ཀྱི་མི་རྗེ་ལྷ་ཕྱིངས་སྲས་སྐལ་བཟང་ཉི་མའི་ཚ་མོ་བསོད་ནམས་སྒྲོལ་མ་གཉིས་ཀྱི་བུ་སྤུན་མཆེད་ཀྱི་རྒྱན་འགོ་ཡེ་ཤེས་སྒྲོལ་མ་འདི་ལ་བསྐྱེད་ལྷ་སྤྲའི་ལུང་བརྟག་ཏུ་བབས་དོན་ལྷ་གཉེར་ཁྲུམ་པ་སྲས་རྒྱུད་སྐྱེར་དགོས་ནན་གསུང་དོན་བཞིན་ཕར་ཚུན་ཕྱོད་སྐྱེར་མོས་མཐུན་གྱི་ངག་འདུན་ཚོད་ཟིན་པས་ཟླ་དུས་གསལ་ཀྱི་ཀྲུལ་ཚེས་རིས་གཟའ་ཟླའི་སྦྱོ་རེས་གྲོགས་རྒྱལ་གྱི་དགའ་མ་དང་བརྩེ་བའི་དུས་ཚེས་མཆོག་ཏུ་དགེ་བར་སྤྱོད་ཚང་དང་། ཞིན་རང་དོན་གཅིག་པའི་རྟེན་འབྲེལ་གྱི་འགོ་འཛིན་ཀྱང་སྐྱབ་ཅིང་ས་གནས་སུ་རྡོ་གཏོང་བསུ་ལེན་མཛད་རྒྱུ་སྐབས་མཚམས་བབས་བསྟུན་གྱིས་འཁྱུངས་མིན་ཞིབ་མོལ་མཛད་རྒྱུ་དང་། དེ་མཚུངས་སྲས་མོར་གོས་རྒྱན་དངོས་ཆས་སྐལ་རྫོང་སོགས་རྡོ་ཐོན་དང་ཚབ་ཅིག་ཕྱེད་གནང་མཛད་རྒྱུ་ཐོ་གཞུང་ཟུར་གསལ་བཞིན་དང་། སྲིད་ནས་ཕན་ཚུན་མཛད་སྒོའི་སྒོར་ལ། གཙོ་བོར་ཕན་ཚུན་ཐབ་ཤེས་གཉིས་ཐད་ནས་མཛའ་བརྩུག་མཐུན་ཞིབ་ཀྱི་འགྲོག་འདྲིས་ལེགས་ལམ་རྒྱུན་འཕྱོངས་མཛད་རྒྱུ་གཞིར་བཟུང་ཐོག་གོང་བཞུགས་ཡབ་ཡུམ་དང་། ས་སྐྱོང་རྒྱལ་སྲས་རྣམ་གཉིས་དབུས་ཚང་མས་ཐུགས་མཐུན་ཞལ་ཆེམ་འདེབ་རྟེན་ལུགས་བཟང་གི་ཐབ་ཤེས་མཛད་པ་མ་ཟད། སྲས་མོས་ཀྱང་ལུས་སྐྱེས་ཡབ་ཡུམ་དང་། ཁང་འཁྲུངས་ཆེ་བའི་ཐེབས་དགོས་བབ་ཡུལ་བཅས་ལ་དགོངས་ཏེ་རྣམ་ཀུན་ཕ་མིང་དང་ཁྱད་མེད་ཀྱི་བྱམས་བརྩེས་ཡོངས་པ་དང་། མཐུན་འགྱུར་ཕན་གྲོགས་ཀྱི་ལེགས་སྒྲོབས་སྐྱལ་ཁོས་གང་ཅི་འདོར་མེད་ཀྱི་བློ་འཕམ་ཡིད་རྩད་དང་། འཕྲུལ་ཡུན་རྟེན་ཆུང་དུ་མི་འགྱུར་བའི་ཕྱུགས་འཚོངས་ཡུན་གནས་མཛད་རྒྱུ་དང་། ཐུགས་འདུན་སྲས་ཀྱང་བོད་ཞུས་ཡབ་ཡུམ་ལ་ལས་བསྔོས་ཀྱི་ཕ་མིང་དང་། རྒྱལ་སྲས་སྐུ་མཆེད་ལའང་མཛའ་གྲོགས་ཀྱི་འདུ་ཤེས་མ་ཐོར་བའི་བཀུར་སྟི་ཀུས་ཞེན་དང་། རྒྱན་ལབ་གཞོན་ཉན་ཀྱི་སྤྱང་བླངས་ལུགས་མཐུན་རྒྱན་འཇོངས་ཀྱི་བློ་ལྷགས་མཚན་ཤས་རིགས་མེད་པའི་འཛིང་མའི་མིག་རྒྱན་དུ་འགྱུར་བ་མཛད་རྒྱུ་བཅས་འདོར་ན་ཕན་ཚུན་གཉིས་ཐད་ནས་ཇི་སྐད་དུ། ལེགས་བཤད་རིན་པོ་ཆེའི་གཏེར་ལས། ཡ་རབ་མ་རབ་སྤྱོད་པས་འགྲེད། རྫོང་པ་ཉམས་ན་རིགས་དོན་མེད། ཅེས་དང་། སྐྱེ་བོ་དམ་པ་རིན་ཆེན་བཞིན། རྣམ་པ་ཀུན་ཏུ་འགྱུར་ལྡོག་མེད། ཅེས་གསུང་པ་ལྟར། ངན་བསྐྱོད་མ་རབ་ཀྱི་དྲི་མས་མ་གོས་ཤིང་། ཡ་རབ་བཟང་སྤྱོད་ཀྱི་ངང་ཚུལ་ལྷུར་བཞེས་དང་འབྲེལ་བའི་གྲོགས་ཤེས་མཐུན་འཇུག་གི་མཛད་བཟང་སྐྱེ་བོ་དམ་པའི་རྣམ་ཐར་བཟང་པོའི་དཔེར་འོས་སུ་འགྱུར་བ་རིན་ཆེན་གསེར་སྦྱངས་ལྷད་བྲལ་བཞིན་རྣམ་ཀུན་འགྱུར་ལྡོག་མེད་པ་ཇི་སྲིད་ནམ་གནས་པར་དུ་སོར་གནས་རྒྱུན་འཁྱོངས་ཕྱུགས་བརྟན་ཡུན་རིང་ནས་བཀྲ་ཤིས་ལུགས་ལེགས་ཡར་ལྡན་དུ་མཛད་དགོས་བཅས་ཀྱི་གཉེན་ཡིག་ཡི་གེ་གཞུང་རྩང་གི་མདུད་བརྒྱ་འདྲ་གཉིས་སུ་བྲིས་བ་འབྲས་ལྡོངས་ས་སྐྱོང་ཡུམ་སྲས་ཀྱི་ཐེའུ། གཉེན་དཔང་ལྷ་གཉེར་ཁྲུམ་པ་སྲས་ཀྱི་ཐེའུ། ཡབ་ཙང་ལྷ་ཕྱིངས་སྲས་སྐལ་བཟང་ཉི་མ་དང་། སྲས་རྣམ་རྒྱལ་རྡོ་རྗེ་གཉིས་ཀྱི་ཐེའུ།

གཉེར་དཔང་ཞོལ་གཉེར་དཀར་ཚང་གི་ཐེའུ། མཆན་མཆན་ལས།

APPENDIX III.

ལམ་ཡིག།

A Passport—Road Bill.

༄༅། །ཨ་ཙར་ཡ་པུ་རེང་གི་རི་འདི་པ། རྒྱ་འབྲུག་གཡུལ་འགྱེད་ཀྱི་དུས་སུ་ཞེགས་རྫིལ་དུ་གཏོང་བ་གནང་བར། དོན་ཆེན་པོ་འགྲུབ་སྟེ་སྐྱོ་བོ་མང་པོ་དུས་མིན་འཆི་བ་ལས་བསྐྱབས་པར་བརྟེན། ཛེ་སྲིད་འཚོ་འི་བར་བཀྲ་རྗེས་ལྡན་པོར་ནམ་ཡོང་གི་དུས་ངོ་གཡོག་གང་ཡོད་ལ། ཛ་མར། འབྲས། ཤ་ཚུམ། ནས། གྲོ་ཕྱེ། ཞོ། འོ་མ། བཞོན་ཁལ་ཡོད་རིགས་ལ་རྩ་བཟན། མི་ཤིང་སོགས་ལྡང་ངེས་སྐྱེར་བ་དང་། ཕྱོགས་སུ་འགྲོ་བའི་དུས་ཁང་ཀུར། བཞོན་ཁལ། ལམ་རྒྱུས་སོགས་ཕན་གྲོགས་སུ་གང་འགྲོ་བྱེད་དགོས་པའི་རྗེ་བཙུན་བློ་བཟང་དཔལ་ལྡན་ཡེ་ཤེས་དཔལ་བཟང་པོ་ནས་གཟིགས་བསྐྱངས་ཀྱིས་བཀའ་ཤོག་བཙན་དམིགས་འདུག་པའི་དགོངས་དོན་ལ་ངོར་བནས་དགོས་པའི་ངོས་ནས་ཀུང་ཐ་མ་ཁ་དྲིན་པ་ཅིན་པས་དྭག་ཞན་ཚང་མ་ནས་ཤུང་སླང་ཡོང་བ་གྱིས། ཤིང་སྦྲུལ་ཟླ་ཚེས་དགེ་བ་ལ།

༦ ༡

Official Seal.

The above pass-port was granted to Purengiri Gosain by the Government of Lhasa in the year *Tree-Serpent* of the 13th cycle རབ་བྱུང་བཅུ་གསུམ་པ།

OFFICIAL ORDER OF THE TASHI LAMA,

Lozaṅ Paldan Yéshé,

sanctioning food allowances, etc., to Ācharya Purnagiri and his servants.

སྐྱབས་མགོན་ཆེན་པོའི་ཞབས་དམ་སྐྱི་སྐྱལ་དགོངས་དོན་བཞིན་ཨ་ཙར་ཡ་པུར་ཎ་གི་རི་སྐོར་ལ་གཉེར་ཚང་ནས་གཏོང་དགོས་ངོ་བོར་ཟླ་ཐོབ་ཚུམ་ཞིབ་བྲེ་ཚང་ཀྱི་ཁལ་གསུམ། གྲོ་ཕྱེ་ཁལ་གཉིས། ཤ་ལུག་ཕོག་བཟང་བ་ཕྱེད་གཉིས། གཡོག་ངོ་ཡོད་ལ་ཞིབ་ཁལ་གཉིས་རེ་དང་གྲོ་ཕྱེ་ཁལ་རེ། ཤ་ལུག་ཕོག་རེ། རྟ་ངོ་ཡོད་ལ་ཉིན་རེར་རྩ་ཟུར་བྲེ་དོ་རེ་བཅས་ངོ་ཐོག་སྒྲུས་ཀ་ཞན་མེད་གཏོང་རྒྱུའི་འཛིན། ཤིང་རྟ་ཟླ་ཚེས་ལ

༡༡ ༢༥

Official Seal.

APPENDIX III

ལམ་ཡིག།

A Passport—Road Bill.

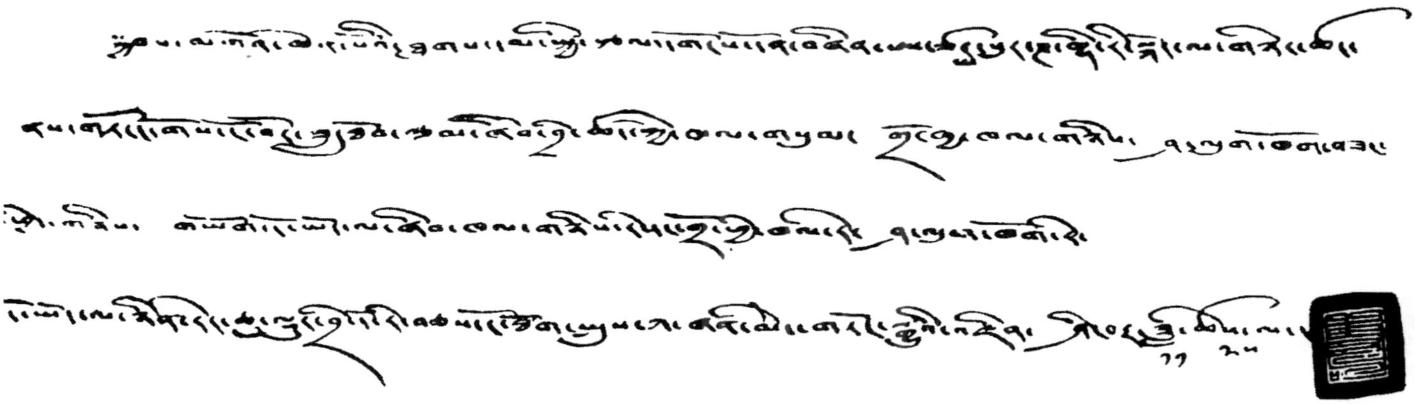

Road-Bill.

༄༅། ལྷ་ས་ནས། བཀྲ་ཤིས་ལྷུན་པོ་དང་། ཕག་རི་རྒྱུད། རྒྱ་གར་ཕྱིན་གྱི་ལམ་འགོད་རྫོང་གཞིས་ཁག་དམངས་བཅས་ནས་ངེས་དགོས། གོང་མ་བདག་པོ་ཆེན་པོའི་བཀའི་འཕྲིན་ལམ་གྱི་གཙོ་བོ་ཉང་ཆུན་ཀུང་ཐང་ཆེན་ངོར་ཀ་ལ་ཀ་ཏའི་ས་ཧེབ་ནས་ཞུ་ཡིག་འབུལ་མི་ཨ་ཙར་ཡ་དྷ་རྗིར་གིར་ངོ་བཤོལ་ནས་ཕྱིར་ལོག་ལ་ཚ་འདུག་པར་བབས་སུ་ཕྱི་ནས་དང་། བཟན་ཤིང་། རྟ་ཐབས་གཡག་གཉིས། རང་སྐྱོལ་གྱི་རྟ་འུལ་ལྔ། རྫས་ཁལ་མ་བཅུ་ཐམ་པ། ས་ཚོགས་ཀྱི་མི་ཧྲང་གཉིས་བཅས་བསྒྱུ་གཏོང་དགོས་པར། འདི་པའི་གཙོང་ཀུང་ཐང་ཆེན་པོ་ནས་ཀ་ལ་ཀ་ཏའི་ས་ཧེབ་ལ་སྐུལ་རྒྱུའི་བཀའ་རྒྱ་གནང་རྟེན་བཅས་རིང་ཁྱུད་ཤིན་ཏུ་ཆེ་བ་ཡོད་འདུག་གཤིས། ལམ་འགོད་རྫོང་གཞིས་དམངས་བཅས་ནས་འགོར་འགྱངས་ཕྲ་མོ་ཙམ་མེད་པ་དགོས་རྒྱུར། གལ་ཆེར་ཁྲིམས་སྐྱུར་རིགས་བྱ་ཆེ་འདི་པའི་ཕྱོན་ཆེས་བོད་བཞུགས་ཨམ་པའི་ཡ་མོན་དུ་གཞུང་ཁྲར་འགོད་སོང་བ་ལེ་ཐོགས་ཤར་ཚེ་རྗེས་གཅོད་གཏོང་ངེས་བཅས་དེ་དོན་ཐུང་བླངས་ཡོང་བ་དང་། སྔེ་ཤན་ངོ་གསོག་ལ་ལྷ་ས་ནས་བཀྲས་ལྷུན་རྒྱུད་ཕག་རི་བར་ལ་ཞར་ཕྱིར་རྫོང་སྐྱོལ་གྱི་རྟ་འུལ་གཉིས། རྫས་ཁལ་གཉིས། ཚ་ཞགས་སར་བཟན་ཤིང་བཅས་དགོས་པ་འང་བསྒྱུ་གཏོང་ཡོང་བ་བཅས་ཀྱིས།

ལྷ་སྐྱོངས་དཀུང་ལོ་ང་བརྒྱད་པའི་ཟླ་ཚེས་ལ། ༢ ༡༣

Official Seal.

གོང་ཞབས་རྒྱལ་དབང་མཆོག་ནས་སྐུལ་བའི་ལམ་ཡིག་བཀའ་ཤོག་གོང་དོན་ལྟར་ཡོང་བ་ཀྱིས། ཆུ་གླང་ཟླ་ཚེས་ལ ༢ ༡༣

Official Seal.

This Road-Bill was granted by the Lhasa Government to Āchārya Dharjirgiri in the 58th year of Emperor Kuenlung, on the 13th of the 2nd Lunar month of the Tibetan year *Water-Ox*.

APPENDIX IV.

ཞུས་ཡིག།།

A letter from His Holiness the DALAI LAMA to His Majesty the King-Emperor EDWARD VII.*

༄༅།། བསོད་ནམས་སྟོབས་ཀྱི་འཁོར་ལོས་བསྒྱུར་བ་གོང་མ་རྒྱལ་པོ་ཆེན་པོ་མཆོག་གི་དྲུང་དུ། ཏཱ་ལའི་བླ་མའི་འབུལ་འབྲས་ངོ་འཕྲོར་ལམ་འགྲོད་བདེ་ལྡན་ཐོག་ཕྱི་གཞུང་ནས་འདི་ཕྱོགས་ཇོད་སྐྱིག་ཡོ་ཆས་ཟབ་བཞེས་གནང་བ་ཐུགས་རྗེ་ཆེ། རྒྱ་ནག་དཔོན་རིགས་དང་འགྲིགས་མིན་བྱུང་ཀཱར་རྒྱལ་ཚབ་ཆེན་པོར་ཞུ་ཐོ་ཕུལ་ཡོད་པ་བཞིན་འཕྲལ་ཕྲུག་ཆོད་པའི་རོགས་སྐྱོང་དམ་དོན་མཛད་ཐུབ་ས་ནས་སྙར་བཀྲིན་སྙིང་བཅངས་ཆོག་པ་ཞུ་རྒྱུར། ད་ལམ་རྟབས་ཐྲེལ་གྱི་འབུལ་འགྱུར་རྟེང་མིན་ཙམ་དུ་ཨ་ཛུས་ནང་མཛོད་དང་། སངས་རྒྱས་ཀྱི་གཟུགས་བརྙན་ནམས་བཅས་ཕྱིན་ཅན། ཧོར་ཟླའི་ཆ་ཚང་གསེར་བཞིའ་མ་ཀར་གླིང་བཟང་གོས་ཁ་ཕྱི་ཆོས་ཚོགས་ཡུག་ཚང་ལྔ།

༡ ༡ ༡༥

* This, with its translation in English, and accompanying presents, was sent direct to King Edward VII, from Calcutta.

A letter from His Serene Holiness the Tashi Lama to the Japanese Lama, Ekai Kawa-guchi.

དད་ལྡན་སྦྱོར་པར་བླ་མ་ལ།།

ཡང་འཚོའི་འདབ་བརྒྱད་ཆོས་སྤྱོད་ཀྱི་ཟེའུ་འབྲུ་འཛུམ་བཞིན་པ་ནས།

ཞིང་སྤྱལ་ཕོ་ཀ་ལ་ཀ་ཏར་ངོས་ལ་བླ་མ་ཉིད་ནས་སྐྱེས་སུ་བསྟར་བའི་ཆོས་དུང་དེ་བཞིན་གྱི་མཆེད་བླ་སྣང་རྣམ་རྒྱུང་དང་བཅས་པ་གཅིག་དང་། བསྟན་བཅོས་འགྱུར་ རོ་ཙོག་གི་སྙིང་པོ་ རྒྱ་ཡིག་མ་དཔེ་གཅིག་བཅས་ཏེ་ལམ་ཀ་སྦྲུག་བུ་ཆུང་རྒྱུད་བསྒྱུར་བ་ཉམས་མེད་འབྱོར་པས་ཡིད་སྨྲའི་སྨན་ཡོད་དུ་གྱུར། ངོས་ཀྱང་འདུ་བ་སྐྱོམས་ཤིང་། རིས་མེད་འགྲོ་ལ་ཕྱམ་པའི་ལྷག་བསམ་དགེ་བར་མཆིས། ཉེ་ལམ། ཇི་ལྟར་གསུང་བ་བཞིན་བཀའ་འགྱུར་ཆ་ཚང་གཅིག འཕྲལ་དུ་བར་གསལ་འདེབས་ཀྱིས་ངེས་པར་ཕུལ་སུ་དེ་ཕྱོགས་གཏོང་དུས་སོགས་འཕྲུལ་གསལ་ཡོང་པ་ཉམས། སྙད་མར། འཚོ་བའི་འདོར་ལན་དང་། ཆོས་སྤྱོད་གོང་འཕེལ་ནས། འཕྲོས་ཚོགས་ཀྱང་རིམ་ལྡན་དུ་འཚོལ། ཞེས་རིན་ཐུགས་མདུད་ངོས་ཀྱིས་མི་རྟག་འཁོར་བའི་སྣང་བརྙན། དམ་རྗེས་ལ་རྟེན། ཁ་བཏགས་བཅས། ཆོས་དགེ།

Official Seal.

པཎ་ཆེན་རིན་པོ་ཆེ་བློ་བཟང་ཆོས་ཀྱི་ཉི་མ་ནས་ཛ་པན་བླ་མ་ཨེ་ཀཱའི་ཀཱ་ཝ་གུ་ཅི་ལ་གནང་བའི་བཀའ་ཤོག་བཏུབ་ས་སོ།།

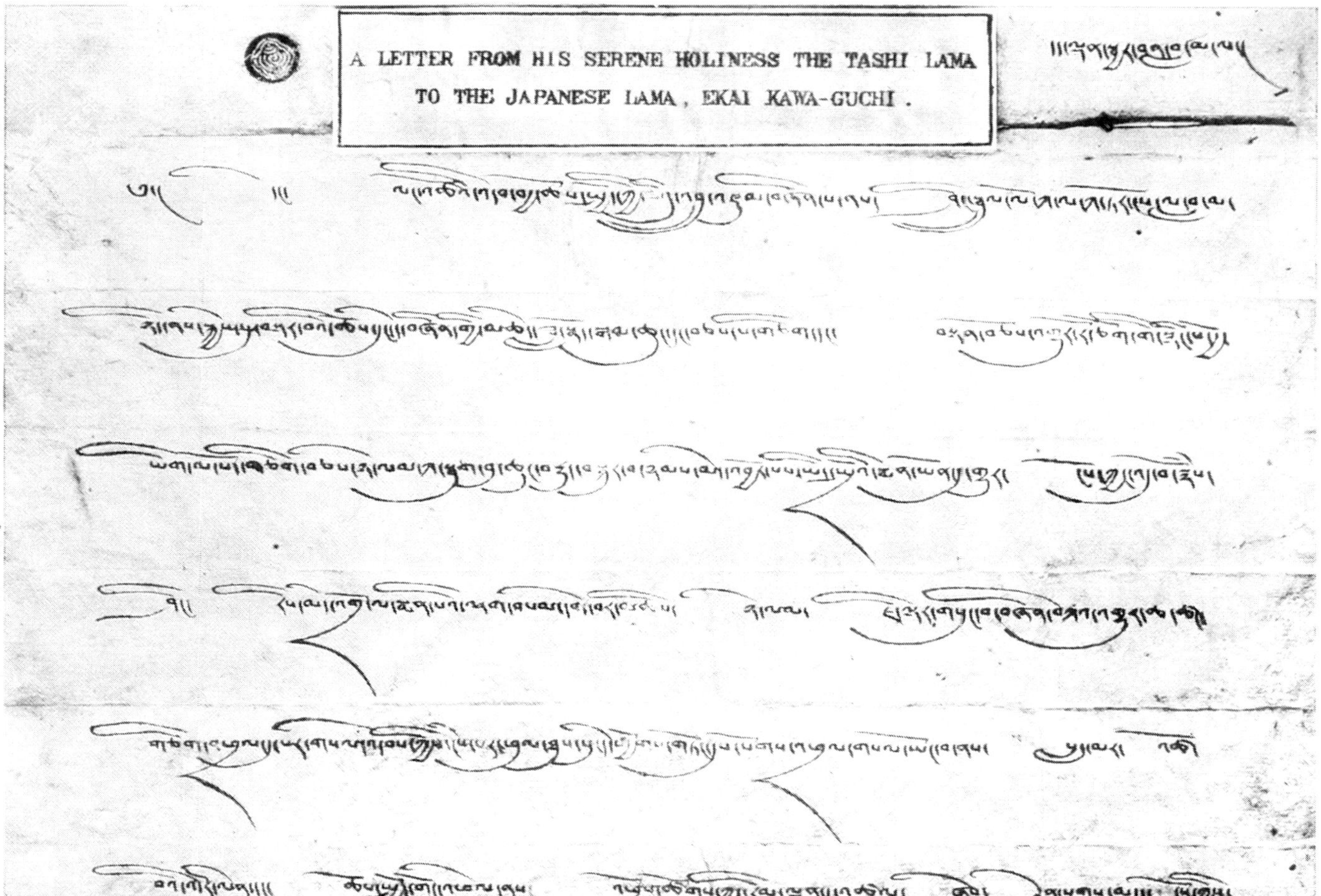

A LETTER FROM HIS SERENE HOLINESS THE TASHI LAMA TO THE JAPANESE LAMA, EKAI KAWA-GUCHI.

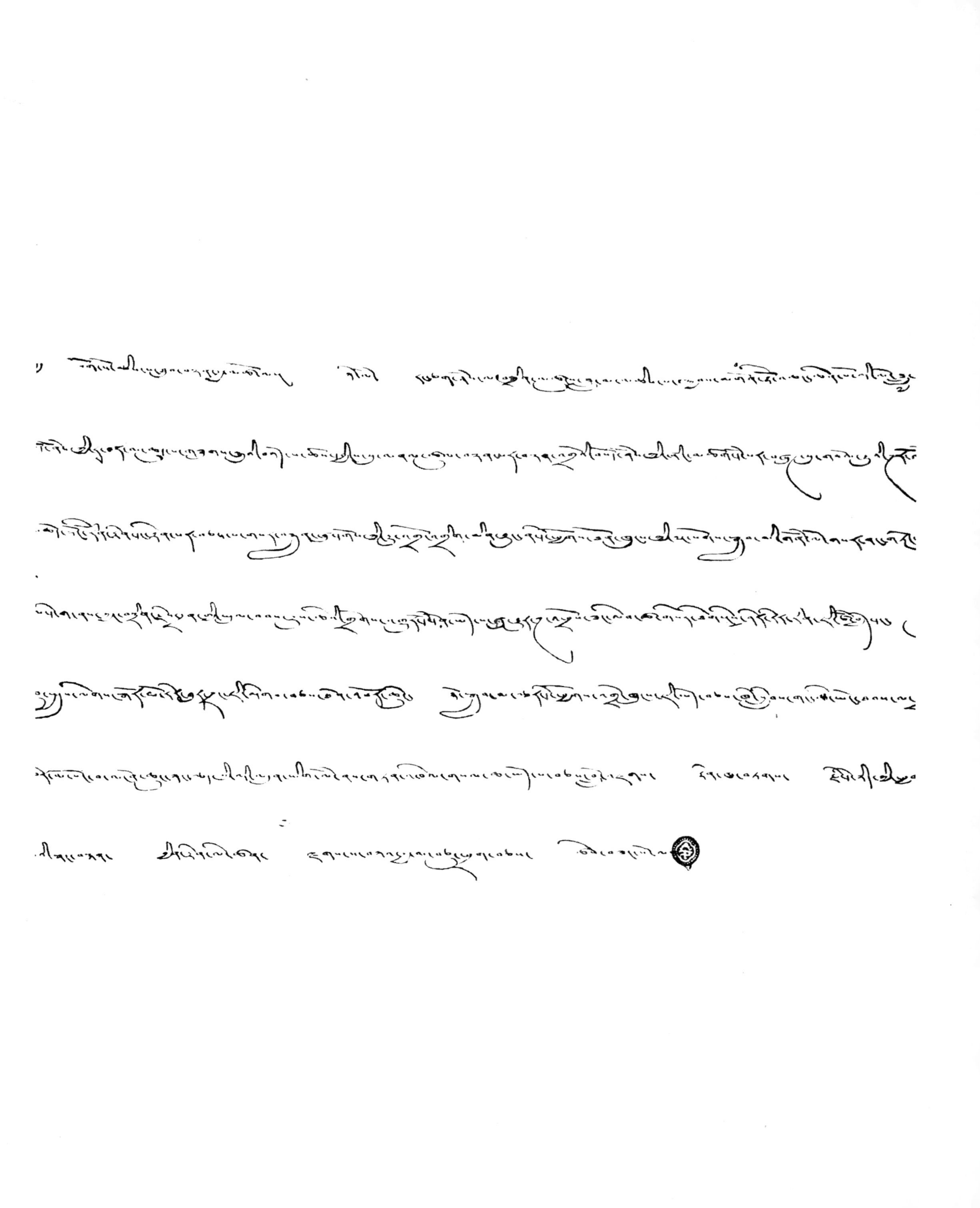

[illegible] [illegible] [illegible]

[illegible]

[illegible]

[illegible]

[illegible] [illegible]

[illegible] [illegible] [illegible]

[illegible] [illegible] [illegible] [illegible]

A letter from Lama Seng-chen Dorje-chang, Chief Khan-po of Thoi-sam-ling College of Tashi-lhun-po to Lama Sherab Gya-tsho of Goom, Yid-gah Choiling Monastery, near Darjeeling.

༄༅། སོག་པོ་རྟེན་པ་ཐུབ་བསྟན་རྒྱ་མཚོ་ལ།

ཉེ་ལམ། རང་ཅག་རྣམས་ལ་བཀྲིན་མཚུངས་བླ་མ་མཆིས་པ། ཧཱུྃ་ སྐྱབས་མགོན་རྡོ་རྗེ་འཆང་ཆེན་པོ་འདི་ཕོ་བླ་བདུན་པ་ནང་། བསོད་ནམས་ཀྱི་དྭ་བར་མ་ཆུད་པ་གཟུགས་སྐུའི་བཀོད་པ་ཆོས་དབྱིངས་སུ་མཉལ་ཚུལ་བསྟན་པར་བསྟན་འགྲོའི་བསོད་ནམས་ཀྱི། ཞིང་མཆོག་དམ་པར་བཞུགས་སུ་གསོལ་རྒྱུའི་སྔོན་ལ་མཆོད་སྡོང་རིན་པོ་ཆེ་རྟེན་དང་རྟེན་པར་བཅས་པ་གསར་བསྐྲུན་བྱ་དགོས་ཀྱི་རྒྱུ་འགྲོ་འགྲིག་མིན་བྱུང་ན་དེ་ཕྱོགས་ཕོན་ཁྱུངས་ཀྱི་ཟང་སོགས་སྐྱབ་མི་གནམ་ལོ་གསར་ནང་གཏོང་འདུན་ལ་དེ་ག་ནས་ཀྱང་བཀྲིན་རྗེས་དྲན་གྱི་ཡུལ་བབས་རྒྱས་ཆེའི་གྲོགས་འགྱུར་དམ་རྡོན་ཡོད་པ་ཞུ་རྒྱུར་སྒ་འཕྲོས་ཟང་ལེབ་ཚ་གསེར་རྡེག་ངེས་ཤེར་རེར་རིན་ཐེ་ཙམ་བྱེད་དང་། དངུལ་རྒྱ་སྲུས་ཞིགས་སྐོར་མོ་རེར་ཕུར་སྲང་ཐེ་འདིགས་བཅས་ཕོན་འབོར་ཆེ་ཆུང་ཇི་སླབ་མ་ཚར་དེ་ཕྱོགས་འགྲོ་ཁྱུངས་ཐེ་ཡོད་བཅས་ཁེ་སྦྱིབས་གང་ཆེ་ཡོད་ཐབས་ལ་གྲུགས་ཆེར་མ་སོང་བ་མདོན་ཆུང་ཟང་རྫོད་ཀྱི་འདི་མདུན་ཡིག་ལམ་ནས་གཏན་འཁེལ་གསལ་ཆ་ཡོད་པ་བཅས་བློ་འཛགས། རྟེན་ཁ་བཏགས། རྗེ་དེ་ཉིད་ཀྱི་ཕྱག་བརྟར་མའི་སྣང་བརྙན། ཕྱིན་ཉིན་ལེ་ཚན། ལྷགས་ས་བཀའ་རྒྱ་མ་བཅུ་ཕྲག་བཅས། ཆོས་བཟང་པོ་ལ།།

* Lama Sherab Gya-tsho, Head Lama of Goom Monastery, near Darjeeling, was tutor to the Tashi Lama Lo zaṅ Choikyi Wangchug, for some years. At Tashi-lhunpo he was known by the name of Thub-tan Gya-tsho.

A letter from Kusho Tung-chen La, Chief Secretary to *Lama Rinpoche* Seng-chen Dorje-chang to *Sri* Sarat Chandra Das.

༄༅ རིགས་གནས་ཀུན་ལ་མཁས་དབང་བསྒྱུར་བ་པཎྜི་ཏ་ཤྲཱི་ཤ་ར་ཏ་ཙན་དྲ་དྲུང་དུ།

ཆེད་འབུལ།

དེ་ཁར་ཉིད་སྐུ་དང་འཚོ་བ་ཡར་ངོའི་ཟླ་བ་ལྟར་གོང་རྒྱས་སུ་ཡོད་པ་ཕྲན་གྱིས་སྣང་བར་ཐོས་ཕྲལ་མི་གཉིས་པའི་དགའ་བ་དང་སྤྲོ་བ་དཔག་མེད་ཐོབ། འདི་ཁ་གཙང་བཀྲས་ལྷུན་དུ། ཧཱུྃ་ སྐྱབས་རྗེ་སེང་ཆེན་རྡོ་རྗེ་འཆང་ཆེན་པོས་དབུས་བསྐོས་པར་བཅས་པ་བདེ་བར་ཐུར་ལྟར་གནས། དྲུང་ཕྲན་ཆོས་མཛད་ནས་རིང་མིན་དངོས་མཇལ་ཞུ་རྒྱུའི་རྟེན་འབྲེལ་མཇལ་མཆོད་དུ་ཁ་བཏགས་ཁལ་ཁ་ཆོས་ལྡན་སེར་དཀར་བཅས་ཕུལ། ཞིབ་ཆའི་ཞུ་དོན་ཕྱུར་ཆུང་མགྲིན་ལམ་ནས་ཞུ་བ་ཡོད། སྨད་ནས་ཕྲན་ལ་ཕྱག་བྲིས་གནང་དགོས་བྱུང་ན་ཕྱུར་རང་ཆུང་བརྒྱུད་མ་རྟོག་མི་གནང་བ་ཞུ།།

A TIBETAN DIPLOMA

བཀའ་ཤོག།

Conferring the dignity of *Don-ñer* མགྲོན་གཉེར། on Lama Ugyen Gya-tsho, *Rai Bahadur.*

༄༅། རང་ཞབས་སུ་འཁོད་པའི་སེར་སྐྱ་མཆོག་དམན་མཐའ་དག་ནས་ངེས་དགོས། དགོན་སབ་ཨོ་རྒྱན་རྒྱ་མཚོ་འདི་པ་རིགས་འཁྲུངས་སོགས་མདོ་སྨད་མི་ཉག་ཕྱོགས་ནས་ལྷ་ས་དང་ས་སྐྱ་བཅས་རིམ་པར་བརྒྱུད་དེ་འབྲས་ལྗོངས་བཞུགས་ཅང་འདིར་ཇི་ལྟར་འགྱུར་པ་ནས་བཟུངས་དེང་ཕན་ཕ་ཇོ་བོ་རྣམས་ཀྱི་སྐབས་ཡུལ་སམ་བཀྲ་ཤིས་སྡིང་དུ་སློབ་ཚོར་བུ་ཁྲིང་འཛིན་དང་། ཕོ་བྲང་རབ་བརྟན་རྩེར་ཕྱག་མཛོད་པདྨ་གང་། བོད་གཞིས་རྫོང་ཁྲ་གཞིས་གཉེར་མཚོ་ཆེན། ཐོ་བྲང་མངའ་པོ་གདན་འཛིན་པ། རྒྱ་དྲུང་རྩིས་པ་སྟག་གཟིག་སོགས་སྐུ་སེར་གང་ས་ནས་ཞབས་འདེགས་ལྷག་བསམ་རྟེས་འདུག་པ་དང་། བརྟན་པའི་ངོགས་ཀྱིས་རབང་། ཀླུ་བུ་རི་ས་ཀྱི་ལོ་བོད་ཕྱི་གཟིངས་དྲིལ་དང་རང་འཁོངས་མི་རིགས་ལོབ་སློན་རན་འཕའ་ཞིག་གིས་འཛིད་དབང་ཆོམ་མེད་གཉིས་བརྩེམས་ཀྱིས་མི་རྟག་ཁབ་རྩིས་རི་ལུང་ཀུན་བསྐོར་པ་བཞིན་ལྗོངས་འདིར་མི་བདེ་སྐྱ་ཚོགས་ཀྱི་ཇོ་མི་ཀུང་བཞུགས་སུ་མ་འཁོད་པའི་ཕྱོད་བ་ཡོལ་མཛད་དགོས་བྱུང་གཉིས་དེ་སྐབས་དང་སྔ་ཕྱིར་ཨོ་རྒྱན་རྒྱ་མཚོ་འདི་པས་དཔོན་འབངས་དད་དམ་འགྱུར་མེད་ཀྱིས་ཞབས་ཞུ་ལྷག་བསམ་འཇོལ་མེད་རྟེས་རྗེས་ལ་བརྟན་བཀྲིན་འཕར་གཟིགས་ཀྱིས་ལས་སྣ་མགྲོན་གཉེར་མིང་འཛིན་གོ་གནས་ལེགས་དར་ལུས་རྣང་བཅས་ཚུལ་ཡོད་པར་མི་བརྗེད་དང་བཅས་པར་སྐུ་སེར་ཚངས་མས་ཕན་འཆར་གང་འགྲོ་ཐྲེད་པ་ལས་གནོད་འཕལ་དུ་འགྲོ་རིགས་བགྱིས་ན་མི་ཐུབ་ཤིང་། ཨོ་རྒྱན་རྒྱ་མཚོ་ནས་ཀྱང་བཀྲིན་བསམ་ཤེས་ཀྱིས་གཙོ་བོར་རྒྱ་འབྲས་ཐབ་མོ་ཉིང་དབུས་སུ་བཙང་དེ་ཇོ་མའི་ངག་བཀོད་ལུང་དུ་འཁྲི་ཞིང་། བརྟན་ཡར་ཞབས་འདེགས་ཞུ་སྒོ་རྣམས་ལྷ་གསམ་གཡོ་མེད་དམ་དོན་དགོས་བརྒྱ་བཅས་དེ་དོན་ལྡང་དོར་འཇོལ་མེད་ཚུལ་བཞིན་དུ་སྤྱོད་པ་བགྱིས། (འབྲས་ལྗོངས་རྒྱལ་པོའི) སྐྱང་ཉོག་ཕོ་བྲང་ཁམས་གསུམ་གཟིལ་གནོན་ནས་རབ་འབྱུང་བཅོ་ལྔའི་ལྷགས་སྤྲང་ཟླ་ ཆོས་དགེ་བར་བྲིས།།

༧༧ ༧༤

Official Seal.

A letter from Dug Bumthang of Bhutan to *Lama* Ekai Kawaguchi of Japan.

༄༅། ཛ་པན་དགེ་སློང་ཆོས་སྤྱོད་ཀྱི་འཛུག་ཞེ་ཡངས་པ་ལ། ཉེ་ལམ། འདི་གའི་གཟིམ་དཔོན་བརྒྱུད་ཡི་གེ་དང་། རྡོ་རེའི་ཆོས་རྟེན་སོགས་ཉམས་བྲལ་འགྱུར་པ་དག་འཕྲེ་ཚེ། དོན་དུ་ཁ་སེང་དྲི་ཞེན་ཇོ་འཕྲད་སྐབས་རྒྱལ་བའི་གསུངས་རབ་དཀའ་འགྱུར་སྡེར་དགའ་རེ་ཕྲར་མ་ཞིག་ཟེར་བ་དེ་བཞིན་སྡེ་དགེའི་ཕྱོགས་སུ་མཆོགས་བཀོད་བྲ་རྣམ་ཡང་རྒྱ་མིའི་ཐྱོ་ཟེང་ཡིས་ཁམས་ཕྱོགས་ནས་མི་རིལ་གཏོག་ཡང་མ་འགྱུར་པས་མངགས་ས་མ་རྙེས་པ་མ་ཟད། འདིར་ཁ་ཐོན་རི་གོ་ཆེ་སྡེ་དགེའི་སྤར་ཁང་ལ་སོགས་སྤར་རྣམས་རྒྱ་མིས་ཚར་བསྒྲིག་འཁྲོས་བྱེད་གོ་བས། གལ་སྲིད་དེ་ལྟར་མ་བདུན་ཡང་རྒྱ་མིའི་བྲོལ་ཟེང་རེ་ཆེག་པ་དང་། ཁམས་ཕྱོགས་ཀྱི་མི་འཁྲུལ་དང་བརྟན་ཏེ་མི་ཉ་པ་མངགས་བཀོད་མ་བཏེས་འདུག་པ་དེ་བཞིན་བགྱིས་འབུལ་བཅས་ཐུགས་མངའ་མཛོད། རྟེན་ལྷ་གོས་བཅས་འབྲུག་བུམ་ཐང་ནས་ཉུལ།

APPENDIX V.

VRIHASPATI CHAKRA, or Cycle of Sixty years, with the corresponding names of the Tibetan years.

༄༅།། ཕྱག་རྡོར་བསྟོད་འགྲེལ་ལས་གསུངས་པའི། རབ་བྱུང་སོགས་ལོ་དྲུག་ཅུའི་མིང་ནི།

No.	Name	Tibetan	Year	Tibetan
1	Prabhava	རབ་བྱུང་།	Fire-hare	མེ་ཡོས།
2	Vibhava	རྣམ་འབྱུང་།	Earth-dragon	ས་འབྲུག།
3	Çukla	དཀར་པོ།	Earth-serpent	ས་སྦྲུལ།
4	Pramodi	རབ་མྱོས།	Iron-horse	ལྕགས་རྟ།
5	Prajāpati	སྐྱེས་བདག།	Iron-sheep	ལྕགས་ལུག།
6	Angira	ཨངྒི་ར།	Water-ape	ཆུ་སྤྲེ།
7	Çrīmukha	དཔལ་གདོང་།	Water-bird	ཆུ་བྱ།
8	Bhāva	དངོས་པོ།	Tree-dog	ཤིང་ཁྱི།
9	Yuvaka	ན་ཚོད་ལྡན།	Tree-hog	ཤིང་ཕག།
10	Dhrita	འཛིན་བྱེད།	Fire-mouse	མེ་བྱི།
11	Içvara	དབང་ཕྱུག།	Fire-ox	མེ་གླང་།
12	Bahu dhānya	འབྲུ་མང་པོ།	Earth-tiger	ས་སྟག།
13	Pramādi	མྱོས་ལྡན།	Earth-hare	ས་ཡོས།
14	Vikrama	རྣམ་གནོན།	Iron-dragon	ལྕགས་འབྲུག།
15	Brisabha	ཁྱུ་མཆོག།	Iron-serpent	ལྕགས་སྦྲུལ།
16	Chitra	སྣ་ཚོགས།	Water-horse	ཆུ་རྟ།
17	Bhānu	ཉི་མ།	Water-sheep	ཆུ་ལུག།
18	Bhanutāra	ཉི་སྒྲོལ་བྱེད།	Tree-ape	ཤིང་སྤྲེ།
19	Bhupāla (Prithvipa)	ས་སྐྱོང་།	Tree-bird	ཤིང་བྱ།
20	Akṣaya	མི་ཟད།	Fire-dog	མེ་ཁྱི།
21	Sarva jita	ཐམས་ཅད་འདུལ།	Fire-hog	མེ་ཕག།
22	Sarva Dhāri	ཀུན་འཛིན།	Earth-mouse	ས་བྱི།
23	Virodhi	འགལ་བ།	Earth-ox	ས་གླང་།
24	Vikriti	རྣམ་འགྱུར།	Iron-tiger	ལྕགས་སྟག།
25	Khara	བོང་བུ།	Iron-hare	ལྕགས་ཡོས།
26	Nanda	དགའ་བ།	Water-hare	ཆུ་འབྲུག།
27	Vijaya	རྣམ་རྒྱལ།	Water-serpent	ཆུ་སྦྲུལ།
28	Jaya	རྒྱལ་བ།	Tree-horse	ཤིང་རྟ།

29 Mada
སྨྱོས་བྱེད།
Tree-sheep
ཤིང་ལུག།

30 Durmukha
གདོང་ངན།
Fire-ape
མེ་སྤྲེ།

31 Hemāvalambi
གསེར་འཕྱང་།
Fire-bird
མེ་བྱ།

32 Vilambi
རྣམ་འཕྱང་།
Earth-dog
ས་ཁྱི།

33 Vikāri
སྒྱུར་བྱེད།
Earth-hog
ས་ཕག།

34 Sarvavati
ཀུན་ལྡན།
Iron-mouse
ལྕགས་བྱི།

35 Sāva
འཕར་བ།
Iron-ox
ལྕགས་གླང་།

36 Çubhakrit
དགེ་བྱེད།
Water-tiger
ཆུ་སྟག།

37 Çobhana
མཛེས་བྱེད།
Water-hare
ཆུ་ཡོས།

38 Krodhi
ཁྲོ་མོ།
Tree-dragon
ཤིང་འབྲུག།

39 Viçva bandhu
སྣ་ཚོགས་དབྱིག།
Tree-serpent
ཤིང་སྦྲུལ།

40 Parābhava
ཟིལ་གནོན།
Fire-horse
མེ་རྟ།

41 Pravanga
སྤྲེའུ།
Fire-sheep
མེ་ལུག།

42 Kīlaka
ཕུར་བུ།
Earth-ape
ས་སྤྲེ།

43 Saumya
ཞི་བ།
Earth-bird
ས་བྱ།

44 Sādhārana
ཐུན་མོང་།
Iron-dog
ལྕགས་ཁྱི།

45 Virodhakrit
འགལ་བྱེད།
Iron-hog
ལྕགས་ཕག།

46 Paridhārī
ཡོངས་འཛིན།
Water-mouse
ཆུ་བྱི།

47 Pramādi
བག་མེད།
Water-ox
ཆུ་གླང་།

48 Ananda
ཀུན་དགའ།
Tree-tiger
ཤིང་སྟག།

49 Rākṣasa
སྲིན་པོ།
Tree-hare
ཤིང་ཡོས།

50 Anala
མེ།
Fire-dragon
མེ་འབྲུག།

51 Pingala
དམར་སེར་ཅན།
Fire-serpent
མེ་སྦྲུལ།

52 Kāla dûti
དུས་ཀྱི་ཕོ་ཉ།
Earth-horse
ས་རྟ།

53 Siddhārtha
དོན་གྲུབ།
Earth-sheep
ས་ལུག།

54 Rudra
དྲག་པོ།
Iron-ape
ལྕགས་སྤྲེ།

55 Durmati
བློ་ངན།
Iron-bird
ལྕགས་བྱ།

56 Dundubhi
རྔ་ཆེན།
Water-dog
ཆུ་ཁྱི།

57 Rudhirura
ཁྲག་སྐྱུག།
Water-hog
ཆུ་ཕག།

58 Raktākṣi
མིག་དམར།
Tree-mouse
ཤིང་བྱི།

59 Krodhana
ཁྲོ་བོ།
Tree-ox
ཤིང་གླང་།

60 Kṣayaka
ཟད་པ།
Fire-tiger
མེ་སྟག།།

APPENDIX VI.

Diary of a Journey to *Lhasa in 1882* *

BY SARAT CHANDRA DAS.

༄༅། ཙ་ཏ་བླ་བ་གསུམ་པའི་ཚེས་ལ། ཕྲན་ཤ་ར་ཏ་ཙནྡ་དཱས་ལྷ་ལྡན་ཕྱོགས་སུ་བཏབས་བསྐོར་འགྲོ་སྐབས་ལ། སྐྱབས་རྗེ་བཀྲིན་གསུམ་ལྡན་ཐུགས་འཆང་ † རྡོ་རྗེ་འཆང་ཆེན་པོ་ནས། མི་རྗེ་ཕ་ལྷའི་ལྷ་ལྕམ་སྐུ་ཞབས་ཆེན་པོར་བཀྲིན་བླ་ན་མ་མཆིས་པས་འདི་རྣམས་ལ་ལམ་བར་སོགས་གང་ཅིའི་ཐད་མགོ་འཛིན་པ་ཅང་རོགས་བསྐྱངས་པས། ལྷ་ལྕམ་སྐུ་ཞབས་ནས་ཀྱང་བཀའ་བཞེས་བཟང་པོ་འཕོབ་སྟེ་ལྷ་ལྕམ་སྐུ་ཞབས་གོང་ཟླའི་ཚེས་ཉེར་གཅིག་ཉིན་རྒྱལ་རྩེར་ཕེབས། དེ་ནས་ལྷ་ལྡན་ཕྱོགས་སུ་ནམ་ཕེབས་ཀྱི་བཀའ་གསལ་རྗེས་སུ་གནང་རྒྱུ་གསུངས་པས། དེའི་བར་ནམ་དུས་ངན་པའི་གངས་རླུང་ཆེན་པོ་རྒྱབ་པར་རྟེན། ཕྲན་ལ་ཚོན་དུ་བླ་ཆམ་ཡོད་པ་དེ་བཞིན་ཙུང་ཞིག་ངན་དུ་སོང་བ་དང་། ཕྱལ་དུ་འགྲོ་མི་ཐུབ་པ་དང་བཀའ་གསལ་རྗེས་སུ་གནང་རྒྱུ་གསུངས་པས། ཕྲན་ཀྱང་སེམས་ཤིན་ཏུ་དགའ་བ་བྱུང་ལ། ཚེས་ཉེར་གཉིས་ཉིན་ཧྲེ་འབྲོང་ཕོ་བྲང་ནས་སྐུ་ཞབས་ ‡ རིན་པོ་ཆེ་དང་། ཕྱག་མཛོད་སྐུ་ཞབས་གཉིས་ལྷན་དུ་ཚེས་སྡེར་ཕེབས། དེ་ནས་ཕྱག་མཛོད་སྐུ་ཞབས་ནས་སྐྱབས་རྗེ་ཆེན་པོ་དཔལ་དུས་ཀྱི་འཁོར་ལོའི་ཚོགས་དབུས་སུ་སྤྱན་འདྲེན་ཏེ་དགེ་འདུན་ལ་གཉེན་བསྐུར་མང་འགྱེད་བཟང་པོ་དང་སྐྱབས་རྗེ་ཆེན་པོར་བཞེ་སྨོན་སྐྱབས་འཛུགས་ཕྱིར་འབུལ་བཟང་པོ་མཛད། དེའི་ཉིན་སྐྱབས་རྗེ་ཆེན་པོ་ནས་འབྲོང་ཚེས་གཙུག་ལག་ཁང་གི་ཡང་རྩེར་རྟེན་པའི་རྒྱལ་མཚན་སྤྱོར་འབུལ་མཛད་རྒྱུའི་ལས་གྲྭ་ཚོགས་པའི་སར་བཟོ་རིགས་པ་རྣམས་ལ་འཚུགས་སྟོན་ཀྱི་གསོལ་རས་བླ་ན་མ་མཆིས་པ་སྩལ་བས་ཕྱག་མཛོད་དྲུང་ཆེན་ལགས་དང་ཞབས་ཞུ་རྣམས་ལ་སྩལ་བ་ཤིན་ཏུ་ཆེ་བ་བྱུང་། ཕྲན་ཀྱང་གཟུགས་ཁམས་མི་བདེ་བས་དེ་ཉིན་དགའ་སྟོན་ལ་ཡོང་ཆོད་མ་ཐུབ། ཚེས་ཉིན་ལྷ་ལྕམ་སྐུ་ཞབས་ནས་ ༢༨ སྐྱབས་རྗེ་ཆེན་པོ་འི་དྲུང་དུ་ལམ་ཆོས་ཀྱི་གསུང་བཏག་ཞུ་མི་ཐུ་ཆར་འགྱུར་པས་ཕྱི་ཕེབས་སུ་ཆོས་ལ་ངེས་པར་ཕེབས་དགོས་ཀྱི་བཀའ་གསལ་ ༢༥

---

* རྒྱ་གར་ཤར་ཕྱོགས་ཕུན་སུམ་ཚོགས་པ་བང་ག་ལའི་ཆུ་བྲག་ཙ་ཏི་ག་ཝོང་ཟེར་བའི་མ་ཏ་དྷེ་རྒྱ་མཚོ་ཆེན་པོའི་འགྲམ་ཀྱི་ས་གནས་པཎ་ཆེན་ན་ར་པའི་བླ་མ་པཎ་ཆེན་ཤེས་རབ་བཟང་པོ་ཏི་ཐོ་པའི་འབྱུངས་སའི་ཙཀ་ཀླ་ལྦ་ལ་བཀྲེས་པ་པཎ་ཆུང་ཤྲཱི་ཤ་ར་ཏ་ཙནྡ་དཱས་ཆོས་ཀྱི་ཞིང་ཁམས་དཔལ་ལྡན་བོད་ཀྱི་གནས་མཆོག་པོ་ཏ་ལ་དང་བསམ་ཡས་སོགས་ལ་འགྲོ་སྐབས་བྲིས་པའི་ལམ་ཡིག་ཐོར་བུ་འདིར་བཞུགས་སོ།།

† འཕགས་པ་ཀླུ་སྒྲུབ་ཀྱི་སློབ་མ་ཀླུའི་བྱང་ཆུབ་ཀྱི་རྣམ་སྤྲུལ་སེང་ཆེན་རིན་པོ་ཆེ། ཀླུའི་བྱང་ཆུབ (Nāga Bodhi) was born in Varendra Bhûmi.

‡ ཧྲེ་འབྲོང་ཕོ་བྲང is ཧྲེ་པ་འབྲོང་རྩེའི་ཕོ་བྲང་། the four storeyed lofty castle of Dong-tse. It was the ancestral residence of *Sha-peh* Lonchen Phalha ཞབས་པད་བློན་ཆེན་ཕ་ལྷ་ཚང་།

སྤྱི་ཤར་རྟ་ཅན་དྲུའི་ལམ་ཡིག།

པོར་ཕེབས་པར་རྟེན། ད་ཕྲལ་ཕྱག་མཛོད་དྲུང་ཆེན་ལགས་ནས་ཕྲན་གྱི་ལམ་བར་དང་གང་སྤྱི་འི་ནེ་མགོ་རྣམས་ཁྲ་བསྡུས་ཀྱི་འདེབས་ཆ་བྱུས་ནས། ཕྲན་དང་ཕྲན་གྱི་ཟླ་བོ་དྲུང་ཆེང་བཀྲས་དང་དཔལ་རྡོར་ལྷམ་སྐུ་ཞབས་ཀྱི་ཞབས་ཕྱུ་སྡེ་རྟོར་རྡོར་འགར་མགོ་རྗེ་ལགས་བཅས་སྡེ་འབྲོང་ཕོ་བྲང་དུ་ཕྱག་མཛོད་ཆེན་པོ་འི་སྐུ་དྲུང་དུ་ཕྱག་འབུལ་ཞུ་བར་བཅར་ཐོག་ཕྲན་ལ་གསོལ་རས་གསོལ་ཞིབ། ཕྱུ་ཚག། གསོལ་མར་བཞེས་འབྲས། གསོལ་ཇ་ཚིག་དངུལ་ཊཾ་གསུམ་མཇལ་དར། ད་མཆུངས་དྲུང་ཆེང་བཀྲས་ལ་ཊཾ་གསུམ་དང་མཇལ་དར། དཔལ་རྡོར་ལ་ཏ་གཉིས་དང་མཇལ་དར་བཅས་གསོལ་རས་སྐྱལ་ཏེ་ཕྲན་གྱི་ཟླ་བོ་གང་དག་དང་གནས་རྣམས་ཕྲལ་མཇལ་གྱིས་མགྱོགས་ཐབས་ཐོག་རྒྱུའི་བཀའ་སློབ་བཟང་པོ་ཡང་ཡང་གནང་། ཆོས་ཉིན་ཐུ་དྲུ་སྐྱབས་རྗེ་ཆེན་པོ་འི་དྲུང་དུ་བཅར་ནས་ཕྱག་འཚལ་ཏེ་ཞུ་བར། བདག་

༢༥

ལ་ལམ་བར་སོགས་དང་བགེགས་བར་བྱ་བ་ཡམ་འགྲོ་ཡོང་མིན་གྱི་སྐྱབས་འདྲུག་ཞུས་པས། སྐྱབས་རྗེ་ཆེན་པོ་ནས་བསྐྱབས་འདྲུག་དང་། གསོལ་རས་སྐྱལ་ནས་མགྱོགས་པར་ཐོག་སོག་བཀའ་ཕེབས་ཤིང་། ད་ནས་ཕྱག་མཛོད་དྲུང་ཆེན་ལགས་ནས་མཇལ་དར་དང་གསོལ་རས་གནང་ཐོག་ཕྱག་འབུལ་ཞུས་ཏེ་ཐོན་པས་ལམ་བར་ལ་མཁར་གསར་ཞིང་གི་ལམ་བྱེད་དང་། ཤིང་སྡོང་ཆེན་པོ་རྒྱ་བན་རྒྱས་ཁྱེངས་པ་སོགས་འཁྱིར་ཡོང་བ་དང་ཕྱག་པས་རྟེན་འབྲེལ་ཀྱང་ཤིན་ཏུ་དགའ་བ་བྱུང་། སྐྱིད་ཆུའི་འགྲམ་རྒྱུད་ནས་རྒྱལ་རྩེར་སློབས། ད་ནས་མི་རྗེ་ཕ་ལྷའི་དགོན་གཞིས་གོང་རྒྱལ་དགའ་དུ་ལྷ་ལྷམ་སྐུ་ཞབས་ཀྱི་དྲུང་དུ་བཅར་ནས་བཀའ་སློབ་ཞུས། ལྷ་ལྷམ་སྐུ་ཞབས་ནས་ངས་ཀྱི་ཕྱག་མཛོད་འདི་པ་ལུས་ནད་ཀྱི་ཟིན་ཏེ། ལོ་མང་པོ་སོང་བས་འདི་ཙན་ཐབས་ཀྱི་སྨན་བཅོས་འདྲ་ཡོད་པ་བསྣམས་ནས་དེ་ཉིན་ཉག་ས་སྐོ་བཞིར་ཡིན་པས་དེར་འཁོར་པ་ཤོག་ཅེས་གསུངས། ད་ནས་ཟླན་རྣམས་རྗེས་སུ་བསྡད་ནས་ཕྱག་མཛོད་ལགས་སུ་གསོལ་སྨན་ཕུལ། ཕྱག་མཛོད་ལགས་ནས་གསོལ་ཇ་གསོལ་ཚིག་ཐོག་མཇལ་དར་དང་སྣམ་རྒྱ་ཐིག་རྫུགས་གཉིས་བཅས་བ་གནང་བྱུང་བ་དེ་རྣམས་རྗེས་སུ་མཇལ་རྒྱུའི་རྟེན་འབྲེལ་དུ་ཕྱིར་འབུལ་ཞུས་ཏེ་ཐོན་པའི་ལམ་བར་གྱི་གཡས་སུ་སྡེ་དཔོན་ཆེན་པོ་ལྷུང་པོ་ཙན་ཟེར་བ་དེ་དང་། ད་ནས་ཤར་དུ་ཕྱིན་པའི་གཡོན་ཕྱོགས་སུ་དགའ་ལྡན་ཆོས་འཕེལ་གླིང་དགེ་ལུགས་པའི་ཆོས་སྡེ། ད་ནས་ཤར་དུ་ཕྱིན་པའི་གཡས་སུ་བླ་བྲང་གི་གཞིས་ཁ་གྲ་ཁྲུད། དའི་བར་གངས་རྒྱུས་བཅད་པའི་ལྷོ་ངོས་ལ་ཕག་རི་འི་ལམ་སྐེ་ཟིན་རྩམ་ལ་ཆོས་སྡེ་ཆེན་པོ་གནས་སྙིང་། ད་ནས་ཕྱིན་པའི་ལམ་གྱི་གཡས་གཡོན་དུ་སྡེ་གྲོང་མང་པོ་དང་། སྔོན་དུས་དམག་ལས་བྱས་པའི་འཛིང་རག་དང་། གྲོང་ཞིག་རལ་མང་པོ་ཡོད། ད་ནས་ཕྱིན་པའི་ལམ་གྱི་གཡས་སུ་སྡེ་གྲོང་མང་པོ་སྟོང་བའི་ས་ཞིག་འདུག་པས་དེ་སྔོན་དུ་སྐྱབས་རྗེ་ཆེན་པོ་ལས་གྲུབ་གྲྭ་ཚང་དུ་ཕེབས་སྐབས་འདི་སྟོན་གྱི་དུས། གཞིས་རྩེ་ཁྲིམ་དང་པོ་ཆགས་ས་དེ་འདི་འདྲ་གསུངས། ད་ནས་ཕྱིན་པའི་ལམ་གྱི་གཡས་གཡོན་ལ་ཡང་དགེ་བསྙེན་གསུམ་གྱི་དགོན་པ་དང་། གྲོང་མང་པོ་ཡོད་པའི་བར་ལམ་འཕྲང་ཀྱང་རྫུང་ཞིག་ངན་པའི་ཐོག་ཏུ་སྐུ་གདུང་ཟམ་པ་ཐོན་ནས། ད་ནས་བྲེལ་སྤུས་ཀྱི་ཕྱིན་པའི་ལྷ་ལྷམ་སྐུ་

བློ་ཤ་ར་ཏ་ཙན་དྲའི་ལམ་ཡིག ༎

ཞབས་དཔོན་འཁོར་རྣམས་ཞྭོ་བཞི་ཀན་པོ་ནས་བཞུགས་གྲྭ་སྒྲིགས་འདུག་པ་རེ་སླུ་རྡུང་དུས་སྒྲོ་ད་མཚམས་སུ་སླེབས་ནས་སྐུ་མདུན་དུ་བཙར། ལྷ་ལྷུམ་སྐུ་ཞབས་ནས་སྔེ་འདི་པ་ཁམས་མི་གཙང་བ་འདུག་པས་རྫོང་ཁུབ་གནས་ཚང་ཡང་བབ་འབྲེལ་ལས་མ་བྱུང་གསུང་། དེར་རྗེན་ནས་ཕྲན་ལ་ཡང་གནས་ཚང་ཞིག་འཚོལ་སླུབ་ཟླ་བོ་གཉིས་ནས་བྱས་རུང་། མ་བྱུང་བས་ཕྲན་ཀྱང་དེའི་ཁུབ་ཏ་ར་འ་ཐོག་འོག་ཏུ་ཉལ་དགོས་བྱུང་ངར་རྗེན་ཇོན་ནས་གཟུགས་ཁམས་མི་བདེ་བའི་ཁར་དེའི་ཁུབ་འཁྱུགས་སྐྱིན་གྱིས་ནད་གཞི་ཡང་སྐྱར་ཐུག་ཏུ་སོང་། ཆོས་ཉིན་ཞྭོ་བཞི་ནས་ཕྱིན་

༢༦

པའི་གཡོན་ཕྱོགས་སུ་རྫོང་ཡིན་ཟེར་བའི་ཁང་པ་མཐོན་པོ་ཞིག་དང་དེའི་འགྲམ་ཆུ་གཉིས་འཛོམས་གཡས་ཆུ་སྦྱང་ཆུ་དང་ཉི་རོ་ཏེའི་ཆུ། དེ་ནས་ཞྭོ་རྒྱུད་ནས་ཕྱིན་པ་རེ་གཡོན་རིའི་འདབས་ལ་ཁ་བོ་དགོན་པ་ཟེར་བ་ཆོས་ལུགས་རྙིང་མ། དེ་ནས་ཕྱིན་པའི་རྭ་ལུང་དུ་སླེབས་ནས་རྭ་སྦྱང་ཆུའི་ལུང་ཀན་པོས་བཞུགས་གྲྭ་སྒྲིགས་འདུག ། ཕྲན་དང་ཟླ་བོ་གཉིས་བཅས་ཁང་པའི་ཟུར་གཅིག་ཏུ་བསྡད། དེ་ཉིན་ལམ་བར་ལ་ཁ་བ་དང་རླུང་ཆེ་བ་དང་། ་སཆ་ཡང་ཁ་མཐོ་བའི་སྐབས་ཀྱི་ནད་གཞི་དེ་ཡང་སྐྱར་ཚ་གྲང་གི་འཕྲུལ་བྱུས་ཏེ་ཐུང་གཞི་ཕྱི་བ་བྱུང་། དེ་ནས་ཆོས་

༢༧

ཉིན་རྭ་ལུང་གི་སྦྱང་ཆུའི་ཞྭོ་རྒྱུད་ནས་ཕྱིན་པའི་གཡས་གཡོན་དུ་འབྲོག་སྡེ་མང་པོ་དང་། བྱམས་བང་ཟེར་པའི་གྲོང་གཅིག་འདུག ། དེ་ནས་ཁ་རོ་ལའི་ལ་མཚམས་ཟིན་པའི་ཆུའི་གཡས་རྒྱུད་ནས་ཕྱིན་པའི་ཆུ་དེ་ཁར་ནང་ཞུ་ཆུ་ཁ་ཤར་བལྟས་ལམ་མཆོར་འདྲེས། ཞྭོ་ནས་རྒྱུག་པའི་ཆུ་དེ་སྦྱང་ཆུར་འདྲེས། ཡང་ཁ་རོ་ལའི་གཡས་རྒྱུད་ཕྱིན་པའི་ཕྱོགས་ན་ལྷ་གཉོད་སྦྱིན་པ་ང་བ་བཟང་པོ་བཙུགས་པའི་གངས་རི་དང་ཙཛལ། གངས་རི་དེ་ཡི་ཆུ་ཁག་གཉིས་འདུག་པས། གཅིག་ཁུབ་ཕྱོགས་སུ་རྒྱུག་པའི་དེ་ཡི་མིང་སྦྱང་ཆུ་དང་། གཅིག་ཤར་ཕྱོགས་སུ་རྒྱུག་པའི་མིང་ཁར་ནང་ཞུ་ཆུ་མིང་གོང་ཆུ་གཉིས་འདྲེ༎ དེ་ནས་ཕྱིན་པའི་འཛོལ་བ་ཟེར་བའི་གྲོང་གཅིག་འདུད་པ་དེར་གསོལ་ཇ་བཞང་། དེ་ནས་ཁར་ནང་ཞུའི་ཆུ་གཡས་རྒྱུད་ནས་ཕྱིན་པའི་ལམ་བར་ལ་སྣིང་ལ་ཟེར་བའི་གྲོང་ཁ་ཤས་ཙམ་འདུག ། དེ་ནས་ཕྱིན་པའི་རྣམ་དཀར་རྩེར་སླེབས་ནས་མཆོད་མཁན་ཟེར་བའི་གྲོང་གཅིག་འདུག་པས་དེར་བཞུགས་སྒྲིགས་དང་། ཕྲན་ཀྱང་ལྷ་ལྷུམ་སྐུ་ཞབས་ཆེན་པོའི་སྐུ་མདུན་དུ་བཙར་ནས་ཐུགས་དགྱེས་པའི་ཞལ་ཤོབ་མང་དག་ཞུས། དེའི་སྐབས་སྦྲོར་རའི་ནང་ལྷ་ཟུན་ཕྱོགས་ནས་ཡོང་བའི་འགྲུལ་པ་འབྲུམ་ནད་ཀྱིས་ཟིན་པའི་མི་ཞིག་འདུག ། དེ་ལ་རིམ་གྲོ་བྱེད་མཁན་དགེ་སློང་གཅིག་དང་ལམ་མཉམ་དུ་དེར་སླེབས་འདུག་པས། དེ་ལྷ་ལྷུམ་སྐུ་ཞབས་ཀྱིས་གཟིགས་པས་ཐུགས་སེམས་ཀྱང་མི་བདེ་བ་བྱུང་བས་དཀོན་མཆོག་རང་གི་ཐུགས་རྗེས་དཔའ་མོ་ཨེ་ཡོང་ངམ་གསུངས། དེ་ཉིན་ཕྲན་ཀྱང་རྭ་ལུང་ནས་བཟུང་ཏེ་ཆིབས་རག་གི་ཞབས་ཕྱིར་མཉམ་དུ་བཙར་བས་ཏ་དྲིལ་འགྲོ་རྒྱུད་རིང་སྐྱངས་ཀྱི་འཁྲུག་སྐྱེན་དང་། མ་ཟད་དེའི་ཁུབ་མཐའ་ཟན་ཞན་པའི་འཁྱུགས་སྐྱིན་དང་། འཁྲུགས་པ་གཉིས་དུས་འཛོམས་ཀྱི་ན་ངར་རྗེན། ཆོས་ཉིན་ལྷ་ལྷུམ་སྐུ་ཞབས་

༢༨

དང་ལྷན་དུ་བཙར་རྟིས་ཡོད་རུང་། ཕྲན་གྱི་ནད་བབ་ཤིན་ཏུ་ཕྱི་བས་བཙར་མ་ཐུབ། དེ་ནས་ཟླ་བོ་གཉིས་ནས་གཏངས་པོར་ལུང་

ཀླུ་ཤ་ར་ཏ་ཙན་དྲའི་ལམ་ཡིག།།

པ་འདི་ལ་སྣང་པ་དང་ལུང་བརྟག་ཕྱ་འདྲ་གནང་མཁན་ཨེ་ཡོད་ཟེར་འདྲི་བས། གནས་པོ་ནས་སྔེ་འདི་ཡི་ནང་ལ་སྤྱི་ཞིག། དེ་འདྲ་མེད་པས། ཡིན་རུང་སྐྱབས་མགོན་རྡོ་རྗེ་ཕག་མོ་བརྒྱུགས་པའི་དགོན་པ་ཕ་གའི་བཙར་ན་དེར་སྔོན་བཙོས་དང་རིམ་གྲོ་རོབ་ས་ཡབ་པོ་ཡོང་ཏེ། དེང་སྐབས་སྐྱབས་མགོན་རྡོ་རྗེ་ཕག་མོའི་མཇལ་ཁ་འདྲ་ཨེ་ཡོད་མེད་ཤེས། ཡིན་ཀྱང་སྔན་པ་ཙན་བ་ཞིན་བ་ཉིས་ཡོད་པས་དེ་བ་ཉིས་ཀྱི་ལྷུང་དུ་བཙར་ནས་རྒྱ་མཚན་དང་གནས་ཚང་སོགས་གསར་པོ་བྱས་ཟེར་བྱུང་། དེ་ནས་ལྷ་ལུམ་སྐུ་ཞབས་ཀྱི་ཞབས་ཕྱི་རྣམས་ནས་དེ་རང་བྱས་ཏེ་ཕེབས་ན། ལྷ་ལུམ་དང་སྐྱབས་མགོན་གཉིས་སྐུ་ཉེར་སོང་བས་ཕྱག་བྲིས་ཞིག་ཞུས་ཆོག་གསུངས། དེ་ནས་ཞབས་ཕྱི་རྣམས་ནས་ལྷ་ལུམ་སྐུ་ཞབས་ལ་ཞུས་ནས་སྐྱབས་མགོན་ལ་འབུལ་རྒྱུའི་རྒྱ་ཡིག་གཅིག་གནང་ཏེ་ཡིག་གེ་འདི་ལ་མཐུས་ཚང་ཡོད་པས་སྐྱབས་མགོན་གྱི་ལྷུང་དུ་བཙར་ནས་སྐྱབས་འཇུག་གསུང་བརྟག་དང་། གཞན་ཡང་དགོས་བྱེད་ཅི་འདྲ་ཡོད་པ་རྣམས་འཆར་མེད་ཞུས་ཆོག་པ་ཡོད་པས་ཞུས་ཤིག་གསུང་། དེ་ནས་ལྷ་ལུམ་སྐུ་ཞབས་དང་ལྷ་སྲས་བསྐྲིས་གཞོན་གཉིས་ལྷན་རྒྱས་ནས་ནད་གཞི་ལྕི་པོ་འདུག་པའི་གྲྭ་པོ་གཉིས་ནས་ཀྱང་བདག་དོན་བདག་བྱེད་ཀྱི་གྲྭ་པོ་ཏུར་ཐག་ཞུས་ཏེ་ནད་པ་དྲག་བསྟན་ལྷ་ལྷན་གཟིམས་ཤག་རང་དུ་ཤོག་ཅེས་གསུང་། དེར་རྟེན་ལྷ་ལུམ་སྐུ་ཞབས་དང་ལྷ་སྲས་རྣམས་གཉིས་ཞབས་ཕྱི་རྣམས་ཀྱི་བསྐྲོན་ལ་བསམས་ན་ཟླན་ཀྱང་ལྷན་དུ་བཙར་ནེ་ཤིན་ཏུ་ནས་འདོད་ཀྱང་། ལུས་སེམས་ངད་བ་ཞི་དྭ་ངོས་བཏུངས་པས་ལྷན་དུ་བཙར་རྒྱུའི་རེ་བ་ནི་ཟད་སོང་། དེ་ནས་གྲྭ་པོ་གཉིས་དང་བསྟུན་བསམ་ཞིང་དུ་དལ་མུས་ཀྱི་ཕྱིན་ནས་ཆོས་སྡེའི་ནུབ་ཕྱོ་འི་འགྲམ་དུ་བསྡད། གྲྭ་པོ་གཅིག་གི་རྒྱ་ཡིག་འཁྱེར་ཏེ་ཨམ་ཅི་ལགས་རྩོ་དཔོན་ཀྱི་གཟིམས་ཤག་ཏུ་བཙར་ནས་ཡིན་ལུགས་ཀྱི་རྒྱ་མཚན་རྣམས་ཞིབ་ཏུ་ཞུས་པ་དང་། མ་ཟད་གྲྭ་པོ་གཅིག་དང་ཨམ་ཅི་གཞོན་པ་གཉིས་ཁྲོན་ངོ་ཤེས་རེད་འདུག་པས། ངོ་ཤེས་ཡོད་པར་ཉིད། ཨམ་ཅི་ལགས་ནས་རོགས་རམ་གྱི་སྐྱབས་མགོན་རྡོ་རྗེ་ཕག་མོར་སྐུ་ཞབས་ལྷ་ལུམ་ནས་གནང་བའི་ཕྱག་བྲིས་དང་གསུང་བརྟག་གི་ས་བོན་དང་སྐྱབས་རྟེན་ཏྲཾ་ཀ་དར་བཅས་ཕུལ། དེ་ནས་ཨམ་ཅི་ལགས་ནས་དགེ་ལེགས་རྣམ་རྒྱལ་ཟེར་པའི་ཤག་ཏུ་གནས་ཚང་གཡར་ནས་དེ་ཕྲུལ་གསོལ་སྨན་ཐུན་གཅིག་བཏང་ནས་སྨན་ཡོན་ཏྲཾ་ཀ་དང་དར་བཅས་ཕུལ། དེ་ནས་སྐྱབས་མགོན་ནས་གསུངས་བརྟག་བཀའ་ཕེབས་གནང་ནས་ནད་བབ་ཕྱི་བས་སྒྲོ་ག་སྐྱོན་གྱི་ཉན་ཁ་ཆེ་བས་ཞབས་རིམ་རྣམས་འཕྲལ་སྒྲུབ་དགོས་རྒྱུ་དང་། གཙོ་ཆེར་བཀྲིས་ལྷུན་པོ་ཡོང་བ་དང་། ཕྱག་པར་ལྷ་ལུམ་སྐུ་ཞབས་ནས་གསུང་བྲིས་སོགས་གནང་བར་དགོས་བྱེད་ཇི་འདྲ་དགོས་པ་རྣམས་འདི་ཁ་ནས་འཆར་མེད་ཡོང་ཞིག་གསུངས། དེ་ནས་ཚོགས་ཆེན་དུ་ཇ་མར་གྱི་ཞལ་འདེབས་དང་ཡུང་རྟག་ཏྲཾ་གཅིག་དང་དར་བཅས་ཕུལ་ནས་ཞབས་བརྟན་ཡང་དག་སྐྱབས། ཆོས་ཉིད་ཚོགས་ཆེན་དུ་མང་རྡོད་ཏྲཾ་སྒང་གང་དང་དགེ་འདུན་བརྒྱ་ཐམ་པ་ལ་རེ་རེར་ཏྲཾ་མེད་ཁ་རེ་ཕུལ་ནས་ཞབས་

༢༨

བརྟན་རྣམས་རིམ་པར་སྒྲུབས། དེའི་ཉིན་སྐྱབས་མགོན་དང་། དགེ་འདུན་ལ་སྐྱབས་འཇུག་ཕྱིར་ཏྲཾ་གཉིས་དང་དར་བཅས་ཕུལ་

ཤྲཱི་ཤ་ར་ཏ་ཙན་དྲའི་ལམ་ཡིག ༎

བའི་བཀའ་ལན་དུ་སངས་རྒྱས་འོད་བསྲུང་གི་རིང་བསྲེལ་ཏྲིན་རླབས་ཆེན་པོ་རེ་རིལ་བུ་གཅིག་གསོལ་རས་གནང་། [༣༠]ཆོས་ཉིད་ཚོགས་ཆེན་དུ་ཞལ་འདེབས་ཇ་མར་དང་ཡུང་ཏག་ཊཾ་གཅིག ། སྐྱབས་རྗེ་ཊཾ་གཉིས་དང་དར་བཅས་ཕུལ། ཡང་རིང་རིལ་བ་ཅིག་གནང་དེ་ནས་ཨམ་ཆི་ལགས་སུ་སྨན་ཡོན་ཊཾ་སྲང་གང་དང་དར་བཅས་ཕུལ། [༡]ཆོས་ཉིད་ཡང་ཚོགས་ཆེན་དུ་ཞལ་འདེབས་གོང་དང་སྐྱབས་རྗེ་ཊཾ་གཅིག་དང་དར་གཅིག་ཕུལ། ཡང་བྱིན་རྟེན་རིལ་གཅིག་གནང་། ཚེ་གླིང་སྤྲུལ་སྐུར་སྐྱབས་རྗེ་ཊཾ་གསུམ་དང་དར། སྐྱབས་མགོན་ལ་ཚེ་སྒྲུབ་རྫོད་ཊཾ་བཅུ་དང་དར། [༢]ཆོས་ཉིད་ཞབས་བརྟན་ཟུར་གསལ་བརྒྱད་སྟོང་པ། ཆ་གསུམ་རྒྱལ་གསོལ། གསེར་སྐྱེམས་འཆི་བསླུ། སྒྲོ་བ་ཞུ་བརྒྱ་བཅས་ཀྱི་ཡོན་ཐེམས་ཊཾ་དགུ་དང་ཞོ་གང་བཅས་སོང་། [༣]ཆོས་ཉིད་ཨམ་ཆི་ལགས་ཀྱི་གསོལ་སྨན་གྱི་ཕན་སྐྱིས་རང་མ་བྱུང་བས། ཨམ་ཆི་རྗེ་དྲུང་ལགས་ཀྱི་གསོལ་སྨན་གྱི་ཡང་ཕན་སྐྱིས་མ་བྱུང་། [༤]ཆོས་ཉིད་ཚེ་གླིང་སྤྲུལ་སྐུ་ནས་ཞགས་རྒྱ་ཕུས་ཏེ་བཏང་ཀྱང་དེ་ཡི་ཡང་ཕན་སྐྱིས་མ་བྱུང་། [༥]ཆོས་ཉིད་སྐྱབས་མགོན་ལ་སྐྱབས་འཇུག་རྟེན་ཊཾ་ལྔ་དང་དར་བཅས་ཕུལ་ནས་སྨན་པ་འདི་རང་རྟེན་ན་ལེགས་སམ་ཞུས་པས། སྐྱབས་མགོན་ནས་ཕྱི་ཐེབས་སུ་འདི་རང་དུ་བསྡད་ནས་སྨན་པ་གཏུགས་ཟུས་རང་བཟང་། ཨམ་ཆི་ལགས་སུ་ཡང་སྐྱར་སྨན་ཡོན་རྒྱ་ཊཾ་ལྔ་དང་དར་བཅས་ཕུལ་ནས་ཡང་སྐར་གསོལ་སྨན་གསར་སྦྱོར་གྱི་གསོལ་རས་ཐུགས་རྗེ་ཆེ་བ་ཞུས། [༦]ཆོས་ནས་བཟུང་སྟེ་ཕྲན་བུའི་སྨན་གྱི་ཕན་སྐྱིས་དང་ནད་བབ་ཡང་ངོ་ཡང་དུ་སོང་། སྐྱབས་མགོན་ནས་ལྷ་རབ་བྱུང་ན་རྟ་ཕྱག་ཁྱུང་གསུམ་གྱི་དབང་། དེ་མིན་རྟ་མགྲིན་གྱི་དབང་མ་བྱུང་བར་ཐབས་མེད་འདུག་གསུང་། ཡང་སྐྱབས་མགོན་ལ་སྐྱབས་རྗེ་ངན་གསོལ་དོད་ཐོམས་ཊཾ་སྲང་གང་ཕུལ་ནས་ཚེ་མདོ་གཟུང་གི་དབང་ཐུགས་རྗེ་ཆེ་བ་ཞུས། ཚེ་གླིང་སྤྲུལ་སྐུ་ནས་ནུབ་ཕྱོགས་ནས་དངོས་རིགས་ཙཾ་ཆེན་གྱི་རྗེས་སུ་རྒྱལ་པོ་འབྲུང་བའི་ལན་འདུག་གསུང་། [༧]ཆོས་ཉིད་ཨམ་ཆི་ལགས་ནས་ད་སྒྲོ་ག་སྐྱོན་གྱི་ཉེན་མེད་འདུག་པས། དེ་རིང་ནས་བཟུང་ཁ་གསོས་གཏོང་གསུང་བསམ་ཤིང་དུ་ཤ་གསར་མེད་པས་ནམ་དཀར་རྩེར་མི་ཞིག་བཏང་ནས་ཁ་གསོས་བཏང་། [༨]ཆོས་ཉིད་ཚེ་རྟ་གཟུང་གི་དབང་ཞུས་ནས་སྐུ་ཡོན་ཊཾ་བཅུ་ཐམ་པ་དང་དར་བཅས་ཕུལ་ནས་ཡང་སྐྱེང་ལྷ་ལྡན་དུ་འགྲོ་རྩིས་ཡོད་པས་ཐུགས་སྨོན་སྐྱབས་འཇུག་ཐུགས་རྗེ་ཆེ་བ་ཞུས། སྐྱབས་མགོན་ནས་ཆོས་བར་འདེར་སྡོད་པ་བཟང་དེ་ནས་བརྟག་བྱེད་ཀྱི་ཕྱིན་ཆོག་གསུང་། ཡང་རིང་བསྲེལ་གསུམ་གནང་། ཕྲན་རང་བདེ་བར་སྡོད་རྩིས་ལ་ཨམ་ཆི་ལགས་ནས་ནད་གཞི་སྐྱོན་བར་མེད་འདུག་པས་འགྲོ་སྒོ་ཆེ་རོགས་ཡིན་པས་སང་ཉིན་སྐྱབས་མགོན་གྱི་བཀའ་བཞིན་

༡༤...༡༥

ཞུད་ན་ཡང་། གནང་ཉིན་ངེས་པར་འགྲོ་རྩིས་བགྱིས་གསུང་། [༩]ཆོས་ཉིད་སྡད་ནས་སྐྱབས་མགོན་ལ་ཨམ་ཆི་ལགས་ནས་ནད་གཞིར་བགེགས་སྐྱོན་མི་ཡོང་གསུང་བྱུང་བས། སང་ཉིན་ཕྱིན་ཆོག་པ་ཞུས། སྐྱབས་མགོན་ནས་བྱིན་རྟེན་སྐུ་འཛོམས་དང་། ཕྱག

ཀླུ་ཤར་ཏ་ཙན་དྲའི་ལམ་ཡིག།།

མདུད་སོགས་གནང་ནས་མར་ལམ་གྱི་དགོས་བྱེད་གང་དགོས་འདི་ནས་ཡོང་ཞིག་མ་ཟད་ཡར་ལམ་ཀྱང་འདིར་ངེས་པར་ཤོག་ཅིག་གསུང་། དེ་
ནས་ཨམ་ཆི་ལགས་ཀྱི་དྲུང་དུ་བཅར་ནས། སང་ཉིན་ཕྱིན་ཆོག་པ་ཡོད་པས་ལམ་བར་གཏོང་བྱེད་སྨན་ཞིག་གསོལ་རས་ཐུགས་རྗེ་ཆེ་བ་ཞུས།
སྐྱབས་མགོན་བཀྲིན་གསུམ་ལྷན་ཐབས་ཟུར་རྡོ་རྗེ་འཆང་ཆེན་པོའི་བཀྲིན་དང་། སྐྱབས་མགོན་རྡོ་རྗེ་ཕག་མོ། ཨམ་ཆི་རྣམས་
བཅོ་འི་ཐུགས་རྗེའི་བྱིན་མཐུར་ཉེན། ཕྱིན་ཀྱང་ལུས་སྒོ་ག་མ་བྲལ་ཙམ་ནས་ཆོས་ཉིད་ལྷ་ལྡན་དུ་ཐོན་པའི་ལམ་མཚོའི་ནུབ་རྒྱུད་ཕྱིན་ནས་
༡༠
ཉམ་དཀར་རྩེ། དེ་ནས་ཏས་ཡོ། དེ་ནས་འདམ་ལུང་། བདེ་ཕུ། དེ་ནས་སྐལ་བཟང་ཟམ་པ་མ་ཟིན་ཙམ་དུ་ཚ་ཐོགས།
དེ་ནས་སྐལ་བཟང་ཟམ་པ་ཐོན་པའི་མཚོའི་ཤར་རྒྱུད་ནས་ཕྱིན་པའི་ཤ་རུའི་འཕྲང་། དེ་ནས་དཔལ་སྡེ་བདེ་ཁང་དུ་ཞབས། ཆོས་
༡༡
ཉིད་དཔལ་སྡེ་ནས་ཕྱིན་པའི་སྟོང་ཆེན་བཅོ་བརྒྱད། དེ་ནས་ཧྲེ་མ་ལུང་ནས་གམ་པ་ལའི་ལ་གཤམ་ཟིན་པའི་ལ་རྐེད་དུ་ཚ་ཐོབ་ས། དེ་
ནས་ལའི་ཕར་རྒྱབ་ཏུ་བར་ཚོས། བྱང་ཐང་སོགས་གྲོང་མང་པོ་འདུག། དེ་ནས་ཕུགས་ཟམ་ཆུ་བོ་རི་ཤུབ་ཐོབ་ཐང་སྟོང་རྒྱལ་པོའི་དགོན་
པ། དེའི་མདུན་དུ་ཆུ་ཆེན་གཙང་པོར་ཕུགས་ཟམ་དང་། གྲུ་གཉིས་ཀ་བ་མང་པོ་འདུག། གྲུ་དབྱིབས་གྲུ་བཞི་པ་གཅིག་ལ་
ཞོན། ཆུ་བོ་ཧ་མཆོག་ཁ་འབབ། རྒྱ་གར་པ་རྣམས་ཀྱིས་ཡོ་ཧི་ཏྲ་ཟེར་བའི་གཙང་པོ་ཆེན་པོ་འདི་ཡིན། དེ་ནས་གྲུ་ས་ནས་གྲུ་བཏང་སྣེ་
ཐོན་པས་དེ་ཉིད་ཛྲུམ་ས་ཁར་དུ་ཞག་ས། ཆོས་ཉིད་ཛྲུམ་ས་ཁར་ནས་ཕྱིན་པའི་ཆུ་བཞུང་དེའི་ལྷོ་འི་ཉེ་འདབས་སུ་ནུབ་ནས་གཙང་པོ་གཅིག
༡༢
ཡོང་། ཤར་ནས་སྐྱིད་ཆུ་གཉིས་འཛོམས་ཏེ་ལྷོ་ཤར་མཚམས་སུ་རྒྱུགས། དེ་ནས་ཙོལ་པ་ནང་། དེ་ནས་ལྷུང་རྫོང་སྨད།
དེ་ནས་རྒྱུག་པ་འཕྲང་། དེ་ནས་གནམ། ལ་ཆེན་ལ་རྒུང་། དེ་ནས་སྣེ་ཐང་རྒྱལ་ལྷ་ཁང་དུ་ཞག་ས། དེར་ཇོ་བོ་རྗེ་
དཔལ་ལྡན་ཨ་ཏི་ཤ (དཱི་པཾ་ཀ་ར་ཤྲཱི་ཛྙཱ་ནའི) སྐུ་གདུང་ཡོད། ཆོས་ཉིད་སྣེ་ཐང་ནས་ཆུ་མིག་རྫིང་སོགས་གྲོང་མང་པོ། དེ་ནས་
༡༣
རྫོང་ལུང་ཁྲིས་ཟམ་སོགས་གྲོང་མང་པོ།།

དེ་ནས་ཤིང་གདོང་དཀར་དུ་ཚ་ཐོགས། དེ་ནས་འབྲས་སྤུངས་ཀྱི་མདའ་དུ་ལྷ་འབབ་དང་དེའི་ཤར་ངོས་ཡ་གནས་ཆུང་གི་ཕོ་བྲང་། དེ་
ནས་ལྷ་ལྡན་གྱི་སྣེ་ཟིན་ནས་སྐྱིད་ཚལ་ཀླུ་སྡིང་དང་། ཀྱང་ཐང་དགའ་ཁ། དེའི་བྱང་ཤར་མཚམས་ཡབ་བཞིས་ལྷ་ཀླུའི་བཀའ་ཞྭན་
གྱི་ཕོ་བྲང་དེ་ནས་བྱེ་རགས་དང་། ཕྱོར་ནོར་བུ་གླིང་ཁ་སྐྱབས་མགོན་རྒྱལ་བའི་དབང་པོ་འི་ཕོ་བྲང་། དེ་ནས་ཀུན་སྡེ་གླིང་རྒྱལ་པའི་སྐུ་ད
ཀྲ་བོད་རྒྱལ་ཁྲི་པ་ཡིན། དེ་ནས་བ་མ་རི་དང་། དེ་ནས་རྒྱ་ལྷ་ཁང་ཡོད། ལྕག་པོའི་རི་དེ་ན་འཚོ་བྱེད་མང་པོ་ཡོད། དེ་ནས་
བར་སྒོ་བཀའ་ཆེ་ཟེར་བའི་མཆོད་རྟེན། དེ་ནས་རྩེ་པོ་ཏ་ལའི་ཕོ་བྲང་། ཞོལ་རྡོ་རིང་ཕྱི་ནང་གཉིས་པོ། དེ་ནས་ཕུང་སྐྱིབ་
ཤར། ཡབ་གཞིས་ས་དབང་གཡུ་ཐོག་པའི་ཕོ་བྲང་། གཡུ་ཐོག་ཟམ་པ་ནས་ཕྱིན་པའི་ལྷ་ལྡན་ཕྱི་བར་སླེབས། དེ་ནས་

སྤྲི་ཤ་ར་ཧ་ཙན་དྲའི་ལམ་ཡིག །།

བཀྲ་ཤིས་ལྷུན་པོའི་བླ་བྲང་གི་ཁང་པ་དཔལ་འཁྱིར་རབ་བརྟན་དང་། སྙིང་བཀོད་ལུང་སྐྱིབ་ཟེར་བའི་ཁང་པ་གཉིས་འདུག་པས་སྙིང་བཀོད་ལུང་སྐྱིབ་ཏུ་གནས་ཚང་གཡར་ནས་ཞག་བཅོ་ལྔ་བར་སྡད། ཆོས་ཉིད[༡༨] ངལ་གསོས་ནས། དེ་ནས་ཕ་ལྷའི་ལྷ་ཕུམ་སྐུ་ཞབས་ཀྱི་དྲུང་དུ་བཅར། དེ་ནས་ལྷ་ཕུམ་སྐུ་ཞབས་ཀྱི་ཟླ་གསོལ་སོགས་གནང་། དེ་ནས་ས་གའི་ཟླ་བའི་ཆོས་བཅོ་ལྔའི་ཉིན་ཇོ་བོ་ཤཱཀྱ་མུ་ནི་དང་རྫས་དཀྱིལ་འཁོར་ཞིང་གི་ལྷ་ཁང་བཅུ་ཤོད་དང་། ཐུགས་རྗེ་ཆེན་པོ་རང་བྱུང་ལྔ་ལྡན་དྭ་མོ་ཆེའི་ཇོ་བོ་མི་བསྐྱོད་རྡོ་རྗེ་སོགས་རྟེན་རྣམས་མཇལ་བར་ཕྱིན་ནས་སྨོན་ལམ་གྱི་སྨོར་བྱུས་ལེགས་པར་མཇལ། དེ་རྣམས་ཀྱི་ཆགས་རྩུལ་སོགས་ཞིབ་ཆ་དཀར་ཆག་ནང་གསལ་དང་། དེ་ནས་གཡས་སྐོར་དུ་བསྟན་རྒྱས་གླིང་སྤྲུལ་པའི་སྐུའི་ཕོ་བྲང་། གཞིས་སྡེ་དྭ་གླིང་སྤྲུལ་པའི་སྐུའི་ཕོ་བྲང་། མཚོ་སྨོན་གླིང་སྤྲུལ་པའི་སྐུའི་ཕོ་བྲང་། དྭ་མོ་ཆེར་ཇོ་བོ་མི་སྐྱོད་རྡོ་རྗེ་བཞུགས། དེ་ནས་ཀྱ་འབུམ་སྒང་ཟེར་བའི་མཆོད་རྟེན་ཆེན་པོ། སྐུ་རུ། ངག་ཕྱོགས། རྒྱུད་སྨད། ཙང་སྐྱབས་པ་སྡེ་དཔོན་གྱི་གྲུས་གནམ་སྡེ་ལེགས། སྲས་ཚུང་། ཡབ་གཞིས་དྲུན་ཁང་། རྡོ་རིང་། མདའ་དཔོན་ཕ་ལྷའི་བང་རྒྱས་ཤར། དེའི་ཤར་ཆོས་སྐྱོང་དཀར་མ་ཤར་གྱི་ཕོ་བྲང་། ཟུར་ཁང་མདའ་དཔོན། ཚ་རོང་། བླ་བྲང་སྙིང་པ། བསམ་གྲུབ་ཕོ་བྲང་དཔྲ་ཡབ་གཞིས། བཤད་སྒྲ། ར་ག་ཤག་དཀའ་བློན། རམ་པ་སོགས་ཀྱི་ཁག་མང་པོ་དང་། གཞན་ཡང་གྲོང་འཁྱིར་ནང་གི་ཁང་ཆེན་མང་པོ་འདུག་པའི་ནང་རྒྱ་བལ་བོད་ཧོར་སྡེ་ཁག་སོགས་ཀྱི་ཚོང་པ་མང་པོ་དང་། རྒྱ་ནག་གི་དཔོན་པོ་ཨམ་བན་གཉིས་སོགས་དཔོན་ཁག་མང་པོ། ལྷ་ལྡན་ནས་ནུབ་ཀྱི་ཉེ་འདབས་སུ་དགོན་ཆེན་འབྲས་སྤུངས་དུ་དགེ་འདུན་ཞལ་གྲངས་འདུན་སྟོང་བདུན་བརྒྱ། དེ་ནས་བྱང་གི་ཉེ་འདབས་སུ་གསེར་ར་དགེ་འདུན་ལྔ་སྟོང་ལྔ་བརྒྱ། དེ་ནས་ཤར་གྱི་ཕྱོགས་དགོན་ཆེན་དགའ་ལྡན་གསུམ་སྟོང་གསུམ་བརྒྱ། གླིང་ཁག་སོ་སོ་དང་། གྲྭ་ཕྱི་དགོན་པ། རྣམ་རྒྱལ་གྲྭ་ཚང་། རྒྱུད་སྟོད་སྨད་སོགས་དགེ་འདུན་སྟོང་ཕྲག་ཉེར་ཡོད། ཆོས་ཉིད[༢༢] གཙུག་ལག་ཁང་དུ་ཇོ་བོ་མཇལ་ཞུས། ཡང་ཆོས་ཉིད[༢༣]། དཀྱིལ་འཁོར་ཞིང་གི་མགོ་གཉིས་དང་གསུམ་གྱི་ལྷ་དང་ལྷ་མོ་དང་ཇོ་བོ་མཇལ། ཆོས་ཉིད[༢༨] ར་མོ་ཆེའི་ཇོ་བོ་མཇལ། ཆོས་ཉིད[༢༥] ལྷ་ཕུམ་སྐུ་ཞབས་ནས་སྐྱས་དབང་རྒྱལ་ཟེར་བ་ཟླ་བོ་ལ་བཏང་གནང་སྟེ་གནས་མཆོག་རྩེ་པོ་ཏ་ལའི་ལྷ་ཁང་གི་མཇལ་ཁ་དང་། ཆབ་གཅིག་སྐྱབས་མགོན་རྒྱལ་བའི་དབང་པོའི་ཞབས་དྲུང་དུ་གསང་ཡུ་དཀྲུར་ཆོས་ཀྱི་ཐོན་འཛུགས་ཞུ་མཁན་དགེ་འདུན་ལྔ་བཅུ་ཙམ་འདུག་པའི་དགེ་འདུན་དང་ཆབ་གཅིག་མཇལ་ཁ་ཞུས། འདི་དུས་རྒྱལ་བའི་དབང་པོའི་སྐུ་འཕྲེང་བཅུ་གསུམ་པས་ངག་དབང་བློ་བཟང་ཐུབ་བསྟན་རྒྱ་མཚོ་མཚན་གསོལ་ནས་དགུང་ལོ་བརྒྱད་ལ་ཕེབས། ཆོས་ཀྱི་ཁྲི་ལ་བཞུགས། ཆོས་ཀྱི་འཆད་པ་གནང་། སྐུ་མདུན་དུ་བཞུགས་གྲལ་ཐོག་གསོལ་ཇ་གཞིས་འབྲས་གནང་། དེ་ནས་ཞབས་བརྟན་དང་གསོལ་འདེབས་མཎྜལ་སོགས་ཕུལ། ཕྲན་ཀྱང་རྒྱལ་བའི་དབང་པོའི་ཕྱག་ལ་གསེར་ཏོ་ལ་༡ ཕུལ། བླ་མ་རིན་པོ་ཆེས་ཀྱང་བདག་གི་སྤྱི་བོར་ཕྱག་དབང་གནང་། ཕྲན་ལ་ཡང་ཕྱག་མདུད་དང་བྱིན་རྟེན་སོགས་གནང་། དེ་ནས་ཟླ་བོ་དབང་རྒྱལ་གྱི་ཕྲུན་རྩེ་རྣམ་རྒྱལ་གྲྭ་ཚང་གི་གྲྭ་པ་གཅིག་འདུག་པའི་དེའི་སར་བཅར་ནས་གསོལ་ཇ་གཞིས་གསོལ་གནང་། དེ་ནས་གནས་ཚང་སྙིང་བཀོད་ལུང་སྐྱིབ་དུ་ལོག་པ་ཡིན་ནོ།། སར་ལྷ་མང་གི་ལམ།།

APPENDIX VII.

རྒྱལ་བའི་འཁྲུངས་རབས།

Dalai Lama's Hierarchy,

ITS ORIGIN, BOTH LEGENDARY AND HISTORICAL.

༄༅། ན་མོ་གུ་རུ་བེ།

༄༅། །སངས་རྒྱས་དང་བྱང་ཆུབ་སེམས་དཔའ་རྣམས་ཀྱི་འབྱུང་ཁུངས་ངེས་པ་ཙམ་ ནི་སོ་སྐྱེའི་སྤྱོད་ཡུལ་ལས་འདས་ཤིང་། འདིར་རིག་པ་ཆེན་པོ་འི་དབང་དུ་བྱས་ཏེ་མདོར་བསྡུས་ཙམ་བརྗོད་ན། ཇི་སྐད་དུ།

ཆོས་སྐུ་ནམ་མཁའ་བཞིན་དུ་དབྱེར་མེད་ཀྱང་། །གཟུགས་སྐུ་འཛའ་ཚོན་བཞིན་དུ་སོ་སོར་གསལ། །
ཐབས་དང་ཤེས་རབ་མཆོག་ལ་མངའ་བརྙེས་པའི། །རིགས་ལྔ་བདེ་བར་གཤེགས་ལ་ཕྱག་འཚལ་ལོ། །

ཞེས་པ་ལྟར་སེམས་ཙམ་གསལ་སྟོང་གཟུང་འཛིན་བྲལ་བ་འདི་ཉིད་ཐོག་མ་ནས་མ་འཁྲུལ་མ་ཉོར་བ་ཆོས་སྐུ་ནམ་མཁའ་རང་རྣམ་པར་ཁྱབ་པ་ཀུན་ཏུ་བཟང་པོ་ཡིན། དེ་ལས་ལོངས་སྐུ་རྒྱལ་བ་རིགས་ལྔའི་སྣང་བ་རྡོ་རྗེ་འཆང་སོགས་སུ་གསལ། དེ་ལས་སྤྲུལ་སྐུ་འགྲོ་དོན་མཛད་པའི་སངས་རྒྱས་རྣམས་བྱུང་། དེ་ཡང་སངས་རྒྱས་ཀུན་གྱི་སྐུའི་སྤྲུལ་པ་འཇམ་སྙིང་རྗེའི་རང་གཟུགས་སྤྱན་རས་གཟིགས་དང་། གསུང་གི་སྤྲུལ་པ་མཁྱེན་པའི་བདག་ཉིད་འཇམ་དཔལ་དབྱངས། ཐུགས་ཀྱི་སྤྲུལ་པ་མཐུ་སྟོབས་ཐུས་པའི་དབང་ཕྱུག་ཕྱག་ན་རྡོ་རྗེས་གསུམ་ཉེ་བའི་སྲས་ཆེན་བརྒྱད་སོགས་བྱང་ཆུབ་སེམས་དཔའ་ཆེན་པོ་གྲངས་ཀྱིས་མི་ཆོད་པ་བྱུང་ནས་འགྲོ་དོན་མཛད་པ་ནི། ཇི་སྐད་དུ། ཤེས་བྱ་ཀུན་ཁྱབ་ལས།

ཇི་སྲིད་ནམ་མཁའི་མཐའ་དང་སེམས་ཅན་ཁམས། །དེ་སྲིད་རྒྱལ་བའི་ཐུགས་རྗེ་འགྲོ་བའི་ལས། །
རྟེན་འབྲེལ་བསམ་ཡེ་ཁྱབ་པར་སྣང་བ་ལས། །གདུལ་བྱའི་རིགས་ཁམས་ཉེ་བར་ཟད་པ་ན། །
འདུལ་བྱེད་ཞིང་དང་སྐུའི་བཀོད་པ་ཤར། །འདུལ་ཐབས་ཚེ་འཕྲུལ་ཚད་ལས་འདས་པ་སྟོན། །

ཞེས་པ་ལྟར་བསམ་བརྗོད་ལས་འདས་ཀྱང་སྤྱི་དོན་མདོ་ཙམ་བསྟན་ནས། བྱེ་བྲག་ཞིང་ཁམས་དང་། སྐུ་ཚེ་མཛད་པ་བསམ་གྱིས་མི་ཁྱབ་པ་ནུབ་ཕྱོགས་བདེ་བ་ཅན་གྱི་མགོན་པོ་འོད་དཔག་མེད་ནི་ཐུགས་བསྐྱེད་སྨོན་ལམ་བཙན་པོས་འགྲོ་འདྲེན་ལ་ཡ་ཡ་གྲངས་མེད་བཀྲི་བའི་ཕ་ཚོ་བོ་ཐུགས་སྲས་སྤྱན་རས་གཟིགས་ཡིན་པ་འདིས་འགྲོ་བ་ཐར་པའི་ལམ་ལ་འགོད་པའི་དོན་དུ་སྐར་ཡང་གདུལ་བྱ་གང་དང་གང་འཚམས་པར་དམན་པའི་སྐྱེ་བ་མང་པོ་འི་ཚུལ་བཞེས་ནས་སེམས་ཅན་རྣམས་ལ་ལམ་སྟོན་པའི་ཐབས་སུ་སེམས་བསྐྱེད་ཀྱི་ནང་ནས་མཆོག་ཏུ་གྱུར་པ་ཕྱུགས་རྫི་ལྟ་བུའི་སེམས་བསྐྱེད་ཀྱི་རྗེས་ཟིན་ཏེ་རྒྱལ་སྲས་ཀྱི་སྤྱོད་པ་རླབས་པོ་ཆེར་སྤྱོབ་ཅིང་། སྔོན་གྱིས་སངས་རྒྱས་མང་པོར་སྤྱི་ཞུ་དང་། འགྲོ་

རྒྱལ་བའི་འཁྲུངས་རབས།

དོན་བཀའ་ཆོས་ཞུ་བསྐུལ་འཆད་ཉན་ཡང་དུ་མ་མཛད། མི་མཇེད་ཀྱི་བསྐལ་པ་འདི་ལ་སྤྱན་རས་གཟིགས་དེས། ཇི་སྐད་དུ།

ཕྱག་སྟོང་འཁོར་ལོ་བསྒྱུར་བའི་རྒྱལ་པོ་སྟོང་། སྤྱན་སྟོང་བསྐལ་པ་བཟང་པོ་འི་སངས་རྒྱས་སྟོང་།

གང་ལ་གང་འདུལ་དེ་ལ་དེར་སྟོན་པའི། བཙུན་པ་སྤྱན་རས་གཟིགས་ལ་ཕྱག་འཚལ་ལོ།

ཞེས་པ་ལྟར་སངས་རྒྱས་སྟོང་རྩ་གཉིས་སྤྲུལ་པ་བཀྱི་བ་ནམ་འདྲེན་བཞི་པ་སངས་རྒྱས་གོ་ཏ་མའི་སྐབས་ རིག་ཆེན་གྱི་ཆོས་གསུངས་དུས་འཁོར་དག་པ་རྣམས་བརྒྱད་ཅེས་ཉེ་བའི་སྲས་ཆེན་བརྒྱད་ཀྱི་ཁོངས་སུ་སྐུ་དངོས་བཞུགས་པ་དང་། ཐེག་པ་ཆུང་ངུའི་ཆོས་གསུངས་སྐབས་ཉན་ཐོས་ལི་ཙ་བྱི་དྲི་མ་མེད་པའི་ཚུལ་བཟུང་ནས་བཀའ་ཆོས་ཞུ་བསྐུལ་དང་། འཆད་ཉན་མཛད། རྒྱ་གར་དུ་ཆོས་རྒྱལ་དགེ་བ་དཔལ་སོགས་བསྟན་འགྲོ་འི་དོན་མཛད་པོ་རྣམས་དང་། བོད་ཡུལ་ཁ་བ་ཅན་སྐྱོང་དགོས་སངས་རྒྱས་ཀྱི་ལུང་བཞིན་གཟུགས་སྐུ་སྣ་ཚོགས་སུ་སྤྲུལ་ནས་བོད་ཡུལ་རྩ་ཡིས་གང་བ་ཁང་པོ་ནས་བཪྩོལ་ཏེ་རྒྱ་མཚོར་དྲངས། ས་གཞིར་ནགས་ཚལ་ཆགས། སྤྱན་རས་གཟིགས་ཀྱི་ཕ་སྤྲེའུ་བྱང་སེམས་དང་། རྗེ་བཙུན་སྒྲོལ་མས་མ་བྲག་སྲིན་གཉིས་སུ་སྤྲུལ་ནས་མིའི་འགྲོ་བ་སྤེལ། ས་གཞི་རི་བྲག་དང་ལྷ་འདྲེ་རྣམས་འདུལ་བའི་སྐད་དུ་དག་པ་དང་མ་དག་པའི་སྐྱེ་བ་མང་པོ་འི་ཚུལ་བཞེས་ཏེ། བོད་ཡུལ་ཆོས་ཀྱི་ཞིང་སར་བྱིན་གྱིས་བརླབས། ཆོས་རྒྱལ་གཉའ་ཁྲི་བཙན་པོ་དང་། སྲོང་བཙན་སྒམ་པོ་སོགས་རིམ་པར་སྤྲུལ་ནས་སངས་རྒྱས་ཀྱི་བསྟན་པ་དར་རྒྱས་སུ་མཛད་དེ་རྒྱ་ནག་ཀྱང་དབང་དུ་གྱུར་བ་ཙམ་བྱུང་བ་སོགས་མ་ཧི་བཀའ་འབུམ་དང་། རྒྱ་བོད་ཆོས་འབྱུང་རྒྱལ་རབས་དེབ་ཐེར་ཁག་ལ་གསལ་བ་ལྟར་ཡང་། བདུད་ཀྱི་སྤྲུལ་པས་མྱོན་ལམ་བཏབ་སྟེ་ཆོས་རྒྱལ་གདུང་རྒྱུད་དུ་བརྫུས་པ་རྒྱལ་པོ་གླང་དར་མས་བསྟན་སྲིད་བཙྣགས་སུ་བཙུག་སྟེ་རིམ་བཞིན་བོད་རྫོངས་སིལ་བུར་བཏང་ཡང་རིགས་གསུམ་མགོན་པོ་འི་སྤྲུལ་པ་མང་པོ་འི་ནང་ཚན་སྤྱན་རས་གཟིགས་ཀྱི་སྤྲུལ་པ་འབྲོམ་སྟོན་རྒྱལ་བའི་འབྱུང་གནས་ཀྱི་ཐུགས་བསྐྱེད་རྒྱལ་རིགས་འདྲེན་པ་ལྷ་བླ་མ་ཡེ་ཤེས་འོད་སྐུ་མཆེད་རྣམས་རྒྱ་གར་དུ་པོ་ཉ་བཏང་ནས་ལྷ་གཅིག་དཱི་པཾ་ཀ་ར་གདན་དྲངས། བསྟན་པ་བསོས་ཤིང་སྐྱེ་འགྲོ་བདེ་བར་བསྐྱངས་པ་སོགས་བཀའ་གདམས་པ་ཆོས་དང་བུ་ཆོས་སུ་གསལ། ལྷག་པར་དུ་འཇམ་དཔལ་དབྱངས་དངོས་རྗེ་ཙོང་ཁ་པ་ཆེན་པོས་རི་བོ་དགེ་ལུགས་པའི་མདོ་སྔགས་བསྟན་པའི་སྲོལ་གཏོད་སྐབས་སྤྱན་རས་གཟིགས་ཀྱིས་རྗེ་དགེ་འདུན་གྲུབ་པར་སྤྲུལ་ནས་དེའི་རིང་ལུགས་དར་རྒྱས་སུ་མཛད་དེ། གདན་ས་བཀྲ་ཤིས་ལྷུན་པོ་ཕྱག་བཏབ། རི་བོ་དགེ་ལུགས་ཅེས་ཤྭ་སེར་གྱིས་བསྟན་པ་འཛིན་པའི་གཙོ་བོ་རྒྱལ་དབང་སྐུ་ཕྲེང་དང་པོ་དེ་ནས། སྐུ་ཕྲེང་གཉིས་པ་རྗེ་དགེ་འདུན་རྒྱ་མཚོས་གདན་ས་ཆོས་འཁོར་རྒྱལ་ཕྱག

ཏཱ་ལའི་བླ་མའི་འབྱུང་རབས།

བཏབ། ལྷ་མོ་འི་བླ་མཚོ་སོགས་གནས་མང་པོ་འི་ཀློ་ཕྱི་དགོན་གྲོང་མང་པོ་གསར་དུ་བཏབ། སྐུ་ཕྲེང་གསུམ་པ་བསོད་ནམས་རྒྱ་མཚོ་འི་སྐབས་གནམ་གྱི་ལྷའི་རིགས་རྒྱུད་མོངྒོལ་ཏེ་སོག་པོ་རྗེན་གར་ཨལ་ཐན་རྒྱལ་པོ་འི་བླ་མ་དོ་རྗེ་འཆང་མཛད་ནས་ཏཱ་ལའི་བླ་མ་ཞེས་མཚན་སྣན་གྱིས་ཁྱབ།* ཕྱི་ནང་སོགས་རིགས་རྒྱལ་ཁག་སུམ་ཅུ་སོགས་ཀྱི་ཡོག་ཆོས་རྣམས་གྲོ་ཏ་མའི་ཆོས་སུ་བསྒྱུར། རྒྱ་ཡུལ་དུ་ཞིངས་གཉིས་ཕེབས་ཏེ། རྒྱ་ནག་པ་རྣམས་དབང་དུ་གྱུར་ནས་བསྐྱངས། དེ་འི་དུས་སུ་སྨུག་ཏུན་དུ་མན་ཧྲུ་ཨུན་རིར་བོག་དའི་བླ་མ་མཛད། དུས་མ་རིངས་པར་རིགས་རྒྱུད་འདི་ནས་གོང་མ་ཆེད་རྒྱུའི་ལུང་བསྟན། སྐུ་ཕྲེང་བཞི་པ་ཡོན་ཏན་རྒྱ་མཚོ་སྐུ་ཡོན་བསམ་གྱིས་མི་ཁྱབ་ཀྱང་དཀྱུང་པོ་ཉིད་གཉིས་ལ་ཆོས་དབྱིངས་སུ་གཤེགས། སྐུ་ཕྲེང་ལྔ་པ་ཆེན་པོ་དང་སངས་རྒྱས་གྲོ་ཏ་མའི་ཉན་ཐོས་རབ་འབྱོར་གྱི་སྐུ་སྐྱེ་རིམ་བརྒྱུད་པཎ་ཆེན་བློ་བཟང་ཆོས་རྒྱན་གཉིས་སྐུ་ན་མ་སོན་པར་ངོ་དུས་དགེ་རྩེང་གསུམ་དང་། གར་ངལྡན་ངབྲི་སྟག་ཅལ་པ་སོགས་ཞྭ་སྨུད་མི་མཐུན་པས་ནང་ཚག་འཁྲུག་པོང་གི་དུས་སུ་ཞུག་རྡོར་ཀྱི་རྒྱལ་པ་སོག་པོ་གོ་ཤྲི་བསྟན་འཛིན་ཆོས་རྒྱལ་གྱིས་ངོད་སིལ་བུར་གྱུར་པའི་རྒྱལ་ཁྲབ་ཐམས་ཅད་དབང་དུ་བསྡུས་ནས། དོན་གྱི་བདག་པོ་རྒྱལ་དབང་སྐུ་ཕྲེང་ལྔ་པ་ཆེན་པོ་འི་ཆོས་འབངས་སུ་ཕུལ། ཏཱ་ལའི་བླ་མ་དང་པཎ་ཆེན་གཉིས་ཐུགས་བསྐྱེད་ཟུར་བཀའ་བགྲོས་ཏེ། སློབ་མ་ཤེས་བྱ་རབ་འབྱམས་ལ་སྨུག་ཏུན་དུ་མཆོད་གནས་སུ་བཏང་ནས་གོང་མའི་རྒྱལ་སྲིད་ལེན་ཐབས་དང་། བླངས་ནས་འབྱུང་འགྱུར་ཡར་རྒྱས་ཕུན་གནས་སོགས་བཀའ་མངགས་ཞིབ་ཏུ་སྩལ་བ་ལྟར་བཀྱིས་པ་ས་དོན་སོན་ཅིང་སྐབས་དེར་རྒྱ་ནག་གོང་མའང་རྒྱལ་དབང་སྐུ་ཕྲེང་གསུམ་པའི་ཕྱིན་རླབས་ལུང་བསྟན་བཞིན་ཆན་ཧྲུའི་རྒྱལ་པོ་ཤུན་ཅེ་ཆེན་བཟུང་པ་དུས་མཐུངས་ཏེ། དབུ་བཟུང་གདན་དྲངས་པར་རྐྱེར་མཇལ་ལ་བརྟེན་རིས་ཀྱིས་མཆོད་ཡོན་འབྲེལ་བ་དམ་ཟབ་པ་ཅིང་ཕོ་བྲང་ནང་རྒྱལ་ཁག་གཉེར་ཀྱི་ས་ཡི་རྟགས་པ་གདུགས་དཀར་ལྷ་ཁང་དང་། ཕྱོགས་ཐམས་ཅད་ལས་རྣམ་པར་རྒྱལ་བའི་ཆེད་དོ་སོལ་རིང་རྣམ་རྒྱལ་མཆོད་རྟེན་ཀུན་གྱི་མཐོང་གསལ་ཡོད། ཕྱི་ནང་ལུགས་རི་ཁག་སོགས་ལ། རྒྱལ་དབང་ལྔ་པ་ཆེན་པོས་རབ་གནས་མཛད་པའི་ཐམས་ཅད་འཆོས་སུ་མཐའ་མེད་པ་ཡོད། རྒྱ་བོད་གཉིས་ཀར་བདེ་སྐྱིད་ཀྱི་ཉི་མ་ཤར། མཛད་ཕྲིན་བསམ་གྱིས་མི་ཁྱབ་པ་ཤ་སྟག་བྱུང་། དེ་ནས་རྒྱལ་དབང་སྐུ་ཕྲེང་རིམ་བྱོན་སྐུ་ཚེ་རིང་ཐུང་སྣ་ཚོགས་ལས། སྐུ་ཕྲེང་དྲུག་པ་ཚངས་དབྱངས་རྒྱ་མཚོ།

---

* **Origin** of the name **Dalai Lama**:—Lama Sonam Gyamtsho, High Priest of the great monastery of Dapûng near Lhasa, was invited by Althan Khan to preach Buddhism in Mongolia. The Lama's name translated, in Mongolian, being *Tālai Poyon* (rgya-mtsho signifying ocean, and bso-nams virtue. Sanskrit, *Puṇya Sāgara*, (Ocean of Virtue). The Mongol Chief addressed him as *Tālai Lama* (or Ocean Lama).

ཏཱ་ལའི་བླ་མའི་འཁྲུངས་རབས།

བདུན་པ་བསྐལ་བཟང་རྒྱ་མཚོ། རྒྱལ་དབང་སྐུ་འཕྲེང་བཅུ་གསུམ་པ་ད་ལྟའི་རྒྱལ་བ་རིན་པོ་ཆེ་འདི་སྐུ་ཕྲེང་གོང་མ་རིམ་བྱོན་ལས་ལྷག་པའི་ལུང་བསྟན་བཞིན་འཁྲུངས། ཡུལ་ཁང་པ་སོགས་ཐེ་ཡོད་ཆོས་འཁོར་རྒྱལ་བླ་མཚོའི་འགྲམ་དུ་སྐུ་སྐྱེ། འཚོལ་མི་བླ་མ་དཔོན་འཁོར་རྣམས་ནས་བདུན་ཕྲག་གསུམ་གྱི་བར་གསོལ་བ་བཏབ་པས་མཚོ་མཐལ་དུ་མེ་ལོང་ནང་གི་གཟུགས་བརྙན་ལྟར་ཚང་མས་མངོན་སུམ་དུ་གསལ་བར་མཐོང་ཞིང་། སྐུ་འཁྲུངས་སྐབས་ཕྱི་ནང་གསང་གསུམ་གྱི་རྟགས་མཚན་བཟང་པོ་བརྗོད་ཀྱིས་མི་ལང་བ་མང་པོ་དང་། སྐུ་ཕྲེང་གོང་མའི་སྐུ་ཆས་ངོས་འཛིན་སོགས་ར་འཕྲོད་ངེས་ཉིད་བྱུང་བ་བཅས་ལ་བརྟེན་པོད་སྐྱོང་སེར་སྐྱ་ཡོངས་རྫོགས་ཡིད་ཆེས་གདིངས་འཕེལ་ཞ་ལད་ཀྱིས་ཐེར་ལམ་གསེར་ཁྲིར་མངའ་གསོལ་ཞུ་རྒྱུ་བོད་འབངས་ལྷ་མི་ཡོངས་ཀྱིས་བསྐོས་མཐུན་གོང་མ་ཡོན་བདག་ལའང་ཀོ་ལྷང་ཤུ་དང་འབྲེལ་དཀྲུང་ལོ་གསུམ་ལ་ལྷ་སར་གདན་དྲངས། པཎ་ཆེན་བསྟན་པའི་དབང་ཕྱུག་མཆོག་གིས་ཏཱ་ལའི་བླ་མ་ངོས་སུ་གཟིགས་ནས་དགེ་སྐྲ་གཙུག་ཕུད་བཞེས་ཏེ་རྗེ་བཙུན་ངག་དབང་བློ་བཟང་ཐུབ་བསྟན་རྒྱ་མཚོ་འཇིགས་བྲལ་དབང་ཕྱུག་ཕྱོགས་ལས་རྣམ་པར་རྒྱལ་བའི་སྡེ་ཞེས་མཚན་གསོལ་དང་། བརྟན་བཞུགས་གསོལ་འདེབས་དོན་ཟབ་ཅིང་རྒྱ་ཆེ་བ་མ་འོངས་ལུང་བསྟན་དང་བྱིན་རླབས་མཚུངས་པ་མཛད། སྐུ་གཞོན་ནུ་ནས་ཐུགས་རྣམ་ཞིང་ཕྱི་ནང་ཐུན་མོང་དང་། ཐུན་མོང་མ་ཡིན་པའི་རིགས་གནས་སོགས་སྐུ་ཡོན་རྣམས་ཡོངས་འཛིན་དགེ་བའི་བཤེས་གཉེན་རྣམས་ཀྱིས་བྱུར་ཙམ་བསྟན་པས་ཐམས་ཅད་བདེ་བླག་ཏུ་མཁྱེན་ཅིང་གསན་བསམ་མཐར་ཕྱིན་པ་དང་། སྡེ་སྣོད་གསུམ་ལ་མཁས་ཤིང་འདུལ་བའི་མཁན་པོ་དང་། རིག་འཛིན་སྔགས་ཀྱི་རྡོ་རྗེ་སློབ་དཔོན་མཛད་དེ། མདོ་སྔགས་བསྟན་པའི་བདག་པོ་མཚན་དོན་དང་མཐུན་པ་ནང་པ་ཡོངས་ཀྱི་གཙུག་རྒྱན་མཆོག་ཏུ་གྱུར། ཤེས་བྱའི་རྣམ་གྲངས་མཐའ་ཡས་པའང་རང་བཞིན་གྱིས་མཁྱེན་པ་ཆེ་བས་བསྟན་སྲིད་ཟུང་འབྲེལ་དུ་བསྐྱངས། ལྷ་ཀླུ་མཁའ་འགྲོ་སོགས་དངོས་མཇལ་མཐོང་ཐོས་ལ་མཚན་བཅས་ཕྱི་ནང་གསང་གསུམ་གྱི་མཛད་པ་རྣམ་ཐར་ངོ་མཚར་རྨད་དུ་བྱུང་བ་བརྗོད་ཀྱིས་མི་ལང་ཞིང་། རྒྱ་སོག་ཡུལ་གྲུར་ཆིབས་བསྐྱོད་དང་འབྲེལ་ཟབ་པ་དང་རྒྱ་ཆེ་བའི་ཆོས་ཀྱི་བདུད་རྩིས་སྐལ་ལྡན་གདུལ་བྱ་གྲངས་ལས་འདས་པ་ཐར་ལམ་ལ་བཀོད། རྒྱ་ནག་རི་བོ་རྩེ་ལྔར་ཡུན་རིང་དུ་ཆོས་ཀྱི་གནས་ལུགས་གཟིགས་ཤར་ཐུབ་རིར་ཕེབས་སྐབས་རྗེ་བཙུན་འཇམ་དཔལ་དབྱངས་ཀ་ཤར་གི་རྣམ་པ་དང་རིགས་ལྔ་མངོན་སུམ་དུ་མཇལ་ཅིང་ངར་རྩེར་སྒྲོལ་འཛམ་མཛད་པ་དང་། རྒྱ་ནག་གོང་མ་ཡུམ་སྲས་མཇལ་འཛོམས་ཙམ་གྱིས་དབུ་བླར་བཞེས་ཏེ་དད་གུས་བཀུར་སྟི་གཟིགས་གཟེངས་ལྷ་པ་ཆེན་པོ་ཕུར་གྱུར། བསྟན་འགྲོའི་དོན་རྒྱ་ཆེན་པོ་མཛད་དགོས་གསུངས་ཏེ། དགོངས་པ་དང་མཐུན་པའི་ཞབས་འདེགས་སྒྲུབ་རྩིས་ཡོད་

ཏཱ་ལའི་བླ་མའི་འཁྲུངས་རབས།

འདུག་ཀྱང་བློན་རིམ་རྣམས་ནས་ངན་གཡོ་འི་ཛུང་སྦྱོར་ལ་བརྟེན་རྟེན་འབྲེལ་ལོག་ཅིང་། སྐྱེ་འགྲོའང་བསོད་ནམས་དམན་པས་གོང་མ་ཡུམ་སྲས་གཤེགས་པ་མ་ཟད། གོང་མ་གསར་པ་ནས་ཀྱང་གཟིགས་པ་དེ་དོན་ལྟར་ཀྱི་བཀའ་དང་བཀའ་ཡིག་སོགས་དངོས་སུ་སྩལ་ཏེ། ལྷ་སའི་བར་གྱི་གདན་ཞུ་སོགས་ཚད་མེད་པས་བསྐྱངས། ཏཱ་ལའི་བླ་མ་ ནས་ཀྱང་གོང་མའི་ཁྲི་ཞབས་མཛད་པ་ལུང་ཟིན་ལྟར་འགྲུབ་པའི་ཐུགས་སྨོན་བདེན་བདར་གྱིས་འཁྲུག་ཟིང་འབྱུང་ཉེར་གྱུར་པའང་རང་མཐའ་དུ་ཞི་ནས་རྒྱལ་ཁབ་ཀྱི་མི་རིགས་ཡོངས་རྣམས་ཡིད་ཆེས་དད་གུས་དང་། གོང་མ་གསར་པ་ནི་ངེས་པ་རྟེན་སྐྱེ་བའི་དོན་ཐོབ་ལེགས་སྐྱེས་དང་། ཐུགས་སྨོན་བདེན་ཚིག་འབུལ་རྒྱུ། ཡུམ་སྲས་གཉིས་ཀྱི་སྨོན་ལམ་དུ་ཞབས་སྐུ་བཅག་གདུང་གི་མཆོད་ཀོང་མར་མེ་འབུལ་སྟོང་བརྒྱ་ཕྲག་ལ་མེ་འབར་བ་དང་། ཕྱོགས་མཚུངས་ཤིང་ཏུན་ཤིང་ཞིང་ཆེན་ནས་ཡི་ཅིང་ཕྱོགས་སུ་ཟླ་བ་བཅུ་པ་ན་འབྲུག་སྒྲ་མངོན་སུམ་བྱུང་བ་སོགས་ཀྱི་མཛད་པ་མང་པོས་བསྐྱངས། བདུན་ཕྲག་ཉེར་གཅིག་བར་ཡི་ཅིང་དགོན་ཁག་རྣམས་ལ་དགོངས་རྫོགས་སྨོན་ལམ་བར་མ་ཆད་པ་གནང་རྒྱ་ཡུལ་ཕྱུན་པའི་གླིང་དུ་ཆོས་ཀྱི་སྒྲོན་མེ་ཤར། ཡར་ཕྱིར་ཕེབས་ཀྱི་སྐུ་འབུམ་རྒྱུད་ནས་ལམ་བར་དུའང་ཆོས་ཀྱི་འཁོར་ལོ་རྒྱ་ཆེར་བསྐོར། ཕེབས་ལམ་དུ་ཆུ་མེད་སར་ཆུ་དང་། ཆུ་ཆེན་ཆུང་ངུར་གྱུར་པ་དང་། ཐང་ཚ་བ་སྒྲི་ག་ཆགས་ཀྱིས་འགྲོ་མི་ཐུབ་པར་གནོད་འཚེ་མེད་པ་བྱུང་ནག་ཆུ་རྭ་སྒྲེང་སོགས་སུ་བདེ་བར་ཕེབས། བསྟན་འགྲོ་འི་དོན་དུ་ཆོས་འཁོར་རྒྱ་ཆེར་མཛད་ནས། ལྷ་སར་ཟླ་བ་བཅུ་གཅིག་པའི་ཚེས་དགུ་ལ་ཕེབས། བོད་སེར་སྐྱ་ཡོངས་ཀྱིས་སྤྱི་བོར་བཀུར་ཏེ་རྟེན་པའི་ཚེ་འཕྲུལ་དུས་ཆེན་ལ་ཆོས་འཁོར་བསྐོར་བའི་མཛད་པ་བསྐྱང་མཚམས་སྐྱེ་འགྲོ་སྤྱི་བློ་འི་བསོད་ནམས་ཞན་པའི་དབང་གིས་ལོག་སྨོན་བདུད་རིགས་རྒྱ་དཔོན་ཕྱི་ནང་འགའ་ཞིག་ངན་མཐུན་གྱིས་གོང་མ་གསར་ཀྱིང་ལ་དབུ་བསྐོར་གཡོ་ཞུས་ཁོ་ནས་བོད་ལ་རྒྱ་དམག་བཏང་སྟེ། + ཁམས་ཕྱོགས་སྡེ་དགོན་མང་པོ་སྟོར་བཅོམ་བྱས། བོད་ཀྱི་སྲིད་དབང་འཕྲོག་ནས་རྒྱལ་བསྟན་ཉམས་ཆག་ཏུ་གཏོང་རྩིས་ཀྱིས་ཞུགས་ཁྲི་ཟླ་བ་དང་པོའི་ཚེས་གསུམ་ཉིན་ལྷ་སར་རྒྱ་དམག་ཕྱིན་འབྱོར་རྣམས་ཀྱིས་མེ་མདའ་གང་བྱུང་འཕངས་པའི་མདའུ་ལྷ་ལྡན་གཙུག་ལག་ཁང་དང་། རྒྱལ་བའི་ཕོ་བྲང་ལའང་བབས་ཏེ། ལམ་བར་བོད་དཔོན་རིགས་བསད་རྨས་སོགས་བྱ་ངན་མང་བས་བོད་མི་རྣམས་བློས་མི་བཟོད་པའི་དུས་

+ བསོད་ནམས་ཞན་པའི་དབང་གིས་སོགས ··· ཁྲིད་པར་དུ་བོད་སྤྱིའི་བསོད་ནམས་དམན་པའི་རྐྱེན་ནི་བྱང་ཆུབ་སེམས་དཔའ་སེང་ཆེན་རྡོ་རྗེ་འཆང་བསད་པ་ལས་བྱུང་།

སྐུ་སྐྱབ་དངོས་སློབ་སྐུ་ཡི་བྱང་ཆུབ་ཡིན། དེ་ཡི་རྣམ་སྤྲུལ་སེང་ཆེན་རྡོ་རྗེ་འཆང་།

བླ་མ་དམ་པའི་ཞབས་ལ་གསོལ་བ་འདེབས།

གཉེན་བརྟན་རབ་འབྱོར་ཉན་ཐོས་དྲི་མེད་སོགས། རྒྱ་གར་པཎ་ཆེན་བོད་ལ་བཀའ་དྲིན་ཆེ།

བློ་བཟང་གྲགས་པའི་ཞབས་ལ་གསོལ་བ་འདེབས། །

ཧུ་ལའི་བླ་མའི་འབྱུངས་རབས་བྱིན།

ཐིང་གིས་མི་རིགས་མང་པོ་ཐི་སྒོ་ག་ལ་ཀོལ་བ་ཡོང་ཞེར་ཐུགས་བརྩེས་མ་བཟོད་པ་དང་། བསྟན་པའི་དོན་དུ་འཕྲུལ་སྣངས་ཀྱི་སྐུ་ངལ་མཛད་དོན་ལ་མ་གཟིགས་པར་གཙང་ཕྱོགས་ཞལ་གཟིགས་རྗེས་སུ་རྒྱ་དམག་གོ་མཆོད་ཐོག་པ་བརྒྱ་ཕྲག་རིམ་རྫོང་རྒྱལ་བློན་གསར་གཟུང་བང་ཐུབ་ཐིད་མཐུན་ཐབས་རྣམས་ཉིན་མཚན་མེད་པར་བྱས་ཀྱང་ཐོན་བཙོམ་ལྡན་འདས་ལ་ལྷས་བྱིན་གྱིས་ཇི་ལྟར་འཁྲུན་པ་བཞིན་མདོན་སུམ་དུ་སྒྱུར་ཏེ་ཧུ་ལའི་བླ་མ་སྐུ་འཁོར་གཅིག་ལའང་སྐྱོན་འགྱུར་མེད་པར་རྒྱ་གར་ཕྱོགས་སུ་ཕེབས་ཐོག་བསྟན་སྲིད་ཀྱི་ཐུག་སྐྱོན་བསང་ཐབས་མཛད་སྨྲས། དེ་ཡང་ཇི་སྐད་དུ།

བྱང་ཆུབ་སེམས་ཀྱི་ནམ་མཁའ་སྐྱེ་མེད་མ། དངོས་པོ་ཀུན་གྱི་རང་བཞིན་དག་པའི་གཏེར།
ཁྱབ་བདག་མཛད་པ་སེམས་ཅན་ཁམས་མ་ཟད། བར་དུ་འཇུག་པ་དམ་བཅས་མ་གཡེལ་སྟོན།

ཞེས་པ་ལྟར་ཆོས་ཀུན་སྐྱེ་འགག་སོགས་མཐའ་བརྒྱད་དང་བྲལ་བ་སྟོང་ཉིད་ནམ་མཁའ་ལྟ་བུའི་ངང་ནས་ལམ་རྒྱུད་རྟག་ཏུ་འཁྲུལ་པའི་གདུལ་བྱ་སེམས་ཅན་གྱི་ཁམས་མ་ཟད་བར་དུ་འདུལ་བྱེད་བྱང་ཆུབ་སེམས་དཔའི་སྤྱོད་པ་ལ་འཇུག་པར་དམ་བཅས་པ་བཞིན་དུ་ནམ་ཡང་མི་གཡེལ་བར་ཕན་བདེའི་མཛད་པ་ཐམས་ཀྱིས་མི་ཁྱབ་པ་སྟོན་པར་འགྱུར།།

བཀྲ་ཤིས་དཔལ་ཡོན་སྐྱེ་བ་ལྔ་པའི་གཟུགས། ལེགས་བྱས་རི་མོ་གཡས་སུ་འཁྱིལ་བ་ཅན།
དགེ་མཚན་ཕྱོགས་བཅུར་སྒྲོགས་པའི་དབྱངས་སྙན་པོས། འགྲོ་ཀུན་མ་རིག་གཉིད་ལས་སློང་གྱུར་ཅིག།

ཛ་ཡན་ཏུ།

---

* པཎ་ཆུང་ཤྲཱི་ཤ་ར་ཏ་ཙནྡ་དྲས་ཡང་ཡང་བསྐུལ་བས་ཧུ་ལའི་བླ་མའི་འབྱུངས་རབས་འདི་བཀའ་བློན་བླ་མ་གུང་ཐང་པས་རྡོར་རྗེ་གླིང་དུ་བཞུགས་སྐབས་བརྩམས།

\+ ཧུ་ལའི་བླ་མ་རིན་པོ་ཆེ་བློན་ཆེན་རྣམས་བཅས་གྲོང་ཁྱེར་ཆེན་པོ་ཀ་ལ་ཀ་ཏར་ཕེབས་ཉིན་རྡུང་ཡི་གེ་བཀྲ་ཤིས་དབང་འདུས་ལགས་ནས་ཕྲན་ཤྲཱི་ཤ་ར་ཏ་ཙནྡ་དྲ་ལ་རྒྱ་གར་རྒྱལ་ཁམས་ཆེན་པོའི་ཡོངས་བདག་རྒྱལ་པོ་ཨེཌ་ཝརཌ་བདུན་པའི་དྲུང་དུ་བཙང་བའི་ཕྱག་ཕྲིས་ཨིང་ཡིག་སྐད་དུ་འགྱུར་དགོས་པའི་བཀའ་བསྒྱུར། སྔོན་ཚུ་ཏུ་ཞོར་ས་ག་ཟླ་བའི་དུས་སུ་ཧུ་ལའི་བླ་མས་པོ་ཏ་ལའི་རྩེ་ཐོག་ན་བཞུགས་སྐབས་བདག་ཤ་ར་ཏ་ཙནྡ་དྲ་ལ་ཕྱག་དང་དང་སོགས་བཀའ་དྲིན་གནང་བ་དྲན་ནས་ཕྱག་ཕྲིས་དེ་ཕྲན་གྱིས་འགྱུར།

བསོད་ནམས་སྟོབས་ཀྱི་འཁོར་ལོས་བསྒྱུར་བ་གོང་མ་རྒྱལ་པོ་ཆེན་པོ་མཆོག་གི་དྲུང་དུ། ཧུ་ལའི་བླ་མའི་འབུལ་འབྲས།
ཇོ་འཁོར་ལམ་འགྲོད་བདེ་ལྡན་ཐོག་ཕྱི་གཞུང་ནས་འདི་ཕྱོགས་ཕྱོད་གླིག་ཡོ་ཆས་ཐབ་བཞེས་གནང་བ་ཐུགས་རྗེ་ཆེ། རྒྱ་ནག་དཔོན་རིགས་དང་འཁྲིགས་མེད་བྱུང་སྐོར་རྒྱལ་ཚབ་ཆེན་པོར་ཞུ་ཡི་ཐུབ་ཡོད་པ་བཞིན་འཁྲུལ་ཕྱག་ཆོད་པའི་རྟགས་རྐྱེན་དམ་དོན་མཛད་ལུགས་ནས་སྤྲུར་བཀྲེན་སྐྱིད་བཙངས་ཚོག་པ་ཞུ་གྱུར། ད་ལམ་རྒྱབས་བྲེལ་ཀྱི་འབུལ་འགྱུར་རྟེང་མེན་ཙམ་དུ་ལྷ་རྫས་ནང་མཛོད་དང་། སངས་རྒྱས་ཀྱི་གཟུགས་བརྙན་རྣམས་བཅས་བྱིན་ཙན་༧། རྡོ་དྲིལ་ཆ་ཚང་༧། གསེར་གསིལ་མ་སྒོར་༧༥ ཐིད་བཟང་གོས་ཁ་ཞི་ཆེས་ཚོགས་ཡུག་ཚང་ལྔ།། རྒྱལ་དབང་རིན་པོ་ཆེའི་ཕྱག་ཕྲིས་མ་དཔེའི་འདྲ་ཞུ་གོང་བཞུགས་འདི་ཡིན། See page 6 Appendix VI.

༄༅ བཅོམ་ལྡན་འདས་ཤཱཀྱ་ཐུབ་པའི་མཛད་པ་ ༡༢༥ བཞུགས་སོ།།

རང་ཅག་གི་སྟོན་པའི་མཛད་པ་ལས་ཆེ་ཡོང་ཙམ་བསྡུས་ན། དང་པོར་དགའ་ལྡན་དུ་དམ་པ་ཏོག་དཀར་པོར་གྱུར་པ་དང་། ༡ རྒྱལ་རིགས་ཙ་ཆོག་ཏུ་སྐུར་པ་ཤཱཀྱའི་རིགས་ཀྱི་ཡབ་ཡུམ་རང་རང་གི་ཡར་གྱི་བདུན་བརྒྱུད་བར་དུ་སྐྱོན་མེད་སོགས་ཀྱི་བརྟག་པ་དང་། ༢ །གཟིགས་པ་ལྷ་ལ་གཟིགས་པ་དང་། ། ༣ །དགའ་ལྡན་ནས་འཕོས་ཏེ་ལྷུམས་སུ་འཇུག་པ་དང་། ༤ །ཡུམ་གྱི་ལྷུམས་སུ་མི་གཙང་བས་མ་གོས་པར་བཞུགས་པའི་གནས་སྐབས་དང་། ༥ །ལུམ་བི་ནིའི་ཚལ་དུ་སྐུ་བལྟམས་པ་དང་། ༦ །གྲོང་ཁྱེར་སེར་སྐྱར་གཤེགས་པ་དང་། ༧ །དྲང་སྲོང་ཉོན་མོངས་མེད་ཀྱིས་ལུང་བསྟན་པ་སོགས་དང་། ༨ །བཟོའི་གནས་ལ་སྦྱངས་པ་དང་། ༩ །སྐུ་རྩལ་གྱི་སྟོབས་བསྟན་པ་དང་། ༡༠ །ཤཱཀྱ་ལག་ན་བེ་ཅོན་གྱི་བུ་མོ་བཙུན་མོ་གྲགས་འཛིན་མ་ཁབ་ཏུ་བསྟེན་པ་དང་། ༡༡ །གྲོང་ཁྱེར་སེར་སྐྱ་དང་ལྷས་བསྟན་གྱི་བར་གྱི་ཆུ་ཀླུང་རོ་ཧི་ཎིའི་འགྲམ་གྱི་ཤིང་ཆེན་པོ་དགེ་བའི་སྙིང་པོ་ཕྱེས་སུ་ཀླུང་གིས་འགྱེལ་ཏེ་གྲོང་ཁྱེར་གཉིས་ལ་གནོད་པ་དོན་ཀུན་གྲུབ་པས་ནམ་མཁར་འཕངས་པས་དུམ་བུ་གཉིས་སུ་སོང་བས་ཆུ་ཀླུང་ཟུར་བཞིན་རོང་བ་ལས་གྲོང་ཁྱེར་བ་བདེ་བར་གྱུར་པའི་གཏམ་དང་། ༡༢ ། ཤཱཀྱ་དྲིལ་བུ་སྒྲའི་བུ་མོ་ས་འཚོ་མ་བཙུན་མོར་ཕྱུར་པ་དང་། ༡༣ །ངེས་པར་འབྱུང་བའི་རྐྱེན་བཞི་གཟིགས་པ་དང་། ༡༤ །ཞིང་པའི་གྲོང་གི་ལམ་དུ་ཞིང་པ་དག་གི་དུཿཁ་གཟིགས་ནས་ཀྱང་སྙིང་རྗེ་ཤིང་ཛམ་བུའི་གྲིབ་མ་ལ་བཞུགས་ནས་བསམ་གཏན་བསྒྲུབས་ཤིང་དུར་ཁྲོད་ལ་གཟིགས་པ་དང་། ༡༥ །ཤཱཀྱ་དུས་འཇིགས་ཀྱི་བུ་མོ་རི་དྭགས་སྐྱེས་ང་འཛིན་མོར་ཐུང་བས་པའི་གཏམ་དང་། ༡༦ །ཞག་བདུན་དུ་སྲུང་མས་བསྐོར་བ་དང་། ༡༧ །ཁྱིམ་ནས་མངོན་པར་བྱུང་བ་དང་། ༡༨ །རབ་ཏུ་བྱུང་ཞིང་དྲང་སྲོང་ངན་སྤོང་གི་བུའི་གནས་སུ་གཤེགས་པ་དང་། ༡༩ །མུ་སྟེགས་ཅན་རིང་འདུར་སོགས་དང་ལྷན་ཅིག་ཐར་ལམ་འཚོལ་བར་བརྟན་པ་དང་། ༢༠ །ཞི་ལྷག་ཆེད་དུ་དཀའ་བ་ནན་པ་བདུན་སྤྱད་པ་དང་། ༢༡ །དཀའ་ཐུབ་གྲོལ་ཏེ་འོ་ཐུག་གསོལ་བས་སྐུ་ལུས་མཐུ་བསྐྱེད་པ་དང་། ༢༢ །བྱང་ཆུབ་སྙིང་པོ་རྡོ་རྗེ་གདན་གྱི་ལམ་དུ་གཤེགས་པའི་གཏམ་དང་། ༢༣ །བདུད་བཏུལ་བ་དང་། ༢༤ །ཟླ་ན་མེད་པའི་ཡེ་ཤེས་བརྙེས་པ་དང་། ༢༥ །ཞགས་ཁྲིད་དུ་ཐུགས་ལས་ཚུང་ཆུས་ངལ་ངར་བཞུགས་པ་དང་། ༢༦ །ཚངས་པ་དང་བརྒྱ་བྱིན་གྱིས་གསོལ་བ་བཏབ་སྟེ་ཝ་ར་ཎ་སིར་གཤེགས་པ་དང་། ༢༧ །ལྔ་སྡེ་ལ་ཆོས་འཁོར་དང་པོ་བསྐོར་བ་དང་། ༢༨ །ཉེ་བའི་སྡེ་ལྔ་ལ་སོགས་པའི་ལོ་རྒྱུས་དང་། ༢༩ །ཝ་ར་ཎ་སི་ནས་མ་ག་དྷར་འགྲོན་པའི་ལམ་དུ་བཟང་སྡེའི་ཚོགས་དྲུག་ཅུ་བདེན་པ་ལ་བཀོད་སོགས་གཏམ་དང་། ༣༠ །རལ་པ་ཅན་སྟོང་བཏུལ་བ་དང་། ༣༡ །རྒྱལ་པོ་གཟུགས་ཅན་སྙིང་པོས་བསུ་ཞིང་བདེན་པ་མཐོང་བ་དང་། ༣༢ །ཉེ་རྒྱལ་དང་པང་ནས་སྐྱེས་ཏེ་མཆོག་ཟུང་གཅིག་འཁོར་དུ་འདུས་པ་དང་། ༣༣ །བྱ་ཨེ་ལའི་འདབ་སྐྱབས་འགྲོ་ལ་བཀོད་དེ་ལུང་བསྟན་ནས་བཏུལ་ཞིང་མི་བྱེན་དགྲ་བཅོམ་ལ་བཀོད་པ་དང་། ༣༤ །ཀཏྱ་ཡ་ན་འཕགས་རྒྱལ་གྱི་རྒྱལ་པོ་གཏུམ་པོ་རབ་སྣང་རིགས་བདུད་བར་ཚགས་པས་བཏུལ་བ་དང་། ༣༥ །སྟོན་པས་གཅེར་བུ་བའི་སྦྱིན་བདག་རབ་བཟང་གི་ཆུང་མ་རྣམ་མ་ལ་ཁྲིད་ལ་བུ་ལྷ་མིའི་དཔལ་འབྱོར་སྤྱོད་ཞིང་དགྲ་བཅོམ་འཐོབ

བཅོམ་ལྡན་འདས་ཤཱ་ཀྱ་ཐུབ་པའི་མཛད་པ།

པ་ཞིག་བཙོ་རེ་ཞེས་ལུང་བསྟན་པ་མི་བདེན་པར་འགྱུར་ཆེད་དུ་གཅེར་བུ་བདག་གིས་ཀྱང་མ་བསད་པའི་རོ་བསྲེགས། ཚོ་ལྷོ་བའི་ཐད་མ་ཚོག་ངར་པད་མ་ལས་ཁྱིམ་བདག་མེ་སྐྱེས་བཙས་པའི་གཏམ་དང་། ༣༦ །འབར་བའི་ཧྲུག་ཏུ་བཀྱེ་ཕྱིན་ལ་སོགས་པ་ལྷ་རྣམས་ལ་ཆོས་བསྟན་པ་དང་། ༣༧ །ཁྱིམ་བདག་མགོན་མེད་ཟས་སྦྱིན་བདེན་པ་ལ་བཀོད་པ་དང་། ༣༨ །དེས་རྒྱལ་བུ་རྒྱལ་བྱེད་ཀྱི་ཚལ་བཞེངས་པ་དང་། ༣༩ །སྟོན་པ་ཉིད་མཉན་ཡོད་དུ་ཀུན་དགའ་ར་བར་སྤྱན་དྲངས་པ་དང་། ༤༠ །ཀོ་ས་ལའི་རྒྱལ་པོ་གསལ་རྒྱལ་དད་པ་ལ་བཀོད་པ་དང་། ༤༡ །ཡབ་རྒྱལ་པོས་འཆར་ཀ་ཆབ། རྫེ་སེར་སྐྱའི་སྐྱིད་ཚལ་གྱི་ནྱ་གྲོ་དྷའི་ཀུན་དགའ་ར་བ་སོགས་སུ་སྤྱན་དྲངས་ཏེ་ཡབ་སྲས་མཇལ་བའི་སྐབས་དང་འདྲིལ་བའི་གཏམ་རྒྱུད་ཆེན་པོ་དང་། ༤༢ །མིང་ཆེན་པོ་རྩང་མ་སོགས་ཤཱཀྱ་རིགས་ཀྱི་བུད་མེད་ཕལ་པ་རྣམས་ལ་ཆོས་བསྟན་ཞིང་སྐྱིད་མ་ཚོ་འཛོམས་ཏེ་བུ་མོ་སྨུ་ཏིག་རྗེ་དཔལ་ཅན་དུ་སྐྱེས་སོགས་ཀྱི་གཏམ་དང་། ༤༣ །གཙུང་དགའ་བོ་རབ་ཏུ་བྱུང་བའི་སྐོར་དང་། ༤༤ །མ་མ་སྐྱེ་དགུའི་བདག་མོ་ལ་བརྟེན་ཏེ་དགེ་སློང་མའི་དགེ་འདུན་ལྔ་བརྒྱ་བྱུང་སྟེ་དགྲ་བཅོམ་པར་གྱུར་པ་དང་། ༤༥ །གྲོང་ཁྱེར་སློབ་མ་ལྔ་བྱུར་གཤེགས་ཏེ་ཁྱིམ་བདག་རི་ཧྣ་ནའི་བྱམས་མའི་བུ་ཁང་པོ་དགྲ་བཅོམ་ལ་བཀོད་སོགས་དང་། ༤༦ །ཐུབ་ཕྱོགས་འོད་ཟེར་ཅན་གྱི་འཇིག་རྟེན་དུ་ཕྱིན་ཏེ་མོའུ་འགལ་གྱི་བུའི་མ་དང་སྐྱེས་པ་རྒྱུན་ཞུགས་ལ་བཀོད་པ་དང་། ༤༧ །བྲམ་ཟེ་པད་མའི་སྙིང་པོ་སོགས་བདེན་པ་མཐོང་བ་ལ་བཀོད་པ་དང་། ༤༨ །སུ་ལྷོ་བ་ཕྱིའུ་གཉིས་དགེ་འདུན་ལ་དཀའ་ཁྲིའི་ལས་མཐོང་ཆོས་ལ་སྨིན་པའི་གཏམ་དང་། ༤༩ །མོའུ་འགལ་བུ་མངོག་ཏེ་གཙུང་དགའ་བོ་ཉེ་དགའ་བཏུལ་བ་དང་། ༥༠ །རྒྱལ་པོ་གསལ་རྒྱལ་ལ་ཁྲུས་མཆོད་ཆའི་ཆར་ཕབ་པ་མོའུ་འགལ་བུས་མི་རྟོག་ཏུ་བསྒྱུར་ནས་སྐྱབས་པ་དང་། ༥༡ །གཟུགས་ཅན་སྙིང་པོའི་དཔའ་བོ་སྙིང་ཐུབ་ཅེས་པ་གནོད་སྦྱིན་འབྲོག་གནས་སུ་སྐྱེས་པ་བཏུལ་བ་དང་། ༥༢ །འབྲོག་གནས་ཀྱི་ལག་ནས་བླངས་པའི་ལག་བརྒྱུད་བདེན་པ་ལ་བཀོད་པ་དང་། ༥༣ །རྒྱལ་པོ་ཨུ་དྲ་ཡ་ཎས་གོ་བྲབ་བསྐུར་ལན་དུ་གཟུགས་ཅན་སྙིང་པོས་རྒྱལ་བའི་སྐུ་གཟུགས་བྲིས་པ་བསྐུར་བས་བདེན་པ་མཐོང་སོགས་གྲོང་ཁྱེར་སྒྲ་སྒྲོགས་པའི་སྐོར་དང་། ༥༤ །གཞན་ཡོད་དང་རྒྱལ་ཁབ་བར་གྱི་སེང་གེ་རལ་པ་ཅན་རྒྱལ་བས་བཏུལ་བས་ལྷར་སྐྱེས་ནས་རྒྱུན་ཞུགས་ཐོབ་པ་དང་། ༥༥ །འོད་སྲུང་གི་དུས་ཀྱི་དགེ་སློང་དག་ལ་ངན་སྨྲས་བྱས་པའི་བྲམ་ཟེ་ཤེད་བུ་སེར་སྐྱ་ཆུ་སྲིན་ཉའི་རིགས་སུ་གྱུར་པ་ལ་ཆོས་བསྟན་ནས་ལྷར་སྐྱེས་ཏེ་རྒྱུན་ཞུགས་ཐོབ་ཅིང་དེ་དྲངས་པ་རེ་ཉ་པ་ལྔ་བརྒྱ་ཡང་དགྲ་བཅོམ་ལ་བཀོད་པའི་གཏམ་དང་། ༥༦ །འོད་སྲུངས་ཆེན་པོ་འཁོར་དུ་འདུས་པའི་གཏམ་དང་། ༥༧ །ཕྱིས་འོད་སྲུངས་ཆེན་པོ་ལ་གསར་བུ་མང་པོས་འཕྱ་བ་སེལ་ཆེད་དུ་སྣམ་ཕྱེད་སྩལ་བ་དང་། ༥༨ །ཀུན་དགའ་བོ་རིམ་འགྲོ་བར་བཀོས་ཏེ་ལྷན་ཅིག་གནས་པར་བསྟན་པ་དང་། ༥༩ །སྦྲེ་འུས་སྦྲང་རྩི་ཕུལ་ཐེས་ཤི་འཕོས་ནས་གནས་འཛིག་གི་བུ་སྦྲང་རྩི་ཅན་དུ་སྐྱེས་དགྲ་བཅོམ་ཐོབ་པ་དང་། ༦༠ །ཆོ་འཕྲུལ་ཆེན་པོས་མུ་སྟེགས་འདུལ་བའི་ལོ་རྒྱུས་དང་། ༦༡ །དྲང་སྲོང་ལྔ་བརྒྱ་དགྲ་བཅོམ་ལ་བཀོད་པ་དང་། ༦༢ །ཕྱོ་བྱུང་

བཅོམ་ལྡན་འདས་ཤཱ་ཀྱ་ཐུབ་པའི་མཛད་པ།

ལྷའི་ལེན་གྱི་རྒྱལ་པོ་གཉིས་བསྡམས་པ་དང་། ༦༣ །ཤ་ར་སྡོང་བཏུལ་ཏེ་སླེབས་འཁྲོར་བཀོད་པ་དང་། ༦༤ །ལྷ་ཀླུ་ལྷ་མིན་མི་སོགས་ཀྱི་འདུས་པ་ཆེན་པོ་ལ་སོགས་པའི་གཏམ་དང་། ༦༥ །ནགས་ཁྲོད་ཀྱི་གནོད་སྦྱིན་དང་རྒྱ་མཚོའི་རླབས་ལས་ཚོང་པ་ལྔ་བརྒྱ་པ་སྐྱེ་བ་ཉིས་སྐྱབས་པ་དང་། ༦༦ །ཚེ་འཕྲུལ་ཆུང་བར་གྲགས་པ་ལྷ་ལས་བབས་པ་དང་། ༦༧ །གྲོང་ཁྱེར་བཟང་བྱེད་དུ་གཤེགས་ཏེ་ཁྱིམ་བདག་ཕྱུགས་སོགས་ས་བདེན་པ་མཐོང་བ་ལ་བཀོད་སོགས་དང་། ༦༨ །ཁྱིམ་བདག་དཔའ་བྱིན་བཏུལ་བ་དང་། ༦༩ །མི་སྐྱེས་རབ་ཏུ་བྱུང་བའི་སྐོར་དང་། ༧༠ །གནོད་སྦྱིན་ས་ཏིའི་བུ་མོ་འཕྲོག་མ་བཏུལ་བ་དང་། ༧༡ །སངས་རྒྱས་འཁོར་ལོས་བསྒྱུར་བའི་ཚུལ་གྱིས་རྒྱལ་པོ་ཀ་ཕི་ན་འཁོར་བཅས་བཏུལ་ཏེ་དགྲ་བཅོམ་པ་ལ་བཀོད་པ་དང་། ༧༢ །ཁྱིམ་བདག་གདེངས་ཅན་དང་དྲང་སྲོང་ལྔ་བརྒྱས་བདེན་པ་མཐོང་བར་མཛད་པ་དང་། ༧༣ །གྲོང་ཁྱེར་ཀཽ་ཤཱམྦྷིར་བྱོན་ནས་རྒྱལ་པོ་ཤར་བ་སོགས་ཀྱི་དོན་མཛད་པ་དང་། ༧༤ །སེང་ག་ལའི་རྒྱལ་པོའི་བུ་མོ་མུ་ཏིག་ཅན་གྱི་ལོ་རྒྱུས་དང་། ༧༥ །མ་ག་དྷ་བཟང་མོས་ཡུལ་བུ་རམ་ཤིང་འཕེལ་དུ་སྤྱན་དྲངས་པ་དང་། ༧༦ །ལྷས་བྱིན་གྱིས་རྫུ་འཕྲུལ་བསླབས་པ་དང་། ༧༧ །དེས་དགེ་འདུན་གྱི་དབྱེན་བྱས་པ་བསྡུམས་པ་དང་། ༧༨ །ལྷས་བྱིན་གྱི་ཕྲ་མས་རྒྱལ་པོ་མ་སྐྱེས་དགྲས་རང་གི་ཕ་ལ་གནོད་པ་བྱས་པ་དང་། ༧༩ །ལྷས་བྱིན་གྱིས་རྒྱལ་པོ་ལ་ཡོབ་རྫུབ་བྱས་ཀྱང་གནོད་པ་མི་མངའ་བ་དང་། ༨༠ །གླང་པོ་ཆེ་སྨྱོས་པ་ནོར་སྐྱོང་བཏུལ་བ་དང་། ༨༡ །འཚོ་བྱེད་གཞོན་ནུས་བདེན་པ་ལ་བཀོད་པ་དང་། ༨༢ །རྒྱལ་ཆེན་བཞི་དང་སྐྱོང་སྡོང་དང་བཅས་པས་བདེན་པ་མཐོང་བ་དང་། ༨༣ །སོར་མོའི་འཕྲེང་བ་ཅན་བཏུལ་ཏེ་དགྲ་བཅོམ་ལ་བཀོད་པ་དང་། ༨༤ །འཕགས་པ་ལེགས་འོད་ཀྱི་རྒྱུས་དང་། ༨༥ །ཆུ་སྦྱིན་བྱིན་པ་གསོད་ཀྱི་རི་ལ་དབྱར་བཞུགས་མཛད་པ་དང་། ༨༦ །རྒྱལ་པོ་གསལ་རྒྱལ་གྱིས་འོད་སྲུངས་ཆེན་པོ་ཙ་ཚོད་པ་དང་། ༨༧ །དབུལ་མོ་སྒྲོན་ཙུགས་པ་སངས་རྒྱས་སུ་ལུང་བསྟན་པ་དང་། ༨༨ །རྒྱལ་པོ་གསལ་རྒྱལ་ང་རྒྱལ་བཅག་པ་དང་། ༨༩ །རྒྱལ་པོ་མ་སྐྱེས་དགྲ་གནོད་པ་ལས་སྐྱབས་པ་དང་། ༩༠ །མ་སྐྱེས་དགྲ་ཚ་བ་མེད་པའི་དད་པ་ལ་བཀོད་པ་དང་། ༩༡ །ལྷས་བྱིན་ཉི་གཏམ་རྒྱུད་འཛིན་པ་དང་། ༩༢ །མཆོག་ཟུང་གིས་དམྱལ་བའི་རྒྱུད་བཟླས་པ་དང་། ༩༣ །ཡངས་པ་ཅན་དུ་གཤེགས་པའི་ལམ་ཁར་བྱུང་བའི་གཏམ་ཡམ་དང་སྤྲེལ་ཞི་རྣས་དང་། ༩༤ །ཡངས་པ་ཅན་པ་རྣམས་བདེ་བར་མཛད་པ་དང་། ༩༥ །ཡུལ་མི་ཕི་ལ་དང་ས་ལའི་གྲོང་དུ་བྱོན་ནས་བདུད་སྐྱིངས་པར་མཛད་སོགས་དང་། ༩༦ །ཡུལ་རྩེབ་པ་ཅན་གྱི་དྲུང་རྣམས་ལ་ཕ་ཡད་ཆ་བཏན་ནས་བཏུལ་བ་དང་། ༩༧ །ཀུ་ཤི་ཧྲའི་གྲོང་སོགས་སུ་གཤེགས་པ་དང་། ༩༨ །བྲམ་ཟེའི་གྲོང་དུ་བྱོན་པ་སོགས་དང་། ༩༩ །ཕྱག་ན་རྡོ་རྗེ་ཁྲིད་དེ་བྱང་ཕྱོགས་ཀྱི་རྒྱུད་དུ་བྱོན་ནས་ཀླུ་སོག་མ་མེད་བཏུལ་ཞིང་མི་མིན་དང་མི་མཐའ་ཡས་པའི་དོན་ཐུན་ཚོད་གཅིག་ལ་མཛད་པ་དང་། ༡༠༠ །སྐྱིན་ལྷ་ལྡན་གྱི་བཅོམ་རྟག་ཏུ་བྱོན་ནས་བྲམ་ཟེ་དང་གནོད་སྦྱིན་དུ་མ་བཏུལ་སོགས་ཀྱི་སྐོར་དང་། ༡༠༡ །ཡུལ་ཨོ་ཏ་འར་བྱོན་པ་ཚོང་པ་ལྔ་བརྒྱས་བདེན་རྟོགས་སོགས་དང་། ༡༠༢ །གྲོང་ཁྱེར་དགྲ་མཐར་དབྱར་བཞུགས་མཛད་

བཅོམ་ལྡན་འདས་ཤཱཀྱ་ཐུབ་པའི་མཛད་པ།

པ་དང་། ༡༠༣ །ལྷོ་ཕྱོགས་ལྷ་ལེན་གྱིས་ལམ་དུ་བྱུང་བའི་གཏམ་དང་། ༡༠༤ །བྲམ་ཟེ་དབྱུལ་པོ་ལ་སོགས་པའི་ལོ་རྒྱུས་དང་། ༡༠༥ །ལས་ཀྱི་རྒྱུ་བ་ལུང་བསྟན་པ་དང་། ༡༠༦ །ཤཱཀྱ་ལྷག་མ་རྣམས་གྲོལ་བ་ལ་བཀོད་པ་དང་། ༡༠༧ །བྲམ་ཟེ་གང་པོ་ལ་སོགས་པ་བྱང་ཆུབ་ཏུ་ལུང་བསྟན་པ་དང་། ༡༠༨ །གྲོང་ཁྱེད་པ་རྣམས་ཡང་ཡང་འདུས་ལ་བྱ་བ་མཐུན་ཞིང་ཁྲིམས་ལ་གནས་པ་དང་རྒན་ལ་གུས་ལ་མི་འོས་པར་མི་བགྱིད་མཆོད་རྟེན་དགེ་བཅོམ་ལ་དད་པ་སྟེ་མི་ཉམས་པའི་རྒྱུ་བདུན་དང་ལྡན་པས་མ་སྐྱེས་དགྲས་ཡམ་མི་ཐུབ་པར་གསུངས་པ་དང་། ༡༠༩ །ཡངས་པ་ཅན་གྱི་ལམ་དུ་བཞུགས་པའི་སྐབས་དང་། ༡༡༠ །འོད་མ་ཅན་གྱི་བྱང་ཕྱོགས་ཤིང་ཤ་པའི་ཚལ་དུ་བཞུགས་པ་དང་། ༡༡༡ །ཁྲིམ་བདག་ནོར་ཅན་གྱི་གཏམ་དང་། ༡༡༢ །སྐུ་ཚེའི་འདུ་བྱེད་བཏང་བ་དང་། ༡༡༣ །ཙུ་ཅན་དུ་བཞུད་པའི་ལམ་གྱི་མཛད་པ་དང་། ༡༡༤ །ཙུ་ཅན་ཉིད་དུ་ཕྱིན་པའི་མཛད་པ་དང་། ༡༡༥ །དྲི་ཟའི་རྒྱལ་པོ་རབ་དགའ་བཏུལ་པ་དང་། ༡༡༦ །ཀུན་ཏུ་རྒྱུ་རབ་བཟང་དགྲ་བཅོམ་ལ་བཀོད་པ་དང་། ༡༡༧ །ཡོངས་སུ་མྱ་ངན་ལས་འདས་པར་བསྟན་པ་དང་། ༡༡༨ ། དེ་ལྟར་བཅོམ་ལྡན་འདས་ཤཱཀྱ་ཐུབ་པའི་མཛད་པ་བརྒྱ་དང་བཅོ་བརྒྱད་དང་། ཟུར་དུ།

སྐུ་གདུང་ཞུགས་ལ་ཞུལ་བ་དང་། ༡༡༩ །སྐུ་གདུང་ཆ་བརྒྱད་དུ་བགོས་པ་དང་། ༡༢༠ །བཀའ་བསྡུ་བ་དང་པོ་འི་གཏམ་དང་། ༡༢༡ །འོད་སྲུང་ཆེན་པོ་མྱ་ངན་ལས་འདས་པ་དང་། ༡༢༢ །ཤཱ་ཎའི་གོས་ཅན་རབ་ཏུ་བྱུང་བ་དང་། ༡༢༣ །ཀུན་དགའ་བོ་འི་མཛད་པ་ཐ་མ་དང་། ༡༢༤ །བཀའ་བསྡུ་པ་གཉིས་པ་ཇི་ལྟར་མཛད་པ་དང་བཅས་ཏེ་བརྒྱ་དང་ཉི་ཤུ་ཙ་ལྔ༔— ༡༢༥། གྲགས་སོ།།

• དཔུང་པོ་བརྒྱད་ཅུའི་བར་གནས་གང་དང་གང་དུ་ལོ་ཐེ་ཙམ་རེ་བཞུགས་པ་ནི། ཅི་བྲག་ཏུ་བཤད་མཛོད་ཆེན་མོ་འི་ལུང་དུམ་བུ་འཕྱུར་པ་ལས།

ཆོས་འཁོར་གནས་དང་ཡངས་པ་ཅན། །ས་དཀར་ཅན་དང་ལྷ་ཡི་གནས །བྱས་པ་གསོད་དང་ཀོ་ཤམ་བྷི།
འབྲོག་གནས་མཆོད་རྟེན་རི་དང་ནི། །འོད་མའི་ཚལ་དང་དགྲར་བཅས་དང་། །སེར་སྐྱ་ཡི་ནི་གྲོང་ཁྱེར་ཏེ།
འདི་རྣམས་སུ་ནི་ཐུབ་པ་ཡི། །སྐྱེས་མཆོག་ལོ་རེ་ལོ་རེ་བཞུགས། །འབར་བའི་ཕུག་གི་གནས་སུ་གཉིས།
མཉན་གྱི་གནས་སུ་ལོ་བཞི་སྟེ། །རྒྱལ་པོ་འི་ཁབ་ཀྱི་གྲོང་དུ་ལྔ། །དཀའ་བ་སྤྱད་པ་ལོ་དྲུག་སྟེ།
ཉི་ཤུ་ཙ་གསུམ་མཉན་ཡོད་དུ། །ཉི་ཤུ་ཙ་དགུ་ཁབ་གནས་སུ། །ཐམས་ཅད་མཁྱེན་པ་བཞུགས་པ་ཡི།
རྒྱལ་བ་དེ་ལྟར་བརྒྱད་ཅུ་ལ། །ཐུབ་མཆོག་དམ་པ་མྱ་ངན་འདས། །སུམ་པ་མཁན་པོས་དཔག་བསམ་ལྗོན་བཟང་ལས།

APPENDIX VIII

༄༅། ཡིག་བསྐུར་རྣམས་གཞག།

I

༈ རྫོང་དཔོན་དང་སྡེ་པ་སོགས་ཀྱི་རིགས་ལ་འབུལ་ཚིག་པ།

རྣམ་ཀུན་ཐུགས་རྗེའི་བཀྲིན་མཚུངས་བྲལ་སྐུ་ཞབས་མཆོག་གི་ཞབས་དྲུང་དུ།

ནང་མ་བཙོས་བདེར་ཞུ་སྙིང་། དེང་རྫོན་སོགས་ལེགས་མཛད་ཁྲུང་རྫོན་སྐྱེས་ཀྱི་ཉེ་བར་དྭངས་པའི་མཆོག་སྐུའི་ཉིན་བྱེད་སྒྲིབ་མེད་དུ་གསལ་ཞིང་། སྨད་བྱུང་མཛད་བཟང་གི་སྣང་བ་མཐའ་ཡུར་ཁྱབ་པ་བཞིན་པ་བཞུགས་རིང་ནས། འདི་པའི་གཙོང་ཐུགས་རྗེས་སྐྱོན་དཀྱུ་ས་ནས་མ་པོར་བའི་བཀའ་མཆིད་ཞིབ་ཟླུག་ནང་སྐྱེས་ལེ་ཚན་བཅས་སྤྲོལ་འབྱོར་བཀྲིན་ཆེ། འདིར་ཕྱུན་ཚུང་ཀྱང་བར་ལམ་གཟུགས་གཞི་བདེ་མིན་བྱུང་བ་ད་ཆ་དྭག་སྐྱེས་ཀྱི་སྐུ་གམ་དུ་བཅར་སྐབས་ན་མཆིས་ལགས། མཚམས་གསོལ། སྤྲད་མར་ཡང་མཆོག་སྐུ་ཟབ་གཉིས་སྦྱོད་དོས། ཕེབས་ཚོགས་ཀྱང་རིམ་ཡོད་མཁྱེན། ཞུ་འདིགས་ལྷ་རིག་བཅས་ཆེས་བཟང་པོར་ཕུལ་བ་ཞུ་ཚུང་།

II

༄༅།། རང་མཉམ་ལ་འབུལ་ན།

༄༅།། སྨད་བྱུང་མཁྱེན་པའི་མངའ་བདག་བརྩེ་ཆེན་མཚུངས་མེད་སྐུ་ཞབས་མཆོག་གི་དྲུང་དུ། ཡང་ན།

༈ ཕྱུལ་བྱུང་མཁྱེན་བརྩེའི་དབང་ཕྱུག་མཚུངས་བྲལ་ཆེན་པོའི་ཞབས་དྲུང་དུ། ཆེད་འབུལ། དེང་ཡང་ལེགས་བྱས་རྒྱ་གཏེར་གྱི་སྙིང་པོ་ལས་ཐོན་པའི་སྐུ་འཚོ་བཅུ་དྲུག་བདག་པོའི་དཀྱིལ་འཁོར་སྒྲིབ་མེད་དུ་གསལ་ཞིང་སྨད་བྱུང་མཛད་འཕྲིན་བཟང་པོའི་འོད་སྣང་འགོག་མེད་དུ་འཚོ་བཞུགས་ནི་བཀྲིན་ཆེ། འདིར་བྲན་ཡང་གོང་ས་ལས་བྱིན་གྱི་ཐུགས་རྗེས་གཟུགས་ཁམས་བདེ་ཞིང་། འཁོར་བསྟུན་གྱི་གསེང་བ་རིམ་སེལ་སྐབས་སུ་གནས་ལགས། མཚམས་ཞུ། སྤྲད་མར་ཡང་སྐུ་འཚོའི་མཐུན། གཞིས་མི་སྦྱོད་དོས། ཕེབས་ཚོགས་ཀྱང་རིམ་ལྡན་ཡོད་པ་མཁྱེན།

ཡང་ན།

༈ མཁྱེན་རབ་ཀྱི་ཡོ་འདབ་ཕྱོགས་བརྒྱར་བཞད་པ་གྲོགས་མཆོག་དམ་པའི་དྲུང་དུ།

འབུལ་འབྲས། དེང་དགེ་མཚན་དུ་མས་ཕྱུག་པའི་སྐུ་འཚོ་འཕྲི་ཤེང་བརྟན་ཅིང་། མཛད་འཕྲིན་གྱི་མེ་ཏོག་གསར་དུ་ཀོད་བཞིན་པར་བཞུགས་གསོལ་གཞིར་བཅས་བཀྲིན་མཆོག་ཏུ་ཆེ། འདིར་ཡང་མཆོག་གསུམ་དམ་པའི་ཐུགས་རྗེའི་བྱིན་མཐུས་བདེ་བར་ལགས། མཚམས་འབུལ། འབྱུང་འགྱུར་གྱི་ཆར་ཡང་མཛེས་སྐུ་ཟབ་གཉིས་ཀྱི་དོས། ཐུགས་ནང་གཤིན་པའི་ཕེབས་ཚོགས་ཀྱང་གོ་ལའི་རྒྱུང་འགྲོས་ལྟར་འགོག་མེད་དུ་ཞུ་སྨྲོ། གཟིགས་རྟེན་རབ་དཀར་ལྷ་རྫས་བཅས་ཕུལ།

ཡིག་བསྐུར་རྣམ་བཞག།

ཡང་ན།

༄༅།། མཁྱེན་ལྡན་ཞལ་ངོ་ལགས་ཀྱི་ཕྱག་ཏུ།

ཆེད་འབུལ། རིང་ཡང་དགེ་ལེགས་ཀྱི་བསྐྱེད་པའི་སྐུ་ཡི་བྲི་རིས་གསལ་ཞིང་། ལེགས་མཛད་ཀྱི་ངོད་དཀར་ཕྲིན་ཡོངས་སུ་སྒྲོ་བ་ནི་སྨན་ཡོད་དུ་གྱུར། སླད་མར་ཡང་བརྩེ་རྒྱུས་སྐུ་འཚོ་འཁྲོད་གཞིས་ནས། རིང་མེད་དགེ་བའི་གསུང་མཆིད་ཀྱང་ཆར་བཞིན་ཡོད་པ་ཞུ།

III

༄༅།། ཚེ་འདིའི་ཕ་མ་ལྷ་བུ་ལ་འབུལ་ན།

ཧཱུྃ ཚེ་རབས་ཀུན་ཏུ་བཀྲིན་འཁོར་མེད་ཕ་མ་ལྷན་རྒྱས་མཆོག་གི་ཞབས་དྲུང་དུ། གུས་པས་མི་ཕྱེད་དྭངས་པ་རྒྱ་གཏེར་བསྒྲུབ་པ་ལས་ཐོན་པའི་སྐུ་མཆོག་ནམ་མཁའི་ཏོར་བུ་མཛོད་པར་དྭངས་ཅིང་། ཕྱི་ནང་མཛད་བཟང་དང་འབྲེལ་བའི་ཀུན་ཏུ་རྟེན་ཡོད་ཀྱི་སྣང་བ་འགོག་མེད་དུ་འཕྱོ་བཞིན་པར་འཚོ་གཞིས་ནས་ཉེ་ལམ་བཅོ་བས་ནམ་ཡང་མི་སྐྱུད་པའི་ཕྱག་བྲིས་རྟེན་ལྡན་ཏོར་འཛིན་གཡང་མོའི་འཁྱུར་དུ་ཀུན་ལ་མཐོ་བའི་ཕོ་ཏོག་བལ་འཛམ་གྱིས་བསྐྱོད་པའི་ཞིང་ས་བསྐྱུང་སྐྱོབ་རྒྱ་བོའི་དྭ་བས་འཁོར་ཡུག་བརྐྱར་བའི་དཔལ་ཡོན་ལས་འཛོངས་མའི་གར་ཉིད་ཀྱི་བསྐྱུན་པའི་དབང་བཞུའི་ཁ་དོག་འཁྲོག་པའི་ཕྱག་པ་རྐྱུས་ལེགས་བཅས་ཕྱག་རྟགས་ཀྱི་རི་ཁས་རྒྱུད་པ་གཏང་འཁྱེར་བ་བཀྲིན་གཞལ་མེད་དུ་ཆེ། ཕྲན་ཡང་གསར་ཆེས་མ་གོས་ཙམ་ནས། ཕྱི་ནང་གསང་གསུམ་གྱི་བཀྱིས་དོས་ཕྱོད་མེད་དུ་ལགས། བཞིན་ནས། མཚམས་ཞུ། སླད་མར་ཡང་། དགེ་ལེགས་ཀྱི་གཞི་རྟེན་སྐུ་འཚོ་འཁྲོད་གཞིས་ནས། རྣམ་དཀར་དོན་ལྡན་ཀྱི་མཛད་པ་ཐུར་བྱམས་བཅོ་ནས་ཡང་མི་སླུད་པའི་ཞབས་ཏོགས་ཀྱང་གསེར་གཞུང་རིང་མོའི་སྐུང་རྒྱུན་ལྟར་སྐྱོལ་བ་མཁྱེན་ལགས།

ཞུ་ཡིག་ལྷ་རིག་དང་དངུལ་སྒང་བཅས་བླ་ཆེས་བཟང་པོར་ཕུལ།

IV

༄༅།། ཉམ་ཆེ་བའི་རིགས་ལ་འབུལ་ན།

ཧཱུྃ སྐད་བྱུང་རྣམ་དཔྱོད་ཀྱི་མཚར་སྣུག་ཆ་ཤས་རྫོགས་པ་མི་རྗེ་ལྷ་ཕྱམ་སྐུ་ཞབས་མཆོག་གི་ཞབས་སོན་པད་མོའི་དྲུང་དུ། ངང་དུས་མཆོག་སྨན་གྱི་སྐྱེ་དགུའི་འདྲེན་བྱེད་བདུད་རྩིའི་དགའ་སྟོན་དུ་གྱུབ་པའི་མཚན་དཔེ་དགེ་མཚན་བྲ་ལྷག་ཏུ་གསལ་ཞིང་། ཕྱི་ནང་ཀུན་དགེའི་བཀའ་འཁོར་རིན་པོ་ཆེ་ཕན་བདེའི་སྤྱི་དཔལ་དུ་བསྒྱུར་བཞིན་པར་བཞུགས་གསལ་ནི་གཞིར་བཅས་བཀྲིན་མཆོག་ཏུ་ཆེ། འདིར་གུས་པའང་འབྱུང་ལུས་བདེ་ཞིང་རྣམ་གཡེང་བཀྱི་བ་རིམ་སེལ་དུ་གནས་ལགས། མཚམས་ཞུ། སླད་མར་ཡང་བཅུ་དྲུག་བདེ་བའི་ཆ་ཤས་ཡོངས་སུ་རྫོགས་པའི་བདག་ཉིད་མཛེས་སྐུ་རིན་ཆེན་ཕུན་བརྟན་གྱི་འཁྲོད་གཞིས་ངོས་ཞབས་ཏོགས་ཀྱང་དུས་བཞིའི་འཕང་ལོ་ལྟར་ཚད་མེད་དུ་སྐྱོལ་བ་མཁྱེན། ཞུ་ཡིག་ལྷ་རྫས་བཅས་གུས་པས་ཕུལ།

V

༄༅།། སྐྱེ་དམན་གྱི་སྤྱི་ཁྱབ་ཏུ་ཡི་གེ་བཏང་ན།

༈ སྤུན་དཀྱུས་ཀྱི་ཨུད་པལ་ཆེ་ཨང་ས་པ་ཨ་ཝེ་ལགས་རིན་པོ་ཆེའི་ཞབས་དྲུང་དུ།

ཆེད་འབུལ། དེང་སྐུ་འཚོ་པད་སོར་མཛད་བཟང་གི་གེ་སར་བཞད་ཅིང་བཀའ་འཁོར་བྱུང་བའི་རྒྱུད་མང་བསྒྲེང་བཞིན་པ་ནི་གཞིར་བཅས་བཀྲིན་ཆེ། འདི་ཡང་གཟུགས་འཚོ་འི་མི་རྟག་དུས་ཀྱི་བ་སོས་བཅོམ་ཙམ་ནས་འཁོས་དཔག་བགྱིས་པ་རིམ་སེལ་དུ་གནས་ལགས། མཚམས་བྲུ། སྤྲད་དུ་འང་དལ་རྟེན་འབྱོད་གཞིས་དང་འབྲེལ་བའི་ཕྱི་ནང་། ཀུན་དགེའི་བཀའ་ཁྱབ་གོང་འཕེལ་ནས། གསུང་མཆིད་ཀྱང་རིམ་པར་བྲུ་སྒྲོ།

VI

རང་གི་ཆུང་མ་ལྷ་བུ་ལ་ཡི་གེ་བཏང་ན།

༈ འཛོའ་བརྩུག་དམ་བཅའི་ཕྱུག་རྒྱས་འབྲེལ་བ་བརྟེ་ལྡན་ཡིད་ཀྱི་ཟེའུ་འབྲུ་གསར་པའི་གམ་དུ།

ཆེད་སྤྲེལ། དེང་དུས་ཡང་ཚོ་འི་རྩ་སྐྱེས་མཚོར་སྡུག་འདབ་རྒྱས་དཔྱིད་དུ་གསལ་ཞིང་། ཕྱི་ནང་ཀུན་དགེའི་མཛད་འོས་མི་དམན་པ་གཞིར་བཅས་པ་ཤིན་ཏུ་སྤྲོ། འདི་ཡང་མཆོག་གསུམ་དམ་པའི་ཐུགས་རྗེའི་བྱིན་མཐུས་བདེ་བར་གནས་ལགས། མཚམས་འབྲས། སྤྲད་དུ་འང་བརྟན་བདེའི་ངང་གནས་སྐུ་འཚོར་འབྱོད་གཞིས་ཀྱི་ཕྱི་དོར་མི་གཡེལ་ངོས། རྗེས་ཆགས་སུ་སེམས་ཀྱི་ཡོལ་སྣོ་ནས་མི་འདོར་བའི་འབྱོད་འོས་ཀྱང་སྣང་བྱེད་བྱུང་གི་བསྒོད་པ་ལྟར་ཡོད་པ་འཚལ། རྟེན་དྲི་བྲལ་ལྷག་བསམ་གྱི་སྤྲིན་བླ་བཅས་ཀླུབ་ཆོས་དགེ་བར་སྤྲེལ།

VII

༄༅། ཡང་སྐྱེ་དམན་ཆུང་བའི་རིགས་ལ་བསྐུར་ན།

༈ བང་འཚོ་འི་ཟླ་རིས་བཀྲ་བ་ཆེ་གེ་མོ་གང་དེར། ཡི་གེ་བྲུས་དོན། དེང་ཟླ་མདོག་བཟང་ཞིང་བགྱིས་ཧོས་མི་དམན་པ་ཡོད་པ་ནི་གཞིར་བཅས་སྤྲོ། འདི་ཡང་བདེ་བ་ཡོད། ཆེད་དོན། སྐབས་འབུལ སྤྲད་དུའང་ཕྱུང་ཁམས་འབྱོད་རྟེན་དང་། འབྲེལ་བའི་མོ་འོས་ཀྱང་རིས་པ་བགྱིས། རྟེན་བཅས་ཆོས་ལ་བསྐུར།

ཡིག་བསྐུར་རྣམ་གཞག།

VIII

༄༅།། རང་གི་གཡོག་རིགས་ལྷ་བུར་བཏང་ན།

༈ བློ་གྲོས་ཀྱི་པོ་ལག་རྫོགས་པ་ཤེས་ལྡན་ཆེ་གེ་མོ་ལ། བློ་བ། དེང་དུ་འབྱུང་ཁམས་བཟང་ཞིང་ཕྱི་ནང་ལར་ཀྱའི་བགྲིས་ངོས་མི་དམན་པ་ཡོད་པ་གཞིར་བཅས། འདིར་ཡང་ལྷ་བློའི་ཕྱིན་མཐུན་བདེ་བར་ཡོད། སྐད་མར་ལུས་འཚོར་འཁྲོད་རྟེན་དང་འབྲེལ་བའི་སོལ་མཆིད་ཀྱང་རིམ་པ་བགྱིས། རྟེན་བཅས་གྲལ་ཆེས་དགེ་བར་སྤྲིངས།

IX

༄༅།། རང་ལས་རྒན་པ་སྤུན་འབྲེལ་རིགས་ལྷ་བུར་བསྐྱི་བཏང་གི་ཡུལ་དུ་གྱུར་པ་ཞིག་ལ་འབུལ་ན།

༈ བརྩེ་ཆེན་བྱམས་པའི་ཐུགས་རྗེས་ནི་བར་འཛིན་པ་བསྐྱིན་འཁོར་མེད་མཆོག་གི་ཞབས་སེན་ཟླ་ཆེས་གསར་པའི་དྲུང་དུ།

མཐོན་མཐིང་རལ་པའི་ཟུར་ཕུད་ཀྱིས་བཏུད་དེ་ཞུ་བ། དེང་དུས་རྒྱབས་ཆེན་ཚོགས་གཉིས་ཀྱི་བཅུད་དུ་སྨིན་པའི་གསང་གསུམ་གཞོམ་མེད་རྡོ་རྗེའི་རང་ཁམས་སུ་བརྟན་ཅིང་མཚུངས་བྲལ་རྣམ་དཔྱོད་ཀྱི་གདུགས་དཀར་སྲིད་རྩེར་འཁོར་བཞིན་པར་བཞུགས་གསོལ་ནི་གཞིར་བཅས་བསྐྱིན་གྱི་ཕྱུང་པོ་གཞལ་དཀའི་རང་བཞིན་གྱུར། འདིར་ཁུས་པའང་བསྐྱིན་མཚུངས་མེད་གང་གི་ཐུགས་རྗེར་བྲིབ་མ་རླུམ་པོར་བདེ་བར་མཆིས་ལགས། མཚམས་ཞུ། འབྱུང་འགྱུར་ཀྱི་ཆར་ཡང་། མཛད་ཡོངས་སུ་རྫོགས་པའི་མཛེས་སྐུ་སྲུན་བརྟན་གྱི་འཁྲོད་གཞེས་མི་གཡེལ་ཞིང་། ཞར་བྱུང་ཁུས་པའང་རྗེས་བརྩེ་ཐུགས་རྗེ་རྗེད་ཁང་ནས་མི་འདོར་བའི་བཀའ་སློབ་ཕེབས་ངོས་ཀྱང་ནི་ཟླའི་བསྐྱོད་པ་ལྟར་སྐྱོལ་བ་མཁྱེན་ལགས།

ཞེས་སྨྲན་རས་ཀྱི་གཟིགས་པ་འབབ་རྟེགས་རབ་དཀར་ལྷ་རྫས་བཅས་ཁུས་པ་ཆེན་པོས་ཕུལ།

X

༄༅།། རང་ལས་གཞོན་པའི་ཉེ་རིགས་ཀྱི་མྱུ་གུ་སོགས་ལ་ཡི་གེ་བཏང་ན།

༈ སྙིང་དབུས་མི་ཞིག་པའི་ཐིག་ལེར་སེམས་པ་ཡིད་ཀྱི་ནོར་བུའི་གང་དེར། དེང་དབྱར་དཔལ་དར་བའི་ཀ་མ་ལ་ལྟར་ཡང་ཚོའི་གཞི་འོད་འཁྲོ་བཞིན་པ་ནས་ལུགས་གཉིས་རྣམ་དཔྱོད་ཀྱི་དགེ་མཚན་གོང་འཕེལ་དུ་ཡོད་པ་གཞིར་བཅས་པས་བློ་དགའི་ཚོར་བ་སྤྲོམ་པོ་ཐོབ། འདིར་ཡང་གཟུགས་ཕུང་ཁྲོ་རེའི་ངང་ནས་འདི་སྣང་གི་གསེང་བ་རིམ་སེལ་ཡོད། མཚམས་འབྲས། སྐད་མའི་དུས་ནའང་རྒྱུ་ལུས་ཡུན་བརྟན་གྱི་འབད་རྩོལ་མི་སྤོང་དོས། ཕོ་བོ་ཡང་དུང་སེམས་རྡོར་རྗེའི་ངོས་ནས་མི་འདོར་བའི་སོལ་ངོས་ཀྱང་ཡང་ཡང་བྱེད། རྟེན་བཅས་ཟླ་ཆེས་དགེ་བར།

ཡིག་སྐུར་རྣམ་གཞག་ཕྲེན།

XI

༄༅༅། །ཕྱུགས་ཉང་གཞིན་པའི་རིགས་ལ་སྤྲིངས་ཡིག་བྱེད་ན།

༈ ནམ་དཔྱོད་མི་རྟག་རྒྱས་པའི་དགའ་ཚལ་ན། བསོད་ནམས་དཔྱིད་ཀྱི་ཞིང་རྟས་ཉེར་དྲངས་པའི། དགེ་མཚན་དབྱངས་སྙན་དྲི་ཟའི་གླིང་བུ་ཅན། གྲོགས་མཆོག་ཁྱུ་བྱུག་གཞོན་ནུའི་ཞབས་དྲུང་དུ། རྙེད་དཀའི་དལ་རྟེན་གདང་བུའི་ཕྲིར་འཛོམས་ཀྱང་། ངེས་པ་འབྱུང་བའི་གསོག་ཐབས་མཐུ་ཞན་པས། མི་ཁྲིམ་འཇོར་ཡོར་ཚུད་པའི་དི་པོར་ཡིས། སྐྱ་རིང་སྣང་བའི་འོག་ཉམས་མཐོང་འདི་རྟེ། ངརྒྱལ་མང་ཤུལ་རིང་ལམ་ནས་ཚོགས་གཉིས་ཀྱི། ཚོང་ཟོག་དུམས་རྙེད་པའི་དལ་བརྟན་ནི། མི་ནུབ་རྒྱལ་མཚན་རྩེ་མོར་ཞབས་བཀོད་ནས། ཕན་བདེའི་ཀུ་ཆར་འབབ་འདི་བཀའ་དྲིན་དཔལ། འདི་ནང་བདག་ཀྱང་རྣམ་གཡེང་ཕ་རྩེའི་རིས། ཟིན་མེད་ཐགས་སུ་འཛིང་པའི་རྒྱུ་སྲིན་གྱིས། མཇུག་ཆུང་ཚེས་འདིའི་རྣམ་བུ་སྐྱབ་པ་ལས། ཡང་དག་ལྷ་བའི་རི་མོས་དབེན་བཞིན་གནས། མཚམས་ཅུས། སྙད་མའི་ཆར་ཡང་ཕྲེད་སྐུ་ཉིན་མོར་བྱེད། ཞིང་འདིར་སྨུན་སེལ་མགོན་པོ་རྟག་བརྟན་ནས། ས་ལ་བདེ་སྐྱིད་རྫོགས་ལྡན་པད་མོའི་ཁ། རྒྱ་ཆེར་བཞད་པའི་དགེ་མཚན་གསལ་བར་མཛོད། དེ་སྐད་ཞུ་མཆིད་གསེར་གྱི་སྦྲེམ་བུ་ནས། རབ་དཀར་དར་གྱི་འདབ་མ་ལྷན་ཅིག་ཏུ། བསྐྱེད་སྦྱིན་གང་གི་དྲུང་དུ་འབུལ་ཏེ་སོང་།།

XII

Letter from De-pa Nor(rgyas)pa, Manager of *Sawang* Phalha's Estates at Gyan-tse to Sarat Chandra Das, in 1883.

བསོ་བ་རིག་པའི་གཞུང་ལུགས་ལ་མཆོག་ཏུ་མཁས་པ་པཎྜི་ཏ་ཤྲཱི་ཤ་ར་ཙནྡ་དཱ་ལགས་མཆོག་གི་སྐུ་ཞབས་སུ། འབུལ་འབྲས། སྐུ་ཉིད་ཞབས་ལམ་བགྲོད་བདེའི་ཐོག་རང་ཡུལ་དུ་ཕེབས་འཁོར་བཅུ་འགྲོ་ལ་ཚ་གདུང་ནད་བསེལ་བགྱི་དོན་མཛད་ཀྱི་བརྟུགས་པ་ངར་སྣང་ཆེ། འདིར་ཕྱིན་བཟའ་མི་བུ་བཅས་ལུས་འཚོ་བདེ་ཐོག་བློ་དཔོན་ཞབས་ཞུས་མཆོད་འཕོས་བསྟུན་བགྱིས་ཆོ་རིམ་བསེལ་དུ་གནས་ལགས། མཚམས་ཞུ། ད་ལམ་སྐྱབས་གཅིག་སེང་ཆེན་རིན་པོ་ཆེ་བརྒྱུད་ཕྱིན་ལ་དེ་ནས་ཕྱག་བྲ་དང་། གནང་སྐྱེས་ཀུ་ཤའི་དཀར་ཡོལ་ཞབས་བཅས། དཀར་སྔེར་ལུགས་སྔེར་ཆ་གཅིག། སོག་བུ་ཁ་ཤས། ཕྱིན་གྱི་བཟའ་བྲར་ལུགས་སྔེར་ཆ་གཅིག་བཅས་གནང་སོགས་བྱུང་བས་མཛངས་ལྡན་ཉ་བར་དབྱར་ཅ་ཆེའི་སྒྲ་ཐོས་ལྟར་དགའ་སྤྲོས་དཔག་མེད་ཐོབ་པས་ཐུགས་རྗེ་ཆེ། སྔ་ལོའི་ཡིག་བསྐུར་ནམ་བཞག་འཕྲོ་བར་འགོ་གསུམ་པོ་གསར་ཤུས་ཀྱི་འབུལ་དགོས་ཐད་ཕྱིན་ནས་འཕྱུར་མེད་ཀྱི་གསར་ཤུ་མ་བྱུས་པ་གཏན་ནས་མིན་ལགས་ཀྱང་། ད་ཕན་བློ་དཔོན་ཞབས་ཞུ་སོགས་ཕྲེལ་ཟིང་ཅི་ཆེ་ཡོད་ནས་གསར་ཤུ་འབུལ་བཙོང་མ་ཐུབ། ད་ལམ་འབུལ་མཆོད་ཀྱང་སྡེ་གཅིག་ཙམ་བྱུང་མ་སོང་དར་དགོངས་འཛིན་མི་བཞེས་པ་དང་། རྗེས་སུ་ཕམ་རིང་ནས་རྡོ་གླིང་བརྒྱུད་ཕྱག་དཔེ་གསར་ཤུ་དང་ཡི་གེ་བཅས་ངེས་འབུལ་ཞུས་ཆོག་པ་ཐུགས་འཛིན་ནས། སྙད་མར་ཡང་། དར་བཀྲུས་འཕྱུར་བཙུས་མཛོད་གྲུབ་པའི་སྐུ་འཚོར་ཟབ་བཞེས་ཐོག་འདི་ཕྱོགས་གནས་ཚུལ་ཀྱང་ཡང་ཡང་ལྷ་ཆུའི་རྟྭན་ལྟར་སྐུལ་བ་མཁྱེན། མཁྱེན། གནང་རྟེན་ལྷ་རིག་བཅས་རྒྱལ་རྩེ་ནས་ནོར་རྒྱས་པས་ཕུལ།།

APPENDIX IX.

The love-songs of the 6th Dalai Lama Tshang-yang Gya-tsho.

༄༅། ཚངས་དབྱངས་རྒྱ་མཚོ་འི་མགུལ་གླུ་སྙན་འཕྲུགས་ཀྱིས་བཀོད་པ་བཞུགས་སོ།།

༄༅། ཤར་ཕྱོགས་རི་བོའི་རྩེ་ནས། དཀར་གསལ་ཟླ་བ་ཤར་བྱུང་། མ་སྐྱེས་ཨ་མའི་ཞལ་རས། ཡིད་ལ་འཁོར་འཁོར་བྱས་བྱུང་།།

ན་ནིང་བཏབ་པས་ལྗང་གཞོན། ད་ལོ་སོག་མའི་ཕོན་ལྕུག། ཕོ་གཞོན་རྒས་པས་ལུས་པོ། ལྷོ་གཞུ་དེ་ལས་རྒྱུང་བའི།།

རང་སེམས་སོང་བའི་མི་དེ། བཏན་ཀྱི་མདུན་མར་བྱུང་ན། རྒྱ་མཚོ་འི་གཏིང་ནས་ནོར་བུ། ཐོན་པ་དེ་དང་མཉམ་བྱུང་།།

འགྲོ་ཞོར་ལམ་བུའི་སྙིང་ཤུབ། ལུས་དྲི་ཞིམ་པའི་བུ་མོ། གཡུ་རྐྱང་གྱུ་དཀར་རྙེད་ནས། སྐྱུར་བ་དེ་དང་འདྲ་བྱུང་།།

མི་ཆེན་དཔོན་པོ་འི་སྲས་མོ། ཁམས་འབྲས་མཚར་ལ་བལྟས་ན། ཁམ་སྡོང་མཐོན་པོ་འི་རྩེ་ན། འབྲས་བུ་སྨིན་པ་འདྲ་བྱུང་།།

སེམས་པ་ཕར་ལ་ཤོར་ནས། མཚན་མོ་འི་གཉིད་ཐེབས་གཅིག་གི། ཉིན་མོ་ལག་ཏུ་མ་ཡོན། ཡིད་ཐང་ཆད་རོགས་ཡིན་པས།།

མེ་ཏོག་ནམ་ཟླ་ཡལ་སོང་། གཡུ་སྦྲང་སེམས་པ་མ་སྐྱོ། བྱམས་པ་ལས་འགྲོ་ཟད་པར། ང་ནི་སྐྱོ་རྒྱུ་མི་འདུག།

རྩི་ཐོག་བ་མོ་འི་ཁ་ལ། སྤྱང་སེར་ལྕུང་གི་ཕོ་ཉ། མེ་ཏོག་སྦྲང་བུ་གཉིས་ཀྱི། འབྲལ་མཚམས་བྱེད་མཁན་ཡོས་ཡིན།།

ངང་པ་འདམ་ལ་ཆགས་ནས། རེ་ཞིག་སྡོད་དགོས་བསམས་ཀྱང་། མཚོ་མོ་དར་ཁ་བསྒྲིགས་ནས། རང་སེམས་ཀོ་ཤག་ཆོད་སོང་།།

གྲུ་ཤན་སེམས་པ་མེད་ཀྱང་། རྟ་མགོས་ཕྱི་མིག་བལྟས་བྱུང་། ཁྲེལ་གཞུང་མེད་པའི་བྱམས་པས། ང་ལ་ཕྱི་མིག་མི་ལྟ།།

ཆུང་འདྲིས་བྱམས་པའི་རླུང་བསྐྱེད། ལྕང་མའི་ཕོགས་ལ་བཙུགས་ཡོད། ལྕང་སྲུང་ཨ་ཇོ་ཞལ་ངོས། རྡོ་ཀ་རྒྱག་པ་མ་གནང་།།

བྲིས་པའི་ཡི་གེ་ནག་ཆུང་། ཆུ་དང་ཐིག་པས་འཇིགས་སོང་། མ་བྲིས་སེམས་ཀྱི་རི་མོ། སུབ་ཀྱང་སུབ་རྒྱུ་མི་འདུག།

རྒྱབ་པས་ནག་ཆུང་ཐེ་འུས། གསུང་སྐད་འཕྲིན་ནི་མི་ཤེས། ཁྲེལ་དང་གཞུང་གི་ཐེའུ། སོ་སོ་འི་སེམས་ལ་སྒྲོན་དང་།།

སྤྲབས་ལྷན་ཏ་ལོ་འི་མེ་ཏོག། མཆོད་པའི་རྫས་ལ་ཕེབས་ན། གཡུ་སྦྲང་གཞོན་ནུ་ང་ཡང་། ལྷ་ཁང་ནང་ལ་ཁྲིད་དང་།།

སེམས་སོང་བུ་མོ་མི་བཞུགས། དམ་པའི་ཆོས་ལ་ཕེབས་ན། ཕོ་གཞོན་ང་ཡང་མི་སྡོད། རི་ཁྲོད་འགྲིམ་ལ་ཐལ་འགྲོ།།

མཚན་ལྡན་བླ་མའི་དྲུང་དུ། སེམས་འཁྲིད་ཞུ་བར་ཕྱིན་པས། སེམས་པ་འཁོར་ཀྱང་མི་ཐུབ། བྱམས་པའི་ཕྱོགས་ལ་ཤོར་སོང་།།

སྒོམ་པ་བླ་མའི་ཞལ་རས། ཡིད་ལ་འཆར་རྒྱུ་མི་འདུག། མ་སྒོམ་བྱམས་པའི་ཞལ་རས། ཡིད་ལ་ལྷ་ལེ་ལྷུ་ལེ།།

སེམས་པ་འདི་ལ་འགྲོ་འགྲོ། དམ་པའི་ཆོས་ལ་ཐེར་ན། ཚེ་གཅིག་ལུས་གཅིག་ཉིད་ལ། སངས་རྒྱས་ཐོབ་པ་འདུག་གོ།།

དག་པ་ཤེལ་རི་གངས་ཆུ། ཀླུ་བདུད་རྡོ་རྗེ་ཟིལ་པ། བདུད་རྩི་སྨན་གྱིས་ཐབ་རྒྱུན། ཆང་མ་ཡེ་ཤེས་མཁའ་འགྲོ།།

དམ་ཚིག་གཙང་མས་བཏུང་ན། ངན་སོང་མྱོང་དགོས་མི་འདུག།

རླུང་རྟ་ཡར་འགྲོ་འི་དུས་ལ། རླུང་བསྐྱེད་དར་ལྕུག་བཙུགས་པས། འཛོང་མ་མ་བཟང་བུ་མོ་འི། མགྲོན་པོ་ལ་བོས་བྱུང་།།

སྙན་འགྱུགས་ཀྱིས་བཀོད་པ།

སོ་དཀར་ཞྭགས་པའི་འཛུམ་མདངས། བཞུགས་གྲལ་སྟེ་ལ་བཀྲམས་ན། མིག་ཟུར་ཕྲ་མོའི་སྒྲིལ་མཚམས། གཞོན་པའི་གདོང་ལ་བཀྲམས་བྱུང་།།

ད་ཅང་སེམས་ལ་སོང་ནས། འཁྲིག་འདྲིས་ཨེ་ཡོང་དྲིས་པས། འཆི་བྲལ་བྱེད་ན་མིན་པ། གསོན་བྲལ་མི་བྱེད་གསུངས་བྱུང་།།

འཛོང་མའི་ཐུགས་དང་བསྟུན་ན། ཚེ་འདི་ཆོས་སྐལ་ཆད་འགྲོ། དབེན་པའི་རི་ཁྲོད་འགྲིམས་ན། བུ་མོའི་ཐུགས་དང་འགལ་འགྲོ།

མཛུམ་དང་སོ་དཀར་སྟོན་ཅིག གཞོན་པའི་བློ་ཁྲིད་ཡིན་འདུག སྙིང་ནས་ཤ་ཚ་ཡོད་མེད། དབུ་མཐའ་ཞེས་རྟོགས་གནང་དང་།།

སྙིང་ཐུབ་ཡིད་འཕྲོག་ལྷ་མོ། རྟོན་པ་ང་རང་ཟིན་ཀྱང་། དབང་ཆེན་མི་ཡི་དཔོན་པོ། ནོར་བཟང་རྒྱ་ལུས་འཕྲོག་སོང་།།

ནོར་བུ་རང་ལ་ཡོད་དུས། ནོར་བུའི་ནོར་ཉམས་མ་ཆོད། ནོར་བུ་མི་ལ་ཤོར་དུས། སྙིང་རྒྱུང་སྟོད་ལ་ཚང་བྱུང་།།

རང་ལ་དགའ་བའི་བྱམས་པ། གཞན་གྱི་མདུན་མར་སླངས་སོང་། ཁོག་ནང་སེམས་པའི་གཅོང་གིས། ལུས་པོའི་ཤ་ཡང་སྐམ་སོང་།།

སྙིང་ཐུབ་ཀུ་ལ་ཤོར་སོང་། མོ་ཆ་རྟེས་འབྲུལ་རན་སོང་། བུ་མོ་དུང་སེམས་ཅན་མ། ཀླུ་ལམ་ནང་ལ་འཁོར་སོང་།།

བུ་མོར་འཆི་བ་མེད་ན། ཆང་ལ་འདོད་པ་མི་འདུག གཞོན་པའི་བརྟན་གྱིས་སྐྱབས་གནས། འདི་ལ་བཙལ་བས་ཐོས་ཆོག།

བུ་མོ་ཨ་མར་མ་སྐྱེས། ཁམ་བུའི་ཤིང་ལ་སྐྱེས་སམ། ཁ་གསར་ཟད་པ་ཁམ་བུའི། མེ་ཏོག་དེ་ལས་མགྱོགས་པས།།

བུ་མོ་རྐྱང་འདྲིས་བྱམས་པ། སྦྲང་གིའི་རིགས་རྒྱུད་མིན་ནམ། ཤ་འདྲིས་ཞྭགས་འདྲིས་བྱུང་ཀྱང་། རི་ལ་ཡར་གྲབ་མཛད་ཀྱིས།།

རྟ་རྒོད་རི་ཡར་རྒྱབ་པ། སྐྱེ་དང་ཞགས་པས་ཟིན་གྱིས། བྱམས་པ་ངོ་ལོག་རྒྱབ་པས། མཐུ་ངོ་ཟིན་པ་མི་འདུག།

སྨག་དང་རྒྱུང་པོ་སྤེབས་ནས། རྐད་པོའི་སྒྲོ་ལ་ཟན་བྱུང་། གཡོ་ཅན་རྫུ་བག་ཅན་གྱིས། ང་ལ་ཟན་པོ་བྱས་བྱུང་།།

སྤྲིན་པ་ཁ་སེར་གཉེར་ནག། སད་དང་སེ་ར་རི་གཉེ་མ། བན་དྷེ་སྐུ་མིན་སེར་མིན། སངས་རྒྱས་བསྟན་པའི་དགྲ་བོ།།

ས་དེ་ཁ་ཞུར་གཏིང་ཁུག། རྟ་ཕོ་གཡོང་ས་མ་རེད། གསར་འགྲོགས་བྱམས་པའི་ཕྱོགས་སུ། སྙིང་གཏམ་བཤད་ས་མ་རེད།།

ཚེས་ཆེན་བཅོ་ལྔའི་ཟླ་བ། ཡིན་པ་འདྲ་བ་འདུག་སྟེ། ཟླ་བའི་དཀྱིལ་གྱི་རི་བོང་། ཚེ་ཟད་ཚར་ནས་འདུག་གོ།

ཟླ་བ་འདི་ནས་ཕར་འགྲོ། གཉིད་མའི་ཟླ་བ་ཚུར་ཡོངས། བཀྲ་ཤིས་ཟླ་བ་དཀར་པོ། ཟླ་སྟོད་ཕྱོགས་ལ་མཇལ་ཡོང་།།

དབུས་ཀྱི་རི་རྒྱལ་ལྷུན་པོ། མ་འགྱུར་བརྟན་པར་བཞུགས་དང་། ཉི་མ་ཟླ་བའི་བསྐོར་ཕྱོགས། ནོར་ཡོང་བསམ་པ་མི་འདུག།

ཚེས་གསུམ་ཟླ་བ་དཀར་བ། དཀར་གོས་ནང་ནས་ཆོད་སོང་། བཅོ་ལྔའི་ནམ་དང་མཉམ་པའི། ཞལ་བཞེས་ཅིག་ཡང་གནང་ཞུ།།

ས་བཅུའི་དབྱིངས་སུ་བཞུགས་པའི། དམ་ཅན་རྡོ་རྗེ་ཆོས་སྐྱོང་། མཐུ་དང་ནུས་པ་ཡོད་ན། བསྟན་པའི་དགྲ་བོ་སྒྲོལ་དང་།།

སྙན་འགྲུགས་ཀྱིས་བཀོད་པ།།

ཁྲུ་བྲུག་མོན་ནས་ཡོངས་པའི། གནམ་ལོ་རི་ས་བཅུད་ཐེབས་སོང་། ང་དང་བྱམས་པ་ཕྲད་ནས། ལུས་སེམས་སྤྲོད་པོར་ཡང་སོང་།།

ཁྲི་དེ་སྟག་ཁྲི་གཟིག་ཁྲི། མདའ་ཁ་སྒྲིར་ནས་འཐྲིས་སོང་། ནང་གི་ཕྱུག་མོ་རས་འཛོམས། འཐྲིས་ནས་མཐུ་རུ་ཡང་སོང་།།

ཤ་འཛམ་ལུས་པོ་འདྲིས་ཀྱང་། བྱམས་པའི་ཞིང་ཆོད་མི་ཡོན། ས་ལ་རི་མོ་བྲིས་པའི། ནམ་མཁའི་སྐར་ཆོད་ཐིག་བྱུང་།།

ང་དང་བྱམས་པའི་སྲིབས་ས། སྐྱོ་རེ་རོང་རྫོན་པའི་ནགས་བཞེབ། སླ་མཁན་དེ་ཙོ་མ་གཏོགས། སུ་དང་གང་གིས་མ་ཤེས།།

སླ་མཁན་དེ་ཙོ་མ་ཤེས། གསང་ཁ་སྟོན་པ་མ་གནང་། ཨ་ས་མི་རྫོགས་མཐུག་ལ། ཀུང་རྒྱལ་མི་གྲུས་དག་པ།།

ང་ལ་ཡོངས་པའི་ཀུང་འདྲིས། ཀུང་རྒྱལ་གཞུང་ན་ཡོད་དེ། ཁྲི་རྐྱན་རྒྱུ་ཟེར་བ། རྣམ་ཤེས་མི་ལས་ཅང་བའི།།

སྒྲོད་ལ་ཡང་སོང་མ་ཟེར། ཐོ་རངས་ཡོག་བྱུང་མ་ཟེར། སྒྲོད་ལ་བྱམས་པ་བཙལ་བའི། ཁ་བ་མང་པོ་འབབ་བྱུང་།།

པོ་ཏ་ལ་རུ་བཞུགས་དུས། རིག་འཛིན་ཚངས་དབྱངས་རྒྱ་མཚོ། ལྷ་ས་ཞོལ་དུ་སྤྱོད་དུས། འཆལ་པོ་དང་བཟང་དབང་པོ།།

གསང་དང་མ་གསང་མི་འདུག། ཞབས་རྗེས་གང་ལ་བཞག་ཉི། ཤ་འཛམ་མཐལ་ས་ནང་གི། སྙིང་ཐུབ་དུང་སེམས་ཅན་མ།།

ཨོ་ཡིས་དགེ་རྐྱེར་འཁྱིག་པའི། གཡོ་སྒྲུ་བཤད་པ་མིན་འགྲོ། དབུ་ཞྭ་དབུ་ལ་བཞེས་སོང་། དབུ་ཞྭ་རྒྱབ་ལ་དགྱེགས་སོང་།།

ག་ལེ་ཐེབས་ཅིག་བྱས་པའི། ག་ལེ་བཞུགས་ཅིག་གསུང་གི། ཐུགས་སེམས་སྐྱོ་ཡོང་བྱས་པའི། མགྱོགས་པོ་འཕྲད་ཡོང་གསུང་བྱུང་།།

བྱ་དེ་ཁྲུང་ཁྲུང་དཀར་མོ། ང་ལ་གཤོག་རྩལ་གཡར་དང་། ཐག་རིང་འགྲུངས་ལ་མི་འགྲོ། ལི་ཐང་བསྐོར་ནས་བསླེབས་ཡོང་།།

ཤི་དེ་དམྱལ་བའི་ཡུལ་གྱི། ཆོས་རྒྱལ་ལས་ཀྱི་མེ་ལོང་། འདི་ནས་ཁྲིག་ཁྲིག་མི་འདུག། རི་ནས་ཁྲིག་ཁྲིག་གནང་ཞུ།།

ཇེ་ཨན་ཏུ།།

མདའ་སོ་འཐེན་ལ་ཐོགས་སོང་། མདེའུ་ས་ལ་འཛུལ་སོང་། ཀུང་འདྲིས་བྱམས་པ་འཕྲད་བྱུང་། སེམས་ཉིད་རྗེས་ལ་འབྲང་སོང་།།

རྒྱ་གར་ཤར་ཀྱི་རྨ་བྱ། ཀོང་ཡུལ་མཐིལ་གྱི་ནེ་ཙོ། འཁྲུངས་ས་འཁྲུངས་ཡུལ་མི་གཅིག། འཛོམས་ས་ཆོས་འཁོར་ལྷ་ས།།

མི་ཚོ་ང་ལ་ལབ་པ། དགོངས་སུ་དག་པ་ཁག་ཐེག། ཨོ་ཡོ་རི་གོམ་གསུམ་སྦྲ་མོ། གནས་མོ་རི་ནང་ལ་ཞལ་སོང་།།

ཕྱུང་མ་བྱི་རུར་སེམས་ཤོར། བྱི་རུ་ཕྱུང་མར་སེམས་ཤོར། སེམས་ཤོར་མཐུན་པ་བྱུང་ན། སྐྱུ་བྲ་ཏོར་པས་མི་ཐུབ།།

ད་སྐྱེའི་ཚེ་འབྱུང་འདི་ལ། དེ་ཁ་ཙམ་ཞིག་ཞུས་ནས། གཉིང་མ་བྲིས་པའི་ཕོ་ལ། མཇལ་འཛོམ་ཨེ་ཡོང་བསྐོར།།

བུ་དེ་སླ་མཁན་དེ་ཙོ། ཁ་རོག་བཞུགས་རོགས་མཛོད་དང་། ཕྱུང་གླིང་ཨ་ཧྲི་འཛོལ་མོ། གསུང་སྙན་སྐྱུར་དགོས་བྱས་བྱུང་།།

རྒྱབ་ཀྱི་བླ་བདུད་བཙན་པོ། འཇིགས་དང་མི་འཇིགས་མི་འདུག། མདུན་གྱི་ཀ་ར་ཀུ་ཤུ། ཐོགས་སུ་དགོས་པ་བྱས་སོང་།།

APPENDIX X.

THE SONG OF THE PRECIOUS REED. *

AS READ OR WRITTEN.

སྨྱུང་མའི་སྨྱུང་བཤད། ལེགས་པ། ཙ་རི་གཞུང་གི་སྨྱུང་མ།།

ཙ་བ་ཉི་ཨ་མ་ཆང་མའི། བྲུང་བཀྲུན་མཉེན་པ་ཡོད་ལ།

བྲུང་བཀྲུན་མི་མཉེན་གསུངས་ན། ཙ་རི་གཞུང་ལ་ཡོག་ནས་འགྲོ།།

སྐྱིད་པ་མགོ་འདྲིན་དཔོན་པོ་འི། ཕྱུས་མདའ་མཉེན་པ་ཡོད་ལ།

ཕྱུག་མདའ་མི་མཉེན་གསུངས་ན། ཙ་རི་གཞུང་ལ་ཡོག་ནས་འགྲོ།།

རྩེ་མོ་མཚན་ལྡན་བླ་མའི། ཕྱུག་སྨྱུག་མི་མཉེན་པ་ཡོད་ལ།

ཕྱུག་སྨྱུག་མི་མཉེན་གསུངས་ན། ཙ་རི་གཞུང་ལ་ཡོག་ནས་འགྲོ།།

AS SUNG.

༄༅།། སྨྱུང་མི་ལ་སྨྱུང་བཤད། ལེགས་ལ་པ། ཙ་རི་གཞུང་གི་སྨྱུང་ལ་མ། ཙ་རི་གཞུང་གི་སྨྱུང་ལ་མ།

ཙ་བ་ཉི་ཨ་མ་ཆང་ལ་མི། བྲུང་བཀྲུན་མཉེན་པ་ཡོད་ལ་ཟེ། བྲུང་བཀྲུན་མཉེན་པ་ཡོད་ལ་ཟེ།

བྲུང་བཀྲུན་མི་མཉེན་གསུངས་ལ་ན། ཙ་རི་གཞུང་ལ་ཡོག་ནས་འགྲོ། ཙ་རི་གཞུང་ལ་ཡོག་ནས་འགྲོ།

སྨྱུང་མི་ལ་སྨྱུང་བཤད་ལེགས་ལ་པ། ཙ་རི་གཞུང་གི་སྨྱུང་ལ་མ། ཙ་རི་གཞུང་གི་སྨྱུང་ལ་མ།

སྐྱིད་པ་མགོ་འདྲིན་དཔོན་ལ་པོ་འི། ཕྱུག་མདའ་མཉེན་པ་ཡོད་ལ་ཟེ། ཕྱུག་མདའ་མཉེན་པ་ཡོད་ལ་ཟེ།

ཕྱུག་མདའ་མི་མཉེན་གསུངས་ལ་ན། ཙ་རི་གཞུང་ལ་ཡོག་ནས་འགྲོ། ཙ་རི་གཞུང་ལ་ཡོག་ནས་འགྲོ།།

སྨྱུང་མི་ལ་སྨྱུང་བཤད་ལེགས་ལ་པ། ཙ་རི་གཞུང་གི་སྨྱུང་ལ་མ། ཙ་རི་གཞུང་གི་སྨྱུང་ལ་མ།

རྩེ་མོ་མཚན་ལྡན་བླ་མའི། ཕྱུག་སྨྱུག་མཉེན་པ་ཡོད་ལ་ཟེ། ཕྱུག་སྨྱུག་མཉེན་པ་ཡོད་ལ་ཟེ།

ཕྱུག་སྨྱུག་མི་མཉེན་གསུངས་ལ་ན། ཙ་རི་གཞུང་ལ་ཡོག་ནས་འགྲོ། ཙ་རི་གཞུང་ལ་ཡོག་ནས་འགྲོ།།

---

* *The slender Bamboo Reed, about a foot long, by means of which* Murwa *beer is drunk in Sikkim and Bhutan.*

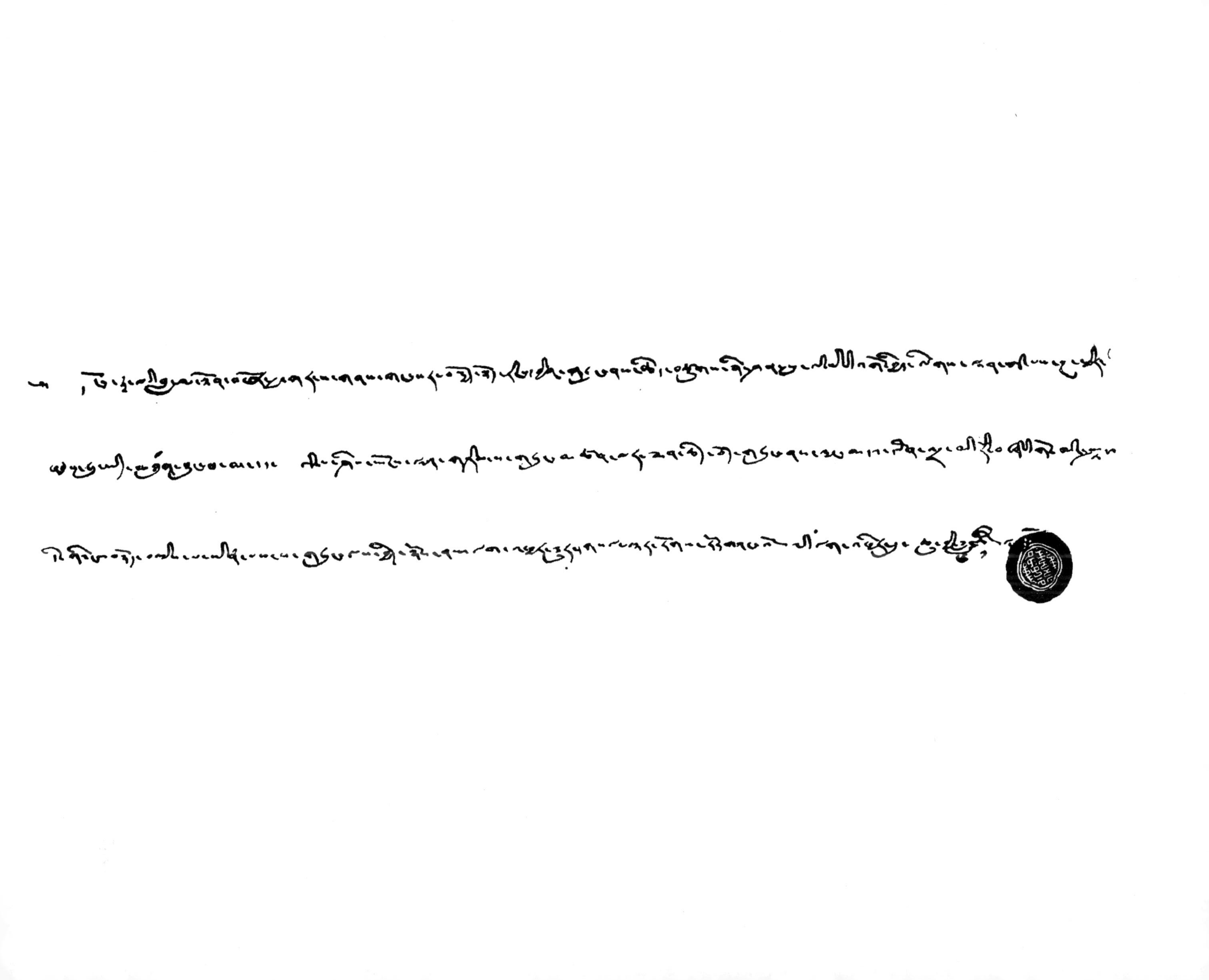

[illegible]

[illegible]

[illegible]

APPENDIX XI.

ལག་འཁྱེར།

བཀའ་ཤོག།

༄༅། ཇོས་ཏཱ་ལའི་བླ་མ་སྟོན་འཁོར་རྒྱ་གར་ས་གནས་གང་སར་བསྐྱོད་སྐོར་རིང་དབྱིན་གཞུང་ * ནས་ཆེད་བཙུགས་སྣེ་ཤན་པུ་ལི་སིའི་འགོ་བྱེད་ལེགས་ལྡན་འདི་པས་ཐ་ཕྱིར་ཞབས་ཞུ་ཡིད་མཐུན་བྱུང་བ་མ་ཟད། འདི་པ་ཤེས་ཡོངས་ལྡན་གཤིས་ས་ †གཞུང་མཚན་ཡར་སྐྱན་(ཡན)ཆེད་བོད་གཞུང་ ‡ནས་ཀྱང་མདའ་དཔོན་འདྲ་བའི་རིམ་པ་བཞིའི་གོ་མིང་སྤྲད་དེ་གཟེངས་བསྟོད་བགྱིས་པ་ཡིན་པས་ས་གཞུང་ལས་བྱེད་རྣམས་ནས་ལག་འཁྱེར་ཟུར་གསལ་ལྟར་རོགས་རམ་གནང་འོས་ཀྱི་ལག་འཁྱེར་དུ། ཆུ་བྱི་ཟླ་ཚེས་ལ། Seal of the Tālai Lama.

(༦ ༡)

Translation.

DIPLOMA.

When I, Tālai Lama with my Court, sojourned in India, to whatever place of pilgrimage I went, Legs-ldan, Head Police Officer, being especially deputed by the British Government as a guide, rendered satisfactory service, from the first to the last. He knows (his work) fully. That he may, for the good name of the (British) Government do better services, the Tibetan Government has complimented him with the 4th class title and (military) rank like that of M̲dah̲-d̲pon. That British Officials may know from this his fitness to deserve their kind help, this diploma, dated the 1st of the 6th month, year *water-mouse*, July 1913 (is granted to him).

---

* དབྱིན་གཞུང་། or ས་གཞུང་། (དབྱིན་ d̲byin stands for English, and ས for *Sarkar*) British Government.

† གཞུང་། literally signifies centre or central, but is ordinarily used to signify Government.

This letter-patent, bearing the red round seal of the Tālai Lama, was granted to Mr. S. W. Laden La, of the Bengal Police. He assisted me in the Press, when my Tibetan-English Dictionary was in the course of being printed.—*Sarat Chandra Das.*

གཤིས is a term of emphasis, signifying 'certainly'.

ལག་འཁྱེར།

བཀའ་ཤོག།

༄༅། *ས་སྟེང་ནང་བསྟན་ཡོངས་ཀྱི་བདག་པོ་ཏཱ་ལའི་བླ་མ་†སྐྱན་འཁོར་བསྟན་དོན་གལ་ཆེའི་སྐོར་དུ་རྡོ་རྗེ་གླིང་དུ་བསྐྱོད་སྐབས་དབྱིན་གཞུང་གིས་ཆེད་འཛུགས་གནང་བ་ཊི་སི་ཀྲིག་སུ་པར་ཨིན་ཊན་ཊན་ཨར་སྭ་ཀྱི་ལི་ལེགས་ལྡན་ནས་ངོས་སྐྱན་འཁོར་རྒྱ་གར་འཕགས་ཡུལ་གྱི་གནས་ཆེན་མཇལ་བསྐྱོད་སྐབས་བབས་རྒྱུས་མངའི་ཞབས་འགྱུར་དང་། འདི་ཕྱོགས་ལོ་ངོ་གསུམ་ཙམ་སྡོད་རིང་དབྱིན་གཞུང་བཀའ་འབྲེལ་སྐོ་ཤན་གྱི་བཀྱིས་སྒོ་གང་ཅིར་ཡིད་མཐུན་འཁྱུར་ཆེ་གང་ལེགས་བྱུང་དོན་ལེགས་སྐྱེས་གཟེངས་བསྟོད་ཆེད་རིན་ཆེན་དང་པོའི་རྟགས་སྨ་སྤྲད་པ་དབྱིན་གཞུང་ལས་དོན་མཛད་པོ་ཁག་ནས་དེ་དོན་ཕན་ཆ་ཡོད་པ་ཆུ་བྱིའི་ལག་འཁྱེར་དུ་རྟ་ཕྱི་བོད་ཟླ་ཚེས་ལ།
༥ ༢༥

Seal of the Tibetan Government.

Translation.

DIPLOMA.

During the visit of the Tālai Lama, Buddha's Vice-Regent on Earth, with his Court, to Darjeeling for an important religious purpose, when (His Holiness) was accorded a most cordial reception by the British Government (Mr.) Legs ldan, District Deputy Superintendent (of Police was on duty). When, under Government orders, he acted as a guide during His Holiness' and party's sojourn extending over two years, including pilgrimage in the sacred-places of *Ärya-deça* India, he behaved becomingly and rendered satisfactory service. In recognition of these (the Tibetan Government) confers on him a gold medal (and hopes) some Government Officers will know from this that Legs-ldan has been useful (to His Holiness). This letter-patent is dated (To-mo), the 25th of the 5th Tibetan month, year *water-mouse*, June 1913.

---

* ནང་བསྟན་ the orthodox Buddhism *i.e.* according to the doctrines of the *Tripiṭaka*; opposed to ཕྱི་བསྟན the religion of the outsiders; heretical.

† སྐྱན་འཁོར། The Court (of the Dalai Lama) comprising, གསོལ་དཔོན། Sol-pon, གཟིམས་དཔོན། Zim-pon, ཆོས་དཔོན། Choi-pon, སྐུ་བཅར་མཁན་པོ། Ku-char khan-po, གཙན་པོ་གུང་། Tsan-po-Kûng, ཛ་སག། Dsa-sag, ཏཱ་བླ་མ། Tālama, བློན་ཆེན་གཉིས། Lon-chen gñis the two Chief ministers (Sha-dā and Shol-khang). (See the Frontispiece).

The first gold medal made at Lhasa and awarded by the Dalai Lama, in 1912, to Mr S.W. Laden La in recognition of services rendered to His Holiness in India.

Analysis of the Appendices.

APPENDIX I.

IDENTIFICATION

(of the soul of a deceased Lama with that of a Child-Pretender).

BY command of the Emperor of China, the 14th Hierarch of the *Karma-pa* (Buddhist Sect of Tibet) was entitled *Shulai Tā-pau-wa Wang-Zi-then tsi-tsā hu-o* Lord over the monasteries of *Szi-then* western country (Tibet). He bore the religious name of Theg-pa M̲chog-gi R̲dorje (in Sanskrit, *Parama Vajra Jñana*). His rescript runs thus :—

Hear and be sure, ye the general public of Jambu dvipa and particularly the clergy and the laity, great and low, the Lamas and the priests, the Ruling King, the ministers, captains and lieutenants, &c. (of Sikkim). Whereas this son of the Ruling King *Dharma-Raja* (of Sikkim) being identified by me as the embodiment of the soul of *Karma* Rin-chen n̂es̲-don b̲s̲tan h̲dsin (the deceased) nephew of Kun-M̲khyen Situ Rin-poche of M̲do-Khams̲, and also installed as High-Priest, has been placed on his seat and given (the religious) name of *Karma* sgrub b̲rgyud̲ b̲s̲tan h̲dsin dar r̲gyas̲ lhun-grub n̂es̲-don d̲van-po. He having duly graduated himself in the (holy) Orders of d̲ge-tshul (*Çramaṇera*) and d̲ge-s̲lon̂ (*Çramaṇa*) and having received consecration and initiation in the deep training of the new and older forms of mysticism, to turn an adept thereunto, has been appointed bishop over the following monasteries of his own sect :—

(1) *Karma* Rab-b̲s̲tan glin̂.
(2) *Karma* B̲kraçis̲ chos̲-h̲khor̲-glin̂.
(3) *Karma* Chos̲-h̲khor̲ glin̂.
(4) *Karma* H̲chi-med̲ r̲gyan d̲ven.
(5) *Karma* Grub-b̲rgyud̲-b̲s̲tan dar glin̂.

The (new) incarnate Lama, by adopting the best means and methods of work, should with unflagging zeal, exert himself to the propagation of the religion of Buddha and work impartially and without prejudice. The religious classes should obey the Lama's behests, observe the customary laws and canonical regulations and act according to the established methods. The faithful believers and alms-givers should also pay him due respect, venerate and obey him.

This letter was issued on an auspicious date in the year *water-tiger* from the great Buddhist College of Hog-min in Tshor-phu.

ཕྱོགས་དུས། abbreviation of དཀོན་མཆོག་གི་ཕྱོགས། དཀར་ཕྱོགས and དུས་གསུམ། present, past and future.

རབ་འབྱམས། same as རབ་འབྱོར, excellent; become supremely good.

འཕྲིན་ལས། high office or commission.

དབང་བསྒྱུར། to endow with power or authority or spiritual sanctity.

གོང་མ་ཆེན་པོ་། The Supreme Ruler; Emperor.

གཙུ་ལའི། གནང་བའི conferring.

རྒྱ་པཙྭ་བ་ལྟར་། ནོར་བུ་འདྲ་བ་དང་། ཆེན་པོ precious like a gem great and kingly.

ཐྲེ་ཐེན། western country, Tibet.

རྗེ་ཙུ་ཏུར། སྐྱེས་བུ་དམ་པ his holiness; saintly personage.

གཏམ statement here signifying rescript or decree.

སེར clergy, priest.

སྐྱ laymen, laity.

འཆད། explaining, རྩོད། disputation, religious controversy; བརྩམ། mis-spelt for རྩོམ composition, writing books.

དྭངས་ལེན taking one's order or wish in the spirit it is delivered; obeying implicitly and cheerfully.

སྐྱེམས mis-spelt for སྐྱེབས

ཡོན as in མཆོད་ཡོན and མཆོད་གནས། ཡོན་བདག lit. gift to Lamas, but ordinarily for སྦྱིན་བདག *dānā-pati*, alms-giver.

APPENDIX II.

(Marriage of *Lha-ding Princess* Yeçes sgrol-ma with the Sikkim Mahārājā Thu-tob Namgyal and his half-brother Hphrin-las Namgyal in 1882.)

In the beginning of the year *water* m. *horse*, 1882, the marriage of Mahārājā Thu-tob Namgayal and his half-brother Thin-leh Namgal with Ye-çe Dolma, Princess Lhading of Lhasa, was definitely arranged for. All preliminaries, according to the customs of Tibet, having been gone through, the marriage took place in the autumn of the same year. The geneology of the Lhading family, on the father's side is given, tracing its origin to the Çākya race of ancient India. This is followed by the account of several ancestors of the bride on the mother's side, and the services the ancestors of the two lines had rendered to Government. Then comes the presentation of what is called the proposal-wine (sloṅ-chaṅ) and the bride's price-wine (*Rin-chaṅ*); these being ceremonially performed on auspicious dates, the bride-groom's party was received in pomp and the marriage was duly celebrated with festive entertainments.

Then comes a description of the jewellery, ornaments, clothes, dresses, &c. (to be given to the bride), in a separate list.

Then follows an enumeration of the duties, both of the bride-groom and the bride, towards each other, and also to their respective fathers-in-law and mothers-in-law, the paying of due respect to them being strictly enjoined on them. Here the name of the Mahārājā's half-brother has been specially mentioned as the bride's joint-husband (thereby legalizing her marriage with him as well, according to the custom of polyandry prevailing in Tibet.) The parents of the bride here exhort their daughter to be equally faithful to her chief and joint-husband. The marriage deed concludes with the signatures and seals of the Mahārājā's mother, half-brother, and also those of Lhading Kusho and his sons, and the marriage witnesses, &c.

ལྷ་སྡིངས a particular family name, ལྷ་ལྕམ princess, a nobleman's wife; equivalent to *Rānee* or *Mahārānee*.

དམ་ཆོས holy religion, Buddhism; in Sanskrit, *Sad-dharma*. དབྱར་སྐྱེས་རྔ་སྒྲ། summer-produced drum-sound, *i.e.*, the rattling thunder of summer. འདོད་པའི་རྒྱལ king of love *i.e.* Cupid, *Kāma-deva*. རྒྱལ་བའི་ཡུམ lit. the mother of all Buddhas; the Goddess Tārā, deliverence or *Nirvāṇa* personified. In the *Ñiṅ-ma* or *Karmapa Tāntrik* School she is called the goddess *Kuru Kullé*. The later *Tāntriks* make her the *Çakti* of the Buddhas. ནོར་སྦྱིན་ལྷ the god who dispenses wealth; he is called མ་ཕམ the conquerable one. འདོད་དགུའི་ཆར the rain of wished for things དགུ signifies, 'many'. དམ་ཅན fearful spirits who used to do mischief to the Buddhist were bound down under solemn oaths to defend Buddhism. དམ་ཅན lit. under vow or oath.

ཕྱག་རྒྱ (*S. mudrā*) mystic configuration, represented by thumb-impression on deeds and contracts of a solemn nature. རབ་བྱུང་། the Cycle of 60 years introduced, in Tibet, in A.D. 1026, from Sanchi (*Çrīdhānya Kaṭaka* in Southern India. Its first year being designated *Prabhava* Rab-byuṅ the Cycle itself came to be known by the name Rab-byuṅ. སྣ་ཚོགས *chitra* the variegated one, it is the 16th year of the Cycle, in Tibetan ཆུ་ཕོ་རྟ་ལོ *Water*-male-*horse* year. (See Appendix V).

ཧོར་ལུགས according to the Calendar that was introduced in China by the early members of Tā-Yuan or the great Tartar dynasty of Mongol Emperors.

དཔྱིད་ར། / སྟག་གི་ཟླ་བ } spring (season) month, *i.e.* April, called the *Tiger* month.

འཕགས་ཆེན་ཐུགས་རྗེའི་གཏེར the most holy mine of mercy, *i.e. Boddhisattva Mahā Kāruṇika* or Avalokiteçvara. གདུལ་ཞིང་། the sphere of Avalokiteçvara's work of converting people into Buddhism. ཆོལ་ཁ་གསུམ the three great Provinces of Tibet. ས་ཚིགས geographical divisions.

ཆོས་ཀྱི་ཆོལ་ཁ the Province (where Buddhism flourished) comprised དབུས and གཙང (U and Tsang).

ལྷོ་རོང the name signifying the Southern country of defiles or ravines, was given to Sikkim and its neighbourhood by the Tibetans.

འབྲས་མོ་ སྨིན་པའི་ འདུན་ས་ སྦ་གནས་ དཀར་མོ་ ལྗོངས

Rice, ripening, lovely land, hidden place, white, cultivated field or cultivation is the full name by which Sikkim is known to the learned of Tibet. Its abbreviation is འབྲས་ལྗོངས། land of rice-cultivation.

ས་ལ་སྤྱོད་པའི་རྒྱལ་པོ lit. the King who subsists on land produce (*Bhû-bhuja*). The Tibetans address the Mahārājā of Sikkim as འབྲས་ལྗོངས་ས་སྤྱོད་པ (in Sanskrit, *Bhû-bhuja*).

ཟབ་ཤེས wife. གནམ་བསྐྱོས Heaven-protected, celestial.

དགའ་བ་བརྒྱ་དང་ལྡན་པ་ཕོ་བྲང་པ་ཆེན་པོ is the pedantic name of the present Lhasa Government. Its common and simple designation is སྡེ་པའི་གཞུང་། *Debā-shûng* the Government under a religious sect *i.e.*, of the *Gelug-pa* or Yellow-Cap Sect; on coins its name is inscribed as དགའ་ལྡན་ཕོ་བྲང་ཕྱོགས་ལས་རྣམ་རྒྱལ། The palace of (*Tuṣita*) victorious in all quarters. *Tuṣita* is the name of the Buddhist Paradise where Maitreya *Bodhisattva* now presides. He is the coming Buddha.

སྲིད་སྐྱ dominion, Government. ཞབས་འདེགས service as in Civil, Medical or Military Service. མདུན་ན་འདོན། (in Sans. *Purohita*) Prime Minister.

གོ་གནས official rank or dignity. བརྒྱད་པ་ཆེན་པ the 8th (Dalai Lama) in succession from བསོད་ནམས་རྒྱ་མཚོ Sonam Gyatsho.

ཞི་དྲག civil or spiritual aud military. ཆེ་ཐོ title or order. ནང་མའི་ལས་ཚན confidential officer of state. ཟམ་མི་ཆད་པ uninterruptedly; without break. རྗེ་དཔོན a chief or district officer. ང་ཕོད་པ name of family.

ཐུ་ཤིའི་གོ་མིང a Chinese title; ཟལ་ནོན་ཏོག་དང་རྨ་མིག decoration of sapphire or ruby button on caps, with peacock's feather thereon.

རྒྱལ་མཆོག་བདུན་པ་ཆེན་པོ the seventh Dalai Lama Kal-zang Gya-tsho བསྐལ་བཟང་རྒྱ་མཚོ།

གོར་བོད་ཐྲེ་གཟར the war between the *Gurkhas* and the Tibetans. *Gor* stands for Gurkha, *Bod* for Tibet; ཐྲེ་གཟར, war; fighting. ཅིའི་ཅིའི hereditary དཔལ་བུ་ལའི་ཆེ་ཐོ་མི་རབ་ཀྱི་དམག་དཔོན་གྱི་གོ་གནས (military rank) n. of a high Chinese hereditary military Order ཆེ་ཐོ, order or dignity.

འབའ་ལི, H̲bah for Bathang and Li for Lithang (two provinces) in Eastern Tibet བར་དགོངས། བར་རྒྱུའི་དགོངས་པ

ཞབས་ཞུར་འགྱུར་རིགས those who were in Government Service. སྤུན་མཆེད brothers and sisters. སློང་སྦྱིར (སློང་། proposal or asking for giving in marriage) སྦྱིར (promise) to give away (in marriage).

མོས by casting lots. ཞིབ་མོལ deliberation; in conference with.

ངོ་ནོན for ཐུགས་ཕན་གསོ་བ, to be of service, or help. ཆབ་ཅིག for ལྷན་ཅིག, together with, in company with.

སྤང་བླངས། སྤང that which is to be avoided or left off; བླངས that is to be taken in earnest, or done or accepted.

གཉན་དཔང་། marriage witness. ཐེཙ also sometimes ཐེཙ, seal or seal impression. ལེགས་བཤད་རིན་པོ་ཆེའི་གཏེར། *Subhāṣita Ratna nidhi* name of a book containing moral sayings, by Çākya Panchen Kungah Gyal-tshan. ཡ་རབ་སྤྱོད་པ། noble deed or conduct; behaviour of the great; high character.

མ་རབ་སྤྱོད་པ mean or sordid action or behaviour. སོར་གནས། སྔར་རྒྱུན་དང་བཞིན as in former custom or procedure.

རྒྱུན་འགྱངས་། at all times, རྟག་པ་རེ་བཞིན། མི་ཤིག cannot be broken. གཡུང་དྲུང་གི་མདུད the knot or tie of marriage solemnized under the symbol of *Swastika*.

སྤྱི་གཉེར the Steward General of Lhasa. དཀར་ཆུང་། name of an individual.

APPENDIX III.

A Pass-port and Road-bill.

This Achārya Purŭñ-giri was sent on a mission for increasing beneficence. During the war between Bhutan and India he saved many souls from untimely death and thereby accomplished a great object. He is hereby granted a life-allowance. Whenever he comes to Tashilhunpo with as many servants as he likes, (he is to get it consisting of) tea, butter, rice, meat, barley-flour, corn-flour, (food for) riding horse, and lade animals he may have with him, all in sufficient quantity. When going to any quarters, he should be furnished with tents, accommodation in houses, ponies or mules for conveyance, beasts of burden and guides, &c., to help him in his journey to any place. His Holiness B̲lo-b̲zañ D̲pal-l̲dan Yeçes d̲pal b̲zañ-po taking a personal interest in his welfare, grants him this letter-patent for his protection and safety, That His Holiness' wish may be honoured by all he has fixed his own seal on it. Accordingly all people great and humble should observe the rule (སྤང་བླང་ཡོང་བ) of "avoiding and doing". (This letter) is dated. (Tashilhunpo) the 1st of the 9th month, year *Tree-serpent* in the 13th cycle (རབ་བྱུང) 1774 A. D.

N.B.—It may be remembered that, at this time, this Tashi Lama was the Supreme Ruler of Tibet.

Official order for Food Allowance, &c., to Purṇagiri.

Conformably to the wish expressed in his holy general order by *Kyab-gon* (Lord-protector) in respect of Achārya Purṇagiri, he will get from the *Government Stores* personal allowance every month in barley flour—3 *Khals* of full *bré* measure; corn-flour 2 *Khals*; one and a half good carcase of sheep (dry or cured in cold air); for his personal attendants, should there be any, 2 *Khals* of barley-flour and 1 *Khal* of corn-flour and one sheep carcase per head. If he has any horse for his personal use, one *bré* measure of bran, for use with water. All these provisions should be of the best (and not of inferior) quality. This order-voucher is dated year *Tree-horse,* the 25th of the 11th month, in the 13th Cycle, 1763 A. D.

Road-bill to Achārya Dharjir-gir.

The *Gan-pos* (village elders or head-men) and the དམངས common people, *Jóng-Pons* and *Shi-Pons* (subordinate *jóngs*) residing on the road from Lhasa *via* Tashilhunpo and Phagri to India, be sure that under order of the Chief High Imperial Commissioner and Confidential Minister *Tûng-thang Chenpo Ácharya* Dharjirgir and his servants bringing letters of the *Shahebs* from Calcutta, while travelling back (to India) at whatever place they may halt or stage, should be supplied with provision for journey, food, fuel, two saddled *yaks*, 5 riding ponies for their conveyance, and ten lade animals with two attendants or *coolies* at every stage.

The letters with enclosures, silk scarves, &c., from *Tung-thang Chenpo* to the *Shahebs* of Calcutta being forwarded by the hand of this (messenger) to a great distance, there should be not the least detention or delay in the transit on the way by the *Jong-Pons, Shi-Pons, Gan-po* and the common people.

It is important that nothing occurs like rambling about on throwing off (of the letter). The date of the starting of this (messenger) being noted in the Register of the *Yasnun* of the Resident Anapa, laziness (on the part of the authorities on the way) will surely necessitate subsequent inquiry. For this reason, do the needful and avoid negligence, &c.

The guide and his servant should be supplied with two *through* relay ponies from Lhasa *via* Tashilhunpho to Phagri and back, besides food and fuel at the halting stages. These should be collected and supplied.

Carry out the above official order of Pass-port and Road-bill issued by the *Gyal-wang-chog* (Dalai Lama). *Water-ox* year, 13th of the 2nd month.

རྒྱ་གར་ཕྱིན་གྱི་ལམ་འཁྱོད lam-ḫkhyod on the road for going to Iudia.

རྫོང་། for *jong* authorities; གཞིས for *shi-kha* authorities.

རྒན for *Gambu* head man (*Panchayit* man). དམངས common people; གོང་མ་བདག་པོ་ཆེན་པོ the Emperor of China.

བཀའི་འཕྲིན་ལས་ཀྱི་གཙོ་བོ the Chief High Commissioner.

ནང་བློན Confidential Minister; ཕྱིར་ཚོག on the return journey.

ཚ་གཞག། ཚ halting at noon and གཞག staying at night.

གྲོ་ཆས་ for འགྲོ་ཆས same as ལམ་ཆས་ provisions &c. for a journey; road-provisions.

རྟ་ཐབས རང་སྐྱེལ relays at every stage; རྟ་ཞུལ ponies supplied by village people, free of cost. རྫས་ཁལ་མ laden animals such as donkeys, yaks, ponies carrying loads; ས་ཚིགས fixed staging or halting places མི་རྗེང cooly without load on his back; བརྫ་གཏོང་། collect man and conveyances for despatching; གཏོང = མདུན།

འདི་པ this man *i.e.*, here this messenger; བཀའ་ཤོ official communication.

གནང་རྟེན enclosure or accompanying presents.

རིང་ཁྱད idiomatically མགྱོགས to expedite despatching.

ལམ་འཕྱོད falling on the way; འགོར་འགྱངས delay and obstruction.

ཟླ་མོ་ཙམ the least, slightest. ཁྱམས for འཁྱམས, rambling about, throwing off.

སྒུར losing; བྱ་ཚེ in the event of doing; ཐོན་ཚེ time of starting or issuing; *Ampa* Chinese Imperial Resident.

ཡ་མོན (Chinese-office); གཞུང་ཁྲ Government Register.

འཁོད་སོང་བ noted down; ལེ་ལོགས laziness or relaxation.

ཤར་ཚེ in the event of occurrence; རྗེས་གཏོན reminder or *Ta-keed*; སྤང what is to be avoided; སྤངས what is to be done as in duty bound, *i.e.*, taken in earnest.

སྣེ་ཤན a guide, one knowing the place; རྫོང་སྐྱེལ through journey from *jong* (district) to another *jong*.

བཀྲིས་ལྷུན for བཀྲ་ཤིས་ལྷུན་པོ Tashilunpho (the grand monastery of).

ལྷ་སྐྱོངས. He protected of Heaven. The name by which Emperor Kuenlung was known to the Tibetans.

APPENDIX IV.

TO HIS MAJESTY THE KING-EMPEROR WHO REIGNETH RIGHTEOUSLY

BY

TURNING THE WHEEL OF GOVERNMENT WITH THE STRENGTH OF HIS MORAL MERITS (*Puṇyabala*).

THE TĀLAĪ LAMA presents his best compliments. Himself and Court, journeying pleasantly, have arrived. Thanks for the excellent arrangements made by the British Government for their residence here. A statement of their difference with the Chinese Ministers has been sent to the Viceroy. Should the Government, taking up the cause in earnest, provide for the present and future (state exigencies) and extend help and protection accordingly, he be tgs to say that these kindnesses will afterwards be gratefully borne in mind.

At present, in the hurry of business, this letter to avoid being sent empty, is accompanied by a long silk-scarf containing holy inscriptions, an image of Buddha of great sanctity, one bell and *Dorje*, gold-dust weighing 15 *Tolas* and 5 pieces of best satin of variegated colours.

ངོ་འཁོར (ངོ self and འཁོར Court or Official retinue); ལམ་འགྲོད journey or travelling; བདེ་ལྡན་ཐོག besides being pleasant; ཕྱི་གཞུང་། British Government; སྡོད་སྒྲིག arrangement for residence; ཡོ་ཆས་ཟབ་བཞེས well furnished; འགྲིགས་མིན disagreement; རོགས་སྐྱོང་། help and protection; དམ་དོན་མཛད espousing the cause earnestly;

བཀྲིན (བཀའ་དྲིན) kindness; སྙིང་བཅངས་ཆོག་པ may be permitted to bear in mind *i.e.* will remember; ལྷ་རྫས lit. divine article *i.e.* silk-scarf; བྱིན་ཅན for བྱིན་རླབས་ཅན possessing sanctity; རྡོ་དྲིལ *i.e.* རྡོ་རྗེ and དྲིལ་བུ signifying thunder-bolt and bell; ཆ་ཚང one pair complete, སྒོར rupee.

TO THE FAITHFUL JAPAN LAMA

WHO IS CHEERFUL IN THE PRACTICE OF BUDDHISM AND SMILING AS THE ANTHERS OF THE EIGHT PETALLED LOTUS OF YOUTH.

IN the year *Tree-serpent*, while at Calcutta, you made me present of a sacred conch-shell encased in a small box. This time you have sent to me the book of the Essence of Buddhist Scriptures in Chinese, through one Buchûng of Kabug (Kalimpong). This having reached here undamaged has pleased me as a medicinal gift. Being in good health, I remain absorbed in the thought about the welfare of all living beings. Now, agreeably to your request, one complete set of *Kahgyur*, cleanly printed will soon be ready for

---

ཛཔ་པན Japan; ངོས lit. by me, here used as 'myself'; མཆེད་ཟླ accompaniment; སྒྲད should be སྒྲོད case or vessel; རོ་ཅོག་གི་སྙིང་པོ the essence or pith which is most delicious. ཉེ་ལམ lately; ཀ་སྦུག (for Kalimpong); བུ་ཆུང་། name of an individual; འདུ་བ constitution, body; འགྲོ་ལ to all living beings, or moving ones; སྨས་པ for སྨན་པ= ཕན་པ to be useful; ངེས་པ་ཕུས་སུ (should be ངེས་པར་ཕུལ་ཕུས་སུ for certainly presenting; རེན་རྫགས་མདུད for རྟེན་རྫགས་མདུད as a symbol of relics and charmed knots; རྫེས (for རྫས article or thing; ལ་ཚན for ལེ་ཚན kinds of things, chapter in books.

presentation to the Buddhist Church of Japan). Please let me know soon when you will come (to take delivery of the same.) Lastly, (I wish) you take care of your health and make progress in doing religious works. You may send me news and topics by and by. This letter of auspicious date is sent with enclosures of a scarf and silken-charmed knot and with several sacred articles together with sanctified relics.

TO THUB-BSTAN RGYA-MTSHO, THE MONGOL ASTROLOGER.

Lately this year in the 7th month our Lord Protector *Dorjechañ*, whose kindness to us all was unrivalled, has passed away. That moral merits may accrue to all living beings, we should offer our prayers for his residence in the holy mansion of *Sakhāvati*, a new sacred *Mausolia* should be erected to enshrine his relics with other like objects, after former precedents. If arrangements for its construction and supply of materials cannot be made here, we shall send orders to that direction for copper sheets &c., where these come from. There, it is hoped, you will, remembering the kindnesses you had received while here, earnestly exert yourself to render assistance, as one knowing the place and the market rate of things.

First (of all) the price per *seer* of copper-sheet which will easily take gold-gilding, should be ascertained, then the price of quick-silver of superior quality in weight, how many ounces or what quantity, in measure, per *rupee* should be ascertained, before purchasing the same. What is the market-price there ; how

---

མཚུངས་ཟླ་མ་མཆིས་པ having no rival or equal ; unrivalled.

རྡོ་རྗེ་འཆང་། *Vajradhara*, the supreme deity of the Lamaic school; his spirit like the Holy Ghost of the Christians is said to descend for inspiring the incarnate Lamas. Hence they are all designated *Dorji-chañ* or Vajradhara.

བསོད་ནམས་ཀྱི་དྭ་བར within the bounds of one's moral merits.

མ་ཆུད་པ=མ་ཤོང་པ could not be contained or kept in.

གཟུགས་སྐུའི་བཀོད་པ mortal frame, in mundane existence.

ཆོས་དབྱིངས་སུ་མནལ་ཚུལ, entering into the spiritual state of existence.

ཞིང་མཆོག་དམ་པར in the paradise of Bde-wa-chan or *Sukhāvati*.

ཐུ་འཕྲོས before all, at the outset.

སྙོན་འཕོར་ཆེ་ཆུང་། much or less in quantity or measure.

ཁེ་སྤྱབས profit arising from.

མཛོན་ཆུང་ཉང་རྩད secretly ascertaining by private inquiry.

གཏན་འཁེལ sure and positive.

སྔགས་མ consecrated with *mantras* or charms.

བཀའ་རྒྱ་མ personal writs.

and with what profit these can be purchased? In ascertaining these less talk and more secrecy and quiet observation should be maintained. Please to send sure and correct information (on these points) by the hand of this man, with enclosure of a *Kha-tag* (silk-scarf) with consecrated relics.

སྔོན་ལམ for སྔར་ལམ according to former precedents.

མཆོད་སྡོང་རིན་པོ་ཆེ the precious holy *Mausolia*, the grand three-storeyed lofty edifices of stone masonry roofed with gold-gilt copper domes, constructed in Chinese style, at Tashi-lhunpo, for enshrining the relics, of the Tashi Lamas.

TO PAṆḌIT *ÇRI* SARAT CHANDRA,

WHO IS WELL VERSED IN ALL THE ARTS.

Presenting special compliments; on hearing that you are in the enjoyment of good health at that place, I got the rarest joy and immense delight. Here, in Tsang, our *Kyab-jé* * *Seng-chen Dorjé-chang* presides over the monastery of Tashi-lhunpo. We all are happy as heretofore. I *Tüng* Choi-dsa<u>d</u>, herewith present, in the auspicious conjunction of events, a light-yellow *Khatag* (silk-scarf) called *Khalkha-choidar* as a sign of my meeting you in no distant time. The details (about here) fit for communication will be conveyed to you by Phurchûng. If you happen to send me any letter, I beg you will kindly do so by the hand of Phurchûng and not through any other person.

ཆེད special; འབུལ offering *i.e.*, compliments; དེ་ཁར there, in that place; ཉིད་སྐུ your person; ཡར་ངོ་ཟླ the increasing moon, crescent. ཕྲན་གྱི་སྣང་བ having come to the knowledge of my humble self.

*མི་གཉིས་པའི་དགའ་དང་། incorrectly written for མི་རྙེད་པའི that can hardly be got.

འདི་ཁ here: བཀྲས་ལྷུན་ for བཀྲ་ཤིས་ལྷུན་པོ; སྐྱབས་རྗེ * is same as སྐྱབས་མགོན one who grants refuge in danger; དབུས་བསྐྱོད་པ become head or president; དྲུང for དྲུང་ཆེན ཕྲན little or humble self; ཆོས་མཛད n. of an individual. དངོས་མཇལ personal interview; མཇལ་མཚོན token of meeting or visit such as a *Khatag*, presentation silk-scarf &c.

Subject-Analysis.

OF

APPENDICES IV—XI.

བཀའ་ཤོག།

THE word མགྲོན་གཉེར། Mgron-gñer literally signifies receiver or entertainers of guests. It is generally applied to an official of the rank of Private Secretary to a great Lama or Chief. Lama Urgyen Gya-tsho, *Rai Bahadur*, while holding the position of Deputy Magistrate at Kalimpong, was appointed to this Honorary Office by His Highness Thutob Namgyal, K.C.I.E. Mahārājā of Sikkim. The Lama belonged to the *Gonsag-pa* sect of Kham which coming from the Do-med District of Mi-ñag, in Ulterior Tibet, had resided for some years at Lhasa and Sakya before finally settling in Sikkim. Several of the Lama's ancestors had rendered good, loyal services to the state for which they were raised to distinction. The Lama had very faithfully served the Mahārājā and his family during the time they were kept as state prisoners at Darjeeling and Kurseong.

THE *Jongpon* of Bumthang in Bhutan འབྲུག་ཡུལ། acknowledges the receipt of a letter and presents comprising of a stone *Chaitya* and other articles sent by the Japanese Buddhist monk, *Ekai* Kawaguchi. He writes him to say that he was pleased with the letter. He was unable to send for the *Kahgyur* (Encyclopœdia of Buddhist Scriptures, in 108 volumes) of Kham, Dergé-print on account of the disturbed state of that country. He has heard from rumour that the printing establishment at Dergé had recently been burnt by the Chinese soldiery. If, however, the rumour proves false, he will send his messenger with *caravans* proceeding to Kham to fetch the *Kahgyur*. He encloses a silk scarf for the Lama's acceptance.

APPENDIX V.

HERE is an enumeration, in Sanskrit, of the names of the cycle of sixty years that was current in Southern India, *i.e.*, in the regions to the south of the River Narmadā. The cycle is called *Vrihaspati Chakra*. It is stated in the *Kala Chakra Tantra* that it was introduced in Uttara Çambhala being taken there from Çridhānya Kaṭaka in very early times. According to Tibetan historians, Chilu *Pandita* introduced the cycle, in Tibet, in 1025 A.D., where it is called Rab-byuñ, in Sanskrit *Prabhava*, from the name of the first year of the cycle. Uttara Çambhala was the name by which the capital of the Bactrian Empire of the Eastern Greeks was known to the Mahāyānā Buddhists. I may identify it with the Sanskrit, Balokshya mentioned in Kṣemendra's *Avadāna Kalpalatā*.

APPENDIX VI.

SARAT CHANDRA made arrangements for his journey, employing Lama Tshering Tashi and Paldor to go with him to Lhasa. Early in the morning of the 25th of the 3rd month, year *Water-horse* 1882, after making reverence to Lama Seng-chen Rimpo-che, he sought refuge in the Three Holies and obtained his blessings. Then, receiving a fare-well scarf from the hands of *Kusho* Tung-chen, he started on his journey. The way lay along the thinly wooded banks of the Myang-chu, a tributary of the Tsang-po. Reaching Gyan-tse, he interviewed Lha-cham *Kusho* in Phala's residential Villa called *Gongyal-gah*. Her ladyship requested him to give some medicine to the *De-pa* of her Gyan-tse estates who was ailing for some times That officer entertained the party with tea, Tibetan dishes, etc., making presents of some fine blankets to Sarat Chandra. These he respectfully returned. Then travelling eastward and keeping the *Shi-kha* of Depon Chang-lo-chan he passed by the *Gelugpa* monastery of Gahdan choi-phelling and Da-khyud village. He then passed a stream coming from the distant snows and the road to Phagri beyond which lay the monastery of Ne-ñing. On both sides of the way there were villages, some of which possessed many deserted roofless houses. He then passed Dsing-rag, formerly a battle-field. Passing by the monastery of Ge-ñen-sum and walking with difficulty on a narrow pathway he crossed the bridge called Kudoong Zampa and arrived at the village of Gobshi where Lha-cham was staging. Here not being able to secure a good lodging, he spent the night in a horse-stall underneath a house. By exposure to cold and snow-storm at night, he fell ill. Next morning, being informed that Lha-chan *Kusho* had left Gobshi, though still very bad in health, he proceeded towards Ralung. Passing by the *Ningma* monastery of Kha-vo, he reached Ra-lung, where, in a corner of the big house where Lha-cham's party was accommodated, he spent a sleepless night. He resumed his journey in the morning, amidst snow-storm and rain. This increased his illness. Passing by the right flank of Kharula, he came to the foot of the snowy mountain called Noijin Khang-zang Then proceeding on his journey, he arrived at a place called Zawa. In the evening, he reached Nagartse. (Nang-kar-tse) Jong situated on the shore of lake Yamdo *Yum-tsho*. Here, his illness having taken a bad turn, he was unable to travel towards Lhasa in the company of Lha-cham. The kind lady gave him a letter of introduction to her cousin, the incarnate Dorje Phagmo (*Vajra-varahi*), the Lady Superior of the great monastery of Samding. He then slowly rode towards Samding. He stayed for a fortnight in the house of one Namgyal, receiving medical treatment from two Tibetan physicians. The incarnate Dorje Phagmo very graciously expressed much anxiety on his account, the illness being acute bronchitis. She sent provisions consisting of barley, flour, tea, butter, mutton, salt, etc., for him. Recovering from his illness he slowly proceeded towards Lhasa and made pilgrimage to the sanctuaries there. He had the audience of the Dalai Lama on the topmost storey of Potala.

APPENDIX VII.

A CLEAR exposition of the doctrine of re-embodiment of the souls of *Bodhisattvas* in general, and incarnations of *Chanre-sig* in the Dalai Lamas. An enumeration of the first six Dalai Lamas. The present Dalai Lama's career delineated, his flight to Mongolia, visit to Peking, and return to Lhasa described. His flight from there and coming to Darjeeling in 1909-10.

An enumeration of the one hundred twenty-five great acts of Buddha Çākya Muni from the time birth of his to his death, and The places where he resided &c.

APPENDIX VIII.

Forms of Correspondence.

I. Letters to be addressed to Jong-pons, De-pa classes &c.
II. Letters to be addressed to one's equals.
III. Letters to be addressed to one's parents.
IV. Letters to be addressed to ladies of high rank.
V. Letters to be addressed to ladies of ordinary rank.
VI. Letters to be addressed to one's wife.
VII. Letters to be sent to women of humbler classes
VIII. Letters to be sent to one's subordinates and servants.
IX. Letters to one's relatives, senior in age and to superiors.
X. Letters to one's relatives, junior in age &c.
XI. Epistles to intimate friends.
XII. A letter from De-pa Nor (gye) pa.

APPENDIX IX.

The love-songs of the sixth Dalai Lama, Tshang-yang Gya-tsho.

APPENDIX X.

The Bhoteas (Tibetan settlers in Sikkim and Bhutan) while picknicking, of which they are very fond, drink *murwa* (half-fermented millet served in bamboo jug, filled with boiled warm water; this they suck through a reed. *Murwa* drink seems more to excite than to debanch the mind.

Sramana Ekai Kawaguchi.
Darjeeling.

An account of the Pilgrimage of Ekai Kawaguchi to the great Sanctuaries of Tibet.

(ཇའ་པན་བླ་མ་ཨེ་ཀའི་ཀ་ཝ་གུ་ཅིའི་བོད་ལ་བསྐྱོད་པའི་རྣམ་ཐར)

༄༅།། བྱང་ཆུབ་གནས་མཇལ།།

༄༅།། ཕྱག་བཙལ་ཐམས་ཅད་བཅོམ་པ་དང་། ཐམས་ལས་འདས་པའི་བདེ་བ་ལྡན།

སེམས་ཅན་གྲོལ་བར་བཙོན་མཛད་པའི། ཤཱཀྱའི་དབང་པོར་ཕྱག་འཚལ་ནས། ༡ ། པཎ་ཊི་ཏ་སྔོན་ཀ་བླ་བ་ལས། *

ཐུགས་དགོས་ཆེན་པོར་གནང་བར་བརྟེན། ཇའ་པན་ཤེས་རབ་རྒྱ་མཚོ་ཡི། † བོད་ལ་འགྲོ་བའི་རྣམ་ཐར་འབྲིས། ༢ །

ༀ འཛམ་གླིང་ཤར་ཕྱོགས་རི་བོ་ཆེ། ཉི་མ་ལ་ཡི་བྱང་ཕྱོགས་ན། སྔོན་རབ་གཟིགས་ཀྱི་དག་པའི་ཞིང་།

དཔལ་ལྡན་བོད་ཡུལ་ཞེས་བྱ་ལ། ༣ །རིག་ཆེན་ཆོས་ཀྱི་རིན་ཆེན་བཞུགས། བྱང་ཆུབ་སངས་རྒྱས་སྤྲུལ་པ་ཡིས།

ཆོས་ཀྱི་མི་རྟག་ས་ལ་བརྒྱན། སྐད་བྱང་འབྲས་བུ་འབྱུང་གནས་ལ། ༤ །བདག་ཉིད་ཇའ་པན་ཨེ་ཀའི་ཡིས།

འགྲོ་བར་སྨོན་པའི་དོན་གཞན་མེད། བོད་སྐད་དམ་ཆོས་བསླབ་པ་དང་། བཀའ་བསྟན་བསྒྲུབ་པའི་སེམས་སྐྱེད་དེ། ༥

ལོ་ནི་བཅུ་བརྒྱད་ཐ་རོལ་ན། མི་བྱ་ལོ་ཡི་ཟླ་དྲུག་པར། ‡ ཇའ་པན་ཡུལ་ནས་གཏོང་ནས་ནི།

རྒྱ་གར་རྡོ་རྗེ་གླིང་དུ་སླེབས། ༦ །གངས་ཅན་མཛོད་ལྔའི་གཟི་བརྗིད་ཀྱིས། རྡོ་རྗེ་ཧོད་ཟེར་འཚར་བའི་གླིང་།

དེར་གནས་པཎ་ཆེན་ཤྲཏ་ཟླ་དང་། སོག་པོ་ཤེས་རབ་རྒྱ་མཚོ་འི་དཔལ། ༧ །ཨ་ས་འི་རྫུང་ཡིག་དབང་ལྡན་དང་།

བཀྲ་ཤིས་ལྷུན་པོ་འི་ཞབས་དྲུང་ལ། བརྟེན་ནས་བོད་སྐད་ལོ་གཉིས་ཙམ། བསླབས་ཤིང་བོད་ལ་འགྲོ་ཐབས་བྱས། ༨

དེ་ལས་རྡོ་རྗེ་གདན་དུ་མཇལ། བདག་གིས་བོད་ལ་འགྲོ་བ་ཡི། རྒྱུན་གྱིས་བོད་ཀྱི་མི་རྣམས་ལ།

བར་ཆད་མ་ཡོང་སྨོན་ལམ་འདེབས། ༩ །དེ་ནས་ཡམ་བུར་འགྲོ་བ་དང་། § མཆོད་རྟེན་རྣམ་གསུམ་མཇལ་བ་དང་།

སངས་རྒྱས་བྱིན་རླབས་ཆེན་པོ་ལ། མིག་རྩ་ཚ་བོ་གཞིན་དུ་བབས། ༡༠ །གངས་ཆེན་པད་མའི་གྲུར་ཕུག་དང་།

གློ་ཡུལ་ཆུ་མིག་བརྒྱ་རྩ་དང་། དྷུ་ལ་གི་རིའི་གངས་ཤར་ལ། མཇལ་ཏེ་སངས་རྒྱས་བྱམས་ཧོད་རྗོམས། ༡༡

ཇ་རངས་ཞུང་པར་བཞུགས་པ་ཡི། དགེ་བཤེས་ཤེས་རབ་རྒྱལ་མཚན་ནས། རིག་གནས་རིག་ཆེན་གསང་སྔགས་རྣམས།

ལོ་གཅིག་ཙམ་ནི་བསླབས་པ་དང་། ༡༢ །དེ་ནས་དབུ་རིའི་བྱང་ངོས་ཀྱི། གངས་ནས་གངས་རིར་ཛོག་པ་དང་།

དཔག་མེད་དཀའ་བ་སྤྱོད་ནས་ནི། ཡེ་ཤེས་གནས་ཆེན་སྤྲོ་པོར་མཇལ། ༡༣ །རི་ལུང་ཆེན་པོ་འི་གངས་འདས་ཏེ།

བྱང་ཐང་བྲག་དཀར་ཐུག་ཏུ་སླེབས། སྒོམ་ཆེན་སྔོ་བཟང་མགོན་པོ་ལས། དམ་ཆོས་ཟབ་དོན་ཐོས་པ་དང་། ༡༤

---

* སྔོན་ཀའི་བླ་བ, ཤ་ར་ཏ་ཙནྡྲ། † ཤེས་རབ་རྒྱ་མཚོ Ekai in Japanese. ‡ མི་བྱ་ལོ 1897 A. D.

§ ཡམ་བུ by this name Katmundu the Capital of Nepal is known to the Tibetans.

མ་ཧེ་ལུང་དང་གསང་སྔགས་ཀྱི། དབང་ཉམས་ཞུས་ཏེ་ཞག་འགའ་འདས། གངས་རིན་པོ་ཆེར་འགྲོ་བ་ཡི།
ལམ་ནི་ཡང་དག་དྲི་བ་ལས། ༡༥ །ལྷོ་རྟ་ཝ་ཤེ་འི་བྱང་ཐང་ལ། རང་ཉིད་གཅིག་བུས་ཕྱི་གོས་ཀྱི།
ཁྲུར་པོ་རྗེ་བ་ཁྲུར་ནས་ནི། ཐང་གཅད་བཞིན་དུ་བགོམས་པ་གཏོར། ༡༦ །དགོན་འབྲོག་བྱང་ཐང་འགྲོ་བ་ལས།
གཡུང་དྲུང་རྒྱ་བོ་ཞལ་བ་ལ། རྒྱ་ཡིས་འཁྱུར་ནས་ཤི་ཀར་ཐུག ལམ་མེད་རི་བོར་རྫོག་པ་ལས། ༡༧
ཁ་བ་ཆེན་པོ་བབས་པ་དང་། མཚན་མོ་སྨུན་ནག་བཀབ་པ་དང་། གངས་ཀྱི་ནང་དུ་མནལ་བ་ལས།
ཤིན་ཏུ་ཁུག་ནས་དྲན་མེད་གྱུར། ༡༨ །སངས་རྒྱས་བྱམས་སྙིང་འོད་ཟེར་གྱིས། དྲན་བྱས་དབང་གིས་གསོས་པར་གྱུར།
དེ་ནས་རྒྱ་མིག་གང་ག་ཡི། ཡོན་ཏན་བརྒྱད་ལྡན་རྒྱ་འབུང་ནས། ༡༩ །ལུས་སེམས་ཤིན་ཏུ་དྭངས་པར་གྱུར།
མ་དྲོས་རྒྱ་ཡིས་མི་ཡོང་ལྟར། སྣང་བའི་མ་ཕམ་ཡུམ་མཚོ་ལ། མཇལ་ཏེ་བདེ་བ་དཔག་མེད་བྱུང་། ༢༠
གླང་ཆེན་ཁ་འབབ་རྒྱ་ངོགས་ཀྱི། ས་ལ་འཆི་མེད་རྒྱ་ཚན་བྱིན། རི་ལ་མཇལ་མཆོད་རྒྱུན་འཁྱུར་བའི།
ཕྲེ་ཏ་པུ་རིའི་གནས་ལ་མཇལ། ༢༡ །འཇིག་རྟེན་ཁམས་ཀྱི་གནས་ཆེན་ཏེ། རིགས་གསུམ་མགོན་པོ་རྣམ་ཐོས་སྲས།
དགྲ་བཅོམ་ལྔ་བརྒྱའི་དཀྱིལ་འཁོར་གྱི། གངས་རིན་པོ་ཆེར་མཇལ་བ་ལས། ༢༢ །རྫོག་པར་དཀའ་བའི་སྒྲོལ་མ་ར།
གངས་ཀྱི་རྩེ་རུ་རྫོག་ཟིན་ནས། དཔག་མེད་དགའ་བ་སྐྱེད་ནས་བསྐྱུད། གནས་བཟང་སྟོབས་ཀྱིས་བདག་མེད་ཤར། ༢༣
བྱིན་རླབས་རྨད་བྱུང་བྱུང་བ་ཡི། ལོ་ནི་ལྕགས་བྱི་ཟླ་དགུ་པ། * ཆོས་བཟང་པོ་དྲ་རང་བཞིན་གྱི།
དཀྱིལ་འཁོར་མཇལ་ཞིང་འཁོར་ཟིན་ནས། ༢༤ །སླར་ཡང་བྱང་ཐང་ཤར་ལ་འགྲོ། དཀོན་རྒྱ་མཚོ་ཡི་རྒྱ་ངོགས་དང་།
དམར་མཚན་རྒྱ་བོ་ཞལ་བ་དང་། ཀྱང་རྒྱ་ཆེན་པོ་གཏོང་བ་ལས། ༢༥ །བཙམ་ཀུན་གྱིས་ནི་ཕྲོག་པ་དང་།
ལྷོ་དང་མཐལ་སྔན་བཤོར་བ་ལས། གངས་ལ་མཉལ་ནས་གངས་ནི་བཟའ། གངས་ཀྱིས་མིག་ཧུང་རྡུག་ཧྐོ་ཆེ། ༢༦
ཡོང་གར་གྱུར་དང་སྦྱུགས་པ་ལས། ལང་ང་ཡོང་ངེར་འགྲོ་གྱུར་ཡང་། ལྷ་སར་འགྲོ་བའི་སྨོན་སེམས་ཀྱིས།
སྙིང་རུས་ཆེན་པོས་འགྲོ་བྱུས་ཀྱང་། ༢༧ །ཞག་གསུམ་ཉིན་གསུམ་ལྟོ་མེད་པས། ལུས་སྟོབས་བཤོར་ཏེ་ཡ་ལབ་ཡ་ལབ་འགྲོ།
གངས་ཀྱི་ཐང་དུ་སྐྱོལ་བ་དང་། ཡང་ཡང་སྐྱོལ་ཏེ་ཡང་སྐྱེ་འགྲོ། ༢༨ །དཀའ་བ་དཔག་མེད་མྱོང་བ་ལས།
བྲག་དཀར་སྒོམ་ཆེན་མདུན་དུ་སླེབས། གཞན་སེམས་ཤེས་པའི་བློ་བཟང་པོས། ཛ་མར་ཕྱེ་གོས་སྦྱིན་པ་ལས། ༢༩
འཆི་བ་དཀའ་བ་ཐར་ཕྱིན་ནས། སླར་ཡང་བྱང་ཐང་འབྲོག་སར་འགྲོ། སངས་རྒྱས་བདུན་གྱི་སྐུ་བདུན་གནས།
མཇལ་ཏེ་སེང་གེའི་ལུང་ནི་འདས། ༣༠ །གཙན་པོ་ཞལ་ཏེ་ལྷ་རྗེ་ནས། ས་སྐྱ་པཎ་ཆེན་དགོན་པ་རུ།
པཎ་ཆེན་དེ་ལ་མཇལ་བ་དང་། ཆོས་ཀྱི་སྐལ་ཆེན་ཐོས་པར་གྱུར། ༣༡ །དེ་ནས་བཀྲ་ཤིས་ལྷུན་པོ་ཡི།

---

* ལྕགས་བྱི 1900, A.D.

དགོན་པར་མཇལ་ཏེ་ཟླ་ཕྱེད་ཙམ།
རིར་བཞུགས་མཁས་པ་རྣམས་ལ་མཇལ།
དམ་ཆོས་ཞུས་ཏེ་དེ་ལས་གཏོང་། ༣༢
དབྱིན་དགོན་གནས་ཀྱི་མཁས་པ་དང་།
རིག་གནས་འཕོར་དུ་རྩོད་པར་བྱས།
རོང་བྱམས་ཆེན་དང་ཚོང་ཁ་པས།
བཞེངས་པའི་མ་ཧེ་ལྷ་ཁང་མཇལ། ༣༣
རོང་རངས་པ་དུ་ཟླ་གསུམ་ཙམ།
བཀའ་བསྒྱུར་ཀློག་ནས་སྤྱོད་པ་དང་།
ལྕགས་གླང་ལོ་ཡི་ཟླ་གསུམ་པར། *
ལྷ་སར་སླེབས་ནས་ཇོ་བོ་མཇལ། ༣༤
། རྒྱ་གར་ཁྲུངས་པའི་སྐུ་འདྲ་སྟེ།
སྲོང་བཙན་སྒམ་པོ་ཆོས་རྒྱལ་གྱིས།
རྒྱ་ཟ་ལྷན་ཅིག་ཇོ་བོ་བཞེས།
བོད་ཡུལ་བསྟན་པའི་གཞི་ལ་འདུད། ༣༥
དེ་ནས་སེ་རའི་དགོན་པ་རུ།
སློབ་གཉེར་དོན་དུ་འཇུག་པ་དང་།
དགེ་བཤེས་རྣམས་ལས་མཚན་ཉིད་བསླབས།
དམ་ཆོས་སླབ་པར་བརྩོན་པར་བྱས། ༣༦
། ཤྲཱ་སྟོང་ཤྲཱ་བརྒྱའི་དགེ་འདུན་གྱི།
ནང་དུ་ཟབ་ཆོས་བསླབས་པ་ལས།
རང་སེམས་རྟག་ཏུ་དགའ་བ་དང་།
སྐལ་བཟང་དེ་ལ་ཐུགས་རྗེ་ཆེ། ༣༧
། སེ་རའི་འདུན་ཁང་རིན་པོ་ཆེས།
བྱང་ཆུབ་སེམས་སྐྱེད་གནང་བ་དང་།
དགའ་ལྡན་ཁྲི་ཡི་རིན་པོ་ཆེས།
དགེ་ཚུགས་སྙིང་གཏམ་གནང་བར་གྱུར། ༣༨
དགེ་འདུན་ཇོ་ཞེས་ནད་པ་ལ།
བདག་གིས་སྨན་རྣམས་བྱིན་པ་དང་།
མྱུར་དུ་ན་ཚ་གསོས་པ་ལས།
བདག་ལ་སྨན་པ་ཆེན་པོར་གྲགས། ༣༩
། ལྷ་ས་གྲོང་ཆེན་སྨོད་རྣམས་ལས།
ནད་པ་མང་པོ་འོངས་པ་དང་།
སེ་རའི་ཨ་མཆི་ཞེས་བྱ་བར།
མིང་ནི་ཆེན་པོར་གྱུར་བ་ལས། ༤༠
། ཏཱ་ལའི་བླ་མ་རྒྱལ་བ་ཡི།
བླ་སྨན་པ་ཡིས་བདག་བོད་དེ།
གསོལ་དཔོན་མཁན་པོའི་ན་ཚ་བསྟན།
ལྷན་གཅིག་སྨན་སྤྱོད་བྱེད་པར་གྱུར། ༤༡
བླ་སྨན་པ་དེ་ད་ལྟ་ཡི།
སྤྱི་ཁྱབ་མཁན་པོར་འགྱུར་བ་དེས།
ཉིན་ཅིག་བདག་ལ་ཟེར་བ་ལ།
ཁྱེད་ནི་ཚེ་གཅིག་བོད་ཡུལ་དུ། ༤༢
། སྨན་སྤྱོད་རྒྱ་ཆེར་བྱེད་ནས་ནི།
སེམས་ཅན་མང་པོའི་ན་ཚ་དང་།
ཟུག་རྔུ་སྡུག་བསྔལ་གྲོལ་བར་དགོས།
དེ་ལ་བདག་གིས་ལན་འདེབས་པ། ༤༣
། ལུས་ནད་གྲོལ་བར་བྱེད་པ་ལས།
སེམས་ནད་གྲོལ་བ་གཙོ་བོ་ཆེ།
སངས་རྒྱས་ཆོས་སློབ་བདག་ཅག་ནི།
ཆོས་ཀྱི་སྨན་གྱིས་ཕན་པར་བྱ། ༤༤
དེས་ན་བདག་ཉིད་རྒྱ་གར་འགྲོ།
ཐེག་ཆེན་བྱུང་ཁྲུངས་ཞིབས་སྦྱར་ཀྱི།
སྐད་རྣམས་སླབ་ཏེ་སངས་རྒྱས་ཀྱི།
དོན་དམ་ཆོས་ནི་བཤད་པར་བྱ། ༤༥
། དེ་ནས་ཏཱ་ལའི་བླ་མ་ལ།
ཐུགས་རྗེ་ཆེན་པོའི་དབང་ནི་ཞུ།
ངོ་མཚར་གསང་ཐབས་གཏམ་ནི་ཐོས།
བྱིན་རླབས་ཆེན་པོས་སེམས་བཀང་སྟེ། ༤༦
། ཟླ་བ་བཅོ་ལྔ་ཙམ་འདས་པར།
ང་དང་བདག་གིས་ལྷ་ས་རུ།
གནས་པར་འགྱུར་ན་བྱིན་བདག་དང་།
གྲོགས་ལ་བར་ཆད་འབྱུང་བར་འགྱུར། ༤༧
དེ་ནི་རྒྱུ་མཚན་གཞན་མེད་དེ།
བདག་ལ་ཕྱི་གླིང་པ་ཡིན་པར།
ཐེ་ཚོམ་ཟ་བའི་མི་བྱུང་བས།
བོད་ཁྲིམས་དང་ནི་འགལ་བ་དང་། ༤༨
། དེས་ན་ཆུ་སྟག་ཟླ་ལྔ་པར། †
ལྷ་ས་ནས་གཏོང་རྒྱལ་རྩེར་མཇལ།

* ལྕགས་གླང, 1901, A. D. † ཆུ་སྟག, 1902, A. D.

ཕག་རི་གྲོ་མོ་འདས་གྱུར་ནས། རྡོ་རྗེ་གླིང་དུ་སླར་ཡང་སླེབས། ༤༩ །ས་རཏ་ཅན་དུ་རྟེན་ཟླ་ཡི།
ཁང་པར་གནས་ཤིང་འདས་པ་ལས། བདག་གི་རྐྱེན་གྱིས་སྡེ་གཞུང་ནས། མི་རར་སྙོ་ཐེ་རྒྱབ་པ་དང་། ༥༠
ཕྱིན་བདག་བྲམས་པ་ཆོས་བཟང་དང་། བདག་གི་ངོ་ཤེས་མང་པོ་ནི། བཙོན་རར་ཐུག་ནས་ཞིབ་ཆོད་བྱས།
ཁྲིམས་གཏང་འགྱུར་བར་ཐོས་པ་ལས། ༥༡ །བདག་ལ་སྡུག་བསྔལ་དཔག་མེད་བྱུང་། དེ་རྣམས་ཐར་བའི་ཐབས་བྱེད་དུ།
རྒྱལ་བར་ཕྲན་ཡིག་ཕུལ་འདོད་པས། ཡམ་བུའི་ཡུལ་དུ་འགྲོ་བ་དང་། ༥༢ །ཡུལ་དེའི་དབང་པོ་ཅན་དྲ་པས།
བོད་ལ་ཡིག་དེ་གཏོང་བར་བཤད། བདག་ནི་ཕྱི་གླིང་པ་མིན་ཏེ། རྒྱ་གར་བ་མིན་ཇའ་པན་ནས། ༥༣
དམ་ཆོས་སྤྱོད་པའི་དོན་གཉེར་ནས། བོད་ལ་སླེབས་པས་ངའི་རྐྱེན་གྱིས། ཁྱེད་ཀྱི་མི་རྣམས་སུ་ལ་ཡང་།
ཁྲིམས་བཏང་དགོས་པའི་དོན་ནི་མེད། ༥༤ །ཅེས་ཡི་གེར་འཇོད་དེ་ཞུ་བ་དང་། མི་རྣམས་ཕལ་ཆེར་བཙོན་ར་ནས།
ཐར་བར་ཐོས་ནས་ཇའ་པན་དུ། * ཆུ་ཡོས་ཟླ་བ་ལྔ་པར་ཕྱིན། ༥༥ །བྱང་ཆུབ་གནས་བཟང་བོད་ལ་མཇལ།
འཆི་ཁར་ཕྲུག་པའི་དཀའ་མང་ཡང་། སངས་རྒྱས་ཐུགས་རྗེ་ཆེན་པོ་ཡིས། རྣམ་པར་ཐར་བས་ཐུགས་རྗེ་ཆེ།། ༥༦ ༎

ལེ་འུ་གཉིས་པ།

༄༅། ལོ་གཅིག་ཟླ་བ་བཞི་ཙམ་ནི། ཕ་ཡུལ་ཇའ་པན་དུ་གནས་ཏེ། བྱང་ཆུབ་གནས་བཟང་བོད་ཡུལ་དུ།
མཇལ་བའི་རྣམ་ཐར་མི་ལ་བཤད། ༡ བདག་ཅག་ཡུལ་དུ་བོད་པར་གྱི། བཀའ་བསྒྱུར་བསྟན་བསྒྱུར་མེད་པ་དང་།
ལེགས་སྦྱར་སྐད་ཀྱི་བཀའ་བསྟན་ཡང་། མེད་པས་དེ་རྣམས་སྒྲུབ་པ་དང་། ༢ །ལེགས་སྦྱར་སྐད་དང་བོད་སྐད་རྣམས།
ཡང་དག་སློབ་པའི་དོན་གྱི་ཕྱིར། རྒྱ་གར་བལ་ཡུལ་བོད་ཡུལ་དུ། སླར་ཡང་འགྲོ་བར་སྨོན་གྱུར་ཏེ། ༣
ཤིང་འབྲུག་ཟླ་བ་ཙུར་ཇའ་པན་ནས། † རྒྱ་ཡིག་བཀའ་བསྟན་དཔེ་ཆ་ཀུན། འཕྲུར་ཏེ་ཐུར་ཁས་ལེན་པ་བཞིན།
བལ་པོའི་ཡུལ་གྱི་དབང་པོར་ཕུལ། ༤ །དབང་པོ་རིས་ཀྱང་ལེགས་སྦྱར་གྱི། བྲི་མའི་དཔེ་རྣམས་གཏང་བར་གྱུར།
ད་དུང་ཡུལ་དེར་ལེགས་སྦྱར་གྱི། བྲི་དཔེ་གསགས་ནས་ཟླ་བརྒྱད་གནས། ༥ །ཀལ་ཀཏྟའི་གྲོང་དང་བལ་ཡུལ་དང་།
ལྷ་ར་ན་ཤིའི་མཁས་རྣམས་ལ། ལོ་དགུ་ལྷག་ཙམ་ལེགས་སྦྱར་སྐད། བསྟན་པའི་དོན་དུ་སློབས་པར་གྱུར། ༦
སློབ་བྱ་དེ་ཡི་བར་མཚམས་སུ། སངས་རྒྱས་འཁྲུངས་ཡུལ་རྒྱ་གར་གྱི། བྱང་ཆུབ་གནས་བཟང་མང་པོར་མཇལ།
སེར་སྐྱའི་གྲོང་དང་ལུམ་བྲིའི་ཚལ། ༧ །རྒྱལ་པོའི་ཁབ་དང་སྤུག་མའི་ཚལ། ན་ལན་དའི་དགོན་ཤུལ་དང་།
ཨོ་ཏནྟ་པུ་རིའི་གནས་རྗེས་དང་། གནས་མཆོག་བྱ་རྒོད་ཕུང་པོའི་རི། ༨ །དཀའ་ཐུབ་ལོ་དྲུག་མཛད་པའི་གནས།

---

* ཆུ་ཡོས 1903, A. D. † ཤིང་འབྲུག, 1905, A. D.

སྔར་ཀྱང་མཚོང་རྒྱ་བ་ཡི་ཕྱག། ན་ལན་ཛ་ནའི་རྒྱུ་ངོགས་ཀྱི། བྱང་ཆུབ་ཤིང་དོག་རྡོ་རྗེ་གདན། ༦༩

ཆོས་འཁོར་དང་པོར་འཁོར་བའི་ས། དྲང་སྲོང་ལྷུང་གནས་རི་དྭགས་ཚལ། ཆོས་ཀྱི་རྒྱལ་བུ་རྒྱལ་བྱེད་ཚལ།

མགོན་མེད་ཟས་སྦྱིན་ཀུན་དགའ་ར། ༧༠ །སྤྱང་ཏན་འདས་གནས་རྩ་མཆོག་གྲོང་། གནས་རྣམས་མཐའ་ཏེ་སངས་རྒྱས་ཀྱི།

བྱམས་པ་སྙིང་རྗེ་ཆེན་པོ་ཡིས། མཛད་པ་བཅུ་གཉིས་གནས་ལ་སྤྱར། ༧༡ །དངོས་སུ་ཞབས་རྗེས་རི་བཞིན་དུ།

མཐའ་དུས་འགྲོ་ཀུན་བུ་བཞིན་དུ། གཅེས་པའི་ཐུགས་དང་མཚན་དཔེ་ཉམས། རང་དབང་མེད་པར་མིག་ཆུ་བབས། ༧༢

གཞན་ཡང་འོད་སྲུང་བྱ་རྐང་རི། ཆོས་སྡུད་གནས་དང་ཡང་པ་ཅན། བཟང་བཟང་ཕྱུག་དང་ཁྲིམས་བཟང་གི།

གནས་རྣམས་མཐའ་ཏེ་ཡོད་པ་ལས། ༧༣ །པཎ་ཆེན་བླ་མས་བཀའ་བསྟན་བསྒྱུར། གནང་བར་འགྱུར་བའི་གཏམ་ཐོས་ཏེ།

ཛ་ར་པན་ཡུལ་ནས་རྒྱ་ཡིག་གི། བཀའ་བསྟན་ལེན་ཏེ་དེ་རྣམས་ནི། ༧༤ །བོད་ལ་རྫར་དུ་བཏང་བ་དང་།

བདག་གིས་བོད་དུ་འགྲོ་དགོས་ལ། རྒྱ་གར་ཡུལ་ནས་བོད་ཀྱི་ལམ། ཕྱི་གླིང་གཞུང་གིས་ཐམས་ཅད་བཀག། ༧༥

སྔར་བཞིན་འགྲོད་པར་མི་ནུས་པས། ཐབས་མེད་བཞིན་དུ་ཐབས་བྱས་ཏེ། ཁྲིམས་ལ་འགལ་བར་ཤེས་བཞིན་དུ།

སངས་རྒྱས་བསྟན་པའི་དོན་གྱིས་པས། ༧༦ །ཕྱི་གླིང་གཞུང་རོག་འབྲས་ལྗོངས་སུ། ཆུ་གླང་ཟླ་བ་བཅུ་གཉིས་པར། +

རྒྱ་གར་གཏོང་སྐྱེ་འགྲོ་བ་ལས། ཉིན་མོར་མཐའ་ནས་མཚན་མོར་འགྲོ ༧༧ །ཤིང་ནགས་སྨུན་ནག་གཅན་ཟན་གྱི།

འཇིགས་ཁྲག་རྣམས་ཀྱང་ཐར་བ་དང་། རི་རྩར་ཛོག་དང་ལུང་ལ་བབས། ཡང་ཡང་དེ་ལྟར་བྱས་པ་ལས། ༧༨

གངས་ཀྱིས་ཁེབ་པའི་རི་བྲར་དང་། ནམ་མཁར་རེག་བཞིན་རི་རྩེ་ཡི། མི་རྟོག་ཉེར་རར་སླེབས་པའི་ཚེ།

ཁ་བ་ལ་ནི་མང་དུ་བབས། ༧༩ །རླུང་ཆེན་གྱིས་ནི་དྲུང་བས་ན། ཡང་དང་ཡང་དུ་རི་ཁར་ཐུག།

བཅོམ་ལྡན་སྙིང་རྗེ་ཉོན་ཆེ་བས། ཕྲག་ནས་མ་ཤི་ཁམས་པ་ནས། ༨༠ །གཞི་ག་རྩེ་རུ་སླེབས་པ་དང་།

པཎ་ཆེན་བླ་མར་བཀའ་བསྟན་ཕུལ། དེ་ནས་ཁོན་གྱིས་བཀའ་བསྒྱུར་དང་། བསྟན་བསྒྱུར་གསུང་འབུམ་གནང་བར་འགྱུར། ༨༡

ཟླ་བ་དྲུག་ཙམ་དེར་གནས་ཏེ། དཔེ་སྙིང་ཕྲི་མ་མང་པོ་སྙེར། དེ་ནས་ལྷ་སར་འགྲོ་བ་དང་།

རྭ་ལའི་བླ་མ་རྒྱལ་བར་མཇལ། ༨༢ །རྒྱལ་བས་ཛ་ར་པན་རྒྱལ་ཁམས་ཀྱི། སློབ་གྲྭ་ཆེན་པོར་ཕྲི་མ་ཡི།

བཀའ་བསྒྱུར་ཚང་པོ་གནང་བར་གྱུར། བདག་ལ་བྱིན་ཆེན་སྐུ་ཡང་གནང་། ༨༣ །སྡོད་ན་གནས་ཚང་བཟང་པོ་དང་།

འགྲོ་ན་རྟ་བོ་གནང་ཀྱང་ཏེ། ཤིན་ཏུ་བདེ་བར་འདས་པ་ལས། ལེགས་སྦྱར་སྐད་ཀྱི་དཔེ་ཆ་རྣམས། ༨༤

ཚོལ་ཆེད་རྭ་སྒྲེང་དུ་སླེབ་ཀྱང་། དཔེ་དེ་གཅིག་ཀྱང་མ་མཐོང་བར། ཤིན་ཏུ་སྐྱོ་ནས་ལྷག་ལམ་དུ།

དགའ་ལྡན་དགེ་ལུགས་རྩ་བའི་གནས། ༨༥ །རྗེ་ཙོང་ཁ་པའི་གསེར་གདུང་དུ། མཐའ་ནས་དགའ་བ་དཔག་མེད་ཐོབ།

+ ཆུ་གླང་ 1913, A. D.

ཤིང་ཡོས་ཟླ་བ་དང་པོ་ལ། * ལྷ་ས་ནས་གཏོང་གཙན་དུ་སྩིབས། ༢༦ །ཁ་བ་ཅན་པོ་ཞིང་འཐབས་པས།
འགྲོ་བར་མ་ནུས་ཟླ་གསུམ་འདས། ཡམ་བུའི་དབང་པོར་ལམ་ཡིག་ཞུ། འོན་ཀྱང་དེ་ནི་མ་གནང་བས། ༢༧
སླར་ཡང་འབྲས་ལྗོངས་ལམ་ལེན་ན། བཙོན་རར་འཇུག་འགྱུར་ངེས་ན་ཡང་། ཐབས་གཞན་མེད་པར་ལམ་དེར་འགྲོ།
ཕྱི་གླིང་གཞུང་ནས་ལམ་དེ་ལ། ༢༨ །ཤིན་ཏུ་དམ་པོར་བཀག་རྒྱུར་ཡང་། དཀའ་བ་ཆེན་པོས་ཐར་བར་གྱུར།
ལོ་དེའི་ཟླ་བ་ལྔ་པ་ལ། རྡོ་རྗེ་གླིང་དུ་སྩིབ་པར་གྱུར། ༢༩ །དེར་གནས་ཕྱི་གླིང་གཞུང་པ་ཡིས།
བདག་ནི་བཙོན་རར་འཇུག་བསམ་ཡང་། རྒྱ་གར་སྤྱི་ཁྱབ་དཔོན་ཆེན་གྱིས། གྲོགས་སེམས་ཡས་ནི་གྲོལ་བར་གྱུར། ༣༠
བདག་གིས་དམ་ཆོས་སྤྱོད་པ་དང་། བཀའ་བསྟན་ཐུབ་པའི་དོན་ཕྱིར་དང་། ལེགས་སྦྱར་བོད་སྐད་སླབ་ཕྱིར་དང་།
བྱང་ཆུབ་གནས་བཟང་མཇལ་བ་ལ། ༣༡ །བཀའ་བ་ཐམས་ཅད་ནམ་ཐར་བས། བཅོམ་ལྡན་འདས་དང་རྒྱལ་བ་དང་།
པཎ་ཆེན་བླ་མ་རྒྱ་གར་གྱི། སྤྱི་ཁྱབ་དཔོན་ལ་ཐུགས་རྗེ་ཆེ། ༣༢ །ཇར་པན་ཡུལ་གྱི་སྦྱིན་བདག་དང་།
བཤེས་གཉེན་གྲོགས་པོས་ལོ་བཅོ་བརྒྱད། གནས་མཇལ་འགྲོ་སོང་ཀུན་སྦྱིན་ནས། ཆོས་སྲུད་སྐྱབས་ལ་ཐུགས་རྗེ་ཆེ། ༣༣
གཞན་ཡང་བོད་ལ་པར་ཡོད་པའི། གསུང་འབུམ་ལོ་བརྒྱུད་རིག་གནས་ཀྱི། དཔེ་ཆ་རྣམས་ཀྱང་ཉོ་ཚོག་གནས།
བོད་ནས་བཏང་བའི་ལམ་དུ་ཡོད། ༣༤ །དམ་ཆོས་ཉི་མ་ཤར་བའི་ཡུལ། དེ་རྣམས་ཇར་པན་དུ་འཁྱུར་ཏེ།
འགྱུར་ཏེ་ཆོས་ཀྱི་མེ་ཏོག་ཤར། ཡང་དག་བྲས་བུ་སྨིན་པར་ཤོག ༎ ༣༥ ༎

དེ་འང་བདག་སྙེ་ཇར་པན་གྱི་དགེ་སློང་ཨེ་ཀའི་ཀ་ཝ་ཀུ་ཙི་སྙེ་ཤེས་རབ་རྒྱ་མཚོས་སླར་ཡང་བོད་ལ་འགྲོ་བ་དང་། ཤིང་ཡོས་ལོ་དེ་ཟླ་ལྔ་པར་བོད་ལས་གཏོང་སྙེ་འདིར་རྒྱ་གར་རྡོ་རྗེ་གླིང་དུ་སྩིབས་ཏེ་སྡོད་པ་དང་། དེར་བདག་གིས་དང་པོར་བོད་སྐད་སློབ་པའི་འཕྲིད་དང་ཟླ་བོ་གནང་བའི་རྒྱ་གར་གྱི་པཎ་ཊི་ཏ་ཆེན་པོ་ཤ་རཏ་ཙན་དྲ་རའི་ཧྲ་རྡོར་སྙེ་མཁས་ཆེན་སྔོན་ཁའི་ཟླ་བ་ནས་ཡང་དང་ཡང་དུ་ནན་ཏན་གྱིས་བྱང་ཆུབ་གནས་མཇལ་ཏེ་བོད་ལ་བསྒྲོད་པའི་རྣམ་ཐར་ཞེས་བྱ་བ་ཞིག་བྲིས་དགོས་པར་བསྐུལ་བས་རང་ལོ་ལྔ་བཅུ་པ་སྙེ་རབ་བྱུང་བཅོ་ལྔ་པའི་ཤིང་ཡོས་ལོ་ཕྱི་ཟླ་དྲུག་པ་ཚེས་བཅུ་གཉིས་སུ་རྡོ་རྗེ་གླིང་གི་ལྷ་ས་ཉེ་ལ་དུ་ཨེ་ཀའི་ཀ་ཝ་ཀུ་ཙིས་བྲིས་པའོ༎ ཀུན་ཏུ་བཀྲ་ཤིས་པར་གྱུར་ཅིག།
༦ ༡༢

* ཤིང་ཡོས 1915, A. D.

BOOK II.

THE GRAMMAR OF THE TIBETAN LANGUAGE.

THE TEXT OF SITU SUM TAG

སུམ་ཅུ་པ་དང་རྟགས་ཀྱི་འཇུག་པ།

BY

SITU PANCHEN

(PAGES 1—88)

BEING

A Commentary on Sum-Chu-pa and Tag-jug-pa of Thon-mi SamBhota

WITH

An Index of Grammatical Terms

BY

SHRAMANA EKAI KAWAGUCHI

(PAGES I—V.)

Page.	༨	Line.	༢༥	For.	འཇམ	Read.	འཛམ
,,	༥	,,	༡༩	,,	མེད་པ་ཡིན	,,	མེད་པ་མིན
,,	༦	,,	༢༠	,,	ཛོ་འཛིན	,,	ཛ་འཛིན
,,	༨	,,	༢༨	,,	སྔན་དུ	,,	སྔོན་དུ
,,	༩	,,	༢༠	,,	དུས་ཕྲལ་གྱི་ཕྲ	,,	དུས་ཕྲལ་གྱི་ཕྲུ
,,	༡༠	,,	༥	,,	པར	,,	ངའི
,,	༡༡	,,	༢	,,	སྤྲ་ཕྱུ	,,	སྤྲ་ཕྱི
,,	༡༡	,,	༡༩	,,	གཉས་པ	,,	གཉིས་པ
,,	༡༡	,,	༡༩	,,	སྦྱོར་རྩལ	,,	སྦྱོར་ཚུལ
,,	༡༢	,,	༧	,,	ལསཔ	,,	ལས
,,	༡༣	,,	༥	,,	ཀེ་ཁར	,,	ཁོ་ཁར
,,	༡༣	,,	༢༦	,,	སྡིག་པ་སྤྱོད་པ་ཞིག	,,	སྡིག་པ་སྤྱོད་པ་ཞིག་ན
,,	༡༩	,,	༡༡	,,	ཇེ་དྲུར	,,	ཛེ་དྲུར
,,	༡༩	,,	༡༩	,,	ཉེས་སོགས	,,	ཉེས་སོགས
,,	༢༥	,,	༨	,,	སྤྲ་ཕྱུ	,,	སྤྲ་ཕྱི
,,	༢༥	,,	༢༣	,,	གང་མང	,,	གང་ཡིང
,,	༢༦	,,	༡༨	,,	རྐུ་བོ	,,	འཁྲུ་བོ
,,	༣༢	,,	༡༠	,,	གང་ལྡན་པའང་ཡིན་ལ	,,	གང་ཡིན་ལ
,,	༣༦	,,	༡༥	,,	སྒོས་ཆོས་མང	,,	སྒོས་མང
,,	༣༧	,,	༩	,,	བརྟག་གི་འདུག་པ	,,	རྟགས་ཀྱི་འདུག་པ
,,	༥༦	,,	༢༨	,,	མཉམ་ཕྱུར་རྫ	,,	མཉམ་ཕྱིར་རྫ
,,	༦༠	,,	༦	,,	ས་དང་ད་ནམཡ	,,	ས་དང་ད་ནམས
,,	༦༥	,,	༢༣	,,	ལཀོ་ལ་བྱེད	,,	འཁོལ་བྱེད
,,	༧༢	,,	༣	,,	བཞིང་པའི	,,	བཞི
,,	༨༢	,,	༡༦	,,	གལ་ཆེར	,,	ཕལ་ཆེར
,,	༨༣	,,	༢༠	,,	རྣམ་པར་མཛེས་པ	,,	རྣམ་པར་མཛེས་པ

སི་ཏུའི་སུམ་རྟགས།

ཤེས་བྱའི་དཀྱིལ་འཁོར་རྣམ་པར་བཀྲ་བ་ནམ་མཁའི་མཐའ་ཡི་སྣ་ཁྲ་ད་ཙམ།
ཅིག་ཅར་འཇལ་བའི་འཕྲུལ་མེད་བློ་མངའ་འཇམ་པའི་དབྱངས་སོགས་དཔའ་རྣམས་ཀྱིས།
རྟག་ཏུ་བརྟེན་འོས་ཞབས་ཀྱི་ཚ་སྐྱེས་ལ་ཆགས་འཁོར་བའི་རྒྱལ་ཕྲན་ཡང་།
དྲན་པ་ཁོ་ནས་སྐྱོངས་པའི་འཇིགས་འཕྲོག་ཤཱཀྱའི་གཙོ་བོ་ལ་བཏུད་ནས།
གངས་རིའི་ཁྲོད་ཀྱི་མཁས་པ་རྣམས། སྨྲ་བའི་ངག་སྒོར་ལ་བརྟེན་ནས།
དོན་གྱི་མཚན་ཉིད་རབ་གསལ་སྣང་། བརྡའ་སྤྲོད་གཞུང་གིས་དགྲོལ་བར་བྱ།

དེའང་འདི་སྐད་ཐོས་ཏེ། བདག་ཅག་གི་སྟོན་པས་འཇམ་དཔལ་རྩ་བའི་རྒྱུད་སོགས་སུ་ཇི་ལྟར་ལུང་བསྟན་པ་བཞིན་ཁ་བ་ཅན་གྱི་ཡུལ་དབུས་སུ་གྱུར་པ་ལྷ་ལྡན་ཉིད་དུ་ཐེ་ཙུ་ཕྱིའི་རིགས་ལས་ཆོས་སྐྱོང་བའི་རྒྱལ་པོ་ཚར་དུ་དངར་བ་རིམ་པར་བྱོན་པ་ལས་ཉི་མ་ལྷ་བུར་གྲགས་པ་རྣམ་པར་གསལ་བ། རྒྱལ་པོ་ཆེན་པོ་མིའི་ལྷའམ་ཡང་ན་སྐྱེ་བོ་མི་བསྒྲུན་པ་གདུལ་དཀའ་བ་རྣམས་ལུགས་གཉིས་ཀྱི་སྒྲོལ་བཟང་པོའི་ལམ་དུ་ནན་གྱིས་སྐྱོང་ཞིང་། མཛའ་བ་དང་མི་མཛའ་བ་དང་བར་མ་རྣམས་ལ་ཐུགས་རབ་ཏུ་སྙོམས་པས་ཕྱོགས་སུ་མ་ལྷུང་བའི་ཕྱིར་ཤིན་ཏུ་དྲང་བའི་བཀའ་ཁྲིམས་བཙན་པོའི་གནས་ལ་མངའ་འོག་པ་རྣམས་འདའ་བའི་སྐབས་མེད་པ་དང་། ཕྱི་དང་ནང་གི་བྱ་བའི་གནས་ཐམས་ཅད་ལ་འཆོལ་ཞིང་འཁྲུགས་པ་མེད་པར་དཔྱད་པ་གསུམ་གྱིས་གཏན་ལ་འབེབས་ཤིང་མཛངས་པར་གྲགས་པ་རྣམས་ཀྱིས་ཀྱང་དགོངས་པའི་གཏིང་དཔོག་པ་མེད་པའི་ཕྱིར་སྲོང་བཙན་སྒམ་པོ་ཉིས་མཚན་རྣན་པར་གྲགས་པ་ཉིད་སྐྱེ་དགུའི་དཔལ་དུ་ཤར་ཏོ། དེའི་ཚེ་དེའི་མདུན་ན་འདོན་མཁས་པར་གྲགས་པ་མང་པོའི་དབུས་སུ་མིང་གི་ཡི་གེ་རབ་ཏུ་བརྗོད་པ་ཐུ་མི་སམ་བྷོ་ཊ་ནས། ཆོས་ཀྱི་རྒྱལ་པོ་བྱང་ཆུབ་སེམས་དཔའི་བཀའ་དང་རང་ཉིད་བྱང་ཆུབ་མཆོག་གི་སྨོན་ལམ་ཁྱད་པར་ཅན་གྱི་མཐུས་འཕགས་པའི་ཡུལ་དུ་བརྫོལ་ཏོ། པཎྜི་ཏ་ལྷ་རིག་པའི་སེང་གེ་དང་། བྲམ་ཟེ་ལི་བི་ཀ་ར་སོགས་བསྟེན་ནས་ཕྱི་ནང་གི་རིག་པ་མང་པོར་སྦྱངས་ཤིང་བསྟན་བཅོས་མང་པོས་མགུལ་པ་བརྒྱན་ནས་སླར་ལྡོག་པའི་ཚེ། སྐུ་མཁར་མ་རུར་ནཱ་ག་རའི་ཡི་གེར་དཔེ་བྱས་ཏེ་བོད་ཡིག་གི་གཟུགས་བརྩམས་ཏེ་ཡིག་ཕུད་དུ། རྒྱལ་པོ་བྱ་དཀའི་ལམ་ལས་དྲངས་པའི་བསྟོད་པས་ཆེད་དུ་བརྗོད་པས་དགྱེས་ཤིང་། རིམ་པར་བསྟན་བཅོས་འདི་ལ་སོགས་བོད་ཀྱི་བརྡའ་ཡང་དག་པར་སྦྱོར་བའི་བསྟན་བཅོས་བརྒྱད་ལ་སོགས་པ་མཛད་པས་ཀླུག་ལ་སྒྲོན་མེ་བཏེག་པ་བཞིན་དུ་ཤཱཀྱའི་བསྟན་པ་བྱང་ཕྱོགས་སུ་རྒྱས་པའི་ལམ་གྱི་ཐོག་མ་སྣང་བར་གྱུར་ཏོ། ཞེས་གྲགས་སོ། དེ་ལས་སུམ་ཅུ་པ་དང་རྟགས་ཀྱི་འཇུག་པ་གཉིས་ཁོ་ན་དེང་སང་གི་བར་དུ་ཡོད་ཅིང་། མཁས་བླུན་མང་པོས་འགྲེལ་བཤད་ཀྱི་ཁུར་བླངས་པས་དོན་གཞན་དང་གཞན་དུ་འདྲེན་པའི་གྲོགས་བྱས་ཀྱི་སྒྲིང་བར་གྱུར་མོད་འོན་ཀྱང་རྣམ་དཔྱོད་དང་ལྡན་པ་ཁ་ཅིག་གིས་རིག་པའི་མདའ་རྣོན་གྱིས་ཕུག་པས་གཞུང་དོན་མང་པོ་ཞིག་དཔྱིས་ཕྱིན་པར་གྱུར་ཅིང་། ཕལ་ཆེར་ནི་བྱང་ཕྱོགས་འདིར་གཙུག་ལག་གཉིས་ཀ་བར་དུ་ཉམས་པའི་དབང་ལས་བཤད་རྒྱུན་དང་བསྟན་བཅོས་ཀྱི་ཡན་ལག་གཞན་མ་ཚང་བའི་ཕྱིར་མི་གསལ་བ་རྣམས་ཁ་ཕྲལ་འཇལ་བ་ཙམ་ལས་དོན་དུ་གནས་པར་མ་མཛོད་པས། བདག་ལྷ་བུས་མཐའ་གཅིག་ཏུ་བཤད་པར་སྤྲོ་བ་མ་ཡིན་ཀྱང་བློ་གྲོས་ཀྱི་ནོར་དང་ལྡན་པ་གཞན་དག་གིས་ཀྱང་ཆེད་དུ་བསྐུལ་བ་དང་། རང་ཉིད་གཞུང་ཁྱད་པར་དུ་འཕགས་པ་འདི་དག་ལ་འཇུག་པར་འདོད་པའི་བློ་བ་བརྟས་པས་ཐེམ་ས་དཔག་གསུམ་གྱིས་ཇི་ལྟར་དཔག་པ་དགྲོལ་བར་བྱའོ། དེ་ལས་ཐོག་མར་སུམ་ཅུ་པའི་གཞུང་འཆད་པ་ལ། བསྟན་བཅོས་རྩོམ་པ་ལ་འཇུག་པའི་ཡན་ལག་དང་བསྟན་བཅོས་དངོས་པོ།

དང་པོ་ལ། མཚན་སྨོས་པ་དང་། འགྱུར་ཕྱག་གོ། དང་པོ་ལ་དངོས་དང་། མཚན་དོན་བཤད་པ། དོགས་གནས་དཔྱད་པ་གསུམ་ལས།

དང་པོ་ནི:—རྒྱ་གར་སྐད་དུ། བྱཱ་ཀ་ར་ཎ་མཱུ་ལ་ཏྲིཾ་ཤཀ་ནཱ་མ། བོད་སྐད་དུ་ལུང་སྟོན་པ་རྩ་བ་སུམ་ཅུ་པ།

ཞེས་བྱ་བ་ཞེས་འབྱུང་བ་སྟེ། བྱཱ་ཀ་ར་ཎ། ལུང་སྟོན་པ། མཱུ་ལ། རྩ་བ། ཏྲིཾ་ཤཀ། སུམ་ཅུ་པ། ནཱ་མ། ཞེས་བྱའོ།།

གཉིས་པ་ནི། སྤྱིའི་མཚན་ཉིད་ལྟར་དུ་རྟེན་ཅིང་ལེའུ་ཕྱི་མ་རྣམས་ཀྱི་བརྟེན་གཞིར་གྱུར་པ་གང་ཞིག་གཞུང་ཚད་མ་ལ་ཀ་སུམ་ཅུར་གནས་པས་ན་དེ་སྐད་ཅེས་བྱའོ།།

གསུམ་པ་ནི། འགའ་ཞིག་འདི་སྐད་དུ་འདི་ལྟར་ལེགས་པར་སྦྱར་བའི་པདའི་མིང་བསྟན་པ་ན་རྒྱ་གར་སྐད་དུ་ཞེས་སྨོས་རིགས་པ་མ་ཡིན་ཏེ། དེ་ལྟར་ན་ལེགས་པར་སྦྱར་བ་དང་བྲལ་བའི་རྒྱ་གར་གྱི་སྐད་ཡུལ་འཁོར་ཆེན་པོ་ལ་གཉེན་པ་རྣམས་སུ་འཕྲུལ་བས་འདི་ལྷའི་སྐད་དུ་རྟོགས་མི་ནུས་པའི་སྐྱོན་འཇུག་གོ། ཞེ་ན་ཞིབ་མོར་དཔྱད་པའི་ལུགས་སུ་དོགས་པ་སྐྱེ་བ་བདེན་མོད། འོན་ཀྱང་ལེགས་པར་སྦྱར་བ་ཉིད་འཕགས་ཡུལ་གྱི་མཁས་པ་རྣམས་ལ་རབ་ཏུ་གསལ་ཞིང་གཞན་དང་གཞན་དུ་དེ་ལྟར་མིན་པས་སྐྱེ་བོ་ཕལ་མོ་ཆེའི་ངོར་གྲགས་པ་ཙམ་གཙོ་བོར་བྱས་བ་དང་། བྱང་ཕྱོགས་འདིར་སངས་རྒྱས་ཀྱི་བསྟན་པ་ཇི་སྙེད་ཅིག་སྣང་བ་ཕལ་ཆེར་འཕགས་པའི་ཡུལ་ནས་འོངས་པ་ཤས་ཆེ་བས་ཡུལ་ཁྲུངས་སུ་བྱས་ཏེ། མཁན་པོ་ཉིད་དང་ཕྱི་ནས་ལོ་ཙཱ་བ་རྣམས་ཀྱིས་ཀྱང་བརྗོད་པ་ཡིན་ཞིང་། མཁན་པོས་འདིར་ནི་ཡི་གེ་དང་སྦྱོར་བས་སུ་སྦྱོར་བ་རྣམས་འཕགས་ཡུལ་པ་དཔེར་མཛད་པ་ཉིད་ཀྱི་ཁུངས་སྟོན་པའི་ཆེད་དུ་འང་ཡིན་པས་སྐྱོན་མེད་དོ། ཡང་ཙ་བ་སུམ་ཅུ་པ་ཞེས་པའི་སྐབས། ཕལ་ཆེར་ཀྱིས་ཀཱ་ལི་སུམ་ཅུ་བརྗོད་བྱའི་གཙོ་བོར་སྟོན་པའི་དོན་དུ་བཀྲལ་ཅིང་།

འགའ་ཞིག་གིས་ནི་ན་ཡས་དུ་སྲུམ་མོ་ལ་ཀ་སུམ་ཅུ་ཙམ་ཞིག་ཡོད་པའི་དོན་དུའང་བཀོད་དེ། ཟླ་མ་ལྟར་ན་རྟགས་འཇུག་ཐའང་སུམ་ཅུ་པའི་མིང་འཇུག་པར་ཐལ་ཏེ་སུམ་ཅུ་པར་ཀཱ་ལི་སུམ་ཅུའི་ཚིག་སྦྲད་རྣམ་དབྱེ་སོགས་བསྟན་ལ། རྟགས་འཇུག་ཏུ་དེ་རི་རྟགས་ཀྱི་དབྱེ་བ་སོགས་བསྟན་པས་གཉིས་ཀར་ཀཱ་ལི་སུམ་ཅུའི་བྱ་བ་རྟེན་པ་མཉམ་པའི་ཕྱིར། གཞན་ཡང་བོད་ཀྱི་བརྡའ་སྦྱོར་བའི་བསྟན་བཅོས་རྩོམ་ན་ཀཱ་ལི་སུམ་ཅུ་བརྗོད་བྱའི་གཙོ་བོར་མེད་པ་ནི་ཆེས་མི་རིགས་པས་ཙ་བ་བརྒྱད་པོ་ཐམས་ཅད་ཀྱང་མིང་དེས་ཁྱབ་པར་བཞེད་ན་ནི་འདིར་དམིགས་ཀྱི་གདགས་དོན་མེད་དོ།། ཕྱི་མས་ཕྱོགས་ཙམ་མཐོང་པར་སྣང་ཡང་། འདིར་མཆོད་བརྗོད་སོགས་ཐམས་ཅད་བསྡུངས་པའི་གཞུང་ཚད་མ་ལ་ཀ་སུམ་ཅུ་མ་གསུམ་འབྱུང་བས་སུམ་ཅུ་པོ་ནར་མ་འགྲིག་སྙེ་སུམ་ཅུ་ཙམ་ཞེས་ལས་སྟོང་བའི་མགྲོན་པོ་ལྟར་ཚོམ་ཚོམ་བྱེད་དགོས་པ་མ་ཡིན་ཏེ། མཆོད་བརྗོད་དང་རྩོམ་པར་དམ་བཅའ་བ་ནི། སྐབས་གཞན་གྱི་ཐུན་མོང་བ་ཡིན་པ་རྟགས་འཇུག་ལ་འདི་མེད་པས་གསལ་ཞིང་། གསུམ་པ་ནི། ཡི་གེ་ཨཱ་ལི་ཀཱ་ལི་གཉིས། སོགས་སྐབས་དང་པོ་ཉིད་ཀྱི་ཐུན་མོང་མིན་པའི་བརྗོད་བྱ་ཚིགས་བཅད་སུམ་ཅུ་ཉིད་ཀྱིས་རྫོགས་པས་གྲངས་ངེས་པའི་མིང་ནས་བཏགས་པའི་ཕྱིར་རོ། དེ་ལྟ་བས་ན་སྔོན་ཚད་འགྲེལ་བྱེད་རྣམས་ཀྱི་བློ་གྲོས་ལྷ་ལ་ཆུད་པའི་ལེགས་བཤད་གསར་པ་འདིས་དཔྱོད་ལྡན་རྣམས་བག་ཕོངས་སུ་རྩིན་པར་མཛོད་ཅིག། གཉིས་པ་འགྱུར་ཕྱག་ལ་དངོས་དང་། མཐའ་དཔྱད་དོ།

དང་པོ་ནི། སྨྲ་བའི་དབང་ཕྱུག་འཇམ་པའི་དབྱངས་ལ་ཕྱག་འཚལ་ལོ།།

ཞེས་སྨོས་ཏེ་བསྟན་བཅོས་འདི་དཔྱད་པ་གསུམ་གྱིས་རྣམ་པར་དག་པས་རྗེས་འཇུག་རྣམས་ཀྱིས་འཕགས་ཡུལ་ནས་བསྒྱུར་བའི་བསྟན་བཅོས་ཁུངས་པར་འཕགས་པ་རྣམས་དང་མཚུངས་པར་ལྷ་ཞིང་དོན་དུ་གཉེར་རིགས་སོ་ཞེས་འདོམས་པའི་དོན་དུ་བྱ་མི་ཉིད་ཀྱིས་བསྒྱུར་བའི་མདོ་རྒྱུད་རྣམས་ཀྱི་འགྱུར་ཕྱག་དང་མཐུན་པར་འཕགས་པ་འཇམ་དཔལ་ལ་ཕྱག་མཛད་པའོ།

གཉིས་པ་ནི། འདིར་ལ་ལ་ཞིག་གིས་བསྟན་བཅོས་བསྒྱུར་བ་སོགས་ལ་བར་ཆད་མི་འབྱུང་བའི་ཆེད་དུ་ལོ་ཙཱ་བ་རྣམས་ཀྱིས་ཕྱག་མཛད་པ་དང་རྗེས་སུ་མཐུན་པར་ཞེས་སྨྲེལ་མོད། སྔོ་ནལ་དུ་གནས་པས་སླུས་པ་མ་ཡིན་ཏེ། དེ་ལྟ་ན་བསྟན་བཅོས་འདི་རྩོམ་པ་དེའི་ཚེ་དེ་ལས་སྔོན་དུ་དཔེར་བྱ་ངེས་པའི་ལོ་ཙཱ་བ་དུ་མ་ཞིག་ཡོད་པར་འདོད་དགོས་ཤིང་། དེ་འདོད་ན་བོད་ཡིག་ཐེབས་སྔོར་དང་བཅས་པའང་བྱ་མིས་བརྩམས་པ་ལས་གཞན་དུ་ཡོད་པར་ཤུགས་ཀྱིས་ཁས་བླངས་པར་སོང་བས་བོད་ཀྱི་དེབ་ཐེར་རྙིང་མ་རྣམས་དང་། ཁྱེད་རང་གིས་རྟེན་ཆེན་གྱི་བློན་པོ་ཐུ་མིང་། སོགས་དྲངས་པའི་རྣམ་བཞག་ཐམས་ཅད་བཤིག་པར་ཐལ་ལོ། རྒྱ་མཚན་འདིས། མཁན་པོས་ཐོག་མར་ཡི་གེ་བརྩམས་པའི་རྗེས་སུ་བརྡའ་སྦྱོར་པའི་གཞུང་ལུགས་རྣམས་བརྩམས་པ་དང་། མདོ་ལ་སོགས་པ་འགྱུར་ཅིང་སློབ་མར་བཤད་པས། ལོ་ཙཱ་བ་རྣམས་བྱུང་བའི་གོ་རིམ་འདི་ལྟར་བར་གྱིས་ཤིག། གཉིས་པ་བསྟན་བཅོས་དངོས་ལ་གཞུང་སྤྱིའི་ཡན་ལག་ཏུ་མཆོད་པར་བརྗོད་ཅིང་བཤད་པར་དམ་བཅའ་བ། སྐབས་དོན་དངོས་ཉིད་སུམ་ཅུ་པ་ཉིད་རྒྱས་པར་བསྟན་པའོ།།

དང་པོ་ལ། མཆོད་བརྗོད་དང་བཤད་པར་དམ་བཅའ་བ་གཉིས། དང་པོ་ཐའང་། དཀོན་མཆོག་གསུམ་ལ་སྤྱིར་ཕྱག་འཚལ་བ། དགོས་པའི་དབང་གིས་རྟག་ཞི་བ་ལ་ཕྱག་འཚལ་བ། དྲིན་བཟོ་བའི་ཕྱིར་མཁས་པ་སྤྱི་དང་བྱེ་བྲག་ལ་ཕྱག་འཚལ་བའོ།།

དང་པོ་ལ་དངོས་དང་མཐའ་དཔྱད་གཉིས་ལས་དང་པོ་ནི།

གང་ལ་ཡོན་ཏན་མཆོག་མངའ་བའི། །དཀོན་མཆོག་དེ་ལ་ཕྱག་འཚལ་ལོ། །

ཞེས་པ་སྟེ། གང་ཞིག་གང་ལ་ནོར་བུ་རིན་པོ་ཆེ་དང་ཆོས་མཚུངས་པའི་ཡོན་ཏན་ཕུན་སུམ་ཚོགས་པ་མངའ་བ་ནི་དཀོན་མཆོག་ཅེས་བྱ་ཞིང་། མཚུངས་ཆོས་ཀྱི་ཡོན་ཏན་ཡང་བསོད་ནམས་མ་བསགས་པ་ལ་སྣང་བ་མིན་པས་འབྱུང་བ་དཀོན་པ་དང་། རང་བཞིན་གྱིས་རྙོག་པའི་ཆོས་ཅན་མ་ཡིན་པས་དྲི་མ་བྲལ་བ་དང་། རང་གཞན་གྱི་དོན་སྒྲུབ་པའི་མཐུ་དང་ལྡན་པ་དང་། འགྲོ་བ་རྣམས་ཀྱི་བསམ་པ་དགེ་བའི་རྒྱུ་ཡིན་པས་འཇིག་རྟེན་གྱི་རྒྱན་དང་། འཇིག་རྟེན་ལས་མཆོག་ཏུ་གྱུར་པ་དང་། རྣམ་པར་བསྒྱུར་བའི་རང་བཞིན་ཅན་མ་ཡིན་པ་རྣམས་ཏེ།

འབྱུང་བ་དཀོན་ཕྱིར་དྲི་མེད་ཕྱིར། །མཐུ་ལྡན་ཕྱིར་དང་འཇིག་རྟེན་གྱི། །

རྒྱན་གྱུར་ཕྱིར་དང་མཆོག་ཉིད་ཕྱིར། །འགྱུར་བ་མེད་ཕྱིར་དཀོན་མཆོག་ཉིད། །

ཅེས་འབྱུང་བས་སོ། དེ་ལ་དབྱེ་ན་སངས་རྒྱས་དང་ཆོས་དང་དགེ་འདུན་ཏེ་དཀོན་མཆོག་རྣམ་པ་གསུམ་ཡིན་ཞིང་། དེའང་སྐྱབས་ཡུལ་དངོས་ཀྱི་དབང་དུ་བྱས་ན། མཐར་ཐུག་གི་སྐྱབས་རྫོགས་པའི་སངས་རྒྱས་སྐུ་གསུམ་གྱི་བདག་ཉིད་ཅན་དང་། གནས་སྐབས་ཀྱི་སྐབས་འགོག་ལམ་གྱིས་བསྡུས་པའི་ཆོས་དང་། སློབ་པ་འཕགས་པའི་དགེ་འདུན་རྣམས་དང་། དེར་མ་ཟད་གང་ལ་བརྟེན་ནས་དཀོན་མཆོག་དངོས་ལ་གུས་པ་འཕེལ་ཞིང་མོས་པས་འཇུག་པར་འགྱུར་བའི་རྐྱེན་ཁྱད་པར་དུ་འཕགས་པ་སངས་རྒྱས་ཀྱི་སྐུ་བརྙན་སོགས་དང་མིང་ཚིག་ཡི་གེའི་ཚོགས་སུ་སྣང་བའི་ལུང་གི་ཆོས་དང་སོ་སོ་སྐྱེ་བོའི་དགེ་འདུན་རྣམས་ལའང་མཁན་པོས་གཞུང་དགོད་པའི་ཐོག་མ་ཉིད་དུ་ལུས་ངག་ཡིད་གསུམ་འདུད་པའི་ཕྱག་མཛད་པ་ཡིན་ནོ། དེ་ལྟར་ཐོག་མ་ཁོ་ནར་དཀོན་མཆོག་གསུམ་ལ་བསྟོད་ཕྱག་མཛད་པ་འདིས་དེའི་ཚེ་བོད་ཡུལ་དུ་བོན་ལས་གཞན་པའི་གྲུབ་མཐའ་སྨྲ་བ་ཐལ་ཀྱིས་ཡོད་པར་མ་འཚལ་ཅིང་། འཕགས་ཡུལ་དུའང་ཕྱི་ནང་གཉིས་ཀ་ཡོད་པས་རྗེས་འཇུག་གི་སྐྱེ་བོ་རྣམས་རྗེས་སུ་བཟུང་བའི་སླད་དུ་གང་ཞིག་དཀོན་མཆོག་གསུམ་ལ་འདུད་ཅིང་སྐྱབས་སུ་འགྲོ་བར་བྱེད་པའི་ལམ་དེ་ནི་ནོར་བ་མེད་ཅིང་ཡང་དག་པའོ། ཞེས་འདོམས་པའང་ཡིན་ནོ། །

གཉིས་པ་ནི། ཁ་ཅིག་གིས། སྐབས་འདིར་གང་ལ་ཞེས་པའི་ལ་ཡིག་ཕྱོགས་སུ་བཀར་ནས་ངོས་བཟུང་བའི་དོན་དང་། དེ་ལ་ཞེས་པའི་ལ་ཡིག་ཆེད་དུ་བྱ་བའི་དོན་དུ་བཤད་མོད།

སྔ་མ་ནི། གཞུང་འདིའི་ལ་དོན་འཆད་པའི་སྐབས་སུ་དེ་འདྲ་ལ་འཇུག་པར་མ་བཤད་པར་མ་ཟད་དོན་གྱིས་ཀྱང་དེ་འདྲར་འཇུག་མི་སྲིད་པས་མི་འཐད་ཅིང་། གང་ཞིག་ལ་ཡོན་ཏན་མཆོག་མངའ་བའམ་ལྡན་པ་ཞེས་སྦྱོར་དགོས་པས་རྣམ་དབྱེ་བདུན་པ་གནས་གཞིའི་དོན་ཉིད་དོ། ཕྱི་མ་ནི་ལེགས་སྦྱར་ཤེས་ཚོམ་ཀྱིས་ཞྭ་དཔེ་ལྷམ་ལ་བཀབ་པར་ཟད་དེ་ཅིའི་ཕྱིར་ན། ཀ་ལྤ་བར། ནམས་སྭ་སྟི། སྭཱ་ཧཱ། སྭ་དྷཱ། ཨ་ལཾ། བ་ཥ་ཊ། སྦྱོར་བ་ལ་བཞི་པའོ་ཞེས་འབྱུང་བར་ནམས་ཀྱི་ཡུལ་ལ་ཕྱིར་བཏང་། དོན་ཐོབ་ཀྱི་སྒོ་ནས་གཉིས་པ་འཇུག་ཀྱང་གྲགས་པ་དམིགས་བསལ་གྱི་སྒོ་ནས་བཞི་པ་སྦྱོར་བར་མཁས་པ་རྣམས་ཀྱིས་བཀྲལ་མོད་ཀྱི། དེ་འདྲའི་བྱེ་བྲག་མ་ཕྱེད་པར། ནམས་ཀྱི་ཡུལ་ལ་བཞི་པ་འཇུག་པར་བཤད་དོ་སྙམ་ནས་ཕྱག་འཚལ་བའི་དོན་ཅན་གྱི་སྒྲ་ཡི་ཡུལ་ཐམས་ཅད་བཞི་པ་འཇུག་པར་བསམ་ཞིང་སྨྲ་བའི་ཕྱིར་རོ། དེས་ན་སྦྱོར་བཏང་གི་སྒྲུབ་པའི་དབང་གིས། ཡྂ་ཊ་ཀྱཾ་སོགས་ཀྲིཏ་ཀྲིན་གཞན་གྱིས་བསྒྲུབས་པ་དང་། ན་མཱ་མི་སོགས་ཏིང་མཐའ་རྣམས་དང་། ཕྱིང་གཞན་ལས་བྱུང་བའི་བཙ་ནཾ་ལྟ་བུ་རྣམས་ཀྱང་འདུད་ཅིང་ཕྱག་འཚལ་བའི་དོན་ཅན་དུ་མཚུངས་ཀྱང་དེ་དག་གི་ཡུལ་ལ་རྣམ་དབྱེ་གཉིས་པ་ལས་གཞན་པའི་རྣམ་དབྱེ་འཇུག་པ་མ་ཡིན་པ་འདི་ཀུན་གྱིས་ཤེས་པར་བྱའོ། རྒྱ་མཚན་དེས་ན་བོད་དུ་དེ་ལྟའི་གྲགས་པ་དམིགས་བསལ་མེད་པའི་ཕྱིར་དོན་ཐོབ་གཙོ་བས། བཞི་པའི་ཕྱིར་བཏང་གི་དོན་སྦྱིན་པའི་ཚོད་ལ་སོགས་པ་བྱ་བ་གང་ཡིན་ཡང་བྱ་ཡུལ་དེའམ་དེ་དང་འབྲེལ་བའི་དོན་དུ་སོང་བ་ཞིག་དགོས་པ་ལས་ཡུལ་ཕྱིར་བར་ཙམ་ལ་ཕྱག་བྱེད་པ་ནི་ཕྱག་བྱེད་པ་པོ་ཉིད་དམ་དེ་དང་འབྲེལ་བའི་དོན་ལས་ཕྱག་ཡུལ་དེའི་ཆེད་དུ་མིན་པ་ནི་གཏན་ཚིགས་ཀྱང་རྟོགས་པར་སླ་བའི་ཕྱིར་ཕྱག་གི་ཡུལ་ལ་རྣམ་དབྱེ་གཉིས་པ་འཇུག་པ་ལས་ངེས་མེད་དོ། །

འོ་ན་གནས་བརྒྱད་འགྲེལ་པ་ལས། བཞི་པ་བྱིན་པ་དང་ཕྱག་འཚལ་བ་ཞེས་བྱ་བ། མིང་གི་ཕྱིར་རྒྱ་འདྲེན་པའང་མིང་ཉིད་རྒྱས་པ་དང་། སྨིན་པའི་ཕྱིར་སྐྱོར་ཡང་དོན་གྱིས་རྒྱ་འདྲེན་པའི་བྱེད་པ་པོའི་ཚེད་ཡིན་པར་འགྱུར་བ་དང་། མཆོད་རྟེན་ལ་ཕྱག་འཚལ་བ་དང་། མཆོད་རྟེན་ཉིད་ཕྱག་གི་ཡུལ་ལས། གནས་སུ་སྐྱུར་ཡང་དོན་གྱིས་ཕྱག་འཚལ་བ་པོའི་ཚེད་ཡིན་པར་འགྱུར་བས་བཞི་ག་བྱ་བའི་ཚེད་ཀྱི་དོན་དུ་དྲང་ངོ་།། ཞེས་བཤད་པ་མ་ཡིན་ནམ་ཞེ་ན། གནས་བརྒྱད་ཙ་འགྲེལ་གྱི་དོན་འགའ་ཞིག་བསྒྲུབ་བྱ་ལས་སྒྲུབ་བྱེད་དུ་མི་འགྲོ་བ་ཡོད་ཅིང་རྣམ་དབྱེ་བཞི་པ་འཇུག་ཚུལ་འདིའང་བརྟག་དགོས་སྙམ། རྒྱ་དྲེན་པའི་བྱེད་པ་པོའི་ཚེད་ཡིན་པའི་རྒྱུ་མཚན་གྱི་མིང་ལ་བཞི་པ་འཇུག་པ་དང་། ཕྱག་འཚལ་ངའི་བྱ་བའི་ཚད་ཡིན་པའི་རྒྱུ་མཚན་གྱིས་མཆོད་རྟེན་ལ་བཞི་པ་འཇུག་པར་འདོད་པ་དེ་ལྟར། བཤན་པས་ཕྱུགས་གསོད། ཚོང་པས་ནོར་སྒྲུབས། ཁ་ཟས་ལ་ལོངས་སྤྱོད། ལྷ་བུ་རྣམས་ལའང་རིམ་པར་གསོད་པ་པོ་དང་སྒྲུབས་པ་པོའི་ཚེད་ཡིན་པས་ཕྱུགས་དང་ནོར་ལ་བཞི་པ་འཇུག་པར་ཐལ་བ་དང་ལོངས་སྤྱོད་པའི་བྱ་བའི་ཚེད་ཡིན་པས་ཁ་ཟས་ལ་བཞི་པ་འཇུག་པར་ཐལ་བ་སོགས་དང་། སྤྲང་པོ་ལ་ཟན་སྦྱིན་ལྷ་བུར་སྦྱིན་བྱ་འམ་སྦྱིན་ཡུལ་ལ་བཞི་པ་མི་འཇུག་པར་ཐལ་བ་སོགས་སྐྱོན་མཐའ་ཡས་མེད་། བརྡའ་སྤྲོད་པའི་བསྟན་བཅོས་ཚད་ལྡན་གང་དུའང་དེ་འདྲའི་རྣམ་བཞག་བཤད་པ་མ་མཐོང་བས་སོ། ཡང་གང་ལ་དང་དེ་ལ་ཞེས་པའི་ལ་དོན་ག་ཉིས་མཐའ་གཅིག་ཏུ་མི་མཚུངས་པར་འཆད་དགོས་པའང་མ་ཡིན་ཏེ། ལེགས་སྦྱར་གྱི་རྣམ་དབྱེ་སྦྱོར་ཚུལ་དང་བསྟུན་ན། གང་ཞེས་པ་སྤྱིའི་སྒྲ། དེ་ཞེས་པ་བྱེ་བྲག་ངེས་གཟུང་གི་སྒྲ་ཡིན་པས། སྤྱིའི་བྱ་བ་བྱེ་བྲག་ལ་ངེས་གཟུང་གིས་སྦྱོར་བ་འདི་འདྲའི་རིགས་ལ་གཉིས་ཀར་རྣམ་དབྱེ་མཚུངས་པར་སྦྱོར་བ་ཡིན་པའི་ཕྱིར་དེ་གཉིས་ཀ་རྣམ་དབྱེ་གཉིས་པའི་དོན་དུ་བྱས་ནའང་རུང་ངོ་། ཕྱག་འཚལ་ལོ།། གང་ལ་ན་ཡོན་ཏན་མཆོག་མངའ་བའི་དཀོན་མཆོག་དེ་ལའོ།། ཞེས་འཆད་པའི་ལུགས་སོ།། གཉིས་པ་ལ་དངོས་དང་ལོག་རྟོག་སེལ་བ་གཉིས།

དང་པོ་ནི།

གང་གིས་སྒྲ་དབྱངས་ཀུན་གསུངས་པའི། །འཇམ་པའི་དབྱངས་ལ་ཕྱག་འཚལ་ལོ།།

ཞེས་པ་སྟེ། གང་ཞིག་གང་གིས་སྒྲ་དབྱངས་བརྗོད་པ་ཐམས་ཅད་མ་ལུས་པར་སྟོན་ཅིང་གསུངས་པས་གསུང་གི་དབང་ཕྱུག་ཆེན་པོར་གྱུར་པ། ཉེས་པའི་ཚུལ་རིག་ཐམས་ཅད་ཡོངས་སུ་སྤངས་པས་འཇམ་པའི་ཡོན་ཏན་དང་ལྡན་པའི་ཕྱིར་འགྲོ་བ་ཐམས་ཅད་ཀྱི་ཁམས་དབང་བསམ་པ་རྣམས་དང་མཐུན་པར་རྗེས་སུ་འཇུག་པའི་དབྱངས་ཀྱི་བདག་ཉིད་དེ་ལ་ཕྱག་འཚལ་ལོ་ཞེས་པའོ། སྒྲ་དབྱངས་ཇི་ལྟར་གསུངས་པའི་ཚུལ་ཡང་འཇམ་པའི་དབྱངས་ཞེས་བྱ་བ་ནི་བསྐལ་པ་དཔག་ཏུ་མེད་པའི་གོང་ནས་མངོན་པར་རྫོགས་པའི་བྱང་ཆུབ་བརྙེས་སུ་ཟིན་ཀྱང་། ས་བཅུ་པའི་བྱང་ཆུབ་སེམས་དཔའ་ལ་སོགས་པའི་ཚུལ་གྱི་སྒྱུ་འཕྲུལ་ཆེན་པོས་འཁོར་བ་ཇི་སྲིད་དུ་སངས་རྒྱས་ཀྱི་འཕྲིན་ལས་མཛད་པ་ཞིག་ཏེ། དོན་དམ་པར་ན་སངས་རྒྱས་ཐམས་ཅད་ཀྱི་ཐུགས་གཉིས་སུ་མེད་པའི་ཡེ་ཤེས་ཀྱི་ངོ་བོ་འཇམ་དཔལ་ཡེ་ཤེས་སེམས་དཔའོ།། དེ་ཉིད་བདེ་བར་གཤེགས་པ་ཐམས་ཅད་ཀྱི་གསུང་མི་ཟད་པ་རྒྱན་གྱི་འཁོར་ལོའི་རྒྱུད་པ་དང་། དེའི་མཐུས་འཇིག་རྟེན་ཐམས་ཅད་ཀྱི་སྒྲ་དབྱངས་བརྗོད་པ་མ་ལུས་པ་གསལ་བར་བྱེད་པའང་ཡིན་ནོ། རྒྱུ་མཚན་དེས་འཇམ་པའི་དབྱངས་ཀྱིས་སྒྲ་དབྱངས་གསུངས་པར་བཤད་དོ། མཚན་ཡང་དག་པར་བརྗོད་པ་ལས།

བཅོམ་ལྡན་འདས་ཀྱི་ཡེ་ཤེས་སྐུ། །གཙུག་ཏོར་ཆེན་པོ་ཚིག་གི་བདག

ཡེ་ཤེས་སྐུ་སྟེ་རང་བྱུང་བ། །འཇམ་དཔལ་ཡེ་ཤེས་སེམས་དཔའ་ཡིན།

ཞེས་གསུངས་ཤིང་དེའི་ཚིག་རྐང་ཐ་མའི་དོན་སླེག་པའི་རྡོ་རྗེའི་འགྲེལ་པར། འཇམ་པ་ནི་མཉེན་པ་དང་དཔལ་དང་ལྡན་པ་གང་ཡིན་པ་དེ་ནི་འཇམ་དཔལ་ལོ། ཡེ་ཤེས་སེམས་དཔའ་ཞེས་བྱ་བ་ནི་དེ་བཞིན་གཤེགས་པ་ཐམས་ཅད་ཀྱི་ཐུགས་ཀ་ན་གནས་པའི་ཕྱིར་རོ། འཇམ་དཔལ་ཡང་དེ་ཡིན་ལ་ཡེ་ཤེས་སེམས་དཔའང་དེ་ཉིད་ཡིན་པས་འཇམ་དཔལ་ཡེ་ཤེས་སེམས་དཔའ་སྟེ། དེས་ས་བཅུའི་དབང་ཕྱུག་གི་བྱང་ཆུབ་སེམས་དཔའ་ནི་མ་ཡིན་ནོ། དེ་ལྟ་ན་དེ་སུ་ཞིག་ཡིན་ན་གཉིས་སུ་མེད་པའི་ཤེས་རབ་ཀྱི་ཕ་རོལ་ཏུ་ཕྱིན་པ་དེ་ཉིད་འཇམ་དཔལ་ཡེ་ཤེས་སེམས་དཔའ་སྟེ་ཞེས་དང་།

རྫོགས་པའི་སངས་རྒྱས་ཨ་ལས་བྱུང་། ཨ་ནི་ཡིག་འབྲུ་ཀུན་གྱི་མཆོག །
དོན་ཆེན་ཡི་གེ་དམ་པ་སྟེ། །ཁོང་ནས་འབྱུང་བ་སྐྱེ་བ་མེད། །
བརྗོད་པ་ཀུན་གྱི་རྒྱུ་ཡི་མཆོག །ཚིག་ཀུན་རབ་ཏུ་གསལ་བར་བྱེད། །

ཅེས་དང་། འགྲེལ་པར་དེས་ན་འདི་སྐད་སྟོན་པར་འགྱུར་ཏེ་ཡི་གེ་ཨ་ནི་མ་སྐྱེས་པའི་རྣམ་ཐར་སངས་རྒྱས་ཐམས་ཅད་ཀྱི་ཡོན་ཏན་རྣམས་ཀྱི་གནས་བྱང་ཆུབ་སེམས་སྔོན་དུ་འགྲོ་བ་རྣམ་པར་མི་རྟོག་པའི་ཡེ་ཤེས་ཀྱི་ངོ་བོ་ཉིད་འཇམ་དཔལ་གྱི་རང་བཞིན་བསྐྱེད་པས་ན་ཆོས་ཀྱི་འཁོར་ལོ་བསྐོར་བར་བྱེད་ཅིང་ཚིག་ཐམས་ཅད་རབ་ཏུ་གསལ་བར་བྱེད་པའི་གསུང་གི་འཁོར་ལོའི་རྒྱུར་གྱུར་པའི་ཕྱིར་བརྗོད་པ་ཐམས་ཅད་ཀྱི་རྒྱུའི་མཆོག་ཡིན་ནོ།། ཞེས་སོགས་རྒྱས་པར་གསུངས་པ་བཞིན་ནོ།།

གཉིས་པ་ནི། སྐབས་འདིར་འགྲེལ་བྱེད་བླ་མ་རྣམས་ཀྱིས་སྒྲ་དབྱངས་ཞེས་པ་ཨཱ་ལི་ཙ་དྲུག་ཁོ་ནར་ངོས་བཟུང་སྟེ་དེ་འཇམ་དཔལ་གྱིས་གསུངས་སོ་ཞེས་བབ་ཅོལ་དུ་སྨྲ་བར་བྱེད་མོད། དེ་དག་གིས་བརྗོད་པ་ཙམ་ལ་བསམས་ན་ནི་སྨྲ་བོ་མཐའ་ཡས་པའི་ཕྱིར་མ་ངེས་སྔོན་དུ་ཨཱ་ལི་བཅུ་དྲུག་ཁོ་ན་གསུངས་པའི་ལོ་རྒྱུས་གཏན་ཚིག་ཡོད་ནའང་བཀོད་རིགས་པ་ལས་མི་སྣང་ཞིང་། འཇམ་དཔལ་ཤེས་རབ་ཀྱི་ལྷ་ཡིན་པས་ཨཱ་ལི་ཁོ་ན་གསུངས་པ་འཐད་དོ། སྙམ་ནའང་རང་བཟོར་རྟོགས་སླ་བར་མ་ཟད། མདོ་རྒྱུད་རྒྱ་མཚོ་རྣམས་གིས་སྒྲ་དབྱངས་བརྗོད་པ་ཐམས་ཅད་ཀྱི་དབང་ཕྱུག་ཏུ་གསུངས་པ་དང་འགལ་ལོ། གསུམ་པ་ལ་དངོས་དང་ལོག་རྟོག་སེལ་བ་གཉིས།

དང་པོ་ནི།

གང་གིས་མིང་གཞི་སྔོན་གསུངས་པ། ཏག་ཞི་བ་ལ་ཕྱག་འཚལ་ལོ།།

ཞེས་པའོ། དེ་འང་འཇིག་རྟེན་གྱི་གྲགས་པ་ཙམ་གྱི་རྗེས་སུ་འབྲང་ནས། བརྡ་ཡང་དག་པར་སྦྱོར་བའི་ཚུལ་འདི་དག་དོག་ནས། བསྟན་པ་ཀུན་གྱི་གཞི་འཛིན་ཅིང་། སོགས་འཆད་འགྱུར་ལྟར་གྲུབ་མཐའ་ཞུགས་མ་ཞུགས་ཕྱི་ནང་ཐམས་ཅད་ཀྱི་བསྟན་བྱར་ཤེས་པའི་ཆེད་དུའམ། ཕྱི་རོལ་པ་རྗེས་སུ་བཟུང་བའི་སླད་དུ་ལྷ་ཆེན་པོ་དབང་ཕྱུག་ལ་བསྟོད་ཕྱག་མཛད་པ་ཡིན་ཞིང་། དབང་ཕྱུག་གི་མཚན་དུ་ཏག་ཞི་བ་ཞེས་པ་ནི་ས་ཏྲ་ཤི་བ་སྟེ་འཕགས་པའི་ཡུལ་དུ་རྒྱང་ལྟར་གྲགས་པ་ཡིན་ནོ།

གཉིས་པ་ནི། དེ་ལྟ་ན་ལྷ་ཆེན་པོས་ཡི་གེ་ཐོག་མར་བཀོད་པའམ་གསུང་བའི་ལོ་རྒྱུས་བཀོད་དུ་མེད་ཅིང་། ཕྱིར་དཀོན་མཆོག་གསུམ་ལ་སྐྱབས་སུ་སོང་ནས་འཇིག་རྟེན་པའི་ལྷ་ཕྱག་བྱེད་པའང་མི་འགྲེལ་བས་མི་འཐད་དོ། ཞེ་ན་ལྷ་ཆེན་པོས་ཡི་གེ་ཐོག་མར་བཀོད་པའི་ལོ་རྒྱུས་དེང་སང་བོད་ཡུལ་འདིར་ཡོངས་གྲགས་སུ་མེད་ཀྱང་སྔོན་དུས་མེད་པར་མ་ངེས་ལ། འཕགས་ཡུལ་དུ་ནི་ཕྱི་རོལ་པ་དག་གིས་དབང་ཕྱུག་འཇིག་རྟེན་གྱི་བྱེད་པོར་ཡང་འདོད་ཅིང་བྲམ་ཟེ་རྣམས་ཀྱི་གཞུང་དུ་བྱེད་པོ་ཉི་ཤུ་རྩ་བཞི་བཤད་པ་ལས་ཡི་གེའི་བྱེད་པོ་དབང་ཕྱུག་ཏུ་གསལ་བར་བསྟན་པ་ཡོད་པར་མ་ཟད། མ་མཐོང་ཕྱིར་ན་མེད་པ་ཡིན་ཞེས་པ་ལྟར་ཁྱོད་རང་གི་མ་མཐོང་བའི་རྟགས་ཀྱིས་མེད་པར་བསྒྲུབ་མི་ནུས་པའི་ཕྱིར་དང་། མཆོག་གསུམ་ལ་སྐྱབས་སུ་སོང་ནས་འཇིག་རྟེན་པའི་ལྷར་ཕྱག་བྱེད་པ་ཕྱིར་མི་རུང་ཀྱང་འདི་དགོས་པ་དང་བཅས་ཤིང་ལྷ་ཆེན་པོ་དེ་འཇིག་རྟེན་དབང་ཕྱུག་གི་རྣམ་རོལ་དུ་འང་ཟ་མ་ཏོག་ལ་སོགས་པའི་མདོ་སྡེ་རྣམས་སུ་བསྟན་པའི་ཚུལ་ཇི་ལྟ་བར་ཐུགས་སུ་ཆུད་ནས་ཕྱག་མཛད་ཀྱི། འཇིག་རྟེན་རང་རྒྱུད་པར་བཟུང་བའམ། འཇིག་རྟེན་གྱི་བྱེད་པོ་སོགས་སུ་ཞེན་པས་ཕྱག་མ་མཛད་པའི་ཕྱིར་སྐྱོན་མེད་དོ། དེས་ན་མཁས་པ་འདིས་ཡི་གེ་དབང་ཕྱུག་གིས་བཀོད་པ་འཕགས་ཡུལ་དུ་བྲམ་ཟེ་རྣམས་ལ་ཡོངས་སུ་གྲགས་པར་དགོངས་ནས་མ་བརྟགས་ཉམས་དགའི་ངོར་འཇིག་རྟེན་གྱི་གྲགས་པ་དང་བསྟུན་ཏེ་དགོས་པའི་དབང་གིས་འདི་ལྟར་བསྟན་པ་ལ་ནི་ཉེས་པའི་ཆ་ཕྲ་མོས་ཀྱང་གོས་པ་མ་ཡིན་ནོ། འདིར་འགྲེལ་བྱེད་གཞན་དང་གཞན་དག་གིས་ཏག་ཞི་བ་ཞེས་པ་སངས་རྒྱས་དང་། སྤྱན་རས་གཟིགས་དང་ཚངས་པ་དང་། ཁྱབ་འཇུག་སོགས་སུ་འདོད་པ་ཡོད་ཀྱང་རིམ་བཞིན་འཐད་པར་མ་མཐོང་སྟེ། སངས་རྒྱས་ནི་དཀོན་མཆོག་གསུམ་གྱི་གཙོ་བོ་ཡིན་པའི་ཕྱིར་དེ་ལ་ཐོག་མར་བསྟོད་ཕྱག་མཛད་པས་འདིར་སླར་ཡང་ཁྱད་པར་དུ་བསྟོད་ཕྱག་མཛད་པར་བསྒྲུབ་པ་ལ་དགོས་པ་འཐད་ལྡན་སྨྲ་རྒྱུ་མ་བྱུང་བའི་ཕྱིར་དང་། ཏག་ཞི་བ་སངས་རྒྱས་ཀྱི་མཚན་དུ་གྲགས་ཆུང་བའི་ཕྱིར་དང་། སྤྱན་རས་གཟིགས་དང་ལྷ་ཚངས་པ་དག་གིས་ཀྱང་ཡི་གེ་ཐོག་མར་བཀོད་པའི་ལོ་རྒྱུས་འཐད་ལྡན་སྨྲ་རྒྱུ་མེད་

པར་མ་ཟད། དེ་དག་ལ་འང་རྟག་ཞི་བའི་མིང་ཡོངས་སུ་མ་གྲགས་པའི་ཕྱིར་དང་། ཁྱབ་འཇུག་གིས་ཡི་གེ་བཀོད་པར་བཤད་པའི་གཞུང་དེ་འང་འཐད་ལྡན་ཡིན་མིན་བརྟག་དགོས་ཤིང་ཁྱབ་འཇུག་ལ་རྟག་ཞི་བར་ཡང་མ་གྲགས་ཏེ་མིང་སྟོང་གིས་ཁྱབ་འཇུག་ལ་བསྟོད་པའི་རྒྱ་དཔེ་ཁོ་བོའི་ལག་ཏུ་སོན་པས་དེའི་ནང་དུ་འང་རྟག་ཞི་བ་ཞེས་པ་མ་བྱུང་བའི་ཕྱིར་དང་། སོ་སོར་འབྲུང་མའི་སྐུང་བའི་སྐབས་སུ། དམངས་རིགས་ཕྱིར་ན་རྟག་ཞི་བ། ཁྱབ་འཇུག་ལེགས་པར་བྲིས་པར་བྱ། ཞེས་འབྱུང་བ་འང་དེ་གཉིས་གཅིག་པར་བརྟན་པ་མ་ཡིན་པའི་ཕྱིར་དང་། དམངས་རིགས་ཀྱི་དོན་དུ་དབང་ཕྱུག་གམ་ཁྱབ་འཇུག་གང་རུང་བྲི་བའི་དོན་དུ་མངོན་པའི་ཕྱིར་ཏེ། དེ་མ་ཐག་ཏུ། རྗེའུ་རིགས་ཕྱིར་ནི་རྣམ་ཐོས་བུ། ལྷ་ཡི་དབང་ཕྱུག་དབང་པོ་བྲིས། ཞེས་འབྱུང་བ་འང་རྣམ་ཐོས་བུའམ་དབང་ཕྱུག་གམ་བརྒྱ་བྱིན་གང་རུང་བྲི་བའི་དོན་དུ་གསལ་བའི་ཕྱིར་རོ། ཡང་འགྲེལ་བྱེད་ཕྱི་མ་ཞིག་གིས་རྟག་ཞི་བ་དབང་ཕྱུག་ཏུ་འདོད་མཁན་དགག་པ་བྱེད་པར་བསམས་སམ་ཏེ། དབང་ཕྱུག་དང་དྲག་པོ་སོགས་སྐབས་འདིར་མཆོད་ཡུལ་དུ་བྱེད་པ་ལ་དགོས་པ་མ་མཆི་ཤིང་ཞེས་སྨྲས་ནས་རང་ལུགས་བཞག་པའི་སྐབས་སུ། གཞན་ཕྱིའི་ངོར་ཚངས་པ་དང་ཁྱབ་འཇུག་སོགས་ལ་བསྟོད་ཕྱག་མཛད་པར་འགྲེལ་རིགས་ཚུལ་ཙམ་རྟོག་གེ་ལུང་རྒྱས་པར་དྲངས་ནས་བསྒྲུབ་འདུག་སྟེ། དེ་དག་དགོས་འགལ་དུ་འགྱུར་རམ་མི་འགྱུར་དབང་ཕྱུག་དང་དྲག་པོ་ཞེས་པའང་མིང་གི་རྣམ་གྲངས་ཡིན་གྱི་ལྷ་ཡི་ངོ་བོ་སོ་སོ་བ་མ་ཡིན་ལགས་སོ། ཡང་འདིར་བརྟན་གྱི་མིང་གཞི་ཞེས་པའང་ཁ་ཅིག་གསལ་བྱེད་ཁོ་ན་ལ་ངོས་བཟུང་བ་ནི། དེ་བས་གོང་དུ་སྨྲ་དབྱངས་ལྷ་ཡི་ཁོ་ནར་བཞེད་པའི་རྐྱབས་ཀྱིས། དེ་དང་འབྲེལ་མཚུངས་པའི་སྐད་དུ་དེ་ལྟར་མི་འཆད་ཀ་མེད་བྱུང་བ་ལས་རྒྱ་མཚན་གཞན་མི་སྣང་ངོ་། མིང་གཞི་ཡི་གེ་ཙམ་ལ་ངོས་འཛིན་པ་ནི་རྒྱ་མཚན་དང་བཅས་པ་སྟེ། ཐོག་ཏུ་མིང་ཚིག་བརྗོད་པ་ཀུན་གྱི་གཞི་ཡི་གེའི་ཞེས་དང་། ཡི་གེ་ལྷ་ཡི་ཀླུ་ཡི་གཉིས། ཞེས་བཤད་པས་མིང་གཞི་ཡི་གེ་ཡིན་པར་གྲུབ་ཅིང་ཡི་གེའང་ལྷ་ཡི་ཀླུ་ཡིའི་བདག་ཉིད་དུ་གྲུབ་པའི་ཕྱིར་རོ།།

བཞི་པ་ནི།

སྡེབ་སྦྱོར་ལེགས་མཛད་མཁས་རྣམས་དང་། བླ་མ་ལ་ཡང་ཕྱག་འཚལ་ནས།

ཞེས་པ་སྟེ། སྒྲ་སྐད་ཀྱི་བརྗོད་པ་དང་དོན་སྡེབ་ལེགས་པར་སྦྱོར་བའི་ཚུལ་སྟོན་པའི་སྒོ་ནས་ཚིག་དོན་གཉིས་ལ་མི་རྨོངས་པའི་ཤེས་རབ་སྐྱེད་པར་བྱེད་ནུས་པའི་གཞུང་རྩོམ་ཞིང་འཇོམས་པར་མཛད་པའི་མཁས་པ་སྤྱི་དང་། བྱེ་བྲག་ཏུ་མཁན་པོ་ཉིད་ལ་དེ་ལྟའི་བྱ་བ་མཛད་པའི་བྲམ་ཟེ་ཝེ་ཝེ་ཀ་ར་ལ་སོགས་པའི་བླ་མ་རྣམས་ལའང་ཕྱག་མཛད་པ་སྟེ། ནས་ཀྱི་སྒྲ་ནི་མཆོད་པར་བརྗོད་ཅིང་མ་ཐག་ཏུ་བཤད་པར་དམ་བཅའ་བའི་ཚིག་འདྲེན་པའི་ཕྱིར་ལྷག་བཅས་ཀྱི་སྒྲའོ།། དེས་ན་སྡེབ་སྦྱོར་ཞེས་པ་སྒྲ་སྐད་ཀྱི་འཇུག་པ་ཕྱིངས་རྐྱེན་རྣམ་འགྱུར་རྣམས་སྡེབ་ལེགས་པར་སྦྱར་བས་ཚིག་དོན་འཁྲུལ་པ་མེད་པར་རྟོན་པའི་ཕྱིར་སྒྲ་རིག་པ་དང་། དེ་ཉིད་ཉན་པ་པོའི་རྣ་བ་དང་ཡིད་དུ་འཇེབས་ཤིང་ངོ་མཚར་བའི་སྐད་དུ་སྦྱེ་ཡང་གི་ཁྲིད་བ་དང་ཚིག་སྦྱོར་ཚུལ་གྱི་ལུས་རྒྱན་མང་པོ་བརྩེགས་ནས་སྦྱོར་བ་སྡེབ་སྦྱོར་དང་། སྙན་ངག་སྟེ་བོད་བརྡའི་དབང་དུ་མཛད་པ་ཡིན་གྱི་ཚནྡཿ་བསྒྱུར་བའི་སྡེབ་སྦྱོར་ཏེ་ཚིགས་བཅད་ཁོ་ན་ནི་འདིར་བསྟན་བྱ་མ་ཡིན་ནོ། གཉིས་པ་རྩོམ་པར་དམ་བཅའ་བ་ལ་དགོས་དང་ཞར་བྱུང་གི་དོན་ནོ།།

དང་པོ་ནི།

བསླབ་པ་ཀུན་གྱི་གཞི་འཛིན་ཅིང་། རིག་བྱེད་སྨྲ་བ་རྣམས་ཀྱི་རྒྱུ།
མིང་ཚིག་བརྗོད་པ་ཀུན་གྱི་གཞི། ཡི་གེའི་སྦྱོར་བ་བཤད་པར་བྱ།

ཞེས་པས་བསྟན་ཏེ། ལྷག་པ་ཚུལ་ཁྲིམས་དང་། བསམ་གཏན་ཤེས་རབ་ཀྱི་བསླབ་པ་སྟེ་སངས་རྒྱས་པའི་བསླབ་པའི་གཞི་ཐམས་ཅད་ཀློག་པའི་སྒོ་ནས་འཛིན་པར་བྱེད་ཅིང་། ཕྱི་རོལ་པའི་ངེས་བརྗོད། མཆོད་སྦྱིན། སྙན་ཚིག། སྲིད་སྲུང་སྟེ་རིག་བྱེད་བཞི་ཡན་ལག་དང་བཅས་པ་རྣམས་དང་། བཟོ་གསོ་སྒྲ་ཚད་ལ་སོགས་པ་ཤེས་བྱ་རིག་པའི་གནས་ཀྱི་གཞུང་ལུགས་མཐའ་དག་སྨྲ་བ་རྣམས་ཀྱི་རྒྱུ་འང་ཡིན་ལ་ཕྱིར་ཡི་གེ་ལས་མེད་། མིང་ལས་ཚིག་འབྱུང་བ་ཡིན་པའི་ཕྱིར་འཇིག་རྟེན་དང་འཇིག་རྟེན་ལས་འདས་པའི་མིང་ཚིག་བརྗོད་པ་ཐམས་ཅད་ཀྱི་གཞིར་འགྱུར་བ་ཡི་གེའི་སྦྱོར་བ་བཤད་པར་བྱའོ། ཞེས་སོ།

གཉིས་པ་ནི། དེ་ལྟར་ཚོགས་སུ་བཅད་པ་འདིས་ཞར་ལ་བསྟན་བཅོས་ཀྱི་དགོས་པ་སོགས་ཆོས་བཞི་པའང་བསྟན་པ་ཡིན་ཏེ། གངས་ཅན་དུ་བདེ་བར་གཤེགས་པའི་གསུང་རབ་ལ་སོགས་པར་འཇུག་པའི་བདའ་དང་སྐད་ཀྱི་འཇུག་པ་ཕལ་མོ་ཆེ་གསལ་བར་བྱེད་པའི་ཡི་གེའི་སྦྱོར་བ་གང་ཡིན་པ་ནི་ཙ་བ་བརྒྱུད་པའི་བསྟན་བཅོས་འདི་རྣམས་ཀྱི་བརྗོད་བྱའོ།། དེ་ཉིད་འཛིན་ཅིང་རྟོགས་པར་བྱས་པ་ལ་བརྟེན་ནས་མིང་ཚིག་བརྗོད་པ་ཐམས་ཅད་ལ་མི་འཁྲུལ་བའི་བློ་གྲོས་སྐྱེ་ཞིང་བསླབ་པ་གསུམ་དང་རིག་བྱེད་སོགས་གཙུག་ལག་གཉིས་ཀར་འཇུག་པའི་ལམ་ཡངས་པོར་འགྱུར་བ་ནི་དགོས་པའོ།། དེ་ལ་བརྟེན་ནས་བྱང་ཆུབ་ཀྱི་ལམ་ལ་སློབས་འཇུག་ཅིང་མཐར་ཀྱིས་རྣམ་པ་ཐམས་ཅད་མཁྱེན་པ་ཉིད་མངོན་དུ་བྱེད་པ་ནི་དགོས་པའི་དགོས་པའོ།། ཉིང་དགོས་དགོས་པར་འབྲེལ། དགོས་པ་བརྗོད་བྱར་འབྲེལ་ཞིང་། བརྗོད་བྱའང་ཡན་ལག་ཕྱི་མ་ཕྱི་མ་སྔ་མ་སྔ་མར་འབྲེལ་པ་ནི་འབྲེལ་པའོ།།

གཉིས་པ་སྐབས་དོན་སུམ་ཅུ་པ་དངོས་ལ་ཡི་གེའི་སྦྱོར་བ་རྒྱས་པར་བཤད་པ་དང་། གདམས་ངག་བརྗོད་པས་འཇུག་བསྡུ་བའོ།

དང་པོ་ལ། སྦྱོར་བྱ་ཡི་གེའི་རྣམ་བཞག་དང་། སྦྱོར་ཚུལ་ཚིག་འཕྲུད་ཀྱི་འཇུག་པ་བཤད་པ་གཉིས།

དང་པོ་ལ། བོད་ཡིག་གི་དབྱངས་གསལ་ངོས་གཟུང་བ་དང་། ཕྱེད་པར་ཀྱི་དབྱེ་བ་བསྟན་པ་གཉིས། དང་པོ་ལ་དངོས་དང་མཐའ་དཔྱད་དོ།

དང་པོ་ནི།

ཡི་གེ་ཨཱ་ལི་ཀཱ་ལི་གཉིས། ཨཱ་ལི་གསལ་བྱེད་ཨི་སོགས་བཞི། ཀཱ་ལི་སུམ་ཅུ་ཐམ་པའོ།

ཞེས་པས་བསྟན་ཏེ། དེའང་ཡི་གེ་ཞེས་བྱ་བ་ལེགས་སྦྱར་གྱི་སྐད་དུ། ཨ་ཀྵ་ར་སྒྲ་མིག་ལྷ་བུར་འདྲེན་བྱེད་ལྷ་བྱེད་ལ་སོགས་པ་མིང་དུ་མས་བསྙད་དུ་ཡོད་ལ། ཀ་ལཱ་བུ་ནི་གཞན་གྱིས་མ་ཡིན་པས་འགྱུར་མེད་དང་། བྱཉྫ་ན་སྟེ་མིང་ཚིག་མཐའ་དག་འདི་གསལ་བས་ན་གསལ་བྱེད་དང་། ཝརྞ་སྟེ། དོན་མཐའ་དག་འདིས་བརྗོད་པའི་ཕྱིར་བརྗོད་བྱེད་ཀྱང་ཡིན་ཞིང་། དེ་ཉིད་ལྷའི་སྐད་ཀྱི་དབང་གིས་དབྱངས་ཡིག་བཅུ་དྲུག་དང་། གསལ་བྱེད་སུམ་ཅུ་རྩ་གསུམ་དུ་བསྡུ་བ་སོགས་སྐད་ཀྱི་བྱེ་བྲག་དང་སྐབས་ཐོབ་ལས་སྣ་ཚོགས་པར་འགྱུར་ནའང་རིགས་མཐུན་ཚོགས་པར་བྱས་པའི། དབྱངས་གསལ་གཉིས་སུ་དབྱེ་བ་ཙམ་གྱི་སྒོ་ནས་ཡི་གེ་མཐའ་དག་བསྡུས་པའི་ཕྱིར་ཨཱ་ལི་སྟེ་ཨ་ཕྲེང་དང་ཀཱ་ལི་སྟེ་ཀ་ཕྲེང་གཉིས་སུ་དབྱེའོ། དེ་ལས་གངས་རིའི་ཁྲོད་འདིར་འཕེལ་བར་བཅོ་བའི་སྐད་ལ་ཡོངས་སུ་གྲགས་ཤིང་ཉེ་བར་མཁོ་བ་ནི་ཨཱ་ལིའི་བྱ་བ་གསལ་བར་མཚོན་པར་བྱེད་པའི་ཡི་གེ་ཨི་ཨུ་ཨེ་ཨོ་བཞི་དང་། ཀཱ་ལི་མཚོན་པར་བྱེད་པ། ཀ་ཁ་ག་ང་། ཅ་ཆ་ཇ་ཉ། ཏ་ཐ་ད་ན། པ་ཕ་བ་མ། ཙ་ཚ་ཛ་ཝ། ཞ་ཟ་འ་ཡ། ར་ལ་ཤ་ས། ཧ་ཨ་སྟེ་སུམ་ཅུ་ཐམ་པ་ཡོད་དོ།

གཉིས་པ་མཐའ་དཔྱད་ནི། འདི་སྐབས་འགྲེལ་བྱེད་ཁ་ཅིག་གིས། ཨ་ཡིག་ཨཱ་ལིར་བགྲངས་པའི་ཨཱ་ལི་ལྔ་དང་ཀཱ་ལི་ཉེར་དགུར་འདོད་པ་བྱུང་མོད་ཀྱི་མཁན་པོའི་དགོངས་པ་མ་རྟོགས་པར་གཟུ་ལུམ་བྱས་པར་སྣང་། རྩ་བ་ལ་དངོས་འགལ་དུ་ཐལ་བའི་ཕྱིར། ཨོ་ན་བདའ་སྦྱོར་བའི་གཙུག་ལག་རྣམས་ལས་བྱུང་བ་བཞིན་དུ་འདིར་ཡང་ཡི་གེ་ཚོགས་པ་མཚུངས་པ་སོ་སོར་བསྡུ་བར་མཛད་ན་ཨ་ཡིག་ཁོ་ན་ཚོགས་པ་མི་མཚུངས་པར་བསྐྱུལ་བའི་དགོས་པ་ཅི་ཞིག། ཅེས་འདྲི་ན་འདི་ལ་སྔོན་ཚད་མཁས་པའི་གོ་སར་བཞུགས་པ་མང་པོས་ངོ་འཛིན་གཡོ་བར་མ་མཛད་ཀྱང་བཤད་པར་བྱ་སྟེ་ལེགས་པར་སྦྱར་བའི་སྐད་ལ་གསལ་བྱེད་སྲོག་ཅན་སྲོག་མེད་གཉིས་སུ་དབྱེ་བའི་སྲོག་དེ་ཡིན་ན་དབྱངས་ཡིན་པས་ཁྱབ་པའི་ཕྱིར་ཀ་ལྷ་བུ་སྲོག་མེད་རྐྱང་པ་བརྗོད་མི་བཏུབ་པ་ཡིན་ཞིང་། བོད་དུའང་། ལེགས་ཟེར་བ་ལྷ་བུ་ལ་ཡིག་ཨ་ཕྲུགས་ཀྱི་རྗེས་སུ་ག་ས་སྲོག་མེད་སྦྱར་བ་སོགས་འགའ་ཞིག་ལ་རིགས་འགྲེ་ནུས་ཀྱང་། མགོ་ཅན། འཕྱུལ་ཅན། འདོགས་ཅན་སོགས་ཀྱི་རྣམ་གཞག་མཛད་པས་མཐའ་གཅིག་ཏུ་སྲོག་ཅན་སྲོག་མེད་ཀྱི་དབྱེ་བ་དེ་བདེ་བླག་མ་ཡིན་ཞིང་འཇུག་པར་དཀའ་བ་དང་། དགོས་ཞེ་ཕལ་ཆེར་བོར་མི་ཆེ་བས་དེ་ལྟའི་རྣམ་གཞག་མ་མཛད་དོ། དེ་བས་ན་བརྗོད་དུ་མེད་པའི་སྲོག་མེད་རྐྱང་པ་འདི་རྣམ་མི་འདོད་ཅིང་ཨ་ཡིག་དེ་ཀ་ལ་སོགས་པར་ཞུགས་པའི་ཞལ་སྐྱོང་བྱར་མེད་པས། ངེས་དེ་དག་ལ་ཨ་ཡིའི་བྱ་བ་གསལ་བར་བྱེད་མ་ནུས་པའི་ཕྱིར་ཀཱ་ལིའི་ཕྱི་ཚན་དུ་འཇུག་པར་མཛད་པ་ཡིན་ནོ།། དེ་ན་མཁས་པ་དག་ཡི་གེ་སྲོག་མེད

ཀྱི་རྣམ་བཞག་མ་མཛད་ན། འོག་ཏུ་དེ་ལ་ཨཱ་ལི་བཞི་པ་སྦྱར་སོགས་ཇི་ལྟར་འགྲེལ་ཅེ་ན། དེ་ནི་སྲོག་མེད་ལ་ཨཱ་ལི་ཞུགས་པའི་དོན་མ་ཡིན་གྱི་ཀཱ་ལི་དེ་དག་ཉིད་ལ་ཨུ་ཏུ་སོགས་སྦྱར་བའི་དོན་ཡིན་ཏེ། གི་གུ། ཞབས་ཀྱུ། འགྲེང་བུ། ཨུ་ཏུ་བཞི་ལ་ཨི་ཨུ་ཨེ་ཨོ་བཞིར་བཏགས་པའི་ཕྱིར་དང་དེ་དག་གིས་ཀ་ལྟ་བུའི་སྒྲའི་ངོ་བོ་དེར་ཀི་ཀུ་ཀེ་ཀོ་སོགས་སྒྲའི་ཁྱད་པར་སྐྱེད་ནུས་པས་ཨཱ་ལིའི་བྱ་བ་གསལ་བར་མཚོན་ནུས་པ་ཙམ་ལ་དགོངས་ནས་ཨཱ་ལིའི་སྒྲ་ཡང་གསུངས་པའི་ཕྱིར་རོ། དེས་ན་ཀཱ་ལི་སུམ་ཅུ་པ་ལ་ཨཱ་ལི་དང་པོ་སྦྱར་བས་ཨེ་ཡིག་ཏུ་འགྱུར་བ་སོགས་ཡིན་པས་དེ་དག་གི་ཨ་ཡིག་ནི་བརྗོད་དོན་རྣམ་འབྲེལ་དུ་བྱས་པའི་ཕྱིར་དབྱེ་བར་བྱ་བ་ཉིད་དོ། འདིར་ཁ་ཅིག་གིས་གི་གུ་ལ་སོགས་པ་ཡོ་ན་འདིར་བསྟན་གྱི་ཨཱ་ལི་ཡིན་ན་དེ་དབྱངས་ཡིག་མ་ཡིན་པར་འགྱུར་ཏེ། དབྱངས་ནི་ང་རོའི་རྣམ་པ་ཙམ་ཡིན་ཞིང་དེ་དག་ནི་གསལ་བྱེད་གཞན་ལ་མ་ལྟོས་པར་འདོན་དུ་མེད་པའི་ཕྱིར་ཞེས་རྟགས་པ་སྐྱེ་བ་སྲིད་ཀྱང་སྐྱོན་མེད་དེ། དངོས་སུ་འདིར་ཨཱ་ལི་སྲོག་ཞུགས་ཀྱི་རྣམ་བཞག་མ་མཛད་ཀྱང་མཚོན་བྱེད་འདི་ཙམ་ལ་བརྟེན་ནས་དབྱངས་ཀྱི་བྱ་བ་གསལ་བར་མཚོན་ནུས་པ་ལ་དགོངས་པའི་ཕྱིར་དང་། དེ་ལྟ་མ་ཡིན་ན་ལེགས་སྦྱར་ལྟར་ཨ་ཨི་འདུས་པས་ཨེ་སོགས་སུ་འགྱུར་བར་ཁས་ལེན་དགོས་པའི་སྐྱོན་ཡང་ཡོད་པའི་ཕྱིར་རོ། དེ་ལྟར་གཞུང་འདིའི་སྐབས་སུ་ཡི་གེ་བརྩི་ཚུལ་ཙམ་དུ་མ་ཟད་གསལ་བྱེད་ཅེས་པ་ལའང་མང་པོས་འབྲུ་གཉེན་ལོག་པར་བྱས་འདུག་པས་ཕོ་མོ་ལེགས་པར་བཤད་པ་འདི་ནི་སྣང་བྱེད་ཀྱི་ཉི་མ་ཆེན་པོ་ལྟར་བརྟེན་པར་འོས་སོ། གཉིས་པ་ཁྱད་པར་གྱི་དབྱེ་བ་བསྟན་པ་ལ། མདོར་བསྟན་པ་དང་། རྒྱས་པར་བཤད་པ་གཉིས། དང་པོ་ནི།

དེ་ལ་རྗེས་འཇུག་བཅུ་ཡིན་ཏེ། དེ་ལས་ལྔ་ནི་སྔོན་དུའང་འཇུག། མི་འཇུག་པ་ནི་ཉི་ཤུའོ།།

ཞེས་པས་བསྟན་ཏེ། བཤད་མ་ཐག་པའི་ཡི་གེ་ཀཱ་ལི་དེ་དག་ལ་དབྱེ་ན་རྗེས་སུ་འཇུག་པ་བཅུ་དང་། རྗེས་འཇུག་རང་ཉིད་ལས་ལྔ་ནི་སྔོན་དུ་འང་འཇུག་པ་ཡིན་པས་སྔོན་འཇུག་ལྔ་དང་སྔོན་རྗེས་གཉིས་ཀར་མི་འཇུག་པའི་ཡི་གེ་ཉི་ཤུ་སྟེ་རྣམ་པ་གསུམ་དུ་དབྱེའོ། གཉིས་པ་རྒྱས་བཤད་ལ་དབྱེ་གཞི་ངོས་བཟུང་བསྟན་པ་དང་། བྱེ་བྲག་སོ་སོར་བཤད་པ་གཉིས།

དང་པོ་ནི།

ཀཱ་ལི་ཕྱེད་དང་བརྒྱད་སྡེ་ནི། བཞི་བཞི་དག་ཏུ་ཕྱེ་བ་ལས།

ཞེས་པས་བསྟན་ཏེ། རྗེས་འཇུག་ལ་སོགས་པར་དབྱེ་བའི་ཐོག་མར་སྡེ་པ་སོ་སོར་ངེས་པར་བྱ་དགོས་པས། ཀཱ་ལི་དེ་རྣམས་སྡེ་པ་ཕྱེད་དང་བརྒྱད་དུ་བགོས་པའི་སྡེ་པ་རེ་རེ་ལ་ཡི་གེ་བཞི་བཞིར་དབྱེ་བ་ཡིན་ཞིང་། དེའང་ཀ་ཁ་ག་ང་སྡེ་པ་དང་པོ་སོགས་ནས་ཧ་ཨ་སྡེ་པ་ཕྱེད་པའི་བར་དུ་སོ་སོའི་མིང་ཤེས་པར་བྱའོ། ལས་ཉེས་པ་ནི། དབྱེ་བ་བྱས་པ་འདི་ལས་འོག་ཏུ་དང་པོ་གསུམ་པ་སོགས་ཀྱི་སྐབས་སུ་སོ་སོའི་ཡི་གེ་རྣམས་དྲན་པར་བྱའོ་ཞེས་པའི་དོན་ཏེ་འབྱུང་ཁུངས་དང་བཅས་པའི་རྒྱུ་མཚན་གྱི་སྒྲོ། གཉིས་པ་བྱེ་བྲག་སོ་སོར་བཤད་པ་ལ། རྗེས་འཇུག་བཤད་པ། སྔོན་འཇུག་བཤད་པ། མི་འཇུག་པ་བཤད་པ་གསུམ།

དང་པོ་ནི།

དང་པོ་གསུམ་པ་བཞི་པ་ཡི། ཅན་གཉིས་དྲུག་པའི་གསུམ་པ་དང་། བདུན་པ་ལ་ནི་ཤ་མ་གཏོགས། རྗེས་འཇུག་ཡི་གེ་བཅུ་རུ་འདོད།།

ཅེས་པས་བསྟན་ཏེ། གོང་དུ་རྗེས་འཇུག་བཅུ་ཞེས་བཤད་པ་དེ་གང་ཞེ་ན། སྡེ་པ་དང་པོ་དང་གསུམ་པ་དང་བཞི་པ་རྣམས་ཀྱི་མཐའ་ཀྱི་ཡི་གེ་གཉིས་གཉིས་ཏེ། ག་ང་ད་ན། བ་མ་རྣམས་དང་། སྡེ་པ་དྲུག་པའི་གསུམ་པ་འ་དང་། བདུན་པའི་ཤ་མ་གཏོགས་པའི་ལྷག་མ་ར་ལ་ས་གསུམ་མོ། དེའང་ཡི་གེ་ཐམས་ཅད་ཀྱི་རྗེས་སུ་འདི་དག་འཇུག་པའི་ཕྱིར་རྗེས་འཇུག་ཅེས་བྱ་ཞིང་ཡི་གེའི་གྲངས་བཅུ་ཉིད་དུ་ངེས་པ་ཡིན་ནོ། གཉིས་པ་སྔོན་འཇུག་བཤད་པ་ནི།

རྗེས་འཇུག་ཡི་གེ་བཅུ་པོ་ལས། དང་པོ་གསུམ་པ་ལྔ་པ་དྲུག། བདུན་པ་རྣམས་ནི་སྔོན་དུའང་འཇུག།

ཅེས་པས་བསྟན་ཏེ། གོང་དུ་སྔོན་འཇུག་ཅེས་པ་གང་ཞེ་ན། རྗེས་འཇུག་ཡི་གེ་བཅུ་པོ་དེ་དག་ཉིད་ལས། དང་པོ་ག། གསུམ་པ་ད། ལྔ་པ་བ། དྲུག་པ་མ།

བདུན་པ་འ་རྣམས་ཡིན་ཞིང་དེ་དག་རྗེས་སུ་འཇུག་པར་མ་ཟད་ཡི་གེ་རྣམས་ཀྱི་སྔོན་དུ་འཇུག་པའང་ཡོད་པས་ན་སྔོན་འཇུག་ཅེས་ཀྱང་བྱ་སྟེ་ཡི་གེའི་གྲངས་ལྔར་ངེས་པ་ཡིན་ནོ། སྔོན་རྗེས་འདི་དག་གི་འཇུག་ཚུལ་ནི་རྟགས་འཇུག་གིས་རྒྱས་པར་འཆད་པར་འགྱུར་རོ། གསུམ་པ་མི་འཇུག་པ་བཤད་པ་ལ། དངོས་དང་། སྐབས་དོན་གྱི་མིང་གཞི་ཁྱད་པར་དུ་བཤད་པ་གཉིས།

དང་པོ་ནི།

མིང་གཞི་གཉིས་སམ་གསུམ་སྦྲེལ་ལམ། །དེ་ལ་དབྱངས་ཀྱི་བཞི་ལྡན་ཡང་། །གང་དུའང་འཇུག་མིན་སྦྱར་བའང་མིན། །

ཞེས་པས་བསྟན་ཏེ། སྔོན་འཇུག་དང་རྗེས་འཇུག་བསལ་བའི་ལྷག་མ་མིང་གཞི་ཁོ་ན་ཡིན་པས། ཀ་ཁ། ཅ་ཆ་ཇ་ཉ། ཏ་ཐ། པ་ཕ། ཙ་ཚ་ཛ་ཝ། ཞ་ཟ་ཡ། ཤ་ཧ་ཨ་སྟེ་ཡི་གེ་ཉི་ཤུ་ཐམ་པ་དེ་དག་ནི་ཚིག་བར་གཅིག་ཏུ་གཉིས་སམ་གསུམ་སྦྲེལ་བའམ་དེ་ལ་དབྱངས་ཨི་སོགས་གང་རུང་རེ་སྦྱར་བས་བཞི་ལྡན་དུ་བྱས་པ། ཅིཀ། ཚུཕ། ཁིཤ། ཛོཡ། ལྟ་བུ་གངས་ལྗོངས་སུ་གྲགས་པའི་ཐ་སྙད་གང་ལའང་འཇུག་པ་མིན་པས་འདི་བཞིན་སྦྱར་བར་རིགས་པའང་མ་ཡིན་ནོ།

གཉིས་པ་ནི། སྦྱོར་གཞུང་འདིའི་སྐབས་སུ་སྔོན་རྗེས་མིང་གསུམ་གྱི་ཟླས་ཕྱེ་བའི་མིང་གཞི་ཞེས་བྱ་བ་ནི་སྔོན་རྗེས་ཀྱི་འཇུག་པའི་ཡི་གེ་རྣམས་གང་ལ་འཇུག་པར་འགྱུར་བ་དེ་ལ་དེ་ལྟར་བརྟགས་པས་གསལ་བྱེད་སུམ་ཅུ་ཐམ་པ་མིང་གཞིར་འགྱུར་མོད་ཀྱི། འོན་ཀྱང་གནས་སྐབས་ཀྱི་དབྱེ་བ་ཡོད་དེ། དཔེར་ན་བསྒྱུབས་ཟེར་བ་ལྟ་བུའི་ཚེ་བཙུགས་མའི་ས་ག་ར་གསུམ་ནི་སྔོན་འཇུག་པ་དང་། རྗེས་འཇུག་པ་ས་དག་གི་འཇུག་ཡུལ་དུ་གྱུར་པའི་ཕྱིར་མིང་གཞིའི་ཐ་སྙད་ཐོབ་ཅིང་རབ་ལྟ་བུ་ལ་ར་ཡིག་མིང་གཞི་བ་ཡིག་རྗེས་འཇུག་དང་། བར་ལྟ་བུ་དེ་ལས་བཟློག་པའང་ཡིན་པའི་ཕྱིར་རོ། ཡང་བསྒྱུབས་ཟེར་བ་ལྟ་བུའི་ཨུ་ཡིག་སོགས་ཨུ་ཡི་བཞི་པོ་རྣམས་ནི་མིང་གཞིར་འོས་ཀྱང་། འདིར་དབྱངས་སྒོག་ཕུགས་ཀྱི་རྣམ་གཞག་མ་མཛད་པའི་ཕྱིར་དེ་འདྲའི་ཐ་སྙད་བྱར་མེད་པས་ཨུ་ཡིག་སོགས་ཀྱི་ཟླས་གསུངས་པའི་ཞབས་ཀྱུ་ལ་སོགས་པ་དེ་རྣམས་འཕུལ་རྟེན་འཇུག་ཡུལ་གྱི་མིང་གཞིའི་ཡན་ལག་ལས་དངོས་མིན་ཏེ། འདིར་བསྟན་གྱི་ཨུ་ཡི་རྐྱང་པ་ཡིན་ན་འཕུལ་རྟེན་གྱི་བྱ་བ་མི་འཇུག་པས་ཁྱབ་པའི་ཕྱིར་རོ། དེས་ན་སྔོན་འཇུག་རྗེས་འཇུག་མིང་གཞི་ཅི་རིགས་པར་འགྱུར་བ་སྔོན་འཇུག་ལྔ། རྗེས་འཇུག་མིང་གཞི་ཅི་རིགས་འགྱུར་བ་རྗེས་འཇུག་བཅུ། མིང་གཞི་ཁོ་ན་ཡིན་པ་ལྷག་མ་མི་འཇུག་པ་ཉི་ཤུ་ཐམ་པ་སྟེ་གསུམ་དུ་དབྱེར་ཡོད་པ་ལས། ཕྱི་བྲག་འདིར་ནི་མི་འཇུག་པ་ཁོ་ན་འཆད་པའི་སྐབས་ཡིན་པའི་ཕྱིར་ཐ་མ་འདི་ཉིད་བཟུང་ནས་བཤད་ཟིན་ཏོ། འདིར་ཁ་ཅིག་གོང་དུ། ཡི་གེ་ཐམས་ཅད་ལ་མིང་གཞིས་ཁྱབ་པར་བསྟན་པ་དང་འགལ་བར་རྟོགས་པ་སྲིད་ཀྱང་སྐྱོན་མེད་དེ། དེ་དག་ཏུ་ནི་སྦྱོར་ཡི་གེ་ཙམ་ལ་དགོངས་པའི་ཡི་གེ་ཡིན་ན། ཡི་གེ་ཨཱ་ལི་ཀཱ་ལི་གཉིས། ཞེས་པའི་སྐབས་ནས་བསྟན་པས་ཁྱབ་ཅིང་། དེ་ལས་འཇིག་རྟེན་འདི་ཉིད་ཀྱི་ཡི་གེ་ཡིན་ན་མཚོན་བརྗོད་གསུམ་པའི་སྐབས་ཀྱི་མིང་གཞི་ཡིན་པས་ཁྱབ་པ་དང་མིང་གཞི་དེ་ནི་མིང་ཚིག་གི་གཞིར་གྱུར་པ་ལ་དགོངས་ཏེ། དཔེར་ན་བོད་ཡུལ་དུ་ཡི་གེ་རྣམས་ལས་འགྲེང་བུ་ཙམ་མེད་པས་ཀྱང་དེས་བརྗོད་པ་ཇི་སྙེད་ཡོད་པ་ཉམས་པར་འགྱུར་བས་ངེས་པར་ཡི་གེ་ཇི་སྙེད་པ་མིང་ཚིག་གི་གཞིར་དགོས་པ་བཞིན་ནོ། དེ་ལྟར་སྔོན་འགྲེལ་བྱེད་འབགས་རྣམས་ལེགས་ཀྱིས་སྐབས་འདིའི་མིང་གཞིའི་ངོས་འཛིན་ཙམ་འགྲིག་ཀྱང་དཔྱིས་ཕྱིན་པའི་ལེགས་བཤད་ནི་དུས་སྙིལ་གྱི་སྦྲ་ལ་འགྲན་ཟླར་སྣང་བའི་ཕྱིར་རང་སྟོབས་ཀྱིས་བཤད་པ་ཡིན་པས་བློ་ལྡན་རྣམས་དགྱེས་པའི་འཛུམ་ཞལ་ངོམ་པར་མཛོད་ཅིག།

གཉིས་པ་སྦྱོར་ཚུལ་ཚིག་ཕྲད་ཀྱི་འཇུག་པ་བཤད་པ་ལ། རྗེས་འཇུག་ལ་ལྟོས་པའི་ཕྲད་རྣམ་དབྱེ་དང་བཅས་པ་དང་། ཕྲད་རང་དབང་ཅན་བཤད་པ་གཉིས། དང་པོ་ལ། སླར་བསྡུ་ལ་དོན། ཨི་ལྡན་གྱི་རྣམ་དབྱེ། རྒྱན་སྡུད། ལྷག་བཅས། འབྱེད་སྡུད། འབྱུང་ཁུངས། བོད་པའི་སྒྲ་བསྟན་པ་སྟེ་བརྒྱད་དོ། དང་པོ་ལ་དངོས་དང་། ལོག་རྟོག་སེལ་བའོ།

དང་པོ་ནི།

རྗེས་འཇུག་ཡི་གེ་བཅུ་པོ་ནི། །མིང་གང་གི་ནི་མཐར་སྦྱར་བ། །དེ་ལ་ཨུ་ཡི་བཞི་པ་སྦྱར། །སླར་བསྡུ་བར་ནི་ཤེས་པར་བྱ། །

ཞེས་པས་བསྟན་ཏེ། སྔར་བཤད་པའི་རྗེས་འཇུག་གི་ཡི་གེ་བཅུ་པོ་དེ་རྣམས་ཉིད་མིང་ཚིག་གང་གི་མཐར་སྦྱར་བ་ཡོད་ཀྱང་རུང་། དེ་དག་ལ་ཨུ་ཡི་བཞི་པ་ཨོ་ཡིག་སྦྱར་ཏེ་སྦྱར་

བ་ནི། སྐབས་བབས་ཀྱི་བརྗོད་བྱའི་དོན་ནས་ཚིག་དེ་ཉིད་དེ་ཙམ་གྱིས་བསྡུ་བར་ཡོད་པས་སླར་བསྡུའི་སྒྲ་ཞེས་སམ་རྫོགས་ཚིག་ཅེས་ཀྱང་བྱའོ། ཞེས་སོ། དེའང་གཞུང་འདིའི་དངོས་བསྟན་གྱི་དབང་དུ་བྱས་ན། གོ། ངོ། དོ། ནོ། བོ། མོ། འོ། རོ། ལོ། སོ་སྐྱེ་ཉིད་ཡིན་ཡང་། ད་དུང་གི་མཐར་ཏོ་འཐོབ་པས་བཅུ་གཅིག་ཏུ་འགྱུར་རོ། འོ་ན་འདིར་ཏོ་ཡི་སྒྲ་མི་བསྟན་པ་ཅི་ཞེ་ན། གཞུང་འདི་གཞི་གཤམ་དུ་རྗེས་འཇུག་བཅུ་ཡི་དོན་ཤེས་ན། ཞེས་དང་། རྗེས་འཇུག་སྦྱོར་བ་མཁས་པ་ན། ཞེས་སོགས་ཀྱི་སྐབས་སུ་འཆད་པར་འགྱུར་བ་བཞིན་གཞུང་འདིས་གཙོ་བོ་རྗེས་འཇུག་གི་བྱ་བ་འཆད་པ་ཡིན་པའི་ཕྱིར། མིང་གཞི་རྐྱང་པའི་སྒྲ་གཙོ་བོར་གྱུར་པའང་ཕྲད་བདག་སྒྲ་ཙམ་ལས་གཞན་འདིར་མ་གསུངས་པ་ཡིན་ནོ། རྒྱ་མཚན་དེའི་སྐབས་འདིས་ཏོ་འི་སྒྲ་གཅིག་པུར་མ་ཟད། ཕྱག་བཅས་ཀྱི་ཏེ་དང་། ཡི་ལྡན་གྱི་ཡི་ཡིས། རྒྱན་སྡུད་ཀྱི་ཡང་། འབྱེད་སྡུད་ཀྱི་ཏམ། ལ་དོན་གྱི་ཏུ་རྣམས་ཀྱང་འདིར་མ་བསྟན་པའི་གནད་ཀ་ཤེས་པར་བྱ་ཞིང་། ཀྱི་ཀྱིས་ཀྱང་སྒྲ་རྣམས་ནི་འཇུག་པའི་ཡི་གེ་དང་ལྡན་ཅིག་པའི་སྒྲ་གཙོ་བོར་གྱུར་པའི་ཕྱིར་འདིར་ཡང་གསུངས་པ་ཉིད་དོ། དེ་ལྟ་ན་ཁྱེད་རང་གིས་སྔར་འཇུག་པའི་ཡི་གེ་རྣམས་ཀྱང་འཕུལ་ཆེན་གྱི་ཡུལ་དུ་སྦྱོར་ཚེ་མིང་གཞི་ཉིད་དུ་ཁས་བླངས་པའི་ཕྱིར་ཕྲད་འདི་རྣམས་ཐལ་མཐའ་ཆེན་འཇུག་པའི་རྒྱ་མཚན་གྱིས་མིང་གཞི་ཉིད་དུ་ཐལ་བས་རྗེས་འཇུག་གི་བྱ་བར་མི་འགྱུར་རོ། སྙམ་ན་སྐྱོན་མེད་དེ། རྗེས་འཇུག་གི་བྱ་བ་ཞེས་པ་ནི་རྗེས་འཇུག་གི་ཡི་གེ་བཅུ་པོ་དེ་ལ་བྱ་བ་འབྱུང་བ་ཙམ་གྱི་ཆ་ནས་ཡིན་གྱི། ཕྲད་སོགས་སུ་གྲུབ་ཟིན་ནས་མིང་གཞི་དང་རྗེས་འཇུག་གང་ཡིན་དཔྱད་པའི་ཆ་ནས་མ་ཡིན་པའི་ཕྱིར་རོ། ད་དུག་ཅན་གྱི་མཐར་ཏོ་ལ་སོགས་པ་ཐོབ་པའི་དོན་ནི།

རྟགས་འཇུག་ཏུ། དེ་ཉིད་རང་གི་སྒྲ་མཐུན་པའི་ཤེས་པའི་སྐབས་སུ་འཆད་པར་འགྱུར་བ་བཞིན་ཕྱིར་བཏང་རྗེས་འཇུག་ལ་སྦྱོར་བའི་རྣམ་དབྱེ་དང་ཕྲད་རྣམས་ལ། སྦྱོར་ཡུལ་མིང་ཚིག་གི་མཐའ་དེ་དང་སྦྱར་བས་བརྗོད་པ་བདེ་ཞིང་སྒྲ་མཐུན་པ་ཡོད་ན་རྟགས་མཚུངས་ཉིད་སྦྱར་བར་བྱ་ཞིང་། དེ་ལྟ་བུ་མེད་ནའམ་ཡོད་ཀྱང་བརྗོད་མི་བདེ་ན་བརྗོད་བདེ་བ་གང་ཡིན་སྦྱར་བར་བྱ་བ་ཡིན་པ་དང་། དེ་དག་ཀྱང་འཇིག་རྟེན་གྱི་གྲགས་པའི་རྗེས་སུ་འབྲང་དགོས་པས་རྗེས་འཇུག་གཞན་རྣམས་རང་རང་ལ་སྟ་དུ་སོགས་སྦྱར་བར་རྟགས་མཚུངས་མིན་ཅི་རིགས་ཡོད་ཀྱང་བརྗོད་བདེ་བ་དང་གྲགས་ཤིང་གྲུབ་པའི་ཕྱིར་ངེས་པ་ཡིན་ལ། ད་དུག་ཅན། བསྟནད། སྒྱུརད། རྒྱལད། ལྟ་བུ་རྣམས་ལ་གྲོག་དག་པའི་དབང་གིས།

རྗེས་འཇུག་གཉིས་ལས་ན་ར་ལ་རྣམས་ཀྱི་སྒྲ་ཤུགས་ཆེ་ཙམ་དང་དའི་སྒྲ་འབྱུང་བར་ཆབ་ཙམ་ལས་མི་གསལ་བའི་ཕྱིར། བསྟནད་དོ། སྒྱུརད་དོ། རྒྱལད་དོ། བསྟནད་ཏམ་སྒྱུརད་ཏམ། རྒྱལད་ཏམ། ལྟ་བུ་ནི་བརྗོད་བདེ་བའང་མ་ཡིན་ཞིང་ཡོངས་སུ་མ་གྲགས་པས་བརྗོད་བདེ་རྟགས་མཚུངས་གཉིས་ཀའི་སྒོ་ནས་སྒྲ་མཐུན་པ་ནི་ཏོ་དང་ཏམ་སོགས་ཁོ་ནར་ངེས་པའི་ཕྱིར་རོ། སླར་བསྡུའི་ཕྲད་དེ་རྣམས་ཀྱི་དཔེར་བརྗོད་པའང་། རྟག་གོ། བཟང་ངོ་། ཡོད་དོ། ཡིན་ནོ། སྒྲུབ་བོ། བསམ་མོ། བྱའོ། འགྱུར་རོ། སེལ་ལོ། བྱས་སོ། ཞེས་སོགས་འབྱམས་ཀླས་པ་ནི་གོ་བར་སླ་ཞིང་། ད་དུག་ཅན་གྱི་མཐར་ཡང་། བསྟནད་ཏོ། སྒྱུརད་ཏོ། རྒྱལད་ཏོ། ཕྱིནད་ཏོ། འཇོནད་ཏོ། ཞེས་སོགས་མང་དུ་འབྱུང་བ་རྣམས་སོ།

གཉིས་པ་ནི། སྐབས་འདིར་འགྲེལ་བྱེད་ཐ་མ་ཁ་ཅིག་གིས་དེར་ཕྱིན་ཏོ་ལྟ་བུ་སླར་བསྡུ་དངོས་ཡིན་ཞིང་རྫོགས་ཚིག་ཀྱང་ཡིན་པ་དང་། རྟག་གོ་ལྟ་བུ་སླར་བསྡུ་ཙམ་པོ་དང་། བྱའོ་ལྟ་བུ་ནས་ཕྱིན་ཏོ་ལྟ་བུ་ཙམ་པོ་བའི་ཁོངས་སུ་གཏོགས་ཙམ་ལས་དོན་དུ་དེའང་མིན་པར་འདོད་པ་ཞིག་འདུག་པ། དེ་ལ་འདི་འདྲི་བར་བྱ་སྟེ། བྱའོ་ཞེས་པའི་འོ་སྒྲ་བརྗོད་པའི་ཚེ་འོ་སྒྲ་དེས་གང་ཞིག་སྡུད་དགོས་པའི་དོན་དེ་བསྡུས་པར་སོང་ངམ་མ་སོང་། སོང་ན་སླར་བསྡུ་དང་རྫོགས་ཚིག་དངོས་མིན་ཞེས་བརྗོད་པའི་རྒྱ་མཚན་ཅི་ཞིག་དེ་ལ་ལྡོམ་ཞིང་འབྲེལ་བའི་ཚིག་དེ་མ་ཐག་ཏུ་འབྱུང་བས་སོ་ཞེ་ན། འོ་ན་ཁྱེད་ཀྱིས་སླར་བསྡུ་དངོས་ཀྱི་མཚན་གཞི་མཐའ་ཆེན་གྱི་རྫོགས་སོ་ལྟ་བུ་ལས་མང་དུ་མི་རྙེད་པར་འགྱུར་ཏེ་ཁྱེད་རང་གིས་རྫོགས་ཚིག་དངོས་སུ་ཁས་བླངས་པའི་དེར་ཕྱིན་ཏོ་ལྟ་བུ་ཡང་ཕྱིན་ནས་ཀྱང་ལྟ་བུའི་ཚིག་གཞན་སྦྲེལ་བའི་ཚེ་དེ་དངོས་མ་ཡིན་པར་འགྱུར་བ་སོགས་གཞུང་འདིར་བསྟན་གྱི་སླར་བསྡུའི་སྒྲའི་འཇུག་པ་ཕལ་མོ་ཆེ་སླར་བསྡུ་དངོས་མ་ཡིན་པར་འགྱུར་བའི་ཕྱིར་རོ། ཡང་མ་སོང་ཟེར་ན་འོ་སྒྲ་ལ་ནུས་པ་མེད་པར་ཐལ་བའི་སྐྱོན་ཡོད་དོ། ཁོ་བོ་ནི་གཞུང་འདིར་བསྟན་གྱི་སླར་བསྡུ་སྒྲ་སྒོ་ནས་བཤད་པའི་ལྷ་སྐད་དེང་སང་རྫོགས་ཚིག་ཏུ་གྲགས་པ་རྣམས་དོན་གཅིག་ཅིང་། བྱའོ་ལྟ་ནས་བྱེད་དོ་ལྟ་བུའི་འོ་སྒྲས་ཀྱང་ཚིག་རྒྱུའི་དོན་དེ་བསྡུས་ཤིང་རྫོགས

པར་གོ་ཙམ་པས་སྒྲར་བསྒྱུ་དངོས་ཡིན་ཏེ། དཔེར་ན་བདའ་སྤྲོད་པའི་གཞུང་དུ། གྲངས་ལས་རྫོགས་པ་ལ་གས་མ་དག་གོ། ཞེས་པའི་རྐྱེན་གྱི་རྗེས་འབེད་ཤ་ཏི་ཏ་མ། ཞེས་པར་ཚིག་གྲོགས་ཨེ་ཏི་བྷཱུ་ཏྭཱ་ཞེས་པ་སྒྲུར་བས་རྫོགས་ཚིག་དངོས་མིན་པར་མི་འགྱུར་བ་བཞིན་དང་། ཀ་རོ་སྨྲྀ་ཏི་ཙིན་ཏ་ན་ཀྲི་ཡ་ཏེ། ཞེས་པར་ཡང་བྱ་ཚིག་ཀྲྀ་ཡཱ་ཤ་བྡ་ཉིད་མཐའ་དངོས་ཡིན་པར་མཚུངས་པ་ལྟ་བུའོ། ཞེས་འཆད་པར་བྱེད་དོ།

ཡང་ཁ་ཅིག་གིས། རྗེས་འཇུག་བ་ཡིག་གི་རྗེས་སུ་པོ་དང་། ད་ས་དག་གི་རྗེས་སུ་ཏོ་སྦྱར་བ་འདོད་པ་དང་། ཁ་ཅིག་གི་བ་ཡིག་འདས་ཚིག་དངོས་ཡིན་པའི་རྗེས་སུ་བོ་སྦྱར་བར་བཤད་མོད། ལྷ་མས་ཞེན་དོན་ཏག་མཚུངས་སྦྱར་ཁྱལ་དུ་འདུག་ཀུང་གོང་སློས་ལྟར་རྟགས་འཇུག་གི་དོན་དཔྱིས་ཕྱིན་པར་མ་རྟོགས་པས་རིགས་འགྲེ་ཐལ་ཆེས་པའི་སྐྱོན་དང་། བུམ་ཏོ་ལྟ་བུ་ཤིན་ཏུ་བརྗོད་མི་བདེ་བའི་ཚིག་གིས་སྦྱར་བ་དོན་མེད་ཅིང་གྲགས་པ་ལ་ལས་ཏ་ཅང་བཀལ་བའི་སྐྱོན་ཡང་ཡོད་དོ། འདོད་པ་ཕྱི་མ་དེའང་རིགས་པ་མ་ཡིན་ཏེ། བ་ཡིག་གི་མཐའ་འདས་ཚིག་ཡིན་དུ་ཟིན་ཀྱང་དེ་ཉིད་དང་སྦྱར་བས་བརྗོད་བདེ་ཞིང་སྒྲ་མཐུན་པ་བ་ཡིག་ཨོ་ལྡན་ཉིད་ཡོད་བཞིན་དུ་གཞན་འཚོལ་བ་ལ་དགོས་པ་མེད་པའི་ཕྱིར། འདས་ཚིག་ཡིན་པ་ཤེས་པའི་ཆེད་དུ་བོ་སྦྱར་ན་འང་མི་འཐད་དོ། དེ་ལྟ་ན་རྡོ་བཅག་གོ། ལྟ་བུ་ལའང་། བཅག་སོ། ཞེས་སྦྱར་དགོས་པར་འགྱུར་བས་ཧ་ཅང་ཐལ་ལོ།

ཡང་འགྲེལ་བྱེད་ཐལ་ཆེར་གྱིས། སྒྲར་བསྒྱུའི་སྒྲ་འདི་རྣམ་དབྱེ་དང་པོའི་དོན་དུ་བཤད་ཀྱང་ཤིན་ཏུ་འཐད་པར་མ་མཐོང་ཞིང་། རྣམ་དབྱེ་དང་པོའི་གཅིག་ཚིག་གིས་ནི་དོན་གྱི་ངོ་བོ་ཙམ་ལས་གཞན་མི་སྟོན་ལ། འདི་ནི་སྡུད་པའི་སྒྲ་ཡིན་པའི་ཕྱིར་དོན་གྱི་ལྡོག་པ་སྟོན་བྱེད་དུ་འགྱུར་བས་ཀྱང་ཁྱད་པར་ཆེ་ཞིང་། ཁྱོད་ལའོ། འདི་ཡིས་སོ། སྡོང་མོ་པར་རོ། འབྱུང་ཁུངས་ནས་སོ། བདག་གིའོ། ཤིང་ལའོ། རྟག་ཏུའོ། ལྟ་བུ་གཉིས་པ་ལ་སོགས་པའི་རྣམ་དབྱེ་ཐམས་ཅད་ཀྱི་མཐར་ཡང་སྒྲར་བསྒྱུ་སྦྱར་བ་ཡོད་པས། ཁྱོད་ལྟར་ན་དེ་རྣམས་ཀུང་རྣམ་དབྱེ་དང་པོའི་དོན་ཅན་དུ་འདོད་དགོས་པའི་ཕྱིར་རོ། སྨྲས་པ།

ལེགས་ལེགས་ལྟར་སྣང་སྨོངས་བློ་ཡི་རྣམ་འགྱུར་གྱིས། བདེན་བདེན་བཅོས་མའི་ཚིག་ཕྲེང་གསེར་འོད་ཅན།
གསལ་གསལ་རིག་པའི་གཞུང་ཆེན་འདྲིས་རེག་ཚེ། ངེས་ངེས་ཡིར་ཏ་ལ་ཡི་རང་ཚུལ་བཟུང་།
གཞན་ཟེར་མཆིང་བུའི་དུམ་བུ་མང་བསྡུས་ནས། འགྲིག་འགྲིག་ཚིག་གི་སྣོད་ཕུར་བརྒྱུས་ན་ཡང་།
འཁྲུལ་མེད་རྣམ་དཔྱོད་ནོར་གིས་ཉེར་བསྒྲུབས་པའི། ལེགས་བཤད་རིན་འདི་དང་བསྡུན་དུ་ཅི།
སྣ་ཚོར་གྱིས་འཐོངས་སླུ་ན་ཀན་སུ་ཏེ་པའི། ཚོགས་སུ་གང་ཞིག་བྲིམ་པ་མ་འཚལ་ཀྱང་།
གཟུར་གནས་མཁས་པ་གནས་པའི་མདུན་ས་དེར། རིག་པའི་སྣང་གིས་ཡོན་ཏན་ཅི་ཤེས་འགྱུར།

གཉིས་པ་ལ་དོན་བཤད་པ་ལ། དངོས་དང་མཐའ་དཔྱད་དོ། དང་པོ་ལ་གཞུང་དོན་འགྲོལ་བ་དང་། སྦྱོར་ཚུལ་བཤད་པའོ།

དང་པོ་ནི།

རྗེས་འཇུག་ཡི་གེ་བཅུ་རྣམས་ལས། གང་མིང་མཐའ་ན་བཅུ་པ་གནས།
དེ་ལ་ཨུ་ཡི་གཉིས་པ་སྦྱར། གང་མིང་མཐའ་ན་བརྒྱད་པ་གནས།
དེ་ལ་གཉིས་པ་ཨུ་ཡང་སྦྱར། གང་མིང་མཐའ་ན་གསུམ་པ་གནས།
དེ་ལ་ཨུ་ཡི་གཉིས་པ་སྦྱར། བཞི་པ་དགུ་པ་དངོས་ཀྱང་སྟེ།
ལས་དང་ཆེད་དང་རྟེན་གནས་དང་། དེ་ཉིད་ཚེ་སྐབས་ལ་སྒྲ་ཡིན

ཞེས་པ་སྟེ། རྗེས་འཇུག་ཡི་གེ་བཅུ་པོ་དེ་རྣམས་ཉིད་ལས། གང་ཡང་རུང་བའི་མིང་གི་མཐའ་ན་ལ་དོན་གྱི་རྣམ་དབྱེ་སྦྱར་བའི་ཆེད་དུ་བཙུ་པ་ས་ཡིག་གནས་པ་དེ་ལ་ཕྱུ་ཡི་གཉིད་པ་ཕྱུ་ཡིག་སྦྱར་བས་སུ་ཞེས་གྲུབ་པ་དང་། དེ་བཞིན་དུ་ཚིག་བར་གཅིག་ཉིད་དུ་མིང་མཐར་བརྒྱུད་པ་ར་ཡིག་སྦྱར་ཏེ་གནས་པ་ལྷག་པར་ལྟ་བུ་དང་། ཡང་ར་ཡི་དེ་ཉིད་ཚིག་བར་ཕྱུས་པ་ལ་ཕྱུ་ཡིག་ཀྱང་སྦྱར་བས་རུ་ཞེས་པ་དང་། རྗེས་འཇུག་གསུམ་པ་ད་ཡིག་གནས་པར་ཕྱུ་ཡིག་སྦྱར་བས་དུ་དང་། རྗེས་འཇུག་བཞི་པ་ན་དང་དགུ་པ་ལ་གཉིས་ནི་དབྱངས་ཀྱིས་མ་བརྒྱན་པའི་དངོས་པོ་ཉིད་དུ་གནས་པའང་སྟེ་དྲུག་པོ་དེ་དག་དང་། འདི་ན་མ་གསུངས་ཀྱང་གོང་བཤད་སྦྱར་བསྡུའི་སྐབས་ལྟར་དོན་གྱིས་ཐོབ་པའི་ཏ་ཡིག་ཕྱུ་ཞུགས་བཅས་ལ་དོན་བདུན་དུ་ངེས་ཤིང་། འདི་དག་ཀྱང་སྐབས་སུ་མཆི་ལྟ་བུ་རྣམ་དབྱེ་གཉིས་པ་ལས་སུ་བྱ་བའི་དོན་ཅན་དུ་སྦྱར་ན་ལས་ཀྱི་སྒྲ་དང་། དབུལ་པོ་ངོམས་ལ་སྦྱིན་པ་གཏོང་ལྟ་བུ་ཆེད་དུ་བྱ་བའི་དོན་ཅན་ཡིན་ན། དགོས་ཆེད་ཀྱི་སྒྲ་དང་། ཤར་ཕྱོགས་སུ་ཡོད་ལྟ་བུ་བདུན་པ་གནས་གཞིའི་དོན་ཅན་ཡིན་ན། རྟེན་གནས་ཀྱི་སྒྲ་དང་། འོད་དུ་གསལ་ལྟ་བུ་སྟེ་བཏང་ལས་ཀྱི་སྒྲ་ཡིན་པ་ལམས། ཁྱད་པར་ལས་དང་བྱ་བ་ཐ་མི་དད་པའི་རང་གི་ངོ་བོ་ཉིད་སྟོན་པའི་དོན་ཅན་ཡིན་ན་དེ་ཉིད་སྒྲ་དང་། ཉེ་མ་ཤར་བ་ན་ཆོས་སྟོན་ལྟ་བུ་དུས་བརྗོད་པའི་བདུན་པ་ཡིན་ན་ཚེ་སྐབས་ཀྱི་སྒྲར་ཤེས་པར་བྱ་དགོས་ཤིང་། དེ་དག་ཐམས་ཅད་རྣམ་དབྱེར་སྦྱོར་པ་ན་ལ་སྒྲའི་འཇུག་པ་དང་ཕལ་ཆེར་མཐུན་པས་ལ་སྒྲ་ཞེས་ཀྱང་བརྗོད་པར་བྱ་བ་ཉིད་དེ་ཞེས་སོ།

གཉིས་པ་ལ་སྒྲ་དང་དོན་གྱི་སྦྱོར་ཚུལ་གཉིས། དང་པོ་ནི། སྐབས་འདིའི་གཞུང་གི་དངོས་བསྟན་དུ་རྣམ་དབྱེའི་རྐྱེན་གྱི་ངོ་བོ་ཙམ་ལས་དེ་དག་མིང་མཐའི་རྗེས་འཇུག་དང་སྦྱོར་ཚུལ་མི་གསལ་ཡང་ཤུགས་ཀྱིས་རྟོགས་ནུས་པའི་དབང་དུ་མཛད་པས་རྗེས་འཇུག་ག་བ་གཉིས་དང་ད་དྲག་ཅན་གྱི་མཐར་སྦྱར་བསྡུའི་སྐབས་སུ་བཤད་པ་བཞིན་འདིར་མ་བསྟན་ཀྱང་དོན་གྱི་ཐོབ་པས་ཏ་ཡིག་ཕྱུ་ལྡན་སྦྱར་བ་དང་། ང་ད་ན་མ་ར་ལ་རྣམས་ཀྱི་རྗེས་སུ་དུ་དང་། ས་མཐར་སུ་དང་། འ་ཡིག་མཐར་ར་ཡིག་རྐྱང་པའམ་རུ་སྦྱར་བར་བྱ་ཞིང་། ལ་ན་དག་ནི་སྐབས་དང་བསྟུན་ཏེ་རྗེས་འཇུག་ཐམས་ཅད་ལ་སྦྱར་བར་བྱའོ། དེ་རྣམས་ཀྱང་རིམ་པ་བཞིན་དཔེར་བརྗོད་ན། ཐག་ཏུ། རབ་ཏུ། ཀུནད་ཏུ། ཕ་རོལད་ཏུ། མཚརད་ཏུ། གང་དུ། ཐམས་ཅད་དུ། གཏན་དུ། ནམ་དུ། ཤར་དུ། དཔལ་དུ། གཡས་སུ། ལྷ་ཆོག་ལ། ཆོག་ན། སྟེང་ལ། སྟེང་ན། ཡོད་ལ། ཡོད་ན། འཛིནད་ལ། འཛིནད་ན། འཛེརད་ལ། འཛེརད་ན། སྐྱལད་ལ། སྐྱལད་ན། གྲུབ་ལ། གྲུབ་ན། ཁྲིམ་ལ། ཁྲིམ་ན། མཐའ་ལ། མཐའ་ན། ཤར་ལ། ཤར་ན། རབ་གསལ་ལ། རབ་གསལ་ན། གཡས་ལ། གཡས་ན། ལྟ་བུ་རྣམས་སོ། དེ་ལ་ཏ་ཡིག་ཕྱུ་ལྡན་གྱི་སྦྱོར་བ་རྣམས་ནི། ཐོས་བོའི་མིང་མཐའ་འདྲེན་པའི་ལུགས་ཏེ་ཀློག་ཚུལ་ཟུར་མི་ཕྱིན་པ་རྣམས་ལ་ཅི་ཆ་ཡོད་ཀྱང་། རྗེས་འཇུག་ཞུགས་པའི་ཀློག་ཚུལ་ཟུར་ཕྱིན་པར་འདོན་པ་རྣམས་ལ་ནི་དེ་ཉིད་བརྗོད་བདེ་བའང་ཡིན་ནོ། དེ་བཞིན་དུ་ང་མ་འདས་རྣམས་ལ་དུ་སོགས་སྦྱོར་བའི་ཚུལ་དེ་ནི་ཆོས་མོ་ཡིག་འདྲེན་པ་དང་ལ་མཐར་དུ་སྦྱོར་བ་ནི་རྟགས་མཚུངས་སུ་སྦྱར་ན་བརྗོད་པ་མི་བདེ་བས་བརྗོད་བདེ་འདྲེན་པ་དང་། ལྷག་མ་ན་ར་ལ་རྣམས་ལ་དུ་སོགས་སྦྱོར་བ་ནི་རྟགས་མཚུངས་དང་དུ་མེད་པས་བརྗོད་བདེ་འདྲེན་པའི་ལུགས་སུ་བྱས་ཤིང་། གོ་དོན་ཟུང་ཟད་བསྡུ་བའི་སྐབས་སུ་སྨོས་པ་བཞིན་ཏེ། འཆད་འགྱུར་རྣམས་ལའང་ཅི་རིགས་སུ་སྦྱར་ཞིང་ཤེས་པར་བྱའོ།

གཉིས་པ་དོན་གྱི་སྦྱོར་ཚུལ་ལ། འདིར་བསྟན་བཤད་པ་དང་། མ་བཤད་པ་ཁ་སྐོང་བ་གཉིས། དང་པོ་ནི། ལ་ན་གཉིས་དེ་ཉིད་ཀྱི་དོན་དུ་མི་འཇུག་ཅིང་གཞན་ལ་འཇུག་པ་དང་། སུ་ར་རུ་དུ་ཏུ་ལྔ་པོ་དེ་རྣམས་ལས་སུ་བྱ་བ་སོགས། དོན་ལྔ་ལ་མཚུངས་པར་འཇུག་པ་ཡིན་པས་དེ་རྣམས་ཇི་ལྟར་སྦྱར་ན། བྱེད་པ་པོས་བྱ་བ་གང་ལ་བྱེད་པའི་ལས་ཀྱི་དོན་དུ་འགྱུར་བ་རྣམ་དབྱེ་གཉིས་པ་ནི། ཤར་ཕྱོགས་སུ་གྲོ། ཇོ་བར་གཟུགས་བརྙན་བྱེད། མཐའ་རུ་འཁྱོལ། རྒྱ་གར་དུ་འགྲོ། རྒྱབ་ཏུ་ཕྱོགས། ཕ་རོལད་ཏུ་ཕྱིན། གཟུགས་ལ་ལྟ། མདུན་ན་རྒྱུ། ཐག་ཏུ་བཟུང་། སྙིང་དུ་བཞག ཤད་དུ་འགྲོ། ལམ་དུ་ཞུགས། ཡུལ་དུ་ཕྱིན། ཞེས་སོགས་མཐའ་ཡས་པར་བསྒྲེས་ནས་སྦྱར་བའོ། དེ་བཞིན་དུ་བྱ་བ་གང་ཞིག་གིས་བྱ་བའི་ཡུལ་དེའམ། དེ་དང་འབྲེལ་བའི་ལས་ལ་ཕན་འདོགས་པར་འགྱུར་བའི་དོན་གྱིས་ཆེད་དུ་བྱ་བའི་ཡུལ་ལ་འཇུག་པ་རྣམ་དབྱེ་བཞི་པ་ནི། ཆོས་ཕྱོགས་སུ་དཀའ་བ་སྤྱད། དམན་པར་བརྩེ། བདུད་རྩི་རུ་བསྒྱུར། ཤིང་གཅོད་དུ་སྟ་རེ་དགོས། གྲུབ་ཏུ་རེ། གར་ལྟ་བ་ལ་སློན་མོ་ཐོགས། ཤིང་ལ་ཆུ་འདྲེན། ཚོགས་ན་ཚེར་འགྱེད། བླ་མ་ལ་ཡོན་འབུལ། ལྷ་ལ་མཆོད་པ་འབུལ། དགེ་འདུན་ལ་བསྙེན་བཀུར་བྱ།

བུལ་པོ་ལ་སྦྱིན་པ་གཏོང་། རྟ་ལ་རྩ་ཆུ་ཕྱིན། ལ་སོགས་པ་རྒྱ་ཆེར་སྤྲོ་བར་བྱ་སྟེ། དེའི་ཆེད་དུ། དེའི་ཆེད་ལ། དེའི་དོན་དུ། དེའི་དོན་ལ། དེའི་ཕྱིར་དུ། ལྟ་བུ་དགོས་ཆེད་གསལ་བྱེད་ཀྱི་སྒྲ་དང་ལྡན་པ་རྣམས་ནི་ཆེད་ཀྱི་དོན་ཡིན་པ་བློས་མ་དགོས་སོ།།

རྟེན་གནས་ཏེ་གང་ཞིག་གང་ལ་བརྟེན་པ་འམ་ཡོད་པའི་དོན་ཅན་དུ་འཇུག་པ་རྣམ་དབྱེ་བདུན་པ་ནི། ཤར་ཕྱོགས་སུ་འོད་སྣང་། མེར་མེ་ལྷ་གནས། ལྷོར་གཤིན་རྗེ། སྤྲེ་བ་ནུ་ཐུང་བཅས། ལྷ་ཁང་དུ་མཆོད་རྟེན་ཡོད། ས་འོག་ཏུ་ཀློབས་ལྡན་གནས། གཟུགས་ཁམས་ན་ཚངས་པ། ཉི་ཟླ་ལ་འོད། ལྕགས་ལ་གསེར་འབྱུག། ལྟ་བུ་སྟེ་གོ་བར་སྦྱོར།། རྣམ་དབྱེ་གཉིས་པའི་བྱེ་བྲག་ཡུལ་གང་ཞིག་ལ་བྱ་བ་གང་ཞིག་བྱེད་པའི་ཚེ།

ལས་ཀྱི་དོན་ལ་འཇུག་པ་ནི། ལས་དེ་ཡོ་ན་ཉིད་ཀྱི་ངོ་བོར་གྱུར་པས་ལས་དང་བྱ་བ་ངོ་བོ་གཅིག་པ་ཡིན་དེ་ལྟ་བུའི་ལས་ཀྱི་དོན་ལ་འཇུག་པ་ནི། མཆོག་གསུམ་ལ་སྐྱབས་སུ་ཤེས། ལྷར་གསོལ། སྨྲ་བར་བྱེད། བརྟན་པར་གྱུར། སློབ་མ་ཚེའི་ལྷ་རུ་བརྟེན། འོད་དུ་འཚེར། གཅིག་ཏུ་གྱུར། མང་དུ་འཕེལ། མེ་རུ་འབར། ཆུ་རུ་འཁྱིལ། རླུང་དུ་འཚུབ། གཟུགས་སུ་སྤྲུལ། སོགས་སུ་ཤེས་པར་བྱ་སྟེ། འདི་ཉིད་རྟོགས་དཀའ་བས་ཅུང་ཟད་བཤད་ན། མཆོག་གསུམ་ལ་སྐྱབས་སུ་ཤེས་ཞེས་པ་ལྟ་བུ་ལ། སྤྱིར་བཏང་སྐྱབས་སུ་ཤེས་པ་ནི་བྱ་བ། མཆོག་གསུམ་ནི་བྱ་བ་དེའི་ཡུལ་ཡིན་པས་དེ་ལ་ལས་ཀྱི་རྣམ་དབྱེ་སྦྱོར་བ་ཡིན་མོད། བྱེ་བྲག་ཏུ་ན་ལས་དང་བྱ་བ་དང་མི་དང་གི་དབང་གིས་ལས་ཀྱི་རྣམ་དབྱེ་འཇུག་པའི་ཡུལ་གཙོ་ཕལ་གཉིས་ལས་གཙོ་བོ་ནི་དེ་ཉིད་དང་། ཕལ་པའམ་འདིར་བསྟན་དེ་ཉིད་ཀྱི་དོན་ཅན་ནི་བྱ་བ་ཉིད་ལ་ལས་དང་བྱ་བ་གཉིས་སུ་དབྱེ་བའི་ཤེས་པ་ནི་བྱ་བ། སྐྱབས་ནི་ཤེས་པར་བྱ་བ་རྒྱུའི་ལས་ཡིན་པས་དེར་ལ་དོན་གྱི་རྣམ་དབྱེ་འཇུག་པ་དེ་ཉིད་དེ། སྐྱབས་དང་ཤེས་པ་གཉིས་སྤྱིར་ཐ་དད་ཡིན་ཡང་བྱ་བ་གཅིག་ལ་སྦྱོར་བ་འདི་འདྲའི་སྐབས་ཤེས་པ་ཉིད་སྐྱབས་ཡིན་ནོ་སྙམ་པའི་ངོ་བོར་ཞེན་པ་བརྗོད་པ་ཡིན་པས། ཤེས་པ་ཡུལ་ཅན་དང་སྐྱབས་ཡུལ་དུ་མི་བཟུང་བར། མཆོག་གསུམ་ཡུལ་དང་། སྐྱབས་དང་ཤེས་པ་བསྡོམས་པའི་ཚིག་ཀུན་ཡུལ་ཅན་གྱི་ངོ་བོ་གཅིག་སྟོན་པ་ཡིནོ། དེས་ན་བྱ་ལས་ངོ་བོ་གཅིག་པའི་ཕྱིར་ལ་དོན་འདི་རིགས་ལ་གཞུང་འདིར་དེ་ཉིད་ཀྱིས་སྒྲ་བསྟན་ཅིང་། ངོ་བོ་གཅིག་ལ་དབྱེ་དངོས་མི་འབྱུང་བས། འཕགས་ཡུལ་པའི་བརྡའ་སྤྲོད་པ་དག་གིས་ལས་ཀྱིས་གཙོ་བོ་མ་ཡིན་པའམ་ཕལ་པ་ཞེས་ཟེར་རོ།། ལ་ན་དག་ནི་དོན་འདི་འདྲ་ལ་ནམ་ཡང་འཇུག་པ་མ་ཡིན་པས། སྒྲ་སྦྱོར་ལ་ན་དག་གི་འཇུག་པ་འཆད་པའི་སྐབས་སུ་འདིར་འཇུག་པ་མ་བཤད་པ་དང་། དུ་ལ་སོགས་པ་ལ་དང་མཐུན། དེ་དག་ལས་ནི་ལྷག་མ་ཡིན། ཞེས་འབྱུང་བ་ནི་ལེགས་པར་བཤད་པའོ།།

ཚེ་སྐབས་ཏེ་རྣམ་དབྱེ་བདུན་པ་ཉིད་དུས་བརྗོད་པའི་དོན་ལ་འཇུག་པ་ནི། ཚེས་གཉིས་སུ་ཉི་མ་ཟློག། ཉི་མ་མ་ཤར་བར་ལྡང་། འཚར་ཁ་རུ་དུས་གདབ། རྒྱུན་དུ་ཁ་ཏོན་བྱེད། རྟག་ཏུ་བདེན་པ་སྨྲ། ནམ་ལངས་པ་ན་ཆོས་སྟོན། སྲོད་ལ་བདུད་བཏུལ། སོགས་མང་དུ་ཤེས་པར་བྱའོ།།

ལས་སུ་བྱ་བའི་རྗེས་མཐུན་ནི། ཡང་སྐབས་འདིར་ལས་ཀྱི་དོན་སོགས་ལ་དགག་སྒྲ་དང་འབྲེལ་བས་ལས་ལ་སོགས་པ་སོ་སོའི་མཚན་ཉིད་དང་མི་ལྡན་པར་གྱུར་པ། གཟུགས་ལ་མི་ལྟ། སྡོང་བ་པོར་སྦྱིན་པར་མི་བྱ། གཟུགས་ཁམས་ན་དྲི་ཟ་མེད། རྟེན་འབྲེལ་པར་མི་བྱེད། ལྟ་བུ་རྣམས་ཀྱི་ལ་དོན་དེ་དག་ལས་ལ་སོགས་པ་སོ་སོའི་རྣམ་དབྱེར་འགྱུར་རམ་སྙམ་ན། རིམ་པ་བཞིན། ལས་དང་། ཆེད་དུ་བྱ་བ་དང་། རྟེན་པ་དང་། དེ་ཉིད་ལས་གཞན་མིན་པའི་ལས་རྣམས་བཀག་པས། དེ་དག་གི་རྒྱུ་མཚན་གྱིས་བཞག་པའི་རྣམ་དབྱེ་དེ་དག་དངོས་སུ་མི་འགྱུར་ཡང་། དགག་བྱའི་ཚིག་དེ་རྣམས་དང་འབྲེལ་པའི་དབང་ལས་རྣམ་དབྱེ་དེ་རྣམས་དང་རྗེས་སུ་མཐུན་པ་ཙམ་དུ་ཤེས་པར་བྱའོ། གཉིས་པ་གཞུང་འདིར་དངོས་སུ་མ་བསྟན་ཀྱང་། བཤད་མ་ཐག་པའི་ལ་སྒྲ་རྣམས་ཀྱི་ནང་ནས་ན་ལ་གཉིས་པོ་དེ་ལ་འཇུག་ཚུལ་གཞན་ཡང་ཡོད་དེ། ནའི་སྒྲ་དམིགས་ཀྱིས་དབྱེ་བའི་དོན་དུ་སྦྱར་བ། དངོས་སུ་ན། མདོར་བསྡུ་ན། ཡིན་ཀྱང་ན། སོགས་དང་། རྒྱུ་མཚན་གྱི་དོན་དུ་སྦྱར་བ། འདི་ཡོད་ན་འདི་འབྱུང་། མེ་ཡོད་ན་དུ་བ་འབྱུང་། ལྟ་བུ་དང་། རྒྱུ་མཚན་དོན་གྱིས་བསྟན་པའི་དོན་དུ་སྦྱར་བ། འདིར་ཤིང་ཡང་མེད་ན་ཤིང་སྐམ་པ་ཇི་ལྟར་ཡོད། འདུས་མ་བྱས་ཡིན་ན་མི་རྟག་པར་རུང་ངམ། ལྟ་བུ་དང་། ཟླ་མ་དེ་ལས་ཚིག་གི་མ་འགལ་བའམ་མ་ཡིན་པ་སོགས་སྟོན་པའི་དོན་དུ་སྦྱར་བ། འདི་སྔོན་དུ་སྡིག་པ་སྤྱོད་པ་ཞིག་ན་ནི་དགེ་བ་ལ་ཡིད་འཇུག་པར་བྱེད་དོ། འདི་སྔོན་ནོར་གྱིས་དབུལ་

བ་ཡིན་ན། ད་ནི་དབྱུལ་པོ་མ་ཡིན་ནོ། ཞེས་པ་ལྟ་བུ་དང་། ངེས་པར་དཀའ་བ་ལྟ་མི་ངེས་པའི་ཚིག་གམ་ཚོད་འཛིན་པའི་སྒོ་ནས་ཚིག་དོན་ཕྱི་མ་ངེས་པའི་དོན་དུ་སྒྱུར་བ། ལྷས་བཏུད་ན་མིས་ལྟ་ཅི་སྨོས། རབ་བྱུང་རྣམས་ཁྲིམས་ལ་འཁྲིན་པར་བྱེད་ན་ཁྲིམ་པ་རྣམས་ལྟ་ཅི་སྨོས། ལྟ་བུ་དང་། ངེས་པ་ནན་གྱིས་བཟུང་ནས་ཕྱི་ཚིག་ངེས་པར་བྱེད་པའི་དོན་དུ་སྒྱུར་བ་ཁྲིམས་པ་ལྟ་འདོད་པ་ལ་སྲིད་ན་རབ་བྱུང་རྣམས་ཀྱང་འདོད་པ་ལ་སྲིད་པར་བྱེད་དོ། དུད་འགྲོ་རྣམས་ལྡན་པ་ཉིད་ན་མིའང་དེ་ལྟ་བུ་དག་མཐོང་ངོ། ལྟ་བུ་དང་།

སྨོན་པའི་དོན་དུ་སྒྱུར་བ། བདག་བྱང་ཆུབ་ཐོབ་ན་ཅི་མ་རུང་! སེམས་ཅན་ཐམས་ཅད་བདེ་བ་དང་ལྡན་ན་ལྷམ་མོ། ལྟ་བུ་དང་།

ཞེ་ཚོམ་གྱི་གཞིའི་དོན་དུ་སྒྱུར་བ། ས་བོན་ནི་བཏབ་ན། འདི་ལས་མྱུ་གུ་འབྱུང་ངམ་མི་འབྱུང་། ཆོས་ནི་བསྟན་ཟིན་ན་གཞན་གྱིས་རྟོགས་སམ་མ་རྟོགས། ལྟ་བུ་མང་དུ་འབྱུང་ཞིང་། ལའི་སྒྲ་ཚིག་ལྷག་མ་འདྲེན་པ་ལྷག་བཅས་ཀྱི་དོན་དུ་སྒྱུར་བ་མཉམ་པར་བཞག་ལ་དེ་ཁོ་ན་ཉིད་སེམས། ལག་པ་བཀྲུས་ལ་ཟས་ཟ་ལྟ་བུ་དང་།

ཚིག་ཕྲ་ཕྱི་མཚམས་སྦྱོར་བ་ཙམ་གྱི་དོན་དུ་སྒྱུར་བ་བདེ་བ་དང་ལྡན་ལ་གནོད་པ་མི་མངའ་བ། གསལ་ཞིང་དྭངས་ལ་དྲི་མ་མེད། ཞེས་སོགས་རྒྱ་ཆེར་འབྱུང་བ་རྣམས་སོ། འདིར་སྨྲ་སྒོ་ལས།

ན་ཞེས་བྱ་བའི་ཚིག་གི་དོན། དམིགས་ཀྱིས་འབྱེད་དང་རྒྱུ་མཚན་དང་། རྒྱུ་མཚན་དོན་གྱིས་བསྟན་པ་དང་། ལས་དང་ཆེད་དང་རྟེན་གནས་དང་། ཕྱི་ཚིག་དེ་གཞན་སོགས་སྟོན་དང་། ངེས་པར་དཀའ་བ་ཚིག་འཛིན་ལས། ཕྱི་ཚིག་ངེས་པར་བྱེད་པ་དང་། དེ་ལས་བཟློག་པ་ཉིད་དང་ནི། འགལ་བཤད་མི་འགལ་སྟོན་པ་དང་། སྨོན་དང་འདྲི་དང་ཞེ་ཚོམ་གཞི། ཚེ་སྐབས་རྣམས་ལ་འདི་མཐོང་ངོ།

ཞེས་དང་།

ལ་ནི་གཉིས་པ་བཞི་པ་དང་། བདུན་པ་སྦྱད་དང་སྦྱོར་བ་དང་། སྨོན་དང་ཚོད་འཛིན་གཞི་དང་ནི། ཚེ་སྐབས་དག་ཏུ་འདོད་པ་ཡིན།

ཞེས་འབྱུང་བའི་དོན་འགྲེལ་པས་བཀྲལ་བ་ལས་འདས་པའི་ཚར་འདུག་སྙམ་པ་རྣམས་བཀོད་ཀྱི། ན་སྒྲ་འགལ་བའང་མི་འགལ་བར་སྟོན་པ་ལ་འཇུག་པ་ནི། དོན་དམ་དུ་དབྱེར་མེད་ན་ཀུན་རྫོབ་ཏུ་དབྱེར་ཡོད་ལྟ་བུ་དཔེར་བརྗོད་པས། ཕྱི་ཚིག་དེ་གཞན་སོགས་སྟོན་དང་།ཞེས་པའི་བསྟན་བྱ་དང་བྲལ་བར་འགྱུར་ཞིང་།

འདྲི་བའི་གཞིར་འཇུག་པ་ནི། གཟུགས་གཟུགས་སུ་རུང་བ་ཡིན་ན་འདི་ཅེས་གཟུགས་སུ་རུང་ལྟ་བུ་དཔེར་བརྗོད་པས། དམིགས་ཀྱི་འབྱེད་པའམ་ཞེ་ཚོམ་གྱི་གཞི་ནང་དུང་ལས་བཙམས་ཏེ་འདྲི་དགོས་པའི་ཕྱིར་དེ་དག་གི་དོན་ལས་ལོགས་སུ་དབྱེ་བ་དགོས་པ་མེད་པ་དང་ལའི་སྒྲ་སྦྱད་པ་དང་སྦྱོར་བ་དང་སྨོན་པ་རྣམས་ལ་འཇུག་པར་བཤད་པ་ནི་སོ་སོའི་དཔེར་བརྗོད་དང་སྒྱུར་ནས་བརྟགས་ན་ལྷག་བཅས་ཉིད་དུ་གསལ་བས་སོ་སོའི་དབྱེ་བ་དོན་མི་ཆེ་བ་དང་། ཚོད་འཛིན་ལ་འཇུག་པར་བཤད་པ་དེ་ནི་ཚོད་བརྗོད་པའི་དོན་ཙམ་དུ་མི་འདུག་པས་དེ་རྣམས་ནི་འདིར་མ་སྨོས་སོ།

གཉིས་པ་མཐའ་དཔྱད་པ་ནི། སྐབས་འདིར་འགྲེལ་བྱེད་སྔ་ཕྱི་རྣམས་ལ་བཞེད་ཚུལ་མི་འདྲ་བ་འགའ་ཞིག་འདུག་པ་དེ་རྣམས་ཀྱི་མཐའ་དཔྱད་པས་འགྲེལ་ཚུལ་འདི་ཉིད་ཁུངས་ངེས་པ་རྙེད་པའི་རྒྱུར་འགྱུར་བའི་ཕྱིར། གཞན་བཞེད་ཀྱི་སྙིང་པོ་བརྟུས་ནས་ཅུང་ཟད་དཔྱད་ན།

གང་མིང་མཐའ་ན་བཅུ་པ་གནས།

སོགས་ཀྱིས་བསྟན་པའི་མིང་མཐར་གནས་པའི་དོན་འགྲེལ་བྱེད་སྔ་མ་ཕལ་ཆེར་གྱིས་རྣམ་དབྱེ་སྒྱུར་ཡུལ་མིང་མཐའི་རྗེས་འཇུག་དེ་ཉིད་དུ་འདོད་ཅིང་། རྒྱུ་མཚན་ནི།

གང་མིང་མཐའ་ན་བརྒྱད་པ་གནས། དེ་ལ་གཉིས་པ་ཀྱུ་ཡང་སྦྱར།

ཞེས་འབྱུང་བས། ར་མཐར་རུ་འཇུག་པ་མི་འདོད་བཞིན་དུ་ཁས་ལེན་པ་དང་། འགའ་ཞིག་གིས། མིང་མཐར་གནས་པའི་དོན་རྣམ་བཞིན་དུ་འདོད་ཅིང་ར་མཐར་རུ་འཇུག་པ་མི་འདོད་པས། དེ་ལ་གཉིས་པར་ཀྱུ་ཡང་སྦྱར ཞེས་ར་ཡིག་བསྟན་ནས། གཉིས་ཞེས་པའང་སྔོན་འཇུག་གཉིས་པར་ངོས་བཟུང་། ཉེ་ར་མཐར་དུ་སྒྱུར་བའི་དོན་ཅན་དུ་འཆད་

པ་དང་། ཁ་ཅིག་གིས་རྟགས་མཚུངས་སྦྱོར་བར་རློམ་ནས་ད་མཐར་ཏུ་འཇུག་པར་འདོད་པ་དང་། ཕལ་ཆེར་གྱིས་ལ་སྒྲའི་འཇུག་ཡུལ་དེ་ཉིད་ཅེས་པ་དངོས་པོའི་དེ་ཁོ་ན་ཉིད་ལ་ངོས་བཟུང་བ་དང་། ཁ་ཅིག་གིས། དེ་ཉིད་ཅེས་པ་ངེས་གཟུང་གི་དོན་དུ་འདོད་པ་དང་། ལ་ལས་ལ་སྒྲ་ཐེར་བའི་རྒྱུ་མཚན་བྱ་ལ་སོགས་པ་རྣམས་ལས་སོགས་དོན་ལྔ་ལ་མཚུངས་པར་འཇུག་པས་སོང་ཞེས་འདོད་ཅིང་རྒྱུ་མཚན་ངེས་ལ་ན་དག་ཀྱང་དེ་ཉིད་ལ་འཇུག་པར་འདོད་པ་རྣམས་ཏེ། དེ་དག་འགའ་དང་འགས་རྗེས་ཟློས་ཀྱི་ཚུལ་དུ་སྨྲ་བར་བྱེད་ཅིང་། འགའ་དང་འགས་ཁྱད་ཆོས་སུ་ངོམ་པར་བྱེད་དོ། དེ་ལ་འདོད་པ་ཐ་མ་དེ་ནི་ཤིན་ཏུ་འཁྲུལ་ཏེ། དེ་ལྟ་ན་རྗེས་འཇུག་ས་ར་ད་གསུམ་གྱི་མཐར་སུ་ཏུ་དུ་རྣམས་འཇུག་ཐེར་བ་ཉི་ཚེ་ཞིག་གཞུང་འདིས་བསྟན་པར་སོང་བས་ཏུ་དང་དུ་གཉིས་ཀྱི་འཇུག་ཡུལ་ད་དུང་གཞན་ཡང་ཡོད་ན་གཞུང་འདིས་མི་སྟོན་པའི་རྒྱུ་མཚན་འཐད་ལྡན་སྨྲ་དགོས་ཤིང་། རྒྱུ་མཚན་མེད་ན་ནི་གཞུང་གི་བསྟན་བྱ་མ་ཚང་བའི་སྐྱོན་དུ་འགྱུར་བའི་ཕྱིར་དང་། ར་མཐར་ཏུ་འཇུག་པའང་ཤིན་ཏུ་བརྗོད་མི་བདེ་བས་ཤིང་མཐའ་རྣམ་དབྱེ་འདྲེན་ཚུལ་གཞུང་འདི་དང་འགལ་བར་མ་ཟད། མེས་དབོན་གྱི་བཀའ་གཅིག་ཞལ་བཤུས་དག་པ་རྣམས་དང་། ཁྲི་ལྡེ་སྲོང་བཙན་དུས་ཀྱི་ཞལ་ཕྱུང་ཅན་བྲག་ལ་བརྐོས་པའི་ལྡ་དང་ཡི་གེ་དུ་མ་ཁམས་ཕྱོགས་སུ་སྣང་བ་རྣམས་དང་། རྡོ་རིང་གི་ཡི་གེ་དང་། གནའ་བོའི་གསུང་རབ་དག་པ་རྣམས་སོགས་གང་དུའང་མི་འབྱུང་བས་མི་འཐད་པར་ངེས་པའི་ཕྱིར་རོ།།

འོ་ན་ལ་དོན་འཆད་པའི་གཞུང་འདི་སྐྱར་བསྒྱུ་དང་འགྲེལ་སྒྲ་སོགས་པའི་སྐབས་ལྟར་བྲུད་དང་མིང་མཐའ་སྦྱོར་ཚུལ་ཞིག་སྟོན་རིགས་པ་ལ། མ་སྟོན་པར་ཐལ་བར་འགྱུར་རོ་ཞེ་ན། སྦྱོར་ཚུལ་དེ་ནི་གཞུང་འདི་ཉིད་ཀྱི་གོང་འོག་གཞན་དང་རྟགས་འཇུག་སོགས་ལས་ཀྱང་རྗེས་སུ་དཔག་ནུས་པར་དགོངས་ནས་གཞུང་ཟུར་ཡངས་པའི་ཚེད་དུ་དངོས་སུ་མ་བསྟན་པར་ཟད་པས་སྐྱོན་དུ་ཅི་ཞིག་འགྱུར། དེ་བས་ཁྱོད་རང་གི་གཞུང་འདིས་བྲུད་དང་མིང་སྦྱོར་ཚུལ་བསྟན་པར་འདོད་པ་ཉིད་སྐྱོན་ཆེ་སྟེ། དེས་རྗེས་འཇུག་ས་ར་ད་གསུམ་ཁོ་ན་ལ་སྦྱོར་ཚུལ་བཤད་ཀྱི་གཞན་ལ་མ་བཤད་པ་དང་། དེ་གསུམ་བཤད་པས་སྦྱོར་ཚུལ་གཞན་གོ་བར་མི་ནུས་པའི་ཕྱིར་ཉན་པ་པོ་ལ་སླར་ཡང་ཞེ་ཚོམ་སྐྱེད་པར་མ་ཟད། གོང་དུ་སྨོས་པ་ལྟར་མཁས་པ་ལ་མ་གྲགས་ཤིང་། གཞུང་དོན་སྤྱིའི་མིང་མཐའ་འདྲེན་ཚུལ་དང་འགལ་བ་ཁས་ལེན་དགོས་པ་དེའང་ཞེ་འདོད་འདིའི་སྐྱོན་གྱིས་བསྐྱེད་པར་སྣང་བའི་ཕྱིར་རོ།། དེས་ན་མིང་མཐར་ས་ཡིག་སོགས་གནས་ཞེས་པ་དེ་མིང་མཐའ་ལ་སྦྲ་ནས་གནས་པའི་དོན་མིན་གྱི། དཔེར་ན། གཡས་དང་། ཤར་ལྟ་བུའི་མིང་མཐར་རྣམ་དབྱེའི་དོན་དུ་ས་ར་ད་རྣམས་བཀོད་དེ་གནས་པ་ལྟ་བུ་ལ་ཕྱུ་ཡིག་སྦྱར་རྒྱུའི་དོན་ཏེ། ལེགས་སྦྱར་ལྟར་ན། དེ་བ་ཞེས་པར་སི་ཏྲིན་ཨི་ཕྱིས་དེ་བས་ཞེས་གནས་པ་ལ་ཐེར་བ་ལྟ་བུར་ཤེས་དགོས་སོ།། དེ་ལྟར་བསྟན་པས་འདོད་པ་གཉིས་པ་དེའི་ལོག་རྟོག་གི་རྩ་བ་སུན་འབྱིན་པར་ནུས་མོད། དོན་ཀྱང་གཞུང་བཅོས་ནས་དོན་མིན་དུ་བཤད་པ་ལ་བརྗོད་པར་བྱ་སྟེ། ཁྱོད་ཅག་གི་ཚུལ་དུ་བསྟན་པའི་བཤད་པ་དེ་ལ་གཉིས་པ་ཞེས་པ་སྔོན་འཇུག་གཉིས་པར་ངོས་འཛིན་པ་སྐབས་དང་མི་འབྲེལ་བ་དང་། གཉིས་པར་ཞེས་བཅོས་ནས་ད་ཡིག་ལ་ཕྱུ་སྦྱར་བའི་དོན་ཅན་དུ་འདོད་པ་དགོས་པ་མེད་པ་དང་། དེ་ལྟར་འདོད་པས་གཞུང་གི་བསྟན་བྱ་གཞན་རྣམས་ཆད་པར་འགྱུར་བ་དང་། ཡང་སྒྲ་བརྗོད་པ་དོན་མེད་དུ་ཐལ་བའི་སྐྱོན་ཡང་ཡོད་དོ།།

སུམ་ཅུ་པའི་གཞུང་ཚིག་འདི་གྲུས་རྣམས་ཀྱི་རྗེས་འཇུག་དང་ལྷ་ཤིའི་གྲངས་སྟོན་པར་སྣང་བ་ལ། སྔ་ཕྱིའི་འབྲེལ་ཅི་ཡང་མེད་པར་འདིར་ལྷ་དོལ་དུ་སྔོན་འཇུག་གི་གྲངས་སྟོན་པ་མཁས་པའི་བསྟན་བཅོས་ཀྱི་ལུགས་སུ་མི་རིགས་པའི་ཕྱིར། གཉིས་པ་གྲུབ་སྟེ།

གང་མིང་མཐའ་ན་གསུམ.པ་གནས།

ཞེས་སོགས་ཁྱོད་རང་ཡང་དུ་སྒྲ་འཆད་པའི་གཞུང་དུ་འདོད་པ་གང་ཞིག ། དེར་འཆད་པར་འགྱུར་བས་འདི་བསྟན་པ་ལ་དགོས་པ་མེད་པའི་ཕྱིར། དེ་ནི་ད་མཐར་དུ་འཇུག་པའི་དོན་དང་། འདིར་ར་མཐར་དུ་འཇུག་པའི་དོན་ཡིན་པས་སོ་སོ་ལ་ཡོད་དོ་ཞེ་ན་དེའང་མི་འཐད་དེ། དེ་ལྟ་ན་ང་ན་མ་ལ་རྣམས་ཀྱི་མཐར་ཡང་དུ་སྒྲ་འཇུག་པས་དེ་རེ་རེ་ནས་འཆད་པའི་གཞུང་འབྱུང་བར་རིགས་པའི་ཕྱིར་ཏེ་ཅང་ཐལ་ལོ།།

གསུམ་པ་གྲུབ་སྟེ། ཁྱོད་འདོད་པ་དེ་ལྟ་ན། ལ་དོན་གཞན་རྣམས་ཀྱི་ཡ་གྱལ་ར་དང་དུའི་སྒྲ་དག་རྐྱེན་བྱེད་ཀྱི་གཞུང་འཆད་པར་འགྱུར་བའི་ཕྱིར་ཏེ། སྐྱར་བསྒྱུའི་སྐབས་སུ་རྒྱུ་མཚན་སྨོས་པ་བཞིན་ཏེ་ཤིག་ཕྱུ་ལྡན་ལྟ་བུ་འདིར་མ་བཤད་པ་སྐྱོན་དུ་མི་འགྱུར་ཡང་སྐབས་དོན་རྗེས་འཇུག་གི་ཡི་གེ་དང་སྦྱར་བའི་ལ་དོན་འཆད་ན་རྩོམ་པ་པོ་མཁས་པའི་,

གསུང་དུ་མི་འགྱུར་བའི་ཕྱིར་རོ། །བཞི་པ་གྲུབ་སྟེ། ཡང་ཞེས་པ་ཚིག་རྐྱང་གཉིས་དང་སྤྱད་པའི་དོན་དུ་འཇུག་པ་ལས་ཚིག་རྐྱང་གི་དོན་མ་ཡིན་པ་ནི་རྟོགས་པར་སླ་བས་སྤྱད་པའི་དོན་ལས་མེད་ཅིང་། སྤྱད་པའི་དོན་ཡང་དབྱེ་གཞི་གཅིག་ལ་དབྱེ་བ་གཉིས་སམ་མང་པོར་མཐུན་པར་བསྡུ་བའམ། ཁྱད་གཞི་གཅིག་ལ་ཁྱད་ཆོས་གཉིས་སམ་མང་པོ་ལྡན་ཅིག་ཏུ་བརྗོད་དགོས་པ་ལྟ་བུར་འདོད་དགོས་པའི་རྒྱུ་མཚན་གྱིས། ཁྱོད་ལྟར་ན། ལྷུ་ཡང་སྦྱར་ཞེས་པའི་ཡང་སྒྲ་དེས། གཞི་གང་ལ་གང་ཞིག་གང་དང་ལྡན་ཅིག་ཏུ་སྤྱད་པའི་དོན་ཅིའང་མི་སྟོན་པར་འགྱུར་བས་མཁན་པོས་འདིར་ཡང་སྒྲ་གསུངས་པ་དགོས་པ་མེད་པར་ཐལ་བའི་ཕྱིར་རོ།། དེས་ན་ཉེས་པ་འདི་ནི་གཞུང་འདིས་དུ་ཡིག་རྐྱང་པ་བརྟན་པར་འདོད་པ་རྣམས་ལའང་འགྱུར་བར་དགོས་སོ།། འདོད་པ་གསུམ་པ་དེའང་འཐད་པར་མ་མཐོང་སྟེ། ད་ཡིག་རྗེས་འཇུག་མོ་ཡིན་པའི་རྒྱུ་མཚན་གྱིས་དེས་ཏུ་འདྲེན་པ་འཐད་དོ་སྙམ་པར་འདུག་ཀྱང་། དེ་ལྟ་ན། ས་ཡིག་ལའང་མཚུངས་པས། གཡས་ཏུ། རྟ་ཏུ། ལྟ་བུ་ཤིན་ཏུ་བརྗོད་མི་བདེ་ཞིང་མ་གྲགས་པ་མང་པོ་ཞིག་གསར་དུ་སྦྱར་དགོས་པར་འགྱུར་ཞིང་། ས་མཐར་སུ་ཐོབ་པ་གཞུང་འདིས་དངོས་སུ་བསྟན་པའི་ལུགས་ཡིན་པས་སྐྱོན་མེད་དོ་སྙམ་པའང་མི་འཐད་དེ། དེ་ལྟ་ན་ད་མཐར་དུ་ཐོབ་པའང་གཞུང་འདིས་དངོས་བསྟན་དུ་འདོད་དགོས་པའི་ཕྱིར་ཏེ། དེ་གཉིས་རིགས་པ་མཚུངས་པའི་ཕྱིར་དང་། ཕྱིར་ཡང་ལུགས་དེ་མི་འཐད་པ་གོང་དུ་སྨྲོས་པ་ལྟ་བུའི་ཕྱིར་རོ།། ཡང་ད་དྲག་གི་མཐར་ཏུ་ཐོབ་པའི་རྒྱུ་མཚན་གྱིས་སོ་སྙམ་ནའང་མི་འཐད་དེ། སྔར་བསྡུའི་སྐབས་སུ་བཤད་པ་བཞིན་དུ་ཡིག་གི་འཇུག་ཡང་འཇུག་གི་མཐའ་གཉིས་ད་ཡིག་ཡིན་པ་ཙམ་དུ་མཚུངས་ཀྱང་ཀློག་ཚུལ་ལ་ཁྱད་པར་ཤིན་ཏུ་ཆེ་བས་ད་དྲག་མཐར་ཏུ་སྒྲ་ཉིད་བརྗོད་བདེ་ཞིང་། གཅིག་ཤོས་ལ་དེ་བས་ཏུ་སྒྲ་ཉིད་བརྗོད་བདེ་བར་མངོན་སུམ་གྱིས་གྲུབ་ཅིང་། ཡོངས་སུ་གྲགས་པའི་ཕྱིར་རོ།།

འདོད་པ་བཞི་པ་དེའང་མི་འཐད་དེ། ཕྱིར་ནའི་ཕྱད་འཆད་འགྱུར་ལྟར་དེ་ཉིད་ལ་མི་འཇུག་ཅིང་། ཁྱད་པར་ཕྱིར་གྱི་ལུགས་སུ་དེ་ཉིད་ཅེས་པ་དངོས་པོའི་དེ་ཁོ་ན་ཉིད་ལ་འདོད་པར་འདུག་པས་དེ་ལ་ནམ་ཡང་འཇུག་པ་མི་སྲིད་པའི་ཕྱིར་དང་། ཁོ་ན་ཞེས་པའི་ན་ཡིག་ཁྱོད་འདོད་པའི་དེ་ཉིད་ཀྱི་དོན་ཡིན་ན་ཉིད་ཅེས་པའི་སྒྲ་ལ་མ་ལྟོས་པར་དངོས་པོའི་དེ་ཉིད་ལ་འཇུག་རིགས་པ་ལ། དེའང་མི་འཇུག་པའི་ཕྱིར་ཏེ། སྒྲ་མོ་ལས། ཁོ་ནའི་སྒྲ་དོན་དྲུག་ལ་འཇུག་པར་བཤད་པ་འཐད་ཅིང་དེ་རྣམས་ཐམས་ཅད་ངེས་གཟུང་གི་དོན་དུ་སྟོང་བའི་ཕྱིར་དང་། དེ་ཁོ་ན་ཉིད་ཅེས་སྦྲེལ་ནས་བརྗོད་པའི་སྒྲ་ཡང་དངོས་པོའི་དེ་ཉིད་ལ་འཇུག་པ་ནི་བདེན་མོད་ཀྱི་དེ་ལ་ངེས་ཁྱབ་པ་ནི་མ་ཡིན་ཏེ། དཔེར་ན་ལྷ་རྣམས་ཀྱི་ནང་ནས་སྐྱིད་མེད་བུ་དེ་ཁོ་ན་མཐུ་ཆེ་འོ།། ལྟ་བུ་ངེས་གཟུང་ལ་འཇུག་པ་ཤིན་ཏུ་མང་བའི་ཕྱིར་ཏེ་ཞེ་འདོད་ཀྱི་དཔེར་བརྗོད་གཅིག་སྟེང་ཁྱབ་དེའང་ཞེ་འདོད་དེར་མ་ངེས་པའི་ཕྱིར་རོ།། དེས་ན་ཁོ་ན་ཞེས་པ་ཚིག་ཕྲད་གཅིག་ཡིན་པ་ལ་ཁོ་དང་ན་སོ་སོར་ཕྲལ་ནས་འཆད་པར་རློམ་པ་ནི། ལ་དོན་དེ་ཉིད་ལ་འཇུག་པར་བཤད་པ་དེ་རྣམ་དབྱེ་གཉིས་པ་དང་མ་འབྲེལ་བ་ཞིག་དགོས་པས་བཟུང་ནས་དཔེར་བརྗོད་བཙལ་ཀྱང་མ་རྙེད་གཏི་མུག་སྟེ་ཟེར་རྒྱུ་ཐོང་བའི་རྟགས་ཟད་མར་བསྟན་པ་ཡིན་ནོ།། འདོད་པ་ལྔ་པ་དེའང་རིགས་པ་མ་ཡིན་ཏེ། ཁྱོད་ཉིད་ཀྱིས་བཀོད་པའི་འདི་ཐད་ཀྱི་དཔེར་བརྗོད་དུ། རྒྱ་གར་དུ་ཤེས། སྟོད་དུ་རིག། འོག་མིན་དུ་ཤེས། དཔལ་དུ་འདུག། ཅེས་འབྱུང་བ་རྣམས་ཀྱི་ལ་སྒྲ་ནི་ལས་དང་བྱ་བ་ངོ་བོ་གཅིག་པའི་ལས་ཀྱི་རྣམ་དབྱེ་ཡིན་པས་ངེད་འདོད་པའི་དེ་ཉིད་ཀྱི་དཔེར་རིགས་ཀྱང་ཁྱོད་རང་གི་ཞེན་དོན་དུ་མི་འགྱུར་ཏེ་དེ་དག་ངེས་གཟུང་གི་སྒྲ་མ་ཡིན་པའི་ཕྱིར་དང་། ཀུན་ལ་དགའ། དེ་རུ་སྐྱིད། རྒྱབ་དུ་ཐོ། ཞེས་འབྱུང་བའི་ལ་སྒྲ་རྣམས་ནི་བྱ་བ་དང་ཐ་དད་པའི་ལས་ཀྱི་དོན་ཡིན་པས་འདིར་བསྟན་གྱི་ལས་ཀྱི་རྣམ་དབྱེ་དངོས་སུ་འགྱུར་བའི་ཕྱིར་ངེས་བཟུང་མ་ཡིན་པ་དང་། རྟག་ཏུ་དགའ། ཕ་རོལ་ཏུ་འདུག། ཅེས་འབྱུང་བའི་ལ་དོན་རྟ་མ་དུས་བརྗོད་པའི་བདུན་པ་ཡིན་པས་འདིར་བསྟན་ཚེ་སྐབས་ཀྱི་སྒྲ་དང་། ཕྱི་མ་རྟེན་གྱི་བདུན་པ་དངོས་ཡིན་པའི་ཕྱིར་དེ་དག་ལ་ངེས་གཟུང་གི་སྒྲའི་དོན་མེད་པས་སོ།། ཅི་སྟེ་དེ་དག་ནན་གྱིས་ངེས་གཟུང་དུ་འདོན་ཅིང་ལ་དོན་འཇུག་ཡུལ་གྱི་དེ་ཉིད་ཀྱང་དེ་དག་ཏུ་འདོད་པ་མི་གནོད་ན་ནི་མཁས་པ་ཉིད་ལ་ཅི་འདྲ་བར་ཆས་པ་སྟེ། དེ་ཉིད་གཅིག་པུ་བསྟན་པས་ཚོག་གི། ལས་དང་ཚེ་སྐབས་དང་རྟེན་གནས་རྣམས་ལ་འཇུག་ཚུལ་སོ་སོར་འཆད་པ་དགོས་པ་མེད་པར་ཐལ་བའི་ཕྱིར་རོ།། དེས་ན་རྣམ་དབྱེ་འདི་དག་སོ་སོར་འཆད་པར་རློམ་བཞིན་དུ་བྱེ་བྲག་མ་ཕྱེད་པ་དང་། ངེས་གཟུང་གི་སྒྲའང་ལན་དུ་མར་སྦྱར་ཞིང་འཆད་བཞིན་དུ་དེ་མ་ཡིན་པ་ལ་དེར་འཁྲུལ་བ་སོགས་བློ་གྲོས་ཀྱི་བཞིན་རས་གསལ་བར་སྟོན་པའི་འགྲེལ་བཤད་སྣང་བྱེད་ནོར་བུ་འདི་ནི་ཤིན་ཏུ་ཡ་མཚན་པའི་གནས་སོ།། འདོད་པ་དྲུག་པ་དེའང་འཐད་པའི་ཕྱོགས་མ་ཡིན་ཏེ། དུ་ལ་སོགས་པ་ལྔའམ་དྲུག་པོ་ཐམས་ཅད་ལས་སོགས་དོན་ལྔ་ལ་ལ་ཡིག་དང་མཚུངས་པར་འཇུག་པ

མ་ཡིན་པའི་ཕྱིར་ཏེ། ལ་ན་གཉིས་དེ་ཉིད་ཀྱི་དོན་ལ་མི་འཇུག་པའི་ཕྱིར་ཏེ། ཁྱེད་རང་གིས་ཀྱང་དཔེར་བརྗོད་འགའ་ཞིག་བཀོད་ནས་འདི་རྣམས་ཕལ་ཆེར་ལ་ལ་ཡིག་སྦྱར་རུང་ངོ། ཞེས་སྨྲ་བ་ཙམ་ལས་དངོས་སུ་ལའི་དཔེར་བརྗོད་བཀོད་མ་ནུས་པ་དང་། ན་ཡིག་འཇུག་པའི་དཔེར་བརྗོད་ཀྱང་འཐད་ལྡན་འགོད་རྒྱུ་མ་སྐྱིད་འདུག་པའི་ཕྱིར་རོ།། དེའང་ཞིབ་མོར་བརྗོད་ན། འདུས་བྱས་སུ་གྲུབ། ཆོས་སུ་གནས། མི་བསྒྱུ་བར་ངེས། ཆོས་ཉིད་དུ་གསལ། དགྲ་བཅོམ་དུ་གྲུབ། སོགས་བཀོད་པ་ནི་དེ་ཉིད་ཀྱི་དཔེར་རུང་ཡང་། དེ་དག་ལ་ཡིག་སྦྱར་དུ་རུང་སྟེ། འདུས་བྱས་ལ་གྲུབ། ཆོས་ལ་གནས། མི་བསྒྱུ་བ་ལ་ངེས། ཆོས་ཉིད་ལ་གསལ། དགྲ་བཅོམ་ལ་གྲུབ་ཅེས་སོགས་སྦྱར་བས་རྟེན་དང་རྟེན་པའམ་བྱ་བའི་ཡུལ་དང་བྱ་བ་ཐ་དད་དུ་གསལ་བའི་ཚིག་ཏུ་གྱུར་བའི་ཕྱིར་འགའ་ཞིག་རྟེན་གནས་དང་འགའ་ཞིག་ལས་དང་འགའ་ཞིག་དགོས་ཆེད་ཀྱི་སྒྲར་ཡང་འགྱུར་ཞིང་། བྱ་ལས་ངོ་བོ་གཅིག་པའི་དེ་ཉིད་ཀྱི་སྒྲར་མི་འགྱུར་བའི་ཕྱིར་རོ།།

དེ་བཞིན་དུ་དེ་རྣམས་ལ་ན་ཡིག་ཀྱང་དེ་ཉིད་ཀྱི་དོན་དུ་སྦྱར་མི་རུང་ཞིང་། དཔེར་བརྗོད་དུ་དེ་རང་ན་འདུག། ཅེས་པ་ཁོ་ན་བཀོད་ཀྱང་དེ་ནི་གནས་གཞིའི་དོན་ཅན་ཡིན་གྱི་དེ་ཉིད་ཀྱི་དོན་ལྟ་ཅི་སྨོས་ལས་ཀྱི་དོན་ཡང་མ་ཡིན་ནོ།། འོ་ན་གཞུང་འདིར་ལ་ན་དག་དམིགས་སུ་མ་ཕྱེ་བར།

ལས་དང་ཆེད་དང་རྟེན་གནས་དང་། དེ་ཉིད་ཚེ་སྐབས་ལ་སྒྲ་ཡིན།

ཞེས་གསུངས་པ་ཅི་ཞེ་ན། དེ་ལྟར་གསུངས་པ་ནི། ལ་སྒྲ་རྣམས་ལས་སོགས་དོན་ལྔ་པོ་ཕལ་ཆེར་ལ་མཚུངས་པར་འཇུག་པ་མང་བའི་དབང་གིས་སྤྱིར་བསྟན་པ་ཡིན་པས་སྐྱོན་མེད་ལ། ལ་སྒྲ་ཞེས་པའི་དོན་ཡང་ལས་སོགས་འཇུག་དོན་ཐམས་ཅད་ལ་ལ་ཡིག་དང་མཚུངས་པར་འཇུག་པའི་ལ་ཡིན་ཏེ། ཏུ་ལ་སོགས་པ་བདུན་ནམ་དུ་ལ་སོགས་པ་དྲུག་པོ་དེའི་ཐ་མ་ལ་ཡིག་ཡིན་པས་དེ་བཟུང་ནས་ཐམས་ཅད་ལ་ལ་སྒྲ་ཞེས་པའི་མིང་གིས་བཏགས་པ་ཡིན་པའི་ཕྱིར་རོ།། དེ་ལྟར་འཐད་པའང་ཡིན་ཏེ་བརྡའ་སྤྲོད་པའི་བསྟན་བཅོས་རྣམས་ན། བརྡའ་ཆད་ཀྱི་སྐབས་སུ། ཙར། ཕལ། ལྟ་བུ་ཡི་གེ་བསྡུས་ནས་མིང་དུ་བྱས་པ་རྣམས་ལ་མིང་དེའི་ཁོངས་སུ་མིང་དེ་བྱ་བ་གང་གི་ཆེད་དུ་བཏགས་པའི་བྱ་བ་དེ་ལ་མི་མཁོ་བའི་ཡི་གེ་འགའ་ཞིག་ཀྱང་ཡོད་མོད་ཀྱི་མཁོ་བ་མང་བའི་ཆ་ནས་དེར་བཏགས་པ་མི་འགལ་བ་དང་། དམིགས་བསལ་ཐམས་ཅད་ལ་མ་ཁྱབ་ཀྱང་ཁྱབ་པ་སྤྱིར་བཏང་བཤད་པ་མི་འགལ་བ་ལྟ་བུར་ངེས་པའི་ཕྱིར་རོ།། དེ་ལྟར་བློར་ལྡན་རྣམས་ཀྱི་བློ་གྲོས་ཀྱི་སྒོ་དབྱེ་བའི་ཕྱིར་མཐའ་དཔྱད་ཅུང་ཟད་ཞིག་བྱས་ཀྱི། གཞན་གྱི་ནོར་བ་མཐའ་དག་ནི་དགག་པར་མི་ལང་ངོ་། སྨྲས་པ།

དོན་མིན་རྟོག་མ་མཐའ་དག་བསླུང་བྱེད་ཅིང་། དོན་གྱི་བཞིན་རས་ཡོངས་རྫོགས་གསལ་མཐོང་བ།

ནོར་བུ་ཀེ་ཏ་ཀ་ཡི་མེ་ལོང་དང་། མཚུངས་པའི་གཏམ་འདི་བློ་ལྡན་དགའ་སྐྱེད་ཡིན། ཞེས་སོ།།

གསུམ་པ་ཨི་ལྡན་གྱི་རྣམ་དབྱེ་འཆད་པ་ལ། མདོར་བསྟན་པ་དང་། རྒྱས་པར་བཤད་པ་གཉིས། དང་པོ་ནི།

རྗེས་འཇུག་ཡི་གེ་བཅུ་པོ་ལ། ཨི་དང་མཐུན་ལུགས་འདི་ཞེས་བྱ།

ཞེས་པ་སྟེ། རྗེས་འཇུག་ཡི་གེ་བཅུ་པོ་དེ་དག་གང་རུང་རྗེས་སུ་ཞུགས་པའི་མིང་རྣམས་ལ། ཨི་ཡིག་དང་སྦྱར་བའི་རྣམ་དབྱེའི་ཁྱད་རྣམས་ཇི་ལྟར་མཐུན་བར་སྦྱོར་བའི་ལུགས་ནི་འདི་དང་འདིའོ་ཞེས་བསྟན་པར་བྱའོ།། ཞེས་སོ།།

གཉིས་པ་ལ་འབྲེལ་སྒྲ་བཤད་པ་དང་བྱེད་པ་པོའི་སྒྲ་བཤད་པའོ།།

དང་པོ་གཉིས་ལ་དང་པོ་མཐུན། གསུམ་ལྔ་བཅུ་ལ་ཀྱི་དང་སྦྱར། བདུན་པ་ཉིད་ལ་བདུན་པ་སྟེ།

ལྷག་མ་རྣམས་ལ་གྱི་སྦྱར་བ། དེ་དག་ཨི་སྦྱར་འབྲེལ་བའི་ས།

ཞེས་གསུངས་ཏེ་རྗེས་འཇུག་བཅུའི་དང་པོ་ག་དང་ང་གཉིས་གང་རུང་རྗེས་སུ་ཞུགས་པའི་མིང་རྣམས་ལ་ནི། རྗེས་འཇུག་དང་པོ་ག་ཉིད་མཐུན་ཞིང་། དེ་བཞིན་དུ་རྗེས་འཇུག་གསུམ་པ་ད། ལྔ་པ་ན། བཅུ་པ་ས་རྣམས་རྗེས་སུ་ཞུགས་པ་ལ་ཀྱི་དང་སྦྱར་བ་དང་། བདུན་པ་བ་ཡིག་གི་མཐའ་ཅན་རྣམས་ལ་དངོས་སུ་བ་ཡིག་ཡོད་དམ་མེད་ཀྱང་རུང་

བདུན་པ་འ་ཉིད་སྦྱར་བ་དང་། འདིར་རྗེས་འཇུག་གི་ཡི་གེའི་བྱ་བ་གཙོ་བོར་བསྟན་པས་དངོས་སུ་མི་འབྱུང་ཡང་འ་ཡིག་གི་མཐར་ཀྲང་པ་ཀ་སྐོང་དགོས་པའི་ཚེ་ལ་ཡིག་སྦྱར་བ་དང་། དེ་དག་ལས་གཞན་ཕྱག་མ་ན་མ་ར་ལ་བཞི་པོའི་མཐའ་ཅན་རྣམས་ལ་ནི་ཀུ་ཉིད་སྦྱར་བ་མཐུན་པ་བཅས། དེ་དག་ཐམས་ཅད་ལ་རིམ་པ་བཞིན་ཨི་ཡིག་ཀྱི་གི་ཀུ་སྦྱར་བས། ཀྱི་ཀྱི་འི་ཡི་ཀྱི་རྣམས་སུ་འགྱུར་བ་དེ་རྣམས་གང་ཞིག་གང་དང་སྒྲ་མཐུན་པའི་མིང་མཐའ་སོ་སོ་དང་སྦྱར་བས། བདག་གི། གང་གི། ཐམས་ཅད་ཀྱི། རབ་ཀྱི། ཕྱོགས་ཀྱི། དེའི། དེ་ཡི། ལམ་གྱི། གསེར་གྱི། དཔལ་གྱི་སོགས་སུ་འགྱུར་ཏེ་དེ་དག་ནི་གཞུང་གཞན་དུ་རྣམ་དབྱེ་དྲུག་པ་ཞེས་འབྱུང་བ་རྟེན་དང་བརྟེན་པའམ་ཡན་ལག་དང་ཡན་ལག་ཅན་སོགས་མིང་དོན་ཐ་དད་འབྲེལ་པ་བརྗོད་པའི་དོན་ཅན་གྱི་སྒྲ་ཡིན་པས་འབྲེལ་པའི་ས་ཞེས་བྱའོ།། ཞེས་པའོ།། འདིར་ཡིག་རྐྱང་དག་པ་རྣམས་སུ་ད་དྲག་ཅན་གྱིས་ཀྱི་ཉིད་དྲངས་པ་མཐོང་མོད་ཀྱི་དེར་སང་ད་དྲག་མི་མཛད་པས་ཐལ་ཆེར་ཀྱི་ཉིད་སྦྱོར་བར་སྣང་ཡང་སྐད་གཞན་དང་བསྟུན་ན་ཀྱི་རང་འདྲེན་པ་བརྗོད་པའི་ཞིང་ལེགས་པར་སེམས་པས། ཀུནྡ་ཀྱི། རབ་འབྱོརད་ཀྱི། བཀའ་སྩལ་ཡོད་ཀྱི་སོགས་སུ་སྦྱར་བར་བྱའོ།།

འབྲེལ་སྒྲ་དེ་དག་ཚིག་གྲོགས་དང་དེ་ལྟར་སྦྱོར་བ་ནི། བདག་གི་ནོར། གང་གི་དྲིན། ཐམས་ཅད་ཀྱི་དོན། རབ་ཀྱི་ཡུལ། ཕྱོགས་ཀྱི་གླང་པོ། དེའི་ཚུལ། དེ་ཡི་ཕྱོགས་སུ་ཅི་ཞིག་ཕྱུང་། གཏན་གྱི་དོན། ལམ་གྱི་ཡོན་ཏན། གསེར་གྱི་རྒྱན། དཔལ་གྱི་བེའུ། ཀུན་གྱི་མཆོག། རབ་འབྱོརད་ཀྱི་ཚུལ། བཀའ་སྩལ་ཡོད་ཀྱི་སྙིང་པོ་སོགས་ཏེ་རྟོགས་པར་སླའོ། གི་ལ་སོགས་པ་དེ་རྣམས་རྣམ་དབྱེའི་དོན་མ་ཡིན་པ་གཞན་ཡང་འཇུག་པ་ཡོད་དེ། འདི་ནི་བདེན་གྱི་གཞན་ནི་གཏི་མུག་གོ། བདག་ཅག་གི་སྐྱབས་ནི་སྟོན་པ་སངས་རྒྱས་ཡིན་གྱི་དྲག་པོ་སོགས་མ་ཡིན་ནོ།། འདི་ལྟར་འཐད་མོད་ཀྱི་དོན་ཀྱང་། ཞེས་པ་ལྟ་བུ་ཚིག་འགལ་བའམ་མི་མཐུན་པར་སྟོན་པའི་ཚིག་གི་རྒྱན་ལ་འཇུག་པའི་ཕྱིར་རོ།། གཉིས་པ་བྱེད་པ་པོའི་སྒྲ་ནི།

དེ་ཉིད་ལ་ནི་བཅུ་པ་སྦྱར། བྱེད་པ་པོ་རུ་ཤེས་པར་བྱ།

ཞེས་བས་བསྟན་ཏེ། སྔར་བཤད་པའི་རྣམ་དབྱེ་དྲུག་པའི་སྒྲ་གི་ལ་སོགས་པ་དེ་དག་ཉིད་ལ་རྗེས་འཇུག་བཅུ་པ་ས་ཡིག་སྦྱར་བས། གིས། ཀྱིས། འིས། ཡིས། ཀྱིས་རྣམས་སུ་གྲུབ་པ་ནི་བྱེད་པ་པོས་བྱ་བ་ལ་སྦྱོར་བ་སྟོན་པས་ན་གཞུང་གཞན་དུ་རྣམ་དབྱེ་གསུམ་པ་ཞེས་འབྱུང་བ་བྱེད་པ་པོའི་ས་རུ་ཤེས་པར་བྱའོ།། ཞེས་སོ།། དེ་རྣམས་མིང་མཐར་སྦྱོར་ཚུལ་ནི་འབྲེལ་སྒྲའི་སྐབས་དང་མཚུངས་པས། བདག་གིས། གང་གིས། ཐམས་ཅད་ཀྱིས། རབ་ཀྱིས། ཕྱོགས་ཀྱིས། དེའིས། དེ་ཡིས། གཞན་གྱིས། ལམ་གྱིས། གསེར་གྱིས། དཔལ་གྱིས། ཀུནད་ཀྱིས། རབ་འབྱོརད་ཀྱིས། ཟླའོད་ཀྱིས། ལ་སོགས་པར་འགྱུར་ཏེ་རྟོགས་པར་སླ་མོད། འོན་ཀྱང་འ་མཐར་འིས་ཞེས་པ་སྐད་གསར་བཅད་ཀྱི་ལུགས་ལ་མི་འབྱུང་བ་ནི་ཡི་གེ་གྲངས་ཡངས་པའི་ཆེད་དུ་འ་མཐར་ཐལ་ཆེར་བསྡུས་པ་བཞིན་འིས་ཞེས་པའི་འི་ཡིག་ཕྱིས་ནས་བསྡུས་པར་ཟད་ཀྱི་ནོར་བ་མེད་པས་ནི་མ་ཡིན་པར་ཤེས་དགོས་སྐྱེ་གཞུང་འདིར་བསྟན་པར་མ་ཟད་ཆོས་རྒྱལ་མེས་དཔོན་དུས་ཀྱི་རྡོ་རིང་གི་ཡི་གེ་སོགས་ལའང་དེ་ལྟར་སྣང་བ་མངོན་སུམ་གྱིས་གྲུབ་པའི་ཕྱིར་རོ།། བྱེད་པ་པོའི་སྒྲ་དེ་རྣམས་ཚིག་གྲོགས་དང་དེ་ལྟར་སྦྱོར་བའང་། བདག་གིས་བསྟན། གང་གིས་བསྒྲུབས། ཐམས་ཅད་ཀྱིས་འདུད། རབ་ཀྱིས་བསྒྱུར། ཕྱོགས་ཀྱིས་དབྱེ། དེའིས་མཛོན། ཞེས་སམ། སྐད་གསར་བཅད་ལྟར་ན། དེས་ཆོན། དེ་ཡིས་ཐམས་ཅད་དབང་དུ་བྱས། གཞན་གྱིས་གསོས། ལམ་གྱིས་འཚོ། གསེར་གྱིས་བྱུགས། དཔལ་གྱིས་བརྒྱན། ཀུནད་ཀྱིས་སྤྱོད། རབ་འབྱོརད་ཀྱིས་གསོལ། ཟླའོད་ཀྱིས་མནན། ཅེས་སོགས་རྒྱ་ཆེར་སྦྱར་ནས་ཤེས་པར་བྱའོ། སྒྲ་སྒོ་ལས་གིས་ལ་སོགས་པ་འདི་རྣམས་མི་མཐུན་པའི་རྒྱན་ལ་འཇུག་པར་བཤད་ཀྱང་འཐད་པར་མ་མཐོང་སྟེ་དེའི་དཔེར་བརྗོད་དུ། དེ་ལྟར་ཡིན་མོད་ཀྱིས་ཞེས་དང་། དོན་གྱིས་ཀྱང་ཞེས་བཀོད་པའི་ཕྱི་མའི་ཤེས་དོན་ལ་བརྟགས་ན། རྟག་པར་ཡོད་ཀྱིས། མི་རྟག་པར་མ་ཡིན་ནོ།། ཞེས་པ་ལྟ་བུ་ལ་བསམས་པར་སྣང་ཡང་། དེ་འདྲའི་ཀྱིས་སོགས་ཀྱི་སྒྲ་དེ་རྒྱ་མཚན་གྱི་དོན་གྱི་བྱེད་པ་པོའི་རྣམ་དབྱེ་ཡིན་གྱི་མི་མཐུན་པའི་རྒྱན་མ་ཡིན་པའི་ཕྱིར་དང་། ཕྱི་མ་དེའི་ཤེས་དོན་ལ་བརྟགས་ན་བསྒྲུབ་ཏུ་རུང་གིས་ཀྱང་མི་བསྒྲུབ་བོ།། ལྟ་བུ་ལ་བསམས་པར་སྣང་ཡང་དེ་འདྲའི་མི་མཐུན་པའི་རྒྱན་དུ་གྱུར་པའི་སྒྲ་ནི་ཀྱང་ཞེས་པ་ཡིན་གྱི་གིས་ཀྱི་སྒྲ་མ་ཡིན་ཏེ། དེའང་རྒྱུ་མཚན་གྱི་དོན་ཅན་ཡིན་པའི་ཕྱིར་རོ། དེས་ན་འདི་འདྲའི་རིགས་རྣམས་

དང་། ཕྱེད་དུ་རུང་གིས་ཀྱིས་ཤིག། ཀྟ་བུའི་ཕྱེད་པ་པོའི་སྒྲ་རྣམས་ཀྱང་རྒྱུ་མཚན་གྱི་དོན་དུ་ཤེས་པར་བྱའོ།། སྐབས་འདིར་འགྲེལ་བྱེད་ཁ་ཅིག་གིས། ཁྲིམས་ཀྱིས་ཀྟ་བུའང་ཕྱེད་པ་པོའི་སྒྲ་རུ་འདུལ་པ་མཐོང་མོད་ཀྱི་ལྷུན་པོའི་ཉམས་སུ་རྟོགས་པར་སླ་བ་ཉིད་དོ།། བཞི་པ་རྐྱན་སྦྱད་ཀྱི་སྒྲ་ནི།

ཨཱུ་ཡི་ཕྱིས་ནས་གཉིས་པ་སྦྱར། ཚིག་རྐྱན་གཉིས་དང་སྦྱད་པར་འགྱུར།

ཞེས་པས་བསྟན་ཏེ། གོང་དུ་བཤད་པའི་འབྲེལ་སྒྲ་དེ་དག་ལས། ཀྱི། འི། གཉིས་ཀྱི་ཨཱུ་ཡི་སྔེ་གི་ཀུ་ཕྱིས་ནས་སོ་སོར་རྗེས་འཇུག་གཉིས་པ་ང་ཡིག་སྦྱར་བས་ཀྱང་འང་། ཞེས་པར་གྲུབ་པ་དང་། འདིར་མ་བསྟན་ཀྱང་དོན་གྱིས་ཐོབ་པའི་ཡང་གི་སྒྲ་དང་བཅས་གསུམ་པོ་དེ་རྣམས་ནི་ཚིག་ཕྱི་མ་མཐུན་པའམ་མི་མཐུན་པར་རྐྱེན་པའི་ཚིག་རྐྱན་གཉིས་དང་། གཞིའམ་དོན་གཞན་ཞིག་ལ་སྦྱད་ཅིང་སྦྱོར་བའི་སྒྲར་འགྱུར་རོ།། ཞེས་སོ།།

དེ་རྣམས་མིང་མཐར་ཇི་ལྟར་སྦྱོར་བའི་ཚུལ་ནི། རྗེས་འཇུག་གི་ཕོ་ཡིག་ག་ད་བ་ས་རྣམས་དང་ད་དྲག་གི་མཐར་རྟགས་མཚུངས་བརྗོད་བདེ་གཉིས་ཀའི་སྒོ་ནས་སྒྲ་མཐུན་པ་ཀྱང་ཉིད་སྦྱར་ཞིང་། དེ་བཞིན་དུ་དངོས་སུ་ཡོད་མེད་ཇི་ལྟར་རུང་འ་མཐའ་ཅན་རྣམས་ལ་འང་དང་། ང་མ་དག་གི་མཐར་ཡང་གི་སྒྲ་འཇུག་པ་དང་། ན་ར་ལ་གསུམ་གྱི་རྗེས་སུ་བརྗོད་བདེ་ཕོ་ནའི་དབང་གིས་ཡང་ཉིད་འཇུག་གོ།། ཚིགས་བཅད་ཀྱི་རྐང་པ་ཁ་སྐོང་དགོས་པའི་ཚེ་ནི་འ་མཐར་ཡང་། ཡང་གི་སྒྲ་སྦྱར་དགོས་སོ།། དཔེར་ན། རྟག་ཀྱང་། བཅད་ཀྱང་། བཀག་ཀྱང་། བྱས་ཀྱང་། བསྟན་ཀྱང་། འགྱུར་ཀྱང་། སྨྲ་ཡང་ཀྱང་། ལྟའང་། ལྟ་ཡང་དུས་སུ་ཆར་འབེབས་ཤིང་། གང་ཡང་། ལམ་ཡང་། ཡིན་ཡང་། ཆར་ཡང་། གསལ་ཡང་། ཀྟ་བུ་རྒྱ་ཆེར། ཞེས་པར་བྱའོ།། དེ་དག་དོན་ལ་ཇི་ལྟར་སྦྱོར་བའི་ཚུལ་ཡང་མཐུན་པའི་ཚིག་རྐྱན་དུ་སྦྱོར་ན། གསལ་ཡང་གསལ། མཛེས་ཀྱང་མཛེས། ཀྟ་བུ་དང་། མི་མཐུན་པའི་རྐྱན་དུ་སྦྱོར་ན། བཏུད་ཀྱང་ཁྲོ། མཛའང་བསླུ། ཀྟ་བུ་དང་། སྦྱད་པའི་དོན་དུ་སྦྱོར་ན། གཟུགས་འདི་ནི་མཛེས་ཤིང་འོད་ཀྱང་འཕྲོ། མིང་མ་ཟད་ལྷས་ཀྱང་བཏུད་དོ། འདི་ནི་ཡུ་ཏྲ་ལ་འང་ཡིན་ལ་སྟོན་པོའང་ཡིན་ནོ། གང་ཡང་ཕྱོགས་བཅུའི་བདེ་གཤེགས་ཐམས་ཅད་ལ། ཞེས་སོགས་སུ་བསྒྲེས་ནས་རྟོགས་པར་བྱའོ། འདིར་ལ་ལ་ཞིག་གིས། མཐུན་པའི་རྐྱན་གྱི་དཔེར། ཡུ་ཏྲ་ལ་འང་ཡིན་པས་སྟོན་པོའང་ཡིན་ཞེས་དང་། གཅིག་ཤོས་ཀྱི་དཔེར། ཇི་ལྟར་པད་མ་ཆུ་ནང་དུ། སྐྱེས་ཀྱང་ཆུ་ཡི་གོས་པ་མེད། དེ་བཞིན་འདི་ནི་འཇིག་རྟེན་དུ། སྐྱེས་ཀྱང་འཇིག་རྟེན་གྱིས་མ་གོས། ཞེས་སོགས་བཀོད་སྣང་། འཐད་པར་མ་མཐོང་སྟེ། སྔ་མ་ནི་གཞི་གཅིག་ལ་མཐུན་པའི་ཆོས་ཡུ་ཏྲ་ལ་དང་སྟོན་པོ་གཉིས་སྦྱད་པའི་དོན་ཡིན་ལ། ཕྱི་མ་ནི་གཞི་གཅིག་ལ་མི་མཐུན་པའི་ཆོས་ཆུ་ནང་དུ་སྐྱེས་པ་དང་ཆུས་མ་གོས་པ་གཉིས་སྦྱད་པ་སོགས་ཀྱི་དོན་ཡིན་པའི་ཕྱིར་དེ་དག་སྦྱད་པའི་དཔེར་འོས་ཀྱི། ཚིག་རྐྱན་གྱི་དཔེར་མི་འོས་པའི་ཕྱིར་རོ། དེས་ན་ངེས་མེད་ཀྱི་དཔེ་དང་། སྦྱད་པའི་དཔེ་སོགས་སྙན་ངག་གི་རྒྱན་འགའ་ཞིག ཚིག་རྐྱན་གཉིས་ཀྱི་དཔེར་སློས་པའང་དེ་དང་འདྲའོ། ཡང་སྒྲ་སྒྲོ་ལས། ཡང་ཞེས་བྱ་ལ་བསྐྱར་བའང་ཡིན། ཞེས་འབྱུང་བར་ཕྱེབས་བཅོས་ནས་བསྟན་པ་ཞེས་སྒྲོན་ཏེ་ཁུངས་སུ་དྲངས་ནས། ཡང་དང་ཡང་དུ་གསུང་བ་གང་། ཞེས་སོགས་བསྐྱར་བའམ་བསྟན་པའི་དོན་དུ་བཤད་མོད། བསྟན་པ་ནི་ངེས་གཟུང་འཛིན་པའི་དོན་ཡིན་པས་བསྐྱར་བ་དང་གཅིག་པའི་སྐབས་མེད་ཅིང་། སྒྲ་སྒྲོ་འི་ཚིག་ཕྱེབས་མ་བཅོས་པ་དེ་ཉིད་དོན་ལ་གནས་པར། ཡང་ཡང་། སླར་ཡང་། དེ་ནས་ཡང་། ཡང་གསུངས་པ། ཀྟ་བུ་རྣམས་བསྐྱར་བའམ་བསྟན་པའི་སྒྲར་འགྱུར་བ་ཡིན་ནོ།། འོན་ཀྱང་ཡང་གི་སྒྲ་དེ་འདྲ་དེ། སྐབས་འདིའི་ཀྱང་སོགས་ཀྱི་སྒྲ་དང་མཚུངས་པ་ནི་མི་སྲིད་དོ།།

ལྔ་པ་ལྷག་བཅས་ཀྱི་སྒྲ་བཤད་པ་ནི།

ལ་དོན་སུ་ལ་ཨུ་ཕྱིས་ནས། དེ་ལ་གསུམ་པའི་དང་པོ་སྦྱར། དེ་ལ་ཨཱུ་ཡི་གསུམ་པ་སྦྱར། དེ་ནི་ལྷག་དང་བཅས་པའོ།

ཞེས་པ་སྟེ། རྟེར་བཤད་པའི་ལ་དོན་གྱི་ནང་ཚན་སུ་ཞེས་པ་དེའི་ཨུ་ཡིག་སྟེ་ཞབས་ཀྱུ་ཕྱིས་ནས་ས་ཞེས་གནས་པ་དེ་ལ་ཀ་ཡི་སྡེ་པ་གསུམ་པའི་དང་པོ་ཏ་ཡིག་སྦྱར་ཞིང་། དེ་ལ་སླར་ཡང་སྔོན་དུ་ཨཱུ་ཡི་གསུམ་པ་སྟེ་འགྲེང་བུ་སྦྱར་བས། སྟེ་ཞེས་གྲུབ་པ་ནི་མིང་ཚིག་གང་གི་མཐར་སྦྱར་ཡང་བསྟན་བྱའི་ལྷག་མ་འདྲེན་པའི་དོན་དུ་འགྱུར་བས་ལྷག་མ་དང་བཅས་པའི་སྒྲ་ཞེས་བྱའོ།། ཞེས་སོ།། དེ་ལྟར་གཞུང་འདིའི་དངོས་བསྟན་ལ་སྟེ་སྒྲ་གཅིག་པུ་ལས་མི་འབྱུང་ཡང་། མིང་མཐའ་སོ་སོ་དང་སྦྱར་བའི་ཚེ་གོང་དུ་སྨོས་པ་རྣམས་ཀྱི་རིགས་པས

བརྗོད་བདེ་བ་གོ་ན་སྦྱོར་གྱི་རྟགས་མཚུངས་ཀྱང་བརྗོད་མི་བདེ་བ་སྲུར་མེད་པས། ཡི་གེ་རྣམས་ཀྱི་ཟུར་ཕྱིན་པར་ཀློག་པའི་དབང་དུ་བྱས་ནི། གང་བ་མ་འ་རྣམས་ཀྱི་མཐར་ནི་ཡིག་མ་སྣ་དང་ལྡན་པ་དེ་བརྗོད་པས་འཇུག་ཀྱང་། ན་ར་ལ་གསུམ་དང་ད་དྲུག་གི་མཐར་ནི་དེ་ཤིན་ཏུ་བརྗོད་མི་བདེ་བའི་ཕྱིར་དང་། མ་ཡིག་གི་མཐར་ནི་ས་སྣ་ཐ་མ་དེ་ཉིད་དང་ནི་ཡིག་གི་ས་སྣ་གཅིག་ཏུ་འདྲེས་པས་སོ་སོར་མི་མངོན་པའི་ཕྱིར་དགོས་པ་མེད་པས། དེ་རྣམས་ཀྱི་མཐར་མ་ཡིག་ཕྱིས་ནས་ཏེ་རྐྱང་ཉིད་སྲུང་བ་གཞུང་འདིའི་དགོངས་པར་དོན་ཐོབ་ཏུ་གནས་ཤིང་། དེ་བཞིན་དུ་ན་མཐར་ཡང་ས་སྣ་ཅན་ཀློག་མི་བདེ་བར་མ་ཟད་དེ་སྣ་འཇུག་ཡུལ་གཞུང་འདིའི་དགོངས་པ་དང་། སྣ་བོ་ཙ་འགྲེལ་མཐུན་པར་སྣང་བས། དེར་དེ་སྣ་ལྷག་བཅས་ས་འཇུག་པར་བཤད་པ། ལ་དོན་གྱི་སྐབས་སུ་ད་མཐར་དུ་སྦྱོར་བ་ལྟར་ད་ཡིག་གི་མཐར་ཟུར་བ་རིགས་པའི་ཕྱིར་ན་རྗེས་འཇུག་གི་ཁྱད་པར་ལ་ལྟོས་པའི་ལྷག་བཅས་ཀྱི་སྣ། ནི། ཏི། དི། གསུམ་དུ་འགྱུར་བ་ཡིན་ནོ།། གོང་དུ་སྨོས་པའི་ལ་དང་འཆད་འགྱུར་གྱི་ནས་དག་ལྷག་བཅས་ལ་འཇུག་པ་ནི་རྗེས་འཇུག་གི་ཁྱད་པར་ལ་མི་ལྟོས་པའི་ཕྱིར་ཕྲད་རང་དབང་ཅན་དུ་ཤེས་པར་བྱའོ།། དེས་ན་ནི་ལ་སོགས་པ་གསུམ་མིང་ཚིག་ཅི་རིགས་པའི་མཐར་ཇི་ལྟར་སྦྱོར་བའི་དཔེར་བརྗོད་པའང་། བཞག་ནི། བྱང་ནི། བཀབ་ནི། ཁྱོད་ཀྱི་ནི་མདུན་ནི། ཡིན་ཏི། འགྱུར་ཏི། གསལ་ཏི། བྱམ་པར་ཏི། བརྟན་ཏི། སྒྱུར་ཏི། བསམ་ཏི། བྱས་ཏི། བསྐྱབས་ཏི། དེ་ཡིས་ཏི། ཡོད་དི་བཤད་དི། ལ་སོགས་པ་རྣམས་ཏེ་རྟོགས་སླ་བར་ཟད་དོ།། སྣ་སྒྲོ་ལས།

ནི་ནི་ལྷག་མ་ཡོད་པ་ནི། མཚམས་སྦྱོར་བ་དང་དམ་བཅས་དང་། གཞན་འདྲེན་པ་དང་གསུམ་དུ་འདོད། བྱེད་དང་བྱ་བའམ་ཡང་ན་ནི།
བྱ་བ་ཉིད་དུ་སྦྱོར་བ་གང་། ཚིག་གཉིས་རིམ་མམ་དུས་གཅིག་ཏུ། སྦྱོར་བར་བྱེད་པ་མཚམས་སྦྱོར་ཡིན། གང་ཞིག་གི་ནི་ཐ་མ་ལ།
གསལ་བར་བྱེད་པ་དམ་འཆའ་བ། ལྷག་མ་ཡོད་ཙམ་རྟོན་འགྱུར་ཞིང་། དེ་ལས་གཞན་ཀྱང་གཞན་འདྲེན་པའོ།།

ཞེས་འབྱུང་བ་ནི་ཚིག་དོན་ལྷག་མ་འདྲེན་ཚུལ་གྱི་དོན་གྱི་དབྱེ་བ་བཤད་པ་ཡིན་ཞིང་། ཡལ་ཆེར་ལེགས་བཤད་དུ་འང་འདུག་པས་འདིར་སྨོས་ན། ནི་ལ་སོགས་པ་དེ་རྣམས་ལྷག་མ་འདྲེན་ཚུལ་གྱི་སྒོ་ནས་དབྱེ་ན་གསུམ་དུ་འགྱུར་ཏེ། མཚམས་སྦྱོར་དང་། དམ་བཅའ་དང་། གཞན་འདྲེན་ནོ།།

དང་པོ་ལ། ཚིག་སྔ་མ་བྱེད་པ་དང་ཕྱི་མ་བྱ་བར་སྦྱོར་བས་འདྲེན་བྱེད་དང་འདྲེན་བྱ་དུས་རིམ་པར་འཇུག་པ་ཞིག་དང་། སྔ་ཕྱི་གཉིས་ཀ་བྱ་བར་སྦྱོར་ཞིང་དུས་རིམ་གྱིས་འཇུག་པ་ཞིག་དང་། དེ་ཉིད་ལ་དུས་སྔ་ཕྱི་མེད་པ་ཞིག་ཏེ་གསུམ་འབྱུང་བའི། སྔ་མ་ནི། མདའ་འཕངས་ཏེ་ཐོག། ལྷ་བསྒྲུབས་ཏེ་གྲུབ། ལྟ་བུ་དང་།

གཉིས་པ་ནི། ལྷ་མཆོད་དེ་ལས་བྱ། ཕྱག་འཚལ་ཏེ་བཤད། ལྟ་བུ་དང་། ཕྱི་མ་ནི། འཇུམ་མུལ་ཏེ་མདངས་ཕྱུང་། འཕུར་ཏེ་འགྲོ། ཚིག་སྦྱ་དང་བཅས་ཏེ་འབར། ལྟ་བུ་ནི་དེ་རྣམས་ནི་ནས་དང་ཅིང་སོགས་ཀྱི་ཕྲད་དང་ཡང་འཇུག་པ་མཐུན་ནོ།། དམ་བཅའ་ཞེས་པ་ནི་ཚིག་སྔ་མ་དམ་བཅས་པ་དེའི་གསལ་བྱེད་དམ་སྒྲུབ་བྱེད་དུ་ཚིག་ཕྱི་མ་འདྲེན་པ་སྟེ། དེའང་དབྱེ་བ་འདྲེན་པ་དང་གཏན་ཚིག་འདྲེན་པ་དང་། ངེས་ཚིག་འདྲེན་པ་དང་། རྒྱས་བཤད་འདྲེན་པ་སོགས་ནང་གསེས་མང་པོར་འགྱུར་རོ།། དཔེར་ན། དངོས་པོ་ནི་རིགས་གསུམ་སྟེ། བེམ་པོ་དང་། ཤེས་པ་དང་ལྡན་མིན་འདུ་བྱེད་དོ།། རྟག་པ་ཡིན་ཏེ་ཡོད་པ་གང་ཞིག་འདུས་བྱས་མ་ཡིན་པའི་ཕྱིར། སངས་རྒྱས་ཏེ་མ་རིག་པའི་གཉིད་སངས་པ་དང་ཤེས་བྱ་ལ་བློ་གྲོས་རྒྱས་པའོ།། བསླབ་པ་ཀུན་གྱི་གཞི་འཛིན་ཅིང་། ཞེས་གསུངས་ཏེ། བསླབ་པ་ནི་ལྷག་པ་ཚུལ་ཁྲིམས་དང་ལྷག་པ་བསམ་གཏན་དང་ལྷག་པ་ཤེས་རབ་ཀྱི་བསླབ་པ་གསུམ་དུ་ནང་པ་ལ་གྲགས་པ་དང་། ཕྱི་རོལ་པ་ལའང་ཚངས་པར་སྤྱོད་པའི་བརྟུལ་ཞུགས་ཀྱི་བསླབ་པ་མང་དུ་འབྱུང་བས་ཞེས་སོགས་རིམ་པར་སྦྱར་བར་བྱའོ།།

གཞན་འདྲེན་ནི་མཚམས་སྦྱོར་དང་དམ་བཅའ་གཉིས་སུ་མི་གཏོགས་པའི་ལྷག་མ་ཡོད་པ་ཙམ་སྟོན་པའི་སྒྲ་གཞན་རྣམས་ཏེ།

ཤར་གྱི་ཕྱོགས་ན་དབང་པོ་སྟེ། ལྷོ་ཡི་ཕྱོགས་ན་འཆི་བདག་གོ། ཁྱོད་ནི་དཔལ་ཏེ་ཁྱོད་ནི་མགོན། ལྟ་བུ་རྣམས་སོ།

སྐབས་འདིར་འགྲེལ་བྱེད་ཁ་ཅིག་གིས། ལྷག་བཅས་ཀྱི་སྒྲ་ནི་ཁོ་ནར་འདོད་པ་ནི་མི་འཐད་དེ། གོང་སྨོས་ལྟར་རྗེས་འཇུག་འགའ་ཞིག་ལ་ནི་ཟུར་བ་ཀློག་དཀའ་བའི་

སྐྱོན་དང་། དེ་ཡིག་ལྷག་བཅས་ཀྱི་དོན་ཅན་འཇུག་པའི་སྐབས་མི་འབྱུང་བའི་ཉེན་དང་། སྔོན་གྱི་གླེགས་བམ་དག་པ་རྣམས་ལ་ཡོངས་སུ་གྲགས་པ་དང་འགལ་བའི་སྐྱོན་ཡང་ཡོད་པའི་ཕྱིར་རོ།

དྲུག་པ་འབྱེད་སྡུད་ནི།

རྗེས་འཇུག་ཡི་གེ་བཅུ་པོ་ལ། དྲུག་པ་སྦྱར་ན་འབྱེད་སྡུད་ཡིན།

ཞེས་པས་བསྟན་ཏེ། རྗེས་འཇུག་ཡི་གེ་བཅུ་པོ་དེ་རྣམས་ལ་དེ་ཉིད་ཀྱི་དྲུག་པ་མ་ཡིག་སྦྱར་བས། གམ། ངམ། དམ། ནམ། བམ། མམ། འམ། རམ། ལམ། སམ། རྣམས་སུ་གྲུབ་པ་དེ་དག་དང་། སྔ་མ་རྣམས་ཀྱི་རིགས་པས་དོན་གྱིས་ཐོབ་པའི། ཏམ་བཅས་བཅུ་གཅིག་པོ་རྣམས་ནི། ཚིག་དོན་སོ་སོར་འབྱེད་པའམ་ཕྱོགས་གཅིག་ཏུ་སྡུད་པའི་སྒྲ་འཇུག་པ་ཡིན་ནོ། ཞེས་སོ། དེ་རྣམས་མིང་ཚིག་གང་གི་མཐར་ཡང་རུང་། སྦྱར་བསྡུའི་སྐབས་དང་མཚུངས་པར་ཕྱིར་བཏང་རྗེས་འཇུག་སོ་སོར་རང་རང་ལ་མ་ཡིག་སྦྱར་བ་ཉིད་འཇུག་པ་མཐུན་པ་ཡིན་ཡང་། དམིགས་བསལ་ད་དྲག་ཅན་རྣམས་ཀྱི་མཐར་ཏམ་ཡིག་སྦྱོར་ཏེ། དེ་དག་རིམ་པས་དཔེར་བརྗོད་ན། རྟག་གམ། མཐོང་ངམ། ཡོད་དམ། ཡིན་ནམ། སྒྲུབ་བམ། སྒོམ་མམ། རིགས་ཀྱི་བུའམ། དེ་ཉིད་དུའམ། གསེར་རམ། མཚལ་ལམ། བྱས་སམ། ཁྱོད་ཀྱིས་སམ། འདོད་ཏམ། གྱུར་ཏམ། འཚལད་ཏམ། སོགས་སོ།

དེ་དག་དོན་ལ་ཇི་ལྟར་སྦྱོར་བའི་ཚུལ་ལ། དབྱེ་གཞི་གཅིག་ལས་བྱེ་བྲག་གཉིས་སམ་མང་པོར་འབྱེད་པ་ཆོས་ནི་གཉིས་ཏེ། འདུས་བྱས་སམ། འདུས་མ་བྱས་སོ། ཕུང་པོ་ནི་ལྔ་སྟེ། གཟུགས་སམ། ཚོར་བའམ། འདུ་ཤེས་སམ། འདུ་བྱེད་དམ། རྣམ་པར་ཤེས་པ་ནི་ཕུང་པོའོ། ལྟ་བུ་དང་།

ཚིག་དོན་གཉིས་སམ་མང་པོ་དོན་གཅིག་ཏུ་སྡུས་པ། འདུས་བྱས་སམ། འདུས་མ་བྱས་ནི་ཆོས་སོ། གཟུགས་སམ། ཚོར་བའམ་འདུ་ཤེས་སམ་འདུ་བྱེད་དམ་རྣམ་པར་ཤེས་པ་ནི་ཕུང་པོའོ། ལྟ་བུ་རྒྱ་ཆེར་ཤེས་པར་བྱའོ། འཇིག་རྟེན་མཐའ་དང་ལྡན་ནམ་མི་ལྡན། རྟག་གམ་མི་རྟག་ལྟ་བུ་དྲི་བ་དང་ནི་ཆོས་ཀྱི་ཚིག་ཅན་རྣམས་ཀྱང་དོན་གྱི་ཁྱད་པར་བརྟག་ཅིང་འབྱེད་པའི་དོན་ཅན་ཡིན་པས། དེ་འདྲའི་འམ་ལ་སོགས་པའི་སྒྲའང་འབྱེད་པའི་སྒྲ་ཉིད་དུ་ངེས་སོ།

ཁ་ཅིག་སྐབས་འདིར་ཡང་། རྗེས་འཇུག་ད་པ་ས་རྣམས་ཀྱི་རྗེས་སུ་ཏམ་འཇུག་པར་འདོད་ཀྱང་། རྟགས་མཚུངས་འདྲེན་པའི་རིགས་འགྲེ་ཐལ་ཆེས་པར་ཟད་དོ།

བདུན་པ་འབྱུང་ཁུངས་ལ། ངོས་དང་། དེ་དག་དགར་སྡུད་ལ་འཇུག་པའི་ཚུལ། མ་བཤད་པ་ཁ་སྐོང་ཞིང་འདོད་པ་གཞན་ལ་ཅུང་ཟད་དཔྱད་པ་སྟེ་གསུམ།

རྗེས་འཇུག་ཡི་གེ་བཅུ་པོ་ཡི། བཞི་པ་དགུ་པ་ལ་བཅུ་པ།

སྦྱར་བ་འབྱུང་ཁུངས་ས་ཡིན་ཏེ།

ཞེས་པས་བསྟན་ལ། རྗེས་འཇུག་ཡི་གེ་བཅུ་པོ་དེའི་བཞི་པ་ན་དང་དགུ་པ་ལ་གཉིས་ལ་སོ་སོར་བཅུ་པ་ས་ཡིག་སྦྱར་བས། ནས། ལས། ཞེས་གྲུབ་པ་ནི་ཆོས་གང་ལས་གང་ཞིག་ཕྱེ་བའམ་བྱུང་བ་སྟོན་པའི་དོན་དུ་མཚུངས་པར་འཇུག་པས་གཞུང་གཞན་དུ་རྣམ་དབྱེ་ལྔ་པ་ཞེས་བཤད་པ་འབྱུང་ཁུངས་ཀྱི་ས་ཡིན་ནོ། ཞེས་སོ། ཏེ་ཞེས་པ་ཚིག་ལྷག་མ་འདྲེན་པའི་དོན་ཏེ། དེ་དག་ཕྲད་རང་དབང་ཅན་ཡིན་པས་སྦྱོར་ཚུལ་རྗེས་འཇུག་ཐམས་ཅད་ཀྱི་མཐར་ཅི་རིགས་པར་སྦྱར་བར་བྱའོ།

འབྱུང་ཁུངས་ཀྱི་དོན་ལ་ཇི་ལྟར་འཇུག་པ་ནི། དཔེར་ན། སངས་རྒྱས་ལས་ཆོས། ཆོས་ལས་འཕགས་པའི་ཚོགས། ཚོགས་ལས་སྙིང་པོ་ཡེ་ཤེས་ཁམས་ཐོབ་མཐར་ཞེས་དང་། གསེར་ཁ་ནས་གསེར། རྒྱ་མཚོ་ནས་ནོར་བུ། བ་ལས་འོ་མ། མཁས་པ་ལས་རིག་པ། ལྟ་བུ་དང་། འབྱུང་ཁུངས་དངོས་མ་ཡིན་ཡང་སྐབས་དེར་དེ་ལས་བྱུང་བས་འབྱུང་ཁུངས་དང་འདྲ་བ། རྟ་ལས་ལྟུང་། རི་ལས་ལྷུང་། སྐས་ནས་བབས། ཤར་ཕྱོགས་ནས་འོད་སྣང་ལྟ་བུ་རྣམས་སུ་ཤེས་པར་བྱའོ། ཡང་མཚན་ཅན་དེ་དུ་བ་མཐོང་བ་སོགས་ཀྱི་རྒྱུ་མཚན་ལས་བྱུང་བའི་ཕྱིར་འབྱུང་ཁུངས་དང་འདྲ་བའི་རྣམ་དབྱེ་ལྔ་པ་ཉིད་དོ།

གཉིས་པ་ནི།

དགར་དང་སྤྱད་པའང་དེ་བཞིན་ནོ།

ཞེས་པས་བརྟན་ཏེ། བཤད་མ་ཐག་པའི་ལས་ནས་ཀྱི་སྒྲ་དེ་དག་འབྱུང་ཁུངས་ཁོ་ནར་མ་ཟད། རྣམ་དབྱེ་སྦྱར་གཞི་དེ་ལས་རིགས་དང་བྱ་བ་ཡོན་ཏན་རྣམས་ཀྱི་ཁྱད་པར་གང་ཡང་རུང་བ་ཚོགས་སུ་དགར་བའི་དོན་ལ་འང་འཇུག་ཅིང་། དེ་ལས་ནས་ཀྱི་སྒྲ་གཅིག་པུ་ནི་ཡུལ་དང་དུས་དང་དངོས་པོ་ལ་སོགས་པ་མཚམས་འཛིན་ཅིང་སྤྱད་པའི་དོན་དུ་འང་དེ་བཞིན་དུ་འཇུག་པ་ཡིན་ནོ། ཞེས་པའོ། །དེ་དག་དབྱེ་བ་དང་བཅས་ཏེ་དཔེར་བརྗོད་ན། རིགས་དང་བྱ་བ་ཡོན་ཏན་རྣམས་ཀྱི་ཁྱད་པར་གྱིས་གཞི་གཅིག་ལས་དགར་བ་ནི། མིའམ་ཅི་ལས་དྲི་ཟ་ཐ་དད་དོ། བཤེས་གཉེན་ངན་པ་བསྐྱུར་ཞི་བྱེད་པ་ལས་ལྷ་མཆོད་པ་ཉིད་ལེགས། ཡང་སོས་ལས་ཐིག་ནག་སྡུག་བསྔལ་ཆེ། ལྷ་ཆེན་པོ་ལས་བདེ་བར་གཤེགས་པ་ཡོན་ཏན་དུ་རྨས་འཕགས་སོ། ཞེས་པ་ལྟ་བུ་སྟེ་འདི་འདྲའི་རིགས་ལ་ལས་ཀྱི་སྒྲ་ཉིད་འཇུག་གོ། དེ་བཞིན་དུ་གཞི་གཉིས་སམ་མང་པོ་ལས་ཀྱང་རུང་། དེ་དག་གི་ནང་ནས་ཕྱུང་བ་ལྟ་བུ་མ་ཡིན་པར་ཚོགས་སུ་དགར་བ་ཙམ་གྱི་དོན་ལའང་ལས་ཀྱི་སྒྲ་ཉིད་འཇུག་སྟེ། རྟག་པ་དང་དངོས་པོའི་ཆོས་ལས་དེ་བཞིན་ཉིད་གཞན་ནོ།། ཟ་བ་དང་སྐོད་པ་དང་སྨྲ་བ་དང་འགྲོ་བ་ལ་སོགས་པ་སྤྱོད་ལམ་ཕལ་པ་རྣམས་ལས་མཆོད་རྟེན་ལ་ཕྱག་དང་སྐོར་བ་བྱེད་པ་ལེགས་སོ། ཁ་དོག་རྣམས་ལས་དཀར་པོ་ཉིད་མཛེས་སོ། ལྟ་བུའོ། རིགས་སོགས་ཀྱི་ཁྱད་པར་གྱི་ཚོགས་ཀྱི་ནང་ནས་འབྱིན་པ་ལྟ་བུར་དགར་བ་ནི་མི་རྣམས་ཀྱི་ནང་ནས་རྒྱལ་རིགས་དཔའ། གསེར་དངུལ་ནང་ནས་གསེར་གོང་ཆེ། རིགས་བཞིའི་ནང་ནས་དམངས་རིགས་དམན། བ་རྣམས་ཀྱི་དཀྱིལ་ནས་ནག་མོ་འོ་མ་མང་། བྱ་བ་རྣམས་ཀྱི་ནང་ནས་སངས་རྒྱས་བཅོམ་ལྡན་འདས་ལ་མཆོད་པ་ནི་ཕུལ་དུ་བྱུང་བའོ། ལྟ་བུ་སྟེ་འདི་འདྲ་ལ་ནས་ཉིད་འཇུག་གོ། ནས་ཀྱི་སྒྲ་སྤྱད་པ་ལ་འཇུག་པ་ནི། ལྷ་ས་ནས་གཞིས་ཀ་རྩེའི་བར། མནར་མེད་ནས་སྲིད་རྩེའི་བར། དེང་ནས་སང་ཉི་མ་མ་ཤར་གྱི་བར། གཅིག་ནས་བརྒྱའི་བར་ལྟ་བུའོ། དེ་ལྟར་དགར་སྤྱད་ལ་འཇུག་པའི་སྒྲ་འདི་རྣམས་ཀྱང་འབྱུང་གནས་མ་ཡིན་པར་རྣམ་དབྱེ་ལྔ་པའི་ཡན་ལག་ཉིད་དུ་ཤེས་དགོས་སོ། དགར་བ་ནི་གང་ལས་དགར་བའི་བ་དེ་དེ་ལས་ཁྱད་པར་དུ་བྱུང་བ་ལྟར་སྣང་བ་དང་། སྤྱད་པ་ནི་ཐོག་མ་གང་ནས་བརྩམས་པ་དེ་ལས་བསྐལ་རྒྱའི་གནས་སྐབས་ཐམས་ཅད་བྱུང་བ་དང་འདྲ་བའི་ཕྱིར་འབྱུང་ཁུངས་ཀྱི་རྣམ་དབྱེ་སྦྱར་བར་སྣང་བའི་ཕྱིར་རོ། འོ་ན་འབྱུང་ཁུངས་ཉིད་སྨོས་པས་ཆོག་གོ་སྙམ་ན། འབྱུང་ཁུངས་ལ་འཇུག་པར་བརྟན་པ་ནི་འབྱུང་ཁུངས་དངོས་དང་། དེ་དང་ཆ་འདྲ་བ་གཙོ་བོ་རྣམས་སྟོན་པའི་དོན་དང་། དགར་སྤྱད་གསུངས་པ་ནི་འབྱུང་ཁུངས་དངོས་དང་ཆ་མཐུན་པ་གཉིས་ཀ་མ་ཡིན་ཡང་ཚིག་སྦྱོར་ཙམ་གྱིས་ཆ་མཐུན་དང་འདྲ་རུང་དུ་ཡོད་པའི་ཕྱིར་ལྔ་པའི་ཡན་ལག་ཕལ་པར་གྱུར་པ་རྣམས་སྤྱད་ཀའི་དོན་ཡིན་པས་སྐྱོན་མེད་དོ།།

གསུམ་པ་ནི། གཞུང་འདིར་མ་བསྟན་ཀྱང་ནས་ཀྱི་སྒྲ་ནི་མཚམས་སྦྱོར་བའི་ལྷག་བཅས་ལའང་འཇུག་པ། ཕྱག་འཚལ་ནས་བཤད། ལྷ་མཆོད་ནས་ལས་བྱ། ལག་པ་བརྐྱངས་ནས་བཟུང་། མིག་ཏུ་ནས་བཏུས་ལྟ་བུ་སྟེ་ལྷག་བཅས་ཀྱི་སྐབས་སུ་འང་ཕྱོགས་ཙམ་སྨོས་པ་བཞིན་ནོ། སྨྲ་སྒོ་ལས།

ལས་ནི་རྒྱུ་དང་འབྱུང་ཁུངས་དང་། དགར་བ་ཡིན་ཏེ་ནས་དེ་བཞིན།

ཞེས་ལས་ནས་ཀྱི་སྒྲ་དག་ཏུ་ལ་འཇུག་པར་བཤད་ཅིང་། འགྲེལ་པར་རྒྱུའི་དོན་ནི་ས་བོན་ལས་མྱུ་གུ་ཞེས་པ་ལྟ་བུའོ། ཞེས་འབྱུང་བ། ཁ་ཅིག་གིས་དེ་འདྲ་དེ་འབྱུང་ཁུངས་དངོས་ཡིན་པར་བྱས་ནས། འབྱུང་ཁུངས་ལས་ཚོགས་སུ་དབྱེ་བ་མི་འཐད་ཅེས་སྨྲས་ཀྱང་། དེ་འབྱུང་ཁུངས་དངོས་ནི་མ་ཡིན་ཏེ། འབྱུང་ཁུངས་ཀྱི་དོན་གོང་སྨོས་ལྟར། རྒྱ་མཚོ་ནས་ནོར་བུ་ལྟ་བུ་ནོར་བུའི་འབྱུང་ཁུངས་རྒྱ་མཚོ་ཡིན་ཞིང་ནོར་བུ་མིའི་ལག་ཏུ་བྱུང་བའི་ཚེ་རྒྱ་མཚོ་ལས་བྱེད་དགོས་པ་དང་། དངོས་སུ་འབྲེལ་པ་བྱེ་མི་དགོས་ཀྱང་རིག་པའི་འབྱུང་ཁུངས་མཁས་པ་ཡིན་ཞིང་དེ་ལས་སློབ་མས་རིག་པ་སློབ་པ་ན་རྒྱུད་ཐ་དད་དུ་གྱུར་པས་བྱེ་བར་སྣང་བར་ལྟ་བུ་ཞིག་སྟེ། བརྡའ་སྤྲོད་པའི་གཞུང་རྣམས་སུ་འབྱུང་ཁུངས་ཀྱི་དོན་འཆད་པ་ན་གང་ལས་འབྲལ་བ་འམ། ལེན་པའམ། ཞེས་དང་། བྱེ་དེང་ལྡང་བ། ཞེས་དང་། ཨ་པཱ་དཱ་ན་ངེས་པར་སྦྱིན་པ་ཞེས་བསྒྱུར་ཀྱང་ཨ་པ་འབྲལ་བ་པྲ་དཱ་ན་ཚིག་ལེན་པ་ཡིན་པས་འབྲལ་བ་ལེན་པ་ཞེས་སོགས་རྒྱས་པར་འབྱུང་ལ། མྱུ་གུ་ནི་ས་བོན་མེད་ན་མི་འབྱུང་གི་འབྲེལ་པར་གྲུབ་ཀྱང་། ས་བོན་ཉིད་མྱུ་གུར་འགྱུར་བས་ས་བོན་གྱི་སྐབས་ན་མྱུ་

ཀུ་མེད་ཅིང་ཀྱུ་ཀུའི་གནས་སྐབས་ན་ས་བོན་གྱི་གནས་སྐབས་བརྗོད་པའི་ཕྱིར་དེ་འདྲའི་འབྱུང་ཁུངས་ཀྱི་དོན་ཆ་ད་པས་སོ། །དེས་ན་དེ་འདྲ་དེ་འབྱུང་ཁུངས་དངོས་མ་ཡིན་ཡང་དེ་ལས་དེ་སྐྱེ་བའམ་འབྱུང་བ་ཡིན་པའི་ཕྱིར་འབྱུང་ཁུངས་དང་འདྲ་བར་རིགས་པས། །གོང་སྨོས་ཤར་ཕྱོགས་ནས་འོད་སྣང་སོགས་དང་ཕྱོགས་མཚུངས་པར་ཤེས་པར་བྱའོ། །

སྐབས་འདིར་འགྲེལ་བྱེད་ཕལ་ཆེར་གྱིས་དཀར་སྤུད་ལ་འཇུག་པའི་ལས་ནས་ཀྱི་སྒྲ་དག་རྣམ་དབྱེ་ལྔ་པར་མི་འདོད་པར་སྣང་ཡང་མི་འཐད་དེ། །རྒྱ་མཚན་གོང་དུ་སྨོས་པ་ལྟར་འཐད་ཕྱིར་ཏེ་ལེགས་སྦྱར་ལའང་ཚོགས་ཀྱི་ནང་ནས་དཀར་བ་ལ། ག་སུཾ་ཀྲྀ་ཤུཀླ་སཾ་པནྣ། ཤུཀླི་ཏ། བ་རྣམས་ལས། ནག་མོ་འི་ཊ་མ་ཕུན་སུམ་ཚོགས། ཀྲྀཥྞ་དམིགས་གསལ་དུ་རྟག་པ་འཇུག་ཀྱང་། ཕྱིར་བཏང་དཀར་བ་ཙམ་ལ། ཏ་སྣཱ་ཏ། ཨ་ཏྲ་ཏྲེ་ན། དེ་ལས་གཞན་ནག་པོ་ཡི་མ་དུ། ཨ་ཏོ་གྲི་ཧ་ཏི་ཧྲར། ཁང་པ་ལས་གཞན་དུ་གཙུག་ལག་ཁང་། ཀྲྀ་བུ་ལྔ་པ་ཉིད་འཇུག་པ་དང་། མཚམས་ངབྱུང་ནས་སྤྲུད་པ་ལའང་། + + + + འདི་ནས་སྐྱ་ཚོགས། ཆོར་བུའི་ཡུལ་གྱི་བར་དུ་ལྷས་ཆར་ཕབ་བས་སོ། ། ཀྲྀ་བུ་རྣམས་དབྱེ་སྦྱོར་ཡུལ་ཐ་ཕྱི་ཙང་ཅན་ལ་འདྲ་བ་ལས། དོན་གྱིས་མཚུངས་པར་ལྔ་པ་འཇུག་པའི་ཕྱིར་དང་། གནས་བརྒྱུད་འགྲེལ་པར་ཡང་ལྔ་པའི་དོན་ནི་གང་ཞིག་ལ་གང་གིས་ཡོད་པ་ལས་དེ་གཞི་དེ་ལས་བྱུང་བ་དང་བྲལ་བ་དང་དཀར་བ་དང་ཁྱད་པར་དུ་བྱེད་ན་གང་ལས་ཞེས་བྱ་བའི་སྒྲ་ཡོད་དེ། །ཞེས་འབྱུང་བ་ལེགས་བཤད་དུ་སྣང་བའི་ཕྱིར་རོ། ། ཡང་ཁ་ཅིག་གིས་ལས་སྒྲ་སྤྱད་པའི་དོན་ལ་འཇུག་པར་བཤད་ཅིང་། དཔེར་བརྗོད་དུ་ལས་སོགས་པ་ཞེས་འགོད་པ་དང་། ལ་སོགས་པ་ཞེས་ཀློག་པ་རྒྱ་མཚན་དུ་ཨས་འགོག་པར་བྱེད་མོད། ལེགས་བཤད་དུ་མ་མཐོང་སྟེ། དེ་ལྟ་ན་གཟུགས་ལས་སོགས་པ་ལྟ་བུར་སོགས་ཀྱི་སྒྲ་ངེས་པར་ལས་སྒྲ་ལ་ལྟོས་པ་ཞིག་འདོད་དགོས་པར་འགྱུར་ན་དེའང་མི་ལྟོས་ཏེ་གཟུགས་སོགས་ཞེས་ལས་སྒྲ་མེད་པས་ཀྱང་དོན་དེ་རྟོགས་པར་མཚུངས་པའི་ཕྱིར། ལ་སོགས་ཞེས་འདོན་པ་མི་འཐད་པའི་སྒྲུབ་བྱེད་དུ་ལས་སྒྲ་དེ་ལ་གཞུང་འདི་དང་སྒྲ་སྙེ་སོགས་ནས་བཤད་པའི་ལ་སྒྲའི་འཇུག་དོན་གྱི་མཚན་ཉིད་ཅེའང་མེད་པའི་རྒྱུ་མཚན་བཀོད་མོད། དེ་ལྟ་ན། ལ་ལ་དག་ཅེས་འདོན་པའང་མི་འཐད་པར་ཐལ། དེ་འདྲའི་ལ་སྒྲ་ལ་གཞུང་འདི་དང་གཞན་ནས་བཤད་པའི་ལ་སྒྲའི་འཇུག་དོན་གྱིས་མཚན་ཉིད་ཅེའང་མེད་པའི་ཕྱིར་རོ། །གཞུང་འདིར།

དཀར་དང་སྤུད་པའང་དེ་བཞིན་ནོ། །

ཞེས་གསུངས་པས་ཀྱང་དཀར་སྤུད་གཉིས་ལ་ལས་ན་ཀྱི་འཇུག་པ་ཁྱབ་མཉམ་དུ་བསྒྲུབ་མི་ནུས་ཏེ། །དེ་དག་ལ་རྣམ་པ་ཀུན་ཏུ་མཚུངས་པར་འཇུག་པ་མ་ཡིན་པ་གོང་སྨོས་ལྟར་གྱི་ཕྱིར་དང་། ལས་ནས་གཉིས་དཀར་སྤུད་ལ་འཇུག་པ་ཡོད་དོ་ཞེས་གསུངས་པས་དེ་གཉིས་སོ་སོ་ནས་དོན་དེ་གཉིས་གང་རུང་ལ་འཇུག་པ་ཡོད་པས་ཚིག་གི་ཁྱབ་མཉམ་དུ་སྟོན་ག་ལ་དགོས་པའི་ཕྱིར་རོ། །དེ་བཞིན་དུ་གསུང་རབ་རྙིང་པ་ལ། ལ་སོགས། ཞེས་པར་ཚིག་མེད་པ་ཡོད་པས་ཀྱང་ལ་སོགས་ཞེས་ཀློག་པ་མི་འཐད་པར་བསྒྲུབ་མི་ནུས་སྟེ། །གསུང་རབ་རྙིང་པ་རྣམས་སུ། རལ་གྱི་སོགས་དང་། སྐྱུ་དང་སྐྱི་སོགས་དང་། ཕྱོགས་སོགས་ཡོད་པས་རལ་གྲི་དང་མེ་དང་ཉི་དང་སོགས་ལ་སོགས་པ་རྣམས་དག་པར་བསྒྲུབ་མི་ནུས་པ་ལྟ་བུའི་ཕྱིར་རོ། །ཡང་ཁ་ཅིག་གིས་དཀར་སྤུའི་སྐབས་སུ་རྫས་དཀར་བའི་དཔེར་བརྗོད་དུ། བུམ་པ་ལས་གསེར་བུམ། ཞེས་དང་། ལ་ལས། ལྷའི་ནང་ནས་རྡོ་རྗེ་ཅན་རྒྱུ་འདོན་པ་ནི་བརྒྱ་བྱིན་ནོ། ། ཞེས་བཀོད་མོད། ཤིན་ཏུ་མི་འཐད་དེ་དེ་གཉིས་ཀ་རིགས་སམ་དངོས་པོ་དཀར་བ་ཉིད་ཡིན་པའི་ཕྱིར་ཏེ་བུམ་ནི་དཀར་གཞི་དཀར་བྱ་གཉིས་ཀ་བུམ་པ། དཀར་བྱེད་དམ་ཁྱད་པར་འབྱེད་བྱེད་ནི་གསེར་ཡིན་པ་དང་། ཕྱི་མ་ནི་དཀར་གཞི་ལྷ་རྣམས་དཀར་བྱ་བརྒྱ་བྱིན། ཁྱད་པར་འབྱེད་བྱེད་རྡོ་རྗེ་ཐོགས་པ་ཡིན་པས་དེ་དག་གི་དཀར་བྱ་རིགས་ཙམ་དུ་ངེས་པའི་ཕྱིར། ཕྱིར་ཡང་དཀར་བྱ་ཞེས་བྱ་བ་ནི་རིགས་དང་བྱ་བ་ཡོན་ཏན་གང་ཡང་རུང་བ་དཀར་བ་ཡིན་གྱི་རྫས་རྐྱང་པ་དཀར་བ་མི་སྲིད་དེ། །རྫས་ནི་རྫས་གཞན་ལྡན་པ་བརྗོད་པ་ཡིན་པས། །དབྱུག་གུ་ཅན་ལས་ཕྱེད་པ་ཅན་མཆོས་ལྟ་བུ་ནི་ཕྱེད་པའི་རྫས་དང་ལྡན་པའི་ཕར་ཅག་ཧྲ་བུ་རིགས་དཀར་བ་སོང་། །དབྱུག་གུ་ཐོགས་པ་ལས་འཕྲེང་བ་ཐོགས་པ་ལེགས། །ལྟ་བུ་ནི་ཕྲེང་བ་ཐོགས་པའི་བྱ་བ་དག་དཀར་བར་སོང་། །དེས་ན་དེས་རིགས་བསྒྲུས་ཏེ་ལེགས་པར་བསམས་པས་རྫས་རྐྱང་པ་དཀར་བ་མི་རྙེད་པའི་ཕྱིར་ཏེ། བརྡ་སྤྲོད་པའི་བསྟན་བཅོས་ཆེན་པོ་རྣམས་སུའང་འཕགས་ཡུལ་གྱི་མཁས་པ་དག་གིས་རྫས་དཀར་བ་མ་བཤད་པའི་ཕྱིར་རོ། ། དེས་ན་འདི་དག་གི་དཔེར་བརྗོད་ཚུལ་བཞིན་འགོད་པར་འདོད་ན་ཐོག་མར་རིགས་སོགས་བཞི་པོ་དེ་ཅི་ལ་ཟེར་མཆོ་བསམ་ཞིབ་མོར་བཏང་ན་མཛེས་སོ། ། སྨྲས་པ།

མཁས་གྲུབ་མང་པོའི་གནས་ངག་འདྲེས་པའི་ཚང་ཚིང་སྦྲུག་ལྡན་འདྲོག་དགོན་དུ། རྣམ་དཔྱོད་རྒྱལ་པོས་འཇུག་པར་རྩོམ་ཡང་གཞུང་དོན་ལས་བཟང་ག་ལ་རྙེད། འདི་ན་དེ་དག་སོ་སོར་འབྱེད་པའི་ལེགས་བཤད་རིགས་པའི་སྒྲུལ་ཡོད་པས། གཟུར་གནས་གང་དག་བདེར་འཇུག་འདོད་རྣམས་ཐབས་འདི་ལེགས་མེད་བརྟེན་མཛོད་ཅིག། བརྒྱད་པ་འབོད་པའི་སྒྲ་ནི།

གང་མིང་བརྗོད་པའི་དང་པོ་རུ། ཀྱེ་སྦྱར་བ་ནི་འབོད་པ་ཡིན།

ཞེས་པས་བསྟན་ཏེ། གང་ཡང་རུང་བའི་མིང་བརྗོད་པའི་ཐོག་མར་ཀྱེ་ཞེས་བྱ་བ་སྦྱར་བ་ནི་འབོད་པའི་རྣམ་དབྱེ་གསལ་བར་བྱེད་པའི་སྒྲ་ཡིན་ནོ།། ཞེས་སོ།། དེའང་རྣམ་དབྱེ་གཉིས་པ་ལ་སོགས་པའི་མཐའ་ཅན་ལ་ནི་མི་འཇུག་ཅིང་འབོད་སྐད་ཀྱི་རྣམ་དབྱེ་དང་པོ་དང་མིང་ཙམ་ལ་ཁྱད་མེད་པས་དེའི་སྔོན་དུ་སྦྱོར་བ། ཀྱེ་ལྷའི་ལྷ། ཀྱེ་ཁ་ལོ་བསྒྱུར་བ། ཀྱེ་ལྷ། ཀྱེ་རྒྱལ་པོ་ཆེན་པོ།། ལྟ་བུ་སྟེ་འདིའང་ཐོག་མར་སྦྱོར་བ་གཙོ་ཆེ་བའི་དབང་གིས་གསུངས་པ་ལས། ཚིགས་བཅད་སོགས་སྦྱོར་བའི་ཚེ། བདག་ལ་དགོངས་ཤིག་མགོན་པོ་ཀྱེ་ཞེས་པ་ལྟ་བུ་མཐར་སྦྱར་བའང་ཡོད་དོ།། འདི་ནས་མ་བསྟན་པ། ཀ་ཡེ་དང་ཀྭའི་སྒྲ་དག་ཀྱང་འབོད་པ་གསལ་བྱེད་ཡིན་མོད་ཀྱི། ཟུར་གྱིས་རྟེན་པ་དང་བསྒྲུལ་བ་དང་སྨྲ་ལེན་པ་དང་འབུ་བ་ལྟ་བུ་སྒྲིག་ཚིག་དང་དྲག་ཤུལ་ལ་སོགས་པར་འབྲེལ་པ་ལས་ཡུལ་ཁྱད་པར་ཅན་ལ་བརྗོད་པ་ནི་ཐུང་ཞིག་མི་མཐོམ་པར་མཛོད་དོ།། སྐབས་འདིར་འགྲེལ་བྱེད་ཕལ་ཆེར་གྱིས། ཀྱེ་ཞེས་པ་འབོད་པའི་རྣམ་དབྱེར་འདོད་ཀྱང་མི་འཐད་དེ། རྣམ་དབྱེ་མིང་གི་ཐོག་མར་སྦྱར་བ་མེད་པ་དང་། འབོད་པའི་རྣམ་དབྱེ་ལེགས་སྦྱར་གྱི་གཅིག་ཚིག་ལ་ཁྱད་པར་ཡོད་པ་ཙམ་མ་གཏོགས་ངོ་བོ་རྣམ་དབྱེ་དང་པོ་ལས་ཐོགས་སུ་དབྱེར་མེད་ཅིང་འབོད་ལ་དང་པོའི་གཅིག་ཚིག་གི་རྗེས་མི་གསལ་ཡང་། གཉིས་ཚིག་དང་མང་ཚིག་གི་རྗེས་ཆ་མཐུན་ཡོད་པར་མ་ཟད་རྣམ་དབྱེ་ཞིག་ངེས་པར་འཇུག་དགོས་ཤིང་གཉིས་པ་སོགས་གཞན་མི་འཇུག་པའི་རྒྱུ་མཚན་ལས་དོན་ཐོབ་གྱིས་དེ་དང་མཚུངས་པར་མིང་མཐའ་རྣམ་དབྱེ་དང་པོ་ཉིད་དུ་ངེས་པ་ལ་སྦྱར་རྣམ་དབྱེ་ཕྱིན་མི་དགོས་པའི་ཕྱིར་རོ།། དེས་ན་ཀྱེ་ཞེས་པ་རྣམ་དབྱེ་མ་ཡིན་ཞིང་འབོད་པ་གསལ་བྱེད་ཀྱི་སྒྲ་ཡིན་ཏེ། ལེགས་སྦྱར་གྱི་ཧེ་བྷོ་ཧྲམ་སོགས་དང་མཚུངས་པར་ཤེས་དགོས་སོ།།

གཉིས་པ་འཕྲད་རང་དབང་ཅན་ཁོ་ན་བཤད་པ་ལ། ནི་སྒྲ། དང་སྒྲ། དེ་སྒྲ། གང་སྒྲ། བདག་སྒྲ། དགག་སྒྲ་བཤད་པ་རྣམ་དྲུག་ལས།

དང་པོ་ནི།

གང་མིང་མཐའ་དང་མཐུན་པ་ཡི། བཞི་པ་ལ་ནི་ཨི་སྦྱར་བ། དགར་དང་བསྟན་པའི་ཚིག་ཏུ་འགྱུར།།

ཞེས་པ་སྟེ། གང་ཡང་རུང་བའི་མིང་ཚིག་གི་མཐའ་དང་མཐུན་པར་སྦྱར་རུང་བའི་སྐད། རྗེས་འཇུག་བཞི་པ་ན་ཡིག་ལ་དབྱངས་ཨི་སྦྱར་བས་ནི། ཞེས་གྲུབ་པ། དེ་ནི་གཞི་ལས་མཆོག་ཏུ། འམ་དམན་པར་རམ་ཐ་དད་ཙམ་དུ་དམིགས་བཟུང་ནས་དགར་བའི་དོན་དང་། དོན་གང་ཡིན་པ་དེ་ཉིད་ལ་ནན་ཏན་དུ་བསྟན་པའི་དོན་གཞང་འཇུག་པའི་ཚིག་ཏུ། འགྱུར་རོ།། ཞེས་སོ།།

དེ་ལ་མཆོག་ཏུ་དགར་བ་ནི། ཁྱབ་འཇུག་ནི་ལྷ་རྣམས་ཀྱི་ནང་ནས་བརྟུལ་ཕོད་པའོ།། དམན་པར་དགར་བ་ནི། རིགས་རྣམས་ལས་ནི་གདོལ་པའི་རིགས་ཐ་ཆད་དོ།། ཐ་དད་པ་ཙམ་དུ་དགར་བ་ནི། མཐིང་ག་ནི་སྔོ་སངས་ལས་གཞན་ནོ།། ཞེས་པ་ལྟ་བུ་རྣམས་སོ།།

སྒྲ་སྒོ་ལས། དགར་གཞི་དངོས་སུ་སྤྲོས་མ་སྤྲོས་ཀྱི་དབྱེ་བས་གཉིས་སུ་བཤད་དེ། ལྷ་རྣམས་ལས་གདོང་བཞི་དང་ལྡན་པ་ནི་ཚངས་པའོ།། མཆོད་སྦྱིན་བརྒྱའི་བདག་ཉིད་ནི་བརྒྱ་བྱིན་ནོ།།

བསྟན་པ་ལ་འཇུག་པ་ནི། ཁྱོད་ནི་གཉེན་དང་ཁྱོད་ནི་བཤེས། སྤང་བར་བྱ་བ་ནི་སྤངས། ཚུབ་པར་བྱ་བ་ནི་ཚུབ། ལྟ་བུ་སྟེ། སྤྲོས་པ་ཐམས་ཅད་ལྡན་པར་ནི་ལྟ་བུ་ཚིག་གི་ཁ་སྐོང་དུ་འཇུག་པའང་ཡོད་མོད་ཀྱི་དོན་ནི་ངེས་གཟུང་གིས་བསྟན་པའི་སྒྲ་ཉིད་ཡིན་ནོ། དེས་ན་ནི་སྒྲ་འདི་ལེགས་སྦྱར་གྱི་ཏུ་དང་ཏུ་བསྒྱུར་བ་ཡིན་པར་བཤད་པའང་ཕྱོགས་འགའ་ཞིག་ནས་ཡིན་གྱི་རྣམ་པ་ཐམས་ཅད་དུ་ནི་མ་ཡིན་ནོ།

གཉིས་པ་དང་སྦྲའི་འཇུག་ཚུལ་ནི།

མིང་གང་དུང་བའི་བར་ཆ་ཚན་སུ། གསུམ་པ་ལ་ནི་གཉིས་པ་སྦྱར།
དེ་ནི་རྫུད་དང་འབྱེད་པ་དང་། རྒྱུ་མཚན་ཚེ་སྐབས་གདམས་ངག་ལྔའོ།།

ཞེས་པས་བསྟན་ཏེ། མིང་ཚིག་གང་ཡང་དུང་བའི་བར་མཚམས་རྣམས་སུ་རྗེས་འཇུག་གསུམ་པ་ད་ཡིག་ལ་གཉིས་པ་ང་ཡིག་སྦྱར་བས། དང་། ཞེས་གྲུབ་པ་དེ་ནི། ཚིག་ཟུ་རྡུ་ཕྱོགས་གཅིག་ཏུ་སྡུད་པ་དང་། སོ་སོར་འབྱེད་པ་དང་རྒྱུ་མཚན་ཉིད་ཀྱི་དོན་དང་དུས་བརྗོད་པ་ཚེ་སྐབས་ཀྱི་དོན་དང་། གཞན་ལ་གདམས་ངག་བརྗོད་པའི་དོན་ཏེ། དོན་ལྔ་ལ་འཇུག་གོ། ཞེས་སོ་དེའང་སྡུད་པའི་དོན་དུ་སྦྱར་བ་འདུས་བྱས་དང་འདུས་མ་བྱས་ནི་ཆོས་སོ། མིག་དང་རྣ་བ་དང་སྣ་དང་ལྕེ་དང་ལུས་རྣམས་ནི་དབང་པོའོ།།

གང་དང་མཚུངས་པར་དེ་དང་ལྡན་ཅིག་འགྲོགས། དགའ་དང་བདེ་དང་འཐུན་པ་འཐོབ་པར་འགྱུར།།

ལྟ་བུ་ཚིག་དོན་གཉིས་སམ་མང་པོ་དོན་གཞན་ཞིག་ལ་སྡུད་ཅིང་བསྡུ་རྒྱུ་ཡོད་པ་རྣམས་དང་། འབྱེད་པ་ལ་སྦྱར་བ་ཆོས་ནི། འདུས་བྱས་དང་འདུས་མ་བྱས་པའོ། དབང་པོ་རྣམས་ནི་མིག་དང་རྣ་བ་དང་སྣ་དང་ལྕེ་དང་ལུས་སོ། ལྟ་བུ་དབྱེ་གཞི་གཅིག་ལས་གཉིས་སམ་དུ་མར་འབྱེད་པའི་དོན་དུ་སྦྱར་བ་རྣམས་དང་།

རྒྱུ་མཚན་ལ་སྦྱར་བ། སྨན་ཟོས་པ་དང་ནད་སོས་སོ། ཆོས་མང་དུ་ཐོས་པ་དང་ལྷག་མཐོང་འཕེལ་ལོ། དུ་བ་མཐོང་བ་དང་མེར་ཤེས་སོ། ལྟ་བུ་རྣམ་དབྱེ་གསུམ་པ་དང་ལྔ་པ་རྒྱུ་མཚན་ལ་འཇུག་པ་བཞིན་དུ་དང་སྒྲ་དེ་ཉིད་རྒྱུ་མཚན་སྟོན་བྱེད་དུ་འགྱུར་བ་རྣམས་དང་། ཚེ་སྐབས་དང་སྦྱར་བ། རྒྱ་སྐར་རྒྱལ་འཆར་བ་དང་ཡུལ་དུ་ཆས་སོ། ཉི་མ་ཤར་བ་དང་ཆོས་སྟོན་དུངས། ལྟ་བུ་དུས་བརྗོད་པའི་སྒྲ་དང་འཇུག་པ་གཅིག་པ་རྣམས་དང་། གདམས་ངག་ལ་སྦྱར་བ། ལེགས་པར་སློབས་དང་། ཁ་ཏོན་གྱིས་དང་། ཡིད་ལ་ཟུངས་དང་། ལྟ་བུ་གཞན་ལ་གདམས་པའམ་བསྐུལ་བའི་ཚིག་དང་འབྲེལ་པ་རྣམས་སོ།།

འདི་སྐབས་འགྲེལ་བྱེད་ཁ་ཅིག་གིས་རྒྱུ་མཚན་ལ་འཇུག་པའི་དཔེར་བརྗོད་དུ། སྒྲ་ཆོས་ཅན་མི་རྟག། སྐྱེ་དངོས་པོ་ཡིན་པའི་ཕྱིར་དང་། སྐྱེ་ལྡན་ཡིན་པའི་ཕྱིར་དང་། རྒྱུ་རྐྱེན་ལས་བྱུང་བའི་ཕྱིར་དང་། ཞེས་པ་ལྟ་བུ་བཀོད་མོད་ཀྱི་དེ་འདྲའི་དང་སྒྲ་དེ་རྣམས་རྒྱུ་མཚན་གྱི་དོན་དུ་མི་འགྱུར་ཏེ་དེ་དག་ལ་རྒྱུ་མཚན་སྟོན་པའི་ནུས་པ་ཅི། འང་མ་མཐོང་བའི་ཕྱིར་གྱི་སྒྲས་རྒྱུ་མཚན་སྟོན་པས། དེ་དང་འབྲེལ་པའི་དང་གི་སྒྲས་ཀྱང་དེ་སྟོན་ཏོ། སྙམ་ན་ཚོར་བ་པོ་དང་མཐོང་བ་པོ་དང་བྱེད་པ་པོ་དང་ཞེས་པ་ལྟ་བུའི་དང་གི་སྒྲ་རྣམས་ཀྱང་བདག་པོའི་དོན་སྟོན་པར་ཐལ་བ་སོགས་ཏེ་ཅང་ཐལ་ལོ། འོ་ན་ཀྱིས་དང་། ལྟ་བུ་ཀྱིས་ཀྱི་སྒྲས་སྒྲུབ་པ་སྟོན་ལ་དེ་དང་འབྲེལ་པའི་དང་གིས་ཀྱང་དེ་སྟོན་པར་འདོད་པ་མ་ཡིན་ནམ་ཞེ་ན། དེ་དང་འདི་མི་མཚུངས་ཏེ། ཀྱིས་དང་ལྟ་བུའི་ཀྱིས་ཀྱི་སྒྲ་དེ་སྒྲུབ་ཚིག་དངོས་དང་དང་སྒྲ་དེའི་ཡན་ལག་ཏུ་འགྱུར་བར་དངོས་སུ་གྲུབ་ཅིང་། དེ་འདྲའི་དང་སྒྲ་དེས་བསྒྲུབ་ཚིག་ལས་གཞན་པའི་དོན་ཅི་ཡང་མི་སྟོན་པ་དང་། ཕྱིར་འདོད་པའི་དང་སྒྲ་དེ་རྣམས་ཀྱིས་རྒྱུ་མཚན་མི་སྟོན་ཅིང་། སྒྲ་མི་རྟག་པར་བསྒྲུབས་པ་ལ་གཏན་ཚིགས་ཀྱི་རྣམ་གྲངས་གཞན་དང་གཞན་ཕྱོགས་གཅིག་ཏུ་སྡོར་ཞིང་སྡུད་པར། སྟོན་པར་སྣང་བའི་ཕྱིར་རོ། འགའ་ཞིག་གིས་དང་སྒྲ་རྒྱུ་མཚན་ལ་འཇུག་པ་ལས་འཕྲོས་ནས་དུས་བརྗོད་པའི་ཚེའམ། སྦྲའང་རྒྱུ་མཚན་ལ་འཇུག་པར་བཤད་མོད། འཐད་པར་མ་མཐོང་ཡང་དོ་གཞལ་མི་ཆེ་བས་དགག་པའི་འབྱུས་པ་མི་བྱེད་དོ།

གསུམ་པ་དེ་སྦྲའི་འཇུག་ཚུལ་བཤད་པ་ལ། དངོས་དང་མཐའ་དཔྱད་དོ།། དང་པོ་ནི།

གང་མང་གི་ནི་ཡ་མཐའ་རུ། གསུམ་པ་ལ་ནི་ཨེ་སྦྱར་བ། ཐ་སྙད་དབང་དུ་གསུམ་ཡིན་ཏེ།
དངོས་པོ་དབང་དུ་བཞི་རུ་འགྱུར། དུས་ཀྱི་དབང་དུ་གཉིས་ཡིན་ནོ།།

ཞེས་པས་བསྟན་ཏེ། གང་ཡང་དུང་བའི་མིང་གི་ཡ་མཐའ་སྐྱེ་ཚིག་མར་རྗེས་འཇུག་གསུམ་པ་ད་ཡིག་ལ་དབྱངས་ཨེ་སྐེ་འགྲེང་བུ་སྦྱར་བས། དེ། ཞེས་གྲུབ་པ་ནི་ཐ་སྙད་ཙམ་གྱི་དབང་དུ་བྱས་ན། རྣམ་གྲངས་གཞན་ནི་སྔོར་རྒྱུ་ཡོད་པར་སྟོན་པའི་དོན་ཅན་དང་། ལྷག་མ་དང་བཅས་པ་དང་། དུས་གསུམ་ལས་འདས་པ་སྟེ་གསུམ་ལ་འཇུག་པ་དང་།

དངོས་པོའི་དབང་དུ་བྱས་ན། བདེན་པ་དང་། གསང་བ་དང་། བདག་གི་བ་དང་། ཡ་ཊོལ་བའི་དངོས་པོ་ལྔ་བཞི་ལ་དུས་གསུམ་གར་འཇུག་པར་འགྱུར་བ་དང་། དུས་དེ་ཉིད་ཀྱི་དབང་དུ་བྱས་ན། འདས་པ་དང་མ་འོངས་པ་གཉིས་ལ་འཇུག་པ་ཡིན་ནོ།། ཞེས་སོ།། དེ་ལྟར་གསུང་ནས་མིང་གི་ཡ་མཐར་གསུངས་པ་ནི་གཙོ་ཆེ་བའི་དོན་ཡིན་གྱི་མཐའ་གཅིག་ཏུ་ངེས་པ་ནི་མ་ཡིན་ནོ།། དེ་དག་སོ་སོའི་དོན་ཡང་འོན་ཆོད་ཙམ་ལས་དཔྱིས་ཕྱིན་པར་ནི་ཐོན་ཆད་སུས་ཀྱང་མ་རྟོགས་པར་སྣང་བས་ཞིབ་ཏུ་བཤད་ན། འདི་སྐབས་དབྱེ་ཚུལ་གསུམ་ལས་ཐ་མ་ཐ་སྙད་ཀྱི་དབྱེ་བས་དེ་སྒྲའི་འཇུག་པ་ཐམས་ཅད་ལ་ཁྱབ་པ་ཡིན་ཏེ། དཔེར་ན། དེ་སྒྲ་དེའི་ཡུལ་དུ་ཚིག་ཟིན་ལ་དངོས་སུ་གསལ་མི་གསལ་ཇི་ལྟར་ཡང་དོན་གྱི་རྣམ་གྲངས་གཞན་ཞིག་བྱུང་ངང་དུ་ཡོད་པའི་ཐ་སྙད་ཀྱི་ཚེ་དེ་བཞིན་གཤེགས་པ། དེ་བཞིན་གང་ཡིན་པ་དེ། དེ་ལས་ཀྱང་གཞན།

ལེགས་སྤྱད་དེས་ནི་འབྲས་བུ་ཆེན་པོར་འགྱུར། དེ་ནི་ཕུན་སུམ་ཚོགས་པའི་འབྱུང་གནས་ཉིད།

ཅེས་པ་ལྟ་བུའི་དེ་སྒྲ་རྣམས་ཀྱིས་རིམ་པ་བཞིན་དུ་གང་ལ་དཔེར་བྱའི་ཡུལ་དེ་དང་། སྤྱི་ལས་དམིགས་སུ་གཟུང་བྱ་དེ་དང་། ལས་ཀྱི་སྦྱས་གང་ལས་དཀར་བའི་གཞི་དེ་དང་། འབྲས་བུ་འབྱིན་བྱེད་ཀྱི་རྒྱུ་དེ་དང་། འབྱུང་གནས་སུ་ངོ་། གཟུང་བྱ་དེ་བཅས་ཀོ་ཞིང་མཚོན་ནུས་པ་ལྟར་ལྷག་བཅས་ཁོ་ནས་གཏོགས་དེ་སྒྲའི་འཇུག་པ་ལྷག་མ་ཐམས་ཅད་རྣམ་གྲངས་གཞན་ཡོད་པར་སྟོན་པ་བའི་དོན་ཙམ་དུ་འདུས་ཤིང་། ལྷག་བཅས་ཀྱི་དེ་སྒྲ་ནི་རང་ཉིད་ཀྱི་ཡུལ་དུ་དོན་གཞན་མི་མཚོན་པས།

དཔེར་ན། ཤིང་བཅད་དེ་ཅི་ཞིག་བྱེད། བཞིན་གྲུབ་ཏུ་ཡོད་དེ་རྟག་པའི་ཕྱིར། ལྟ་བུ་བརྗོད་བྱ་ལྷག་མ་འདྲེན་པ་ཙམ་དུ་ཟད་པའི་ཕྱིར། དགེ་བ་བྱུར་དུ་མཛད་པ་དང་། འཇུག་པ་དེ་གཉིས་ཀའང་བརྗོད་བྱ་སྤྱིར་དོན་ལ་མ་དཔྱད་པར་བརྗོད་ཚུལ་དེ་ཉིད་ལ་ཐད་ཀར་བཏགས་པའི་དུས་ཀྱི་ཐ་སྙད་ཀྱི་དབང་དུའམ། ཡ་ཡང་ཚིག་དོན་གཉིས་ཀའི་དབང་དུ་བྱས་ནའང་འདས་པ་ཁོ་ན་ཡིན་ཏེ་དཔེར་ན་རྣམ་གྲངས་གཞན་སྟོན་ལ། དེ་སྒྲ་དང་སྦྱོར་རྒྱུའི་དོན་དེ་དངོས་སུ་ཚིག་ཟིན་དུ་ཡོད་ན་དེ་ཕྱིན་དུ་བརྗོད་ཟིན་པ་མཚོན་པར་བྱེད་པའི་འགྲུབ་ཡིན་པས་འདས་པར་འགྱུར་བ། མ་འོངས་པ་ན་འཁོད་ཡོས་སྦྱང་བའི་རྒྱལ་པོ་དུང་ཞེས་བྱ་བ་འབྱུང་བར་འགྱུར་བ་དེ་ནི་བསྐལ་བཟང་གི་སངས་རྒྱས་དྲུག་པ་སེང་གེའི་སྐྲར་འགྱུར་རོ།། མང་གི་ཁ་ཟས་དེ་དེ་རིང་ཐ་གོན་གྱིས་ཤིག། ཞེས་པ་ལྟ་བུ་དང་། ཚིག་ཟིན་དུ་མེད་ཀྱང་དེ་བཞིན་གཤེགས་པ་ལྟ་བུའི་དེ་སྒྲས་བསྟུས་པའི་དོན་དེ་རྗེན་དུ་སོང་བའམ་བརྗོད་ཟིན་པ་ཞིག་ལ་མི་བསམས་པ་མི་སྲིད་པས་འདས་པར་འགྱུར་ཞིང་། ལྷག་བཅས་ནི་ཚིག་ཙམ་བརྗོད་ཟིན་གྱི་འདས་པ། ད་མོར་བྱེད་དེ་བསྒྱུར་ཀྱིར་ཡང་བྱེད་དོ། ལྟ་བུ་དང་།

ཚིག་དོན་གཉིས་ཀ་འདས་མ་ཐག་པ། ཕྱིར་བསྐྱོད་དེ་འགྲོ། ཤིང་བཅད་དེ་འབུད། ཀྱ་བུ་འདས་པ་ཉིད་ཀྱིས་ཁྱབ་པའི་ཕྱིར་རོ།། དེས་ན་ཐ་སྙད་ཀྱི་དབང་གིས་དབྱེ་བ་མཚན་ཉིད་པ་གཉིས། དབྱེ་གཞི་ཕྱུ་ཏུ་དུས་ད་ལྟ་དང་མ་འོངས་པ་གསལ་བའི་འཇུག་ཚུལ་གཅིག་བཅས་གསུམ་དུ་གྲངས་ངེས་ཤིང་། དབྱེ་བ་འདི་ཐ་སྙད་ཀྱི་དབང་གིས་བཞག་པའི་རྒྱུ་མཚན་ཡང་རྣམ་གྲངས་གཞན་སྟོན་གྱི་དེ་ནི་དོན་གཞན་ལ་དེ་ཞེས་ནན་གྱིས་བཏགས་པ་ཙམ་དང་། ལྷག་བཅས་ཀྱི་དེ་ནི་ལྷག་མ་འདྲེན་པར་ཐ་སྙད་བྱས་པ་ཙམ་དང་དུས་འདས་པའི་ངེའང་དོན་ལ་ཇི་ལྟར་ཡང་བརྗོད་པ་ཙམ་གྱི་དབང་དུ་བྱས་པའི་ཕྱིར་ཏེ་ཐ་སྙད་ཅེས་པའི་གོ་བའང་།

གནས་བརྒྱད་རྩ་བར། ཐ་སྙད་ནི་དངོས་པོ་མེད་པ་ལ་དངོས་པོར་བཏགས་པ་སྟེ། དེའང་བཏགས་པ་དང་འཇུག་པ་དང་བརྗོད་པར་བཅས་པ་ཐམས་ཅད་དོ།། དེ་ལ་བརྡ་ནི་གོ་བར་བྱེད་པའི་བདག་ཉིད་ཅན་ཡིན་ལ། ཐ་སྙད་ནི་འཇུག་པར་བྱེད་པའི་བདག་ཉིད་ཅན་ཡིན་ནོ།། ཞེས་དང་།

འགྲེལ་པར། ཐ་སྙད་ནི་དངོས་པོ་ལ་ཐ་སྙད་མེད་པ་ལ་ནན་གྱིས་བཏགས་པ་སྟེ། དེའང་བཏགས་པའི་ཤེས་པ་ནི་ དེ་ཀ་བ་ཡིན་ནོ་སྙམ་པ་ལ་སོགས་པའི་ཤེས་པའོ།། བརྗོད་པ་ནི་འདི་ཀ་བའོ་ཞེས་བྱ་བའི་སྒྲའོ།། འཇུག་པ་ནི་ཀ་བ་ཡིན་པས་ཁང་ཁྱིམ་བྱེད་པར་རྩོམ་པ་ལ་སོགས་པའོ།།

ཐ་སྙད་ཅེས་བྱ་བ་ནི་འཇུག་པའི་རྒྱུ་མཚན་ཡིན་ནོ།། ཞེས་ལྷག་པར་བཀྲལ་ནས་བསྟན་པ་བཞིན་ནོ།།

དབྱེ་ཚུལ་གཉིས་པ་ངེས་ནི། ལྷག་བཅས་ཁོ་ན་དངོས་པོར་ནི་འཇུག་པས་ཐམས་ཅད་མ་གཏོགས་དེ་སྒྲའི་འཇུག་པ་ཐམས་ཅད་ལ་ཁྱབ་སྟེ། དེ་ཁོ་ན་ཉིད་དོ། དེ་དེ

་བཞིན་པ་སོགས་པ་ལྟ་བུ་བདེན་པའི་དངོས་པོ་སྟོན་པ་དང་། གཞན་གྱིས་ཤེས་ཀྱིས་རྟོགས་ནས་དོན་དངོས་སུ་མི་སླ་བར་ཟུར་གྱིས་གོ་བར་བྱེད་པའི་ཚིག་ཕྲད་ཀྱིས་དེ་ལེགས་པར་བསྒྲུབ་པས། ཞེས་པ་ལྟ་བུ་གསང་བའི་དངོས་པོ་སྟོན་པར་བྱེད་པ་དང་།

བདག་ཉིད་དང་འབྲེལ་བ། བདག་གི་ལྟ་དེ། ཁོ་བོའི་ནོར་དེ། ཞེས་པ་ལྟ་བུ་བདག་གི་བའི་དངོས་པོ་སྟོན་པ་དང་། དེ་ནི་ཡོད་དོ། དེ་ནི་མེད་དོ། ཀ་བ་དེ་ལྟ་བུ། ཁྱོད་ཀྱི་དེ། དེས་བརྟན་པ་དེ་ནི། ཞེས་པ་ལ་སོགས་ལྟ་བུ་ཕ་རོལ་པོའམ། གཞན་གྱི་དངོས་པོ་སྟོན་པར་འདུ་བའི་ཕྱིར་ཏེ། དེ་བཞི་གང་རུང་དུ་མ་འདུས་པའི་འབྲུ་འདིས་དངོས་པོ་བསྟན་པ་མེད་ཅིང་དངོས་མི་སྟོན་པའི་སྒྲ་དེ་སྒྲའང་ལྷག་བཅས་ཙམ་དུ་ཟད་པའི་ཕྱིར་རོ།། དེས་ན་དབྱེ་བ་འདི་ཕྱིའི་དངོས་པོའི་དོན་གཙོ་བོའི་སྒོ་ནས་ཕྱེས་པས་དུས་གསུམ་གར་ལ་ཡོད་དེ།

འདས་པ་ལ་དམིགས་ནས་བརྗོད་པ། སྟོན་གྱི་ཚེ་འཕགས་པའི་ཡུལ་དེ་ན། ཞེས་པ་ལྟ་བུ་དང་།

ད་ལྟ་བ། རྡོ་རྗེ་ཁྱོད་ཀྱིས་འདེགས་ནུས་སམ། ལྟ་བུ་དང་།

འབྱུང་འགྱུར་ལ། འཚང་རྒྱ་བར་འགྱུར་བ་དེ། ཞེས་པ་ལྟ་བུ་ཚིག་གྲོགས་ཀྱི་དོན་ལས་རིག་པར་བྱ་ཞིང་།

མི་འཇུག་པ་ནི། རང་ལ་དེ་ཞེས་མི་བརྗོད་པའི་ཕྱིར། བདག་ཉིད་ཀྱི་དངོས་པོ་ལ་འཇུག་པ་མ་ཡིན་ནོ།།

དབྱེ་ཚུལ་གསུམ་པ་དེ་ནི། དེ་སྒྲ་སྤྱིའི་དབང་དུ་མ་བྱས་པར་དུས་ཁོ་ན་བརྗོད་པ་དང་འབྲེལ་བའི་དེ་སྒྲ་ལ་དབྱེ་བ་བྱས་པར་ཟད་དེ། འདས་པའི་དུས་བརྗོད་པ་དང་འབྲེལ་བ། སྟོན་དེ་བཞིན་གཤེགས་པ་འཁོར་བ་འཇིག་འཇིག་རྟེན་དུ་བྱོན་པ་དེའི་ཚེ། ན་ཉིང་གི་ལོ་དེ་ལ། ཁ་སང་གི་ཉི་མ་ཤར་བ་དེའི་ཚེ། སྔད་ཅིག་མ་དེར། ཞེས་པ་ལྟ་བུ་དང་། མ་འོངས་པའི་དུས་པ་བརྗོད་པ་དང་འབྲེལ་བ། དེའི་དུས་ན་འཁོར་ལོས་བསྒྱུར་བའི་རྒྱལ་པོ་དུང་ཞེས་བྱ་བ་འབྱུང་བར་འགྱུར་རོ།། སང་ཉི་མ་ཤར་བའི་དུས་དེར་ཤོག། ཞེས་པ་ལྟ་བུ་འདས་དང་མ་འོངས་པ་གཉིས་ལ་འཇུག་པ་ཉིད་དོ།།

ད་ལྟར་བའི་དུས་ལ་ནི། ནམ་ཡང་མི་འཇུག་ད་ལྟའི་བསྐལ་པ་འདིར། ད་ལྟའི་ལོ་འདིར། དེ་རིང་གི་དུས་འདིར་ཞེས་སོགས་སྦྱོར་བ་ལས། ད་ལྟའི་བསྐལ་པ་དེར་སོགས་མི་སྦྱོར་བ་ཆ་ཚོད་སུམ་གྱིས་གྲུབ་པ་ཕྱིར་རོ།། དེས་ན་སླ་གྲོ་ལས།

དེ་ཞེས་བྱ་བའི་ཚིག་གི་དོན། ཐ་སྙད་དངོས་དང་དུས་འཇུག་གསུམ། འདས་དང་ནམ་གྲངས་གཞན་ཚན་དང་། ལྷག་མ་དག་དང་བཅས་པའོ།།

བདེན་པ་གང་དང་གསང་བ་དང་། བདག་གི་པ་དང་ཕ་རོལ་པོ།། དངོས་པོ་དག་ལ་འཇུག་པ་བཞི། འདས་པ་དང་ནི་མ་འོངས་པའི།

དུས་གཉིས་ལ་ནི་འཇུག་པ་ཡིན། བདག་ཉིད་ད་ལྟ་ཉིད་ལ་སྤང་། དངོས་པོའི་དུས་ནི་མི་འདོར་ཏེ། ཀུན་ལ་རབ་ཏུ་སྦྱར་བར་བྱ།

ཞེས་འབྱུང་བའི་དོན་རང་འགྲེལ་ལས་ཀྱང་ཤིན་ཏུ་གསལ་བ་གཞུང་འདིའི་དགོངས་པ་དང་ཡང་ལེགས་པར་འགྲོར་བར་སྣང་བའི་ཕྱིར་རྣམ་པར་ཕྱེས་ནས་བཤད་པ་ཡིན་པས་བློས་ཀྱི་རྟགས་པ་སོགས་མི་བདེ་བ་མང་པོས་མ་བཅིངས་པའི་ཕུ་ཡངས་སུ་བློ་ལྡན་རྣམས་རྟེན་པར་མཛོད་ཅིག།

གཉིས་པ་ནི། འགྲེལ་བྱེད་ཐ་མ་འགའ་ཞིག་གིས། ཐ་སྙད་ཀྱི་དབང་དུ་བྱས་པའི་གསུམ་ལ་ཀུན་བརྟགས་གཞན་དབང་ཡོངས་གྲུབ་གསུམ་དང་། བྱ་བྱེད་ལས་གསུམ་ལུས་ངག་ཡིད་གསུམ་སོགས་སུ་འདོད་པ་དང་དངོས་པོའི་དབང་གིས་རིག་དང་བྱ་བ་ཡོན་ཏན་རྫས་བཞིན་འདོད་པ་སོགས་སྣང་ཡང་ཐ་སྙད་ལ་མི་མཁས་པའི་མཚན་མ་གསལ་བར་བསྟན་པ་ཡིན་ཏེ། དེ་ལྟ་ན་ཁམས་གསུམ་སྲིད་གསུམ་འཇིག་རྟེན་གསུམ་མཚན་མཚོན་གཞི་གསུམ་སོགས་དང་ལུག་རྒྱ་བ་དེ་སོགས་གསུམ་ཕྱེ་བ་བཞི་ཕྱེ་ཡོད་དཔག་ཚིག་ཐམས་ཅད་ལ་རྟོག་རིགས་པ་ལ་དེ་དག་ཡོན་ངེས་པར་གཟུང་བ་ཅི་རིགས། དེ་དག་ཐ་སྙད་བཏགས་པ་ཙམ་དང་། དངོས་པོ་ཙམ་ཡིན་པའི་ཕྱིར་རོ་ཞེ་ན་གཞན་ལའང་ཅིར་མི་མཚུངས། དེ་བས་ན་འདི་སྐབས་སུ་གལ་ཆེ་བའི་སྐྱུད་ཀྱིས་འཇུག་ཚུལ་འཆད་དུ་མེད་པར་དབྱུ་ཡེར་སོགས་ཀྱི་བཤད་ཡས་རྒྱས་པས་ནི་གང་དུའང་མི་འགྱུར་རོ།། ཡང་ཕལ་མོ་ཆེས་སྐྱ་སྒོའི་ལུགས་སུ་བྱས་ཀྱང་གཞུང་འགྲེལ་གྱི་

དོན་ལེགས་པར་མ་བྲིས་པས་དོན་མ་མཐོང་སྟེ། ། བཀའ་རིག་གིས་ཁ་སྐད་ཀྱི་འཇུག་ཚུལ་ལ་དབྱེ་གཞི་དབྱེ་བའི་ཡ་གྱལ་དུ་གྲངས་པ་མ་ཤེས་པས་ངེས་གཟུང་གི་དེ་སྒྲ་འདས་པར་ཁས་བླངས་ནས་རྣམ་གྲངས་གཞན་སྐོར་གྱི་དེ་སྒྲ་ངེས་གཟུང་དང་ལྷག་བཅས་མ་ཡིན་པ་ཞིག་འདོད་ཀྱང་མ་རྙེད་པས། །ཇི་ལྟ་ཇི་ལྟར་མཐུན་འདོད་པ་དེ་དེ་ལ་དོན་དེ་དང་དེ། སོགས་བཀོད་པ་དང་།

དངོས་པོའི་སྐབས་སུ། བདག་གི་བ་དང་གསང་བ་དང་བདེན་པའི་དངོས་པོ་བརྗོད་པ་ལས་གཞན་པའི་དངོས་པོ་ལ་ལྟོས་པའི་དེ་སྒྲ་ཐམས་ཅད་ཕ་རོལ་པོའི་དངོས་པོར་སྟོན་པར་འཇུག་པ་མ་གོ་བས། དེའི་དཔེར་ཁྱོད་ཀྱིས་དེ་སྒྲ་ཁོ་ན་སྦྱར་ནས་བཀོད་པ་སོགས་དང་། བཀའ་རིག་གིས་རྣམ་གྲངས་གཞན་སྐོར་ཞེས་པའི་རྣམ་གྲངས་དེ་དོན་ནས་མིང་གི་རྣམ་གྲངས་མང་པོར་བསམས་ནས། དེ་འདུ་གོ་བར་བྱེད་པའམ་དངོས་སུ་བརྗོད་པ་དང་འབྲེལ་པའི་དེ་སྒྲ་རྣམས་རྣམ་གྲངས་གཞན་སྐོར་གྱི་དོན་དུ་འདོད་པ་སོགས་སོ།། འོ་ན་དེ་ལྟར་འདོད་པ་དེ་དག་ལ་སྐྱོན་ཅི་ཞིག་ཡོད་ཅེ་ན། འདོད་པ་དང་པོ་དེའི་སྐྱོན་ནི་རྣམ་གསལ་གྱི་དཔེར་བརྗོད་འབའ་ཞིག་མ་རྙེད་པ་དེར་ཟད་དེ། དཔེར་བརྗོད་དེ་རྣམས་ཁྱོད་རང་གི་ཞེན་དོན་དུ་མ་སོང་བའི་ཕྱིར་ཏེ། དེ་རྣམས་ཀྱི་དེ་སྒྲ་དེ་ངེས་གཟུང་ཁོ་ནར་སྣང་བའི་ཕྱིར་གྲུབ་སྟེ། ཁྱོད་རང་གི་ངེས་གཟུང་གི་དཔེར་དགོད་པའི་ལུས་བུ་དེ་ཞེས་པ་དང་། དཔེར་བརྗོད་ཕྱི་མའི་ཇི་ལྟར་མཐུན་འདོད་པ་དེ། ཞེའམ། དོན་དེ། ཞེའམ། སངས་རྒྱས་ཀྱང་དེ། ཞེས་པ་རྣམས་ཀྱི་དེ་སྒྲའི་འཇུག་པ་མཐུན་པའི་ཕྱིར་ཏེ། ཕྱི་མའི་དེ་རྣམས་ཀྱང་ཇི་ལྟར་མཐུན་པ་དང་དོན་དང་སངས་རྒྱས་རྣམས་ངེས་པར་གཟུང་བའི་སྒྲ་ཡིན་པའི་ཕྱིར་རོ།།

འདོད་པ་གཉིས་པ་དེ་ལའང་། ལེགས་པར་མ་བཤད་པ་དང་བསྟན་བྱ་མ་ཚང་བའི་སྐྱོན་ཡོད་དེ། བདག་གི་བ་མ་ཡིན་པའི་དངོས་པོ་གཞན་ཐམས་ཅད་ལ། ཕ་རོལ་པོ་ལས་གཞན་གྱི་དངོས་པོ་ཞེས་བརྗོད་པར་རིགས་པ་བཞིན་དུ། ཁྱོད་ཅེས་པའི་སྒྲ་ཉིད་ཚིག་དང་འབྲེལ་པ་ཕ་རོལ་པོའི་དོན་དུ་ཞེན་པར་སྣང་བའི་ཕྱིར།

འདོད་པ་ཕྱི་མ། དེ་ལའང་ཕྱིར་རྣམ་གྲངས་ཀྱི་སྒྲ་དོན་ལ་འཁྲུལ་པ་དང་། རྒྱུ་དེས་སྐབས་དོན་གྱི་རྣམ་གྲངས་ལེགས་པར་མ་བཤད་པའི་སྐྱོན་ཡོད་དེ། ཁྱོད་དག་གིས་རྣམ་གྲངས་ཞེས་པའི་སྒྲ་དེ་གྲངས་མང་པོར་འཇུག་པར་དོན་གྱིས་ཞེན་པས་མི་འཐད་པའི་ཕྱིར་དང་། སྐབས་འདིའི་རྣམ་གྲངས་ཞེས་པའི་དོན་ཀྱང་དེ་མ་ཡིན་པའི་ཕྱིར་རོ།

དང་པོ་གྲུབ་སྟེ། རྣམ་གྲངས་ཞེས་པ་ལེགས་སྦྱར་གྱི་སྐད་དུ་པར་ཡཱ་ཡ་ཞེས་པ་ཡིན་ཏེ། དེ་ནི་གནས་སྐབས་དང་རིམ་པ་དང་སྒྱུར་བ་དང་རྣམ་པ་རྣམས་ལ་འཇུག་པར་མངོན་བརྗོད་ཀྱི་བསྟན་བཅོས་རྣམས་སུ་བཤད་ལ། དེ་རྣམ་གྲངས་སུ་བསྒྱུར་བ་ནི་རྣམ་པ་ལ་འཇུག་པའི་རྒྱུ་མཚན་གྱིས་ཡིན་པས། རྣམ་གྲངས་དང་རྣམ་པ་དོན་གཅིག་ཏུ་གྲུབ་པའི་ཕྱིར་ཏེ། དཔེར་ན།

མིང་གི་རྣམ་གྲངས་གཞན་མེད་དོ།། དོན་གྱི་རྣམ་གྲངས་མང་པོའོ།། དོན་གྱི་རྣམ་གྲངས་གཅིག་པོ། འདི་ནི་རྣམ་གྲངས་ཙམ་མོ།།

རྣམ་གྲངས་ཀྱི་དོན་དམ་བདེན་པའོ།། ཞེས་པ་ལྟ་བུ་རྣམས་ལ་གྲངས་མང་ཉུང་གི་ཁྱད་པར་མེད་པར།

མིང་གི་རྣམ་པ་གཞན་མེད་དོ།། དོན་གྱི་རྣམ་པ་མང་པོའོ།། དོན་གྱི་རྣམ་པ་གཅིག་པོ། འདི་ནི་རྣམ་པ་ཙམ་མོ།།

རྣམ་པའི་དོན་དམ་བདེན་པའོ།། ཞེས་ཐམས་ཅད་རྣམ་པའི་སྒྲ་དང་འཇུག་པར་གཅིག་པར་སྣང་བའི་ཕྱིར་རོ།།

ངེས་ན་ཕྱི་མའང་གྲུབ་སྟེ། སྐབས་འདིར་སྒྲ་སྦྱོར་གྱི་གཞུང་དུ་རྣམ་གྲངས་གཞན་ཅན་ཞེས་དང་འབྲེལ་པར་རྣམ་གྲངས་གཞན་ཡོད་དེར་སྐོར་བ་ཞེས་འབྱུང་བར་རྣམ་གྲངས་ཀྱི་སྒྲས་ནི་རྣམ་པ་ཙམ་ལས་གཞན་མ་བསྟན། དེ་ལས་གཞན་དུ་འང་མང་པོ་དགོས་པ་རྒྱས་བྱེད་ཀྱི་ཚིག་མ་བྱུང་ཞིང་རྒྱུ་མཚན་གཞན་ཡང་མེད་པས། དེ་སྒྲ་དེའི་ཤུལ་དུ་དོན་གྱི་རྣམ་པ་གཞན་སྐོར་རྒྱུ་ཡོད་པས་ཆོག་པ་ལ། དགོས་མེད་ཀྱི་འབྲུ་དོན་ལྷག་པར་གཉེར་བར་སྣང་བའི་ཕྱིར་རོ།།

གཞན་ཡང་འགྲེལ་བྱེད་ཕྱི་མ་རིག་གིས། ཁ་སྐད་ལ་བྱའི་ཁ་སྐད་དང་། མིང་ཚིག་ཁ་སྐད་གཉིས་སུ་ཕྱེས་ཤིང་འདིར་བཤད་ཀྱི་ཁ་སྐད་ཕྱི་མར་འདོད་པ་དང་། དངོས་པོ་ཞེས་པ་སྐབས་འདིར་བརྗོད་བྱའི་དོན་ཙམ་ལ་ངོས་བཟུང་མོད། ཅུ་མ་ཕྱི་འཐད་དེ། མིང་ཚིག་ལ་མ་བརྟེན་པར་བྱ་ཁོ་ནས་ཁ་སྐད་བྱར་མི་རུང་ཞིང་། སྔོ་ལ་མ་བརྟེན་པར

ཡང་མིང་ཚིག་ཁོ་ནས་ཐ་སྙད་གདགས་སུ་མེད་པས་དེ་གཉིས་ཀྱི་དབྱེ་བ་འདུལ་པའི་ཕྱིར་ཏེ། ཐ་སྙད་ལ་ཞེས་བརྗོད་འཇུག་གསུམ་དང་བཅས་པ་ཞེས་མཁས་པའི་བསྟན་བཅོས་ལ་ལྷུང་ལྟར་གྲགས་པའི་ཕྱིར་རོ།། ཕྱི་མ་འཆད་མི་འཐད་དེ། དེ་ལྟ་ན། ལྷག་བཅས་ཀྱི་དེ་བྲ་དེ་ཚེ་ཙན། དངོས་པོ་རྐྱེན་བྱེད་དུ་ཐལ། བརྗོད་བྱའི་དོན་རྐྱེན་བྱེད་ཡིན་པར་འདོད་ན་དེ་འདྲ་དེས་བདེན་པ་ལ་སོགས་པ་དངོས་པོ་བཞི་ལས་གང་ཞིག་རྐྱེན་པ་བཤད་དགོས་ཤིང་། མ་གྲུབ་ན་ལྷག་བཅས་ཀྱི་བྲ་མཚམས་སྦྱོར་སོགས་དོན་མང་པོ་ལ་འཇུག་པར་བཤད་པ་དང་དངོས་སུ་འགལ་ལོ། འདིར་སྨྲས་པ།

ལ་ལས་ལོ་བརྒྱུར་ཕྱུངས་པ་གང་། ལ་ལས་ཡུད་ཙམ་གཅིག་ལ་ཤེས། ལ་ལས་ཚོགས་ཀྱིས་བསྒྲུབ་པ་ཡང་། ལ་ལས་བདེ་བླག་ཉིད་དུ་བྱེད།
ལ་ལས་མཁས་པར་རྨོངས་པ་གང་། ལ་ལས་མོངས་པའི་གནས་སུ་བགོད། ལ་ལར་སྨྲ་བའི་དབང་ཕྱུག་ཀྱང་། ལ་ལར་ལྐུག་པའི་བརྟུལ་ཞུགས་འཛིན།
བློ་ལྡན་ཙམ་དུ་མཚུངས་ན་ཡང་། བློ་གྲོས་མཆོག་གི་ཁྱད་པར་ཕྱེས། བློ་གཏེར་དབང་པོ་ཡི་བློ་མཚོ་ལས། བྱུང་བའི་བློ་ཙན་ང་མིན་སུ།

བཞི་པ་གང་སྒྲའི་འཇུག་ཚུལ་ནི།

གང་མིང་བརྗོད་པའི་དང་པོར་ནི། དང་པོ་ལ་ནི་གཉིས་པ་སྦྱར། ཧྱི་ལ་ཁྱབ་པ་ཉིད་དུ་འགྱུར།

ཞེས་པས་བསྟན་ཏེ། གང་ཡང་རུང་བའི་མིང་བརྗོད་པའི་དང་པོར་རྗེས་འཇུག་དང་པོ་ག་ལ། གཉིས་པ་ང་སྦྱར་བས། གང་ཞེས་གྲུབ་པ་དེ་ནི་གཙོ་བོར་དོན་གྱི་བྱེ་བྲག་དམིགས་སུ་མི་འཛིན་པར་སྤྱི་ལ་ཁྱབ་པའི་དོན་ཅན་གྱི་སྒྲ་ཉིད་དུ་འགྱུར་རོ།། ཞེས་སོ།། དེའང་དཔེར་ན།

གང་ཞིག་རྟག་ཏུ་སྙིང་པོའི་དོན་བསམ་པས། གང་ཡང་དམན་པར་འགྱུར་བའི་གནས་དེ་ཙི། ཞེས་པ་ལྟ་བུ་སྤྱི་སྒྲ་དངོས་དང་།
ཕྱིར་རོ།། ཕྱི་མ་གྲུབ་སྟེ།

གང་ཞིག་བརྟེན་ན་ཡོན་ཏན་ཀུན། འདོད་དགུར་འབྱིན་པ་ཁོ་བོའི་རྗེ། ཞེས་པ་ལྟ་བུ། བྱེ་བྲག་ལ་འཇུག་པའི་སྤྱིའི་སྒྲ་དང་། འདིའི་སྐབས་ཚིགས་གང་། ཁྱོད་ཀྱི་ལྷ་གང་ཡིན། གང་བྱེད། ལྟ་བུ་སྤྱི་སྒྲ་འདྲི་བའི་དོན་དུ་སྦྱར་བ་སོགས་སྐབས་ཐོབ་ཀྱི་སྒོ་ནས་ཤེས་པར་བྱ་ཞིང་། འདིར་མིང་ཐོག་ཏུ་སྦྱར་བ་གསུངས་པའང་གཙོ་ཆེ་བའི་དོན་ལ་དགོངས་ཀྱི་མིང་མཐར་མི་འཇུག་པ་ནི་མ་ཡིན་ཏེ། སྔོན་དུ་འདྲི་བའི་དཔེར་བརྗོད་ལ་སོང་བ་ལྟར་དང་དེ་འདྲར་མ་ཟད་དེ་ཐོབ་བྱ་ཕྱིར་གང་དང་བསྟན་བཅོས་གང་། ཞེས་སོགས་མང་དུ་འབྱུང་བ་ལྟར་རོ།།

འདི་ནས་མ་བསྟན་ཀྱང་ཅི་དང་ཇི་དང་སུའི་སྒྲ་རྣམས་གང་དང་སྐབས་ཕལ་ཆེར་ལ་འཇུག་པ་མཚུངས་པ་ཡིན་ཏེ། དེ་དག་ཐམས་ཅད་གང་ཅིའང་རུང་། ཇི་ལྟར་སུ་དག་འགྲོ་བ་རྣམས། ལྟ་བུའི་ཅི་སོགས་སྤྱི་སྒྲ་ལ་འཇུག་པ་དངོས་དང་།

ཅི་ཞིག་བསམ་པ་དེ་གྲུབ་ནས། ཇི་ལྟར་བདེ་བ་དེ་ལྟར་བ། སྐལ་བཟང་སུ་ཡིན་དེ་འགྲོ་འགྱུར།

ཞེས་པ་ལྟ་བུ་བྱེ་བྲག་ལ་འཇུག་པའི་སྤྱི་སྒྲ་དང་།

དངོས་པོ་དེ་ཅི་ཇི་ཙམ་ཞིག། བདག་པོ་ཁྱོད་སུ་ལེགས་པར་སྨྲོས།

ལྟ་བུ་འདྲི་བ་འཇུག་པ་རྣམས་སོ།། ཅི་ལ་སོགས་པ་དེ་རྣམས་རྣམ་པ་ཐམས་ཅད་དུ་གང་དང་འཇུག་པ་མཚུངས་པའང་མ་ཡིན་ཏེ་སུའི་སྒྲ་གང་ཟག་ཁོ་ན་ལ་སྦྱོར་གྱི་བེམ་པོ་སོགས་དངོས་པོ་གཞན་ལ་མི་འཇུག་པའང་ཇི་སྐད་དང་། ཇི་སྲིད་ལྟ་བུ་ལའང་གང་སྒྲ་མི་འཇུག་པ་དང་། ཅེས་ཀྱང་ལྟ་བུ་ལའང་གང་དང་ཇིའི་སྒྲ་མི་འཇུག་པ་སོགས་འཇིག་རྟེན་པའི་ཉེར་སྤྱོད་དང་བསྟུན་ནས་སྐབས་ཐོབ་ཀྱིས་ཤེས་པར་བྱའོ།།

ལྔ་པ་བདག་སྒྲ་བཤད་པ་ལ། དངོས་དང་། མཐའ་དཔྱད་དོ།།

དང་པོ་ནི།

གང་མིང་གི་ནི་མཐའ་ར་ན།། ཕུ་ཊིཀྐ་ཡི་སྒྲ་ཅན་པ།། དེ་ལ་ཕུ་ཊིཀྐ་སྒྲར་ན།། བདག་པོ་འི་སྐད་ནི་ཤེས་པར་བྱ།།

ཞེས་པ་སྟེ། གང་ཡང་རུང་བའི་མིང་གི་མ་མཐའ་རྣམས་སུ་ཕུ་ཊིཀྐ་ཏེ་ཏྲེས་བུའི་རྟགས་མངོན་པར་བྱེད་པའི་སྒྲ་རྐྱང་མེད་པ་ཞིག་ཡིན་ན། དེ་ལ་ཕུ་ཊིཀྐའི་སྒྲ་སྦྱར་བར་བྱས་པས་དེའི་བདག་པོའི་དོན་གསལ་བར་ནུས་པའི་ཕྱིར་བདག་པོའི་སྐད་ཤེས་པར་བྱའོ།། ཞེས་སོ།། དེ་ལ་ཕུ་ཊིཀྐའི་སྒྲ་ནི་བདག་པོའི་དོན་རྟོན་པར་བྱེད་པའི་པ་དང་པོའི་སྒྲ་གཉིས་ཡིན་ཏེ། དེ་དག་རྐྱང་མེད་པ་ལ་གསར་དུ་སྦྱར་བས། རྟ་པ། གསེར་པ། ཁ་ལོ་པ། བྱེད་པོ།། གཏོང་བ་པོ་སོགས་སོ་སོའི་བདག་པོ་གོ་བར་བྱེད་པ་རྣམས་སོ།། དེ་བཞིན་དུ། ཡོད་པ་པ། མེད་པ་པ། བྱེད་པ་པོ།། ཤེས་པ་པོ།། ལྟ་བུ་རྣམས་ཀྱང་སྔོན་ནས་ཡོད་ཡོད་པའི་པ་སྒྲ་རྣམས་བདག་པོའི་དོན་མི་སྟོན་པའི་ཕྱིར་ཕུ་ཊིཀྐའི་སྒྲ་མིན་པས་སྦྱར་ཕུ་ཊིཀྐའི་སྒྲ་སྦྱར་ཏེ་བདག་པོའི་དོན་ཅན་དུ་སོང་བ་ཡིན་ནོ།། བདག་པོ་ཞེས་པའང་རྟ་དང་གསེར་སོགས་དང་བྱེད་པ་དང་ཤེས་པ་སོགས་གང་ལ་ཡོད་པའི་གང་ཟག་དེར་ཤེས་དགོས་ཏེ། ཐེམ་པོ་སོགས་ལ་བདག་པོའི་ཐ་སྙད་མི་འཇུག་པའི་ཕྱིར་རོ།། འདིར་ཕུ་ཊིཀྐ་དང་ སྟྲཱི་ཊིཀྐ་ཞེས་པའི་དོན་ཀྱང་བོད་ཡུལ་དུ་གྲགས་པའི་ཐ་སྙད་ལ་བྱེད་པ་པོ།། འཕྲིན་པ་པོ།། ཞི་བ་པོ། ལྷ་པ། ཚོས་པ། ལྷ་བུའི་པ་དང་པོའི་སྐབས་སྐྱེས་པར་མཚོན་ཞིང་དེ་ལས་ལྡོག་ཏེ། བྱེད་པ་མོ།། འཕྲིན་པ་མོ།། ཞི་བམ། ལྷ་མ། ཚོས་མ་ལྷ་བུའི་མ་དང་མོའི་སྐབས་བུད་མེད་དུ་མཚོན་པར་བྱེད་པའི་རྒྱུ་མཚན་གྱིས་སྒྲ་དེ་དང་དེ་དག་ལ་སྐྱེས་པའི་རྟགས་དང་བུད་མེད་ཀྱི་རྟགས་ཀྱི་མིང་གིས་བརྟན་པར་ཤེས་པར་བྱའོ།།

གཉིས་པ་ནི། སྐབས་འདིར་འགྲེལ་བྱེད་ཁ་ཅིག་གིས། བ། ཅན། ལྡན། རྣམས་ཀྱང་ཕུ་ཊིཀྐའི་སྒྲར་འདོད་པར་སྣང་བ་འཐད་པར་མ་མཐོང་སྟེ། དེ་དག་ལ་བ་ཤད་མ་ཐག་པ་ལྟར་གྱི་ཕུ་ཊིཀྐའི་སྒྲ་འཇུག་པའི་རྒྱུ་མཚན་མེད་པའི་ཕྱིར་དང་། ཅན་དང་ལྡན་གྱི་སྒྲ་གཉིས་གང་ཞིག་གང་ལ་ཡོད་པ་སྟོན་པའི་ཚ་ནས་བདག་སྒྲ་དང་མཚུངས་པ་ཡོད་ཀྱང་དེ་དག་ཐེམ་པོ་ལ་འང་འཇུག་པས་བདག་སྒྲར་མ་ངེས་པའི་ཕྱིར་དང་། བ་ཡིག་ནི་ཕུ་ཊིཀྐའི་སྒྲ་དངོས་སུ་འགྱུར་བ་ལྟ་ཅི་སྨོས། ཕྱིར་བདག་རྟོན་བྱེད་ཙམ་དུ་འང་མི་འཇུག་པའི་བ་ཡིག་བདག་སྒྲར་འཇུག་པའི་དཔེར་བརྗོད་དུ། འཕོར་ལོས་སྒྱུར་བ། ལྷས་བ། སེར་ར་བ། ལྟ་བུ་དུ་མ་བཀོད་པ་རྣམས་ཀྱང་མི་འཐད་ཅེང་འཐད་ལྡན་གྱི་དཔེར་བརྗོད་གཞན་ཡང་དགོད་རྒྱུ་ཆེད་པའི་ཕྱིར་ཏེ། འཁོར་ལོས་སྒྱུར་བ། ལྟ་བུའི་བ་ཡིག་གིས་བདག་པོ་མངོན་པ་ལྟར་སྣང་ཡང་དེ་འདྲ་ནི་འཁོར་ལོས་སྒྱུར་བ་པོ་ཞེས་པའི་པོ་སྒྲ་བསྡུས་པའི་རྗེས་ཙམ་ཡིན་པས་པོ་ཡིག་དངོས་སུ་མེད་ཀྱང་མིང་སྤྱི་འི་ཁོག་ནས་བདག་པོའི་དོན་གསལ་བ་ཡིན་གྱི་བ་ཡིག་ཕོ་ནའི་ནུས་པ་མ་ཡིན་པ། བ་ཡིག་མེད་པའི། འཁོར་སྒྱུར། ལྷ་སྦྱིན་ཀྱང་བདག་པོ་གོ་ནུས་པ་སོགས་ཀྱིས་མཚོན་ལ། ལྷས་བ། སེ་ར་བ། ལྟ་བུ་རྣམས་ནི་གྲོང་པའི་སྐད་ཕལ་བ་ཙམ་དུ་ཟད་པས་དཔེར་མི་རོས་ཏེ། དེ་འདྲ་ལ་ཡིད་བརྟན་འཛའ་ན་ཉེར་པ་མང་པོ་འང་ཁས་ལེན་དགོས་པར་འགྱུར་ཞིང་། དེ་དག་དག་པར་འདོད་ན། ལྷས་པ། སེར་པ་ལྷ་བུ་བརྗོད་རིགས་པའི་ཕྱིར་རོ།། ཡང་རྗེས་འཇུག་འ་ཡིག་མཐར་འདོད་པ་རྣམས་ཀྱིས་དེ་འདྲ་དེ་རྟགས་མཚུངས་འདྲེན་ཚུལ་དུ་བསམས་པ་ཡོད་སྲིད་ཀྱང་། བདག་སྒྲ་འདི་རྗེས་འཇུག་གི་ཁྱད་པར་ལ་མི་ལྟོས་པའི་སྒྲ་རང་དབང་ཅན་ཡིན་པས་དེ་འདྲར་མི་འགྱུར་བར་མ་ཟད། རྟ་པ། གྲྭ་པ། ཡོད་པ་པ། ཞི་བ་བ་ལ་སོགས་པ་སྔོར་ཚུལ་མ་ལོག་པའི་དཔེར་བརྗོད་རྣམས་ལ་བརྟགས་པས་ཀྱང་འཐུལ་པ་སེལ་བར་འགྱུར་རོ།།

ཡང་འགའ་ཞིག་གིས། པ་བ་ཅན་རྣམས་འཇུག་པ་མཚུངས་པའི་སླུབ་བྱེད་དུ། པ་བ་ཅན་ནི་བདག་པོ་འམ། ལྡན་པའི་དོན་དུ་སྦྱར་བར་བྱ། ཞེས་སྒྲ་སྒྲོའི་ལུང་འདྲེན་མོད། དེའི་དཔེ་དག་པ་རྣམས་སུ་པ་འམ་ཅན་ནི་བདག་པོ་འམ། ཞེས་འབྱུང་ཞིང་འགྲེལ་པ་ཡང་གསེར་པ་དང་གསེར་ཅན་ཞེས་དཔེར་བརྗོད་པ་ལས་བ་ཡིག་གི་དཔེར་བརྗོད་མ་བྱུང་བར་མ་ཟད།

གསུམ་པ་ནི་དེ་མ་ཐག་ཏུ།

བ་ནི་ཕྱི་རུ་བཞག་པ་སྟེ། ཡུལ་དུས་ངེས་པར་མ་བཟུང་བའོ།། ཟ་བ་བཟའ་དང་ཟ་པོ་བཞིན། མ་ཞིང་དག་ཏུ་བཞག་པར་བྱ།

ཞེས་ཟ་བ་ལྟ་བུའི་བ་ཡིག་དེ་བྱ་བྱེད་བདག་གཞན་དུས་གསུམ་གང་ལའང་བྱེ་བྲག་ཏུ་མི་འཇུག་པར་བཤད་པས་ཕྱིད་རང་གིས་དཔེ་མ་དག་པ་ཞིག་མཐོང་བའམ་བསྒྱུག་ཉེས་པའམ་རང་འདོད་

གྱིས་བཅོས་པར་བྱས་ཀྱི། ལུང་དེ་ནི་ཁྱེད་ཀྱི་འདོད་པ་དེའི་གནོད་བྱེད་ཡང་དག་ཏུ་ཡོད་དོ།། ཡང་འགའ་ཞིག་གིས། ཛ་མ། ཚང་མ་སོགས་མ་ཡིག་བུ་ཡིཎྜར་འགྱུར་བ་ཡོད་ཅེས་ཟེར་བ་ཐོས་ཀྱང་། གཞུང་དོན་ལ་ཅུང་ཟད་ཀྱང་མ་དཔྱད་པའི་རྟགས་སུ་ཟད་དོ། དེ་འདྲ་དེ་བདག་པོའི་དོན་བརྟན་དུ་ཚུག་ཀྱང་བུ་ཡིཎྜའི་ཚིག་ཕྱོགས་ཀླུ་ཡིཎྜའི་སྐད་ཡིན་པའི་ཕྱིར་རོ།།

རྡུག་པ་དགག་སྒྲ་བཤད་པ་ལ། དངོས་དང་མཐའ་དཔྱད་གཉིས། དང་པོ་ནི།

གང་མིང་བརྗོད་པའི་ཡ་མཐའ་ན།། ཀླུ་ཡི་ཎྜ་ཡི་སྒྲ་མེད་པ།། དེ་ལ་ཀླུ་ཡི་ཎྜ་སྦྱར་ན།། དགག་པའི་གནས་སུ་ཤེས་པར་བྱ།།

ཞེས་པ་སྟེ། གང་ཡང་རུང་བའི་མིང་བརྗོད་པའི་ཡ་མཐར་སྔ་ཐོག་མར་ཀླུ་ཡིཎྜ་སྟེ། མོ་རྟགས་ཀྱི་སྒྲ་མེད་པ་རྣམས་ལ་ཀླུ་ཡིཎྜའི་སྒྲ་སྦྱར་བ་བྱས་ན་སྔོར་ཡུལ་གྱི་དོན་དེ་མ་ཡིན་པའམ་མེད་པར་སྟོན་པའི་ཕྱིར་དགག་པའི་གནས་སུ་ཤེས་པར་བྱའོ། ཞེས་སོ།། དེ་ལ་ཀླུ་ཡིཎྜའི་སྒྲ་དངོས་ནི། མ་དང་མི་གཉིས་ཁོ་ན་ཡིན་པ་གོང་སྨོས་ལྟར་ལས་མོ་ཡིག་དགག་སྒྲ་ལ་མི་འཇུག་པས་འདིར་མ་ཡིག་ཉིད་བཟུང་བར་བྱ་ཞིང་། དེ་དང་འབྲེལ་བའི་མི་ཡིག་ཀྱང་ཞར་གྱིས་ཐོབ་པས་དེ་དག་དགག་སྒྲར་སྦྱོར་ཚེ་དགག་བྱའི་མིང་ཐོག་ཁོ་ནར་ངེས་པ། དཔེར་ན། མ་ཡིན། མ་ལུས། མ་ཤེས། མ་མཐོང་། མ་ངལ། མ་བྱེད། མ་རྟོན། མི་རིགས། མི་འགྱུར། མི་རྟག། མི་འགལ། མི་བྱ། ལ་སོགས་པ་ལྟ་བུའོ།།

གཉིས་པ་ནི། སྐབས་འདིར་འགྲེལ་བྱེད་ཕལ་ཆེར་གྱིས་འདིར་བསྟན་མོ་རྟགས་ཀྱི་དགག་སྒྲ་མིང་མཐར་ཡང་འཇུག་པ་ཡོད་པར་འདོད་ཅིང་། དེའི་དཔེར་བརྗོད་དུ། གཟུགས་མེད། སྒྲ་མེད། ཡོད་མིན། མེད་མིན། རྒྱ་མ་ཡིན་སོགས་བཀོད་པ་དང་། ལ་ལས། བྱམས་པས་སྟོང་པ། བྱམས་པས་དག་པ། ལྷ་བྱའང་འདིའི་དཔེར་བརྗོད་དུ་བྱས་སྣང་བ་སྒྲ་གྲོས་རྩིང་པོར་ཤོར་བའི་སྐྱོན་དུ་ངེས་སྟེ། མེད་དང་མིན་དག་ནི་མ་ཡིག་དང་འབྲེལ་བའི་དགག་སྒྲར་གྱུར་པ་དང་དོན་དང་ལྡན་པའི་ཕྲད་ཀྱང་ཡིན་པས་རྟགས་འཇུག་གི་སྐབས་སུ་འཆད་འགྱུར་ལྟར་ཀླུ་ཡིཎྜའི་སྒྲའི་ཆ་ཤས་སུ་གཏོགས་མོད་ཀྱི་འདི་དག་མིང་གི་ཐོག་མར་མི་འཇུག་པས་སྐབས་འདིའི་བསྟན་བྱ་མ་ཡིན་པ་དང་། མ་ཡིན་ཞེས་པ་ནི་དགག་བྱ་ཡིན་ཞེས་པའི་མིང་དེའི་སྟོན་དུ་འགོག་བྱེད་མོ་རྟགས་སྦྱར་བ་ཡིན་པས་ཕོ་རང་གི་ཞེན་དོན་གྱི་དཔེར་མི་རུང་བ་དང་། སྟོང་པ་དང་དག་པ་སོགས་ཀྱང་ཕྲད་མོ་རྟགས་གཉིས་ཀ་མིན་པའི་ཕྱིར་ཏེ། དགག་པའི་དོན་ཅན་གྱི་སྒྲ་ཡོད་ཚད་གཏི་ཐུག་རིགས་འགྲེས་ཀྱིས་འདིར་བསྡུ་བར་རྟོམ་པ་གཞུང་དོན་ལ་ཤིན་ཏུ་མ་ཞུགས་པར་འདུག་པའི་ཕྱིར་རོ།། འདི་སྐབས་ཕྲད་ཁོ་ན་མ་ཡིན་པར་མིང་གི་འཇུག་པ་གཞན་བསྟན་པས་ཅི་ཞིག་ཉེས་ཤེ་ན། ཕྱིར་མིང་གི་འཇུག་པ་རྟོན་པ་ནི་མངོན་བརྗོད་ཀྱི་བསྟན་བཅོས་སོགས་སུ་གཙོ་བོར་མིན་ཞིང་། བརྡ་དག་གི་བསྟན་བཅོས་རྣམས་སུ་ནི་མིང་ཚིག་དེ་དག་གི་ཡི་གེའི་སྦྱོར་ཚུལ་ཕྲད་དང་རྣམ་དབྱེ་ལ་སོགས་པར་གཙོ་བོར་འབྱུང་བ་ཤེས་དགོས་ལ། ཁྱད་པར་གཞུང་འདིར་ནི་ཕྲད་དང་རྣམ་དབྱེ་ཁོ་ན་བསྟན་པ་མངོན་སུམ་གྱིས་གྲུབ་བཞིན་དུ་དེའི་སྐབས་དོན་དང་མི་མཐུན་པའི་མིང་དོན་ལྷག་པོ་ཁ་ཤས་བསྣན་ནས་དགོས་མེད་ཀྱི་བཤད་ཡམ་བྱེད་པ་ནི་རིགས་པར་སྨྲ་བའི་མཁས་པ་རྣམས་ཀྱི་མདུན་སར་མཛེས་པ་མ་ཡིན་ནོ།། གཞན་ཡང་སྒྲ་སྒོ་རྩ་འགྲེལ་དུ་འདིར་མ་བསྟན་པའི་ཕྲད་སོགས་མང་དུ་བཤད་ཅིང་ཕལ་ཆེར་ལེགས་བཤད་དུའང་ཡོད་ལ་སྐྱོན་དུ་མཐོང་བའང་དུ་མ་མཐོང་མོད། འདིར་ནི་ཡི་གེ་མངས་པའི་འཇིགས་པས་སྤྲོ་བར་མི་བྱ་ཞིང་བློ་ལྡན་རྣམས་ཀྱིས་ཤེས་པར་འདོད་ན་དེ་ཉིད་དུ་རྟོགས་ཤིག།

གང་མིང་གི་ནི་ཡ་མཐའ་རུ།། གསུམ་བ་ལ་ནི་ཨ་སྦྱར་བ།

ཐ་སྙད་དབང་དུ་གསུམ་ཡིན་ཏེ། དངོས་པོ་ཡི་དབང་དུ་བཞི་རུ་འགྱུར། དུས་ཀྱི་དབང་དུ་གཉིས་ཡིན་ནོ།

གཉིས་པ་གདམས་ངག་བརྗོད་པས་འཇུག་པ་བསྡུ་བ་ལ་བཞི་སྟེ། ཚིག་བཅད་འགྲོལ་ཚུལ་འདོམས་པ། ཉན་པ་པོ་བློ་བསྐྱེད་པའི་སྒོ་ནས་འདོམས་པ། བསླབ་ཚུལ་གྱི་གོ་རིམ་ལ་འདོམས་པ། གདམས་ངག་སྤྱོད་ཆུང་ལ་བསྟན་དགོས་པར་འདོམས་པའོ།།

དང་པོ་ནི།

ཚིགས་སུ་བཅད་པའི་མཚམས་སྦྱོར་རྣམས། །ཉུང་ཟད་བསྡུས་པ་ཡོད་ན་ཡང་། །

དེ་ཉིད་དེ་བཞིན་སྦྱར་བར་བྱ། །

ཞེས་པ་སྟེ། །དེའང་བདེ་བར་གཤེགས་པའི་བཀའ་དང་བཀའི་དགོངས་འགྲེལ་གྱི་བསྟན་བཅོས་དེ་དག་དང་རྗེས་སུ་འབྲེལ་པའི་རིག་གནས་ཐུན་མོང་བའི་བསྟན་བཅོས་རྣམས་ལ་ཚིགས་སུ་བཅད་པ་ཡང་དག་པར་སྦྱར་བས་རྣམ་དབྱེ་དང་ཚིག་ཕྲད་ལ་སོགས་པའི་མཚམས་སྦྱོར་མང་དུ་བསྡུས་པ་ཡོད་ན་ལྟ་ཅི་སྨོས། །ཉུང་ཟད་བསྡུས་པར་གྱུར་པ་ཡོད་ནའང་། །དེ་ནི་འདིར་སྟོན་དུ་བསྟན་པའི་སྦྱར་བསྡུ་ལ་སོགས་པ་ཇི་སྐད་བཤད་པ་དེ་བཞིན་དུ་བསྟུན་ཅིང་སྦྱར་ཏེ་བཤད་པས་དོན་ཁོང་དུ་ཆུད་པར་བྱ་སྟེ། །དཔེར་ན། །ཟག་བཅས་ཟག་པ་མེད་ཆོས་རྣམས། །ཞེས་པ་ལྟ་བུར་ཟག་པ་དང་བཅས་པའི་ཆོས་རྣམས་དང་ཟག་པ་མེད་པའི་ཆོས་རྣམས་ཞེས་སྡུད་པའི་སྒྲ་དང་འབྲེལ་སྒྲ་སོགས་བསྟུན་ནས་དོན་རང་གི་བསམ་པ་དང་གཞན་ལ་འཆད་དགོས་པ་བཞིན་ནོ། །

དེའང་ཚིགས་བཅད་ལ་ཚིག་སྡུད་མང་བའི་རྒྱ་མཚན་གྱི་གཙོ་བོར་གསུངས་པ་ལས་ཚིག་ལྷུག་པར་ཡང་ཕྲད་སོགས་མཚམས་སྦྱོར་བསྡུས་པ་རྣམས་ལ་འདི་ལྟར་སྦྱར་ཏེ་ཤེས་པར་བྱ་བ་ཉིད་དོ། །

གཉིས་པ་ནི། རྗེས་འཇུག་མེད་མི་རུང་དུ་བསྟན་པ། རྗེས་འཇུག་ཤེས་པའི་དགོས་པ་བསྟན་པ། དེ་དོན་ལ་དབབ་པའི་ཚུལ་བསྟན་པའོ། །

དང་པོ་ནི། །

སྔོན་འཇུག་ཡོད་དམ་མེད་ཀྱང་རུང་། །མིང་བཞིའི་ཡི་གེ་གང་ལྡན་པའང་ཡིན་ལ། །གཉིས་འབྲེལ་ཡོད་དམ་གསུམ་འབྲེལ་ཡོད། །

ཨ་ཡི་བཞི་ལས་གང་འབྲེལ་ཡང་། །རྗེས་འཇུག་བཅུ་པོ་མ་ཞུགས་ན། །མིང་གཞན་སྦྱོར་བ་ཡོད་མི་སྲིད། །

ཅེས་པ་སྟེ། མིང་ཚིག་གི་སྦྱོར་བ་རྣམས་ལ་གོང་དུ་བཤད་པའི་སྔོན་འཇུག་གི་ཡི་གེ་རྣམས་སྔོན་དུ་ཞུགས་པ་ཡོད་དམ་མེད་ཀྱང་རུང་སྟེ། བསྒྲུབས། སྒྲུབ། ལྟ་བུ་ཅི་རིགས་པར་སྣང་ཞིང་འཕུལ་རྟེན་གྱི་འཇུག་ཡུལ་མིང་གཞིའི་ཡི་གེ་རྣམས་ནི། ལྷ། ལྟ་བུ་གཉིས་འབྲེལ་ཡོད་དཔ་སྒྲ་རྒྱ་ལྟ་བུ་གསུམ་འབྲེལ་ཡོད་དམ། དེ་དག་ལ་ཨ་ཡི་བཞི་ལས་གང་ཡང་རུང་བ་ལྡན་པ། ལྷུ། སྒྲོ། ལྟ་བུ་རྣམས་ལའང་རྗེས་འཇུག་བཅུ་པོ་གང་ཡང་རུང་བ་ཞིག་མ་ཞུགས་ན་ཡི་གེའི་གཟུགས་དེ་ཉིད་ལས་མིང་དོན་གཞན་ལ་འཇུག་ཅིང་སྦྱོར་བ་ནི་ཚུལ་འདི་ལ་ནམ་ཡང་སྲིད་པ་མ་ཡིན་ནོ། །ཞེས་སོ། །དེས་ན་དཔེར་སྦྱོར་བ་དེ་དག་ལ་རིམ་པ་བཞིན་རྗེས་འཇུག་སྦྱར་བས། ལྷན། ལྷག། སྒྲག། རྒྱན། ལྷུར། སྒྲོན། ལྟ་བུར་སོ་སོར་དོན་དང་བཅས་པར་འགྱུར་བ་སྟེ། སྒྲ་སྦྱོར་བྱེ་མ་རྣམས་ཀྱིས་སྐད་གསར་བཅད་ཀྱི་ཚེ། དཔའ། འདའ། དགའ་སོགས། དགོས་དཔང་གིས་དམིགས་གསལ་ཁ་ཤས་མ་གཏོགས་འ་མཐའ་ཕལ་ཆེར་ཐོར་ཡང་བའི་ཆེད་དུ་བསྡུ་བར་མཛད་པས་དེང་སང་དངོས་སུ་མེད་ནའང་རྣམ་དབྱེ་དང་ཕྲད་ཀྱི་སྐབས་སུ་དོན་གྱིས་ཐོབ་པ་དེ་གསལ་བར་མཚོན་པ་གོང་བཤད་ལྟར་རོ། །འདི་སྐབས་འགྲེལ་བྱེད་ཁྲ་མ་འགར་ཞིག་གིས། རྗེས་འཇུག་གང་རུང་མ་ཞུགས་པའི་མིང་གི་སྦྱོར་བ་ཡོད་པར་འདོད་པ་སོགས། འཁྱོག་བཤད་མང་དུ་བྱས་པ་མཐོང་མོད་ཀྱི་སྐད་ནས་དཔྱོད་ལྡན་ཁ་ཅིག་གིས་སུན་འབྱིན་པར་མཛད་འདུག་པས་དགག་པ་མ་སྤྲོས་སོ། །

གཉིས་པ་ནི། །

རྗེས་འཇུག་བཅུ་ཡི་དོན་ཤེས་ན། །འབྲི་དང་ཀློག་དང་བཤད་རྣམས་ཀྱི། །མཚམས་སྦྱོར་སླ་ལ་ཐོགས་མེད་ཅིང་། །

འབྲེལ་པར་སླ་བའི་མཆོག་ཏུ་འགྱུར། །གཞན་ཡང་རྗེས་འཇུག་ཤེས་པ་ཡིས། །དོན་གྱི་སྦྱོར་བ་མ་མཐོང་ཡང་། །

དོན་དང་མཐུན་པའི་སྦྱོར་བ་ཤེས། །

ཞེས་པ་སྟེ། དེ་ལྟར་རྗེས་འཇུག་གི་ཡི་གེ་བཅུའི་བྱ་བ་དང་གཙོ་བོར་འབྲེལ་པའི་ཕྲད་དང་རྣམ་དབྱེ་ལ་སོགས་པའི་སྒྲ་དོན་གྱི་འཇུག་ཚུལ་ལེགས་པར་ཤེས་ནས། མདོ་རྒྱུད་བསྟན་བཅོས་རྣམས་ཡི་གེ་འབྲི་བ་དང་ཡི་གེར་བྲིས་ཟིན་པ་རྣམས་བརྗོད་པ་དག་པར་ཀློག་པ་དང་། ཚིག་དོན་རྒྱ་བཀྲོལ་ནས་བཤད་པ་བྱེད་པ་དང་། དེར་མ་ཟད། བསྟན་བཅོས་

སོགས་སྙོམ་པ་དང་། གཞན་གྱི་རྩོལ་བ་ཚར་གཅོད་པའི་ཕྱིར་རྩོད་པ་བྱེད་པ་ལ་སོགས་པའི་ཚེ་ཚིག་དོན་ལྡན་གྱི་མཚམས་སྦྱོར་བའི་སྒྲ་དོན་རྣམས་ལ་བློ་གྲོས་ཀྱི་སྣང་བ་འཇུག་པར་སོགས་པ་མེད་ཅིང་ཚིག་དང་དོན་ལྡན་གྱི་གོ་ལོག་པ་དང་། མི་འབྲེལ་པ་དང་ འགར་བ་ལ་སོགས་པའི་སྐྱོན་མེད་པར་འཆད་པ་དང་ལྡན་ཞིང་འབྲེལ་ཆགས་པ་ཕོ་ནས་སྨྲ་བའི་མཆོག་ཏུ་འགྱུར་བ་དང་། གཞན་ཡང་རྗེས་འཇུག་གི་དོན་རྒྱུ་ཤེས་པ་དེས། ཡི་གེར་བྲིས་པ་མཐོང་བ་འམ་གཞན་གྱིས་ཀློག་པ་ཐོས་ཀྱང་ཐུང་ངང་ཉིད་ཀྱིས་ངེའི་དོན་གྱི་སྦྱོར་བ་ལྟར་མ་མཐོང་ང་སྐྱེ་དཔྱོད་ཡུལ་དུ་མ་གྱུར་པ་ཞིག་ཡིན་ནའང་བརྗོད་པ་དེའི་སྐད་སོགས་ཀྱི་རྣམ་པས་དོན་དང་མཐུན་པའི་སྦྱོར་བ་གང་ཡང་རྗེས་སུ་དཔག་སྟེ་ཤེས་པར་ནུས་པ་ཡིན་ནོ།། ཡང་ན་ཚིག་རྐང་ཕྱི་མ་གཉིས་ཀྱི་དོན། བསྟན་བཅོས་ལ་སོགས་པའི་དོན་རྣམ་པར་འབྱེད་པའི་སྦྱོར་བ་སྟེ། དེའི་འགྲེལ་བཤད་སོགས་སྟོན་ཚད་མ་མཐོང་ཡང་འགྲེལ་བཤད་སོགས་ཀྱི་དོན་ནི་མངོན་པའི་ཚིག་གི་སྦྱོར་བ་ཤེས་པར་འགྱུར་རོ།། ཞེས་པའོ།། གསུམ་པ་ནི།

རྗེས་འཇུག་སྦྱོར་བ་མཁས་པ་ཡིན།། ལུང་གི་དོན་དང་སྦྱོར་བ་དང་།། བླ་མའི་མན་ངག་གསུམ་སྦྱར་ནས།། དོན་གྱི་ཐོག་ཏུ་དབབ་པར་བྱ།།

ཞེས་པ་སྟེ། རྗེས་འཇུག་གི་སྦྱོར་བ་རྣམས་ལ་མཁས་པར་གྱུར་པའི་གང་ཟག་གིས་རང་ཉིད་ཐུན་མོང་དང་ཐུན་མོང་མ་ཡིན་པའི་ཤེས་བྱ་རིག་པའི་གནས་གང་དང་གང་ལ་འཇུག་ཅིང་ཤེས་པར་འདོད་པ་ན་དེ་དང་དེའི་རང་རང་གི་ཁུངས་སུ་ཆེ་བའི་ལུང་ཐུན་མོང་བར་དྲང་སྲོང་དང་པཎྜི་ཏས་བྱས་པའི་བསྟན་བཅོས་དང་། ཐུན་མོང་མིན་པར་བཅོམ་ལྡན་འདས་ཀྱི་གསུང་རབ་དང་། དེའི་དགོངས་འགྲེལ་ཚད་ལྡན་རྣམས་ལས་འབྱུང་བ་དག་གི་དོན་སྐབས་སུ་ཇི་ལྟར་འཚམ་པར་སྦྱོར་བར་བྱེད་པ་དང་། བསྒྲུབ་པར་བྱ་བ་གང་ཡིན་དེ་ལ་མཁས་ཤིང་དོན་རྩལ་བཞིན་དུ་འདོམས་པའི་བླ་མའི་མན་ངག་དག་ཀྱང་མཉན་ནས་རྗེས་འཇུག་གི་སྦྱོར་བ་ལུང་དོན། བླ་མའི་མན་ངག་གསུམ་ཕྱོགས་གཅིག་ཏུ་སྦྱར་ཏེ་ཤེས་པར་འདོད་པའི་དོན་དེའི་སྙིང་དུ་དབབ་པས་བདེ་བླག་ཏུ་རྟོགས་པར་འགྱུར་བ་དེ་ལྟར་བྱའོ།། ཞེས་སོ།། དེའང་ངག་དོན་རྟོགས་པར་སླ་བ་རྣམས་ནི་བརྡ་ལ་སོགས་པའི་དོན་ཤེས་པས་ཀྱང་འགྲོལ་བར་ནུས་ལ། རྟོགས་པར་དཀའ་ཞིང་འཁྲུལ་གཞི་དང་བཅས་པ་རྣམས་ལ་ནི་དེར་མ་ཟད་ལུང་དོན་ཀྱང་སྦྱོར་དགོས་པ་དང་ལུང་གི་དོན་ཀྱང་ཟབ་ཅིང་རྒྱ་ཆེ་བ་དག་འཁྲུལ་མེད་དུ་ཤེས་པ་བླ་མའམ་སློབ་དཔོན་ལ་རག་ལས་པའི་ཕྱིར་དེ་སྐད་གསུངས་ཀྱི། ཚིག་སྦྱོར་ཕྲ་མོ་རེའི་དོན་ལའང་དེ་གསུམ་ག་ངེས་པར་ཚོགས་དགོས་པའི་དོན་ནི་མ་ཡིན་ནོ།།

ཙནྡྲ་པའི་ཡི་གེའི་མདོར། གནས་དང་བྱེད་པ་དང་རྩོལ་བ་ཞེས་གསུམ་དུ་བཤད་པ། བོད་ཀྱི་ཡི་གེ་རྣམས་ལ་སྦྱོར་བའི་ཚེ། སོ་སོའི་གནས་ནི། ཀ་ཁ་ག་ང་འ་ཧ་ཨ་རྣམས་ཀྱི་སྐྱེ་གནས་མགྲིན་པ། ཙ་ཚ་ཛ་ཉ་ཅ་ཆ་ཇ་ཞ་ཡ་ཤ་ཨི་ཨེ་རྣམས་ཀྱི་སྐྱེ་གནས་རྐན། ཏ་ཐ་ད་ན་ཟ་ལ་ས་རྣམས་ཀྱི་སྐྱེ་གནས་སོ། པ་ཕ་བ་མ་ཝ་ཨུ་ཨོ་འདི་སྐབས་ཁ་ཅིག་གིས། དོན་གྱི་ཐོག་ཏུ་ཞེས་པའི་དོན་དེ་སྒྲུབ་པའི་ཉམས་ལེན་ཁོ་ནར་བཤད་པ་ནི་ཁྲུལ་ཆུང་ངོ་།།

གསུམ་པ་བསྟན་བཅོས་ཀྱི་གོ་རིམ་ལ་འདོམས་པ་ནི།

བསྟན་པ་ལ་བརྩོན་པའི་གང་ཟག་གིས།། དང་པོར་ང་རོ་རྣམས་ལ་སྦྱང་།

སྔོན་འཇུག་རྗེས་འཇུག་མིང་གཞི་གསུམ། བློ་ཡི་ཆེད་དུ་བསླབ་པ་ཡིན།

རྗེས་འཇུག་བཞི་ཡི་སྦྱོར་བ་ནི། མཉན་པས་བརྟན་པའི་ཆེད་དུ་སྦྱར། མན་ངག་དེ་དག་མཐུ་ཡིས་ནི།

འབྲས་བུའི་ཆེད་དུ་དོན་ལ་དབབ། བསླབ་པའི་རིམ་པ་འདི་ཡིས་ནི། གང་ཞིག་འདོད་པ་ཆུང་ངུས་ཀྱང་།

ཤེས་རབ་མྱུར་དུ་གྲོལ་བར་འགྱུར། དེ་ཕྱིར་དང་པོར་འདི་ཉིད་བསླབ། དེ་ནས་རྒྱས་པར་མཉན་བྱས་སྟེ།

བསླབ་པ་པ་གང་ལ་དད་པ་ཡི། གཞུང་ཉིད་བླ་མ་དག་ལས་མཉན།

ཞེས་པས་བསྟན་ཏོ།། རིགས་པའི་ཚུལ་གང་ཞིག་བསླབ་པར་བྱ་བ་ལ་བརྩོན་པས་འཇུག་པར་བྱེད་པའི་གང་ཟག་ལས་དང་པོ་པ་དེས་ནི་ཐོག་མ་ཉིད་དུ་ང་རོ་ཞེས་བྱ་བ་ཡི་གེ་ཀྲུང་པ་རྣམས

རང་རང་གི་སྐྱེ་གནས་དང་མཐུན་པ་དང་། དབྱངས་ལྡན་རྣམས་ཀྱང་སོ་སོའི་ང་རོ་འབྱུང་ཚུལ་བཅས་ཡི་གེ་རེ་རེ་ནས་ཀློག་པའི་སྒྲ་གདངས་ལ་སྦྱར་བར་བྱ་ཞིང་། དེ་ནས་སྔོན་འཇུག་ལྔ་དང་འཕུལ་རྗེས་ཀྱི་འཇུག་ཡུལ་མིང་གཞི་སུམ་ཅུ་དང་རྗེས་འཇུག་བཅུ་སྟེ། དེ་གསུམ་ཅི་རིགས་པ་ཚེག་བར་གཅིག་ཏུ་སྦྱོར་བའི་ཚུལ་ཡང་ཀློག་ལེགས་པར་ཤེས་པའི་ཆེད་དུ་བསླབ་པར་བྱ་བ་ཡིན་པ་དང་། ཀློག་ལ་བྱང་ནས་རྗེས་འཇུག་སྔ་དེར་སྔོན་འཇུག་ཀྱང་འདུས་པ་དེ་དག་རྟགས་འཇུག་ནས་བཤད་པ་ལྟར་སྒྲ་དོན་གང་ལ་འཇུག་པ། ཡི་གེ་གང་གིས་འཇུག་པ། ཚུལ་ཇི་ལྟར་འཇུག་པ། དགོས་པ་ཅིའི་ཕྱིར་འཇུག་པ་སྟེ་རྣམ་པ་བཞིའི་སྦྱོར་བ་རྣམས་ནི། རང་ལ་སློབ་ཅིང་འདོམས་པར་བྱེད་པ་པོ་བླ་མ་སོགས་ལས་ལེགས་པར་བཤད་པ་མཉན་པ་དང་། ཉན་པ་དེའི་དོན་རང་ཉིད་ཀྱིས་ཚུལ་བཞིན་དུ་བསམས་པ་དང་། དོན་དེ་རང་ཉིད་ཀྱིས་ཁོང་དུ་ཆུད་ནས་གཞན་ལ་བསྟན་པ་རྣམས་ཀྱི་དོན་དུ་སྦྱར་ཏེ་མཁས་པར་བསླབ་པར་བྱའོ།། ཀློག་དང་བརྡ་དག་གི་ཡན་ལག་དེ་གཉིས་ཀྱི་མཐུས་ནི་གང་བསླབ་པར་བྱ་བ་དེ་ཤེས་པའི་འབྲས་བུ་ཐོབ་པར་བྱ་བའི་སླད་དུ་དོན་ལ་དབབ་ནས་ཉམས་སུ་བསྟར་བར་བྱའོ།། དེ་ལྟར་བསླབ་པའི་རིམ་པ་འདིས་ནི་སྐྱེས་བུ་གང་ཞིག་ཐོས་བསམ་ལ་བརྩོན་འགྲུས་ཆེན་པོ་དང་ལྡན་པ་རྣམས་སློས་ཅི་དགོས་ཏེ། འབད་པ་ཆུང་ངུ་ཙམ་བྱས་པས་ཀྱང་ཚིག་དོན་ལ་རྨོངས་པ་མེད་པའི་ཤེས་རབ་རྒྱ་ཆེར་དུ་འཕེལ་བར་འགྱུར་རོ།། རྒྱ་མཚན་དེའི་ཕྱིར་མཁས་པར་འདོད་པ་རྣམས་ཀྱིས་ཐོག་མར་སུམ་ཅུ་པའི་གཞུང་འདི་ཉིད་བསླབ་པར་བྱ་ཞིང་འདི་ཤེས་ནས་རྟགས་འཇུག་ལ་སོགས་པ་འདིའི་སྐབས་ཕྱི་མ་རྣམས་དང་། དེ་ནས་བར་སྐོར་པའི་གཞུང་ཆུས་པ་གཞན་དང་གཞན་རྣམས་ཀྱང་མཉན་པར་བྱས་ནས་ཁོང་དུ་ཆུད་པ་ན། ཐེག་པ་གསུམ་ཀྱི་གཞིར་གྱུར་པའི་བསླབ་པ་གང་ལ་དད་ཅིང་སློབ་པར་འདོད་པ་དེའི་གཞུང་ལུགས་ཡན་ལག་དང་བཅས་པ་ཉིད་བླ་མ་རྣམས་ལས་མཉན་པར་བྱའོ།། ཞེས་སོ།། དེ་ན་འདིར་ཐོག་མར་ཡི་གེའི་ང་རོ་དང་ཕྱི་ནས་སྦྱོར་ཀློག་ལ་སྦྱངས་དགོས་པར་གསུངས་པ་དེའི་ཚུལ་བོད་ཡུལ་དུ་ཆུང་ཟད་གྲགས་པ་ཉིད་ཡིན་མོད་ཀྱི་འོན་ཀྱང་དེ་དག་དག་པར་འདོན་པ་ནི་ཞིབ་དགོས་པར་སྣང་བས་ཅུང་ཟད་བཤད་ན།

རྣམས་ཀྱི་སྐྱེ་གནས་མཆུ། ར་ཡིག་གི་སྐྱེ་གནས་ལྕེ་རྩེ་དང་ཉེ་བའི་སྙི་བོ་ལྕེ་རྩེའི་སྟེང་ཕྱོགས། ང་ཉ་ན་མ་རྣམས་རང་རང་གི་གནས་སུ་མ་ཟད་སྣ་དང་བཅས་པའོ།། བྱེད་པ་ནི་མགྲིན་པ་དང་མཆུ་ལས་སྐྱེས་པ་རྣམས་རང་རང་གི་གནས་ཀྱི་བྱེད་པ་ཅན་དང་། རྐན་ལས་བྱུང་བ་རྣམས་ལྕེའི་དབུས་ཀྱི་བྱེད་པ་ཅན་དང་། སོ་ལས་བྱུང་བ་རྣམས་ལྕེ་རྩེའི་བྱེད་པ་ཅན་དང་། ར་ཡིག་ནི་ལྕེ་རྩེ་དང་ཉེ་བའི་བྱེད་པ་ཅན་ནོ།།

རྩོལ་བ་ལ་ཕྱི་ནང་གཉིས་ལས་ཕྱིའི་རྩོལ་བ་ནི།། ཕྱི་རོལ་དུ་སྒྲ་ཐོན་པ་ལྟ་བུའི་བྱེད་རྩོལ་དང་ལྡན་པའི་ཕྱིར་ཏེ། དེའང་གདངས་འཐོན་ཆེ་ཆུང་གི་དབྱེ་བས། ག་ང་ཇ་ཉ་ད་ན་བ་མ་ཛ་ཝ་ཞ་འ་ཡ་ར་ལ་ཧ་ཨ་ཨི་ཨུ་ཨེ་ཨོ་རྣམས་སྒྲ་ལྡན་དང་། ཀ་ཁ་ཙ་ཆ་ཏ་ཐ་པ་ཕ་ཚ་ཞ་ཟ་ཤ་ས་རྣམས་སྒྲ་མེད་དང་། སྒྲ་ཕྱིར་དབྱུང་ཚེ་དབུགས་ཆེ་ཆུང་གི་ཁྱད་པར་གྱིས། ཁ་ཆ་ཐ་ཕ་ཚ་ཞ་ཤ་ས་ཧ་ཨ་ཨི་ཨུ་ཨེ་ཨོ་རྣམས་སྲོག་ཆེན་དང་། ཡི་གེ་ལྷག་མ་རྣམས་སྲོག་ཆུང་དང་། དེ་དག་ལས་ཁ་ཐ་ཤ་ས་ཧ་རྣམས་བརྗོད་པའི་ཚེ་དབུགས་དུ་བར་འབྱིན་པས་དྲོ་བའང་ཡིན་ནོ།།

ནང་གི་རྩོལ་བ་ནི། མགྲིན་པ་གདངས་ནས་བརྗོད་དགོས་པའི་ཕྱིར་ཨ་ཡིག་མ་གཏོགས་པའི་སྲོག་ཆེན་གྱི་ཡི་གེ་རྣམས་ཕྱེ་བའི་རྩོལ་བ་ཅན་དང་། ཨ་ཡིག་མགྲིན་པ་མ་ཕྱེ་བར་བརྗོད་པའི་ཕྱིར་བཙུམ་པའི་རྩོལ་བ་ཅན་དང་། ཡི་གེའི་གནས་རྣམས་འདུ་འཕྲོད་ཀྱི་རྩོལ་བ་ཆེ་བའི་ཕྱིར་ཡ་མ་གཏོགས་པའི་རྗེ་པ་ལྟའི་ཡི་གེ་རྣམས་ཐུད་པའི་རྩོལ་བ་ཅན་དང་། འདུ་འཕྲོད་ཀྱི་རྩོལ་བ་འདི་དག་ལས་ལྷོད་པའི་ཕྱིར་ཡ་ར་ལ་བ་རྣམས་ཅུང་ཟད་ཐུད་པའི་རྩོལ་བ་ཅན་ནོ།། ངེས་ན་ཡི་གེ་དེ་རྣམས་སོ་སོར་ཀློག་པའི་ཚེ་སོ་སོའི་གནས་དང་བྱེད་པ་དང་རྩོལ་བ་རྣམས་དང་མཐུན་པ་ཞིག་གལ་ཆེ་ཞིང་གསལ་བྱེད་ལ། དབྱངས་ཡིག་སྦྱོར་བའི་ཚེའང་། ༄།ཀ་ལྟ་བུ་མགྲིན་པའི་སྐྱེ་གནས་ཅན་ལ་ཨི་ཨེ་མཚོན་བྱེད་གི་གུ་དང་འགྲེང་བུ་སྦྱར་བས་རྐན་ཀྱི་སྐྱེ་གནས་དང་ཡང་ལྡན་པར་འགྱུར་བ་སོགས་ཤེས་པར་བྱས་ནས་དེ་དང་མཐུན་པའི་ཀློག་ཚུལ་ཐོན་པ་དགོས་སོ། ཁྱད་པར་དབྱངས་སྦྱར་བའི་ཀློག་ཚུལ་ནི་དཀའ་བ་ཤིན་ཏུ་གཅེས་བར་མཐོང་སྟེ། ཁམས་ཕྱོགས་ཀྱི་ཡུལ་གྲུ་འགའ་རེ་ལ་ན་རོ་དང་འགྲེང་བུ་ཡོད་མེད་ཀྱི་ཀློག་ཚུལ་ཐ་དད་དུ་མི་འབྱུང་བ་དང་། འགའ་ཞིག་ན་ཞབས་ཀྱུ་དང་ན་རོ་ཀློག་ཚུལ་གཅིག་ཏུ་བྱེད་པ་སོགས་ཀྱིས་མཚོན་མ་དག་པར་འདོན་པ་མང་ཞིང་། དེས་ཡི་གེ་འབྲི་བ་ནའང་མ་དག་པ་ཁོ་ནར་འགྱུར་བའི་ཕྱིར་རོ།།

སྦྱོར་ཀློག་གི་སྐབས་སུའང་། འཕུལ་རྟེན་དང་མགོ་འདོགས་ཀྱི་ཡི་གེ་རྣམས་སོ་སོའི་སྒྲ་འདོན་དགོས་པ་ནི།

རྗེ་བཙུན་བསོད་ནམས་རྩེ་མོ།།

གང་དང་གང་ལ་གང་བཏགས་པ། །གོ་རིམ་བཞིན་དུ་གནས་ནས་དབྱུང་། །དེ་ལ་ར་མགོ་ལྕེ་རྩེ་འདར། །ལ་མགོ་ལྕེ་ཀློད་རྒྱ་ཡངས་བསྐྱེད། །

ས་མགོ་སོ་ཡི་བར་ནས་དབྱུང་། །ལྷག་མ་རྣམས་ཀྱང་དེ་བཞིན་ཞེས།། གལ་ཏེ་མ་ཕྱིན་ཕྱུར་པ་ནི། །ཡི་གེ་ཕྲལ་ཞིང་བརྗོད་པར་བྱ།།

དཔེར་ན་གྲུ་ལ་ག་ར་འམ། །དགྲ་ལ་ད་ག་ར་ཇི་བཞིན་དུ། །དེ་ནས་འཕུལ་བ་བསྟན་པར་བྱ། །གས་འཕུལ་ཐོག་མར་རྐན་ནས་དབྱུང་། །

དས་འཕུལ་ལྕེ་རྩེ་ཀློད་པ་ལས། །བ་མས་འཕུལ་བ་ཐོག་མར་ནི། །མཆུ་བཙུམ་པ་ལས་ཕྲུད་པར་སྣང་། །འས་འཕུལ་གྲེ་བའི་ཕུག་ནས་དབྱུང་། །

འཕུལ་ཞིང་བརྩེགས་པའི་ཡི་གེ་ཡང་། །གོ་རིམ་བཞིན་དབྱུང་མ་ཕྱིན་ན། །འདི་ཡང་ཕྲལ་ཞིང་བཀླག་པ་སྟེ། །འཕྲུ་ལ་ཁ་ར་ཇི་བཞིན་ནོ།།

ཞེས་སོགས་གསུངས་པས་ཀྱང་གྲུབ་མོད། སྔོན་འབྲི་ཁྲིད་དུ་སློབ་པ་རིན་པོ་ཆེ་བཞུགས་པའི་ཚེ་གནའ་བོའི་དུས་བཞིན་དུ་ཡིག་ཀློག་སྐྱོན་ཆད་ཀྱང་བརྩེགས་འཕུལ་སོགས་ཀྱི་སྒྲ་ཟུར་ཕྱིན་པར་འདོན་པའི་སློབ་བཟང་པོ་དབྱུང་བར་གྲགས་པ་དང་ཁམས་ཕྱོགས་ཀྱི་མཐའ་ཁུལ་མདོ་དང་རྒྱལ་མོ་རོང་སོགས་བྱང་ཤར་གྱི་ཆ་རྣམས་སུ་འཁོད་པའི་སྐྱེ་བོ་དག་ལའང་གནའ་བོའི་དུས་སུ་བོད་ཡུལ་དབུས་ནས་བྱུང་བའི་ཀློག་རྒྱུན་མ་ཉམས་པ་ཡིན་པར་གྲགས་པའི་ཡི་གེ་ཀློག་རྒྱུན་དང་། དེ་དག་གི་ཡུལ་སྐད་བཅས་ལའང་སྐྱོང་ཉམས་ཆེ་ཚམ་ལས་འཕུལ་རྟེན་སོགས་ཀྱི་ཟུར་དག་པར་འདོན་པ་འབྱུང་བར་མངོན་སུམ་གྱིས་གྲུབ་པ་སོགས་ཀྱིས་ཀྱང་མཚོན་ནུས་སོ། །གཞན་ཡང་བོད་ཡིག་གི་སྡེབ་ཇི་ལྟར་སྦྱོར་བའི་ཚུལ་ནི་སྔོན་གྱི་བོད་སྐད་དག་པ་ཉིད་ལ་བརྗོད་པའི་སྒྲ་ཇི་ལྟར་འབྱུང་བ་དེ་ལྟར་མཁན་པོ་འདེམས་སྒྱུར་བ་ཡིན་པས། སྐད་ལ་འཕུལ་རྟེན་སོགས་ཀྱི་ཟུར་གསལ་བ་མེད་ན་ཡི་གེ་ལ་དེ་ལྟར་སྦྱོར་བ་རྒྱུ་མཚན་གང་ཞིག་གིས་རྟོགས་པར་ནུས། དེས་ན་གནའ་བོའི་དུས་སུ་ཡིག་ཀློག་ཙམ་དུ་མ་ཟད་བོད་སྐད་ཉིད་ལའང་སྒྲ་ཟུར་ཐམས་ཅད་མ་ཉམས་པར་འདོན་པ་ཞིག་ཡོད་པར་ངེས་ཀྱང་། དེང་སང་བོད་ཡུལ་དབུས་དང་མཐའ་འཁོབ་ཕལ་ཆེར་ལ་རང་སྐད་དང་ཡིག་ཀློག་གཉིས་ཀ་སྒྲ་དག་པར་འདོན་པ་མེད་པ་ལ་བརྟེན་ནས་མཁས་པའི་ཁྲོད་ནའང་ཡིག་གཟུགས་ཀྱི་སྡེབ་དག་ཕྱིན་ཀློག་ཚུལ་དེ་དང་ངེས་པར་བསྟུན་མི་དགོས་བསམས་པའམ། །སྡེབ་སྦྱོར་ནི་ཡི་གེ་འབྲི་བའི་དབང་དུ་བྱས་ཀྱི་བརྗོད་པའི་དབང་དུ་མ་བྱས་སྙམ་པའམ། ཀློག་ཚུལ་ཡིག་སྡེབ་དང་བསྟུན་དགོས་ཀྱང་ཕྱོགས་ཙམ་ལས་ཡིག་སྡེབ་ཇི་ལྟ་བར་སྒྲ་ཟུར་ཐོན་པ་ནི་སྔར་ཡང་མ་བྱུང་ཞིང་ད་ལྟ་ཡང་འདོན་པར་མི་ནུས་སོ་སྙམ་པ་མང་དུ་ཡོད་པར་རྟོགས་པ་དང་།

ལེགས་སྦྱར་གྱི་སྐད་ཡའང་། གངས་ཅན་གྱི་བོད་སྤྱོད་ཞེས་པར་རློམ་པ་ཕྱིས་བྱུང་རྣམས་ཀྱིས་ཐུགས་ཀྱི་ཀློག་ཚུལ་ཞེས་བོད་སྤྱོད་ཀྱི་གཞུང་དང་གཏན་འགལ་བ་རེ་ལ་ཡིད་བརྟན་འཆའ་ཞིང་དབྱངས་གསལ་གྱི་མཚམས་སྦྱོར་ལས་བྱུང་བའི་རྣམ་འགྱུར་དེ་རྣམས་ཡིག་གཟུགས་ཀྱི་སྐབས་སུ་མ་གཏོགས་བརྗོད་པ་ལ་ཇི་ལྟ་བར་སྦྱོར་མི་ནུས་སྙམ་པར་འདུག་པ་ནི་ཡ་མཚོ།། དེ་བས་ན་རང་ཉིད་ཀྱིས་སྒྲ་དག་པར་བཀླག་མ་ཤེས་པའམ་མ་ནུས་ནའང་ཀློག་ཚུལ་དག་པ་མེད་དོ་ཞེས་བརྗོད་པར་མི་བྱའོ།།

སྦྱོར་ཀློག་དངོས་ཇི་ལྟར་བྱ་བའང་། འཕུལ་ཅན་རྣམས་ལ་བཤད་མ་ཐག་པ་ལྟར་འཕུལ་བྱེད་ཀྱི་ཡི་གེ་རང་རང་གི་སྐྱེ་གནས་དང་མཐུན་པའི་ཐོག་མར་འབྱུང་དགོས་ཤིང་། མགོ་ཅན་དང་འདོགས་ཅན་རྣམས་ལའང་མགོ་དང་འདོགས་ཀྱི་ཡི་གེ་སོ་སོའི་གནས་དང་མཐུན་པའི་བརྗོད་པ་སོ་སོར་འབྱུང་དགོས་པ་དཔེར་ན་སྐྲ་ལྕུག་ལ་ས་ག་ར་རྣམས་རིམ་པར་རང་སྒྲ་ཐོན་ཙམ་དུ་སྒྱུར་བ་ཀློག་པ་ལྟ་བུ་དང་། འ་མཐའ་ཅན་ཕལ་ཆེར་ཞིག་གི་རྟེན་བྱེད་ཀྱི་སྒྲ་མི་གསལ་བས་དེ་དག་མ་གཏོགས་གསལ་བར་སྣང་བའི་མཐའ་རྟེན་ཅན་ཡང་ཡང་འཇུག་མེད་པ་རྣམས་ནི་རྟེན་ཡིག་སོ་སོའི་གནས་དང་མཐུན་པའི་སྒྲ་རྗེས་སུ་འབྱུང་བ་དང་། ཡང་རྗེས་འཇུག་ཅན་ལ་ས་ཡིག་གི་ཡང་འཇུག་ཅན་ནི་ཕ་རོལ་དུ་ཚིག་གྲོགས་གཞན་མེད་ན་ས་སྒྲ་དངོས་སུ་མི་གསལ་ཡང་སྒྲ་དེ་འབྱུང་བར་ཉེ་བ་ལྟར་བཀླག་ཅིང་། ཚིག་གྲོགས་ཡོད་ན་རྗེས་འཇུག་ཐ་མ་དེའི་སྒྲ་ཟུར་གྱི་རྗེས་སུ་ས་སྒྲའང་ཐོན་པར་འབྱུང་དགོས་པ་དང་། ད་ཡིག་གི་ཡང་འཇུག་ཅན་ནི་ཚིག་གྲོགས་ལ་ལྟོས་མི་དགོས་པར་རྗེས་འཇུག་ཐ་མའི་སྒྲའི་མཐར་དའི་སྒྲ་འབྱུང་བ་ཁད་ཙམ་སྒྲ་མཉམ་དུ་བཀྲ་བར་བཀླག་པ་ཡིན་ནོ།། དེས་ན་སྐད་གསར་བཅད་ཀྱི་དུས་སུ་ཨ་མཐའ་ཕལ་ཆེར་དང་ད་དྲག་མ་ཕྲིས་པའང་དེ་དག་གི་སྒྲ་བརྗོད་པ་ལ་ཧ་ཅང་མ་གསལ་བས་ཡིན་པར་སྣང་ངོ་།། དེ་ལྟར་ཡི་གེ་ཀློག་ཚུལ་དག་པར་འདོན་པ་རྣམས་ལ་ཕྱོགས་ཙམ་སློས་པར་

ཟད་ཀྱི་རྒྱུ་བར་སྨྲོས་ཕྱི་མ་ཁངས་ཤིང་། འདི་ཙམ་གྱིས་ཀྱང་། ཀུ་ཁུ་གུ་རྣམས། ཙ་ཚ་ཛ་རྣམས་དང་། ཊུ་ཋུ་ཌུ་རྣམས་ཕྱོགས་མཚུངས་པར་སྦྱག་པ་དང་། བསྐྱ་བཀྱུ་ཀྱུ་སྨུ་དགུ་སྨུ་ཛ་རྣམས་མཚུངས་པར་སྦྱག་པ་དང་། ཛ་ཛྷ་དངའ་རྣམས་མཚུངས་པར་སྦྱག་པ་སོགས་འདུལ་བ་འབུམས་སུ་གྲུས་པ་རྣམས་ཀྱི་མཚང་རིག་པར་ནུས་སོ།། སྐབས་འདིར་འགྲེལ་བྱེད་སྔ་མ་འགའ་རེག་གིས་རྗེས་འཇུག་བཞི་ཡི་སྦྱོར་བ་ནི། ཞེས་དང་། གཞན་ཡང་ཀྱུག་བཤད་བྱས་པ་འགའ་ཞིག་ཡོད་ཀྱང་འགྲེལ་པ་གཞན་དང་གཞན་དུ་ལེགས་པར་བཀག་པའང་མཐོང་བས་འདིར་དགག་པའི་སྤྲོས་པ་མ་བྱས་སོ།། བཞི་པ་དོན་ཐུང་ལ་གདམས་ངག་བསྟན་དགོས་པར་འདོམས་པ་ནི།

སློབ་དཔོན་དེ་ཉིད་དུ་འཛིན་ཅིང་། ལེ་ལོ་གཡེང་བ་རྣམ་པར་སྤངས། ཚེ་བཟང་དད་པ་ལ་བརྟེན་པ།
སྐྱེས་བུ་དེས་ནི་སྒྱུར་རྟབས་ཏེ། དེ་ལ་དུས་སུ་འདོམས་པར་བྱ། ཅིག་ཤོས་དེས་ལས་ལྡོག་པའོ།།

ཞེས་པ་སྟེ། བརྡའི་སྦྱོར་བ་ལ་མཁས་པར་བྱེད་པའི་བསྟན་བཅོས་འདི་ལྷ་བུའི་གདམས་ངག་བསྟན་དུ་རུང་བའི་དོན་ནི། གདམས་ངག་སྟོན་མཁན་གྱི་སློབ་དཔོན་དེ་ལ་སློབ་དཔོན་དུ་འཛིན་ཅིང་ཞེ་ས་དང་བཅས་པས་བྱིན་དུ་བཙོ་བ་དང་། རིག་པ་སློབ་པའི་མི་མཐུན་ཕྱོགས་བསྐྱབ་པར་བྱ་བ་དེ་ལ་སྤྱོ་བ་ཞན་པའི་ལེ་ལོ་དང་། བྱ་བ་གཞན་ལ་འཇུག་པའི་གཡེང་བ་གཉིས་སྤངས་པ་སྟེ་དེ་དག་གིས་གླགས་མི་རྙེད་པའི་རྟག་སྦྱོར་གྱི་བརྩོན་འགྲུས་དང་ལྡན་པ་དང་། རིག་པ་སློབ་པའི་མཐུན་རྐྱེན་ཚེ་སྔོ་རང་བཞིན་ནམ་ངང་ཚུལ་བཟང་ཞིང་བསླབ་པར་བྱ་བའི་གནས་ལ་མཆོག་ཏུ་དད་པ་ལ་བརྟེན་པའི་ཀུན་སྦྱོར་གྱི་བརྩོན་འགྲུས་དང་ལྡན་པ་སྟེ་མཚན་ཉིད་གསུམ་དང་ལྡན་པ་དེ་ལྟ་བུའི་སྐྱེས་བུ་དེས་ནི་བསླབ་པར་བྱ་བ་གང་ཡིན་དེ་སྒྱུར་དུ་རྟོགས་པར་འགྱུར་བས་དེ་ལ་དུས་ཤེས་པར་བྱས་ནས་དུས་སུ་འདོམས་པར་བྱ་ཞིང་། ཅིག་ཤོས་གཞན་ནི་དེ་ལས་ལྡོག་པ་སྟེ། སློབ་དཔོན་ལ་མི་གུས་པ་དང་། ལེ་ལོ་དང་གཡེང་བ་ཅན་དང་། རང་བཞིན་ངན་ཞིང་དད་པ་མེད་པ་རྣམས་ལ་ནི་རྒོད་དང་མི་ལྡན་པས་རེ་ཞིག་འདོམས་པར་བྱ་བ་མ་ཡིན་མོད། འོན་ཀྱང་ཕྱི་ནས་དོན་དུ་གཉེར་ཅིང་འདུན་པར་འགྱུར་ན་ལེགས་པར་རྗེས་སུ་བསྟན་པར་ཡང་བྱའོ།། ཞེས་སོ།། འདིར་སྨྲས་པ།

གང་གི་ཐུགས་རྗེས་སྐྱོར་བསྐྱལ་བས། བདག་བློ་ཞི་གདེངས་རན་གོ་ད་སང་རེ། ལེགས་བཤད་སྦྲང་རྩིའི་ཆར་འབབ་པས། དོན་རབ་གསལ་བའི་དབྱར་ཁ་བྱུང་།
བྱ་མིའི་གཞུང་བཟང་ཉེར་འཛིན་མར། ཚིག་དོན་རྩལ་ཚོགས་དངེབས་བྱེད་པའི། བཤད་སྒྲོས་སྒྲོས་མང་ཇ་རི་གློ་བུར་གྱིས། དཀྲིགས་ལྡན་དཔྱིད་ཀ་ཤར་བའི་ཚེ།
ད་སྙེ་བློ་གསལ་གཞོན་ནུ་རྣམས། འདྲུལ་མེད་ཉམ་དཔྱོད་སྨྱུ་གུ་གསར། ཅི་ཡང་རྒྱས་པའི་ཞང་ག་འདིར། བག་ཡངས་ཉིད་དུ་རྩེན་པར་རོམས།

དེ་ལྟར་སུམ་ཅུ་པའི་གཞུང་གི་ཚིག་དོན་གྱི་ཆ་རང་བློས་ཇི་ལྟར་དཔོག་པ་རེ་ཞིག་བཤད་ཟིན་ཏོ།། ང་ལྟར་བཤད་རེས་ངང་ནས་འདིར། ཀུན་གྱིས་དེ་ལྟར་རྟོགས་གྱུར་ཅིག།

རྟགས་འཇུག་གི་འགྲེལ་པ།

སི་ཏུ་རིན་པོ་ཆེས་མཛད་པ་བཞུགས་སོ།

རྒྱ་གར་སྐད་དུ། ལྟྲྀ་ཀ་ར་ཎ་ཨཝེང་ཤཱ་བ་ཊཱི་ཀཱ་ནཱ་མ། བོད་སྐད་དུ། ལུང་དུ་སྟོན་པ་རྟགས་ཀྱི་འཇུག་པ་ཞེས་བྱ་བ། བྱཱ་ཀ་ར་ཎའི་དབང་ཕྱུག་ལ་ཕྱག་འཚལ་ལོ།

སྨྲ་བའི་སྐྱེས་མཆོག་སྨྲ་བའི་རྒྱལ། ཐམས་ཅད་མཁྱེན་ལ་ཕྱག་འཚལ་ལོ།

༄༅། སྐད་ཅིག་ཙམ་ཞིག་ཡིད་མཁར་ཤར་བས་ཀྱང་། ནང་གི་སྨུན་སྤྲུག་རྣམ་པར་སེལ་བྱེད་པ།

འཇམ་དཔལ་དཔའ་བོའི་བྱིན་རླབས་ཉིན་མོར་བྱེད། བྱང་ཆུབ་བར་དུ་སྒོ་གསུམ་སྙིང་པོར་བརྟེན།

ཞེས་ཤིས་པའི་ཚིག་སྔོན་དུ་བཏང་ནས་ད་ནི་རྟགས་ཀྱི་འཇུག་པ་ཞེས་ཡོངས་སུ་གྲགས་པའི་གཞུང་གི་ཚིག་དོན་ལ་རྣམ་པར་དཔྱད་ནས་ཅུང་ཟད་འགྲོལ་བར་བྱའོ།། དེ་ལ་རེ་ཞིག་གཞུང་འདིར་སྤྱི་སྡོམ་གྱིས་དཔྱད་ན་མིང་གཞིའི་ཡི་གེ་སྤྱིའི་རྟགས་ཀྱི་དབྱེ་བ་བཤད་པ་དང་། སྔོན་འཇུག་གི་རྟགས་ཀྱི་འཇུག་པ་བཤད་པ་དང་རྗེས་འཇུག་གི་རྟགས་ཀྱི་འཇུག་པ་བཤད་པ་སྟེ་གསུམ་དུ་རིག་པར་བྱའོ།། དང་པོ་ནི།

ཨ་ཡི་ཡི་གེ་འབའ་ཞིག་ལ། སྡེ་པ་ཕྱེད་དང་བརྒྱད་གནས་པའང་། སྡེ་ཚན་ལྔ་རུ་དྲིལ་བྱས་ལ།
ཕོ་དང་མ་ནིང་མོ་དང་ནི། ཤིན་ཏུ་མོ་དང་བཞི་བཞི་རུ། སྡེ་པ་བཞི་པ་ཡན་ཆད་དབྱེ།
ལྷག་མ་བཅུ་བཞི་གནས་པ་ལ། ཙ་སོགས་གསུམ་ནི་ཙ་སོགས་སྦྱར། ཝ་ནི་བ་དང་སྦྱར་བར་བྱ།
ལྷག་མ་དྲུག་ནི་མོ་རུ་སྦྱར། ར་ལ་ཧ་ནི་མོ་གཤམ་སྟེ། ཨ་ནི་མཚན་མེད་ཅེས་ཀྱང་བྱ།

ཞེས་པས་བསྟན་ཏེ། ཕྱིར་བོད་ཀྱི་སྐད་ལ་ཉེ་བར་གྲགས་པའི་ཡི་གེ་རྣམས་ལ་ཕོ་མོ་གཉིས་སུ་དབྱེ་བའི་དབང་དུ་བྱས་ན་དབྱངས་ཡིག་མཚོན་བྱེད་ཨི་ཨུ་ཨེ་ཨོ་བཞི་ཤེས་རབ་ཀྱི་རང་བཞིན་མོ་དང་། ཀ་ནས་ཨའི་མཐར་ཐུག་པ་གསལ་བྱེད་སུམ་ཅུ་པོ་རྣམས་ནི་ཐབས་ཀྱི་རང་བཞིན་ཕོར་ཤེས་པར་བྱའོ།། དེས་ན་ཨའི་ཡི་གེ་འབའ་ཞིག་སྟེ་གསལ་བྱེད་སུམ་ཅུ་པོ་ཁོ་ན་ལ་སྡེ་པ་ཕྱེད་དང་བརྒྱད་དུ་གནས་ཏེ། སྡེ་པ་དང་པོ། ཀ་ཁ་ག་ང་། གཉིས་པ། ཙ་ཚ་ཇ་ཉ། གསུམ་པ། ཏ་ཐ་ད་ན། བཞི་པ། པ་ཕ་བ་མ། ལྔ་པ། ཙ་ཚ་ཛ་ཝ། དྲུག་པ། ཞ་ཟ་འ་ཡ། བདུན་པ། ར་ལ་ཤ་ས། ཕྱེད་པ། ཧ་ཨ། རྣམས་སོ། དེ་རྣམས་སྡེ་ཚན་ལྔ་རུ་དྲིལ་བ་ནི་ཕོ་དང་མ་ནིང་དང་མོ་དང་ཤིན་ཏུ་མོ་དང་མོ་གཤམ་སྟེ་རྣམ་པ་ལྔའོ།། དེའང་། སྡེ་པ་བཞི་པོ་རྣམས་ཀྱི་དང་པོ་ཀ་ཅ་ཏ་པ་རྣམས་ཕོ་དང་། གཉིས་པ་ཁ་ཆ་ཐ་ཕ་ཚ་རྣམས་མ་ནིང་དང་། གསུམ་པ་ག་ཇ་ད་བ་རྣམས་མོ་དང་། བཞི་པ། ང་ཉ་ན་མ་རྣམས་ཤིན་ཏུ་མོར་དབྱེ་བར་བྱའོ།། དེར་མ་ཟད་པའི་ལྷག་མ་ཙ་སྟེ་ཕྱིན་ཡི་གེ་བཅུ་བཞིར་གནས་པ་ལ། ཙ་ལ་སོགས་པ་ཙ་ཚ་ཛ་གསུམ་ནི་རིམ་པ་བཞིན་སྔར་བསྟན་པའི་ཙ་ལ་སོགས་པ་གསུམ་ལ་སྦྱར་བར་བྱ་སྟེ། ཙ་ཕོ། ཚ་མ་ནིང་། ཛ་མོར་ཤེས་པར་བྱའོ།། དེ་བཞིན་དུ་ཝ་ནི་བ་དང་སྦྱར་བས་མོ་དང་། ལྷག་མ་ཞ་ཟ་འ་ཡ་ཤ་ས་དྲུག་ཀྱང་མོའི་ཡི་གེར་སྦྱར་བར་བྱའོ།། ར་ལ་ཧ་གསུམ་ནི་མོ་གཤམ་གྱི་ཡི་གེ་ཞེས་བྱ་ཞིང་། ཨ་ཡིག་ནི་མོ་གཤམ་གྱི་ཡི་གེ་ཡིན་པར་མ་ཟད་མཚན་མེད་ཀྱི་ཡི་གེ་ཞེས་ཀྱང་བྱའོ།། ཞེས་པའི་དོན་ཏོ།། འདིར་མིང་གཞིའི་ཡི་གེ་རྣམས་ཕོ་ལ་སོགས་པར་རྒྱུ་མཚན་གང་གི་སྒོ་ནས་བཞག་པའང་འདི་ལྟར་ཤེས་དགོས་སོ། ཡི་གེ་རྣམས་སོ་སོར་ངག་ནས་བརྗོད་པའི་ཚེ་སོ་སོའི་སྐྱེ་གནས་མགྲིན་སོ་མཆུ་རྐན་སོགས་ལ་བྱེད་རྩོལ་གྱི་ཤུགས་ཆེ་ཆུང་ངམ་གྲིམས་ལྷོད་ཀྱི་དབང་གིས་ཤུགས་ཆེ་བའམ་གྲིམས་པ་རྣམས་ཕོ་ཡིག་དང་། རན་པ་རྣམས་མ་ནིང་དང་། ཆུང་ཟད་ཆུང་བའམ་ལྷོད་པ་རྣམས་མོ་དང་། དེ་ལས་ཀྱང་ཆུང་བའམ་ལྷོད་པ་རྣམས་ཤིན་ཏུ་མོ་དང་། ཤིན་ཏུ་ཆུང་བ

བསྐྱོད་ཅིང་ཞན་པ་རྣམས་སོ་གཉིས་སུ་བཞག་པའོ།། དེས་ན་ཨ་ཡིག་རྩོལ་བ་ཤིན་ཏུ་སྐྱོད་པའི་སྒོ་ནས་སོ་གཉིས་སུ་བཞག་མོད་ཀྱི་ར་ལ་ཧ་གསུམ་ལ་ལྟོས་པའི་དེ་ལས་ཀྱང་རྩོལ་བ་ཞན་པའི་ཕྱིར་མཚན་མེད་དུ་འང་བཞག་གོ།། དེ་ལྟར་ཡིན་པ་ཅེས་ཤེས་ན་འདི་ཉིད་དུ་ཚོ་ཐེ་དག་པའི་ཚུལ་གྱིས་འཇུག། ཅེས་སོགས་ཀྱི་ཤུགས་ལས་ཀྱང་རྟོགས་ཤིང་། ཡི་གེ་རྣམས་ཀྱི་ཀློག་ཚུལ་རང་གིས་ཀྱང་བདེ་བླག་ཏུ་གོ་བར་ནུས་ཏེ། ཀ་ཕྲེ་སོགས་བཞི་པོའི་ཕྱེ་པ་སོ་སོའི་དང་པོ་ལས་གཉིས་པ་སོགས་རིམ་པར་རྩོལ་བ་བསྐྱོད་པ་དང་། ཙ་ཚ་ཛ་གསུམ་ཡང་དེ་དག་གི་རིམ་པ་དང་མཚུངས་ཤིང་ཝ་ཞ་ཟ་འ་ཡ་ཤ་ས་རྣམས་ག་སོགས་དང་འདྲ་བ་དང་། ར་ལ་ཧ་ཨ་རྣམས་དེ་ལས་ཀྱང་ཅུང་ཟད་རྩོལ་བ་སྐྱོད་པར་མངོན་སུམ་གྱིས་གྲུབ་པའི་ཕྱིར་དང་། ཨ་ཡིག་ནི་ཀློག་ཚུལ་གྱིས་སོ་གཉིས་གཞན་ལས་སྐྱོད་པར་གྲུབ་ཅིང་། དེར་མ་ཟད་ཡི་གེའི་མདོར་སྡོམ་ཆེན་གྱི་ཡི་གེ་གཞན་རྣམས་བྱེ་བའི་རྩོལ་བ་ཅན་དུ་བྱས་ཤིང་ཨ་ཁོ་ན་མགྲིན་པ་བཙུམ་པའི་རྩོལ་བ་ཅན་དུ་བཞག་པས་ཀྱང་གྲུབ་པའི་ཕྱིར་རོ།། སྐབས་འདིར་འགྲེལ་བྱེད་ཕྲ་མ་ཁ་ཅིག་ཨ་ཡིག་རྟགས་མེད་དུ་འདོད་པ་དང་། ཁ་ཅིག་སོ་གཉིས་མམ་མ་ནིང་དུ་འདོད་པ་དང་། ཁ་ཅིག་མོ་རྟགས་སུ་འདོད་པ་རྣམས་བྱུང་ཡང་། ལུགས་དང་པོ་ལྟར་ན་ཐུ་མི་ཉིད་ཀྱིས་ཕྱེ་བ་བྱེད་དང་བརྒྱད་པོ་ཕྱེ་ཚན་ལྟར་ཕྱེ་བར་བསྟན་པ་དང་དངོས་སུ་འགལ་ཏེ་ཕྱེ་ཚན་ལྟར་མི་གཏོགས་པའི་རྟགས་མེད་ཀྱི་ཨ་ཡིག་ཁས་བླངས་པའི་ཕྱིར་རོ།། འདོད་པ་གཉིས་པ་ལྟར་ཡང་མི་ལེགས་ཏེ་འཆད་འགྱུར་ལྟར་གཞུང་གི་ཡི་གེ་ཉམས་པ་ཉིད་ཚད་མར་བཟུང་ནས་ཨ་ཡིག་ལ་ཧོལ་ཚོད་ཀྱིས་རིགས་འགྲེ་སྦྱར་བ་ཙམ་དུ་སྣང་བའི་ཕྱིར་རོ།། ལུགས་གསུམ་པ་ལ་འང་སྐྱོན་ཡོད་དེ་གཞུང་ཉིད་དུ་དམིགས་བསལ་གྱི་མོ་ཡིག་བོར་བསྒྲུབས་པའི་ཕྱིར་རོ།། ཡང་སྐབས་འདིར་འགྲེལ་བྱེད་ཕལ་ཆེར་མགྲིན་གཅིག་ཏུ་ར་ལ་ཧ་རྣམས་སོ་གཉིས་ཡིན་པར་མ་ཟད་མ་ནིང་མཚན་མེད་ཀྱང་ཡིན་པར་སྨྲ་བའང་འཐད་པར་མ་གོ་སྟེ། དེ་དག་གིས་ར་ལ་ཧ་ནི་སོ་གཉིས་སྟེ། མ་ནིང་མཚན་མེད་ཅེས་ཀྱང་བྱ། །ཞེས་གཞུང་གི་ཡི་གེ་ཉམས་པ་ཉིད་སྒྲ་དང་དོན་དུ་བཟུང་བས་ནོངས་པར་འདུག་པའི་ཕྱིར་རོ།། གཞུང་དེ་ལྟར་བསྒྲགས་པས་སྐྱོན་དུ་འགྱུར་བའི་ཕྱིར་རོ།། ཚུལ་ཇི་ལྟ་བུ་ཞེ་ན། སོ་གཉིས་དང་མ་ནིང་གི་གཞི་མཐུན་ཁས་ལེན་དགོས་པའི་ཕྱིར་དེ་ཉིད་དང་། ཕྱེ་བ་བྱེད་དང་བརྒྱད་པོ་ཕྱེ་ཚན་ལྔ་དུ་དབྱེ་དགོས་པ་ལ་དབྱེ་མི་ནུས་པའི་སྐྱོན་དུ་འང་འགྱུར་རོ།། དེ་ལ་སོ་གཉིས་དང་མ་ནིང་གི་གཞི་མཐུན་ཁས་བླངས་པས་ཅིར་འགྱུར་ཞེ་ན་བཤད་པར་བྱ་སྟེ། ཕྱིར་ག་ཡིག་ལྟ་བུ་ཕྱིར་བཏང་གསལ་བྱེད་རྣམས་མོ་ཡིག་ཏུ་བྱས་པའི་མོ་ཡིན་པ་དང་། ནང་གསེས་ཕྱེ་ཚན་ལྟར་དབྱེ་བའི་མོ་ཡིན་པ་ལྟ་བུ་མི་འགལ་ཡང་དབྱེ་སྒོ་གཅིག་ཉིད་ཀྱི་ཚེ་ནི་ཡི་གེའི་ལྗེ་གནས་ཀྱི་རྩོལ་བ་ཆེ་ཆུང་ངམ་སྒྲ་གྲིམས་སྐྱོད་སོགས་འབྱེད་ཆོས་ཐ་དད་པས་རྣམ་པར་བཞག་པའི་དབྱེ་བ་ཐ་དད་པ་རྣམས། ཆོས་ཅན་བྱེ་བྲག་པ་གཅིག་གི་སྟེང་དུ་འདུ་བར་རུང་བ་མ་ཡིན་ཏེ་དཔེར་ན་རྩོལ་བ་ཆེ་བའི་སྒྲ་གྲིམས་པའི་སྒོ་ནས་བཞག་པའི་ཕོ་ཡིག་ཀ་ལྟ་བུ་ལ། སྐབས་དེའི་མ་ནིང་དང་མོ་སོགས་ཀྱི་འབྱེད་ཆོས་བྱེད་པ་དང་རྩོལ་བ་མཉམ་པ་དང་སྐྱོད་པ་སོགས་ལྷན་ཅིག་ཏུ་འགལ་བ་འདུ་བའི་སྐབས་མེད་པ་བཞིན་ནོ།། དེས་ན་མ་ནིང་བྱེད་རྩོལ་བ་མཉམ་པའི་སྒོ་ནས་བཞག་པ་དང་། སོ་གཉིས་བྱེད་རྩོལ་བ་ཤིན་ཏུ་སྐྱོད་ཅིང་ཞན་པའི་སྒོ་ནས་བཞག་པ་གཉིས་དབྱེ་སྒོ་གཅིག་གི་ཚེ་ནས་ཡང་མི་འགྲིག་སྟེ། དཔེར་བྱས་པའི་མོ་གཉིས་དང་མ་ནིང་སོགས་ཀྱང་གཞི་གཅིག་ལ་གཉིས་ཀ་དང་གསུམ་ག་སོགས་ཡིན་པའི་མི་སྲིད་ཅིང་དེ་ལྟར་སྲིད་དོ་ཞེས་སྨྲ་བའང་འཇིག་རྟེན་གྱིས་གྲགས་པ་དང་འགལ་བ་བཞིན་དཔེ་ཅན་ཡང་མཚུངས་པའི་ཕྱིར་རོ།། ཡང་ཕྱེ་ཚན་ལྟར་དབྱེ་མི་ནུས་པའི་སྐྱོན་མེད་དེ། ར་ལ་ཧ་གསུམ་སོ་གཉིས་སུ་བཤད་པས་ཨ་ཡིག་སོ་གཉིས་སུ་ཤུགས་ཀྱིས་གོ་ནུས་པའི་ཕྱིར། རྣམ་ནའང་མི་འཐད་དེ་ཡི་གེ་གཞན་ཐམས་ཅད་ཞིབ་མོར་ཕྱེ་ནས་བཤད་ཅིང་ཨ་ཡིག་གཅིག་བུ་ཤུགས་བསྟན་དུ་བཞག་པ་ལ་ཉན་པ་པོ་ལ་ཐེ་ཚོམ་སྐྱེ་བ་སོགས་ཀྱི་རྒྱུ་ལས་དགོས་པ་གཞན་ཅིའང་མེད་པའི་ཕྱིར་རོ།། དེས་ན་གོང་དུ་བཀོད་པ་བཞིན། ཨ་ནི་མཚན་མེད་ཅེས་ཀྱང་བྱ། ཞེས་ཀློག་པ་ཉིད་དོན་དང་འབྱོར་ཏེ། ཀྱང་སྒྲས་བསྡུས་པས་ཨ་ཡིག་ར་ལ་ཧ་བཞིན་དུ་སོ་གཉིས་ཡིན་པར་གྲུབ་ཅིང་། མཚན་མེད་ཅེས་པས་དེ་སོ་གཉིས་ཡིན་ཡང་སོ་གཉིས་ཀྱི་ཡི་གེ་གཞན་གྱི་བྱེད་རྩོལ་གྱི་མཚན་ཉིད་ཏུ་ཀྱང་གསལ་བར་མངོན་མི་ནུས་པའི་རྒྱུ་མཚན་གྱིས་མཚན་མེད་ཅེས་ཀྱང་མིང་དུ་གདགས་པར་བྱའོ་ཞེས་པ་འདི་གྲུབ་པོ།། དེ་སྐ་ནའང་མཚན་མེད་ཅེས་པས་མ་ནིང་མཚན་མེད་ཉིད་བསྟན་པར་སོང་ངས་ཟླར་སྦྱོར་བའི་སྐྱོན་མི་ཤེས་སོ།། སྙམ་ན་རྟགས་པ་ལྟ་མི་དགོས་ཏེ། མ་ནིང་ལ་འགྱུར་བ་དང་། མཚན་གཉིས་དང་མཚན་མེད་གསུམ་དུ་དབྱེ་བ་རྟགས་འཇུག་གི་སྐབས་སུ་ཡིན་གྱི་འདིར་མི་འཁྲུག་བཞིན་དུ་དེ་ལྟར་ཚིགས་ཀྱིས་སྐྱོན་བ་དགོས་པ་མེད་པའི་ཕྱིར་རོ།། དེ་ལྟར་འདིར་ཡི་གེ་རྣམས་པའི་ཚུལ་དོན་གྱིས་རྒྱུ་མཚན་དེ་དག་གི་སྒོ་ནས་ཤེས་པར་མ་ཟད་ཡིག་གཟུགས་ལས་ཀྱང་མ་ནིང་དང་ཨ་ནི་ཞེས་པ་ལ་འཁྲུལ་གཞི་འབྱུང་རིགས་པར་རྟོགས་སླ་བ་ཡིན་གྱི། འགའ་ཞིག

ཏུ་ར་ལ་ཏ་ཡ་མོ་ག་ཤམ་སྟེ། ཞེས་དག་པར་འདོན་པའི་ཁྲུལ་བྱེད་པ་རྣམས་ནི་བརྟགས་པ་ཉིད་དོ།། འདིར་སྨྲས་པ།

ཐེ་ཚོམ་མཚན་མོ་བརྟན་བཞིན་དུ། ཐུ་མིའི་གཞུང་ལུགས་བལྟ་འདོད་རྣམས། སྔོན་ཆད་མཁས་པའི་ཁུར་འཛིན་པའི། འགྲེལ་བྱེད་འགའ་འགའི་ཡིད་མཁའ་ན། ནམ་ཡང་ཤར་ཞེས་མ་ཐོས་པའི། ཁོ་བོའི་ལེགས་བཤད་ཟླ་སྣང་འདི། གེགས་མེད་བསྟེན་ནས་རིགས་པའི་ལམ། དྭང་པོ་ཕྱོགས་སུ་འཇུག་པར་གྱིས།

གཉིས་པ་སྔོན་འཇུག་གི་རྟགས་ཀྱི་འཇུག་པ་བཤད་པ་ལ། མིང་གཞི་ལས་སྔོན་རྗེས་དབྱུང་བའི་ཚུལ། སྔོན་འཇུག་གི་རྟགས་ཀྱི་དབྱེ་བ། དེའི་འཇུག་ཚུལ་བཤད་པ་དང་གསུམ་གྱི་དང་པོ་ནི།

མོ་ཡི་ཡི་གེ་ནང་ནས་ནི། འཇུག་པའི་ཡི་གེ་བཅུ་དབྱུང་བྱ། འཇུག་པ་བཅུ་ཡི་ནང་ནས་ནི། སྔོན་འཇུག་ཡི་གེ་ལྔ་དབྱུང་བྱ།

ཞེས་པས་བསྟན་ཏེ། མོའི་ཡི་གེ་ལ་བཤད་མ་ཐག་པ་ལྟར་མོ་ཙམ་དང་ཤིན་ཏུ་མོ་དང་མོ་གཤམ་དང་གསུམ་དུ་གནས་པ་ས་སོ་སོར་མ་ཕྱེ་བའི་ནང་ནས་སྔར་སུམ་ཅུ་པར་བཤད་པ་ལྟར་རྗེས་འཇུག་གི་ཡི་གེ། ག་ང་ད་ན་བ་མ་འ་ར་ལ་ས་སྟེ་བཅུ་པོ་རྣམས་དབྱུང་བར་བྱ་ཞིང་། དེའི་ནང་ནས་ཀྱང་སྔོན་འཇུག་གི་ཡི་གེ། ག་ད་བ་མ་འ་ལྔ་པོ་རྣམས་དབྱུང་བར་བྱའོ།། ཞེས་སོ།།

གཉིས་པ་སྔོན་འཇུག་གི་རྟགས་ཀྱི་དབྱེ་བ་བཤད་པ་ནི།

སྔོན་འཇུག་ཡི་གེ་ལྔ་པོ་ལ། ཕོ་དང་མ་ནིང་མོ་དང་ནི། ཤིན་ཏུ་མོ་དང་བཞི་རུ་དབྱེ།

ཞེས་པས་བསྟན་ཏེ། བཤད་མ་ཐག་པའི་སྔོན་འཇུག་གི་ཡི་གེ་ལྔ་པོ་དེ་ལ། ཕོ་བ་ཡིག་དང་། མ་ནིང་ག་ད་གཉིས་མོ་འ་ཡིག ཤིན་ཏུ་མོ་མ་ཡིག་བཅས་བཞིར་དབྱེ་བར་བྱའོ། ཞེས་སོ། འདི་སྐབས་དབྱེ་ཚུལ་ལ་འབྲེལ་གཞི་མེད་པས་འགྲེལ་བྱེད་རྣམས་ཀྱང་དག་མཐུན་པར་སྣང་ལ། རྟགས་དེ་ལྟར་དབྱེ་བའི་རྒྱུ་མཚན་ནི། མིང་གཞི་ལྟར་སྔོན་འཇུག་གི་ཡི་གེ་རང་རང་ཀློག་པའི་སྒྲ་གྲིམས་ལྷོད་སོགས་ལས་ནི་མ་ཡིན་ཏེ་འཆད་འགྱུར་ལྟར་དེ་དག་འཇུག་ཡུལ་གྱི་མིང་གཞིའི་ཡི་གེའི་དང་སྦྱར་ནས་ཀློག་པའི་ཚེ་སྒྲ་གདངས་ཤུགས་ཆེ་ཆུང་དུ་འགྱུར་བའི་ཆ་ནས་བཞག་པའོ།།

གསུམ་པ་དེའི་འཇུག་ཚུལ་བཤད་པ་ལ། འཇུག་ཚུལ་རྟགས་བྱེད་ཀྱི་ཡན་ལག་རྣམས་མདོར་བསྟན་པ་དང་། དྲི་ལན་གྱི་སྒོ་ནས་རྒྱས་པར་བཤད་པ་གཉིས་ཀྱི།

དང་པོ་ནི།

དེ་དག་རེ་རེའང་བཞི་བྱེད་དེ། གང་ལ་འཇུག་བྱེད་གང་གིས་འཇུག ཇི་ལྟར་འཇུག་བྱེད་ཅི་ཕྱིར་འཇུག

ཅེས་པས་བསྟན་ཏེ། སྔོན་འཇུག་དེ་དག་གི་ཕོ་སོགས་རེ་རེའི་འཇུག་ཚུལ་ཡང་རྣམ་པ་བཞི་བཞིར་བྱེད་པ་སྟེ་བྱེད་པ་བཞི་བཞིའི་སྒོ་ནས་རྟོགས་པར་བྱེད་དགོས་སོ།། དེའང་འཇུག་ཡུལ་མིང་གཞིའི་ཡི་གེ་གང་དང་གང་ལ་འཇུག་པར་བྱེད་པ་དང་། འཇུག་པ་པོ་སྔོན་འཇུག་གང་གིས་འཇུག་པར་བྱེད་པ་དང་། སྦྱོར་ཚུལ་ཇི་ལྟ་བུས་འཇུག་པར་བྱེད་པ་དང་། དགོས་པ་ཅིའི་ཕྱིར་དུ་འཇུག་པ་པོར་བྱེད་པ་རྣམས་སོ།།

གཉིས་པ་དྲི་ལན་གྱི་སྒོ་ནས་རྒྱས་པར་བཤད་པ་ལ། གང་ལ་འཇུག་པར་བྱེད་པ་དང་གང་གིས་འཇུག་པར་བྱེད་པ་ཐུན་མོང་དུ་བསྟན་པ། ཇི་ལྟར་འཇུག་པར་བྱེད་པ་བསྟན་པ། ཅི་ཕྱིར་འཇུག་པར་བྱེད་པ་བསྟན་པ་སྟེ་གསུམ་མོ།། དང་པོ་ལ་དྲི་བས་མཚམས་སྦྱར་བ་དང་། ལན་གྱིས་བསྟན་པའོ།།

དང་པོ་ནི།

གང་ལ་འཇུག་པར་བྱེད་ཅེ་ན།

ཞེས་པའོ།། གཉིས་པ་ལན་ལ། ལན་དངོས་དང་། ཞར་བྱུང་གི་འཇུག་པ་བཤད་པ་གཉིས་ཀྱི་དང་པོ་ནི།

ཕོ་ནི་ཕོ་དང་མོ་ལའང་འཇུག། མོ་ནི་མོ་དང་མ་ནིང་ལ། མ་ནིང་ཡང་ནི་ཕོ་མོ་ལའང་།

ཤིན་ཏུ་མོ་ནི་མ་ནིང་དང་། མོ་དང་ཤིན་ཏུ་མོ་ཉིད་ལའོ།

ཞེས་པས་བསྟན་ཏེ། དེ་ལ་གང་གིས་འཇུག་པར་བྱེད་པ་པོ་སྔོན་འཇུག་གི་ཕོའི་ཡི་གེ་བ་དང་། རང་གི་རྗེ་པ་མ་ཡིན་པའི་མིང་གཞིའི་ཕོ་ཡིག་ཀ་ཅ་ཏ་ཙ་རྣམས་དང་། མོ་ཡིག་ག་ང་ཇ་ཉ་ད་ན་ཛ་ཞ་ཟ་ར་ཤ་ས་རྣམས་ལ་འཇུག་གོ། དེའང་། ཀ་ག་གཉིས་ལ་བརྟགས་འདོགས་རྐྱང་གསུམ་ཀར་དང་། ཙ་ད་གཉིས་ལ་རྐྱང་བརྟགས་གཉིས་ཀར་དང་། ང་ཇ་ཉ་ན་ཛ་རྣམས་ལ་བརྟགས་མ་ཡོ་ནར་དང་། ཙ་ཤ་གཉིས་ལ་རྐྱང་པ་ཡོ་ནར་དང་། ཞ་ས་གཉིས་ལ་རྐྱང་འདོགས་གཉིས་དང་། ར་འདོགས་ཅན་ཡོ་ན་རྗེ་དེ་རྣམས་ལ་འཇུག་པ་ཡིན་ནོ།། དེས་ན་འདི་སྐབས་སུ་རྐྱང་འཇུག་གི་དབང་དུ་བྱས་ནས་ཕོ་ལ་བ་ཡིག་འཇུག་ཚུལ་ནི། བཀའ། བཅས། བཏགས། བཙུགས། ལྟ་བུ་དང་།

མོ་ལ། བགོས། བདག། བཞེད། བཟང་། བཤད། བསམ། ལ་སོགས་པ་ལྟ་བུ་རྣམས་དཔེར་བརྗོད་པར་བྱའོ།། དེ་བཞིན་དུ་བརྟགས་འཇུག་གི་དབང་གིས། དཔེར་ན་ཕོ་ལ། བཀོ། བསྐོན། བཏམ། བསྐལ། བསྟོད། བརྟགས། སོགས་དང་།

མོ་ལ། བརླལ། བརླ། བརྡལ། བརྡུགས། བརྗོད། བརྡུས། བརྙེན། བདའ། བཞུད། བརྙོག། བརྡོག། བསྟུན། བརྗིང་ ལྟ་བུ་དང་། འདོགས་ཚུལ་གྱི་དབང་གིས། ཕོ་ལ། བཀྲི། བཀྱང་། བཀྱེད། བཀྲག། བཀྲུན། བཀྲུགས། སོགས་དང་།

མོ་ལ། བགྲུད། བགྲིངས། བགྲད། བགྲགས། བསྲང་། བཟླས། བརླབས། བསྲིངས། ལྟ་བུས་མཚོན་ཏེ་ཤེས་པར་བྱའོ།། དེ་བཞིན་དུ་སྦྱར་ཏེ།

སྔོན་འཇུག་གི་མོ་འ་ཡིག་ནི། མིང་གཞི་མོ་ག་ཇ་ད་བ་ཛ་རྣམས་དང་མ་ནིང་ཁ་ཆ་ཐ་ཕ་ཚ་རྣམས་ལ་རྐྱང་འཇུག་གིས་འཇུག་ཅིང་། དེ་རྣམས་ལས། ག་བ་ཁ་ཕ་རྣམས་ལ་འདོགས་འཇུག་དུའང་འཇུག་གོ།།

དཔེར་ན། རྐྱང་འཇུག་ལ། འགོད། འཇམ། འདམ། འབོལ། འཛོམ། འཁོར། འཆམ། འཐད། འཕགས། འཚལ་ལྟ་བུ་དང་།

འདོགས་འཇུག་ལ། འགྱེད། འབྱེད། འཁུར། འགྲོལ། འབྲེལ། འཁྲིན། འཕྲད། ལྟ་བུའོ།། སྔོན་འཇུག་གི་མ་ནིང་ག་ཡིག་ནི་མིང་གཞིའི་ཕོ་ཙ་ཏ་རྣམས་དང་། མོ་ཉ་ད་ན་ཞ་ཟ་ཡ་ཤ་ས་རྣམས་ལ་རྐྱང་འཇུག་ཡོ་ནར་འཇུག་གོ།

དཔེར་ན། གཅིག། གཏམས། གཙང་། གཉེར། གདངས། གནས། གཞལ། གཟུགས། གཡས། གཤམ། གསལ།

ལ་སོགས་པ་ལྟ་བུའོ།།

སྔོན་འཇུག་གི་མ་ནིང་ད་ཡིག་ནི། མིང་གཞིའི་ཕོ་ཀ་པ་གཉིས་དང་། མོ་ག་བ་གཉིས་ཏེ་བཞི་ལ་རྐྱང་འདོགས་གཉིས་ཀར་འཇུག་ཅིང་། མོ་ཡིག་ང་མ་གཉིས་ལ་རྐྱང་འཇུག་ཡོ་ནར་འཇུག་གོ།

དཔེར་ན། རྐྱང་ཚུལ་ལ། དཀོན། དཔའ། དགའ། དབང་། དངར། དམར། ལྟ་བུ་དང་།

འདོགས་ཅན་ལ། དཀྱིལ། དཔྱད། དཀྲིས། དབྱངས། དཀྲོགས། དགྲམ། དབྱིག་ལྟ་བུའོ།།

སྔོན་འཇུག་གི་ཤིན་ཏུ་མོ་མ་ཡིག་ནི། མིང་གཞིའི་མ་ནིང་ཁ་ཆ་ཐ་ཚ་རྣམས་དང་། མོ་ཡིག་ག་ཇ་ད་ཛ་རྣམས་དང་། ཤིན་ཏུ་མོ་ང་ཉ་ན་རྣམས་ལ་རྐྱང་འཇུག་གིས་འཇུག་ཅིང་། དེ་ལས་ཁ་ག་གཉིས་ལ་འདོགས་འཇུག་དུའང་འཇུག་གོ།

དཔེར་ན། རྐྱང་འཇུག་ལ། མཁའ། མཆན། མཐོང་། མཚན། མགུ། མཇེད། མདོག། མཛད། མངོན། མཉེས། མནབས། ལྟ་བུ་དང་།

འདོགས་འཕུལ་ལ། མཆིན། མཐྲངས། མཇུགས། མགྲིན་ལྷ་བུའོ།། སྐབས་འདིར་འབྲེལ་བྱེད་ཕྱི་མ་ཁ་ཅིག་གིས། ཕོ་ནི་ཕོ་དང་མོ་ལ་འཇུག། ཅེས་པའི་གཞུང་གིས་རྐྱང་བརྩེགས་གཉིས་ཀའི་འཕུལ་འཇུག་བསྟན་པར་འདོད་བཞིན་དུ་ང་ཇ་ཉ་ན་ཛ་རྣམས་ལ་བརྩེགས་འཕུལ་དང་། ར་ཡིག་ལ་འདོགས་འཕུལ་གྱི་འཇུག་ཚུལ་ཐོག་མར་འཆད་པར་མི་བྱེད་ཅིང་། ངག་དོན་གྱི་ཟུར་ཚིག་འགོད་པའི་ཚེ་དེ་དག་ལས་ན་ར་གཉིས་ལ་འཇུག་ཚུལ་བཤད་པ་དང་། ཅི་ཕྱིར་འཇུག་གི་སྐབས་སུ་དེ་རྣམས་ཐམས་ཅད་ཀྱི་དཔེར་བརྗོད་རྒྱས་པར་འགོད་པའི་འགལ་བའི་ཕུང་པོ་ཆེན་པོ་སྤྲོ་བར་བྱེད་པ་ནི་ཤིན་ཏུ་མི་རིགས་སོ། ཕྱིར་རྒྱས་བཤད་དང་དེའི་ངག་དོན་བསྡུས་པའི་ཟུར་ཚིག་མཐུན་དགོས་ཤིང་དེ་དག་དང་། དེ་དག་ཉིད་ཀྱི་རྣམ་གཞག་གི་དཔེར་བརྗོད་མཐུན་དགོས་པའི་ཕྱིར་དང་། རྒྱུ་དེས་མོ་ལ་ཞེས་པའི་མོ་ཡིག་རིགས་ཀྱི་ལ་མི་འདོད་པར་ག་ཛ་བ་ད་སོགས་མོ་ཡིག་བཅུ་གཉིས་པོ་ཁོ་ནར་བསམས་ནང་། ཁྱེད་རང་གི་ཟུར་ཚིག་ཏུ་ན་ར་གཉིས་བྱུང་བ་དང་འགལ་བར་མ་ཟད་གཞུང་གི་དཔེར་བརྗོད་དང་འགལ་བའི་ཕྱིར་དང་།

ཕོ་ནི་ཕོ་དང་མོ་ལ་འཇུག།

ཅེས་པས་སྔོན་འཇུག་གི་ཕོའི་འཇུག་ཡུལ་ཐམས་ཅད་བསྡུས་ནས་བསྟན་པར་འདོད་དགོས་པ་གང་ཞིག། དེའི་འཇུག་ཡུལ་འགའ་ཞིག་མ་ཚང་བར་བཤད་པས་གཞུང་དོན་དང་ཡང་འགལ་བའི་ཕྱིར་རོ། དང་པོ་གྲུབ་སྟེ། གཞུང་འདིར་སྔོན་འཇུག་གི་མོ་དང་མ་ནིང་སོགས་ཀྱི་འཇུག་ཡུལ་ཐམས་ཅད་བསྟན་པར་ཁྱེད་རང་ཡང་འདོད་ཅིང་། དེ་ལས་ཕོ་ཡིག་གི་འཇུག་ཡུལ་ཚང་བར་མ་བསྟན་པར་འདོད་པ་ལ་དགོས་པ་སོར་ཅི་ཡང་བཤད་དུ་མེད་པའི་ཕྱིར་རོ།། ཁ་ཅིག་འདིར་བསྟན་རྐྱང་འཕུལ་ཁོ་ནར་འདོད་པ་ཡོད་ཀྱང་གཞུང་གི་བསྟན་ཚུར་རྫོགས་པར་མི་འགྱུར་བའི་ཕྱིར་ཁྱབ་ཆུང་བ་ཉིད་དུ་ཟད་ཅིང་། དེ་སྐད་འདོད་པའང་མོ་ལ་ཞེས་པ་མོ་ཡིག་གི་ཚིག་ལ་མ་བརྟགས་པའི་སྐྱོན་ཉིད་དུ་གསལ་ལོ། དོན་ཀྱང་དེ་དག་གིས་མ་ནིང་གི་འཇུག་པ་འཆད་པའི་ཚེ་ནི་མོ་ལ་ཞེས་པ་མོ་ཡིག་ཁྱེར་ཤེ་འདོད་ཀ་མེད་བྱུང་སྣང་ངོ་།། ཡང་ཕྱི་དུས་གངས་ཅན་དུ་བོད་དག་གི་སློབ་ཆེན་བརྗོད་པ་པོ་རྣམས་མགྲིན་གཅིག་ཏུ་ཡ་ར་ལ་གསུམ་གྱི་འདོགས་དང་འབྲེལ་བའི་ཀ་ལ་སོགས་པ་མིང་གཞིའི་ཡི་གེ་གཉིས་འབྲེལ་ཅན་རྣམས་འཕུལ་བྱེད་གང་གིས་ཕུལ་རྐྱང་འཕུལ་དུ་བཞེད་ཀྱང་། ཡང་ཞིབ་མོར་དཔྱད་ན་དེ་ལྟར་འཐད་པ་མ་ཡིན་ཏེ། སྐབས་འདིར་རྐྱང་པའི་གོ་དོན་སྔོན་འཇུག་གི་འཇུག་ཡུལ་དུ་རྗེས་འཇུག་མི་བརྩེ་བའི་མིང་གཞིའི་ཡི་གེ་ཉིད་རེ་རེ་ཡིན་ན་རྐྱང་པ་དང་། གཉིས་གསུམ་འབྲེལ་པ་ཡིན་ན་བརྩེགས་མའི་ཐ་སྙད་འཇུག་ཅིང་། འདོགས་ཅན་ཞེས་ཐ་སྙད་ཙམ་དུ་བྱེད་པའང་བརྩེགས་མའི་དབྱེ་བ་ཉིད་ཡིན་པའི་ཕྱིར། བཀྱེ། བསྒྲན། བཀླས། བཙན་སོགས་མིང་གཞི་གཉིས་འབྲེལ་ཅན་རྣམས་ལ་རྐྱང་པའི་སྒྲས་བརྗོད་ཚེ་ཐ་སྙད་ལ་མ་ཤོང་བའི་དགག་ཏུ་འགྱུར་ཞིང་། ཡ་ར་ལ་གསུམ་ཀ་ཡའི་ཡ་ཀྱང་དུ་བསྟན་བཞིན་དུ་འདིར་ལྷ་ཡི་མཆོད་བྱེད་ཀྱི་གི་གུ་དང་ཞབས་ཀྱུ་སོགས་དང་མཚུངས་པར་ཡི་གེའི་ཡན་ལག་ཙམ་ལས་ཡི་གེ་དངོས་ཡིན་པར་བྱས་ནས་དེ་རྣམས་ལྡན་པའི་ཡི་གེ་ལ་རྐྱང་པར་བརྩིས་པས་དོན་ལ་འཐད་འཁྲུལ་པ་དང་། དེ་ལྟ་ན་བརྩེགས་འཕུལ་གཞན་རྣམས་ལའང་རྒྱུ་མཚན་མཚུངས་པས་ཁྱད་པར་མེད་པར་རྐྱང་འཕུལ་དུ་བརྗོད་དགོས་པར་ཡང་འགྱུར་རོ།། ཡང་སྐབས་འདིར་བརྩེགས་མ་དང་། འདོགས་ཅན་རྣམས་ལ་འཕུལ་ཡིག་འཇུག་པའི་ཚེ་མགོ་འདོགས་ཀྱི་ཡི་གེ་རྣམས་འཕུལ་ཡིག་གི་ཡུལ་ཡིན་མིན་ལ་སྔོན་ཚད་སུས་ཀྱང་དངོས་སུ་དཔྱད་པ་མ་མཐོང་མོད། གཞན་དོན་ལ་བརྟགས་ན་མགོ་ཅན་དང་འདོགས་ཅན་གྱི་ཡི་གེ་དངོས་གཞི་དེ་ཉིད་ལས་གཞན་རྣམས་འཕུལ་འཇུག་གི་ཡུལ་དུ་མི་འདོད་པར་སྣང་བ། གཙོ་ཆེ་ཆུང་གི་དབང་དུ་བྱས་ན་ནི་དེ་བཞིན་འཐད་པ་ཡང་ཡིན་ཏེ། བ་ཡིག་གི་འཇུག་ཡུལ་གྱི་རྗེས་འཇུག་མི་བརྩེ་བའི་མིང་གཞིའི་ཡི་གེ་གཉིས་གསུམ་འབྲེལ་པ། བཀྱེ། བཀལ། བརྒྱད། ལྟ་བུ་ལ་རིམ་པར་ཀ་ཡ་དང་ར་ག་དང་ས་ག་ལ་རྣམས་སོ་སོར་གཞིའི་ཡི་གེ་རང་སྒྲ་ཐུབ་པ་རེ་ཡིན་པར་མཚུངས་ཀྱང་བརྗོད་པའི་ཚེ་དེ་དག་ལས། རང་སྡེའི་ཀ་དང་ག་དང་ག་རྣམས་ཀྱི་སྒྲ་གཙོ་བོར་འབྱུང་བའི་ཕྱིར་གཞུང་འདིར་ཡང་དེའི་དབང་དུ་མཛད་ནས་སྔོན་འཇུག་རྣམས་ཡི་གེ་གང་འཇུག་ཚུལ་གསུངས་པར་སྣང་བ་རང་གི་སྡེ་དང་འཕྲད་པ་ན།

མི་འཇུག་པ་ནི་འདི་ལྟ་སྟེ། ཕོ་ཡང་མོ་ལ་འཇུག་མི་འགྱུར།

ཞེས་བསྟན་པས་ཤེས་པར་ནུས་པའི་ཕྱིར་ཏེ། གཞན་དུ། འགྱེད་ཅེས་པ་ལྟ་བུ་འ་ཡིག་རང་སྡེའི་ཡ་ལ་འཇུག་པར་འགྱུར་བའི་ཕྱིར་རོ། ཕྱིར་ནི་དེ་འདྲའི་མགོ་འདོགས་ཀྱི་

ཡི་གེ་རྣམས་འཕུལ་ཡིག་གི་འཇུག་ཡུལ་ཙམ་ཡིན་པར་འདོད་པ་འགལ་བ་མེད་པར་མ་ཟད་ངེས་པར་ཁས་ལེན་དགོས་སོ། །ཙམ་པ་ལྟ་བུའི་བ་ཡིག་སྔོན་འཇུག་དང་ད་ཡིག་རྗེས་འཇུག་དང་། ས་ཀ་ཡ་གསུམ་མེད་གཉེར་འགྱུར་ཞིང་། མིང་གཞི་དེ་གསུམ་ག་སྔོན་རྗེས་དེ་དག་གི་འཇུག་ཡུལ་ཡིན་པ་ཙམ་དུ་མཚུངས་པའི་ཕྱིར་ཏེ་མིང་གཞིའི་ཡི་གེ་ཡིན་ན་སྔོན་རྗེས་གཉིས་ཀའམ་གང་རུང་གི་འཇུག་ཡུལ་ཡིན་པས་ཁྱབ་པའི་ཕྱིར་རོ། །དེ་ལྟ་བུའི་ས་ཡ་གཉིས་པོ་དེ་རྗེས་འཇུག་གི་ཡུལ་དུ་རུང་གི་སྔོན་འཇུག་གི་ཡུལ་དུ་མི་རུང་ངོ་ཞེ་ན་འང་གོང་སྨོས་ལྟར་འདིར་བསྟན་གཙོ་ཆེ་རུང་གི་འཇུག་ཚུལ་གྱི་དབང་དུ་བྱས་ན་བདེན་མོད། ཕྱིར་བཏང་ཙམ་ལ་མི་རུང་བའི་རྒྱུ་མཚན་ཅིའང་བཤད་དུ་མེད་དོ།

གཉིས་པ་ཞར་བྱུང་དུ་མི་འཇུག་པ་བཤད་པ་ནི།

ཕོ་ནི་མ་ནིང་ལ་མི་འཇུག། མོ་ཡང་ཕོ་ལ་འཇུག་མི་འགྱུར། མ་ནིང་རང་ལ་རང་མི་འཇུག།
རང་གི་སྡེ་དང་ལྡན་པ་ན། ཕོ་ཡང་མོ་ལ་འཇུག་མི་འགྱུར། མ་ནིང་མོ་ཡང་དེ་བཞིན་ནོ།།

ཞེས་བསྟན་ཏེ། སྔོན་འཇུག་གི་ཕོ་བ་ཡིག་ནི་མིང་གཞིའི་མ་ནིང་ཁ་ཆ་ཐ་ཕ་ཚ་རྣམས་ལ་མི་འཇུག་ཅིང་། སྔོན་འཇུག་གི་མོ་འ་ཡིག་དང་དེའི་ཤུགས་ཀྱིས་ཤིན་ཏུ་མོ་མ་ཡིག་དག་ནི་མིང་གཞིའི་ཕོ་ཀ་ཅ་ཏ་པ་ཙ་རྣམས་མི་འཇུག་པ་དང་། དེ་བཞིན་དུ་སྔོན་འཇུག་གི་མ་ནིང་ག་ད་གཉིས་ཀྱང་རང་སྡེའི་ཕོ་མོ་དག་ལ་མི་འཇུག་པས་ག་ཡིག་མིང་གཞིའི་ཀ་ཁ་ག་ང་རྣམས་དང་། ད་ཡིག་ཏ་ད་ན་རྣམས་ལ་མི་འཇུག་ཅིང་། སྔོན་འཇུག་གི་མོ་ཡིག་འ་ནི་རང་སྡེའི་མིང་གཞིའི་མོ་འ་ཡ་གཉིས་དང་མ་ནིང་ཛ་ཡིག་ལ་མི་འཇུག་པ་དང་། ཡང་སྔའི་ཤུགས་ཀྱིས་སྔོན་འཇུག་གི་ཤིན་ཏུ་མོ་མ་ཡིག་ནི་རང་སྡེ་ཡི་མིང་གཞིའི་མོ་དང་མ་ནིང་ཕ་བ་མ་རྣམས་ལ་འཇུག་པ་མ་ཡིན་ནོ་ཞེས་སོ།

འགྲེལ་བྱེད་ཁ་ཅིག་གིས། སྐབས་འདིར་གང་གིས་འཇུག་བྱེད་འཇུད་པའི་གཞུང་འཇུད་པར་འདོད་པ་ཡོད་ཀྱང་གོང་སྨོས་བཞིན་འདིར་འཇུག་བྱེད་དང་འཇུག་ཡུལ་ལྷན་ཅིག་ཏུ་གསལ་བར་བསྟན་པ་མཐོང་བཞིན་དེ་ལས་ལྡོག་སྟེ་སྦྱ་བ་ལ་དགོས་པ་ཅི་ཞིག་ཡོད་བསམས་དགོས་ཤིང་། མ་བཅད་ཟུར་པ་ཞིག་ངེས་པར་དགོས་སོ་སྙམ་ནའང་འཇུག་བྱེད་ཀྱི་དོན་གསལ་བར་མཚོན་པའི་ངག་བཀོད་ཟིན་ནས་སྐྱར་ཡང་དེ་ཉིད་སྐུར་བ་ནི་ཟློས་པའི་སྐྱོན་དུ་འགྱུར་རོ།

གཉིས་པ་ཇི་ལྟར་འཇུག་པར་བྱེད་པ་བསྟན་པ་ལ་དྲི་བས་མཚམས་སྦྱར་བ་དང་། ལན་གྱིས་བསྟན་པ་གཉིས། དང་པོ་ནི།

ཇི་ལྟར་འཇུག་པར་བྱེད་ཅེ་ན།

ཞེས་པའོ། །གཉིས་པ་ནི།

ཕོ་ནི་དྲག་པོའི་ཚུལ་གྱིས་ཏེ། མ་ནིང་རན་པར་འཇུག་པ་ཡིན། མོ་ནི་ཞན་པས་ཚུལ་གྱིས་ཏེ།
ཤིན་ཏུ་མོ་ནི་མཉམ་པས་སོ། རང་ཡུལ་ཡི་གེ་ཐམས་ཅད་ལ། འཇུག་པའི་ཚུལ་གྱིས་གནས་པའོ།

ཞེས་གསུངས་ཏེ། སྔོན་འཇུག་གི་ཕོ་ཡིག་བ་ནི་མིང་གཞིའི་ཡི་གེ་རང་གི་འཇུག་ཡུལ་དུ་གྱུར་པ་རྣམས་ལ་སྒྲ་དང་བྱེད་རྩོལ་དྲག་པོའི་སྒོ་ནས་འཇུག་པ་དང་། མ་ནིང་ག་ད་གཉིས་ནི་སྒྲ་རྩོལ་རན་པས་འཇུག་པ་དང་། མོ་ཡིག་འ་ནི་སྒྲ་རྩོལ་ཞན་པས་འཇུག་པ་དང་། ཤིན་ཏུ་མོ་མ་ནི་སྒྲ་རྩོལ་མཉམ་པ་སྟེ་ཤིན་ཏུ་ལྷོད་པའི་ཚུལ་གྱིས་འཇུག་པར་བྱེད་དོ། ཞེས་སོ། གཞན་དག་འདིར་མཉམ་པ་ཞེས་པ་དྲག་ཞན་མཉམ་པར་འདོད་པ་ཡོད་ཀྱང་། དེ་ལྟ་ན་མ་ནིང་གི་འཇུག་ཚུལ་དང་ཟློས་པར་འགྱུར་ཞིང་། ཕྱིར་གོང་དུ་བཤད་པ་ལྟར་ཤིན་ཏུ་མོ་ཞེས་པ་མོ་ཡིག་ཏུ་འདོད་དགོས་པས་སྒྲ་རྩོལ་ཞན་པས་འཇུག་པ་ལས་ཁྱད་མེད་ཅིང་ལྷག་པར་ཤིན་ཏུའི་སྒྲས་སྒྲ་རྩོལ་ཤིན་ཏུ་ཞན་པས་འཇུག་པ་ཉིད་དེ་མཉམ་པ་ཞེས་པ་ཉམ་ཆུང་བ་ལ་འཇུག་པ་ཡོད་ཅིང་ད་ལྟ་ཡུལ་འགའི་སྐྱེ་བོ་ལ་དེ་ལྟ་བུའི་བརྡ་ཆགས་པའང་མཐོང་ངོ་། །འགྲེལ་བྱེད་ཕལ་མོ་ཆེས་སྐབས་འདིའི་འཇུག་ཚུལ་དྲག་ཞན་སོགས་སྒྲ་གདངས་ཁོ་ནའི་སྒོ་ནས་བཤད་པར་འདོད་ཀྱང་ལེགས་པ་མ་ཡིན་ཏེ། ཕོ་དང་མ་ནིང་གི་འཇུག་ཚུལ་ལ་སྒྲ་དྲག་ཞན་གྱི་དབྱེ་བ་ཆེར་མེད་ཀྱང་གཙོ་བོར་བྱེད་རྩོལ་ཆེ་ཆུང་གི་སྒོ་ནས་འབྱེད་དགོས་ཤིང་། གཞན་རྣམས་ཀྱང་སྒྲ་གདངས་དྲག་ཞན་དུ་མ་ཟད་བྱེད་རྩོལ་ཆེ་ཆུང་གི་ཁྱད་པ་རེའང་ཞིབ་མོའི་བློས་དཔྱད་ན་མངོན་སུམ་གྱིས་གྲུབ་པའི་ཕྱིར་རོ།

གསུམ་པ་ཅི་ཕྱིར་འཇུག་པར་བྱེད་པ་བསྟན་པ་ལ་དྲི་བས་མཚམས་སྦྱར་བ་དང་ལན་གྱིས་བཤད་པའོ། །དང་པོ་ནི།

ཅི་ཕྱིར་འཇུག་པར་བྱེད་ཅེ་ན།

ཞེས་པའོ།

གཉིས་པ་ལ། གཞུང་དོན་བདེ་བླག་ཏུ་རྟོགས་པའི་ཕྱིར་འདིར་བསྟན་གྱི་བདག་གཞན་དང་དུས་གསུམ་ཕྱིར་བཤད་པ་དང་གཞུང་དོན་གྱི་ལན་དངོས་བཤད་པ་སྟེ་གཉིས་ལས།

དང་པོ་ལ། དངོས་དང་མཐའ་དཔྱད་གཉིས། དང་པོ་ནི། འཆད་པར་འགྱུར་བ།

ཕོ་ནི་འདས་དང་གཞན་བསྒྲུབ་ཕྱིར།

ཞེས་སོགས་ཀྱི་གོ་དོན་དཔྱིས་ཕྱིན་པར་བྱ་བར་ལ། ཐོག་མར་འདིར་ཤེས་དགོས་སྟེ། ལས་གང་ཞིག་བྱེད་པ་པོ་གཞན་དང་དངོས་སུ་འབྲེལ་བའི་དབང་དུ་བྱས་ནས། བྱེད་པ་པོའི་དངོས་པོ་དེ་ཉིད་དང་དེའི་བྱེད་པ་དང་བཅས་པ་ལ་ནི་བདག་ཅེས་བྱ་ཞིང་། དེས་བསྒྲུབ་པར་བྱ་བའི་ཡུལ་གྱི་དངོས་པོ་བྱ་བ་དང་བཅས་པ་ལ་ནི་གཞན་ཞེས་བྱའོ།། དེ་བཞིན་དུ་བྱེད་པ་གཞན་དང་དངོས་སུ་འབྲེལ་མ་འབྲེལ་ཇི་ལྟར་ཡང་རུང་བྱ་བ་བྱས་ཟིན་པ་ནི་དུས་འདས་པ་དང་། བྱ་བ་བྱེད་པར་འགྱུར་བ་ནི་དུས་མ་འོངས་པ་དང་། བྱ་བ་བྱེད་བཞིན་པ་ནི་དུས་ད་ལྟ་བ་ཡིན་ནོ། གཞན་དུ་བྱེད་པའི་ལས་དང་བྱ་བའི་ལས་ཞེས་ལས་ཀྱི་ཚིག་ལ་གཉིས་སུ་དབྱེ་བའང་དབྱེ་བ་དེ་དག་ཏུ་འདུས་ཏེ་དུས་གསུམ་གྱི་དབང་གིས་བྱེད་པའི་ལས་ནི་དུས་ད་ལྟ་བ་དང་བྱ་བའི་ལས་ནི་དུས་མ་འོངས་པར་འདུ་ཞིང་བདག་གཞན་གྱི་དབང་གིས་བྱེད་པོ་གཞན་དང་དངོས་སུ་འབྲེལ་བའི་བྱེད་པ་བདག་དང་བྱ་བ་གཞན་ཡིན་པ་བཤད་མ་ཐག་པ་ལྟར་རོ།། རྒྱུ་མཚན་འདིས་དུས་གསུམ་གྱི་དབྱེ་བས་ནི་བྱེད་ལས་དང་འབྲེལ་བའི་ངག་གི་སྦྱོར་བ་ཐམས་ཅད་ལ་ཁྱབ་ཅིང་། བདག་གཞན་གྱི་དབྱེ་བས་ནི་དེ་ཙམ་དུ་ཁྱབ་པ་མ་ཡིན་ཡང་། གཞུང་འདིར་བྱེད་པ་པོ་དང་བྱ་བའི་ཡུལ་གྱི་སྒྲ་རྣམས་བསྒྲུབ་པའི་ཕྱིར་བདག་གཞན་གྱི་དབྱེ་བ་ཟུར་དུ་མཛད་པ་ཡིན་ཞིང་དེའི་ཞར་ལས་བདག་གཞན་དང་འབྲེལ་བའི་བྱ་བྱེད་ཀྱི་ཚིག་ཕན་ཚུན་ཤེད་མཚུངས་པ་རྣམས་ཀྱང་བསྡུས་པ་ཡིན་ནོ། དེས་ན་ཅི་ཕྱིར་རྟགས་འཇུག་གི་གཞུང་འདི་འཆད་པའི་སྐབས་སུ་དུས་གསུམ་གྱི་དབྱེ་བས་བཤད་པ་རྣམས་ནི། བདག་གཞན་གྱི་དབྱེ་བས་མ་ཁྱབ་པའི་ལྷག་མ་རྣམས་བསྡུ་བའི་དོན་དུ་བལྟ་བར་བྱའོ། དེ་ལྟར་ངེས་པར་བྱས་ནས་དབྱེ་བ་དེ་དག་གི་དཔེར་བརྗོད་རྒྱས་པར་གཤམ་དུ་འཆད་འགྱུར་རྣམས་མ་འཛིངས་པར་རྟོགས་པར་བྱ་དགོས་མོད་ཀྱི། འདིར་ཡང་གོ་བདེ་བའི་ཕྱིར་རྣམ་གསལ་གྱི་དཔེར་བརྗོད་ཅུང་ཟད་འགོད་ན།

བྱེད་པ་པོ་བདག་གི་དངོས་པོའི་སྒྲ་ནི། སྒྲུབ་པ་པོ། སྟོན་པ་པོ། གཅོད་པ་པོ། འདྲེན་པ་པོ། སྒྲུབ་བྱེད། སྟོན་བྱེད། གཅོད་བྱེད། འདྲེན་བྱེད་ལྟ་བུ་དང་། དེའི་བྱེད་པའི་ཚིག་གསལ་བར་བྱེད་པ། སྒྲུབ་པར་བྱེད། སྟོན་པར་བྱེད། གཅོད་པར་བྱེད། འདྲེན་པར་བྱེད། སྒྲུབ་པོ། སྟོན་ཏོ། གཅོད་དོ། འདྲེན་ནོ། ལྟ་བུ་དང་།

བྱ་བའི་ཡུལ་གཞན་གྱི་དངོས་པོའི་སྒྲ་ནི། བསྒྲུབ་པར་བྱ་བ། བསྟན་པར་བྱ་བ། གཅད་པར་བྱ་བ། དྲང་བར་བྱ་བ། བསྒྲུབ་བྱ། བསྟན་བྱ། གཅད་པར་བྱ། དྲང་བར་བྱ། ལྟ་བུ་དང་།

དེའི་བྱ་བའི་ཚིག། བསྒྲུབ་པར་བྱ། བསྟན་པར་བྱ། དྲང་བར་བྱ། སྒྲུབ་བོ། བསྟན་ཏོ། གཅད་དོ། དྲང་ངོ། ལྟ་བུ་དང་། དབྱེ་བ་དེ་གཉིས་སུ་མ་འདུས་པའི་དུས་གསུམ་ལས་བྱུང་བ་ཞིན།

འདས་པའི་སྒྲ་ནི། བསྒྲུབས། བསྟན། བཅད། བྱུང་། གྲུབ། ཆད། བྱུང་། ལྟ་བུ་དང་།

བྱེད་བཞིན་ད་ལྟ་བའི་སྒྲ་ནི། ད་ལྟ་སྒྲུབ་བཞིན་པ། སྟོན་བཞིན་པ། གཅོད་བཞིན་པ། འདྲེན་བཞིན་པ། འགྲུབ་པར་བྱེད། འཆད་པར་བྱེད། འབྱུང་བར་བྱེད། འགྲུབ་བཞིན་པ། འཆད་བཞིན་པ། འབྱུང་བཞིན་པ་ལྟ་བུ་དང་།

བྱ་འགྱུར་མ་འོངས་པའི་སྒྲ་ནི། འགྲུབ་པར་འགྱུར། འཛད་པར་འགྱུར། འབྱུང་བར་འགྱུར། འགྲུབ་བོ།། འཛད་དོ།། འབྱུང་ངོ་།། འགྲུབ་པར་བྱ། འབྱུང་བར་བྱ་ལྟ་བུ་སྟེ། འདི་དག་གིས་མཚོན་ནས་ཀུན་ལ་བསྒྲེ་བར་བྱའོ།

འདིར་བྱེད་པ་པོ་གཞན་དང་དངོས་སུ་འབྲེལ་མ་འབྲེལ་ངེས་སྦྱོར་བ་ནི། དངོས་པོ་གང་ཞིག་ལ་ལས་གང་ཞིག་བྱེད་པ་པོ་གཞན་གྱིས་དངོས་སུ་བསྒྲུབ་པར་བྱེད་པ་དེ་ནི་བྱེད་པ་པོ་གཞན་དང་དངོས་སུ་འབྲེལ་བའི་ལས་སྟེ། དཔེར་ན། ལྕགས་གསེར་དུ་བསྒྱུརད་ཟེར། བསྒྱུར་བར་བྱ། སྒྱུར་བར་བྱེད། ཤིང་བཅད་ཟེར། བཅད་པར་བྱ། གཅོད་པར་བྱེད། འབྲུ་ཁུངས་ནས་ཕྱུང་ཟེར། དབྱུང་བར་བྱ། འབྱིན་པར་བྱེད་ཅེས་པ་དུས་གསུམ་གྱི་དབྱེ་བས་ཤེས་པར་བྱ་ཞིང་། དངོས་པོ་གང་ཞིག་ལ་ལས་གང་ཞིག་བྱེད་པ་པོ་གཞན་དངོས་སུ་མེད་པར་རང་གིས་རང་གིས་གྲུབ་པར་སྣང་བ་འདི་ནི་བྱེད་པ་པོ་གཞན་དང་དངོས་སུ་མ་འབྲེལ་བའི་ལས་ཏེ། དཔེར་ན། ལྕགས་གསེར་དུ་གྱུརད་ཟེར། འགྱུར་བཞིན་པ། འགྱུར་བར་འགྱུར་རོ། ཤིང་ཆད་ཟེར། འཆད་བཞིན་པ། འཆད་པར་འགྱུར་རོ། གནས་ནས་བྱུང་། འབྱུང་བཞིན་པ། འབྱུང་བར་འགྱུར་རོ། ཞེས་སོགས་ཀྱི་བྱེ་བྲག་ནས་རྟོགས་པར་བྱའོ།།

དེ་ལས་ཐ་མའི་དོན་ནི་རྟོགས་སླ་ལ། ཕྱི་མ་ནི་དཔེར་ན་སྐྱེས་བུ་ཞིག་གི་མདུན་དུ་ལྕགས་དོང་རང་བཞིན་གྱིས་གསེར་དུ་གྱུར་པའི་ཚེ་ལྕགས་རང་ཉིད་ལ་ཡོད་པའི་འགྱུར་བ་རྣམས་ཀྱི་བྱེད་པས་དེ་བཞིན་དུ་འགྱུར་ཀྱང་གཞན་གྱིས་མ་ཡིན་པ། སྐྱེས་བུ་དེ་ཡི་བློ་ངོ་ན་ལས་ཀྱིས་དེ་བཞིན་དུ་གྲུབ་ཅེས་བརྗོད་ནམས་ཉིད་བྱེད་པ་པོ་གཞན་ཡིན་མོད་ཀྱི་དེ་ནི་དངོས་སུ་མི་སྣང་བ་ལྟ་བུ་དང་། སྐྱེས་བུ་གང་ཞིག་གནས་ནས། འབྱིན་པ་པོ་མེད་པར་རང་ཉིད་གནས་འབྱུང་བའི་ཚེ་རང་ཉིད་བྱེད་པ་པོ་ཡིན་མོད་ཀྱི་བྱེད་པ་པོ་གཞན་མེད་པ་སོགས་ཀྱིས་མཚོན་ནས་ཞིབ་མོའི་བློས་ངེས་པར་བྱའོ།།

གཉིས་པ་ནི། སྐབས་འདིར་འབྲེལ་བྱེད་ཀྱི་ཚ་ཕལ་ཆེར་གྱིས་ངེས་པ་རྟོགས་པ་རེ་ཞིབ་བཤད་ན་མཛད་ལ་ཅུང་ཟད་བཤད་པ་རྣམས་ཀྱང་དོན་དང་མི་འཕྲོད་པ་མང་ཞིང་། བཤད་པ་འགྲིག་ཏུ་རུང་བ་རྣམས་ཀྱང་བློ་ཅི་གདད་མཚམས་ཀྱི་དཔེར་བརྗོད་པོ་རེ་བར་བཀོད་པ་ཙམ་དང་བས། དེ་དག་གི་སོ་སོ་ནས་ཞིབ་མོར་བཤད་ན་ཡི་གེ་མང་བས་འཇིགས་པའི་ཆེད་ཀྱི་ཕྱོགས་མཐོང་བའི་སླད་དུ་བསྡུས་ཏེ་ཅུང་ཟད་བརྗོད་ན། འགའ་ཞིག་གིས། འདིར་བཙན་བདག་གཞན་གྱི་ཆམས་ཀྱི་བའི་གནས་དང་བྱ་བའི་སྒྲ་གཉིས་དབྱེ་བའི་ཡ་ཀྱལ་རེ་རེ་བར་འདོད་ཅིང་གསལ་ཀྱི་ངོས་འཛིན་གསལ་པོར་མ་བྱས་པ་དང་། འགའ་ཞིག་གིས་བདག་བྱེད་པ་དང་གཞན་བྱ་བ་གཉིས་ཉིད་དུ་ཁོ་ན་བཅད་པ་དང་། འགའ་ཞིག་གིས་མིང་རྐྱང་རྣམས་ཀྱང་འདི་སྐབས་སུ་བསྟན་པའི། དུས་གསུམ་གྱི་དབྱེ་བའི་ཁོངས་སུ་སྡུད་པ་རྣམས་མཐོང་བ་ལས་འདོད་པ་དང་པོ་དེ་མི་འཐད་དོ། བྱ་བའི་སྒྲ་ལ་བྱེད་པོ་གཞན་དང་དངོས་སུ་འབྲེལ་མི་འབྲེལ་གཉིས་ཡོད་པའི་ཚུལ་ལ་དངོས་པོ་གཞན་གྱི་མཚན་གཞི་མི་ཕྱེད་ན་དེ་ལས་གཞན་དུ་མཚན་གཞི་འཐད་ལྡན་རྙེད་པར་མི་འགྱུར་ཞིང་། དེ་ལ་དབྱེ་ན་གཞན་དང་དེ་བྱ་བའི་སྒྲ་གཉིས་པོ་སོ་སོ་རང་ཆེ་ཐང་དུ་དབྱེ་བ་བྱེད་པ་འགལ་བའི་ཕྱིར་དང་། ཡང་ན་བྱེད་པོ་གཞན་དང་དངོས་སུ་འབྲེལ་བའི་བྱ་བའི་སྒྲ་ལ་གཞན་དང་གཅིག་ཤོས་ལ་བྱ་བ་ཉིད་དུ་ཐ་སྙད་འདོགས་ན་ནི་ཐ་མ་ཕྱོགས་གཅིག་ནས་འགྲིགས་ཀྱང་། ཕྱི་མ་གཞུང་འདིའི་དངོས་བསྟན་དང་། དོན་འཐོབ་གཉིས་ཀ་པོ་ཡིག་གི་འཇུག་ཡུལ་དུ་མ་བྱུང་ཞིང་འབྱུང་བའང་མི་སྲིད་པས་འབྲེལ་མེད་དུ་གྱུར་བའི་ཕྱིར་དང་། དཔེར་བརྗོད་པོ་ཡིག་གི་འཇུག་ཡུལ་གཞན་གྱི་ངོས་འཛིན་གསལ་པོ་བྱེད་རྒྱུ་མེད་བཞིན་དུ། མ་བསྟན་པའི་བྱ་བའི་དབྱེ་བ་གསར་དུ་བསྟན་པ་ལ་དགོས་པ་ཅི་ཡང་མེད་པའི་ཕྱིར། འདོད་པ་གཉིས་པ་དེ་འང་མི་འཐད་དེ། དེ་ལྟར་ན་བྱེ་བྲག་ཟེས་ནས་མ་བཤད་པས་བྱེད་པའི་སྒྲ་ཡིན་ཚད་བདག་དང་། བྱ་བའི་སྒྲ་ཡིན་ཚད་གཞན་དུ་ཁས་བླངས་པར་སོང་བས། འདིར་བསྟན་དུས་གསུམ་གྱི་ད་ལྟ་བ་དང་མ་འོངས་པའི་སྒྲ་འཆད་པའི་ཚེ་ཟློས་པའི་ཉེན་དུ་འགྱུར་བ་མ་ཟད་དབྱེ་བ་དེ་དག་ཕན་ཚུན་འཛིངས་པས་དབྱེ་བ་དགོས་མེད་དུ་ཐལ་བའི་ཕྱིར་དང་། རྒྱ་མཚན་དེས་མཁས་པའི་གཞུང་ལུགས་ཆུད་གསན་པར་འགྱུར་བའི་ཕྱིར་དང་། བསྟན་བྱའི་གཙོ་བོ་བྱེད་པ་པོ་དང་བྱ་བའི་ཡུལ་གཉིས་ཆད་པའི་ཉེན་ཡོད་པའི་ཕྱིར།

འདོད་ཚུལ་གསུམ་པ་དེ་འང་མི་འཐད་དེ། སྐབས་འདིའི་དུས་གསུམ་གྱི་དབྱེ་བ་ནི་བྱེད་ལས་སམ་བྱ་ཚིག་གི་སྒོ་ནས་འབྱེད་དགོས་ཤིང་། མིང་རྐྱང་ལ་བྱ་བྱེད་ཀྱི་

ཐ་སྙད་མི་འཇུག་པས་བྱ་བྱེད་མེད་པ་བྱ་བྱེད་ཙམ་དུ་སྣང་བ་ལས་མཚང་ཆེ་བ་ཅི་ཞིག་ཡོད། ཁྱད་པར་མིང་རྐྱང་རྣམས་བདག་གཞན་གྱིས་ཟླས་ཕྱེ་བའི་བདག་ཡིན་པར་བསམ་ནས་མ་ཞེན་དང་མོའི་སྔོན་འཇུག་གི་འཇུག་པ་འཆད་པའི་ཚེ་གད་འའི་འཕུལ་ཅན་གྱི་མིང་རྐྱང་རྣམས་བདག་གི་དཔེར་བརྗོད་དུ་བཀོད་འདུག་པ་དེ་ལྟ་ན་ཐ་ཡིག་བས་འཕུལ་ཅན་གྱི་མིང་རྐྱང་ཡང་མང་པོ་ཡོད་ན་སློབ་དཔོན་ཐུ་མིས་ཐ་ཡིག་བདག་རྐྱང་བ་ལ་འཇུག་པར་མ་གསུངས་པའི་རྒྱུ་མཚན་ཅི་ཡོད། སེམས་ཉལ་དུ་ཕབ་ནས་ལེགས་པར་བསམ་དགོས་སོ། དེས་ན་མཁས་པ་གཞན་གྱིས་མིང་ལ་བདག་དང་དུས་གསུམ་ལ་གཞན་གྱི་ཐ་སྙད་བྱས་པ་དང་། མིང་རྐྱང་ཉིད་དུས་གསུམ་ལས་ད་ལྟ་བར་འདོད་པ་སོགས་ཡོད་པ་ནི་གཞུང་གཞན་དང་གཞན་གྱི་འཆད་ཚུལ་ཡིན་གྱི་སྐབས་འདི་དང་འབྲེལ་བའི་དོན་མེད་ལ། མི་འབྲེལ་བཞིན་དུ་བསྒྲིག་པར་སྨྲས་པ་ནི་གཡག་གི་རྭ་རྟའི་མགོ་ལ་སྦྱོར་བ་དང་མཚུངས་སོ། གཞན་ཡང་འགའ་ཞིག་གིས་བདག་བྱེད་པ་པོ་ཁོ་ནར་འདོད་པ་དང་། ལ་ལས་བྱེད་པ་ཁོ་ནར་འདོད་པ་མཐོང་བས་དེ་དག་ལ་ནི་གང་བཤད་པ་དཔྱིས་མ་ཕྱིན་པ་དང་གཞུང་གི་བསྟན་བྱ་མ་རྟོགས་པའི་སྐྱོན་ཡང་འཇུག་གོ། ཡང་འགའ་ཞིག་གིས། བྱེད་པ་པོ་ལ་ཡོད་པའི་ལས་ཐམས་ཅད་ལ་བདག་དང་། བྱ་བའི་གཞི་ལ་ཡོད་པའི་ལས་ཐམས་ཅད་ལ་གཞན་དུ་ངོས་བཟུང་ཞིང་། ཕྱི་མ་ལ་དུས་གསུམ་གྱི་དབྱེ་བ་བྱེད་པར་འདུག་མོད། ལས་དེ་དག་ཀུན་ངོས་མ་ཟིན་པས་དཔེར་བརྗོད་དུ་མིང་རྐྱང་སྒྲིག་པར་བྱེད་པ་རྣམས་ལ་ནི་དཔྱད་དུ་ཅི་ཞིག་ཡོད་དེ།

འཕེན་ཟན་རིན་ཆེན་ལ་བལྟ་ཡི། །འགལ་དུ་མལ་ནི་སུ་ཞིག་དཔྱོད། །

ཅེས་པ་ལྟར་བས་པའི་ཕྱིར། དོན་ཀུན་སྐྱོན་གྱི་ཕྱོགས་མཚོན་པ་ཙམ་ཞིག་ཤོག་ཏུ་འཆད་པར་བྱ་ཞིང་། གཉན་དུ་ན། བདག་གཞན་གྱི་འཆད་ཚུལ་དེའང་ལེགས་པར་བསམ་པའི་ངག་མ་ཡིན་ཏེ། ལས་དེ་དག་སྟོན་པའི་ཚིག་ཐམས་ཅད་ལ་འདིར་བསྟན་བདག་གཞན་གྱི་སྒྲ་འཇུག་པས་མ་ཁྱབ་པའི་ཕྱིར་ཏེ། སྐབས་འདིའི་བདག་གཞན་གྱི་སྒྲ་ནི་དངོས་སུ་བྱེད་པོ་དང་བྱ་བ་ངེས་པར་ཐ་དད་པ་ཞིག་གི་སྒོ་ནས་བཞག་དགོས་པ་བཤད་ཟིན་དང་འཆད་འགྱུར་ལྟར་ངེས་པའི་ཕྱིར། དངོས་སུ་བྱེད་པོ་དང་བྱ་བ་ཐ་མི་དད་པའི་ལས་ཀྱི་ཚིག་རྣམས་ལ་ནི་ལས་དེ་དག་གང་རུང་སྟོན་པའི་ཚིག་ཡིན་པས་ཁྱབ་ཀྱང་ངོ་བོ་གཅིག་པ་ལ་བདག་གཞན་གྱི་དབྱེ་བ་མི་རུང་བས་འདིར་བསྟན་བདག་གཞན་གྱི་སྒྲ་མི་འཇུག་པའི་ཕྱིར་རོ།། ཁྱེད་རང་གིས་གཞན་དུ་ངོས་འཛིན་ཀྱི་བྱ་བ་གཞིའི་ལས་ལ་དུས་གསུམ་དུ་དབྱེ་བའང་ཆེས་མི་འཐད་དེ།། དེ་ལྟ་ན་ཐ་ནི་འདས་དང་གཞན་བསྒྲུབ་ཕྱིར། ཞེས་པའི་གཞུང་འདི་འཆད་པའི་སྐོར་རྗེས་ཀྱི་ཐ་ཡིག་བྱེད་ལས་ཀྱིས་དབྱེ་བའི་དུས་གསུམ་ག་ལ་འཇུག་པ་ཞིག་ཁས་མི་ལེན་ཀ་མེད་དུ་སོང་བས་འདས་དང་ཞེས་སོགས་སུ་བཀར་ནས་གསུངས་པ་དགོས་མེད་དུ་ཐལ་བའི་ཕྱིར་དང་། དེའི་ལུགས་ཀྱིས་མ་ཞེད་གད་གཉིས་ཀྱང་དུས་གསུམ་ག་ལ་འཇུག་པར་འདོད་དགོས་པ་སོགས་ཀྱིས་དབྱེ་བ་ཕལ་ཆེར་བྱེ་བྲག་མེད་པར་འགྱུར་བའི་ཕྱིར་རོ།། ཕྱིར་ཡང་བྱ་བ་གཞི་ལ་ཡོད་པའི་ལས་ལ་དུས་གསུམ་དུ་དབྱེར་རུང་བ་མ་ཡིན་ཏེ། ཤིང་གཅོད་པར་བྱ། གཅོད་པར་བྱེད། བཅད་ཟིན། ལྟ་བུར་མཚོན་ན་གཅོད་བྱ་མ་འོངས་པ་དང་བཅད་ཟིན་འདས་པ་གཉིས་བྱ་བའི་གཞི་དང་འབྲེལ་མོད་ཀྱི། གཅོད་བྱེད་ད་ལྟ་བ་བྱེད་པ་པོ་དང་འབྲེལ་བ་ལས་བྱ་བའི་གཞིར་འབྲེལ་བའི་སྐབས་མེད་དོ།།

འདིར་བྱ་གཞིའི་ལས་ད་ལྟ་བའི་དཔེར་བརྗོད་དུ། ཆུ་དགག། བུམ་པ་དཀང་། བཅིངས་པ་དཀྲོལ། གདུགས་དབུབ། ཁྱིམ་དུ་གདེག། བསྟོད་པ་གདོན། གསལ་གདབ་སོགས་བཀོད་པ་མཐོང་བ་ནི་བྱ་གཞིའི་ལས་ཀྱི་ཚིག་ཡིན་མོད་ཀྱང་དུས་མ་འོངས་པ་ཡིན་གྱི་ད་ལྟ་བར་ནམ་ཡང་མི་འགྱུར་ཏེ།

དེ་རྣམས་ལ་དུས་གསུམ་དུ་དབྱེ་བའི་ཚེ། བཀག། འགེགས། དགག། བཀང་། འགེངས། དགང་། བཀྲོལ། འཁྲོལ། དཀྲོལ། ཕུབ། འབུབས། དབུབ། བཏེག། འདེག། གདེག། བཏོན། འདོན། གདོན། བཏབ། འདེབས། གདབ་སོགས་རིམ་པ་བཞིན་འདས་ད་ལྟ་མ་འོངས་གསུམ་གྱི་དཔེར་བརྗོད་དུ་མཁས་པ་རྣམས་ལ་ཡོངས་སུ་གྲགས་པའི་ཕྱིར་རོ།།

ཡང་འགྲེལ་བྱེད་སྔ་མ་ཐམས་ཅད་ཀྱིས་འདི་སྐབས་ལས་ཀྱི་ཚིག་ལ་བྱེད་པ་པོ་གཞན་དང་དངོས་སུ་འབྲེལ་མ་འབྲེལ་གྱི་རྣམ་དབྱེ་མ་མཛད་པ་ནི་ཤིན་ཏུ་མི་ལེགས་ཏེ། དེ་མ་ཤེས་ན་བྱེད་པོ་དང་བྱ་བ་ཐ་དད་པ་དང་ཐ་མི་དད་པའི་ལས་ཀྱི་ཚིག་སོ་སོར་ངོས་མི་ཟིན་ཅིང་། དེ་མ་ཟིན་པས་འདིར་བསྟན་བདག་གཞན་གྱི་ཐ་སྙད་གང་ལ་འཇུག་པ་ཚུལ་བཞིན་མ་རྟོགས་པར་ལོང་བའི་འཁར་བ་བཞིན་གར་འཛུག་མེད་པའི་ཅལ་ཅོལ་མང་པོ་བྱུང་བར་སྣང་ངོ་།། དེས་ན་གནད་འདི་རྟོགས་པ་གཞུང་དོན་ཇི་བཞིན་མ་འཛིངས་པར་འཆད་པའི་བར་འགྱུར་

བའི་ཕྱིར་གལ་ཤིན་ཏུ་ཆེ་ཞིང་། བཀའ་རིག་གིས། བྱེད་པོ་དང་བྱ་ཡུལ་ངོ་བོ་གཅིག་པའི་ལས་ཀྱི་ཚིག་ཀྱང་འཕྲད་དམ་སྐབས་པ་སྲིད་ན་དེ་འདྲ་མང་དུ་བྱུང་སྟེ། གོང་དུ་སྨོས་ཟུ་ཕར་ལ་དོན་དེ་ཉིད་ལ་འཇུག་ཚུལ་གྱི་སྐབས་སུའང་ཕྱོགས་ཙམ་སྨོས་པ་ལྟར། དཔེར་ན། ངང་ཀ་འགྲོ་བོ། ཞེས་པའི་འགྲོ་བའི་སྒྲ་དེ་བྱ་བའི་ལས་ཀྱི་ཚིག་ཡིན་ཡང་། བྱེད་པ་པོ་དང་བྱ་བའི་གཞི་ཐ་དད་དུ་མེད་དེ་འགྲོ་བར་བྱེད་པ་པོ་བདག་ཡིན་ཞིང་འགྲོ་བར་བྱ་བའང་བདག་ཉིད་ཡིན་པ་དང་། ལྕགས་རང་བཞིན་གྱིས་གསེར་དུ་འགྱུར། ཞེས་པ་འགྱུར་བྱེད་དང་འགྱུར་བྱ་གཉིས་ཀ་ལྕགས་ཉིད་ལས་གཞན་དུ་མི་དམིགས་པ་ལྟ་བུ་རྒྱ་ཆེར་ཤེས་པར་བྱ་ཞིང་ཤིན་ཏུ་ཞིབ་མོར་དཔྱོད་པའི་ཚེ་དངོས་པོ་རྣམས་ཀྱི་རང་མཚན་སོ་སོ་ནས་རང་གིས་རང་ལ་བྱ་བ་འགལ་ཡང་། སྨྲ་སྒོག་རགས་པ་ནས་ཐ་སྙད་ཙམ་ལ་འཇིག་རྟེན་གྱི་གྲགས་པ་དང་མཐུན་པར་རང་གིས་རང་ལ་བྱ་བ་འབྱུང་བའང་གོ་དགོས་སོ།། དེ་དག་ཏུ་དཔེར་བརྗོད་ཐོག་པ་ནི་ཤིན་ཏུ་མང་བས་སྨོས་ཀྱིས་མི་ལང་མོད། འོན་ཀྱང་སྔོན་དུ་བཀའ་རིག་གི་མཚང་བརྟོལ་ཟིན་ཅིང་འདིར་ཡང་ཕྱོགས་ཙམ་སྨོས་ན།

སྔོན་འཇུག་གི་བོ་ཡིག་བ་བྱ་བའི་ཡུལ་ལ་འཇུག་པའི་དཔེར་བརྗོད་ལ། སྤྲ་བཀོད། མགོ་བཀད། སོགས་བྱ་བའི་ཡུལ་དང་འབྲེལ་བའི་བྱ་ཚིག་དང་། རྡོང་བཀང་། ཤིང་བཀས། ཆུ་བཀག། སོགས་འདས་ཚིག་དང་། རྣམས་པར་བཀྲ། སྨན་བཀུ། སོགས་མིང་རྐྱང་རྣམས་བཀོད་པ་ལས། བྱ་བའི་ཡུལ་ཉིད་ཀྱི་དཔེར་བརྗོད་སྒྲ་གཅིག་ཀྱང་མེད་པ་དང་།

མ་ནིང་ག་ཡིག་བྱེད་པ་པོ་ལ་ཡོད་པའི་ལས་ཀྱི་དོན་ལ་འཇུག་པའི་དཔེར་བརྗོད་དུ། རང་ཉིད་གཅིག་པུ། གཅུད་ལ་བོར་བ། ཡིད་གཙུགས་པ། འཕངས་པའི་གཅེས་སོགས་ལས་ཀྱི་ཚིག་མ་ཡིན་པའི་མིང་རྐྱང་ཁོ་ན་བཀོད་པ་དང་།

ག་ཡིག་བྱ་བ་གཞི་ལ་ཡོད་པའི་ལས་ལ་འཇུག་པའི་དཔེར་ཡང་། གཅན་གཟན། ལ་གཅན་པ། སྒྲ་གཅན། རུས་ཀྱི་གཉེས། དུད་འགྲོ་གཉན་སོགས་ཕལ་ཆེར་མིང་རྐྱང་ཁོ་ན་བཀོད་པ་ལྟ་བུས་མཚོན་མ་བརྟགས་པའི་བབ་ཅོལ་མང་དུ་སྨྲས་པའི་རྗེ་བ་རྣམས་བློ་གྲོས་ཀྱི་པད་མ་རྒྱས་པ་རྣམས་ཀྱིས་ཅུང་ཟད་དཔྱད་པས་འཇིག་པར་འགྱུར་བ་ཉིད་ན་ཇི་སྐྱིད་པ་འདིར་ཡི་གེ་སྤྲོལ་བའི་དཀའ་ཚེགས་ཀྱིས་ཅི་ཞིག་བྱ། འདིར་སྨྲས་པ།།

ཐུ་མིའི་གཞུང་ལུགས་རྟོགས་པར་དཀའ་བ་རིན་པོ་ཆེ་ཡི་གཏེར་གྱི་སྒོ། །ཕྱི་དུས་འདི་ན་བློ་མིག་མི་གསལ་བློ་ལྡན་ཚུལ་ཅན་དུ་མ་ཡིས། །
དགེ་བར་རློམ་ནས་དོན་མིན་ཚིག་ཕྲེང་སྤྲོག་ཅི་རྒྱལ་ངོམས་གནས་མིན་དུ། །ལན་བརྒྱར་བརྟགས་ཀྱང་རང་ཉིད་ངལ་ལས་གཞུང་དོན་རིན་ཆེན་རྙེད་དོས་ཅི། །

དེང་དུས་ལེགས་བཤད་གཏེར་སྟོན་འདི་བྱུང་ནས། །གཞན་གཞུང་ཚར་གཅོད་རིགས་པའི་ཐུགས་ཅན་གྱིས། །
ལོག་བཤད་ཚང་ཚིང་སྦུག་པོ་རྣམ་པར་བསྲེགས། །འཐད་ལྡན་རྣམ་དཔྱོད་གཞོན་ནུན་ལེགས་སོགས་ཏེ། །
དཀའ་གནས་པོར་མའི་བུ་ག་གསལ་བྱས་པས། །ད་ལྟ་བློ་གསལ་གཞུང་ལུགས་དོན་གཉེར་དག །
ལ་ཟུར་སྦྱོན་ལ་རྟགས་ཀྱི་འཇུག་པ་ཡི། །གཞུང་དོན་ནོར་བུའི་ཚོགས་ལ་ཅི་གར་རོལ། །ཅེས་སོ།།

གཉིས་པ་བོ། བོ་ཡིག་གི། མ་ནིང་གི། མོ་ཡིག་གི། ཤིན་ཏུ་མོའི་འཇུག་དོན་བཤད་པ་སྔ་བཞི་ལས།

དང་པོ་སྔོན་འཇུག་གི་བོ་ཡིག་དགོས་པ་ཅིའི་ཕྱིར་འཇུག་པ་ནི།

བོ་ནི་འདས་དང་གཞན་བསྒྲུབ་ཕྱིར། །

ཞེས་པས་བསྟན་ཏེ་སྔོན་འཇུག་གི་བོ་ཡིག་བ་ནི་དགོས་པ་དུས་གསུམ་ལས། བྱེད་པ་པོ་གཞན་དང་དངོས་སུ་འབྲེལ་བའི་བྱ་བ་བྱས་ཟིན་འདས་པ་བསྒྲུབ་པའི་ཕྱིར་དང་། དངོས་པོ་བདག་གཞན་གཉིས་ལས་གཞན་ཏེ་བྱེད་པ་པོ་གཞན་དང་དངོས་སུ་འབྲེལ་བའི་བྱ་བའི་ཡུལ་དང་བྱ་བ་བསྒྲུབ་པའི་ཕྱིར་འཇུག་པ་ཡིན་ནོ། །ཞེས་སོ།།

དེ་ལས་འདས་པ་ལ་འཇུག་པ་ནི་དཔེར་ན། ཆུས་བཀང་། གོས་བཀབ། ཕོགས་སུ་བཀར། ལམ་བཀག། ལག་པ་བཀན། ཁལ་བཀལ།

ཤིང་བཀས། སྣོད་དུ་བཀལ། ཁྲལ་བཀལ། གཞུ་བཀང་། གོང་དུ་བཀུར་ཏོ། ཤིང་བཀུག། སྐན་བཀུམ། སྨོག་བཀུམས། ཟླ་བཀོང་།། རྩ་བ་བཀོག། ཀླས་བཀོད། ཟུར་དུ་བཀོལ་ཏོ། གཡོག་ཏུ་བཀོལ་ཏོ། ཐག་པས་བཀྱིགས། སྒྲུལ་པ་བཀྲིས། ཀྱི་བཀྲེད། མི་ཏོག་བཀྲུམ། དགོངས་པ་བཀྲལ། ཁྲལ་བཀྲལ། རྒྱལ་པོས་བཀྲབས། ཞར་པར་བཀྲིས། དྲི་མ་བཀྲུས། དགྲ་བཅོམ་བཀྲོངས། ཚིག་གིས་བཀྲོས། མདོ་བཀླགས། འདོད་པ་ལ་བཀམ། ནོར་བཀྲུས། ལག་པ་བཀྱངས། ས་བཀོས། ཁ་བསྐངས། ཐུགས་དམ་བསྐངས། ཆུ་བསྐམས། ཡང་ཡང་བསྐྱར། སྨོག་བསྐྱབས། ཆུ་བསྐྱུམས། དྲིན་གྱིས་བསྐྱངས། ནུ་བ་བསྐྱུས། གནས་སུ་བསྐྱལ་ཏོ། ཕྱིར་བསྐྱུད། ཆུ་བསྐྱིལ་ཏོ། ནོར་བསྐྱིས། སྐམ་བསྐུས། དབང་བསྐུར་ཏོ། ལག་བསྐུམས། ནོར་བསྐུངས། ཆོས་ལ་བསྐུལ་ཏོ། རྒྱབ་ཏུ་བསྐུར་ཏོ། སེམས་ཀྱིས་བསྐུད་དོ། གཅོམ་བསྐུངས།། ཁོངས་པ་བསྐུངས། ཟས་བསྐུས། ལོ་ཏོག་བསྐྲུན་ཏོ། སེམས་བསྐྱེད། སྐྱུ་བསྐྱེད། སྐན་བསྐོལ་ཏོ། རྒྱལ་སར་བསྐོས། འཁོར་གྱིས་བསྐོར་ཏོ། གོས་བསྐོན་ཏོ། ཏར་བསྐྱོན་ཏོ། ཀླུང་གིས་བསྐྱོད་དོ།།

གད་མོ་བགད། ལམ་བགགས། ཚོད་བགམ། གཡང་ལ་བགྱིལ། གོ་བགོས། གོས་བགོས། གོམ་པ་བགོམས། སྐལ་བ་བགོས། ལམ་དུ་བགོར་ཏོ། དུས་བགྱངས། ལས་བགྱིས། མིག་བགྲད། ཕྲེང་བ་བགྲངས། གྲངས་བགྲངས། ཆུ་བགྲུངས། འབྲས་བགྲུས། བཀའ་བརྗོས། ལམ་བགྲོད། ཆུ་བཅལ། རྒྱན་གྱིས་བརྒྱན་ཏོ། དྲན་མེད་བརྒྱལ་ཏོ། མཚོན་བརྒྱབ། ངོ་བརྒྱལ་ཏོ། ནོར་གྱིས་བརྒྱགས། ཀོ་བ་བརྒྱངས། རྒྱུད་མར་བརྒྱུད། ཕྲེང་བ་བརྒྱུས། བང་བརྒྱུགས། བུ་རམ་བརྔར། མནར་བསྔགས། ནོར་གྱིས་བསྔབ། ལམ་དུ་བསྒུགས། ལག་པས་བསྒུལ་ཏོ། དྲིས་བསྒོས། བསམ་གཏན་བསྒོམས། ཟན་བསྒོངས། བཀའ་བསྒོས། རྣམ་པར་བསྒྲིངས། ལེགས་པར་བསྒྱུར་ཏོ། ཕྱིར་བསྒྱིལ་ཏོ། ཆོས་བསྒྲགས་ཆུ་བསྒྲལ་ཏོ། ཐང་བསྒྲངས། གྲལ་བསྒྲིགས། ཟློ་བསྒྲིམས། སྐུད་པ་བསྒྲིམས། སྒྲོན་བསྒྲིབས། ཤི་ཀུ་བསྒྲིལ་ཏོ། ད་ཡིས་བསྒྲུན་ཏོ། དོན་བསྒྲུབས། ཇོ་བསྒྲུབས། རིགས་བསྒྲེས། རྒྱེན་དུ་བསྒྲེངས། བུད་མེད་བསྒྲོད།

༈ ནོར་གྱིས་བརྔན་ཏོ། བཙོས་མ་བརྔས། དུ་བ་བརྔུབས། རི་དྭགས་བརྔོན་ཏོ། བུད་མེད་བརྔོད། ཡོན་ཏན་བསྔགས། དགེ་བ་བསྔོས། མཆིང་བསྔོགས། ༈ ལོགས་སུ་བཅར་ཏོ། ཕྱག་བཅབས། ཞབས་ཀྱིས་བཅགས། ཤིང་བཅག། དུམ་བུར་བཅད། མིག་བཅར། འཁྲུལ་འཁོར་བཅམས། དམ་བཅས། བློས་བཅལ། ནོར་བཅལ། ལག་ཏུ་བཅངས། ཕྱིར་བཅིལ། ཞགས་པས་བཅིངས། ཆིབ་བཅིབས། རྡོད་དུ་བཅུག། ཆུ་བཅུས། སྣང་དུ་བཅུར་ཏོ། ཤིང་གཅེར་ཏོ། ནོར་བཅོལ། དགྲ་བཅོམ། ཡུར་བ་བཅོས། ལས་བཅོལ། ༈ ཕན་ཚུན་བརྗེས། མཆོད་ཅིང་བརྗོད་དོ། བདག་གིས་བརྗོད་ཟེར། ༈ གོས་བརྙན་ཏོ། རྗེས་སུ་བསྙེགས། ལག་པས་བསྙབས། འཕྲེང་ལ་བསྙལ་ཏོ། ཚང་བསྙལ་ཏོ། ཁོད་བསྙམས། གཞན་ལ་བསྙད། ཕྱིར་བསྙིལ་ཏོ། མར་ཁུ་བསྙུགས། ཡོ་ཐུད་བསྙུངས། ནད་ཀྱིས་བསྙུན་ཏོ། ཉེ་བར་བསྙེན་ཏོ། ཚངས་པར་བསྙེམས། གནས་སུ་བསྙེངས། ཆུ་བསྙོགས། གཞན་ལ་བསྙོན་ཏོ། ༈ རྒྱན་བཏགས། ཁ་བཏགས། ནོར་བཏག། རྒྱས་བཏབ། ཞལ་དུ་བཏབ། ཞིག་པ་བཏིག། གདན་བཏིང་། མེ་ཏོག་བཏུས། རྡུགས་བཏུས། ཆང་བཏུངས། སྤྱི་བོས་བཏུད། ཕྱིས་སུ་བཏེག། བདུད་བཏུལ། ཕུར་མས་བཏུར། རྒྱེན་དུ་བཏེག། སྣང་ལ་བཏེག། བཙོན་ལས་བཏོན། མགོ་བཏོན། སྒྲ་བཏོགས། སྨོལ་བཏོད། ལྟས་བཏགས། ཐིགས་པ་ལ་བཏབས། ཕྱུ་བ་བཏུལ། དེར་བཏེན་ཏོ། ཐག་པས་བཏད། གནས་སུ་བཏོལ། ཏག་བཏོལ་ཏོ། སྐྱ་བརྟམས། བཅུད་ཀྱིས་བརྟམས། མིག་གིས་བརྟས། གོས་བརྟབས། ས་དི་བརྟར། ཆོས་བརྟན་ཏོ། འགྲོ་ཚམས་བརྟད། ཁ་ཟས་བརྟབས། ལྷ་བརྟེམས།

ཚིག་གིས་བསྒྲིངས། ཐག་བསྲིངས། གྲོས་བསྡུར། བཤེས་གཉེན་བསྟེན་ཏོ། མངོན་པར་བསྟོད། ༈ མདུན་དུ་བདར་ཏོ། རྗེས་སུ་བདས། ཕྱག་བདར་ཏོ། ཕྱི་མར་བདར་ཏོ། ནོར་བདལ། བདུག་པས་བདུགས། གཞུ་བདུངས། ཐང་མར་བརྡལ་ཏོ། མཚོན་བརྡར་ཏོ། ལག་པ་བརྡབས། རྫ་བརྡུངས། སྦྲ་བརྡུངས། དུལ་མོ་བརྡུལ་ཏོ། ཡང་ཡང་བསླབས། ཀློ་མ་བསླགས། ཁ་ཟས་བཟད། སར་བཟུད། ཉེས་པ་བསྡམས། ཐག་པས་བསྡམས། འཛིགས་ཚུལ་གྱིས་བརྫིགས། དབང་དུ་བསྡུས། ཕན་ཚུན་བསྡུར་ཏོ། འགྲུས་པ་བསྡུམས། ཕན་ཚུན་བརྡེབས། སྣ་ཐག་བརྡོགས། ཕྱ་ཁོན་བརྡོགས། གྲོགས་དང་བསྡོངས། ཕྱོགས་གཅིག་བསྡོམས། སྡོག་དང་བསྡོམས། དཀྲ་ལ་བསྡོམས། ༈ ནན་གྱིས་བནན་ཏོ། ཡིད་ལ་བནགས། ཟས་ཀྱིས་བནངས། ནོར་བནོག། རྫས་ལ་བནབས། སྙིང་དུ་བསྣར་ཏོ། མཇུག་བསྣར་ཏོ། ཕྱག་ཏུ་བསྣམས། གནད་དུ་བསྣུན་ཏོ། སྣེ་བསྣམས། དུས་ཚོད་བསྣུར་ཏོ། སྣག་ཚ་བསྣུར་ཏོ། སྤོལ་བསྣུབས། ཉམ་པར་བསྙམས། ཧོང་ཐོག་བསྙོར་ཏོ། ཕན་ཚུན་བསྙོལ་ཏོ། ཟན་བསྙེམས། ༈ བྱ་བཙོས། ནོར་བཙོལ་ཏོ། ཚགས་ཀྱིས་བཙགས། རྩམ་པ་བཙབས། གསེབ་ཏུ་བཙངས། གཅེས་པར་བཙམས། སོ་བཙེམས། དམ་པོར་བཙིར་ཏོ།། ཤིང་བཙུགས། སྡོད་དུ་བཙུད། མིག་བཙུམས། ལྭ་བ་བཙེམས། གནོད་པས་བཙེས། ཚོས་ཀྱིས་བཙོས། ནོར་བཙོངས། རྗེས་བཙོགས། བསྟན་བཅོས་བརྩམས། དྲིས་ཤིང་བརྩད། འགོ་བརྩམས། རྩིག་པ་བརྩིགས། གྲངས་བརྩིས། སྟེང་དུ་བརྩེགས། རྩེད་མོ་བརྩེས། ༈ གཞན་དུ་བརྫངས། ཕྱོད་དུ་བརྫངས། རྐང་པས་བརྫིས། ཟན་བརྫིས། ཁྲོ་བོར་བརྫུས། རལ་པ་བརྫེས། ༈ དལ་བུས་བཞབས། གནས་སུ་བཞག། སྒྲ་བཞར་ཏོ།། ཁྲུ་བ་བཞིབས། ལམ་དུ་བཞུད། གདན་ལ་བཞུགས། མར་ཁུ་བཞུར་ཏོ། ཞུག་གིས་བཞུས། རྫུན་ལས་བཞེངས། བཟའ་བ་བཞེས། ཤིང་བཞོགས། བཞོན་མ་བཞོས།

ཟས་བཟས། ཞབས་ཏོག་བཟབས། ཕྱག་པར་བཟར། སྔགས་བཟླས། ལ་བཟླས། ལག་པས་བཟུང་། འཕྲང་ལམ་བཟུར། ཟ་བར་བཟླུགས། ཚོགས་བཟླུམས། གཅིག་ཏུ་བཟླུམས། སྣོད་བཟེད། ཤིང་བཟོས། གཡུལ་བཟློག། ༈ བྱིན་གྱིས་བརླབས། ཆུས་བརླན་ཏོ། འབྱུང་པོས་བརླམས། དགྲ་བརླག། ༈ སྦུབས་བཤངས། ཆུས་བཤལ། ཁྲིས་བཤར། འཕྱང་ལ་བཤར། ཕྱག་བཤམས། སྡིག་པ་བཤགས། ཞིབ་པར་བཤད། བཀོད་པ་བཤམས། ཤིང་བཤགས། མཉམས་ངོར་བཤིབས། མཁར་བཤིག། པགས་པ་བཤུས། མེས་བཤུར་ཏོ། སྐྱོ་བས་བཤུམས། ནོར་བཤུགས། དཔེ་བཤུས། ཕན་ཚུན་བཤུད། གཏམ་བཤེར་ཏོ། ཕྱིར་བཤོས། རི་དྭགས་བཤོར་ཏོ། འཁྲུས་བསྲོལ་ཏོ། ༈ ཚོགས་བསགས། དྲི་མ་བསངས། སྐྱོན་བསལ་ཏོ། དོན་བསམས། དྲིན་ལན་བསབས། སྲོག་ཆགས་བསད། ཡོ་བྱད་བསར་ཏོ། ལག་གིས་བསིགས། མདེའུ་བསིར། དུམ་བུར་བསིལ་ཏོ། རྗེས་བསུབས། ཁ་བསུམ། མདུན་བསུས། ཞིབ་མོར་བསེད། ནོར་བསོགས། ངལ་བསོས། སྒྲིབ་པ་བསྲབས། ཡོ་བ་བསྲངས། གཞུང་བསྲུངས། ཡི་གེ་བསྲིངས། སེམས་ཀྱིས་བསྲན་ཏོ། ཚེ་བསྲིངས། ནོར་བསྲེས། ཞོ་བསྲུབས། བསྲུང་བྱ་བསྲུངས། ཚུང་མ་བསྲིལ་ཏོ། ཕན་ཚུན་བསྲེས། མེས་བསྲེགས། ཤེད་བསྲོམས། རིག་པ་བསླབས། ནོར་བསླངས། གཞན་གྱིས་བསླད། ཕྱོགས་སུ་བསླན་ཏོ། ཁྱིན་དུ་བསྲངས། བསླུ་བྲ་བསླུས། ཕྱིར་བསློག། ཅེས་པ་ལ་སོགས་པ་རྣམས་ཏེ་དེ་དག་ལ་སྦྱར་བསྡུའི་སྒྲ་སྦྱར་བ་རྣམས་ད་ཡིག་གི་ཡང་འཇུག་ཡོད་པར་ཤེས་དགོས་སོ།།

དེ་རྣམས་ཀྱང་དཔེར་ན། བུམ་པ་རྒྱས་བཀང་། ལྟ་བུ་སྔོན་འཇུག་ཁོ་ནའི་བྱེད་པས་འདས་ཚིག་ཏུ་གྱུར་པ་དང་། ཐུགས་དམ་བསྐངས་ལྟ་བུ་སྔོན་འཇུག་བ་ཡིག་དང་འབྲེལ་པ་ཙམ་ལས་གཞི་བོར་རྗེས་འཇུག་གི་བྱེད་པས་འདས་ཚིག་ཏུ་གྱུར་པ་སོགས་བྱེ་བྲག་ཕྱེས་ནས་ཤེས་པར་བྱའོ།།

བ་ཡིག་གཞན་ཏུ་བའི་ཡུལ་བསྒྲུབ་པའི་ཕྱིར་འཇུག་པ་ནི། དཔེར་ན། བཀན་བྱའི་ལག་པ། བཀྱིག་བྱའི་དགྲ། བཀོལ་བྱའི་དོན། བཀྱོན་བྱའི་

ཨབངས། བཀབ་བྱའི་འབངས། བཀྲུ་བྱའི་རས། བཀྲག་བྱའི་ཡི་གེ། བསྐམ་བྱའི་དངོས་པོ། བཀྱེ་བྱའི་ནོར། བཀོ་བྱའི་ས། བཀྲུང་བྱའི་ཐག་པ། བསྐང་བྱའི་དམ་ཚིག། བསྐུ་བྱའི་སྣུམ། བསྐུལ་བྱའི་ལས། བསྐོར་བྱའི་འཁོར་ལོ། བསྐོན་བྱའི་ཞྭ། བསྐྱུམ་བྱའི་སྤྱོད། བསྐྱུ་བྱའི་ནོར། སྐྱུར་བྱའི་ཐིག། བསྐྱེ་བྱའི་དངོས་པོ། བསྐྱིལ་བྱའི་རྫིང་། བསྐྱུར་བྱའི་ཉེས་པ། བསྐྱེད་བྱའི་འདྲེ། བསྲུན་བྱའི་བསོད་ནམས། ༄ བགམ་བྱའི་ཚོད། བགད་བྱའི་གད་མོ། བགོ་བྱའི་གོས། བགེ་བྱའི་ལས། བགྲང་བྱའི་གྲངས། བགྲད་བྱའི་འདོམས། བགྲུ་བྱའི་འབྲུམ། བསྒྲི་བྱའི་སྒྲོམ། བསྒྲོད་བྱའི་ལམ། བརྒལ་བྱའི་ལ། བརྒྱན་བྱའི་གཟུགས། བརྒྱལ་བར་བྱ་བའི་དགྲ། བརྒྱང་བྱའི་ཐག་པ། བརྒྱུག་བྱའི་རྟ། བརྒྱུད་བྱའི་ཕྲེང་བ། བསྒྲག་བྱའི་བུག། བསྒབ་བྱའི་གཉེན། བསྒར་བྱའི་བུ་རམ། བསྒུག་བྱའི་མགྲོན། བསྒུལ་བྱའི་རྡོ་བ། བསྒོ་བྱའི་ངག། བསྒང་བྱའི་ཟན། བསྒྱུར་བྱ། བསྒྱེལ་བྱ། བསྒྲུག་བྱའི་ཚོས། བསྒྲིམ་བྱའི་བློ། བསྒྲིབ་བྱའི་སྒྲོན། བསྒྲིག་བྱའི་གྲལ། བསྒྲིལ་བྱའི་ཤོག་གུ། བསྒྲུབ་བྱའི་དོན། བསྒྲུན་བྱའི་དཔེ། བསྒྲུག་བྱའི་རྫ། བསྒྲི་བྱའི་ཆོས་མཚུངས། བསྒྲེང་བྱའི་རྒྱལ་མཚན། བསྒྲོད་བྱའི་བུད་མེད། ༄ བརྔན་བྱའི་གྲོགས། བརྔབ་བྱའི་ལོ་ཏོག། བརྔུབ་བྱའི་སྨན། བརྔོད་བྱའི་ནས། བསྔག་བྱའི་ཡོན་ཏན། བསྔོ་བྱའི་དགེ་བ། བསྔོག་བྱའི་མཚང་། ༄ བཅར་བྱའི་མིག། བཅང་བྱའི་སྣན། བཅག་བྱའི་ས། བཅལ་བྱའི་འདྲུལ་འཁོར། བཅབ་བྱའི་བྱང་བ། བཅིངས་བྱའི་ཀུན་པོ། བཅིབ་བྱའི་རྟ། ། བཅུར་བྱའི་འཐུང་། བཅུ་བྱའི་ཆུ། བཅོལ་བྱའི་ནོར། བཅོ་བྱའི་གཏོར་མ། ༄ བརྗེ་བྱའི་དངོས་པོ། བརྗེད་བྱའི་དམ་པ། བརྗོད་བྱའི་གཏམ། ༄ བརྙན་བྱའི་གོས། བསྙག་བྱའི་བུ་མོན། བསྙབ་བྱའི་དངོས་པོ། བསྙལ་བྱའི་ཤིང་། བསྙམ་བྱའི་རིང་ཐུང་། བསྙད་བྱའི་གཏམ། བསྙིལ་བྱའི་བྲག། བསྙུག་བྱའི་མར་ཁུ། བསྙུང་བྱའི་ཡོ་བྱད། བསྙུན་བྱའི་ལུས། བསྙེན་བྱའི་ལྷ། བསྙེམ་བྱའི་ཡོན་ཏན། བསྙོག་བྱའི་ཆུ།།

གཏིག་བྱའི་ཞིག་པ། བཏུ་བྱའི་སྤྲགས། བཏུང་བྱའི་ཆང་། བརྟག་བྱའི་ལྟས། བལྟར་བྱའི་ལུས། བརྟེན་བྱའི་ཡུལ། བརྟོད་བྱའི་རྟ། བརྟོལ་བྱའི་ནག། བལྟ་བྱའི་གཟུགས། བལྟམ་བྱའི་གནས། བལྟབ་བྱའི་གོས། བསྟན་བྱའི་ཆོས། བསྟད་བྱའི་ཕྱུགས། བསྟད་བྱའི་སྦྲ། བསྟིམ་བྱའི་ལྷ། བསྟུང་བྱའི་ཐག། བསྟེན་བྱའི་བཤེས་གཉེན། བསྟོད་བྱའི་ཡོན་ཏན།།

མདུན་དུ་བདར་བྱའི་རྡུམ། བདའ་བྱའི་ཕྱུགས། བདར་བྱའི་ཙན་དན། བདས་བྱའི་ནོར། བདུག་བྱའི་སྤོས། བདུང་བྱའི་གཞུ། བརྡལ་བྱའི་ཁྲུ་མ། བརྡར་བྱའི་མཚོན། བརྡབ་བྱའི་ཐལ་མོ། བརྡུང་བྱའི་རྔ། བལྡབ་བྱའི་ཚིག། བལྡག་བྱའི་སྐྱུ་མ། བལྡད་བྱའི་ཟས། བསྡམ་བྱའི་ཟམ། བསྡམ་བྱའི་ཉེས་པའམ་ངག། བསྡིག་བྱའི་སྐྱེ་བོ། བསྡུ་བྱའི་འཁོར། བསྡུམ་བྱའི་མཁོན། བསྡུར་བྱའི་དངོས་པོ། བསྡེབ་བྱའི་གྲོགས། བསྡོག་བྱའི་ཐག་པ། བསྡོག་བྱའི་ཆས་དགོས། བསྡོང་བྱའི་གྲོགས། བསྡོམ་བྱའི་གྲངས། བསྡོ་བྱའི་དགྲ།།

བརྣན་བྱའི་དོན། བརྣག་བྱའི་དོན། བསྣན་བྱའི་ནོར། བསྣམ་བྱའི་དྲིའམ་ཕྱག་མཚན། བསྣར་བྱའི་མཐུག། བསྣུན་བྱའི་མཚོན་ནམ་རྒྱུ་མ། བསྣུབ་བྱའི་སྣོལ་ངན། བསྣུར་བྱའི་དུས། བསྣོར་བྱའི་གོ་རིམ། བསྣོལ་བྱའི་གོ། བསྣོ་བྱའི་ཟན།

བཙའ་བྱའི་བུ། བཙལ་བྱའི་ནོར། བཙག་བྱའི་ཆུ། བཙན་བྱའི་སྙིང་སྡུག། བཙུམ་བྱའི་ཁ། བཙིར་བྱའི་གཡོག། བཙེམ་བྱའི་གོས། བཙོ་བྱའི་གསེར། བཙོང་བྱའི་ཚོང་། བཙོག་བྱའི་མཛེག། བརྩམ་བྱའི་བྱ་བ། བརྩད་བྱའི་ཞལ་ལྕེ། བརྩིག་བྱའི་ཛི། བརྩི་བྱའི་གྲངས། བརྩེ་བྱའི་གྲོགས།།

བརྫང་བྱའི་ཕོ་ཉ། སྔོན་དུ་བརྫང་བྱའི་ནོར། བརྫི་བྱའི་གདན་ནམ་ཟན། རྫུབ་བྱའི་བྲོ་བོ། བརྫེ་བྱའི་སྨྲ།།

བཞར་བྱའི་སྐྲ། བཞབ་བྱའི་ནོར། བཞུ་བྱའི་མར། བཞུར་བྱའི་ཤིང་། བཟུར་བྱའི་སྐྲ། བཞོག་བྱའི་ཤིང་། བཞོ་བྱའི་འོ་མ།། བཟའ་བྱའི་ཟས། བཟབ་བྱའི་མགྲོན། བཟླ་བྱའི་སྔགས། བཟླུག་བྱའི་གཏམ། བཟེད་བྱའི་ཟས། བཟློག་བྱའི་བྱད། བཟློ་བྱའི་གཏམ། བཟོ་བྱའི་ཤིང་།། བྱིན་གྱིས་བརླབ་བྱ། བརླན་བྱའི་དགྲ། བརླམ་བྱའི་ཁོག་པ། བརླན་བྱའི་རྫས། བརླིང་བྱའི་མང།།

བཤའ་བྱའི་ལུག། བཤད་བྱའི་ཆོས། བཤལ་བྱའི་སྣོད། བཤར་བྱའི་ནས། བཤང་བྱའི་སྦུབས། བཤགས་བྱའི་སྡིག། བཤམ་བྱའི་སྟན་མོ། བཤིག་བྱའི་རྫོང་། བཤུ་བྱའི་པགས་པ། མེར་བཤུར་བྱའི་རྫས། བཤུམ་བྱའི་སྡུག་བསྔལ། བཤུད་བྱའི་མཁུར་ཚོས། བཤུག་བྱའི་ནོར། བཤེར་བྱའི་ཚིག། བཤོལ་བྱའི་འགྲུལ། བཤོར་བྱའི་རི་དྭགས།།

བསང་བྱའི་དྲི་མ། བསམ་བྱའི་དོན། བསག་བྱའི་ཚོགས། བསལ་བྱའི་སྐྱོན། བསར་བྱའི་ཆས། བསབ་བྱའི་དྲིན། བསིག་བྱའི་རལ་པ། བསིར་བྱའི་མདེའུ། བསུབ་བྱའི་རྗེས། བསུམ་བྱའི་ཁ། བསུ་བྱའི་མགྲོན། བསེད་བྱའི་བལ། བསོག་བྱའི་ནོར། བསྲང་བྱའི་མདའ། བསྲབ་བྱའི་བག་ཆགས། བསྲན་བྱའི་རྒྱན། བསྲིང་བྱའི་འཐེན། བསྲིང་བྱའི་ཚེ། བསྲི་བྱའི་ཟས། བསྲུབ་བྱའི་ཞོ། བསྲུང་བྱའི་མི། བསྲེལ་བྱའི་ཆུང་མ། བསྲི་བྱའི་རྫས། བསྲེག་བྱའི་བུད་ཤིང་། བསྒོ་བྱའི་ཚོད་མ། བསླབ་བྱའི་རིག་པ། བསླང་བྱའི་ཟས། བསླང་བྱའི་བསོད་སྙོམས། བསླན་བྱའི་ཕྱོགས། རྒྱན་དུ་བསླང་བྱའི་ཤིང་། བསླུ་བྱའི་སྲོག། ཕྱིར་བསློག་བྱ། ཞེས་པ་ལ་སོགས་པ་རྣམས་སོ།།

དེ་ལྟར་བྱ་བའི་ཡུལ་ལ་འཇུག་པའི་སྒྲ་འདི་རྣམས་ལ་ཚིག་གྲོགས་དང་སྦྱར་ནས་དཔེར་བརྗོད་པ་ནི་གོ་སླ་བའི་ཕྱིར་ཏེ་གཞན་དུ། བཀན་བྱ། བཀོལ་བྱ། བགམ་བྱ། བགད་བྱ། བཙར་བྱ། བཙང་བྱ། ཞེས་སོགས་སྨོས་པ་ཉིད་ཀྱིས་བྱ་བའི་ཡུལ་གྱི་སྒྲ་ཡིན་པ་རྟོགས་པར་ནུས་པའི་ཕྱིར་སྐབས་ཐོབ་ཀྱི་དཔེར་བརྗོད་དངོས་ནི་དེ་རྣམས་ཉིད་ཡིན་ནོ།།

དེ་བཞིན་དུ་འཆད་འགྱུར་གྱི་འཇུག་པ་ཕྱི་མ་རྣམས་ཀྱི་སྐབས་སུའང་ཤེས་པར་བྱའོ།། ཡང་སྐབས་འདི་དག་ཏུ་བྱ་ཚིག་གིས་གསལ་མི་དགོས་པར་ཡུལ་གྱི་སྒྲ་མཚོན་ནུས་པ། གོས་སོགས་ལ་བགོ་བ་དང་། རྟ་ལ་བཅིབ་པ། ཆང་སོགས་ལ་བཏུང་བ། ཁྲིམས་ལ་བཏུག་པ། བྱ་བ་ལ་བརྩམ་པ། ཟས་ལ་བཟའ་བ། བསླབ་བྱ་ལ་བསླབ་པ་སོགས་དང་། འཆད་འགྱུར་མ་ནིང་གི་འཇུག་པའི་སྐབས་སུ། གདམ་བྱ་ལ་གདམས་པ། རྩྭ་ལ་གཟན་པ། ཡུལ་ལ་གཟུང་བ་སོགས་དང་། མོ་དང་ཤིན་ཏུ་མོའི་འཇུག་པའི་སྐབས་སུའང་དེ་འདྲ་མང་དུ་འབྱུང་བ་གོ་དགོས་སོ།།

དེ་བཞིན་དུ་བ་ཡིག་དངོས་པོ་གཞན་བྱ་བའི་ཡུལ་དང་འབྲེལ་བའི་བྱ་བ་ཉིད་ལ་འཇུག་པ་ནི། བཀལ་བར་བྱའོ། བཀལ་ལོ། བཀོལ་བར་བྱ། བཀོལ་ལོ། བཀན་པར་བྱ། བཀན་ནོ། བཀྲིག་པར་བྱ། བཀྲིག་གོ། ཀྲོན་པར་བྱ། བཀྲོན་ནོ། བཀྲབ་པར་བྱ། བཀྲབ་བོ། བཀྲུ་བར་བྱ། བཀྲུའོ། བཀླག་པར་བྱ། བཀླག་གོ། བསྐམ་པར་བྱ། བསྐམ་མོ། བརྐུ་བར་བྱ། བརྐུའོ། བརྐོ་བར་བྱ། བརྐོའོ། བསྐྱང་བར་བྱ། བསྐྱང་ངོ་། བསྐང་བར་བྱ། བསྐང་ངོ་། བསྐུ་བར་བྱ། བསྐུའོ། བསྐུལ་བར་བྱ། བསྐུལ་ལོ། བསྐོར་བར་བྱ། བསྐོར་རོ། བསྐོན་པར་བྱ། བསྐོན་ནོ། བསྐུམ་པར་བྱ། བསྐུམ་མོ། བསྐྱ་བར་བྱ། བསྐྱའོ། བསྐྱུར་བར་བྱ། བསྐྱུར་རོ། བསྐྱི་བར་བྱ། བསྐྱིའོ། བསྐྱིལ་བར་བྱ། བསྐྱིལ་ལོ། བསྐྱུར་བར་བྱ། བསྐྱུར་རོ། བསྐྱེད་པར་བྱ། བསྐྱེད་དོ། བསྐྱུན་པར་བྱ། བསྐྱུན་ནོ།།

དེ་བཞིན་དུ། བགམ་བྱ། བགད་བྱ་སོགས་ཊཱིར་སྨོས་པ་རྣམས་དང་གཞན་ལའང་སྦྱར་ནས། བགམ་པར་བྱ། བགམ་མོ། བགད་པར་བྱ། བགད་དོ། སོགས་རྒྱས་པར་དཔེར་བརྗོད་པར་བྱ་ཞིང་།

འདི་སྐབས། བརྒྱན། བསྒྱར། བརྒྱལ་ལྟ་བུ་ན་ར་ལའི་མཐའ་ཅན་རྣམས་ནི་འདས་ཚིག་མ་ཡིན་པའི་ཕྱིར་ད་དྲག་མི་འཐོབ་པས། བརྒྱན་ནོ། བསྒྱར་རོ། བརྒྱལ་ལོ་ཞེས་བརྗོད་པར་བྱའི། བརྒྱན་ཏོ་ཞེས་སོགས་སུ་མི་འགྱུར་བར་ཤེས་པར་བྱའོ།།

དེ་བཞིན་དུ་མ་ནིང་གི་འཇུག་པའི་སྐབས་སོགས་འཆད་འགྱུར་གྱི་བྱེད་པ་དང་བྱ་བའི་ཚིག་རྣམས་ཀྱི་སྟེང་བསྡུའི་སྒྲ་ཐའང་དེ་དག་གི་ན་ར་ལའི་མཐའ་རྟེན་གྱིས་རྗེས་སུ་འབྲོན་ཏོ། ལྟ་བུ་དམིགས་བསལ་འགའ་ཞིག་ལས་ཕལ་ཆེར་ལ་ད་དྲག་མི་འཐོབ་པར་ངེས་པས་ཏོ་ཡིག་གི་སྒྲ་བརྗོད་པ་མེད་པ་ཉིད་དུ་ཤེས་པར་བྱ། ཞིང་འདི་རིགས་ཀྱི་རྣམ་དབྱེ་དང་འབྲུད་གཞན་རྣམས་སྦྱོར་བའི་ཚེའང་འདིས་མཚོན་ནས་རྗེས་སུ་དཔག་པར་བྱའོ།།

གཉིས་པ་སྔོན་འཇུག་གི་མ་ནིང་དགོས་པ་གང་གི་ཕྱིར་འཇུག་པ་ནི།

མ་ནིང་གཉིས་ཀ་ད་ལྟར་ཆེད།

ཅེས་པས་བསྟན་ཏེ། སྔོན་འཇུག་གི་མ་ནིང་ག་ད་གཉིས་ནི་དངོས་པོ་བདག་དང་གཞན་གཉིས་ཀ་ལ་འཇུག་པ་དང༌། དེར་མ་གཏོགས་པའི་དུས་གསུམ་ལས་ད་ལྟ་བ་སྟོན་པའི་ཕྱིར་འཇུག་གོ།

དེ་དག་ཀྱང་རིམ་པ་བཞིན་དཔེར་བརྗོད་ན། ག་ཡིག་བདག་བྱེད་པ་པོ་ལ་འཇུག་པ་ནི། ཡོགས་སུ་གཅོར་བ་པོ། གཅོར་བྱེད། གཅིན་གཅི་བ་པོ། གཅི་བྱེད། བར་དུ་གཅེར་བ་པོ། གཅེར་བྱེད། སྣང་དུ་གཅུར་བ་པོ། གཅུར་བྱེད། ལག་པ་གཅུ་བ་པོ། གཅུ་བྱེད། ཤིང་གཅོད་པ་པོ། གཅོད་བྱེད། རྡོ་བ་གཅོག་པ་པོ། གཅོག་བྱེད། ཡྃ བཟང་ངན་གཉུལ་བ་པོ། གཉུལ་བྱེད། དོན་གཉེར་བ་པོ། གཉེར་བྱེད། བཟའ་ཕྱིར་གཉོག་པ་པོ། གཉོག་བྱེད། ཡྃ ཁྲག་གཏར་བ་པོ། གཏར་བྱེད། ནོར་གཏམ་པ་པོ། གཏམ་བྱེད། ཆུ་གཏིག་པ་པོ། གཏིག་བྱེད། མགོ་གཏུམ་པ་པོ། གཏུམ་བྱེད། ཤིང་གཏུབ་པ་པོ། གཏུབ་བྱེད། ཞབས་ལ་གཏུག་པ་པོ། གཏུག་བྱེད། སེ་གོལ་གཏོག་པ་པོ། གཏོག་བྱེད། གཞན་ལ་གཏོད་པ་པོ། གཏོད་བྱེད། ནོར་གཏོང་བ་པོ། གཏོང་བྱེད། དཔེགས་པ་གཏོད་པ་པོ། གཏོད་བྱེད། ཡྃ ཁ་གདང་བ་པོ། གདང་བྱེད། གདུང་བ་པོ། གདུང་བྱེད། ཐུག་པ་གདུ་བ་པོ། གདུ་བྱེད། མཆོན་གདེང་བ་པོ། གདེང་བྱེད། ཡྃ འོག་ཏུ་གནོན་པ་པོ། གནོན་བྱེད། ཡྃ གཙག་བུས་གཙག་པ་པོ། གཙག་བྱེད། ཤིང་གཙུབ་པ་པོ། གཙུབ་བྱེད། གནོད་པས་གཅོར་བ་པོ། གཅོར་བྱེད། ཡྃ བློས་གཞིག་པ་པོ། གཞིག་བྱེད། ལམ་དུ་གཞུག་པ་པོ། གཞུག་བྱེད། ཤ་གཞུར་བ་པོ། གཞུར་བྱེད། ལྕུག་གིས་གཞུ་བ་པོ། གཞུ་བྱེད། ཡྃ ཕྲུག་ལ་གཟར་བ་པོ། གཟར་བྱེད། གཟེར་བ་པོ། གཟེར་བྱེད། ལམ་དུ་གཟུར་བ་པོ། གཟུར་བྱེད། གཡེང་བ་པོ། གཡེང་བྱེད། གཡབ་གཡུག་གཡོབ་པ་པོ། གཡོབ་བྱེད། ཟས་གཡོ་བ་པོ། གཡོ་བྱེད། གོས་གཡོག་པ་པོ། གཡོག་བྱེད། མིག་གཡོར་བ་པོ། གཡོར་བྱེད། ཡྃ གྲལ་གཤིབས་པ་པོ། གཤིབས་བྱེད ཡྃ ཆུ་གཤོ་བ་པོ། གཤོ་བྱེད། ཤིང་གཤོག་པ་པོ། གཤོག་བྱེད། བྲིས་གཤོར་བ་པོ། གཤོར་བྱེད། མཆོད་པ་གཤོམ་པ་པོ། གཤོམ་བྱེད། ཡྃ རྡིལ་བུ་གསིལ་བ་པོ། གསིལ་བྱེད། ལུས་གསིག་པ་པོ། གསིག་བྱེད། གསུང་བ་པོ། གསུང་བྱེད། ཤིང་གསེ་བ་པོ། གསེ་བྱེད། ནོར་གསོག་པ་པོ། གསོག་བྱེད། གསོད་པ་པོ། གསོད་བྱེད། མདུང་གསོར་བ་པོ། གསོར་བྱེད། གསང་གཏམ་གསོང་བ་པོ། གསོང་བྱེད། ཆུད་གསོན་པ་པོ། གསོན་བྱེད། ཅེས་པ་ལ་སོགས་པ་རྣམས་སོ།།

དེ་བཞིན་དུ་ག་ཡིག་བྱེད་པ་པོ་བདག་ལ་ཡོད་པའི་ལས་སམ་བྱེད་པ་ཙམ་ལ་འཇུག་པ་ནི། གཅར་བར་བྱེད། གཅར་རོ། གཅི་བར་བྱེད། གཅིའོ། གཅེར་བར་བྱེད། གཅེར་རོ། གཅུར་བར་བྱེད། གཅུར་རོ། གཅུ་བར་བྱེད། གཅུའོ། གཅོད་པར་བྱེད། གཅོད་དོ། གཅོག་པར་བྱེད། གཅོག་གོ། ཡྃ གཉུལ་བར་བྱེད། གཉུལ་ལོ། གཉེར་བར་བྱེད། གཉེར་རོ། ཞེས་སོགས་རིམ་པ་བཞིན་དུ་སྦྱར་ཏེ་དཔེར་བརྗོད་པར་བྱའོ།།

ག་ཡིག་གཞན་བྱ་བའི་ཡུལ་ཉིད་ལ་འཇུག་པ་ནི། གཅད་བྱའི་ཤིང་། གཅི་བྱའི་རྩ། གཅེར་བྱའི་ཐུམ། གཅོག་བྱའི་རྡོ། ཉོ གཉག་བྱའི་ཉམ། གཉལ་བྱའི་གྲོན། གཉེར་བྱའི་དོན། ཉོ གཏད་བྱའི་ཐུམ། གཏང་བྱའི་ནོར། གཏམས་བྱའི་སྣོད། གཏིགས་བྱའི་ཆུ། གཏིབ་བྱའི་སྤྲིན། གཏུབ་བྱའི་ཤིང་། གཏུམ་བྱའི་མགོ། གཏུར་བྱའི་ཐུམ། གཏུག་བྱའི་ཞབས། གཏོར་བྱའི་མེ་ཏོག། ཉོ གསོལ་བ་གདབ་བྱའི་ཡུལ། རྒྱས་གདབ་བྱའི་དངོས་པོ། གདབ་བྱའི་དངོས་པོ། གདགས་བྱའི་མིང་། གདབ་བྱའི་ས་བོན། གདམས་བྱའི་ཁྲིམས། གདམ་བྱའི་ནོར། གདིང་བྱའི་སྟན། གདུལ་བྱའི་སེམས་ཅན། གདུ་བྱའི་ཕྱུགས། མེས་གདུང་བྱ། སྣང་ལ་གདེག་བྱ། ངན་སོང་ལས་གདོན་བྱའི་སེམས་ཅན། གདོན་བྱའི་གདོན་པ། ཉོ བཙོག་བྱའི་ཤ། གཙུབ་བྱའི་མེ། གཙོད་བྱའི་དགྲ། ཉོ གཞལ་བྱའི་ཚད། གཞག་བྱའི་དངོས་པོ། གཞིག་བྱའི་དོན། གཞིབ་བྱའི་ཕྲུ་བ། གཞིལ་བྱའི་ནད། གཞིབས་བྱའི་གྲལ། ནང་དུ་གཞུག་བྱའི་མི། གཞུར་བྱའི་དངོས་པོ། ཕྱིར་དུ་གཞུག་བྱའི་ལས། ལྷག་གིས་གཞུ་བྱ། གཞོམ་བྱའི་དགྲ། གཞོག་བྱའི་ཤིང་། གཞོལ་བྱའི་ལམ། ཉོ གཟར་བྱའི་གོས། གཟབ་བྱའི་ལས། གཟན་བྱའི་གཟན་པ། གཟད་བྱའི་གོས། གཟགས་བྱའི་བཅུད། གཟེར་བྱའི་བགེགས། གཟུགས་བྱའི་གཟེར་བུ། གཟུང་བྱའི་ཡུལ། ཆོས་ལ་གཟུད་བྱའི་སྐྱེ་བོ། ལམ་གཟུར་བྱ། གཟོད་བྱའི་གཟན། ཉོ གཡབ་བྱའི་གཡབ་མོ། གཡེར་བྱའི་ཡིད། གཡོ་བྱའི་ཉམ། གཡོག་བྱའི་གོས། གཤག་བྱའི་ཤིང་། གཤིབས་བྱའི་གྲལ། གསད་བྱའི་བགེགས། གསང་བྱའི་སྔགས། གསིལ་བྱའི་དྲིལ་བུ། དུམ་བུར་གསིལ་བྱ། གསོ་བྱའི་བུ། ལ་སོགས་པ་རྣམས་སོ།།

ག་ཡིག་གཞན་བྱ་བའི་གཞི་དང་འབྲེལ་བའི་ལས་སམ་བྱ་བ་ཙམ་ལ་འཇུག་པ་ནི། གཅད་པར་བྱ། གཅད་དོ། གཅི་བར་བྱ། གཅིའོ། གཅེར་བར་བྱ། གཅེར་རོ། གཅོག་པར་བྱ། གཅོག་གོ། གཉག་པར་བྱ། གཉག་གོ། གཉལ་བར་བྱ། གཉལ་ལོ། གཉེར་བར་བྱ། གཉེར་རོ། གཏད་པར་བྱ། གཏད་དོ། གཏང་བར་བྱ། གཏང་ངོ་། སོགས་རིམ་བཞིན་སྦྱར་ནས་དཔེར་བརྗོད་པར་བྱའོ།།

ད་ཡིག་བདག་བྱེད་པ་པོ་ལ་འཇུག་པ་ནི། སྐལ་མས་དགྲི་བ་པོ། དགྲི་བྱེད། རྟ་དཀྲུ་བ་པོ། དཀྲུ་བྱེད། ཉོ གཞན་དུ་དགར་བ་པོ། དགར་བྱེད། གང་ཞིག་དགོད་པ་པོ། དགོད་བྱེད། ཉོ ངར་དཔྱོང་བ་པོ། དཔྱོང་བྱེད། མཚན་མར་དཔྱོད་པ་པོ། དཔྱོད་བྱེད། གཏིང་དཔོག་པ་པོ། དཔོག་བྱེད། ཉོ དཔྱིག་གིས་དཔུར་བ་པོ། དཔུར་བྱེད། རལ་གྲི་དཔྱུག་པ་པོ། དཔྱུག་བྱེད། པགས་པ་དཔྲོལ་བ་པོ། དཔྲོལ་བྱེད། ཉོ སྙིང་ནས་དམོད་པ་པོ། དམོད་བྱེད་ལ་སོགས་པའོ། ཉོ ད་ཡིག་བྱེད་པ་ཙམ་ལ་འཇུག་པ་ནི། དགྲི་བར་བྱེད། དགྲིའོ། དགར་བར་བྱེད། དགར་རོ། སོགས་སྔ་མ་བཞིན་དུ་སྦྱར་རོ།།

དེ་བཞིན་དུ་ད་ཡིག་གཞན་བྱ་བའི་ཡུལ་ལ་འཇུག་པ་ནི། དགྲི་བྱའི་མདོས་རིམ། དཀྲུ་བྱའི་རྟ། དགར་བྱའི་གནས། དགག་བྱའི་སྐྱོན། དགས་བྱའི་ཤིང་། དགལ་བྱའི་ཁལ་མ། དགབ་བྱའི་སྣོད། དཀྲམ་བྱའི་རྡོང་། དགང་བྱའི་བུམ་པ། དཀྲུག་བྱའི་མཚོན། དགོད་བྱའི་ཡི་གེ། དགྲོལ་བྱའི་མདུད་པ། ཉོ དཔག་བྱའི་ཕྲོག་སྦྱར། དཔྱང་བྱའི་དར། དཔྱད་བྱའི་ཡུལ། དཔྱལ་བྱའི་སྐྱོན། ཉོ དབྲལ་བྱའི་པགས་པ། དབབ་བྱའི་ཆར། དབྱི་བྱའི་གྱངས། དབྱེ་བྱའི་རི་མོ། དབྱུང་བྱའི་ཚེར་མ། དབུག་བྱའི་ཤིང་། དབུལ་བྱའི་ཐུམ། དབུབ་བྱའི་ཁྱིམ། དབུབ་བྱའི་གདུགས། དབྱུག་བྱའི་རལ་གྲི། དབུར་བྱའི་རས། དབྱེ་བྱའི་ཁ། དཔོ་བྱའི་རྩ། དགྲོག་བྱའི་ནོར། དབོག་བྱའི་ལུང་། དམད་བྱའི་ཉམ། ལ་སོགས་པ་རྣམས་སོ།།

ད་ཡིག་གཞན་བྱ་བ་ཙམ་ལ་འཇུག་པ་ནི། དགྲི་བར་བྱ། དགྲིའོ།། དཀྲུ་བར་བྱ། དཀྲུའོ།། དགར་བར་བྱ། དགར་རོ། དགག་པར་བྱ། དགག་གོ། དགལ་བར་བྱ། དགལ་ལོ། དཀྲོལ་བར་བྱ། དཀྲོལ་ལོ། སོགས་སྔ་མ་བཞིན་དུ་སྦྱར་ནས་རྟོགས་པར་བྱའོ།།

མ་ནིང་གི་སྔོན་འཇུག་གཉིས་པ་དེ་བཤད་མ་ཐག་པའི་བདག་གཞན་གཉིས་པོ་དེར་མི་གཏོགས་པའི་དུས་ད་ལྟ་བ་ལ་འཇུག་པའི་ཚུལ་ནི། བྱེད་པ་པོ་བདག་དང་འབྲེལ་བའི་བྱེད་པའི་ཚིག་གི་དཔེར་བརྗོད་པ་དེ་རྣམས་ཉིད་ཚིག་གྲོགས་ཀྱིས་བསྒྱུར་བ་ལས་ཤེས་པར་བྱའོ།།

དེའང་དཔེར་ན། གཅར་བར་བྱེད། གཅར་རོ། དགྲི་བར་བྱེད། དགྲི་འོ།།

ལྟ་བུ་ད་ལྟ་བའི་སྒྲ་ཡིན་མོད་ཀྱི། གཟུང་བར་བྱ། གཟུང་ངོ་། དགང་བར་བྱ། དགང་ངོ་། ལྟ་བུ་གཞན་གྱི་སྒྲ་ཐའང་དེ་དང་ཤེས་མཚུངས་ཡོད་པས་ཕྱར་སྟོབས་མཚུངས་ཀྱིས་བདག་གཞན་དུ་ཟླས་ཕྱེ་བའི་བདག་སྒྲའི་ཁོངས་སུ་བསྡུས་ནས་བརྗོད་ཟིན་པས་འདིར་ནི་དོན་གྱིས་བདག་བྱེད་པའི་ཚིག་ཡིན་ཡང་གཞན་གྱི་སྒྲ་ལ་དེ་དང་ཤེས་མཚུངས་སྦྱར་རྒྱུ་མེད་པས་གོང་སློས་བདག་སྒྲའི་ཁོངས་སུ་སྡུད་པར་མི་དགོས་པའི། གཅར་གྱིན་སྣང་ངོ་། གཅར་བཞིན་པའོ།། དགྲི་ཡིན་འདུག་གོ། དགྲི་བཞིན་པའོ།། ལྟ་བུ་ཕྱར་སློས་པའི་བདག་སྒྲའི་བྱེད་ཚིག་དེ་རྣམས་ཉིད་བརྗོད་ཚུལ་ཚིག་གྲོགས་ཀྱི་ཁྱད་པར་དང་བཅས་པས་དཔེར་བརྗོད་པར་བྱའོ།།

གསུམ་པ་སྔོན་འཇུག་གི་མོ་ཡིག་དགོས་པ་གང་གི་ཕྱིར་འཇུག་པ་ནི།

མོ་ནི་བདག་ད་མ་འོངས་ཕྱིར།

ཞེས་པས་བསྟན་ཏེ།

སྔོན་འཇུག་གི་མོ་ཡིག་འ་ནི། དངོས་པོ་བདག་དང་། དུས་ད་ལྟ་བ་དང་མ་འོངས་པ་དག་བསྒྲུབ་པའི་ཕྱིར་འཇུག་གོ།

དེ་ལ་བདག་བྱེད་པ་པོ་ལ་འཇུག་པ་ནི། སྐུད་པ་འཁལ་བ་པོ། འཁལ་བྱེད། ཁུར་འཁུར་བ་པོ། འཁུར་བྱེད། ལུས་ལ་འཁྲུད་པ་པོ། འཁྲུད་བྱེད། ཐག་པས་འཁྱིད་པ་པོ། འཁྱིག་བྱེད། གཞན་དུ་འཁྱེར་བ་པོ། འཁྱེར་བྱེད། གནས་སུ་འཁྲ་བ་པོ། འཁྲ་བྱེད། བྲོ་འཁྲབ་པ་པོ། འཁྲབ་བྱེད། ལམ་དུ་འཁྲིད་པ་པོ། འཁྲིད་བྱེད། ཤིང་ལ་འཁྲིལ་བ་པོ། འཁྲིལ་བྱེད། ཆགས་པས་འཁྲིག་པ་པོ། འཁྲིག་བྱེད། དྲི་མ་འཁྲུད་པ་པོ། འཁྲུད་བྱེད། ཁྲིམ་ལ་འཁྲིན་པ་པོ། འཁྲིན་བྱེད། ༈ ཕྱེ་འགམ་པ་པོ། འགམ་བྱེད། འགུགས་པ་པོ། འགུགས་བྱེད། སྣོད་འགེངས་པ་པོ། འགེངས་བྱེད། མགོ་འགེམས་པ་པོ། འགེམས་བྱེད། འགོག་པ་པོ། འགོག་བྱེད། འགོད་པ་པོ། འགོད་བྱེད། འོད་འགྱེད་པ་པོ། འགྱེད་བྱེད། གཡུལ་འགྱེད་པ་པོ། འགྱེད་བྱེད། ཕྱིན་དུ་འགྱུག་པ་པོ། འགྱུག་བྱེད། ཆ་འགྲེམ་པ་པོ། འགྲེམ་བྱེད། མདུད་པ་འགྲོལ་བ་པོ། འགྲོལ་བྱེད། ༈ ཆོས་འཆད་པ་པོ། འཆད་བྱེད། ཉེས་པ་འཆབ་པ་པོ། འཆབ་བྱེད། གནས་འཆའ་བ་པོ། འཆའ་བྱེད། འཆང་བ་པོ། འཆང་བྱེད། ཁྲིམས་འཆལ་བ་པོ། འཆལ་བྱེད། ཞགས་པས་འཆིང་བ་པོ། འཆིང་བྱེད། ༈ དལ་གྱིས་འཆུ་བ་པོ། འཆུ་བྱེད། ཁས་འཆེ་བ་པོ། འཆེ་བྱེད། ལས་འཆོལ་བ་པོ། འཆོལ་བྱེད། རྒྱུད་འཆོས་པ་པོ། འཆོས་བྱེད། ༈ བློའམ་ཚད་ཀྱིས་འཇལ་བ་པོ། འཇལ་བྱེད། ཁུ་བ་འཇིབ་པ་པོ། འཇིབ་བྱེད། མཆོད་རྟེན་འཛེག་པ་པོ། འཛེག་བྱེད། ཟོས་ལ་འཇུ་བ་པོ། འཇུ་བྱེད། ནང་དུའང་བྱེད་དུ་འཇུག་པ་པོ། འཇུག་བྱེད། ཐབས་ཀྱིས་འཇུན་པ་པོ། འཇུན་བྱེད། སྣང་དུ་འཇུར་བ་པོ། འཇུར་བྱེད། འོ་མ་འཇོ་བ་པོ། འཇོ་བྱེད། གནས་སུ་འཇོག་པ་པོ། འཇོག་བྱེད། ཤིང་འཇོག་པ་པོ། འཇོག་བྱེད། དགྲ་འཇོམས་པ་པོ། འཇོམས་བྱེད།

དགྲ་ལ་འཐབ་པ་པོ། འཐབ་བྱེད། ཕྱེ་མར་འཐག་པ་པོ། འཐག་བྱེད། ཐམ་ལ་འཐུ་བ་པོ། འཐུ་བྱེད། དུམ་བུར་འཐུབ་པ་པོ། འཐུབ་བྱེད། ཆུ་འཐུང་བ་པོ། འཐུང་བྱེད། ཐུན་བུ་འཐུ་བ་པོ། འཐུ་བྱེད། ཐག་པས་འཐེན་པ་པོ། འཐེན་བྱེད། ཤ་འཐོག་པ་པོ། འཐོག་བྱེད། ཆ་འཐོར་བ་པོ། འཐོར་བྱེད། ༈ སྐྱ་མ་འདག་པ་པོ། འདག་བྱེད། ནོར་འདམ་པ་པོ། འདམ་བྱེད། འདུན་པ་པོ། འདུན་བྱེད།

འདུད་པ་པོ། འདུད་བྱེད། འདུལ་བ་པོ། འདུལ་བྱེད། འདུ་བ་པོ། འདུ་བྱེད། འདེགས་པ་པོ། འདེགས་བྱེད། རྗེས་སུ་འདེད་པ་པོ། འདེད་བྱེད། འདེབས་པ་པོ། འདེངས་བྱེད། སྣད་དུ་འདོགས་པ་པོ། འདོགས་བྱེད། ཕྱིར་འདོན་པ་པོ། འདོན་བྱེད། གདམས་ངག་འདོམས་པ་པོ། འདོམས་བྱེད། གོམ་པའམ་དྲི་མ་འདོར་བ་པོ། འདོར་བྱེད། དྲ་བ་འདྲལ་བ་པོ། འདྲལ་བྱེད། ཁ་སྐད་འདྲི་བ་པོ། འདྲི་བྱེད། ནོར་གྱིས་འདྲིད་པ་པོ། འདྲིད་བྱེད། ཤིང་འདྲུད་པ་པོ། འདྲུད་བྱེད། ཁུང་འདྲུ་བ་པོ། འདྲུ་བྱེད། སྐྲ་འདྲེག་པ་པོ། འདྲེག་བྱེད། གནས་ནས་འདྲེན་པ་པོ། འདྲེན་བྱེད།

ཕྱིར་འཕུལ་བ་པོ། འཕུལ་བྱེད། མདའ་འཕེན་པ་པོ། འཕེན་བྱེད། དར་འཕྱུར་བ་པོ། འཕྱུར་བྱེད། གཞན་ལ་འཕྱ་བ་པོ། འཕྱ་བྱེད། ཐལ་བ་འཕྱག་པ་པོ། འཕྱག་བྱེད། ནོར་འཕྲོག་པ་པོ། འཕྲོག་བྱེད།

ལམ་ལ་འབད་པ་པོ། འབད་བྱེད། སྐྲ་འབལ་བ་པོ། འབལ་བྱེད། ཤིང་འབིགས་པ་པོ། འབིགས་བྱེད། ནོར་འབུལ་བ་པོ། འབུལ་བྱེད། ཁྱིམ་འབུབ་པ་པོ། འབུབ་བྱེད། དུང་དམ་རྒྱང་འབུད་པ་པོ། འབུད་བྱེད། ཆར་འབེབས་པ་པོ། འབེབས་བྱེད། གདམས་ངག་འབོགས་པ་པོ། འབོགས་བྱེད། མིང་ནས་འབོད་པ་པོ། འབོད་བྱེད། ཕྱིར་འབོར་བ་པོ། འབོར་བྱེད། རི་མོ་འབྲིད་པ་པོ། འབྲིད་བྱེད། གནས་ནས་འབྱིན་པ་པོ། འབྱིན་བྱེད། ཚོན་འབྱུག་པ་པོ། འབྱུག་བྱེད། སྒོ་འབྱེད་པ་པོ། འབྱེད་བྱེད། འབྱེད་བ་པོ། འབྱེ་བྱེད། ལྕེས་འལྡག་པ་པོ། འལྡག་བྱེད། ཆུ་འབྱོ་བ་པོ། འབྱོ་བྱེད། ས་ལ་འབྲད་པ་པོ། འབྲད་བྱེད། གྲངས་འབྲིད་པ་པོ། འབྲིད་བྱེད། ཡི་གེ་འབྲི་བ་པོ། འབྲི་བྱེད། མཚང་འབྲུ་བ་པོ། འབྲུ་བྱེད། ཁུང་བུ་འབྲུད་བ་པོ། འབྲུད་བྱེད། རྗེས་སུ་འབྲེང་བ་པོ། འབྲེང་བྱེད།

ཕྱག་འཚལ་བ་པོ། འཚལ་བྱེད། སྐྱིན་པ་འཚབ་པ་པོ། འཚབ་བྱེད། ཆུ་འཚག་པ་པོ། འཚག་བྱེད། ཉིལ་འཚེར་བ་པོ། འཚེར་བྱེད། ཟས་འཚེད་པ་པོ། འཚེད་བྱེད། གཞན་ལ་འཚེ་བ་པོ། འཚེ་བྱེད། ནོར་འཚོལ་བ་པོ། འཚོལ་བྱེད། ཚོང་འཚོང་བ་པོ། འཚོང་བྱེད། ཕྱུག་འཚོ་བ་པོ། འཚོ་བྱེད། རྡོ་བས་འཚོག་པ་པོ། འཚོག་བྱེད། ལུས་འཚོ་བ་པོ། འཚོ་བྱེད། རྗོ དངོས་པོ་འཛིན་པ་པོ། འཛིན་བྱེད། སྐོད་དུ་འཛུད་པ་པོ། འཛུད་བྱེད། ཚང་འཛུག་པ་པོ། འཛུག་བྱེད། ཁུང་དུ་འཛུལ་བ་པོ། འཛུལ་བྱེད། སྐོད་འཛེད་པ་པོ། འཛེད་བྱེད། ཁྱིན་དུ་འཛོག་པ་པོ། འཛོག་བྱེད། ལ་སོགས་པ་རྒྱ་ཆེར་ཤེས་པར་བྱའོ།།

དེ་ལྟར་བཀོད་པ་རྣམས་ནི་གོང་སྨོས་ལྟར་གང་ཞིག་ལས་སམ་བྱ་བ་དེ་ལས་ངེས་པར་ཐ་དད་པར་གྱུར་པའི་བདག་བྱེད་པ་པོའི་ཚིག་སྐྱེ། འདིར་བརྟན་གྱི་དཔེར་བརྗོད་དངོས་ཡིན་ལ། ཞར་ལས་གང་ཞིག་ལས་སམ་བྱ་རྒྱུ་དེ་དང་ཐ་མི་དད་པ་ལྟར་སྣང་བའི་བྱེད་པ་པོའི་ཚིག་རྣམས་ཀྱང་ཕལ་ཆེར་འདས་འཕྲུལ་ཅན་དུ་ཤེས་དགོས་ཏེ།

དཔེར་ན། རྟེན་ལ་འཁར་བ་པོ། འཁར་བྱེད། ངག་འཁྲུན་པ་པོ། འཁྲུན་བྱེད། གདན་ལ་འཁོད་པ་པོ། འཁོད་བྱེད། འཁོར་བར་འཁོར་བ་པོ། འཁོར་བྱེད། ལུས་འཁྱུར་བ་པོ། འཁྱུར་བྱེད། ཡུལ་དུ་འཁྱམས་པ་པོ། འཁྱམས་བྱེད། སྐྱུར་བར་འཁྱུག་པ་པོ། འཁྱུག་བྱེད། གཡས་སུ་འཁྱིལ་བ་པོ། འཁྱིལ་བྱེད།

སྟོད་འགྱིང་བ་པོ། འགྱིང་བྱེད། རྟོག་པ་འགྱུ་བ་པོ། འགྱུ་བྱེད། གནས་འགྱུར་བ་པོ། འགྱུར་བྱེད། ཁྱིམ་དུ་འགྲིམ་པ་པོ། འགྲིམ་བྱེད། ལམ་དུ་འགྲོ་བ་པོ། འགྲོ་བྱེད།

འཆག་སར་འཆག་པ་པོ། འཆག་བྱེད། ཤར་ནས་འཆར་བ་པོ། འཆར་བྱེད། འཆི་བ་པོ། འཆི་བྱེད། འཇུག་པ་པོ། འཇུག་བྱེད། ཕྱིར་འཐོན་པ་པོ། འཐོན་བྱེད། ཧཱུྃ མྱ་ངན་འདའ་བ་པོ། འདའ་བྱེད། ཚོགས་སུ་འདུ་བ་པོ། འདུ་བྱེད། སྟན་ལ་འདུག་པ་པོ། འདུག་བྱེད། ལྡོངས་སུ་འདེང་བ་པོ། འདེང་བྱེད། སྒྲོ་འདོག་པ་པོ། འདོག་བྱེད།

གནས་ལས་འཕག་པ་པོ། འཕག་བྱེད། འཕར་བ་པོ། འཕར་བྱེད། གནམ་དུ་འཕུར་བ་པོ། འཕུར་བྱེད། གོང་དུ་འཕོ་བ་པོ། འཕོ་བྱེད། ལྡོངས་སུ་འཕྱན་པ་པོ། འཕྱན་བྱེད། རྐང་མེད་འབྱེ་བ་པོ། འབྱེ་བྱེད། ནམ་མཁར་འཕྱོ་བ་པོ། འཕྱོ་བྱེད།

སར་འབབ་པ་པོ། འབབ་བྱེད། རང་ཉིད་འབར་བ་པོ། འབར་བྱེད། འབྱུང་བ་པོ། འབྱུང་བྱེད། འབྱོན་པ་པོ། འབྱོན་བྱེད། གཞན་དུ་འབྱོལ་བ་པོ། འབྱོལ་བྱེད། རྗེས་སུ་འབྲང་བ་པོ། འབྲང་བྱེད། འབྲོས་པ་པོ། འབྲོས་བྱེད།

འཛུལ་བ་པོ། འཛུལ་བྱེད། བཞིན་འཛུམ་པ་པོ། འཛུམ་བྱེད། ལ་སོགས་པ་ལྟ་བུའོ༎ དེའང་དཔེར་ན་འཁོར་བར་འཁོར་རྒྱུ་སེམས་ཅན་རྣམས་ཡིན་ཞིང་། འཁོར་བ་པོའམ་འཁོར་བྱེད་ཀྱང་། འཁོར་བཞིན་པའི་གནས་སྐབས་དེར་སེམས་ཅན་ཉིད་ལས་གཞན་དུ་མི་དམིགས་པས་བྱེད་པོ་དང་བྱ་བ་ཐ་མི་དད་པའི་ཆ་ནས་འཁོར་བ་པོའམ་འཁོར་བྱེད་ཅེས་འ་འཕྲུལ་ཅན་དུ་གྲུབ་པ་ཡིན་གྱི་བྱེད་པ་པོ་གཞན་ཞིག་ཡོད་པའི་ཆ་ནས་ནི་དེ་ལྟར་གྲུབ་པ་མ་ཡིན་ནོ༎

དེ་བཞིན་དུ་རྫ་མཁན་གྱིས་འཁོར་ལོ་བསྐོར་བའི་ཚེ་སྤྱི་ལྡོག་ནས་འཁོར་བ་བྱེད་པ་པོ་ལ་ལྟོས་ཀྱང་དེ་མི་བརྗོད་པར་འཁོར་བཞིན་པའི་གནས་སྐབས་ཙམ་བརྗོད་པའི་ཚེ་བྱེད་པོ་དང་བྱ་བ་གཉིས་ཀ་ཐ་མི་དད་པའི་དབང་གིས་རྫ་མཁན་གྱི་འཁོར་ལོ་འཁོར་བ་ཞེས་བརྗོད་པ་ཡིན་ནོ། དེས་མཚོན་ནས་བརྗོད་བྱའི་གནས་སྐབས་དང་བསྟུན་ཏེ་རྗོད་བྱེད་ཀྱི་ཚིག་སྦྱོར་བའི་ཚུལ་རྣམས་ཁོང་དུ་ཆུད་པར་བྱ་དགོས་སོ།

སྔོན་འཇུག་མ་ཡིག་བདག་དང་འབྲེལ་པའི་བྱེད་པ་ཙམ་ལ་འཇུག་པ་ནི། སྐུད་པ་འཁལ་བར་བྱེད། འཁལ་ལོ། འཁུར་བར་བྱེད། འཁུར་རོ། འཁྱུད་པར་བྱེད། འཁྱུད་དོ། འཁྱིག་པར་བྱེད། འཁྱིག་གོ། འཁྱེར་བར་བྱེད། འཁྱེར་རོ། འཁྲབ་པར་བྱེད། འཁྲབ་བོ། འཁྲིད་པར་བྱེད། འཁྲིད་དོ། འཁྲིལ་བར་བྱེད། འཁྲིལ་ལོ། འཁྲིག་པར་བྱེད། འཁྲིག་གོ། འཁྲུད་པར་བྱེད། འཁྲུད་དོ། འཁྲེན་པར་བྱེད། འཁྲིན་ནོ། འགམ་པར་བྱེད། འགམ་མོ། འགུགས་པར་བྱེད། འགུགས་སོ༎ ཞེས་སོགས། སྔ་མ་བཞིན་ཐམས་ཅད་ལ་རིག་འགྲེ་བར་བྱའོ༎

སྔོན་འཇུག་གི་མ་ཡིག་སྦྱར་བཤད། བདག་གཞན་གྱི་དབྱེ་བ་མ་སྨོས་པའི་དུས་ད་ལྟ་བར་འཇུག་པ་ནི། མ་ནིང་གི་འཇུག་པའི་སྐབས་སུ་བཤད་པ་ལྟར་སྔོན་མ་ཐག་པའི་བྱ་བྱེད་ཐ་དད་པ་དང་ཐ་མི་དད་པ་གཉིས་ཀའི་བྱེད་ཚིག་རྣམས་ལ་ཚིག་གྲོགས་ཀྱིས་བསྒྱུར་བ། སྐུད་པ་འཁལ་བཞིན་པ། འཁལ་གྱིན་སྣང་། འཁུར་བཞིན་པ། འཁུར་གྱིན་སྣང་། འཁྱུད་བཞིན་པ། འཁྱུད་གྱིན་འདུག་སོགས་དང་། འཁར་བཞིན་པ། འཁར་གྱིན་འདུག། འཁྲུན་བཞིན་པ། འཁྲུན་གྱིན་འདུག། འཁོད་བཞིན་པ། འཁོད་གྱིན་སྣང་། སོགས་སྔ་མ་བཞིན་རྒྱས་པར་སྦྱར་ནས་རྟོགས་པར་བྱའོ༎

སྔོན་འཇུག་གི་མ་ཡིག་སྦྱར་བཤད་བདག་གཞན་གྱི་དབྱེ་བ་མ་སྨོས་པའི་དུས་མ་འོངས་པའི་དོན་ལ་འཇུག་པ་ནི། རང་གི་ངང་གིས་འབྱུང་བ་ལྟ་བུ་བྱེད་པོ་གཞན་མེད་པ་དང་རགས་པར་བྱ་བྱེད་ཐ་དད་དུ་མི་སྣང་བའི་འབྱུང་འགྱུར་གྱི་ཚིག་རྣམས་ཏེ།

དཔེར་ན། ཁྱིམ་ལ་འཁར་བར་འགྱུར། གཞན་དུ་འཁྱུར་བར་འགྱུར། ཡུལ་དུ་འཁྱམ་པར་འགྱུར། འོད་འཁྱིམས་པར་འགྱུར། ཆུ་འཁྱིལ་བར་འགྱུར། གོས་ལ་འཁྲི་བར་འགྱུར། གཡོག་ཏུ་འཁོལ་བར་འགྱུར། རང་བཞིན་འཁྲུན་པར་འགྱུར། བག་འཁྲུམས་པར་འགྱུར། གལ་གྱིས་འཁྲུ་བར་འགྱུར། སྒྲོག་འཁྲུག་པར་འགྱུར། དྲི་མ་འཁྲུ་བར་འགྱུར། སྐུ་འཁྲུང་བར་འགྱུར། ལུས་ལ་འཁྲིམ་པར་འགྱུར། འཁོར་བར་འཁོར་བར་འགྱུར།

གདན་ལ་འཁོད་པར་འགྱུར། ཁྲན་དུ་འཁོར་བར་འགྱུར། ཤིང་འཁྱུག་པར་འགྱུར། ལུས་འཁྱོར་བར་འགྱུར། རྒྱ་མཚོ་འཁྱུམ་པར་འགྱུར། གནས་སུ་འཁྱོལ་བར་འགྱུར། རིལ་མོ་འཁྲིལ་བར་འགྱུར། སོགས་དང་།

དེ་བཞིན་དུ། འགག། འགས། འགྲིམ། འགྲིབ། འགྲིལ། འགུལ། འགུམས། འགྱུ། འགྱུར། འགྱུབ། འགྱེས། འགྱེལ། འགྲེ། འགོ། འགྲོ།

འཆར། འཆད། འཆག། འཆབ། འཆི། འཆུས།

འཛགས། འཛེག། འཛུ། འཛུག། འཛེ།

འཐོན། འཐོབ། ཉོ འདའ། འདག། འདུ། འདུག། འདོང་།

འཕར། འཕག། འཕུན། འཕུང་། འཕྲད། འཕྱི། འཕྱུག། འཕྱེ། འཕྱོ། འཕྲོ།

འབབ། འབུམ། འབུར། འབུང་། འབྲལ། འབྲང་། འབྱིང་། འབྱི། འབྲི། འབྲིམ། འབྱུང་། འབྱེད། འབྱེར། འབྱོངས། འབྱོར། འབྲོས།

འཚོལ། འཚོ། འཚོག། ཉོ འཛག། འཛུར། འཛོམ། ལ་སོགས་པ་རྒྱ་ཆེར་ཤེས་པར་བྱ་ཞིང་། དེ་དག་ལའང་འགའ་ཞིག་ནི་ཚིག་གྲོགས་མམ་བུ་ཚིག་གིས་གསལ་མི་དགོས་པར་སྐབས་འདིའི་དཔེར་བརྗོད་དུ་རུང་བ། དཔེར་ན། འགག། འགྱུར། འགྱུབ། འདུ་ལྟ་བུ་སྟེ་དེ་དག་བྱེད་པ་པོ་གཞན་དང་དངོས་སུ་འབྲེལ་པ་ཡིན་ན། དགག། བསྒྱུར། བསྒྱུབ། བསྡུ་ལྟ་བུ་ཐེབ་སྐོར་གཞན་འཐོབ་ཅིང་། བྱེད་པ་དང་ལྟ་བ་བརྗོད་ན། འགོག་པར་བྱེད། འགྱུར་བར་བྱེད། འགྱུབ་པར་བྱེད་སོགས་ཐོབ་པས་འབྲུལ་གཞི་མེད་པ་དང་། འགའ་ཞིག་ནི་ཚིག་གྲོགས་མམ་བུ་ཚིག་དང་བཅས་པས་འདི་སྐབས་ཀྱི་དཔེར་རུང་བ། དཔེར་ན། འཁྲུན། འཆག། འདག། ལྟ་བུ་སྟེ། དེ་དག་ལ་རང་བཞིན་གྱིས་འཁྲུན་པར་འགྱུར། རང་ཉིད་འཆག་པར་འགྱུར། རང་འདག་པར་འགྱུར། ཞེས་པ་ལྟ་བུར་སྦྱར་ན་བྱེད་པོ་གཞན་མི་མངོན་པ་སོགས་གསལ་བའི་ངག་ཏུ་འགྱུར་བས་སྐབས་འདིའི་དཔེར་རུང་ཞིང་གཞན་དུ་དེ་རྣམས་ཚིག་གྲོགས་མེད་པ་ཉིད་དུ་ཚིག་ཕྲི་ཙམ་དུ་སྦྱར་བས་དཔེར་མི་རུང་བ་དང་། ནད་ཀྱིས་འཁྲུན་པར་བྱེད། རྐང་པས་འཆག་པར་བྱེད། འདག་ཆལ་གྱིས་འདག་པར་བྱེད། སོགས་སྦྱར་ནའང་མི་རུང་བ་ལྟ་བུར་ཞིབ་མོར་བྱེ་བྲག་ཕྱེ་ནས་རྟོགས་དགོས་ཤིང་། འདིར་ས་སོའི་དཔེར་བརྗོད་རྒྱས་པར་འགོད་པ་ཡི་གེ་འཇིགས་པས་བློས་པ་སྤང་ངོ་།།

འདིར་གཞུང་གི་ཡིག་ཆ་རྣམས་སུ། མོ་ནི་བདག་དང་མ་འོངས་ཕྱིར། ཞེས་པ་ཡོད་ཅིང་འགྲེལ་བྱེད་བླ་མ་རྣམས་ལའང་དོགས་པ་མ་ཤར་མོད། དེ་ནི་འདིར་བསྟན་གྱི་བདག་གཞན་དང་དུས་གསུམ་གྱི་དབྱེ་བ་གཞུང་གི་དགོངས་པ་བཞིན་མ་ཕྱེད་པས་ནོངས་ཏེ། བདག་གི་ཐ་སྙད་ཀྱིས་མ་བསྟན་པའི་ད་ལྟ་བའི་ཚིག་འ་འཕྲུལ་ཅན་མང་དུ་ཡོད་པ་སྐབས་འདིར་བསྟན་དགོས་པ་མ་ཤེས་པར་འདུག་པའི་ཕྱིར་རོ།། དེས་ན་གཞུང་དེ་ལྟར་བཀླགས་པ་གཞུང་གི་བསྟན་བྱ་མ་རྫོགས་པའི་སྐྱོན་དུ་འགྱུར་བས་ཡིག་ནོར་བརྒྱུད་པར་ཤེས་པར་བྱས་ལ་དཀྱུས་སུ་བཀོད་པ་བཞིན་གཟུང་བར་བྱའོ།།

བཞི་པ་སྟོན་འཇུག་གི་ཤིན་ཏུ་མོ་དགོས་པ་གང་གི་ཕྱིར་འཇུག་པ་ནི།

ཤིན་ཏུ་མོ་ནི་མཉམ་ཕྱིར་རོ།།

ཞེས་པས་བསྟན་ཏེ། སྟོན་འཇུག་གི་ཤིན་ཏུ་མོ་མ་ཡིག་ནི་སྔར་བཤད་པའི་བདག་གཞན་དང་དུས་གསུམ་གྱི་བྱེ་བྲག་མེད་པར་ཐམས་ཅད་ལ་མཉམ་པ་སྟེ་མཚུངས་པ་ཉིད་བསྒྲུབ་པའི་ཕྱིར་འཇུག་གོ། དེས་ན་དཔེར་བརྗོད་ཀྱང་བདག་གཞན་དང་དུས་གསུམ་ལ་སོ་སོར་མི་དགོས་པས་ཅི་རིགས་པར་ཚིགས་གཅིག་ཏུ་དགོད་ན།

མཉམ་པར་བྱས། མཉམ་པ། མཉམ་པར་བྱེད། མཉམ་བྱ། མཉམ་པར་བྱ། མཉམ་པར་གྱུར། མཉམ་བཞིན་པ། མཉམ་པར་འགྱུར།

ཀླུ་བུ་ཀུན་ལ་སྨྲར་ཏེ། མཁང་། མཁྲང་། མཁྱེན། འཁྲིགས། མཁོ། ༈ མགར། མགུ། མགྱོགས།

མངའ། མངག། མངགས། མངོན། ༈ མཆི། མཆིས། མཆེད། མཆོད། ༈ མཇལ། ༈ མཉན།
མཉམ། མཉེས། མཉེན། མཉེ།

མཐུན། མཐུད། མཐོ། མཐོལ། མཐོང་། ༈ མདུད། ༈ མཚན། མཚར། མཚུངས། མཛོན། ༈ མཛད།
མཛའ། མཛངས། མཛེས། ལ་སོགས་པ་རྣམས་སོ།། དེར་ཡང་མངགས་དང་མཆིས་སོགས་འདས་ཚིག་ལ་ཁྱད་པར་ཡོད་པ་རྣམས་ནི་རྗེས་འཇུག་གི་བྱེད་པ་ཡིན་པས་སྔོན་འཇུག་མ་ཡིག་གི་འཇུག་པ་མི་མཉམ་པར་ཐལ་བའི་སྐྱོན་མེད་དོ།།

གསུམ་པ་རྗེས་འཇུག་གི་རྟགས་ཀྱི་འཇུག་པ་བཤད་པ་ལ་གཉིས། རྟགས་སོ་སོར་ངོས་འཛིན་པ་དང་། དེའི་འཇུག་པ་རྒྱས་པར་འཆད་པའོ།། དང་པོ་ལ་གཞུང་དོན་འཆད་པ་དང་བཅས་ནས་བཤད་པ་དང་། གཞན་གྱི་ནོར་བ་འགོག་པ་གཉིས།

དང་པོ་ལ། ཕྱིར་རྟགས་གསུམ་དུ་དབྱེ་བ་དང་། ནང་གསེས་བརྒྱད་དུ་དབྱེ་བ་གཉིས་ཀྱི་དང་པོ་ནི།

རྗེས་འཇུག་ཡི་གེ་བཅུ་པོ་ལ། ཕོ་མོ་མ་ནིང་གསུམ་དུ་དབྱེ།

ཞེས་པས་བསྟན་ཏེ། རྗེས་འཇུག་གི་ཡི་གེ་ག་ང་ད་ན་བ་མ་འ་ར་ལ་ས་སྟེ་བཅུ་པོ་དེ་རྣམས་ལའང་ཕོ་མོ་མ་ནིང་གསུམ་དུ་དབྱེ་བར་བྱའོ།། ཞེས་སོ།།

དེ་ལ་ཕོ་ནི་ག་ད་བ་ས་བཞིའོ།།

མོ་ནི་ང་མ་འ་གསུམ་མོ།།

མ་ནིང་ནི་ན་ར་ལ་གསུམ་མོ།།

དེ་ལྟར་ཡིན་པ་ཙམ་ཞེས་ཅེ་ན་བཤད་པར་བྱ་སྟེ། རྗེས་འཇུག་ལ་ཕོ་མོ་མ་ནིང་གསུམ་དུ་དབྱེ་བ་ནི་རྗེས་འཇུག་དེ་ཉིད་མིང་གཞིའི་ཡི་གེ་གང་ལ་ཞུགས་པ་ལས་བརྗོད་པའི་སྒྲ་གདངས་དྲག་ཞན་བར་མར་འགྱུར་བའི་ཆ་ནས་བཞག་དགོས་ཏེ།

ཕོ་གསུམ་མོ་གཉིས་མ་ནིང་གསུམ། དྲག་ཞན་བར་མ་གསུམ་དུ་འཇུག།

ཅེས་གཞུང་འདིར་དངོས་སུ་བསྟན་པའི་རྒྱུ་མཚན་གྱིས་སོ།། དེ་ལྟར་བཞག་པའི་ཚེ་མིང་གཞི་གང་གི་མཐར་ཡང་རུང་ག་ད་བ་ས་རྣམས་ཞུགས་པ་སྒྲ་དྲག་པ་དང་། ང་མ་འ་རྣམས་ཞུགས་པ་སྒྲ་ཞན་པ་དང་། ན་ར་ལ་རྣམས་ཞུགས་པ་སྒྲ་བར་མར་འགྱུར་བ་ཞིབ་མོའི་བློས་བརྟགས་ན་མངོན་སུམ་གྱིས་གྲུབ་ཅིང་། དེའང་བརྗོད་པ་ལྷུབ་ཕྱིབ་མ་ཡིན་པར་ཡི་གེའི་སྐྱེ་གནས་བྱེད་རྩོལ་སོགས་དང་མཐུན་པར་ཟུར་ཕྱིན་པར་བགྲགས་པ་ལས་སོ།།

འདིར་ཁ་ཅིག་ཕོ་གསུམ་ཞེས་སོགས་ཀྱི་གཞུང་གིས་སྒྲའི་འཇུག་པ་ཙམ་བསྟན་གྱི་རྟགས་གསུམ་དུ་དབྱེ་བའི་རྒྱུ་མཚན་ནི་གཙོ་བོར་མིང་མཐའ་འདྲེན་ཚུལ་སོགས་ལས་ངེས་དགོས་སོ། སྙམ་པ་སྲིད་ཀྱང་གཞུང་དེས་སྒྲ་འཇུག་བསྟན་པ་ཉིད་ཀྱིས་རྟགས་ཀྱི་དབྱེ་བ་བྱེད་པའི་རྒྱུ་མཚན་བསྟན་པར་གྲུབ་སྟེ། རྟགས་ཀྱི་དབྱེ་བ་སྒྲའི་འཇུག་པ་ལ་ལྟོས་ཀྱི་སྒྲ་འཇུག་ཙམ་རྟགས་ལ་ལྟོས་པ་མ་ཡིན་པའི་ཕྱིར་དང་། མིང་མཐའ་འདྲེན་ཚུལ་སོགས་ཀྱང་རྟགས་ཀྱི་རྒྱུ་མཚན་དུ་མི་འགྱུར་ཏེ། དེ་རྣམས་རྗེས་འཇུག་གི་རྟགས་ལ་ལྟོས་པ་ཡོད་ཀྱང་རྗེས་འཇུག་དེ་རྣམས་ལ་མི་ལྟོས་པའི་ཕྱིར་རོ།།

གཉིས་པ་དེའི་ནང་གསེས་ཀྱི་དབྱེ་བ་ནི།

ཕོ་ལ་སྐྱེས་བུ་རབ་འབྲིང་གསུམ། མོ་ལ་མོ་དང་ཤིན་ཏུ་མོ།

མ་ནིང་འགྱུར་དང་མཚན་གཉིས་དང་། མཚན་མེད་དག་དང་གསུམ་དུ་འདོད།

ཅེས་པས་བསྟན་ཏེ། དེ་ལྟར་རྗེས་འཇུག་ལ་རྟགས་གསུམ་དུ་ཕྱེས་པ་དེ་ལ་སྔར་ཡང་ནང་གསེས་ཀྱི་སྒོ་ནས་རྣམ་པ་བརྒྱད་དུ་དབྱེ་སྟེ། ཕོ་ལ་སྐྱེས་བུ་རབ་འབྲིང་ཐ་གསུམ་དང་། མོ་ལ་མོ་ཙམ་དང་ཤིན་ཏུ་མོ་གཉིས་དང་། མ་ནིང་ལ་འགྱུར་བ་མ་ནིང་མཚན་གཉིས་མ་ནིང་མཚན་མེད་མ་ནིང་གསུམ་དུ་དབྱེ་བར་འདོད་དོ། ཞེས་སོ། །

དེའང་རྗེས་འཇུག་གི་ཕོ་ག་ཡིག་ལ་ཡང་འཇུག་ས་ཡིག་ཞུགས་པ་ནི་རྗེས་འཇུག་ནང་ཚན་གྱི་སྟོབས་ལས་སྒྲ་དྲག་པའི་དྲག་པར་འགྱུར་བས་སྐྱེས་བུ་རབ་ཡིན་ནོ། དེ་བཞིན་དུ་རྗེས་འཇུག་བ་ལ་ས་ཡིག་ཞུགས་པ་ནི་སྒྲ་དྲག་པའི་འབྲིང་དུ་འགྱུར་བས་སྐྱེས་བུ་འབྲིང་པོའོ། །

ག་བ་གཉིས་ཀྱི་མཐར་ཡང་འཇུག་མ་ཞུགས་པ་དང་ས་དའི་མཐའ་རྣམས་ནི་སྒྲ་དྲག་པའི་ཞན་པར་གྱུར་བས་སྐྱེས་བུ་ཐ་མའོ། །

མོ་ཡིག་ང་མ་གཉིས་ལ་ཡང་འཇུག་ཞུགས་པ་ནི་སྒྲ་ཞན་པའི་དྲག་པར་འགྱུར་བས་མོ་ཙམ་དང་། དེ་གཉིས་ལ་ཡང་འཇུག་མ་ཞུགས་པ་དང་འ་ཡིག་གི་མཐའ་རྣམས་ནི་སྒྲ་ཤིན་ཏུ་ཞན་པར་འགྱུར་བས་ཤིན་ཏུ་མོའོ། །

མ་ནིང་གི་ཡི་གེ་ན་ར་ལ་གསུམ་ནི་མིང་གཞིའི་ཕོ་ཡིག་གི་མཐར་ཡང་འཇུག་ཡོད་མེད་གང་རུང་དང་མོ་ཡིག་གི་རྗེས་སུ་ཡང་འཇུག་མེད་པར་ཞུགས་པའི་ཚེ་ནི་སྒྲ་བར་མའི་དྲག་པའམ་ཞན་པར་འགྱུར་བས་འགྱུར་བ་མ་ནིང་དང་། མིང་གཞིའི་མོ་ཡིག་གི་མཐར་ཞུགས་ཤིང་ཡང་འཇུག་དང་བཅས་པར་གྱུར་པའི་ཚེ་ནི་སྒྲ་བར་མ་ལས་དྲག་ཞན་གཉིས་ཀའི་ཆ་དང་ལྡན་པར་འགྱུར་བས་མ་ནིང་མཚན་གཉིས་པ་དང་། མིང་གཞིའི་མ་ནིང་གི་མཐར་ཞུགས་པའི་ཚེ་ཡང་འཇུག་ཡོད་མེད་ཇི་ལྟར་རུང་སྒྲ་བར་མ་ཙམ་ལས་དྲག་ཞན་གང་དུའང་མི་འགྱུར་བའི་ཕྱིར་མཚན་མེད་མ་ནིང་ངོ། །

དེ་ལྟར་སྔོན་ཚད་འགྲེལ་བྱེད་སུས་ཀྱང་མ་བསྟན་པའི་སྤྱི་ཚོལ་འདི་ནི་འབྱུང་མའི་བུ་བཞིན་དུ་སུ་ཞིག་ཡིད་ཆེས་པར་འགྱུར་སྙམ་ན། རྫར་ཕྱིར་བཏང་རྟགས་ཀྱི་དབྱེ་བའི་རྒྱུ་མཚན་བློས་པ་བཞིན་དུ་གཞུང་འདི་ཉིད་ལས། དྲག་པ་གསུམ་ནི་ནང་ཕྲད་དམ། ཞེས་སོགས་འཆད་འགྱུར་ལྟར་ནང་གསེས་ཀྱི་དབྱེ་བ་འདིའི་རྒྱུ་མཚན་གསལ་པོར་གསུངས་པ་ཉིད་ཁུངས་སུ་བྱས་ནས་བཤད་པ་ཡིན་པས་ཡིད་རྟོན་དུ་ངེས་པར་རུང་བ་ཡིན་གྱི། སྔ་འགྲེལ་རྣམས་ཀྱིས་གཞུང་གི་དངོས་བསྟན་གསལ་བ་རྣམས་རང་རང་གི་ཀློག་བཤད་ཀྱིས་སྒྲིབས་ནས་གར་འགྲོ་གཏོལ་མེད་ཀྱི་སྨན་པར་ཞུགས་ཏེ་སྙི་སྤྲུགས་ཀྱི་སྦྲང་བར་ཐོན་ལུག་ཐོན་དུ་སྤྲོ་བར་བྱེད་པ་རྣམས་ལ་དེ་བས་ཀྱང་སུ་ཞིག་ཡིད་ཆེས་པར་འགྱུར། ལེགས་པར་བསམ་དགོས་སོ། །

གཉིས་པ་གཞན་གྱི་ནོར་བ་འགོག་པ་ནི། རྗེས་འཇུག་གི་རྟགས་ཀྱི་དབྱེ་བ་བཤད་པའི་སྐབས་འདིར་འགྲེལ་བྱེད་རྣམས་མི་མཐུན་པ་མང་ཡང་བསྒྲུབ་བྱ་དང་སྒྲུབ་བྱེད་ཀྱི་ཚིག་གི་སྦྲེང་བ་ཕལ་ཆེར་མི་འཐད་པའི་ཕྱོགས་ཤས་ཆེ་བར་མཐོང་སོང་། འོན་ཀྱང་དེ་རྣམས་སོ་སོར་ངོས་འཛིན་ཅིང་སུན་འབྱིན་པ་ནི་ཡི་གེའི་ལས་སུ་ཆེ་ཞིང་དགོས་པའང་ཆེར་མེད་པས་བཞག་ལ། བློ་གསལ་རྣམས་ཀྱིས་མི་ཤེས་སུ་མི་རུང་བའི་མཚང་འགའ་ཞིག་འཆད་འགྱུར་རྣམས་ལས་ཀྱང་གསལ་བར་འགྱུར་མོད་ཀྱི་འདིར་ཡང་ཕྱོགས་ཙམ་མཚོན་པའི་ཕྱིར་ཅུང་ཟད་དཔྱད་ན། ཕྱིར་གོང་བློས་ལྟར་སྐབས་འདིའི་སྤྱི་བྱེ་བྲག་གི་རྟགས་ཀྱི་ངོས་འཛིན་སྒྲའི་འཇུག་ཚུལ་གྱི་སྒོ་ནས་རྟོགས་ནུས་པ་ལ་དེའི་གོ་བ་ངེས་ཅན་མ་ཕྱེད་པས་རྟགས་འགའ་ཞིག་མིང་མཐའ་དང་རྣམ་དབྱེ་སོགས་འཛིན་ཚུལ་གྱི་སྒོ་ནས་དང་། འགའ་ཞིག་སྔོན་འཇུག་བཞིན་དུ་འདས་པ་དང་གཞན་སྒྲུབ་སོགས་ཀྱི་དོན་སྟོན་ཚུལ་གྱི་སྒོ་ནས་དང་། འགའ་ཞིག་སྒྲ་འཇུག་དྲག་ཞན་གྱི་སྒོ་ནས་ཀྱང་འབྱེད་པར་ཀློམ་ཞིང་དེར་ཡང་འབྱེད་ཚུལ་འདྲ་མིན་མང་དུ་སྣང་ངོ། ། དེ་ལ་སྔ་མ་མིང་མཐའ་སོགས་འཛིན་ཚུལ་གྱིས་འབྱེད་པ་དེ་ནི་སྐབས་འགར་འགྲིག་ཏུ་རུང་ཡང་ཕལ་ཆེར་ལ་མི་འགྲིག་པ་མང་བས་མི་འཐད་དོ། །

དཔེར་ན་པེར་མཐའ་འཛིན་ཚུལ་གྱིས་འབྱེད་པའི་ཚེ། གཞུང་ལྟ་བུ་གཞན་དང་།

ཕོ་ཡིས་ཕོ་ཡི་མིང་མཐའ་དྲང་།

ཞེས་སོགས་ཀྱི་དགོངས་པ་ལེན་ཚུལ་མ་ནོར་བའི་སྒོ་ནས་དཔྱད་པ་ན། རྟག་པ། བཅད་པ། སྒྲུབ་པ། བྱས་པ། བཟང་བ། བྱ་བ་སོགས་ཕོ་མོའི་རྟགས་ཕལ་ཆེར་ལ་དཔེར་བསལ་ཁ་ཤས་མ་གཏོགས་འགྲིག་ཀྱང་མོ་ཡིག་མ་མཐའ་ཅན་དང་མ་ནིང་གི་མཐའ་ཅན་རྣམས་ལ་འགྲིག་མི་འགྲིག་ཅི་རིགས་སུ་འགྱུར་བ་འཆད་འགྱུར་ལྟར་དང་། ཕོ་མོ་མ་ནིང་གི་ངོས་འཛིན་གཞན་དང་གཞན་བྱེད་པ་རྣམས་ལའང་དེ་བཞིན་དུ་མོས་ཕོའམ་མོས་མ་ནིང་ངམ་མ་ནིང་གིས་མོའི་མིང་མཐའ་དྲངས་པ་སོགས་སུ་འགྱུར་བ་དང་། རྣམ་དབྱེ་དྲུག་སྒྲ་ཕོ་ཡིག་ཅན་དང་མཐུན་པའི་སྒྲུབ་བྱེད་ཀྱིས་ད་བ་ས་གསུམ་ཕོར་སྒྲུབ་པ་སོགས་རྣམ་དབྱེ་འདྲེན་ཚུལ་གྱི་སྒོ་ནས་འབྱེད་པའི་ཚེའང་། རང་རང་གི་རྟགས་ངོས་འཛིན་ཚུལ་དང་མི་འགྲིག་པའི་འགལ་བ་མང་དུ་འབྱུང་སྟེ། ད་བ་ས་གསུམ་ཕོ་དང་། ག་ང་ན་མ་ར་ལ་མོར་འདོད་པ་རྣམས་གསུམ་པ་དང་དྲུག་པའི་སྒྲ་ལ་འགྲིག་ཀྱང་ལ་དོན་རྣམས་ལ་མི་འགྲིག་པ་མང་བ་དང་། འ་མ་ནིང་དུ་འདོད་པ་ནི་གསུམ་ག་ལ་མི་འགྲིག་པ་དང་། ག་ཡིག་ཕོར་འདོད་པ་ལ་དོན་ལ་འགྲིག་ཀྱང་གསུམ་པ་དྲུག་པ་ལ་མི་འགྲིགས་པ་དང་། ག་ང་ན་མ་ར་མ་ནིང་དུ་འདོད་པ་ནི་རྣམ་དབྱེ་ཐམས་ཅད་ལ་མི་འགྲིག་པ་སོགས་སྐྱོན་གྱིས་མི་ལང་ཞིང་། འཕྲད་འདྲེན་ཚུལ་གྱིས་འབྱེད་པའི་ཚེའང་། ཅིང་ཅེས་ཤིང་ཞེས་སོགས་ག་ད་བ་ཕོར་འདོད་པ་དང་ང་ན་མ་འ་ར་ལ་མོར་འདོད་པ་རྣམས་ཀྱི་ཕྱོགས་ལ་འགྲིག་ཀྱང་ས་ཕོ་དང་ང་ན་མ་འ་ར་ལ་མ་ནིང་དུ་འདོད་པ་རྣམས་ལ་མི་འགྲིག་པ་དང་དེ་བཞིན་དུ་ཀྱུན་སྤྱད་སྦྱར་བསྡུ་ལྷུག་བཅས་སོགས་དང་སྦྱོར་བའི་ཚེའང་འགྲིག་མི་འགྲིག་ཅི་རིགས་སུ་འགྱུར་བ་ཞིབ་མོར་དཔྱད་ནས་ཤེས་པར་བྱའོ།། ཅི་སྟེ་ཐམས་ཅད་ནས་མ་འགྲིག་ཀྱང་གང་འགྲིག་འགྲིག་གི་ཐད་ནས་རྟགས་ངོས་བཟུང་བས་ཅི་ཕྱི་སྙམ་ན། ཁྱེད་ཅག་གི་དགོངས་པ་དེ་བཞིན་དུ་ཡིན་པ་ངེས་ཀྱིས་ཀྱང་འཁྲུམས་མོད་ཀྱི། བསྒྲུབ་བྱ་སྒྲུབ་བྱེད་ངེས་པ་ལ་ལྟོས་པ་རིགས་པ་མཁྱེན་པ་རྣམས་ཀྱི་གཞུང་ལུགས་བཞིན་དུ་མཁན་པོའི་བསྟན་བཅོས་ལ་བཀུར་སྟི་བྱ་བར་འདོད་པ་ལས། སྒྲུབ་བྱེད་མ་ངེས་པས་བསྒྲུབ་བྱ་འདུ་མིན་མང་པོ་སྤྲོས་ཏེ་མཁས་པའི་བསྟན་བཅོས་རྩུད་གསན་པར་མི་བྱེད་དོ།། སྦྱོར་ཡང་རྣམ་དབྱེ་དང་འཕྲད་རྣམས་རྟགས་མཚུངས་ཕོ་ནས་འདྲེན་པར་འདོད་པ་གཞུང་གི་དགོངས་པར་ཡི་འགྱུར་ཏེ་རྒྱ་མཚན་སྔར་སུམ་རྟ་པར་ཡང་བཤད་ལ་གཞན་དུ་འང་འཆད་པར་འགྱུར་རོ། གཉིས་པ་སྔོན་འཇུག་བཞིན་དུ་དོན་ལ་འཇུག་ཚུལ་གྱིས་འབྱེད་པ་རེའང་མི་ལེགས་ཏེ། ཚུལ་དེས་རྟགས་འབྱེད་པར་མི་ནུས་པའི་ཕྱིར་ཏེ། རྗེས་འཇུག་གི་དོན་གྱི་འཇུག་ཚུལ་ཕྱོགས་གཅིག་ལ། སྔ་མ་སྔོན་འཇུག་ལྟ་བཞིན་སྦྱར། ཞེས་གསུངས་པའམ་རྗེས་འཇུག་རྣམས་སྔོན་འཇུག་ལྟར་གཙོ་བོར་རང་དབང་གིས་འདས་དང་གཞན་སྒྲུབ་སོགས་ཀྱི་དོན་སྟོན་བྱེད་སོ་སོར་ངེས་པ་ཅན་དུ་འཇུག་པར་འཆད་པའི་གཞུང་མ་ཡིན་པ་ག་ཤམ་དུ་བརྗོད་པར་འགྱུར་བ་ལྟར་ཡིན་པས་རྗེས་འཇུག་གི་བདག་གཞན་དང་དུས་གསུམ་གྱི་དོན་ཐམས་ཅད་རང་དབང་དུ་སྟོན་པའི་ལུང་མེད་ཅིང་རིགས་པས་ཀྱང་མི་འགྲུབ་པའི་ཕྱིར་ཏེ། དཔེར་ན་འདས་དང་གཞན་སྒྲུབ་ལ་འཇུག་པའི་རྒྱུ་མཚན་གྱིས་ཕོ་ཡིག་ཏུ་སྒྲུབ་པར་བྱེད་པ་རྣམས་ཀྱིས་ད་བ་ས་གསུམ་ཕོ་ཡིག་ཏུ་ངོས་འཛིན་པ་ན། ས་ད་གཉིས་ཀྱིས་འདས་པ་རང་དབང་དུ་སྒྲུབ་པ་མང་དུ་ཡོད་ཀྱང་བ་ཡིག་གིས་འདས་པ་སྒྲུབ་པ་མེད་ཅིང་། དེ་གསུམ་གིས་བྱ་བ་གཞན་སྒྲུབ་པའང་མེད་པས་ཐབ་ཆོལ་དུ་སྨྲས་པར་ཟད་པའི་ཕྱིར་རོ།། དེ་ལ་བ་ཡིག་འདས་ཚིག་གི་མཐར་འབྱུང་བ་བཀབ་བཏབ་ལྟ་བུ་དང་། བ་ས་ད་གསུམ་ག་གཞན་བྱ་བ་ལ་འཇུག་པ། གཟབ་བྱ། གཙུབ་བྱ། གདགས་བྱ། གདམས་བྱ། གཅད་བྱ། གསད་བྱ་སོགས་འབྱུང་བས་སྐྱོན་མེད་སྙམ་ན་འང་མི་འཐད་དེ། དེ་དག་ཐམས་ཅད་སྔོན་འཇུག་གི་ནུས་པས་འདས་པ་དང་དངོས་པོ་གཞན་སྒྲུབ་ལ་འཇུག་པ་ཡིན་གྱི་རྗེས་འཇུག་གི་ནུས་པས་མ་ཡིན་པའི་ཕྱིར་རོ།། རྗེས་འཇུག་གི་ནུས་པས་དེ་ལྟར་བསྒྲུབས་པ་མ་ཡིན་ཀྱང་འདས་ཚིག་དང་གཞན་སྒྲུབ་ལ་དེ་དག་བྱུང་བ་ཉིད་ཀྱིས་དོན་འགྲུབ་པོ་སྙམ་ནའང་མི་འཐད་དེ། དེ་ལྟར་ན། འདོགས། གཅོད། འཛིན། ལྟ་བུ་བྱེད་པ་བདག་གི་ཚིག་ཅན་གྱི་ད་བ་སའི་མཐར་དུ་མ་འབྱུང་བ་རྣམས་རྒྱ་མཚན་དུ་བྱས་ནས་རྗེས་འཇུག་དེ་རྣམས་བདག་སྒྲུབ་ལ་འཇུག་པར་རང་དབང་དུ་སྨྲས་ཀྱང་སྐྱོན་ཅི་ཞིག་ཡོད་དེ་རྒྱ་མཚན་མཚུངས་པའི་ཕྱིར་རོ། དེ་བཞིན་དུ་བདག་གཞན་གཉིས་ག་དང་ད་ལྟ་བ་བསྒྲུབ་པའི་ཕྱིར་འཇུག་པའི་རྟགས་ཀྱིས་མ་ནིང་དང་། བདག་དང་མ་འོངས་པ་བསྒྲུབ་པའི་ཕྱིར་འཇུག་པའི་རྟགས་ཀྱིས་མོར་སྒྲུབ་པ་དག་ཀྱང་མི་འཐད་དེ། འ་ཡིག་བདག་དང་མ་འོང་པའི་སྒྲུབ་བྱེད་དུ་འཇུག་པ་ཙམ་མཐོང་གི་གཞན་དེ་དག་དེ་དང་དེའི་སྒྲུབ་བྱེད་དུ་ངེས་པར་འཇུག་པ་མ་མཐོང་ཞིང་དོན་དེ་དག་དང་ལྡན་པའི་ཚིག་གི་མཐར་རྗེས་འཇུག་དེ་དག་བྱུང་བ་ཙམ་གྱིས་ཀྱང་ཉེན་དོན་མི་འགྲུབ་པའི་ཕྱིར་ཏེ། དེ་ལྟ་ན། བཀང་། གང་། བདར། བརྟར། ཤར། བཅལ། ཉལ། བཀྲམ་སོགས་མོའམ་མ་ནིང་དུ་འདོད་པའི་ཡི་གེའི་མཐའ་ཅན་གྱི་འདས་ཚིག་མང་དུ་འབྱུང་བས

ཡི་གེ་དེ་རྣམས་འདས་པ་བསྒྲུབ་པའི་ཕྱིར་འཇུག་པའང་མི་འཐད་བཞིན་དུ་ཁས་ལེན་དགོས་པར་འགྱུར་བའི་ཕྱིར་རོ། །དེ་བཞིན་དུ་ཁ་གཅིག་ནང་གསེས་ཀྱིས་རྟགས་ངོས་འཛིན་པར་དོན་ལ་འཇུག་ཚུལ་གྱི་སྒོ་ནས་རྒྱས་བཤད་བྱེད་པ་དག་སྣང་ཡང་། རྟགས་ཀྱིས་བསྒྲུབ་བྱ་བདག་གཞན་དང་དུས་གསུམ་གྱི་དོན་རྣམས་རྟགས་ཉིད་དུ་འདྲིལ་ནས། ཕོ་མོའི་རྟགས་སྟོན་པ་ཕོ་མོའི་རྟགས་སྟོན་པ་ཞེས་སོགས་རང་བཟོའི་གཟུ་ལུམ་གྱིས་བསྟན་བཅོས་ལ་དབང་ཟ་བར་ཟད་དེ། བཤད་པ་དེ་ལ་ལེགས་པར་བརྟགས་པའི་ཚེ་འཐད་པའི་ཕྱོགས་ཆུང་ཟད་ཀྱང་མི་སྣང་ངོ། །འོན་ཀྱང་ཐམས་ཅད་དཔྱད་པ་ཡི་གེའི་ལས་སུ་ཆེ་བས་ཕྱོགས་ཙམ་མཚོན་ན་ཕྱོགས་སྔ་དེས་མིང་ལས་གཞན་པ་བྱ་བྱེད་ལས་གསུམ་མི་སྟོན་པ་ལ་ཕོ་མོ་གཉིས་ཀའི་རྟགས་མེད་པའི་སྒྲུབ་བྱེད་ཀྱིས་རང་ཉིད་ཀྱིས་མ་ནིང་དུ་ཁས་བླངས་པའི་རྗེས་འཇུག་རྣམས་མིང་རྐྱང་གི་མཐར་སྦྱར་བ་མཚན་མེད་མ་ནིང་དུ་བསྒྲུབ་མོད། དེ་ལྟ་ན་མིང་རྐྱང་གི་འ་མཐའ་རྣམས་ཤིན་ཏུ་མོར་འདོད་པ་དང་འགལ་ཞིང་། ས་དའི་མཐའ་ཅན་གྱི་མིང་རྐྱང་ཡང་ཡོད་པས་དེ་འདྲའི་ས་དང་ད་རྣམས་མ་ནིང་མཚན་མེད་དུ་ཐལ་བར་འགྱུར་རོ། །ཡང་ན་དེས་མིང་རྐྱང་གི་མཐའི་ས་ད་ལ་རྟགས་ཀྱི་ངོས་འཛིན་ཚིགས་སུ་མ་བྱས་པས་དེ་དག་ལ་ཕོ་མཚན་མེད་ཅེས་པ་ལྟ་བུའི་རྣམ་གཞག་གསར་པ་ཞིག་མཛད་པ་ར་བཞེད་ཀྱང་ལུས་པ་ཡིན་འདུ་སྙམ་མོ། །དེ་དེ། །དེས་མཚོན་ནས་ལྷག་གཞན་ཡང་རྟོགས་པར་བྱའོ། །གསུམ་པ་ཁ་ཅིག་སྒྲ་འཇུག་དྲག་ཞན་གྱི་སྒོ་ནས་རྟགས་འབྱེད་པ་ནི་རིགས་པ་ཡིན་ཡང་། དེ་དག་གི་སྒྲ་འཇུག་དྲག་ཞན་ཉིད་མ་ཕྱེད་པས་ནོར་ནས་ཏེ། ད་བ་ས་གསུམ་ཕྱིར་སྒྲ་འཇུག་དྲག་པར་ངོས་འཛིན་པ་ཙམ་འགྲིག་ཀྱང་། ག་ཡིག་སྒྲ་འཇུག་དྲག་པར་མངོན་སུམ་དུ་གྲུབ་བཞིན་དུ་མ་ནིང་དང་བསྲུལ་བ་དང་། ན་ར་ལ་རྣམས་ལས་ང་འ་མ་རྣམས་ཀྱི་འཇུག་པ་སྒྲ་ཞན་པར་རྟོགས་སླ་བ་ཡིན་ཡང་དེ་དག་གི་དབྱེ་བ་འཕྲུགས་པ་དང་། གཞན་ཡང་ནོར་པ་མང་ཞིང་རྒྱུ་མཚན་དེ་རྣམས་ཀྱིས་དང་། ནང་གསེས་སྟོན་བྱེད་ཀྱི་གཞུང་ལོག་པར་བཀྲལ་བའི་དབང་གིས་ནང་གསེས་ཀྱི་སྒྲ་འཇུག་རྣམས་ལའང་འཁྲུལ་པའི་ཕྱིར་རོ། །

གཉིས་པ་རྟགས་དེ་རྣམས་ཀྱི་འཇུག་པ་རྒྱས་པར་འཆད་པ་ལ་མདོར་བསྟན་པ་དང་། རྒྱས་པར་བཤད་པ་གཉིས། དང་པོ་ནི།

དེ་ཡང་བྱེད་པ་བཞི་བྱེད་དེ། །གང་ལ་འཇུག་བྱེད་གང་གིས་བྱེད། །ཇི་ལྟར་འཇུག་བྱེད་ཅི་ཕྱིར་བྱེད། །

ཅེས་པས་བསྟན། དེའང་རྗེས་འཇུག་ཕོ་མོ་མ་ནིང་གསུམ་རེ་རེ་ལའང་བྱེད་པ་བཞི་བཞིའི་སྒོ་ནས་འཇུག་ཚུལ་ཤེས་པར་བྱ་སྟེ། འཇུག་ཡུལ་ཡི་གེ་གང་ལ་འཇུག་པར་བྱེད་པ་དང་། འཇུག་པ་པོ་གང་གིས་འཇུག་པར་བྱེད་པ་དང་། ཚུལ་ཇི་ལྟར་འཇུག་པར་བྱེད་པ་དང་། དགོས་པ་ཅིའི་ཕྱིར་འཇུག་པར་བྱེད་པ་རྣམས་ཀྱིས་སོ། །

གཉིས་པ། དེ་དག་རྒྱས་པར་བཤད་པ་ལ། རྣམ་པ་བཞི་ལས། དང་པོ་གང་ལ་འཇུག་པ་ནི།

གང་ལ་ཡི་གེ་ཐམས་ཅད་ལ། །

ཞེས་པས་བསྟན་ཏེ། རྗེས་འཇུག་གི་ཡི་གེ་བཅུ་པོ་དེ་དག་འཇུག་ཡུལ་ཡི་གེ་གང་དང་གང་ལ་འཇུག་ན་མིང་གཞིའི་ཡི་གེ་ཐམས་ཅད་ལ་ཁྱད་པར་མེད་པར་འཇུག་གོ། ཞེས་སོ། །

དཔེར་ན། བགག །བགང་། བགད། བགན། བགབ། བགུམ། བགའ། བགར། བགལ། བགས་ལྟ་བུ་ཀ་ཡིག་གི་མཐར་རྗེས་འཇུག་ཐམས་ཅད་འཇུག་པ་སོགས་ཀུན་ལ་བསྒྲེ་བར་བྱའོ། །སྐབས་འདིར་རྗེས་འཇུག་གི་འཇུག་ཡུལ་གྱི་ཡི་གེ་ཡིན་ན་འདིར་བསྟན་མིང་གཞིའི་ཡི་གེ་ཡིན་པས་ཁྱབ་བམ་ཞེ་ན་མ་ཁྱབ་སྟེ། ས་ཡིག་རྗེས་འཇུག་ག་ང་བ་མ་རྣམས་ཀྱི་མཐར་ཡང་འཇུག་ཅིང་། ད་ཡིག་ན་ར་ལ་རྣམས་ལ་འཇུག་པའི་ཕྱིར་རོ། །

གཉིས་པ་གང་གིས་འཇུག་པ་ནི།

གང་གིས་བཅུ་པོ་དེ་དག་གིས། །

ཞེས་བསྟན་ཏེ། ཡི་གེ་ཐམས་ཅད་ཀྱི་རྗེས་སུ་འཇུག་པ་པོ་ཡི་གེ་གང་དང་གང་ཞིག་གིས་འཇུག་པར་བྱེད་ཅེ་ན་སྔར་བཤད་པའི་རྗེས་འཇུག་ཡི་གེ་བཅུ་པོ་དེ་དག་གིས་འཇུག་གོ། ཞེས་སོ། །འདིར་འགྲེལ་བྱེད་ཁ་ཅིག་གིས་གཞན་གྱིས་ནི་མ་ཡིན་པར་རྗེས་འཇུག་ཉིད་ཁོ་ནས་དུས་གསུམ་དང་བླང་དོར་གྱིས་གནད་ཐམས་ཅད་སྟོན་བྱེད་དུ་འཇུག་གོ། ཞེས་ཟེར་ཡང་བབ་ཅོལ་དུ་སྨྲས་པར་ཟད་དེ། སྔོན་འཇུག་སོགས་གཞན་གང་ཡང་མ་ལྟོས་པར་རྗེས་འཇུག་ཁོ་ནས་རང་དབང་གིས་ཕྱེད་འདོད་པའི་རྗེས་འཇུག་དང་རང་གི་བསྟན་བྱ་ཐམས་ཅད་སྟོན་པའི་ཕྱིར་

འཇུག་པ་མེད་པའི་ཕྱིར་ཏེ། གོང་དུ་སྨོས་པ་བཞིན་སྔོན་འཇུག་ལ་མ་ལྟོས་པར་ས་ད་གཉིས་ཀྱི་འཇུག་པས་འདས་པ་དང་སླུལ་ཚིག་སྟོན་པ་དང་། འ་ཡིག་གིས་མ་འོངས་པའི་ཁྱད་པར་འགའ་ཞིག་སྟོན་པ་ཙམ་མཐོང་ཡང་དེ་རྣམས་མིང་གཞི་ལ་མི་ལྟོས་པ་ནི་མི་སྲིད་པས་རང་སྟོབས་དང་གཞན་དབང་གཉིས་ཀས་ཡིན་ལ་དེ་རྣམས་ཀྱིས་དེ་དག་ལས་གཞན་པ་མི་སྟོན་ཅིང་རྗེས་འཇུག་ལྷག་མ་རྣམས་ཀྱིས་ནི་རང་སྟོབས་གཙོ་བོར་གྱུར་པས་གང་ཡང་བསྟན་པ་མ་མཐོང་བའི་ཕྱིར་རོ།། གསུམ་པ་ཇི་ལྟར་འཇུག་པ་འཆད་པ་ལ་མདོར་བསྟན་དང་རྒྱས་བཤད་གཉིས།

དང་པོ་ནི།

ཇི་ལྟར་རྣམ་པ་གཉིས་ཡིན་ཏེ། སྒྲ་ཡི་འཇུག་ཚུལ་དོན་གྱི་ཚུལ།

ཞེས་པས་བསྟན་ཏེ་རྗེས་འཇུག་རྣམས་ཚུལ་ཇི་ལྟར་འཇུག་པའང་རྣམ་པ་གཉིས་ཀྱི་སྒོ་ནས་ཤེས་པར་བྱ་སྟེ། རྗེས་འཇུག་ཞུགས་ཚུལ་གྱིས་སྒྲ་དྲག་ཞན་དུ་འགྱུར་བ་སྒྲའི་འཇུག་ཚུལ་དང་། དེ་ལྟར་ཞུགས་པས་དོན་ཅི་ཞིག་སྟོན་པ་དོན་གྱི་འཇུག་ཚུལ་ལོ། ཞེས་སོ།།

འདིར་ཡང་ཁ་ཅིག་རྗོད་བྱེད་སྒྲ་དང་བརྗོད་བྱ་དོན་ཞེས་གསལ་བཏགས་པ་ཡོད་མོད། སྒྲའི་འཇུག་པ་རྣམས་བརྗོད་བྱེད་ཡིན་དུ་ཆུག་ཀྱང་། སྐབས་འདིའི་དོན་གྱི་འཇུག་ཚུལ་གྱི་དོན་ཡིན་ན་བརྗོད་བྱ་ཡིན་པས་མ་ཁྱབ་སྟེ། རྟགས་མཚུངས་དང་སྒྲ་མཐུན་འདྲེན་ཚུལ་གྱི་སྐབས་སུ་དོན་འདྲེན་བྱ་དང་འདྲེན་བྱེད་ཡི་གེ་མཐུན་མི་མཐུན་སྟོན་པ་ཡིན་པས་དེ་སྐབས་ཀྱི་དོན་གྱི་འཇུག་པ་དེ་སྐབས་ཡི་གེའི་འཇུག་པ་ཡིན་གྱི། མིང་ཚིག་དེ་དག་གིས་དོན་གང་ཞིག་བརྗོད་པར་འགྱུར་བའི་བརྗོད་བྱ་མ་ཡིན་པའི་ཕྱིར་རོ།།

གཉིས་པ་རྒྱས་བཤད་ལ་སྒྲའི་འཇུག་ཚུལ་དང་དོན་གྱི་འཇུག་ཚུལ་གཉིས། དང་པོ་ལ་དྲག་ཞན་སྤྱིར་འཇུག་ཚུལ། ནང་གསེས་ཞིབ་ཏུ་འཇུག་ཚུལ། ཐུན་མོང་དུ་དེ་དག་གི་དཔེར་བརྗོད་བསྟན་པའོ།

ཕོ་གསུམ་མོ་གཉིས་མ་ནིང་གསུམ། དྲག་ཞན་བར་མ་གསུམ་དུ་འཇུག།

དང་པོ་ནི།

ཅེས་པ་སྟེ། རྗེས་འཇུག་གི་ཡི་གེ་བཅུ་ལས་ཕོ་སྐྱེས་བུ་རབ་འབྲིང་ཐ་གསུམ་དང་། མོ་མོ་ཙམ་དང་ཤིན་ཏུ་མོ་གཉིས། མ་ནིང་འགྱུར་དང་མཚན་གཉིས་མཚན་མེད་གསུམ་སྟེ་འཇུག་ཚུལ་གྱི་སྒོ་ནས་དབྱེ་བ་དེ་རྣམས་རིམ་པ་བཞིན་དུ་ཕོ་གསུམ་མིང་གཞིའི་ཡི་གེ་གང་ལ་ཞུགས་ཀྱང་བརྗོད་པའི་སྒྲ་གདངས་དྲག་པར་འགྱུར་བས་དྲག་པར་འཇུག་པ་དང་། དེ་བཞིན་དུ་མོ་གཉིས་ཞན་པར་འཇུག་པ་དང་། མ་ནིང་བར་མ་སྟེ་རན་པར་འཇུག་པ་ཡིན་ནོ། ཞེས་སོ།། དེ་ལྟར་དྲག་ཞན་བར་མ་གསུམ་དུ་འཇུག་པའི་རྒྱུ་མཚན་དེས། སྤྱིར་བཏང་རྗེས་འཇུག་ལ་ཕོ་མོ་མ་ནིང་གསུམ་དུ་རྣམ་པར་བཞག་པའང་ཡིན་ནོ། ཞེས་ཞར་ལས་བསྟན་པར་གྲུབ་བོ།།

གཉིས་པ་ནང་གསེས་ཀྱི་འཇུག་ཚུལ་ནི།

དྲག་པ་གསུམ་ཉིད་ནང་ཕྲད་དམ། གལ་ཏེ་ཞན་པ་ནང་ཕྲད་ན། དེ་ལ་ངང་ནང་གི་ཆ་ཤས་ཀྱིས།
དེ་ཡང་དྲག་ཞན་གཉིས་སུ་དབྱེ། མ་ནིང་གསུམ་དུ་གང་གཏོགས་པ། དྲག་དང་ཕྲད་ན་དྲག་པར་འགྱུར།
ཞན་དང་ཕྲད་ན་ཞན་པར་འགྱུར། གཉིས་ཀ་དང་ནི་ཕྲད་གྱུར་ན། དེ་ནི་གཉིས་ཀ་ཅན་དུ་འགྱུར།
གཉིས་ཀ་དག་དང་མ་ཕྲད་ན། གང་དུ་ཡང་ནི་མི་འགྱུར་རོ། དེས་ན་འགྱུར་དང་མཚན་གཉིས་དང་།
མཚན་མེད་དག་དང་གསུམ་དུ་འདོད། དེ་ནི་སྒྲ་ཡི་འཇུག་ཚུལ་ལོ།

ཞེས་ཤོ་ལོ་ཀ་གསུམ་དང་རྐང་པ་གཉིས་ཀྱིས་བསྟན་ཏེ། དེ་ལ་གཉིས། གཞུང་དོན་ཇི་ལྟ་བ་བཤད་པ་དང་། དེའི་འཐད་པ་སྒྲུབ་པའོ།།

དང་པོ་ནི། རྟགས་ངོས་འཛིན་གོང་དུ་སོང་བ་ལྟར་རྗེས་འཇུག་ལ་ནང་གསེས་ཀྱིས་རྟགས་བརྒྱད་དུ་དབྱེ་བ་ནི་སྒྲའི་འཇུག་ཚུལ་གྱི་དབང་གིས་ཡིན་པས། དེ་རྣམས་

ས་སྤྱིའི་འཇུག་ཚུལ་ཐ་དད་པ་བརྗོད་དུ་ཇི་ལྟར་དབྱེ་ཞེ་ན། དག་པ་གསུམ་སྟེ་ཕོ་ཡིག་རྐྱེན་བྱ་རབ་འབྱེད་ཐ་གསུམ་ནི་རྗེས་འཇུག་ཉིད་ནང་ཁྲད་དུ་ཤུར་པ་ལ་ལྟོས་ནས་དབྱེ་སྟེ། མིང་གཞི་གང་གི་མཐར་ཡང་རུང་རྗེས་འཇུག་གི་ཕོ་ཡིག་རྣམས་ཡང་འཇུག་དང་བཅས་ཤུགས་པས་སྒྲ་དག་པ་གཉིད་གཞག་པའི་ནང་གསེས་དག་འབྱེད་གང་རུང་དུ་འགྱུར་བའི་ཆ་ནས་རྐྱེན་བྱ་རབ་འབྱེད་གཉིས་སུ་འབྱེད་ཅིང་། ཡང་འཇུག་མེད་པ་ཤུགས་པས་སྒྲ་དག་པའི་ཞན་པར་འགྱུར་བའི་ཆ་ནས་རྐྱེན་བྱ་ཐ་མར་འབྱེད་པའི་ཕྱིར། འདིར་དམ་ཞེས་པ་སྐད་པའི་ཚིག་ཕྲད་དེ་ག་ཤམ་དུ་དབྱེ་ཞེས་གསུངས་པ་དང་སྦྱོལ་བའི་སྐད་དུའོ། དེ་བཞིན་དུ་གལ་ཏེ་ཞན་པ་སྟེ་མོ་ཡིག་རྣམས་རྗེས་འཇུག་ནང་ཁྲད་ཀྱིས་མིང་གཞིར་ཤུགས་པ་ཡོད་ན་དེར་ལྟོས་པས། དེ་དག་ལ་ནང་གི་ཆ་ཤས་སྒྲ་འཇུག་དག་ཞན་གྱི་དབང་གིས་ཕྱིར་ཞན་པ་དེ་ལའང་ནང་གསེས་དག་ཞན་གཉིས་སུ་དབྱེ་སྟེ། ཡང་འཇུག་དང་བཅས་པའི་མོ་ཡིག་ཤུགས་པ་མོ་ཙམ་དང་། ཡང་འཇུག་མེད་ན་ཤིན་ཏུ་མོར་འབྱེད་པའི་ཕྱིར། དེ་བཞིན་དུ་འགྱུར་བ་སོགས་མ་ནིང་གསུམ་དུ་གང་རིག་གཏོགས་པར་གྱུར་པའི་རྗེས་འཇུག་གི་ཡི་གེ་དེ་རྣམས་ནི་མིང་གཞིར་འཇུག་ཚུལ་དང་རྗེས་འཇུག་ནང་ཁྲད་གཉིས་ཀ་ལ་ལྟོས་ནས་དབྱེ་སྟེ། དེ་རྣམས་མིང་གཞིའི་ཡི་གེ་དག་པ་དང་འདྲ་ན་ཡང་འཇུག་ཡོད་མེད་ཇི་ལྟར་རུང་སྒྲ་དག་པར་འགྱུར་ཞིང་། ཞན་པ་དང་ཁྲད་ན་ཡང་འཇུག་མེད་པའི་ཚེ་ཞན་པར་འགྱུར་བ་དང་། མིང་གཞི་ཞན་ཅིང་ཡང་འཇུག་དག་པའི་བར་དུ་ཆུད་པས་དག་ཞན་གཉིས་ཀ་དང་ཁྲད་པར་གྱུར་ན། མ་ནིང་དེ་རྣམས་སྒྲ་དག་ཞན་གཉིས་ཀ་ཅན་དུ་འགྱུར་བ་དང་། མིང་གཞི་དག་ཞན་གཉིས་ཀ་དང་མ་ཁྲད་པ་སྟེ་བར་མ་མ་ནིང་གི་ཡི་གེ་རྣམས་ལ་ཤུགས་པའི་ཚེ་ཡང་འཇུག་ཡོད་མེད་ཇི་ལྟར་རུང་སྒྲ་དག་ཞན་གང་དུའང་མི་འགྱུར་བར་བར་མ་ཉིད་དུ་གནས་པ་སྟེ། དེ་ལྟར་གསུམ་དུ་འགྱུར་བའི་རྒྱུ་མཚན་གྱིས་རིམ་པ་བཞིན་དུ། འགྱུར་བ་མ་ནིང་། མཚན་གཉིས་མ་ནིང་། མཚན་མེད་མ་ནིང་གསུམ་དུ་འབྱེད་པར་འདོད་པའི་ཕྱིར་རོ། ཞེས་སོ།

གཉིས་པ་ནི། སྔོན་གྱི་འགྲེལ་བྱེད་ཕལ་མོ་ཆེས། སྐབས་འདིར་དག་པ་གསུམ་ནང་ཁྲད་པ་ནི། སྔོན་འཇུག་མིང་གཞི་རྗེས་འཇུག་གསུམ་གྱི་ཕོ་ཡིག་འདུས་པ་དང་། ཞན་པ་ནང་ཁྲད་ཀྱང་དེ་གསུམ་གྱི་མོ་ཡིག་འདུས་པ་ལ་འདོད་མོད། དེ་ནི་ངེས་པར་ཁས་བླང་དུ་རུང་བ་མ་ཡིན་ཏེ། དེ་འཆད་པའི་སྐབས་མ་ཡིན་པ་དང་། བཤད་པ་མི་འཐད་པ་དང་། སྐབས་དོན་ཆད་པའི་སྐྱོན་གསུམ་ཡོད་པའི་ཕྱིར་རོ། དེ་ལ་སྐྱོན་དང་པོ་ཡོད་དེ། འདི་སྐབས་ཕྱིར་རྗེས་འཇུག་གི་འཇུག་པ་འཆད་པའི་སྐབས་དང་ཁྱད་པར་སྒྲའི་འཇུག་པ་འཆད་པའི་སྐབས་དང་། དེ་ལས་ཀྱང་ནང་གསེས་འཆད་པའི་སྐབས་ཡིན་པས་འདིར་བླ་ཐོལ་དུ་སྔོན་རྗེས་མིང་གསུམ་གཞི་ཐུན་མོང་གི་སྒྲ་འཇུག་འཆད་པ་མི་འབྲེལ་བའི་ཕྱིར་རོ།།

སྐྱོན་གཉིས་པའང་ཡོད་དེ། ཁྱོད་དག་གི་འགྲེལ་ཚུལ་གྱི་དབང་དུ་བྱས་ནས་གཞུང་དོན་ལ་བརྟགས་པའི་ཚེ། དག་པ་གསུམ་དང་ཞན་པ་གསུམ་ནང་ཁྲད་པ་གཉིད་བཞག་ནས་དེ་དག་ལ་ནང་གསེས་དག་ཞན་གཉིས་སུ་དབྱེ་བ་ཙམ་ཞིག་ལས་མ་བསྟན་པས། དངོས་བསྟན་དེ་ལྟར་དུ་འདོད་ན་ནི་སྔོན་རྗེས་མིང་གསུམ་འདུས་པའི་སྒྲ་འཇུག་ཕྱིར་བསྟན་པའང་སྐབས་འདིར་དགོས་པ་མེད་ན། ཉེ་རྩེ་བ་དེ་དག་བསྟན་པ་ལྷག་པར་ཡང་དགོས་མེད་དུ་འགྱུར་བའི་ཕྱིར་དང་། སྔོན་རྗེས་མིང་གསུམ་དག་ཞན་བར་མ་སྦྱོར་ཚོགས་འཆད་པའི་དབང་དུ་བྱས་ནས། དག་པའི་དག་ཞན་འབྲིང་གསུམ་སོགས་དབྱེ་བ་མང་པོ་བྱེད་པ་ནི་རང་བཟོ་ཉིད་དུ་ཟད་པས་རང་འདོད་ཀྱི་གཞུང་དོན་འགྲེལ་ཚུལ་དང་ཡང་འགལ་བའི་ཕྱིར་ཏེ་དག་ཞན་བར་མ་སྦྱོར་ཚོགས་འདུས་པ་དབྱེ་གཞིར་བཟུང་བས་ནང་ཁྲད་ཅེས་པའི་ཚིག་གི་ནུས་པ་དང་འགལ་ཞིང་། རྣམ་པ་མང་པོར་ཕྱེས་པས་གཉིས་སུ་དབྱེ་ཞེས་པ་དང་འགལ་བའི་ཕྱིར།།

སྐྱོན་མེད་དེ་སྔ་མ་ཤུགས་བསྟན་གྱི་དབང་དུ་བྱས་ཤིང་། ཕྱི་མ་སྔོན་རྗེས་དག་ལ་མིང་གཞི་ཞན་པ་སོགས་མང་པོར་ཕྱེ་ནའང་དག་ཞན་སོ་སོར་དག་ཞན་གཉིས་གཉིས་སུ་ཕྱེ་བས་བསྡུས་པའི་ཕྱིར། སྙམ་ནའང་རིམ་པ་བཞིན་མི་འཐད་དེ་གཞུང་དུ་ནང་ཁྲད་ཅེས་ངེས་གཟུང་མཛད་པ་ལ་ནང་མི་མཐུན་ཤུགས་བསྟན་དུ་འབྱུང་བ་འགལ་བའི་ཕྱིར་དང་། སྔོན་རྗེས་མིང་གསུམ་སོ་སོར་ཕོ་མོ་མ་ནིང་གསུམ་གསུམ་དུ་རྒྱུ་མཚན་དང་བཅས་ནས་གསུངས་པ་ལས་བཀལ་ནས་དེ་དག་གི་མོ་དང་མ་ནིང་དག་སྒྲ་ཞན་པར་ཕྱོགས་གཅིག་ཏུ་བསྡུས་ནས་དག་ཞན་གཉིས་གཉིས་སུ་དབྱེ་བ་དེ་སྐབས་འདིར་མ་འབྲེལ་པས་རང་བཟོ་མི་བྱེད་ཀ་མེད་དུ་ཤོར་བ་ལས་རྒྱུ་མཚན་གང་ཡང་མེད་པའི་ཕྱིར་རོ།།

སྐྱོན་གསུམ་པའང་ཡོད་དེ། གཞུང་འདིའི་གོང་དུ་རྗེས་འཇུག་གི་རྟགས་གསུམ་ཕྱིར་དབྱེ་བའི་སྒྲ་འཇུག་བཤད་ཅིང་། མཇུག་ཏུ་ནང་གསེས་མ་ནིང་ལ་གསུམ་དུ་

དབྱེ་བའི་སྒྲ་འཇུག་གསུངས་པའི་བར་དུ་ཕོ་མོ་གཉིས་ཀྱི་ནང་གསེས་ཀྱི་སྒྲ་འཇུག་ངེས་པར་རྟེན་རིགས་པ་ལ་དེ་མ་བཤད་པའི་ཕྱིར་རོ།།

རྟེན་མེད་དེ། ཕོ་གསུམ་མོ་གཉིས་ཀྱི་ཡི་གེ་དེ་རྣམས་ཉིད་ཕྲིན་འཇུག་དང་མིང་གཞི་ལ་སྦྱོར་བས་སྒྲ་གདངས་འབྱུང་ཚུལ་ཉིད་འཆད་པའི་ཕྱིར་རོ། རྣམ་དབང་མི་འཐད་དེ་གཉིས་སུ་དབྱེ་ཞེས་ངེས་གཟུང་མཛད་པ་ལས་བཀལ་བའི་རྐྱེན་དང་ཐུན་མོང་གི་འཇུག་པ་བསྟན་པའི་རྐྱེན་གཉིས་སེལ་བར་མི་ནུས་པའི་ཕྱིར་རོ།།

དེ་ལྟར་གཞན་གྱི་འདོད་པ་ལ་དཔྱད་པས་རང་ལུགས་འཐད་པར་གྲུབ་ཅེ་སྐབས་དོན་ཡིན་པ་དང་། བཤད་པ་གཞུང་དོན་དང་མཐུན་པ་དང་། གཞུང་གི་བསྟན་བྱ་རྫོགས་པར་གྲུབ་པའི་ཕྱིར་རོ།།

གསུམ་པ་ཐུན་མོང་དུ་དེ་དག་གི་དཔེར་བརྗོད་བསྟན་པ་ནི། རྟགས་གསུམ་ཕྱིར་འཇུག་ཚུལ་གྱི་དཔེར་བརྗོད་ཞར་ལ་རྟོགས་པའི་དབང་དུ་བྱས་ནས་འདིར་ནང་གསེས་བརྒྱད་ཀྱི་འཇུག་ཚུལ་གྱི་དཔེར་བརྗོད་ཕྱོགས་ཙམ་འགོད་པ་ལ།

སྐྱེས་བུ་རབ་ནི། སྐྱོགས། དཀྲིགས། དཀྲོགས། དཀྲུགས། བསྐྱགས། བཀྲིགས། འཁྲུགས། འཁྲུགས། ཁྲགས། ཁྲོགས། སྐྲོགས། བསྐྲགས། འགགས། ངོགས། བསྔགས། ལྕུགས། བཅགས། འཆགས། འཇགས། འཇིགས། གཉགས། སྙོགས། བསྙེགས། སྙིགས། ཏགས། ཏོགས། བཏགས། གཏོགས། གཏུགས། བཏགས། སྟེགས། ཐོགས། ཐེགས། ཐུགས། དོགས། འདོགས། འདེགས། གདགས། ནགས། པགས། བཏོགས། ཕྲགས། སྤྲགས། སྤུགས། ཕུགས། འཕྱུགས། བགས། བོགས། བླུགས། བླགས། དབུགས། སྦྲགས། བྲིགས། དབགས། སྦགས། སྨུགས། དམིགས། དམུགས། སྨུགས། གཙིགས། གཙུགས། བཙགས། བརྩིགས། བརྩེགས། ཚོགས། ཚགས། ཚེགས། འཛུགས། ཛོགས། ཞབས། ཞུགས། གཞོགས། བཞུགས། གཟུགས། གཟིགས། གཟགས། བཟླུགས། གཡོགས། གཡེགས། རིགས། རྒྱུགས། ལེགས། ལགས། ཤགས། གཤེགས། གཤགས། བཤགས། སོགས། བསྲིགས། ཧྲགས། ཞེས་སོ།།

སྐྱེས་བུ་འབྲིང་ནི། སྐབས། སྐུབས། བསྐྲབས། སྐྱབས། བསྐྱབས། སྐྱོབས། འཁོབས། བསྐྱུབས། སྒྲུབས། བརྒྱབས། བཅབས། བཅིབས། ཆབས། ཆེབས། འཇབས། འཇེབས། བསྙབས། སྙོབས། སྙབས། སྟབས། གཉེབས། བསྟབས། ཐབས། འཐེབས། ཐུབས། འབྲེབས། བསྲུབས། སྡུབས། སྡུབས། སྤུབས། མནབས། སྦྲབས། ཕེབས། བྱབས། དབབས། སྦྲུབས། སྲུབས། གཙུབས། རྩིབས། རྩུབས། ཚབས། འཚབས། ཞབས། གཞིབས། གཞབས། གཟབས། གཡབས། རབས། བརླབས། རློབས། ཤུབས། གཤིབས། སྲུབས། བསྲུབས། བསབས། ལ་སོགས་པ་རྣམས་སོ།།

སྐྱེས་བུ་ཐ་མ་ནི། སྐམས། སྐད། བཀག། བཀབ། མཁས། འཁྲིད། ཁྲག། ཁྲབ། འགས། བརྒྱད། རྒྱག། སྒྲུབ། སྡམས། ངེད། ངག། ཇབ། ལ་སོགས་པའོ།།

མོ་ཙམ་ནི། བསྐྲངས། བསྐུམས། ཁོངས། ཁམས། གངས། བགོམས། དངངས། བཅམས། ལ་སོགས་པའོ།།

ཤིན་ཏུ་མོ་ནི། བསྐྲང་། ཀོང། སྐོམ། བཀའ། ཁོང་། ཁམ། མཁའ། གང་། སྒོམ། འགའ། ངང་། དངོམ། ཇའ། ལ་སོགས་པའོ།།

འགྱུར་བ་མ་ཞིང་ནི། བསྐྱེད། སྐུན། བསྐོར། བསྐུར། ཀུ་ཁད། བཅོལ། འདྲེན། འགོར། འགྱུལ། ལ་

སོགས་པའོ། །

མཚན་གཉིས་པ་ནི། འཛིན་ད། བསྒྱུར་ད། བྱུར་ད། འགྱུར་ད། རིལ་ད། བསལ་ད། ལ་སོགས་པའོ། །

མཚན་མེད་ནི། ཕྱིན་ད། མཐུན། ཐར་ད། འཁོར། འབྱུང་ད། འཕྲུལ་ལ་སོགས་པ་རྣམས་ཏེ་དེ་དག་གིས་མཚོན་ནས་རྒྱ་ཆེར་ཤེས་པར་བྱའོ། །

གཉིས་པ་དོན་གྱི་འཇུག་ཚུལ་ལ། མདོར་བསྟན་དང་རྒྱས་བཤད་གཉིས། དང་པོ་ནི།

ནི་རྣམ་པ་གཉིས་ཡིན་ཏེ། ཐ་མ་གང་ལྟར་གྱུར་པ་དང་། ཕྱི་མ་གང་ལྟར་འགྱུར་བའོ།

ཞེས་པས་བསྟན་ཏེ། རྗེས་འཇུག་རྣམས་དོན་གང་དང་གང་ལ་འཇུག་པར་འགྱུར་བའི་ཚུལ་ནི་རྣམ་པ་གཉིས་ཡིན་ཏེ། ཐ་མ་རྗེས་འཇུག་ཉིད་གང་ལ་ཞུགས་ཤིང་གནས་པའི་མིང་དེའི་དོན་གང་ལྟར་ཏེ་ཇི་ལྟ་བུ་ཞིག་ཏུ་འགྱུར་བ་དང་། ཕྱི་མ་རྗེས་འཇུག་གམ་མཐའ་རྟེན་མིང་མཐའ་ལ་སོགས་པ་འདྲེན་ཚུལ་གྱིས་དོན་གང་ལྟར་འགྱུར་བའོ། ། ཞེས་སོ། །

གཉིས་པ་དེ་རྒྱས་པར་འཆད་པ་ལ་གཉིས་ལས། དང་པོ་ཐ་མ་གང་ལྟར་འགྱུར་བ་འཆད་པ་ལ། གཞུང་དོན་དཔེར་བརྗོད་དང་བཅས་དགོས་པ་དང་། གཞན་གྱི་འདོད་པ་ཉོར་བར་བསྟན་པ་གཉིས་སོ། ། དང་པོ་ནི།

ཐ་མ་སྔོན་འཇུག་ལྟ་བཞིན་སྦྱར།

ཞེས་པས་བསྟན་ཏེ། རྗེས་འཇུག་རྣམས་གང་ལ་ཞུགས་པའི་མིང་དེ་ཉིད་མིང་མཐའ་སོགས་ལ་ལྟོས་ནས་ཐ་མར་གྱུར་པས་དེས་བདག་གཞན་སོགས་དོན་ཅི་ཞིག་སྟོན་པ་ནི་མིང་དེའི་སྔོན་དུ་གནས་པ་སྔོན་འཇུག་ལྔ་ལས་གང་ཞིག་ཡིན་པ་དེའི་དོན་དང་ཇི་ལྟ་བ་བཞིན་དུ་སྦྱར་ནས་རྟོགས་པར་བྱའོ། ། ཞེས་པའོ། །

དེས་ན་གཙོ་བོར་སྔོན་འཇུག་གི་ནུས་པ་དང་སྦྱར་ནས་རྗེས་འཇུག་རྣམས་ཀྱིས་ཀྱང་ཅི་རིགས་པར་བདག་གཞན་དང་དུས་གསུམ་གྱི་དོན་རྣམས་དེ་དང་མཚུངས་པར་སྟོན་པར་འགྱུར་བ་ཡིན་གྱི་སྐབས་འགའ་ཞིག་ཏུ་མ་གཏོགས་པར་རྗེས་འཇུག་གི་ནུས་པ་གཙོ་ཆེ་བས་ནི་མ་ཡིན་ནོ། ། ཞེས་པ་ནི་འདིར་ཤེས་པར་བྱ་བའི་གནད་དམ་པའོ། །

འདིར་ཁ་ཅིག་སྔོན་འཇུག་ལ་མི་ལྟོས་པར། བྱས། ཟོས། གྲགས། ཆད། ཐར་ད། ཐོན་ད། ཐོག། དག། ཐབ། ལྟ་བུ་ཡིག་གིས་འདས་པ་སྟོན་པ་དང་།

ཀྱིས། ཀྱོས། ཁོས། ནོན་ད། རིལ་ད། ཆོད། རྒྱབ། ཤོག། ལྟ་བུ་ཡིག་གིས་སྐུལ་ཚིག་སྟོན་པ་དང་། སྔོན་འཇུག་ལ་ལྟོས་ཀྱང་རྗེས་འཇུག་གི་ནུས་པ་གཙོ་བ། བསྐངས། བསྒྲུབས། བསམས། བསགས། བསད། བཅད། བརྟན་ད། བསྒྱུར་ད། བསལ་ད། ལྟ་བུ་ཡིག་གིས་འདས་པ་སྒྲུབ་པ་སོགས་མང་དུ་ཡོད་པས་འདིར་རྗེས་འཇུག་གི་ནུས་པ་གཙོ་བོར་མི་འཆད་པ་མི་ལེགས་སོ་སྙམ་པ་དག་ཡོད་པར་མངོན་ཡང་། དགག་པ་མི་དགོས་ཏེ། སྐུལ་ཚིག་གི་འཇུག་ཚུལ་ནི་གཞུང་འདིར་དངོས་ཤུགས་གང་དུའང་མ་བསྟན་པ་དེར་ཟད། སྔོན་འཇུག་ལ་མ་ལྟོས་པར་རྗེས་འཇུག་རྣམས་ཉིད་བདག་གཞན་དང་དུས་གསུམ་སོགས་བྱ་བྱེད་དང་འབྲེལ་པའི་མིང་ཚིག་ཐམས་ཅད་ལ་འཇུག་པ་ཡོད་ཀྱང་སྔོན་འཇུག་ཅན་ལ་ལྟོས་ན་ཤས་ཆུང་བས་ཞར་ལ་གོ་བའི་དབང་དུ་མཛད་ཅིང་། སྔོན་འཇུག་ལས་རྗེས་འཇུག་གི་ནུས་པ་གཙོ་བོ་འདས་པ་སྒྲུབ་པའི་ས་ཡིག་གི་འཇུག་ཡང་འཇུག་གཉིས་ཀ་དང་ད་ཡིག་གི་ཡང་འཇུག་ཁོ་ན་ཙམ་ལ་ཡོད་ཀྱི་གཞན་རྣམས་སྔོན་འཇུག་གི་ནུས་པ་གཙོ་བོ་ཁོ་ན་ཡིན་པའི་ཕྱིར་སྔོན་འཇུག་གི་འཇུག་པས་བདག་གཞན་སོགས་སྟོན་པ་ཁྱབ་ཆེ་བས་གཙོ་བོར་གྱུར་པ་ལ་དགོངས་ནས་འདིར་སྔོན་འཇུག་ལྟ་བཞིན་སྦྱར་ཞེས་ངེས་གཟུང་གིས་གསུངས་པ་ལྟར་ཁོ་བོས་ལེགས་པར་བཤད་པ་ཡིན་པའི་ཕྱིར་རོ། །

སྔོན་འཇུག་མེད་པར་རྗེས་འཇུག་གིས་དོན་བསྟན་པ་ཅེས་མང་ཀྱི་མིང་ཀྲུང་ཐལ་ཆེར་དེ་འདྲ་ཡིན་པའི་ཕྱིར་སྙམ་ན། དེ་འདྲའི་མིང་ཀྲུང་རྣམས་རྗེས་འཇུག་གིས་མིང་དུ་

སྒྲུབ་པ་ཡིན་ཀྱང་ དེས་བདག་གཞན་དང་དུས་གསུམ་སོགས་བསྟན་པ་མེད་པས། ཕྱིར་རྟགས་འཇུག་གི་གཞུང་འདིའི་བསྟན་བྱའི་གཙོ་བོ་མ་ཡིན་ལ། ཁྱད་པར་སྔོན་འཇུག་ལྔ་བཞིན་སྦྱར། ཞེས་པའི་སྦྱར་བྱ་མ་ཡིན་པར་ངེས་པས་སྐྱོན་དུ་མི་འགྱུར་རོ།།

དེས་ན་སྐབས་འདིའི་དངོས་བསྟན་གྱི་དབང་དུ་བྱས་པའི་དཔེར་བརྗོད་ནི་སྔོན་འཇུག་གི་སྐབས་སུ་རྒྱས་པར་བསྟན་པ་ཉིད་ལས་ཤེས་སུ་མི་དགོས་ནའང་ཕྱོགས་མཚོན་པའི་ཕྱིར་རྗེས་འཇུག་གི་རྟགས་ཀྱི་གོ་རིམ་དང་མཐུན་པར་ཅུང་ཟད་བཀོད་པས་གོ་བདེ་བ་ལ་བསམས་ནས་དཔེར་བརྗོད་ན།

སྐྱེས་བུའི་རྟགས་རབ་འབྲིང་ཐ་གསུམ་ཅི་རིགས་པར་དུས་འདས་པ་ལ་འཇུག་པ་ནི། བརྟགས། བཏགས། བཅགས། བསགས། བསྐྱབས། བསྒྲུབས། བསྡུབས། བཀག། བརྡུས། བརྒྱབ། བཅད་ལྟ་བུ་དང་།

དེ་རྣམས་བྱེད་པ་བདག་ལ་འཇུག་པ་ནི། འདོགས་བྱེད། འདེགས་བྱེད། འཇུག་བྱེད། འགུགས་བྱེད། གཞིབས་བྱེད། གཉིབས་བྱེད། བསྡུབ་བྱེད། འཇོག་བྱེད། འགགས་བྱེད། འགྲུབ་བྱེད། གཅོད་བྱེད་ལྟ་བུ་དང་།

དེ་རྣམས་བྱ་བ་གཞན་ལ་འཇུག་པ་ནི། གདགས་བྱ། བརྡེགས་བྱ། བསྡོགས་བྱ། གཏུབས་བྱ། དགག་བྱ། བརྡུར་བྱ། གཞབ་བྱ། བསྒྲུབ་བྱ། བསྡུབ་བྱ། བརྒྱབ་བྱ། བསྐྱེད་བྱ་ལྟ་བུ་དང་།

དེ་རྣམས་བྱ་བ་གཞན་ལ་འཇུག་པ་ནི། གདགས་བྱ། བརྡེགས་བྱ། བསྡོགས་བྱ། གཏུབས་བྱ། དགག་བྱ། བརྡུས་བྱ། གཞབ་བྱ། བསྒྲུབ་བྱ། བསྡུབ་བྱ། བརྒྱབ་བྱ། བསྐྱེད་བྱ་ལྟ་བུ་དང་།

དེ་རྣམས་བདག་གཞན་གྱི་དབྱེ་བས་མ་བསྡུས་པའི་ད་ལྟ་དང་མ་འོངས་པ་ཅི་རིགས་པར་འཇུག་པ་ནི། འདེགས་བཞིན་པ། འདོགས་བཞིན་པ། གཏུབས་བཞིན་པ། འགོག་བཞིན་པ། གཅོད་བཞིན་པ། རང་བཞིན་གྱིས་གཤེགས་པར་འགྱུར། རང་བཞིན་གྱིས་འགྲུབ་པར་འགྱུར། འཆད་པར་འགྱུར། འཐས་པར་འགྱུར། ལྟ་བུ་རྣམས་སོ།།

དེ་བཞིན་དུ་མོ་རྟགས་གཉིས་འདས་པ་ལ་འཇུག་པ། བསྐངས། བརྐྱངས། བསྒྲུམས། བཀང་། བཀྲམ་ལྟ་བུ་དང་།

བདག་ལ་འཇུག་པ། འདོམས་བྱེད། འགེངས་བྱེད། འཆིངས་བྱེད། འདོད་བྱེད། འཁྱོམ་བྱེད། གསོལ་བྱེད་ལྟ་བུ་དང་།

གཞན་ལ་འཇུག་པ། གདམས་བྱ། འཁྲུམས་བྱ། བསྐང་བྱ། དགང་བྱ། གཏམས་བྱ། བཟའ་བྱ་ལྟ་བུ་དང་།

ད་ལྟ་དང་མ་འོངས་པར་འཇུག་པ། འདོམས་བཞིན་པ། འགེངས་བཞིན་པ། བརྡོད་བཞིན་པ། གསོལ་བཞིན་པ། རང་བཞིན་གྱིས་འདོམས་པར་འགྱུར། འགྲོ་བར་འགྱུར། འགོང་བར་འགྱུར། འདམ་པར་འགྱུར་ལྟ་བུའོ།།

མ་ནིང་གསུམ་འདས་པ་ལ། བསྟན། བཀན། བཀར། བསྟར། བཅལ། མནན། བགར། བསལ། མཁྱེན། མཆར། འཁྱལ། ལྟ་བུ་དང་།

བདག་ལ། བསྟུན་བྱེད། བརྩོན་བྱེད། གཏོན་བྱེད། གཏོར་བྱེད། གསོར་བྱེད། འཁོལ་བྱེད། འགྲོལ་བྱེད། འདུན་བྱེད། འཛེར་བྱེད། གསོལ་བྱེད། མཐར་བྱེད། འཕོར་བྱེད། འཕེན་བྱེད། མཐུན་བྱེད། འཐུལ་བྱེད། ལྟ་བུ་དང་།

གཞན་ལ། བརྟེན་བྱ། བསྐྱུར་བྱ། དགར་བྱ། བསྔལ་བྱ། བསྐུལ་བྱ། མཁྱེན་བྱ། འཆོར་བྱ། འཕོལ་བྱ། ལྟ་བུ་དང་།

ད་ལྟ་དང་མ་འོངས་པར། བསྟུན་བཞིན་པ། གཏོན་བཞིན་པ། གཏོར་བཞིན་པ། འཛིན་བཞིན་པ། གསོལ་བཞིན་པ། འཁྱོལ་བཞིན་པ།

འཐོརད་བཞིན་པ། མཁྲིནད་བཞིན་པ། རང་བཞིན་གྱིས་དགོནད་པར་འགྱུར། འདུནད་པར་འགྱུར། མཐུན་པར་འགྱུར། གསལ་བར་འགྱུར། འཕྲུལ་བར་འགྱུར་ལྟ་བུ་རྒྱ་ཆེར་ཤེས་པར་བྱའོ།། དེ་ལྟར་སྔོན་འཇུག་ལ་ལྟོས་པ་གཙོ་བོར་གསུངས་པའི་ཞར་ལས་སྔོན་འཇུག་མེད་པའི་མིང་དོན་རྣམས་ལ་ཡི་ལྟར་འཇུག་པའང་ཤེས་པར་བྱ་སྟེ།

དཔེར་ན། སྐྱེས་པའི་རྟགས་འདས་པ་ལ་འཇུག་པ། བཀུགས། ཐོགས། བཏུགས། བཏབས། བཏུམ། བསམ། བཏྲམ། བསམ། བརྣམ། བསྒྲམ། བརྩམ། བཙོག། བརྙག། བཞབ། བསྐབ། བསྒྲད། བཅད། བཀོད། བརྡད། སོགས་དང་།

བདག་ལ། སྐོགས་བྱེད། སྐོགས་བྱེད། སྐྱབས་བྱེད། སྒྲུབས་བྱེད། སྒྲིབས་བྱེད། སྒྲུབ་བྱེད། སྐྲོད་བྱེད། སྤྲོད་བྱེད། རྫད་བྱེད། རྩིག་བྱེད། རིག་བྱེད། སྤྲོས་བྱེད་སོགས་དང་།

གཞན་ལ། རྟོགས་བྱ། བཀབས་བྱ། ཤེས་བྱ། བསྒྲུག་བྱ། བསྒྲོད་བྱ་སོགས་དང་།

དེ་དག་ལས་གཞན་ད་ལྟ་དང་མ་འོངས་པར་འཇུག་པ། རྟོག་བཞིན་པ། ཤེས་བཞིན་པ། སྤྱོད་བཞིན་པ་སོགས་དང་། རྟོག་པར་འགྱུར། སྒྲུབ་པར་འགྱུར། ཤེར་པར་འགྱུར། ཞེས་སོགས་ཀྱིས་མཚོན་པར་བྱའོ།།

དེ་བཞིན་དུ་མོ་གཉིས་འདས་པ་ལ་འཇུག་པ། བསྲངས། ཁངས། བཞངས། བསམས། བསྒྲིམས། བཟང་། སོང་། བསམ། བསུམ། ཆོམ། ཞིམ་སོགས་དང་།

བདག་ལ། སྐྱངས་བྱེད། འཛངས་བྱེད། སྐྱེམས་བྱེད། ཉམས་བྱེད། སྤྱོང་བྱེད། སྐང་བྱེད། བརྙི་བྱེད། སྲབ་བྱེད། རྒྱབ་བྱེད།

གཞན་ལ། བསྲུངས་བྱ། བསྲང་བྱ། བསྲིང་བྱ། བསྲང་བྱ། བཙོམ་བྱ། བསྲབ་བྱ། སོགས་དང་།

ད་ལྟ་མ་འོངས་པར། འཛངས་བཞིན་པ། སྐྱེམས་བཞིན་པ། སྤྱོང་བཞིན་པ། བརྙིར་བཞིན་པ། ངང་གིས་སྐྱོང་བར་འགྱུར། ཉམས་པར་འགྱུར། གང་བར་འགྱུར། དམ་པར་འགྱུར། སྲབ་བར་འགྱུར། སོགས་སོ།།

མ་ནིང་གསུམ་འདས་པར་འཇུག་པ། སྤྲལད། ཟིལད། དུལ། ཤར། བོར། བསྐྱནད། བཀནད། ཟིནད། སྐྱིནད། ཕྱིནད། ཕྱིནད། ཐརད། ཚརད། ཚོར། ཐལ། སོགས་དང་།

བདག་ལ། སྐྱོནད། སྐྱེནད། རྟེནད། སྒྲིན། སྒྲུན། སྒྲོན། སྐྱུརད། སྒྲུལད། སྒྲུར། སྒྲིལ། འཕེནད། སྒྲོནད། སེལད། ཉནད། ཁྲུར། ཕན་བྱེད་སོགས་དང་།

གཞན་ལ། བསྒྲར་བྱ། བསྒྲིལ་བྱ། བསྒྲོར་བྱ། བསྒྲིན་བྱ། བསྐུལ་བྱ། བསྒྲོན་བྱ། ཉལ་བྱ་སོགས་དང་།

ད་ལྟ་དང་མ་འོངས་པར་འཇུག་པ་ཡང་། སྐྱོནད་བཞིན་པ། སྐྱེནད་བཞིན་པ། སྒྲུར་བཞིན་པ། སྒྲིལ་བཞིན་པ། སྐུལ་བཞིན་པ། སྒྲོལ་བར་འགྱུར། སྐྱན་པར་འགྱུར། ཕྱིན་པར་འགྱུར། ཐར་པར་འགྱུར། སོགས་ཏེ་འདི་དག་གིས་རིགས་ཐམས་ཅད་ལ་མཚོན་པར་བྱའོ།།

དེ་ལྟར་དཔེར་བརྗོད་པ་དེ་དག་ལས་སྔོན་འཇུག་གི་ཤིན་ཏུ་མོ་བདག་གཞན་སོགས་ཐམས་ཅད་ལ་མཉམ་པར་འཇུག་པར་གསུངས་པ་བཞིན་དུ་སྔོན་འཇུག་ལ་ལྟོས་པར། མཐུན་མཁྲིན་སོགས་མང་པོ་དང་། སྔོན་འཇུག་མེད་པ་ཡང་། རྟོགས། བསྲུངས། སྐང་། སྐྱེམས། རངས། སྒྲུལ་སོགས་མང་པོ་བདག་གཞན་དུས་གསུམ་ཀུན་ལ་གཟུགས་ཐ་དད་མེད་པར་འཇུག་པས་འཇུག་ཡུལ་བདག་གཞན་སོགས་གང་ཡིན་ཚིག་གྲོགས་ལས་ཤེས་པར་བྱ་དགོས་པ་རྣམས་ཀྱང་བློ་གྲོས་དང་ལྡན་པ་རྣམས་ཀྱིས་རྟོགས་པར་བྱའོ།།

གཞན་ཡང་གཞུང་འདིར་དམིགས་གསལ་དུ་མ་བསྟན་ཀྱང་རྗེས་འཇུག་ས་ཡིག་གི་འཇུག་ཡང་འཇུག་གཉིས་ཀ་དང་། ད་ཡིག་གིས་ཡང་འཇུག་གིས་དུས་འདས་པ་སྟོན་པ་ཤིན་ཏུ་མང་ཞིང་། འ་ཡིག་འདས་པ་ལ་མི་འཇུག་པའི་ཁྱད་པར་ཙམ་ནི་གསལ་བར་མཐོང་བ་སྔོན་རྗེས་ཀྱི་དཔེར་བརྗོད་བཀོད་པ་རྣམས་སུ་གསལ་ཞིང་། ཀླུགས་ཆེ་བ་དེར་ཟད། རྗེས་འཇུག་རྣམས་སྐྱེལ་ཚིག་ལ་འཇུག་པའི་ཚུལ་ནི། གཞུང་འདིའི་དངོས་ཤུགས་གཉིས་ཀར་མ་བསྟན་པས་བཤད་བྱར་མ་གྱུར་མོད། འོན་ཀྱང་དེའི་རྣམ་གཞག་ཞར་ལས་རྟོགས་པར་བྱ་བའི་ཕྱིར་དཔེར་བརྗོད་ན།

ས་ད་གཉིས་དང་ཁྱད་པར་ས་ཡིག་སྐྱེལ་ཚིག་ལ་འཇུག་པ་མང་བར་མཐོང་སྟེ། སྐྱོགས་ཤིག། གླུགས་ཤིག། སྦྲོགས་ཤིག། རྟོགས་ཤིག། ཐིགས་ཤིག། ཐུགས་ཤིག། སྲིགས་ཤིག། ཚུགས་ཤིག། ལྡོགས་ཤིག། ལྡོབས་ཤིག། སློབས་ཤིག། སྐྲུབས་ཤིག། ཐིམས་ཤིག། གྲིམས་ཤིག། ཐུམས་ཤིག། ཁྲུས་ཤིག། ཛོས་ཤིག། སྤོས་ཤིག། ཕྱོས་ཤིག། ཉོས་ཤིག། ཟློས་ཤིག། ཀུས་ཤིག། ཁོས་ཤིག། ཚོས་ཤིག། རྡུངས་ཤིག། སྦོངས་ཤིག། ཆིངས་ཤིག། སྲུངས་ཤིག། དྲངས་ཤིག། སྐྱུངས་ཤིག། སྡོམས་ཤིག། སྐྱོམས་ཤིག། སོམས་ཤིག། རྩམས་ཤིག། སྐོནད་ཅིག། ཐོནད་ཅིག། ཆེནད་ཅིག། སོལད་ཅིག། ཉནད་ཅིག། སྐྱནས་ཅིག། སྐྱེནད་ཅིག། རོལད་ཅིག། རྩལད་ཅིག། སྦྲོལད་ཅིག། སྐྲོལད་ཅིག། སྐུརད་ཅིག། སྦྲོརད་ཅིག། སྐོརད་ཅིག། ཆོད་ཅིག། སོད་ཅིག། ཁོད་ཅིག། སྦོད་ཅིག། སྦྲོད་ཅིག། ཅེས་པ་ལ་སོགས་པ་དང་།

རྗེས་འཇུག་གཞན་དེར་འཇུག་པ་ན། ཤོག་ཅིག། ཁོག་ཅིག། བློབ་ཅིག། ཐོབ་ཅིག། སྦོབ་ཅིག། སྐྱོབ་ཅིག། སྐོང་ཞིག། ཟུང་ཅིག། སོང་ཞིག། མ་སླའ་ཞིག། མ་ཕྲའ་ཞིག། མ་བླའ་ཞིག། སྣན་ཞིག། སྒྲུན་ཞིག། ཕྱུར་ཞིག། སྐྱུར་ཞིག། ཚོལ་ཞིག། སྐྱོལ་ཞིག། ལྟ་བུ་སྟེ་འདི་རྣམས་ཀྱིས་མཚོན་ནས་རྒྱ་ཆེར་ཤེས་པར་བྱའོ།།

དེས་ན་སྐྱེལ་ཚིག་ཕལ་ཆེར་ལ་སྔོན་འཇུག་མེད་པ་མང་ཞིང་སྔོན་འཇུག་སྦྱར་དགོས་པའང་ཡོད་དེ། བཀྲུས་ཤིག། བསྐོད་ཅིག། བརྟེན་ཞིག། བསྡོམས་ཤིག། གཏོརད་ཅིག། གདུངས་ཤིག། གསོངས་ཤིག། དཀུགས་ཤིག། དགོངས་ཤིག། དཔྱོད་ཅིག། མཆོད་ཅིག། མཆོང་ཞིག། མཛོད་ཅིག། འཇོམས་ཤིག། མ་འགྲོའ་ཞིག། མ་འཚོའ་ཞིག། ཅེས་པ་ལྟ་བུ་རྣམས་སོ།།

གཉིས་པ་གཞན་གྱི་འདོད་པ་ཞར་ལ་བསྟན་པ་ནི། སྐབས་འདིར་འགྲེལ་བྱེད་ཐ་མ་ཕལ་ཆེར་གྱིས། ཐ་མ་སྔོན་འཇུག་ལྟ་བཞིན་སྒྱུར། ཞེས་པའི་དོན་སྔོན་འཇུག་ལྟར་རྗེས་འཇུག་གི་ཡི་གེ་རྣམས་འདས་པ་དང་། གཞན་སྒྲུབ་ལ་འཇུག་པ་སོགས་རྟགས་ཀྱི་བྱ་ཚིག་གིས་འཇུག་ཡུལ་སོ་སོར་སྒྱུར་རྒྱུ་འདོད་མོད། དེ་ལྟར་སྦྱོར་བ་སྐབས་རེ་གཉིས་ལ་འགྲིག་པ་ལྟར་སྣང་ཡང་ཕལ་མོ་ཆེར་ངེས་པ་མེད་པའི་སྦྱོར་ཚུལ་དུ་འགྱུར་བས་མི་འཐད་པའི་ཚུལ་གོང་དུ་རྟགས་ངོས་འཛིན་གྱི་སྐབས་སུ་བཤད་ཟིན་ཅིང་། གཞན་ཡང་དེ་ལྟར་འདོད་པ་ལ་བསྒྱུན་མང་དུ་ཡོད་དེ། གཞུང་གི་ཚིགས་བཅད་དང་མི་འགྲིག་པ་དང་། བྱ་ཚིག་མདོར་བསྟན་དང་འགལ་བ་དང་། ཉིན་དོན་གྱི་དཔེར་བརྗོད་མི་འཐད་པའི་སྐྱོན་རྣམས་ཡོད་པའི་ཕྱིར། དང་པོ་གྲུབ་སྟེ། ཐ་མ་སྔོན་འཇུག་སོགས་ཀྱི་གཞུང་འདི། ཕྱིའི་ས་དཔྱད་ཇི་ལྟར་འཇུག་བྱེད་འཆད་པའི་སྐབས་དང་། དེ་ལས་གྱུར་དོན་གྱི་ཇི་ལྟར་འཇུག་བྱེད་འཆད་པའི་སྐབས་ཡིན་པ་ལ། དེ་དང་མི་འགྲིག་པའི་ཅི་ཕྱིར་འཇུག་བྱེད་བཤད་པའི་ཕྱིར་ཏེ། རྗེས་འཇུག་རྣམས་སྔོན་འཇུག་གི་ཅི་ཕྱིར་འཇུག་པ་བཤད་པ་ལྟར། རྟགས་ཀྱི་ཁྱད་པར་གྱིས་བདག་གཞན་དང་དུས་གསུམ་གྱི་ཁྱད་པར་ངེས་པར་སྟོན་པའི་སླད་དུ་འཇུག་པར་བཤད་པའི་ཕྱིར། ཐ་མ་མ་གྲུབ་སྟེ། ཇི་ལྟར་འཇུག་པ་དང་ཅི་ཕྱིར་འཇུག་པ་གཉིས་ཀ་དང་མཐུན་པར་བཤད་དུ་ཡོད་པའི་ཕྱིར། སྐམ་ནའང་མ་ཡིན་ཏེ། ཅི་ཕྱིར་འཇུག་པ་ནི་དོན་དེ་སྟོན་བྱེད་དུ་ངེས་པར་འཇུག་པ་ཞིག་དགོས་ལ། ཇི་ལྟར་འཇུག་པ་ནི། སྒྲ་དོན་དེ་དང་དེར་འཇུག་པ་ཙམ་དུ་ཟད་པའི་ཕྱིར་རོ།

གཞན་ཡང་ཇི་ལྟར་དང་ཅི་ཕྱིར་གྱི་འཇུག་པ་གཉིས་སྐབས་འདིར་མཐུན་པར་བཤད་ན། གཞུང་དུ་ཅི་ཕྱིར་འཇུག་པ་གསུངས་པ་ལྟོས་པས་དབྱེ་བ་འདྲུགས་པའི་སྐྱོན་དུ་འགྱུར་ཞིང་། གལ་ཏེ། ཕོ་ནི་འདས་དང་གཞན་བསྒྲུབ་ཕྱིར། སོགས་སྔོན་འཇུག་གི་སྐབས་ཅི་ཕྱིར་འཇུག་འཆད་བྱེད་ཡིན་ཡང་འདིར་མིན་ནོ་ཞེར་ནའང་། མ་བཅད་མ་འཁྲིག་པས་ཅི་བྱ་གཏོལ་མེད་ཀྱིས་བྱུང་རྒྱལ་དུ་སླུས་པར་ཟད་དེ། རྒྱུ་མཚན་མེད་པར་མ་ཟད་དོན་ཅིའི་ཕྱིར་འཇུག་པ་འཆད་བཞིན་པ་དང་དངོས་སུ་འགལ་བའི་ཕྱིར་རོ༎

གཉིས་པ་གྲུབ་སྟེ། བྱེ་བྲག་དོན་གྱི་འཇུག་ཚུལ་ལ་གཉིས་སུ་དབྱེ་བའི་ཐ་མ་གང་ལྟར་འགྱུར་བ་ཞེས་མཛད་བསྟན་པ་འཆད་པའི་སྐབས་ཡིན་པ་གང་ཞིག། དེ་ལ་ཁྱེད་ཀྱིས་རྗེས་འཇུག་རྣམས་རང་དབང་གིས་དོན་རྐྱེན་བྱེད་དུ་འཇུག་པར་བཤད་པ་འགལ་བའི་ཕྱིར་ཏེ། འགྱུར་བ་ཞེས་པའི་དོན་རྗེས་འཇུག་རྣམས་རང་དབང་མི་བཙན་པར་སྔོན་འཇུག་ལ་སོགས་པའི་དོན་བཞིན་དུ་འགྱུར་འགྲོ་བ་ལ་འཆད་དགོས་པའི་ཕྱིར། དེ་མ་གྲུབ་སྙམ་ན། དེ་ལྟར་འཆད་རིགས་ཏེ་ཐ་མ་རྗེས་འཇུག་གི་དོན་གཙོ་བོར་སྔོན་འཇུག་གི་རྗེས་སུ་འགྲོ་ཞིང་ཕྱི་མ་མིང་མཐའ་དང་རྣམ་དབྱེ་སོགས་ཀྱི་དོན་རྗེས་འཇུག་དང་ཚིག་ཕྱི་མ་དག་གི་རྗེས་སུ་འགྲོ་བ་གཞུང་དུ་གང་ལྟར་འགྱུར་བ་ཞེས་པའི་སྒྲས་མཚུངས་པར་བསྟན་པའི་ཕྱིར་ཏེ། དེ་ལྟར་མ་བཤད་པས་ཐར་སློས་པའི་སྐྱོན་དེ་རྣམས་ཀྱང་སྤོང་མི་ནུས་པའི་ཕྱིར་རོ༎

གསུམ་པ་གྲུབ་སྟེ། ཁྱེད་རྣམས་ཀྱིས་སྐབས་འདིར་ད་བ་ས་གསུམ་གྱིས་འདས་པ་སྟོན་པའི་དཔེར་བཀོད་པ། བཅད། བཀབ། བཀས། ཞེས་པ་རྣམས་ལས་ཕྱི་མ་ས་ཡིག་གིས་འདས་པ་བསྟན་དུ་རུང་ཀྱང་། སྔ་མ་གཉིས་འདས་ཚིག་ཏུ་གྲུབ་པ་རྗེས་འཇུག་གི་ནུས་པས་མ་ཡིན་པའི་ཕྱིར་ཏེ། དེ་གཉིས། གཅད། གཅོད། དཀབ། འགེབ་ཅེས་བྱ་བྱེད་ཀྱི་ཚིག་ལ་སྦྱར་བའི་ཚེ་ནའང་རྗེས་འཇུག་དེ་ཕོ་ན་ལས་གཞན་དུ་མི་འགྱུར་བའི་ཕྱིར་ཏེ། སྔོན་འཇུག་གི་ནུས་པ་ཕོ་ནས་བྱ་བྱེད་ཀྱི་ཚིག་ཏུ་གྲུབ་པའི་ཕྱིར་རོ། དེས་ན་དཔེར་བརྗོད་དེ་ཙམ་ལའང་ཡིད་བརྟན་ཐེར་བ་མ་བྱུང་ན། རང་ཉིད་ཀྱིས་བཤད་པ་དང་མཐུན་པའི་དཔེར་བརྗོད་གཞན་རྣམས་འགོད་པ་ར་ལྟ་ག་ལ་ནུས་པས་འགོད་མ་ནུས་པ་དེར་ཟད་དོ༎

གཞན་ཡང་། ལུགས་དེ་ཁས་ལེན་པའི་ཕྱིས་བྱུང་ཤིག་གིས་སྐབས་འདིར་དཔེར་བརྗོད་ཐུང་ཟད་མང་བར་འགོད་པའི་ཁྲུལ་དུ་བྱས་ཏེ། བྱ་བ་བྱས། ཆར་པ་ཕབ། མེ་ཏོག་ཐོག། ན་ཚ་ཆད་ཅེས་སོགས་འདས་པ་ལ་འཇུག་པ་དང་། བྲམ་ཟེ། སྦབ། སྦོག། སྤྱོད་ལྟ་བུ་དངོས་པོ་གཞན་དང་། གདམས་པར་བྱ། བསྒྲུབ་པར་བྱ། བསྒྲག་པར་བྱ། བརྗོད་པར་བྱ་ལྟ་བུ་བྱ་ཚིག་དང་དངོས་འབྲེལ་པ་དང་། རྒྱས་པར་བྱས། ས་བོན་བཏབ། ལམ་འགོག། རྟོད་འདོད་ལྟ་བུ་དངོས་སུ་མ་འབྲེལ་ཡང་བྱ་བ་བསྒྲུབ་པ་ལ་འཇུག་པ་དང་། ནམ་མཁའ་ལྟ་བུ་གཞན་དང་། ཡོད་པའི་གདའ་སོགས་ད་ལྟར་བ་སྟོན་པ་དང་། འགྱུར། འཇལ། འབྱུང་། འདྲེན། འཁྲུམ། སྔོ་གསར། ཚ་སྒོར། བཀྲང་ཕྲེང་། མདུན། མཚལ་སོགས་བདག་དང་མ་འོངས་པ་འཇུག་པ་ལྟ་བུའོ༎

ཞེས་བྲིས་མོད། དེ་རྣམས་ཟེར་རྒྱུས་ཐོངས་པ་འམ་བློ་ནལ་དུ་མི་གནས་པའི་རྒྱུན་ཉིད་ཀྱིས་བྱུང་རྒྱལ་དུ་སླུས་པ་སྟེ། འདས་པའི་དཔེར་སྐྱུར་ཚིག་བྲིས་པ་དང་། གཞན་གྱི་དཔེར་མིང་རྐྱང་དང་འདས་ཚིག་དང་བྱེད་ཚིག་བཀོད་པ་དང་། བདག་དང་མ་འོངས་པའི་དཔེར་མིང་རྐྱང་བཀོད་པ་སོགས་ཐལ་ཆེར་འགལ་བ་ཁོ་ནར་སྣང་བའི་ཕྱིར་རོ༎

ཁྱད་པར་མིང་རྐྱང་རྣམས་འདིའི་དཔེར་བརྗོད་དུ་བཀོད་པ་ནི་ཤིན་ཏུ་མཚར་ཆེ་སྟེ། མིང་རྐྱང་ཙམ་དེ་འདིར་བསྟན་གྱི་བདག་གཞན་དང་དུས་གསུམ་གྱིས་མ་བསྡུས་པ་སྔོན་འཇུག་གི་སྐབས་སུ་བཤད་པ་ལྟ་བུའི་ཕྱིར་དང་། མིང་རྐྱང་རྣམས་ལ་རྗེས་འཇུག་ཐམས་ཅད་ཀྱི་བྱེ་བྲག་མེད་པར་འཇུག་པ་ཡིན་པས་རྟགས་ཀྱི་འཇུག་དོན་གྱི་དབང་གིས་ཐ་དད་དུ་འབྱེད་པའི་རྒྱུ་མཚན་ཅིའང་མེད་པའི་ཕྱིར་རོ། སྐྱེས་དབང་གིས་དཔེར་བརྗོད་འཁྲིག་པ་དེ་རྣམས་ཀྱང་གོང་བློས་བཞིན་རང་གི་ཞེན་དོན་གྱི་སྒྲུབ་བྱེད་དུ་མི་འགྲོ་སྟེ། འ་ཡིག་འདས་པ་ལ་མི་འཇུག་པ་དང་། ས་ད་གཉིས་འདས་པ་ལ་འཇུག་པ་མང་བ་ཙམ་ལས་གཞན་བྱེ་བྲག་ཆེར་མེད་པར་རྗེས་འཇུག་རྣམས་བདག་གཞན་དང་དུས་གསུམ་ཐམས་ཅད་ལ་འཇུག་པའི་ཕྱིར་རོ༎

འདིར་སྨྲས་པ།

མཁས་རློམ་ཐལ་ཆེར་རི་བོང་ཅལ་རྗེས་སློགས། སྨིག་རྒྱུའི་ཆུ་སྤྱོད་བྲག་ཅའི་སྒྲ་དབྱངས་ལེན། མཁས་པ་རྣམས་ཀྱང་དེ་འདྲའི་འཕྱས་སྨོགས་ལ།

གཞོལ་ཞིང་ངལ་བ་ཅི་ཡང་བརྙེན་པ་མཐོང་། འདི་དང་འདི་འདྲའི་ཚུལ་ལ་བརྟགས་པའི་ཚེ། ནམ་ཡང་གཞན་དྲིང་ཁོ་ནར་མི་བརྙེན་ཅིང་།
གཞན་ཐེར་ཁོ་ནའི་ལྟད་མོའང་མི་བློ་བས། ཁོ་བོའི་བློ་གྲོས་སྐལ་བ་བཟང་སྙམ་བསྐྱེད། མཁས་པའི་བསྟན་བཅོས་རང་བཞིན་དག་པའི་དངོས།
གསལ་བྱེད་མཁས་པ་ཉིད་ལ་རག་ལས་ཏེ། འཇོད་སྦྱིན་དབྱིག་མཆོག་ནོར་བུ་བཻ་ཌཱུརྱ། དེད་དཔོན་མཁས་པས་ཡོངས་སུ་སྦྱངས་ལ་ལྟོས། ཞེས་སོ།།

གཉིས་པ་ཕྱི་མ་གང་ལྟར་འགྱུར་བ་འཆད་པ་ལ་གཉིས། མདོར་བསྟན་པ་དང་རྒྱས་པར་བཤད་པའོ།། དང་པོ་ནི།

ཕྱི་མ་དག་གིས་འདྲེན་ཚུལ་ནི།

ཞེས་པ་སྟེ། ཕྱི་མ་མིང་མཐའ་དང་རྣམ་དབྱེ་སོགས་ཀྱི་ཐོབ་ཐང་གི་དོན་དེ་ལྟར་འཇུག་པར་འགྱུར་བའི་ཚུལ་ནི་སྔ་མའི་རྗེས་འཇུག་དང་ཕྱི་མའི་བརྗོད་བྱ་དག་པ་ལ་ཅི་རིགས་པར་ལྟོས་པའི་སྒོ་ནས་འདྲེན་པའི་ཕྱིར་དེའི་ཚུལ་སྨོས་པ་ནི། ཞེས་མདོར་བསྟན་པའོ།།

གཉིས་པ་རྒྱས་བཤད་ལ་མིང་མཐའ་འདྲེན་ཚུལ་དང་། རྣམ་དབྱེ་སོགས་འདྲེན་ཚུལ་འཆད་པ་སྟེ་གཉིས་སོ། དང་པོ་ནི།

ཕོ་ཡིས་ཕོ་ཡི་མིང་མཐར་དྲང་། མོ་ཡིས་མོ་ཡི་མིང་མཐར་དྲང་། མ་ནིང་གིས་ནི་མ་ནིང་ངོ་།།

ཞེས་པས་བསྟན་ཏེ། མིང་སྔ་མའི་མཐའི་རྗེས་འཇུག་ཕོ་ཡིག་གིས། དེ་ཉིད་ཀྱི་མིང་མཐའ་གཞན་གྱི་མིང་གཞིའི་ཕོ་ཡིག་དྲང་བར་བྱ་ཞིང་། དེ་བཞིན་དུ་མོ་ཡིག་གིས་མོའི་མིང་མཐའ་དྲང་བ་དང་། མ་ནིང་གི་མ་ནིང་གི་མིང་མཐའ་དྲང་བར་བྱའོ།། ཞེས་སོ།།

དེས་ན་མིང་སྔ་མའི་མཐའི་རྗེས་འཇུག་རྣམས་ཀྱང་མིང་མཐའ་ཡིན་མོད་ཀྱི་འདིར་བསྟན་གྱི་མིང་མཐའ་ཞེས་པ་ནི་རྗེས་འཇུག་གིས་མིང་དུ་གྲུབ་པའི་མིང་སྔ་མ་དེ་ཉིད་ཀྱི་ཆ་ཤས་མིང་དེའི་མཐར་སྦྱར་རྒྱུ་ཞིག་ལ་ངོས་འཛིན་དགོས་སོ།།

དེ་དག་གི་དཔེར་བརྗོད་པ་ནི།

ཕོ་ཕོའི་མིང་མཐའ་དྲངས་པ། དཔྱིད་ཀ། སྟོནད་ཀ། ཐད་ཀ། སྟོད་ཀོར། ཀླད་ཀོར། ཐེརད་ཀ། བསྟོད་པ། མཁྱེནད་པ། བཅད་པ། ཕནད་པ། ཕྱེནད་པ། སྐྱེནད་པ། སྡོད་པ། རྩོད་པ། ནོད་པ། སྒྲོད་པ། ཁྲབ་པ། ཚུབ་པ། གྲུབ་པ། སྒྲུབ་པ། སྐྱོབ་པ། གདབ་པ། བདས་པ། ཐོབ་པ། འགྲུབ་པ། ཐུབ་པ། སོས་ཀ། གཉིས་ཀ། བྲུས་པ། བསྒྲུབས་པ། བརྟགས་པ། དགོངས་པ། གཏམས་པ། དངོས་པོ། དགོས་པ། གོམས་པ། བཀླམས་པ། དམིགས་པ། ཆགས་པ། མཁྲིས་པ། པགས་པ། སྐྲུས་པ། རྟག་པ། འཕྲུག་པ། ཟག་པ། ལྷག་པ། དག་པ། རིག་པ། ལག་པ། བདུག་པ། གདུག་པ། གཅིག་བུ། ཅིག་ཅར། བདག་ཅག་སོགས་པ་ཤིན་ཏུ་མང་ངོ་།

མོ་མོའི་མིང་མཐའ་དྲངས་པ་ནི། གང་བ། བྱུང་བ། མཐོང་བ། གསུང་བ། འབྱུང་བ། འདྲེང་བ། གཏོང་བ། བསླང་བ། དགང་བ། བཟང་བ། སྐྱིང་ག། མཐོང་ག། མཆིང་ག། ལྷུང་ག། སྤྲང་མ། དང་མ། གདུང་མ། གསིང་མ། འདུང་མ། འདེམ་ག། གསུམ་ག། ཐམ་ག། ཟླ་བ། འདྲ་བ། དཔའ་བ། སྨྲ་བ། དགའ་བ། འཚའ་བ། བདེ་བ། རེ་བ། བཙའ་བ། བཀྲ་བ། གདའ་བ། ཉི་མ། དགའ་མ། གཏའ་མ། འདའ་ག། ཡ་ག། ཉ་ག། འདི་ག། གྲོ་ག། ཁྱི་གུ། ལུ་གུ་སོགས་སོ།།

མ་ནིང་གིས་མ་ནིང་དྲངས་པ་ནི། སྟོན་ཁ། དཔུན་ཁ། མོན་ཁ། དབྱར་ཁ། སེར་ཁ། གཏར་ཁ། ཤར་ཁ། སྒུར་ཁ།

རལ་ཁ། ཉལ་ཁ། མཚལ་ཁ། རྒྱལ་ཁ། གསལ་ཁ། དཔལ་ཁ། སོགས་སོ།།

དེ་ལྟར་མིང་མཐའ་རྟགས་མཚུངས་ཕོ་ན་འདྲེན་པ་ལྟ་བུར་གསུངས་པ་ནི་ཕོ་མོའི་རྟགས་ཕལ་ཆེར་གྱིས་དེ་ལྟར་འདྲེན་པས་གཙོ་ཆེ་བ་ཙམ་ལ་དགོངས་པ་སྟེ། འཆད་འགྱུར་ལྟར། དེ་ཉིད་རང་གི་སྒྲ་མཐུན་པའི། ཞེས་གསུངས་པ་དང་སྦྱར་ན་འདྲེན་ཚུལ་གཞན་ཡང་ཡོད་པར་གྲུབ་ཅིང་། མངོན་སུམ་གྱིས་ཀྱང་འགྲུབ་པའི་ཕྱིར་རོ།།

དེས་ན་མ་ནིང་གི་རྟགས་རྣམས་ཀྱིས་རྟགས་མཚུངས་འདྲེན་པ་དཔེར་བརྗོད་བཀོད་པ་འདི་འདུ་ཤོར་བུ་ལས། ཕལ་ཆེར་བརྗོད་བདེ་བས་སྒྲ་མཐུན་པ་མོ་རྟགས་ཉིད་དྭངས་པ་མཐོང་སྟེ། མངོན་བ། མཐུན་བ། བསྟར་བ། ཤར་བ། དར་བ། འབྱུལ་བ། གསལ་བ། རྒྱལ་བ། ཞེས་པ་ལྟ་བུ་དང་། མོ་རྟགས་མ་ཡིག་གིས་ཀྱང་བརྗོད་བདེ་རང་སྡེའི་རྗེས་པའི་རྟགས་དྭངས་པ། དམ་པ། བསམ་པ། རྫམ་པ། སྙམ་པ། རམ་པ། རིམ་པ། ལྷུམ་པ། ནམ་པ། བུམ་པ། ལྟ་བུ་མང་དུ་སྣང་བས་ཕྱི་བྲག་སོ་སོར་མ་འཛིངས་པར་རྟོགས་པར་བྱའོ། གཞན་དུ་རྐང་པ། ཁང་པ། སྟོང་པ། སོགས་ང་ཡིག་གིས་ཕོ་དྭངས་པ་འགའ་ཞིག་སྣང་བ། ཁ་ཅིག་གིས། བདག་པོའི་སྒྲ་ཡིན་པར་འདོད་ཀྱང་མི་འཐད་པ་རྟོགས་སྒྲ་བས་དེ་དག་དང་། གཞན་ཡང་། ལྷམ་མ། བཙམ་མ། ལྟད་མོ། སྒྲུག་མ་སོགས་ཕོ་མོ་དྭངས་པ་ལྟ་བུ་དམིགས་གསལ་དེ་འདྲ་བར་ཤོར་ལ་ངེས་པ་མེད་དེ།

ཀ་ལཱ་པར། ལྷག་མ་འཇིག་རྟེན་པའི་ཉེར་སྤྱོད་ལས་འཇོན་པ་གྲུབ་པོ།། ཞེས་གསུངས་པ་བཞིན་འཇིག་རྟེན་པའི་གྲགས་པ་དང་བསྟུན་དགོས་པའི་ཕྱིར་རོ།།

འདིར་ཁ་ཅིག ཁྱོད་ཀྱིས་རྟགས་མཚུངས་འདྲེན་པའི་དཔེར་བཀོད་པ་འདི་རྣམས་ལ་ཁྱོད་ཉིད་ཀྱིས་ཁས་བླངས་པ་དང་འགལ་བ་ཡོད་དེ། སྔར་ཡང་འཇུག་དང་བཅས་པའི་ན་ར་ལ་རྣམས་མ་ནིང་དང་། ང་མ་ཡང་འཇུག་ཅན་རྣམས་མོ་རྟགས་སུ་ཁས་བླངས་པ་གང་ཞིག འདིར་དེ་རྣམས་ཀྱིས་ཕོ་ཡིག་དྭངས་པ། ཕོས་ཕོའི་མིང་མཐའ་དྭངས་པའི་དཔེར་བརྗོད་དུ་བཀོད་པའི་ཕྱིར། སྨྲས་ན་སྐྱོན་མེད་དེ། རྫོགས་སྒྲ་གདངས་དྲག་ཞན་གྱི་འཇུག་ཚུལ་གྱི་དབང་གིས་བཤད་ཅིང་། འདིར་ཡང་འཇུག་མེད་ན་མིང་མཐའི་རྗེས་འཇུག་དེ་ཉིད་དང་ཡོད་ན་ཡང་འཇུག་ཉིད་ཀྱི་རྟགས་གང་ཡིན་པ་དང་སྦྱར་ནས་མིང་མཐའ་ཕྱི་མ་འདྲེན་ཚུལ་ཙམ་འཆད་པ་ཡིན་གྱི། རྫ་མ་ལྟར་འཇུག་ཡང་འཇུག་གཉིས་ཀ་བརྩེགས་པའི་སྒྲ་གདངས་དེའི་ཚུལ་པ་འཆད་པའི་སྐབས་མ་ཡིན་པའི་ཕྱིར་རོ།།

སྐབས་འདིར་འགྲེལ་བྱེད་སྔ་མ་རྣམས་ཀྱིས་མིང་གཞི་ཕྱི་མས་མིང་མཐའ་སྔ་མ་འདྲེན་པར་འདོད་ཀྱང་། ཤིན་ཏུ་མི་འཐད་དེ། སྐབས་འདིའི་རྡེན་ཚུལ་ནི་ངག་གི་བརྗོད་པ་དང་སྦྱར་ནས་རྟོགས་དགོས་པའི་ཕྱིར་འདྲེན་བྱེད་སྔོན་དུ་མ་བརྗོད་པ་དེ་ལ་ལྟོས་པའི་འདྲེན་བྱའི་བརྗོད་པ་འབྱུང་བ་མི་སྲིད་དེ།

དཔེར་ན། རྟག་ལྟར་བུའི་ངག་སྔོན་དུ་ཡོད་ན་དེའི་མཐའ་ག་ལ་ལྟོས་པའི་མིང་མཐའ་ཕྱི་མ་པ་ཡིག་འདྲེན་པར་འགྱུར་བ་ལྟ་བུ་ཕོ་ན་ཡིན་པའི་ཕྱིར་ཏེ། ཁྱེད་རྣམས་ལྟར་ན་ལྟོས་ས་མ་བྱུང་བའི་སྔོན་དུ་ལྟོས་ཆོས་གྲུབ་ཟིན་པ་དང་། འདྲེན་བྱེད་མ་བྱུང་བའི་སྔོན་དུ་དེར་ལྟོས་པའི་འདྲེན་བྱ་གྲུབ་ཟིན་པ་སོགས་ཕྱིན་ཅི་ལོག་མང་པོ་ཁས་ལེན་དགོས་པར་འགྱུར་བའི་ཕྱིར་ཏེ། འདྲེན་བྱེད་རྣམ་དབྱེ་དང་ཚིག་ཕྲད་སོགས་སུ་བྱས་ཤིང་། འདྲེན་བྱ་མིང་སྔ་མའི་མཐར་འདོད་པ་དེ་ལས། མིང་མཐའ་དེ་དག་ཉིད་ཀྱིས་ཀྱང་། སོགས་ཀྱི་གཞུང་འཆད་པའི་ཚེ་དངོས་འགལ་དུའང་སྨྲ་དགོས་པར་བྱུང་སྣང་བའི་ཕྱིར་རོ།།

སྤྱིར་ཡང་མིང་མཐའ་སྔ་མས་ཕྱི་མ་འདྲེན། མིང་མཐའ་སྔ་ཕྱི་གཉིས་ཀས་རྣམ་དབྱེ་སོགས་འདྲེན་པ་འདིའི་རྒྱུ་མཚན་ངེས་པ་མ་རྙེད་པས། འདྲེན་བྱའི་མིང་མཐའ་ངེས་མ་ཉེན་པ་དང་། འདྲེན་ཚུལ་གོ་ལྡོག་དང་རྣལ་མ་གཉིས་ཐོན་པ་འདི་ལགས་སོ། གཞན་ཡང་སྐད་གཉིས་སྨྲ་བ་འགའ་ཞིག་གིས། དགོནད་ཅིག རིནད་ཅིག ཐབས་ཅིག ལྷནད་ཅིག ཡུངས་དཀར་ལ་སོགས་པ་རྣམས། དེ་དག་གི་སྐད་དོད་ལེགས་སྦྱར་ལ་དཀོན་པའི་མཆོག་དང་། རིན་ཐང་ཆེན་པོ་དང་གྲངས་ཀྱི་གཅིག་དང་ཁ་དོག་དཀར་པོ་སོགས་ཀྱི་དོན་མེད་པས་དེ་དང་དེའི་དོན་དུ་མི་འགྲུབ་པའི་ཕྱིར་ཞེས་ཕོའི་མིང་མཐའ་དྭངས་པར་བཞེད་པ་མཁས་པའི་གསུངས་ཡིན་ཡང་ཞིབ་མོར་དཔྱད་ན་གོ་བ་མི་བཟང་སྟེ། སྤྱིར་ཟུར་བོད་དུ་མ་གྲགས་པའི་བརྡ་གསུང་རབ་སྒྱུར་བ་ན་དགོས་པར་བྱུང་ནས་ལེགས་སྦྱར་གྱི་སྐད་དང་སྦྱར་ཏེ་གསར་དུ་བཏགས་པ་རྣམས་ལ་ལེགས་སྦྱར་གྱི་ཕྱིང་མ་སོགས

དང་བསྟུན་ནས་དཔྱད་པས་སྣང་ལ་མ་ངེས་པའི་དགོས་པ་སེལ་ཞིང་བརྗོད་དོན་ཇི་བཞིན་དུ་རྟོགས་པར་འགྱུར་བ་ཡིན་མོད། འོན་ཀྱང་ཐམས་ཅད་ལ་ངེས་མ་ཁྱབ་སྟེ། སྒྲ་དོན་དང་སྦྱར་ནས་བརྟགས་པ་མ་ཡིན་པར་མཚོན་དོན་གྱི་སྒོ་ནས་མིང་གསར་དུ་སྦྱར་བ་དག་ཀྱང་ཡོད་ཅིང་དེ་འདྲ་ལ་སྐད་དོད་ཡོད་མེད་དང་ཁམས་དང་རྐྱེན་གྱི་ནུས་པས་འགྱུར་མི་འགྱུར་དཔྱད་དུ་མེད་པའི་ཕྱིར་ཏེ། ཀཱ་རི་ཀཱ། ཞེས་པ་ཚིག་ལེའུར་བྱས་པར་བསྒྱུར་ན་དེར་ཚིག་དང་ལེའུ་གཉིས་ཀའི་སྐད་དོད་མེད་པ་དང་། པཉྫི་ཀཱ། དཀའ་འགྲེལ་དུ་བསྒྱུར་ན་དེར་དཀའ་བ་དང་འགྲེལ་པ་གཉིས་ཀའི་སྐད་དོད་མེད་པ་སོགས་ཤིན་ཏུ་མང་བའི་ཕྱིར་རོ།།

གཞན་དུ་བོད་ཉིད་ལ་སྔར་ནས་གྲགས་པའི་བརྡ་འདོད་རྒྱལ་དང་རྗེས་སྒྲུབ་གང་ཡིན་ཡང་རུང་། དེ་འདྲའི་སྐབས་སྐོར་ལ་ལེགས་སྦྱར་གྱིས་ཞུས་དག་བགྱིད་མི་བཏུབ་སྟེ། དེ་འདྲ་དེ་ལེགས་སྦྱར་ནས་བསྒྱུར་བ་ཡིན་ཡང་སྐད་གཉིས་པའི་འཇུག་ཡུལ་མཚུངས་ཕྱིན། སྒྲ་དོན་གྱི་ཟུར་ཡན་ཆད་གཅིག་ནོར་ལ་གང་ཡོད་གཅིག་ནོར་ལ་ཡོད་པའི་པར་བཀབ་ཅིའང་མི་དགོས་པའི་ཕྱིར་རོ།།

དེས་ན་རཏྣ་ཞེས་པ་དཀོན་ཅོག་ཏུ་བསྒྱུར་བ་ནི། བོད་དུ་དམ་ཆོས་མ་དར་གོང་དུ་དཀོན་མཆོག་གི་བརྡ་མེད་པ་ལ་ནོར་བུ་བས་རིན་ཅེན་དུ་བསྒྱུར་ན་དབྱིག་གི་མཆོག་དང་ཐུན་མོང་དུ་འགྱུར་བའི་ཕྱིར་ཐུན་མོང་མིན་པའི་དོན་མཚོན་པར་འདོད་ནས་ལུང་དང་སྦྱར་ཏེ་དཀོན་པ་དང་སྒྲ་དོན་དང་སྦྱར་ནས་མཆོག་ཅེས་བསྡེབས་ནས་མིང་གཅིག་ཏུ་མཛད་པ་ཡིན་ནོ།།

དེ་ལྟར་ན་དཀོན་ཅོག་ཅེས་འདོན་པར་རུང་ངམ་ཅེ་ན། དེ་ལྟར་ཤིན་ཏུ་རུང་སྟེ་དཀོན་ཅོག་ཅེས་མིང་གཅིག་ཏུ་བྱེད་པའི་ཚེ་མཆོག་གི་སྒྲ་མིང་མཐར་འགྱུར་བས་སྡོམས་པའི་མིང་མཐའ་དྲང་བའི་ཕྱིར་སྔོན་འཇུག་མ་ཡིག་ཕྱིས་ནས་མིང་གཉིའི་མ་ཞིང་རང་སྡེའི་ཐ་ཡིག་ཏུ་བསྒྱུར་བར་ཟད་ཀྱི་དོན་བསྒྱུར་བ་མ་ཡིན་པའི་ཕྱིར། ལེགས་སྦྱར་ལ་ཏྲ་ཧི་སྤྱི་དུ་བསྒྱུར་བ་བཞིན་ནོ།།

དེས་ན་དཀོན་པ་དང་མཆོག་སྒྲ་དོན་ལུང་ལ་བརྟེན་ནས་བཤད་དུ་ཡོད་པའི་ཕྱིར་དཀོན་མཆོག་ཅེས་འདོན་པ་འཐད་ཀྱི་དཀོན་ཅོག་ཅེས་མི་རུང་ངོ་ཞེར་བའང་གནད་འདི་མ་རྟོགས་པའི་ཅལ་ཅོལ་ཙམ་མོ།།

རཏྣའི་སྒྲ་མཆོག་ལ་མི་འཇུག་པའང་མ་ཡིན་ཏེ། རང་རིགས་ཀྱི་མཆོག་ལ་འཇུག་པའི་ཕྱིར་ཏེ། རཏྣ་ན་རང་རིགས་གཙོ་བོ་ལ། ཞེས་འབྱུང་བའི་ཕྱིར་རཏྣ་ནའི་སྒྲ་ལ་མཆོག་གི་སྐད་དོད་དངོས་སུ་མེད་ཟེར་བ་དང་། ཙན་དྲ་པའི་ཀོ་ཥ་སོགས་སུ་རཏྣ་ནི་གང་མཆོག་ཏུ་གྱུར་པ་དེའོ།།

ཞེས་འབྱུང་བ་ལུང་འདྲེན་པའང་འགལ་བ་ཡིན་ཏེ། རཏྣ་ནའི་སྒྲ་མཆོག་གི་སྐད་དོད་དངོས་སུ་འགྱུར་བར་ལུང་དེ་ཉིད་ཀྱིས་གྲུབ་པའི་ཕྱིར། དཀོན་ཅོག་ཅེས་པའང་བོད་ཀྱི་འདོད་རྒྱལ་ཡིན་ཟེར་བའང་མི་འཐད་དེ། དེ་བོད་དུ་ཐོག་མ་ནས་མ་གྲགས་ཤིང་མཁས་པ་དག་གིས་དོན་དང་བསྟུན་ནས་རྒྱ་མཚན་དང་བཅས་པར་གསར་དུ་བཏགས་པའི་མིང་ཡིན་པའི་ཕྱིར་རོ།།

དེ་བཞིན་དུ་རིན་པོ་ཆེའི་སྒྲ་བསྡུས་པས་རིན་ཅེན་ཞེས་པ་ནི་བོད་བརྡ་རྙིང་པ་ཡིན་ཞིང་རིན་ཐང་ཆེ་བའི་དོན་ཡང་ཡིན་མོད། དེའི་སྐད་དོད་ཀྱང་རཏྣ་ཡིན་པས་དེ་ལ་རིན་ཆེ་བའི་སྒྲ་བཤད་བྱེད་དུ་མེད་ཀྱང་དེ་དག་གི་འཇུག་ཡུལ་རང་རིགས་ཀྱི་གཙོ་བོ་ཡིན་པར་མཚུངས་པས་རིན་ཅེན་དུ་བསྒྱུར་བ་མི་འགལ་ཞིང་རིན་ཐང་ཆེ་བའི་དོན་ཉིད་མི་གཏོང་བར་སྡོམས་ཚིའི་མིང་མཐའ་དྲངས་པའི་དགོས་པས་རིན་ཅེན་དུ་གྲུབ་པའང་ཡིན་ནོ།།

བོད་སྐད་རིན་ཐང་ཆེ་བ་ཙམ་རང་རིགས་ཀྱི་མཆོག་ལ་མི་འཇུག་པའང་མ་ཡིན་ཏེ། དཔེར་ན། སྐྱེས་བུ་འགང་ཆེན་བུད་མེད་འགང་ཆེན་རྟ་འགང་ཆེན་ཞེས་སྐྱོང་པ་ལ་གྲགས་པའང་རིན་ཐང་ཆེ་བའི་ཚིག་ཙམ་ཡིན་པ་བཞིན་ནོ།།

ཐབས་ཅིག་གམ། ལྷན་ཅིག་གི་སྒྲའང་དེའི་སྐད་དོད་ལ་གྲངས་གཅིག་གི་དོན་མེད་རུང་། བོད་བརྡ་རྙིང་པ་ཕྱོགས་གཅིག་གམ་ཚོམ་གཅིག་གི་དོན་ཅན་ཡིན་པས་

གྲངས་ཀྱི་སྒྲར་ངེས་པ་དང་། ཡུངས་ཀར་ཞེས་པའང་ཡུང་དཀར་ནག་གི་རྣམ་བྱེ་བའི་ཡུངས་གཉིས་དཀར་པོ་ཡིན་པས་དཀར་ཞེས་པ་ཁ་དོག་ཉིད་དུ་གོར་མ་ཆག་པས་དེ་དག་གི་གཅིག་དང་དཀར་ལ་འཁྲུལ་བྱེད་དོར་བའང་མིང་མཐའ་འདྲེན་ཚུལ་ཉིད་དོ།།

རྒྱ་མཚན་འདིས། སྐད་དོད་དང་བོད་སྐད་གཉིས་ཀ་མཐུན་པའི་སློ་ནས་གྲངས་སུ་ངེས་པ་ལ་ནད་ཅིག་ཕྱ་བྱ་ལའང་ག་འཁྲུལ་མི་འབྱུང་བཞིན་བའི་གནད་ཀ་དང་། སྐད་ཅིག་གི་ད་ཡིག་འབྲིད་མི་དགོས་པ་སོགས་ཀྱང་ཤེས་པར་འགྱུར་རོ།།

གཞན་ཡང་རྒྱ་གར་ཞེས་པ་རྒྱ་ཡས་ཁོངས་སུ་གར་བའི་དོན་ཡིན་ཞེས་འཆད་ཅིང་རྒྱ་དཀར་པོའི་དོན་དུ་འདོད་པ་རྣམས་གཉི་ཕྱག་ལུང་མེད་དུ་ཐོ་བར་མཛད་ཀྱང་། ལེགས་པར་བརྟགས་ན་ཅི་འགྱུར་མི་ཤེས་ཏེ། རྒྱ་ནག་པོ་ཞེས་ཡུལ་དེའི་མི་རྣམས་ཞ་གོས་སོགས་ནག་པོ་ཤས་ཆེ་བ་ལས་གྲགས་ཤིང་གཅིག་ཤོས་དེ་ལས་བཟློག་པའི་ཕྱིར། རྒྱ་ནག་གི་རྣམ་དྭངས་པའི་རྒྱ་དཀར་པོ་ཞེས་བོད་དུ་གྲགས་པར་ཟད་མོད། དོན་ཀྱང་མིང་མཐའ་འདྲེན་ཚུལ་གྱིས་ཁྲོན་འཇུག་མ་ཤེས་ད་ཡིག་ཕྱིས། མིང་གཞི་རང་སྡེའི་མོ་ཡིག་ཏུ་བསྒྱུར་བས་རྒྱ་གར་ཞེས་གྲུབ་པར་འཁྲུམས་པས་སོ།།

དེ་བཞིན་དུ། ཀླད་ཀོར། རྡེད་ཀོར། པད་ཀོར་སོགས་ཀྱང་སྐོར་བའི་དོན་ལ། ཟླ་མའི་རྗེས་འཇུག་གི་དབང་ལས་ས་མགོ་མོ་ཡིག་ཡིན་པས་ས་ཕྱིས་པ་ཏེ་སྐོར་བའི་སྐད་དོད་ཡོད་མེད་ཅུད་གཅོད་མི་དགོས་ཤིང་ཐོ་སྐོར་ཏེ་སྐོར་སོགས་ལ་ས་མགོ་ངེས་པར་རྒྱུར་དགོས་པ་ལྟ་བུའང་གོ་བར་བྱའོ།།

དེས་ན་འདི་འདྲའི་རིགས་མིང་མཐའ་རྟགས་མཚུངས་འདྲེན་ཚུལ་ཁྲོན་གྱི་བརྡའ་རྙིང་ལ་ཤིན་ཏུ་མང་བ་ཞིག་ཡོད་པ་འདྲའང་གསར་བཅད་ཀྱི་ཕྱུམ་དག་མངས་པས་ད་ལྟ་ཕལ་ཆེར་ཤུས་པར་གདོན་མི་ཟ་བས་དཔེར་བརྗོད་ཀྱང་ཆེར་མི་སྣང་ལ། འདིས་ཐམས་ཅད་ལ་རིགས་འགྲེ་སྦྱར་ཆོག་པའང་མིན་པར་མངོན་ཏེ། འདི་རིགས་མིང་མཐའ་འདྲེན་ཚུལ་རྟགས་མཚུངས་བརྗོད་བདེ་མི་བདེ་སོགས་དང་བསྟུན་པའི་ཚིག་སྦྱོང་ལས་བྱུང་བའི་དམིགས་བསལ་གྱི་ཡི་གེའི་རྣམ་འགྱུར་ཞིག་ཏུ་མངོན་པའི་ཕྱིར་རོ།།

དེས་ན། པད་ཅེས་པའི་ད་ཡིག་ཕོ་ཡིན་པས་ས་མགོ་མི་ཐོབ་ཅེ་ནའང་མི་འཐད་དེ། སྒྲུབ་སྐོར་དང་། བཤད་སྒྲུབ་དང་། མདོད་རྫོད་སོགས་མཐའ་ཡས་པ་ཞིག་ལ་ས་མགོ་མི་ཐོབ་པར་ཐལ་བའི་ཕྱིར་རོ།། ཞེས་ཟེར་བའང་སྙིང་པོས་དཔེན་པར་རྟོགས་སོ།།

གཉིས་པ་རྣམ་དབྱེ་སོགས་འདྲེན་ཚུལ་ལ། སྤྱིར་འདྲེན་ཚུལ་དང་། ནང་གསེས་འཇུག་ཚུལ་བཤད་པ་གཉིས།

དང་པོ་ནི།

མིང་མཐའ་དེ་དག་ཉིད་ཀྱིས་ནི། དེ་ཉིད་རང་གི་སྒྲ་མཐུན་པའི། ཆོས་དངོས་ལས་དང་བྱེད་པ་དང་།
སྦྱིན་དང་འབྱུང་ཁུངས་འབྲེལ་པ་དང་། གནས་དང་བོད་པའི་སྒྲ་ཡང་དྲང་། གཞན་ཡང་སྒྲར་བསྡུ་ལྷག་བཅས་དང་།
འབྱེད་སྡུད་བསྣན་དང་བདག་པོ་དང་། དགག་སྒྲུབ་རྒྱན་དང་དུས་ལའང་འཇུག། དེ་དག་ཐ་ཤུགས་འདྲེན་པས་འབྱུང་།

ཞེས་པས་བསྟན་ཏེ། བཤད་མ་ཐག་པའི་མིང་མཐའ་ཐ་ཕྱི་དེ་དག་ཉིད་ཀྱིས། མིང་མཐའ་དེ་དག་ཉིད་རང་གི་རྟགས་མཚུངས་པའམ་བརྗོད་པ་བདེ་བས་སྒྲ་མཐུན་པར་གྱུར་པའི་རྣམ་དབྱེ་དང་པོ་ཆོས་དངོས་སྨྲ་ངོ་བོ་ཙམ་བརྗོད་པ་དང་། གཉིས་པ་ལས་སུ་བྱ་བ་དང་། གསུམ་པ་བྱེད་པ་པོ་འམ་བྱེད་པ་ཙམ་དང་། བཞི་པ་སྦྱིན་པའི་ཡུལ་གྱིས་མཚོན་ནས་ཆེད་དུ་བྱ་བ་དང་། ལྔ་པ་འབྱུང་ཁུངས་དང་། དྲུག་པ་འབྲེལ་པ་དང་། བདུན་པ་གནས་གཞི་དང་། བརྒྱད་པ་བོད་པའི་སྒྲ་རྣམས་ཀྱང་དྲང་བར་བྱ་ཞིང་། དེ་བཞིན་དུ་གཞན་ཡང་རྣམ་དབྱེའི་ཡན་ལག་ཏུ་གྱུར་པའམ་མ་གྱུར་པའི་ཚིག་ཕྲད། སྒྲར་བསྡུ་དང་། ལྷག་བཅས་དང་། འབྱེད་སྡུད་དང་། བསྣན་པ་དང་། བདག་པོ་དང་། དགག་པ་དང་། སྒྲུབ་པ་དང་། ཚིག་རྒྱན་དང་། དུས་ཏེ་ཚེ་སྐབས་ལ་འཇུག་པའི་སྒྲ་ལ་སོགས་པ་དེ་དག་རྣམས་ཀྱང་ཐ་མ་མིང་མཐའི་ཤུགས་ཀྱིས་འདྲེན་པར་བྱེད་པ་ན་སྦྱོར་ཚུལ་ལེགས་པར་འབྱུང་བ་ཡིན་ནོ།། ཞེས་སོ།།

དེ་རྣམས་ཀྱི་དཔེར་བརྗོད་པ་ནི་སུམ་བཅུ་པའི་སྐབས་སུ་རྒྱས་པར་སྨོས་ཟིན་པ་དང་། ག་ཤས་དཀའ་ཕྱོགས་ཙམ་འཆད་པར་འགྱུར་བས་འདིར་མི་སྤྲོ་ཞིང་། སྐབས་འདིར་སྒྲ་མཐུན་ཞེས་པའི་དོན་རྟགས་མཚུངས་ཁོ་ན་ལ་ཕལ་ཆེར་ཀྱིས་བཞེད་ཀྱང་། རྣམ་དབྱེ་དང་ཕྲད་སོགས་རྟགས་མཚུངས་ཁོ་ནས་འདྲེན་པར་མ་ངེས་ཤིང་གཙོ་བོར་བརྗོད་བདེ་བའི་སྒྲ་མཐུན་འདྲེན་པ་ཤས་ཆེ་བར་སྣང་བ་དང་།

སུམ་བཅུ་པར། དང་པོ་གཉིས་ལ་དང་པོ་མཐུན། གསུམ་ལྔ་བཅུ་ལ་ཀྱ་དང་སྦྱར། བདུན་པ་ཉིད་ལ་བདུན་པ་སྟེ། ལྷག་མ་རྣམས་ལ་ཀྱ་སྦྱར་བ། དེ་དག་ཡི་སྦྱར་འབྲེལ་པའི་ས། ཞེས་སྒྲ་མཐུན་ཚུལ་གསལ་བར་གསུངས་པའང་། ད་བ་ས་ང་རྣམས་ཀྱི་མཐར་རྟགས་མཚུངས་འདྲེན་པ་འགྲིག་ཀྱང་གཞན་རྣམས་བརྗོད་བདེ་བ་ཙམ་ལ་དགོངས་པར་སྣང་བས། རྒྱུ་མཚན་འདི་རྣམས་དང་སྦྱར་ན་ཁོ་བོའི་འགྲེལ་ཚུལ་འདི་ཉིད་ལེགས་བཤད་དུ་རྟོགས་པར་འགྱུར་རོ།།

གཉིས་པ་ནང་གསེས་ཀྱི་འཇུག་ཚུལ་འཆད་པ་ལ། མདོར་བསྟན། རྒྱས་བཤད་གཉིས་ལས། དང་པོ་ནི།

དེ་དག་ནང་གསེས་གང་འཇུག་པ། མཐར་སྦྱར་འོག་མའི་མིང་དོན་ལས།

ཞེས་པ་སྟེ། དེ་ལྟར་རྣམ་དབྱེ་དང་ཚིག་ཕྲད་དེ་དག་གི་ནང་གསེས་གང་དང་གང་ཞིག་འཇུག་པ་ནི་གཙོ་བོར་རྣམ་དབྱེའམ་ཕྲད་དང་བཅས་པའི་མིང་ཚིག་དེའི་མཐར་སྦྱར་རྒྱུའི་མིང་དོན་འོག་མ་ལས་ཤེས་པར་བྱའོ།། ཞེས་སྤྱིར་བསྟན་པའོ།།

གཉིས་པ་རྒྱས་བཤད་ལ་གཞུང་དོན་དང་། འཕྲོས་དོན་ནོ། དང་པོ་ལ། རྣམ་དབྱེའི་ནང་གསེས་གང་ཞིག་འཇུག་པ་དང་། ཕྲད་ཀྱི་ནང་གསེས་གང་ཞིག་འཇུག་པ་གཉིས།

དང་པོ་ནི།

སྤྱི་འཇུག་ཡོད་དམ་བྱེད་པ་ཡོད། དེ་བཞིན་ཆེད་བྱེད་རྟེན་བྱེད་དང་།
ལས་བྱ་བླང་བྱ་བསྒྲུབ་པར་བྱ། རྫོན་དུ་འོས་པ་གནས་པ་འམ།

ཞེས་པས་བསྟན་ཏེ། དེ་ལ་རྣམ་དབྱེའི་ནང་གསེས་གང་དང་གང་འཇུག་པ་ནི་རྣམ་དབྱེ་སྦྱར་སའི་མིང་བདུད་རྩི་ལྟ་བུ་ལ་དེའི་རྗེས་སུ་སྤྱི་ལ་འཇུག་པའི་སྒྲ་གང་ཞིག་ལྟ་བུ་ཡོད་ན་མིང་ཕྲ་མ་ལ་རྣམ་དབྱེ་དང་པོ་འཇུག་པ་ཡིན་ཡང་བོད་སྐད་ལ་མིང་ཀྱང་དང་རྣམ་དབྱེ་དང་པོ་སོ་སོར་མཚོན་མི་རུས་པས་མིང་ཀྱང་དེ་གར་གནས་པ་བདུད་རྩིས་གང་ཞིག་ལྟ་བུར་འགྱུར་བ་དང་། མིང་དེའི་མཐར་འཚོ་བར་བྱེད་ལྟ་བུ་བྱེད་པའི་སྒྲ་ཡོད་ན་རྣམ་དབྱེ་གསུམ་པ་འཇུག་པས་བདུད་རྩིས་འཚོ་བར་བྱེད། ཅེས་པར་འགྱུར་བ་དང་། དེ་བཞིན་དུ་སྦྱར་ཏེ་མིང་དེའི་མཐར་ཆེད་དུ་བྱེད་པའི་སྒྲ་སྨོས་པ་ལྟ་བུ་ཡོད་ན་རྣམ་དབྱེ་བཞི་པ་ལ་འཇུག་པས་བདུད་རྩི་ལ་སྨོས་པ་ཞེས་སུ་འགྱུར་བ་དང་། བརྟེན་ལྟ་བུ་རྟེན་བྱེད་ཀྱི་སྒྲ་ཡོད་ན་བདུན་པ་འཇུག་པས་བདུད་རྩི་ལ་བརྟེན་ཅེས་དང་། བསྒྱུར་བ་ལྟ་བུ་ལས་སུ་བྱ་བའི་སྒྲ་ཡོད་ན་གཉིས་པ་ཐོབ་པས་བདུད་རྩིར་བསྒྱུར་ཅེས་དང་། བླང་བར་བྱ་ལྟ་བུ་བླང་བྱའི་སྒྲ་ཡོད་ན་ལྔ་པ་འཇུག་པས་བདུད་རྩི་ལས་བླང་བར་བྱ་ཞེས་དང་། བསྒྲུབ་བྱ་རྒྱ་མཚོ་ལྟ་བུའི་སྒྲ་ཡོད་ན་དྲུག་པ་འཇུག་པས་བདུད་རྩིའི་རྒྱ་མཚོ་ཞེས་དང་། རྫོན་དུ་འབོད་པར་འོས་པའི་མིང་བདུད་རྩི་མ་ལྟ་བུ་ཡོད་ལ་དེ་ལའང་ལས་བཙལ་ཀྱེ་ལྟ་བུ་འབོད་པར་འོས་པའི་དོན་ཡོད་ནའང་རྣམ་དབྱེ་དང་པོ་འཇུག་ཅིང་བོད་པ་གསལ་བྱེད་ཀྱི་ཀྱེ་འང་སྦྱར་བར་བྱ་སྟེ། བདུད་རྩི་མ་ཀྱེ་བདག་ལ་བརྩེ་མེད་སྩོལ། ཞེས་པར་འགྱུར་བ་སོགས་ཤེས་པར་བྱའོ།། ཞེས་པའོ།།

འམ་ཞེས་པ་ནི་ཕྱི་མ་དང་སྦྲེལ་བའི་ཕྱིར་སྡུད་པའི་ཚིག་ཕྲད་དོ།།

དེ་དག་ལ་དཔེར་བརྗོད་གཞན་ཡང་། མིང་མཐའ་ཙམ་གྱིས་རྣམ་དབྱེ་དྲངས་པ་དང་མིང་མཐས་མིང་མཐའ་གཞན་དྲངས། དེས་རྣམ་དབྱེ་དྲངས་པའི་དབྱེ་བས་སོ་སོར་གཉིས་གཉིས་ཏེ། ལྷ་གང་། རྟག་པ་གང་། ལྷས་བྱུང་། དཀོན་ཅོག་གིས་སྐྱོབ། འཚོལ་དུ་འགྲོ། སློང་བ་པ་སྦྱིན། ཤིང་ལ་གནས།

བརྟན་པ་ལ་གནས། ཚུར་འཚུ། གསལ་བར་བྱེད། ཐབས་ལས་འབྲས་བུ་འབྱུང་། བདེ་བ་ལས་དགའ་བ་སྐྱེ། གསེར་གྱི་བུམ་པ། རྟག་པའི་གོ་འཕང་། ཞེས་སོགས་རྒྱ་ཆེར་སྦྱར་བར་བྱའོ།།

དེ་ལྟར་འདིར་གཉིས་པ་བཞི་པ་དྲུག་པ་བརྒྱད་པ་རྣམས་ཀྱི་འཇུག་རྟེན་མ་གཏོགས་པའི་ཕྱི་འཇུག་དང་བྱེད་པ་སོགས་གསུངས་པ་ནི་རྣམ་དབྱེ་དེ་རྣམས་ཉིད་ཀྱི་འཇུག་རྟེན་ཕྱོགས་རེའི་ཆ་ནས་དཔེར་བརྗོད་པའི་ཚེད་དུ་གསུངས་པ་ཡིན་གྱི་མཐའ་དག་པ་ནི་མ་ཡིན་ཏེ་དེ་དག་ཏུ་མི་གཏོགས་པའི་འཇུག་རྟེན་གཞན་ཡང་ཡོད་པའི་ཕྱིར་རོ།།

དཔེར་ན། བདུད་རྩི་ཞེས་པའི་མིང་མཐར་ངེས་གཟུང་སོགས་ཀྱི་སྒྲ་ཡོད་ནའང་ཕྲ་མར་དང་པོ་འཇུག་པས་མིང་རྐྱང་ཉིད་དུ་གནས་པ། བདུད་རྩི་དེ། བདུད་རྩི་འདི། ལྟ་བུ་དང་། མིང་ཕྲ་མ་ངེས་བསྒྲུབ་པར་བྱ་བའི་མིང་དོན་ཐོག་ཏུ་གནས་པ་ལ་ཕྲ་མར་བྱེད་པ་པོ་དང་མཚུངས་པའི་རྒྱུ་མཚན་གྱི་གསུམ་པ་འཇུག་པ། བརྗོད་པས་ཉེ་མ་དང་མཚུངས། དུ་བའི་རྟགས་ཀྱིས་མེ་ཡོད་པར་གྲུབ། ལྟ་བུ་དང་། མིང་མཐར་དེ་ལས་བྱུང་བའི་སྐབས་དཀར་བུའི་སྐབས། བསྒྲུབ་བྱའི་སྒྲ་ཡོད་ན་འབྱུང་ཁུངས་སོགས་ཀྱི་ལྔ་པ་འཇུག་པ། ས་གཞི་ལས་མྱུ་གུ་འཁྲུངས། རྒྱ་མཚོ་ནས་རིན་པོ་ཆེ་འབྱུང་། ཚངས་པ་ལས་སངས་རྒྱས་ཁྱད་པར་འཕགས། ནག་པ་ལས་སྲིད་སྒྲུབ་འཕོང་སྐྱེན། མི་རྟག་པ་ལས་དངོས་པོར་གྲུབ། ལྟ་བུ་དང་། མིང་མཐར་རྟེན་བྱེད་ཀྱི་སྒྲ་དངོས་མ་ཡིན་ཡང་རྟེན་བྱེད་ལྟར་སྣང་བའི་བུ་བའི་ཚིག་ལ་སོགས་པ་འགའ་ཞིག་ལའང་བདུན་པ་འཇུག་པ། མདུན་རྩེར་སྤྲང་ཅན་མཐོང་། མཚོན་ཁར་བབས། ལྟ་བུ་སྟེ་འདིས་མཚོན་ནས་འཇུག་རྟེན་དང་སྦྱོར་ཚུལ་གཞན་ཡང་རྒྱས་པར་རྟོགས་པར་བྱའོ།།

སྐབས་འདིར་ཡང་། ཁ་ཅིག་གིས། ཕྱི་འཇུག་གང་ལྟ་བུར་ངོས་བཟུང་ནས་ངེས་རྣམ་དབྱེ་འདྲེན་པ་དང་། དྲུག་པ་མ་གཏོགས་པའི་བྱེད་པ་ལ་སོགས་པའི་སྒྲ་རྣམ་དབྱེར་ངོས་བཟུང་ནས་དེས་ཕྱི་ཚིག་འདྲེན་པར་འདོད་པ་ནི་ཤིན་ཏུ་མི་རིགས་ཏེ། གཞུང་དོན་དང་དངོས་སུ་འགལ་བའི་ཕྱིར་ཏེ། མཐར་སྦྱར་རྒྱུའི་ཐོག་མའི་མིང་དོན་ཕྱི་འཇུག་ནས་བསྒྲུབ་བྱའི་བར་གང་ཡང་རུང་བ་ཡིན་པར་དེ་ལས་མིང་ཕྲ་མའི་མཐར་རྣམ་དབྱེ་དང་པོ་ནས་དྲུག་པའི་བར་གང་ཡང་རུང་བ་འཇུག་པར་དཀྱུས་གཅིག་ཏུ་གསལ་བར་བསྟན་པ་ལས་ཕྱིན་ཅི་ལོག་ཏུ་སྨྲས་པའི་ཕྱིར། གཞན་དེ་ལྟར་འདོད་ན། དེ་དག་ནང་གསེས་གང་འཇུག་པ། ཞེས་པ་དང་འགལ་ཏེ། ཕྱི་འཇུག་གིས་རྣམ་དབྱེ་འདྲེན་བྱེད་པ་ཙམ་དང་། བྱེད་པ་སོགས་རྣམ་དབྱེས་རང་རང་དང་འབྲེལ་བའི་ཕྱི་ཚིག་འདྲེན་བྱེད་པ་ཙམ་ལས་རྣམ་དབྱེའི་ནང་གསེས་གང་འཇུག་ཕྱོགས་ཙམ་ཡང་མ་བསྟན་པར་ཐལ་བའི་ཕྱིར་རོ།།

གཞན་ཡང་ཁྱེད་ལྟར་ན། གཞུང་འདིར་བྱེད་པའི་སྒྲས་བསྟན་པའི་བྱེད་ལས་དེ་བྱེད་པ་པོ་དང་། ཆེད་དུ་བྱེད་པའི་ལས་དེ་ཆེད་དུ་བྱ་བ་དང་། རྟེན་པར་བྱེད་པ་དེ་བརྟེན་བྱ་དང་། ལས་ཀྱི་བྱ་བ་དེ་ལས་བྱ་རྒྱུ་དང་། བྱུང་བྱ་དེ་གང་ལས་བྱུང་བའི་གནས་སུ་ཁས་བླངས་པར་སོང་བས། གཞུང་འདི་དང་འགལ་བ་བརྒྱ་ཅི་སྨོས་ན་སྐད་ཀྱི་གཙུག་ལག་ཕྱོགས་ཙམ་ཡང་མ་རྟོགས་པའི་རྫོ་བ་ཐམས་ཅད་བསྟན་པར་ཟད་དོ།།

གཞན་ཡང་སྔོན་དུ་བོད་པ་གནས་པའམ། ཞེས་པར། བོད་པའི་སྒྲ་ཀྱེ་སོགས་སྔོན་དུ་གནས་པས་འབོད་རྒྱུའི་མིང་འདྲེན་པར་འབྲུ་གཉེར་བཟང་མི་འཐད་དེ་ཕྱིར་སུམ་རྟ་པར་འབོད་པའི་སྒྲ་མིང་གི་སྔོན་དུ་སྦྱར་བ་ཤས་ཆེ་བར་གསུངས་ཀྱང་། འདིར་དམིགས་བསལ་དུ་མིང་གི་མཐར་སྦྱར་ཚུལ་གསུངས་པ་ཡིན་པའི་ཕྱིར། གྲུབ་སྟེ་འདིར་མིང་མཐའི་སྦྱོར་འཇུག་གིས་རྣམ་དབྱེ་བརྒྱད་ཀ་འདྲེན་ཚུལ་འཆད་པའི་སྐབས་ཡིན་པ་གང་ཞིག། སྔོན་དུ་བོས་པ་ཞེས་པའང་གང་ལ་འབོད་པར་བོས་པའི་མིང་སྔོན་དུ་གནས་པ་ལ་དགོངས་པའི་ཕྱིར། ཕྱི་མ་གྲུབ་སྟེ། རྣམ་དབྱེ་གཞན་རྣམས་མཐར་སྦྱར་རྒྱུའི་མིང་དོན་ལ་ལྟོས་དགོས་ཀྱང་བོད་པའི་སྒྲ་དེ་རྣམས་དང་མི་མཚུངས་པའི་དམིགས་བསལ་བསྟན་པའི་ཕྱིར་དེ་ལྟར་གསུངས་པར་ངེས་པའི་ཕྱིར་རོ།།

གཉིས་པ་ཕྲད་ཀྱི་ནང་གསེས་གང་ཞིག་འཇུག་པ་ནི།

གཞན་ཡང་ཚིག་དོན་འོག་མ་ལས། །བསྡུ་རྒྱུ་ཡོད་དམ་ཉིད་པ་དང་། །གོང་མ་ལས་ཀྱང་དེ་བཞིན་ཏེ། །

རྣམ་གྲངས་དག་ཀྱང་བཀོད་པ་ལས། །བསྒྱུར་བ་ཡོད་དམ་མེད་པ་དང་། །ཕོ་སྒྲ་དང་ནི་མོ་སྒྲ་དག །
མིང་གི་མཐའ་ན་ཡོད་མེད་དང་། །རྒྱན་དུ་གྱུར་པ་རྣམས་ལ་ཡང་། །དོན་ལ་བསྐྱེགས་པ་ཡོད་མེད་དང་། །
བསྟན་བྱ་ཨཱ་ག་མ་ཡོད་མེད་དང་། །ཚིག་དོན་རྫོགས་དང་མ་རྫོགས་ཀྱིས། །དེ་དག་ནང་གསེས་རྣམ་པར་དབྱེ། །

ཞེས་པ་བསྟན་ཏེ་གཞན་ཡང་མིང་མཐའ་ཚིག་ཕྲད་ཀྱི་བྱེ་བྲག་གང་ཞིག་འདྲེན་པར་འགྱུར་བ་ནི་ཕལ་ཆེར་མིང་དེའི་མཐར་སྦྱར་རྒྱུའི་ཚིག་དོན་འོག་མ་ལས་ཤེས་དགོས་ཤིང་ཕྱི་ཚིག་ལ་ལྟོས་མ་དགོས་པར་བརྗོད་འདོད་ཙམ་གྱི་འགྲུབ་པའང་ཡོད་པ། །དཔེར་ན་ཚིག་དོན་འོག་མ་གང་ཡིན་དེ་ཉིད་དང་མཚུངས་པ་ལས་སྔ་མ་བསྡུ་རྒྱུ་ཡོད་པ་ཡིན་ན། །མིང་སྔ་མ་སྔ་མའི་མཐར་སྔ་མ་སྡུད་པའི་ཚིག་ཕྲད་སྦྱར་བར་བྱ་སྟེ། །ལྷ་དང་མི་དང་ལྷ་མ་ཡིན་དང་དྲི་ཟར་བཅས་པའི་འཇིག་རྟེན་ཡིད་རང་སྟེ། །ལྟ་བུ་དང་། །དེ་བཞིན་དུ་ཚིག་དོན་སྔ་མ་དེ་ཉིད་དང་མཚུངས་པ་ལས་ཕྱི་མ་བསྡུ་རྒྱུ་ཡོད་པ་ཡིན་ན་ཕྱི་མ་བསྡུ་པའི་ཚིག་ཕྲད་འཇུག་སྟེ། །ལྷས་ཀྱང་བཏུད་ན་མིས་ལྟ་ཅི་སྨོས། །ལྷས་ཀྱང་འདེགས་ན་བགེགས་ལྟ་ཅི་སྨོས། །དེ་དག་ཀྱང་བདག་དང་ལྷན་ཅིག་དགའོ། །ལྟ་བུ་དང་། །མཐུག་ཏུ་བྱ་ཚིག་ལྟ་བུར་ལྷན་ཅིག་ཏུ་སྦྲེལ་ཕྱིར་ཚིག་དོན་སྔ་མ་ལ་ཕྱི་མ་བསྟན་དགོས་པ་ཡོད་ནའང་སྐྱད་པའི་བྱེ་བྲག་བསྟན་པའི་ཕྲད་སྦྱར་ཏེ། །སངས་རྒྱས་པའི་གྲུབ་མཐར་མ་ཟད། །ཕྱི་རོལ་པའང་ཤེས་པར་བྱ། །གསེར་དངུལ་ཟངས་ལྕགས་ག་ཤའ་ཅེའང་སྦྱར། །ལྟ་བུ་དང་། །ཕྱི་མར་མིང་ཚིག་གི་རྣམ་གྲངས་གཅིག་གམ་གཉིས་སམ་མང་པོ་བཀོད་པ་ལས། །དེ་དག་ཀྱང་གལ་ཏེ་བསྒྱུར་བ་ཡིན་ན་སྔ་མ་སྔ་མར་རྣམ་གྲངས་ཀྱིས་འབྱེད་པའམ་སྡུད་པའི་ཕྲད་སྦྱར་བར་བྱ་སྟེ། །དོན་བསྒྱུར་བ་ལ། །ཉི་འོད་ནི་གསལ་བའམ། །སྣང་བའོ། །འཆི་མེད་དམ། །རྣམ་སད་དམ། །མིག་མི་འཛུམ་ནི་ལྷའོ། །འགྲོ་བ་དང་། །འདོད་པ་དང་། །མཆི་བ་ཞེས་བྱའོ། །ཞེས་པ་ལྟ་བུ་དང་།

ཚིག་དོན་གཉིས་ཀ་བསྒྱུར་བ་ལ། །སྔོར་ཞིང་སྔོར་ཞིང་སྨྲར་ཡང་དེ་རུ་འབབ། །གཏུབས་ཤིང་གཏུབས་ཤིང་དུག་ཏུ་གསོལ་བར་བྱེད། །ལྟ་བུ་དང་། །མིང་གི་མཐར་ཕོ་སྒྲ་པ་པོ་བ་བོའི་སྒྲ་གསར་དུ་སྦྱར་བ་ཡོད་ན་མིང་མཐའ་དེ་ཉིད་བདག་པོའི་སྒྲར་འགྱུར་བ། །རྟ་པ། །གསེར་པ། །རྟག་པ་པ། །ཡོད་པ་པ། །བྱེད་པ་པོ། །སྒྲུབ་པ་པོ། །ལྟ་བུ་དང་། །བདག་པོའམ་དགག་པའི་དོན་དུ་གསར་དུ་སྦྱར་བ་མ་ཡིན་པའི་མིང་མཐའ་ཉིད་པ་བ་མ་ཕོ་མོ་གནས་པ་ནི་ངོ་བོའམ་བྱ་བ་གང་ཡིན་དེ་དེ་ཉིད་དུ་སྒྲུབ་པའི་སྒྲར་འགྱུར་བ། །རྟག་པ། །དམ་པ། །བསྙོད་པ། །མཛེས་པ། །ཡག་མ། །གསར་མ། །རྙིང་མ། །གོང་མ། །ལྟ་བུ་དང་། །མིང་གི་མཐར་དགག་དོན་དུ་སྦྱར་བའི་མོ་སྒྲ་མ་མི་མིན་མེད་ཀྱི་སྒྲ་གཏོགས་པ་ཡོད་ན་ངོ་བོའམ་བྱ་བ་གང་ཡིན་དེ་ཉིད་དགག་པའི་སྒྲར་འགྱུར་བ། །འཇིག་མེད། །འཆི་མེད། །ཡོད་མིན། །མེད་མིན། །གཟུགས་མེད། །སྒྲ་མེད། །ལྟ་བ་དང་།

ཚིག་དོན་སྔ་མ་དང་ཆོས་མཐུན་པའི་ཕྱི་ཚིག་གཞི་གཅིག་ཏུ་བསྡུ་རྒྱུ་ཡོད་ན། །སྔ་མ་ལ་མཐུན་པའི་རྒྱན་དུ་གྱུར་པའི་ཕྲད་སྦྱར་ཏེ། །མཛེས་ཀྱང་མཛེས་ལ་འོད་ཀྱང་འཚེར། །ལྟ་བུ་དང་། །སྔ་ཕྱི་ཆོས་མི་མཐུན་པ་གཞི་གཅིག་ཏུ་བསྡུ་ན། །སྔ་མར་མི་མཐུན་པའི་རྒྱན་འཇུག་སྟེ། །ལྷ་ཉིད་ཡིན་ཡང་བདུད་ཀྱི་བདུད། །བློ་བ་སྲུངས་ཀྱང་དགྲ་འཛོམས་པ། །ལྟ་བུ་སྟེ་རྒྱན་དུ་གྱུར་པའི་ཚིག་ཕྲད་དེ་དག་ཀྱང་ངེས་པར་དོན་ལ་ལྟོས་པ་ཡོད་ན་ཡི་སྐྱར་དུ་མི་རུང་ཞིང་ཚིག་མཛེས་པར་བྱེད་པའི་རྒྱན་ཙམ་ཁོ་ན་ཡིན་ན་སྦྱོར་རམ་མི་སྦྱོར་ཅི་རིགས་བྱེད་པ་རུང་བ་དང་། །ཚིག་དོན་སྔ་མའི་འཕྲོས་དེ་མ་ཐག་ཏུ་བསྟན་བྱ་ཨཱ་ག་མ་ཡོད་ན་སྔ་མ་ལ་ཨཱ་ག་མ་བཅས་ཀྱི་ཕྲད་འཇུག་སྟེ། །རྟག་སྟེ་འཇིག་པ་མེད་པའི་ཕྱིར། །རྒྱུ་བཅས་སྐྱེ་བཞག །ལྟ་བུ་དང་། །ཚིག་གི་དོན་དེ་ཉིད་ཀྱི་འཕྲོས་དེ་མ་ཐག་ཏུ་བསྟན་བྱ་མེད་པར་རྫོགས་པ་ཡིན་ན་ཐ་མར་བསྡུའི་ཕྲད་སྦྱར་ཏེ། །རྟག་གོ། །རྫོགས་སོ། །བསྟན་ཏོ། །བྱའོ། །འགྲུབ་བོ། །ལྟ་བུ་རྣམ་དབྱེ་དང་ཕྲད་དེ་དག་གི་ནང་གསེས་གང་དང་གང་ཞིག་འཇུག་ཚེ་དོན་ཅི་འདྲ་ཞིག་སྟོན་པ་རྣམ་པར་དབྱེ་བར་བྱའོ། །ཞེས་སོ།

སྐབས་འདིར་ཡང་འགྲེལ་བྱེད་སྔ་མ་རྣམས་ཀྱིས་མ་བརྟགས་པ་ཡོད་དེ། ཕྱིར་འདི་སྐབས་མིང་མཐའ་ཕྲད་དང་རྣམ་དབྱེ་སོགས་འདྲེན་ཚུལ་འཆད་པའི་སྐབས་ཡིན་པ་ལ། པ་ར། སཾ། ཕྱུ་པ་སོགས་ཀྱི་ཉེ་སྒྱུར་དང་ སྐྱེའི་ཡིཀྵའི་སྒྲ་དག་མིང་གི་ཐོག་ཏུ་སྦྱར་ནས་ཚིག་རྒྱན་དང་། དགག་སྒྲའི་དཔེར་བརྗོད་པ་དང་། མིང་གི་རྣམ་གྲངས་བཀོད་པ་ལ་ཚིག་དོན་བསྒྱུར་བ་ཡོད་མེད་ཀྱི་ཁྱད་པར་གྱིས་ཕྲད་ཀྱི་སྦྱོར་ཚུལ་ཤེས་པར་བྱ་དགོས་པ་ལ་ཕྲད་སྦྱོར་ཚུལ་སོགས་ཀྱི་དོན་འདི་ཡིན་མེད་པའི། ལེགས་སོ་ལེགས་སོ་དང་། ཨ་ལ་ལ་ཆོས་ཨ་ལ་ལ་ཆོས། སོགས་ཀྱི་དཔེར་བརྗོད་བཀོད་པ་དང་། དེ་དག་ནང་གསེས་གང་འདུག་པ། ཞེས་པའི་དེ་དག་གི་སྒྲས། བཤད་མ་ཐག་པའི་ཆོས་དངོས་ལས་དང་སོགས་ནས། དུས་ལ་འཇུག་ཅེས་པའི་བར་བསྟན་ཅིང་། མཐར་ཕྱུར་འོག་མའི་མིང་དོན་ལས། ཞེས་པའི་མིང་དོན་དེ། ཕྱི་འཇུག་ཡོད་དམ་སོགས་ནས། མ་རྫོགས་ཀྱིས། ཞེས་པའི་བར་གྱི་བསྟན་བྱ་ཡིན་པས་འོག་མ་ཤས་ཆེ་བའི་མིང་དོན་གང་ཡོད་ཀྱི་རྒྱུ་མཚན་ལས་མིང་མཐར་རྣམ་དབྱེ་དང་ཕྲད་གང་འཐོབ་ལྟ་དགོས་པ་གསལ་པོར་གསུང་གིས་ཟིན་པ་ལ། དེ་འདྲའི་རྣམ་བཞག་གང་ཡང་མེད་པའི་འགྲེལ་མེད་ཀྱི་ལུང་འདྲེན་དང་བཤད་པ་མང་དུ་ཐུམ་པ་སོགས་སོ།།

གཉིས་པ་འཕྲོས་དོན་ནི། སྐབས་འདིར་ཕྱིར་རྣམ་དབྱེ་དང་ཕྲད་ཀྱི་དོན་ཤེས་པ་གལ་ཆེ་བར་སྣང་བས་ཅུང་ཟད་བཤད་ན། རྣམ་དབྱེ་ཞེས་པ་ནི་ལེགས་སྦྱར་གྱི་སྐད་ལ་མིང་གི་མཐར་སྦྱར་བས་ཚིག་ཏུ་འགྲུབ་པར་བྱེད་པའི་རྐྱེན་སི་སོགས་བདུན་གསུམ་ཉི་ཤུ་རྩ་གཅིག་པོ་རྣམས་ཏེ། དོན་སྟོབས་ཀྱི་དབང་གིས་དོན་རྗོད་པར་བྱེད་པའི་སྐད་རིགས་ཐམས་ཅད་ལ་རྣམ་དབྱེ་དེ་རྣམས་མེད་པ་མི་སྲིད་པས་མཁས་པ་འདྲིས་བོད་ཀྱི་སྐད་ལའང་ལེགས་སྦྱར་དང་བསྟུན་ནས་རྣམ་དབྱེ་དེ་རྣམས་ཀྱི་འཇུག་པ་གསལ་བར་མཛད་པ་ཡིན་ནོ།།

དེ་འང་ལེགས་སྦྱར་ལ་ཨོཾ་གཉིས། ཆུམ་གསུམ་ཆུམ་གཉིས། ཡོས་གཉིས་རྣམས་སྦྱོར་ཡུལ་དོན་སྟོབས་ཀྱིས་དབྱེ་བ་ལས་རྐྱེན་གྱི་ངོ་བོ་གཉིས་སུ་མེད་པས་རྐྱེན་གྱི་ངོ་བོ་བཅུ་དྲུག་ཏུ་ངེས་པ་ཡིན་ཡང་བོད་སྐད་ལ་དེ་དང་མི་མཚུངས་པས། ལ་དོན། འབྲེལ་པ། བྱེད་པ་སྒྲ་རྣམ་དབྱེའི་རྐྱེན་གྱི་ངོ་བོ་གསུམ་དུ་ངེས་ཤིང་གཉིས་ཚིག་དང་མང་ཚིག་མཚོན་པའི་སྒྲ་དག་ཀྱང་རྣམ་དབྱེའི་ཡན་ལག་ཏུ་འདུག་པའི་ཕྲད་ཙམ་མོ།།

ལ་ན་ཏུ་དུ་ལ་སོགས་པ་རྐྱེན་དེ་རྣམས་ཀྱི་ནང་གསེས་ནི་མིང་མཐའ་ཕྲད་པའི་རྣམ་འགྱུར་ཙམ་ལས་རྐྱེན་གྱིས་ངོ་བོ་སོ་སོ་བ་མ་ཡིན་ཏེ། ལེགས་སྦྱར་ལ་ཟླས་ཨེས་སུ་བསྒྱུར་བ་དང་། ཊཱ་བྷིཾ་དང་ཊེ་བྷྱཾ་དང་ང་ལྷན་རྣམས་ཡི་ཡཱམ྄་ཡཱམ྄་ཡཱམ྄་དུ་བསྒྱུར་བ་སོགས་དང་མཚུངས་པའི་ཕྱིར་རོ།།

རྣམ་དབྱེ་དེ་རྣམས་ཀྱང་དོན་ལ་སྦྱོར་ཚུལ་གྱི་སྒོ་ནས་དབྱེ་ན་ལེགས་སྦྱར་དང་མཐུན་པར་རིགས་བདུན་དང་རེ་རེའང་གཅིག་ཚིག་གཉིས་ཚིག་མང་ཚིག་གིས་བསྒྱུར་བས་ཉི་ཤུ་རྩ་གཅིག་ཉིད་དུ་འགྱུར་རོ།།

དེའང་མི་ཟད་པ་མ་གཏོགས་པའི་ལེགས་སྦྱར་གྱི་མིང་ཐམས་ཅད་རྟགས་ཀྱི་དབྱེ་བ་ཡོད་པས་དེའི་ཆེད་དུ་རྣམ་དབྱེ་དང་པོ་སྦྱིན་པ་ཡིན་ཡང་འདིར་དེ་མེད་པས་མིང་དོན་ཙམ་ལ་རྣམ་དབྱེ་དང་པོ། ལས་ཀྱི་དོན་ལ་གཉིས་པ། བྱེད་པ་པོའི་དོན་ལ་གསུམ་པ། ཆེད་དུ་བྱ་བའི་དོན་ལ་བཞི་པ། འབྱུང་ཁུངས་སམ་གང་ལས་འབྲལ་བའི་དོན་ལ་ལྔ་པ། འབྲེལ་པའི་དོན་ལ་དྲུག་པ། གནས་གཞིའི་དོན་ལ་བདུན་པ་རྣམས་འཇུག་ཅིང་། བརྒྱད་པ་བོད་པ་ཞེས་ཟེར་བ་ཡང་བོད་པའི་ཡུལ་ལ་རྣམ་དབྱེ་དང་པོ་ཉིད་འཇུག་ཅིང་ཀྱེ་དང་ཀྭ་སོགས་ནི་བོད་པ་གསལ་བྱེད་ཀྱི་སྒྲ་ཡིན་གྱི་རྣམ་དབྱེ་མ་ཡིན་པས་ཁོངས་སུ་དབྱེར་མེད་དོ།།

དེ་ལ་རྣམ་དབྱེ་དང་པོའི་གཅིག་ཚིག་གིས་མིང་དོན་གྱི་ངོ་བོ་ཙམ་ཞིག་སྟོན་པ་ནི། བུམ་པ། རྟག་པ། བསྟན་པ། བྱས་པ། བསྒྲུབས། བསྒྲུབ། སྒྲུབ། ལྷ་བུ་སྐྱེ། བོད་སྐད་ལ་རྣམ་དབྱེའི་རྗེས་ཤོགས་པ་མེད་པས་མིང་ཙམ་དེ་ཉིད་ཡིན་ཞིང་མིང་ལ་ནི་བདག་གཞན་དང་དུས་གསུམ་གྱི་དབྱེ་བ་ཅན་རྣམས་དང་མིང་རྐྱང་ཡང་ཙང་སྐྱི་ཁྱད་པར་མེད་དོ།།

དཔེར་ན་ལེགས་སྦྱར་གྱི་སྐད་དུ། ཀྲྀ་ཏ། ཀ་ར་ཎ། ཀྲྀ་ཙ། ལྷ་བུ་དུས་གསུམ་དང་བདག་གཞན་གྱི་དབྱེ་བ་ཅན་ཡོད་པས་སྒྲ་རྣམས་ཀྱང་མིང་ཙམ

ཉིད་དུ་མཚུངས་པ་ལ་རྣམ་དབྱེ་ཚིག་ཏུ་བསྒྲུབ་དགོས་པ་བཞིན་ནོ།།

དང་པོའི་གཉིས་ཚིག་དང་མང་ཚིག་དག་གིས་ནི་ལྡོག་པ་ཙམ་ཅན་དང་བཅས་པའི་མིང་དོན་གྱི་ངོ་བོ་ཙམ་སྟོན་ཏེ། ལྷ་དག ལྷ་རྣམས། བུམ་པ་དག བུམ་པ་རྣམས། བསྒྲུབ་པ་དག བསྒྲུབ་པ་རྣམས། སྒྲུབ་བྱེད་དག སྒྲུབ་བྱེད་རྣམས། དྷ་བ་ཝོ།།

འདིར་དག་དང་རྣམས་ཞེས་པའི་སྒྲའང་ཚིག་ཕྲད་ཙམ་ལས་རྣམ་དབྱེའི་རྟེན་དངོས་མ་ཡིན་ཏེ། ད་དུང་དེ་དག་གི་མཐའ་ལ་རྣམ་དབྱེ་གཞན་འཇུག་པའི་ཕྱིར། དེས་ན་ཕྲད་འདི་དག་མིང་གང་གི་མཐར་སྦྱར་ཡང་དུང་རྣམ་དབྱེ་དང་པོའི་གཉིས་ཚིག་གམ་མང་ཚིག་མཚོན་ནུས་ཤིང་རྣམ་དབྱེའི་རྟེན་གཞན་རྣམས་ཀྱང་འདི་དག་གི་འཇུག་ཏུ་སྦྱར་དགས་སོ་སོའི་གཉིས་ཚིག་གི་མང་ཚིག་ཏུ་འགྱུར་རོ།།

དག་ཅེས་པའི་སྒྲའང་ཕྱིར་གཉིས་ཚིག་ཁོ་ན་ལ་འཇུག་པའི་ངེས་པ་མེད་དེ་ཕལ་ཆེར་མང་ཚིག་ལ་སྦྱོར་བ་ཤས་ཆེ་ཞིང་། གཉིས་ཁོ་ན་ལ་འཇུག་པའི་སྦྲད་པོད་སྐད་ལ་མེད་པས་དེའི་དོན་དུ་གཅིག་ལ་མི་འཇུག་ཅིང་གཉིས་ཡན་ཆད་ལ་འཇུག་པའི་སྤྱི་ཡི་ཙྭ་བ་རྣམས་ཀྱིས་ཕྱིའི་སྒྲ་བྱེ་བྲག་ལ་སྦྱར་ནས་གཉིས་ཚིག་ཏུ་མཛད་པ་ཡིན་ནོ།།

དེས་ན་དག་གི་སྒྲ་མང་ཚིག་ལ་སྦྱོར་བ་མི་འཐད་ཅེས་སྨྲ་བ་ནི་ལེགས་སྦྱར་གྱི་ལུགས་མ་ཐལ་ཤེས་པའི་གཡུང་དྲུང་ངོ།། འགར་རིག་གིས་ཐམས་ཅད་དང་ཀུན་དང་། མཐའ་དག་སོགས་ཀྱང་རྣམ་དབྱེའི་མང་ཚིག་ཏུ་འདོད་ཀྱང་མིང་དང་རྣམ་དབྱེ་མ་ཕྱེད་པར་ཟད་དོ།། རྣམ་དབྱེ་གཉིས་པ་ལ་སོགས་པས་ནི་དོན་གྱི་ལྡོག་པ་ཁོ་ན་སྟོན་གྱི་ངོ་བོ་ནི་ནམ་ཡང་མི་སྟོན་ཏེ།

དཔེར་ན། བུམ་པ་ལ། ཞེས་པས་དེའི་བྱ་བའམ་ཆེད་དོན་ནམ་རྟེན་གཞན་ལྡན་པའི་དོན་དག་བུམ་པའི་ཞེས་པས་དེ་དང་འབྲེལ་པའི་དོན་དང་། བུམ་པས་ཞེས་པས་དེའི་བྱེད་པའི་དོན་སྟོན་པས་ཚིག་དེ་དག་གིས་བུམ་པ་རང་གི་ངོ་བོ་ཙམ་མ་ཡིན་པར་དེའི་ལྡོག་པ་སྟོན་པ་ལྟ་བུར།།

དེ་ལ་ལ་དོན་རྣམས་རྣམ་དབྱེ་གཉིས་པ་ལས་ལ་འཇུག་པའི་ཚུལ་ནི། དཔེར་ན། ལྷ་ལ་ཕྱག་འཚལ། གཟུགས་ལ་ལྟ། ཤར་དུ་འགྲོ། ཏྲ་བྲེ། ལྷ། གཟུགས། ཤར་རྣམས་ནི་ཕྱག་འཚལ་བ་དང་། ལྟ་བ་དང་། འགྲོ་བ་རྣམས་ཀྱི་བྱ་བ་འཇུག་པའི་ཡུལ་ཡིན་པས་དེ་དག་ལ། ལས་ཀྱི་རྣམ་དབྱེ་འཇུག་པ་ཡིན་ནོ།།

ཞིབ་མོར་དཔྱད་ན། གཟུགས་ལ་ལྟ་བར་བྱེད་ལྟ་བུ། གཟུགས་ལ་ལས་ཀྱི་དོན་དང་། ལྟ་བ་ལ་བྱ་བའི་དོན་དུ་སྟེ་གཉིས་ཀ་ལ་རྣམ་དབྱེ་གཉིས་པ་འཇུག་ཅིང་ཕྱི་མ་ལ་གཞུང་འདིར་དེ་ཉིད་ཀྱི་སྒྲས་གསུངས་སོ།།

དེ་བཞིན་དུ་བུམ་པར་ཆུ་ལྷུགས་ཞེས་པ་ལྟ་བུ་བུམ་པ་ལ་བྱ་བ་ལྷུགས་པའི་ཡུལ་ཡིན་པས་གཉིས་པའམ་ཏུ་བརྗོད་པའི་ཚ་ནས་གནས་གཞི་སྟེ་རྣམ་དབྱེ་གཉིས་གང་རུང་འཇུག་ཅིང་། ཆུ་ནི་ལྷུགས་པར་བྱ་རྒྱུའི་ལས་ཉིད་ཡིན་པས་དེ་ཉིད་ཀྱི་དོན་ལ་གཉིས་པ་ཁོ་ན་འཇུག་མོད། ཕྱིས་འདི་རིགས་ཀྱི་རྣམ་དབྱེ་བོད་སྐད་ལ་མེད་པ་ཆ་ར་དོ།།

རྣམ་དབྱེ་གསུམ་པ་བྱེད་པ་པོ་ལ་འཇུག་པ་ནི། ལྷས་བརྟན། རྡོ་རྗེས་བསྒྲུབ། ཁྱོད་ཀྱིས་སྐྱོང་། བདག་གིས་བརྗོད་ཅེ་དེ་སྟེ། བརྟན། བསྒྲུབ། སྐྱོང་། བརྗོད། རྣམས་བྱ་བ་ཡིན། པས་དེ་བྱེད་མཁན་གྱི་དོན་དུ་རིམ་པར། ལྷ། རྡོ་རྗེ། ཁྱོད། བདག་རྣམས་ལ་རྣམ་དབྱེ་གསུམ་པ་བྱེད་པ་པོའི་ཚིག་འཇུག་པ་ཡིན་ནོ།།

དེའང་ཞིབ་མོར་དཔྱད་ན། བདག་གིས་རིགས་ཐུགས་ཀྱིས་ཚེ་རྒྱལ་ལྷ་བུར་བདག་དང་རིགས་ཐུགས་གཉིས་ཀ་བྱེད་བྱེད་པ་པོ་ཡིན་པས་གཉིས་ཀ་ལ་རྣམ་དབྱེ་གསུམ་པ་ལ་འཇུག་ཀྱང་། བདག་བྱེད་པ་པོ་གཙོ་བོ་དང་རིགས་ཐུགས་བྱེད་པོ་ཕལ་པ་ཡིན་པའི་དབྱེ་བ་ཡོད་ཅིང་། ཡང་ན་བདག་བྱེད་པ་པོ་དང་རིགས་ཐུགས་ནི་བྱེད་པ་ཙམ་ཡིན་པའི་བྱེ་བྲག་ཤེས་པར་བྱ་དགོས་སོ།

རྒྱུ་མཚན་གྱི་དོན་ལ་གསུམ་པ་འཇུག་པའང་རྒྱུ་མཚན་དེས་དེ་ལྟར་འགྲུབ་པར་བྱེད་པས་བྱེད་པ་པོ་དང་མཚུངས་པའི་ཕྱིར་རོ།།

རྣམ་དབྱེ་བཞི་པ་ཆེད་དུ་བྱ་བའི་དོན་ལ་འཇུག་པ་ནི། ལོ་ཏོག་ལ་ཆུ་འདྲེན། ནོར་འཚོང་དུ་འགྲོ། སློང་མོ་པ་ལ་ཟན་སྦྱིན། ལྟ་བུ། ཆུ་འདྲེན་པ་དང་། འགྲོ་བ་དང་། ཟན་སྦྱིན་པ་རྣམས་བྱ་བ་ཡིན་ཞིང་། དེ་གང་གིས་དོན་ནམ་ཆེད་དུ་བྱ་བའི་ཡུལ། ལོ་ཏོག ནོར་འཚོང་། སློང་མོ་པ་རྣམས་ལ་བཞི་པ་དགོས་ཆེད་ཀྱི་རྣམ་དབྱེ་འཇུག་པ་ཡིན་ནོ། དེས་ན་བྱ་བ་གང་ཞིག་བྱ་བའི་དོན་གྱི་ཡུལ་དེ་ལ་ཕན་བཏགས་པའི་ཆེད་དུ་འཇུག་པའི་ལ་དོན་དྲུག་པོ་རྣམས་ནི་རྣམ་དབྱེ་བཞི་པ་ཞེས་བྱ་བ་ཡིན་ལ། དཔེར་ན་ཤའི་ཆེད་དུ་ཕྱུགས་གསོད་པ་བྱེད། ལྟ་བུ་ལ་མཚོན་ན། གསོད་པ་བྱ་བ། ཕྱུགས་ནི་ལས། ཤ་ནི་བྱ་བའི་དོན་གྱི་ཡུལ་ཡིན་པས་གསོད་པའི་བྱ་བས་ཤ་ཐོབ་པ་ལ་ཕན་འདོགས་པར་བྱེད་པ་དང་། སློང་མོ་པར་ཟན་སྦྱིན་ཟེར་བ་ལ། སྦྱིན་པ་ནི་བྱ་བ། ཟན་ནི་ལས། སློང་མོ་པ་བྱ་བའི་དོན་གྱི་ཡུལ་ཡིན་པའི་ཕྱིར་སྦྱིན་པས་སློང་མོ་པར་ཕན་འདོགས་པ་སོགས་ཀྱི་དགོས་ཆེད་ཀྱང་། བར་དུ་ལས་ཀྱི་ཚིག་མེད་ཀྱང་ཤའི་ཆེད་དུ་གསོད། སློང་མོ་པར་སྦྱིན་སོགས་ཀྱང་བཞི་པའི་དོན་དེ་ཉིད་ལས་མི་འདའ་འོ།།

འོ་ན་ལེགས་སྦྱར་ལ་བྱ་བའི་དོན་གྱི་ཡུལ་དེར་ཕན་འདོགས་པ་མ་ཡིན་པར་ཡང་བཞི་པ་འཇུག་པ་མང་དུ་མཐོང་བ་ཅི་སྙམ་ན། ལེགས་སྦྱར་ལའང་སྤྱིར་བཏང་གི་འཇུག་ཡུལ་འདི་དང་མཐུན་ཀྱང་དམིགས་བསལ་མི་མཐུན་པ་ནི།

མགོ་བོར་དབྱུག་པས་བརྡུང་བའི་དོན་ལ། མཱུརྡྷཱ་ཡ་དཎྜཾ་དད་ཏི། མགོ་བོར་དབྱུག་པ་སྦྱིན་ཞེས་དང་། བྲམ་པར་ཆུ་གླུགས་པའི་དོན་ལ། ཀླཱ་ཏཱ་ཡ་ཛཾ་ལཾ་དད་ཏི། བྲམ་པར་ཆུ་སྦྱིན། ཞེས་པ་ལྟ་བུ་ཡོད་པ་ནི་སྦྱིན་པའི་ཡུལ་ལ་བཞི་པ་འཇུག་པ་སྤྱིར་བཏང་བས། འདིར་བསྟན་པ་དང་། གླུགས་པ་ལ་སྦྱིན་པའི་སྒྲས་བརྗོད་པའི་ཚེ་ཚིག་ཙམ་གཙོ་བོར་བྱས་ནས་དེའི་ཡུལ་ལ་བཞི་པ་སྦྱར་བ་ཡིན་གྱི་སྐབས་དེའི་སྦྱིན་པ་སྦྱིན་པ་དངོས་མ་ཡིན་པ་བཞིན་དུ་དེའི་ཡུལ་གྱི་རྣམ་དབྱེ་བཞི་པའང་བཞི་པ་དངོས་མ་ཡིན་ཏེ། སྔ་མ་གཉིས་པ་དང་ཕྱི་མ་བདུན་པར་དོན་གྱིས་འཐོབ་པ་ལ་བཞི་པ་སྦྱར་བ་ཙམ་ཡིན་པའི་ཕྱིར་རོ།།

དེ་བཞིན་དུ་ན་མས་སོགས་ཀྱི་ཡུལ་ལ་བཞི་པ་འཇུག་པའང་དོན་ཐོབ་ཀྱི་བཞི་པའི་འཇུག་ཡུལ་དངོས་མ་ཡིན་ཡང་། འཇིག་རྟེན་པའི་ཉེར་སྤྱོད་ལས་དེ་བཞིན་དུ་འཇུག་པ་སྟེ་སྐབས་འདིར་མ་ཟད་རྣམ་དབྱེ་གཞན་དང་གཞན་ལའང་འདི་འདྲའི་རིགས་མང་དུ་འབྱུང་བ་རྣམས་རྣམ་དབྱེ་དེ་དངོས་ཀྱི་དོན་དུ་མི་འགྱུར་བས་ཚམ་པོ་པ་ཞེས་བྱའོ།།

བོད་འདིར་ནི་དཔེ་ལེགས་བསམ་དེ་འདྲ་དབྱེ་བ་ལ་དགོས་པ་ཆེད་པས་དོན་འཐོབ་ཉིད་ཀྱི་དབང་དུ་བྱེད་དགོས་པ་ཡིན་ནོ།།

ཡང་གསོད་པའི་ཕྱིར་དུ་མཚོན་བརྣར། ཞེས་པ་ལྟ་བུར་མཚོན་བརྣར་བས་གསད་བྱ་ལ་ཕན་བཏགས་ཟེར་བའི་དོན་མ་ཡིན་གྱི། མཚོན་བརྣར་པའི་བྱ་བས་བྱ་བའི་དོན་གྱི་ཡུལ་གསོད་པ་བ་ཕན་འདོགས་པར་བྱེད་པ་ཡིན་ནོ།

སྐབས་འདིར་འགའ་ཞིག་གིས་དོན་དང་ཆེད་དང་ཕྱིར་ཞེས་པའི་སྒྲ་རྣམས་རྣམ་དབྱེ་བཞི་པར་བྱས་པ་མི་འཐད་དེ། དེ་རྣམས་རྣམ་དབྱེ་འཇུག་ཡུལ་གྱི་མིང་ཙམ་ཡིན་པའི་ཕྱིར་ཏེ་དེ་དག་ལ་རྣམ་དབྱེ་ཚུགས་པས། དོན་དུ། དོན་གྱི། དོན་གྱིས། ལྟ་བུར་འགྱུར་བའི་ཕྱིར། དཔེར་ན་ལེགས་སྦྱར་ལ་དེའི་ཆེད་དུ་ཞེས་པར། ཏ་དརྠ་ཡ། ཞེས་འབྱུང་བའི་ཨརྠ་ནི་སྒྲ་དེ་རྣམ་དབྱེ་མ་ཡིན་པ་བཞིན་ནོ།།

རྣམ་དབྱེ་ལྔ་པ་འབྱུང་ཁུངས་ལ་འཇུག་པ་ནི། སངས་རྒྱས་ལས་ཆོས། གསེར་ཁ་ནས་གསེར། རྒྱ་མཚོ་ལས་ཆུ་བོ་འབྱུང་། དྲག་རི་ནས་ཐབ་ལྷུང་། མཛོད་ནས་ནོར་བླངས། ལྟ་བུ་སྟེ། ཆོས། གསེར། ཆུ་བོ། ཐབ། ནོར་རྣམས་ཀྱི་འབྱུང་ཁུངས་རིམ་པ་བཞིན། སངས་རྒྱས། གསེར་ཁ། རྒྱ་མཚོ། དྲག་རི། དཀོར་མཛོད་རྣམས་ཡིན་པས་དེ་དག་ལ་རྣམ་དབྱེ་ལྔ་པ་འཇུག་པ་ཡིན་ཞིང་། ཆུ་ལས་ལྷུང་། འཇིག་རྟེན་ལས་འདས། ཤར་ཕྱོགས་ནས་འོད་ཤར། ལྟ་བུ་ལྷུང་བ་དང་། བབས་པ་དང་། འོད་རྣམས་ཀྱི་འབྱུང་ཁུངས་དངོས་ཏེ་དང་། སྐྱེས་དང་། ཤར་རྣམས་མ་ཡིན་ཡང་འཕྲུལ་དུ་དེ་དག་ལས་འབྱུང་བའི་རྒྱུ་མཚན་གྱིས་རྣམ་དབྱེ་ལྔ་པ་སྦྱར་བ་དང་། དུ་བའི་རྟགས་ལས་མེ་ཡོད་པར་རྗེས་སུ་དཔག་གོ། ལྟ་བུ་རྒྱུ་མཚན་གྱི་དོན་ལའང་རྟགས་དེ་ལས་རྗེས་སུ་དཔག་པའི་ཚད་མ་སྐྱེ་

ཐམས་འབྱུང་ཁུངས་ལྟར་སྣང་བའི་ཕྱིར་ལྷ་པ་སྦྱར་བ་དང་། བུད་མེ་རྣམས་ལས་སྤྲོ་བསངས་མཛེས། ལྟ་བུ་ཡོན་ཏན་སོགས་ཀྱི་སྒོ་ནས་ཕོགས་སུ་བཀར་བ་སྐྱེ་བུད་མེད་རྣམས་ཀྱི་ནང་ནས་གློས་ཁྱད་པར་བྱེ་ནས་ཕྱུང་བ་ཡིན་པའི་ཕྱིར་འབྱུང་ཁུངས་དང་འདྲ་བའི་དོན་གྱིས་ལྷ་པ་སྦྱར་བ་སོགས་ཤེས་པར་བྱའོ།།

ལེགས་སྦྱར་ལ་ནི་གང་ལས་འབྲལ་བའི་དོན་ལ་ལྔ་པ་བཤད་ཅིང་དོན་དེས་ལྔ་པའི་འཇུག་ཡུལ་ཐམས་ཅད་ལ་ཁྱབ་པར་ཡང་བཤད་པ་མཐོང་བས་བོད་སྐད་ལའང་ཞིབ་མོར་བརྟགས་ན་འཆད་ཚུལ་དེ་འགྱུར་བར་སེམས་སོ།།

རྣམ་དབྱེ་དྲུག་པ་འབྲེལ་པའི་དོན་ལ་འཇུག་པ་ནི། ཕྱུག་པོའི་ནོར། ཁྱིམ་ཀྱི་ལྷ། ཆོས་ཀྱི་སྐུ། བདག་གི་དོན། ཤིང་གི་ཡལ་ག། ལྟ་བུ། ནོར། ལྷ། སྐུ། དོན། ཡལ་ག་རྣམས་རིམ་པ་བཞིན། ཕྱུག་པོ། ཁྱིམ། ཆོས། བདག ཤིང་རྣམས་དང་འབྲེལ་པ་ཡིན་པའི་ཕྱིར། དེ་དག་ལ་རྣམ་དབྱེ་དྲུག་པ་འཇུག་ཅིང་འདིར་གོང་དུ་བསྒྲུབ་བྱ་ཞེས་གསུངས་པས་ཞིབ་མོར་བརྟགས་ན་དྲུག་སྒྲ། འི། ཀྱི། ཀྱི་རྣམས་བསྒྲུབ་བྱ་ནོར་དང་། ལྷ་དང་། སྐུ་རྣམས། བདག་པོ། ཕྱུག་པོ་དང་། རྟེན་གནས་ཁྱིམ་དང་། ཞི་བའི་ཆོས་རྣམས་དང་འབྲེལ་པའི་སྒྲུབ་བྱེད་དུ་འགྲོ་བ་ལྟ་བུར་གོ་དགོས་སོ།།

འབྲེལ་པའང་བདག་ཉིད་གཅིག་པའི་འབྲེལ་པར་བརྗོད་པ། ཆོས་ཀྱི་སྐུ། རྒྱ་མཚོའི་ཆུ། གསེར་གྱི་བུམ་པ་ལྟ་བུ་དང་། ཕྱུག་པོའི་ནོར་ལྟ་བུ། བདག་པོ་དང་ཡུལ་གྱི་འབྲེལ་པ། ཁྱིམ་ཀྱི་ལྷ་ལྟ་བུ་རྟེན་དང་བརྟེན་པའི་འབྲེལ་པ། ཤིང་གི་ཡལ་ག་ལྟ་བུ་ཡན་ལག་དང་ཡན་ལག་ཅན་གྱི་འབྲེལ་པ་སོགས་དུ་མར་འགྱུར་བ་སྟེ་རྟོགས་པར་སླའོ།།

ལ་དོན་དྲུག་པོ་རྣམ་དབྱེ་བདུན་པ་གནས་གཞི་ལ་འཇུག་པ་ནི། ཤིང་ལ་བྱ། ཁྱིམ་དུ་མི། བུམ་པར་ཆུ། གདན་ལ་འདུག ས་ལ་ཉལ། རྒྱབ་ཏུ་རི་ཡོད། ལྟ་བུ། བྱ། མི། ཆུ། འདུག ཉལ། རི་རྣམས་ཀྱི་རྟེན་གནས་སམ་གནས་པའི་གཞི་ནི། ཤིང་། ཁྱིམ། བུམ་པ། གདན། ས། རྒྱབ། ཕྱོགས་རྣམས་ཡིན་པས་དེ་དག་ལ་རྣམ་དབྱེ་བདུན་པ་འཇུག་པ་ཡིན་ཞིང་། དེ་བཞིན་དུ་ཆུ་ལ་ཞུགས། ཁུང་དུ་འཛུལ། གཡུལ་དུ་གོ་བགོས། གཡུལ་དུ་བསད། ལྟ་བུ་རྣམས་ཀྱང་ཞུགས་པ་དང་འཛུལ་བ་དང་གོ་བགོས་པ་དང་བསད་པ་རྣམས་ཀྱི་བྱ་བ་དེ་དག་གི་རྟེན་རིམ་བཞིན་དུ་ཆུ་ལ་སོགས་པ་དེ་དག་ཡིན་པས་ལ་དོན་གྱི་རྣམ་དབྱེ་དེ་རྣམས་བདུན་པའི་དོན་དུ་འགྱུར་བ་ཡིན་གྱི་རྣམ་དབྱེ་གཉིས་པ་ལས་ཀྱི་དོན་མ་ཡིན་པར་ཤེས་པར་བྱའོ།།

ཡང་སྐྱེས་བུ་ཞིག་གིས་སྐྱེས་བུ་གཞན་ཞིག་ལ་མཚུབ་མོས་བརྡས་བསྟན་ནས་མཚུབ་མོའི་རྩེ་འདི་ལ་གླང་པོ་ཆེ་བརྒྱ་ཡོད་དོ་ཞེར་བ་ལྟ་བུ་ལ་མཚུབ་མོའི་རྩེ་དེར་གླང་པོ་ཆེ་དེ་རྣམས་བརྟེན་པ་མ་ཡིན་ཀྱང་མཚུབ་མོའི་རྩེ་དེས་མཚོན་པའི་ཡུལ་ཕྱོགས་དེར་གླང་པོ་ཆེ་མཐོང་བའི་ཡིད་ཤེས་སྐྱེ་བའི་རྐྱེན་བྱེད་པའི་ཆ་ནས་རྟེན་དང་འདྲ་བའི་ཕྱིར་བདུན་པ་འཇུག་པ་དང་། སྡིག་པ་ལ་འཛེམས། སེང་གེ་ལ་སྐྲག་སོགས་གང་ལས་འཇིགས་པ་འབྱུང་བའི་གནས་དེ་ལ་རྣམ་དབྱེ་ལྔ་པ་འཇུག་པ་ལེགས་སྦྱར་གྱི་ལུགས་ཡིན་ཡང་། བོད་སྐད་ལ་འཇུག་པ་སྐྱེ་བའི་ཡུལ་ལས་རྟེན་དུ་གྱུར་པའི་ཆ་ནས་བདུན་པ་ཉིད་སྦྱོར་བ་དང་། སྨུག་ལ་ཀུན་མ་འབྱུང་། ཉི་མ་ཤར་བ་ན་གཉིད་སད་ལྟ་བུ་གནས་སྐབས་དེ་དང་དེར་བརྟེན་ནས་དེ་འདྲ་འབྱུང་བས་དངོས་སུ་མ་བརྗོད་ཀྱང་དོན་ཐོབ་ཀྱིས་དུས་བརྗོད་པ་ལ་བདུན་པ་སྦྱར་བ་དང་། ཚེས་གསུམ་ལ་ལྷ་མཆོད། དབྱིད་ལ་ཁུ་བྱུག་གྲགས། སྟོན་དུས་སུ་བཙས་མ་བཟའ་ལྟ་བུ། དུས་དངོས་སུ་བརྗོད་པ་ལ་བདུན་པ་སྦྱར་བ་སྟེ་འདི་དག་གིས་མཚོན་ནས་འཇུག་ཡུལ་གྱི་བྱེ་བྲག་ཐམས་ཅད་ཞིབ་མོར་རྟོགས་པར་བྱའོ།།

དེ་ལྟར་རྣམ་དབྱེའི་འཇུག་ཚུལ་ཕྱོགས་ཙམ་བསྟན་ནས་ཚིག་གི་ཕྲད་ཅེས་བྱ་བ་ནི་སྤྱིར་མིང་ཚིག་གཉིས་སམ་དུ་མར་སྦྲེལ་བའི་ཚེ་བར་དུ་མཚམས་སྦྱོར་བའམ་དོན་གསལ་བ་ལ་ཕན་འདོགས་པར་བྱེད་ཅིང་འགའ་ཞིག་དེ་འདྲའི་ཕྲག་མཐའ་གཉིས་དང་མིང་རྐྱང་ཙམ་ལའང་དོན་གསལ་བའམ་བརྗོད་བདེ་བ་ལ་ཕན་འདོགས་པར་བྱེད་པའི་སྒྲའི་རྣམ་པ་ཞིག་སྟེ་དེའང་། མིང་ངམ་ཚིག་གཞན་ལ་མ་སྦྱར་ན་དེ་ཉིད་རྐྱང་པ་བརྗོད་པས་དོན་གསལ་བར་མི་མཚོན་པའི་ཕྲད་ནི། བཤད་མ་ཐག་པའི་རྣམ་དབྱེའི་རྐྱེན། ལ། ན། ཏུ། དུ། སུ། རུ། ཀྱི། གྱི། གི། འི། སོགས་དང་རྣམ་དབྱེ་ལ་མི་གཏོགས་པར། ལ། ན། ཀྱི། གྱི། གི། ཡི། ནས་

རྣམས་དང་། ཀོ། ཛོ། ཇ། ཉོ། ཐོ། སྨོ། འོ། ར། ཡོ། ཟ། ཧོ། པ། ཟ། ཚོ། མ།
ཨི། ཙན། ནི། ཕྱིར། ཀྱི། ཀྱ། ཅིང་། ཞིང་། ཤིང་། ཅེས། ཞེས། ཤེས། ཅིག། ཞིག། ཤིག།
ཅེའོ། ཞེའོ། ཤེའོ། ཅེ་ན། ཞེ་ན། ཤེ་ན། གུ། ཀྱང་། འང་། ཡང་། གམ། ངམ། དམ། ནམ།
བམ། མམ། འམ། རམ། ལམ། སམ། དག། རྣམས། ཏེ། སྟེ། དེ།● ལྟ། ལྟར། བཞིན། ཏྲེད།
དང་། ལོ། ལ་སོགས་པ་རྣམས་ཡིན་མོད་ཀྱི་རྣམ་དབྱེ་རྣམས་ཡོགས་སུ་བཤད་པས་ལྷག་མ་རྣམས་གཟུང་བར་བྱའོ།།

དེ་རྣམས་ཀྱང་མིང་ཚིག་ལ་ཇི་ལྟར་སྦྱོར་ན།

དག་ལ་གསལ་ན་ལེགས་མོད་ཀྱི། བརྟན་གྱི་འཇུག་གི་འཆད་བྱ་ཡི། མཁས་པར་བྱས་ནས་ཚུལ་བརྟག་གོ།
བྱ་བ་བཟང་ངོ་ལེགས་བཀོད་དོ། འགྱུར་ཏོ་འགྲུབ་བོ་དོན་བསམ་མོ། བྱའོ་ཕྱར་རོ་ལྷ་རྒྱལ་ལོ།
བསྟུས་སོ་བསྟན་ཏོ་ལྷ་ཆོས་པ། སྐྱབ་པོ་དགའ་བོ་གསར་མ་པ། མཆོག་མི་ལྷུང་དགེ་བ་ཙམ།
ད་ནི་ཅི་ཕྱིར་ཀྱི་ཀྱི་བུ། ཀྱ་ཡི་ཕྲུགས་དག་བསྟོད་ཅིང་མཛེས། བདེ་ཞིང་དཀྱིས་ཤིང་ཡོད་ཅེས་ཛོས།
གསལ་ཞེས་མཛེས་ཤེས་* ཞད་ཅིག་མདའ། ནམ་ཞིག་གྲོས་ཤིག་གདབ་ཅེའོ། སུ་ཡོད་ཅེ་ན་གང་ཞེ་ན།
མ་བྱས་ཤེ་ན་གྲོས་ཤིག་གུ། འཁོད་ཀྱང་འགྲོ་བའང་དུན་ན་ཡང་། རྒྱུག་གམ་འཛིང་ངམ་རྫོད་དམ་ཅི།
མདུན་ནམ་རྒྱབ་བམ་ལེགས་བསམ་མམ། བྱའམ་འཛར་རམ་ཙང་ཐལ་ལམ། རྒྱས་སམ་དེ་དག་དཔལ་འབྱོར་རྣམས།
མཁས་ཏེ་འཆད་དེ་ཀུན་རྟུབ་སྟེ། དེ་ལྟ་དེ་ལྟར་དེ་བཞིན་སྨྲད། ཇི་སྙེད་བདེ་དང་ལྡན་ནོ་ལོ།

ལྟ་བུ་དང་། ཡང་སྒྲར་ཡུལ་ལ་མི་ལྟོས་པར་ཡང་རང་ཉིད་ཀྱི་བརྗོད་དོན་གསལ་བར་མཚོན་པ་རྣམ་ཀྱི་སྐད་ནི། གང་། ཅི། དེ། འདི། སུ། ཡང་། ནམ། སྔར། འོ་ན། ལ་ལ། ཇི། ཞེས་པ་ལྟ་བུ་ཕྲད་རྐྱང་པ་རྣམས་དང་། ཕྲད་གཉིས་གསུམ་སོགས་འདུས་པ། གང་དག། དེ་དག། གང་རྣམས། དེ་རྣམས། ཇི་སྙེད། དེ་སྙེད། གང་ལྟར། ཇི་ལྟར། གལ་ཏེ་ན། གལ་ཏེ། ཅི་ཞིག། སུ་ཞིག། ཅི་ཕྱིར། གང་ཕྱིར། དེ་སྐད། དེ་ལྟ་ན། འོན་ཀྱང་། ཅིའང་། ཅི་ནས་ཀྱང་། ཡང་ཡང་། སྔར་ཡང་། ཅི་ཞིག་ན་དེ། ནམ་ཞིག། སུའང་། ཅི་ཞེ་ན། ཞེས་པ་ལྟ་བུ་རྣམས་དང་། འོ་ན་ཞེས་པ་བསྡུས་པས་འོན་དང་། ཇིའང་ཞེས་པ་བསྡུས་ཙང་དང་། གང་ལ་ལ་ཞེས་པ་བསྡུས་པས་གལ་ཞེས་པ་ལྟ་བུ་རྣམས་སོ།། དེས་ན་ཚིག་ཕྲད་ཀྱི་རིགས་འདི་འདྲ་ཤིན་ཏུ་མང་བས་འདིར་ཕྱོགས་ཙམ་མཚོན་པའི་ཕྱིར་ཆུང་ཟད་བཀོད་ཀྱི་ཞིབ་མོར་ཡི་གེར་འབྲིར་མ་ལངས་སོ།།

འདིར་འགའ་ཞིག་གིས་ལེགས་སྦྱར་གྱི་སྐད་ནི་པྲ་ཏ་བསྒྱུར་བ་ཚིག་ཕྲད་ཡིན་པའི་རྒྱུ་མཚན་གྱིས་བོད་སྐད་ཀྱི་ཚིག་ཕྲད་གང་ཡིན་པ་རྣམས་ཀྱང་ལེགས་སྦྱར་གྱི་ནི་པྲ་ཏ་རྣམས་དང་བསྒྲིག་རྩང་བ་ཞིག་དགོས་སོ་སྙམ་དུ་བསམ་ནས་སྒྲ་སྒྲོ་ཅོ་འཁྱོལ་ལ་དགག་པ་བརྗོད་པའི་ཞར་དུ་གཞུང་འདི་ལའང་རྫུར་ཟ་བ་དང་། ཅི་བྲག་ཅོགས་བྱེད་ཆེན་མོ་ལའང་ཀྱོན་གདགས་པར་བྱེད་མོད། དགོངས་པ་ཅན་ཞིག་ཡིན་ན་མ་གཏོགས་མཁས་པའི་གསུང་དུ་མ་མཛོད་སྙམ། ཕྱིར་ཙོ་ཐུ་བ་རྣམས་ཀྱིས་ནི་པྲ་ཏ་ཞེས་པ་ཚིག་ཕྲད་དུ་བསྒྱུར་མོད་ཀྱི་ལེགས་སྦྱར་གྱི་ནི་པྲ་ཏ་ཡིན་ཚད་བོད་སྐད་ཀྱི་ཚིག་ཕྲད་ཡིན་དགོས་པ་དང་། བོད་སྐད་ཀྱི་ཕྲད་ཡིན་ཚད་ནི་པྲ་ཏ་ཡིན་དགོས་པའི་ཁྱབ་པ་སུ་ཞིག་གིས་ཁས་བླངས། ཁྱེད་ཉིད་ཀྱིས་ཁས་བླངས་པས་ནི་གཞན་ལ་གནོད་བྱེད་དུ་མི་འགྱུར་ཏེ། ད་དུང་དམ་བཅའ་དེ་བསྒྲུབ་དགོས་ཤིང་བསྒྲུབས་ཀྱང་མི་འགྲུབ

* ས་མཐར་ཤེས་ཞེས་སྦྱོར་བ་འདི་བཞིན་འཐད་ཀྱང་འདུལ་གཞི་འབྱུང་བར་གཡིགས་ནས་མཁས་པ་ཕྱི་མ་རྣམས་ཀྱིས་མ་མཛད་པ་བཞིན་ད་ལྟར་ལག་རྒྱུན་ལ་མི་བྱེད་དོ།

བའི་ཕྱིར་རོ། །ཅིའི་ཕྱིར་ན་སྔོན་གྱི་མཁས་པ་རྣམས་ཀྱིས་ནི་པཱ་ཏ་ཚིག་ཕྲད་དུ་སྒྱུར་བའི་དགོངས་པ་ནི། ལེགས་སྦྱར་གྱི། ཙ། ཝཱ། ཨེ་བ་ལ་སོགས་པ་ནི་པཱ་ཏ་རྣམས་ཕལ་ཆེར་ཚིག་ཕྲད་ལ་འབྱུང་བ་ཤས་ཆེ་བས་ཡིན་གྱི་བོད་སྐད་ཀྱི་ཚིག་ཕྲད་དང་ནི་པཱ་ཏ་གཉིས་ཡིན་ཁྱབ་མཉམ་དུ་དགོངས་པས་དེ་བཞིན་དུ་བསྒྱུར་བ་མ་ཡིན་པའི་ཕྱིར་ཏེ། ལེགས་སྦྱར་ནི་པཱ་ཏ་ལ་ཡོད་པའི། སྭར྄། སྭཱ་ཧཱམ྄། ཏྲུར་ཊ་ཊམ྄། ཀཱཏ་ཐཾ། སྭསྟི། མིཐུཝི། ཧྱུཏྨས྄། ལྟ་བུ་རྣམས་རིམ་བཞིན་བསྒྱུར་བའི། མཐོ་རིས། མགྱོགས་པ། ཀླུར་པོ། ཐུ་བ། བདེ་ལེགས། བརྫུན། མཐོན་པོ་ལྟ་བུ་རྣམས་བོད་སྐད་ཀྱི་ཚིག་ཕྲད་མ་ཡིན་པ་དང༌། བོད་ཀྱི་སྐད་ལ་ཚིག་ཕྲད་དུ་འདང་བགྲང་ཚོག་པའི་རྣམ་དབྱེའི་རྐྱེན་གྱི་གྱི་ལ་ན་ལྟ་བུ་ཡོད་ཀྱང༌། ལེགས་སྦྱར་ལ་དེའི་དོད། སྱ། ཡཱས྄། ཡཱམ྄། ལྟ་བུ་རྣམས་རྣམ་དབྱེའི་རྐྱེན་གྱི་རྗེས་ཙམ་ལས་ནི་པཱ་ཏ་མ་ཡིན་པའི་ཕྱིར་རོ།།

སྤྱིར་ཡང་ནི་པཱ་ཏ་ཞེས་པ་སྒྲ་ཤར་ཕྱོག་ཏུ་བསྒྱུར་ན་ངེས་ཚིག་ཅེས་བྱ་ཞིང་ངེས་པའི་དོན་ཡང་ནི་པཱ་ཏ་ཡིན་པ་རྣམས་ལ་རྟགས་གསུམ་གྱི་དབྱེ་བ་མེད་པ་དང༌། རྣམ་དབྱེ་རྣམ་འགྱུར་ཕལ་ཆེར་མེད་པས་སྐྱའི་གཟུགས་ངེས་པའི་དོན་ཡིན་ཞིང་དེ་དག་ལ་མིང་གི་རྣམ་གྲངས་གཞན་ཞི་ཟད་བ་ཞེས་ཀྱང་བྱ་ལ། བོད་ཀྱི་ཚིག་ཕྲད་ཅེས་བཏགས་པ་ནི་ཚིག་གི་བར་བར་དུ་མཚམས་སྦྱོར་བའི་འཕྲད་དུ་འབྱུང་བ་ཤས་ཆེ་བའི་རྒྱུ་མཚན་གྱིས་དེ་སྐད་ཅེས་བྱ་བའི་མིང་དོན་གྱི་རྒྱུ་མཚན་ཡང་མཚུངས་པ་མ་ཡིན་ནོ།།

དེས་ན་བྱེ་རྟོགས་སུ་བོད་བརྡའ་ཉིད་ཀྱི་དབང་དུ་བྱས་ནས་སྐབས་སྐབས་ནས་ཚིག་གི་འཕྲད་དུ་འབྱུང་བ་ཞེས་མདོར་བསྟན་ནས་འཕྲད་དུ་འབྱུང་བ་རྣམས་བཀོད་པ་ལ་ནི་པཱ་ཏ་མ་ཡིན་པ་འགའ་ཞིག་མཐོང་བ་ལ་ཀློན་དུ་སླ་བ་ནི་ཡ་ཆའོ།།

དེ་བཞིན་དུ་སྒྲ་སྒོ་ཙ་འགྲེལ་དུ་གང་ལ་ཞེས་པ་བརྟུས་པས། གལ་དང་ཅི་ཞིག་ན་ཞེས་པ་སྐྱེ་ནར་བསྒྱུར་ནས་སྒྱུར་བས་གལ་ཏེ་ན་ཞེས་གྲུབ་པར་བཤད་པ་སུན་འབྱིན་པའང་ལེགས་བཤད་ཡིན་མིན་བརྟག་དགོས་ཏེ། གལ་ཏེ་ཞེས་པ་དེའི་སྐད་དོད་ཡ་དི་དང་ངེས་པར་སྦྱར་དགོས་ན། ཡ་དི་ཞེས་པ་ཡ་ཏ་ལ་དུས་བརྗོད་པའི་དོན་དུ་རྣམ་དབྱེ་བདུན་པའི་ཌི་ཕྱིན་ནས་ཚིག་ཕྲད་ཀྱི་ལུགས་སུ་བསྒྲུབས་ཤིང་ཚིག་ཕྲད་དུ་གྱུར་པ་ཏ་དི་དང་ཏདི་ལྟ་བུ་ཡིན་པས་བོད་སྐད་གང་ལ་ཞེའམ་གང་ཚེ་ཞེས་པར་འགྱུར་བས་སྒྲ་སྒོ་འི་འཆད་ཚུལ་དེ་ཕྱོགས་གཅིག་ནས་འགྲིག་པ་མ་ཡིན་ནམ། དེ་བས་ཡ་དིའི་འཐད་དེ་སྒྲུབ་ཚུལ་ཅི་ཡིན་མ་མཁྱེན་པའི་ཚུལ་བརྗོད་པ་དེ་ག་མཚར་ཆེ་བར་རྟོགས་སོ།།

ཡང་ལེགས་སྦྱར་ལ་རྣམ་དབྱེའི་རྐྱེན་དང་ནི་པཱ་ཏ་མི་མཚུངས་པ་ཁྱུགས་མོད་ཀྱང་བོད་སྐད་གཉིས་བཞག་གི་རྣམས་དབྱེའི་རྐྱེན་ལ་ཚིག་ཕྲད་དུ་བརྗོད་པ་མི་འགལ་ཏེ་རྐྱེན་དེ་དག་ཚིག་ཕན་ཚུན་མཚམས་སྦྱོར་བའི་ཕྲད་ཀྱི་དོན་ལས་མི་འདའ་བའི་ཕྱིར་རོ།།

རྣམ་དབྱེ་རྐྱེན་ཙམ་དང་ཚིག་ཕྲད་མིང་ངམ་ཚིག་ཡིན་པས་ཁྱད་ཆེར་སྣམ་པ་སྲིད་ཀྱང་གོང་སློས་སྦྱོར་ཡུལ་གཞན་མེད་པར་རང་ཉིད་གཅིག་པུ་བརྗོད་ན་དོན་མི་གསལ་བའི་ཕྲད་རྐྱང་དེ་རྣམས་ཀྱང་རྐྱེན་ཙམ་ཡིན་གྱི་མིང་ཚིག་གང་ཡང་མ་ཡིན་ནོ།།

འོ་ན་ལེགས་སྦྱར་གྱི་རྩ་དང་ཙིཏ྄་བསྒྱུར་བའི་དང་དང་ན་ལྟ་བུའང་རྐྱེན་དུ་འདོད་དགོས་པས་ཏ་ཙང་ཐལ་ལོ་སྙམ་ན་གོང་སློས་ཕྲད་སྐད་གཉིས་དོན་ཐོག་ཏུ་དབབ་དུས་མཚུངས་ཕྱིན་རྐྱེན་དང་མིང་སོགས་ཡིན་མཉམ་དགོས་པར་བསམས་པ་ནི་དེ་བས་ཀྱང་ཐལ་ཆེས་ཏེ། དཔེར་ན། ན་རཱ་ཡ་ཎ་ཞེས་པར་ན་ར་སྲི་དུ་མེད་དང༌། ཞྭ་ཡ་ན་ནཊ་ཀྱི་རྐྱེན་དོན་ཕྱུར་བསྒྱུར་བ་ན་བོད་སྐད་བུ་ཞེས་པ་མིང་ཡིན་གྱི་རྐྱེན་མ་ཡིན་པ་དང༌། ས་ཀྲྀ་ཡ་ཞེས་པར་སརྦ་ཀུན་དང་ཨི་ཡའི་དོན་ཕན་པར་བསྒྱུར་བ་ན་ཕན་པ་རྐྱེན་མ་ཡིན་པ་སོགས་མཐའ་ཡས་པའི་ཕྱིར་རོ།།

ལེགས་སྦྱར་གྱི་ལུགས་ལའང་ཀཏྭཱ་དང་ཏ་བཻ་དང་ཏུ་མུན་ལ་སོགས་པ་རྐྱེན་ཡིན་མོད་ཀྱི་དེའི་མཐའ་ནི་པཱ་ཏའང་ཡིན་པས་རྐྱེན་དང་ནི་པཱ་ཏ་རྣམ་པ་ཀུན་ཏུ་འགལ་བར་བསམས་ནའང་མི་རུང་ངོ།།

ཡང་སྐད་དོད་ལ་རྣམ་དབྱེ་དབྱེ་བར་མིང་ངེས་པའི་རྒྱུ་མཚན་གྱིས་གང་ཅི་དེ་སོགས་ཚིག་ཕྲད་མིན་ཞེས་གསུངས་པའང་བྱེ་བྲག་མ་ཕྱེད་པའི་གསུངས་སྒོ་དེ་དག་གི་སྐད་དོད་ཡར

ཏཏ྄་ཀིམ་སོགས་རྒྱུ་མཚན་སོགས་ཀྱི་དོན་ལ་འཇུག་པའི་ཚེ་ནི་ཕླུ་ཏ་ཡིན་པ་འཆི་མེད་མཛོད་སོགས་སུ་གསལ་ཞིང་སཱ་རསྭ་ཏའི་སྐབས་སུ་ནི་ཕླུ་ཏ་མ་ཡིན་པའང་སྒྲ་གཞུང་རྣམས་སུ་གསལ་བས་དེ་དག་མ་ཕྱེད་པར་སློབ་ཡོང་ཀྱིས་གཞན་ལ་གོལ་བར་སྣང་བའི་ཕྱིར་རོ། །

དེས་ན་འཆི་མེད་མཛོད་སོགས་གཟིགས་པའི་ཞལ་ཟད་ཀྱང་དེ་ཙམ་དུ་བས་སོ། ། ཡང་དོན་དམ་པར་དབྱེར་མེད་ན། ཞེས་པ་ལྟ་བུའི་ན་དེ་ལ་དོན་འཆད་པའི་ཀུམ་པ་མེད་པར་བཤད་འདུག་པ། ཕྱི་ཚིག་མི་མཐུན་པར་སྟོན་པའི་ཀུས་པ་ནའི་སྒྲ་དེ་ལ་མེད་ན་དོན་དམ་དུ་དབྱེར་མེད་ཅེས་ཚིག་ཟླ་མ་དེར་ཀུན་རྫོབ་ཏུ་དབྱེར་ཡོད་ཅེས་ཚིག་ཕྱི་མ་དག་སོ་སོའི་ངོ་བོ་བརྗོད་པ་ཙམ་ཡིན་པའི་ཕྱིར་དེ་གཉིས་ལ་མི་མཐུན་པར་སྟོན་པའི་ཀུས་པ་དེ་བས་ཀྱང་མེད་དོ། ། གཞན་ཡང་མི་འཐད་པ་དུ་མ་ཞིག་སྣང་ཡང་དགག་པའི་སྤྲོས་པ་མ་བྱས་ལ།

སྒྲ་མོ་ཙ་འགྲེལ་དང་སྒྲ་བ་ཀུན་ལ་འཇུག་པའི་སྒྲའི་བསྟན་བཅོས་ཙ་འགྲེལ་འདི་རྣམས་ལའང་མི་འཐད་པ་ཤིན་ཏུ་མང་ཞིང་མཁས་པ་གཞན་ཀྱིས་གནོད་བྱེད་བརྗོད་པ་གནང་དུ་སོང་བའང་མང་བར་སྣང་བས་འཕགས་ཡུལ་མཁས་པའི་ལེགས་བཤད་ནི་མིན་པར་ངེས་སོ། ། འོན་ཀྱང་སུམ་ཅུ་པའི་སྐབས་སུ་འགའ་ཞིག་དྭངས་པ་སོགས་གཞུང་འདིའི་དོན་དང་སྐབས་འགར་མཐུན་པའི་ལེགས་བཤད་མང་དག་ཀྱང་འདུག་པས་རྣམ་པ་ཀུན་ཏུ་འདོར་བྱ་ནི་མ་ཡིན་ནོ། །

དེ་ལྟར་གལ་ཆེ་བའི་འཕྲོས་དོན་ཅུང་ཟད་བཤད་ནས། བཞི་པ་རྗེས་འཇུག་གི་ཡི་གེ་རྣམས་དགོས་པ་ཅིའི་ཕྱིར་འཇུག་པ་འཆད་པ་ལ། རྗེས་འཇུག་གི་དགོས་པ་དངོས་བཤད་པ་དང་། ཞར་བྱུང་ཡི་གེའི་འཇུག་པ་ཕྱིའི་དགོས་པ་བཤད་པ་གཉིས།

དང་པོ་ནི།

ཅི་ཕྱིར་འཇུག་པར་བྱེད་ཅེ་ན། །ཡི་གེའི་ཁོངས་ནས་མིང་འབྱུང་སྟེ། །
མིང་གི་ཁོངས་ནས་ཚིག་ཕྱུང་ནས། །ཚིག་གིས་དོན་རྣམས་སྟོན་པར་བྱེད། །

ཅེས་པས་བསྟན་ཏེ། རྗེས་འཇུག་ཡི་གེ་བཅུ་པོ་དེ་རྣམས་དགོས་པ་ཅིའི་ཕྱིར་དུ་འཇུག་པར་བྱེད་ཅེ་ན། སྔོན་འཇུག་ཡོད་མེད་གང་ཡང་རུང་བའི་མིང་གཞིའི་ཡི་གེ་གཅིག་གམ་གཉིས་སམ་དུ་མ་འདུས་པ་ཡིན་ཡང་རུང་རྗེས་འཇུག་ཡི་གེ་གང་རུང་ཞིག་མ་ཞུགས་པར་དོན་གྱི་ངོ་བོ་སྟོན་པའི་མིང་དུ་འགྲུབ་པ་མི་སྲིད་པས་ཡི་གེའི་ཁོངས་ནས་མིང་འབྱུང་བར་བྱ་བའི་ཕྱིར་དང་། མིང་གཅིག་གམ་གཉིས་སམ་དུ་མ་སྦྲེལ་དུ་ཟིན་ཀྱང་མཚམས་སྦྱོར་བར་བྱེད་པའམ་དོན་གསལ་བར་བྱེད་པའི་རྣམ་དབྱེ་དང་ཕྲད་སོགས་གལ་ཆེར་རྗེས་འཇུག་ལས་བྱུང་ཞིང་རྗེས་འཇུག་ལ་ལྟོས་པ་དེ་རྣམས་མ་ཞུགས་ན་དོན་གྱི་ཁྱད་པར་བརྗོད་པའི་ཚིག་ཏུ་འགྲུབ་པ་མི་སྲིད་པས་མིང་གི་ཁོངས་ནས་ཚིག་འབྱུང་བའི་ཕྱིར་འཇུག་སྟེ། དེ་ལྟ་བུ་ཚིག་གིས་འཇིག་རྟེན་དུ་དོན་རྣམས་རྟོགས་པར་བྱེད་པའི་ཕྱིར་དོན་མཚོན་པའི་བརྗོད་པ་ཇི་སྙེད་པའང་རྗེས་འཇུག་གི་ཡི་གེ་རྣམས་འཇུག་པའི་དགོས་པར་གྲུབ་བོ་ཞེས་སོ། །

སྐབས་འདིར་མིང་ཚིག་བརྗོད་པ་གསུམ་པོ་ཇི་ལྟར་དབྱེ་བའི་ཚུལ་ནི། སྒྲ་ཀ་ར་ཎའི་ལུགས་ལ་རྣམ་དབྱེའི་མཐའ་ཅན་ནི་ཚིག་གོ། རྣམ་དབྱེ་མེད་པ་ནི་མིང་ངོ། །ཞེས་འབྱུང་ཡང་། བོད་སྐད་ལ། རྣམ་དབྱེ་དང་ཕྲད་གཅིག་ཚིག་མིང་ཙམ་ལས་ལོགས་སུ་དབྱེར་ཆེད་ཅིང་། དག་དང་རྣམས་ཀྱི་ཕྲད་ཀྱིས་གཉིས་ཚིག་དང་མང་ཚིག་མཚོན་ཡང་ད་རུང་དེ་དག་གི་མཐར་རྣམ་དབྱེ་གཞན་འཇུག་པ་སོགས་ཀྱིས་རྣམ་བཞག་དེ་ལྟ་བུ་སྦྱར་དུ་མི་རུང་བ་དང་། ཆོས་མངོན་པའི་ལུགས་ཀྱི་ཡི་གེ་དུ་མ་འདུས་པ་ལས་མིང་། མིང་དུ་མ་འདུས་པ་ལས་ཚིག ཅེས་གསུངས་པའང་སྤྱིར་བཏང་རགས་ཙམ་ཡིན་པས་འདིར་ཟླ་བའི་དབང་དུ་བྱས་ན་མི་འགྱུར་བས་སྐབས་འདིར་ནི་བོད་སྐད་གཞིར་བཞག་གིས་གང་ཞིག་ཡི་གེ་གཉིས་སམ་མང་པོ་འདུས་པའང་རུང་དོན་གྱི་ངོ་བོ་ཙམ་སྟོན་པའི་སྒྲ་ནི་མིང་ཡིན་ཞིང་། མིང་དེ་ཉིད་རྣམ་དབྱེའམ་ཕྲད་གང་རུང་དང་ལྡན་པས་དོན་གྱི་ཁྱད་པར་སྟོན་པར་བྱེད་པ་རྣམས་ནི་ཚིག་དང་། ཚིག་མང་པོ་སྦྲེལ་ནས་དོན་དང་ལྡན་པའི་ངག་གི་ཕྲེང་བར་གྲུབ་པ་ནི་བརྗོད་པ་ཞེས་བྱའོ། །

དེའང་བསྟན་བཅོས་འདི་ཡི་ལུགས་ཀྱིས་དབྱངས་ཡིག་སྔོག་ཐུགས་མི་བཞེད་པ་དེ་ལྟ་བུ་ཡི་གེ་གཅིག་ཡིན་ཡང་བཤད་མ་ཐག་པ་ལྟར་རྗེས་འཇུག་དངོས་སུ་མེད་ཀྱང་དོན་ཀྱིས་ཐོབ་པས་ངར་ཞེས་ཡི་གེ་གཉིས་སུ་འགྱུར་བ་དེ་ལྟ་བུ་ནི་ཡི་གེ་གཉིས་ཚོགས་པའི་མིང་གི་མཚན་གཞི་དང་། དེ་བཞིན་དུ། དཔལ། དཀར་བ། སྒྲུབ་པ། བསོད་

རྣམས་ལྷ་བུ་རིམ་བཞིན་ཡི་གེ་གསུམ་བཞི་ལྔ་དྲུག་འདུས་པའི་མིང་དུ་ཤེས་པར་བྱ་ཞིང་ཡི་གེ་དེ་ལས་མང་བ་འདུས་པའི་མིང་རྣམས་ཀྱང་མཚོན་པར་བྱའོ།

ཡང་། རྒྱ་འཕྲུལ་ཆེན་མོ། རྡོ་རྗེ་འཛིན་དབང་། སྒྲིད་མེད་བུ། ལྟ་བུ་རྣམས་ནི་ཚིག་གཉིས་སམ་མང་པོ་བསྡུས་ནས་མིང་གཅིག་ཏུ་བྱས་པ་སྟེ། དོན་གྱི་ཁྱད་པར་དེ་དག་དང་ལྡན་པའི་མིང་ཅན་དེའི་ངོ་བོ་ཙམ་བརྗོད་པའི་ཕྱིར་མིང་ལས་མི་འདའོ།།

འདི་འདྲ་ཕལ་ཆེར་ལ་བར་གྱི་རྣམ་དབྱེ་དང་ཕྲད་རྣམས་བསྡུས་པ་མང་ཡང་མ་བསྡུས་པ་འང་། དེ་བཞིན་གཤེགས་པ། ཀུན་ཏུ་བཟང་པོ། འཁོར་ལོའི་དབང་ཕྱུག། ལྟ་བུ་ཅི་རིགས་པར་འབྱུང་བས་དེ་འདྲ་རྣམས་ལ་ཕྲད་དང་རྣམ་དབྱེ་ཡོད་པས་ཚིག་ཏུ་འཁྲུལ་བར་མི་བྱ་སྟེ་ཕྱི་ལྡོག་ནས་མིང་ཅན་དེའི་དོན་གྱི་ངོ་བོ་ཙམ་སྟོན་པས་མིང་ཉིད་ཡིན་པའི་ཕྱིར། དཔེར་ན་ལེགས་སྦྱར་ལ། ཀེ་ཤ་ཞེས་པ་མགོ་རལ་ཏེ་མིང་དེའི་ནང་ན་དོན་གྱི་ཁྱད་པར་སྟོན་པའི་ཚིག་མཚོན་གྱུར་དུ་ཡོད་ཀྱང་ཕྱི་ལྡོག་ནས་སྤྱིའི་ངོ་བོ་ཙམ་རིག་ལས་མི་སྟོན་པའི་ཕྱིར་མིང་ཡིན་པ་ལྟ་བུའོ།།

ཡང་ལྷ་མོ་དང་སྤྲིན་ཕྱིས་ལྟ་བུ་ནི་ལེགས་སྦྱར་ལ་མིང་གཅིག་ཉིད་ལ་མོ་རྟགས་དང་བུ་རྒྱུད་ཀྱི་རྐྱེན་སོགས་ཀྱིས་བསྒྱུར་བ་ཡོད་ཀྱང་བོད་སྐད་ལ་དེ་འདྲའི་རྐྱེན་མེད་པས་མིང་གཉིས་བསྡུས་པ་ཡིན་ཞིང་། བདེ་བ་ཅན་ལྟ་བུ་ཕྲད་ཀྱི་མཐའ་ཡིན་ཡང་ཞིང་ཁམས་ཀྱི་མིང་དུ་བྱེད་པའི་ཚེ་དོན་གྱི་ངོ་བོ་སྟོན་པའི་ཆ་ནས་མིང་ཡིན་ཞིང་། བདེ་བ་དང་ལྡན་པ་ཙམ་བརྗོད་རྒྱུ་ཡིན་ན་དོན་གྱི་ཁྱད་པར་སྟོན་བྱེད་ཡིན་པས་ཚིག་ཏུ་འགྱུར་ཏེ་སྐབས་ཐོབ་ཀྱིས་ཤེས་པར་བྱའོ།།

དེ་བཞིན་དུ་ཕྲད་རྣམས་ལའང་། གང་། དེ། འདི། ལྟ་བུ་རྣམས་ལ་མིང་ཙམ་དང་། གང་དག། གང་ཕྱིར། དེ་ལྟ་བུ། འོན་ཀྱང་། དེ་ལྟ་ན། ལྟ་བུ་རྣམས་ཚིག་དང་། ན། ལ། སྟེ། ལྟ་བུ་རྣམས་མིང་ཚིག་གང་ཡང་མ་ཡིན་པར་གོ་དགོས་ཤིང་། རྣམ་དབྱེ་གཉིས་པ་ནས་བདུན་པའི་བར་དང་། གཉིས་དང་མང་པོའི་ཚིག་ཕྲད་དང་། བོད་ཀྱི་སྒྲ་སོགས་སྦྱར་བ་རྣམས་ནི་ཚིག་ཁོ་ན་ཡིན་ནོ།།

དེས་ན་ཕྲད་ཙམ་གྱིས་ཚིག་ཏུ་གྲུབ་པ་རྣམས་ཀྱི་མཐར་ནི་སླར་ཡང་ཕྲད་དང་རྣམ་དབྱེ་ཅི་རིགས་པར་འཇུག་པ་ཡོད་ལ་རྣམ་དབྱེས་ཚིག་ཏུ་གྲུབ་པ་རྣམས་ཀྱི་མཐར་ནི་སླར་རྣམ་དབྱེ་འཇུག་པ་མ་ཡིན་ཞིང་ཕྲད་འགའ་ཞིག་འཇུག་པ་ཡོད་དེ། དཔེར་ན། དེ་ཡིས་ཀྱང་། ཁྱོད་ཀྱི་ནི་ལྟ་བུ་རྣམས་སོ།།

ཚིག་བསྡུས་ནས་མིང་དུ་གྱུར་པ་དེ་རྣམས་ཀྱི་མཐར་ཡང་ཕྲད་དམ་རྣམ་དབྱེ་སྦྱར་བས་དོན་གྱི་ཁྱད་པར་སྟོན་པར་བྱེད་ན་ཚིག་ཏུ་འགྱུར་བ་སོགས་ཞིབ་མོའི་བློས་དཔྱད་པར་བྱ་སྟེ། ཁྱད་པར་མཐའ་དག་ནི་འདིར་འབྲི་བར་མ་ལངས་སོ།།

ཡང་བརྗོད་པ་ཞེས་བྱ་བའང་སྤྱིར་མིང་ཚིག་ཡི་གེ་གང་ཡང་རུང་ངག་གི་བརྗོད་པས་ཐམས་ཅད་ལ་སྦྱར་དུ་རུང་ཡང་། སྙན་ངག་གི་གཞུང་དུ་བརྗོད་པ་དང་། གཏམ་གཉིས་རིགས་གཅིག་པར་བཤད་པ་བཞིན་མིང་ཚིག་བརྗོད་པ་གསུམ་དུ་དབྱེ་བའི་བརྗོད་པ་ནི་ཚིག་དུ་མ་འདུས་པའི་ངག་གི་ཕྲེང་བ་ཉིད་ཡིན་ཞིང་། དེ་ལ་མིང་གཞན་གཏམ་ཞེས་ཀྱང་བྱ་སྟེ། པདྨ་དཀར་པོ་ལྟར་རྣམ་པར་མཛེས་པའི་བྱང་ཆུབ་སེམས་དཔའ་མཁས་པ་རྣམས་ནི་འཇིག་རྟེན་གྱི་རྒྱན་དུ་གྱུར་པ་ཡིན་ནོ།། ཞེས་པ་ལྟ་བུའོ།།

འདི་ཐད་ཀྱི་ཞ་ལུའི་འགྲེལ་པར་གནས་བརྒྱད་ཆེན་མོའི་རྗེས་སུ་འབྲང་བའི། སྒྲ་དང་སྐད། མིང་དང་མཚན་མ། བརྡའ་དང་ཐ་སྙད། ཚིག་དང་དོན་ཏེ་ཡི་གེ་འཇུག་པའི་གནས་བརྒྱད་ཀྱི་བཤད་པ་ཞིག་འབྱུང་བ་ཕལ་ཆེར་ལེགས་པར་བཤད་དུ་ཡོད་ཀྱང་། བོད་སྐད་ཟུར་ཆག་ཏུ་མཛད་པ་ཙམ་མི་ལེགས་ཏེ་སྐད་རིགས་བཞི་ནི་འཕགས་ཡུལ་གྱི་དབང་དུ་བྱས་ནས་བཞག་ལ། སྐད་ངན་མི་ཤོང་དུ།

བསྟན་བཅོས་རྣམས་ལ་ལེགས་སྦྱར་ལས། གཞན་པ་ཟུར་ཆག་ཉིད་དུ་བརྗོད།

ཅེས་འབྱུང་བ་འང་འཕགས་ཡུལ་གྱི་དབང་དུ་བྱས་པའི་ཕྱིར། ཀོ་ཊ་ལ་སོགས་པ་ཡུལ་འཁོར་ཆེན་པོ་ལ་བརྟེན་པའི་རང་བཞིན་གྱི་སྐད་རྣམས་ནི། ཏྲམ་ལ་ཏུ་མི་དང་། ཨཱ་དྷྲ་ལ་ཏ་མི་དང་། སུ་དྲི་ཤ་ལ་ས་རི་ཁ་དང་། ཨ་གྣི་ལ་ཨ་གིན་དང་། རཏྣ་ལ་ར་ཏན་ལྟ་བུ་ལེགས་སྦྱར་གྱི་ཟུར་ཉམས་པ་ཁོ་ན་ཡིན་པ་དང་། རྒྱ་གར་མཐའ་འཁོབ

ཀྱི་བ་ཡང་ཧཱི་ལ་སོགས་པའི་སྐད་རྣམས་ནི་རང་བཞིན་གྱི་སྐད་རྣམས་ཉིད་ལས་གྱུར་ཉམས་པར་འདོད་པ་ཙམ་ཡིན་པ་དང་། ཤ་ཟའི་སྐད་ཅེས་པའང་གློས་གར་གྱི་བསྟན་བཅོས་སུ་འབྱུང་སྟེ། ཕཙྪ་པུ་ཏ་ཞེས་པར། ཨརྫ་ཛ་ཀྲུཏ་དང་། ཡ་ཏྲི་པཾ་ཞེས་པར། ཛ་ཨི་ཨེ་ཌཱི་དང་། ཀུ་ལ་པྲ་སྟོ་ཞེས་པར། ཀུ་ལ་པ་པ་ཏུ་ཊོ་ཞེས་པ་ལྟ་བུ་ལེགས་སྦྱར་གྱི་གྱུར་ཤེད་དུ་ཉམས་པ་ཙམ་ཡིན་པས་སྐད་རིགས་དེ་དག་ཐམས་ཅད་ལེགས་སྦྱར་ལས་གྱུར་ཆག་པ་ཉིད་དུ་མཚུངས་པའི་ཕྱིར་ལེགས་སྦྱར་ལས་གཞན་པའི་སྐད་ཐམས་ཅད་གྱུར་ཆག་ཏུ་གསུངས་པ་ཡིན་གྱི། བོད་དང་རྒྱ་ནག་ལྷོ་བུའི་སྐད་རྣམས་ནི་ལེགས་སྦྱར་གྱི་གྱུར་ཆག་པ་མ་ཡིན་པའི་ཕྱིར་གྱུར་ཆག་ཏུ་འཇོག་པའི་རྒྱུ་མཚན་ཅིའང་མེད་དོ།།

འོན་ཀྱང་བོད་དང་རྒྱ་ནག་སོགས་ཀྱི་ཡུལ་དབུས་པའི་སྐད་བསྟན་བཅོས་སུ་གྲགས་པ་རྣམས་ལ་ལྟོས་ནས་མི་སོའི་མཐའ་ཁོབ་པའི་སྐད་སོགས་དེ་ལས་མ་དག་པར་འདོད་པ་རྣམས་ཡུལ་དེ་དང་དེའི་གྱུར་ཆག་གི་སྐད་ཡིན་ནོ་ཞེས་སྨྲ་ན་ནི་འོས་པ་ཙམ་མོ།།

དེས་བོད་སྐད་རྒྱ་གར་གྱི་སྐད་རིགས་བཞིའི་ཁོངས་སུ་ཚུད་པས་སྐད་རིགས་དེ་བཞི་ལས་འདི་ཡིན་ཞེས་ངོས་གཟུང་མི་དགོས་ཀྱང་མཐུན་རྐྱེར་ན་རང་བཞིན་གྱི་སྐད་ཡིན་བྱམ་པས་ཚིག་ཀྲྀ་པྲཱ་ཀྲྀ་ཏ་ཞེས་པ་ཕལ་པ་ལ་འཇུག་པས། རྒྱ་གར་གྱི་ཡུལ་འཁོར་ཆེན་པོར་གྲགས་པའི་ཕལ་སྐད་བཞིན་དུ། བོད་ཡུལ་གྱི་ཕལ་སྐད་དམ་རང་བཞིན་གྱི་སྐད་ཡིན་པའི་ཕྱིར་རོ།།

ཡང་མེད་གི་སྐབས་སུ་བརྡ་སྤྲོ་བའི་ལུགས་ཀྱིད་རྣམ་དབྱེའི་མཐའ་ཅན་ཞེས་བྱུང་ཡང་ཡིག་ནོར་དུ་གོར་མ་ཆག་སྟེ། ཁོང་ཞྭ་ལུའི་མཁས་པ་ཆེན་པོ་ལ་དེ་ཙམ་གྱི་འཁྲུལ་པ་ག་ལ་འབྱུང་། ཞ་ལུའི་གསུང་གི་རྗེས་ཟློས་མཛད་པར་ཟློས་མཁན་ཕྱིས་ཀྱི་འགྲེལ་བྱེད་ཅིག་གིས་ནི་དེ་ཙམ་ལའང་རྟོག་དཔྱོད་མ་ཞུགས་པར་ཚིག་དེ་ཉིད་བསྐུས་ཤིང་མེད་གི་ངེས་ཚིག་ནུ་མའི་སྒྲ་ལས་དྲངས་ཏེ་ལེགས་པར་བཤད་པ་མ་རྟོགས་ནས་གཞན་དུ་དྲངས་པ་དང་། སྒྲ་བར་བྱེད་པའི་དུས་ཅན་གྱི་བདག་ཉིད་ཅེས་པའི་འབྲུ་དོན་མ་གོ་བར་སྒྲ་བར་བྱེད་པའི་འདུས་བྱས་ཀྱི་བདག་ཉིད་ཅེས་འདོན་པ་དང་། ཐ་སྙད་ཀྱི་དོན་ལ་འགལ་བ་མང་པོ་སྤྲོས་པ་སོགས་རྗེས་ཟློས་བྱེད་ཕྱིན་རྗེས་ཟློས་ཤུར་སོད། ལུགས་དེ་ལེགས་པ་ལ་དེའང་ཞེན་པའི་མཁས་ཁྲིད་འདོད་པས་རྗེས་ཟློས་ཀྱང་མ་འཕྱོར་བ་དེར་གདའ་འོ།།

གཉིས་པ་ཞར་བྱུང་ཡི་གེའི་འདུག་ཕྱིའི་དགོས་པ་བཤད་པ་ལ། ཡི་གེའི་འདུག་པ་རྣམས་ཀྱི་རང་བཞིན་གྱི་དགོས་པ་བཤད་པ་དང་། ཡི་གེའི་འདུག་པ་ཇི་ལྟར་སྦྱོར་བའི་ཚུལ་གྱི་བསྟན་བཅོས་འདི་ཉིད་བརྩམས་པའི་དགོས་པ་བཤད་པ་གཉིས། དང་པོ་ལ་དགོས་པ་ཟློག་ཕྱོགས་ནས་བསྟན་པ་དང་། ཉིང་དགོས་ཟློག་ཕྱོགས་ནས་བསྟན་པའོ།།

དང་པོ་ནི།

མོ་ཡི་ཡི་གེ་མེད་པ་ན། ཕོ་ཡིག་བརྗོད་པ་མེད་པར་འགྱུར།
ཕོ་ཡིག་དེ་དག་རྣམས་ལ་ཡང་། འདུག་པར་བཅས་པ་མེད་ན་ནི།
མིང་དང་ཚིག་ཀྱང་གསལ་མི་ནུས། མིང་ཚིག་གསལ་བ་མེད་ན་ནི།
དོན་རྣམས་བརྗོད་པར་མི་འགྱུར་རོ།།

ཞེས་པ་བསྟན་ཏེ། མོ་ཡི་ཡི་གེ་གི་ཀུ་སོགས་ཨ་ཡི་བཞི་པོ་མེད་ན་ཕོ་ཡིག་ཀ་ཡི་རྣམས་ཁོ་ན་བརྗོད་པ་མེད་པར་འགྱུར་ཏེ། ཨ་ཡི་རྣམས་ལ་ལྟོས་པའི་བརྗོད་པ་དེ་ཉིད་མི་རུང་བར་འགྱུར་བའི་ཕྱིར་དང་། ཕོ་ཡིག་ཀ་ཡི་དེ་དག་རྣམས་ལའང་ཨ་ཡི་དང་ལྡན་མི་ལྡན་ཇི་ལྟར་ཡང་འདུག་པར་བཅས་པ་སྟེ་འདུག་པའི་ཡི་གེ་བཅུ་མེད་པར་གྱུར་ན་ནི་དོན་གྱི་ངོ་བོ་སྟོན་པའི་མིང་དང་དོན་གྱི་ཁྱད་པར་སྟོན་པའི་ཚིག་ཀྱང་གསལ་བར་མི་ནུས་ཏེ། ཡི་གེའི་ཁོངས་ནས་མིང་ཕྱུང་སྟེ། ཞེས་སོགས་བཤད་མ་ཐག་པ་ལྟ་བུའི་རྒྱུ་མཚན་གྱི་ཕྱིར་དང་། མིང་དང་ཚིག་གསལ་བར་གྱུར་པ་མེད་ན་ནི་དོན་གྱི་རྣམ་པ་རང་དང་གཞན་ལ་མཚོན་ཞིང་གོ་བར་བྱེད་པའི་བརྗོད་པ་རྣམས་ཀྱང་མེད་པར་འགྱུར་རོ།།

དེས་ན་ཨ་ཡི་རྣམས་ནི་ཀ་ཡིའི་ཡི་གེ་རྣམས་ཀྱི་བརྗོད་པའི་ཡན་ལག་ཡོངས་སུ་རྫོགས་པའི་ཕྱིར་དང་། འདུག་པའི་ཡི་གེ་རྣམས་ནི་མིང་ཚིག་གསལ་བར་བྱ་བའི་ཕྱིར་དང་། ཡི་གེའི་འདུག་པ་མཐའ་དག་དང་ལྡན་པའི་མིང་ཚིག་རྣམས་ནི་དོན་ཇི་སྙེད་པ་དག་མཚོན་ཅིང་བརྗོད་པའི་ཕྱིར་འདུག་པར་མཁས་པ་རྣམས་ལ་རབ་ཏུ་གྲགས་ཤིང་གྲུབ་པའང་ཡིན་པས་ཡི་གེ་དང་ཡི་གེའི་ཚོགས་དང་སྦྱོར་བ་དེ་རྣམས་ནི་རང་གི་ངང་གིས་དོན་ནམ་དགོས་པ་དང་པ་དང་བཅས་པ་ཡིན་ནོ་ཞེས་པའོ།།

འདིར་འགྲེལ་བྱེད་ཁ་ཅིག་གིས་མོ་ཡིག་ཅེས་པ་མིང་གཞི་ལ་ཕོ་མོ་མ་ནིང་གསུམ་དུ་དབྱེ་བའི་མོ་ཡིག་རྣམས་ལ་ངོས་བཟུང་ནས་དེ་ནས་ཕྱུང་བའི་འདུག་པའི་གི་རྣམས་མེད་ན་མིང་གཞིའི་ནང་ཚན་ཕོ་ཡིག་རྣམས་ཀྱི་བརྗོད་པ་དོན་མེད་པར་འགྱུར་ཞེས་བཀྲལ་སོང་། ཤིན་ཏུ་མི་འཐད་དེ་ཕྱིར་མོ་ཡིག་རྣམས་ཞེས་ཟེར་ཡང་ཡང་ཏིག་འདུག་པའི་ཡི་གེ་བཅུར་དམིགས་རྩེ་གཏད་པས་དེ་དག་མེད་ན། ཕོ་ཡིག་ཀ་ཙ་ཏ་པ་ཙ་ཞླ་པོའི་བརྗོད་པ་དོན་མེད་པར་འགྱུར་ཞེས་འདུག་པའི་ཡི་གེ་རྣམས་མེད་པའི་ཉེས་པ་དེ་འདུག་ཡུལ་གྱི་ཡི་གེ་ཐམས་ཅད་དང་སྦྱར་རིགས་པ་ལ་ཕོ་ཡིག་ཉི་ཚེ་བ་དེ་རྣམས་ཁོ་ན་དང་སྦྱར་བ་ལ་དམིགས་བསལ་གྱི་དགོས་པ་ཅིའང་མེད་པའི་ཕྱིར་དང་། མོ་ཡིག་འདུག་པ་བཅུར་ཁས་བླངས་ནས་ཕོ་ཡིག་ཀ་ཡི་ཐམས་ཅད་ལ་འདོད་ནའང་མི་རུང་སྟེ་འཆད་འགྱུར་ལྟར། འདུག་པར་བཅས་པ་མེད་ན་ནི། མིང་དང་ཚིག་ཀྱང་གསལ་མི་ནུས། ཞེས་པ་དང་ཟློས་པར་འགྱུར་བའི་ཕྱིར་རོ།། འདི་ལྟར་འཆད་མཁན་ཕྱི་མ་ཞིག་གིས་ཞ་ལུ་བའི་གསུང་རྒྱབ་སྐྱོར་དུ་དྲངས་སོང་ཀྱི། ཞ་ལུ་བས་ནི་འདིར་བསྟན་གྱི་ཕོ་མོ་མ་ནིང་གང་ཡིན་ངོས་བཟུང་བ་མི་འདུག

ཀྱང་ཁོ་རང་གིས་ཤཱ་ལོ་ཀ་ཏྲ་ཡིའི་འགྲེལ་པའི་མཚམས་མ་ཕྱེད་པས་ནོངས་པར་སྣང་བ། རྒྱས་འགྲེལ་དེ་ཙམ་གྱི་ཐུགས་ཁུར་བཞེས་པ་ལ་ཁུངས་སུ་མཛད་རྒྱུའི་ཕྱག་དཔེ་དེར་ཐུགས་རྟོག ཞིབ་མོ་ཙམ་ཡང་མི་མཛད་པ་ནི་ཡ་མཚན་པའི་གནས་སོ།།

འགྲེལ་བྱེད་འདིས་མོ་ཡིག་འདིར་བསྟན་གྱི་ཨ་ཝི་བཞི་པ་ངོས་འཛིན་མཁན་ཚོར་དགག་པ་མང་དུ་མཛད་མོད།། ཕྱོགས་སྔ་དེ་རྣམས་ཀྱིས་དབྱངས་ཡིག་སྔོག་ཐུགས་ཀྱི་ཐ་སྙད་བོད་ཡིག་ལ་སྦྱར་བ་ཡོད་ན་ནི་སྐྱོན་དེ་དག་འགྲོ་བར་སྣང་ཡང་ཕལ་ཆེར་གྱིས་ཨ་ཝི་ཞེས་པ་གི་གུ་སོགས་ལ་བསམས་པ་འདྲ་བས། དེ་ལྟ་ན་ཕྱོགས་སྔའི་ནམ་མ་ལངས་པར་དགག་བཞག་གི་ཉི་མ་ཤར་ཟེར་བ་དེ་བྱུང་སྣང་ངོ་།།

གཉིས་པ་ཉེར་དགོས་ལྡོག་ཕྱོགས་ནས་བསྟན་པ་ནི།

དེ་ལྟར་གྱུར་ན་འཇིག་རྟེན་དུ། །དོན་མཚོན་བརྗོད་པ་ཀུན་ཀྱང་མེད། །
རིག་བྱེད་སྨྲ་བའང་ཡོད་མི་འགྱུར། །ཉན་ཐོས་རང་རྒྱལ་སངས་རྒྱས་ཀྱི། །
བསྟན་པ་རྣམས་ཀྱང་མེད་པར་འགྱུར། །

ཞེས་པས་བསྟན་ཏེ། དེ་ལྟར་མིང་ཚིག་བརྗོད་པ་ཐམས་ཅད་མེད་པར་གྱུར་ན་འཇིག་རྟེན་འདིར་དོན་མཚོན་པར་བྱེད་པའི་བརྗོད་པ་སྒྲ་ཡུང་དུ་སྟོན་པའི་སྨྲ་སྐད་ཐམས་ཅད་མི་འབྱུང་བས། དེ་ལ་བལྟོས་པའི་འཇིག་རྟེན་པ་དང་ཐུན་མོང་བའི་བཟོ་གནས་རྩིས་དང་སྨན་དཔྱད་སོགས་རིག་བྱེད་སྨྲ་བ་རྣམས་ཀྱང་ཡོད་པར་མི་འགྱུར་ཞིང་། འཇིག་རྟེན་ལས་འདས་པར་འདུག་པའི་ཤེས་བྱ་ཐུན་མོང་མིན་པ་ཉན་ཐོས་དང་རང་སངས་རྒྱས་དང་རྫོགས་པའི་སངས་རྒྱས་ཀྱི་བསྟན་པ་རྣམས་སྟོན་ཞིང་སྨྲ་བའང་མེད་པར་འགྱུར་བ་དེའི་ཕྱིར། མིང་ཚིག་བརྗོད་པ་ཐམས་ཅད་ལེགས་པར་སྦྱར་བ། འཇིག་རྟེན་དུ་ཡོད་པའི་རང་བཞིན་གྱི་དགོས་པ་ནི་འཇིག་རྟེན་དང་འཇིག་རྟེན་ལས་འདས་པའི་ཤེས་བྱ་དང་བསྒྲུབ་བྱ་མཐའ་དག་ཅི་རིགས་པར་སྟོན་ཅིང་སྨྲ་བ་འབྱུང་བ་དང་། དེ་དག་ལ་ཞུགས་ཤིང་བླང་དོར་ཕྱིན་ཅི་མ་ལོག་པར་བྱས་པ་ལ་བརྟེན་ནས་འདི་དང་གཞན་གྱི་བདེ་བ་དམ་པ་ཕུན་སུམ་ཚོགས་པར་འབྱུང་བ་རྣམས་ཡིན་ནོ། ཞེས་པའི་དོན་ཏོ།།

འདིར་རིག་བྱེད་ཅེས་པ་མཆོད་སྦྱིན་སོགས་རིག་བྱེད་བཞི་པོ་ཁོ་ན་ལ་འདོད་པ་ནི་ཁྱབ་ཆུང་བས་མི་ལེགས་ཏེ། བོད་བཟའ་སོར་བཞག་གིས་ཐུན་མོང་བའི་ཤེས་བྱ་རིག་གནས་ཐམས་ཅད་ལའང་རིག་བྱེད་ཅེས་པའི་སྒྲ་འཇུག་པའི་ཕྱིར་རོ།། ཡང་ན།། མོ་ཡི་ཡི་གེ་མེད་ན་ནི། སོགས་ནས། བསྟན་པ་རྣམས་ཀྱང་མེད་པར་འགྱུར། ཞེས་པའི་བར་གྱི་གཞུང་འདིས་གོང་སློས་ལྟར་རྗེས་འཇུག་ཁོ་ནར་མ་ཟད་ཡི་གེའི་འཇུག་པ་སྤྱིའི་དགོས་པ་བསྟན་པ་ཡིན་མོད་ཀྱི།

ཡི་གེའང་བོད་ཡུལ་ཁོ་ནའི་དབང་དུ་མ་བྱས་པར་སྤྱི་ཁྱབ་ལ་སྦྱར་དུ་རུང་བའི་དབྱངས་སམ་ང་རོ་ཙམ་ལ་མོ་ཡིག་དང་། གསལ་བྱེད་དམ་ང་རོས་འདྲེན་པའི་ཡི་གེའི་རྣམས་ཆ་ཐ་དད་པ་རྣམས་ལ་ཕོ་ཡིག་དང་ཡི་གེ་དེ་རྣམས་དོན་མཚོན་པའི་བརྗོད་པ་ལ་ཇི་ལྟར་འཇུག་པ་དེ་ལྟར་སྦྱོར་བ་ལ་འཇུག་པར་བཅས་པ་ཞེས་དགོངས་པའི་དབང་དུ་བྱས་ནས། ཚིག་དོན་ལྷག་མ་རྣམས་དང་སྦྲེལ་ཏེ་བཤད་ནའང་དཔྱོད་ལྡན་དག་གི་བློ་ལ་འཐེབས་པར་འགྱུར་རོ།།

གཉིས་པ་ཡི་གེའི་འཇུག་པ་སྟོན་པའི་བསྟན་བཅོས་འདིའི་དགོས་པ་བསྟན་པ་ལ་དངོས་དང་། དགོས་པ་དེ་འགྲུབ་པར་སྟོན་པའོ།།

དང་པོ་ནི།

ཇི་ལྟར་འཇིག་རྟེན་སེམས་ཅན་རྣམས། །ཕུང་པོ་ཁམས་དང་སྐྱེ་མཆེད་དང་། །
གྲུབ་མཐའ་གཞན་ཡང་ཡོད་ན་ཡང་། །རང་ཉིད་ཀྱིས་ནི་མི་ཤེས་བཞིན། །
དེ་བཞིན་ཡི་གེའི་འཇུག་ཚུལ་རྣམས། །སྨྲ་བ་ཀུན་ལ་གནས་གྱུར་ཀྱང་། །

རང་རྒྱལ་དེ་ཉིད་མི་ཤེས་པས། །དོན་ལ་སྦྱོར་བ་ག་ལ་ཤེས།
དེ་ཕྱིར་སྨྲ་བའི་དབང་ཕྱུག་གི། །རྗེས་ཟླས།

ཞེས་གསུང་ཏེ། ཇི་ལྟར་ན་འཇིག་རྟེན་གྱི་སེམས་ཅན་རྣམས་ལ། གཟུགས་ཕུང་ལ་སོགས་པའི་ཕུང་པོ་དང་། མིག་གི་ཁམས་ལ་སོགས་པའི་ཁམས་དང་། མིག་གི་སྐྱེ་མཆེད་ལ་སོགས་པའི་སྐྱེ་མཆེད་རྣམས་རང་རང་ལ་ཡོད་པར་མ་ཟད། ཐུབ་པའི་ཐབས་བཞག་པ་གཞན་ཡང་གྲངས་ཅན་པའི་དེ་ཉིད་ཉེར་ལྔ་དང་། ནང་པའི་ཐེག་ཆེན་ལུགས་རྣམ་ཤེས་ཚོགས་བརྒྱད་སོགས་གཞན་དང་གཞན་ཡང་ཡོད་ཅིང་། ཐོག་མ་མེད་པའི་དུས་ནས་ལྷན་ཅིག་ཏུ་འགྲོགས་པ་ཡིན་ཡང་ཐོག་མ་ནས་དེ་ལྟ་བུའི་རྣམ་བཞག་རང་ཉིད་ཀྱིས་ཤེས་པ་མེད་པ་དེ་བཞིན་དུ། རང་རང་གི་ཡི་གེ་རྣམས་ཇི་ལྟར་འདུག་པའི་ཚུལ་ཡང་ཡུལ་སོ་སོའི་ལུང་སྟོན་པའི་སྒྲ་སྐད་ཀྱི་སྒྲ་བ་ཐམས་ཅད་ལ་རང་བཞིན་གྱིས་གནས་པ་སྔོ་ཚོད་པ་མི་སྲིད་ཀྱང་གཞན་གྱིས་བརྡ་སྤྲོད་པ་ལ་སོགས་པའི་རྐྱེན་མེད་པར་ཐོག་མ་ནས་ཡི་གེ་རྣམས་མིང་ཚིག་སོགས་ལ་ཇི་ལྟར་འདུག་པའི་རང་རྒྱུ་དེ་ཉིད་ཀྱང་མི་ཤེས་ན་མིང་ཚིག་ལ་སོགས་པ་དེ་རྣམས་ཀྱི་བྱ་བྱེ་ནས་དོན་ལ་ཇི་ལྟ་བར་སྦྱོར་བའི་ཚུལ་ག་ལ་ཤེས་ཏེ་མི་ཤེས་སོ།།

དེ་བས་ན། བུ་ཡི་བདག་གིས་གངས་ཅན་པ་རྣམས་ལ་རབ་ཏུ་བརྩེ་བའི་བློས་འདི་དང་གཏན་གྱི་བདེ་བ་སྒྲུབ་པའི་ཐབས། ཐུན་མོང་དང་ཐུན་མོང་མིན་པའི་རིག་བྱེད་དང་བསྟན་བཅོས་དང་བསླབ་པ་གསུམ་དང་ཐོས་བསམ་སྒོམ་གསུམ་སོགས་ལེགས་པར་སློབ་ཅིང་ཞེས་སུ་དུང་བ་བཏུབ་ཇི་ལྟར་སྦྱོར་བའི་ཚུལ། ཡི་གེ་དང་མིང་དང་ཚིག་གི་འདུག་པ་རྣམས་ཚུལ་བཞིན་དུ་རྟོགས་པ་ལ་རག་ལུས་པར་མཐོང་ནས་དགོས་པ་ཁྱད་པར་ཅན་དེ་ལྟ་བུའི་ཆེད་དུ་ཡུལ་འདི་ཉིད་ཀྱི་སྐད་དང་རྗེས་སུ་འཚམས་པའི་ཡི་གེའི་འདུག་པ་གསལ་བར་བྱེད་པའི་བསྟན་བཅོས་འདི་འཕགས་ཡུལ་ལ་སོགས་པའི་སྨྲ་བའི་དབང་ཕྱུག་མཁས་པ་རྣམས་ཀྱི་བརྡ་སྤྲོད་པའི་བསྟན་བཅོས་འཆད་པའི་ཚུལ་གྱི་རྗེས་སུ་འབྲང་ནས་སྨྲས་པ་ཡིན་ནོ་ཞེས་སོ།།

གཉིས་པ་ནི།

འདི་ཀུན་རྟོགས་ཀྱུར་ཅིག།

ཅེས་པ་སྟེ། དེ་ལྟར་ཡི་གེའི་འདུག་པ་ལེགས་པར་སྤྲུར་བའི་ཚུལ་འདི་གངས་ཅན་གྱི་སྐྱེ་བོ་ཀུན་གྱིས་རྟོགས་ནས་མིང་ཚིག་བརྗོད་པ་ཐམས་ཅད་ལ་རྨོངས་པ་མེད་པར་སྨྲ་བའི་དབང་ཕྱུག་ཆེན་པོར་གྱུར་ཅིག། ཅེས་པ་སྟེ། ཞར་ལ་རྫར་སློས་པའི་ཉིང་དགོས་དེ་རྣམས་ཀྱང་འགྲུབ་པའི་སྨོན་ལམ་མཛད་པ་ཡིན་ནོ།།

དེ་ལྟར་རྟགས་ཀྱི་འཇུག་པའི་གཞུང་གི་ཚིག་དོན་གྱི་ཆ་རྣམས་ཇི་ལྟར་དཔོག་པ་རི་ཞིག་བཤད་ཟིན་ཏོ།།

འདིར་སྨྲས་པ།

གང་དག་ཐར་མཆོག་བདེ་ཆེན་དབྱིག་ཐོབ་ཕྱིར། །ངེས་དོན་སྙིང་པོའི་རྒྱ་མཚོར་འཇུག་འདོད་ན། །མིང་ཚིག་བརྗོད་གཞི་ཡི་གེའི་སྦྱོར་བའི་གྲུ། །

བློ་ལྡན་དེད་དཔོན་ཚོགས་ཀྱིས་བརྟེན་བྱ་ཡིན། །གྲགས་པའི་གཏེར་གྱུར་ཡོན་ཏན་བྱེ་བའི་མཛོད། །མཁས་པའི་ཁང་བཟང་རྩེ་མོར་འཛེག་འདོད་ན། །

བདེའ་དང་ཐ་སྙད་རྣམ་པར་སྦྱོར་བ་ཡི། །འཛེག་སྐས་འདི་ལ་མི་བརྟེན་ཐབས་གཞན་ཅི། །ལྷ་དང་མི་མཆོག་རྣམས་ཀྱི་དཔལ་གང་ཡིན། །

དཔག་ངམས་ཟླ་བ་བདུད་རྩི་ཡི་རྗེས་འགྲོ་བ། །དེ་དག་ལེགས་བྱས་རྒྱ་གཏེར་ལས་འབྱུང་མོད། །དེ་ཡང་རིགས་ལམ་རི་དབང་འདིར་རྟོས་སོ། །

དེང་དུས་ཆེར་སྙེམས་སྨྲ་བརྩོལ་ཅན་འགའ་ཞིག། །ཡིག་རྡེབ་ཙམ་ལའང་བློ་མིག་ལྡོང་བཞིན་དུ། །འཆད་ཉན་བྱིས་པའི་བློས་གར་སྐྱུར་བ་ལ། །

མཁས་རློམ་དེ་དག་གི་ནར་མ་གྱུར་ཏམ། །བརྡ་སྤྲོད་ཤེས་པས་དོན་ལ་མི་རྨོངས་དང་། །ཐ་སྙད་ལ་བརྟེན་དོན་ལ་རྟོགས་པ་དང་། །

རྟོགས་པའི་བསྟན་པ་ལུང་ལ་རག་ལུས་ནས། །རིགས་པར་སྨྲ་བའི་བྲག་ཙ་ཟློ་བཞིན་དུ། །གཙུག་ལག་དང་འགལ་ལུང་དོན་འཆད་རློམས་དང་། །

ལུང་དང་འགལ་བའི་སྒོམ་སྒྲུབ་བྱེད་པ་རྣམས། །བསམས་ཀྱི་ཕོང་ནས་གད་མོ་འཆོར་ན་ཡང་། །སྙིགས་མའི་རང་མདངས་བཙོས་སུ་ཅི་ཞིག་ཡོད། །

དེ་ཕྱིར་རྣམ་བཤད་སུ་ཏིག་ཕྲེང་མཛེས་འདི་འདང་། །མཁས་མཆོག་བུ་ཡིད་དགོངས་པ་གསལ་བྱེད་པའི། །རྒྱན་དུ་སྤྲ་འགྲེལ་གཞན་གྱིས་བསྒྲུན་མིན་པར། །

གྲུབ་པ་གཟུར་གནས་རྣམས་ཀྱིས་མཁྱེན་འགྱུར་མོད། ཕལ་ཆེར་བླུན་པོས་དོན་དུ་མི་གཉེར་ཞིང་། བློ་ལྡན་འགའ་ཡང་ཕྱོགས་ཞེན་རྫུང་རྫུག་ཏུ་ཞུད།
དེ་འདྲས་གཞན་ལ་ཕན་པར་མི་འགྱུར་ཡང་། རང་ཉིད་ལྷག་བསམ་དཀར་བའི་རྒྱུན་བྱེད་དོ། འདི་ན་མཁས་པ་དག་གིས་རྣམ་བཤད་པར།
རིགས་དང་མི་རིགས་ཅུང་ཟད་དཔྱད་པ་ཡང་། སྡང་དང་ཕྲག་དོག་དབང་གིས་མ་ལགས་ཏེ། བློ་ལྡན་རྣམས་ཀྱི་བློ་གྲོས་འཕེལ་སླད་དུའོ།
དེ་ཕྱིར་ཇི་ལྟར་དཔྱོད་པའི་ཚུལ་འདི་ལས། བརྩམས་ཏེ་གཟུ་བོར་གནས་པའི་མཁས་རྣམས་ཀྱིས། རིགས་པའི་སྣང་བྱེད་འབུམ་ཕྲག་སྤྲར་སྤྲོས་ནས།
མཁན་པོའི་དགོངས་དོན་ཡིད་མ་འཁྲིད་པར་མཛོད། གང་འདིར་བདག་བློ་དམན་པའི་དབང་གྱུར་པས། མ་བཤད་པ་དང་ལོག་པར་བཤད་པ་སོགས།
མཁྱེན་ལྡན་ཡངས་པ་རྣམས་ཀྱིས་བཟོད་མཛོད་ལ། ཉོངས་པའི་དྲི་མ་རྣམ་པར་སྦྱང་དུ་གསོལ། གཞན་གྱིས་ལན་མོ་ཤེན་པར་རང་སྟོབས་ཀྱིས།
ལེགས་པར་བཤད་པ་པུཎྜ་རཱི་ཀའི་ཕྲེང་། འགའ་ཞིག་བརྟག་པར་རྩོམ་པའང་མཁས་རྣམས་ཀྱི། མགུལ་དང་སྙན་གྱི་རྒྱན་དུ་མཛེས་གྱུར་ཅིག།

ཅེས་སུམ་ཅུ་པ་དང་རྟགས་ཀྱི་འཇུག་པའི་གཞུང་གི་རྒྱས་འགྲེལ་མཁས་པའི་མགུལ་རྒྱན་མུ་ཏིག་ཕྲེང་མཛེས་འདི་ནི་དོན་གཉེར་དུ་མས་སྔོན་དུ་ཡང་ཡང་བསྐུལ་བ་ལ་བརྟེན་ནས་ཡོམ་བུ་པ་གཙུག་ལག་ཆོས་ཀྱི་སྣང་བ་ཞེས་བྱ་བས་རང་ལོ་སུམ་ཅུ་པ་ལ་གཞུང་ཕྲ་མའི་འགྲེལ་པ་བརྩམས་པ་ལ་གཡེང་བའི་རྐྱེན་དུ་མས་འཕྱོར་ལུས་ཤིང་། སླར་རང་ལོ་སུམ་ཅུ་རྩ་བདུན་དུ་རན་པའི་མེ་འབྲུག་ལོར། གྲུབ་པའི་རིགས་སུ་འཁྲུངས་ཤིང་གཙུག་ལག་མང་པོར་གཟིགས་པའི་སྨྲ་རས་པད་མའི་འདབ་མ་ལྟར་ཡངས་པ་གདངས་ཅན་གྱི་སའི་དབང་ཕྱུག་དམ་པའི་བཀའི་འདུན་ན་འདོན་ཆེན་པོའི་ཆེན་པོར་གྱུར་པ་ཞབས་དྲུང་མདོ་མཁར་པ་ཚེ་རིང་དབང་རྒྱལ་གྱི་ཞལ་སྔ་ནས་མེ་ཏོག་དང་བཅས་ཏེ་དངོས་སུ་སྐུལ་བར་མཛད་པ་དང་། སླར་ཡང་བཀའ་དྲིན་གྱི་སྒོ་ནས་ཡང་ཡང་སྐུལ་བར་མཛད་པས་བཀའ་བཞིན་བགྱིད་པར་ཡིད་ལ་བཅགས་ཀྱང་སྐབས་འགར་བསྙེན་སྒྲུབ་སོགས་ཆོས་ལྡན་གྱི་བྱ་བ་དང་ཕལ་ཆེར་བཟློག་ཏུ་མེད་པའི་གཞན་དབང་གི་འཁོལ་བ་ཉིད་དུ་འཕྱུན་པའི་རྣམ་པར་གཡེང་བ་བར་མེད་དུ་གཉེར་བས་པས་རེ་ཞིག་འགྱངས་ཡང་། རང་ལོ་བཞི་བཅུ་རྩ་ལྔ་པར་སོན་པ་རབ་བྱུང་བཅུ་གཉིས་པ་ཤིག་དམར་ཤིང་མོ་བྱི་བའི་ལོར་སྔར་བརྩམས་ཟིན་པ་རྣམས་ལ་དག་ཞེར་དང་། སྒྲ་མའི་འཕྲོས་དང་རྟགས་འཇུག་གི་འགྲེལ་པ་བཅས་སྐྲ་ཟླའི་དབང་ཕྱུག་ཟླ་བ་སྨྲ་ཉིན་གྱི་འགྲུབ་སྦྱོར་དང་ལྡན་པའི་རྒྱལ་བའི་ཆོས་ཀྱི་ནམ་ཡངས་འཁྲུལ་མེད་བདུད་རྩི་ཐུབ་མཚམས་དང་ལྡན་པའི་དུས་དགེ་བར་སྒྲུབ་བསྟན་ཆོས་འཁོར་གྱི་གཙུག་ལག་ཁང་དུ་ཡོངས་སུ་གྲུབ་པ་འདིའི་དགེ་བས་བདེ་བར་གཤེགས་པའི་བསྟན་པ་རིན་པོ་ཆེ་ཕྱོགས་དུས་གནས་སྐབས་ཐམས་ཅད་དུ་དར་ཞིང་རྒྱས་ལ་ཡུན་རིང་དུ་གནས་པ་དང་། ལུས་ཅན་མཐའ་དག་སྨྲ་བའི་དབང་ཕྱུག་ཐམས་ཅད་མཁྱེན་པའི་གོ་འཕང་ཐོབ་པར་གྱུར་ཅིག། སརྦ་མངྒ་ལཾ། ཕུན་ཚོགས་ལེགས་བྱས་རྒྱ་མཚོས་མི་ངོམས་ཤིང་།། སྔོན་མེད་ལེགས་བཤད་དགེ་མཚན་འབུམ་འཛིན་པའི།། ངོ་མཚར་བདེ་དགའ་སྣང་བས་གདངས་སྤྲོས་ཀྱི།། བསྟན་འགྲོའི་དཔལ་འཛིན་བུ་མོ་ལོ་ཚུར་བཏེགས།། གང་གི་ཕྲིན་ལས་ཟབ་བསྐྱེད་གཉའ་ཆེར།། ཉེར་གནས་རྣམ་དཔྱོད་དེད་དཔོན་གྱི་དབང་གིས།། དཀར་གཙང་ཆོས་ཀྱི་བུའི་སྐྱེས་བཟང་ཕྱིལ་བ་འདི།། མཁས་ཀུན་སྙན་དང་མགུལ་བར་མཛེས་གྱུར་ཅིག།

སརྦ་ཀཱ་ལེ་ཤྲི་ཡོ་བྷ་བ་ཏུ།། ༎

D. B. Press 502—1,000—17-7-1912.

INDEX OF GRAMMATICAL TERMS.

Page.

BOOK III.

ON SPELLING.

DAG-JE SAL-WAI MELONG

དག་བྱེད་གསལ་བའི་མེ་ལོང་། Pages 1—27.

MIRROR OF CLEAR (CORRECT) SPELLING.

IN this work, the different methods of spelling have been clearly illustrated, almost all the root-words with their meanings being metrically arranged according to the rules of spelling, which are peculiar to the Tibetan language. Words of similar sound, conveying different significations, have been explained and, where necessary, they are differentiated, by elucidation in the manner of their spelling.

Contents.

བོད་ཀྱི་བརྡའི་ཡི་ཕྲག་སོ་སོར་ཕྱེ་བ

དག་ཡིག་གསལ་བའི་མེ་ལོང་།

༄༅། ན་མོ་གུ་རུ་མཉྫུ་ནེ་ཨིནྡྲ་ཡ།།

ངག་གི་དབང་ཕྱུག་རྗེ་བཙུན་འཇམ་དབྱངས་དང་། སྒྲ་དབྱངས་ལྷ་མོ་དབྱངས་ཅན་མ་ལ་འདུད།
བསྟན་པའི་ཆ་རྐྱེན་ཡི་གེའི་དག་ཡིག་གཞུང་། བློ་ལྡན་གཞོན་ནུ་དོན་གཉེར་ཅན་རྣམས་ལ།
ཕན་ཕྱིར་མཁས་པའི་ལེགས་བཤད་ལས་བཏུས་ནས། མདོ་ཙམ་བཀོད་ལ་བདག་བློ་རྒྱས་པར་མཛོད།།

གསུང་རབ་བརྡ་ལ་མ་སྦྱངས་ན།

རྗོད་བྱེད་ཚིག་གི་སྒྲ་འདྲ་ཡང་། བརྗོད་བྱ་དོན་ལ་ཁྱད་པར་ཡོད།། དེ་ཕྱིར་ཡི་གེའི་དག་ཡིག་དགོས།།
དེ་ཡང་ཀ་སོགས་གསལ་བྱེད་ལ། དབྱངས་ཨ་ཨི་ཨུ་ཨེ་ཨོ་དང་། ཡ་ར་ལ་ཝའི་སྔོན་འཇུག་རྣམས།
གང་དུ་ཡོད་ཀྱང་འཕུལ་དང་མགོ། མེད་ན་ཐམས་ཅད་རྐྱང་པ་ཡིན། རྗེས་འཇུག་ག་ད་བ་མ་འ།
ཡོད་པ་ཐམས་ཅད་འཕུལ་ཅན་ཡིན། ཐོད་དུ་ར་ལ་ས་གསུམ་པོ། ཡོད་པ་ཐམས་ཅད་མགོ་ཅན་ཡིན།
དེ་དག་ངེས་པར་ཤེས་པ་ལ། རྐྱང་པ་འཕུལ་ཅན་མགོ་ཅན་གསུམ། ཀ་ནས་རིམ་བཞིན་སྦྱོར་བར་བྱ།

I

ཐོག་མར་ཀའི་བརྡ་བཤད་པ་ལ།

དང་པོ་རྐྱང་པ་འདི་ལྟ་སྟེ།

ཀ་བ་ཀ་ཙ་ཀ་ར་དང་། ཀ་མ་ལ་དང་ཀ་པྲ་ལ། *ཀ་ཙ་ཀ་ཏན་ཀ་ཤིག་ཀ། ཀོ་ཙུ་ཤིག་ཀ་ཀེ་ལ་ཤ།
ཙེ་ཤིང་ཀ་ཤ་ཀུ་ཤ་དང་། †ཀ་ཙུ་ཀུན་རྡོང་མང་ཚིག་ཀུན། ཀ་ལ་པིངྐ་ཀླིང་ཀླིང་ཀ།
ཙི་ཙུ་ཚིག་ཀ་ཀུར་ཀུར་སློག། ཀེ་རེ་ལངས་དང་ཀུ་ཅོ་འདོན། ‡ཀྱལ་ཀ་བློན་ཀ་ཀུ་རེ་བྱེད།
འཐབ་ཀྲོལ་ཕྱུང་ཀྲོལ་ཀྲག་ཀྲོག་སྒྲ། སྔང་མིན་ཀྱོག་པོ་ཀྲབ་ཀྲབ་འཕྲབ། ཀོང་པོ་ཡི་ཀོང་ཙ་འདི་ཀོ་དང་།
སྟོད་ཀོར་ཕྲད་ཀོར་ཕྲད་ཀྱི་དོན། འབྲས་བུ་ཀུ་ཤུ་ཀུར་ཀུམ་དང་།

---

* ཀ་ཊ=ནོར་སྦྱིའི་མིང་། † ཀ་ཙུ=སློག་པའི་བྱེ་བྲག ‡ ཀྱལ་ཀ=ཀུ་རེའི་མིང་།

+ ལན་ཀན་ཝན་ཤོར་ཉེན་ཤོར་འཁོར། རུས་ཀྲང་སྐྱལ་ཀྲུང་ཀྲང་ཊེ་སྟོད། མར་མེའི་ཤོང་བུ་ཨུགས་ཀྱུ་དང་།
ཞབས་ཀྱུ་གེང་རུས་ཀླད་པ་ཟ། ཤ་བ་ཨྰམ་ཁྱི་ཀྲད་པ་ཡིན། ནགས་ཀླུང་ཆུ་ཀླུང་ཐ་ཀློང་དང་།
† ཀླུ་དང་ཀླ་ཀློ་ཀླག་ཅོར་ཆེ། ཡི་གེ་ཀླག་དང་གོས་ཀྱིས་ཀླུབས། ‡ ཀྲིག་ཀྲིག་ཀློང་ཡངས་ཀློང་དུ་གྱུར། §
ཀྱེ་ཧོ་ཀྭ་ཡེ་འོད་པའི་ཚིག། འབྲུམས་ཀླས་མཐས་ཀླས་རྡོ་ཀར་ཅན། ‖ ཀྱོང་མོ་ཡུངས་ཀར་ཐལ་ཀར་མདོག།
ཐུགས་ཀ་ལ་སོགས་ཀ་ཀྱང་ཡིན།།

དས་འཕྲུལ་ཀ་ཡིག།

གཉིས་པ་འཕྲུལ་ཅན་འདི་ལྟ་སྟེ།

ཞྭ་ཡིག་དཀར་ཆག་དཀོར་ན་ཉོར། དཀར་ཡོལ་ཆག་དཀྲུམ་ཁ་མདོག་དཀར། མི་ནུས་དཀའ་དང་མི་ཉིད་དཀོན།
དཀྲང་བསྐྱེད་དཀྱིལ་འཁོར་དབུས་ཀྱི་དཀྱིལ། སྨྲུན་དཀྲུས་རིང་དང་དཀྲུས་མ་དང་། རྒྱུག་སར་རྒྱུགས་པའི་དཀྱུ་སར་དཀྲུས།
ཕན་རྩན་དཀྲུགས་དང་ཁྲག་ཁྲུག་དཀྲུགས། * དཀོས་ཐག་ཀུན་དཀྲགས་ཉོན་མོངས་མེད་། གོས་ཀྱིས་དཀྲིས་དང་འཁྲིགས་པའི་དཀྲགས།
ཉེ་སོགས་དཀྲོགས་དང་རོལ་མོ་དཀྲོལ། སྣ་ཟུར་དཀྲུ་དང་རི་གཟར་དཀན། ཁོང་ཡངས་པ་ཡི་དཀྱུལ་ཆེ་སོགས།
ད་ཡིས་འཕྲུལ་བའི་ཀ་ཡིག་ཡིན།།

བས་འཕྲུལ་ཀ་ཡིག།

ཉམ་བཀྲ་བཀྲ་ཤིས་བཀྲག་མདངས་དང་། ཆལ་མར་བཀྲམ་དང་དྲི་མ་བཀྲུས། བལ་བཀལ་ཁྲལ་བཀལ་ཁལ་སོགས་བཀལ།
རྒྱལ་བའི་བཀའ་དང་ཁྲལ་སོགས་བཀྲལ། ཡོགས་སུ་བཀར་དང་གོང་དུ་བཀུར། སྣོད་བཀང་གཞུ་བཀང་ཐུགས་དམ་བཀང་།
བཤད་པའི་བཀུམ་དང་བཀྲོངས་པ་དང་། བཙེམས་པའི་བཀྱིགས་དང་ཚ་བ་བཀོག། བདེ་ལ་བཀོད་དང་དཔེ་སོགས་བཀོད།
བཀུར་སྟི་ཞུས་དང་འོད་སོགས་བཀྱེ། ཉོར་མེད་བཀྲིན་དང་རྐྱེགས་པའི་བཀྲིས། ཟུར་དུ་བཀོལ་དང་ཟླན་དུ་བཀོལ།
མཉན་དུ་བཀུག་དང་ཉམ་ཉུར་བཀས། ༔ གཉང་བཀག་སྐན་བཀུ་བཀུམ་ཏེ་བོར། བཀའ་དྲིན་བཀའ་བཀྱོན་བཀྱུད་བཀག་གཉང་།།
ལུས་སོགས་བཀད་དང་གོས་སོགས་བཀབ། ལམ་སོགས་བཀག་དང་ཤ་གོང་བཀོང་། འཁྲིད་པའི་བཀྲ་དང་བཙེམས་པ་བཀྲལ།

+ ལན་ཀན་=བུ་ཤུ། † ཀླག་ཅོར་=ཀུ་ཅོ་ཆེ། ‡ ཀྲིག་ཀྲིག་=ནར་ནར། § ཀློང་དུ་གྱུར་=དབང་དུ་གྱུར། ‖ རྡོ་ཀར་ཅན་=སོར་ཅོག་ཅན།
* དཀོས་ཐག་=ཉམས་ཐག་པའི་མིང་། ༔ བཀུམ་ཏེ་བོར་=ཁྲུར་འདོན་པ་སྒྲོན་པའི་མིང་།

ངག་བཀྱལ་མདོ་སྡེ་བསྒྲགས་པ་སོགས། བ་ཡིས་འཛུལ་བའི་ཀ་ཡིག་ཡིན།

གསུམ་པ་མགོ་ཅན་འདི་ལྟ་སྟེ།

ར་མགོ་ལྡན་པའི་ཀ།

རྐང་བཞི་རྐང་པ་ཡ་རྐན་དང་། *

ཅིག་རྐྱང་རྐན་པོའི་རྐུབ་ཆོས་རྐུབ། རྩ་ལ་རྐྱལ་དང་རི་དྭགས་རྐྱང་། † རྔ་རྐྱལ་གན་རྐྱལ་རྐོང་པའི་ནད།

རྐྱུ་རྐྱེ་ན་རྣོད་རྐྱན་རྐེད་པ་རྐྱོང་། རྩ་ཡི་རྐ་དང་ས་རྐོ་སོགས། ར་མགོ་ལྡན་པའི་ཀ་ཡིག་ཡིན།།

ལ་མགོ་ལྡན་པའི་ཀ།

‡ མགྲིན་པ་རི་ལྐོག་མ་ལྐོག་ཤལ་དང་། ངག་ལྐུགས་ལྐུ་ཕྱིད་ལྐོག་གྱུར་རྣམས། ལ་མགོ་ལྡན་པའི་ཀ་ཡིག་ཡིན།

ས་མགོ་ལྡན་པའི་ཀ།

སྐྱལ་བའི་སྐུ་དང་སྐུར་འདེབས་དང་། སྐར་མ་སྐ་རགས་པོ་ཡི་སྐག། འཛིན་བྱེད་སྐམ་པ་སྐུད་པ་དང་།

ཐོད་སྐམ་སེམས་སྐྱོ་སྐྱོ་མ་སྐུགས། ཁ་སྐོམ་སྐོམ་བཏུང་ཇ་སོགས་སྐེལ། + སྐྱང་ནུལ་ཆུ་སྐྱོར་སྐྱོགས་ཀྱིས་སྐྱོམ།

དགེ་སྐོས་མཐའ་སྐོར་སྐོར་བ་བྱེད། སྐྱེ་ཤིང་སྐྱེར་པ་སྐྱེད་ཙལ་དང་། སྐྱི་དཀར་སྐྱ་བོ་སྐྱུར་ཁ་མདོག།

ཆོས་སྐྱོང་འཛིགས་སྐྲག་སྐྱོན་ལས་སྐྱོབ། འཚོ་སྐྱོང་ཉེར་སྐྱོང་ས་སྐྱོང་དང་། འདབ་ཆགས་ཆུ་སྐྱར་སྐྱུར་གའི་སྐད།

མཐེབ་སྐྱུ་རོ་སྐྱུར་སྐྱིད་སྐྱུར་དང་། གོས་སྐེན་ཁ་སྐེང་རི་བ་སྐེང་། མགོ་ཡི་སྐྲ་དང་སྐྲན་གྱིས་སྐྲངས།

སྐེ་དང་སྐེད་པ་འཇོག་པའི་སྐས། སྐྱལ་གྱི་སྐུགས་དང་སྦ་བའི་སྐུངས། རང་སྐབ་བདེ་སྐྱིད་སྐྱོས་མ་སྐྲོད།

འཛིགས་སེལ་སྐྱེ་ལ་མ་སྐྱེས་ཆེན་འདེགས། ཇི་སྐད་སྐད་ཅིག་སྐྱ་རིངས་དང་། སྐུ་ཡི་སྐྱ་བ་སྐྲབ་ཀྱི་སྐྱོགས།

མཀྱགས་པའི་སྐྱིན་དང་རྐྱ་སྐྱེགས་ཆོས། ངོ་ཚའི་སྐྱེངས་དང་བྱ་སྐྱིབས་དང་། སྐབས་སུ་སྐྱབས་འགྲོ་སྐྱོར་བྱང་བྱེད།

སྐྱེས་བུ་སྐྱག་ཡར་གསེར་སྐྱེམས་སྐྱོལ། སྐམ་བྱེད་ཤ་སྐམ་སྐྱེལ་ཀྱང་སོགས། ས་མགོ་ལྡན་པའི་ཀ་ཡིག་ཡིན།།

བས་འཕུལ་ར་མགོ་ལྡན་པའི་ཀ།

འདོད་པའི་བརྐམ་དང་བརྐུ་བྱ་བརྐུས།

སྒྲ་བརྐྱང་བོས་དང་ལག་སོགས་བརྐྱངས། བརྐོ་བྱ་ས་བརྐོས་ཤིང་ལ་བརྐོས། བས་འཕུལ་ར་མགོ་ལྡན་པའི་ཀརོ།།

---

* དཀན་ཡང་ཟེར། † ཀུལ་ཡང་ཟེར། ‡ གྲོང་ཚིག་ཏུ་ཨོག་ཞལ་ཟེར། + སྐྱང་ནུལ = ཞལ་བ།

བས་འཕྲུལ་ས་མགོ་ལྡན་པའི་ཀ།

ཡན་ལག་བསྐུམས་དང་ཆོས་ལ་བསྐུལ། དྲིན་གྱིས་བསྐྱངས་དང་གནས་སུ་བསྐྱལ།
བྱུག་པ་བསྐུ་བསྐུས་བྱ་བ་བསྐྱངས། བསྐྱེད་པའི་བསྐུན་དང་གར་བའི་བསྐ། དབང་བསྐུར་འཕྲིན་ཡིག་འབན་སོགས་བསྐུར།།
རྩ་སོགས་བསྐྱིལ་དང་ཚོར་བསྐྱིས་བསྐྱེན། གོས་བཀེན་རྟར་བསྐྱོན་རྩ་སོགས་བསྐམས།། ཕྱིར་བསྐྲད་རྐྱང་བརྐྱར་འཚོ་བརྐྱས་བྱེད།
དུས་ཀྱི་བསྐལ་པ་ཡང་བསྐྱར་དང་། སེམས་བསྐྱེད་རྐྱར་བསྐྱེད་བརྗོད་པའི་བརྒྱུད། མཐའ་ནས་བཀོར་དང་རྒྱལ་སར་བཀས
ཁ་བསྐང་ཐུགས་དམ་བསྐངས་པ་སོགས། བས་འཕྲུལ་ས་མགོ་ལྡན་པའི་ཀོར། ཀ་ཡི་བརྡ་རྣམས་མདོར་བསྡུས་རྫོགས།།

II

༄༅ ཁའི་བརྡ་བཤད་པ་ལ།

དང་པོ་རྐྱང་པ་འདི་ལྟ་སྟེ། འདབ་ཆགས་ཁྭ་དང་ཁྲུང་ཁྲུང་ཁྲ།
ཁྲ་བོ་ཁྲི་ཁྲག་ཁྲག་ཁྲིག་གྲངས། ཁ་ཁྲམ་ཁྲལ་འཇལ་ཁག་ཁྲུག་དཀྲུག། གོ་ཁྲབ་ཁྲམ་ཤིང་ཁྲིམས་བོ་ཆེར།
ཁྲོ་བོ་ཁྲོས་དང་ཁྲོན་པ་དང་། དག་བྱེད་ཁྲུས་དང་འཇལ་བྱེད་ཁྲུ། ཁྲོལ་ཙ་གས་སིལ་ཁྲོལ་ཚོགས་པའི་ཁྲོམ།
རི་ཁྲོད་ཁྲལ་མེད་རྩ་སོགས་ཁྲིམས། ཡུལ་ཁྲིམས་རྒྱལ་ཁྲིམས་སྐར་མ་ཁྲུམས། རྩིས་ཀྱི་ཁྲམ་ཁ་འབྲུ་ཡི་ཁྲི།
གདན་ཁྲི་སྐྱ་ཁྲིད་ཁོང་ཁྲོ་ཁྲག། ཟངས་ཁྲོལ་སོགས་ཁ་རྐྱང་ཡིན།།

མས་འཕྲུལ་ཁ།

གཉིས་པ་འདུལ་ཅན་འདི་ལྟ་སྟེ།
མཁན་པོ་མཁས་པ་ཀུན་མཁྱེན་དང་། དཔེ་མཁུད་ས་མཁར་མཁང་དང་མཁྲིགས། * ལྷ་མཁན་ཉེར་མགོ་མཁལ་གཤམ་དང་།
ནང་ཁྲོལ་མཁལ་མ་མཁྲིས་པའི་ནད། ལག་པའི་མཁྲིག་མ་ནམ་མཁའ་སོགས། མ་ཡིས་འདུལ་བས་ཁ་ཡིག་ཡིན།།
འཁར་བ་འཁར་གསིལ་འཁར་ཏ་དང་། དཀྱིལ་འཁོར་དུ་འཁོར་འཁོད་དང་འཁྲུལ། མཐའ་འཁོབ་ལཁོབས་ཆེ་དུ་ཐུན་འཁོལ།
ཐོས་པའི་འཁྲུམས་དང་ཟླ་སོགས་འཁུམས། † ཞེ་ནས་འཁུ་དང་འཁང་ཞིང་འཁོན། གྱང་བའི་འཁྱགས་དང་འཁྱམས་ཤིང་འཁྱར།
ཤིང་སོགས་འཁྱོམ་དང་འཁྱོར་ཞིང་འཁྱོག། སྐྲན་འཁྲིགས་ཕན་རྩུན་འཁྲུད་དང་འཁྲིལ། ཆོར་འཁྲུལ་སེམས་འཁྲུགས་འཐབ་འཁྲུག་འཁྲུགས།

---

* དཔེ་མཁུད = ཆོས་ལ་སེར་སྣ་བྱེད་པའི་དོན། † འཁུ = ཞུང་བའི་མིང་།

བལ་འབིལ་འཁོས་རྒྱུང་འབྲི་བ་ཆོད། འབྲ་སར་འབྲུས་དང་དྲི་མ་འབྲུད། གླག་འཕྲུག་གདུགས་སོགས་འཕྲིར་དང་འཕྲིལ།

སྐུ་འབྲུངས་བྲོ་འབྲབ་དཀྲལ་བའི་འཁྲོལ། བསྒྲད་པའི་འབྲང་དང་བསྐྲུར་བའི་འཕྲུར། རྡོར་ལ་འབྲན་དང་ལྷག་མ་འབྲི།

ན་བའི་འབྲུན་དང་འཁྲིག་པ་ཀྲུ། སྐུམ་འཕྲུར་འཕྲུར་འཕྲིར་རྗེ་འཁྲིམས་སོགས། འ་ཡིས་འཛུལ་བའི་ཁ་ཡིག་ཡིན།

ཁ་ཡི་བརྡ་རྣམས་མདར་བསྡུས་རྫོགས།།

III

༄ གའི་བརྡ་བཤད་པ་ལ།

དང་པོ་རྐྱང་པ་འདི་ལྟ་སྟེ། གྲོགས་པོ་གྲོས་མཁས་ཀྱང་ལ་གྲིམས།

ཀྱབ་ཐབ་ཀྱབ་མཐའ་ཀྱགས་པ་ཆེ། ཆོས་ཀྱར་དངོས་ཀྱབ་ཀྱུ་ཆར་འབེབས། རིམ་གྱོ་ཀྱལ་དུ་གྱོ་མས་བྱུས། རྐྱི་ཤིང་ཀྱམ་ཀྱུ་བཞི་དང་།

རལ་ཀྲི་གྱོ་གས་ཀྲིལ་ཞེས་ཀྱག། ཀྱུ་ཁའི་ཀྱམ་པ་ངམ་གྲོག་གཡང་། གཟུགས་ཀྱི་ཀྲིབ་མ་མི་གཙང་ཀྲིབ། རྐྱེ་མོའི་ཀྱ་དང་འབྲུ་ཡི་གྲོ།

གླ་ག་ཆགས་གྲོག་མ་ཀྱུལ་བུམ་དང་། ཀྲིབ་གཙོན་ཀྱངས་མེད་ཤི་བའི་གྲོངས། ཀྱང་ནད་ཀྱུམ་བུའི་ནད་ལས་གྲོལ། གྲོད་པ་ཆག་ཀྱུམ་ཀྱབས་གསོམ་ཀྲིར།

སྐར་མ་ནམ་ཀྱུ་གྲོ་བཞིན་ཀྲི། ལག་པའི་ཀྱུ་མོ་ཀྲི་བ་འཛེར། ཡུལ་ཀྱུ་གྲོང་ཁྱེར་ཐབས་གླགས་རྙེད། གླིང་གཞི་བགྲོ་གླིང་གླིང་བུ་གླུ།

འཛོམ་གླིང་རྒྱ་གླིང་གཟུགས་ཀྱི་གླུད། གླ་རྩེ་གླ་བ་གླང་ཆེན་གླིན། * གླ་ངན་ལན་གླན་ལྔན་པ་གླན།

ཤིབ་མོར་གླིབས་དང་གླིས་ཕབ་གླིད། གླིགས་བམ་ཀློ་གླིགས་སྲང་མའི་གླུམ། ནང་ཁྲིལ་གླ་བ་ཆམ་ལུད་གླ།

གཞོགས་ཀྱི་གློ་དང་ནམ་མཁའི་གློག། མ་ངེས་གློ་བུར་གསལ་བའི་གླལ། † ཐོ་གླང་གླང་ཤུ་ག་རྐྱང་ཡིན།

གཉིས་པ་འཛུལ་ཅན་འདི་ལྟ་སྟེ། དགེ་སློང་དཀུན་དུས་དགོན་པ་ལ།

དཀར་ཞིང་དཀྱེས་པ་དགེ་ལ་དགོངས། དགོངས་དགྲོལ་བཅིངས་གཀྲོལ་མདུད་པ་དཀྲོལ། ཕྱི་ཧྣཱ་འི་དགོང་དང་དབྱིབས་དཀྱེད་དཀྲུར།

རི་དྭགས་དགོ་བ་གད་མོ་དགོད། རྐྱན་དགོད་གོས་དཀབ་ཐེང་སོགས་དཀྲམ། ཚོགས་སུ་དཀར་དང་དུམ་བུར་དག

མཚན་དང་ནམ་མཁའ་ཡོའི་མིང་དཀུང་། མདུན་དུ་དཀུག་དང་དཀུ་ཚོགས་དཀུ། སྐད་དགང་དགང་གཟར་སྐྱི་དཀུ་དང་།

འདད་དཀུ་ལ་སོགས་མང་ཚོག་དང་། མཛའ་མིན་དགྲ་དང་དགག་སྒྲུབ་སོགས། ད་ཡིས་འཛུལ་བའི་ག་ཡིག་ཡིན།

བཀའ་བཀྲོ་གསུང་བཀྲོས་གད་མོ་བགད། བྱ་བའི་བཀྱི་དང་བཀྱིས་དང་བཀྱེད། གོས་བགོ་བགོས་དང་བགྲོད་ལམ་བགགས།

---

* གླན་ཡང་ཟེར † ནད

* ཚོད་བགམ་དུས་བཀྲུངས་གཞོད་བྱེད་བགེགས། ཀས་པའི་བཀྲིས་དང་མིག་སོགས་བཀྲད།

བཀྲུང་འཕྲེང་བཀྲུངས་དང་འབྲས་སོགས་བཀྲུས † བགོ་བཤའ་བགོས་པའི་བགོ་སྐལ་སོགས། བ་ཡིས་འཛུལ་བའི་ག་ཡིག་ཡིན།

ཁུས་ཀྱི་མགོ་དང་མཀུལ་མཀུར་མགོན།

བཟོ་བོའི་མགར་བ་དགའ་བའི་མགུ། ཡ་མགལ་མཀལ་མི་མགལ་དུམ་དང་། མགྲིན་བུ་གཏོར་མགྲོན་སྒྱུར་བའི་མཀྱཱ་ས།

མ་ཡིས་འཛུལ་བའི་ག་ཡིག་ཡིན།། ཐོག་མའི་འགོ་དང་གཤམ་གྱི་འགབ། འགག་དང་རི་འགའ་འགྲམ་དུ་འཀྱིལ།

འགྲིམ་འཁྲུལ་འགྲོ་འགྲེང་འཁྲིང་འགྲོས་བྱེད། འཁྲུབ་འཁྲུར་སེམས་འཁྲུ་སྙིང་ནས་འགེམ། ཕན་ཚུན་འགྲན་འགྲུས་འཁྱིད་དང་འཁྲུད།

གཡོ་འཀུལ་སྐབས་འགོལ་ཟས་ཀྱིས་འཁྲུངས། ལམ་གྱི་འཁྲུལ་པ་འཁྲུངས་འགོར་ཆེ། འགན་ཁུར་ནང་འཁུགས་བདེ་ལ་འགོད།

འཕེལ་འགྲིབ་འགལ་དང་བརྩོན་འགྲུས་འགྲེབ། ‡ འགོང་པོའི་འགོ་ནད་འགོས་ན་འཀུམ། འགྲོད་གར་བློ་འགྲེ་སྣོད་འགེང་འགགས།

འགྲམ་པ་འགྲམ་གཞི་ནད་ཀྱི་འགྲམ། དགོངས་འགྲེལ་འགྲོལ་དང་རྒྱ་སྒགས་འགྲིམ། རིགས་འགྲེ་འགྲོགས་དང་འགྲུས་འགེམས་སོགས།

ང་ཡིས་འཛུལ་བའི་ག་ཡིག་ཡིན།།

གསུམ་པ་མགོ་ཅན་འདི་ལྟ་སྟེ།

རྒྱལ་བ་སངས་རྒྱས་རྒྱལ་མཚན་རྒྱན། བྱ་རྐད་རྐད་མ་དགྱེ་ཀོ་ད་དང་།

འཕྲོ་རྐད་གན་པོ་པོ་རྐོད་ཀས། ངར་རྐྱང་ཕས་ཀོལ་རྩྭ་ལ་ཀོལ། ཞེས་རྒྱུད་འཕྲེང་རྒྱུད་ལུ་ཀུ་རྒྱུད། གཏམ་རྒྱུད་ལོ་རྒྱུས་རྒྱུད་མང་དང་།

རྒྱུད་སྡེ་རྒྱུགས་ལེན་ཟས་ཀྱི་རྒྱུགས། ལུས་ཀྱི་རྒྱབ་དང་ཕྱག་རྒྱ་རྒྱབ། ང་རྒྱལ་རྒྱགས་ནས་རྒྱང་རིང་རྒྱག། རྫོངས་རྒྱ་རྒྱ་ཚྭ་རྒྱགས་ཕྱིའི་རྒྱུ།

ཉ་རྒྱ་རྒྱ་གྲམ་རྒྱན་པོ་རྒྱ། རྒྱ་མ་རྒྱས་པ་རྒྱངས་ཤིང་རྒྱངས། སྨིག་རྒྱུའི་རྒྱ་རྒྱན་རྒྱ་ཡུལ་དང་། § རྒྱ་པ་རྒྱ་ཆེ་རྒྱན་འབྲུ་སོགས།

ར་མགོ་ལྡན་པའི་ག་ཡིག་ཡིན། ནང་གྲོལ་སྣང་པ་སྣན་གྱི་སྣ། ⁊ ལ་མགོ་ལྡན་པའི་ག་ཡིག་ཡིན། སྟོན་གློམ་གློམ་གློམ་གློམ་ཆེན་གྱི།

གློ་དུ་ཆོས་སྒྲ་སྒྲག་པ་སྒྲུབ། ཟབ་པའི་གློམ་དང་ཤིང་གི་སྒོམ། མཁས་པའི་སྒྲན་དང་འགྲན་པའི་སྒྲོན། སྒྲོལ་ཚིགས་ཏའི་སྒྲ་ས་ཡི་སྒང་།

གོང་བུར་སྒོང་དང་བུ་རམ་སྒོར། སྒོར་མོར་སྒྲམ་དང་ཕྱོགས་སུ་སྒྲལ། སྒོག་པ་སྒོང་ཆས་ཀྱིས་སྒེག། མཐའ་མའི་སྒྲུག་མོ་སྒྲིད་ལུག་དང་།

ཐབ་ཀྱི་སྒྲིད་བུ་སྒྲོལ་སྒྲོད་སྒྲིལ། གཡོ་སྒྲུ་སྒྲུ་ཙོལ་སྒྲུ་མ་སྒྲུང་། སྒྲིག་བྱེད་སྒྲི་ཀུ་ཤུགས་སྒྲིག་དང་། བྱ་སྒྲོ་སྒྲོ་སྒྲེ་སྒྲིཨུ་ཚུགས་སྟོད།

ཀླུ་སྒྲུབ་སྒྲུབ་ཐབས་སྒྲུབ་པར་བྱེད། རིག་སྔགས་སྒྲོན་མི་སྒྲབ་བྱེད་དང་། སྒྲ་སྒྲོས་ད་སྒྲོས་ཕྱོགས་གཅིག་སྒྲག། དབང་སྒྱུར་འཁོར་སྒྱུར་སྒྱུར་བྱེད་དང་།

---

* ཉིམ་སད་པ། † སྒྲུས་ཀྱང་ཟེར། ‡ འཆི། § ཁྱི་བའི་མིང་ཡིན། ⁊ སྣ་ཡང་ཟེར།

སྐྱུགས་པའི་སྦྲིགས་པ་དུས་པའི་སྦྲོམ། གཙེར་བུའི་སྦྲིན་མོ་ཆུ་ལས་སྤྲོལ། མཐུན་པར་སྦྲག་དང་སྦྲ་སྐད་སྦྲོག།
ལུས་ཀྱི་སྙིད་པ་སྦྱོགས་ཇ་སོགས། ས་མགོ་ལྡན་པའི་ག་ཡིག་ཡིན།

ཆུ་བཀལ་བཀལ་ལན་ལེ་བཀན་དར། ཕྲེང་བ་བརྒྱ་ཕྲག་བརྒྱུས་པས་བརྒྱན། བརྒྱད་ཅུ་བརྒྱད་དང་དྲན་མེད་བརྒྱལ།
འོ་བརྒྱལ་ལམ་བརྒྱགས་ཕྱུར་བར་བརྒྱགས། བྲོ་བརྒྱུད་གད་བརྒྱངས་བརྒྱུད་མར་འབྱུང་། བརྒྱད་བཀག་དབྱུག་པ་བརྒྱབ་པ་སོགས།
བས་འཕྱལ་ར་མགོ་ལྡན་པའི་གཏོ།།

མནའ་བསྐགས་ལམ་བསྐགས་བྱ་བའི་བསྐང་། བུ་རམ་བསྐར་དང་གཅིག་ཏུ་བསྒྲོངས། * གྲངས་སུ་བསྒྲངས་དང་རྒྱལ་མཚན་བསྒྲེངས།
ཆུ་བསྐྱལ་ཆོས་བསྐྱགས་ཉིང་འཛིན་བསྒོམས། བཀའ་བསྒོ་བསྒོས་དང་བག་ཆགས་བསྒོས། ཆོས་བསྒྱུར་མཛོག་བསྒྱུར་རིགས་པ་བསྒྲི།
སྐྲིབ་པས་བསྒྲིབས་དང་འོད་སོགས་བསྒྲིབས། གཅིག་ཏུ་བསྒྲིགས་དང་སྤུད་བུ་བསྒྲུམས། བྲོ་བསྒྲུམས་བསྒྲུབ་བྱ་བསྒྲུན་མི་ནུས།
གཞན་ཀྱིས་མི་བསྐུལ་གན་རྒྱལ་བསྐྱེལ། བས་འཕྱལ་ས་མགོ་ལྡན་པའི་གཏོ།། ག་ཡི་བཟ་རྣམས་མདར་བསྡུས་རྫོགས།།

IV

ༀ ངའི་བརྡ་བཤད་པ་ལ།

དང་པོ་རྐྱང་པ་བཤད་མི་དགོས། གཉིས་པ་འཕྱལ་ཅན་འདི་ལྟ་སྟེ།

† སྔན་དངགས་དངངས་སྔག་དངོམ་ཆེ་དང་། དངོས་མེད་དངོས་དོན་དངོས་གཞི་དང་། དངོས་བཤགམས་དངོས་གྲུབ་རིན་ཆེན་དངུལ།
༡ ཚོར་དུ་དངར་དང་དངན་འཐན་དང་། ༢ ཆུའི་ངོགས་དངོ་དང་གྲི་ཡི་དངོ། ད་ཡིས་འཕྱལ་བའི་ང་ཡིག་ཡིན།
མངའ་རིས་མངའ་ཞབས་མངའ་ཐང་དང་། མངའ་མཛོད་མངའ་བདག་ཐུགས་ལ་མངའ། མངོན་སུམ་མངོན་གྱུར་མངོན་མཚན་ཅན། ༣
མངོན་ཤེས་མངའ་བརྙེས་མངོན་སྤྱོད་ལས། ༤ མངག་གཞུག་ནན་ལ་བྲོ་བ་མངགས། ༥ མངོན་པའི་སྔེ་སྣོད་མངན་མིབ་གྲང་།
སྐྱེ་གནས་མོའི་མངལ་རྫ་མངར་སོགས། ༦ མ་ཡིས་འཕྱལ་བའི་ང་ཡིག་ཡིན།

གསུམ་པ་མགོ་ཅན་འདི་ལྟ་སྟེ།

ཕྱུགས་ཀྱི་ཛ་མ་ཛ་ཡབ་དང་། འཁར་ཛ་ལ་སོགས་བཙུང་བུའི་ཛ། སྦྲ་ཛན་བཀྲིས་ཛབ་དམ་པའི་ཛམ།

---

* གྲངས་སུ་བཙུག་པའི་དོན་ཏེ་བགྲངས་ཀྱང་ཐེར † སྔངས་ཀྱང་ཐེར ༡ འཕྲེང་དའམ་བསྒྲིགས་པའི་མིང་ཡིན། ༢ ཆཞན་གྱི་ཆོར་ཕྱིར་མི་བྱོད་པའི་མིང་དོ། ༣ བྱུན་སྦྱོད
༤ དྲག་ལས ༥ མཐུ་མི་བཟུང་། ༦ དངར་ཡང་ཐེར

༡ ངམ་བརྗིད་རྩམ་ངམ་ནས་ཡོས་ངད། ༢ ཏ་ཡི་ངག་མ་དྲིའུ་ངོག་སྟན། ངན་ཆན་དབུགས་ངུབ་ལུས་ཀྱི་ངུལ།

ངུལ་གཟན་མཐུག་ངམས་ནད་ཀྱི་ང། ངོན་པ་ཚྭ་ང་ང་མི་ཐོགས། ར་མགོ་ལྡན་པའི་ང་ཡིག་ཡིན། གྲངས་ཀྱི་ལྔ་ཉི་ལ་ལྔར་ངེས།

༣ ཞལ་ངེ་སྨིན་ངེ་ངེ་སོར་ངུན། སྔོན་ཆེ་གསང་ངགས་ངེ་ཕྱི་ངོ། ངེ་ཧྲི་ངས་ལ་ངུར་སླ་ཆེ།

༤ ཁ་དོག་ངོ་ སྔོན་སྐྱོ་ ངོགས་ཅིད། ས་མགོ་ལྡན་པའི་ང་ཡིག་ཡིན། འདྲིད་པའི་བརྗོད་དང་བཙོས་མ་བངས།

འགབ་ཀྱི་བངབ་དང་ཆང་འཐུངས་བཙུབས། བས་འཕྲུལ་ར་མགོ་ལྡན་པའི་ངའོ༎ ཕྱག་བངལ་བངགས་བརྗོད་བངོ་བྱ་བངོས།

བངོ་བཀྲང་ཁ་དོག་རྣམ་པར་བངོས། བས་འཕྲུལ་ས་མགོ་ལྡན་པའི་ངའོ༎ ང་ཡི་བརྡ་རྣམས་མ ར་བསྡུས་རྫོགས༎

V

༄༅ ཙའི་བརྡ་བཤད་པ་ལ།

དང་པོ་རྐྱང་པ་འདི་ལྟ་སྟེ། ༥ ཙ་ཙོ་སྨུ་ཙོར་ཙོད་པན་དང་།

སྒྲ་མེད་སྐྱུ་ཙེར་ཙེར་ཙོག་ཙན། ཙེ་ཙད་ཙང་ཤེས་ཙིག་ཤོས་དང་། ༦ བབ་ཙོལ་ཐོ་ཙོ་ཙང་ཏེའུ་རྐྱོག།

ཏ་ཙང་ཙུང་ཟད་ཙོ་འདྲི་དང་། ༧ བེ་ཙོན་ཙོག་པུར་ཙིག་ཙར་འཛོག། སྐད་ཙིག་ཐང་ཙིག་ལན་ཙིག་དང་།

ལྷན་ཙིག་ཆབས་ཙིག་ཐབས་ཙིག་ཏུ། ལ་ཙིག་ཙས་ཙུས་ཙམ་མི་ཤེག། སུམ་ཙུ་དྲུག་ཙུ་བདུན་ཙུ་དང་།

བརྒྱད་ཙུ་ཙི་སླས་ཡོད་ད་ཙོག། ༨ ཁྱིད་ཙག་བདག་ཙག་མིག་ཙེ་རེ། ཙི་སྟེ་ཙིས་ཀྱང་ཙལ་སླ་སློག།

གང་ཙི་རྣམ་གྲངས་འདྲི་བའི་ཙི། ཙིའི་ཕྱིར་ལ་སོགས་ཙ་རྐྱང་ཡིན། གཉིས་པ་འཛུལ་ཙན་འདི་ལྟ་སྟེ། ༩ གཙན་གཟན་སྒྲ་གཙན་ལ་གཙན་པ།

ཡིད་ལ་གཙགས་ནས་ནང་དུ་གཙུན། ཕྱག་ཏུ་གཙུར་ནས་ལག་པ་གཙུས། གཙང་བྱ་ཤིང་གཙོད་དུམ་བུར་གཙོག

གཙལ་དུ་བཀྲམ་དང་གཙུད་ལ་བོར། གཙེས་འཛིན་གཙོང་ནད་གྲངས་ཀྱི་གཙིག། འཁོན་བཙུགས་ཡིད་གཙུགས་གཙམ་བུའི་ཚིག། ༡༠

༡༡ གཙོམ་བསྐུངས་གསོས་གཙོམ་གཙོང་རང་གཡང་། ཚར་གཙོད་གཙུ་གལ་གཙིན་གཙི་བ། +

རྣམ་གཙོད་ཡོངས་གཙོད་ཁྲིམས་གཙོད་དང་། ༡༢ སྔོན་སྐྱེས་གཙེན་དང་རྗེས་སྐྱེས་གཙུང་། ༡༣ ར་གཙིག་གོས་མེད་གཙེར་བུ་སོགས།

ག་ཡིས་འཕྲུལ་བའི་ཙ་ཡིག་ཡིན། བཙོམ་ལྡན་དགྲ་བཙོམ་འཁོར་བཅས་ཀྱིས། ཁྲིམས་བཙས་བཙའ་ཡིག་ལག་ཏུ་བཙངས།

---

༡ འཛིག་རྡངས ༢ བྲ་བོ་སྙི་གྲུམ་རྩི་སོགས ༣ མདུན ༤ འཁྲུག་གོང་སྐྱིད་པའི་མིང་། ༥ ཁ་ཟེར་བ ༦ མ་བརྟགས་པ ༧ མཐོ་འཚམས་པ ༨ མཐའ་དག

༩ ཡའི་རྩུགས་པ ༡༠ གཙོས་མའི་ཚིག ༡༡ ཁྱིངས་ཆག་ནས་ཁ་དོག་འདུག་པའི་དོན། + དྲི་ཙུ ༡༢ ཨ་ཇོ ༡༣ ཙུ་བོ

༡ ཉེས་པ་བཅབས་དང་རྩུ་བཙུར་བཙུག། ནང་དུ་བཙུག་བཙུམ་བཅིང་བས་བཅིང་། བཅའ་གཞི་བསྣན་བཅོས་ལས་བཅོལ་བཅོས།

བཅུད་ལྡན་བཟའ་བཅའ་སོ་ཡིས་གཅམ། ཞིང་སོགས་བཅད་བཅག་ཚིགས་སུ་བཅད། རྣམ་བཅད་མིག་བཅར་ཡོགས་སུ་བཅར།

དྲི་མ་ཕྱིར་བཅིལ་ཞབས་ཀྱིས་བཅགས། བཅུ་དང་བཞི་བཅུ་ལྔ་བཅུ་དང་། དགུ་བཅུ་བཅོ་ལྔ་བཅོ་བརྒྱད་སོགས།

བ་ཡིས་འཛུལ་བའི་ཙ་ཡིག་ཡིན། གསུམ་པ་མགོ་ཅན་འདི་ལྟ་སྟེ། གཉེན་ལྩུག་ལྩང་མ་ལྩུག་ཕྲན་དང་།

བརླུལ་ལྩུག་མགོ་ལྩོགས་བླ་ཡིས་ལྩོགས། དུད་འགྲོའི་ལྩུ་བ་ལྩིད་ལྩི་བ། ལྩགས་རི་ཀྲིའི་ལྩུགས་ལྩུག་མ་ལྩགས།

མི་ལྩི་ལྩི་འབབ་འཆི་ཕྱིར་ལྩེབ། བྲ་ལྩུག་ལྩུམ་པ་ཟློ་རི་ལྩིབས་ཐུར། ཉ་ལྩིབས་སྦྲལ་ལྩོང་ཁ་ནང་ལྩི། ལྩུམ་སྲང་ལྩོག་རྩེ་ལྩུང་པོ་ཅན།

ཁག་ལྩིབས་སླ་ཡི་ལྩང་པོ་སོགས། ལ་མགོ་ལྡན་པའི་ཙ་ཡིག་ཡིན། ཙ་ཡི་བརྡ་རྣམས་མདོར་བསྡུས་རྫོགས།།

VI

༄༅ ཆའི་བརྡ་བཤད་པ་ལ།

དང་པོ་རྐྱང་པ་འདི་ལྟ་སྟེ། ༢ ཆེ་བོའི་རྩུན་པོ་ཆན་པས་ཆོད། ༣ ཆོལ་ཟངས་ནད་ཆིངས་རྩུ་ཞིང་ཆེ།

སྨུས་འགྱུར་ཆང་དང་ཆམ་ལ་ཕང་། ཆམ་ནད་ཟན་ཆང་འབྲས་ཆན་དང་། ཆབ་འོག་ཆབ་རོམ་ཆལ་ཆིལ་ཆོག།

སྤྲོག་ཆགས་ཚ་གའི་ཁ་ཆེམ་ཆུབ། ཆར་རྩུ་ཆབ་སོགས་ཆ་བད་མང་། ༤ ཆིབ་པ་ཆིབས་སོགས་ཆ་རྐྱང་ཡིན།

གཉིས་པ་འཛུལ་ཅན་འདི་ལྟ་སྟེ། ༥ དཀོན་མཆོག་མཆོད་དང་བཀའ་མཆིད་དང་། འགྲོ་བའི་མཆི་དང་ཡོད་པའི་མཆིས།

སྐྱེ་མཆེད་སྐྱ་མཆད་ཨེ་མཆད་དང་། ཆོར་བུ་མཆིང་བུ་ཀྱ་མཆོའི་མཆིང་། ༦ ནང་གྲོལ་མཆིན་པ་མཆེར་པ་དང་།

མིག་གི་མཆི་མ་ཁའི་མཆིལ་མ། ༧ མཆིག་དང་མཆིག་གུ་རྩོལ་གྱིས་མཆོང་། ༨ མཆིས་བྲང་མཆོང་གི་རྐྱན་གྱིས་མཆོར།

༩ མཆིལ་ལྷམ་གཞུ་མཆོག་ཡི་གེའི་མཆན། ཕྱགས་ཀྱུའི་མཆིལ་བ་ཁ་མཆུ་སོགས། མ་ཡིས་འཛུལ་བའི་ཆ་ཡིག་ཡིན།

འཆག་སར་འཆག་དང་ལག་ཏུ་འཆང་། ཆོས་འཆད་གར་འཆམ་རྩུལ་འཆོས་དང་། འཆར་བློ་སྒྲོས་འཆམས་གནས་འཆའ་དང་།

ཉི་མ་འཆར་དང་གསོ་འཆད་འཆི། ཞགས་པས་འཆིང་དང་སྟོབས་ཀྱིས་འཆུན།

༡༠ འཆོད་ལ་འཆུམས་དང་ཁས་འཆེ་འཆེས། ༡༡ ལས་འཆོལ་རྒྱུ་འཆོར་གནས་སུ་འཆུར།

---

༡ གསང་བའི་མིང་། ༢ ཁྱི་བོའི་ཁྱི་ཕྲུག། ༣ རྡེ་ཆུའི་སྡོང ༤ ཆ་བད་ཞེས་སྨྲོ།། ༥ ཅོག་ཙུང་ཟེར། ༦ དབུས་སམ་དཀྱིལ།

༧ བམ་གཏུན་དང་མམ་གཏུན། ༨ ཚུང་མ ༩ ཀྱུ་མའི་མཆན་བུ་ཡང་འདི་ཡིན། ༡༠ ཆགས་བཞམ་པ་ཉེན། ༡༡ ལེན་དང་བླངས།

གཏད་མེད་འཆལ་འཚོལ་ཤིང་འརྒྱུས་སོགས། འ་ཡིས་འཛུལ་བའི་ཆ་ཡིག་ཡིན། ཆ་ཡི་བརྡ་རྣམས་མདོར་བསྡུས་རྫོགས།།

VII

༄ ཇའི་བརྡ་བཤད་པ་ལ།

དང་པོ་རྐྱང་པ་འདི་ལྟ་སྟེ།

ཇི་ལྟར་ཇི་ ད་ཇི་སྐད་དང་། ཇི་ལྟ་ཇི་སྙེད་ཇི་བཞིན་གཟིགས། དང་པོ་རེ་ཇེ་དང་ཇེ་མཐོང་སོང་།

ཇོ་བོ་ཇོ་མོ་ཇོ་ཇོ་དང་། རྐུ་བའི་ཇག་པ་བཀུང་ཟྭའི་ཇ། ཇི་འོས་ལ་སོགས་ཇ་ཀྱང་ཡིན།

གཉིས་པ་འཕྲུལ་ཅན་འདི་ལྟ་སྟེ། འཕྲད་པའི་མཇལ་དང་གོ་བའི་མཇལ། ལུས་ཀྱི་མཇིང་པ་རྗེས་ཀྱི་མཇུག།

མི་མཇེད་ཞིང་དང་མཇུག་མ་མཇེ། མ་ཡིས་འཛུལ་བའི་ཇ་ཡིག་ཡིན། སྐྱེ་ཤིང་འཇག་མ་ཁྲིམས་འཇགས་དང་།

མཚོར་འཇབ་དང་རིག་བྱ་འཇམ། ༡ འཇིག་རྟེན་འཇིག་འཇིགས་ཐོབ་འཇལ་འཇོམས།

ལྟས་འཇལ་ཚད་འཇལ་ནམ་མཁའི་འཇའ། དབྱིབས་འཇོང་འཇོལ་འཇོལ་འཇོ་བཞེག་དང་། སེར་སྣའི་འཇུངས་དང་འཇོད་པ་འཇོ།

སྲད་བུའི་འཇུར་དང་ཁྲུང་དུ་འཇུག། འདམ་གྱི་འཇི་བ་འཇིམ་པ་འཇགས། ལག་པ་འཇུ་འཇུས་གནས་སུ་འཇོག།

ཟས་འཇུ་མཇུས་འཇིབས་རྒྱ་མཚོའི་འཇིངས། ༢ སྙན་འཇེབས་ཤ་འཇུམས་ཞི་བའི་འཇིལ། རྩ་འཇིང་གཉེན་དང་མཁས་པའི་འཇེམ།

ཁྲིམས་འཇལ་སྐྱད་འཚོང་འཇུད་མཐུན་སོགས། ༣ འ་ཡིས་འཛུལ་བའི་ཇ་ཡིག་ཡིན།

གསུམ་པ་མགོ་ཅན་འདི་ལྟ་སྟེ། རྗེ་བཙུན་རྗེ་དཔོན་ལྷ་རྗེ་དང་།

རྗེ་རྗེ་རྗེས་འཇུག་བཀུར་སྟིའི་རྗེད། རྗེད་བྱེད་སྙིང་རྗེ་ལག་རྗེས་དང་། ཤ་རྗེན་རྗེ་ངར་རྒྱུད་པའི་རྗུད།

བང་བའི་རྗིང་དང་རྗེའུ་རིགས་དང་། རྗེ་སུ་འགྲོ་དང་རྗེད་བྱེད་སོགས། ར་མགོ་ལྡན་པའི་ཇ་ཡིག་ཡིན།

ཡུལ་ལྗོངས་སྨན་ལྗོངས་ལྗོན་ཤིང་དང་། ༤ ལྗང་བུ་ལྗན་ལྗིན་ལྕི་བའི་ལྗིད། ཁ་དག་ལྗང་ཁུ་རོ་འཛིན་ལྗགས།

ལ་མགོ་ལྡན་པའི་ཇ་ཡིག་ཡིན། རབ་བརྗིད་གཟི་བརྗིད་བརྗིད་ཆགས་དང་། བརྗེད་ངས་མི་བརྗེད་བརྗོད་བྱ་བརྗོད།

བན་རྒྱུན་བརྗེ་དང་བརྗེས་པ་སོགས། བས་འཛུལ་ར་མགོ་ལྡན་པའི་ཇའོ།། ཇ་ཡི་བརྡ་རྣམས་མདོར་བསྡུས་རྫོགས།།

VIII

༄ ཉའི་བརྡ་བཤད་པ་ལ།

---

༡ གཞན་གྱི་ནོར་ཐབས་ཀྱིས་འཕྲོག། ༢ དབྱུས ༣ བཟང་འཇོད་མ་དང་གཟུགས་འཚོ་མ་དང་ཚོགས་ཅན་མ་རྣམས་དོན་འདྲ། ༤ མི་གཙང་བ།

ངང་པོ་རྒྱང་པ་འདི་ལྟ་སྟེ། ཉ་དང་ཉུང་མ་ཉུང་ངུ་ཉེ། ཉིང་ཁྲུ་ཉག་ཅིག་ཉལ་ཉིལ་དང་།

སྙོས་ཉུག་རྒྱུ་ཉོག་ལག་པ་ཉབ། ཉ་ག་ཉིང་དགོས་ཉག་ཕྲན་མདའ། ཉམ་ཉེས་ཉོན་མོངས་ཉིང་ཤ་དང་།

ཉིང་ལག་ལ་སོགས་ཉ་རྒྱང་ཡིན། ༡ གཉིས་པ་འཕྲུལ་ཅན་འདི་ལྟ་སྟེ། གཉའ་ཤིང་གཉེར་པ་བྲོ་གཉེར་དང་།

བཤེས་གཉེན་དཔུང་གཉེན་ཉེ་འབྲེལ་གཉེན། དབང་པོའི་གཉའ་པོ་དོན་གཉེར་དང་། བཀའ་གཉན་གཉན་ནད་དུད་འགྲོ་གཉན།

གཉིད་ཀྱི་གཉེན་པོ་གཉུག་མ་གཞིས། ནང་འབྲིལ་གཉེ་མ་གཉིས་ལ་སོགས། ག་ཡིས་འཕྲུལ་པའི་ཉ་ཡིག་ཡིན༎

བསྙུ་མཉེ་ཀོ་བ་མཉེད་མཉེས་མཉེན། མཉན་པ་ཐུགས་མཉེས་ཉ་བས་མཉན། མཉན་ཡོད་གནས་དང་ངལ་བའི་མཉེལ།

མཉེས་གཤིན་པ་དང་མཚུངས་པའི་མཉམ། མཉམ་གཉག་མཉམ་མེད་ཤིང་གཉན་སོགས། མ་ཡིས་འཕྲུལ་བའི་ཉ་ཡིག་ཡིན༎

གསུམ་པ་མགོ་ཅན་འདི་ལྟ་སྟེ། རྙོར་རྙེད་རྙེད་བཀུར་གསར་རྙིང་དང་། རྒྱ་རྙིག་སོའི་རྙིལ་རྙེ་དང་རྙོང་། ༢ ར་མགོ་ལྡན་པའི་ཉ་ཡིག་ཡིན།

སྙིང་པོ་གཏམ་སྙན་སྙན་ཤལ་དང་ ཐ་སྙད་སྙན་ཚིག་ཟེ་སྙམ་སེམས། རིག་བྱ་སྙེ་དང་ཁྲུས་ལ་སྙེས། གཉེན་གྱི་སྙེད་མོ་གོ་སྙོད་སྨན།

སྨྲ་སྙོལ་ཆང་སྙོལ་རྒྱལ་མཚན་སྙོལ། ༣ བཏང་སྙོམས་སྙམ་འདུག་སྙོམ་ལས་དང་། བསོད་སྙོམས་སྙུགས་སྤྲོངས་སྙིབ་སར་སྙོགས།

སྙིགས་དུས་སྙུན་ནད་སྙུད་པ་སྙོད། འབྲུ་ཡི་སྙེ་མ་སྙེམ་པ་སོགས། ༤ ས་མགོ་ལྡན་པའི་ཉ་ཡིག་ཡིན།

གཟུགས་བརྙན་སྙང་བརྙན་སྐྲ་བརྙན་དང་། གཉན་ལ་བརྙས་སྤྱོད་མངའ་བརྙེས་དང་། གཡར་པོའི་བརྙན་པོ་བརྙས་པ་སོགས།

བས་འཕྲུལ་ར་མགོ་ལྡན་པའི་ཉ་རོ༎ དགེ་བསྙེན་བསྙེན་གནས་བསྙེན་རྫོགས་དང་། ཟས་བསྙོད་བསྙོན་དོར་ནས་སོགས་བསྙོར།

བཤད་པའི་བསྙད་དང་བརྗོད་པའི་བརྙལ། ཡན་རྩུན་བསྙམས་དང་ཐང་ལ་བསྙལ། ཕར་ལ་བསྙབས་དང་སྨུན་གཞིས་བསྙུན།

བསྙེན་སྒྲུབ་བསྙེན་བཀུར་སྦྱི་མར་བསྙེལ། ཕྱིར་བསྙད་བསྙེལ་དང་འཛིགས་པའི་བསྙེངས། ཁྱུང་བཟེད་བསྙོགས་དང་རྗེས་བསྙེགས་སོགས།

བས་འཕྲུལ་ས་མགོ་ལྡན་པའི་ཉ་རོ༎ ཉ་ཡི་བརྡ་རྣམས་མདོར་བསྡུས་རྫོགས༎

IX

༄༅ ཏའི་བརྡ་བཤད་པ་ལ།

ངང་པོ་རྒྱང་པ་འདི་ལྟ་སྟེ། གཙུག་ཏོར་ཏེ་མོའི་ཐོར་ཏོ་དང་། ཏོལ་ཅེ་ཏྲ་ཏོར་དབྱུག་ཏོ་ཏིའི་ཏོག། ༥

སྨུ་ཏིག་ཏིང་འཛིན་ཟ་མ་ཏོག། ཏེ་ཏོག་པོ་ཏོག་རྩེ་ཏོག་དང་། ༦ ཞབས་ཏོག་ཏེ་པོར་ནན་ཏར་བཟང་། ༧

---

༡ སོར་མོ། ༢ གཡལ ༣ ང་རྒྱལ་དི་བ། ༤ ཐལ་མོ ༥ རྩི་ཐོག་ཀྲུང་ཟེར། ༦ རྩུག་ཏོར ༧ ཤིན་ཏུའམ་རབ་ཏུ་ལེགས་པའི་དོན།

ཞལ་ཏ་ཁ་ཏོན་ནན་ཏན་དང་། ཏིལ་འབྲུ་ཡོན་ཏན་ཏ་ལའི་ཤིང་། ཏིང་ལོ་ཏིང་ཤགས་ཏབ་བེ་སྟོད།

ཏི་ཏུག་ཏང་ཏོང་ཏོག་ཏོག་སྦ། ཏིག་ཏ་སྨན་སོགས་ཏ་ཀྲུང་ཡིན། གཉིས་པ་འཇུལ་ཅན་འདི་ལྟ་སྟེ།

བསམ་གཏན་གཏན་ཚིགས་གཏན་ལ་འབེབས། གཏུན་བུ་གཏུན་ཤིང་དུམ་བུར་གཏུབས། གཏང་རག་གཏོར་མ་སྦྱིན་གཏོང་གཏང་།

བཙོལ་བའི་གཏམས་དང་གང་བའི་གཏམས། གཏེར་མཛོད་གཉེར་གཏོད་ལག་ཏུ་གཏད། འཐེམ་ལ་གཏོད་དང་དམིགས་པ་གཏོད།

ཟད་པའི་གཏུགས་དང་ཞབས་ལ་གཏུགས། གཏི་མུག་གཏམ་སྙ་གཏོལ་མེད་དང་། ༡ ཁྲག་གཏར་རྩ་གཏིགས་སེ་གོལ་གཏོགས།

སྒོ་གཏན་གཏིང་ཟབ་མུན་པ་གཏིབས། བྲོ་བའི་གཏུམ་དང་ཐུམ་པོར་གཏུམ། ནོར་གྱི་གཏའ་མ་གཏུར་བུ་སྟོད། ༢

དུ་བ་གཏུལ་དང་ཁོངས་སུ་གཏོགས། རི་བོའི་གཏོས་དང་ཚང་གཏོལ་སོགས། ག་ཡིས་འཇུལ་བའི་ཏ་ཡིག་ཡིན།

མིང་བཏགས་ཕན་གཏགས་ཁ་བཏགས་བཏགས། ཕྱི་མར་བཏགས་དང་རྒྱགས་བཏུ་བཏུས། བཏང་སྙོམས་བློས་བཏང་སྤུར་བཏང་དང་།

དཀྲི་བཏུལ་སྤྲོལ་བཏོད་ཏུང་བའི་བཏུབ། བཟའ་བཏུང་གདན་བཏིང་བྱིས་སུ་བཏེག། གསོལ་བཏབ་ཀྲུས་བཏབ་ས་བོན་བཏབ།

ཀུན་དུ་བཏེག་དང་ཞབས་ལ་བཏུད། ཤ་བཏོགས་རྩ་བ་བཏོན་པ་སོགས། བ་ཡིས་འཇུལ་བའི་ཏ་ཡིག་ཡིན།

གསུམ་པ་མགོ་ཅན་འདི་ལྟ་སྟེ།

མི་རྟོག་རྣམ་རྟོག་རྟོགས་ལྡན་དང་། གོ་བའི་རྟོགས་དང་རྟོག་ག་བ།

རྟག་ཏུ་རྟག་དང་མི་རྟག་རྟགས། དབང་རྟུལ་རྟུལ་ཕོད་བྲིད་པའི་རྟབ། ༣ ཁང་པའི་རྟེང་པ་རྟེམ་གྱི་རྟེང་།

རྟ་དང་རྟོད་ཕུར་མི་གཙང་རྟུག། འཇིག་རྟེན་ལྷ་རྟེན་མཆོད་རྟེན་དང་། མཐའ་རྟེན་ཡིད་རྟོན་རྟ་བབས་སོགས། ༤

ར་མགོ་ལྡན་པའི་ཏ་ཡིག་ཡིན། བུར་ལྡང་འགྲང་ལྡོགས་མཚན་ལྡས་དང་། ལྡིང་ཀྲུས་ལྡིང་ཀ་ལྡེམ་གྱིས་གང་།

ལུས་ཀྱི་ལྡག་པ་ལྡེ་བ་ལྡ། ལྡོ་འབྱེ་ལྡོས་འགྲོ་ལྡད་མོ་ལྡ། ཛ་ལྡིར་ལྡོ་ཟ་མདའ་ཡི་ལྡོང་། རི་ལྡོས་བྱེད་དང་འོག་ཏུ་ལྡུང་།

ཛི་ལྡར་དི་ལྡར་དི་ལྡ་བུ། ད་ལྡ་ལྡ་ཞག་ལྡ་ཅི་ལྡོས། གོས་སོགས་ལྡེབས་དང་ལྡག་ཆོས་སོགས།

ལ་མགོ་ལྡན་པའི་ཏ་ཡིག་ཡིན། བཀུར་སྟི་སྟབས་དང་སྟངས་སྟབས་དང་། ཆོས་སྟོན་དུས་སྟོན་སྟོན་མོ་སྟེར།

སྟེགས་བུ་མུ་སྟེགས་བྱད་སྟེམས་དང་། སྟབས་ཆེན་སྟག་དང་སྟག་པ་ཤིང་། དགྲ་སྟ་སྟ་རེ་སྟེ་འུས་བཞོགས།

གཞོགས་སྟེགས་སྟེས་དབང་སྟབས་ལེགས་དང་། ༥ སྟེང་ཕྱོགས་སྟོང་ཉིད་ཟད་པའི་སྟངས།

༡ཆ་མེད། ༢ གཏེབ་དང་གཏིང་པ་ཡང་ཟེར། ༣སྟེང་སྟབས་ཆེ་བ། ༤རྗེས་སུ་འབྲང་བ། ༥ཕུར་གཡེང་ངམ་ཟུར་མིག།

གྲོགས་ཀྱི་སྟོངས་དང་སྐྱོན་མི་སྟ། གདིང་བའི་སྟན་དང་མཐུག་པའི་སྟུག། མི་སྟག་སྟ་གོན་ཏོ་སྟུག་དང་། ༡

བོར་བའི་སྟོར་དང་སྟོར་ཁུང་དང་། ཤ་སྟག་སྟ་ཟུར་སྟར་ཁ་འབྲུ། ༢ འཕྲེང་བའི་སྟར་དང་སྟང་ཟེལ་སོགས། ༣

ས་མགོ་ལྡན་པའི་ཏ་ཡིག་ཡིན། བརྟག་དཔྱད་གནས་བརྟན་ཀུན་བརྟགས་དང་། མི་འགྱུར་བརྟན་དང་མཚན་ཉིད་བརྟགས།

ཡིད་བརྟན་བརྟུལ་ཞུགས་རྟེན་ལ་བརྟེན། གློ་བུར་བརྟད་པ་ལུས་སེམས་བརྟས། རྟབས་བརྟོལ་སྦུ་བརྟོལ་ཅན་ལ་སོགས། ༤

བས་འཕྲུལ་ར་མགོ་ལྡན་པའི་ཏའོ།། བལྟས་ས་བལྟོས་ཚོས་བལྟ་ལྟུང་བལྟས། བལྟ་ལྟ་ལྟུ་བལྟམས་གོས་སོགས་བལྟབ།

བས་འཕྲུལ་ལ་མགོ་ལྡན་པའི་ཏའོ།། བསྟོད་འོས་གཟེངས་བསྟོད་མངོན་པར་བསྟོད། ཐུབ་བསྟན་དང་བསྟུན་མཁས་པ་བསྟེན།

བསྟི་སྟང་བསྟི་གནས་ལེགས་པར་བསྟར། ༥ ཐག་བསྟངས་སྟ་བསྟད་འགྲོ་ཆས་བསྟད། ཆོས་བསྟན་སྟར་བསྟུད་ཕྲིན་ལེན་པ་སྟབས།

བསྟིར་མེད་བསྟིང་ཚིག་སྨྲ་བ་སོགས། ༦ བས་འཕྲུལ་ས་མགོ་ལྡན་པའི་ཏའོ།། ཏ་ཡི་བརྡ་རྣམས་མདོར་བསྡུས་རྫོགས།།

X

༄ ཐའི་བརྡ་བཤད་པ་ལ།

ཀྱང་པ་ཐྲག་ཐྲིག་ལྷམ་ལྷུར་ཅེས།

གཉིས་པ་འཕྲུལ་ཅན་འདི་ལྟ་སྟེ། མཐོ་རིས་མཐར་ཐུག་མཐའ་དག་དང་། ནུས་མཐུ་མཐའ་ཡས་མཐུན་མི་མཐུན། ༧

ལག་མཐིལ་མཐེ་བོང་མཐེའུ་ཆུང་དང་། བརྒྱ་མཐོང་དཔངས་མཐོ་མཐང་གོས་མཐུག། ༨ མཐོ་ཡོར་མཐོ་གང་མིག་གིས་མཐོང་།

ཐ་ཡི་མཐུར་དང་ཕན་ཚུན་མཐུད། མཐར་ཆགས་མཐོ་འཚམ་མཐོལ་བཤགས་སོགས། ༩ མ་ཡིས་འཕྲུལ་བའི་ཐ་ཡིག་ཡིན།

ཐྲན་འཐིབ་མགོ་འཐོམས་ཆུ་འཐུང་འཐོར། འཐེང་པོ་སྤྲ་འཐས་དུ་བ་འཐུལ། ཕན་ཚུན་འཐེན་དང་འཐོབ་པ་དང་།

ཐུ་མར་འཐག་དང་དུམ་བུར་འཐུབ། ཟས་འཐུ་ཐོར་འཐེབ་གོས་ཀྱིས་འཐུམ། འཐད་དང་སྨྲོད་ཚིག་འཐེང་སྨྲད་སོགས།

འ་ཡིས་འཕྲུལ་བའི་ཐ་ཡིག་ཡིན། ཐ་ཡི་བརྡ་རྣམས་མདོར་བསྡུས་རྫོགས།།

XI

༄ དའི་བརྡ་བཤད་པ་ལ།

དང་པོ་ཀྱང་པ་འདི་ལྟ་སྟེ། མ་དྲོས་མཚོ་ཡི་ཤིང་དྲུང་དུ། དྲང་སྲོང་དྲུག་ལ་དྲི་བ་དྲིས། སྔ་དྲོ་ཕྱི་དྲོ་བཀའ་དྲིན་དྲན།

---

༡ གྲབས་གསོམ། ༢ དཔྱི་མགོ ༣ དངུལ་རྡོ། ༤ དཔྲལ་གྱི་ཐུག་པོ། ༥ ངལ་བསོའི་གནས། ༦ ངལ་བསོ་མེད་པ། ༧ འཐུན་ཡང་ཟེར། ༨ སྐད་ཀྱི་གོས། ༩ འཐོལ་ཡང་ཟེར།

ཡ་རབས་དྭ་མ་དྲི་མས་སྦགས། དྲེད་པོ་ཁ་དྲག་མི་ཟློད་ཟློ། གཞན་དྲིང་མི་འཇོག་དྲང་དོན་རྟོགས།

ཐལ་བའི་དྭགས་དང་ཉོར་གྱིས་དྭགས། དྲག་པོ་དྲག་ཤུལ་དྲག་ནད་དང་། དྲིས་མས་དྭགས་དྲུད་དྲུང་ནས་ཕྱུང་། *

དྭ་བ་དྭ་ཕྱིད་དྲིལ་བུས་བཀྲུན། གཡུང་དྲུང་དྲང་པོར་དྲས་ནས་དྲུབས། † ཟས་དང་གནས་སུ་དྲངས་དང་ངས།

‡ ཁྲིམས་དྲལ་ལྷམ་དྲལ་དྲཱུ་རྡོག་ཀྱན། ཁྲུར་དྭགས་དྲེད་ཀྱིས་དྲཱུ་ཏ་དེད། དྲག་པ་དྲིལ་ཕྱིས་གཅིག་ཏུ་དྲིལ།

དྭ་ཕྲུག་དྭངས་གསལ་ད་ཀྲུང་ཡིན། §

གཉིས་པ་འཕྲུལ་ཅན་འདི་ཀྱཻ་ཧྲེ། ཤླུག་གདུང་གདུང་བརྒྱུད་གདུང་འཛིན་དང་། མཆོད་རྫས་གདུགས་དང་ཉིན་མོའི་གདུགས།

གདོད་ནས་གདུལ་བྱ་དམ་ལ་གདགས། མིང་གདགས་གདངས་སྙན་བསྒྲང་བ་གདངས།

༡ གདམ་ང་འབྱེད་དང་གདམས་ངག་སྟོན། གདིང་བ་སྟན་དང་ས་བོན་གདབ། སྔས་ཀྱི་གདང་བུ་གོས་འགེལ་གདང་།

ཁ་གདངས་མཆོན་གདེངས་གདུང་བས་གདུངས། གདུ་བུ་གདུབ་ཀོར་ཞེ་སའི་གདའ། གསོལ་གདབ་གསལ་གདབ་ཐྲག་དེང་རྗེད།

བྱད་ཀྱི་གདོང་པ་ཉོར་ལ་གདུ། ༢ སྣང་ལ་གདེག་དང་གདོན་མི་ཟ། ༣ གདོན་དང་གདོལ་པ་གདུག་པ་ཆེ། ༨

གདགས་གཞི་གདུང་མ་གདེངས་ཀ་སོགས། ག་ཡིས་འཛུལ་བའི་ད་ཡིག་ཡིན། བདེ་གཤེགས་བདེ་ཆེན་བདེན་གཉིས་དང་།

མ་དུན་དུ་བདར་དང་བདེན་པ་བདར། ཕྱག་པ་ཕྱི་བདར་ཕྱི་མར་བདར། སེམས་པའི་བདེ་དང་དར་བའི་པ་རྡོ།

ཉོར་ཀྱི་བདོག་པ་གྲངས་ཀྱི་བདུན། བདུད་དང་བདུད་རྩི་བདུག་སྤོས་དང་། གཞུ་བདུངས་ཟས་འདའ་ཡོད་པའི་བདོག།

བདག་པོས་ཕྱུགས་བདས་བདའ་དེད་སོགས། བ་ཡིས་འཛུལ་བའི་ད་ཡིག་ཡིན། མདའ་མདུང་མདེའུ་དུས་ཀྱི་མདང་།

བཀྲག་མདངས་མི་མདག་ལུས་ཀྱི་མདུན། གྲོས་ཀྱི་མདུན་མ་ལུང་པའི་མདའ། མདོ་སྡེ་མདོར་བསྡུས་དཔྲལ་བའི་མདངས།

མདུད་པ་ཆོན་མདོག་ར་མདའ་འབྱེད། སྒྲུད་མདོས་ལམ་མདོ་གསུམ་མདོ་སོགས། མ་ཡིས་འཛུལ་བའི་ད་ཡིག་ཡིན།

དགེ་འདུན་འདུས་ནས་འདུལ་བ་འདོན། འདོད་ཆགས་མ་འདྲེས་སྐྱང་འདས་འདའ། འདབ་ཆགས་འདམ་ཟན་འདི་རུ་འདུག

འདུ་བྱེད་འདུས་བྱས་འདྲིས་པ་འདྲ། གནས་སུ་འདྲེན་དང་གསོལ་འདེབས་འདུད། ལྷ་འདྲེ་ཤིང་འདྲུད་ཁྲུང་བུ་འདྲུ།

༥ ཁྲིམས་འདྲལ་ཁྲམ་འདྲེ་ཤེ་གེ་དྲེ། རྫས་འདེད་གློ་འདུན་གོ་འདུན་ཚོགས། བང་འདུར་དུལ་སློང་རྐྱེན་དུ་འདེགས།

འདབ་མ་འདུ་འཛོ་ཞབས་འདྲེད་འདྲད། ༦ ཐབ་འདྲིལ་ལྡགས་དྲིལ་ཡིལ་ཡང་རྗེར་སླུ་བའི་འདྲེད། ༧

---

* ཙ་བ་ནས་ཐོན། † བཙེམས། ‡ བཙེམས། § འདི་དང་ཡི་དྭགས་དང་ལྷུལ་དྭགས་པ་རྣམས་ལ་ལྷ་ཟུར་བཏགས་པའི་དཔེ་མང་པོ་སྣང་ངོ་།

༡ འདམ་ག་ཕྱེད་ཟེར་བ་ཕྱང་ཚིག། ༢ ཟག། ༣ ཟེ་ཚོམ་མེད། རིགས་ངན། ༨ འཛེམས། ༥ འཕྲད་ཀྱང་ཟེར། ༦ འགྲིལ་ཀྱང་ཟེར། ༧

འདྲིག་མཁན་ལུས་འདར་འདག་ཆལ་འཛིན།	འགྲོ་བའི་འཛོང་དང་པོར་བའི་འཛོར།	འཛ་མེད་བྱ་འདག་འཛོམ་གང་འགཛོས།
ས་འཛོལ་རྒྱ་འདལ་སྒྱུ་མ་འདལ།	འཁོར་འདབ་ནང་འཛོམ་ཚོས་འཛོམས་སོགས།	འ་ཡིས་འཕྲུལ་བའི་ད་ཡིག་ཡིན།
གསུམ་པ་མགོ་ཅན་འདི་ལྟ་སྟེ།	གྲོང་རྡལ་ཐོག་རྡེབ་རྡོ་རྗེའི་རྡུལ།	རིག་བྱེད་ཐབས་རྟགས་རྗེའུ་རྟོག་པོ།
རྟོག་པས་རྡུང་བྱེད་རྡར་རྡོས་རྡོར།	ཐིག་རྡིབ་རྡོས་ཆེ་ལག་རྡུམ་སོགས།	ར་མགོ་ལྡན་པའི་ད་ཡིག་ཡིན།
མཆོད་རྫས་ལྡ་ ལྡི་མིག་དང་།	མཁའ་ལྡང་འབྲུག་འདིར་ལྡབ་ ལྡིབ་སྐད	འཇུག་ལྡོག་མགོ་ལྡིག་ཕྱིར་མི་ལྡོག།
ཤེས་སླར་སྟོབ་སྤྲིན་ཡོད་པའི་ལྡན།	བྱད་ཀྱི་ལྡན་པ་ལྡེར་བཟྡེའི་ལྡ།	མི་ལྡེ་སེང་ལྡེང་ལྡུམ་ལྡེམ་དང་།
ར་ལྡེ་ཤེག་ལྡོངས་ཡོགས་ཀྱི་ལྡེབས།	ལྡང་ཤེད་ལྡེམ་པོ་ལྡེམ་དགོངས་དང་།	ལྡུམ་རའི་ལྡུམ་ལྡུམ་ལྡིས་ལན་ལྡོན། *
ཧ་ལྡིར་ཀོམ་ལྡུད་སྐད་དུ་ལྡུགས།	ལྡེ་གུ་ལྡར་ལྡུར་ངད་ལྡང་ལྡན།	འཁོབ་པའི་ལྡངས་དང་སྐན་ལས་ལྡང་།
བསྐུར་ལྡབ་ཉིས་ལྡབ་ལྡེམ་བུ་སྨ་ད། †	ཉེ་ཝ་ལྡངས་དང་ལྡང་ཚད་སོགས། ‡	ལ་མགོ་ལྡན་པའི་ད་ཡིག་ཡིན།
ཞི་སྣང་སྣང་མིག་སྣིགས་རྩབ་དང་།	དགེ་སྣིག་བདེ་སྡུག་སྣེ་ཚན་སྣེབས།	ག་ཆགས་སྣོམ་སྣིག་སྣེར་མོ་སྣོ།
མཛེས་སྡུག་སྡུག་བསྔལ་སྡིག་ཏོ་ཅན།	ནོར་སྡུད་སའི་སྡིངས་བྲིད་པའི་སྣར།	སྡོམ་པ་བསྲུང་སྡོམ་སྣག་དང་སྡོ།
བཀའ་སྣད་སྡེ་སྣད་མང་པོ་འི་སྡེ།	སྡོད་སྙུད་སྡེར་མ་ཕུག་སྡར་དང་།	ཤིང་སྡང་མཆོད་སྡོང་གནས་སུ་སྡོད།
སྡེབ་སྦྱོར་ཕྱོགས་གཅིག་སྡམས་ཤིག་སོགས།	ས་མགོ་ལྡན་པའི་ད་ཡིག་ཡིན།	’ཆལ་བདབ་ཆལ་མར་བདལ་བ་དང་།
གྲི་བདར་ཁ་བདར་གོ་བྱེད་བདར།	ཛ་བདུང་གྲོ་བདུང་བདེག་བྱ་བདགས།	བདུང་བྱ་བདུངས་དང་བདེག་འཆོས་སོགས།
བས་འཕྲུལ་ར་མགོ་ལྡན་པའི་དའོ།།	བཟུག་པ་བཟུག་དང་སྨུར་བའི་བཟུད།	བས་འཕྲུལ་ལ་མགོ་ལྡན་པའི་དའོ།།
དབྱིན་བསྡུམ་མདོར་བསྡུས་བསྡུ་བྱ་བསྡུས།	གཅིག་ཏུ་བསྡོམས་དང་པན་རྩུན་བསྡུད།	སྡོག་དང་བསྡམས་ནས་ཉེས་པ་བསྡམས།
གྲོགས་དང་བསྡོངས་བསྡེབས་ཉེར་བསྡོགས་དང་།	ལྡམ་གྱི་བསྡོགས་པ་གྲབས་ཀྱི་བསྡེགས།	གནས་སུ་བསྡད་དང་གཞན་ལ་སྡིགས།
རྡོ་རྗེ་བསྡམས་པ་དམ་དུ་བསྡམས།	བས་འཕྲུལ་ས་མགོ་ལྡན་པའི་དའོ།	ད་ཡི་བདུ་རྣམས་མདོར་བསྡུས་རྫོགས།།

XII

ཀྲྀ ནའི་བད་བཤད་པ་ལ།

དང་པོ་རྐྱང་པ་བཤད་མི་དགོས། གཉིས་པ་འཕྲུལ་ཅན་འདི་ལྟ་སྟེ།

---

* ལ་ཕུག་སོགས། † བསོད་སྙོམས། ‡ ཉ་སོ་མཉམ་པའི་མིང་།

གནས་འཛིན་ཉེར་གནས་གནས་ཁང་དུ། གནས་ནས་གནོད་བྱེད་ཟློག་གྱིས་གནོན། གནས་སྐབས་ཕན་གནོད་གཞན་བཀག་བྱེད།
ཞི་གནས་གནས་འགྱུར་གནས་ལུགས་རྟོགས། གནོད་སྦྱིན་མདོག་གནག་གནས་ངན་ལེན། གནག་ཕྱུགས་བནད་གཅོད་ཞི་ནས་གནོང་།
གནངས་བཞེས་དུས་དང་གནམ་སྔོང་སོགས། ག་ཡིས་འཕྲུལ་བའི་ན་ཡིག་ཡིན། མནལ་གཟིམས་མནའ་མ་འོག་ཏུ་མནན།
མནའ་བསྐྱལ་དྲི་མནམ་བསམ་མནོ་མནོས། * ཟས་མནོག་མནོག་ཆུང་མན་ངག་མནོས། † གོས་མནབས་མནར་སེམས་མནར་མེད་མནར། ‡
མ་ཡིས་འཕྲུལ་བའི་ན་ཡིག་ཡིན། གསུམ་པ་མགོ་ཅན་འདི་ལྟ་སྟེ། § ན་བའི་ནམ་ཤེས་ནོན་པོ་ནམས།
ནམ་རྟོག་ནམ་གྲངས་ནམ་པ་མང་། ༡ ནལ་མའི་ནལ་འབྱོར་རྡོ་མོ་ནོ། ༢ ཞིང་གི་ནང་མ་ཁྲུག་ན་དང་། ༣
ནག་ཁྲག་ཆིག་ཕྲད་ནམ་པར་སོགས། ར་མགོ་ལྡན་པའི་ན་ཡིག་ཡིན། རྣག་ཚ་རྣ་ཚོགས་རྣ་ཡི་རྣབས།
རྣམ་སྣྲར་རྣམ་བུའི་རྒྱུ་རྣལ་མ། མནོ་རྣང་བར་རྣང་ལྷར་རྣང་དང་། རྣང་གསལ་སྣེ་མོ་སྣོལ་ཞིབ་ཕྲེད།
སེར་སྣ་ལམ་སྣ་སྣ་མངདང་། རྒྱབ་ཀྱི་རྣམ་ཕོགས་རྣད་བཙུད་སྣུམ། ལུས་རྣང་དྲི་རྣོམ་སྣུར་ཞིག་སོགས།
ས་མགོ་ལྡན་པའི་ན་ཡིག་ཡིན། འགགས་པའི་བནངས་དང་ནན་ཏན་བནན། སྲས་པའི་བནོགས་དང་བསམ་པའི་བནག།
བནབ་སེམས་བཟོད་དཀའི་བནག་དཀའ་སོགས། བས་འཕྲུལ་ར་མགོ་ལྡན་པའི་ནའོ།།
གནད་དུ་བསྣུན་དང་ཉུ་མ་བསྣུན། མཆེན་བསྣུན་དྲི་བསྣམས་ཕྱག་ཏུ་བསྣམས། གོང་འོག་བསྣོར་དང་ཕན་རྣུན་བསྣལ།
མང་དུ་བསྣན་དང་སྣུས་སོགས་བསྣུབས། དུས་བསྣུར་ཞིབ་མོར་བསྣུར་བ་སོགས། བས་འཕྲུལ་ས་མགོ་ལྡན་པའི་ནའོ།།
ན་ཡི་བརྡ་རྣམས་མདོར་བསྡུས་རྫོགས།།

༄ པའི་བརྡ་བཤད་པ་ལ།

དང་པོ་རྐྱང་པ་འདི་ལྟ་སྟེ།

མཁར་གྱི་པུ་ཤུ་པང་ལེབ་ཤིང་། ⸪ འདབ་ཆགས་པུ་ཤུད་པར་པར་འཕར། པང་པར་པི་ཕང་པིར་གྱིས་བྲིས།
ཟེ་བྲོག་བྲོག་ཚུ་འོག་པག་རྒྱན། པོ་ཏིའི་པར་དང་གཟའ་པ་སངས། པུར་ཁང་པུས་གཙུགས་པྲ་ཕབ་དང་།
པགས་པ་སྐྱག་གི་པགས་པ་ཞེས། ཞིག་དང་མ་འབྲེལ་བ་དང་ནི། རྡུག་པྲ་ཡོད་སོགས་པ་རྐྱང་ཡིན།
གཉིས་པ་འཕྲུལ་ཅན་འདི་ལྟ་སྟེ། དཔལ་ལྡན་དཔག་མེད་སེམས་དཔའ་ཆེ། རྫས་དཔག་དཔག་ཚད་དཔག་བྱ་དཔོག།

---

* རྡིད་པ། † ཁ་ཆུང་བ། ‡ རྒྱན་པའི་མིང་། § སྣ་འཛིན། ༡ ཡང་དག་པའི། ༢ གྲོང་ཚིག་ཏུ་ལྷག་ཟེར ༣ དབུ་ན། ⸪ སྤྲན་བད་ལྷ་བུན།།

དབྱུང་པ་དབྱུང་རྒྱན་དཔོན་སློབ་དང་། ཛ་དཔོན་དམག་དཔོན་དཔའ་བོ་དཔའ། དཔེར་ན་དཔེ་བྱད་དཔེ་ཆ་དང་།
དཔང་པོ་དཔངས་མཐོ་དཔག་བསམ་ཤིང་། རྣམ་དཔྱོད་རྟོག་དཔྱོད་བརྟག་དཔྱད་དཔྱད། *འཚོ་དཔྱད་དཔྱིས་ཕྱིན་དཔྱས་མི་འདོགས། †
དབྱིད་དུས་དབྱལ་བ་སྟ་ཐུར་དབྱི། དར་དབྱངས་དབྱང་ཞག་དབྱ་ཁྲལ་སོགས། ད་ཡིས་འཕུལ་བའི་པ་ཡིག་ཡིན།།
གསུམ་པ་མགོ་ཅན་འདི་ལྟ་སྟེ། སྒང་བུ་སྒངས་དང་ལ་སྒོད་སྒྲུན། སྒ་དགུག་སྒང་སྒོས་སྒར་སྨོར་སྒྲུད།
ཙེ་ཤིང་སྲིན་མ་སྲ་མ་དང་། རྒྱན་གྱི་སྲིན་ཧྲོག་བརྒྱན་པའི་སྲུད། མཛེས་བའི་སྲ་དང་རིན་ཆེན་སྲུག།
སྲུ་སྲུར་གནས་སྲོར་གཞན་དུ་སྲགས། མཐའ་ལ་སྲུག་སྲུགས་ཟས་ཀྱི་སྲགས། སྲིལ་མར་ནོར་སྲིལ་གཟའ་སྲིན་པ།
མཁར་གྱི་སྲི་འུ་སྲོབས་པ་ཆེ། ‡ བ་སྲུ་སྲི་བོ་རྒྱན་གྱིས་སྲུས། + དཀའ་སྲུད་ཆོས་སྲུད་སྤྲུལ་པ་འགྱུར།
ཆུ་འཛིན་སྲིན་སྲོས་སྲིལ་བོ་སྲོ། § སྲོང་ཐག་སྲང་བ་སྲོང་བ་པ། ÷ སྲི་སྲུགས་ཁ་སྲུང་ཆུ་ལ་སྲིང་། མིག་གི་སྲུན་དང་འབྲུར་བྱེད་སྲིན།
སྤྲ་བ་སྤྲ་ཚོལ་སྤྲ་ཆལ་དང་། ༡ ཉི་ཡི་སྤྲིས་མ་ཐགས་ཀྱི་སྤྲུན། སྤྲ་དང་སྤྲི་འུ་སྤྲང་གི་དང་། སྤྲང་པོ་སྤྲོང་སར་འཐབ་མོ་སྤྲད། ༢
སྤྲང་པོ་སྤྲི་གྲོས་དགེ་མི་སྤྲོམས། དངོས་སྤྲུད་ཞེ་སྤྲོགས་ཕྱུང་པོར་སྤྲུངས། ཡོངས་སྤྱོད་སྤྱོད་དང་གཞི་བའི་སྤྱོ།
༢ སྤྲབས་རྟུལ་སྤྲུག་སྤྲུགས་སྤྲུན་སྤྲུལ་དང་། ༣ སྤྲ་བཀོང་གཅེས་སྤྲས་རྩུར་སྤྱོར་སོགས། ས་མགོ་ལྡན་བའི་པ་ཡིག་ཡིན།
སྤག་སྤགས་ཤུན་སྤགས་ཞེས་རྟག་སྤྲ། མེད་པ་ལ་ཡི་མགོ་ཅན་ཡིན། པ་ཡི་བརྡ་རྣམས་མདོར་བསྡུས་རྫོགས།།

ཕའི་བརྡ་བཤད་པ་ལ།

དང་པོ་རྐྱང་པ་འདི་ལྟ་སྟེ། ཕྲ་མ་ཕྲག་དོག་ཕྲན་ཚེགས་དང་། ༤ ཕྲེང་བ་བརྒྱ་ཕྲག་དུལ་ཕྲན་ཕྲ།
ཕྲག་གོང་ཕུར་བ་ཕུག་གིས་ཕུར། ༥ ཕུ་མཁན་ཕུལ་ན་ཕྱིང་པ་ཕྱུར། ༦ རྒྱན་གྱི་ཕུང་ཕྲུལ་ཕུང་ངེ་བ། ༧
ཕྱུགས་ཀྱི་ཕྱིར་དུ་ཕྱོགས་བཙུར་ཕྱིན། ༨ དབུལ་ཕོངས་ཕྱི་སྤོངས་ཕྲུ་བ་ཕྲོགས། ༩ ནམ་ཕྱེད་ཕྲུ་གུ་དྲི་ཕྱིན་གཏོང་།
ཕྱག་དར་ཕྱི་ས་ཕྱི་ལ་ཕྱུང་། ༡༠ ཕྱི་ཕྱིར་ཕྱུག་པོ་འི་སྒོ་ཕྱི་ནས། ༡༡ ཕྱིན་ཅི་ལོག་པ་ཕྱུགས་མས་ཕྱུགས།
ཚ་རྣན་ཕྱི་མས་དྲིལ་ཕྱིས་ཕྱིས། ཕྲ་མན་ཕྲིན་ལས་ས་ཕྱོད་ཆེ། ༡༢ ཚིག་ཕྲད་ཐ་ཕྱི་རྣམ་དབྱེ་ཕྱེད།
མངལ་དང་དམག་གི་ཕྲུ་མ་དང་། ༡༣ སྲུ་ཕྲུག་ཕྲུགས་ཐེབས་གཡན་པ་ཕྲུགས། ༡༤ ༡༥ ཕོག་གི་ཕྱམ་སོགས་ཕ་རྐྱང་ཡིན།

---

*གཏིང་ཕྱིན་བ། †འཕྱས་མ་འདོགས། ‡ བློ་གྲོས་ཆེ་བ། + བརྒྱན། § སྦྲུབ་ཁང་། ÷ མི་འཇིགས་པའི་མིང་སྐྲ་ཕྲང་བའི་སྐད་བྱེད་ཀྱང་ངོ་།
༡ སྤྲང་གི་ཚོགས་མ། ༢ སྤྲབས་རྟུལ་ཡང་ཟེར་བ་སྣང་ངོ་། ༣ དགེ་བ་མི་རྫོགས་པ། ༤ འཕྲེང་བ་ཡང་ཟེར། ༥ ཕྱི་མཁན། ༦ གྲོད་པའི་ཞེ་ས།
༧ འཇོལ་ལེ་བ། ༨ རྡོན་དུ། ༩ རྩམ་པ། ༡༠ མི་གཙང་བ་ཕྱོན། ༡༡ སྐྱར་ཡང་། ༡༢ འཕྲིན་ལས་ཀྱང་ཟེར། ༡༣ སྐར
༡༤ འདུད་པའི་མིང་། ༡༥ འཕུམ་དང་ཕྱུམ་ཡང་ཟེར་བ།

གཉིས་པ་འཕྲུལ་ཅན་འདི་ལྟ་སྟེ། ནམ་འཕང་ཁྲི་འཕང་གོ་འཕང་དང་། གོང་དུ་འཕགས་དང་ཕྱིན་དུ་འཕྱུར།
ཚོར་འཕྲོག་འཕལ་ཀ་ཕན་ཚུན་འཕྲད། སྙིང་འཕྱོ་སེམས་འཕྱེང་འོད་འཕྲོ་འཕྲོས། གཞན་ལ་འཕྲ་འཕྲུས་ཡན་པའི་འཕྲུན།
ཀང་མེད་འཕྱེ་བོ་སྦྲེ་འཕྱེ་དང་། སེམས་ཅན་འཕྱེ་བ་དུས་འཕྱི་འཕྱིས། ཕྱི་འཕྱུར་དར་འཕྱུར་འབུར་དུ་འཕྱུང་།
† འཕྲལ་དུ་འཕོང་གི་མདའ་འཕེན་འཕངས། ‡ འཕྱིན་མའི་འཕངས་བདེ་འཕོངས་དུལ་འཕྱུག། § ཕྲུད་འཕྱོད་ཁྱུ་འཕྲུར་ལམ་ཕྱུག་འཕྱུགས།
ནམ་འཕྲུལ་སྤྲུ་འཕྲུལ་དར་འཕན་སོགས། འ་ཡིས་འདུལ་བའི་ཕ་ཡིག་ཡིན། ཕ་ཡི་བརྡ་རྣམས་མདོར་བསྡུས་རྫོགས།།

༄༅ བའི་བརྡ་བཤད་པ་ལ།

དང་པོ་རྐྱང་པ་འདི་ལྟ་སྟེ། སྦྱིན་བླ་བླ་མེད་བདེ་བླག་དང་། བླ་མའི་བྱིན་རླབས་བླ་རེ་བྲེས།
༡ བླ་གབ་བླ་དྭགས་སྦྱི་བླུགས་དང་། ༢ བློན་པོ་བློ་གྲོས་རྣ་བ་བླགས། ༣ བླང་དོར་ཁས་བླངས་བླ་ཐབས་བསྟན།
བློ་དང་རིག་པ་བློང་བློང་དང་། ༤ ཐབས་བྲལ་བླུན་པོ་བླུས་ཀྱང་བླ། ༥
སླ་བྲིགས་རབ་བྱུང་བླ་གོས་བྱིན། ༦ བྱ་དང་བྱེའུ་བྱི་ལ་དང་། ཕྱི་བྱུན་བྱང་གི་བྲགས་སུ་བྱུབས།
རི་བྲགས་བྲིས་རྩུ་སྙིང་མི་བྲ། ཕྲག་ལ་བྲམ་ཟེས་ཡི་གེ་བྲིས། བྱིས་ནས་སྦྱོན་བྱུང་བྱུག་པ་བྱ།
བྱིས་པའི་བྲན་དང་བྱ་ར་སྦྱོས། བྲང་འགྲོ་བྲེ་ཡི་བྱེ་མས་བྲབ། བྱད་དང་བྱུར་རྣམས་བྱབས་པས་བྱེར༔
བྱམས་པས་ཟམ་བྲིམས་བྱུག་མཁན་བྲེལ། སྐྱུག་བྲོ་རྒྱུས་བྲན་ས་ལ་བྲལ། བྲོ་གར་བྲོ་བོར་བྲོ་ཉད་དང་། ༧
སྦྱལ་སོང་བྱེ་བྲག་བྲུ་བ་ཙམ། ༨ ཚ་བླུད་སོས་བླད་འདམ་དུ་བྱིང་། བྱིང་རྒོད་སྦྱིའི་བྱིངས་ནང་བྱན་ཚུད།
ཡོ་བྱད་ཆ་བྱད་བྱད་བཞིན་གདོང་། སྦྱིན་བྲལ་བྱ་རུ་བྱི་དོར་བྱེད། སྦྲུ་ཕྱི་བྱིལ་མོར་བ་བླ་བྱུགས།
བྱ་ག་རིས་གྲལ་ནས་བྲིས་ལ་སྦྱལ། བྱ་ན་རོ་བྲི་བྱུར་བུར་གང་། སྦྲབས་བྲི་བློ་བྲོད་ཕྱི་བོ་བྲན། ༩
བཙོ་བླག་མཁན་སོགས་བ་རྐྱང་ཡིན། གཉིས་པ་འཕྲུལ་ཅན་འདི་ལྟ་སྟེ། དབང་ཕྱུག་དབང་ལྡན་དབང་ཐང་དང་།
དབང་པོ་དབང་བསྐུར་ཨེ་ཤེས་དབབ། ༡༠ ༡༡ རྒྱ་ཡི་དབར་རླབས་དབུ་བ་དང་། ༡༢ ཞེ་ས་རི་དབར་དང་ཏོག་གི་དབལ།
ཟས་དབུལ་གདུགས་དབུབ་ཁ་ནང་དབུགས། བུག་པ་དབུག་དང་ཚོར་གྱིས་དབུལ། དབུས་དང་དབུང་ནི་དཀྱིལ་གྱི་མིང་།

---

† མདའ། ‡ བུད་མེད་གཡེང་མའི། § རྟབ་རྒྱ་ཕོངས་ཀྱང་ཟེར། ༡ སྟེང་གཡོགས། ༢ རྣམ་གྲངས། ༣ གཉད། ༤ མི་གསལ་བའི་མིང་།
༥ རིན་ཐིས་བླུས་ཀྱང་བཟང་དམ་ངང་། ༦ སྟེང་གོས། ༔ བྲིས ༧ མཐའ་བོར། ༨ ལྐོགས། ༩ ཕོ་འཕྱུར་པའི་མིང་། ༡༠ ཕབ། ༡༡ ཐ་རླབས། ༡༢ བླུ་བ།

དབུ་མའི་ལྟ་བ་གདན་ལ་དབབ། དབུགས་དབྱུང་ཕྱིར་དབྱུང་སྤྱན་དབྱུང་ཕྱུང་། རྫང་དབོལ་ཆུ་དབོ་སྐར་མ་དབོ།

ཕྱུང་དབོག་ནོར་དབོག་དབོན་པོ་འི་དབུ། ཆོས་དབྱིངས་དབྱིབས་དང་དབྱེར་མེད་དང་། འབྱེད་པའི་དབྱེན་དང་སེམས་ཅན་དབྱི།

རིན་ཆེན་དབྱིག་དང་རི་མོ་དབྱི། དབྱུག་པ་དབྱུག་དབྱུགས་དབྱུ་གུ་ཤིང་། * དབྱར་དུས་དབེན་པར་དབྱངས་སྙན་སྒྲོག།

བཙོག་པའི་དབྲི་དང་དབྲལ་དཀར་སོགས། ད་ཡིས་འདུལ་བའི་བ་ཡིག་ཡིན། དཔལ་འབྱོར་ཕྱིས་འབྱུང་འབྲོམ་སྟོན་འབྱོན།

རབ་འབྱམས་ཚེ་འབྱིད་འབེལ་གཏམ་འབྱིན། མཚོང་ནས་འབུ་དང་འབྲས་བུ་འབུ། འབྲས་ཆེན་ཧྲིས་འབྲུག་ས་ལ་འབྲོ།

སྦུར་བའི་འབུར་དང་བར་མའི་འབྲང་། དུད་འགྲོ་འབྲོང་འབྲི་འབྲོག་ཏུ་འབྲོས། འབྲུམ་ནད་འབྲུག་གི་རྫས་འབྲང་འབྱེར། †

འབྲང་པོ་འབྲུབ་ཁྲུང་འདམ་དུ་འབྲིང་། ཆོན་འབྲུག་ཐོ་འབྱེད་ཆུ་འབྲུབ་འགྱེལ། ‡ འབྲལ་མེད་འབྱུང་བཞི་སྤྲུལ་བའི་འབྲལ།

སྦྲོང་སའི་འབྲང་དང་འབྲེང་པ་རྒྱན། ཁ་འབྲ་ལས་འགྲོངས་འབྲང་བ་སོགས། འ་ཡིས་འདུལ་བའི་བ་ཡིག་ཡིན།

གསུམ་པ་མགོ་ཅན་འདི་ལྟ་སྟེ། ཁྲི་ཐོད་ཐབ་སྦལ་ཐད་གཏོང་ཐ། § ཁ་ཐད་ཐད་ཆོད་སྐྱ་ཐབ་ནད།

ར་མགོ་ལྡན་པའི་བ་ཡིག་ཡིན། མཁྲིན་པའི་སྦྲ་བ་ཆུའི་སྦྲུ་བ། ལ་མགོ་ལྡན་པའི་བ་ཡིག་ཡིན།

ནོར་སྦྱིན་གནོད་སྦྱིན་སྦྱིན་བདག་དང་། དགེ་སྦྱོང་གསོ་སྦྱོང་གཙང་སྦྲ་སྦྱོར། སྡིག་ཆགས་སྦལ་སྦྲུལ་སྒྲིག་སྦུར་སྦྲེ།

ཤ་སྦྲང་སྦྲང་བུ་སྦྲང་རྩི་སྦྲོས། སྦྲུན་མ་ཆང་གི་སྦྲང་མས་སྦྲངས། སྦྲུ་ཆལ་ནང་སྦྲུབས་སྦྱིད་དོས་སྐོར།

དུད་འགྲོ་འི་སྦྲང་སྦྲགས་གཅིག་ཏུ་སྦྲམས། སྦྲོམ་པོ་ཉིས་སྦྲག་སྦྱར་ནས་སྦྲེལ། མི་སྦྲར་སྦྲུད་པ་ཁྲུར་དུ་སྦྲགས། ꞉

ལུས་སྦྲིད་སྦྲིད་པ་ཆུ་རྒྱུན་སྦྲེངས། གསང་བའི་སྦྲ་བ་གཏེར་སྦྲ་སྦྲས། བུད་མེད་སྦྲུམ་མ་གྲང་བའི་སྦྲིབ།

སྦྲུ་སྦྲུབས་གྲོགས་སྦྲན་ར་མདའ་སྦྲན། ས་ལེ་སྦྲམ་གསེར་སྦྲུག་སྦྲལ་བཙོན། ཟས་སྦྲུས་སྦྲང་བྱེ་སྦྱོང་ཕྱིད་སྦྲངས།

ས་མགོ་ལྡན་པའི་བ་ཡིག་ཡིན། བ་ཡི་བརྡ་རྣམས་མདོར་བསྡུས་རྫོགས།།

༄ མའི་བརྡ་བཤད་པ་ལ།

དང་པོ་རྐྱང་པ་འདི་ལྟ་སྟེ། སྨང་འདས་རྫ་སྨང་བའི་པ་སྨོང་། སྨ་ཅན་སྨུག་སྨིག་རོ་སྨྲུགས་འདམ།

སྨུར་དུ་ནགས་སྨུལ་སྨྲ་ངམ་ཐང་། ཉམས་སྨོང་སྨ་ཀུ་ཆང་གིས་སྨོས། སྨང་སྨང་སྨུག་སྨུག་མ་རྐྱང་ཡིན།

གཉིས་པ་འབྱུལ་ཅན་འདི་ལྟ་སྟེ། དམག་གི་ཉེས་དམིགས་དམིགས་བསམ་དང་། དམངས་རིགས་རིགས་དམའ་དམན་པར་དགས།

---

* ཆུ་ཚོད་ཀྱི་མིང་ཡང་ཡིན། † འགྲོས། ‡ རྒྱལ་བའི། § ཆུའི། ꞉ ཆེ་ཆས།

གཙང་དམི་འཛུམ་དམུལ་དམིགས་པ་གཏོད། * དམི་བོ་དམུས་ཡོངས་དམིགས་བུ་མེད། † དམུ་རྒོད་དམུ་ཅུ་འདྲི་སྲིན་དམུ།
ཉམས་དམས་དམུས་བྱུང་ཁ་གདོག་དམར། བུག་པའི་དམིག་དང་ཟློ་དམུན་བླུན། དམོད་བཙུགས་དཔྱལ་བ་དམོད་པ་འཛེར།
དཔེས་འཕུལ་བའི་མ་ཡིག་ཡིན། གསུམ་པ་མགོ་ཅན་འདི་ལྟ་སྟེ། རྨད་བྱུང་རྨད་པའི་རྨི་ལམ་རྨིས། ‡
§ རྨུགས་འཛིན་ཁྲིས་རྨུར་རྨུགས་པའི་རྨ། རྨ་བྱ་ཁམས་སྨྱོ་བྱ་སྨྱོང་བྱད། + སྨིན་པ་ཞིང་སྨོ་སྨོན་དོར་སྨོས། ཐན་མོ་འི་རྨ་མོ་བལ་རྨེལ་དང་།
འདྲེ་བའི་རྨེད་དང་དྲིས་པའི་རྨས། ཕྱུགས་ཀྱི་རྨིག་པ་རྨ་ཡི་རྨིད། ‖ རྨང་གཞི་རྨངས་ཆེར ༔ རྨིག་མེད་བཙོམ། ༡
སེམས་རྨོངས་བྱིང་རྨུགས་སྨུན་པའི་རྨུས། གོ་ཆའི་རྨོག་དང་དབུ་རྨོག་སོགས། ༢ ར་མགོ་ལྡན་པའི་མ་ཡིག་ཡིན།
གདོང་གི་སྣ་ར་སྣིན་མ་དང་། སྣེ་བ་སྣུག་ཅེ་ཁ་དོག་སྣུག ཕན་པའི་སྨན་དང་སུག་སྨེལ་སྨན། སྨིག་རྒྱུ་སྨུག་རྣུ་ཐྲང་མིན་སྨར། ༣
ཚེ་སྨད་སྨ་ཕབ་སྨད་རས་སྨོད། སྐར་མ་སྨིན་དྲུག་སྨལ་པོ་དང་། སྨིན་དྲུག་བུ་དང་སྨེ་ཤ་ཅན། ༨
ཤིང་གི་སྨྱིག་མ་སྨུག་མ་དང་། གདམ་སྨས་སྨོས་དང་འབྲས་བུ་སྨིན། དྲུར་སྨྱིག་སྨན་རྫོངས་སྨྲི་ཐགས་འཛིན།
སྨན་ལམ་ནམ་སྨིན་སྨོན་འདྲིན་གྲོགས། བུ་སྨད་མིང་སྨོས་སྨྱོན་ཀ་བྱེད། སྨྲང་གནས་དུས་སྨྲུར་སྨྱོན་པོ་སྨྱོ།
མགོ་སྨུང་ལྟ་ཅི་སྨོས་ཞེས་སོགས། ས་མགོ་ལྡན་པའི་མ་ཡིག་ཡིན། མ་ཡི་བརྡ་རྣམས་མདོར་བསྡུས་རྫོགས། ‖

༄༅ ཙའི་བརྡ་བཤད་པ་ལ།

དང་པོ་རྐྱང་པ་འདི་ལྟ་སྟེ། ཙབ་ཙུབ་མི་བྱ་དེ་ཙུག་ལགས། ཙནྡན་དེ་ཙོ་ཙོག་པུར་འདུག
༥ ཙ་ན་ཀ་དང་ཙམ་པ་ཀ། ཙུག་ཙུག་སླ་སོགས་ཙ་རྐྱང་ཡིན། གཉིས་པ་འཕྱུལ་ཅན་འདི་ལྟ་སྟེ།
སྤྱི་གཙུག་གཙུག་ཏོར་གཙུག་ལགས་ཁང་། གཙང་སྦྲ་གཙོ་བོ་དྲི་གཙང་ཁང་། གཙོང་རོ་ཀྱུ་གཙང་གཙང་ཕྱོགས་ཡུལ།
མཆེ་བ་གཙིགས་དང་མི་གཙིགས་ཆེ། ཁྲག་འཛིན་གཙག་བུས་གཙག་པ་དང་། གཙོར་བ་གདོན་གྱིས་གཙེས་ཤིང་གཙེ།
གཙུབ་ཤིང་བཙུང་ཕྲན་གཙུབས་པ་སོགས། ག་ཡིས་འཕུལ་བའི་ཙ་ཡིག་ཡིན། བཙན་པོ་བཀའ་བཙན་རྫོང་བཙན་དང་།
བཙུན་མོ་བུ་བཙས་བཙོན་རར་བཙུད། བཙུན་པ་མིག་བཙུམ་བཙོ་བླག་མཁན། ༦ བཙག་དང་བཙོད་ཀྱིས་གོས་བཙོས་བཙེམས།
ཨུ་ཀ་པ་ཀྱི་བཙའ་དང་ཉོད་སོགས་བཙལ། འབགས་པའི་བཙོག་དང་རིག་བཙོག་བྱེད། གནོག་བཙོང་བཙོངས་ནས་བཙན་དུག་ཉོ།
བཙན་རྒོད་ཞབས་བཙན་གསེར་བཙོ་མ། ཚོགས་ཀྱིས་བཙགས་དང་འཆོར་པའི་བཙིར། མཐེ་བཙེམས་བཙོད་པོ་བཙོས་མ་བཟང་།

---

* གཏོག་པ། † དུས་གཅིག་པ་བཤད་པའི་ཕྱོགས་འགྲེད་མེད་པ། ‡ དོ་མཚར་བའི། § གནོད་སྦྱིན་ཇམ་བྷ་ལ། + ཉམས་པ ‖ བཀྲམ་གཞི།
༔ སྟའི་སྤུ་འཐོག་སྤུད་དེ་སྣང་ཡང་ཟེར། ༡ གཏན་མེད། ༢ བུ་འཕང་། ༣ སྟན་པ། ༨ བཤད་པ། ༥ སྣན་མ། ༦ ཆོས་མཁན།

སྤྱོལ་དང་ཤིང་སོགས་བཙུགས་པ་དང་། ལ་བཙས་ཀྱི་བཙས་པ་ལ་སོགས། བ་ཡིས་འཕྲུལ་བའི་ཚ་ཡིག་ཡིན།

གསུམ་པ་མགོ་ཅན་འདི་ལྟ་སྟེ། རྩ་བ་རྩེ་མོ་རྩ་ལག་གཉེན། ལུས་ཀྱི་རྩ་དང་རྩོན་རྩེ་རྩེང་།

རྩི་ཤིང་རྩྭ་དང་རྩི་མར་དང་། རྩེ་ཐོག་རྩངས་པ་རྩོད་ནས་གཅོད། འཐབ་རྩོད་རྩེད་མོ་རྩེ་དང་རྩེས།

རུས་པའི་རྩིབ་མ་འཁོར་ལོ་འི་རྩིབས། བརྟང་བའི་རྩབ་དང་བྲུ་རྩིང་རྩུབ། རྩིས་མཁན་རྩིས་བྱེད་ཐབས་རྩལ་ཆེ།

ཁ་རྩང་རྩམ་པའི་རིན་ལ་རྩིག ། * ལྷས་རྩེན་སྲུམ་རྩེན་རྩེན་དེ་སྲིད། འབད་རྩོལ་སྒྲོག་རྩོལ་བྱ་བ་རྩོམ།

རྩེ་རྒོད་རྩིག་པ་རྩིག་མཁན་སོགས། † ར་མགོ་ལྡན་པའི་ཚ་ཡིག་ཡིན། བཀའ་སྩལ་ལྷུན་པ་སྩལ་བཀྱི་དང་།

བཀྱིད་དུ་སྩལ་དང་དངོས་གྲུབ་སྩལ། སྩོལ་དང་སྩལ་དུ་གསོལ་ལ་སོགས། ས་མགོ་ལྡན་པའི་ཚ་ཡིག་ཡིན།

བརྩོན་འགྲུས་སྙིང་བརྩེ་བརྩེ་བ་ཅན། བརྩད་ཅིང་དྲིས་ནས་བརྩམ་བྱ་བརྩམས། ཁང་བརྩིགས་བརྩིགས་དང་བརྩི་བྱ་བརྩིས།

སོ་བརྩི་ཉ་ཅང་བརྩེངས་པའི་གོས། ‡ བས་འཕྲུལ་ར་མགོ་ལྡན་པའི་ཚའོ།།

ཙ་ཡི་བརྡ་རྣམས་མདོར་བསྡུས་རྫོགས།།

༄༅ ཚའི་བརྡ་བཤད་པ་ལ།

དང་པོ་རྐྱང་པ་འདྲེ་བྱེད་ཚྭ། འོད་ཟེར་ཚ་ཚྭ་འཕྲོ་བའོ།། § གཉིས་པ་འཕྲུལ་ཅན་འདི་ལྟ་སྟེ།

---

* ཁ་སང་ཟེར། † ལྷ་འབངས། ‡ སོ་རྩི་དང་རྩེངས་ཀྱང་ཟེར། § མང་ལ་ཕ་ཟུར་བཏབ་པའི་དཔེ་མང་དུ་སྣང་ངོ་།།

ཕྱུགས་མཚམས་མཚམས་མེད་མཚན་ཉིད་དང་། ཛོ་མཚར་མཚན་དཔེ་མཚོ་དང་ཚེའུ།

མཆེ་མ་མཚམས་བཙད་མཚན་གཞི་དང་། རྒྱལ་མཚན་མཚར་སྦུག་མཚན་མས་མཚན།

མཆོད་བྱེད་ཕྱག་མཚན་མཆོད་ཆ་དང་། མཚུར་སྔོན་ཁ་མཚུལ་མཚལ་དང་མཚུངས། སྤྱི་བོ་འི་མཆོག་མ་མིང་གི་མཚན།

དྲེའུ་རྟ་མཚལ་ལུ་སྨྱོན་གྱི་མཚང་། རྒྱ་མཚན་ཁྲིམ་མཆེས་དུར་དུ་མཆེད། མ་ཡིས་འཛུལ་བའི་ཚ་ཡིག་ཡིན།

ཟས་ཀྱི་འཚལ་མ་ཟོས་པའི་འཚལ། ཤེས་དང་ཚིག་པའི་འཚོལ་སོགས་དང་། ཕྱག་འཚལ་འཚང་རྒྱ་བློ་དང་འཚམས།

དུས་འཚམས་བློ་འཚབས་ཡོངས་པའི་འཚར། * རིག་འཚོག་གདུང་འཚོབ་འཚོག་ཆས་འཚེང་།

གནོད་འཚེ་ལུས་འཚོ་རྒྱལ་བའི་འཚེངས། འཚོམ་པའི་འཚག་དང་ལུས་འཚག་བཟང་། †

ནོར་འཚོལ་ཕྱུགས་འཚོ་འཚོ་བྱེད་དང་། ངལ་འཚོ་འོད་འཚེར་ནད་དུ་འཚངས། ‡ ཚུ་སོགས་འཚག་དང་ཟས་འཚོད་སོགས།

འ་ཡིས་འཛུལ་བའི་ཚ་ཡིག་ཡིན། ཚ་ཡི་བརྡ་རྣམས་མདོར་བསྡུས་རྫོགས།། §

༄ ཛའི་བརྡ་བཤད་པ་ལ།

དང་པོ་རྐྱང་པ་བཤད་མི་དགོས། གཉིས་པ་འཛུལ་ཅན་འདི་ལྟ་སྟེ། དཔའ་མཛངས་མཁས་མཛངས་ཡ་རབས་མཛངས།

གནོད་མཛེས་མཛའ་བོ་འི་མཛད་པ་མཛོད། བང་མཛོད་མཛུབ་མོ་མཛོད་སྤྲུས་མཛེས། དུད་འགྲོ་མཛོ་དང་མཛེ་ནད་སོགས།

མ་ཡིས་འཛུལ་བའི་ཛ་ཡིག་ཡིན། ཕན་རྫུན་འཛིངས་དང་ཆུ་འཛག་འཛེར། སྡོད་འཛིད་གོས་འཛེར་ལག་པས་འཛིན།

འཛམ་གླིང་ནོར་འཛོམ་སྡོད་དུ་འཛུད། བཞིན་འཛུམ་རྩུད་འཛེར་འདུ་འཛེར་འཛེམ། ནོར་བའི་འཛོལ་དང་འོག་ཏུ་འཛུལ།

འཁྲུགས་པའི་འཛིག་འཛོག་ཟད་པའི་འཛད། སྐད་འཛེར་ཡོགས་སྐྱེས་འཛེར་པ་དང་། བཟུར་བའི་འཛུར་དང་རྡོ་ཡི་འཛེར།

སྤོལ་དང་རྒྱལ་མཚན་འཛུགས་པ་སོགས། འ་ཡིས་འཛུལ་བའི་ཛ་ཡིག་ཡིན། གསུམ་པ་མགོ་ཅན་འདི་ལྟ་སྟེ།

རྫུན་གྱི་རྫབ་རྫུབ་ཀུན་རྫོབ་དང་། རྫས་སྐྱེས་རྫང་བུ་འདམ་རྫབ་རྫོབ། བུ་ཛ་ཕྱུགས་ཛ་ཛ་མེད་དང་།

མིག་གི་ཛ་མ་ལྷུང་གི་ཛ། མཁར་རྫིང་ནོར་རྫས་རྫུ་འཕྲུལ་དང་། སྣོད་ཀྱི་རྫ་མ་འབུལ་པའི་རྫོངས།

ལས་རྫོགས་རྫོགས་སངས་རྒྱས་ལ་སོགས། ར་མགོ་ལྡན་པའི་ཛ་ཡིག་ཡིན། ཟས་བརྫས་ཀྱིན་བ ས་སྒྲིག་ཆགས་བརྫས།

གཞན་གྱིས་མི་བརྫེ་སྲུན་པོར་བརྫ ས། བརྫུན་ཟླས་ཡུལ་གཞན་བརྫངས་པ་སོགས། བས་འཛུལ་ར་མགོ་ལྡན་པའི་ཛའོ།།

---

* གདུང་འཛིན་ནམ་བརྒྱུད་འཛིན། † མདངས་བཟང་བའམ་ཤ་རྒྱས་པ། § བསྡུས། ‡ ངལ་བསོ།།

ཛ་ཡི་བརྡ་རྣམས་མཛོད་བསྡུས་རྫོགས།།

༄ ཕྱིའི་བརྡ་འདི་ལྟ་སྟེ།

ཕ་སྐྱེས་རྒྱ་ཡི་ཕ་ཁ་དང་། ཕ་ཕང་འགིའུ་ཕང་ཕི་ཕང་དང་། ཡིད་པ་ཕལ་ལེ་ལ་སོགས་པའོ།།

༄ ཞའི་བརྡ་བཤད་པ་ལ།

དང་པོ་རྐྱང་པ་འདི་ལྟ་སྟེ། ཞ་པོ་རྟར་ཞོན་ཞྭ་མོ་རྒྱོན། ཟླ་རྟེན་ཞོལ་པོ་ཛ་ཞོལ་ཆེ།

ཞག་གི་ཟུན་མར་ཞོ་ཟན་ཞིམ། ཞོན་ཟུ་ཟུས་དང་ཟོད་དུ་ཟུ། ཞེམས་ཟུམ་གཟིགས་ཞི་ཟླུད་ཞིའི་ཞབས།

ཞིབ་རྩིང་ཞེང་ཆེ་ཞར་ཟུང་ཞོག། ཞང་པོ་ཞེན་ཆེ་ཟློ་ནུས་ཞན། ཛེས་ཛོགས་བརྟུལ་ཞུགས་ཛ་ཡི་ཛོགས།

ཞོམས་པར་ཞུགས་སོགས་ཞ་རྐྱང་ཡིན། གཉིས་པ་འདྲུལ་ཅན་འདི་ལྟ་སྟེ། རྣམ་གཞག་ཞུན་པ་ཉིར་བཞག་དང་།

མཉམ་གཞག་གཞལ་བྱ་གཞལ་མེད་ཁང་། ནམ་གཞག་གཏན་དུ་བཏག་གཞིག་གཞུག། ཀུན་གཞི་གཞི་གཞུབ་གཞུང་ལུགས་གཞུང་།

གནས་གཞི་གཞོང་པ་གཡང་གཞི་དང་། གཞོན་ནུ་གཞུང་བཟང་ཆོས་ལ་གཞོལ། གཞོགས་སློང་བདུད་གཞོམས་གཞོམ་དུ་མེད།

* ཡིད་གཞུངས་གཞོབ་ཟེ་ནང་དུ་གཞུག། ཞྲོ་གཞོགས་ནད་གཞི་གཞང་འབྲུམ་གཞིལ།

གཞིས་ཀ་གླུ་གཞས་གཞེན་བསྐུལ་འདེབས། † ‡ གཞིག་པོ་གཞོངས་སྤྱོད་གཞའ་ཛོན་གཞུ། §

འཛིབ་པའི་གཞིབ་དང་མཛུག་གཞུག་ཟྲན། འཚོ་ཞིང་བཞུགས་པའི་གཞིས་པ་སོགས།

ག་ཡིས་འཛུལ་བའི་ཞ་ཡིག་ཡིན། གནས་སུ་བཞག་དང་ནང་བྲོལ་བཞག། སྐྱ་བཞར་བཞད་གད་འདབ་ཆགས་བཞད།

བཞབས་ནས་ཞུག་བཟུས་ལྡན་གྱི་བཞར། བཞམས་བཞྲོ་གསོལ་བཞིའི་དགོངས་བཞེད་བཞིན།

འདི་བཞིན་མར་བཞུ་བཞུར་ནས་བཞེས་ + ཁྲུར་བཞེས་བྱུད་བཞིན་ཤིང་སོགས་བཞོགས། ༦

བཞེངས་བཞུགས་འབྱོན་བཞུད་བཞོན་པ་རྟ། དཔང་པོ་ཞི་ཆེ་བཞི་གྲངས་ཀྱི་བཞི། བཞོན་མ་བཞོ་བཞོས་གཡོག་བཞེན་སོགས།

བ་ཡིས་འཛུལ་བའི་ཞ་ཡིག་ཡིན། ཞ་ཡི་བརྡ་རྣམས་མཛོད་བསྡུས་རྫོགས།།

༄ ཟའི་བརྡ་བཤད་པ་ལ།

དང་པོ་རྐྱང་པ་འདི་ལྟ་སྟེ། ཛྭ་ཚོད་ཟས་ཟོ་ཟད་པ་མེད། གང་ཟག་ཟག་མེད་ཟབ་དོན་སྒོམ། ༧

---

* མཁས་པ། † དྲན་བསྐུལ། ‡ ལོངས་སྤྱོད་པ། § འཇའ་ཚོན། + ཟོ་བ་ཟ་བྱེད་པའི་ཞེ་སའོ།། ༦ ལོངས་སྤྱོད་པའི་ཞེ་སའོ།། ༧ ཉོན་མོངས་མེད་པ།

ཟང་ཟིང་ཟོལ་ཟོག་གཉིས་ཀྱི་ཟུང་། ཆང་ཟུངས་ལུས་ཟུངས་རྫོགས་ཟིན་ཟུངས།

ཁྲི་ཟུག་ཟོར་འཛིན་ཟུད་ཟོས་ཟོབ། * ཛྭ་ངའི་ཟོར་བ་ཟོ་བ་ཟོམ། སྨར་མིན་ཟོང་དང་རིན་ཆེན་ཟངས།

ཛྭ་ཛེ་འི་ཟིལ་པ་ཟིལ་གྱིས་གནོན། ཟལ་པོ་འི་ཟྲུ་ཟགས་ཟར་མ་ཟོས། ཤིང་ཟན་ཟུང་ཟད་ཟླུས་ཟིན་ཟེར།

འོད་ཟེར་ཟེའུ་འབྲུ་ཟུག་ཙོ་ནད། ཟམ་ཟིམ་ཁ་ཟུམ་ཟམ་པའི་ཟུར། ཟུང་དུ་ཐོགས་ཟླ་གཞན་ལ་ཟླ།

ཟླ་བ་ཟླུམ་པོ་ཟློས་གར་བྱེད། ཟླ་མེད་ཟླ་གམ་ཟླས་དབྱེ་དང་། ཟླ་གྲོགས་ཕོ་ཟླ་སྒྲ་ངན་ཟློ།

རྫས་ཟློས་ཟློག་པ་ཟ་རྐྱང་ཡིན། གཉིས་པ་འཛུལ་ཅན་འདི་ལྟ་སྟེ། དགང་གཟར་གླུགས་གཟར་གཟར་བུ་སྒྲོགས།

རྫུལ་གཟན་གཟར་ཐག་ཕྲག་པར་གཟར། † རི་གཟར་གཟའ་སྐར་གཟི་བརྗིད་ཅན།

གཅན་གཟན་གཟན་ཟ་ཕྱན་གྱི་གཟར། གཟན་ཕྱན་གཟན་ཆེ་བརྡེག་པར་གཟས། གཟུ་གཟིངས་གཟི་འོད་ནོར་བུ་གཟི།

ཕྱག་གཟིག་སྣུན་གཟིགས་གཟུགས་བརྙན་གཟིགས། གཟུངས་ཐོགས་གསུངས་གདབ་དགེ་ལ་གཟུད། ‡

ད་གཟོད་ཟིན་གཟོ་ཆུད་མི་གཟོན། གཟུ་ལུམ་གཟུང་འཛིན་གཟེར་ནད་ཆེ། §

འོད་གཟེར་གཟེར་བུ་སྟོད་ཀྱི་གཟེབ། || ཀོ་བའི་གཟོང་དང་གཟོད་མའི་དུས། ¶

གཟུང་བྱེད་གཟུ་བོ་མཐའ་དུ་གཟིམས། ᴗ ཤ་གཟུག་ལ་གཟིར་ཤིང་སོགས་གཟེར།

བགྲོ་བ་རྣར་གཟོན་གཟིངས་བསྐྱོད་དང་། ᐱ ཚེར་མ་གཟངས་རིང་གཟུང་སྒྲིབས་སོགས།

ག་ཡིས་འཛུལ་བའི་ཟ་ཡིག་ཡིན། ལྷུང་བཟེད་བཟེད་ཞལ་བཟེད་ནས་བཟུར། གཟའ་བ་བཟབས་རྒྱུས་ཕྱིན་པ་བཟས།

བཟོ་བོ་བཟའ་མི་ཚང་གིས་བཟི། ན་བཟའ་བཟང་པོ་ལག་པས་བཟུང་། བཟུང་བྱ་ཚུལ་གཟུང་ངེས་བཟས་རན།

དེང་ནས་བཟུངས་ཏེ་རྗེས་སུ་བཟུངས། གཏུམ་པའི་མི་བཟད་བཟེ་རེ་ཅན། ᴖ

བཟོད་པ་དཔྱིན་བཟླུམས་གཅིག་ཏུ་བཟླུམས། གསང་ཐོགས་བཟླ་བཟླས་སྒྲ་ངན་བཟླ།

མི་བཟློག་པ་དང་གཡུལ་བཟློག་སོགས། བ་ཡིས་འཛུལ་བའི་ཟ་ཡིག་ཡིན། ཟ་ཡི་བརྡ་རྣམས་མདོར་བསྡུས་རྫོགས།།

འ་ཡི་བརྡ་ནི་བཤད་མི་དགོས།

༄ ཡའི་བརྡ་བཤད་པ་ལ།

---

* ཏུ་ཟུག་ཟུད་པ། † དཔུང་ཐག། ‡ ནམ་རྟེན་བྱིན་རླབས་སུ་གཟུངས་གདབ་པོ་ཟེར་བ་ལྷ་བུའོ།། § རང་བཟོ་ཅན། || འོད་ཟེར་ཡང་རྩང་།

¶ དང་པོའི་དུས། ᴗ ནད་པོ། ᐱ སྒྲུབ་པ་ལ་མི་ཉན་པའི་མིང་། ᴖ བཟོད་བསྲན་ཆུང་པ།

དང་པོ་རྐྱང་པ་བཤད་མི་དགོས། གཉིས་པ་འཕྲུལ་ཅན་འདི་ལྟ་སྟེ།

གཡར་རྡོ་གཡར་ཁྲོལ་གཡར་དམ་དང་། * གཡས་གཡོན་གཡང་གཞི་གཡབ་གཡུབ་གཡོབ།

གཡང་ས་གཡི་གཡོ་གཡུང་དྲུང་དང་། དཔལ་གྱི་གཡང་དང་དྲུག་དམར་གཡུ། སྐྱི་གཡའ་གཡའ་སྐྱོག་ཞྭགས་གཡའ་དང་།

གཡོ་སྒྱུ་ས་གཡོ་ཟས་གཡོ་གཡོས། མི་བརྩོན་གཡེལ་དང་གཡེང་པས་གཡེངས། གཞན་ལ་ཁ་གཡར་གཡམ་ལ་རྒྱུག †

གཡེར་མ་གཡིགས་བྱེད་སེམས་ཅན་གཡི། རིགས་ངན་གཡུང་མོ་ཡོགས་གཡེམ་སྤྱོད། ‡

གཡུལ་ས་གཡུལ་འཁྲུག་དུད་འགྲོ་གཡག། གཡེར་ཁ་གཡུར་ཟ་གཡན་པ་ནད། མིག་གཡོར་བྲན་གཡོག་གོས་ཀྱིས་གཡོགས།

§ གསེང་གཡབས་བསིལ་གཡབས་གཡར་པོ་གཡོར། ‖ རླུང་གཡོར་གཡེར་ ༦ པོ་སྣང་གཡེལ་ཅན། ༧

ག་ཡིས་འཕྲུལ་བའི་ཡ་ཡིག་ཡིན། ཡ་ཡི་བརྡ་རྣམས་མདོར་བསྡུས་རྫོགས།།

ༀ རའི་བརྡ་བཤད་པ་ལ།

དང་པོ་རྐྱང་པ་འདི་ལྟ་སྟེ། མགོ་སྐྲས་རྭ་དང་ཁྲག་རླངས་དང་། ཁ་རླངས་རླུང་གིས་རླག་བྱེད་རློག།

རོལ་བུའི་རྙིད་བུ་ཁྲུང་བུའི་རྒྱབས། འཛོམས་ཀྱི་རྙིག་པ་ཟས་ཕྱིར་རྒྱུགས། རླབས་ཆེན་དབའ་རླབས་ཕྱིན་རླབས་རློབས། ༨

མདོན་རྙོམ་རྙོམ་སེམས་རྣན་རྙོན་ཆང་། ད་སོགས་རྐྱང་པ་འཕྲུལ་མེད་ཡིན། གཉིས་པ་འཕྲུལ་ཅན་འདི་ལྟ་སྟེ།

ལུས་ཀྱི་བཀྲ་ཤ་རྩ་ཡིས་བཀྲན། བརྟན་པའི་བརྙིང་དང་བྱིན་གྱིས་བརླབས། བཙོམ་བརླག་བརླག་བྱ་དགྲ་བོ་བརླག།

རྩུབ་ཚིག་བརྙང་བོ་གདོན་གྱིས་བརླམས། རྙིང་པོ་མེད་པའི་ཨ་མ་བརྙ། བས་འཕྲུལ་ར་ལ་ལ་བརྟགས་ཡིན།

ར་ཡི་བརྡ་རྣམས་མདོར་བསྡུས་རྫོགས།། ཞྭ་བ་གོས་ཀྱི་བྱེ་བྲག་གོ

ༀ ཤའི་བརྡ་བཤད་པ་ལ།

དང་པོ་རྐྱང་པ་འདི་ལྟ་སྟེ། ཤང་ཤང་ཤུག་པའི་ཤིང་བར་ཤི།

ཤུལ་དུ་ཤིད་ཟན་ཤུབ་བུར་སྦྲ། ༩ ཤེས་ལྡན་ཤམ་ཐབས་ཤུར་བྲུས་བཅིངས། ཤེད་བུ་ཤེད་བདག་ཤེད་ལས་སྐྱེས།

ཤད་སྒྲུངས་ཚིག་ཤད་རྟོར་བུ་ཤེལ། རྡོ་ཤལ་སོག་པུ་སྣ་ཡི་ཤངས། ཆ་ཤས་ཤུགས་དྲག་དྲག་ཤུལ་ཆེ།

གྲི་ཤུབ་རྟིང་ཤགས་ཤབ་སོབ་རྫུན། ཤག་པོ་ཤར་ཤར་ཤུགས་བླུ་སོད། ཤན་ཞུགས་ཤན་འབྱེད་མི་འགྱུར་ཤིགས།

---

* རྡོ་ཁྲོལ་དང་དམ་བཙའ། † ཞར་ལ། ‡ འདོད་ལོག། § བུད་མེད་གཡེར་མོ། ‖ གཡོར་མོ་ཡང་ཟེར། ༦ ཁྲིམས་པའམ་ཐར་པོ།། ༧ དྲུའི་ནང་། ༨ ཐ་རླབས། ༩ སྣ་རགས་ཀྱི་བྱེ་བྲག་གཅིག་གི་མིང་།

ཤྭ་ཧོད་ཤར་སོགས་ཤ་རྒྱུད་ཡིན།

གཉིས་པ་འཕྲུལ་ཅན་འདི་ལྟ་སྟེ། འགབ་ཀྱི་གཤམ་དང་མོ་གཤམ་དང་། * ཡང་དག་གཤའ་མ་ཡིན་ལུགས་གཤའ།
དེ་བཞིན་གཤེགས་པ་གཤིས་ལུགས་གནས། གཤིན་པོ་བདེ་བར་སོང་བའི་གཤེགས། གཤིན་རྗེ་གཤེད་དང་ཞིང་ས་གཤིན།
གཤན་རབས་གཤང་དཀྱིལ་ཁ་གཤགས་འགྱེད། གཤིས་ངན་གཡུལ་གསོམ་སྒྱུ་བའི་གཞི། ཐུན་གཤེར་སྨོད་པའི་གཤུང་བ་དང་།
རྒྱ་གསོ་བྲིས་གསོར་འཕྲང་ལ་གཤར། ཡུར་བའི་གསོར་དང་ཐོང་གསོལ་དང་། †
ཤིང་གསོག་གཤགས་དང་འདབ་གསོག་གཤིབས། དམའ་བའི་གཤོང་དང་ཐང་གཤོངས་སོགས།
ག་ཡིས་འཕྲུལ་བའི་ཤ་ཡིག་ཡིན། ཚོས་བཤད་བྲིར་བཤར་འཕྲང་ལ་བཤར། ཐིག་བཤགས་བཤང་གཙི་བཀོད་པ་བཤམས། ‡
བཤུལ་ལམ་བཤར་དང་རི་དྭགས་བཤོར། རྒྱ་བསོར་རྒྱུས་བཤལ་བཤལ་བ་རྡུད། མཛའ་བཤེས་དགེ་བཤེས་ལྷ་བསོས་བཤམས།
ཕྱི་བསོལ་བཤགས་ནས་བགོ་བཤའ་བྱེད། རྒྱབ་བཤུལ་བཤུས་ནས་བཤན་པས་བཤས། མཁར་བཤིག་ཐྲུབས་བཤངས་ནང་དུ་བསོང་།
ཅུ་བའི་བཤུམ་དང་གཏམ་བཤེར་སོགས། བ་ཡིས་འཕྲུལ་བའི་ཤ་ཡིག་ཡིན
ཤ་ཡི་བརྡ་རྣམས་མདོར་བསྡུས་རྫོགས།།

ༀ སའི་བརྡ་བཤད་པ་ལ།

དང་པོ་རྐྱང་པ་འདི་ལྟ་སྟེ། སངས་རྒྱས་སོར་མོ་སེན་མོ་སོ། སེལ་སྣན་སིལ་སིལ་སེ་མོ་ཧ།
སོག་པོའི་ཕྱུག་པ་སོག་པ་དང་། ༤ སག་ཐག་སིང་ཐེར་སྦྲི་སིང་ཏེ། གཉིད་སད་ཉམས་སད་སོམ་ཉི་སོལ། §
སད་དང་སེར་བ་སོ་ནམས་ལས། བདེ་བའི་སིམ་དང་ཕྱིན་པའི་སོན། སེཀྲིའི་སེད་སྒྲོག་སེམས་སྲུན་འཛིན།
སེ་འབྲུ་སལ་ཕུལ་སོལ་བ་སོད། ༥ གདུང་སེལ་སྨན་སེལ་བར་ཆད་སེལ།
མདོན་སུམ་ཕྱུན་སུམ་ཁ་དོག་སེར། སེག་ཧར་སོག་ལེ་སེར་ཁ་ཅན། སེལ་པོ་སྲོག་ཆགས་སྲི་མོ་སྲུམ།
སྲིག་པ་སྲིན་བྱ་སྲི་མ་ཞིག། སྲིན་བུ་སྲིལ་དང་ཚོས་སྲུང་དར། ༦ འོད་སྲུང་སྲུས་དང་ས་སྲུང་བུ། ༧
དྲང་སྲོང་སྲིད་པ་སྲུལ་པོར་བྱེད། ཡིད་སྲུབས་སྲུབ་ཤིང་སྲུབ་ཐག་དང་། སྲིན་པོ་ལུས་སྲུལ་ཚེ་སྲོག་སྲ།
སྲིག་བྱེད་སྲིག་བླུགས་ལམ་སྲང་སྲབ། རྒྱལ་སྲིད་ཚོས་སྲིད་སྨན་སྲིབས་སྲིད། ༨ སྲད་བུའི་སྲུང་བས་སྲད་མ་སྲུངས།

---

* རབ་ཆད་མོ།། † རྒྱ་ལམ། ‡ ཧུག་གཙེར། ༤ ལག་པ། § ཐེ་ཚོམ། ༥ སོག་བ་དང་གོས་སོགས་ཀྱི་ཕུལ། ༦ སྨུག་པ།
༧ གླང་པོ་ཆེ། ༨ ཐུད་པའི།

འཇལ་བྱེད་སྲང་དང་སྲིད་དུ་སྲིངས། ཏ་ཡི་སྲབ་དང་སྲན་མ་སྲུས།

སྲིད་དུས་ས་སྲིས་ལུགས་སྲོལ་སྲིངས། གཉེན་གྱི་སྲིང་མོ་སྲུ་མོ་དང་། འདོད་སྲིད་སྲི་ཞུ་སྲི་ཙུའི་སྲི། *

སློབ་དཔོན་སློབ་གཉེར་སློབ་པ་སློ། སློབ་པ་སློབ་མ་སློང་མོ་སློང་། † ཀུན་སློང་གྱིན་དུ་སློང་དང་སློག།

སྲིའུ་སློག་པ་ཕྱི་ནང་སློག། ‡ སྣ་ངའི་སྣད་རོལ་ཕྱུགས་སུ་སྣོན། § སྣད་ཚར་སྣད་ནས་དུག་རོ་སྣོང་། =||

གནས་སུ་བསྣེས་དང་ངན་པར་སྣོད། སྣར་ཡང་སྣུ་གུའི་རྩུ་སྣ་མོ། སྣུ་མེད་སྣི་འདམ་ཅན་ལ་སོགས། ⸪

ས་ཡིག་རྐྱང་པ་འཕུལ་མེད་ཡིན། གཉིས་པ་འཕུལ་ཅན་འདི་ལྟ་སྟེ། གསར་བུ་འོད་གསལ་གསང་སྔགས་པ།

འཁར་གསིལ་གསར་ནས་སྟན་གསན་འཇེབས། ཁ་གསག་གསོག་འཛོག་གསད་བྲ་གསོད།

ཏ་གསེབ་གསུམ་དང་སྲོ་ག་ཆགས་གསར། གསང་གཏམ་གསོང་དང་གསོང་པོར་སྣ། +

བསོན་དང་གསོལ་འདེབས་གསུང་རབ་གསུངས། གསོན་པོ་སྟན་གསང་སྐད་ཀྱང་གསང་། གསང་གི་གསུར་བཏང་དྲིལ་བུ་གསིལ།

འཚིགས་བྱེད་གསོར་གྱིས་ཤིང་གསོམ་གསིལ། གསུམ་པ་གསོ་ཕྱིར་རྩུད་མ་གསོན། གསིག་མ་གསབ་གསིང་གསོ་ཀའི་དུས།

ནང་གསེས་ཙེའུ་གསིང་རིན་ཆེན་གསེར། གསོ་རས་གསིང་གསིང་གསོ་མ་གསོད། གསོ་སྦྱོང་གསལ་ཤིང་གསེགས་ཀ་ཙན།

གསོག་གསོབ་ལུས་གསིག་རྩུ་གསིལ་ནད། ག་ཡིས་འཕུལ་བའི་ས་ཡིག་ཡིན། ཁ་དོག་སྔོ་བསངས་འབགས་པ་བསངས།

བགེགས་བསངས་བསོད་ནམས་བསག་དང་བསགས། དམིགས་བསལ་སྐྱོན་བསལ་བཀག་པ་བསལ།

ཚོར་བསྲི་ཚ་བསྲིངས་རྒྱང་རིང་བསྲིངས། བསྐུར་བའི་བསྲིངས་དང་འཆང་བའི་བསྲིལ།

རིང་བསྲིལ་བསོད་པའི་ཟས་བསྲི་བསྲིས། ‹ ངལ་བསོ་བསྒོ་ཁང་མི་ལ་བསྒོ། དྲི་བསུང་གིས་བསུས་བསེ་རུ་བསད།

ཀོ་བའི་བསེ་དང་བསོད་སྙོམས་བསོགས། དྲིན་ལན་བསབས་དང་བསམ་བློ་བསམས། བསྙུང་བྲོ་བསྙུངས་དང་འཁྲིག་རྫས་བསྙིགས།

ཞོ་བསྲུབས་འཛིག་བསེལ་བཟོད་བསྲན་ཆེ། བློ་བསླལ་ཆེ་དང་གྲང་བའི་བསིལ། བསེར་བུ་ཁ་བསྲུབ་ཞབས་བསིལ་སོགས། ~

བ་ཡིས་འཕུལ་བའི་ས་ཡིག་ཡིན། ཟས་སོགས་བསླངས་དང་གྱེན་དུ་བསླངས། བསླབ་བྱ་ཀུན་ནས་བསླངས་ནས་བསླབས།

རྗེས་སུ་བསླབས་དང་སླུ་བ་མེད། བློ་ལ་བསླན་དང་ངན་པར་བསླད། བས་འཕུལ་ས་ལ་ལ་བཏགས་ཡིན།

ས་ཡི་བརྡ་རྣམས་མདོར་བསྡུས་རྫོགས།། ཊུལ་པོ་ཊིང་ཊང་ཊིམ་ཊུལ་ཊེལ། ཊག་ཊིག་བཊ་དང་ཊུམ་ཊུམ་གཊུབས།

དེ་ལྟར་རྐྱང་པ་འཕུལ་ཅན་དང་། མགོ་ཅན་བརྡ་རྣམས་མདོར་བསྡུས་རྫོགས།། སརྦ་མངྒ་ལམ།

---

* བུ་ཆུང་ངུའི་དུས་སྲི། † ཉན་ཐོས། ‡ ཕྱི་རོལ། § སྣོར། ||=ཕྱིས་ནས། ⸪ མཆན་མ་ཚད་པ། + དང་པོར།
‹ བཟང་པོའི་ཟས། ~ སྐྱུང་།

BOOK IV.

SITUI SHAL LUNG

སི་ཏུའི་ཞལ་ལུང་། Pages 1—35.

A LECTURE (ཞལ་ལུང་།) *i.e.* ESSAY ON SITU SUM-TAG.

IN this work, Lama Dharma Bhadra, High Priest of the Monastery of Gahdan-tse, in Tsang, Ngul-Chu, has simplified Situ Panchen's elaborate commentary on Thon-mi SamBhota's *Sum-chu-pa* and *Tag-ki-jug-pa*. Readers should begin with this.

Page		Line		For		Read	
Page	༡	Line	༡༠	For	པསྟན་བཅོས	Read	བསྟན་བཅོས
,,	༡	,,	༡༨	,,	སུམ་བཅུར་གནས་པ	,,	སུམ་ཅུར་གནས་པས
,,	༨	,,	༧	,,	དབྱེ་ན་རྗེ་སུ	,,	དབྱེ་ན་རྗེས་སུ
,,	༤	,,	༣	,,	དང་དུ་འཇུག	,,	གང་དུའང་འཇུག
,,	༤	,,	༡༡	,,	རྣམས་དབྱེ	,,	རྣམ་དབྱེ
,,	༦	,,	༨	,,	གང་མིན་མཐར	,,	གང་མིང་མཐར
,,	༦	,,	༥	,,	དེ་ལ	,,	དེ་ལ
,,	༧	,,	༡༠	,,	གསུམ་པ་ང	,,	གསུམ་པ་ད
,,	༧	,,	༡༠	,,	བཅུ་བ	,,	བཅུ་པ
,,	༧	,,	༡༥	,,	ར་ཡི	,,	ད་ཡི
,,	༧	,,	༡༨	,,	དངོས་སུམ	,,	དངོས་སུ་མ
,,	༧	,,	༢༠	,,	ཞེས་བར	,,	ཞེས་པར
,,	༨	,,	༩	,,	ལ་དོན་སུ་ཡི	,,	ལ་དོན་སུ་ལ
,,	༨	,,	༡༠	,,	ལྷག་མ་དང	,,	ལྷག་དང
,,	༩	,,	༡༣	,,	མཐོང་ལས	,,	མཐོང་བ་ལས
,,	༩	,,	༡༨	,,	འཇུག་བའི	,,	འཇུག་པའི
,,	༩	,,	༡༨	,,	སྤྱད་པའམ	,,	སྤྱད་པའང
,,	༩	,,	༡༦	,,	ཡའམ	,,	ཡའང
,,	༩	,,	༡༧	,,	མཐུན་པ་ལ་གནས	,,	མཐུན་པ་ལ་ནས
,,	༩	,,	༢༠	,,	དེ་ལཔ	,,	དེ་ལས
,,	༡༠	,,	༡	,,	ཀྱི་སྒྲར་ན་ནི	,,	ཀྱི་སྒྲར་བ་ནི
,,	༡༠	,,	༣	,,	ང་ཡི	,,	ཀ་ཡི
,,	༡༠	,,	༦	,,	བདག་བཤད་པ	,,	བདག་སྒྲ་བཤད་པ
,,	༡༡	,,	༥	,,	འདྲི་གཞི	,,	འབྲི་གཞི
,,	༡༡	,,	༡༡	,,	བདག་གི་བ་ལག	,,	བདག་གི་བ་ལས

Page	༡༢	Line	༡	For	བདག་པོའི་གསར	Read	བདག་པོའི་སར
,,	༡༢	,,	༡༢	,,	སྠི་རི་ཐེཛ	,,	ས་ཏྲི་ཐེཛ
,,	༡༢	,,	༡༢	,,	དེ་ལ་སྠི་རི	,,	དེ་ལ་ས་ཏྲི
,,	༡༢	,,	༡༨	,,	མར་ཏྲི	,,	མར་ས་ཏྲི
,,	༡༢	,,	༡༩	,,	བཅད་སའི་མཚམས་སྦྱར	,,	བཅད་པའི་མཚམས་སྦྱོར
,,	༡༣	,,	༡༤	,,	འགྲེལ་བར་སྦྱ་བ	,,	འགྲེལ་བ་སྦྱ་བ
,,	༡༨	,,	༦, ༧	,,	རྗེས་སུ་དཔགས་ཏྲི	,,	རྗེས་སུ་དཔག་སྐྲི
,,	༡༨	,,	༡༢	,,	མཐུན་མོན་མིན་པ	,,	མཐུན་མོང་མིན་པ
,,	༡༩	,,	༥, ༧	,,	གནས་པ་ལས	,,	གནས་པ་ལ
,,	༢༠	,,	༧	,,	མོ་ཞན་ན་པའི	,,	མོ་ནི་ཞན་པའི
,,	༢༢	,,	༡༧	,,	གསུམ་རྗེས་འཇུག	,,	གསུམ་པ་རྗེས་འཇུག
,,	༢༣	,,	༨	,,	བརྒྱད་ད་དུ	,,	བརྒྱད་དུ
,,	༢༣	,,	༨	,,	ག་མཐའ་སའི	,,	ག་མཐར་སའི
,,	༢༣	,,	༥	,,	བ་མཐའ་སའི	,,	བ་མཐར་སའི
,,	༢༣	,,	༦	,,	ད་མ་སའི་ཡང་འཇིག	,,	ང་མ་ལ་སའི་ཡང་འཇུག
,,	༢༣	,,	༦, ༧	,,	ད་མ་འའི་མཐའ་ཅན	,,	ང་མ་འའི་མཐའ་ཅན
,,	༢༣	From line	༦	,,	མ་ནིང་གསུམ་ནི	Up to line	དབྱེ་བར་འདོད་དོ་ཞེས་སོ

According to the Situ Sumtag run as follows:—

༄ མ་ནིང་གི་ཡི་གེ་ན་ར་ལ་གསུམ་ནི་མིང་གཞིའི་མོ་ཡིག་གི་མཐར་ཡང་འཇུག་ཡོད་མེད་གང་རུང་དང་། མོ་ཡིག་གི་རྗེས་སུ་ཡང་འཇུག་མེད་པར་ཞུགས་པའི་ཚེ་ནི་སྒྲ་བར་མའི་དག་པའམ་ཞན་པར་འགྱུར་བས་འགྱུར་བ་མ་ནིང་དང་། མིང་གཞིའི་མོ་ཡིག་གི་མཐར་ཞུགས་ཤིང་ཡང་འཇུག་དང་བཅས་པར་འགྱུར་བའི་ཚེ་ནི་སྒྲ་བར་མ་ལས་དག་ཞན་གཉིས་ཀའི་ཆ་དང་ལྡན་པར་འགྱུར་བས་མ་ནིང་མཚན་གཉིས་པ་དང་། མིང་གཞིའི་མ་ནིང་གི་མཐར་ཞུགས་པའི་ཚེ་ཡང་འཇུག་ཡོད་མེད་ཇི་ལྟར་རུང་སྒྲ་བར་མ་ཙམ་ལས་དག་ཞན་གང་དུའང་མི་འགྱུར་བའི་ཕྱིར་མཚན་མེད་མ་ནིང་ངོ༎

Page	༢༥	Line	༡	For	སྐྱུད་པའི་ཚེས	Read	སྐྱུད་པའི་ཚེག
,,	༢༥	,,	༥	,,	སྐྱོབག	,,	སྐྱོབས
,,	༢༦	,,	༦	,,	ནམ་དབྱུ་གཉིས་པ	,,	ནམ་དབྱེ་གཉིས་པ
,,	༣༡	,,	༨	,,	ཞེག་སོ	,,	ཞེས་སོ
,,	༣༢	,,	༡༩	,,	དེབས་ན	,,	དེ་བས་ན
,,	༡༨	,,	༡༦	,,	གསྒྲུ	,,	སྒྲུག

ན་མོ་གུ་རུ་མཉྫུ་གྷོ་ཥཱ་ཡ།།

ཡོན་ཏན་མཆོག་མངའ་སྨྲ་མེད་རིན་ཆེན་གསུམ། ཡེ་ཤེས་མི་ཟད་གཙུག་ན་ཟླ་བ་དང་།
ཧ་དབྱངས་བཅུ་ན་པ་ཟླ་བ་སམ་བྷོ་ཊ། ལ་སོགས་འཕགས་བོད་མཁས་པའི་ཚོགས་སྤྱི་དང་།།
ཁྱད་པར་དམ་ཆོས་ཙོ་མའི་རྒྱན་བཟང་གིས། མང་ཐོས་ལུང་གི་ལུས་སྟོབས་ཆེར་བསྐྱེད་ནས།
རྟོགས་པའི་བསམ་འཕེལ་ལག་རྩེར་སྨིན་མཛད་པའི། དྲིན་ཅན་བླ་མའི་ཚོགས་ལ་གུས་བཏུད་ནས།
མིང་ཚིག་རིན་ཆེན་འབྱུང་གནས་སིན་དྷུའི་བདག། རིག་བྱེད་རྣམ་བཞི་སྨྲ་བའི་གཉེར་ལེན་རྒྱུ།
བསླབ་གསུམ་མྱུ་གུ་སྐྱེད་བྱེད་རྒྱ་མཚོའི་གོས། གང་དེ་མདོར་བསྡུས་ཚིག་གིས་བཤད་པར་བྱ།།

དེ་ལ་འདིར་ཡུལ་གངས་ཅན་གྱི་སྐད་ཀྱིས་བརྡ་སྤྲོད་པའི་བསྟན་བཅོས་ཀུན་གྱི་མ་ཕྱིར་གྱུར་པ། སུམ་རྟགས་གཉིས་ཀྱི་ཚིག་དོན་ཅུང་ཟད་ཙམ་བཤད་པ་གཉིས། སུམ་ཅུ་པ་བཤད་པ་དང་། རྟགས་ཀྱི་འཇུག་པ་བཤད་པ་པོ། དང་པོ་ལ་གཉིས། བསྟན་བཅོས་རྩོམ་པ་ལ་འཇུག་པའི་ཡན་ལག་དང་། བསྟན་བཅོས་དངོས་སོ།།

དང་པོ་ལ་གཉིས། མཚན་དོན་དང་། འགྱུར་ཕྱག་གོ། དང་པོ་ནི། རྒྱ་གར་སྐད་དུ། བྱཱ་ཀ་ར་ཎ་མཱུ་ལ་ཏྲིམ་ཤཏ་ཀཱ་མ། བོད་སྐད་དུ། ལུང་སྟོན་པ་རྩ་བ་སུམ་ཅུ་པ་ཞེས་བྱ་བ། ཞེས་པ་སྟེ། བྱཱ་ཀ་ར་ཎ་ལུང་སྟོན་པ། མཱུ་ལ་རྩ་བ། ཏྲིམ་ཤཏ་སུམ་ཅུ་པ། ཀཱ་མ་ཞེས་བྱ་བའོ། དེ་ཡང་སྒྲའི་མཚན་ཉིད་ལུང་དུ་སྟོན་ཅིང་ལེའུ་ཕྱི་མ་རྣམས་ཀྱི་རྟེན་གཞིར་གྱུར་པ་གང་ཞིག་གཞུང་ཚད་ཤོ་ལོ་ཀ་སུམ་བཅུར་གནས་པ་དེ་སྐད་ཅེས་བྱའོ། འདིར་རྒྱ་སྐད་སྨོས་པ་ནི་རྒྱ་གར་མཁས་པའི་བསྟན་བཅོས་ལ་དཔེར་མཛད་བགྲོ་བའི་ཆེད་དང་། གཞུང་ཚད་ཤོ་ལོ་ཀ་སུམ་ཅུ་སོ་གསུམ་ཡོད་པ་ལ་སུམ་ཅུ་པ་ཞེས་བཏགས་པ་ནི། མཆོད་བརྗོད་དང་རྩོམ་པར་དམ་བཅའ་སྐབས་གཞན་དང་མཐུན་མོང་བ་ཡིན་པ་ལ་དགོངས་སོ།།

གཉིས་པ་འགྱུར་ཕྱག་ནི། ངག་གི་དབང་ཕྱུག་འཇམ་པའི་དབྱངས་ལ་ཕྱག་འཚལ་ལོ། ཞེས་པ་སྟེ། བསྟན་བཅོས་འདི་འཕགས་ཡུལ་ནས་བསྒྱུར་བའི་བསྟན་བཅོས་ཁུངས་མ་རྣམས་དང་མཚུངས་པར་འདོམས་པའི་དོན་དུ་ཐོན་མི་ཉིད་ཀྱིས་བསྒྱུར་བའི་མདོ་རྒྱུད་རྣམས་དང་མཐུན་པར་འཕགས་པ་འཇམ་དཔལ་ལ་འགྱུར་ཕྱག་མཛད་པའོ།།

གཉིས་པ་བསྟན་བཅོས་དངོས་ལ། གཞུང་སྤྱིའི་ཡན་ལག་ཏུ་མཆོད་པར་བརྗོད་ཅིང་། བཤད་པར་དམ་བཅའ་བ་དང་། སྐབས་དོན་སུམ་ཅུ་པ་ཉིད་རྒྱས་པར་བཤད་པའོ། དང་པོ་ལ་གཉིས། མཆོད་པར་བརྗོད་པ་དང་། བཤད་པར་དམ་བཅའ་བའོ།། དང་པོ་ལ་བཞི། དཀོན་མཆོག་གསུམ་ལ་སྤྱིར་ཕྱག་འཚལ་བ། ཕྱི་བྲག་ཏུ་འཇམ་པའི་དབྱངས་ལ་ཕྱག་འཚལ་བ། དགོས་པའི་དབང་གིས་རྟག་ཞི་པ་ལ་ཕྱག་འཚལ་བ། དྲིན་བཟོ་བའི་ཕྱིར་མཁས་པ་སྤྱི་དང་ཕྱེ་བྲག་ལ་ཕྱག་འཚལ་བའོ།

དང་པོ་ནི། གང་ལ་ཡོན་ཏན་མཆོག་མངའ་བའི། དཀོན་མཆོག་དེ་ལ་ཕྱག་འཚལ་ལོ། ཞེས་པ་སྟེ། གང་ཞིག་གང་ལ་རིམ་པ་བཞིན་དོན་གཉིས་མཐར་ཕྱིན་པ་དང་། འགོག་ལམ་གྱི་བདེན་པ་གཉིས་དང་། རིག་གྲོལ་གྱི་ཡོན་ཏན་མཆོག་ཏུ་གྱུར་པ་མངའ་བའི་སངས་རྒྱས་དང་། ཆོས་དང་། དགེ་འདུན་ཏེ་དཀོན་མཆོག་གསུམ་པོ་དེ་རྣམས་ལ་སྒོ་གསུམ་གུས་པས་ཕྱག་འཚལ་ལོ།། ཞེསཔའམ། ཡང་ན། ཕྱག་འཚལ་ལོ།། གང་ལ་ན་ཡོན་ཏན་མཆོག་མངའ་བའི་དཀོན་མཆོག་དེ་ལའོ།། ཞེས་བཤད་ཀྱང་རུང་ངོ་།། གཉིས་པ་ཕྱེ་བྲག་ཏུ་འཇམ་པའི་དབྱངས་ལ་ཕྱག་འཚལ་བ་ནི། གང་གིས་སྒྲ་དབྱངས་ཀུན་གསུངས་པའི། འཇམ་པའི་དབྱངས་ལ་ཕྱག་འཚལ་ལོ། ཞེས་པ་སྟེ། གང་གིས་སྒྲ་དབྱངས་བརྗོད་པ་ཐམས་ཅད་གསུངས་པས་གསུང་གི་དབང་ཕྱུག་ཏུ་གྱུར་པ། ངག་གི་ཉེས་པའི་རྩུབ་རིག་དང་བྲལ་བའི་འཇམ་པའི་ཡོན་ཏན་དང་ལྡན་པའི་གསུང་དབྱངས་ཀྱི་བདག་ཉིད་དེ་ལ་ཕྱག་འཚལ་ལོ། ཞེས་པའོ།། དེ་ཡང་རྗེ་བཙུན་ཉིད་རྒྱལ་བ་ཐམས་ཅད་ཀྱི་མཁྱེན་རབ་ཀྱི་ངོ་བོ་ཡིན་པ་དང་། མཁྱེན་རབ་དེ་གསུང་དབྱངས་ཀྱི་རྒྱུ་ཡིན་པ་དང་། གསུང་ནི་སྒྲ་དབྱངས་བརྗོད་པ་ཐམས་ཅད་ཀྱི་འབྱུང་ཁུངས་ཡིན་པས་འཇམ་པའི་དབྱངས་ཉིད་སྒྲ་དབྱངས་གསུང་བ་པོར་བསྟན་ཏོ། །གསུམ་པ་དགོས་པའི་དབང་གིས་རྟག་ཞི་བ་ལ་ཕྱག་འཚལ་བ་ནི། གང་གིས་མིང་གཞི་སྟོན་གསུངས་པའི། །རྟག་ཞི་བ་ལ་ཕྱག་འཚལ་ལོ།། ཞེས་པ་སྟེ། གང་གིས་མིང་ཚིག་བརྗོད་པ་ཀུན་གྱི་གཞིར་གྱུར་བའི་དབྱངས་གསལ་གྱི་ཡི་གེ་སྟོན་དུ་གསུང་བ་པོར་འཇིག་རྟེན་ན་གྲགས་པ་ལྷའི་དབང་པོ་རྟག་ཏུ་ཞི་བ་སྟེ་དབང་ཕྱུག་ཆེན་པོ་ལ་ཕྱག་འཚལ་ལོ།། ཞེས་པའོ།། དེ་ཡང་བྲམ་ཟེ་རྣམས་ཀྱི་གཞུང་དུ་བྱེད་པོ་ཅི་ཤུ་ཏ་བཞི་བཤད་པ་ལས་ཡི་གེའི་བྱེད་པ་པོ་དབང་ཕྱུག་ཆེན་པོར་གྲགས་པ་དང་སློབ་བསྟུན་ནས་ཕྱི་རོལ་པ་རྣམས་རྗེས་སུ་གཟུང་བའི་སླད་དུ་ཡིན་པར་གསུངས་སོ།། བཞི་པ་དྲིན་གཟོ་བའི་ཕྱིར་མཁས་པ་སྤྱི་དང་ཕྱེ་བྲག་ལ་ཕྱག་འཚལ་བ་ནི།

སྡེབ་སྦྱོར་ལེགས་མཛད་མཁས་རྣམས་དང་། བླ་མ་ལ་ཡང་ཕྱག་འཚལ་ནས།

ཞེས་པ་སྟེ། སྒྲ་སྐད་ཀྱི་བརྗོད་པ་དང་དོན་སྡེབ་ལེགས་པར་སྦྱོར་བའི་ཚུལ་སྟོན་པའི་སྒོ་ནས་ཚིག་དོན་གཉིས་ལ་མི་རྨོངས་པའི་ཤེས་རབ་སྐྱེད་ནུས་པའི་གཞུང་རྩོམ་ཞིང་འདོམས་པར་མཛད་པའི་མཁས་པ་སྤྱི་དང་། བྱེ་བྲག་ཏུ་མཁན་པོ་ཉིད་ལ་དེ་ལྟའི་བྱ་བ་མཛད་པའི་བྲམ་ཟེ་ལི་བི་ཀ་ར་ལ་སོགས་པའི་བླ་མ་རྣམས་ལ་འང་ཕྱག་མཛད་པ་སྟེ། ནས་ནི་ལྷག་བཅས་ཀྱི་སྒྲའོ། གཉིས་པ་བཤད་པར་དམ་བཅའ་བ་ནི།།

བསྟན་པ་ཀུན་གྱི་གཞི་འཛིན་ཅིང་། རིག་བྱེད་སྨྲ་བ་རྣམས་ཀྱི་རྒྱུ།
མིང་ཚིག་བརྗོད་པ་ཀུན་གྱི་གཞི། ཡི་གེའི་སྦྱོར་བ་བཤད་པར་བྱ།།

ཞེས་བ་སྟེ། སངས་རྒྱས་པའི་ཚུལ་ཁྲིམས་དང་། ཏིང་ངེ་འཛིན་དང་། ཤེས་རབ་ཀྱི་བསླབ་པའི་གཞི་ཐམས་ཅད་ལྟོས་པའི་སྒོ་ནས་འཛིན་པར་བྱེད་ཅིང་། ཕྱི་རོལ་པའི་ངེས་བརྗོད་དང་། མཆོད་སྦྱིན་དང་། སྙན་ཚིག་དང་། སྲིད་སྲུང་སྐྲོ་རིག་བྱེད་བཞི་ཡན་ལག་དང་བཅས་པའི་གཞུང་ལུགས་མཐའ་དག་སྨྲ་བ་རྣམས་ཀྱི་རྒྱུ་འང་ཡིན་ལ། སྦྱོར་ཡི་གེ་ལས་མིང་དང་། མིང་ལས་ཚིག་དང་ཚིག་ལས་བརྗོད་པ་འབྱུང་བའི་ཕྱིར་འཇིག་རྟེན་ལས་འདས་པའི་མིང་ཚིག་བརྗོད་པ་ཐམས་ཅད་ཀྱི་གཞིར་གྱུར་པ་ནི་ཡི་གེ་འི་སྦྱོར་བ་ཡིན་པས་དེ་བཤད་པར་བྱའོ། ཞེས་པའོ། དེ་ཡང་བོད་ཀྱི་ཡི་གེའི་སྦྱོར་བ་ནི་བརྗོད་བྱ་དང་། གཙུག་ལག་གཉིས་ཀྱི་བླང་དོར་ལ་མ་རྨོངས་པ་ནི་དགོས་པ་དང་། མཐར་ཐུག་རྣམ་མཁྱེན་ཐོབ་པ་ནི་ཉིང་དགོས་དང་། སྔ་ཕྱི་འབྲེལ་ཆགས་པ་འབྲེལ་བའོ།

གཉིས་པ་སྐབས་དོན་སུམ་ཅུ་པ་ཉིད་རྒྱས་པར་བཤད་པ་ལ་གཉིས། ཡི་གེའི་སྦྱོར་བ་རྒྱས་པར་བཤད་པ་དང་། གདམས་ངག་བརྗོད་པས་མཇུག་བསྡུ་བའོ། དང་པོ་ལ་གཉིས། སྒྲར་བྱ་ཡི་གེའི་རྣམ་བཞག་བཤད་པ་དང་། སྦྱོར་ཚུལ་ཚིག་ཕྲད་ཀྱི་འཇུག་པ་བཤད་པའོ།

དང་པོ་ལ་གཉིས། བོད་ཡིག་གི་དབྱངས་གསལ་ངོས་གཟུང་བ་དང་། ཁྱད་པར་གྱི་དབྱེ་བ་བསྟན་པའོ། དང་པོ་ནི། ཡི་གེ་ཨཱ་ལི་ཀཱ་ལི་གཉིས། ཨཱ་ལི་གསལ་བྱེད་ཨི་སོགས་བཞི། ཀཱ་ལི་སུམ་ཅུ་ཐམ་པའོ། ཞེས་པ་སྟེ། སྦྱོར་ཡི་གེ་ལ་ཨཱ་ལི་སྟེ་ཨ་ལ་སོགས་པའི་འཕྲེང་བ་དབྱངས་ཡིག་དང་། ཀཱ་ལི་སྟེ་ཀ་ལ་སོགས་པའི་འཕྲེང་བ་གསལ་བྱེད་

ཀྱི་ཡི་གེ་གཉིས་སུ་ཡོད་ལ། ཕྱི་བྲག་ཏུ་བོད་ཡིག་ལ་ནི། ལེགས་སྦྱར་གྱི་ཨཱ་ལིའི་བྱ་བ་གསལ་བར་མཚོན་པར་བྱེད་པའི་ཡི་གེ་ཨི་ཨུ་ཨེ་ཨོ་བཞི་དང་། ཀཱ་ལི་མཚོན་པར་བྱེད་པ། ཀ་ཁ་ག་ང། ཙ་ཚ་ཛ་ཉ། ཏ་ཐ་ད་ན། པ་ཕ་བ་མ། ཙ་ཚ་ཛ་ཝ། ཞ་ཟ་འ་ཡ། ར་ལ་ཤ་ས། ཧ་ཨ། སྟེ་སུམ་ཅུ་ཐམ་པ་ཡོད་དོ། ཞེས་པའོ།

གཉིས་པ་ཁྱད་པར་གྱི་དབྱེ་བ་བསྟན་པ་ལ་གཉིས། མདོར་བསྟན་པ་དང་། རྒྱས་པར་བཤད་པའོ། དང་པོ་ནི། དེ་ལས་རྗེས་འཇུག་བཅུ་ཡིན་ཏེ། དེ་ལས་ལྔ་ནི་སྔོན་དུའང་འཇུག། མི་འཇུག་པ་ནི་ཉི་ཤུའོ། ཞེས་པ་སྟེ། བཤད་མ་ཐག་པའི་ཡི་གེ་ཀཱ་ལི་དེ་དག་ལ་དབྱེ་ན་རྗེ་སུ་འཇུག་པ་བཅུ་དང་། རྗེས་འཇུག་དེ་ཉིད་ལས་ལྔ་ནི་སྔོན་དུ་འང་འཇུག་པ་ཡིན་པས་སྔོན་འཇུག་དང་། སྔོན་རྗེས་གཉིས་ཀར་མི་འཇུག་པའི་ཡི་གེ་ཉི་ཤུ་སྟེ་ཚན་བ་གསུམ་དུ་དབྱེའོ། ཞེས་པའོ། གཉིས་པ་རྒྱས་པར་བཤད་པ་ལ་གཉིས། དབྱེ་སྒོ་སྤྱིར་བསྟན་པ་དང་། ཕྱེ་བྲག་སོ་སོར་བཤད་པའོ། དང་པོ་ནི། ཀཱ་ལི་ཕྱེད་དང་བརྒྱད་སྡེ་ནི། བཞི་བཞི་དག་ཏུ་ཕྱེ་བ་ལས། ཞེས་པ་སྟེ། ཀཱ་ལི་སུམ་ཅུ་པོ་དེ་རྣམས་ཀ་སྡེ་དང་། ཙ་སྡེ་དང་། ཏ་སྡེ་དང་། པ་སྡེ་དང་! ཙ་སྡེ་དང་། ཞ་སྡེ་དང་། ར་སྡེ་སྟེ་སྡེ་པ་རྣམས་པོ་བདུན་དང་། ཧ་སྡེ་ཕྱེད་དུ་བྱས་ནས་ཕྱེད་དང་བརྒྱད་ཀྱི་སྡེ་ཚན་དུ་བགོས་པ་ནི། སྡེ་པ་རེ་རེ་ལ་ཡི་གེ་བཞི་བཞི་རུ་ཕྱེ་བ་ཡིན་ཅིང་། ལས་ནི་འབྱུང་ཁུངས་ཀྱི་སྒྲའོ།

གཉིས་པ་ཕྱེ་བྲག་སོ་སོར་བཤད་པ་ལ་གསུམ། རྗེས་འཇུག་བཤད་པ། སྔོན་འཇུག་བཤད་པ། མི་འཇུག་པ་བཤད་པའོ།། དང་པོ་ནི། དང་པོ་གསུམ་པ་བཞི་པ་ལས། མཐས་གཉིས་དྲུག་པའི་གསུམ་པ་དང་། བདུན་པ་ལ་ནི་ཤ་མ་གཏོགས། རྗེས་འཇུག་ཡི་གེ་བཅུ་རུ་འདོད། ཅེས་པ་སྟེ། གོང་དུ་རྗེས་འཇུག་བཅུ་ཞེས་བཤད་པ་དེ་གང་ཞེ་ན། སྡེ་པ་དང་པོ་དང་། གསུམ་པ་དང་། བཞི་པ་རྣམས་ཀྱི་མཐས་ཀྱི་ཡི་གེ་གཉིས་གཉིས་ཏེ། ག་ང་། ད་ན། བ་མ། རྣམས་དང་། སྡེ་པ་དྲུག་པའི་གསུམ་པ་འ་དང་། བདུན་པའི་ཤ་མ་གཏོགས་ལྷག་མ་ར་ལ་ས་གསུམ་མོ། དེའང་ཡི་གེ་ཐམས་ཅད་ཀྱི་རྗེས་སུ་འདི་དག་འཇུག་པའི་ཕྱིར་རྗེས་འཇུག་ཅེས་བྱ་ཞིང་ཡི་གེའི་གྲངས་བཅུ་ཉིད་དུ་ངེས་པ་ཡིན་ནོ།

གཉིས་པ་སྔོན་འཇུག་བཤད་པ་ནི། རྗེས་འཇུག་ཡི་གེ་བཅུ་ཉིད་ལས། དང་པོ་གསུམ་པ་ལྔ་པ་དྲུག། བདུན་པ་རྣམས་ནི་སྔོན་དུའང་འཇུག། ཅེས་པ་སྟེ། གོང་དུ་སྔོན་འཇུག་ལྔ་ཞེས་བཤད་པ་དེ་གང་ཞེ་ན། རྗེས་འཇུག་ཡི་གེ་བཅུ་པོ་དེ་དག་ཉིད་ལས་དང་པོ་ག གསུམ་པ་ད། ལྔ་པ་བ། དྲུག་པ་མ། བདུན་པ་འ་རྣམས་ཡིན་ཅིང་། དེ་དག་རྗེས་སུ་

འཇུག་པར་མ་ཟད་སྔོན་དུ་འཇུག་པའང་ཡོད་པས་སྔོན་འཇུག་ཅེས་ཀྱང་བྱ་སྟེ། ཡི་གེའི་གྲངས་ལྔ་ཉིད་དུ་ངེས་པ་ཡིན་ནོ།

གསུམ་པ་མི་འཇུག་པ་བཤད་པ་ནི་མིང་གཞི་གཉིས་སམ་གསུམ་སྦྲེལ་ལམ། དེ་ལ་དབྱངས་ཀྱི་བཞི་ལྡན་ཡང་། གང་དུ་འཇུག་མིན་སྦྱོར་བའང་མིན། ཞེས་པ་སྟེ། སྔོན་འཇུག་དང་རྗེས་འཇུག་གསལ་བའི་ལྷག་མ་མིང་གཞི་ཁོ་ན་ཡིན་པ། ཀ་ཁ། ཅ་ཆ་ཇ་ཉ། ཏ་ཐ། པ་ཕ། ཙ་ཚ་ཛ་ཝ། ཞ་ཟ་ཡ། ཤ་ཧ་ཨ་སྟེ་ཡི་གེ་ཉི་ཤུ་ཐམ་པ་ནི། ཚིག་བར་གཅིག་ཏུ་གཉིས་སམ་གསུམ་སྦྲེལ་བའམ། དེ་ལ་དབྱངས་ཨི་སོགས་གང་རུང་རེ་སྦྱོར་བའི་བཞི་ལྡན་དུ་བྱས་པ། ཙཀ། ཚཁ། ཀྲིཡ། ལྟ་བུ་གངས་ལྗོངས་སུ་གྲགས་པའི་ཐ་སྙད་གང་ལའང་འཇུག་པ་མིན་པས་འདི་བཞིན་སྦྱོར་བར་རིགས་པའང་མ་ཡིན་ནོ། དེ་ཡང་སྐབས་འདིའི་མིང་གཞི་ནི་སྔོན་རྗེས་གཉིས་ཀྱི་འཇུག་ཡུལ་དུ་གྱུར་པའི་གསལ་བྱེད་ཀྱི་ཡི་གེ་ཡིན་ལ། དེས་ན་སྔོན་རྗེས་མིང་གསུམ་ཅི་རིགས་པར་འགྱུར་བ་སྔོན་འཇུག་ལྔ། རྗེས་མིང་གཉིས་ཅི་རིགས་པར་འགྱུར་པ་རྗེས་འཇུག་ལྷག་མ་ལྔ། མིང་གཞི་ཁོ་ན་ཡིན་པ་མི་འཇུག་པ་ཉི་ཤུ་ཐམ་པ་སྟེ་གསུམ་དུ་དབྱེར་ཡོད་པ་ལས་འདིར་ནི་ཕྱི་མ་འཆད་པའི་སྐབས་སོ།

གཉིས་པ་སྦྱོར་ཚུལ་ཚིག་ཕྲད་ཀྱི་འཇུག་པ་བཤད་པ་ལ་གཉིས། རྗེས་འཇུག་ལ་ལྟོས་པའི་ཕྲད་རྣམས་དབྱེ་དང་བཅས་པ་བཤད་པ་དང་། རྗེས་འཇུག་ལ་མ་ལྟོས་པའི་ཕྲད་རང་དབང་ཅན་བཤད་པའོ། དང་པོ་ལ་བརྒྱད། སླར་བསྡུ་བཤད་པ། ལ་དོན་བཤད་པ། ཨི་ལྡན་གྱི་རྣམ་དབྱེ་བཤད་པ། རྒྱན་སྡུད་བཤད་པ། ལྷག་བཅས་བཤད་པ། འབྱེད་སྡུད་བཤད་པ། འབྱུང་ཁུངས་བཤད་པ། བདག་པའི་སྒྲ་བཤད་པའོ།

དང་པོ་ནི། རྗེས་འཇུག་ཡི་གེ་བཅུ་པོ་ནི། མིང་གང་གི་ནི་མཐར་སྦྱོར་བ།

དེ་ལ་ཨོ་ཡི་བཞི་པ་སྦྱར། སླར་བསྡུ་བར་ནི་ཤེས་པར་བྱ།

ཞེས་པ་སྟེ། སྔར་བཤད་པའི་རྗེས་འཇུག་གི་ཡི་གེ་བཅུ་པོ་དེ་རྣམས་ཉིད་མིང་ཚིག་གང་གི་མཐར་སྦྱར་བ་ཡོད་ཀྱང་རུང་། དེ་དག་ལ་ཨོ་ཡི་བཞི་པ་ཨོ་ཡིག་སྟེ་སྔ་དུ་སྦྱར་བ་ནི། སྐབས་བབ་ཀྱི་བརྗོད་བྱའི་དོན་དེ་ཉིད་དེ་ཙམ་གྱིས་བསྡུ་བར་སོང་བས་སླར་བསྡུའི་སྒྲ་ཞེས་སམ། རྫོགས་ཚིག་ཅེས་ཀྱང་བྱའོ། དེ་ཡང་གཞུང་གི་དངོས་བསྟན་ཏག་གོ། བཟང་ངོ། ཡོད་དོ། ཡིན་ནོ། སྒྲུབ་བོ། བསམ་མོ། བྱའོ། འགྱུར་རོ། སེལ་ལོ། བྱས་སོ། ཞེས་པ་ལྟ་བུ་བཅུ་དང་། ད་དྲག་གིས་ཐོབ་པའི་ཤུགས་བསྟན། གྱུརད་ཏོ། ལྟ་བུ་གཅིག་སྟེ་བཅུ་གཅིག་ཡོད་དོ།

གཉིས་པ་ལ་དོན་བཤད་པ་ནི།

སྡེས་འཇུག་ཡི་གེ་བཅུ་རྣམས་ལས། གང་མིང་མཐའ་ན་བཅུ་པ་གནས།
དེ་ལ་ཨཱུ་ཨི་གཉིས་པ་སྦྱར། གང་མིང་མཐའ་ན་བརྒྱད་པ་གནས།
དེ་ལ་གཉིས་པ་ཨུ་ཡང་སྦྱར། གང་མིན་མཐའ་ན་གསུམ་པ་གནས།
རི་ལ་ཨཱུ་ཨི་གཉིས་པ་སྦྱར། བཞི་པ་དགུ་པ་དངོས་ཀྱང་སྟེ།
ལས་དང་ཆེད་དང་རྟེན་གནས་དང་། དེ་ཉིད་ཚེ་སྐབས་ལ་སྒྲ་ཡིན།

ཞེས་པ་སྟེ། སྡེས་འཇུག་ཡི་གེ་བཅུ་པོ་དེ་རྣམས་ཉིད་ལས། གང་ཡང་རུང་བའི་མིང་གི་མཐའ་ན་ལ་དོན་གྱི་རྣམ་དབྱེ་སྦྱར་བའི་ཚེད་དུ་བཅུ་པ་ས་ཡིག་གནས་པ་དེ་ལ་ཨཱུ་ཨི་གཉིས་པ་ཨུ་ཡིག་སྦྱར་བས། སུ། ཞེས་གྲུབ་པ་དང་། དེ་བཞིན་དུ་ཚིག་བར་གཅིག་ཉིད་དུ་མིང་མཐར་བརྒྱད་པ་ར་ཡིག་སྦྱར་ཏེ་གནས་པ་ལྷག་པར་ལྡ་བུ་དང་། ཡང་ར་ཡིག་དེ་ཉིད་ཚིག་བར་ཕྲེས་པ་ལ་ཨུ་ཡིག་ཀྱང་སྦྱར་བའི་རུ་ཞེས་པ་དང་། སྡེས་འཇུག་གསུམ་པ་ད་ཡིག་གནས་པར་ཨུ་ཡིག་སྦྱར་བའི་དུ་དང་། སྡེས་འཇུག་བཞི་པ་ན་དང་། དགུ་པ་ལ་གཉིས་དབྱངས་ཀྱིས་མ་བརྒྱན་པའི་དངོས་པོ་ཉིད་དུ་གནས་པའང་སྟེ་དངོས་བསྟན་དྲུག་དང་། ཤུགས་བསྟན་ཏ་ཡིག་ཨུ་ཞུགས་ཀྱི་ཏུ་བཅས་བདུན་པོ་འདི་རྣམས་ནི། ཤར་ཕྱོགས་སུ་འགྲོ་ལྟ་བུ་བྱེད་པ་པོས་བྱ་བ་གང་ལ་བྱེད་པའི་དོན་ཅན་དུ་སྦྱར་ན་རྣམ་དབྱེ་གཉིས་པ་ལས་སུ་བྱ་བའི་སྒྲ་དང་། རྟར་ཙྭ་ཁྲིད་ལྟ་བུ་བྱ་བ་གང་ཞིག་གིས། བྱ་བའི་ཡུལ་དེའམ། དེ་དང་འབྲེལ་བའི་ལས་ལ་ཕན་འདོགས་པར་འགྱུར་བའི་དོན་ཅན་དུ་སྦྱར་ན་རྣམ་དབྱེ་བཞི་པ་དགོས་ཆེད་ཀྱི་སྒྲ་དང་། དཔལ་པ་རུ་སླེ་བ་ཡོད་ལྟ་བུ་གང་ཞིག་གང་ལ་བརྟེན་པའི་དོན་ཅན་དུ་སྦྱར་ན་རྣམ་དབྱེ་བདུན་པ་རྟེན་གནས་ཀྱི་སྒྲ་དང་། ཤོད་དུ་འཚོར་ལྟ་བུ་ཡུལ་གང་ཞིག་ལ་བྱ་བ་གང་ཞིག་བྱེད་པའི་ཚེ་ལས་དང་བྱ་བ་ངོ་བོ་གཅིག་པའི་དོན་ཅན་དུ་སྦྱར་ན་རྣམ་དབྱེ་གཉིས་པའི་བྱེ་བྲག་དེ་ཉིད་ཀྱི་སྒྲ་དང་། ཉི་མ་ཤར་བ་ན་ཆོས་སྟོན་ལྟ་བུ་དུས་བརྗོད་པའི་དོན་ཅན་དུ་སྦྱར་ན་རྣམ་དབྱེ་བདུན་པའི་བྱེ་བྲག་ཚེ་སྐབས་ཀྱི་སྒྲར་ཤེས་དགོས་ཤིང་། དེ་དག་ཐམས་ཅད་རྣམ་དབྱེར་སྦྱོར་བ་ན་ལ་སྒྲའི་འཇུག་པ་དང་ཐལ་ཆེར་མཐུན་པ་དང་མཐའི་གསལ་བྱེད་ཡིན་པས་ལ་སྒྲ་ཞེས་ཀྱང་བརྗོད་པར་བྱ་སྟེ། འོན་ཀྱང་ན་ལ་གཉིས་དེ་ཉིད་ཀྱི་དོན་ཅན་ལ་ནི་འཇུག་པར་མི་རུང་ངོ་། སྒྲ་སྒྲོ་ལས་ནའི་འཇུག་པ་བཅུ་བཞི་ཙམ་བཤད་པའི་སྐབས་སུ་དེ་ཉིད་ལ་འཇུག་པ་མི་འབྱུང་བ་དང་། དུ་ལ་སོགས་པ་ལ་དང་མཐུན། དེ་ཉིད་དག་ནི་ལྷག་པ་ཡིན། ཞེས་གསུངས་པའི་ཕྱིར་རོ།

གསུམ་པ་ཨི་ལྡན་གྱི་རྣམ་དབྱེ་བཤད་པ་ལ་གཉིས། མདོར་བསྟན་པ་དང་། རྒྱས་པར་བཤད་པའོ། །དང་པོ་ནི། རྗེས་འཇུག་ཡི་གེ་བཅུ་པོ་ལ། ཨི་དང་མཐུན་ལུགས་འདི་ཞེས་བྱ། ཞེས་པ་སྟེ། རྗེས་འཇུག་ཡི་གེ་བཅུ་པོ་དེ་དག་གང་རུང་རྗེས་སུ་ཞུགས་པའི་མིང་རྣམས་ལ། ཨི་ཡིག་དང་སྦྱར་བའི་རྣམ་དབྱེའི་ཕྲད་རྣམས་ཇི་ལྟར་མཐུན་པར་སྦྱོར་བའི་ལུགས་ནི་འདི་དང་འདི་འོ་ཞེས་བསྟན་པར་བྱའོ། ཞེས་སོ། །གཉིས་པ་རྒྱས་པར་བཤད་པ་ལ་གཉིས། འབྲེལ་སྒྲ་བཤད་པ་དང་། བྱེད་པ་པོའི་སྒྲ་བཤད་པའོ།

དང་པོ་གཉིས་ལ་དང་པོ་མཐུན། །གསུམ་ལྔ་བཅུ་ལ་ཀྱ་དང་སྦྱར། །
བདུན་པ་ཉིད་ལ་བདུན་པ་སྟེ། །ལྷག་མ་རྣམས་ལ་གྱ་སྦྱར་བ། །
དེ་དག་ཨི་སྦྱར་འབྲེལ་བའི་སྒྲ། །

ཞེས་པ་སྟེ། རྗེས་འཇུག་བཅུའི་དང་པོ་ག་དང་ང་གཉིས་གང་རུང་རྗེས་སུ་ཞུགས་པའི་མིང་རྣམས་ལ་ནི། རྗེས་འཇུག་དང་པོ་ག་ཉིད་མཐུན་ཞིང་། དེ་བཞིན་དུ་རྗེས་འཇུག་གསུམ་པ་ད་དང་། ལྔ་པ་བ་དང་། བཅུ་བ་ས་རྣམས་རྗེས་སུ་ཞུགས་པ་ལ་ཀྱ་དང་སྦྱར་བ་དང་། བདུན་པ་འ་ཡིག་གི་མཐའ་ཅན་རྣམས་ལ་དངོས་སུ་འ་ཡིག་ཡོད་དམ་མེད་ཀྱང་རུང་བདུན་པ་འ་ཉིད་སྦྱར་བ་དང་། ཤུགས་བསྟན་འ་མཐའ་ཅན་ལ་རྐང་པ་ཁ་སྐོང་ཚེ་ཡ་ཡིག་སྦྱར་བ་དང་། དེ་དག་ལས་གཞན་ལྷག་མ་ན་མ་ར་ལ་བཞི་པོའི་མཐའ་ཅན་རྣམས་ལ་གྱ་ཉིད་སྦྱར་བ་མཐུན་པ་བཅས། དེ་དག་ཐམས་ཅད་ལ་རིམ་པ་བཞིན་ཨི་ཡིག་སྟེ་གི་གུ་སྦྱར་བས། གི། ཀྱི། འི། ཡི་གྱི་རྣམས་སུ་གྲུབ་དེ་རྣམས་གང་ཞིག་གང་དང་སྒྲ་མཐུན་པའི་མིང་མཐའ་སོ་སོ་དང་སྦྱར་བས། བདག་གི། གང་གི། ཁྱོད་ཀྱི། རྒྱབ་ཀྱི། གཡས་ཀྱི། དེའི། དེཡི། མདུན་གྱི། ལམ་གྱི། གསེར་གྱི། དངུལ་གྱི་སོགས་སུ་འགྱུར་ཏེ། དེ་དག་ནི་རྗེན་པའམ། ཡན་ལག་དང་ཡན་ལག་ཅན་སོགས་མིང་དོན་ཐ་དད་ཀྱང་འབྲེལ་བ་བརྗོད་པའི་དོན་ཅན་གྱི་སྒྲ་ཡིན་པས་རྣམ་དབྱེ་དྲུག་པ་འབྲེལ་བའི་ས་ཞེས་བྱའོ། གི་སོགས་དེ་དག་མི་མཐུན་པའི་ཚིག་རྒྱན་ལ་འཇུག་པ་ལྟ་བུ་གཞུང་འདིར་དངོས་སུ་མ་བསྟན་པའི་དོན་གཞན་དང་གཞན་ལ་འཇུག་པ་སྣ་ཕྱིར་མང་དུ་སྣང་ཡང་འདིར་གཞུང་གི་དངོས་བསྟན་ཙམ་ལས་མི་འཆད་པས་སྒྲ་སྒོ་སོགས་གཞུང་གཞན་དུ་རྟོགས་པར་བྱའོ།

གཉིས་པ་བྱེད་པ་པོའི་སྒྲ་བཤད་པ་ནི། དེ་ཉིད་ལ་ནི་བཅུ་པ་སྦྱར། བྱེད་པ་པོ་རུ་ཤེས་པར་བྱ། ཞེས་པ་སྟེ། སྔར་བཤད་པའི་རྣམ་དབྱེ་དྲུག་པའི་སྒྲ། གི། ཀྱི། འི། ཡི། གྱི་སྟེ་ལྔ་པོ་དེ་དག་ཉིད་ལ་རྗེས་འཇུག་བཅུ་པ་ས་ཡིག་སྦྱར་བས། གིས། ཀྱིས། འིས། ཡིས། གྱིས་རྣམས་སུ་གྲུབ་པ་ནི་བྱ་བ་ལ་སྦྱོར་བར་སྟོན་པས་ན་རྣམ་དབྱེ་གསུམ་

པ་བྱེད་པ་པོ་ནི་ས་རྭ་ཤེས་པར་བྱ་སྟེ། དཔེར་ན་བདག་གིས་བསྟན། ཁྱོད་ཀྱིས་ཉན། དེའིས་ཕྱིན། འདི་ཡིས་བླངས། གསེར་གྱིས་རྗེས་ལྷ་བུའོ། བཞི་པ་རྒྱན་སྦྱད་བཤད་པ་ནི། ཨཱ་ཡི་ཕྱིས་ནས་གཉིས་པ་སྦྱར། །ཚིག་རྒྱན་གཉིས་དང་སྦྱད་པར་འགྱུར། ཞེས་པ་སྟེ། གོང་དུ་བཤད་པའི་འབྲེལ་སྒྲ་དེ་དག་ལས། ཀྱི། འི། ཡི། གསུམ་གྱི་ཨཱ་ཡི་རྟེ་གི་གུ་ཕྱིས་ནས་སོ་སོར་རྗེས་འཇུག་གཉིས་པ་ང་ཡིག་སྦྱར་བས། ཀྱང་། འང་། ཡང་། ཞེས་གྲུབ་པ་དེ་རྣམས་ནི། གསལ་ཡང་གསལ། མཛེས་ཀྱང་མཛེས། ལྟ་བུ་ཚིག་སྔ་ཕྱི་མཐུན་པར་སྟོན་པའི་རྒྱན་དང་། བཏུད་ཀྱང་ཁྲོ། མཛའང་སྒྲུ་ལྟ་བུ་ཚིག་སྔ་ཕྱི་མི་མཐུན་པར་སྟོན་པའི་རྒྱན་གཉིས་དང་། མིར་མ་ཟད་ལྷས་ཀྱང་བཏུད་དོ།* ལྟ་བུ་གཞི་འམ་དོན་གཞན་ཞིག་ལ་སྦྱད་ཅིང་སྦྱོར་བའི་སྒྲར་འགྱུར་རོ། ཞེས་སོ།

ལྔ་པ་ལྷག་བཅས་བཤད་པ་ནི།

ལ་དོན་སུ་ཡི་ཨུ་ཕྱིས་ནས། དེ་ལ་གསུམ་པའི་དང་པོ་སྦྱར།
དེ་ལ་ཨཱ་ཡི་གསུམ་པ་སྦྱར། དེ་ནི་ལྷག་མ་དང་བཅས་པའོ།

ཞེས་པ་སྟེ། སྔར་བཤད་པའི་ལ་དོན་གྱི་ནང་ཚན་སུ་ཞེས་པ་དེའི་ཨུ་ཡིག་རྟེ་ཞབས་ཀྱུ་ཕྱི་ནས་ས་རྐྱང་གནས་པ་དེ་ལ་ཀླུ་ཡིའི་སྡེ་པ་་གསུམ་པའི་དང་པོ་ཏ་ཡིག་སྦྱར་ཞིང་། དེ་ལ་སྔར་ཡང་རྟེང་དུ་ཨཱ་ཡི་གསུམ་པ་རྟེ་འགྲེང་བུ་སྦྱར་བས། སྟེ་ཞེས་གྲུབ་པ་དང་རོག་ནས་འབྱུང་བའི་དེ་དང་། ཤུགས་བསྟན་གྱི་ཏེ་རྐྱང་བཅས་གསུམ་པོ་དེ་རྣམས་ནི། མིང་ཚིག་གང་གི་མཐར་སྦྱར་ཡང་བསྟན་བྱའི་ལྷག་མ་འདྲེན་པའི་དོན་དུ་འགྱུར་བས་ལྷག་མ་དང་བཅས་པའི་སྒྲ་ཞེས་བྱ་སྟེ། དེ་ཡང་། མདའ་འཕངས་ཏེ་ཐོག། ཕྱག་འཚལ་ཏེ་བཤད། འཕར་ཏེ་འགྲོ་ལྟ་བུ་ནས་དང་ཅིང་སོགས་ཀྱི་སྒྲད་དང་འདྲ་བ་མཐུན་པ་ནི་མཚམས་སྦྱོར་དང་། དངོས་པོ་ནི་གསུམ་སྟེ། ཐམ་པོ་དང་། ཤེས་པ་དང་། ལྡན་མིན་འདུ་བྱེད་དོ་ལྟ་བུ་ཚིག་སྔ་མའི་གསལ་བྱེད་དུ་ཕྱི་མ་འདྲེན་པ་ནི་དམ་བཅའ་དང་། ཁྱོད་ནི་དཔལ་ཏེ་ཁྱོད་ནི་མགོན། ལྟ་བུ་ལ་དང་འདྲ་བ་མཐུན་ཅིང་ལྷག་མ་ཡོད་པ་ཙམ་སྟོན་པ་ནི་གཞན་འདྲེན་ཏེ་རགས་པ་ཙམ་དབྱེ་ན་གསུམ་དུ་འགྱུར་རོ།།

དྲུག་པ་འབྱེད་སྡུད་བཤད་པ་ནི། རྗེས་འཇུག་ཡི་གེ་བཅུ་པོ་ལ། དྲུག་པ་སྦྱར་ན་འབྱེད་སྡུད་ཡིན། ཞེས་པ་སྟེ། རྗེས་འཇུག་གི་ཡི་གེ་བཅུ་པོ་དེ་རྣམས་ལ་དེ་ཉིད་ཀྱི་དྲུག་པ་མ་ཡིག་སྦྱར་བ། གམ། ངམ། དམ། ནམ། བམ།

*འདི་འདྲའི་བཏུད་དོ། འདས་དང་མ་འོངས་ད་ལྟ་གསུམ་གང་ལ་ཡང་ མི་འཇུག་པའི་ཕྱིར་མ་དག་པ་ཡིན་ནམ། འདས་པ་ལ་བཏུད་ཏོ། ད་ལྟ་མ་འོངས་གཉིས་ལ་ འདུད་དོ། ཞེས་དགོས་པས་དེ་གཉིས་པོ་གང་རུང་ངོ།།

མམ། འམ། རམ། ལམ། སམ་རྣམས་སུ་གྲུབ་པ་དེ་དག་དང་། ཤུགས་བསྣན་ཏམ་བཅས་བཅུ་གཅིག་པོ་རྣམས་ནི། ཕུང་པོ་ནི་ལྔ་སྟེ་གཟུགས་སམ། ཚོར་བའམ། འདུ་ཤེས་སམ། འདུ་བྱེད་དམ། རྣམ་པར་ཤེས་པའོ་ལྟ་བུ་དབྱེ་གཞི་གཅིག་ལས་བྱེ་བྲག་སོ་སོར་འབྱེད་པ་དང་། གཟུགས་སམ། ཚོར་བའམ། འདུ་ཤེས་སམ། འདུ་བྱེད་དམ། རྣམ་པར་ཤེས་པ་ནི་ཕུང་པོ་འོ་ལྟ་བུ་ཚིག་དོན་མང་པོ་ཕྱོགས་གཅིག་ཏུ་སྡུད་པའི་སྒྲར་འཇུག་པ་ཡིན་ནོ། ཞེས་སོ། དེ་ཡང་ཡོད་དམ་མེད་ལྟ་བུ་དྲི་ཚིག་རྣམས་ཀྱང་ཡོད་མེད་ཀྱི་ཁྱད་པར་འབྱེད་པའི་ཚིག་ཡིན་པས་འབྱེད་པའི་སྒྲ་ཉིད་དུ་ངེས་སོ།

བདུན་པ་འབྱུང་ཁུངས་བཤད་པ་ལ་གཉིས། འབྱུང་ཁུངས་དངོས་བཤད་པ་དང་། དེ་དགར་སྡུད་ལ་འཇུག་པའི་ཚུལ་ལོ། དང་པོ་ནི། རྫས་འཇུག་ཡི་གེ་བཅུ་པོ་ཡི། བཞི་པ་དགུ་པ་ལ་བཅུ་པ། སྦྱར་བ་འབྱུང་ཁུངས་ས་ཡིན་ཏེ། ཞེས་པ་སྟེ། རྫས་འཇུག་ཡི་གེ་བཅུ་དེའི་བཞི་པ་ན་དང་། དགུ་པ་ལ་གཉིས་སོ་སོར་བཅུ་པ་ས་ཡིས་སྦྱར་བས། ནས། ལས་ཞེས་གྲུབ་པ་ནི། ས་ནས་རྩྭ་སྐྱེས། བ་ལས་འོ་མ་འཇོ། ལྟ་བུ་ཆོས་གང་ལས་གང་ཞིག་བྱུང་བའམ་འབྱུང་བ་སྟོན་པའི་དོན་དུ་མཚུངས་པར་འཇུག་པས་རྣམ་དབྱེ་ལྔ་པ་འབྱུང་ཁུངས་ཀྱི་ས་ཡིན་ཅིང་། ཏེ་ནི་ལྷག་བཅས་སོ། ཡང་དུ་བ་ལས་མེར་ཤེས་ལྟ་བུ་ལས་ཀྱི་སྒྲ་ཁོ་ན་རྒྱུ་མཚན་ལ་འཇུག་པ་ཡོད་ཀྱང་རྣམ་དབྱེ་ལྔ་པ་ལས་མ་འདས་ཏེ། མེར་ཤེས་པའི་རྒྱུ་མཚན་དེ་དུ་བ་མཐོང་ལས་བྱུང་བས་སོ།

གཉིས་པ་དེ་དགར་སྡུད་ལ་འཇུག་པའི་ཚུལ་ནི། དགར་དང་སྡུད་པའམ་དེ་བཞིན་ཡིན། ཞེས་པ་སྟེ། བཤད་མ་ཐག་པའི་ནས་དང་ལས་ཀྱི་སྒྲ་དེ་དག་འབྱུང་ཁུངས་ཁོ་ནར་མ་ཟད། དགར་གཞི་ལས་ཐོགས་སུ་དགར་བའི་དོན་ལའམ་འཇུག་ཅིང་། དེ་ལས་ནས་ཀྱི་སྒྲ་གཅིག་པུ་ནི་མཚམས་འཛིན་ཅིང་སྡུད་པའི་དོན་དུའང་དེ་བཞིན་དུ་འཇུག་པ་ཡིན་ཏེ། ལྷ་རྣམས་ཀྱི་ནང་ནས་བརྒྱ་བྱིན་མཛེས་ལྟ་བུ་དགར་གཞི་དང་དགར་ཆོས་རིས་མཐུན་པ་ལ་གནས་དང་། ལྷ་ལས་མི་དམན་ལྟ་བུ་དགར་གཞི་དང་དགར་ཆོས་རིས་མི་མཐུན་པ་ལ་ལས། གཟུགས་ནས་རྣམ་མཁྱེན་གྱི་བར་ལྟ་བུ་སྡུད་པ་ལ་ནས་འཇུག་ཅིང་དགར་སྡུད་གཉིས་ཀ་ཡང་རྣམ་དབྱེ་ལྔ་པའི་ངོར་དུ་གཏོགས་ཏེ། དགར་བ་ནི་དགར་གཞི་ལས་དགར་ཆོས་བྱེ་བ་ལྟར་སྣང་བ་དང་། སྡུད་པ་ནི་ཐོག་མ་གང་བརྩམས་པ་དེ་ཡན་བསྡུ་བྱ་རྣམས་བྱུང་བ་ལྟར་སྣང་བས་སོ།

བརྒྱད་པ་བོད་པའི་སྒྲ་བཤད་པ་ནི། གང་མིང་བརྗོད་པའི་དང་པོ་རུ། ཀྱི་སྦྱར་ན་ནི་བོད་པ་ཡིན༎ ཞེས་པ་སྟེ། གང་ཡང་རུང་བའི་མིང་བརྗོད་པའི་ཐོག་མར་ཀྱི་ཞེས་སྦྱར་བ་ནི། ཀྱི་རྒྱལ་པོ་ཆེན་པོ་ལྟ་བུ་ཡུལ་ཁྱད་པར་ཅན་ལ་བོད་པ་གསལ་བར་བྱེད་པའི་སྒྲ་ཡིན་ལ། ཤུགས་བསྟན་ཀྭ་ཡེ་དང་ཀྭ་དང་ང་ཡེ་ལྟ་བུ་ནི་ཡུལ་དམན་པ་ལ་བོད་པ་གསལ་བྱེད་ཀྱི་སྒྲ་ཡིན་ནོ།

གཉིས་པ་རྗེས་འཇུག་ལ་མ་ལྟོས་པའི་ཁྱད་རང་དབང་ཅན་བཤད་པ་ལ་དྲུག། ནི་སྒྲ་བཤད་པ། དང་སྒྲ་བཤད་པ། དེ་སྒྲ་བཤད་པ། གང་སྒྲ་བཤད་པ། བདག་བཤད་པ། དགག་སྒྲ་བཤད་པའོ།

དང་པོ་ནི། གང་མིང་མཐའ་དང་མཐུན་པ་ཡི། བཞི་པ་ལ་ནི་ཨི་སྦྱར་བ། དགར་དང་བརྣན་པའི་ཚིག་ཏུ་འགྱུར། ཞེས་པ་སྟེ། གང་ཡང་རུང་བའི་མིང་ཚིག་གི་མཐའ་དང་མཐུན་པར་སྦྱར་རུང་བའི་ཁྱད་རྗེས་འཇུག་བཞི་པ་ན་ཡིག་ལ་དབྱངས་ཨི་སྦྱར་བས། ནི་ཞེས་གྲུབ་པ་དེ་ནི་སྦྱོར་དངོས་འཇུག་གསུམ་གྱི། དང་པོ་ནི། ལྟ་བུ་དགར་གཞི་ལས་ཐ་དད་དུ་དམིགས་གསལ་ནས་དགར་བའི་དོན་དང་། དཔལ་བའི་རྟེན་བཟང་པོ་ནི་ཐོབ། དགེ་བའི་བཤེས་གཉེན་དང་ནི་མཇལ། བློ་གྲོས་ཀྱི་མིག་དང་ནི་ལྡན་ལྟ་བུ་དོན་གང་ཡིན་པ་དེ་ལ་ངེས་བཟུང་ངམ་ནན་ཏན་དུ་བརྣན་པའི་དོན་ལ་འང་འཇུག་པའི་ཚིག་ཏུ་འགྱུར་ལ། སྡོམ་པ་ཐམས་ཅད་ལྡན་པར་ནི། ལྟ་བུ་ཚིག་གི་ཁ་སྐོང་དུ་འཇུག་པ་རྣམས་ཀྱང་བརྣན་པའི་སྒྲ་ཉིད་ཡིན་ནོ།

གཉིས་པ་དང་སྒྲ་བཤན་པ་ནི། མིང་གང་རུང་བའི་བར་མཚམས་སུ། གསུམ་པ་ལ་ནི་གཉིས་པ་སྦྱར། དེ་ནི་སྡུད་དང་འབྱེད་པ་དང་། རྒྱུ་མཚན་ཚེ་སྐབས་གདམས་ངག་ལྔོ། ཞེས་པ་སྟེ། མིང་ཚིག་གང་ཡང་རུང་བའི་བར་མཚམས་རྣམས་སུ་རྗེས་འཇུག་གསུམ་པ་ད་ཡིག་ལ་གཉིས་པ་ང་ཡིག་སྦྱར་བས། དང་ཞེས་གྲུབ་པ་དེ་ནི། མིག་དང་། རྣ་བ་དང་། སྣ་དང་། ལྕེ་དང་། ལུས་སོ་ལྟ་བུ་སོ་སོར་འབྱེད་པ་དང་། དུ་བ་མཐོང་བ་དང་མེར་ཤེས་སོ་ལྟ་བུ་རྒྱུ་མཚན་ཉིད་ཀྱི་དོན་དང་། ཉི་མ་ཕྱིད་པ་དང་ཆོས་སྟོན་དྲངས་ལྟ་བུ་དུས་བརྗོད་པ་ཚེ་སྐབས་ཀྱི་དོན་དང་། ཡིད་ལ་གཟུངས་དང་། ལྟ་བུ་གཞན་ལ་གདམས་ངག་བརྗོད་པའི་དོན་ཏེ། དོན་ལྔ་ལ་འཇུག་གོ། ཞེས་སོ།

གསུམ་པ་དེ་སྒྲ་བཤད་པ་ནི། གང་མིང་གི་ནི་ཡ་མཐའ་རུ། གསུམ་པ་ལ་ནི་ཨེ་སྦྱར་བ། ཐ་སྙད་དབང་

དུ་གསུམ་ཡིན་ཏེ། དངོས་པོའི་དབང་དུ་བཞི་རུ་འགྱུར། དུས་ཀྱི་དབང་དུ་གཉིས་ཡིན་ནོ། ཞེས་པ་སྟེ། གང་ཡང་རུང་བའི་མིང་གི་ཡ་མཐའ་སྟེ་ཐོག་མར་རྗེས་འཇུག་གསུམ་པ་ད་ཡིག་ལ་དབྱངས་ཨེ་སྟེ་འབྲེང་བུ་སྦྱར་བས། དེ་ཞེད་གྲུབ་པ་ནི། སྦྱར་མེད་ལ་གསར་དུ་ནན་གྱིས་བཏགས་པའི་ཐ་སྙད་ཙམ་གྱི་དབང་དུ་བྱས་ནས་དབྱེ་ན། དབྱེ་གཞི་ཀ་བ་རིང་པོའོ། དེ་ཕྲའོ། དེ་ལ་ཟུར་ཡོད་དོ། ལྟ་བུ་བརྗོད་བྱ་སྤྱིའི་དོན་ལ་མ་དཔྱད་པར། བརྗོད་ཚུལ་དེ་ཉིད་ལ་ཐད་ཀར་བརྟགས་པའི་དུས་འདས་པ་དང་། དེ་ལས་དབྱེ་བའི་ཡ་གྱལ། དེ་ལ་ཡི་གེ་བྲིས་ཤིག ལྟ་བུ་འདྲི་གཞི་དངོས་སུ་མི་གསལ་ཡང་དེ་ལྟའི་ཤུལ་དུ་ཤོག་བུ་ལྟ་བུ་དོན་གྱི་རྣམ་གྲངས་གཞན་ཞིག་སྦྱོར་རྒྱུ་ཡོད་པར་སྟོན་པའི་དོན་ཅན་དང་། ཤིང་བཅད་དེ་མེ་ལ་འབུད། ལྟ་བུ་རང་ཉིད་ཀྱི་ཤུལ་དུ་དོན་གཞན་མི་མཚོན་ཀྱང་བརྗོད་བྱ་ལྷག་མ་འདྲེན་པ་ཙམ་སྟེ་གསུམ་ལ་འཇུག་ཅིང་། དབྱེ་ཚུལ་དེས་དེ་ལྟའི་འཇུག་པ་ཐམས་ཅད་ལ་ཁྱབ་པ་ཡིན་ནོ། ཡང་ཆོས་སྤྱིའི་དངོས་པོའི་དོན་གཙོ་ཆེ་བའི་དབང་དུ་བྱས་ནས་དབྱེ་ན། དེ་རང་ཡིན་ནོ། ལྟ་བུ་བདེན་པའི་དངོས་པོ་དང་། དེ་མ་སྟོན་ཅིག། ལྟ་བུ་གསང་བའི་དངོས་པོ་དང་། ཁོ་བོའི་གླེགས་བམ་དེ་ཀློགས་ཤིག། ལྟ་བུ་བདག་གི་བའི་དངོས་པོ་དང་། རྡོ་བ་དེ་འདེགས་ནུས་སམ། ལྟ་བུ་བདག་གི་བ་ལས་གཞན་པ་ཕ་རོལ་པོའི་དངོས་པོ་སྟེ་བཞི་ལ་དུས་གསུམ་གར་འཇུག་པར་འགྱུར་ཞིང་། དབྱེ་ཚུལ་དེས་ལྷག་བཅས་ལས་གཞན་པའི་དེ་ལྟའི་འཇུག་པ་ཐམས་ཅད་ལ་ཁྱབ་པོ། ཡང་དུས་ཉིད་ཀྱི་དབང་དུ་བྱས་ནས་དབྱེ་ན། ན་ནིང་གི་ལོ་དེ་ལ། ལྟ་བུ་འདས་པ་དང་། སང་ཉི་མ་ཤར་བའི་དུས་དེར་འགྲོའོ། ལྟ་བུ་མ་འོངས་པ་གཉིས་ལ་འཇུག་པ་ཡིན་ཅིང་། དབྱེ་ཚུལ་དེས་དུས་ཁོ་ན་བརྗོད་པ་དང་འབྲེལ་བའི་དེ་ལྟའི་འཇུག་པ་ཙམ་ལ་ཁྱབ་པ་ཡིན་ནོ།

བཞི་པ་གང་སྒྲ་བཤད་པ་ནི། གང་མིང་བརྗོད་པའི་དང་པོ་རུ། དང་པོ་ལ་ནི་གཉིས་པ་སྦྱར། སྤྱི་ལ་ཁྱབ་པ་ཉིད་དུ་འགྱུར། ཞེས་པ་ན། གང་ཡང་རུང་བའི་མིང་བརྗོད་པའི་དང་པོར་རྗེས་འཇུག་དང་པོ་ག་ལ་གཉིས་པ་ང་སྦྱར་བས། གང་ཞེས་གྲུབ་པ་དེ་ནི། གང་ཞིག་དང་། གང་དག་དང་། གང་བྱེད། ལྟ་བུ་གཙོ་བོར་དོན་གྱི་བྱེ་བྲག་དམིགས་སུ་མི་འཛིན་པར་སྤྱི་ལ་ཁྱབ་པའི་དོན་ཅན་གྱི་སྒྲ་ཉིད་དུ་འགྱུར་ཏེ། ཅི་དང་། ཇི་དང་སུའི་སྒྲ་རྣམས་དང་ཡང་འཇུག་པ་ཕལ་ཆེར་མཐུན་ནོ།

ལྔ་པ་བདག་སྒྲ་བཤད་པ་ནི། གང་མིང་གི་ནི་མ་མཐའ་ན། ཕུཾ་ཡིཀྐ་ཡི་སྒྲ་མེད་པ། དེ་ལ་ཕུཾ་ཡིཀྐ་སྦྱར་ན། བདག་པོའི་གསར་ནི་ཤེས་པར་བྱ། ཞེས་པ་སྟེ། གང་ཡང་རུང་བའི་མིང་གི་མ་མཐའ་རྣམས་སུ། ཙནྡྲ་པ་ལས། ཨུཎ་ཀྱི་སྡེ་དང་བཅས་པའོ། ཞེས་པ་ལྟར། ཕུཾ་ཞེས་པ་པ་སྡེ་དང་། ཡིཀྐ་ཞེས་པ་རྟགས་ཏེ། པ་སྡེ་ནས་འབྱུང་བའི་ཕོ་རྟགས་པ་དང་། མོ་རྟགས་མ་དང་མ་ནིང་གི་རྟགས་བ་གསུམ་གྱི་སྒྲ་སྔར་མེད་པ་དེ་ལ་གསར་དུ་ཕུཾ་ཡིཀྐའི་སྒྲ་གསུམ་པོ་གང་རུང་སྦྱར་བ་ན། དེ་ནི་བདག་པོའི་དོན་གསལ་བར་བྱེད་པའི་སར་ནི་ཤེས་པར་བྱ་སྟེ། དཔེར་ན། ཛ་པ། ཚང་མ། ཁ་ཡོ་སྦྱར་བ་ལྟ་བུ་དང་། གཞན་ཡང་། གྱོས་པོ། སྐྱུག་མོ། ཟླ་བོ་ཞེས་པ་རྣམས་ཀྱང་རྟགས་གསུམ་ལྡན་པའི་བདག་སྒྲ་ཡིན་ལ། བློ་ཅན་དང་། ཤེས་ལྡན་ལྟ་བུ་ནི་གང་ཞིག་གང་ལ་ཡོད་པར་སྟོན་པའི་ཆ་ནས་བདག་སྒྲ་དང་འདྲ་བར་སྣང་ཡང་། སྒྲ་དེ་གཉིས་ཐེམ་པོ་ལའམ་འཇུག་པས་བདག་སྒྲ་དངོས་ནི་མ་ཡིན་ནོ། འོ་ན་པ་དང་མ་གཉིས་ཕོ་མོའི་རྟགས་ཡིན་པར་གྲུབ་ཀྱང་། བ་ཡིག་མ་ནིང་གི་རྟགས་ཡིན་པ་གང་གི་སྒྲུབ་ཅེ་ན། སྒྲ་སྒོ་ལས། བ་ནི་སྤྱི་རུ་བཞག་པ་སྟེ། ཡུལ་དུས་ངེས་པར་མ་བཟུང་པའོ། ཟ་བ་བཟའ་མ་ཟ་པོ་བཞིན། མ་ནིང་དག་ཏུ་བཞག་པར་བྱ། ཞེས་པས་སོ།

དྲུག་པ་དགག་སྒྲ་བཤད་པ་ནི། གང་མིང་བརྗོད་པའི་ཡ་མཐའ་ན། སྟྲི་ཡིཀྐ་ཡི་སྒྲ་མེད་པ། དེ་ལ་སྟྲི་ཡིཀྐ་སྦྱར་ན། དགག་པའི་གནས་སུ་ཤེས་པར་བྱ། ཞེས་པ་སྟེ། གང་ཡང་རུང་བའི་མིང་བརྗོད་པའི་ཡ་མཐའ་སྣེ་ཐོག་མར་ཏྲི་ཡིཀྐ་སྟེ། མོ་རྟགས་ཀྱི་སྒྲ་སྔར་བཤད་ཟིན་པ་མ་ཡིག་དང་ཞར་ཀྱིས་ཐོབ་པ་མི་ཡིག་གཉིས་སྔར་མེད་པ་དེ་ལ་གསར་དུ་སྟྲི་ཡིཀྐ་སྦྱར་ན་སྦྱོར་ཡུལ་གྱི་དོན་དེ་མ་ཡིན་པའམ་མེད་པར་སྟོན་པའི་དགག་པའི་གནས་སུ་ཤེས་པར་བྱ་སྟེ། དཔེར་ན། མ་མཐོང་། མི་རིགས། ཞེས་པ་ལྟ་བུའོ། གཉིས་པ་གདམས་ངག་བརྗོད་པས་འཇུག་བསྡུ་བ་ལ་བཞི། ཚིགས་བཅད་འགྲེལ་ཚུལ་ལ་འདོམས་པ། ཉན་པ་པོ་སྤྲོ་བསྐྱེད་པའི་སྒོ་ནས་འདོམས་པ། སློབ་ཚུལ་གོ་རིམ་ལ་འདོམས་པ། གདམས་ངག་སྣོད་རུང་ལ་བསྟན་དགོས་པར་འདོམས་པའོ།

དང་པོ་ནི། ཚིགས་སུ་བཅད་པའི་མཚམས་སྦྱར་རྣམས། ཆུང་ཟད་བསྒྱུས་པ་ཡོད་ན་ཡང་། དེ་ནི་དེ་བཞིན་སྦྱར་བར་བྱ། ཞེས་པ་སྟེ། རྒྱལ་བའི་བཀའ་བསྟན་ཡན་ལག་དང་བཅས་པ་རྣམས་ལ། ཚིགས་སུ་བཅད་པ

ཡང་དག་པར་སྦྱར་བའི་ཚེ་ཚིག་སྦྱད་མང་བ་ཡིན་པས་རྣམ་དབྱེ་དང་ཚིག་ཕྲད་ལ་སོགས་པའི་མཚམས་སྦྱར་མང་དུ་བསྡུས་པ་ཡོད་ན་ལྟ་ཅི་སྨོས། ཙུང་ཟད་བསྡུས་པར་གྱུར་པ་ཡོད་ན་ཡང་། དེ་ནི་འདིར་སྔོན་དུ་བསྟན་པའི་སྐབས་བསྡུ་ལ་སོགས་པ་ཇི་སྐད་བཤད་པ་དེ་བཞིན་དུ་བསྒྲན་ཅིང་སྦྱར་ཏེ་བཤད་པའི་དོན་ཁོང་དུ་ཆུད་པར་བྱ་སྟེ། དཔེར་ན། ཟག་བཅས་ཟག་པ་མེད་ཆོས་རྣམས། ཞེས་པ་ལྟ་བུར། ཟག་པ་དང་བཅས་པའི་ཆོས་རྣམས་དང་། ཟག་པ་མེད་པའི་ཆོས་རྣམས། ཞེས་སྦྱད་པའི་སྒྲ་དང་འབྲེལ་སྒྲ་སོགས་བསྣན་ནས་དོན་རང་གིས་བསམ་བ་དང་གཞན་ལ་འཆད་དགོས་པ་བཞིན་ནོ།

གཉིས་པ་ཉན་པ་པོ་བློ་བ་སྤྲེང་བའི་སྒོ་ནས་འདོམས་པ་ལ་གསུམ། རྗེས་འཇུག་མེད་མི་རུང་དུ་བསྟན་པ། རྗེས་འཇུག་ཤེས་པའི་དགོས་པ་བསྟན་པ། དེ་དོན་ལ་འབབ་པའི་ཚུལ་བསྟན་པའོ།

དང་པོ་ནི། སྔོན་འཇུག་ཡོད་དམ་མེད་ཀྱང་རུང་། མིང་གཞིའི་ཡི་གེ་གང་ཡིན་ལ། རྗེས་འབྲེལ་ཡོད་དམ་གསུམ་འབྲེལ་ཡོད། ཨཱུ་ཡི་བཞི་ལས་གང་ལྡན་ཡང་། རྗེས་འཇུག་བཅུ་པོ་མ་ཞུགས་ན། མིང་གཞན་སྦྱོར་བ་ཡོད་མི་སྲིད། ཅེས་པ་སྟེ། མིང་ཚིག་གི་སྦྱོར་བ་རྣམས་ལ་གོང་དུ་བཤད་པའི་སྔོན་འཇུག་གི་ཡི་གེ་རྣམས་སྔོན་དུ་ཞུགས་ཡོད་དམ་མེད་ཀྱང་། རུང་སྟེ། དཔེར་ན། བཀ་དང་ཀ་ལྟ་བུ་དང་། འཕུལ་རྟེང་གི་འཇུག་ཡུལ་མིང་གཞིའི་ཡི་གེ་གང་ཡིན་པ་རྣམས་ལ་སྐྱ་ལྟ་བུ་ཉིས་འབྲེལ་ཡོད་དམ། སྐྲུ་ལྟ་བུ་གསུམ་འབྲེལ་ཡོད་པ་དང་། དེ་དག་ལ་ཨཱུ་ཡི་བཞི་ལས་གང་ཡང་རུང་བ་དང་ལྡན་པ། བགི། ཀུ། སྐེ། སྐྱོ། ལྟ་བུ་རྣམས་ལའང་རྗེས་འཇུག་བཅུ་པོ་གང་ཡང་རུང་བ་ཞིག་མ་ཞུགས་ན། ཡི་གེའི་གཟུགས་དེ་ཉིད་ལས་མིང་དོན་གཞན་ལ་འཇུག་ཅིང་སྦྱོར་བ་ནི་ཚུལ་འདི་ལ་ནམ་ཡང་སྲིད་པ་མ་ཡིན་ཏེ། ད་ལྟ་སྐྱོ་ལྟ་བུས་དོན་ལ་འཇུག་པ་སྣང་ཡང་སྐྱོའ་ཞེས་པའི་འ་མཐའ་སྐད་གསར་བཅད་ཀྱི་ཚེ་ཡི་གེ་ཟུར་ཡང་བའི་ཆེད་དུ་ཕྱིས་པ་ཡིན་གྱི་དོན་ལ་ཐོབ་ཐང་མེད་པ་ནི་མ་ཡིན་ནོ།

གཉིས་པ། རྗེས་འཇུག་ཤེས་པའི་དགོས་པ་བསྟན་པ་ནི། རྗེས་འཇུག་བཅུ་ཡི་དོན་ཤེས་ན། འབྲི་དང་ཀློག་དང་བཤད་རྣམས་ཀྱི། མཚམས་སྦྱོར་སྒྲ་ལ་ཐོགས་མེད་ཅིང་། འབྲེལ་བར་སྨྲ་བའི་མཆོག་ཏུ་འགྱུར། གཞན་ཡང་རྗེས་འཇུག་ཤེས་པ་ཡིས། དོན་གྱི་སྦྱོར་བ་མ་མཐོང་ཡང་། དོན་དང་མཐུན་པའི་སྦྱོར་བ་ཤེས། ཞེས་པ་སྟེ། དེ་ལྟར་རྗེས་འཇུག་བཅུའི་བྱ་བ་དང་གཙོ་བོར་འབྲེལ་བའི་ཕྲད་དང་རྣམ་དབྱེ་ལ་སོགས་པའི་སྒྲ་དོན་གྱི་འཇུག་ཚུལ་ལེགས་པར་ཤེས་ན། མདོ་རྒྱུད་བསྟན་བཅོས་རྣམས་ཡི་གེར་འབྲི་བ་དང་། གྲིས་ཟིན་པ་རྣམས་བརྗོད་པ་དག་པར་ཀློག་པ་དང་། ཚིག་དོན་

རྒྱ་ཆེར་བཀྲོལ་ནས་བཤད་པ་བྱེད་པ་དང་། དེར་མ་ཟད་བསྟན་བཅོས་སོགས་རྩོམ་པ་དང་། གཞན་གྱི་རྩོལ་བ་ཚར་གཅོད་པའི་ཕྱིར་རྩོད་པ་བྱེད་པ་ལ་སོགས་པའི་ཚེ། ཚིག་དོན་སྤྱི་མཚམས་སྦྱོར་བའི་སྐབ་དོན་རྣམས་ལ་བློ་གྲོས་ཀྱི་སྣང་བ་འཇུག་པར་ཐོགས་པ་མེད་ཅིང་། ཚིག་དོན་སྤྱི་ཕྱི་གོ་ལོག་པ་དང་། མི་འབྲེལ་བ་དང་། འགལ་བ་ལ་སོགས་པའི་སྐྱོན་མེད་པར་འཆད་པ་དང་ལྷན་ཅིག་འབྲེལ་ཆགས་པ་ཁོ་ན་སྨྲ་བའི་མཆོག་ཏུ་འགྱུར་བ་དང་། གཞན་ཡང་རྗེས་འཇུག་གི་དོན་ཚུལ་བཞིན་ཤེས་པ་དེས་བསྟན་བཅོས་ལ་སོགས་པའི་དོན་རྣམ་པར་འབྱེད་པའི་སྦྱོར་བ་སྟེ། དེའི་འགྲེལ་བཤད་སོགས་སྟོན་ཚད་མ་མཐོང་ཡང་། འགྲེལ་བཤད་སོགས་ཀྱི་དོན་དང་མཐུན་པའི་ཚིག་གི་སྦྱོར་བ་རྗེས་སུ་དཔགས་ཏེ་ཤེས་པར་འགྱུར་རོ། ཞེས་སོ།

གསུམ་པ་དེ་དོན་ལ་དབབ་པའི་ཚུལ་བསྟན་པ་ནི། རྗེས་འཇུག་སྦྱོར་བ་མཁས་པ་ན། ལུང་གི་དོན་དང་སྦྱོར་བ་དང་། བླ་མའི་མན་ངག་གསུམ་སྦྱར་ནས། དོན་གྱི་ཐོག་ཏུ་དབབ་པར་བྱ། ཞེས་པ་སྟེ། རྗེས་འཇུག་གི་སྦྱོར་བ་རྣམས་ལ་མཁས་པར་གྱུར་ཅིང་། མཐུན་མོང་མིན་པའི་རིག་གནས་ལ་སློབ་པར་འདོད་པ་དེའི་ཚེ་ན། རིག་གནས་མཐུན་མོང་བ་དྲུང་སྔོང་དང་པཎྜི་ཏས་བྱས་པའི་སྐད་ཚད་བཟོ་གསོ་རྩིས་སྙན་མངོན་ཛེབ་ཟློས་གར་གྱི་བསྟན་བཅོས་དང་། མཐུན་མོང་མིན་པ་བཅོམ་ལྡན་འདས་ཀྱི་གསུང་རབ་དགོངས་འགྲེལ་དང་བཅས་པའི་ལུང་གི་དོན་དང་། རྗེས་འཇུག་གི་སྦྱོར་བ་ལ་མཁས་པའི་རིགས་པ་དང་། བསླབ་བྱའི་དོན་ལ་མཁས་པའི་རིགས་དང་། བསླབ་བྱའི་དོན་ལ་མཁས་པའི་བླ་མའི་མན་ངག་ལེགས་པར་མཉན་པ་སྟེ་གསུམ་པོ་དེ་ཕྱོགས་གཅིག་ཏུ་ལེགས་པར་སྦྱར་ཏེ། ཞེས་པར་འདོད་པའི་གཞུང་དོན་གང་ཡིན་པ་དེའི་སྟེང་དུ་དབབ་པ་སྟེ་བདེ་བླག་ཏུ་རྟོགས་པར་འགྱུར་བ་དེ་ལྟར་བྱའོ། ཞེས་སོ། དེའང་གཞུང་དོན་རྟོགས་དཀའ་ཞིང་འཁྲུལ་གཞི་ཡོད་པ་རྣམས་ལུང་དོན་དང་སྦྱོར་དགོས་པ་དང་། ལུང་དོན་ཟབ་ཅིང་རྒྱ་ཆེ་བ་རྣམས་མན་ངག་གིས་འགྲོལ་དགོས་པའི་དོན་ཏེ། ཚིག་སྦྱོར་ཕྲ་མོ་རེ་ལའང་གསུམ་ག་ཚོགས་དགོས་པ་ནི་མ་ཡིན་ནོ། གསུམ་པ་བསླབ་ཚུལ་གོ་རིམ་ལ་འདོམས་པ་ནི།

བསླབ་ལ་བརྩོན་པའི་གང་ཟག་གིས། དང་པོར་ང་རོ་རྣམས་ལ་སྦྱང་།

སྔོན་འཇུག་མིང་གཞི་རྗེས་འཇུག་གསུམ། ཀློག་གི་ཆེད་དུ་བསླབ་པ་ཡིན།

རྗེས་འཇུག་བཞི་ཡི་སྦྱོར་བ་ནི། མཉན་བསམ་བསྟན་པའི་དོན་དུ་སྦྱར།

ཡན་ལག་དེ་དག་མཐུ་ཡིས་ནི། །འབྲས་བུའི་ཚེད་དུ་དོན་ལ་དབབ། །
བསྒྲུབ་པའི་རིམ་པ་འདི་ཡིས་ནི། །གང་ཞིག་འབད་པ་ཆུང་ངུས་ཀྱང་། །
ཤེས་རབ་སྒྱུར་དུ་གྲོལ་བར་འགྱུར། །དེ་ཕྱིར་དང་པོར་འདི་ཉིད་བསྒྲུབ། །
དེ་ནས་རྒྱས་པའང་མཉན་བྱས་ཏེ། །བསྒྲུབ་པ་གང་ལ་དད་པ་ཡི། །
གཞུང་ཉིད་བླ་མ་དག་ལས་མཉན། །

ཞེས་པ་སྟེ། །རིག་པའི་གནས་གང་ཞིག་བསྒྲུབ་པར་བྱ་བ་ལ་བརྩོན་པས་འཇུག་པར་བྱེད་པའི་གང་ཟག་ལས་དང་པོ་པ་དེས་ནི། །ཐོག་མ་ཉིད་དུ་ང་རོ་ཞེས་བྱ་བ་ཡི་གེ་རྐྱང་པ་རྣམས། །ཡི་གེའི་མདོ་ལས་འབྱུང་བ་ལྟར་རང་རང་གི་སྐྱེས་གནས་དང་། །བྱེད་པ་དང་། །ཕྱི་ནང་གི་རྩོལ་བ་རྣམས་དང་མཐུན་པ་དང་། །དབྱངས་ལྡན་རྣམས་ཀྱང་སོ་སོའི་ང་རོ་དབྱུང་ཚུལ་དང་བཅས་རེ་རེ་ནས་ཀློག་པའི་སྒྲ་གདངས་ལ་སྦྱང་བར་བྱ་ཞིང་། །དེ་ནས་སྔོན་འཇུག་ལྔ་དང་། །འཕུལ་རྟེན་གྱི་འཇུག་ཡུལ་མིང་གཞི་སུམ་ཅུ་དང་། །རྗེས་འཇུག་བཅུ་སྟེ། །དེ་གསུམ་ཅི་རིགས་ཚིག་བར་གཅིག་ཏུ་སྦྱོར་བའི་ཚུལ་ཡང་། །བྱིས་པ་བདེ་འཇུག་ནས་འབྱུང་བ་ལྟར་ཀློག་ལེགས་པར་ཤེས་པའི་ཚེད་དུ་བསྒྲུབ་པར་བྱ་བ་ཡིན་པ་དང་། །ཀློག་ལ་བྱང་ནས་རྗེས་འཇུག་སྟེ་དེར་སྔོན་འཇུག་ཀྱང་འདུས་པས། །དེ་དག་རྟགས་འཇུག་ནས་བཤད་པ་ལྟར། །སྒྲ་དོན་གང་ལ་འཇུག་པ་དང་། །ཡི་གེ་གང་གིས་འཇུག་པ་དང་། །ཚུལ་ཇི་ལྟར་འཇུག་པ་དང་། །དགོས་པ་ཅིའི་ཕྱིར་འཇུག་པ་སྟེ་རྣམ་པ་བཞིའི་སྦྱོར་བ་རྣམས་ནི། །བླ་མ་ལས་ལེགས་པར་བཤད་པ་མཉན་པ་དང་། །དེའི་དོན་རང་ཉིད་ཀྱིས་ཚུལ་བཞིན་དུ་བསམ་པ་དང་། །རང་གིས་ཁོང་དུ་ཆུད་ནས་གཞན་ལ་བསྟན་པ་རྣམས་ཀྱི་དོན་དུ་སྦྱར་ཏེ་མཁས་པར་བསྒྲུབ་པར་བྱའོ། །ཀློག་དང་བརྡ་དག་གི་ཡན་ལག་དེ་གཉིས་ཀྱི་མཐུས་ནི། །གང་བསྒྲུབ་པར་བྱ་བ་དེ་ཤེས་པའི་འབྲས་བུ་ཐོབ་པར་བྱ་བའི་སླད་དུ་དོན་ལ་དབབ་ནས་ཉམས་སུ་བསྟན་པར་བྱའོ། །དེ་ལྟར་བསྒྲུབ་པའི་རིམ་པ་འདི་ནི། །སྐྱེས་བུ་གང་ཞིག་ཐོས་བསམ་ལ་བརྩོན་འགྲུས་ཆེན་པོ་དང་ལྡན་པ་རྣམས་སློས་ཅི་དགོས་ཏེ། །འབད་པ་ཆུང་ངུ་ཙམ་བྱས་པས་ཚིག་དོན་ལ་རྨོངས་པ་མེད་པའི་ཤེས་རབ་སྒྱུར་དུ་གྲོལ་བར་འགྱུར་རོ། །རྒྱུ་མཚན་དེའི་ཕྱིར་མཁས་པར་འདོད་པ་རྣམས་ཀྱིས་ཐོག་མར་སུམ་ཅུ་པའི་གཞུང་འདི་ཉིད་བསྒྲུབ་པར་བྱ་ཞིང་། །འདི་ནི་ཤེས་ནས་རྟགས་འཇུག་ལ་སོགས་པ་འདིའི་སྐབས་ཕྱི་མ་རྣམས་དང་། །དེ་ནས་བརྡ་སྤྲོད་པའི་གཞུང་རྒྱས་པ་གཞན་དང་གཞན་

རྣམས་ཀྱང་མཉན་པར་བྱས་ནས་ཁོང་དུ་ཆུད་པ་ན། ཐེག་པ་གསུམ་གྱི་གཞིར་གྱུར་པའི་བསླབ་པ་གང་ལ་དང་ཅིང་སློབ་པར་འདོད་པ་དེའི་གཞུང་ལུགས་ཡན་ལག་དང་བཅས་པ་ཉིད་བླ་མ་རྣམས་ལས་མཉན་པར་བྱའོ། ཞེས་སོ།

བཞི་པ་གདམས་ངག་སྙིང་རུང་ལ་བསྟན་དགོས་པར་འདོམས་པ་ནི།

སློབ་དཔོན་དེ་ཉིད་དུ་འཛིན་ཅིང་། ལེ་ལོ་གཡེང་བ་རྣམ་པར་སྤངས།

ཞེ་བཟང་དད་པ་ལ་བརྟེན་པ། སྐྱེས་བུ་དེས་ནི་མྱུར་རྟོགས་ཏེ།

དེ་ལ་དུས་སུ་འདོམས་པར་བྱ། ཅིག་ཤོས་དེ་ལས་ལྡོག་པའོ།

ཞེས་པ་སྟེ། བསྟན་བཅོས་འདི་ཉིད་ཀྱི་གདམས་ངག་བསྟན་དུ་རུང་བའི་སྣོད་ནི། གདམས་ངག་སྟོན་མཁན་གྱི་སློབ་དཔོན་དེ་ལ་སློབ་དཔོན་དུ་འཛིན་ཅིང་། ཞེ་ས་དང་བཅས་པས་དྲིན་དུ་བཟོ་བ་དང་། འགལ་རྐྱེན་བསླབ་པར་བྱ་བའི་གནས་དེ་ལ་སྒྲིབ་བྱེད་པའི་ལེ་ལོ་དང་། བྱ་བ་གཞན་ལ་འཇུག་པའི་གཡེང་བ་གཉིས་སྤངས་པ་སྟེ། སྐྱོན་དེ་དག་གིས་གླགས་མི་རྙེད་པའི་རྟག་སྦྱོར་གྱི་བརྩོན་འགྲུས་དང་ལྡན་པ་དང་། མཐུན་རྐྱེན་ཞེ་སྡེ་རང་བཞིན་བཟང་ཞིང་། བསླབ་བྱའི་གནས་ལ་མཆོག་ཏུ་དད་པའི་གུས་སྦྱོར་གྱི་བརྩོན་འགྲུས་དང་ལྡན་པ་སྟེ། མཚན་ཉིད་གསུམ་དང་ལྡན་པའི་སྐྱེས་བུ་དེས་ནི། བསླབ་པར་བྱ་བ་གང་ཡིན་པ་མྱུར་དུ་རྟོགས་པར་འགྱུར་བས། དེ་ལ་དུས་ཤེས་པར་བྱས་ནས་འདོམས་པར་བྱ་ཞིང་། གོང་དུ་བཤད་པའི་སྣོད་ལྡན་གྱི་ཅིག་ཤོས་སློབ་དཔོན་ལ་མི་གུས་པ་དང་། ལེ་ལོ་དང་གཡེང་བ་ཅན་དང་། རང་བཞིན་ངན་ཅིང་དད་པ་མེད་པ་རྣམས་ནི་སྣོད་དང་མི་ལྡན་པས། དུས་སུ་འདོམས་པ་དེ་ལས་ལྡོག་སྟེ་རེ་ཞིག་འདོམས་པར་བྱ་བ་མ་ཡིན་མོད། འོན་ཀྱང་ཕྱི་ནས་དོན་དུ་གཉེར་ཞིང་འདུན་པར་འགྱུར་ན་ལེགས་པར་རྗེས་སུ་བསྟན་པར་ཡང་བྱའོ་ཞེས་སོ། སྨྲས་པ།

ཨ་འདུས་རིག་བྱེད་སྨྲར་བུ་ལ་བཀྲུས་པའི། ཀ་འཕྲེང་མཁའ་མེའི་གྲངས་འཕྲུད་ཨཀྵ་ར།

མིང་གཞིའི་སྔོན་རྗེས་འཇུག་པའི་རྣམས་འགྱུར་ཅན། ཚིག་ཕྲད་རྣམ་དབྱེའི་མགུལ་རྒྱན་སྤེལ་རྩེན་ནས།

སྤྱི་དང་བྱེ་བྲག་རྟགས་ཀྱི་དབྱེ་བ་ཡིས། དུས་གསུམ་བདག་གཞན་བྱ་བྱེད་སྒྲ་དོན་ལ།

འཇུག་ཚུལ་སྔོན་མེད་ལེགས་བཤད་མ་ཧེ་ཀའི། ངོ་ཤལ་གཏུར་གཟུམ་སྐྱེ་བོའི་རྒྱན་དུ་དགོད།

རྟགས་ཀྱི་འཇུག་པ།

༄༅། །གཉིས་པ་རྟགས་ཀྱི་འཇུགས་པ་བཤད་པ་ལ་གསུམ། མིང་གཞིའི་ཡི་གེ་སྤྱིའི་རྟགས་ཀྱི་དབྱེ་བ་བཤད་པ། སྔོན་འཇུག་གི་རྟགས་ཀྱི་འཇུག་པ་བཤད་པ། རྗེས་འཇུག་གི་རྟགས་ཀྱི་འཇུག་པ་བཤད་པའོ།

དང་པོ་ནི། ཕོ་ཡི་ཡི་གེ་འབའ་ཞིག་ལ། སྡེ་པ་ཕྱེད་དང་བརྒྱད་གནས་པའང་། སྡེ་ཚན་ལྔ་རུ་དྲིལ་བྱས་ལ། ཕོ་དང་མ་ནིང་མོ་དང་ནི། ཤིན་ཏུ་མོ་དང་བཞི་བཞི་རུ། སྡེ་པ་བཞི་པ་ཡན་ཆད་དབྱེ། ལྷག་མ་བཅུ་བཞི་གནས་པ་ལས། ཙ་སོགས་གསུམ་ནི་ཙ་སོགས་སྦྱར། ཝ་ནི་བ་དང་སྦྱར་བར་བྱ། ལྷག་མ་དྲུག་ནི་མོ་རུ་སྦྱར། ར་ལ་ཧ་ནི་མོ་གཤམ་སྟེ། ཨ་ནི་མཚན་མེད་ཅེས་ཀྱང་བྱ། ཞེས་པ་སྟེ། སྤྱིར་བོད་ཀྱི་ཡི་གེ་རྣམས་ལ་ཕོ་མོ་གཉིས་སུ་དབྱེ་བའི་དབང་དུ་བྱས་ན། དབྱངས་ཡིག་མཚོན་བྱེད་ཨི་ཨུ་ཨེ་ཨོ་བཞི་ནི་ཤེས་རབ་ཀྱི་རང་བཞིན་མོ་དང་། ཀ་ནས་ཨའི་མཐར་ཐུག་པའི་གསལ་བྱེད་སུམ་ཅུ་པོ་རྣམས་ནི་ཐབས་ཀྱི་རང་བཞིན་ཕོར་ཤེས་པར་བྱའོ། དེས་ན་ཕོ་འི་ཡི་གེ་འབའ་ཞིག་སྟེ་གསལ་བྱེད་སུམ་ཅུ་པོ་ཁོ་ན་ལ། སྡེ་པ་ཕྱེད་དང་བརྒྱད་དུ་གནས་ཏེ། སྡེ་པ་དང་པོ། ཀ་ཁ་ག་ང་། གཉིས་པ། ཅ་ཆ་ཇ་ཉ། གསུམ་པ། ཏ་ཐ་ད་ན། བཞི་པ། པ་ཕ་བ་མ། ལྔ་པ། ཙ་ཚ་ཛ་ཝ། དྲུག་པ། ཞ་ཟ་འ་ཡ། བདུན་པ། ར་ལ་ཤ་ས། ཕྱེད་པ། ཧ་ཨ་རྣམས་སོ། དེ་རྣམས་སྡེ་ཚན་ལྔ་རུ་དྲིལ་བ་ནི། སྒྲ་དྲག་པ་ཕོ་དང་། རན་པ་མ་ནིང་དང་། ཆུང་ཟད་ཞན་པ་མོ་དང་། དེ་ལས་ཀྱང་ཆུང་ཟད་ཞན་པ་ཤིན་ཏུ་མོ་དང་། ཤིན་ཏུ་ཞན་པ་མོ་གཤམ་སྟེ་རྣམ་པ་ལྔའོ། དེའང་སྡེ་པ་དང་པོ་བཞི་པོ་རྣམས་ཀྱི་དང་པོ། ཀ་ཅ་ཏ་པ་རྣམས་ཕོ་དང་། གཉིས་པ། ཁ་ཆ་ཐ་ཕ་རྣམས་མ་ནིང་དང་། གསུམ་པ། ག་ཇ་ད་བ་རྣམས་མོ་དང་། བཞི་པ། ང་ཉ་ན་མ་རྣམས་ཤིན་ཏུ་མོར་དབྱེ་བར་བྱའོ། དེར་མ་ཕྱེ་བའི་ལྷག་མ་ཙ་སྡེ་ཕྱིན་ཆད། ཡི་གེ་བཅུ་བཞི་གནས་པ་ལ། ཙ་ལ་སོགས་པ་སྟེ་ཙ་ཚ་ཛ་གསུམ་ནི། རིམ་བཞིན་སྔར་བསྟན་པའི་ཙ་ལ་སོགས་པ་གསུམ་དང་སྦྱར་བར་བྱ་སྟེ། ཙ་ཕོ་དང་། ཚ་མ་ནིང་དང་། ཛ་མོར་ཤེས་པར་བྱའོ། དེ་བཞིན་དུ་ཝ་ནི་བ་དང་སྦྱར་བས་མོ་དང་། ལྷག་མ། ཞ་ཟ་འ་ཡ་ཤ་ས་དྲུག་ཀྱང་མོ་འི་ཡི་གེར་སྦྱར་བར་བྱའོ། ར་ལ་ཧ་གསུམ་ནི་མོ་གཤམ་གྱི་ཡི་གེ་ཞེས་བྱ་ཞིང་། ཨ་ཡིག་ནི་མོ་གཤམ་གྱི་ཡི་གེ་ཡིན་པར་མ་ཟད་ར་ལ་ཧ་གསུམ་ལས་ཀྱང་རྩལ་བ་ཤིན་ཏུ་ཞན་པའི་ཕྱིར་ན་མཚན་མེད་ཀྱི་ཡི་གེ་ཞེས་ཀྱང་བྱའོ་ཞེས

སོ། དེ་ཡང་གཞུང་ཐལ་མོ་ཆེར། མ་ཉིང་མཚན་ མེད་ཅེས་ཀྱང་བྱ། ཞེས་འབྱུང་བ་ནི་ཡི་གེ་ཉམས་པའོ།

གཉིས་པ་སྔོན་འཇུག་གི་རྟགས་ཀྱི་འཇུག་པ་བཤད་པ་ལ་གསུམ། མིང་གཞི་ལས་སྔོན་རྗེས་དབྱུང་ཚུལ་བཤད་པ། སྔོན་འཇུག་གི་རྟགས་ཀྱི་དབྱེ་བ་བཤད་པ། སྔོན་འཇུག་གི་རྟགས་ཀྱི་འཇུག་ཚུལ་བཤད་པའོ། དང་པོ་ནི། མོ་ཡི་ཡི་གེའི་ནང་ནས་ནི། འཇུག་པའི་ཡི་གེ་བཅུ་དབྱུང་བྱ། འཇུག་པ་བཅུ་ཡི་ནང་ནས་ནི། སྔོན་འཇུག་ཡི་གེ་ལྔ་དབྱུང་བྱ། ཞེས་པ་སྟེ། མོ་འི་ཡི་གེ་ལ་བཤད་མ་ཐག་པ་ལྟར་མོ་ཙམ་དང་། ཤིན་ཏུ་མོ་དང་མོ་གཤམ་སྟེ་གསུམ་དུ་གནས་པ་སོ་སོར་མ་ཕྱེ་བའི་ནང་ནས། སྔར་སུམ་ཅུ་པར་བཤད་པ་ལྟར། རྗེས་འཇུག་གི་ཡི་གེ་ག་ང་ད་ན་བ་མ་འ་ར་ལ་ས་སྟེ་བཅུ་པོ་རྣམས་དབྱུང་བར་བྱ་ཞིང་། དེའི་ནང་ནས་ཀྱང་སྔོན་འཇུག་གི་ཡི་གེ་ག་ད་བ་མ་འ་སྟེ་ལྔ་པོ་རྣམས་དབྱུང་བར་བྱའོ། ཞེས་སོ།

གཉིས་པ་སྔོན་འཇུག་གི་རྟགས་ཀྱི་དབྱེ་བ་བཤད་པ་ནི། སྔོན་འཇུག་ཡི་གེ་ལྔ་པོ་ལ། ཕོ་དང་མ་ཉིང་མོ་དང་ནི། ཤིན་ཏུ་མོ་དང་བཞི་རུ་དབྱེ། ཞེས་པ་སྟེ་བཤད་མ་ཐག་པའི་སྔོན་འཇུག་གི་ཡི་གེ་ལྔ་པོ་དེ་ལ། མིང་གཞི་དང་སྦྱར་ནས་གློག་པའི་ཚེ་སྒྲ་གདངས་དྲག་ཞན་དུ་འགྱུར་བའི་ཆ་ནས་ཕོ་བ་ཡིག་དང་། མ་ཉིང་ག་ད་གཉིས་དང་། མོ་འ་ཡིག་དང་། ཤིན་ཏུ་མོ་མ་ཡིག་སྟེ་བཞིར་དབྱེ་བར་བྱའོ་ཞེས་སོ།

གསུམ་པ་སྔོན་འཇུག་གི་རྟགས་ཀྱི་འཇུག་ཚུལ་བཤད་པ་ལ་གཉིས། མདོར་བསྟན་པ་དང་། རྒྱས་པར་བཤད་པའོ། དང་པོ་ནི། དེ་དག་རེ་རེའང་བཞི་བྱེད་དེ། གང་ལ་འཇུག་བྱེད་གང་གིས་བྱེད། ཇི་ལྟར་འཇུག་བྱེད་ཅི་ཕྱིར་བྱེད། ཅེས་པ་སྟེ། སྔོན་འཇུག་གི་ཡི་གེ་ཕོ་སོགས་དེ་དག་རེ་རེའི་འཇུག་ཚུལ་ཡང་རྣམ་པ་བཞི་བྱེད་པ་སྟེ་བྱེད་པ་བཞི་བཞིའི་སྒོ་ནས་རྟོགས་དགོས་ཏེ། འཇུག་ཡུལ་མིང་གཞིའི་ཡི་གེ་གང་ལ་འཇུག་པར་བྱེད་པ་དང་། འཇུག་པ་པོ་སྔོན་འཇུག་གི་ཡི་གེ་གང་གིས་འཇུག་པར་བྱེད་པ་དང་། སྒྲའི་འཇུག་ཚུལ་ཇི་ལྟ་བུས་འཇུག་པར་བྱེད་པ་དང་། དགོས་པ་ཅིའི་ཕྱིར་འཇུག་པར་བྱེད་པ་རྣམས་སོ། ཞེས་པའོ།

གཉིས་པ་རྒྱས་པར་བཤད་པ་ལ་གསུམ། གང་ལ་འཇུག་པ་དང་གང་གིས་འཇུག་པ་མཐུན་མོང་དུ་བཤད་པ། ཇི་ལྟར་འཇུག་པ་བཤད་པ། ཅི་ཕྱིར་འཇུག་པ་བཤད་པའོ། དང་པོ་ལ་གཉིས། དྲི་བས་མཚམས་སྦྱར་བ་དང་། ལན་གྱིས་བསྟན་པའོ། དང་པོ་ནི། གང་ལ་འཇུག་པར་བྱེད་ཅེ་ན། ཞེས་པའོ། གཉིས་པ་ལན་གྱིས་བསྟན་པ་ལ་གཉིས། ལན་གྱིས་བསྟན་པ་དངོས་དང་། ཞར་བྱུང་མི་འཇུག་པ་བཤད་པའོ།

དང་པོ་ནི། ཕོ་ནི་ཕོ་དང་མོ་ལ་འཇུག། མོ་ནི་མོ་དང་མ་ནིང་ལ། མ་ནིང་ཡང་ནི་ཕོ་མོ་འདོར། ཤིན་ཏུ་མོ་ནི་མ་ནིང་དང་། མོ་དང་ཤིན་ཏུ་མོ་ཉིད་འདོར། ཞེས་པ་སྟེ། དེ་ལ་གང་གིས་འཇུག་པར་བྱེད་པ་པོ་ཕོའི་ཡི་གེ་བ་ནི། རང་གི་སྡེ་པ་མ་ཡིན་པའི་མིང་གཞིའི་ཕོ་ཀ་ཅ་ཏ་ཙ་བཞི་དང་། མོ་ཡིག། ག་ང་ཛ་ཉ་ད་ན་ཛྷ་ཞ་ཟ་ར་ཤ་ས་བཅུ་གཉིས་ཏེ་བཅུ་དྲུག་ལ་འཇུག་གོ་དེ་བཞིན་དུ། སྔོན་འཇུག་གི་མོ་འ་ཡིག་ནི། མིང་གཞིའི་མོ་ཡིག། ག་ཛ་ད་བ་ཛ་ལྷ་དང་། མ་ནིང་། ཁ་ཆ་ཐ་ཕ་ཚ་ལྷ་སྟེ་བཅུ་ལ་འཇུག་གོ། སྔོན་འཇུག་གི་མ་ནིང་ག་ཡིག་ནི། མིང་གཞིའི་ཕོ་ཡིག་ཅ་ཏ་ཙ་གསུམ་དང་། མོ་ཡིག། ཉ་ད་ན་ཞ་ཟ་ཡ་ཤ་ས་བརྒྱད་དེ་བཅུ་གཅིག་ལ་འཇུག་ཅིང་། ད་ཡིག་ནི། མིང་གཞིའི་ཕོ་ཡིག། ཀ་པ་གཉིས་དང་། མོ་ཡིག། ག་ང་བ་མ་བཞི་སྟེ་དྲུག་ལ་འཇུག་གོ། སྔོན་འཇུག་གི་ཤིན་ཏུ་མོ་མ་ཡིག་ནི། མིང་གཞིའི་མ་ནིང་། ཁ་ཆ་ཐ་ཚ་བཞི་དང་། མོ་ཡིག། ག་ཇ་ད་ཛ་བཞི་དང་། ཤིང་ཏུ་མོ། ང་ཉ་ན་གསུམ་སྟེ་བཅུ་གཅིག་ལ་འཇུག་གོ། ཞེས་སོ། དེའང་བསྒྲེད་ཅེས་པ་ལྟ་བུའི་འཕྲུལ་རྟེན་གྱི་བ་དང་དའི་འཇུག་ཡུལ་སྒྲིར་ས་ཀ་ཡ་གསུམ་ག་ཡིན་ཀྱང་འཇུག་ཡུལ་གཙོ་བོ་ནི་ཀ་ཡིག་ཉིད་ཡིན་པས་སྐབས་འདིར་ཡང་གང་ལ་འཇུག་པ་དེ་འཇུག་ཡུལ་གཙོ་བོ་དེ་ལ་བྱེད་དགོས་ཏེ། དེ་ལྟ་མ་ཡིན་ན་འགྱེད་ཅེས་པ་ལྟ་བུའི་ཚེའ་ཡིག་རང་སྡེའི་ཡ་ཡིག་ལ་འཇུག་པར་ཁས་ལེན་དགོས་སོ།

གཉིས་པ་ཞར་བྱུང་མི་འཇུག་པ་བཤད་པ་ནི། ཕོ་ནི་མ་ནིང་ལ་མི་འཇུག། མོ་ནི་ཕོ་ལ་འཇུག་པ་མེད། མ་ནིང་རང་ལ་རང་མི་འཇུག། རང་གི་སྡེ་དང་འཕྲད་པ་ན། ཕོ་ཡང་མོ་ལ་འཇུག་མི་འགྱུར། མ་ནིང་མོ་ཡང་དེ་བཞིན་ནོ། ཞེས་པ་སྟེ། སྔོན་འཇུག་གི་ཕོ་བ་ཡིག་ནི། མིང་གཞིའི་མ་ནིང་ཁ་ཆ་ཐ་ཕ་ཚ་རྣམས་ལ་མི་འཇུག་ཅིང་། སྔོན་འཇུག་གི་མོ་འ་ཡིག་དང་། དེའི་ཤུགས་བསྟན་ཤིན་ཏུ་མོ་མ་ཡིག་དག་ནི། མིང་གཞིའི་ཕོ། ཀ་ཅ་ཏ་ཙ་རྣམས་ལ་མི་འཇུག་པ་དང་། སྔོན་འཇུག་གི་མ་ནིང་ག་ད་གཉིས་ནི། མིང་གཞིའི་ཡི་གེ་མ་ནིང་། ཁ་ཆ་ཐ་ཕ་ཚ་རྣམས་ལ་མི་འཇུག་གོ། ཡང་སྔར། ཕོ་ནི་ཕོ་དང་མོ་ལ་འཇུག། ཅེས་སོགས་ཀྱི་དམིགས་བསལ། སྔོན་འཇུག་རྣམས་བཞི་ཚན་དུ་ཕྱེ་བའི་མིང་གཞི་རྣམས་དང་འཕྲད་པའི་ཚེ་ན། སྔོན་འཇུག་གི་ཕོ་བ་ཡིག་ནི། མིང་གཞིའི་མོ་བ་མ་དག་ལ་མི་འཇུག་ཅིང་། ཡང་སླས་ཕོ་ཡིག་པ་ལའང་མི་འཇུག་པར་བསྟན་པ་དང་། དེ་བཞིན་དུ་སྔོན་འཇུག་གི་མ་ནིང་ག་ད

གཉིས་ཀྱང་རང་སྡེའི་ཕ་མོ་དག་ལ་མི་འཇུག་པས། ག་ཡིག་མིང་གཞིའི་ཀ་ག་ང་རྣམས་དང་། ད་ཡིག་མིང་གཞིའི་ཏ་ད་ན་རྣམས་ལ་མི་འཇུག་ཅིང་། སྔོན་འཇུག་གི་མོ་ཡིག་འ་ནི། རང་སྡེའི་མིང་གཞིའི་མོ། ཞ་ཟ་འ་ཡ་རྣམས་ལ་མི་འཇུག་པ་དང་། ཡང་སླས་སྔོན་འཇུག་གི་ཤིན་ཏུ་མོ་མ་ཡིག་ནི། རང་སྡེའི་མིང་གཞིའི་མ་ནིང་ཕ་དང་། མོ་བ་དང་། ཤིན་ཏུ་མོ་མ་རྣམས་ལ་འཇུག་པ་མ་ཡིན་ནོ། ཞེས་སོ། གཉིས་པ་ཇི་ལྟར་འཇུག་པ་བཤད་པ་ལ་གཉིས། དྲི་བས་མཚམས་སྦྱར་བ་དང་། ལན་གྱིས་བསྟན་པའོ། དང་པོ་ནི། ཇི་ལྟར་འཇུག་པར་བྱེད་ཅེས་ན། ཞེས་པ་འོ། གཉིས་པ་ལན་གྱིས་བསྟན་པ་ནི། ཕོ་ནི་དྲག་པའི་ཚུལ་གྱིས་ཏེ། མ་ནིང་རན་པར་འཇུག་པ་ཡིན། མོ་ཞན་ན་པའི་ཚུལ་གྱིས་ཏེ། ཤིན་ཏུ་མོ་ནི་མཉམ་པས་སོ། ཞེས་པ་སྟེ། སྔོན་འཇུག་གི་ཕོ་ཡིག་བ་ནི། མིང་གཞིའི་ཡི་གེ་རང་གི་འཇུག་ཡུལ་དུ་འགྱུར་བ་རྣམས་ལ་སྒྲ་དང་བྱེད་རྩོལ་དྲག་པའི་སྒོ་ནས་འཇུག་པ་དང་། མ་ནིང་ག་ད་གཉིས་ནི་སྒྲ་རྩོལ་རན་པར་འཇུག་པ་དང་། མོ་ཡིག་འ་ནི། སྒྲ་རྩོལ་ཞན་པས་འཇུག་པ་དང་། ཤིན་ཏུ་མོ་ཡིག་མ་ནི། སྒྲ་རྩོལ་མཉམ་པ་སྟེ་ཤིན་ཏུ་ལྷོད་ཅིང་ཉམ་ཆུང་བའི་ཚུལ་གྱིས་འཇུག་པར་བྱེད་དོ་ཞེས་སོ།

གསུམ་པ་ཅི་ཕྱིར་འཇུག་པ་བཤད་པ་ལ་གཉིས། དྲི་བས་མཚམས་སྦྱར་བ་དང་། ལན་གྱིས་བསྟན་པའོ། དང་པོ་ནི། ཅི་ཕྱིར་འཇུག་པར་བྱེད་ཅེ་ན། ཞེས་པའོ། གཉིས་པ་ལན་གྱིས་བསྟན་པ་ནི། ཕོ་ནི་འདས་དང་གཞན་བསྒྲུབ་ཕྱིར། མ་ནིང་གཉིས་ཀ་ད་ལྟར་ཆེད། མོ་ནི་བདག་ད་མ་འོངས་ཕྱིར། ཤིན་ཏུ་མོ་ནི་མཉམ་ཕྱིར་རོ། ཞེས་པ་སྟེ། སྔོན་འཇུག་གི་ཕོ་ཡིག་བ་ནི། དགོས་པ་དུས་གསུམ་ལས། ལྷ་བསྒྲུབས་སོ། ཕྱུགས་གསེར་དུ་བསྒྱུརད་ཏོ། ལྟ་བུ་བྱེད་པ་པོ་གཞན་དང་དངོས་སུ་འབྲེལ་བའི་བྱ་བ་བྱས་ཟིན་པ་འདས་པ་བསྒྲུབ་པའི་ཕྱིར་དང་། དངོས་པོ་བདག་གཞན་གཉིས་ལས། གཞན་ཏེ། བཏུང་བ། བདུག་པ། བསྒྲུབ་བྱ། བསྒྲུབ་པར་བྱ་བ། བསྒྲུབ་བྱའི་ལྷ། བསྒྱུར་བྱ། བསྒྱུར་བར་བྱ་བ། བསྒྱུར་བྱའི་ཕྱུགས་ལྟ་བུ་བྱེད་པ་པོ་གཞན་དང་དངོས་སུ་འབྲེལ་བའི་བྱ་བའི་ཡུལ་གྱི་དངོས་པོ་དང་། བསྒྲུབ་པར་བྱ། བསྒྲུབ་བོ། བསྒྱུར་བར་བྱ། བསྒྱུར་རོ། ལྟ་བུ་བྱ་བའི་ཡུལ་དང་འབྲེལ་བའི་བྱ་བ་གསལ་བྱེད་ཀྱི་སྒྲ་ཉིད་བསྒྲུབ་པའི་ཕྱིར་འཇུག་གོ། སྔོན་འཇུག་གི་མ་ནིང་ག་ད་དག་ནི། ཤིང་གཅོད་པ་པོ། གཅོད་བྱེད། སྐྱོན་དགག་པ་པོ། དགག་བྱེད་ལྟ་བུ་བྱེད་པ་པོའི་དངོས་པོ་དང་། གཅོད་པར་བྱེད། གཅོད་དོ། དགག་པར་

དཔེ། དགག་གོ། ལྷ་བུ་བྱེད་པ་པོ་དང་འབྲེལ་བའི་བྱེད་ལས་གསལ་བྱེད་ཀྱི་སྒྲ་གཉིས་བདག་གི་དངོས་པོ་དང་གདམ་པ། གཟུང་བ། གཅད་བྱ། གཅད་པར་བྱ་བ། གཅད་བྱའི་ཞིང་། དགག་བྱ། དགག་པར་བྱ། དགག་བྱའི་སྐྱོན་ལྷ་བུ་བྱེད་པ་པོ་གཞན་དང་དངོས་སུ་འབྲེལ་བའི་བྱ་བའི་ཡུལ་གྱི་དངོས་པོ་དང་། གཅད་པར་བྱ། གཅད་དོ། དགག་པར་བྱ། དགག་གོ། ལྷ་བུ་བྱ་བའི་ཡུལ་དང་འབྲེལ་བའི་བྱ་བ་གསལ་བྱེད་ཀྱི་སྒྲ་གཉིས་གཞན་གྱི་དངོས་པོ་སྟེ། དངོས་པོ་བདག་དང་གཞན་གཉིས་ཀ་བསྒྲུབ་པའི་འཇུག་པ་དང་། དེར་མ་གཏོགས་པའི་དུས་གསུམ་ལས། གཏོད་ཀྱིན་འདུག། གཏོད་བཞིན་པའོ། དགག་གིན་འདུག། དགག་བཞིན་པའོ། ལྷ་བུ་བྱེད་པ་པོ་གཞན་དངོས་སུ་འབྲེལ་བའི་བྱ་བ་བྱེད་བཞིན་པ་ད་ལྟར་བ་བསྒྲུབ་པའི་ཚེད་དུ་འཇུག་སྟེ། ད་ལྟར་བ་ནི། བྱེད་ལས་གསལ་བྱེད་ཀྱི་སྒྲ་ཉིད་ཚིག་གྲོགས་ཀྱིས་བསྒྱུར་བའོ། སྔོན་འཇུག་གི་མོ་ཡིག་འ་ནི། མདུད་པ་འགྲོལ་པ་པོ། འགྲོལ་བྱེད། ཡོས་འཐག་པ་པོ། འཐག་བྱེད་ལྷ་བུ་བྱ་བྱེད་ཐ་དད་དུ་སྣང་བའི་བྱེད་པ་པོའི་དངོས་པོ་དང་། མདུད་པ་འགྲོལ་བར་བྱེད། འགྲོལ་ལོ། ཡོས་འཐག་པར་བྱེད། འཐག་གོ་ལྷ་བུ་བྱེད་པ་པོ་དང་འབྲེལ་བའི་བྱེད་ལས་གསལ་བྱེད་ཀྱི་སྒྲ་སྟེ། དེ་རྣམས་དངོས་པོ་བདག་ཡིན་པས་དེ་བསྒྲུབ་པའི་ཕྱིར་དང་། འགྲོལ་ཀྱིན་འདུག། འཐག་བཞིན་པའོ། འགྱུར་གྱིན་འདུག་འགྲུབ་བཞིན་པའོ། ལྷ་བུ་བདག་གཞན་གྱི་དབྱེ་བས་མ་བསྡུས་པའི་དུས་ད་ལྟར་བ་བསྒྲུབ་པའི་ཕྱིར་དང་། འཁོར་ལོ་འཁོར་བར་འགྱུར། དོན་འགྲུབ་པར་འགྱུར། ལྷ་བུ། བྱེད་པ་པོ་གཞན་དངོས་སུ་མེད་པར་བྱ་བྱེད་ཐ་མི་དད་པ་ལྟ་བུར་སྣང་བའི་བྱ་བ་བྱེད་འགྱུར་མ་འོངས་པའི་དུས་བསྒྲུབ་པ་རྣམས་ཀྱི་ཕྱིར་འཇུག་གོ། སྔོན་འཇུག་གི་ཞིན་ཏུ་མོ་མ་ཡིག་ནི། མཁས་པར་བྱས། མཁས་པ། མཁས་པར་བྱེད། མཁས་བྱ། མཁས་པར་བྱ། མཁས་པར་གྱུར། མཁས་བཞིན་པ། མཁས་པར་འགྱུར། ལྷ་བུ་སྔར་བཤད་པའི་བདག་གཞན་དང་། དུས་གསུམ་གྱི་བྱེ་བྲག་མེད་པར་ཐམས་ཅད་ལ་མཉམ་པ་སྟེ་མཚུངས་པ་ཉིད་བསྒྲུབ་པའི་ཕྱིར་འཇུག་གོ། དེ་ཡང་དུས་གསུམ་གྱི་དབྱེ་བས་ནི། བྱ་བྱེད་ཀྱི་ལས་དང་འབྲེལ་བའི་ངག་གི་སྦྱོར་བ་ཐམས་ཅད་ལ་ཁྱབ་སྟེ། བྱ་བའི་ལས་ཐམས་ཅད་མ་འོངས་པ་དང་། བྱེད་པའི་ལས་ཐམས་ཅད་ད་ལྟར་བ་ཡིན་པས་སོ། བདག་གཞན་གྱི་དབྱེ་བས་ནི། བྱ་བྱེད་ཀྱི་ལས་ཐམས་ཅད་ལ་མ་ཁྱབ་སྟེ། བྱེད་པ་པོ་གཞན་དང་དངོས་སུ་མ་འབྲེལ་བའི་བྱ་བྱེད་ཀྱི་ལས་རྣམས་ལ་མ་ཁྱབ་པའི་ཕྱིར་རོ། དེས་ན་

བདག་གཞན་གྱི་དབྱེ་བ་མཛད་པ་ནི། བྱེད་པ་པོ་དང་། བྱ་བའི་ཕྲུལ་གྱི་སྒྲ་རྣམས་བསྡུས་པའི་ཕྱིར་དུ་ཡིན་ཅིང་། དེའི་ཞོར་ལ་བདག་གཞན་དང་འབྲེལ་བའི་བྱ་བྱེད་ཀྱི་སྒྲ་ཕན་ཚུན་ཤེད་མཚུངས་པ་རྣམས་ཀྱང་བསྡུས་པ་ཡིན་ལ།

དུས་གསུམ་གྱི་དབྱེ་བ་མཛད་པ་ནི། བདག་གཞན་གྱི་དབྱེ་བ་མཛད་པ་ན། བདག་གཞན་གྱི་དབྱེ་བས་མ་ཁྱབ་པའི་བྱ་བྱེད་ཀྱི་སྒྲ་ལྷག་མ་རྣམས་བསྡུ་བའི་ཕྱིར་དུ་ཡིན་ནོ། འོ་ན་བྱེད་པ་པོ་མེད་པའི་བྱ་བྱེད་ཐ་མི་དད་པ་དེ་གང་ཡིན་ཅེ་ན། བྱ་བ་བྱེད་པའི་གནས་སྐབས་སུ་བྱེད་པ་པོ་གཞན་དངོས་སུ་མི་སྣང་བ་ཞིག་སྟེ། དེ་ཡང་བྱེད་པ་པོ་གཞན་མི་སྣང་ཞེས་པས། དཔེར་ན། བདག་འགྲོ་འོ། ལྟ་བུའི་ཚེ། འགྲོ་བ་དེ་བྱ་ཚིག་ཡིན་ཀྱང་། འགྲོ་བྱ་འགྲོ་བྱེད་གཅིག་ཀ་བདག་ཡིན་པས། འགྲོ་བྱ་ལས་གཞན་པའི་འགྲོ་བྱེད་མེད་པས་ན་འདི་ལ་བདག་གཞན་གྱི་དབྱེ་བའང་མི་བྱེད་པ་ཡིན་ནོ། ཡང་བྱ་བ་བྱེད་པའི་གནས་སྐབས་སུ་བྱེད་པ་པོ་གཞན་མི་སྣང་ཞེས་པས། དཔེར་ན། རྫ་མཁན་གྱི་འཁོར་ལོ་འཁོར་རོ། ལྟ་བུའི་ཚེ། དང་པོར་སྐོར་བྱེད་གཞན་ཡོད་ཀྱང་། འཁོར་བཞིན་པའི་གནས་སྐབས་སུ་སྐོར་བྱེད་གཞན་མེད་པར་རང་གི་ངང་གིས་འཁོར་བས་གནས་སྐབས་དེར་བྱ་བྱེད་ཐ་མི་དད་པའི་ཆ་ནས་བསྐོར་ཞེས་མི་བརྗོད་པར་འཁོར་ཞེས་བརྗོད་པ་ཡིན་ནོ། ཡང་བྱེད་པ་པོ་གཞན་དངོས་སུ་མི་སྣང་ཞེས་པས། དཔེར་ན། སྐྱེས་བུ་ཞིག་གི་མདུན་དུ་ལྕགས་ཤིག་རང་བཞིན་གྱིས་གསེར་དུ་གྱུར་པའི་ཚེ། སྐྱེས་བུ་དེའི་བསོད་ནམས་ཉིད་བྱེད་པ་པོ་གཞན་ཡིན་མོད་ཀྱི་དེ་དངོས་སུ་མི་སྣང་བ་དང་ལྕགས་རང་ཉིད་ཀྱི་འབྱུང་བ་རྣམས་ཀྱི་བྱེད་པས་འགྱུར་བའི་ཆ་ནས། ལྕགས་གསེར་དུ་བསྒྱུར་ཅེས་མི་བརྗོད་པར་གྱུར་ཅེས་བརྗོད་པ་སྟེ། དེ་ཡང་ཞིབ་ཏུ་དཔྱོད་པའི་ཚེ་དངོས་པོའི་རང་བཞིན་སོ་སོ་ནས། རང་གིས་རང་ལ་བྱ་བ་བྱེད་པ་འགལ་ཡང་། སྤྱི་ལྡོག་རིགས་པ་ནས་ཐ་སྙད་ཙམ་ལ་འགལ་བ་མེད་དོ། དེ་དག་གིས་མཚོན་ནས་སྐབས་འདིར་ཕྲ་ཞིང་ཞིབ་པའི་བློས་བརྟག་དགོས་པ་མང་དུ་སྣང་ངོ་།

གསུམ་རྗེས་འཇུག་གི་རྟགས་ཀྱི་འཇུག་པ་བཤད་པ་ལ་གཉིས། རྗེས་འཇུག་གི་རྟགས་ཀྱི་དབྱེ་བ་བཤད་པ་དང་། རྗེས་འཇུག་གི་རྟགས་ཀྱི་འཇུག་ཚུལ་བཤད་པའོ། དང་པོ་ལ་གཉིས། སྤྱིར་རྟགས་གསུམ་དུ་དབྱེ་བ་དང་། ནང་གསེས་བརྒྱད་དུ་དབྱེ་བའོ། དང་པོ་ནི། རྗེས་འཇུག་ཡི་གེ་བཅུ་པོ་ལ། ཕོ་མོ་མ་ནིང་གསུམ་དུ་དབྱེ། ཞེས་པ་སྟེ། རྗེས་འཇུག་གི་ཡི་གེ། ག་ང་ད་ན་བ་མ་འ་ར་ལ་ས་སྟེ་བཅུ་པ་དེ་རྣམས་ལ། ཕོ་ཡིག ག་ད་བ་ས་བཞི་དང་།

མོ་ཡིག། ང་མ་འ་གསུམ་དང་། མ་ནིང་། ན་ར་ལ་གསུམ་སྟེ་གསུམ་དུ་དབྱེ་བར་བྱའོ། ཞེས་སོ། གཉིས་པ་ནང་གསེས་བརྒྱད་དུ་དབྱེ་བ་ནི། ཕོ་ལ་སྐྱེས་བུ་རབ་འབྲིང་གསུམ། མོ་ལ་མོ་དང་ཤིན་ཏུ་མོ། མ་ནིང་འགྱུར་དང་མཚན་གཉིས་དང་། མཚན་མེད་དག་དང་གསུམ་དུ་འདོད། ཅེས་པ་སྟེ། རྗེས་འཇུག་ལ་རྟགས་གསུམ་དུ་ཕྱེས་པ་དེ་ལ། སྔར་ཡང་ནང་གསེས་ཀྱིས་བརྒྱད་ད་དུ་དབྱེ་སྟེ། ཕོ་ཡིག་བཞི་ལ་ག་མཐའ་སའི་ཡང་འཇུག་ཅན་སྐྱེས་བུ་རབ་དང་། བ་མཐའ་སའི་ཡང་འཇུག་ཅན་སྐྱེས་བུ་འབྲིང་དང་། ག་ད་བ་སའི་མཐའ་ཅན་ཡང་འཇུག་མེད་པ་སྐྱེས་བུ་ཐ་མ་སྟེ་གསུམ་དུ་འདོད་པ་དང་། མོ་ཡིག་གསུམ་ལ། ད་མ་སའི་ཡང་འཇུག་ཅན་མོ་ཙམ་དང་། ད་མ་འའི་མཐའ་ཅན་ཡང་འཇུག་མེད་པ་ཤིན་ཏུ་མོ་སྟེ་གཉིས་སུ་འདོད་པ་དང་། མ་ནིང་གསུམ་ནི། མིང་གཞིའི་ཕོ་ཡིག་གི་མཐར་དའི་ཡང་འཇུག་ཡོད་མེད་གཉིས་ཀ་དང་། མོ་ཡིག་གི་མཐར་ཡང་འཇུག་མེད་པ་ཕོ་ན་དང་། མ་ནིང་གི་མཐར་ཡང་འཇུག་ཡོད་པ་ཕོ་ན་སྟེ། གསུམ་ནི་འགྱུར་པ་མ་ནིང་དང་། མིང་གཞིའི་མོ་ཡིག་གི་མཐར་ཡང་འཇུག་ཡོད་པ་ནི་མཚན་གཉིས་མ་ནིང་དང་། མིང་གཞིའི་མ་ནིང་གི་མཐར་ཡང་འཇུག་མེད་པ་ནི་མཚན་མེད་མ་ནིང་སྟེ་གསུམ་དུ་དབྱེ་བར་འདོད་དོ་ཞེས་སོ།

གཉིས་པ་རྗེས་འཇུག་གི་རྟགས་ཀྱི་འཇུག་ཚུལ་བཤད་པ་ལ་གཉིས། མདོར་བསྟན་པ་དང་། རྒྱས་པར་བཤད་པའོ། དང་པོ་ནི། དེ་ཡང་བྱེད་པ་བཞི་བྱེད་དེ། གང་ལ་འཇུག་བྱེད་གང་གིས་བྱེད། ཇི་ལྟར་འཇུག་བྱེད་ཅི་ཕྱིར་བྱེད། ཅེས་པ་སྟེ། དེའང་རྗེས་འཇུག་ཕོ་མོ་མ་ནིང་གསུམ་པོ་རེ་རེ་ལའང་བྱེད་པ་བཞི་བཞིའི་སྒོ་ནས་འཇུག་ཚུལ་ཤེས་པར་བྱ་སྟེ། འཇུག་ཡུལ་ཡི་གེ་གང་ལ་འཇུག་པར་བྱེད་པ་དང་། འཇུག་པ་པོ་གང་གིས་འཇུག་པར་བྱེད་པ་དང་། ཚུལ་ཇི་ལྟར་འཇུག་པར་བྱེད་པ་དང་། དགོས་པ་ཅིའི་ཕྱིར་འཇུག་པར་བྱེད་པ་རྣམས་ཀྱིས་སོ། ཞེས་པའོ། གཉིས་པ་རྒྱས་པར་བཤད་པ་ལ་བཞི། གང་ལ་འཇུག་པ་བཤད་པ། གང་གིས་འཇུག་པ་བཤད་པ། ཇི་ལྟར་འཇུག་པ་བཤད་པ། ཅི་ཕྱིར་འཇུག་པ་བཤད་པའོ། དང་པོ་ནི། གང་ལ་ཡི་གེ་ཐམས་ཅད་ལ། ཞེས་པ་སྟེ། རྗེས་འཇུག་གི་ཡི་གེ་བཅུ་པོ་དེ་དག་འཇུག་ཡུལ་གྱི་ཡི་གེ་གང་ལ་འཇུག་ན་ཀ་ནས་ཨའི་བར་གྱི་མིང་གཞིའི་ཡི་གེ་ཐམས་ཅད་ལ་ཐྱི་བྲག་མེད་པར་འཇུག་གོ། འོ་ན་རྗེས་འཇུག་གི་འཇུག་ཡུལ་ཡིན་ན། འདིར་བསྟན་མིང་གཞིའི་ཡི་གེ་ཡིན་

པས་ཕྱུབ་བམ་ཞེ་ན། མ་ཕྱུབ་སྟེ། ཆོས་རྗེས་པཎ་གྱིས། མཁས་པའི་ཁ་རྒྱན་དུ། ད་ས་དག་ནི་ཡང་འཇུག་པ་དག་གོ། ད་ནི་ན་ར་ལ་རྣམས་ཀྱིའོ། ས་ནི་ག་ང་བ་མ་རྣམས་ཀྱིའོ། ཞེས་གསུངས་པའི་ཕྱིར་རོ།

གཉིས་པ་གང་གིས་འཇུག་པ་བཤད་པ་ནི། གང་གིས་བཅུ་པོ་དེ་དག་གིས། ཞེས་པ་སྟེ། ཡི་གེ་ཐམས་ཅད་ཀྱི་རྗེས་སུ་འཇུག་པ་པོ་ཡི་གེ་གང་དང་གང་ཞིག་གིས་འཇུག་པར་བྱེད་ཅེ་ན། སྔར་བཤད་པའི་རྗེས་འཇུག་གི་ཡི་གེ་བཅུ་པོ་དེ་དག་གིས་འཇུག་གོ་ཞེས་སོ།

གསུམ་པར། ཇི་ལྟར་འཇུག་པ་བཤད་པ་ལ་གཉིས། མདོར་བསྟན་པ་དང་། རྒྱས་པར་བཤད་པའོ། དང་པོ་ནི། ཇི་ལྟར་རྣམ་པ་གཉིས་ཡིན་ཏེ། སྒྲ་ཡི་འཇུག་ཚུལ་དོན་གྱི་ཚུལ། ཞེས་པ་སྟེ། རྗེས་འཇུག་རྣམས་ཚུལ་ཇི་ལྟར་འཇུག་པའང་རྣམ་པ་གཉིས་ཀྱི་སྒོ་ནས་ཤེས་པར་བྱ་སྟེ། རྗེས་འཇུག་ཞུགས་ཚུལ་གྱི་སྒྲ་དྲག་ཞན་དུ་འགྱུར་བ་སྒྲའི་འཇུག་ཚུལ་དང་། དེ་ལྟར་ཞུགས་པས་དོན་ཅི་ཞིག་སྟོན་པ་དོན་གྱི་འཇུག་ཚུལ་ལོ། ཞེས་སོ། གཉིས་པ་རྒྱས་པར་བཤད་པ་ལ་གཉིས། སྒྲའི་འཇུག་ཚུལ་བཤད་པ་དང་། དོན་གྱི་འཇུག་ཚུལ་བཤད་པའོ། དང་པོ་ལ་གཉིས། དྲག་ཞན་སྤྱིར་འཇུག་ཚུལ་བཤད་པ་དང་། ནང་གསེས་ཞིབ་ཏུ་འཇུག་ཚུལ་བཤད་པའོ། དང་པོ་ནི། ཕོ་གསུམ་མོ་གཉིས་མ་ནིང་གསུམ། དྲག་ཞན་བར་མ་གསུམ་དུ་འཇུག། ཅེས་པ་སྟེ། རྗེས་འཇུག་གི་ཡི་གེ་བཅུ་ལས། ཕོ་སྐྱེས་བུ་རབ་འབྲིང་ཐ་གསུམ། མིང་གཞིའི་ཡི་གེ་གང་ལ་ཞུགས་ཀྱང་བརྗོད་པའི་སྒྲ་གདངས་དྲག་པ་དང་། དེ་བཞིན་དུ་མོ་ཅམ་དང་ཤིན་ཏུ་མོ་གཉིས་ཞུགས་ན་ཞན་པ་དང་། འགྱུར་བ་དང་མཚན་གཉིས་དང་མཚན་མེད་མ་ནིང་གསུམ་ཞུགས་ན་བར་མ་སྟེ་རན་པར་འཇུག་པ་ཡིན་ནོ་ཞེས་སོ། གཉིས་པ་ནང་གསེས་ཞིབ་ཏུ་འཇུག་ཚུལ་བཤད་པ་ནི། དྲག་པ་གསུམ་ཉིད་ནང་ཕྲད་ནས། གལ་ཏེ་ཞན་པ་ནང་ཕྲད་ན། དེ་ལའང་ནང་གི་ཆ་ཤས་ཀྱིས། དེ་ཡང་དྲག་ཞན་གཉིས་སུ་དབྱེ། མ་ནིང་གསུམ་དུ་གང་གཏོགས་པ། དྲག་དང་ཕྲད་ན་དྲག་པར་འགྱུར། ཞན་དང་ཕྲད་ན་ཞན་པར་འགྱུར། གཉིས་ཀ་དྲག་དང་ཕྲད་གྱུར་ན། དེ་ནི་གཉིས་ཀ་ཅན་དུ་འགྱུར། གཉིས་ཀ་དྲག་དང་མ་ཕྲད་ན། གང་དུ་ཡང་ནི་མི་འགྱུར་རོ། དེས་ན་འགྱུར་དང་མཚན་གཉིས་དང་། མཚན་མེད་དག་དང་གསུམ་དུ་འདོད། དེ་ནི་སྒྲ་ཡི་འཇུག་ཚུལ་ལོ། ཞེས་པ་སྟེ། གོང་དུ་བཤད་པ་ལྟར་སྒྲ་གདངས་དྲག་པ་རྗེས་འཇུག་ཕོ་ཡིག་ལ་སྐྱེས་རབ་འབྲིང་ཐ་གསུམ་ཉིད་དུ་དབྱེ་བ་ནི

རྗེས་འཇུག་ཕན་ཚུན་ནང་འཕྲད་ཀྱིས་ཡིན་ཏེ། དམ་ཞེས་པ་སྦྱུད་པའི་ཚིག་ཡིན་པས་གང་སྦྱུད་ན་ཅང་གི་ཆས་དྭག་ཞན་གཉིས་སུ་དབྱེ་བསྡུད་པས། དབྱེ་ཚུལ་ནི། སྐྱེས་བུ་རབ་འབྲིང་གཉིས་ལ་ཅང་འཕྲད་ཡོད་པས་སྒྲ་དྭག་པའི་དྭག་པ་དང་། སྐྱེས་བུ་ཐ་མ་ལ་ཅང་འཕྲད་མེད་པས་སྒྲ་དྭག་པའི་ཞན་པ་གཉིས་སུ་དབྱེ་ཞིང་། དང་པོ་ལ་འང་སྐྱེས་བུ་རབ་སྒྲ་ཤིན་ཏུ་དྭག་པ་དང་། འབྲིང་དེ་ལས་ཅུང་ཟད་ཞན་པ་གཉིས་སུ་དབྱེ་བས་ཅང་གཟེས་གསུམ་དུ་འགྱུར་ཏེ། དཔེར་ན། སྐྱོབས། སྐྱབས། སྐས། སྐད། བཀག། བཀབ། ལྷ་བུའོ། དེ་བཞིན་དུ་གལ་ཏེ་སྒྲ་གདངས་ཞན་པ་རྗེས་འཇུག་མོ་ཡིག་ལ་མོ་ཙམ་དང་། ཤིན་ཏུ་མོ་གཉིས་སུ་དབྱེ་བའང་རྗེས་འཇུག་ཕན་ཚུན་ཅང་ཕྲད་ན་སྔེ་འཕྲད་མ་འཕྲད་ཀྱིས་ཡིན་པས། དེ་ལའང་ཅང་གི་ཆ་ཤས་ཀྱིས་མོ་ཙམ་ལ་ཅང་འཕྲད་ཡོད་པས་སྒྲ་ཞན་པའི་དྭག་པ་དང་། ཤིན་ཏུ་མོ་པ་ཅང་འཕྲད་མེད་པས་སྒྲ་ཞན་པ་གཉིས་སུ་དབྱེ་སྟེ། དཔེར་ན། བསྐངས། བསྐུམས། སྐོང་། སྐོམ། བཀའ། ལྷ་བུའོ། སྒྲ་གདངས་བར་མ་རྗེས་འཇུག་མ་ཉིང་ལ་འགྱུར་བ་དང་། མཚན་གཉིས་དང་། མཚན་མེད་གསུམ་དུ་གང་གཏོགས་པའི་དབྱེ་བ་བྱས་པ་ནི། མིང་གཞིར་འཇུག་ཚུལ་དང་། རྗེས་འཇུག་ཕན་ཚུན་ནང་འཕྲད་མ་འཕྲད་གཉིས་ཀའི་སྒོ་ནས་ཡིན་ཏེ། བསྟནད། བསྒོརད། སྒྲལད། རྒྱུན། བསྟུར། བཙལ། ལྷ་བུ་མིང་གཞི་ཕོ་ཡིག་གི་མཐར་ཡང་འཇུག་ཡོད་མེད་གཉིས་ཀ་དང་། ཕྱིརད། ཐརད། འཁྲུལད། ལྷ་བུ། མ་ཉིང་གི་མཐར་ཡང་འཇུག་ཡོད་པ་གཉིས་ནི། སྒྲ་གདངས་དྭག་པ་དང་འཕྲད་པའི་དབང་གིས་དྭག་པར་འགྱུར་བ་དང་། འགྲན། འགོར། འགྱུལ། ལྷ་བུ་མོ་ཡིག་གི་མཐར་ཡང་འཇུག་མེད་པ་ནི། སྒྲ་གདངས་ཞན་པ་དང་འཕྲད་པའི་དབང་གིས་ཞན་པར་འགྱུར་བ་སྟེ། དེས་ན་དེ་གཉིས་ནི་འགྱུར་མ་ཉིང་དང་། འཛིནད། འབྱོརད། བསལད། ལྷ་བུ་མོ་ཡིག་གི་མཐར་ཡང་འཇུག་ཡོད་པ་ནི་སྒྲ་གདངས་དྭག་ཞན་གཉིས་ཀ་འཕྲད་པའི་དབང་གིས་དྭག་ཞན་གཉིས་ཀ་ཅན་དུ་འགྱུར་བས་མཚན་གཉིས་མ་ཉིང་དང་། མཐུན། མགོར། འཁྲུལ། ལྷ་བུ་མ་ཉིང་གི་མཐར་ཡང་འཇུག་མེད་པ་ནི། སྒྲ་གདངས་དྭག་ཞན་གཉིས་ཀ་དང་མ་འཕྲད་པའི་དབང་གིས་དྭག་ཞན་གང་དུའང་མི་འགྱུར་བར་སྒྲ་གདངས་མཉམ་པར་གནས་པས་མཚན་མེད་མ་ཉིང་སྟེ་དབྱེ་བ་གསུམ་དུ་འདོད་དེ། དེ་དག་ནི་སྒྲ་གདངས་དྭག་ཞན་བར་མ་གསུམ་དུ་འཇུག་ཚུལ་གྱི་དབྱེ་བ་ཡིན་ནོ། ཞེས་སོ།

གཉིས་པ་དོན་གྱི་འཇུག་ཚུལ་བཤད་པ་ལ་གཉིས། མདོར་བསྟན་པ་དང་། རྒྱས་པར་བཤད་པའོ། དང་པོ་ནི། དོན་ནི་རྣམ་པ་གཉིས་ཡིན་ཏེ། སྔ་མ་གང་ལྟར་འགྱུར་པ་དང་། ཕྱི་མ་གང་ལྟར་འགྱུར་པའོ། ཞེས་པ་སྟེ། རྗེས་འཇུག་རྣམས་དོན་གང་དང་གང་ལ་འཇུག་པར་འགྱུར་བའི་ཚུལ་ནི་རྣམ་པ་གཉིས་ཡིན་ཏེ། སྔ་མ་རྗེས་འཇུག་ཉིད་གང་ལ་ཞུགས་ཤིང་གནས་པའི་མིང་དེའི་དོན་གང་སྟར་ཏེ། ཇི་ལྟ་བུ་ཞིག་ཏུ་འགྱུར་བ་དང་། ཕྱི་མ་རྗེས་འཇུག་གམ་མཐའ་དེས་མིང་མཐའ་ལ་སོགས་པ་འདྲེན་ཚུལ་གྱིས་དོན་གང་ལྟར་འགྱུར་པའོ་ཞེས་སོ། གཉིས་པ་རྒྱས་པར་བཤད་པ་ལ་གཉིས། སྔ་མ་གང་ལྟར་འགྱུར་བ་བཤད་པ་དང་། ཕྱི་མ་གང་ལྟར་འགྱུར་བ་བཤད་པའོ། དང་པོ་ནི། སྔ་མ་སྔོན་འཇུག་ལྟ་བཞིན་སྦྱར། ཞེས་པ་སྟེ། རྗེས་འཇུག་རྣམས་གང་ལ་ཞུགས་པའི་མིང་དེ་ཉིད་མིང་མཐའ་སོགས་ལ་ལྟོས་ནས་སྔ་མར་གྲུབ་པས། དེས་བདག་གཞན་སོགས་དོན་ཅི་ཞིག་སྟོན་པ་ནི། མིང་དེའི་སྔོན་དུ་གནས་པ་སྔོན་འཇུག་ལྟ་ལས་གང་ཞིག་ཡིན་པ་དེའི་ནུས་པ་དང་ཇི་ལྟ་བ་བཞིན་དུ་སྦྱར་ནས་བདག་གཞན་དང་དུས་གསུམ་སོགས་གང་ཡིན་རྟོགས་དགོས་ཏེ། དཔེར་ན། འཇོག་བྱེད། བཞག་བྱ། བཀག་གོ། འགག་པར་འགྱུར། དགག་བཞིན་པ། བདག། བསྡོད་ཅིག། ལྟ་བུའོ། འོ་ན་ཏེ་སྔོན་འཇུག་མེད་ཀྱང་། རྗེག་བྱེད། སྒྲུབ་བྱ། ཕྲོག་གོ། སྒྲུབ་པར་འགྱུར། རྗེག་བཞིན་པ། རྟག་པ། ཤོག་ཅིག། ལྟ་བུ་རྗེས་འཇུག་རྣམས་བདག་གཞན་དང་དུས་གསུམ་ལ་འཇུག་པ་ལྟ་བུར་སྣང་མོད་ཀྱི། ཞུགས་སོ། གས་སོ། ཕྱིན་ཏོ། ཧ་བུ་སའི་འཇུག་ཡང་འཇུག་ཀ་དང་དའི་ཡང་འཇུག་ཙམ་ཁོ་ནས་འདས་པར་རང་དབང་དུ་སྒྲུབ་པ་དང་། འ་མཐའ་འདས་པ་ལ་གཏན་ནས་མི་འཇུག་པའི་ཁྱད་པར་ཙམ་ལས་གཞན་མ་ཚིག་གྲོགས་ཀྱིས་བསྒྱུར་བའི་ནུས་པས་མ་གཏོགས་རྗེས་འཇུག་གིས་རང་དབང་དུ་བདག་གཞན་དང་དུས་གསུམ་ལ་འཇུག་པ་ནི་མེད་དོ།

གཉིས་པ་ཕྱི་མ་གང་ལྟར་འགྱུར་བ་བཤད་པ་ལ་གཉིས། མདོར་བསྟན་པ་དང་། རྒྱས་པར་བཤད་པའོ། དང་པོ་ནི། ཕྱི་མ་དག་གི་འདྲེན་ཚུལ་ནི། ཞེས་པ་སྟེ། ཕྱི་མ་མིང་མཐའ་དང་རྣམ་དབྱེ་སོགས་ཀྱི་ཐོབ་ཐང་གི་དོན་ཇི་ལྟར་འཇུག་པར་འགྱུར་བའི་ཚུལ་ནི། སྔ་མའི་རྗེས་འཇུག་དང་། ཕྱི་མའི་བརྗོད་བྱ་དག་ལ་ཅི་རིགས་པར་ལྟོས་པའི་སྒོ་ནས་འདྲེན་པའི་ཕྱིར་དེའི་ཚུལ་སློས་པ་ནི། ཞེས་སོ། གཉིས་པ་རྒྱས་པར་བཤད་པ་ལ་གཉིས། མིང་

མཐའ་འདྲིན་ཚུལ་བཤད་པ་དང་། རྣམ་དབྱེ་སོགས་འདྲིན་ཚུལ་བཤད་པའོ། དང་པོ་ནི། ཕོ་ཡིས་ཕོ་ཡི་མིང་མཐའ་དྲང་། མ་ནིང་གིས་ནི་མ་ནིང་ངོ་། ཞེས་པ་སྟེ། དེ་ཡང་། ཅིག་ཅར། ཐད་ཀ། སྒྲུབ་པ། གཉིས་ཀ། མཁྱེན་ད་པ། འགྱུར་ད་པ། བསྐལ་ད་པ། ཐུགས་ཀ། བསྒྲུབས་པ། དགོངས་པ། བསམས་པ། ལྟ་བུ། མིང་སྔ་མའི་མཐའི་རྗེས་འཇུག་ཕོ་ཡིག་གིས་མིང་དེ་ཉིད་ཀྱི་ཆ་ཤས་ཡིན་པས་མཐར་སྦྱོར་དགོས་པའི་མིང་མཐའ་གཞན་གྱི་མིང་གཞིའི་ཕོ་ཡིག་དྲང་བར་བྱ་ཞིང་། དེ་བཞིན་དུ། གསིང་མ། ཐམ་ག། དགའ་བ། ལྟ་བུ་མ་ཡིག་གིས་མིང་གཞིའི་མོ་འི་མིང་མཐའ་དྲང་བ་དང་། དགུན་ཁ། དབྱར་ཁ། གསལ་ཁ། ལྟ་བུ་མ་ནིང་གི་མིང་མཐའ་དྲང་བར་བྱའོ་ཞེས་སོ། དེ་ཡང་མིང་མཐའ་རྟགས་མཚུངས་ཁྲིན་འདྲིན་པ་ལྟ་བུར་གསུངས་པ་ནི། གཙོ་ཆེ་བ་ཙམ་ལ་དགོངས་པ་ཡིན་པས་དེ་ཁོ་ནར་མ་ངེས་ཏེ། སྟག་མ། ཚད་མ། ཚབ་མ། ལྷས་མ། ལྟ་བུ་ཕོས་མོ་དང་། ཀང་པ། དམ་པ། མདའ་པ་ལྟ་བུ་མོས་ཕོ་དང་། སྟོན་མོ། བསྐོར་བ། རྒྱལ་བ། ལྟ་བུ་མ་ནིང་གིས་མོ་དྲངས་ཡང་མང་དུ་འབྱུང་ཞིང་། དེ་ཉིད་རྟགས་མ་མཐུན་ཀྱང་བརྗོད་བདེ་གཙོ་བོར་བྱས་ནས་སྒྲ་མཐུན་དྲངས་པ་ཡིན་པས་སུམ་རྟགས་གཉིས་ཀའི་དངོས་བསྟན་གྱི་དགོངས་པར་གནས་སོ། གཞན་ཡང་སྔར་ན་ར་ལ་གསུམ་ཡང་འཇུག་ཅན་མ་ནིང་དང་། ང་མ་ཡང་འཇུག་ཅན་མོར་བཞག་པ་ནི། འཇུག་ཡང་འཇུག་བརྗོད་པའི་སྒྲ་གདངས་ཀྱི་ནུས་པ་འཆད་པའི་སྐབས་དང་། འདིར་དེ་རྣམས་ཕོ་རྟགས་སུ་བཞག་པ་ནི། ཡང་འཇུག་གི་རྟགས་ཀྱིས་མིང་མཐའ་འདྲིན་པ་སྐབས་དོན་ཡིན་པས་མི་འགལ་ལོ། གཞན་ཡང་དཀོན་ཅིག། རིན་ཅན། ལྷན་ཅིག། ཐབས་ཅིག། ཆབས་ཅིག། སྟོད་ཀོར། སྨད་ཀོར། བད་ཀོར། ཡུངས་ཀར། རྒྱ་གར། ལྟ་བུ་བརྡ་སྙིང་ལ་རྟགས་མཚུངས་འདྲིན་པ་ཤིན་ཏུ་མང་ཡང་ཐལ་ཆེར་སྐད་གསར་བཅད་ཀྱི་ཞུས་དག་མང་བས་ནུབ་པར་མངོན་ནོ།

གཉིས་པ་རྣམ་དབྱེ་སོགས་འདྲིན་ཚུལ་བཤད་པ་ལ་གཉིས། སྤྱིར་འདྲིན་ཚུལ་བཤད་པ་དང་། ཉེར་གསེས་འཇུག་ཚུལ་བཤད་པའོ། དང་པོ་ནི། མིང་མཐའ་དེ་དག་ཉིད་ཀྱིས་ནི། དེ་ཉིད་རང་གི་སྒྲ་མཐུན་པའི། ཚིག་དོན་ལས་དང་བྱེད་པ་དང་། སྦྱིན་དང་འབྱུང་ཁུངས་འབྲེལ་པ་དང་། གནས་དང་བོད་པའི་སྒྲ་ཡང་དྲང་གཞན་ཡང་སྒྲར་བསྡུ་ལྷག་བཅས་དང་། འབྱེད་སྡུད་བསྟན་དང་བདག་པོ་དང་། དགག་སྒྲུབ་རྒྱན་དང་དུས་འདའ་འཇུག།

དེ་དག་ཕྱི་ཤུགས་འདྲེན་པས་འབྱུང་། ཞེས་པ་སྟེ། བཤད་མ་ཐག་པའི་མིང་ཕྱི་ཕྱི་དེ་དག་ཉིད་ཀྱིས། མིང་མཐའ་དེ་དག་ཉིད་རང་གི་རྟགས་མཚུངས་པའམ་བརྗོད་པ་བདེ་བས་སྒྲ་མཐུན་པར་སྒྱུར་བའི་རྣམ་དབྱེ་དང་པོ་ཚོས་དངོས་ཏེ་ངོ་བོ་ཙམ་བརྗོད་པ་དང་། གཉིས་པ་ལས་སུ་བྱ་བ་དང་། གསུམ་པ་བྱེད་པ་པོའམ་བྱེད་པ་ཙམ་དང་། བཞི་པ་སྦྱིན་པའི་ཡུལ་གྱིས་མཆོད་ནས་ཆེད་དུ་བྱ་བ་དང་། ལྔ་པ་འབྱུང་ཁུངས། དྲུག་པ་འབྲེལ་པ་དང་། བདུན་པ་གནས་གཞི། བརྒྱད་པ་བོད་པའི་སྒྲ་རྣམས་ཀྱང་དྲང་བར་བྱ་ཞིང་། དེ་བཞིན་དུ་གཞན་ཡང་རྣམ་དབྱེའི་ཡན་ལག་ཏུ་གྱུར་པའམ། མ་གྱུར་པའི་ཚིག་ཕྲད་སླར་བསྡུ་དང་། ལྷག་བཅས་དང་། འབྱེད་སྡུད་དང་། བསྣན་པ་དང་། བདག་པོ་དང་། དགག་པ་དང་། སྒྲུབ་པ་དང་། ཚིག་རྒྱན་དང་། དུས་ཏེ་ཚེ་སྐབས་ལ་འཇུག་པའི་སྒྲ་ལ་སོགས་པ་དེ་དག་རྣམས་ཀྱང་ཕྱི་མ་མིང་མཐའི་ཤུགས་ཀྱིས་འདྲེན་པར་བྱེད་པ་ན་སྦྱོར་ཚུལ་ལེགས་པར་འབྱུང་བ་ཡིན་ནོ་ཞེས་པ་སྟེ། དེ་དག་ལས་དྲུག་པ་འདྲེན་ཚུལ་སུམ་ཅུ་པར་ཡང་འབྱུང་ང་ལ། གཞན་ཡང་ཨི་ལྡན་དང་། ལ་དོན་དང་། སླར་བསྡུ་དང་། ལྷག་བཅས་དང་། འབྱེད་སྡུད་དང་། བདག་པོ་དང་། ཚིག་རྒྱན་དང་། རིང་སོགས་ཀྱི་ཚིག་ཕྲད་རྣམས་མིང་ཕྱི་མའི་རྗེས་འཇུག་གི་ཤུགས་ཀྱིས་སྒྲ་རྟགས་བ་ང་རུང་མཐུན་པ་ཇི་ལྟར་འདྲེན་ཚུལ་གྱི་རྣམ་ཚིག་མཛོད་ལྡེབས་ཤིག་ཁོ་བོས་རང་ལོ་ཉེར་གསུམ་གྱི་ཚེ་བཀོད་ཟིན་པས་དེར་ཤེས་པར་བྱའོ།

གཉིས་པ་ནང་གསེས་འཇུག་ཚུལ་བཤད་པ་ལ་གཉིས། མདོར་བསྟན་པ་དང་། རྒྱས་པར་བཤད་པའོ། དང་པོ་ནི། དེ་དག་ནང་གསེས་གང་འཇུག་པ། མཐར་སྦྱར་འོག་མའི་མིང་དོན་ལས། ཞེས་པ་སྟེ། རྣམ་དབྱེ་དང་ཚིག་ཕྲད་དེ་དག་གི་ནང་གསེས་གང་དང་གང་ཞིག་འཇུག་པ་ནི། གཙོ་བོར་རྣམ་དབྱེའི་ཕྲད་དང་བཅས་པའི་མིང་ཚིག་དེའི་མཐར་སྦྱར་རྒྱུའི་མིང་དོན་འོག་མ་ལས་ཤེས་པར་བྱའོ། ཞེས་སོ། གཉིས་པ་རྒྱས་པར་བཤད་པ་ལ་གཉིས། རྣམ་དབྱེའི་ནང་གསེས་གང་ཞིག་འཇུག་པ་བཤད་པ་ལ་གཉིས། རྣམ་དབྱེའི་ནང་གསེས་གང་ཞིག་འཇུག་པ་དང་། ཕྲད་ཀྱི་ནང་གསེས་གང་ཞིག་འཇུག་པ་བཤད་པའོ། དང་པོ་ནི། སྤྱི་འཇུག་ཡོད་དམ་བྱེད་པ་ཡོད། དེ་བཞིན་ཆེད་བྱེད་རྟེན་བྱེད་དང་། ལས་བྱ་སྣང་བྱ་བསྒྲུབ་པར་བྱ། སྔོན་དུ་ངེས་པ་གནས་པ་འམ། ཞེས་པ་སྟེ། དེ་ལ་རྣམ་དབྱེའི་ནང་གསེས་གང་དང་གང་ཞིག་འཇུག་པ་ནི། མིང་བདུད་རྩི་ལྟ་བུའི་རྗེས་སུ་གང་ཞིག་ལྟ་བུ་སྤྱི་ལ་འཇུག་པའི་སྒྲ

*སོགས་ཡོད་ན་མིང་སྔ་མ་ལ་རྣམ་དབྱེ་དང་པོ་འཇུག་པ་ཡིན་ཀྱང་བོད་སྐད་ལ་དང་པོ་མཚོན་བྱེད་ཀྱི་སྒྲ་མེད་པ་ཤ་ཆེ་བས་བདུད་རྩི་བུང་ཞིག་ཟླ་བུ་འམ། སྦྱོར་ན་བདུད་རྩི་ཉིད་གང་ཞིག་ལྷ་བུ་དང་། ཡང་མིང་དེའི་མཐར་འཚོ་བར་བྱེད་ལྷ་བུ་བྱེད་པའི་སྒྲ་སོགས་ཡོད་ན་རྣམ་དབྱེ་གསུམ་པ་འཇུག་པས་བདུད་རྩིས་འཚོ་བར་བྱེད་ལྷ་བུ་དང་། དེ་བཞིན་དུ་སྦྱར་ཏེ། མོས་པ་ལྷ་བུ་ཆེད་དུ་བྱེད་པའི་སྒྲ་ཡོད་ན་རྣམ་དབྱེ་བཞི་འཇུག་པས་བདུད་རྩི་ལ་མོས་པ་ལྷ་བུ་དང་། ཡང་རྟེན་ལྷ་བུ་རྟེན་བྱེད་ཀྱི་སྒྲ་སོགས་ཡོད་ན་རྣམ་དབྱེ་བདུན་པ་འཇུག་པས་བདུད་རྩི་ལ་རྟེན་ལྷ་བུ་དང་། ཡང་བསྒྱུར་ལྷ་བུ་ལས་སུ་བྱ་བའི་སྒྲ་ཡོད་ན་རྣམ་དབྱེ་གཉིས་པ་འཇུག་པས་བདུད་རྩིར་བསྒྱུར་ལྷ་བུ་དང་། ཡང་བླང་བར་བྱ། ལྷ་བུ་བླང་བྱའི་སྒྲ་སོགས་ཡོད་ན་རྣམ་དབྱེ་ལྔ་པ་འཇུག་པས་བདུད་རྩི་ལས་བླང་བར་བྱ་ལྷ་བུ་དང་། ཡང་རྒྱ་མཚོ་ལྷ་བུ་བསྒྲུབ་པར་བྱ་བའི་སྒྲ་ཡོད་ན་རྣམ་དབྱེ་དྲུག་པ་འཇུག་པས་བདུད་རྩིའི་རྒྱ་མཚོ་ལྷ་བུ་དང་། ཡང་སྔོན་དུ་མིང་བདུད་རྩི་མ་ལྷ་བུ་ཡོད་ན་དེ་ཡའང་བདག་ལ་འཆི་མེད་སྐྱོལ་ལྷ་བུ་འབོད་པར་འོས་པའི་དོན་ཡོད་ན་རྣམ་དབྱེ་དང་པོ་འཇུག་རིང་བོད་པ་གསལ་བྱེད་ཀྱི་སྒྲའང་སྦྱར་དགོས་པས། བདུད་རྩི་མ་ཀྱི་བདག་ལ་འཆི་མེད་སྐྱོལ། ལྷ་བུར་འགྱུར་བ་སོགས་ཤེས་པར་བྱ་སྟེ། འམ་ནི་སྡུད་པའི་ཚིག་ཕྲད་དོ། གཞན་ཡང་མིང་མཐའ་ཙམ་གྱིས་རྣམ་དབྱེ་འདྲེན་པ་དང་། མིང་མཐས་མིང་མཐར་གཞན་དྲངས། དེས་རྣམ་དབྱེ་འདྲེན་པའང་ཡོད་དོ། གཞན་ཡང་། ངེས་གཟུང་གི་སྒྲ་སོགས་ཡོད་ན་སྔ་མར་དང་པོ་དང་། བསྒྲུབ་བྱའི་སྒྲ་སོགས་ཡོད་ན་སྔ་མར་གསུམ་པ་དང་། མིང་མཐའ་དེ་ལས་བྱུང་བའི་སྒྲའམ། དགར་བྱའི་སྒྲའམ། བསྒྲུབ་བྱའི་སྒྲ་སོགས་ཡོད་ན་སྔ་མར་ལྔ་པ་དང་། རྟེན་བྱེད་ལྟར་སྣང་གི་བྱ་ཚིག་སོགས་ཡོད་དེ། དཔེར་ན། བདུད་རྩི་དེ། བརྗིད་པས་ཉི་མ་དང་མཚུངས། ས་ལས་རྩྭ་སྐྱེས། མི་ལས་ལྷ་བཟང་། མི་རྟག་པ་ལས་དངོས་པོར་གྲུབ། མཚོན་ཁར་བསད་ཅེས་པ་ལྷ་བུའོ།

གཉིས་པ་ཕྲད་ཀྱི་ཉང་གསེས་གང་ཞིག་འཇུག་པ་བཤད་པ་ནི། གཞན་ཡང་ཚིག་དོན་འོག་མ་ལས། བསྡུ་རྒྱུ་ཡོད་དམ་མེད་པ་དང་། ཕོང་མ་ལས་ཀྱང་དེ་བཞིན་ཏེ། རྣམ་གྲངས་དག་ཀྱང་བཀོད་པ་ལས། བསྒྱུར་བ་ཡོད་དམ་མེད་པ་དང་། ཕོ་སྒྲ་དང་ནི་མོ་སྒྲ་དག། མིང་གི་མཐའ་ན་ཡོད་མེད་དང་། རྒྱན་དུ་རྒྱུར་པ་རྣམས་ལ་ཡང་། དོན་ལ་བརྟགས་པ་ཡོད་མེད་དང་། བསྟན་བྱ་ལྷག་མ་ཡོད་མེད་དང་། ཚིག་དོན་རྫོགས་དང་མ་རྫོགས་ཀྱིས།

*ལྷ་བུ་ཡི་ལ་འཇུག་ངའི་སྒྲ།

དེ་དག་ཙང་གསེལ་རྣམ་པར་དབྱེ། ཉིས་པ་སྟེ། གཞན་ཡང་མིང་མཐའི་ཚིག་ཕྲད་ཙང་གསེལ་གང་ཉིག་འདྲེན་པར་འགྱུར་པ་ནི། བརྗོད་འདོད་ཙམ་གྱིས་གྲུབ་པ་རེ་གཉིས་ཡོད་པ་མ་གཏོགས་ཕལ་ཆེར་མིང་དེའི་མཐར་སྦྱར་རྒྱུའི་ཚིག་དོན་འོག་མ་ལས་ཤེས་དགོས་ཏེ། ཚིག་དོན་འོག་མ་བོང་མ་དང་མཚུངས་པ་ལས། བོང་མ་བསྡུ་རྒྱུ་ཡོད་ན། མིང་སྔ་མའི་མཐར་སྦྱོད་པའི་ཚིག་ཕྲད་སྦྱར་དགོས་ཏེ། ལྷ་དང་། མི་དང་། ལྷ་མ་ཡིན་དང་། དྲི་ཟར་བཅས་པའི་འཇིག་རྟེན་ཡི་རང་སྟེ། ལྷ་བུ་དང་། དེ་བཞིན་དུ་ཚིག་དོན་བོང་འོག་མཚུངས་པ་ལས་འོག་མ་བསྡུ་རྒྱུ་ཡོད་ན་འོག་མ་སྦྱོང་པའི་ཚིག་ཕྲད་སྦྱར་དགོས་ཏེ། ལྷས་ཀྱང་བཏུད་ན་མིས་ལྷ་ཅི་སྨོས། ལྷ་བུ་དང་། མཐུག་ཏུ་བྱ་ཚིག་ཕྲད་ལྷ་བུར་ལྷན་ཅིག་སྦྲེལ་བའི་ཕྱིར། ཚིག་དོན་སྔ་མ་རྣམས་ལ་ཕྱི་མ་བསྡན་དགོས་ཙའང་། སྦྱོད་པའི་བྱེ་བྲག་བསྟན་པའི་ཕྲད་སྦྱར་དགོས་ཏེ། གསེར་དངུལ་ཟངས་ལྕགས་གཤའ་ཚོའང་སྦྱར། ལྷ་བུ་དང་། ཕྱི་མར་མིང་ཚིག་གི་རྣམས་གྲངས་གཅིག་གམ་གཉིས་སམ་མང་པོ་བཀོད་པ་ལས། དེ་དག་ཀྱང་གལ་ཏེ་དོན་བསྒྱུར་བ་ཡོད་ན། སྔ་མའི་སྔ་མར་རྣམ་གྲངས་ཀྱི་འབྱེད་པའི་ཕྲད་དགོས་ཏེ། འཆི་མེད་དམ། རྣམ་སད་དམ། མིག་མི་འཛུམ་ནི་ལྷའོ། ལྷ་བུ་དང་། ཚིག་དོན་གཉིས་ཀ་བསྒྱུར་བ་ཡོད་ན་རྣམ་གྲངས་ཀྱི་སྦྱོད་པའི་ཕྲད་སྦྱར་དགོས་ཏེ། གཏུབ་རིང་གཏུབ་རིང་དྲང་ཏུ་གསོལ་བར་བྱེད། ལྷ་བུ་དང་། མིང་གི་མཐར་པ་ལྷ་བུའི་ཕོ་སྒྲ་གསར་དུ་སྦྱར་ཡོད་ན་མིང་མཐའ་དེ་ཉིད་བདག་པོའི་སྒྲར་འགྱུར་བ། རྟ་པ། སྒྲུབ་པ་པོ། ལྷ་བུ་དང་། མིང་གི་མཐར་མེད། མིན་ལྷ་བུའི་མོ་སྒྲར་གཏོགས་པ་གསར་དུ་སྦྱར་ཡོད་ན། མིང་མཐའ་དེ་ཉིད་དགག་པའི་སྒྲར་འགྱུར་བ། འཆི་མེད། ལྷ་མིན། ལྷ་བུ་དང་། གསར་དུ་སྦྱར་བ་མ་ཡིན་པར་དང་པོ་ནས་མིང་གི་ཆ་ཤས་སུ་ཡོད་ན་ཕོ་མོའི་སྒྲ་དེ་བདག་སྒྲ་དང་དགག་སྒྲར་མི་འགྱུར་བར། ཛ་བོ་གང་། ཡིན་པ་དེ་ཉིད་དུ་སྒྲུབ་པའི་སྒྲར་མི་འགྱུར་བར། ཛ་བོ་གང་ཡིན་པ་དེ་ཉིད་སྒྲུབ་པའི་སྒྲར་འགྱུར་བ། དམ་པ། བླ་མ་ལྷ་བུ་དང་། ཚིག་དོན་སྔ་མ་དང་ཆོས་མཐུན་པའི་ཕྱི་ཚིག་གཞི་གཅིག་ཏུ་བསྡུ་རྒྱུ་ཡོད་ན། སྔ་མ་ལ་མཐུན་པའི་རྒྱན་དུ་རྒྱུར་པའི་ཚིག་ཕྲད་སྦྱར་དགོས་ཏེ། མཛེས་ཀྱང་མཛེས་ལ་འོད་ཀྱང་འཚེར། ལྷ་བུ་དང་། སྔ་ཕྱི་ཆོས་མི་མཐུན་པ་གཞི་གཅིག་བསྡུ་ན། སྔ་མར་མི་མཐུན་པའི་རྒྱན་འཇུག་སྟེ། བྲོ་བ་སྤྲངས་པར་ཀྱང་དགྲ་འཛོམས་པ། ལྷ་བུ་སྟེ། རྒྱན་དུ་རྒྱུར་པའི་ཚིག་ཕྲད་དེ་དག་ཀྱང་ངེས་པར་དོན་ལ་བསྟེགས་ཡོད་ན་མི་སྦྱར་དུ་མི་རུང་ཞིང་། ཚིག་མཛེས་བྱེད་

ཚམ་ཡིན་ན་མ་སྦྱར་ཀྱང་རུང་བ་དང་། ཚིག་དོན་སྤྱི་མའི་དེ་མ་ཐག་ཏུ་བསྟན་བྱ་ལྷག་མ་ཡོད་ན་སྤྱི་མ་ལ་ལྷག་བཅས་ཀྱི་ཕྲད་སྦྱར་དགོས་ཏེ། རྒྱས་བཏབ་སྟེ་བཞག་ལྟ་བུ་དང་། ཚིག་དོན་སྤྱི་མའི་དེ་མ་ཐག་ཏུ་བསྟན་བྱ་ལྷག་མ་མེད་པར་རྫོགས་ན་སྒྲར་བསྡུའི་ཕྲད་སྦྱར་དགོས་ཏེ་རྫོགས་སོ། ལྟ་བུ་རྣམ་དབྱེ་དང་ཚིག་ཕྲད་དེ་དག་གི་ཚང་གསེས་གང་དང་གང་ཞིག་འཇུག་རིང་དོན་ཅི་འདྲ་ཞིག་སྟོན་པ་རྣམ་པར་དབྱེ་བར་བྱའོ་ཞིག་སོ། དེ་ཡང་རྣམ་དབྱེ་ནི་ལེགས་སྦྱར་གྱི་སྐད་ལ། མིང་གི་མཐར་སྦྱར་བས་ཚིག་ཏུ་འགྱུར་བར་བྱེད་པའི་རྐྱེན་སེ་སོགས་ཉེར་གཅིག་སྟེ། བོད་སྐད་ལ་འང་ལེགས་སྦྱར་དང་བསྟུན་ནས་སྔར་གྱི་རྣམ་དབྱེ་བདུན་པོ་དེ་རྣམས་གཅིག་ཚིག་ཉིད་དང་། གཉིས་ཚིག་དག་དང་། མང་ཚིག་རྣམས་ཀྱི་དབྱེ་བས་ཉེར་གཅིག་ཏུ་འགྱུར་ཞིང་། འདི་རྣམས་ཀྱི་ཁྱད་པར་ཕྲ་མོ་རྣམས་ཤིན་ཏུ་འབྱེད་དཀའ་བར་སྣང་ཡང་ཡི་གེས་འཇིགས་པས་མ་སྤྲོས་སོ།

ཚིག་ཕྲད་ནི། མིང་ཚིག་ལ་མ་སྦྱར་ན་རང་སྟོབས་ཀྱིས་དོན་མི་སྟོན་ཅིང་། མིང་གི་ཐོག་མཐའ་དང་བར་དུ་སྦྱར་ན་བརྗོད་བདེ་བ་དང་། མཚམས་སྦྱོར་བ་དང་། དོན་གསལ་བ་ལ་ཕན་འདོགས་པ་ཞིག་སྟེ། འདི་དག་ཕལ་ཆེར་ལེགས་སྦྱར་གྱི་ནི་པཱ་ཏ་སྟེ་ངེས་ཚིག་གམ་མི་ཟད་པར་གྲགས་པ་དང་འདྲའོ། དེ་ཡང་དོན་གྱི་ལྡོག་པ་ཁོ་ན་སྟོན་པའི་རྣམ་དབྱེ་ཡིན་ན་ཚིག་ཕྲད་ཡིན་པས་ཁྱབ་ཀྱང་། ཚིག་ཕྲད་ཡིན་ན་དོན་གྱི་ལྡོག་ཁོ་ན་སྟོན་པའི་རྣམ་དབྱེ་ཡིན་པས་མ་ཁྱབ་བོ།

བཞི་པ་ཅི་ཕྱིར་འཇུག་པ་བཤད་པ་ལ་གཉིས། རྗེས་འཇུག་གི་དགོས་པ་དངོས་བཤད་པ་དང་། ཞར་བྱུང་ཡི་གེའི་འཇུག་པ་སྤྱིའི་དགོས་པ་བཤད་པའོ། དང་པོ་ནི། ཅི་ཕྱིར་འཇུག་པར་བྱེད་ཅེ་ན། ཡི་གེའི་ཚོགས་ནས་མིང་འབྱུང་སྟེ། མིང་གི་ཚོགས་ནས་ཚིག་བྱུང་ནས། ཚིག་གིས་དོན་རྣམས་སྟོན་པར་བྱེད། ཅེས་པ་སྟེ། རྗེས་འཇུག་ཡི་གེ་བཅུ་པོ་དེ་རྣམས། དགོས་པ་ཅིའི་ཕྱིར་དུ་འཇུག་པར་བྱེད་ཅེ་ན། སྔོན་འཇུག་དང་དབྱངས་ཡོད་མེད་གང་ཡང་རུང་བའི་མིང་གཞིའི་ཡི་གེ་གཅིག་གམ་གཉིས་སམ་དུ་མ་འདུས་པ་ཡིན་ཡང་རུང་། རྗེས་འཇུག་གི་ཡི་གེ་གང་རུང་ཞིག་མ་བཞུགས་ན། དོན་གྱི་ངོ་བོ་སྟོན་པའི་མིང་དུ་འགྱུར་པ་མི་སྲིད་པས་ཡི་གེའི་ཚོགས་ནས་མིང་འབྱུང་བར་བྱ་བའི་ཕྱིར་དང་། མིང་གཅིག་གམ་གཉིས་སམ་དུ་མ་སྦྲེལ་དུ་ཟིན་ཀྱང་མཚམས་སྦྱོར་བར་བྱེད་པའོ། དོན་གསལ་བར་བྱེད་པའི་རྣམ་དབྱེ་དང་ཚིག་ཕྲད་སོགས་ཕལ་ཆེར་རྗེས་འཇུག་ལས་འབྱུང་ཞིང་རྗེས་འཇུག་ལ་ལྟོས་པ་དེ་རྣམས་མ་ཞུགས་

ན། དོན་གྱི་ཁྱད་པར་སྟོན་པའི་ཚིག་ཏུ་འགྱུབ་པ་མི་སྲིད་པས་མིང་གི་ངོས་ནས་ཚིག་དབྱུང་བའི་ཕྱིར་འཇུག་སྟེ། དེ་ལྟ་བུའི་ཚིག་གིས་འཇིག་རྟེན་དུ་དོན་རྣམས་བརྗོད་པ་བྱེད་པའི་ཕྱིར་དོན་མཚོན་པའི་བརྗོད་ཇི་སྙེད་པའང་རྗེས་འཇུག་གི་ཡི་གེ་རྣམས་འཇུག་པའི་དགོས་པར་གྲུབ་པོ་ཞེས་པ་སྟེ། འདིར་ཡི་གེ་དང་མིང་དང་ཚིག་དང་བརྗོད་པ་རྣམས་ཀྱི་ཁྱད་པར་བོད་སྐད་ཀྱི་དབང་དུ་བྱས་ནས་དབྱེ་བར་བྱའོ།

གཉིས་པ་ནར་བྱུང་ཡི་གེའི་འཇུག་པ་སྤྱིའི་དགོས་པ་བཤད་པ་ལ་གཉིས། ཡི་གེའི་འཇུག་པ་རྣམས་ཀྱི་རང་བཞིན་གྱི་དགོས་པ་བཤད་པ་དང་། ཡི་གེའི་འཇུག་པ་སྟོན་པའི་བསྟན་བཅོས་འདི་ཉིད་བཙམས་པའི་དགོས་པ་བཤད་པའོ། དང་པོ་ལ་གཉིས། དགོས་པ་ལྡོག་ཕྱོགས་ནས་བསྟན་པ་དང་། ཉིང་དགོས་ལྡོག་ཕྱོགས་ནས་བསྟན་པའོ། དང་པོ་ནི། སྔོ་ཡི་ཡི་གེ་མེད་པ་ན། ཐོ་ཡིག་བརྗོད་པ་མེད་པར་འགྱུར། ཐོ་ཡིག་དེ་དག་རྣམས་ལ་ཡང་། འཇུག་པར་བཅས་པ་མེད་ན་ནི། མིང་དང་ཚིག་ཀྱང་ཤེས་པ་མི་ནུས། མིང་ཚིག་གསལ་བ་མེད་ན་ནི། དོན་རྣམས་བརྗོད་པར་མི་འགྱུར་རོ། ཞེས་པ་སྟེ། སྔོ་ཡི་ཡི་གེ་ཀ་ཁ་སོགས་ཨཱ་ལི་བཞི་པོ་མེད་ན། ཐོ་ཡིག་ཀཱ་ལིའི་རྣམས་ཁོ་ནས་བརྗོད་པ་མེད་པར་འགྱུར་ཏེ། ཨཱ་ལི་རྣམས་ལ་ལྟོས་པའི་བརྗོད་པ་དེ་སྙེད་མི་ཚང་བར་འགྱུར་བའི་ཕྱིར་དང་། ཐོ་ཡིག་ཀཱ་ལི་དེ་དག་རྣམས་ལའང་ཨཱ་ལི་དང་ལྡན་མིན་ཇི་ལྟར་ཡང་འཇུག་པར་བཅས་པ་སྟེ། འཇུག་པའི་ཡི་གེ་བཅུ་མེད་པར་གྱུར་ན་ནི། དོན་གྱི་ངོ་བོ་སྟོན་པའི་མིང་དང་། ཁྱད་པར་སྟོན་པའི་ཚིག་ཀྱང་གསལ་བར་མི་ནུས་པར་གོང་དུ་བཤད་ཟིན་པའི་ཕྱིར་དང་། མིང་དང་ཚིག་གསལ་བར་གྱུར་པ་མེད་ན་ནི་དོན་གྱི་རྣམ་པ་རང་དང་གཞན་ལ་མཚོན་ཞིང་གོ་བར་བྱེད་པའི་བརྗོད་པ་རྣམས་ཀྱང་མེད་པར་འགྱུར་རོ། དེས་ན་ཨཱ་ལིའི་རྣམས་ནི་ཀཱ་ལིའི་བརྗོད་པ་ཡོངས་སུ་རྫོགས་པའི་ཕྱིར་དང་། འཇུག་པ་རྣམས་ནི་མིང་ཚིག་གསལ་བའི་ཕྱིར་དང་། མིང་ཚིག་རྣམས་ནི་དོན་བརྗོད་ཕྱིར་འཇུག་པས་ཡི་གེའི་སྦྱོར་བ་རྣམས་ནི་དགོས་པ་ཆེན་པོ་དང་བཅས་པ་ཡིན་ནོ་ཞེས་སོ།

གཉིས་པ་ཉིང་དགོས་ལྡོག་ཕྱོགས་ནས་བསྟན་པ་ནི། དེ་ལྟར་གྱུར་ན་འཇིག་རྟེན་དུ། དོན་མཚོན་བརྗོད་པ་ཀུན་ཀྱང་མེད། རིག་བྱེད་སྨྲ་བའང་ཡོད་མི་འགྱུར། ཉན་ཐོས་རང་རྒྱལ་སངས་རྒྱས་ཀྱི། བསྟན་པ་རྣམས་ཀྱང་མེད་པར་འགྱུར། ཞེས་པ་སྟེ། དེ་ལྟར་མིང་ཚིག་བརྗོད་པ་ཐམས་ཅད་མེད་པར་གྱུར་ན། འཇིག་རྟེན་འདིར་དོན་མཚོན་པར་

བྱེད་པའི་བརྗོད་པ་སྐྱེ་ལུང་དུ་སྟོན་པའི་སྒྲ་སྐད་ཐམས་ཅད་མི་འབྱུང་བས། དེ་ལ་རྟོགས་པའི་འཇིག་རྟེན་པ་དང་མཐུན་མོང་བའི་བརྡ:གཏན་དང་། ཅི་ས་དང་། སྐར་ངག་སོགས་རིག་བྱེད་སྒྲ་བ་རྣམས་ཀྱང་ཡོད་པར་མི་འགྱུར་ཞིང་། འཇིག་རྟེན་དང་མཐུན་མོང་མིན་པའི་ཤེས་བྱ་ཉན་ཐོས་དང་། རང་སངས་རྒྱས་དང་། རྫོགས་པའི་སངས་རྒྱས་ཀྱི་བསླབ་པ་རྣམས་སྟོན་རིང་སྒྲ་བཟང་མེད་པར་འགྱུར་བ་དེའི་ཕྱིར། མིང་ཚིག་བརྗོད་པ་ཐམས་ཅད་འཇིག་རྟེན་དུ་ཡོད་ན་ནི། འཁོར་འདས་ཀྱི་བླང་དོར་མཐའ་དག་སྟོན་རིང་སྒྲ་བ་འབྱུང་ལ། བླང་དོར་ལ་ཞུགས་ན་ནི་གནས་སྐབས་དང་མཐར་ཐུག་གི་དོན་ཐམས་ཅད་འགྲུབ་པ་ཡིན་ནོ་ཞེས་སོ།

གཉིས་པ་ཡི་གེའི་འཇུག་པ་བསྟན་པའི་བསྟན་བཅོས་འདི་ཉིད་བརྩམས་པའི་དགོས་པ་བཤད་པ་ལ་གཉིས། དགོས་པ་དངོས་བཤད་པ་དང་། དགོས་པ་དེ་འགྲུབ་པར་སྟོན་པའོ། དང་པོ་ནི། ཇི་ལྟར་འཇིག་རྟེན་སེམས་ཅན་རྣམས། ཕུང་པོ་ཁམས་དང་སྐྱེ་མཆེད་དང་། གྲུབ་མཐའ་གཞན་ཡང་ཡོད་ན་ཡང་། རང་ཉིད་ཀྱིས་ནི་མི་ཤེས་བཞིན། དེ་བཞིན་ཡི་གེའི་འཇུག་ཚུལ་རྣམས། སྒྲ་བ་ཀུན་ལ་གནས་གྱུར་ཀྱང་། རང་ཚུལ་དེ་ཉིད་མི་ཤེས་པས། དོན་ལ་སྦྱོར་བ་ག་ལ་ཤེས། དེ་ཕྱིར་སྒྲ་བའི་དབང་ཕྱུག་གི། རྗེས་སློས། ཞེས་པ་སྟེ། དཔེ་ཇི་ལྟར་ན་འཇིག་རྟེན་གྱི་སེམས་ཅན་རྣམས་ལ། གཟུགས་སོགས་ཕུང་པོ་དང་། མིག་གི་ཁམས་སོགས་ཁམས་དང་། མིག་གི་སྐྱེ་མཆེད་རྣམས་རང་རང་ལ་ཡོད་པར་མ་ཟད། གྲུབ་པའི་མཐའ་བཞག་པ་བཞན་ཡང་གྲངས་ཅན་པའི་དེ་ཉིད་ཉེར་ལྔ་དང་། ཐེག་ཆེན་པའི་རྣམ་ཤེས་ཚོགས་བརྒྱད་སོགས་ཀྱང་ཡོད་རིང་། སྟོན་ནས་ལྷན་ཅིག་ཏུ་འགྲོགས་པ་ཡིན་ཀྱང་། དེ་ལྟ་བུའི་རྣམ་གཞག་གཞན་གྱིས་མ་བསྟན་ན། རང་ཉིད་ཀྱིས་མི་ཤེས་པ་དེ་བཞིན་དུ། རང་རང་གི་ཡི་གེ་རྣམས་ཇི་ལྟར་འཇུག་པའི་ཚུལ་ཡང་ཡུལ་སོ་སོའི་ལུང་སྟོན་པའི་སྒྲ་སྐད་ཀྱི་སྒྲ་བ་ཐམས་ཅད་ལ་རང་བཞིན་གྱིས་གནས་པ་སྐྱེ་མེད་པ་མི་སྲིད་ཀྱང་། གཞན་གྱིས་བརྡ་མ་སྤྲད་པར་རང་ཉིད་ཀྱིས་ཡི་གེ་རྣམས་མིང་ཚིག་སོགས་ལ་འཇུག་པའི་ཚུལ་དེ་ཉིད་ཀྱང་མི་ཤེས་ན། མིང་ཚིག་ལ་སོགས་པ་དེ་རྣམས་བྱེ་བྲག་ཏུ་ནས་དོན་ལ་ཇི་ལྟར་སྦྱོར་བའི་ཚུལ་ག་ལ་ཤེས་ཏེ་མི་ཤེས་སོ། དེའས་ན་བླང་དོར་མཐའ་དག་ཤེས་པའི་རྒྱུ་མིང་ཚིག་ཡི་གེའི་སྦྱོར་བ་རྣམས་གསལ་བར་བྱེད་པའི་བོད་སྐད་ལ་མཛད་པའི་བསྟན་བཅོས་འདི་ཉིད་འཕགས་ཡུལ་ལ་སོགས་པའི་སྒྲ་བའི་དབང་ཕྱུག་མཁས་རྣམས་ཀྱི་བརྡ་སྤྲོད་པའི་བསྟན་བཅོས་ཀྱི་རྗེས་

སྒྲ་འབྲངས་ནས་བྲུ་ཨི་བདག་གིས་བཅོ་བས་སླས་པ་ཡིན་ནོ། །ཞེས་སོ།

གཉིས་པ་དགོས་པ་དེ་འགྲུབ་པར་སྨོན་པ་ནི། འདི་ཀུན་རྟོགས་གྱུར་ཅིག་ཅེས་པ་སྟེ། དེ་ལྟར་ཡི་གེའི་འཇུག་པ་ལེགས་པར་སྦྱར་བའི་ཚུལ་འདི་གངས་ཅན་སྐྱེ་བོ་ཀུན་གྱིས་རྟོགས་ནས་མིང་ཚིག་བརྗོད་པ་ཐམས་ཅད་ལ་རྨོངས་པ་མེད་པར་སྨྲ་བའི་དབང་ཕྱུག་ཆེན་པོར་གྱུར་ཅིག་ཅེས་ཉིང་དགོས་དེ་རྣམས་འགྲུབ་པའི་ཐུགས་སྨོན་མཛད་པའོ། །སླས་པ། ཤཱཀྱ་སེངྒེའི་བསྟན་ལ་རབ་ཞུགས་ཤིང་། །ལག་པའི་མིག་ལ་དབྱངས་འཇུག་བཞི་བཅུ་དང་།

མཚམས་ཀྱི་བསྒྲོད་པར་འཕུལ་རྟེན་རྩེ་ཟུང་གིས། །བརྒྱན་པའི་འབོད་བྱ་ལྡན་པ་གང་དེ་ཡིས།
གངས་ཅན་མིག་གཅིག་སམ་བྷོ་ཊ་ཡི་གཞུང་། །གངས་ཅན་བརྡ་སྤྲོད་ཕྱི་མོ་སུམ་རྟགས་དོན།
གངས་ཅན་མཁས་པ་ཀུན་གྱི་ལེགས་བཤད་བཞིན། །གངས་ཅན་བསྟན་འགྲོའི་དོན་དུ་སྦྱར་མོད་ཀྱི།
རྒྱལ་བསྟན་སྣང་གཏེར་དུས་རིམ་གྲིབ་ལ་ཉེ། །དབང་གྱུར་མཁས་པའི་མཚོ་སྐྱེས་ཐལ་ཆེར་ཟུམ།
གཟུ་ལུམ་སྤྱོད་པའི་འབྱུང་བྱ་རང་དགར་རྒྱུ། །བསིལ་ལྗོངས་སྐྱེ་བོའི་གདོང་མཐུན་ཇི་ལྟར་སེལ།
གདུང་སྤྲུལ་ཐལ་ཆེར་འདོད་ཡོན་སྤྱོད་ལ་ཡེངས། །སྒོམ་ཆེན་ཐལ་ཆེར་ཟློག་རྫུན་བྱ་བས་བྲེལ།
མཁས་རློམ་ཐལ་ཆེར་ཚོང་ཞིང་ལས་ལ་སྤྱོད། །ཀྱི་མ་ཐུབ་བསྟན་སུ་ཡིས་འཛིན་པར་འགྱུར།
དོན་གཉེར་འདུན་པའི་ཀུན་གཏིང་ནས་འགགས། །ལེགས་ཉེས་དེ་བའི་རྩ་འགྲིབ་ཀྱིས་ནོར།
ཕྱུགས་ལྷུང་གདོན་གྱིས་མ་ན་ཆེར་བརླམས་པ། །དེ་དག་ལེགས་བཤད་ཉ་དས་ཅི་ཞིག་བྱ།
འོན་ཀྱང་གཟུར་གནས་དཔྱོད་ལྡན་མཁའ་ནོར་གྱིས། །བསླུལ་ཚིག་ཚ་ཟེར་ལན་མང་སློས་པའི་ཚེ།
ལེགས་བཤད་སྣང་རྩེ་སྐྱུག་དང་མི་གསྐྱུ་གི། །རང་དབང་འདབ་སྟོང་ཚན་ལ་ཡོད་མ་ཡིན།
དེ་ཕྱིར་འདིར་དབང་ལེགས་བྱས་འབབ་ལྡན་མ། །བརྒྱ་ཕྲག་གཅིག་ཏུ་བསྡོམས་པའི་རྣམ་སད་ཚུས།
རབ་རྨོངས་ཁྲིབ་འཇུག་རྐང་དྲི་བཀྲུས་ལས་སྨར། །བྱང་ཆེན་རྒྱ་མཚོའི་གསོས་སུ་འཇུག་གྱུར་ཅིག

ཅེས་ཡུལ་གངས་ཅན་གྱི་སྐད་ཀྱིས་བརྡ་སྤྲོད་པའི་བསྟན་བཅོས་སུམ་ཅུ་པ་དང་། །རྟགས་ཀྱི་འཇུག་པའི་རྣམ་བཤད་མཁས་མཆོག་སི་ཏུའི་ཞལ་ལུང་ཞེས་དཔེ་འདི་ནི། །སྡོམ་བརྩོན་མང་དུ་ཐོས་པའི་དགེ་སློང་ཛྙཱ་ན་མི་ཏྲས་ནན་ཆེན་པོས་བསྒྲུབ་

མ་མཛོད་པ་ལ་བརྟེན་ནས་མཁས་གྲུབ་དམ་པ་ངག་དབང་རྡོ་རྗེ་དཔལ་བཟང་པོའི་ཞབས་དྲུལ་ཀྱི་ཐོས་རིག་རིང་། སྤེལ་ཁང་པ་ཎྜི་ཏ་ཆེན་པོའི་ཞལ་གྱི་བདུད་རྩི་ཆ་ཤས་ཙམ་མྱངས་པས་བོད་ཀྱི་བརྡ་དག་གི་བསྟན་བཅོས་ཡལ་མོ་ཆེའི་དགོངས་དོན་སྨྲ་བ་ལ་མཁས་པའི་མདུན་སར་མི་ཉམས་པའི་ཕྲིབས་པ་ཅུང་ཟད་ཕྱིབ་པའི་ཤཱཀྱའི་དགེ་སློང་ཛམྦྷ་ཟླ་ད་ཞེས་བྱ་བས་སུམ་རྟགས་དང་སྒྲ་སྒྲོ་དང་མཁས་པའི་ཁ་རྒྱན་ལ་སོགས་པའི་བོད་ཀྱི་བརྡ་སྤྲོད་པའི་བསྟན་བཅོས་རྩ་འགྲེལ་མང་པོ་ལ་ཞིབ་ཏུ་དཔྱད་དེ། དེ་དག་གི་ལེགས་ཆ་མཐའ་དག་ཕྱོགས་གཅིག་ཏུ་བཏུས་ནས་རང་ལོ་སོ་ལྔ་པ་ཟད་པ་ཞེས་པ་མེ་སྟག་ལོའི་ཀྲོ་བཞིན་ཟླ་བའི་དཀར་ཆོས་དགའ་བ་བྱེད་པོའི་ཉིན། གཙང་གཡས་རུ་བཞད་ཀྱི་བྱེ་བྲག་དཔལ་ཁུའི་རི་ཁྲོད་དགའ་ལྡན་རྩེའི་སྒྲོང་ཁང་དུ་སྦྱར་བ་འདིས་ཀྱང་རྒྱལ་བའི་བསྟན་པ་རིན་པོ་ཆེ་གངས་ཅན་གྱི་ལྗོངས་སུ་ཡུན་རིང་དུ་གནས་པའི་རྒྱུ་བྱེད་ནུས་པར་གྱུར་ཅིག།

མཁས་མང་རྣམས་ཀྱི་གསུང་གི་གནད་བཏུས་པའི། མཁས་མཆོག་སི་ཏུའི་ཞལ་ལུང་འདི་ཉིད་ལ།
བཙ་ཆུང་ཟློ་ཤ་ར་ཏ་ཙནྡྲ་ཡིས། མཁས་འདོད་ཀུན་ལ་ཕན་ཕྱིར་སྤར་བསྒྲུབས་དགོས།
གནས་སྐབས་བོད་ཡིག་དཀའ་གནད་བདེ་རྟོགས་ཅིང་།
མཐར་ཐུག་རྣམ་མཁྱེན་ཐོབ་པའི་རྒྱུར་གྱུར་བསྔོ།།

D. B. Poona—906—1000—3-8 1912